*The Editor*

JANE MCAULIFFE, the inaugural director of National and International Outreach at the Library of Congress, is the editor of the six-volume *Encyclopaedia of the Qurʾān* and the *Cambridge Companion to the Qurʾān*. She is a former president of Bryn Mawr College and a former dean of arts and sciences at Georgetown University.

# NORTON CRITICAL EDITIONS
## ANCIENT, CLASSICAL, AND MEDIEVAL ERAS

AQUINAS, St. Thomas Aquinas on Politics and Ethics
The Arabian Nights
ARISTOTLE, Poetics
Beowulf (prose)
Beowulf (verse)
The Bhagavad Gita
BOCCACCIO, The Decameron
BOETHIUS, The Consolation of Philosophy
CHAUCER, The Canterbury Tales
CHAUCER, Dream Visions and Other Poems
CHAUCER, Troilus and Criseyde
CONFUCIUS, The Analects
DANTE, Inferno
The English Bible, Vol. One: The Old Testament
The English Bible, Vol. Two: The New Testament
The Epic of Gilgamesh
HERODOTUS, The Histories
HOMER, The Odyssey
JULIAN, The Showings of Julian of Norwich
KEMPE, The Book of Margery Kempe
LANGLAND, Piers Plowman
MALORY, Le Morte Darthur
MARIE DE FRANCE, Marie de France's Poetry
Middle English Lyrics
Middle English Romances
OVID, Metamorphoses
ST. PAUL, The Writings of St. Paul
PIZAN, The Selected Writings of Christine de Pizan
The Qur'ān
Sir Gawain and the Green Knight
SOPHOCLES, Oedipus Tyrannus
THUCYDIDES, The Peloponnesian War

For a complete list of Norton Critical Editions, visit
wwnorton.com/nortoncriticals

A NORTON CRITICAL EDITION

# THE QUR'ĀN

A REVISED TRANSLATION

ORIGINS

INTERPRETATIONS AND ANALYSIS

SOUNDS, SIGHTS, AND REMEDIES

THE QUR'ĀN IN AMERICA

*Edited by*

JANE McAULIFFE

LIBRARY OF CONGRESS

W • W • NORTON & COMPANY • *New York* • *London*

W. W. Norton & Company has been independent since its founding in 1923, when William Warder Norton and Mary D. Herter Norton first published lectures delivered at the People's Institute, the adult education division of New York City's Cooper Union. The firm soon expanded its program beyond the Institute, publishing books by celebrated academics from America and abroad. By midcentury, the two major pillars of Norton's publishing program—trade books and college texts—were firmly established. In the 1950s, the Norton family transferred control of the company to its employees, and today—with a staff of four hundred and a comparable number of trade, college, and professional titles published each year—W. W. Norton & Company stands as the largest and oldest publishing house owned wholly by its employees.


Printed in the United States of America
First Edition

Manufacturing by LSC Communications
Book design by Antonina Krass
Production manager: Elizabeth Marotta

Library of Congress Cataloging-in-Publication Data

Names: McAuliffe, Jane, editor.
Title: The Qur'an : A Revised Translation : Origins : Interpretations and Analysis : Sounds, Sights, and Remedies : The Qur'an in America / edited by Jane McAuliffe, Library of Congress.
Description: New York : W. W. Norton & Company, Inc., [2017] | Series: A Norton Critical Edition | Includes bibliographical references.
Identifiers: LCCN 2016049586 | **ISBN 9780393927054 (pbk.)**
Subjects: LCSH: Qur'an—History. | Qur'an—Criticism, Textual. | Qur'an—Criticism, interpretation, etc.—History. | Qur'an—Study and teaching—United States.
Classification: LCC BP130 .Q625 2017 | DDC 297.1/22521—dc23
LC record available at https://lccn.loc.gov/2016049586

W. W. Norton & Company, Inc., 500 Fifth Avenue, New York, N.Y. 10110
www.wwnorton.com
W. W. Norton & Company Ltd., 15 Carlisle Street, London W1D 3BS

1 2 3 4 5 6 7 8 9 0

To my brothers and sisters, especially
Thomas Martin Dammen (1953–2010)

# Contents

# Introduction

This book presents, in English translation, the sacred scripture of 1.6 billion people. Encountering the Qur'ān first as a printed text, however, reverses the experience of most of the world's Muslims. Muslims hear the Qur'ān before they read it, and many never read it at all. But the sounds of qur'ānic recitation fill Muslim spaces, both public and private, bathing the believers in the blessing (*baraka*) of God's own word. The Qur'ān also surrounds Muslims visually. They see its words beautifully carved into the façades of buildings both ancient and modern, or decorating the walls and arches of massive urban mosques and smaller community prayer halls. Framed calligraphy of qur'ānic verses decorates homes and offices; and sometimes, special verses are worn or even ingested as a protection against misfortune or as a prayer for health and prosperity. A few examples may illustrate this point.

(1) A group of small children in Dhaka or Damascus or Dakar or Detroit—fidget quietly as they listen intently to the strange sounds being repeated over and over by their patient teacher: "*bis mil law ar rah maan ar rah heem.*" "Now recite after me," the teacher urges, "*bis mil law ar rah maan ar rah heem.*" Back and forth it goes, the teacher speaking slowly and distinctly, the children struggling to mimic the sounds and the stresses.

The phrase they are reciting, rendered in English as "In the name of God, the beneficent, the merciful," stands at the beginning of every chapter (*sūra*) of the Qur'ān but one. Learning and memorizing it launches a child into a language use that is utterly different from the speech of daily discourse. For most such students Arabic is not their native tongue, and even those who speak Arabic do not speak qur'ānic Arabic. Yet this is where their introduction to the Qur'ān begins. Soon these children embark upon the recitation and memorization of short sūras (chapters) and, for the most dedicated among them, the slow, patient progression to learning the whole Qur'ān by heart.

(2) The moment of stepping from the blazing Indian sun into the cool, dim interior of the Taj Mahal remains etched in any tourist's memory. The white marble of the mausoleum seems to glow from within, and its perfect symmetry reflects the harmonious proportionality of the entire complex. Shah Jahan (1592–1666) commissioned this magnificent tomb for his beloved wife, Mumtaz Mahal. Overwhelmed with grief at her death, he built an earthly vision of her place in paradise, inscribing her cenotaph with the promise found in the eighty-third sūra of the Qur'ān: "The righteous are in delight, / On couches, gazing, / You will know in their faces the radiance of delight" (Q 83:22–24).

The Taj Mahal envelops its visitors with eloquent inscriptions. The four exterior arches of the tomb carry all eighty-three verses of Sūra *Yā Sīn*, which fittingly concludes: "Therefore glory be to Him in Whose hand is the dominion over all things! To Him you will be brought back" (Q 36:82). Three complete sūras (Q 48, 67, and 76) frame the inner arches and the upper register of the interior. From every angle and level, magnificent qurʾānic calligraphy catches the eye.

(3) An elderly woman in Indonesia, seeking a remedy for the persistent pain in her back and sides, approaches a traditional healer. The healer listens intently, taking careful note of the symptoms she describes. Drawing on manuals of time-honored medical practice, the healer then takes saffron ink and writes some verses of the Qurʾān on the interior of a drinking bowl. The bowl is next filled with fresh water, and the woman drinks as the healer recites additional verses and prayers for her health.

These three sketches capture some of the different ways in which believers encounter the Qurʾān. They are offered to underscore a simple but important assertion: in the lives of Muslims, the Qurʾān is experienced before it is studied. To approach the Qurʾān as simply a book among books, as simply a text to be read, ignores the full qurʾānic phenomenon of the Muslim believer. For Muslims, the Qurʾān is sound and sight before it is paper and print.

Few readers come to the Qurʾān for the first time with no prior awareness or preconceptions. Muslim believers bring the perspective of a religious tradition and, for many, lifelong familiarity with these words. Those who do not share this faith formation, who are not Muslims, have often been exposed to denigrations or dismissals of the Qurʾān, to misinformed or even antagonistic misperceptions, well before they encounter the work itself. Especially in recent years it has been hard to dodge the deluge of attacks on the Qurʾān generated by simplistic patriotism, religious chauvinism, or racist malice. Not infrequently, professors will begin a class on the Qurʾān with a word association game, asking students to call out the first term that comes to mind when they hear the word "Qurʾān." While its results are often disheartening, such an exercise can expose the unrecognized or unacknowledged stereotypes that frequently attach themselves to this text.

A more benign form of this phenomenon is the puzzlement that frequently follows an initial attempt to read the Qurʾān. I cannot count the number of friends, colleagues, and acquaintances who, upon hearing that I have focused much of my scholarly work and writing on the Qurʾān, confess that they found it hard going. When they are pressed to explain, a familiar litany of complaint and confusion quickly surfaces: The text jumps from one topic to another. The genres are jumbled. The voice or speaker moves from the first to the third to the second person without warning. There are no "stories"—that is, there are few extended narratives with developed plot lines. Such reactions are not simply a function of contemporary sensibilities: non-Muslim reception of the Qurʾān records a long history of such reproaches.

Even those who have devoted themselves to the academic study of Islam are not immune. One British Arabist lamented that the Qurʾān "is confused in its progression and strangely mixed in its contents." The German author of an important nineteenth-century history of the Qurʾān complained of "the awful dreariness of the book." Yet another scholar, a biographer of the prophet Muḥammad, cited the view of a colleague who opined that "none—except an Arabic Scholar—had ever succeeded *in wading through* the whole body of the Holy Book."[1]

The Anglican cleric John Medows Rodwell prefaced his 1861 translation of the Qur'ān with a quote from one of the greatest literary figures of modern times, Johann Wolfgang von Goethe (1749–1832), that captures the mix of exasperation and admiration aroused by the Qur'ān in many of its readers. Goethe wrote in his *West-Oestlicher Divan* (1819): "However often we turn to it, at first disgusting us each time afresh, it soon attracts, astounds, and in the end enforces our reverence. . . . Its style, in accordance with its contents and aim, is stern, grand, terrible—ever and anon truly sublime. . . . Thus this book will go on exercising through all ages a most potent influence."[2] Forthrightly acknowledging that the Qur'ān is not an immediately accessible text may ease the frustration and annoyance that so many first-time readers feel.

## Two Trajectories of Textual Study

In addition to a translation of the Qur'an, this volume offers an introduction to centuries of scholarship on the text. A glance at that scholarship immediately exposes a persistent division. Much work has been produced by Muslim scholars and much has been produced by those who do not share this faith tradition. There are, in other words, two trajectories of qur'ānic study, analysis, and interpretation, which begin from different starting points and, not unexpectedly, often reach quite different conclusions. While they may have points of convergence, it is simpler to imagine these two trajectories as parallel conversations, each one self-replicating and producing its own scholarly lineage and literature. In order to make sense of the selections in this volume, the reader needs a more than passing acquaintance with each.

### *Traditional Accounts of the Qur'ān's Origins, Collection, and Codification*

Muslim scholars have written countless commentaries on the Qur'ān, and every area of Islamic thought—law, philosophy, theology, mysticism, ethics—has been erected upon a qur'ānic foundation. All together, this literature spans more than a millennium of intellectual activity that all goes back to a single starting point or, more specifically, a starting person: an Arab prophet from the seventh century. Muslim scholarship on the Qur'ān builds from a basic theological assertion: the Qur'ān is divine revelation. God, through an angelic intermediary, spoke the words of the Qur'ān in Arabic to Muḥammad ibn ʿAbdallāh. Muḥammad, in turn, recited and preached these words to his early followers, and they have been passed

1. Stanley Lane Poole, introduction to *Selections from the Kur'án*, by Edward William Lane (1879; reprint, New Delhi: Asian Educational Services, 2003), p. civ; Theodor Nöldeke, *Geschichte des Qorāns* [*History of the Qur'ān*], 2nd ed., ed. Friedrich Schwally (1909–38; reprint, Hildesheim: Georg Olms, 1981), 2:219; Hartmut Bobzin, "'A treasury of heresies': Christian Polemics against the Koran," in *The Qur'an as Text*, ed. Stefan Wild (Leiden: Brill, 1996), p. 157.
2. Quoted on the title page of J. M. Rodwell, trans., *The Koran: Translated from the Arabic, the Suras Arranged in Chronological Order* (London: Williams and Norgate, 1861).

down to all subsequent generations in an unbroken chain of complete and accurate transmission.

Muslim narratives of the Qur'ān's revelation, while varying greatly in scope and detail, sketch the basic story of a young man from a trading center on the western side of the Arabian Peninsula who, in periods of prayer and religious retreat, began to hear voices for which he could not account. Initially frightened by the experience, he sought confirmation from a few intimates that his auditions were divine, not diabolical. Their reassurance bolstered his spiritual self-confidence and growing self-awareness as a prophet, a vehicle of God's revelation to humankind.

According to early biographies (*sīrāt*), Muḥammad ibn ʿAbdallāh was born in Mecca about 570 CE to a widowed mother who died when he was six. His grandfather assumed care of the orphan; and at his grandfather's death that guardianship passed to an uncle, Abū Ṭālib (d. 619) who regularly took his nephew on trading journeys. As a young adult, Muḥammad was hired by an older widow, Khadīja bint al-Khuwaylid (ca. 554–619), to oversee her own caravans. Eventually, Khadīja married her successful manager.

Mecca could not boast the agricultural advantages of some other oasis towns in the Arabian Peninsula, but its economy prospered through the caravans that crossed its borders and the cultic rituals performed at its major shrine. As stewards of that shrine and enforcers of its sacred precincts (*ḥaram*), the dominant Quraysh tribe enjoyed a prestige that extended well beyond the city limits. Muḥammad, though only a member of one of its lesser clans, benefited from this kinship and cachet.

Muḥammad's first experience of revelation dated to 610 CE. The angel Gabriel served the role of intermediary agent, a function affirmed by Q 2:97: "Say (O Muḥammad, to mankind): 'Who is an enemy to Gabriel! For he it is who has revealed (this scripture) to your heart by God's permission, confirming what was (revealed) before it, and a guidance and glad tidings to believers.'" While the Prophet clearly understood God to be the real source of his revelations, the Qur'ān denies direct vision or audition of the divine: "And it was not (given) to any mortal that God should speak to him unless (it be) by revelation or from behind a veil, or (that) He sends a messenger to reveal what He will by His leave" (Q 42:51). Receiving God's word was not an easy experience. Many accounts describe the physical torment that Muḥammad underwent during periods of intense revelatory activity.

Later doctrinal development of the Qur'ān's disclosure speaks of its "descent" from "a preserved tablet" (*al-lawḥ al-maḥfūz*) as both a single event and a sequence. In this cosmology, the Qur'ān first descends to the lower heaven and from there is progressively revealed to the Prophet over a period of twenty-two or twenty-three years. In his encyclopedic work on the Qur'ān, the Egyptian scholar Jalāl al-Dīn al-Suyūṭī (1445–1505) cites scholars who envision this period of prolonged, progressive revelation as a series of falling stars that God sends gently down.

Muḥammad's initial efforts to preach the message he was receiving—a call to submit oneself to the one God, to act with integrity and justice, and to prepare for the last judgment—attracted some followers but also aroused the wrath of Mecca's leading oligarchs. After eventually losing clan support, Muḥammad and his supporters felt compelled to leave the city and to accept the invitation of leaders of Yathrib, to the north, to establish themselves there. This 200-mile emigration (*hijra*) from Mecca to Yathrib—soon thereafter renamed Medina—transformed Muḥammad from a powerless preacher into the political and military leader of an increasingly dynamic community.

From the date of the *hijra* in 622—the first year of the Muslim calendar—until his death in 632, the Prophet continued to receive and to relay revelations, but he also undertook commerce-disrupting forays and major military moves against Mecca. Names of these battles—Badr, Uḥud, the Trench—live in Muslim memory as critical moments in the early history of emergent Islam. A treaty concluded at Hudaybiya on the outskirts of Mecca stabilized relations between Mecca and Medina for a few years, but in 630 Muḥammad conquered his birthplace with an overwhelming armed force. Throughout these years of conflict with Mecca, concurrent campaigns and expeditions to other parts of the Arabian Peninsula consolidated the Prophet's power and laid the foundation for the extraordinary years of conquest that followed his death in 632.

During his decade in Medina, Muḥammad shaped the city as the first Muslim theocracy. A long-settled date palm oasis, Medina was a mixed society of Jewish and pagan clans. Those who had emigrated with the Prophet and those who had assisted the emigrants soon formed the core elite. Loyalty and willingness to fight opposing tribes were key values. Betrayal and conspiring with enemies could result in deportation or execution, the fate of several prominent Jewish tribes. Reinforcing his religious leadership of the city, Muḥammad instituted the forms of prayer, fasting, pilgrimage, and charity that would define Muslim religious practice. Everything the Prophet said and did—his *sunna*, or way of living—became the model for Muslim life. His closest companions and followers remembered these acts and words, and their collective memory was eventually recorded in the compilations of *ḥadīth*, the second major source of Muslim religious literature.

This traditional account of the Qur'ān's revelation and of Islam's origins embeds itself within a theological narrative, a "salvation history" that begins with God's creation of the world and his primordial covenant with humankind. In the continuous sequence of messengers and prophets that God sent to guide human beings through the ages, Islam looks back to Abraham as the monotheist who brought his religion to people of Arabia. Abraham built a sanctuary, the Kaʿba, in Mecca, and his son Ismāʿīl became the ancestor of the Arabs. In the early seventh century, Muḥammad's role as prophet was not to found a new religion but to restore the religion of Abraham.

The Muslim understanding of the pre-Islamic past fits within this theological perspective. A single, derogatory term summarizes the qur'ānic and post-qur'ānic attitude toward the existing religious practices in Arabia: *jāhiliyya*, an Arabic adjective commonly translated as "Age of Ignorance." Both the Qur'ān and the Prophet's biography depict a polytheist society centered on clan and household idols, stone and star worship, divination by arrows and entrails, and pilgrimage rituals involving animal sacrifice and circumambulation of a sacred space.

When he finally conquered Mecca and overcame his Meccan opponents, Muḥammad restored its sacred sanctuary to the worship of the one God (*al-ilāh* or *Allāh*) and expanded his theocratic federation to encompass not just his birthplace but, through both conquest and compacts, much of the Arabic Peninsula. With his death, the leadership of this community (*umma*) passed to a succession of caliphs. The line began with Abū Bakr (573–634) and continued—with enormous variation of geographical reach and effective power—until the early twentieth century, when Mustafa Kemal Atatürk (1881–1938), the first Turkish president, abolished the institution of the caliphate.

But while the caliphs inherited political, military, and religious authority from Muḥammad, they did not assume his status as a prophet. With Muḥammad's death, God's revelation to humans ceased. Muḥammad is the last prophet, the "seal of the prophets," and the Qurʾān contains God's complete and final guidance for his creation. But how did that divine guidance, verbal disclosures transmitted over two decades, achieve its written and final form? Most accounts assume that while some parts of the Qurʾān may have been written down before Muḥammad's death, most of it circulated orally from memory. The traditional Muslim history of the collection, codification, and canonization of the text as we now have it must be drawn from sometimes divergent reports, but a basic outline is as follows: Perhaps during the caliphate of Abū Bakr but certainly during that of ʿUthmān ibn ʿAffān (d. 656), a complete version of the Qurʾān was assembled from oral and written sources and arranged in the order of sūras and verses now presented by the text. The writing was of a sort that we might call shorthand and what scholars term a *scriptio defectiva*—"defective" because it lacked the markings that distinguish Arabic consonants of similar form as well as the signs that indicate vowels. This skeletal inscription (*rasm*) functioned chiefly as an aide-mémoire for oral recitation. ʿUthmān's promulgation of this collected, written version as the official one was, according to the standard reports, a decisive step toward the Qurʾān's canonization. Since the *scriptio defectiva* could support different readings—and a number of them emerged—the final stage in the Qurʾān's canonical fixation was the production of a fully marked and vocalized written codex (*muṣḥaf*). This occurred, again according to the traditional histories of the Qurʾān, largely through the work of the Baghdadi scholar Abū Bakr ibn Mujāhid (859/60–936). While an accepted number of variant versions continue to coexist, today the most common printed and recited version in the world follows the reading of the Kūfan ʿĀṣim ibn Abū al-Najūd (d. 745), as transmitted by his student Ḥafs ibn Sulaymān (708–796).

## *Challenges to the Traditional Accounts*

This brief recapitulation of the revelation, collection, and codification of the Qurʾān summarizes more than a millennium of Muslim scholarship on the sacred text. It forms the foundational narrative for all of its subsequent interpretation and analysis. In the contemporary world this narrative coexists, often uneasily, with approaches to the study of the Qurʾān that are not built upon belief. The second scholarly conversation, therefore, begins from different perspectives and presuppositions. It presumes a human author, or authors, of the Qurʾān. While it often—but not always—speaks respectfully of the theological claims of believing scholars, it does not share them. Consequently, it treats the Qurʾān like any other major work of world literature and feels free to apply the same techniques and methods of literary scholarship to this text that it would to any other.

This research trajectory lies deeply rooted in nineteenth-century academic environments that began to study the Qurʾān with strategies drawn from the cognate field of biblical studies. Such work received renewed emphasis in the twentieth century with some seminal—and controversial—contributions. In 1938, the Australian Semiticist Arthur Jeffery published *The Foreign Vocabulary of the Qurʾan*, a work whose implications have yet to be fully assessed. Some forty years later, the British scholar John Wansbrough proposed an alternative theory of qurʾānic, and Islamic, origins. Building on earlier work that had questioned the historicity of foundational sources in the areas of the prophetic biography (*sīra*), the traditions of Muḥammad and his Companions (*ḥadīth*), and the exegesis (*tafsīr*) of the Qurʾān, Wansbrough concluded that a fixed text of the Qurʾān cannot be dated earlier than the end of the eighth century and that the area of its genesis was more likely to have been Mesopotamia than Mecca and Medina.

In the same year that Wansbrough's *Qurʾanic Studies* (1977) appeared, another British scholar, John Burton, published a monograph that also challenged the traditional narratives of the Qurʾān's origins and codification but from the opposite direction. According to Burton, Muḥammad himself accomplished a complete collection of the Qurʾān. Accepting the premises of Ignaz Goldziher (1850–1921) and Joseph Schacht (1902–1969), Burton judged the reports that place the Qurʾān's compilation after the Prophet's death to be hypothetical reconstructions by later legal scholars seeking to shore up existing practices for which they could find no qurʾānic grounding. More recently, Angelika Neuwirth has also argued—while not making claims as comprehensive as those of Burton—that many of the Qurʾān's sūras were definitively shaped during Muḥammad's lifetime. She focuses on the structure and composition of individual sūras, with painstaking analysis of rhyme patterns, verse groupings, and shifts of theme and topic.

Others, drawing more heavily on lexical and philological analysis, have redirected attention to the search for Christian influences on the genesis of the Qurʾān. Positing a significant Christian presence in pre-Islamic Arabia, these scholars suggest that Christian liturgical texts form a primitive layer of the Qurʾān, a textual nucleus to which Muḥammad and his disciples added. In a variation of this hypothesis, some argue that a Syro-Aramaic lexicon and syntax underlie many qurʾānic passages that have generated divergent interpretations.

These kinds of literary analysis, often built on biblical models, are not the only lines of inquiry that have taken a searching look at the sources upon which the traditional consensus was constructed. The other big shift in Western scholarship on the Qurʾān in the past fifty years has been a geographical expansion. Classical and postclassical Muslim study of the Qurʾān puts a laser-like focus on the tightly circumscribed area of western Arabia and depends, almost exclusively, on Arabic sources. In the past several decades, scholars of late antiquity have begun to scour their own Greek and Syriac texts for evidence that could support—or disprove—the received consensus. They have looked for attestations to the early seventh-century figure of Muḥammad and to his community's military excursions in the region of western Arabia. These investigations have made scholars increasingly aware that there is far more continuity between the periods of late antiquity and the early Islamic centuries than had previously been acknowledged. The sense of "Islamic exceptionalism" that marked earlier periods of historical research is crumbling before an emergent understanding that Arabia was integrated into, and influenced by, patterns of change within the whole eastern Mediterranean world.

Some textual segments selected for this volume point to narrative intersections that can be found in the vast corpus of extant Near Eastern literature. Within an apocryphal gospel, a Syriac liturgical text, and an example of rabbinical exegesis are echoes of qurʾānic material that stimulate source-critical scholarship. Of course, the largest repository of such narrative intersections is the Bible itself. It is worth, for example, taking a look at the book of Genesis, the first book of the Torah (one of three parts of the Hebrew Bible) and also the first book of the Old Testament, the Christian version of the Hebrew Bible. In its fifty chapters, Genesis recounts God's creation of the world and of Adam and Eve, the flood that destroyed all creation except Noah and those he saved on the ark, and God's call to Abraham and his covenant with Abraham and his descendants. These and many other narrative strands from Genesis may be found in the Qurʾān and in the genre of post-qurʾānic Islamic literature known as the "stories of the prophets" (*qiṣaṣ al-anbiyāʾ*). Abraham (Ibrāhīm) figures prominently among Islam's succession of prophets and messengers and is revered as the "friend of God" (*khalīl Allāh*). His role in espousing a primordial monotheism prefigures that of Muḥammad, and Abraham's service in building the Kaʿba links him to the annual pilgrimage (*ḥajj*) ritual. Genesis 22 and Q 37:99–111 tell the dramatic story of Abraham's attempted sacrifice of his son, a divine testing that is commemorated every year at the end of the *ḥajj* rituals with the Muslim festival of ʿĪd al-Aḍḥā.

For several reasons, the two scholarly conversations that I have just summarized are likely to remain parallel discourses for some time to come. We have virtually no documents from the first decades of Islamic history. What exists are literary works composed long after the events they purport to describe, clearly shaped to present a form of "salvation history." While a great deal of pre-Islamic epigraphic evidence has been uncovered, it is not conclusive, and to date relatively little serious archaeological investigation of seventh-century western Arabia has been undertaken. Nevertheless, recent decades have witnessed far more exchange and interchange between scholars of diverse orientations. Conferences and symposia across the globe now host a plurality of perspectives, offering many opportunities for fruitful academic dialogue.

This brings me to a concluding remark on terminology: These parallel discussions about the Qurʾān's origins are commonly designated as "Muslim" versus "Western"—meaning non-Muslim—labels widely recognized as inaccurate and clumsy. There are many Western scholars, past and present, who accept and transmit the standard story, or stories, of the Qurʾān's genesis. Conversely, there are a number of Muslim scholars, particularly those educated in European and American universities, who question that account and adopt a historical-critical stance in their studies. Still others, in the words of Tim Winter, a prominent convert to Islam, "hold that the entire Western culture of scriptural criticism, whether conservative or skeptical, is a reductionist Enlightenment or Protestant project which is apt to be culturally oppressive as well as philologically inappropriate when applied to Muslim sources."[3]

Today, most university departments or faculties of Islamic studies in Muslim-majority countries would align themselves with the traditional narrative. In American and European universities, as well as those in many other non-majority-Muslim regions, some version of a "revisionist" approach has become either the norm or an important voice in the conversation.

## The Text and Its Analysis, Interpretation, and Intellectual Amplification

The Qur'ān is not a particularly long book. Compared to the full library of Hindu sacred literature, the canonical texts of Theravada Buddhism, or even the sixty-six books of the Protestant Bible, the Qur'ān is of modest size, assembled from 114 separate textual units called sūras (*suwar*). Each sūra has a specific name (or names), and each but one (the ninth) is prefaced with an invocation known as the *basmala*: "In the name of the God, the beneficent, the merciful." These sūra units span from a few to several hundred lines and, except for the opening one, they are arranged in roughly descending order of length. Thus the chronology of revelation does not function as the Qur'ān's ordering principle. To the contrary, the earliest revelations tend to be those found in the shorter sūras, those that fall toward the end of the book.

Each sūra is composed of verses (*āyāt*; sing. *āya*), and these, too, can be very short or quite lengthy. The rhythmic prose patterns created by the cadence and closing syllables of many *āyāt* lend great power and beauty to the oral recitation (*tajwīd, tartīl*) of the Qur'ān. Indeed, the text has also been divided into several recitational sequences: into sevenths (*manāzil*; sing. *manzila*) to facilitate recitation of the whole Qur'ān in a week; into thirtieths (*ajzā'*; sing. *juz'*) for recitation in a month, particularly the month of Ramaḍān; and into sixtieths (*aḥzāb*; sing *ḥizb*) for a month's twice-daily recitation—again, especially during Ramaḍān.

Throughout its 114 suras, the Qur'ān advances a variety of self-designations. The most prominent of these is, of course, the term *qur'ān*, an Arabic verbal form that is derived from the verb *qara'a* (a cognate of the Hebrew *kārā*) meaning "to read" or "to recite." The imperative form introduces Q 96, a sūra that many believe to have been the first revealed: "Recite (*iqra'*): In the name of your Lord." Contemporary Muslims often use the phrase *al-Qur'ān al-karīm* (the Noble Qur'ān) as a respectful reference to the scripture, but dozens of other epithets have been drawn from the text itself and from the lists compiled in the medieval compendia of the "qur'ānic sciences." Some of the most common are the Book (*al-kitāb*), the Wisdom (*al-ḥikma*), the Guidance (*al-hudā*), the Distinguisher or Criterion (*al-furqān*), the Straight Path (*al-ṣirat al-mustaqīm*), the Truth (*al-ḥaqq*), the Exalted (*al-majīd*), the Firm Handle (*al-'urwa al-wuthqā*), and the Light (*al-nūr*).

3. Tim Winter, "Qur'ānic Reasoning as an Academic Practice," *Modern Theology* 22 (2006): 454.

Another group of phrases marks the concept of the "heavenly book" and the cosmology of the Qur'ān as positioned in the presence of God: for example, Q 43:4, *umm al-kitāb*/mother of the book; Q 56:78, *kitāb maknūn*/hidden book; and Q 85:22, *lawḥ maḥfūẓ*/guarded tablet. The heavenly book records all that has happened and all that will happen from creation to the final resurrection. It is also the ontological wellspring of all revelation, whether that be given to Moses, Jesus, Muḥammad, or any in a long list of other prophets and messengers.

Although the sūras are not arranged chronologically, classical scholars were keenly interested in determining the temporal order of certain verses and in linking particular passages to the life and times of the prophet Muḥammad. The first of these interests was motivated by legal concerns, which form the basis for the intra-qur'ānic exegetical exercise known as "the abrogating and the abrogated" (*al-nāsikh wa-l-mansūkh*). Certain verses that were disclosed in subsequent stages of revelation are thought to have canceled the commands of earlier verses. The quintessential example is the progressive prohibition of alcohol: Q 5:90's connection of strong drink with Satan is understood as overriding the more lenient stance of Q 2:219 and Q 4:43.

A second target of exegetical interest took classical Muslim scholars beyond the Qur'ān as they sought to uncover the circumstances in the Prophet's lifetime that could have served as "occasions of the revelation" (*asbāb al-nuzūl*) for specific verses. Probing the ḥadīth, the biography of Muḥammad, and the accounts of his campaigns (*maghāzī*), they looked for linkages that could illuminate particular passages of the Qur'ān. In another form of chronological analysis, these scholars assessed whether a sūra had been revealed in Mecca, before the Prophet's emigration in 622, or in Medina after it. While there were some differences in the lists generated, a stable consensus—with accepted variation—emerged in the late medieval period. Printed Qur'āns, such as the Egyptian standard edition published in 1923, ordinarily specify at the beginning of the sūra whether it is Meccan or Medinan and signal instances of interpolation (i.e., places where a Meccan verse has been inserted in a Medinan sura and vice versa). By this calculation, most of the sūras—86 of the 114—are counted as Meccan.

## *The "Sciences" of the Qur'ān*

The three ways mentioned above (abrogating and abrogated, occasions of revelation, and Meccan/Medinan) to classify sūras constitute fundamental categories within the developed intellectual discipline known as the "sciences of the Qur'ān" (*'ulūm al-Qur'ān*). In Muslim universities around the world, graduate programs devoted to the study of the Qur'ān expound particular topics of these "sciences" in semester-long courses. Such traditional disciplines draw their importance from qur'ānic verses like Q 16:89, "And We reveal the scripture to you as an exposition of all things," and Q 6:38, "We have neglected nothing in this book." If the Qur'ān contains all knowledge, then everything that contributes to its comprehension counts as an important intellectual pursuit. Abū al-Faraj 'Abd al-Raḥmān ibn al-Jawzī (1116–1200), a renowned scholar and preacher, expresses this sentiment perfectly. He introduces his commentary on the Qur'ān with the argument that "since the mighty Qur'ān is the noblest fund of knowledge, understanding its ideas is the most perfect form of understanding. This is because the degree of eminence of the act of knowing lies in the eminence of that which is known."

Two compendia of the qur'ānic sciences, one written in the fourteenth century and the other in the fifteenth, provide the scope and span of these "sciences" and remain standard sources: *The Proof in the Qur'ānic Sciences* (*al-Burhān fī 'ulūm al-Qur'ān*), by Badr al-Dīn al-Zarkashī (d. 1392), and *The Perfection in the Qur'ānic Sciences* (*al-Itqān fī 'ulūm al-Qur'ān*), by Jalāl al-Dīn al-Suyūṭī (1445–1505). Al-Suyūṭī's work, which drew heavily on al-Zarkashī's, comprises eighty individual chapters that, taken together, demonstrate the minute and multifaceted analysis of the qur'ānic text to which centuries of Muslim scholarship has devoted itself. For example, chapters in the first section of *The Perfection* examine how particular verses were revealed, whether in Mecca or Medina, whether during the day or the night, whether during the prophet Muḥammad's travels or when he was at home, whether in summer or winter. They not only designate the first and the last verses revealed but also include the various opinions on those designations. In addition, as noted above, they devote attention to the "occasions of revelation." *The Perfection* treats the rules of recitation as well: where pauses are possible or mandatory, when consonants are elided or assimilated, and those instances when vowel pronunciation must be prolonged or shortened. It even contains a section on the character and comportment of those who recite the Qur'ān, detailing the etiquette appropriate to its sacredness.

Al-Suyūṭī devotes almost half of *The Perfection* to linguistic and rhetorical scrutiny of the text: identifying words of multiple signification, distinguishing literal and metaphorical language use, and classifying qur'ānic utterances as oaths, parables, and argumentation. Because linguistic classifications carry legal consequences, qur'ānic verses are categorized on multiple levels. The distinction between "abrogating" and "abrogated" verses has already been mentioned; other binaries include those verses with universal applicability and those that pertain to a particular period or set of circumstances, verses that are clear and those that are ambiguous, verses that are concise and those that are elaborated, and verses that must be understood literally and those that may be taken metaphorically.

Balancing the focus on language and law are sections of al-Suyūṭī's work that discuss the "meritorious qualities" (*faḍā'il*) of the Qur'ān. The idea of being "meritorious" applies to both people and text. Statements (*ḥadīth*) attributed to Muḥammad and his Companions praise those who study, teach, and recite the Qur'ān, identifying the moral qualities and defining personal behavior required to perform these functions. Other statements list the special benefits that accrue from the recitation of certain sūras and verses, particularly the first (*al-Fātiḥa*), second (*al-Baqara*), and the 112th (*al-Ikhlāṣ* or *al-Tawḥīd*). For example, "[Recitation of] the sūra beginning with these words 'Say: He is God, the one!' [Q 112] is equal to [recitation of] a third of the Qur'ān." As in his other sections, al-Suyūṭī here summarizes an extensive literature that includes individual works dedicated to this topic, as well as chapters devoted to it in the major collections of ḥadīth. Other passages are highlighted for their ability to promote healing or to ward off misfortune. Al-Zarkashī's earlier work includes a statement from Muḥammad that conveys a sense of such assessments:

"Truly the mightiest verse in the Qur'ān is 'God! There is no god except Him, the alive, the eternal, etc.' (Q 2:255); the most justice-assuring verse in the Qur'ān is 'God enjoins justice and kindness, etc.' (Q 16:90); the most fear-inspiring is 'And whoever does an atom's weight of good will see it then, And whoever does an atom's weight of ill will see it then' (Q 99:7–8); and the most hope-inspiring verse in the Qur'ān is 'O My servants who have been prodigal to their own hurt! Do not despair of the mercy of God, etc.' (Q 39:53)."[4]

This emphasis on the Qur'ān's spiritual effectiveness and its aesthetic superiority generated the fully developed theology of its inimitability, a reflective discourse spurred by verses that dared those who mocked Muḥammad and his prophecy to produce something of equal perfection. These have come to be known as the Challenge Verses (*āyāt al-taḥaddī*) and include Q 2:23–24, 10:39, 11:13, 17:88, and 52:33–34. An entire genre of classical Islamic literature devoted itself to painstaking demonstration of the Qur'ān's formal perfection, an exhaustive literary analysis that generated the major works on Arabic poetics—which, in turn, shaped and structured all subsequent literary study. The Qur'ān's perfection, a perfection unattainable by mortal effort, is miraculous proof of Muḥammad's prophethood and confirms its divine origin.

Close acquaintance with the compendia of al-Zarkashī and al-Suyūṭī, and with the dozens of earlier works that they recap, inspires awe at the level of attention and analysis lavished on the qur'ānic text. A final example of this painstaking and reverential scrutiny can be drawn from al-Zarkashī. He relates the story of an Umayyad general who asked the best Qur'ān reciters for a tally of textual statistics. After four months they arrived at the totals: 323,015 letters and 77,439 words. Subsequent calculations produced verse totals (which vary from 6,104 to 6,236), identification of the longest sura (Q 2, with 286 verses), the longest verse (Q 2:282, with 128 words), and the shortest verses (Q 89:1 or Q 93:1, each a one-word verse).

## *Qur'ānic Commentaries*

The most expansive and enduring expressions of the "sciences of the Qur'ān" are the hundreds—perhaps thousands—of full-length commentaries that have been produced over more than a millennium. Any sizable Muslim library or university will house a collection of the major works, most of which are regularly reprinted by publishing houses in Egypt, Lebanon, and Saudi Arabia. These enormous exegetical repositories can trace themselves back to the first efforts to clarify and comprehend the qur'ānic utterances. As many of the sayings attributed to Muḥammad and his Companions attest, questions greeted almost every new verse proclaimed. Some of the early exegetical materials that eventually found their way into the encyclopedic commentaries were simple word glosses, synonyms, or short phrases to explain unfamiliar terms.

With the passage of time and the vast expansion of Muslim territory, later generations of scholars addressed the qur'ānic text from a chronological and geographical distance. Much like its accounts of the Qur'ān's genesis, traditional Muslim scholarship has a well-established narrative

4. Jalāl al-Dīn al-Suyūṭī, *al-Itqān fī 'ulūm al-Qur'ān*, ed. M. A. Ibrāhīm (Cairo: Dār al-Turāth, 1967), 4:129. Al-Suyūṭī cites this from Abū Dharr al-Haraqī's (d. 1044) *Faḍā'il al-Qur'ān*.

about the stages of interpretive development. It begins with Muḥammad's own exegetical explanations and expands to include first those of his Companions and then those of the two generations who followed them. A Companion who figures prominently in this standard account is ʿAbdallāh ibn al-ʿAbbās (ca. 619–687/88), often dubbed "the Doctor" or "the Sea" for his vast knowledge of the Qurʾān.

Particularly in the modern and contemporary periods, efforts to categorize and characterize this exegetical output have been made by both Western and Muslim scholars. Two works published within the last century can be regarded as representative of this endeavor: *Schools of Koranic Commentators* (1920, *Die Richtungen der Islamischen Koranauslegung*), by Ignaz Goldziher, and *Commentary and the Commentators* (1961, *al-Tafsīr wa-l-mufassirūn*), by Muḥammad Ḥusayn al-Dhahabī. In the lectures issued as *Die Richtungen*, Goldziher describes the earliest periods of exegetical development and then characterizes commentaries according to five "orientations" or schools: traditional (based primarily on ḥadīth), rationalist (drawing on dialectical theology), mystical (with esoteric insights), sectarian (chiefly Shīʿī), and modern. Al-Dhahabī, who refers to Goldziher's volume in his own, uses both chronological and thematic classifications. Chronologically, he stays with the standard narrative by identifying the first stage with the lifetime of Muḥammad and the second with the two generations that immediately followed. Stage three covers a vast span of more than a millennium—containing such notables as Abū Jaʿfar Muḥammad ibn Jarīr al-Ṭabarī (ca. 839–923), Aḥmad ibn Muḥammad al-Thaʿlabī (d. 1035), Abū al-Qāsim Maḥmūd ibn ʿUmar al-Zamakhsharī (1075–1144), Fakhr al-Dīn al-Rāzī (1149–1210), and Ismāʿīl ibn ʿUmar ibn Kathīr (ca. 1300–1373)—while the final stage is that of modern and contemporary commentary. At the same time, al-Dhahabī recognizes both sectarian (Shīʿī, Khārijī) and thematic categories (philosophical, legal, mystical, scientific).

In his *Qurʾanic Studies*, John Wansbrough adopted a typology derived from biblical scholarship to argue that the formative period of qurʾānic exegesis proceeded through consecutive phases: narrative (haggadic), legal (halakhic), lexical (masoretic), rhetorical, and allegorical. But Wansbrough failed to make a persuasive case for the chronological sequence of these modes of exegetical activity; and more recent scholarship on the history of qurʾānic commentary questions the utility of creating such categories, observing that individual commentaries often blend several perspectives and employ multiples modes of interpretation.

Nevertheless, qurʾānic commentaries (*tafāsīr*; sing. *tafsīr*) do share certain formal features. They follow the canonical order of the Qurʾān, beginning with the first verse of the first sūra and continuing methodically until the last sūra and verse, in what is often labeled a "linked" (*musalsal*) approach. In the multivolume print editions of many of the largest commentaries, consecutive passages of the Qurʾān—usually individual verses—are set at the very top of the page. Traditional commentaries also tend to be cumulative, with each new effort incorporating masses of material from earlier centuries. The ninth-century scholar al-Ṭabarī is credited with the first of these encyclopedic undertakings. His *Comprehensive Clarification of the Interpretation of the Verses of the Qurʾān* (*Jāmiʿ al-bayān ʿan taʾwīl āy al-Qurʾān*) subsumes much of the first two centuries of exegetical comment: in its frequently reprinted modern edition, it runs to thirty large volumes.

Al-Ṭabarī prefaces the material he collects and collates, whether statements from Muḥammad and his early followers or narrative elaborations, with the names of those who transmitted each account from one generation to another. The scale is astonishing: 13,026 such "chains of transmission" are provided for the 35,400 pieces of transmitted information. Subsequent encyclopedic commentaries compiled on al-Ṭabarī's foundation include al-Thaʿlabī's *The Unveiling and Clarification Concerning the Qurʾān* (*al-Kashf wa-l-bayān ʿan tafsīr al-Qurʾān*), al-Zamakhsharī's *Unveiler of the Real Meanings of the Hidden Matters of What Was Sent Down* (*al-Kashshāf ʿan ḥaqāʾiq ghawāmiḍ al-tanzīl*), Fakhr al-Dīn al-Rāzī's *The Keys of the Unseen* (*Mafātīḥ al-ghayb*), Abū ʿAbdallāh al-Qurṭubī's (1214–1273) *The Comprehensive Clarification of the Legal Stipulations of the Qurʾān* (*al-Jāmiʿ li aḥkām al-Qurʾān*), and Ibn Kathīr's *Interpretation of the Mighty Qurʾān* (*Tafsīr al-Qurʾān al-ʿaẓīm*). Not surprisingly, continued expansion created a need for concision and summary commentaries became popular—they include *Provisions for the Journey into the Science of Exegesis* (*Zād al-maṣīr fī ʿilm al-tafsīr*), by Ibn al-Jawzī; and *Interpretation of the Two Jalāls* (*Tafsīr al–Jalālayn*), by Jalāl al-Dīn al-Maḥallī (1389–1549) and Jalāl al-Dīn al-Suyūṭī. Although the current print edition of Ibn al-Jawzī's work totals nine volumes, he expected his students to memorize it and to have learned all the detail that stood behind his condensation.

The leading Shīʿī commentaries, such as that of ʿAlī ibn Ibrāhīm al-Qummī (d. 919), share many characteristics with those of Sunnī authors, but they give special prominence to statements from the Shīʿī imāms and to verses of the Qurʾān that can be understood to support Shīʿī theological claims. Sūfī commentaries—one by Sahl al-Tustarī (818–896) is an early example—often represent a more marked departure from the comprehensive, linked model of the major Sunnī works. While continuing to reproduce much traditional material, they probe deeper, more hidden, textual meanings that both point to and ratify the levels of spiritual insight sought in the mystic's journey.

Several of the questions that commentators regularly address cut across such sectarian divisions. Any given verse may be subject to philological and grammatical analysis, as commentators strive to understand unfamiliar words or unusual grammatical constructions. They often express an appreciation of literary tropes such as metaphors and similes and of rhetorical strategies such as repetition, concision, and elaboration. If there are variant readings, these will be cited along with ḥadīth attestations. A verse's possible legal implications, and the extent to which they may apply, will be assessed. The related question of where a verse falls within the chronology of revelation—that is, whether it is Meccan or Medinan—will be examined, and any reports that speak about the circumstances of its revelation will be noted. A broader historicization may draw on the stories of earlier prophets to illuminate aspects of Muḥammad's life.

Comprehensive Qurʾān commentaries have continued to be written in the modern and contemporary periods, sustaining a deep and unbroken tradition. But new emphases and new methods have also entered the exegetical arena, and diversity in many forms has grown. The most pressing issue addressed by many commentators is modernity itself. As emigration and colonization increased exposure to post-Enlightenment thinking, intellectuals such as the Indian Sayyid Ahmad Khan (1818–1898), the Egyptian Muḥammad ʿAbduh (1849–1905) and his student Rashīd Riḍā (1865–1935), and the Iranian Abū al-Qāsim al-Khūʾī (1889–1992) took a rationalist approach to the Qurʾān that could account for scientific advances and new forms of political, social, and economic organization.

Other authors strove to go beyond an accommodation with modern science, insisting that its new discoveries had all been anticipated in the Qurʾān. Such "scientific exegesis" (*tafsīr ʿilmī*) found support in the classical claims that the Qurʾān contains all knowledge and in the doctrine of the Qurʾān's miraculous inimitability (*iʿjāz*). While this claim has been dismissed by most scholars of the Qurʾān, it was widely disseminated and achieved a measure of popular notoriety.

Much like some biblical scholarship, another modern approach to the Qurʾān drew on the methods of literary studies, acknowledging the Qurʾān's position as a major piece of world literature. Treating the text as literature was not without risks, however. Several scholars who embarked on such forms of analysis, like Naṣr Ḥāmid Abū Zayd (1943–2010), ran afoul of both religious and university authorities. Their work was censured and, in at least a few cases, they were dismissed from their positions.

Dismay with postcolonial Muslim societies and a strong sense that they had gone too far in seeking accommodation with Western ideas and mores drove other commentators, such as Sayyid Quṭb (1906–1966) and Abū al-Aʿlāʾ Mawdūdī (1903–1979), to purge their commentaries of those parts of the accumulated exegetical tradition that went well beyond ḥadīth-based interpretation. A particular target was the inclusion of *Isrāʾīliyyāt*, narrative material drawn largely from Jewish and Christian sources. For example, rather than attempt to harmonize Islam with modernity, Quṭb insisted that Muslims should re-create the pristine practice of the prophet Muḥammad and his first followers.

The new exegetical emphases that followed upon the encounters with post-Enlightenment rationalism, with colonialism and postcolonialism, with scientific advances, and with literary studies broadened the scope of the commentary tradition and brought the Qurʾān into conversation with new ideas and intellectual currents. Concurrently, another type of commentary began to emerge, one characterized as "thematic interpretation" (*tafsīr mawḍūʿī*). Rather than following the textual sequence of sūra and verse from beginning to end, as in the traditional linked pattern, thematic exegesis focuses on key concepts or issues as the commentator draws together material from throughout the Qurʾān deemed relevant to the topic under consideration.

## *The Qurʾān's Impact on Islamic Thought*

Such thematic commentaries blur the boundaries between *tafsīr* as a distinct genre and the exegetical analysis found in every field of Islamic religious scholarship. As a number of the selections in this volume demonstrate, the Qurʾān and its interpretation permeate all areas of Muslim learning. Scholars of ḥadīth such as Muslim ibn al-Ḥajjāj and Yaḥyā al-Nawawī devoted entire sections of their compendia to exegetical traditions and all areas of the qurʾānic sciences. The prominent historian and proto-sociologist ʿAbd al-Raḥmān ibn Muḥammad ibn Khaldūn (1332–1406) pays considerable attention in the first two volumes of his *Muqaddima* (*Introduction*) to the nature of prophecy and inspiration and to the scholarly exercise of Qurʾān interpretation. More than three hundred years earlier, ʿAbd al-Malik ibn Muḥammad al-Juwaynī (1028–1085), known as the "leading master of the two holy cities" (*Imām al-Ḥaramayn*), developed theological arguments about those miracles, such as the inimitability of the Qurʾān, that authenticate the divine mandate of Muḥammad's mission. Earlier still, Abū Ḥātim al-Rāzī (d. ca. 934) rebutted challenges not only against the Qurʾān's inimitability but also against the validity of pre-qurʾānic scriptures, such as the Torah and the Gospels.

The most famous figure from the world of medieval Islamic thought, Abū Ḥāmid Muḥammad al-Ghazālī (1058–1111), referred frequently to the Qurʾān in his theological, philosophical, and legal writings. In his magnum opus, *The Revival of the Religious Sciences* (*Iḥyāʾ ʿulūm al-dīn*) al-Ghazālī offers a detailed discussion of the practices of qurʾānic recitation and reading and their spiritual benefits. In a similar fashion—but on quite a different topic—the Ṣūfī Abū al-Qāsim ʿAbd al-Karīm al-Qushayrī (986–1072) ties a reflective meditation on trust of God to three key verses of the Qurʾān. A later master, Jalāl al-Dīn Rūmī (1207–1273), places the intrinsic meaning of the Qurʾān at the center of Ṣūfī spiritual formation.

These renowned figures are among the most prestigious in Islamic intellectual history, but many more have contributed to the almost limitless store of insight and erudition produced by attention to the Qurʾān. Every period of Islam's history, from the earliest days to the most recent, has produced important scholarly work in theology, philosophy, law, ethics, and mysticism that draws its premises and arguments from qurʾānic reasoning. Within this ever-growing intellectual reservoir, the tradition of qurʾānic commentary and of the associated qurʾānic sciences has remained central. Exegetical production, including full-scale commentaries, continuously absorbs and incorporates the insights and conclusions of contemporary Qurʾān-based scholarship.

Over the centuries, as the Qurʾān found its way into all areas of Islamic intellectual inquiry, it also shaped the spiritual sensibilities of an ever-wider range of peoples and places. Arabic words and phrases infiltrated languages from Ethiopia to Indonesia. While military action expanded the frontiers of the Muslim world in its first centuries, the outward momentum was later sustained by trading and commerce, fostering settlements across the globe, attracting missionaries and migrants, and eventually infusing the local culture with Islamic ideals and values. Trade, unfortunately, was not in goods and materials alone. Ships could carry human cargo, and it was slave ships from west Africa that first bore countless Muslims to the Americas. Despite efforts by some to depict Islam as a "foreign" religion, Muslims have been part of the American social fabric since well before the signing of the Declaration of Independence. The autobiography of Omar ibn Said (ca. 1770–1864) introduces readers to a literate and educated west African who, like many before him, was captured into slavery and forced to live his Muslim life in a deeply alien environment.

One of the nation's founding fathers and most prominent intellectuals, Thomas Jefferson, has left evidence of his interest in Islam and the Qurʾān. His personal library—carefully selected and quite extensive—became the core collection of the Library of Congress, the oldest federal cultural institution of the United States. Among Jefferson's acquisitions, which are now on permanent display at the Library of Congress, is a translation of the Qur'ān done by the English scholar George Sale (ca. 1697–1736). Because Sale prefaced his translation with a lengthy explanation of Islamic thought and practice, we can assume that America's third president was not unfamiliar with the tenets of this global faith.

In the generations since Jefferson, Islam and its scripture have proven to be a source of fascination to American intellectuals, social reformers, and spiritual seekers as, for example, Washington Irving's (1850) biography of the Prophet attests. The twentieth-century appearance of Elijah Muhammad and the Nation of Islam, as well as the perennial popularity of Ṣūfī teachers and teachings, further exemplify how Islam has woven itself into the fabric of American life.

## Sounds, Sights, and Remedies

Important as these forms of interpretation, analysis, and intellectual amplification are for understanding the Qur'ān and its place in the entire tradition of Islamic thought, attention must also be paid to all the other ways in which the Qur'an is experienced in Muslim lives and communities.

### *Reciting the Qur'ān*

Voicing the Qur'ān, reciting parts of it, listening to professional recitation—this immersion in the sounds and rhythms of the text marks the lives of Muslims around the world. An observant Muslim recites the first sūra (*al-Fātiḥa*) and other verses of the Qur'ān during each of the five daily prayers. In total, the ritual prayer encompasses seventeen recitations from the Qur'an. These recitations are always in Arabic, regardless of the reciter's native tongue. In the communal mosque prayer on Fridays, the preacher invariably invokes pertinent passages to accentuate his message. During Ramaḍān, the month of fasting, many Muslims read or recite one-thirtieth (*juz'*) of the Qur'ān each day. Falling within the last ten days of the month, the Night of Power (*laylat al-qadr*; see Q 97:1) commemorates the first stage of the Qur'ān's revelation, giving the evening prayers and recitations made during this period particular importance.

Listening to Qur'ān recitation can produce an enduring fascination. Countless stories underscore the irresistible attraction of the voiced Qur'ān, and early Islamic history records spontaneous conversions prompted by such beautiful sounds. With the advent of the electronic age, exposure to qur'ānic recitation has exploded across the Muslim world. What had once been available only in special settings and on special occasions has suddenly become nearly omnipresent. Television channels broadcast the best reciters twenty-four hours a day. First cassettes, then CDs, and now MP3 players and smartphones make it possible to listen to the Qur'ān anywhere and anytime. These same media have also spawned a global marketplace in Qur'ān recitation, enabling individual reciters, through websites and social media, to build a worldwide audience. Concurrently, variations in recitational style no longer reflect local boundaries. Indonesian recitation—such as that of the famed female reciter Maria Ulfah—travels electronically to Indianapolis, just as Saudi voices resound in Singapore.

But recitation runs a spectrum from the humble to the exalted, from the faltering efforts of many ordinary Muslims to the consummate artistry of the trained professional. Correct recitation of the Qurʾān is far from easy (as one who studied it for a semester with minimal success knows too well). The discipline known as "the science of recitation" (*ʿilm al-tajwīd*) requires years of study and practice. To master it, the student must rehearse pronunciations, prolongations, and pauses; must learn the multiple accepted readings of the Qurʾān; must understand the idiosyncratic spellings of some qurʾānic vocabulary, and must master the many other technicalities encompassed in the rules of *tajwīd*.

Traditionally, a student was dependent on a skilled teacher. But here, too, the digital age is leaving its mark. Anyone with online access can locate websites or download apps that offer *tajwīd* tutorials. The more sophisticated of these learning aids color-code the Arabic text according to the articulation required. Click on the highlighted passage, and you will hear it recited. These opportunities for self-instruction are democratizing a learning system that has been stratified for centuries.

As the voice engages the sacred text through recitation, the body encounters it through touch. Q 80:13–14 speaks of the Qurʾān as being "on honored leaves / Exalted, purified," so reverence for the Qurʾān is also expressed in practices of ritual purification. An individual who wishes to touch, read, or recite the Qurʾān must be ritually pure. Various physical functions create conditions of impurity, classified as either minor or major. Minor ritual impurity (*ḥadath*) results from lesser bodily emissions or from contact with an impure substance. Major impurity (*janāba*) is caused by sexual intercourse and menstruation. Purification can be achieved through ablutions (*wuḍūʾ*), full immersion (*ghusl*), or, in the absence of water, the rubbing of body parts with clean sand or dust. According to some schools of Islamic law, this mandate for ritual purity extends to other books, such as commentaries on the Qurʾān, that contain significant portions of the Qurʾānic text. As non-Muslims do not practice such purification, many Muslims consider them to be in a permanent state of impurity that should preclude their touching the Qurʾān.

It is not only the purity of the person that matters in handling the Qurʾān. As a venerated physical object, the Qurʾān should never be placed on the ground or near dirt or dust. Nothing should be set on top of it, nor should it be carried or transported in a fashion that might compromise its purity. In Muslim homes the Qurʾān is housed on a high shelf or set on a special book stand, often beautifully decorated.

Many Muslims will kiss the Qurʾān and raise it above their heads as an act of reverence, despite disagreements about whether such acts are authorized by the words and deeds (*sunna*) of the Prophet. Many will weep at the sound of the recited Qurʾān, encouraged by Q 17:109, an oft-cited textual warrant for this custom: "They fall down on their faces, weeping, and it increases humility in them."

Multiple therapeutic and prophylactic uses of the Qurʾān have become deeply entrenched in a number of Muslim cultures. While these remain the subject of theological and legal controversy, they are common among populations both rural and urban. Examples include wearing verses encased in an amulet or talisman, drinking and eating from cups and bowls etched with specific qurʾānic phrases, wrapping an inscribed cloth around a baby's arm to protect the child from harm, and drinking inked verses dissolved in water to promote healing or ward off illness. When such practices verge on foretelling the future or invoking sympathetic magic—to ensure marital fidelity or to foil business rivals—they have drawn more strenuous opposition from orthodox scholars.

History even records the Qurʾān's use in times of conflict, most famously during the Battle of Ṣiffīn in 657: the governor of Syria, Muʿāwiya ibn Abū Sufyān (ca. 602–680), raised a Qurʾān on the tip of his spear to signal a request for arbitration. Centuries later, several classical chronicles note that the codex sent to Damascus by the caliph ʿUthmān ibn ʿAffān would be brought forth when the city was under siege and carried in procession as prayers for victory were offered. Moreover, the codex over many years was periodically displayed so that people could seek blessing simply by seeing and touching it.

### *The Qurʾān in Art and Architecture*

While hearing, voicing, and touching the Qurʾān are fundamental features of Muslim life, seeing its words writ large also plays a prominent role. Monumental inscriptions from the Qurʾān in beautifully ornate scripts embellish major mosques across the globe. They are a signature element of Islamic religious art, much as icons and statues are characteristic of Christian churches. Numerous ḥadīth proscribe the depiction of living beings, and these have been understood as forbidding the creation of any object that might attract the veneration due only to God. Consequently, public art in Islam uses calligraphy, geometric patterns, and stylized floral elements, often in combination and often to stunning effect. Inscribed verses from the Qurʾān decorate spaces large and small, continually pulling the eye toward the divine word. The Dome of the Rock in Jerusalem, dated to 691, carries about 820 feet of inscriptions. The golden letters in Kufic, an early qurʾānic script, inscribe the *basmala* and the profession of faith (*shahāda*), as well as various other citations, most of which—but not all—are from the Qurʾān.

But the use of such inscription is not limited to religious buildings or objects. Quite early, coinage with qurʾānic phrases began to circulate, the first examples being the gold and silver dirhams struck by the Umayyad caliph ʿAbd al-Malik (r. 685–705)—a symbolic use of the Qurʾān to legitimate the power of the Muslim polity. Phrases from Q 48:29 and 9:33, with their references to Muḥammad as God's messenger, became common on coinage in many parts of the Muslim world.

Within the first three centuries of Islam, such inscriptions became somewhat standardized, with particular qurʾānic passages regularly used for specific objects. Many mosques, for example, contain citations of Q 9:18: "He only shall tend God's sanctuaries (*masājid*) who believes in God and the last day." The epitaphs on tombstones and other funerary structures, frequently the earliest remaining evidence of Muslim settlement, often include the Throne Verse (Q 2:255) and Sūra 112. The *miḥrāb*—the alcove or indentation in a mosque that indicates the direction of Mecca, toward which worshippers pray—is regularly embellished with Q 17:78, a verse that refers to the times of prayer. Mosque lamps, especially from the Mamluk period, evoke the Light Verse (Q 24:35) with its image of a glowing lamp enclosed in glass. Inscribed verses in the great Mughal mausoleums, such as the Taj Mahal in Agra, bear witness to the link between earth and paradise and to the eternal awards awaiting the deceased.

The ʿAbbāsid caliph al-Mutawakkil (r. 847–61) achieved another noteworthy use of qurʾānic inscription when he ordered the rebuilding of the Fusṭāṭ Nilometer (*miqyās al-nīl*), the ancient stone-lined shaft that measured the river's flood heights. At the caliph's command, portions of the Nilometer were etched with qurʾānic passages describing God's mercy in sending rain—for example Q 50:9: "And We send down from the sky blessed water whereby We give growth to gardens and the grain of crops."

But not all qurʾānic calligraphy is monumental. It also finds a place in the decoration of domestic architecture. Modest homes in Muslim countries and in the Muslim diaspora frequently display framed qurʾānic passages or posters of the entire Qurʾān written in miniature script. Many also showcase a particularly fine copy of the Qurʾān on a special easel or stand. The combination of such wall art with the aural immersion provided by Qurʾān recitation on television, radios, and recording devices is believed to infuse the home with the blessing (*baraka*) of God's word.

While architectural inscription and artistic display prominently visualize the Qurʾān, so do the countless manuscripts and printed editions produced over more than a millennium. In Q 39:23 the Qurʾān makes an aesthetic argument for itself, declaring: "God has (now) revealed the fairest of statements, a scripture consistent, (in which are promises of reward) paired (with threats of punishment), with which the flesh of those who fear their Lord creep (*taqshaʿirru*)." As noted earlier, doctrinal declarations of the Qurʾān's miraculous inimitability (*iʿjāz*) prompted the exhaustive study of its literary qualities. They also motivated the artistic use of qurʾānic verses and the fabrication of Qurʾāns as works of art. Although the material culture of the Islamic world shows considerable variation over time and over its vast geographic distances, certain commonalities can be found throughout. Chief among these is the care and attention given to producing, using, and preserving copies of the Qurʾān in all their individual beauty and variety. The results of this attention can be found in major museums and libraries around the world. Any important collection of Islamic art, whether in New York, Toronto, Dublin, or Doha, will include a selection of exquisite Qurʾān manuscripts. Exhibition catalogues and, more recently, digital reproductions online now make it possible to view and enjoy these incomparable treasures as never before.

## Translations

For Muslims, the act of translating the Qurʾān involves both linguistic and theological issues. In multiple passages, the Qurʾān describes itself as "a qurʾān in Arabic" (*qurʾānan arabiyyan*), and the developed doctrine of the Qurʾān's inimitability (*iʿjāz*) reinforced the belief that only in Arabic could the Qurʾān express the divine revelation. Consequently, recitation of the Qurʾān, whether of the mandated verses in the ritual prayer or of more extensive sections, is always in Arabic.

Nevertheless, full and partial translations of the Qurʾān have been produced from the earliest periods of Islamic history. A Persian paraphrase was the first such effort, and from it a Turkish version was soon prepared. In the interests of increasing understanding of the Qurʾān's message among non-Arabic speakers, the Sāmānid ruler Abū Ṣāliḥ Manṣūr ibn Nūḥ (r. 961–74) even commissioned a Persian translation of the multivolume commentary by al-Ṭabarī. As Islam spread, so did translation activity. Spain and India, the western and eastern ends of Islamic expansion in the premodern period, were each the site of numerous translations. The expansion of printing technology, particularly in the nineteenth century, accelerated the production of translations across the Muslim world.

Translations produced in non-Muslim countries were created for a different purpose, motivated by a desire not to promote the Qurʾān but to contest it. Early translations into the neighboring languages of Greek and Syriac are known only from citations in polemical tracts. Full translations into Latin, however, can be dated to the twelfth century. Peter the Venerable (ca. 1092–1156), the French abbot of Cluny, authorized an English Arabist, Robert of Ketton (active 1141–57), to undertake the translation of the Qurʾān and several other Islamic texts. Working with a Muslim collaborator in Spain, Ketton completed his Latin rendition, which he titled *Lex Mahumet pseudoprophete* (*The Law of Muḥammad, the False Prophet*), in 1142/43. It enjoyed immediate success and wide circulation. Its popularity was magnified when it was published in Basel exactly four centuries later by Theodore Bibliander; a second printing in 1550 bore a preface by Martin Luther. In the early thirteenth century in Spain, Mark of Toledo (d. ca. 1216) produced another Latin translation, which was more literal and less periphrastic.

Although a few other Latin translations appeared in subsequent centuries, the next big advance in accuracy arrived in 1698 with the appearance at Padua of Fr. Ludovico Marracci's *Alcorani Textus Universus Arabice et Latine* (*The Entire Text of the Alcoran in Arabic and Latin*). Marracci used Arabic Qurʾān manuscripts from the Vatican Library as his textual base and also drew on major classical commentaries of the Qurʾān to refine his renderings of particular words and phrases. This translation, quickly recognized for its scholarly worth, itself later became the source of derivative translations in European vernaculars.

The history of Qurʾān translations in the English-speaking world begins in 1649, when the Scottish writer Alexander Ross published an English version of the 1647 French translation by André du Ryer, a linguist and diplomat who had held posts in Cairo, Alexandria, and Istanbul. Ross's perspective is clearly conveyed by the title of an essay he added: "A needful Caveat or Admonition for them who desire to know what use may be made of, or if there be danger in reading the *Alcoran*." In 1806, this translation became the first Qurʾān to be published in America (in Springfield, Massachusetts).

By that time, the Ross translation had been superseded in England by the 1737 work of George Sale, the British legal scholar and Arabist mentioned earlier. While Sale drew directly from the Arabic text, he frequently consulted both classical works of qurʾānic exegesis and Ludovico Marracci's Latin translation. Before his translation Sale placed a lengthy prelude, or "preliminary discourse," that introduced the history, doctrines, and practices of Islam to generations of English speakers. Ensuing editions of this work, which remains in print (and freely available on the Internet), were produced in the late eighteenth century by Elwood Morris Wherry, an American missionary in India, and in the early twentieth century by Edward Denison Ross, the first director of the School of Oriental and African Studies at the University of London.

In the nineteenth century the European study of the Qurʾān was increasingly undertaken by scholars schooled in the disciplines of Semitic philology and biblical studies, a reorientation that benefited subsequent English translations. Post-Enlightenment critiques of religion and the cultural curiosity fueled by European trade and colonization intensified this trend, resulting in fewer apologetic attacks and more interest in cross-cultural scriptural comparison. Among the noted twentieth-century English translations by non-Muslims are those by J. M. Rodwell, E. H. Palmer, Richard Bell, and A. J. Arberry.

English-speaking Muslim scholars in South Asia (particularly Pakistan), in the Middle East, in Britain, and in the United States have produced several generations of English translations. A recent inventory puts the output at about sixty, including a number translated not directly from Arabic but from Urdu, Persian, and Turkish. The most prominent versions are by Abdullah Yusuf Ali, Muhammad Taqui al-Din al-Hilali (in collaboration with M. Muhsin Khan), M. A. S. Abdel Haleem, and Tarif Khalidi.

Translations by converts to Islam constitute yet another category among the growing number of English-language Qurʾāns. Thomas Ballantyne Irving was born in Canada, received a PhD from Princeton, and converted to Islam in his forties. An academic who taught at universities in both the United States and Canada, in 1985 he published *The Quran: The First American Version*. Five years earlier, Muhammad Asad had released *The Message of the Qurʾān*. Asad was born Leopold Weiss to an Orthodox Jewish family in Poland. He chose to be a journalist rather than a rabbi, and as a young man his travels to the Middle East and North Africa set the stage for his conversion, which he chronicled in his best-selling autobiography, *The Road to Mecca* (1954).

## *Muhammad Marmaduke Pickthall and* The Meaning of the Glorious Qurʾān

Two generations before Asad, Muhammad Marmaduke Pickthall published *The Meaning of the Glorious Qurʾān* (1930), a translation that quickly won broad acclaim across the English-speaking Muslim world. Unlike many who have since made English translations of the Qurʾān, Pickthall was not an academic and did not hold a university position. Rather, he was a writer—a journalist, columnist, editorialist, and novelist. Several of his novels gained a wide readership, particularly *Saïd the Fisherman* (1903), published in both London and New York (reprinted in 1925) and described by D. H. Lawrence as "a curious mixture of Arabian Nights and modern realism."[5]

5. D. H. Lawrence, "Review of *Saïd the Fisherman*" (1915), reprinted in his *Introductions and Reviews*, ed. N. H. Reeve and John Worthen (Cambridge: Cambridge University Press, 2005), p. 246.

Marmaduke Pickthall was born in 1875, the son of an Anglican clergyman, and he enjoyed the advantages of a countryside childhood in rural Suffolk. As a boarder at Harrow, one of the most prestigious independent schools in Britain, he was a schoolmate of Winston Churchill. Travels to Jerusalem, Cairo, Damascus, Aleppo, and beyond began before he turned twenty and introduced him to a language and culture that captured him completely. In his review of *Saïd the Fisherman*, Lawrence places Pickthall in the company of fellow expatriates like Lady Hester Stanhope (1776–1839) and T. E. Lawrence (1888–1935), opining that "there seems always to have been some more or less fantastic Englishman, or woman, Arabizing among the Arabs."[6]

Pickthall's interest in Islam was nurtured in his trips to the Middle East, but his formal conversion took place on English soil. In the weeks before Britain wrested Jerusalem from Turkish control, Pickthall gave a series of lectures titled "Islam and Progress" to the Muslim Literary Society in Notting Hill, West London. During the last of these lectures, on 29 November 1917, he publicly declared his acceptance of Islam and began to use "Muhammad" as his first name. Pickthall quickly rose to leadership within the community of British Muslims, both native-born and expatriate, often preaching and leading Friday prayer at the mosque in London. He wrote for Muslim periodicals and, for a time, served as the acting editor of the *Islamic Review*. His frequent inclusion of qur'ānic citations in his sermons and lectures, first recited in Arabic and then rendered in English, created the nucleus of the work for which he would become best known—a full English translation of the Qur'ān.

Pickthall's very brief foreword in the first edition of his translation succinctly summarizes his intention and the attitudes with which he approached this work. First, he argues that no nonbeliever can produce a faithful translation of any scripture and proudly declares his to be "the first English translation of the Qur'ân by an Englishman who is a Muslim." Second, he acknowledges the Muslim doctrine that nothing can take the place of the Qur'ān in Arabic. In a phrase that has been frequently quoted, Pickthall asserts that no translation can claim to be "the Glorious Qur'ân, that inimitable symphony, the very sounds of which move men to tears and ecstasy." Next, he explains that he has tried to make his rendering as literal as possible, "to choose befitting language" and to convey "something of the charm" of the original.

In a 1924 letter to his literary agent quoted by Anne Fremantle, the writer and journalist who would later become his biographer, Pickthall describes how his approach to translating the Qur'ān differs from that in earlier efforts. In the latter

> certain words are left untranslated so as to give quite a wrong impression of the book. Thus the words "Islam" and "Muslim" are left untranslated, this implying that they had at the time of revelation the technical meaning that they acquired afterwards. I translate those words, as any Arab hearing them understands them, as "surrender" or "submission," "those who surrender" or "submit" (i.e. to Allah). For example the text which has always been translated "the religion with Allah is Islam" in my translation reads "religion with Allah consists in the surrender unto

6. Ibid., p. 245.

> Him," which, besides being the accurate rendering, is a statement of a universal truth instead of a sectarian assertion.[7]

The setting for this translation project was neither Britain nor the Middle East but South Asia. Shortly after the end of the First World War, Pickthall set sail for Bombay to assume the editorship of the *Bombay Chronicle*, having agreed to hold that post for six months. Yet he was to remain in India for fifteen years—five in Bombay, followed by a decade in Hyderabad. The Nizamate of Hyderabad, which was created in the first quarter of the eighteenth century as an entity independent of the Mughal Empire, had evolved into a major center of culture and education. Sir Usman Ali Khan Bahadur (r. 1911–48), the nizam of Hyderabad and one of the richest men who ever lived, initially invited Pickthall to take the headship of a boys school but soon turned to him for other services as well.

Pickthall again assumed an editorial position, this time of *Islamic Cultural*, a quarterly journal whose patron was the nizam. The authors attracted to this periodical, which continued to publish until 2004, included many notable scholars, such as D. S. Margoliouth, A. L. Tibawi, Sayed Vahiduddin, Joseph Somogyi, Leon Zolondek, Wilfred Cantwell Smith, Annemarie Schimmel, Franz Rosenthal, Helmer Ringgren, Solomon Pines, R. A. Nicholson, and Abdullah Yusuf Ali.

Most significantly, the nizam underwrote Pickthall's living expenses for two years so that he could concentrate fully on his translation of the Qur'ān. Pickthall embraced the opportunity, seeking consultations with European scholars and collecting sources, such as the works of Theodor Nöldeke (1836–1930), that would serve as important references. He would also keep close to hand the biographies of the prophet Muḥammad by Ibn Isḥāq (ca. 704–767; in the recension of Ibn Hishām [d. 833]) and by Ibn Khaldūn. Pickthall also frequently referred to other standard classical works, named in his foreword: Maḥmūd ibn ʿUmar al-Zamakhsharī, *al-Kashshāf*; ʿAbdallāh ibn ʿUmar al-Bayḍāwī (d. 1286), *Anwār al-tanzīl was asrār al-taʾwīl*; Jalāl al-Dīn al-Suyūṭī and Jalāl al-Dīn al-Maḥallī, *Interpretation of the Noble Qurʾān* (*Tafsīr al-Qurʾān al-karīm*, i.e. *Tafsīr al-Jalālayn*); ʿAlī ibn Aḥmad al-Wāḥidī (d. 1076), *Occasions for the Sending Down of the Qurʾān* (*Asbāb nuzūl al-Qurʾān*); and Muḥammad ibn Ismāʿīl al-Bukhārī (810–870), *The Trustworthy Collection [of Hadīth]* (*al-Jāmiʿ al-ṣaḥīḥ*).

For the next major stage of his work, Pickthall traveled to Egypt in 1929 with two aims in mind. He wanted educated native speakers of Arabic to vet the more complicated passages in his translation and he wanted to secure the imprimatur of al-Azhar, the ancient university in Cairo that served as the center of intellectual orthodoxy. Pickthall accomplished his first goal but not his second, for King Fuad's reported resistance to any translation of the Qur'ān made al-Azhar's leaders reluctant to officially affiliate themselves with the project. Yet he did win the support of such prominent Muslim intellectuals as Muḥammad Rashīd Riḍā, author (along with Muḥammad ʿAbduh), of *Tafsīr al-Manār* (1948), one of the most important modern commentaries on the Qur'ān, and Shaykh Muṣṭafā al-Marāghī, former rector of al-Azhar.

7. Anne Fremantle, *Loyal Enemy* (London: Hutchinson, 1938), p. 389.

The completed translation, first published in New York by Alfred A. Knopf in December 1930, has never gone out of print. It has been reissued in both hardcover and paperback by publishing houses in the United States, Britain, India, Lebanon, and Tunisia; it is now available online at many websites; and it can be purchased as an e-book. Yet Pickthall did not live to see it published with the Arabic and English on facing pages, as he preferred. The first such bilingual edition was produced in 1938, two years after Pickthall's death, by the government press in Hyderabad; others, issued by other publishers, have appeared since.

This publication history attests to the immediate and sustained success of Pickthall's translation. In *Translating the Untranslatable* (2011), a survey of translations done by English-speaking Muslims, Abdur Raheem Kidwai praises Pickthall's for "its faithfulness to the original" and judges it to be "free from any dogmatic interpolations."[8] Nevertheless, it has not avoided critical comment, including a quite negative 1931 review in *The Muslim World*, a journal (originally intended for missionaries) that then bore the subtitle "A Christian Quarterly Review of Current Events, Literature & Thought among Mohammedans."[9] In the early 1980s, accusations appeared in the Pakistani press that Pickthall's command of Arabic was inadequate. Supporters and former students responded quickly and sharply, pointing both to his fluency in the language and to the prepublication work that he had done in Cairo.

Pickthall's attitude toward the Qur'ān in Arabic—he held the orthodox view that only in Arabic is the Qur'ān actually the Qur'ān—is reflected in his choice of title. Recognizing that every act of translation is an act of interpretation, Pickthall called his work "The *Meaning* of the Glorious Qur'ān." In revising his translation for this critical edition, I have abided by some but not all of his original editorial decisions. Pickthall's translation has long been praised for adhering closely to a "literal" rendering of the original Arabic, and I have respected that approach. For several generations, English-speaking Arabists have benefited from the clarity of Pickthall's decisions about word choice and syntactical construction, and I hope that this reworking will continue to aid them.

As the earlier account of the commentary tradition underscores, the Qur'ān, like so many other complicated texts, has spawned multiple—and sometimes competing—interpretations of many of its verses. Choices among these interpretations are inevitably reflected in any translation. Again, I have respected Pickthall's decisions and have not radically departed from them. In one obvious change, I have translated the Arabic *Allāh* with the English word "God." For native speakers of Arabic, whether Muslim, Christian, or Jew, the ordinary word for "God" is *Allāh*. Not rendering the Arabic term with its English equivalent ignores this linguistic fact and perpetuates the misperception that Jews, Christians, and Muslims do not worship the same God.

What I have mostly done, however, is to take a cue from Pickthall's foreword and his expressed desire "to choose befitting language." For Pickthall, this meant a linguistic register congruent with the King James version of the Bible. The audience for which he prepared his translation,

8. Abdur Raheem Kidwai, *Translating the Untranslatable: A Critical Guide to 60 English Translations of the Quran* (New Delhi: Sarup, 2011), p. 10.
9. W. G. Shellabear, "Can a Moslem Translate the Koran?" *The Muslim World* 21 (1931): 287–303.

whether Muslim or non-Muslim, would have found the formality of Elizabethan English most appropriate for a scriptural text. Pickthall's rendering was thus replete with "thee" and "thou," with "lo" and "verily," with "haply" and "forsooth," with "hast" and "doth," with "speaketh" and "giveth." For the twenty-first-century reader, such language sounds odd and antiquarian, and retaining it does a disservice to a text whose first hearers found it fresh, original, and arresting. I have therefore recast Pickthall's translation in a more contemporary idiom without, I hope, sacrificing his tone of reverence and respect.

With regard to the annotations to his translation, I have both subtracted and added. Some of Pickthall's original footnotes have been shortened or, when redundant, eliminated; in many cases his citations have been updated to more recent editions. New annotations have been incorporated to identify unfamiliar terms or to clarify ambiguities. I have also kept Pickthall's sūra introductions, although with reductions and modifications. My purpose has been to produce an accessible text with glosses that assist readers but do not overwhelm them with unnecessary information.

The Arabic text from which Pickthall worked was a lithograph produced in 1830 at the behest of the Ottoman Sultan Maḥmūd II (r. 1808–39). Some of its verse numbers and its ascription of Meccan and Medinan sūras differ slightly from what has become the most popular printed edition (produced in Cairo in 1923).

### *Acknowledgments*

Above all, I am grateful to the editors at W. W. Norton, especially Carol Bemis and Rachel Goodman for their remarkable patience and their elastic deadlines as I worked intermittently on this volume during the years that I was dean of one school and president of another. I would like to acknowledge the generous support of both institutions, Georgetown University and Bryn Mawr College, and to offer special thanks to the dedicated staff of the John W. Kluge Center at the Library of Congress, where I spent a sabbatical year as a distinguished visiting scholar—a year that enabled me to bring this book to completion. Several research associates—Clare Wilde, Robert Tappan, Sayeed Rahman, and Carolyn Baugh—worked with me on this project over its multiyear span. I am grateful to each one of them and look forward to watching their careers flourish. Norton's extraordinary copyeditor, Alice Falk, made countless improvements to this volume. Most ardently, I would like to thank my husband, Dennis McAuliffe, whose occasional query, "So how's it going?" signaled support at just the right moments.

# THE QUR'ĀN

## Sūra 1

*Al-Fātiḥa*, "The Opening," or *Fātiḥat al-kitāb*, "The Opening of the Book," or *Umm al-Qur'ān*, "The Essence of the Qur'ān," as it is variously named, has been called the Lord's Prayer of the Muslims. It is an essential part of all Muslim worship, public and private, and no solemn contract or transaction is complete unless it is recited. The date of revelation is uncertain, but the fact that it has always, from the very earliest times, formed a part of Muslim worship, there being no record or remembrance of its introduction, or of public prayer without it, makes it clear that it was revealed before the fourth year of the Prophet's Mission (the tenth year before the *hijra*[1]); because we know for certain that by that time regular congregational prayers were offered by the little group of Muslims in Mecca. In that year, as the result of insult and attack[2] by the idolaters, the Prophet arranged for the services, which had until then been held out of doors, to take place in a private house.

This sūra is also often called *Saba'an min al-mathānī*, "Seven of the Oft-Repeated" ("verses" being understood), Q 15:87, words which are taken as referring to this sūra.[3]

## The Opening

### *Revealed at Mecca*

1. In the name of God, the beneficent, the merciful.[4]
2. Praise be to God, Lord of the worlds,
3. The beneficent, the merciful.
4. Owner of the day of judgment,
5. You (alone) do we worship; You (alone) do we ask for help.
6. Show us the straight path,
7. The path of those whom You have favored; not the (path) of those who earn Your anger nor of those who go astray.

## Sūra 2

*Al-Baqara*, "The Cow," is so named from the story of the yellow heifer (verses 67–71). As is the case with many other sūras, the title is taken from some word or incident which surprised the listeners. All suggestions to the contrary notwithstanding, it seems probable that the whole of this sūra was revealed during the first four years after the *hijra*, and that by far the greater portion

1. Literally, "emigration": the emigration of the prophet Muḥammad and his early companions from Mecca to Medina in 622 CE.
2. Alfred Guillaume, *The Life of Muhammad: A Translation of Ibn Isḥāq's "Sīrat Rasūl Allāh"* (1955; reprint, Karachi: Oxford University Press, 1987), p. 118 [Pickthall's note].
3. Theodor Nöldeke, *Geschichte des Qorâns* [*History of the Qur'ān*], 2nd ed., ed. Friedrich Schwally (1909–38; reprint, Hildesheim: Olms, 1981), part 1, pp. 110ff. [Pickthall's note].
4. This phrase, known as the *basmala*, occurs at the beginning of each sūra except the ninth. Scholars differ about its scriptural status: some consider it to be a qur'ānic verse, others deem it part of the Qur'ān but not a verse, and still others insist that it simply serves as a divider between or a benediction before sūras. Muslim scholarly consensus holds that the *basmala* counts as a verse in this sūra.

of it was revealed in the first eighteen months of the Prophet's reign at Medina—that is to say, before the battle of Badr.[1]

The Jewish tribes, once paramount in Yathrib, had, not very long before the coming of Islam, been reduced by the pagan Arab tribes of Aws and Khazraj, each Jewish tribe becoming an adherent of one or the other. But they had preserved a sort of intellectual ascendancy owing to their possession of the scripture and their fame for occult science, the pagan Arabs consulting their rabbis on occasions and paying heed to what they said. Before the coming of Islam,[2] these Jewish rabbis had often told their neighbors that a Prophet was about to come, and had often threatened them that, when he came, they (the Jews) would destroy the pagan Arabs as the tribes of ʿĀd and Thamūd had been destroyed of old.[3] So plainly did they describe the coming prophet that pilgrims from Yathrib recognized the Prophet, when he addressed them in Mecca, as the same whom the Jewish doctors had described to them. But the Jewish idea of a prophet was one who would give them dominion, not one who would make them brethren of every pagan Arab who chose to accept Islam. When they found that they could not make use of the newcomer, they opposed him and tried to bewilder him with questions from their theology, speaking to him as men who possessed superior wisdom; failing to perceive that, from a prophet's standpoint, theology is childish nonsense, the very opposite of religion, and its enemy; religion, for the prophet, being not a matter of conjecture and speech, but of fact and conduct.

Ibn Isḥāq[4] states definitely that verses 1–141 were revealed concerning these Jewish rabbis and such of the new converts to Islam as were half-hearted and inclined to them. There follows the order to change the *qibla* (the place toward which the Muslims turn their face in prayer) from Jerusalem to the Kaʿba at Mecca, which was built by Abraham, the choice of Jerusalem having led to a misunderstanding on the part of the Jews that the Prophet was groping his way toward their religion and stood in need of their guidance and instruction.

All through the sūra runs the note of warning, which sounds indeed throughout the whole Qur'ān, that it is not the mere profession of a creed, but righteous conduct, which is true religion. There is the repeated announcement that the religion of Abraham, to which Judaism and Christianity (which springs from Judaism) trace their origin, is the only true religion, and that that religion consists in the surrender of man's will and purpose to the will and purpose of the Lord of creation as manifested in His creation and revealed by way of guidance through successive prophets. Of sincerity in that religion the one test is conduct, and the standard of that religion is for all alike.

At the time when this sūra was revealed at Medina, the Prophet's own tribe, the pagan Quraysh at Mecca, were preparing to attack the Muslims in their place of refuge. Cruel persecution was the lot of Muslims who had stayed in Meccan territory or who journeyed there, and Muslims were being prevented from performing the pilgrimage. The possible necessity of fighting had been foreseen in the terms of the oath, taken at al-ʿAqaba by the Muslims of Yathrib before the flight, to defend the Prophet as they would their own wives and children, and the first commandment to fight was revealed to the Prophet before his flight from Mecca; but there was no actual fighting by the Muslims until the battle of Badr. Many of them were reluctant, having before

1. Nöldeke, *Geschichte des Qorâns*, part 1, pp. 173ff. [Pickthall's note]. The battle of Badr (624 CE) was the first military victory of the prophet Muḥammad.
2. *Al-islām* means "the surrender"—i.e. man's surrender to God's will and purpose [Pickthall's note].
3. Guillaume, *Life*, pp. 93–95 [Pickthall's note].
4. Guillaume, *Life*, pp. 247–70 [Pickthall's note].

been subject to a rule of strict non-violence. It was with difficulty that they could accept the idea of fighting even in self-defense, as can be seen from several verses in this sūra; which contains also rules for fasting and the pilgrimage, bequests, almsgiving, divorce and contracts, and verses which discountenance usury, strong drink and gambling. It concludes with a statement of the universal character of Islam, the religion of God's sovereignty, and a prayer for the forgiveness of shortcomings.

This sūra might be described as the Qur'ān in little. It contains mention of all the essential points of the revelation, which are elaborated elsewhere. This accounts for the precedence given to it in the arrangement of the book.

The period of revelation is the years 1 and 2 AH[5] for the most part, certain verses of legislation being considered as of later date.

## The Cow

*Revealed at Medina*

In the name of God, the beneficent, the merciful.

1. Alif. Lām. Mīm.[6]

2. This is the scripture of which there is no doubt, a guidance to those who ward off (evil).

3. Who believe in the unseen, and establish worship, and spend of what We have bestowed upon them;

4. And who believe in what is revealed to you (Muḥammad) and what was revealed before you, and are certain of the hereafter.

5. These depend on guidance from their Lord. These are the successful.

6. As for the disbelievers, whether you warn them or you do not warn them, it is all one for them; they do not believe.

7. God has sealed their hearing and their hearts, and on their eyes there is a covering. Theirs will be an awful doom.

8. And of mankind are some who say: "We believe in God and the last day," when they believe not.

9. They think to beguile God and those who believe, and they beguile none but themselves; but they perceive not.

10. In their hearts is a disease, and God increases their disease. A painful doom is theirs because they lie.

11. And when it is said to them: "Do not make mischief on the earth," they say: "We are peacemakers only."

12. Are not they indeed the mischief-makers? But they perceive not.

5. *Anno hegirae* (in the year of the *hijra*; Latin), the years in the Islamic calendar; 1 coincides with 622 CE.

6. Three letters of the Arabic alphabet. Many sūras begin thus with letters of the alphabet. Opinions differ as to their significance, the prevalent view being that they indicate some mystic words. Some have opined that they are merely the initials of the scribe. They are always included in the text and recited as part of it [Pickthall's note]. Muslim scholars consider these letters to be part of the Qur'ānic revelation. They are thought to represent the names of God or his attributes, or are signs with symbolic meanings, though the consensus is that their full meaning is known only by God. Some Western scholars argue that the letters are not part of the Qur'ān itself but represent either the names of God or the *basmala* (or both), notes on the ordering of the text, or the initials of early Muslims consulted about possible ways to read the sūra in question.

13. And when it is said to them: "Believe as the people[7] believe," they say: "Shall we believe as the foolish believe?" Are not they indeed the foolish? But they know not.

14. And when they fall in with those who believe, they say: "We believe"; but when they go apart to their devils they declare: "We are with you; we were only mocking."

15. God (Himself) mocks them, leaving them to wander blindly on in their defiance.

16. These are they who purchase error at the price of guidance, so their commerce doth not prosper, neither are they guided.

17. Their likeness is as the likeness of one who kindles fire, and when it sheds its light around him God takes away their light and leaves them in darkness, where they cannot see,

18. Deaf, dumb, and blind; and they do not return.

19. Or like a rainstorm from the sky, in which is darkness, thunder, and the flash of lightning. They thrust their fingers in their ears by reason of the thunderclaps, for fear of death. God encompasses the disbelievers (in His guidance).

20. The lightning almost snatches away their sight from them. As often as it flashes forth for them they walk in it, and when it darkens against them they stand still. If God willed, He could destroy their hearing and their sight. God is able to do all things.

21. O mankind! Worship your Lord, Who has created you and those before you, so that you may ward off (evil);

22. Who has appointed the earth a resting-place for you, and the sky a canopy; and causes water to pour down from the sky, thereby producing fruits as food for you. And do not set up rivals to God when you know (better).

23. And if you are in doubt concerning what We reveal to Our servant[8] (Muḥammad), then produce a sūra the like of it, and call your witnesses beside God if you are truthful.

24. And if you do not do it—and you can never do it—then guard yourselves against the fire prepared for disbelievers, whose fuel is of men and stones.

25. And give glad tidings (O Muḥammad) to those who believe and do good works; that theirs are gardens underneath which rivers flow; as often as they are regaled with food of its fruit, they say: "This is what was given us before";[9] and it is given to them in resemblance. There for them are pure companions; there forever they abide.

26. God does not disdain to coin the similitude even of a gnat. Those who believe know that it is the truth from their Lord; but those who disbelieve say: What does God wish (to teach) by such a similitude? He misleads many by it, and He guides many by it; and He misleads by it only the iniquitous;

7. I.e. the people of Medina, most of whom were Muslims. Verses 8 to 19 refer to the "Hypocrites," or lukewarm Muslims of Medina, whose leader was ʿAbdallāh ibn Ubayy [d. 631]. They pretended that their aim was to make peace between the Muslims and the Jewish rabbis, but they only embittered the controversy [Pickthall's note].

8. Pickthall regularly translated the Arabic *ʿabd* as "slave," arguing that "to be the slave of God is the proudest boast of the Muslim." I have preferred the more common English rendering, "servant."

9. The joys of paradise will recall, in a rapturous degree, the joys the righteous tasted in their life on earth [Pickthall's note].

27. Those who break the covenant of God after ratifying it, and sever what God ordered to be joined, and (who) make mischief on the earth: Those are they who are the losers.

28. How do you disbelieve in God when you were dead and He gave life to you! Then he will give you death, then life again, and then to Him you will return.

29. He it is who created for you all that is on the earth. Then He turned to the heaven, and fashioned it as seven heavens. And He is knower of all things.

30. And when your Lord said to the angels: "I am about to place a viceroy[1] in the earth," they said: "Will You place on it one who will do harm there and will shed blood, while we, we hymn Your praise and sanctify You?" He said: "Surely I know what you know not."

31. And He taught Adam all the names,[2] then showed them to the angels, saying: "Inform me of the names of these, if you are truthful."

32. They said: "Be glorified! We have no knowledge except what You have taught us. You, only You, are the knower, the wise."

33. He said: "O Adam! Inform them of their names," and when he had informed them of their names, He said: "Did I not tell you that I know the secret of the heavens and the earth? And I know what you disclose and what you hide."

34. And when We said to the angels: "Prostrate yourselves before Adam," they fell prostrate, all except Iblīs.[3] He demurred through pride, and so became a disbeliever.

35. And We said: "O Adam! Dwell with your wife in the garden, and eat[4] freely from it (of the fruits) where you will; but do not come near this tree for fear that you become wrongdoers."

36. But Satan caused them to slip from it and expelled them from the (happy) state in which they were; and We said: "Fall down,[5] one of you a foe to the other! There shall be for you on earth a habitation and provision for a time."

37. Then Adam received from his Lord words (of revelation), and He relented toward him. He is the relenting, the merciful.

38. We said: "Go down, all of you, from here; but there comes to you from Me a guidance; and whoever follows My guidance, no fear shall come upon them neither shall they grieve."

39. But they who disbelieve, and deny Our revelations, such are rightful owners of the Fire. They will abide there.

40. O Children of Israel! Remember My favor with which I favored you, and fulfill your (part of the) covenant, I shall fulfill My (part of the) covenant, and fear Me.

41. And believe in what I reveal, confirming what you possess already (of the scripture),[6] and do not be first to disbelieve in it, and do not part with My revelations for a trifling price, and keep your duty to Me.

1. *Khalīfa* (caliph), a term that connotes one who exercises authority delegated from another (in this case, God).
2. Some, especially Ṣūfīs, hold "the names" to be the attributes of God; others, the names of animals and plants [Pickthall's note].
3. Satan, or the devil. Muslim scholars have debated about whether Iblīs was a fallen angel or a jinn (an invisible being for whom salvation is possible; see Q 55:15).
4. Here the command is in the dual, as addressed to Adam and his wife [Pickthall's note].
5. Here the command is in the plural, as addressed to Adam's race [Pickthall's note].
6. Usually understood as referring to previous revelations (e.g., the Bible).

42. Do not confound truth with falsehood, nor knowingly conceal the truth.
43. Establish worship, pay the poor tax,[7] and bow your heads with those who bow (in worship).
44. Do you enjoin righteousness upon mankind while you yourselves forget (to practice it)? And you are readers of the scripture! Have you then no sense?
45. Seek help in patience and prayer; and truly it is hard except for the humble-minded,
46. Who know that they will have to meet their Lord, and that to Him they are returning.
47. O Children of Israel! Remember My favor with which I favored you and how I preferred you to (all) creatures.
48. And guard yourselves against a day when no soul will avail another in anything, nor will intercession be accepted from it, nor will compensation be received from it, nor will they be helped.
49. And (remember) when We delivered you from Pharaoh's people, who were afflicting you with dreadful torment, slaying your sons and sparing your women: That was a tremendous trial from your Lord.
50. And when We brought you through the sea and rescued you, and drowned the people of Pharaoh in your sight.
51. And when We appointed for Moses forty nights (of solitude), and then you chose the calf,[8] when he had gone from you, and were wrongdoers.
52. Then, even after that, we pardoned you in order that you might give thanks.
53. And when We gave to Moses the scripture and the criterion[9] (of right and wrong), that you might be led rightly.
54. And when Moses said to his people: "O my people! You have wronged yourselves by your choosing of the calf (for worship) so turn in penitence to your creator, and kill (the guilty) yourselves. That will be best for you with your creator and He will relent toward you. He is the relenting, the merciful."
55. And when you said: "O Moses! We will not believe in you until we see God plainly"; and even while you gazed the lightning seized you.
56. Then We revived you after your extinction, that you might give thanks.
57. And We caused the white cloud[1] to overshadow you and sent down on you the manna and the quails, (saying): "Eat of the good things with which We have provided you"—We did not wrong them, but they wronged themselves.
58. And when We said: "Go into this township and eat freely of what is in it, and enter the gate prostrate, and say: 'Repentance.'[2] We will forgive you your sins and will increase (reward) for the right-doers."

7. *Al-zakāt*, a tax at a fixed rate in proportion to the worth of property, collected from the well-to-do and distributed among the poor Muslims [Pickthall's note]. This obligatory almsgiving is a religious duty for Muslims.
8. The golden calf created and worshipped by the Israelites while Moses was receiving the tablets of law on the mountain (see Exodus 32:1–8).
9. In Arabic, *furqān*, which conveys a sense of salvation through discernment and of the revelatory guidance which provides that awareness.
1. A cloud that guided or shaded the Israelites during the exodus (see Exodus 13:21–22; 40:38). On the manna and quails, see Exodus 16:11–15.
2. According to a tradition of the Prophet, *ḥittatun* is a word implying submission to God and repentance. The evildoers changed it for a word of rebellion—i.e. they were disobedient [Pickthall's note].

59. But those who did wrong changed the word which had been told them for another saying, and We sent down upon the evildoers wrath from heaven for their evildoing.

60. And when Moses asked for water for his people, We said: "Strike with your staff the rock."[3] And there gushed out from it twelve springs (so that) each tribe knew their drinking-place. Eat and drink of what God has provided, and do not act corruptly, making mischief on the earth.

61. And when you said: "O Moses! We are weary of one kind of food; so call upon your Lord for us that he bring forth for us of what the earth grows—of its herbs and its cucumbers and its corn and its lentils and its onions." He said: "Would you exchange what is higher for what is lower? Go down to settled country, thus you shall get what you demand." And humiliation and wretchedness were stamped on them and they were visited with wrath from God. That was because they disbelieved in God's revelations and slew the prophets wrongfully. That was for their disobedience and transgression.

62. Those who believe (in what is revealed to you, Muḥammad), and those who are Jews, and Christians, and Sabaeans[4]—whoever believes in God and the last day and does right—surely their reward is with their Lord, and no fear shall come upon them neither shall they grieve.

63. And (remember, O Children of Israel) when We made a covenant with you and caused the mountain to tower above you, (saying): "Hold fast what We have given you, and remember what is in it, that you may ward off (evil)."

64. Then, even after that, you turned away, and if it had not been for the grace of God and His mercy you would have been among the losers.

65. And you know of those of you who broke the sabbath, how We said to them: "Be apes, despised and hated!"

66. And We made it an example to their own and to succeeding generations, and an admonition to the God-fearing.

67. And when Moses said to his people: "God commands that you sacrifice a cow,"[5] they said: "Do you make fun of us?" He answered: "God forbid that I should be among the foolish!"

68. They said: "Pray for us to your Lord that He make clear to us what (cow) she is." (Moses) answered: "He says, 'She is not a cow with calf nor immature; (she is) between the two conditions'; so do what you are commanded."

69. They said: "Pray for us to your Lord that He make clear to us of what color she is." (Moses) answered: "He says: 'She is a yellow cow. Bright is her color, gladdening beholders.'"

70. They said: "Pray for us to your Lord that He make clear to us what (cow) she is. Cows are much alike to us; and if God wills, we may be led rightly."

71. (Moses) answered: "He says: 'she is a cow unyoked; she neither ploughs the soil nor waters the fields; whole and without mark.'" They said:

3. See Exodus 17:6.
4. A designation (also "Sabians") that has been applied historically to a number of different groups, including the Harranians and the Mandeans. It is not clear exactly who the Qurʾānic Sabians are.
5. See Numbers 17:1–10.

"Now you bring the truth." So they sacrificed her, though they almost did not.

72. And (remember) when you killed a man and disagreed concerning it and God brought forth what you were hiding.

73. And We said: "Strike him with some of it." Thus God brings the dead to life and shows you His signs so that you may understand.[6]

74. Then, even after that, your hearts were hardened and became as rocks, or worse than rocks, for hardness. For indeed there are rocks from which rivers gush, and indeed there are rocks which split apart so that water flows from them. And indeed there are rocks which fall down for the fear of God. God is not unaware of what you do.

75. Have you any hope that they will be true to you when a party of them used to listen to the word of God, then used to change it, after they had understood it, knowingly?

76. And when they fall in with those who believe, they say: "We believe." But when they go apart one with another they say: "Talk to them of what God has disclosed to you that they may contend with you before your Lord concerning it? Have you then no sense?"

77. Are they then unaware that God knows what they keep hidden and what they proclaim?

78. Among them are unlettered people who do not know the scripture except from hearsay. They only guess.

79. Therefore woe be to those who write the scripture with their hands and then say, "This is from God," that by it they may purchase a small gain. Woe to them for what their hands have written, and woe to them for what they earn thereby.

80. And they say: "The fire (of punishment) will not touch us except for a certain number of days." Say: "Have you received a covenant from God—God will not break His covenant—or do you tell concerning God what you do not know?"

81. No, but whoever has done evil and his sin surrounds him, such are rightful owners of the fire; they will abide in it.

82. And those who believe and do good works: such are rightful owners of the garden. They will abide in it.

83. And (remember) when We made a covenant with the Children of Israel, (saying): "Worship none except God (only), and be good to parents and to relatives and to orphans and the needy, and speak kindly to mankind; and establish worship and pay the poor-tax." Then, after that, you slid back, except a few of you, being averse.

84. And when We made a covenant with you (saying): "Do not shed the blood of your people nor turn (a party of) your people out of your dwellings." Then you ratified (Our covenant) and you were witnesses (to it).[7]

85. Yet you are those who slay each other and drive out a party of your people from their homes, supporting one another against them by sin and

6. The old commentators tell various stories by way of explaining verses 72 and 73; one of them concerning a miracle that happened at Medina [Pickthall's note]. An early account by the exegete Muqātil ibn Sulaymān (d. 767) speaks of a murder victim who is struck with part of a slaughtered cow, rises from the dead, and names his killer.

7. Verse 83 is generally taken as referring to the biblical covenant and verse 84 as referring to the solemn treaty which the Jews of Medina made with the Prophet in the year 1 AH [622 CE; Pickthall's note].

transgression[8]—and if they came to you as captives you would ransom them, whereas their expulsion was itself unlawful for you. Do you believe in part of the scripture and disbelieve in part of it? And what is the reward of those who do so except ignominy in the life of the world, and on the day of resurrection they will be consigned to the most grievous doom. For God is not unaware of what you do.

86. Such are those who buy the life of the world at the price of the hereafter. Their punishment will not be lightened, neither will they have support.

87. And We gave to Moses the scripture and We caused a train of messengers to follow after him, and We gave to Jesus, son of Mary, clear proofs (of God's sovereignty), and We supported him with the holy spirit.[9] Is it ever so, that, when there comes to you a messenger (from God) with what you yourselves do not desire, you grow arrogant, and some you disbelieve and some you slay?

88. And they say: "Our hearts are hardened." No, but God has cursed them for their unbelief. Little is what they believe.

89. And when there comes to them a scripture from God, confirming that in their possession—though before that they were asking for a victory over those who disbelieved—and when there comes to them what they know (to be the truth) they disbelieve in it. The curse of God is on disbelievers.

90. Evil is that for which they sell their souls: that they should disbelieve in what God has revealed, grudging that God should reveal of His bounty to whom He will of His servants. They have incurred anger upon anger. For disbelievers there is a shameful doom.

91. And when it is said to them: "Believe in what God has revealed," they say: "We believe in what was revealed to us." And they disbelieve in what comes after it, though it is the truth confirming what they possess. Say (to them, O Muḥammad): "Why then did you slay the prophets of God before, if you are (indeed) believers?"

92. And Moses came to you with clear proofs (of God's sovereignty), yet, while he was away, you chose the calf (for worship) and you were wrongdoers.

93. And when We made with you a covenant and caused the mountain to tower above you, (saying): "Hold fast by what We have given you, and hear (Our Word)," they said: "We hear and we rebel." And (worship of) the calf was made to sink into their hearts because of their rejection (of the covenant). Say (to them): "Evil is what your belief enjoins on you, if you are believers."

94. Say (to them): "If the abode of the hereafter in the providence of God is indeed for you alone and not for others of mankind (as you pretend), then long for death (for you must long for death) if you are truthful."

95. But they will never long for it, because of what their own hands have sent before them. God is aware of evildoers.

8. The reference is to the wars between the Arab tribes of Medina in which the Jews used to take part as allies of one side and the other, so that Medinan Jews warred against each other [Pickthall's note].

9. "The holy spirit" is a term for the angel of revelation, Gabriel [Pickthall's note]. Gabriel delivered the word of God to Muḥammad. In the New Testament, he also announced to Mary that she would bear Jesus (Luke 1:26–38).

96. And you will find them greediest of mankind for life and (greedier) than the idolaters. (Each) one of them would like to be allowed to live a thousand years. And to live (a thousand years) would by no means remove him from the doom. God is observer of what they do.

97. Say (O Muḥammad, to mankind): "Who is an enemy to Gabriel! For he it is who has revealed (this scripture) to your heart by God's permission, confirming what was (revealed) before it, and a guidance and glad tidings to believers";

98. Who is an enemy to God, and His angels and His messengers, and Gabriel and Michael! Then, God (Himself) is an enemy to the disbelievers.

99. We have revealed to you clear signs, and only the iniquitous will disbelieve in them.

100. Whenever they make a covenant do a party of them set it aside? The truth is, most of them do not believe.

101. And when there comes to them a messenger from God, confirming what they possess, a party of those who have received the scripture fling the scripture of God behind their backs as if they did not know.

102. And follow what the devils falsely related against the kingdom of Solomon. Solomon did not disbelieve; but the devils disbelieved, teaching mankind magic and what was revealed to the two angels in Babel, Hārūt and Mārūt. They (the two angels) did not teach it to anyone until they had said: "We are only a temptation, therefore do not disbelieve (in the guidance of God)." And from these two (angels) people learn that by which they cause division between man and wife; but by it they injure no one except by God's permission. And they learn what harms them and does not profit them. And surely they do know that he who trades in it will have no (happy) portion in the hereafter; and surely evil is the price for which they sell their souls, if they only knew.[1]

103. And if they had believed and kept from evil, a recompense from God would be better, if they only knew.

104. O you who believe, do not say (to the Prophet): "Listen to us"[2] but say "Look upon us," and be listeners. For disbelievers there is a painful doom.

105. Neither those who disbelieve among the People of the Book[3] nor the idolaters love that there should be sent down to you any good thing from your Lord. But God chooses for His mercy whom He will, and God is of infinite bounty.

106. Such of Our revelations as We abrogate or cause to be forgotten, we bring (in place) one better or the like of it. Do you not know that God is able to do all things?

1. The reference is to the occult science practiced by the Jews, the origin of which was ascribed to Solomon [Pickthall's note]. In rabbinical literature and legend, the biblical King Solomon is said to have controlled demons and spirits.
2. A word which the Muslims used to call the Prophet's attention respectfully, *rā'ina*, the Jews could change into an insult by a slight mispronunciation. It is not clear in which language the insult was made but it was probably a double entendre in Hebrew, Syriac, or Aramaic [Pickthall's note].
3. I.e. Jews and Christians [Pickthall's note]. This expression, used chiefly in the Qur'ān for Jews and Christians as recipients of earlier revelations, was extended in later Islamic thought to certain other religious communities.

107. Do you not know that it is God to whom belongs the sovereignty of the heavens and earth; and you have not, beside God, any friend or helper?

108. Or would you question your messenger as Moses was questioned before? He who chooses disbelief instead of faith, truly he has gone astray from a plain road.

109. Many of the People of the Book long to make you disbelievers after your belief, through envy on their own account, after the truth has become manifest to them. Forgive and be indulgent (toward them) until God gives his command. God is able to do all things.

110. Establish worship, and pay the poor tax; and whatever of good you send before (you) for your souls, you will find it with God. God is observer of what you do.

111. And they say: "None enters Paradise unless he be a Jew or a Christian." These are their own desires. Say: "Bring your proof (of what you state) if you are truthful."

112. No, but whoever surrenders his purpose to God while doing good, his reward is with his Lord; and no fear shall come upon them neither shall they grieve.

113. And the Jews say the Christians follow nothing (true), and the Christians say the Jews follow nothing (true); yet both are readers of the scripture. Thus speak those who do not know. God will judge between them on the day of resurrection concerning that in which they differ.

114. And who does greater wrong than he who forbids the approach to the sanctuaries of God for fear that His name should be mentioned there, and strives for their ruin. As for such, it was never meant that they should enter them except in fear. Theirs in the world is ignominy and theirs in the hereafter is an awful doom.

115. To God belong the east and the west, and wherever you turn, there is God's countenance. God is all-embracing, all-knowing.

116. And they say: "God has taken to Himself a son. Be He glorified!" No, but whatever is in the heaven and the earth is His. All are subservient to Him.

117. The originator of the heavens and the earth! When He decrees a thing, He says to it only: "Be!" and it is.

118. And those who have no knowledge say: "Why does not God speak to us, or some sign come to us?" Even thus, as they now speak, those (who were) before them spoke. Their hearts are all alike. We have made clear the revelations for people who are sure.

119. We have sent you (O Muḥammad) with the truth, a bringer of glad tidings and a warner. And you will not be asked about the owners of hellfire.

120. And the Jews will not be pleased with you, nor will the Christians, until you follow their creed. Say: "The guidance of God (Himself) is guidance." And if you should follow their desires after the knowledge which has come to you, then you would have from God no protecting friend nor helper.

121. Those to whom We have given the scripture, who read it with the right reading, those believe in it. And whoever disbelieves in it, those are they who are the losers.

122. O Children of Israel! Remember My favor with which I favored you and how I preferred you to (all) creatures.

123. And guard (yourselves) against a day when no soul will avail another in anything, nor will compensation be accepted from it, nor will intercession be of use to it; nor will they be helped.

124. And (remember) when his Lord tried Abraham with (His) commands, and he fulfilled them, He said: "I have appointed you a leader for mankind." (Abraham) said: "And of my offspring (will there be leaders)?" He said: "My covenant does not include wrongdoers."

125. And when We made the house (at Mecca)[4] a resort for mankind and a sanctuary, (saying): "Take as your place of worship the place where Abraham stood (to pray)." And We imposed a duty upon Abraham and Ishmael, (saying): "Purify My house for those who go around and those who meditate there and those who bow down and prostrate themselves (in worship)."

126. And when Abraham prayed: "My Lord! Make this a region of security and bestow upon its people fruits, such of them as believe in God and the last day," He answered: "As for him who disbelieves, I shall leave him in contentment for a while, then I shall compel him to the doom of fire—an unfortunate journey's end!"

127. And when Abraham and Ishmael were raising the foundations of the house, (Abraham prayed): "Our Lord! Accept from us (this duty). You, only You, are the hearer, the knower.

128. "Our Lord! And make us submissive to You and of our seed a nation submissive to You, and show us our ways of worship, and relent toward us. You, only You, are the relenting, the merciful.

129. "Our Lord! And raise up in their midst a messenger from among them who shall recite to them Your revelations, and shall instruct them in the scripture and in wisdom and shall make them grow. You, only You, are the mighty, the wise."

130. And who forsakes the religion of Abraham except him who fools himself? We chose him in the world, and in the hereafter he is among the righteous.

131. When his Lord said to him: "Surrender!" he said: "I have surrendered to the Lord of the worlds."

132. The same did Abraham enjoin upon his sons, and also Jacob,[5] (saying): "O my sons! God has chosen for you the (true) religion; therefore do not die except as men who have surrendered (to Him)."

133. Or were you present when death came to Jacob, when he said to his sons: "What will you worship after me?" They said: "We shall worship your God, the God of your fathers, Abraham and Ishmael and Isaac, one God, and to Him we have surrendered."

134. Those are a people who have passed away. Theirs is what they earned, and yours is what you earn. And you will not be asked about what they used to do.

135. And they say: "Be Jews or Christians, then you will be rightly guided." Say (to them, O Muḥammad): "No, but (we follow) the religion of Abraham, the upright, and he was not of the idolaters."[6]

4. The Ka'ba, the stone shrine whose foundation is credited to Abraham.
5. Abraham's grandson, whose father was Isaac, his son born to his wife, Sarah; Ishmael was Abraham's older son, born to her servant Hagar (see Genesis 15–16, 21).
6. Abraham was called a *ḥanīf*—that is, an independent, "natural" monotheist, neither Jew nor Christian. The Qur'ān presents Islam as the continuation of this natural monotheism.

136. Say (O Muslims): "We believe in God and what is revealed to us and what was revealed to Abraham, and Ishmael, and Isaac, and Jacob, and the tribes, and what Moses and Jesus received, and what the prophets received from their Lord. We make no distinction among any of them,[7] and to Him we have surrendered."

137. And if they believe in the like of what you believe, then they are rightly guided. But if they turn away, then they are in schism, and God will suffice you (for defense) against them. He is the hearer, the knower.

138. (We take our) color[8] from God, and who is better than God at coloring? We are His worshippers.

139. Say (to the People of the Book): "Do you dispute with us concerning God when He is our Lord and your Lord? Ours are our works and yours your works. We look to Him alone.

140. "Or do you say that Abraham, and Ishmael, and Isaac, and Jacob, and the tribes were Jews or Christians?" Say: "Do you know best, or does God?" And who is more unjust than he who hides a testimony which he has received from God? God is not unaware of what you do.

141. Those are a people who have passed away; theirs is what they earned and yours what you earn. And you will not be asked about what they used to do.

142. The foolish of the people will say: "What has turned them from the *qibla*[9] which they formerly observed?" Say: "To God belong the east and the west. He guides whom He will to a straight path."

143. Thus We have appointed you a middle nation, that you may be witnesses against mankind, and that the messenger may be a witness against you. And We appointed the *qibla* which you formerly observed only that We might know him who follows the messenger, from him who turns on his heels. In truth it was a hard (test) except for those whom God guided. But it was not God's purpose that your faith should be in vain, for God is full of pity, merciful toward mankind.

144. We have seen the turning of your face to heaven (for guidance, O Muḥammad). And now We shall make you turn (in prayer) toward a *qibla* which is dear to you. So turn your face toward the inviolable place of worship,[1] and you (O Muslims), wherever you may be, turn your faces (when you pray) toward it. Those who have received the scripture know that (this revelation) is the truth from their Lord. And God is not unaware of what they do.

145. And even if you brought to those who have received the scripture all kinds of signs, they would not follow your *qibla*, nor can you be a follower of their *qibla*; nor are some of them followers of the *qibla* of others. And if you should follow their desires after the knowledge which has come to you, then surely you would be of the evildoers.

146. Those to whom We gave the scripture recognize (this revelation) as they recognize their sons. But a party of them knowingly conceal the truth.

7. The prophets.
8. The Arabic *ṣibgha* has the sense of "baptism," "color," or "dye." Though Qur'ānic commentators have speculated on its meaning, the ultimate interpretation remains unclear.
9. I.e. the place toward which the face is turned at prayer. The first *qibla* of the Muslims was Jerusalem, which gave rise to a misunderstanding on the part of the Jews of Medina, who wished to draw the Muslims into Judaism. This was the cause of the Prophet's anxiety mentioned in the next verse but one [Pickthall's note].
1. The Ka'ba at Mecca [Pickthall's note].

147. It is the truth from your Lord (O Muḥammad), so do not be of those who waver.

148. And each one has a goal toward which he turns; so vie with one another in good works. Wherever you may be, God will bring you all together. God is able to do all things.

149. And whenever you come forth (for prayer, O Muḥammad) turn your face toward the inviolable place of worship. It is the truth from your Lord. God is not unaware of what you do.

150. Whenever you come forth turn your face toward the inviolable place of worship; and wherever you may be (O Muslims) turn your faces toward it (when you pray) so that men may have no argument against you, except such of them as do injustice—fear them not, but fear Me!—and so that I may complete My grace upon you, and that you may be guided.

151. Even as We have sent to you a messenger from among you, who recites to you Our revelations and causes you to grow, and teaches you the scripture and wisdom, and teaches you what you did not know.

152. Therefore remember Me, I will remember you. Give thanks to Me, and do not reject Me.

153. O you who believe! Seek help in steadfastness and prayer. God is with the steadfast.

154. And do not call those who are slain in the way of God "dead." No, they are living, only you perceive not.[2]

155. And surely We shall try you with something of fear and hunger, and loss of wealth and lives and crops; but give glad tidings to the steadfast,

156. Who say, when a misfortune strikes them: "We are God's and to Him we are returning."

157. Such are they on whom are blessings from their Lord, and mercy. Such are the rightly guided.

158. (The mountains) al-Ṣafā and al-Marwa are among the indications of God. It is therefore no sin for him who is on pilgrimage to the house (of God)[3] or visits it, to go around them (as the pagan custom is). And he who does good of his own accord, (for him) God is responsive, aware.

159. Those who hide the proofs and the guidance which We revealed, after We had made it clear to mankind in the scripture: such are accursed of God and accursed of those who have the power to curse.

160. Except such of them as repent and amend and make manifest (the truth). These are they toward whom I relent. I am the relenting, the merciful.

161. Those who disbelieve, and die while they are disbelievers; on them is the curse of God and of angels and of men combined.

162. They dwell forever in it. The doom will not be lightened for them, neither will they be reprieved.

2. The Qur'ān presents those who died in the cause of God as martyrs. This verse is traditionally understood to indicate that such martyrs go directly to paradise, though others believed the martyrs merely abide near heaven until the day of judgment, at which time they will be admitted to paradise.

3. The pilgrimage, or *ḥajj*, to the Ka'ba in Mecca, which each Muslim is required to do once in his or her lifetime, if possible.

163. Your God is one god; there is no god except Him, the beneficent, the merciful.

164. In the creation of the heavens and the earth, and the difference of night and day, and the ships which run upon the sea with that which is of use to men, and the water which God sends down from the sky, thereby reviving the earth after its death, and dispersing all kinds of beasts in it, and (in) the ordinance of the winds, and the clouds obedient between heaven and earth: are signs (of God's sovereignty) for people who have sense.

165. Yet of mankind are some who take to themselves (objects of worship which they set as) rivals to God, loving them with a love like (what is the due) to God (only)—Those who believe are stauncher in their love for God—Oh, that those who do evil had only known, (on the day) when they behold the doom, that power belongs wholly to God, and that God is severe in punishment!

166. (On the day) when those who were followed disown those who followed (them), and they behold the doom, and all their aims collapse with them.

167. And those who were only followers will say: "If a return were possible for us, we would disown them even as they have disowned us." Thus will God show them their own deeds as anguish for them, and they will not emerge from the fire.

168. O mankind! Eat of what is lawful and wholesome on the earth, and do not follow the footsteps of the devil. He is an open enemy for you.

169. He enjoins on you only the evil and the foul, and that concerning God you should tell what you do not know.

170. And when it is said to them: "Follow what God has revealed," they say: "We follow that in which we found our fathers." What! Even though their fathers were wholly unintelligent and had no guidance?

171. The likeness of those who disbelieve (in relation to the messenger) is as the likeness of one who calls to what hears nothing except a shout and cry. Deaf, dumb, blind, therefore they have no sense.

172. O you who believe! Eat of the good things with which We have provided you, and render thanks to God if it is (indeed) He whom you worship.

173. He has forbidden you only carrion, and blood, and swine-flesh, and what has been immolated to (the name of) any other than God. But he who is driven by necessity, neither craving nor transgressing, it is no sin for him. God is forgiving, merciful.

174. Those who hide anything of the scripture which God has revealed, and thereby purchase a small gain, they eat into their bellies nothing else than fire. God will not speak to them on the day of resurrection, nor will He make them grow. Theirs will be a painful doom.

175. Those are they who purchase error at the price of guidance, and torment at the price of pardon. How constant are they in their strife to reach the fire!

176. That is because God has revealed the scripture with the truth. Those who find (a cause of) disagreement in the scripture are in open schism.

177. It is not righteousness that you turn your faces to the east and the west; but righteous is he who believes in God and the last day and the angels and the scripture and the prophets; and gives his wealth, for love of Him, to

kin and to orphans and the needy and the wayfarer and to those who ask, and to set slaves free; and observes proper worship and pays the poor tax. And those who keep their treaty when they make one, and the patient in tribulation and adversity and time of stress. Such are they who are sincere. Such are the God-fearing.

178. O you who believe! Retaliation is prescribed for you in the matter of the murdered; the freeman for the freeman, and the slave for the slave, and the female for the female. And for him who is forgiven somewhat by his (injured) brother, prosecution according to usage and payment to him in kindness. This is an alleviation and a mercy from your Lord. He who transgresses after this will have a painful doom.

179. And there is life for you in retaliation, O men of understanding, that you may ward off (evil).

180. It is prescribed for you, when death approaches one of you, if he leave wealth, that he bequeath to parents and near relatives in kindness. (This is) a duty for all those who ward off (evil).

181. And whoever changes (the will) after he heard it—the sin of it is only on those who change it. God is hearer, knower.

182. But he who fears from a testator[4] some unjust or sinful clause, and makes peace between the parties, (it shall be) no sin for him. God is forgiving, merciful.

183. O you who believe! Fasting is prescribed for you, even as it was prescribed for those before you, that you may ward off (evil);

184. (Fast) a certain number of days; and (for) him who is sick among you, or on a journey, (the same) number of other days; and for those who can afford it there is a ransom: the feeding of a man in need—But whoever does good of his own accord, it is better for him: and that you fast is better for you if you did but know—

185. The month of Ramaḍān in which was revealed the Qur'ān, a guidance for mankind, and clear proofs of the guidance, and the criterion (of right and wrong). And whoever of you is present, let him fast the month, and whoever of you is sick or on a journey, (let him fast the same) number of other days. God desires ease for you; He does not desire hardship for you; and (He desires) that you should complete the period, and that you should magnify God for having guided you, and that perhaps you may be thankful.

186. And when My servants question you concerning Me, then surely I am near. I answer the prayer of the suppliant when he cries to Me. So let them hear My call and let them trust in Me, in order that they may be led aright.

187. It is made lawful for you to go in to your wives on the night of the fast. They are garments for you and you are garments for them. God is aware that you were deceiving yourselves[5] in this respect and He has turned in mercy toward you and relieved you. So hold intercourse with them and seek what God has ordained for you, and eat and drink until the white thread becomes distinct to you from the black thread of the dawn. Then

4. A person who makes bequests.
5. Until this verse was revealed, the first Muslims used to fast from the evening meal of one day till the evening meal of the next. If they fell asleep before they had taken that meal they had considered it their duty to abstain from it, with the result that men fainted and came near to death. Intercourse with their wives had been similarly restricted [Pickthall's note].

strictly observe the fast until nightfall and do not touch them, but be at your devotions in the mosques. These are the limits imposed by God, so do not approach them. Thus God expounds His revelations to mankind that they may ward off (evil).

188. And do not eat up your property among yourselves in vanity, nor seek by it to gain the hearing of the judges that you may knowingly devour a portion of the property of others wrongfully.

189. They ask you, (O Muḥammad), of new moons. Say: "They are fixed seasons for mankind and for the pilgrimage." It is not righteousness that you go to houses by their backs (as do the idolaters at certain seasons), but the righteous man is he who wards off (evil). So go to houses by their gates, and observe your duty to God, that you may be successful.

190. Fight in the way of God against those who fight against you, but do not begin hostilities. God does not love aggressors.

191. And slay them wherever you find them, and drive them out of the places from which they drove you out, for persecution is worse than slaughter. And do not fight with them at the inviolable place of worship until they first attack you there, but if they attack you (there) then slay them. Such is the reward of disbelievers.

192. But if they desist, then God is forgiving, merciful.

193. And fight them until persecution is no more, and religion is for God. But if they desist, then let there be no hostility except against wrongdoers.

194. The forbidden month for the forbidden month, and forbidden things in retaliation.[6] And one who attacks you, attack him in like manner as he attacked you. Observe your duty to God, and know that God is with those who ward off (evil).

195. Spend your wealth for the cause of God, and do not be cast by your own hands to ruin; and do good. God loves the beneficent.

196. Perform the pilgrimage[7] and the visit (to Mecca)[8] for God. And if you are prevented, then send such gifts as can be obtained with ease, and do not shave your heads until the gifts have reached their destination. And whoever among you is sick or has an ailment of the head must pay a ransom of fasting or almsgiving or offering. And if you are in safety, then whoever contents himself with the visit for the pilgrimage (shall give) such gifts as can be had with ease. And whoever cannot find (such gifts), then a fast of three days while on the pilgrimage, and of seven when you have returned; that is, ten in all. That is for him whose people are not present at the inviolable place of worship. Observe your duty to God, and know that God is severe in punishment.

197. The pilgrimage is (in) the well-known months, and whoever is minded to perform the pilgrimage in them (let him remember that) there is (to be) no lewdness or abuse or angry conversation on the pilgrimage. And whatever good you do God knows it. So make provision for yourselves (hereafter); for the best provision is to ward off evil. Therefore keep your duty to Me, O men of understanding.

6. Certain months were considered sacred in the pre-Islamic society, and fighting was forbidden in them. This verse gave permission to Muslims to fight if attacked during the sacred months.
7. See also Q 22:26ff. [Pickthall's note].
8. The ʿ*umra*, or minor pilgrimage, which can be performed at any time of year and which takes place within the boundaries of the Great Mosque of Mecca.

198. It is no sin for you that you seek the bounty of your Lord (by trading). But, when you press on in the multitude from 'Arafāt,[9] remember God by the sacred monument. Remember Him as He has guided you, although before you were of those astray.

199. Then hasten onward from the place from which the multitude hastens onward, and ask forgiveness of God: God is forgiving, merciful.

200. And when you have completed your devotions, then remember God as you remember your fathers[1] or with a more lively remembrance. But of mankind is he who says: "Our Lord! Give to us in the world," and he has no portion in the hereafter.

201. And of them (also) is he who says: "Our Lord! Give to us in the world what is good and in the hereafter what is good, and guard us from the doom of fire."

202. For them there is in store a goodly portion out of what they have earned. God is swift at reckoning.

203. Remember God through the appointed days. Then whoever hastens (his departure) by two days, it is no sin for him, and whoever delays, it is no sin for him; that is for him who wards off (evil). Be careful of your duty to God, and know that to Him you will be gathered.

204. And of mankind there is he whose conversation on the life of this world pleases you (Muḥammad), and he called God to witness as to what is in his heart; yet he is the most rigid of opponents.

205. And when he turns away (from you) his effort in the land is to make mischief in it and to destroy the crops and the cattle; and God does not love mischief.

206. And when it is said to him: "Be careful of your duty to God," pride takes him to sin. Hell will settle his account, an evil resting-place.

207. And of mankind is he who would sell himself, seeking the pleasure of God; and God has compassion on (His) servants.

208. O you who believe! Come, all of you, into submission (to Him); and do not follow the footsteps of the devil. He is an open enemy for you.

209. And if you slide back after the clear proofs have come to you, then know that God is mighty, wise.

210. Do they wait for nothing else than that God should come to them in the shadows of the clouds with the angels? Then the case would be already judged. All cases go back to God (for judgment).

211. Ask of the Children of Israel how many clear revelations We gave them! He who alters the grace of God after it has come to him, God is severe in punishment.

212. The life of the world is beautified for those who disbelieve; they make a jest of the believers. But those who keep their duty to God will be above them on the day of resurrection. God gives without stint to whom He will.

213. Mankind was one community, and God sent (to them) prophets as bearers of good tidings and as warners, and with them revealed the scripture with the truth that it might judge between mankind concerning that in which they differed. And only those to whom (the scripture) was given

9. A plain and low mountain about 13 miles east of Mecca; it is a key station in the pilgrimage ritual.

1. It was the custom of the pagan Arabs to praise their forefathers at the conclusion of the pilgrimage [Pickthall's note].

differed concerning it, after clear proofs had come to them, through hatred of one another. And God by His will guided those who believe to the truth of that concerning which they differed. God guides whom He will to a straight path.

214. Or do you think that you will enter paradise while there has not yet come to you the like of (what came to) those who passed away before you? Affliction and adversity befell them, they were shaken as with earthquake, until the messenger (of God) and those who believed along with him said: "When does God's help come?" Now surely God's help is near.

215. They ask you, (O Muḥammad), what they shall spend. Say: "What you spend for good (must go) to parents and near relatives and orphans and the needy and the wayfarer. And whatever good you do, God is aware of it.

216. "Warfare is ordained for you, though it is hateful to you; but it may happen that you hate a thing which is good for you, and it may happen that you love a thing which is bad for you. God knows, you do not know."

217. They question you (O Muḥammad) with regard to warfare in the sacred month. Say: "Warfare in it is a great (transgression), but to turn (men) from the way of God, and to disbelieve in Him and in the inviolable place of worship, and to expel His people from there, is a greater (transgression) with God; for persecution is worse than killing." And they will not cease from fighting against you until they have made you renegades from your religion, if they can. And whoever becomes a renegade and dies in his disbelief: such are they whose works have fallen both in the world and the hereafter. Such are rightful owners of the fire: they will abide there.

218. Those who believe, and those who emigrate (to escape the persecution) and strive in the way of God, these have hope of God's mercy. God is forgiving, merciful.

219. They question you about strong drink and games of chance. "Say: In both is great sin, and (some) utility for men; but the sin of them is greater than their usefulness." And they ask you what they ought to spend. Say: "That which is superfluous." Thus God makes plain to you (His) revelations, that perhaps you may reflect

220. Upon the world and the hereafter. And they question you concerning orphans. Say: "To improve their lot is best. And if you mingle your affairs with theirs, then (they are) your brothers." God knows him who spoils from him who improves. Had God willed He could have overburdened you. God is mighty, wise.

221. Do not wed idolatresses until they believe; for a believing slave woman is better than an idolatress though she please you; and do not give your daughters in marriage to idolaters until they believe, for a believing slave is better than an idolater though he please you. These invite to the fire, and God invites to the garden, and to forgiveness by His grace, and expounds thus His revelations to mankind that perhaps they may remember.

222. They question you (O Muḥammad) concerning menstruation. "Say: It is an illness,[2] so let women alone at such times and do not go in to them until they are cleansed. And when they have purified themselves, then go in to them as God has enjoined upon you." Truly God loves those who turn to Him, and loves those who have a care for cleanness.

2. A translation of *adhan*, which conveys a range of meanings from "harm" to "nuisance."

223. Your women are a tilth for you (to cultivate) so go to your tilth as you will, and send (good deeds) before you for your souls, and fear God, and know that you will (one day) meet Him. Give glad tidings to believers, (O Muḥammad).

224. And by your oaths, do not make God a hindrance to your being righteous and observing your duty to Him and making peace among mankind. God is hearer, knower.

225. God will not take you to task for what is unintentional in your oaths. But He will take you to task for what your hearts have garnered. God is forgiving, clement.

226. Those who renounce their wives must wait four months; then, if they change their mind, God is forgiving, merciful.

227. And if they decide upon divorce (let them remember that) God is hearer, knower.

228. Women who are divorced shall wait, keeping themselves apart, three (monthly) courses. And it is not lawful for them that they should conceal what God has created in their wombs if they are believers in God and the last day. And their husbands would do better to take them back in that case if they desire a reconciliation. And they (women) have rights similar to those (of men) over them in kindness, and men are a degree above them.[3] God is mighty, wise.

229. Divorce must be pronounced twice and then (a woman) must be retained in honor or released in kindness. And it is not lawful for you that you take from women anything of what you have given them; except (in the case) when both fear that they may not be able to keep within the limits (imposed by) God.[4] And if you fear that they may not be able to keep the limits of God, in that case it is no sin for either of them if the woman ransom herself. These are the limits (imposed by) God. Do not transgress them. For whoever transgresses God's limits: such are wrongdoers.

230. And if he has divorced her (the third time), then she is not lawful to him thereafter until she has wedded another husband. Then if he (the other husband) divorce her it is no sin for both of them that they come together again if they consider that they are able to observe the limits of God. These are the limits of God. He manifests them for people who have knowledge.

231. When you have divorced women, and they have reached their term, then retain them in kindness or release them in kindness. Do not retain them to their harm so that you transgress (the limits). He who does that has wronged his soul. Do not make the revelations of God a jest (by your behavior), but remember God's grace upon you and what He has revealed to you of the scripture and of wisdom, by which He does exhort you. Observe your duty to God and know that God is aware of all things.

232. And when you have divorced women and they reach their term, do not place difficulties in the way of their marrying their husbands if it is agreed between them in kindness. This is an admonition for him among you who believes in God and the last day. That is more virtuous for you, and cleaner. God knows: you know not.

3. The word here translated as "degree above" (*daraja*) has generated disagreement among commentators: some stress innate gender differences, while others refer to the heavier financial responsibilities that men ordinarily incurred.

4. That is, in the Qur'ān, the limits of acceptable behavior, particularly in marital or family relationships.

233. Mothers shall suckle their children for two whole years; (that is) for those who wish to complete the suckling. The duty of feeding and clothing nursing mothers in a seemly manner is upon the father of the child. No one should be charged beyond his capacity. A mother should not be made to suffer because of her child, nor should he to whom the child is born (be made to suffer) because of his child. And on the (father's) heir is incumbent the like of that (which was incumbent on the father). If they desire to wean the child by mutual consent and (after) consultation, it is no sin for them; and if you wish to give your children out to nurse, it is no sin for you, provided that you pay what is due from you in kindness. Observe your duty to God, and know that God is observer of what you do.

234. Such of you as die and leave behind them wives, they (the wives) shall wait, keeping themselves apart, four months and ten days. And when they reach the term (prescribed for them) then there is no sin for you in anything that they may do with themselves in decency. God is informed of what you do.

235. There is no sin for you in what you proclaim or hide in your minds concerning your marriage proposal with women. God knows that you will remember them. But do not propose marriage with women except by uttering a recognized form of words. And do not consummate the marriage until (the term) prescribed is run. Know that God knows what is in your minds, so beware of Him; and know that God is forgiving, clement.

236. It is no sin for you if you divorce women while you have not yet touched them, nor appointed for them a portion. Provide for them, the rich according to his means, and the poor according to his means, a fair provision. (This is) a duty for those who do good.

237. If you divorce them before you have touched them and you have appointed to them a portion, then (pay the) half of what you appointed, unless they (the women) agree to forgo it, or he agrees to forgo it in whose hand is the marriage tie.[5] To forgo is nearer to piety. And do not forget kindness among yourselves. God is observer of what you do.

238. Be guardians of your prayers, and of the middle prayer,[6] and stand up with devotion to God.

239. And if you go in fear, then (pray) standing or mounted. And when you are again in safety, remember God, as He has taught you what (before) you did not know.

240. (In the case of) those of you who are about to die and leave behind them wives, they should bequeath to their wives a provision for the year without turning them out, but if they go out (of their own accord) there is no sin for you in what they do of themselves within their rights. God is mighty, wise.

241. For divorced women a provision in kindness: a duty for those who ward off (evil).

242. Thus God expounds to you His revelations so that you may understand.

243. Do you think (O Muḥammad) of those of old, who went forth from their habitations in their thousands, fearing death,[7] and God said to

5. I.e. the bridegroom [Pickthall's note].
6. Meaning, probably, the best amid all forms of prayer; but some authorities think the reference is to the *'asr* (afternoon) prayer, which Muslims are most apt to forget [Pickthall's note].
7. The reference is to the Israelite Exodus from Egypt [Pickthall's note].

them: "Die"; and then He brought them back to life? God is a Lord of kindness to mankind, but most of mankind do not give thanks.

244. Fight in the way of God, and know that God is hearer, knower.

245. Who is it that will lend to God a goodly loan,[8] so that He may give it manifold increase? God restricts and enlarges. To Him you will return.

246. Do you think of the leaders of the Children of Israel after Moses, how they said to a prophet[9] whom they had: "Set up for us a king and we will fight in God's way?" He said: "Would you then refrain from fighting if fighting were prescribed for you?" They said: "Why should we not fight in God's way when we have been driven from our dwellings with our children?" Yet, when fighting was prescribed for them, they turned away, all except a few of them. God is aware of evildoers.

247. Their prophet said to them: "God has raised up Saul to be a king for you." They said: "How can he have kingdom over us when we are more deserving of the kingdom than he is, since he has not been given wealth enough?" He said: "God has chosen him above you, and has increased him abundantly in wisdom and stature." God bestows His sovereignty on whom He will. God is all-embracing, all-knowing.

248. And their prophet said to them: "The sign of his kingdom is that there shall come to you the ark in which is peace of reassurance from your Lord, and a remnant of what the house of Moses and the house of Aaron left behind, the angels bearing it. In this shall be a sign for you if (in truth) you are believers."

249. And when Saul set out with the army, he said: "God will try you by (the ordeal of) a river. Whoever therefore drinks of it he is not of me, and whoever does not taste it, he is of me, except him who takes (of it) in the hollow of his hand." But they drank of it, all except a few of them. And after he had crossed (the river), he and those who believed with him, they said: "We have no power this day against Goliath and his hosts." But those who knew that they would meet their Lord exclaimed: "How many a little company has overcome a mighty host by God's leave!" is with the steadfast.

250. And when they went into the field against Goliath and his hosts they said: "Our Lord! Bestow on us endurance, make our foothold sure, and give us help against the disbelieving people."

251. So they routed them by God's leave and David slew Goliath;[1] and God gave him the kingdom and wisdom, and taught him of what He wills. And if God had not repelled some men by others the earth would have been corrupted. But God is a Lord of kindness to (His) creatures.

252. These are the signs of God which We recite to you (Muḥammad) with truth, and you are one of (Our) messengers;

253. Of those messengers, some of whom We have caused to excel others, and of whom there are some to whom God spoke, while some of them He exalted (above others) in degree; and We gave Jesus, son of Mary, clear proofs (of God's sovereignty) and We supported him with the holy spirit.[2] And if God had so willed it, those who followed after them would not have fought one another after the clear proofs had come to them. But they differed, some of

8. A loan without interest—i.e. without thought of gain [Pickthall's note].
9. Traditionally held to be Samuel.
1. See 1 Samuel 17.
2. I.e. the angel Gabriel [Pickthall's note]. See Luke 1:26–38.

them believing and some disbelieving. And if God had so willed it, they would not have fought one another; but God does what He will.

254. O you who believe! Spend of what We have provided you before a day comes when there will be no buying and selling, nor friendship, nor intercession. The disbelievers, they are the wrongdoers.

255. God! There is no god except Him, the alive, the eternal. Neither slumber nor sleep overtakes Him. To Him belongs whatever is in the heavens and whatever is on the earth. Who is he that intercedes with Him except by His leave? He knows what is in front of them and what is behind them, while they encompass nothing of His knowledge except what He will. His throne includes the heavens and the earth, and He is never weary of preserving them. He is the sublime, the tremendous.

256. There is no compulsion in religion. The right direction is distinct from error. And he who rejects false deities[3] and believes in God has grasped a firm handhold[4] which will never break. God is hearer, knower.

257. God is the protecting friend of those who believe. He brings them out of darkness into light. As for those who disbelieve, their patrons are false deities. They bring them out of light into darkness. Such are rightful owners of the fire. They will abide in it.

258. Think of him who had an argument with Abraham about his Lord, because God had given him the kingdom; how, when Abraham said: "My Lord is He who gives life and causes death," he answered: "I give life and cause death." Abraham said: "God causes the sun to rise in the east, so do you cause it to come up from the west." Thus was the disbeliever abashed. And God does not guide wrongdoing people.

259. Or (think of) one who, passing by a township which had fallen into utter ruin, exclaimed: "How shall God give this township[5] life after its death?" And God made him die a hundred years, then brought him back to life. He said: "How long have you lingered?" (The man) said: "I have lingered a day or part of a day." (He) said: "No, but you have lingered for a hundred years. Just look at your food and drink which have not rotted! Look at your donkey!" And, that We may make you a sign to mankind, look at the bones, how We adjust them and then cover them with flesh! And when (the matter) became clear to him, he said: "I know now that God is able to do all things."

260. And when Abraham said (to his Lord): "My Lord! Show me how You give life to the dead," He said: "Do you not believe?" Abraham said: "Yes, but (I ask) in order that my heart may be at ease." (His Lord) said: "Take four of the birds and cause them to incline to you, then place a part of them on each hill, then call them, they will come to you in haste. And know that God is mighty, wise."

261. The likeness of those who spend their wealth in God's way is as the likeness of a grain which grows seven ears, in every ear a hundred grains. God gives manifold increase to whom He will. God is all-embracing, all-knowing.

3. Arabic *ṭāghūt*.
4. The phrase *Al-ʿurwa al-wuthqā* (*Firm Handhold* or *Firm Handle*) was used as the title of a noted Egyptian modernist journal in the first part of the 20th century.
5. Most of the commentators agree that the reference here is to Jerusalem in ruins, while the following words tell of the vision of Ezekiel [Pickthall's note]. See Ezekiel 37.

262. Those who spend their wealth for the cause of God and afterward do not make reproach and injury to follow what they have spent; their reward is with their Lord, and no fear shall come upon them, neither shall they grieve.

263. A kind word with forgiveness is better than almsgiving followed by injury. God is absolute, clement.

264. O you who believe! Do not render your almsgiving vain by reproach and injury, like him who spends his wealth only to be seen by men and does not believe in God and the last day. His likeness is as the likeness of a rock on which is dust of earth; a rainstorm strikes it, leaving it smooth and bare. They have no control of anything of what they have gained. God does not guide the disbelieving people.

265. And the likeness of those who spend their wealth in search of God's pleasure, and for the strengthening of their souls, is as the likeness of a garden on a height. The rainstorm strikes it and it brings forth its fruit twofold. And if the rainstorm does not strike it, then the shower. God is observer of what you do.

266. Would any of you like to have a garden of palm trees and vines, with rivers flowing underneath it, with all kinds of fruit for him in it; and old age has stricken him and he has feeble offspring; and a fiery whirlwind strikes it and it is (all) consumed by fire. Thus God makes plain His revelations to you, in order that you may give thought.

267. O you who believe! Spend of the good things which you have earned, and of what We bring forth from the earth for you, and do not seek the bad (with intent) to spend of it (in charity) when you would not take it for yourselves except with disdain; and know that God is absolute, owner of praise.

268. The devil promises you destitution and enjoins on you lewdness. But God promises you forgiveness from Himself with bounty. God is all-embracing, all-knowing.

269. He gives wisdom to whom He will, and he to whom wisdom is given, he truly has received abundant good. But none remember except men of understanding.

270. Whatever alms you spend or vow you take, God knows it. Wrong-doers have no helpers.

271. If you publish your almsgiving, it is well, but if you hide it and give it to the poor, it will be better for you, and will atone for some of your ill deeds. God is informed of what you do.

272. The guiding of them is not your duty (O Muḥammad), but God guides whom He will. And whatever good thing you spend, it is for yourselves, when you spend only in search of God's countenance; and whatever good thing you spend, it will be repaid to you in full, and you will not be wronged.

273. (Alms are) for the poor who are restricted for the cause of God, who cannot travel in the land (for trade). The unthinking man counts them wealthy because of their restraint. You shall know them by their mark: They do not beg of men with importunity. And whatever good thing you spend, God knows it.

274. Those who spend their wealth by night and day, by stealth and openly, truly their reward is with their Lord, and no fear shall come upon them, neither shall they grieve.

275. Those who swallow usury cannot rise up except as he whom the devil has prostrated by (his) touch arises. That is because they say: Trade is just like usury; whereas God permits trading and forbids usury. He to whom an admonition from his Lord comes, and (he) refrains (in obedience of it), he shall keep (the profits of) what is past, and his affair (thereafter) is with God. As for him who returns (to usury)—Such are rightful owners of the fire. They will abide there.

276. God has blighted usury and made almsgiving fruitful. God does not love the impious and guilty.

277. Those who believe and do good works and establish worship and pay the poor tax, their reward is with their Lord and no fear shall come upon them neither shall they grieve.

278. O you who believe! Observe your duty to God, and give up what remains (due to you) from usury, if you are (in truth) believers.

279. And if you do not, then be warned of war (against you) from God and His messenger. And if you repent, then you have your principal (without interest). Do not wrong, and you shall not be wronged.

280. And if the debtor is in restricted circumstances, then (let there be) postponement to (the time of) ease; and that you remit the debt as almsgiving would be better for you if you only knew.

281. And guard yourselves against a day in which you will be brought back to God. Then every soul will be paid in full what it has earned, and they will not be wronged.

282. O you who believe! When you contract a debt for a fixed term, record it in writing. Let a scribe record it in writing between you in (terms of) equity. No scribe should refuse to write as God has taught him, so let him write, and let him who incurs the debt dictate, and let him observe his duty to God his Lord, and diminish nothing of it. But if he who owes the debt is of low understanding, or weak, or unable himself to dictate, then let the guardian of his interests dictate in (terms of) equity. And call to witness, from among your men, two witnesses. And if two men are not (at hand) then a man and two women, of such as you approve as witnesses, so that if the one errs (through forgetfulness) the other will remember. And the witnesses must not refuse when they are summoned. Do not be averse to writing down (the contract) whether it be small or great, with (record of) its term. That is more equitable in the sight of God and more sure for testimony, and the best way of avoiding doubt between you; except in the case when it is actual merchandise which you transfer among yourselves from hand to hand. In that case it is no sin for you if you do not write it. And have witnesses when you sell to one another, and let no harm be done to scribe or witness. If you do (harm to them) it is a sin in you. Observe your duty to God. God is teaching you. And God is knower of all things.

283. If you are on a journey and cannot find a scribe, then a pledge in hand (shall suffice). And if one of you entrusts to another let him who is trusted deliver what is entrusted to him (according to the pact between them) and let him observe his duty to God his Lord. Do not hide testimony. He who hides it, his heart is sinful. God is aware of what you do.

284. To God (belongs) whatever is in the heavens and whatever is on the earth; and whether you make known what is in your minds or hide it, God will bring you to account for it. He will forgive whom He will and He will punish whom He will. God is able to do all things.

285. The messenger believes in what has been revealed to him from his Lord and (so do) the believers. Each one believes in God and His angels and His scriptures and His messengers—we make no distinction between any of His messengers—and they say: "We hear, and we obey. (Grant us) Your forgiveness, our Lord. To You is the journeying."

286. God does not task a soul beyond its scope. For it (is only) what it has earned, and against it (only) what it has deserved. Our Lord! Do not condemn us if we forget, or miss the mark! Our Lord! Do not lay on us such a burden as You laid on those before us! Our Lord! Do not impose on us what we have not the strength to bear! Pardon us, absolve us and have mercy on us, You, our protector, and give us victory over the disbelieving people.

## Sūra 3

*Al ʿImrān* takes its title from verse 33, where "the family of ʿImrān" (the father of Moses) occurs as a generic name for all the Hebrew prophets from Moses to John the Baptist and Jesus Christ. This, with the mention of the mother of Mary as "the wife of ʿImrān" (verse 35), and the words "sister of Aaron" addressed to Mary (Q 19:28), has given rise to a charge of anachronism—absurd because the whole of the rest of the Qur'ān is against it—by Muir[1] and other non-Muslim writers, who say that the Prophet confused Mary, the mother of Jesus, with Miriam, the sister of Moses. Most Muslims believe, on the authority of the Qur'ān, that the grandfather of Jesus Christ was named ʿImrān, which may also have been the name of the father of Moses. In Q 19:28, where Mary is addressed as "sister of Aaron," they hold the ancestral sense to be the more probable, while denying that there is any reason to suppose that the Virgin Mary did not have a brother named Aaron.

If verses 1 to 34 were, as tradition states, revealed on the occasion of the deputation from the Christians of Najrān, which took place in the tenth year of the *hijra* ("the year of deputations," as it is called), then they are of much later date than the rest of the sūra, but it seems possible that they were only recited by the Prophet on that occasion, having been revealed before.

The Jews have become bolder and more bitter in opposition which, as Nöldeke[2] points out, cannot have been the case, after the signal victory of Badr, until after the Muslims suffered a reverse at Uḥud, a battle to which verses 120 to 188 largely refer.

In the third year of the *hijra* (625) the Meccans came against Medina with an army of 3,000 men to avenge their defeat at Badr in the previous year, and to wipe out the Muslims. The Prophet, against his own first plan, which was to defend Medina, at the insistence of his Companions, went out to meet them on Mt. Uḥud, posting his men carefully. He led an army of 1,000 men, a third of whom under ʿAbdallāh ibn Ubayy (the "Hypocrite" leader) deserted him before the battle, and said afterward that they did not think there would be any fighting that day. The battle began well for the Muslims but was changed to something near defeat by the disobedience of a band of fifty archers placed to guard a certain point. Seeing the Muslims winning, they feared that they might lose their share of the spoils, and ran to join the others, leaving a way open for the Meccan cavalry. The idolaters then rallied and inflicted considerable loss upon the Muslims, the Prophet himself being wounded in the struggle. A cry arose that the Prophet had been slain, and the Muslims

1. William Muir (1819–1905), Scottish Islamicist and colonial administrator in India.
2. Theodor Nöldeke (1836–1930), German Orientalist and author of *The History of the Qur'an* (1860).

were in despair until someone recognized the Prophet and cried out that he was living. The Muslims then rallied to his side, and retired in some sort of order. The army of Quraysh also retired after the battle.

In this battle the wives of the leaders of Quraysh, who had been brought with the army to give courage by their presence and their chanting, mutilated the Muslim slain, making necklaces and bracelets of ears and noses. Hind, the wife of Abū Sufyān, plucked out the liver of the Prophet's uncle, Ḥamza, publicly, and tried to eat it. The Prophet, when he saw the condition of the slain, was moved to vow reprisals. But he was relieved of his vow by a revelation, and mutilation was forbidden to the Muslims.

On the day after the battle of Mt. Uḥud, the Prophet again went out with such of the army as survived, in order that Quraysh might hear that he was in the field and perhaps be deterred from any project of attacking Medina in its weakened state. On that occasion many wounded men went out with him. Tradition tells how a friendly nomad met the Muslims and afterward met the army of Quraysh. Questioned by Abū Sufyān, he said that the Prophet was seeking vengeance with an overwhelming force; and that report determined Abū Sufyān to march back to Mecca.

The period of revelation is the third and fourth years of the *hijra*.

## The Family of ʿImrān

*Revealed at Medina*

In the name of God, the beneficent, the merciful.

1. Alif. Lām. Mīm.

2. God! There is no god except Him, the alive, the eternal.

3. He has revealed to you (Muḥammad) the scripture with truth, confirming what was (revealed) before it, even as He revealed the Torah and the Gospel

4. Before, for a guidance to mankind; and has revealed the criterion (of right and wrong). Those who disbelieve the revelations of God, theirs will be a heavy doom. God is mighty, able to requite (the wrong).

5. Nothing on the earth or in the heavens is hidden from God.

6. He it is who fashions you in the wombs as pleases Him. There is no god except Him, the almighty, the wise.

7. He it is who has revealed to you (Muḥammad) the scripture in which are clear revelations—they are the substance of the book—and others (which are) allegorical. But those in whose hearts is doubt pursue what is allegorical seeking (to cause) dissension by seeking to explain it. None knows its explanation except God. And those who are of sound instruction say: "We believe in it; the whole is from our Lord"; but only men of understanding really heed.[3]

8. Our Lord! Do not cause our hearts to stray after You have guided us, and bestow upon us mercy from Your presence. You, only You are the bestower.

9. Our Lord! It is You who gathers mankind together to a day of which there is no doubt. God does not fail to keep the meeting.

3. This is among the most important verses in the Qurʾān for establishing the principles of its interpretation. Commentators have paid particular attention to the terms here translated as "clear" and "allegorical," and to the location of the break between the final two sentences. Some prefer the reading: "None knows its explanation except God and those who are of sound instruction."

10. (On that day) neither the riches nor the progeny of those who disbelieve will avail them anything with God. They will be fuel for fire.

11. Like Pharaoh's people and those who were before them, they disbelieved Our revelations and so God seized them for their sins. And God is severe in punishment.

12. Say (O Muḥammad) to those who disbelieve: "You shall be overcome and gathered to hell, an evil resting-place."

13. There was a sign for you in two hosts which met:[4] one army fighting in the way of God, and another disbelieving, whom they saw as twice their number, clearly, with their very eyes. Thus God strengthens with His succor whom He will. In this is a lesson for those who have eyes.

14. Beautified for mankind is love of the joys (that come) from women and offspring, and stored-up heaps of gold and silver, and horses branded (with their mark), and cattle and land. That is comfort of the life of the world. God! With Him is a more excellent abode.

15. Say: "Shall I inform you of something better than that? For those who keep from evil, with their Lord, are gardens underneath which rivers flow, and pure companions, and contentment from God. God is observer of His servants,

16. "Those who say: 'Our Lord! We believe. So forgive us our sins and guard us from the punishment of fire';

17. "The steadfast, and the truthful, and the obedient, those who spend (and do not hoard), those who pray for pardon in the watches of the night."

18. God (Himself) is witness that there is no god but Him. And the angels and the men of learning (too are witness). Maintaining His creation in justice, there is no god but Him, the almighty, the wise.

19. Religion with God (is) the surrender[5] (to His will and guidance). Those who (formerly) received the scripture differed only after knowledge came to them, through transgression among themselves. Whoever disbelieves the revelations of God (will find that) God is swift at reckoning.

20. And if they argue with you, (O Muḥammad), say: "I have surrendered my purpose to God and (so have) those who follow me." And say to those who have received the scripture and those who do not read: "Have you (too) surrendered?" If they surrender, then truly they are rightly guided, and if they turn away, then it is your duty only to convey the message (to them). God is observer of (His) servants.

21. Those who disbelieve the revelations of God, and slay the Prophets wrongfully, and slay those of mankind who enjoin equity: promise them a painful doom.

22. Those are they whose works have failed in the world and the hereafter; and they have no helpers.

23. Have you not seen how those who have received a portion of the scripture invoke the scripture of God (in their disputes) that it may judge between them; then a faction of them turn away, being opposed (to it)?

24. That is because they say: "The fire will not touch us except for a certain number of days." What they used to invent has deceived them regarding their religion.

4. The reference is to the battle of Badr [623 CE; Pickthall's note].
5. This is a translation of the Arabic *al-islām*, which is also frequently translated as "submission" [Pickthall's note].

25. How (will it be with them) when We have brought them all together to a day of which there is no doubt, when every soul will be paid in full what it has earned, and they will not be wronged?

26. Say: "O God! Owner of sovereignty! You give sovereignty to whom You will, and You withdraw sovereignty from whom You will. You exalt whom You will, and You abase whom You will. In Your hand is the good. You are able to do all things.

27. "You cause the night to pass into the day, and You cause the day to pass into the night. And You bring forth the living from the dead, and You bring forth the dead from the living. And You give sustenance to whom You choose, without stint."

28. Let not the believers take disbelievers for their friends in preference to believers. Whoever does that has no connection with God unless (it be) that you only guard yourselves against them, taking (as it were) security. God bids you beware (only) of Himself. To God is the journeying.

29. Say, (O Muḥammad): "Whether you hide what is in your breasts or reveal it, God knows it. He knows what is in the heavens and what is on the earth, and God is able to do all things."

30. On the day when every soul will find itself confronted with all that it has done of good and all that it has done of evil (every soul) will long that there might be a mighty space of distance between it and that (evil). God bids you beware of Him. And God is full of pity for (His) servants.

31. Say, (O Muḥammad, to mankind): "If you love God, follow me; God will love you and forgive you your sins. God is forgiving, merciful."

32. Say: "Obey God and the messenger." But if they turn away, God does not love the disbelievers (in His guidance).

33. God preferred Adam and Noah and the family of Abraham and the family of 'Imrān[6] above (all His) creatures.

34. They were descendants of one another. God is hearer, knower.

35. (Remember) when the wife[7] of 'Imrān said: "My Lord! I have vowed to You what is in my belly as a consecrated (offering). Accept it from me. You, only you, are the hearer, the knower!"

36. And when she was delivered she said: "My Lord! I am delivered of a female—God knew best of what she was delivered—the male is not as the female; and I have named her Mary, and I crave Your protection for her and for her offspring from Satan the outcast."

37. And her Lord accepted her with full acceptance and granted to her a goodly growth; and made Zachariah her guardian. Whenever Zachariah went into the sanctuary where she was, he found that she had food. He said: "O Mary! From where does this (food) come to you?" She answered: "It is from God. God gives without stint to whom He will."

38. Then Zachariah prayed to his Lord and said: "My Lord! Bestow on me of Your bounty goodly offspring. You are the hearer of prayer."

39. And the angels called to him as he stood praying in the sanctuary: "God gives you glad tidings of (a son whose name is) John,[8] (who comes) to confirm a word from God, lordly, chaste, a prophet of the righteous."

6. The biblical 'Amrām, father of Moses and Aaron.
7. The identities of 'Imrān, of his wife, of Zachariah (i.e. Zechariah), and of Mary in these and subsequent verses are debated. Muslim scholars have argued for several different figures who shared these names, while Western scholars have suggested figures from other biblical accounts with whom they might be conflated.
8. Arabic Yaḥyā [Pickthall's note].

40. He said: "My Lord! How can I have a son when age has overtaken me already and my wife is barren?" (The angel) answered: "So (it will be). God does what He will."

41. He said: "My Lord! Appoint a sign for me." (The angel) said: "The sign to you (shall be) that You shall not speak to mankind three days except by signs. Remember your Lord much, and praise (Him) in the early hours of night and morning."

42. And when the angels said: "O Mary! God has chosen you and made you pure, and has preferred you above (all) the women of creation.[9]

43. "O Mary! Be obedient to your Lord, prostrate yourself and bow with those who bow (in worship)."

44. This is of the tidings of things hidden. We reveal it to you (Muḥammad). You were not present with them when they threw their pens (to know) which of them should be the guardian of Mary,[1] nor were you present with them when they quarreled (about it).

45. (And remember) when the angels said: "O Mary! God gives you glad tidings of a word from Him, whose name is the Messiah, Jesus, son of Mary, illustrious in the world and the hereafter, and one of those brought near (to God).

46. "He will speak to mankind in his cradle and in his manhood, and he is of the righteous."

47. She said: "My Lord! How can I have a child when no mortal has touched me?" He said: "So (it will be). God creates what He will. If He decrees a thing, He says to it only: 'Be!' and it is.

48. "And He will teach him the scripture and wisdom, and the Torah[2] and the Gospel.

49. "And will make him a messenger to the children of Israel, (saying): "I come to you with a sign from your Lord. I fashion for you out of clay the likeness of a bird, and I breathe into it and it is a bird, by God's permission. I heal him who was born blind, and the leper, and I raise the dead, by God's permission.[3] And I announce to you what you eat and what you store up in your houses. In this is a sign for you, if you are to be believers.

50. "And (I come) confirming what was before me of the Torah, and to make lawful some of what was forbidden to you. I come to you with a sign from your Lord, so keep your duty to God and obey me.

51. "God is my Lord and your Lord, so worship Him. That is a straight path."

52. But when Jesus became conscious of their disbelief, he cried: "Who will be my helpers in the cause of God?" The disciples said: "We will be God's helpers. We believe in God, and bear you witness that we have surrendered[4] (to Him).

53. "Our Lord! We believe in what You have revealed and we follow him whom You have sent. Enroll us among those who witness (to the truth)."

54. And they (the disbelievers) schemed, and God schemed (against them): and God is the best of schemers.

9. Shī'ī commentators use this verse to extol the virtues of Fātima, daughter of Muḥammad and wife of the first imām, 'Alī ibn Abī Ṭālib (ca. 599–661).
1. Lots were cast by the temple priests. As a result, her uncle, the prophet Zechariah (also father of John the Baptist), became her guardian.
2. The first five books of the Hebrew Bible, traditionally ascribed to Moses.
3. These accounts are related to those in certain noncanonical gospels.
4. Or "are Muslims" [Pickthall's note].

55. (And remember) when God said: "O Jesus! I am gathering you and causing you to ascend to Me, and am cleansing you of those who disbelieve and am setting those who follow you above those who disbelieve until the Day of Resurrection. Then to Me you will (all) return, and I shall judge between you about that in which you used to differ.

56. "As for those who disbelieve I shall chastise them with a heavy chastisement in the world and the hereafter; and they will have no helpers."

57. And as for those who believe and do good works, He will pay them their wages in full. God does not love wrongdoers.

58. This (which) We recite to you is a revelation and a wise reminder.

59. The likeness of Jesus with God is as the likeness of Adam. He created him of dust, then He said to him: "Be!" and he is.

60. (This is) the truth from your Lord (O Muḥammad), so be not of those who waver.

61. And whoever disputes with you concerning him, after the knowledge which has come to you, say (to him): "Come! We will summon our sons and your sons, and our women and your women, and ourselves and yourselves, then we will pray humbly (to our Lord) and (solemnly) invoke the curse of God upon those who lie."[5]

62. This is the true narrative. There is no god but God, and God is the mighty, the wise.

63. And if they turn away, then God is aware of (who are) the corrupters.

64. Say: "O People of the Book![6] Come to an agreement between us and you: that we shall worship none but God, and that we shall ascribe no partner to Him, and that none of us shall take others for lords beside God." And if they turn away, then say: "Bear witness that we are they who have surrendered (to Him)."

65. O People of the Book! Why will you argue about Abraham, when the Torah and the Gospel were not revealed until after him? Have you then no sense?

66. You are those who argue about that of which you have some knowledge: Why then do you argue concerning that of which you have no knowledge? God knows. You know not.

67. Abraham was not a Jew, nor yet a Christian; but he was an upright man who had surrendered (to God), and he was not of the idolaters.

68. Those of mankind who have the best claim to Abraham are those who followed him, and this Prophet and those who believe (with him); and God is the protecting friend of the believers.

69. A party of the People of the Book long to make you go astray; and they make none to go astray except themselves, but they perceive not.

70. O People of the Book! Why do you disbelieve in the revelations of God, when you (yourselves) bear witness (to their truth)?

71. O People of the Book! Why do you confound truth with falsehood and knowingly conceal the truth?

5. In 632 CE a delegation of Christians from the south Arabian city of Najrān came to Medina to dispute with Muḥammad over the divine nature of Jesus. He proposed setting the dispute by *mubāhala*—a method whereby disputants pray to God to curse the untruthful party—but the Christians decided to withdraw from the contest. Muḥammad struck a peace treaty with them, the first between Muslims and Christians, guaranteeing their freedom of worship but demanding an annual tribute.

6. Jews and Christians [Pickthall's note].

72. And a party of the People of the Book say: "Believe in what has been revealed," to those who believe at the opening of the day, and disbelieve at the end of it, in order that they may return;[7]

73. And do not believe except in one who follows your religion—Say (O Muḥammad): "The guidance is God's guidance—that any one is given the like of what was given to you or that they may argue with you in the presence of their Lord." Say (O Muḥammad): "The bounty is in God's hand. He bestows it on whom He will. God is all-embracing, all-knowing.

74. "He selects for His mercy whom He will. God is of infinite bounty."

75. Among the People of the Book there is he who, if you trust him with a weight of treasure, will return it to you. And among them there is he who, if you trust him with a piece of gold, will not return it to you unless you keep standing over him. That is because they say: "We have no duty to the gentiles." They speak a lie concerning God knowingly.

76. No, but (the chosen of God is) he who fulfills his pledge and wards off (evil); for God loves those who ward off (evil).

77. Those who purchase a small gain at the cost of God's covenant and their oaths,[8] they have no portion in the hereafter. God will neither speak to them nor look upon them on the day of resurrection, nor will He make them grow. Theirs will be a painful doom.

78. And there is a party of them who distort the scripture with their tongues, that you may think that what they say is from the scripture, when it is not from the scripture. And they say: "It is from God," when it is not from God; and they speak a lie concerning God knowingly.

79. It is not (possible) for any human being to whom God had given the scripture and wisdom and the prophethood that he should afterwards have said to mankind: "Be servants of me instead of God"; but (what he said was): "Be faithful servants of the Lord by virtue of your constant teaching of the scripture and of your constant study of it."

80. And he did not command you that you should take the angels and the prophets for lords. Would he command you to disbelieve after you had surrendered (to God)?

81. When God made (His) covenant with the prophets, (He said): "Behold what I have given you of the scripture and knowledge. And afterward there will come to you a messenger, confirming what you possess. You shall believe in him and you shall help him." He said: "Do you agree, and will you take up My burden (which I lay on you) in this (matter)?" They answered: "We agree." He said: "Then bear witness. I will be a witness with you."

82. Then whoever after this shall turn away: they will be the iniquitous.

83. Do they seek other than the religion of God, when to Him submits whoever is in the heavens and the earth, willingly or unwillingly, and to Him they will be returned?

84. Say (O Muḥammad): "We believe in God and what is revealed to us and what was revealed to Abraham and Ishmael and Isaac and Jacob and the tribes, and what was granted to Moses and Jesus and the prophets

7. The reference is to some Jews of Medina, who feigned an interest in Islam only in the hope of detaching some of the Muslims by their subtle arguments [Pickthall's note].

8. The Jews of Medina had made a solemn treaty with the Prophet in the year 1 AH [Pickthall's note].

from their Lord. We make no distinction between any of them, and to Him we have surrendered."[9]

85. And whoever seeks as religion other than the surrender[1] (to God) it will not be accepted from him, and he will be a loser in the hereafter.

86. How shall God guide a people who disbelieved after their belief and (after) they bore witness that the messenger is true and after clear proofs (of God's sovereignty) had come to them? And God does not guide wrong-doing people.

87. As for such, their recompense is that on them rests the curse of God and of angels and of men combined.

88. They will abide in it. Their doom will not be lightened, neither will they be reprieved;

89. Except those who afterward repent and do right. God is forgiving, merciful.

90. Those who disbelieve after their (profession of) belief, and afterward grow violent in disbelief: their repentance will not be accepted. And such are those who are astray.

91. Those who disbelieve, and die in disbelief, the (whole) earth full of gold would not be accepted from such a one if it were offered as a ransom (for his soul). Theirs will be a painful doom and they will have no helpers.

92. You will not attain to piety until you spend of what you love. And whatever you spend, God is aware of it.

93. All food was lawful to the Children of Israel, except what Israel forbade himself, (in days) before the Torah was revealed. Say: "Produce the Torah and read it (to us) if you are truthful."

94. And whoever shall invent a falsehood after that concerning God, such will be wrongdoers.

95. Say: "God speaks truth. So follow the religion of Abraham, the upright. He was not of the idolaters."

96. The first sanctuary appointed for mankind was that at Becca,[2] a blessed place, a guidance to the peoples;

97. In which are plain memorials (of God's guidance); the place where Abraham stood up to pray; and whoever enters it is safe. And pilgrimage to the House[3] is a duty to God for mankind, for him who can find a way there. As for him who disbelieves, (let him know that) God is independent of (all) creatures.

98. Say: "O People of the Book! Why do you disbelieve in the revelations of God, when God (Himself) is witness of what you do?"

99. Say: "O People of the Book! Why do you drive believers back from the way of God, seeking to make it crooked, when you are witnesses (to God's guidance)? God is not unaware of what you do."

100. O you who believe! If you obey a party of those who have received the scripture they will make you disbelievers after your belief.

101. How can you disbelieve, when God's revelations are recited to you, and His messenger is in your midst? He who holds fast to God, he indeed is guided to a right path.

9. Almost identical with Q 2:136 [Pickthall's note].
1. Arabic *al-islām* [Pickthall's note].
2. Mecca [Pickthall's note].
3. The Kaʿba.

102. O you who believe! Observe your duty to God with right observance, and die only as those who have surrendered (to Him);

103. And hold fast, all of you together, to the rope of God, and do not separate. And remember God's favor to you: how you were enemies and He made friendship between your hearts so that you became as brothers by His grace; and (how) you were upon the brink of an abyss of fire, and He saved you from it. Thus God makes clear His revelations to you, that perhaps you may be guided,

104. And there may spring from you a nation who invite to goodness, and enjoin right conduct and forbid indecency. Such are they who are successful.

105. And do not be as those who separated and disputed after the clear proofs had come to them. For such there is an awful doom,

106. On the day when (some) faces will be whitened and (some) faces will be blackened; and as for those whose faces have been blackened, it will be said to them: "Did you disbelieve after your (profession of) belief? Then taste the punishment because you disbelieved."

107. And as for those whose faces have been whitened, in the mercy of God they dwell forever.

108. These are revelations of God. We recite them to you in truth. God wills no injustice to (His) creatures.

109. To God belongs whatever is in the heavens and whatever is on the earth; and to God all things are returned.

110. You are the best community that has been raised up for mankind. You enjoin right conduct and forbid indecency; and you believe in God. And if the People of the Book had believed it would have been better for them. Some of them are believers; but most of them are transgressors.

111. They will not harm you except a trifling hurt, and if they fight against you they will turn and flee. And afterward they will not be helped.

112. Ignominy shall be their portion wherever they are found except (where they grasp) a rope from God and a rope from men.[4] They have incurred anger from their Lord, and wretchedness is laid upon them. That is because they used to disbelieve the revelations of God, and slayed the prophets wrongfully. That is because they were rebellious and used to transgress.

113. They are not all alike. Of the People of the Book there is a staunch community who recite the revelations of God in the night season,[5] falling prostrate (before Him).

114. They believe in God and the last day, and enjoin right conduct and forbid indecency, and vie with one another in good works. These are of the righteous.

115. And whatever good they do, they will not be denied its recompense. God is aware of those who ward off (evil).

116. The riches and the progeny of those who disbelieve will not avail them anything against God; and such are rightful owners of the fire. They will abide there.

117. The likeness of what they spend in this life of the world is as the likeness of a biting, icy wind which strikes the harvest of a people who have

4. I.e. when they keep the covenant which the Prophet had made with the Jews of Medina [Pickthall's note].

5. That is, during the night.

wronged themselves, and devastates it. God did not wrong them, but they wronged themselves.

118. O you who believe! Do not take for intimates others than your own people, who would spare no pains to ruin you; they love to hamper you. Hatred is revealed by (the utterance of) their mouths, but what their breasts hide is greater. We have made plain for you the revelations if you will understand.

119. You are those who love them though they do not love you, and you believe in all the scripture. When they fall in with you they say: 'We believe; but when they go apart they bite their fingertips at you, for rage. Say: "Perish in your rage! God is aware of what is hidden in (your) breasts."

120. If a lucky chance befalls you, it is evil to them, and if disaster strikes you they rejoice at that. But if you persevere and keep from evil their guile will never harm you. God is surrounding what they do.

121. And (remember) when You set forth at daybreak from your household to assign to the believers their positions for the battle,[6] God was hearer, knower.

122. When two parties of you almost fell away, and God was their protecting friend. In God do believers put their trust.

123. God had already given you the victory at Badr, when you were contemptible. So observe your duty to God in order that you may be thankful.

124. And when You said to the believers: "Is it not sufficient for you that your Lord should support you with three thousand angels sent down (to your help)?

125. "No, but if you persevere, and keep from evil, and (the enemy) attack you suddenly, your Lord will help you with five thousand angels sweeping on."

126. God ordained this only as a message of good cheer for you, and that by it your hearts might be at rest—victory comes only from God, the mighty, the wise—

127. That He may cut off a part of those who disbelieve, or overwhelm them so that they retire, frustrated.

128. It is no concern at all of you (Muḥammad) whether He relents toward them or punishes them; for they are evildoers.

129. To God belongs whatever is in the heavens and whatever is on the earth. He forgives whom He will, and punishes whom He will. God is forgiving, merciful.

130. O you who believe! Do not devour usury, doubling and quadrupling (the sum lent). Observe your duty to God, that you may be successful.

131. And ward off (from yourselves) the fire prepared for disbelievers.

132. And obey God and the messenger, that you may find mercy.

133. And vie with one another for forgiveness from your Lord, and for a paradise as wide as are the heavens and the earth, prepared for those who ward off (evil);

134. Those who spend (of what God has given them) in ease and in adversity, those who control their wrath and are forgiving toward mankind; God loves the good;

6. The battle at Mt. Uḥud near Medina in the third year of the hijra (see the introduction to this sūra) [Pickthall's note].

135. And those who, when they do an evil thing or wrong themselves, remember God and implore forgiveness for their sins—Who forgives sins except God only?—and will not knowingly repeat (the wrong) they did.

136. The reward of such will be forgiveness from their Lord, and gardens underneath which rivers flow, in which they will abide forever—a bountiful reward for workers!

137. Customary ways[7] have passed away before you. Only travel in the land and see the nature of the consequence for those who did deny (the messengers).

138. This is a declaration for mankind, a guidance and an admonition to those who ward off (evil).

139. Do not faint or grieve, for you will overcome them if you are (indeed) believers.

140. If you have received a blow, the (disbelieving) people have received a blow the like of it.[8] These are (only) the vicissitudes which We cause to follow one another for mankind, to the end that God may know those who believe and may choose witnesses[9] from among you; and God does not love wrongdoers.

141. And that God may prove those who believe, and may blight the disbelievers.

142. Or did you think that you would enter paradise without God knowing those of you who really strive, nor knowing those (of you) who are steadfast?

143. And you used to wish for death before you met it (in the field). Now you have seen it with your eyes!

144. Muḥammad is but a messenger, messengers (the like of whom) have passed away before him. Will it be that, when he dies or is slain, you will turn back on your heels? He who turns back does no hurt to God, and God will reward the thankful.[1]

145. No soul can ever die except by God's leave and at a term appointed. Whoever desires the reward of the world, We give of it to him; and whoever desires the reward of the hereafter, We give of it to him. We shall reward the thankful.

146. And with how many a prophet have there been a number of devoted men who fought (beside him). They did not quail for anything that befell them in the way of God, nor did they weaken, nor were they brought low. God loves the steadfast.

147. Their cry was only that they said: "Our Lord! Forgive us for our sins and wasted efforts, make our foothold sure, and give us victory over the disbelieving people."

7. The word translated here is *sunan* (sing. *sunna*). Generally it refers to the good or bad actions of peoples of the past; in the Qur'ān, it typically indicates the negative behavior of those who refused to submit to the earlier messengers. Later Islamic scholarship used *sunna* as a technical term to indicate the exemplary actions of Muḥammad and his companions.

8. At Badr [Pickthall's note].

9. Or martyrs [Pickthall's note].

1. On the morning when the Prophet died, Abū Bakr came into the mosque at Medina and found the people all distracted, and 'Umar telling them that it was a sin to say that he was dead. Abū Bakr went and ascertained the truth, and coming back into the mosque, cried: "Lo! as for him who worshipped Muḥammad, Muḥammad is dead, but as for him who worships God, God is alive and does not die." Then he recited this verse "and it was as if the people had not known until then that such a verse had been revealed" [Pickthall's note]. Abū Bakr (573–634), Muḥammad's chief adviser and father-in-law, and the first caliph. 'Umar ibn al-Khaṭṭāb (ca. 586–644), the second caliph.

148. So God gave them the reward of the world and the good reward of the hereafter. God loves those whose deeds are good.

149. O you who believe! If you obey those who disbelieve, they will make you turn back on your heels, and you turn back as losers.

150. But God is your protector, and He is the best of helpers.

151. We shall cast terror into the hearts of those who disbelieve because they ascribe to God partners,[2] for which no warrant has been revealed. Their habitation is the fire, and wretched the abode of the wrongdoers.

152. God made good His promise to you when you routed them by His permission, until (the moment) when your courage failed you, and you disagreed about the order and you disobeyed, after He had shown you that for which you long.[3] Some of you desired the world, and some of you desired the hereafter. Therefore He made you flee from them, that He might try you. Yet now He has forgiven you. God is a Lord of kindness to believers.

153. When you climbed (the hill) and paid no heed to anyone, while the messenger, in your rear, was calling you (to fight). Therefore He rewarded you grief for (his) grief, that (He might teach) you not to sorrow either for what you missed or for what befell you. God is informed of what you do.

154. Then, after grief, He sent down security for you. As slumber it overcame a party of you, while (the other) party, who were anxious on their own account, thought wrongly of God, the thought of ignorance. They said; "Have we any part in the cause?" Say (O Muḥammad): "The cause belongs wholly to God." They hide within themselves (a thought) which they do not reveal to you, saying: "Had we had any part in the cause we should not have been slain here." Say: "Even though you had been in your houses, those appointed to be slain would have gone forth to the places where they were to lie." (All this has been) in order that God might try what is in your breasts and prove what is in your hearts. God is aware of what is hidden in the breasts (of men).

155. Those of you who turned back on the day when the two hosts met, Satan alone it was who caused them to backslide, because of some of what they have earned. Now God has forgiven them. God is forgiving, clement.

156. O you who believe! Do not be as those who disbelieved and said of their brother who went abroad in the land or were fighting in the field: "If they had been (here) with us they would not have died or been killed"; that God may make it anguish in their hearts. God gives life and causes death; and God is observer of what you do.

157. And though you be slain in God's way or die in it? Surely pardon from God and mercy are better than all that they amass.

158. What does it matter if you are slain or die, when to God you are gathered?

159. It was by the mercy of God that you were lenient with them (O Muḥammad), for if you had been stern and fierce of heart they would have dispersed from round about you. So pardon them and ask forgiveness for them and consult with them about the conduct of affairs. And when you are resolved, then put your trust in God. God loves those who put their trust (in Him).

2. *Shirk*, the association of partners with God, violates the Islamic conception of monotheism and is considered the only sin that cannot be forgiven.
3. When the archers deserted their post to share in the spoils, thinking that the day was won [Pickthall's note].

160. If God is your helper none can overcome you, and if He withdraws His help from you, who is there who can help you after Him? In God let believers put their trust.

161. It is not for any prophet to deceive (mankind).[4] Whoever deceives will bring his deceit with him on the day of resurrection. Then every soul will be paid in full what it has earned; and they will not be wronged.

162. Is one who follows the pleasure of God as one who has earned condemnation from God, whose habitation is the fire, a wretched journey's end?

163. There are degrees (of grace and reprobation) with God, and God is observer of what they do.

164. God has shown grace to the believers by sending to them a messenger of their own who recites to them His revelations, and causes them to grow, and teaches them the scripture and wisdom; although before (he came to them) they were in flagrant error.

165. And was it so, when a disaster struck you, though you had struck (them with a disaster) twice (as great),[5] that you said: "How is this?" Say (to them, O Muḥammad): "It is from yourselves. God is able to do all things."

166. What befell you, on the day when the two armies met, was by permission of God; that He might know the true believers;

167. And that He might know the hypocrites, to whom it was said: "Come, fight in the way of God, or defend yourselves." They answered: "If we knew anything of fighting we would follow you." On that day they were nearer disbelief than faith. They utter with their mouths a thing which is not in their hearts. God is best aware of what they hide.

168. Those who, while they sat at home, said of their brethren (who were fighting for the cause of God): "If they had been guided by us they would not have been slain." Say (to them, O Muḥammad): "Then avert death from yourselves if you are truthful."

169. Do not think of those, who are slain in the way of God, as dead. No, they are living. With their Lord they have provision.

170. Jubilant (are they) because of what God has bestowed upon them of His bounty, rejoicing for the sake of those who have not joined them but are left behind: that no fear shall come upon them neither shall they grieve.

171. They rejoice because of favor from God and kindness, and that God does not waste the wage of the believers.

172. As for those who heard the call of God and His messenger after the harm befell them (in the fight): for such of them as do right and ward off (evil), there is great reward,

173. Those to whom men said: "The people have gathered against you, therefore fear them." (The threat of danger) only increased the faith of them and they cried: "God is sufficient for us! Most excellent is He in whom we trust!"

174. So they returned with grace and favor from God, and no harm touched them. They followed the good pleasure of God, and God is of infinite bounty.

175. It is only the devil who would make (men) fear his partisans. Do not fear them; fear Me, if you are true believers.

4. After one of the early Muslim battles, some believed that Muḥammad had improperly divided the spoils. This verse is understood to be a response to those accusations.

5. At Badr [Pickthall's note].

176. Do not let their conduct grieve you, who run easily to disbelief, for they do not injure God at all. It is God's will to assign them no portion in the hereafter, and theirs will be an awful doom.

177. Those who purchase disbelief at the price of faith do not harm God at all, but theirs will be a painful doom.

178. And do not let those who disbelieve imagine that the rein We give them bodes good to their souls. We only give them rein that they may grow in sinfulness. And theirs will be a shameful doom.

179. It is not (the purpose) of God to leave you in your present state until He shall separate the wicked from the good. And it is not (the purpose of) God to let you know the unseen. But God chooses of His messengers whom He will, (to receive knowledge of it). So believe in God and His messengers. If you believe and ward off (evil), yours will be a vast reward.

180. And do not let those who hoard up what God has bestowed on them of His bounty think that it is better for them. No, it is worse for them. What they hoard will be their collar on the day of resurrection. God's is the heritage of the heavens and the earth, and God is informed of what you do.

181. God heard the saying of those who said, (when asked for contributions to the war): "God is poor, and we are rich!"[6] We shall record their saying with their slaying of the prophets wrongfully and We shall say: "Taste the punishment of burning!"

182. This is on account of what your own hands have sent before (you to the judgment). God is no oppressor of (His) servants.

183. (The same are) those who say: "God has charged us that we shall not believe in any messenger until he bring us an offering which fire (from heaven) shall devour." Say (to them, O Muḥammad): "Messengers came to you before me with miracles, and with that (very miracle) which you describe. Why then did you slay them? (Answer that) if you are truthful!"

184. And if they deny you, even so did they deny messengers who were before you, who came with miracles and with the Psalms and with the scripture giving light.

185. Every soul will taste of death. And you will be paid on the day of resurrection only what you have fairly earned. Whoever is removed from the fire and is made to enter paradise, he indeed is triumphant. The life of this world is but comfort of illusion.

186. Assuredly you will be tried in your property and in your persons, and you will hear much wrong from those who were given the scripture before you, and from the idolaters. But if you persevere and ward off (evil), then that is of the steadfast heart of things.

187. And (remember) when God laid a charge on those who had received the scripture (He said): "You are to expound it to mankind and not to hide it." But they flung it behind their backs and bought thereby a little gain. Evil is what they have gained by that.

188. Do not think that those who exult in what they have given, and love to be praised for what they have not done—do not think they are in safety from the doom. A painful doom is theirs.

189. To God belongs the sovereignty of the heavens and the earth. God is able to do all things.

6. A saying of some Jews of Medina [Pickthall's note].

190. In the creation of the heavens and the earth and (in) the difference of night and day are signs (of His sovereignty) for men of understanding,

191. Such as remember God, standing, sitting, and reclining, and consider the creation of the heavens and the earth, (and say): "Our Lord! You did not create this in vain. Glory be to You! Preserve us from the doom of fire.

192. "Our Lord! Whom You cause to enter the fire: him indeed You have confounded. For evildoers there will be no helpers.

193. "Our Lord! We have heard a crier calling to faith: 'Believe in your Lord!' So we believed. Our Lord! Therefore forgive us our sins, and remit from us our evil deeds, and make us die the death of the righteous.

194. "Our Lord! And give us what You have promised to us by Your messengers. Do not confound us on the day of resurrection. You do not break the meeting."

195. And their Lord has heard them (and He says): I do not permit the work of any worker, male or female, to be lost. You proceed from one another.[7] So those who fled and were driven forth from their homes and suffered damage for My cause, and fought and were slain, I shall remit their evil deeds from them and I shall bring them into gardens underneath which rivers flow—A reward from God. And with God is the fairest of rewards.

196. Do not let the vicissitude (of the success) of those who disbelieve, in the land, deceive you (O Muḥammad).

197. It is but a brief comfort. And afterward their habitation will be hell, an ill abode.

198. But those who keep their duty to their Lord, for them are gardens underneath which rivers flow, in which they will be safe for ever. A gift of welcome from their Lord. What God has in store is better for the righteous.

199. And of the People of the Scripture there are some who believe in God and what is revealed to you and what was revealed to them, humbling themselves before God. They do not purchase a trifling gain at the price of the revelations of God. Their reward is with their Lord, and God is swift to take account.

200. O you who believe! Endure, outdo all others in endurance, be ready, and observe your duty to God, in order that you may succeed.

## Sūra 4

*Al-Nisā'*, "Women," is so called because it deals largely with women's rights. The period of revelation is the months following the battle of Uḥud, or, as Nöldeke, a careful critic, puts it, "between the end of the third year and the end of the fifth year"[1] of the Prophet's reign at Medina. As the sūra contains no reference to the siege of Medina ("the War of the Trench") by the allied tribes, which took place in the fifth year, I should rather say, between the end of the third year and the beginning of the fifth year.

Many Muslims were killed at the battle of Uḥud, hence the concern for orphans and widows in the opening verses which lead on to a declaration of some rights of women of which they were deprived among the pagan Arabs.

7. This expression, which recurs in the Qur'ān, is a reminder to men that women are of the same human status as themselves [Pickthall's note].

1. Nöldeke, *Geschichte des Qorâns*, Part 1, p. 195 [Pickthall's note].

The defection of the Hypocrites—as the lukewarm or purely time-serving adherents were called—had been the chief cause of the reverse at Uḥud; and after that reverse some of the Jewish tribes, who had until then observed the letter of their treaty with the Prophet, became avowed supporters of the enemy, even going so far as to declare that the old Arab idolatry was preferable to Islam as a religion, and giving help and information to Quraysh, so that in the end the Muslims were obliged to make war on them. Both the Hypocrites and the rebellious Jews are dealt with incidentally in this sūra, the former at some length. There is a reference to Christian beliefs in verses 171–72.

The period of revelation is the fourth year of the *hijra*.

## Women

*Revealed at Medina*

In the name of God the beneficent, the merciful.

1. O mankind! Be careful of your duty to your Lord who created you from a single soul and from it created its mate and from the two has spread abroad a multitude of men and women. Be careful of your duty toward God in whom you claim (your rights) of one another, and toward the wombs (that bear you). God has been a watcher over you.

2. Give to orphans their wealth. Do not exchange the good for the bad (in your management of it) or absorb their wealth into your own wealth. That would be a great sin.

3. And if you fear that you will not deal fairly by the orphans, marry of the women, who seem good to you, two or three or four; and if you fear that you cannot do justice (to so many) then one (only) or (the captives) that your right hands possess.[2] Thus it is more likely that you will not do injustice.

4. And give to the women (whom you marry) free gift of their marriage portions; but if they of their own accord remit to you a part of it, then you are welcome to absorb it (in your wealth).

5. Do not give to the foolish (what is in) your (keeping of their) wealth, which God has given you to maintain; but feed and clothe them from it, and speak kindly to them.

6. Test orphans until they reach the marriageable age; then, if you find them of sound judgment, deliver over to them their fortune; and do not devour it by squandering and in haste for fear that they should grow up. Whoever (of the guardians) is rich, let him abstain generously (from taking of the property of orphans); and whoever is poor let him take of it in reason (for his guardianship). And when you deliver up their fortune to orphans, have (the transaction) witnessed in their presence. God suffices as a reckoner.

7. To the men (of a family) belongs a share of what parents and near kindred leave, and to the women a share of what parents and near kindred leave, whether it be little or much—a legal share.

8. And when relatives and orphans and the needy are present at the division (of the heritage), bestow on them from it and speak kindly to them.

2. Typically understood as referring to female slaves made to serve as concubines.

9. And let those fear (in their behavior toward orphans) who if they left behind them weak offspring would be afraid for them. So let them mind their duty to God, and speak justly.

10. Those who devour the wealth of orphans wrongfully, they only swallow fire into their bellies, and they will be exposed to burning flame.

11. God charges you concerning (the provision for) your children: to the male the equivalent of the portion of two females, and if there be more than two women, then theirs is two-thirds of the inheritance, and if there be one (only) then the half. And to each of his[3] parents a sixth of the inheritance, if he has a son; and if he has no son and his parents are his heirs, then to his mother appertains the third; and if he has brothers, then to his mother appertains the sixth, after any legacy he may have bequeathed or debt (has been paid). Your parents or your children: You do not know which of them is nearer to you in usefulness. It is an injunction from God. God is knower, wise.

12. And to you belongs a half of what your wives leave, if they have no child; but if they have a child then to you the fourth of what they leave, after any legacy they may have bequeathed or debt (they may have contracted has been paid). And to them belongs the fourth of what you leave if you have no child, but if you have a child then the eighth of what you leave, after any legacy you may have bequeathed or debt (you may have contracted has been paid). And if a man or a woman has a distant heir (having left neither parent nor child), and he (or she) has a brother or a sister (only on the mother's side), then to each of the two (the brother and the sister) the sixth, and if they are more than two, then they shall be sharers in the third, after any legacy that may have been bequeathed or debt (contracted) has been paid, not injuring (the heirs by willing away more than a third of the heritage). A commandment from God. God is knower, indulgent.

13. These are the limits (imposed by) God. Whoever obeys God and His messenger, He will make him enter gardens underneath which rivers flow, where such will dwell forever. That will be the great success.

14. And whoever disobeys God and His messenger and transgresses His limits, He will make him enter fire, where such will dwell forever; his will be a shameful doom.

15. As for those of your women who are guilty of lewdness, call to witness four of you against them. And if they testify (to the truth of the allegation) then confine them to the houses until death take them or (until) God appoint for them a way (through new legislation).[4]

16. And as for the two of you who are guilty of it, punish them both. And if they repent and improve, then let them be. God is relenting, merciful.

17. Forgiveness is only incumbent on God toward those who do evil in ignorance (and) then turn quickly (in repentance) to God. These are they toward whom God relents. God is ever knower, wise.

18. The forgiveness is not for those who do ill deeds until, when death attends upon one of them, he says: "I repent now"; nor yet for those who die while they are disbelievers. For such We have prepared a painful doom.

19. O you who believe! It is not lawful for you forcibly to inherit the women (of your deceased kinsmen), nor (that) you should put constraint

3. The deceased [Pickthall's note].
4. See Q 24:2–10 [Pickthall's note].

upon them that you may take away a part of what you have given them, unless they be guilty of flagrant lewdness. But consort with them in kindness, for if you hate them it may happen that you hate a thing in which God has placed much good.

20. And if you wish to exchange one wife for another and you have given to one of them a sum of money (however great), take nothing from it. Would you take it by the way of calumny and open wrong?

21. How can you take it (back) after one of you has gone in to[5] the other, and they have taken a strong pledge from you?

22. And do not marry those women whom your fathers married, except what has already happened (of that nature) in the past. It was ever lewdness and abomination, and an evil way.

23. Forbidden to you are your mothers, and your daughters, and your sisters, and your father's sisters, and your mother's sisters, and your brother's daughters and your sister's daughters, and your foster-mothers, and your foster-sisters, and your mothers-in-law, and your stepdaughters who are under your protection (born) of your women to whom you have gone in—but if you have not gone in to them, then it is no sin for you (to marry their daughters)—and the wives of your sons who (spring) from your own loins. And (it is forbidden to you) that you should have two sisters together, except what has already happened (of that nature) in the past. God is ever forgiving, merciful.

24. And all married women (are forbidden to you) except those (captives) whom your right hands possess. It is a decree of God for you. Lawful to you are all beyond those mentioned, so that you seek them with your wealth in honest wedlock, not debauchery. And those of whom you seek enjoyment (by marrying them), give to them their portions as a duty. And there is no sin for you in what you do by mutual agreement after the duty (has been done). God is ever knower, wise.

25. And whoever is not able to afford to marry free, believing women, let them marry from the believing slave girls whom your right hands possess. God knows best (concerning) your faith. You (proceed) one from another;[6] so wed them by permission of their people, and give to them their portions in kindness, they being honest, not debauched or of loose conduct. And if when they are honorably married they commit lewdness they shall incur the half of the punishment (prescribed) for free women (in that case). This is for him among you who fears to commit sin. But to have patience would be better for you. God is forgiving, merciful.

26. God would explain to you and guide you by the examples of those who were before you, and would turn to you in mercy. God is knower, wise.

27. And God would turn to you in mercy; but those who follow vain desires would have you go tremendously astray.

28. God would make the burden light for you, for man was created weak.

29. O you who believe! Do not squander your wealth among yourselves in vanity, except it is a trade by mutual consent, and do not kill one another. God is ever merciful to you.

5. Has had sexual intercourse with.
6. This expression, which recurs in the Qur'ān, is a reminder to men that women are of the same human status as themselves [Pickthall's note].

30. Whoever does that through aggression and injustice, We shall cast him into fire, and that is ever easy for God.

31. If you avoid the great (things) which you are forbidden, We will remit from you your evil deeds and make you enter at a noble gate.

32. And do not covet the thing in which God has made some of you excel others. To men a fortune from what they have earned, and to women a fortune from what they have earned. (Do not envy one another) but ask God of His bounty. God is ever knower of all things.

33. And to each We have appointed heirs of what parents and near kindred leave; and as for those with whom your right hands have made a covenant, give them their due. God is ever witness over all things.

34. Men are in charge of women, because God has made the one of them to excel the other,[7] and because they spend of their property (for the support of women). So good women are the obedient, guarding in secret what God has guarded. As for those from whom you fear rebellion, admonish them and banish them to beds apart, and scourge them.[8] Then if they obey you, do not seek a way against them. God is ever high exalted, great.

35. And if you fear a breach between the two (the man and wife), appoint an arbiter from his people and an arbiter from her people. If they desire amendment God will make them of one mind. God is ever knower, aware.

36. And serve God. Ascribe nothing as partner to Him. (Show) kindness to parents, and to near kindred, and orphans, and the needy, and to the neighbor who is related (to you) and the neighbor who is not related, and the fellow traveler and the wayfarer and (the slaves) whom your right hands possess. God does not love such as are proud and boastful,

37. Who hoard their wealth and enjoin avarice on others, and hide what God has bestowed on them of His bounty. For disbelievers We prepare a shameful doom;

38. And (also) those who spend their wealth in order to be seen of men, and do not believe in God or the last day. Whoever takes Satan for a comrade has a bad comrade.

39. What have they (to fear) if they believe in God and the last day and spend (rightly) of what God has bestowed upon them, when God is ever aware of them (and all they do)?

40. God does no wrong even of the weight of an ant; and if there is a good deed, He will double it and will give (the doer) from His presence an immense reward.

41. But how (will it be with them) when We bring of every people a witness, and We bring you (O Muḥammad) as a witness against these?

42. On that day those who disbelieved and disobeyed the messenger will wish that they were level with the ground, and they can hide no fact from God.

43. O you who believe! Do not draw near to prayer when you are drunken,[9] until you know what you utter, nor when you are polluted, except when journeying on the road, until you have bathed. And if you are ill, or on a

7. Male superiority has been variously identified, including in physical strength, financial capacity, and essence.
8. This is ordinarily understood as a gradual series of chastisements. "Scourging" or "beating," a physical reprimand, has been variously interpreted on a range from slight to severe.
9. The prohibition of alcohol is generally understood to have been implemented gradually in the Qur'ān. Islamic law extends the prohibition to all intoxicants.

journey, or one of you comes from the toilet, or you have touched women, and you do not find water, then go to high clean soil and rub your faces and your hands (with it). God is benign, forgiving.

44. Do you not see those to whom a portion of the scripture has been given, how they purchase error, and seek to make you (Muslims) err from the right way?

45. God knows best (who are) your enemies. God is sufficient as a friend, and God is sufficient as a helper.

46. Some of those who are Jews change words from their context and say: "We hear and disobey; hear as one who hears not" and "Listen to us!"[1] distorting with their tongues and slandering religion. If they had said: "We hear and we obey: hear, and look at us" it would have been better for them, and more upright. But God has cursed them for their disbelief, so they do not believe, except a few.

47. O you to whom the scripture has been given, believe in what We have revealed confirming what you possess, before We destroy countenances so as to confound them, or curse them as We cursed the sabbath-breakers. The commandment of God is always executed.

48. God does not forgive that a partner should be ascribed to Him. He forgives (all) except that to whom He will. Whoever ascribes partners to God, he has indeed invented a tremendous sin.

49. Have you not seen those who praise themselves for purity? No, God purifies whom He will, and they will not be wronged even the hair on a date stone.[2]

50. See, how they invent lies about God! That of itself is flagrant sin.

51. Have you not seen those to whom a portion of the scripture has been given, how they believe in idols and false deities, and how they say of those (idolaters) who disbelieve: "These are more rightly guided than those who believe?"

52. Those are they whom God has cursed, and he whom God has cursed, you (O Muḥammad) will find for him no helper.

53. Or have they even a share in the sovereignty? Then in that case, they would not give mankind even the speck on a date stone.

54. Or are they jealous of mankind because of what God of His bounty has bestowed on them? For We bestowed on the house of Abraham (of old) the scripture and wisdom, and We bestowed on them a mighty kingdom.

55. And of them were (some) who believed in it and of them were (some) who turned away from it. Hell is sufficient for (their) burning.

56. Those who disbelieve Our revelations, We shall expose them to the fire. As often as their skins are consumed We shall exchange them for fresh skins that they may taste the torment. God is ever mighty, wise.

57. And as for those who believe and do good works, We shall make them enter gardens underneath which rivers flow—to dwell there forever; there for them are pure companions—and We shall make them enter plentiful shade.

1. Devices of some of the Jews of Medina to annoy the Muslims by distorting words of Scripture. *Rāʿinā* (meaning "listen to us"), by which the Muslims used to call the Prophet's notice, they turned by slight mispronunciation into a Hebrew word of insult (cf. Q 2:104, footnote) [Pickthall's note].
2. The Qurʾān mentions dates and the date palm frequently. Here the Arabic expression means "the tiniest amount."

58. God commands you that you restore deposits to their owners, and, if you judge between mankind, that you judge justly. How good is this which God admonishes you! God is ever hearer, observer.

59. O you who believe! Obey God, and obey the messenger and those of you who are in authority;[3] and if you have a dispute concerning any matter, refer it to God and the messenger if you are (in truth) believers in God and the last day. That is better and more seemly in the end.

60. Have you not seen those who pretend that they believe in what is revealed to you and what was revealed before you, how they would go for judgment (in their disputes) to false deities when they have been ordered to abjure them? Satan would mislead them far astray.

61. And when it is said to them: "Come to what God has revealed and to the messenger," you see the hypocrites turn from you with aversion.

62. How would it be if a misfortune struck them because of what their own hands have sent before (them)? Then they would come to you, swearing by God that they were seeking nothing but harmony and kindness.

63. Those are they, the secrets of whose hearts God knows. So oppose them and admonish them, and address them in plain terms about their souls.

64. We sent no messenger except that he should be obeyed by God's permission. And if, when they had wronged themselves, they had only come to you and asked forgiveness of God, and asked forgiveness of the messenger, they would have found God forgiving, merciful.

65. But no, by your Lord, they will not believe (in truth) until they make you judge of what is in dispute between them and find within themselves no dislike of what you decide, and submit with full submission.

66. And if We had decreed for them: "Lay down your lives or go forth from your dwellings," only a few of them would have done it; though if they did what they are exhorted to do it would be better for them, and more strengthening;

67. And then We would bestow on them from Our presence an immense reward,

68. And would guide them to a straight path.

69. Whoever obeys God and the messenger, they are with those to whom God has shown favor, from among the prophets and the true-hearted and the martyrs and the righteous. The best of company are they!

70. Such is the bounty of God, and God suffices as knower.

71. O you who believe! Take your precautions, then advance the proven ones, or advance all together.

72. Among you there is he who loiters; and if disaster overtook you, he would say: "God has been gracious to me since I was not present with them."

73. And if a bounty from God befell you, he would surely cry, as if there had been no love between you and him: "Oh, would that I had been with them, then I should have achieved a great success!"

74. Let those fight in the way of God who sell the life of this world for the other. Whoever fights in the way of God, be he slain or be he victorious, on him We shall bestow a vast reward.

3. Arabic *ulū l-amr.* Sunnis have often understood "those of you who are in authority" to mean scholars, military commanders, Muḥammad's companions, the four caliphs, or the actual rulers of Muslim lands. For Shīʿīs it usually means the infallible imāms.

75. How should you not fight for the cause of God and of the feeble among men and of the women and the children who are crying: "Our Lord! Bring us forth from this town[4] of which the people are oppressors! Oh, give us from Your presence some protecting friend! Oh, give us from Your presence some defender!"

76. Those who believe do battle for the cause of God; and those who disbelieve do battle for the cause of idols. So fight the minions of the devil. The devil's strategy is ever weak.

77. Have you not seen those to whom it was said: "Withhold your hands, establish worship and pay the poor tax," but when fighting was prescribed for them behold! a party of them fear mankind even as they fear God or with greater fear, and say: "Our Lord! Why have you ordained fighting for us? If only You would give us respite for a while!" Say (to them, O Muḥammad): "The comfort of this world is scant; the hereafter will be better for him who wards off (evil); and you will not be wronged the down upon a date stone.

78. "Wherever you may be, death will overtake you, even though you were in lofty towers." Yet if a happy thing befalls them they say: "This is from God"; and if an evil thing befalls them they say: "This is of your doing (O Muḥammad)." Say (to them): "All is from God." What is amiss with these people that they do not come near to understand a happening?[5]

79. Whatever of good befalls you (O man) it is from God, and whatever of ill befalls you it is from yourself. We have sent you (Muḥammad) as a messenger to mankind and God is sufficient as witness.

80. Whoever obeys the messenger obeys God, and whoever turns away: We have not sent you as a caretaker over them.

81. And they say: "(It is) obedience"; but when they have gone forth from you a party of them spend the night in planning other than what you say. God records what they plan by night. So oppose them and put your trust in God. God is sufficient as trustee.

82. Will they not then ponder on the Qur'ān? If it had been from other than God they would have found in it much incongruity.

83. And if any tidings, whether of safety or fear, come to them, they spread it abroad, whereas if they had referred it to the messenger and such of them as are in authority, those among them who are able to think out the matter would have known it. If it had not been for the grace of God upon you and His mercy you would have followed Satan, except a few (of you).

84. So fight (O Muḥammad) in the way of God—You are not taxed (with the responsibility for anyone) except for yourself—and urge on the believers. Perhaps God will restrain the might of those who disbelieve. God is stronger in might and stronger in inflicting punishment.

85. Whoever intervenes in a good cause will have the reward of it, and whoever intervenes in an evil cause will bear the consequence of it. God oversees all things.

86. When you are greeted with a greeting, greet with one better than it or return it. God takes count of all things.

4. Mecca [Pickthall's note].
5. The reference is to the reverse which the Muslims suffered at Mt. Uḥud which was caused by their own disobedience to the Prophet's orders [Pickthall's note].

87. God! There is no god except Him. He gathers you all to a day of resurrection of which there is no doubt. Who is more true in statement than God?

88. What ails you that you are two parties regarding the hypocrites,[6] when God cast them back (to disbelief) because of what they earned? Do you seek to guide him whom God has sent astray? He whom God sends astray, for him you (O Muḥammad) cannot find a road.

89. They long that you should disbelieve even as they disbelieve, that you may be upon a level (with them). So do not choose friends from them until they forsake their homes in the way of God; if they turn back (to enmity) then take them and kill them wherever you find them, and choose no friend nor helper from among them,

90. Except those who seek refuge with a people between whom and you there is a covenant, or (those who) come to you because their hearts forbid them to make war on you or make war on their own people. Had God willed He could have given them power over you so that assuredly they would have fought you. So, if they hold aloof from you and do not wage war against you and offer you peace, God allows you no way against them.

91. You will find others who desire that they should have security from you, and security from their own people. So often as they are returned to hostility they are plunged into it. If they keep not aloof from you nor offer you peace nor hold their hands, then take them and kill them wherever you find them. Against such We have given you clear warrant.

92. It is not for a believer to kill a believer unless (it be) by mistake. He who has killed a believer by mistake must set free a believing slave, and pay the blood money to the family of the slain, unless they remit it as a charity. If he (the victim) is of a people hostile to you, and he is a believer, then (the penance is) to set free a believing slave. And if he comes of a people between whom and you there is a covenant, then the blood money must be paid to his people and (also) a believing slave must be set free. And whoever does not have the wherewithal must fast two consecutive months. A penance from God. God is knower, wise.

93. Whoever slays a believer of set purpose, his reward is hell forever. God is angry against him and He has cursed him and prepared for him an awful doom.

94. O you who believe! When you go forth (to fight) in the way of God, be careful to discriminate, and do not say to one who offers you peace: "You are not a believer," seeking the chance profits of this life (so that you may despoil him). With God are plenteous spoils. Even thus (as he now is) were you before; but God has since then been gracious to you. Therefore take care to discriminate. God is ever informed of what you do.

95. Those of the believers who sit still, other than those who have a (disabling) hurt, are not equal with those who strive in the way of God with their wealth and lives. God has conferred on those who strive with their wealth and lives a rank above the sedentary. To each God has promised

6. According to tradition, the reference here is not to the lukewarm section of the Muslims of Medina, but to a particular group of alleged converts from among the Arabs, who afterward relapsed into idolatry, and concerning whom there were two opinions among the Muslims [Pickthall's note].

good, but He has bestowed on those who strive a great reward above the sedentary;

96. Degrees of rank from Him, and forgiveness and mercy. God is ever forgiving, merciful.

97. As for those whom the angels take (in death) while they wrong themselves, (the angels) will ask: "In what were you engaged?" They will say: "We were oppressed in the land." (The angels) will say: "Was not God's earth spacious that you could have migrated there?" As for such, their habitation will be hell, an evil journey's end;

98. Except the feeble among men, and the women, and the children, who are unable to devise a plan and are not shown a way.

99. As for such, it may be that God will pardon them. God is ever clement, forgiving.

100. Whoever migrates for the cause of God will find much refuge and abundance on the earth, and whoever forsakes his home, a fugitive to God and His messenger, and death overtakes him, his reward is then incumbent on God. God is ever forgiving, merciful.

101. And when you go forth in the land, it is no sin for you to curtail (your) worship if you fear that those who disbelieve may attack you. In truth the disbelievers are an open enemy to you.

102. And when you (O Muḥammad) are among them and arrange (their) worship for them, let only a party of them stand with you (to worship) and let them take their arms. Then when they have performed their prostrations let them fall to the rear and let another party come that has not worshipped and let them worship with you, and let them take their precaution and their arms. Those who disbelieve long for you to neglect your arms and your baggage that they may attack you once for all. It is no sin for you to lay aside your arms, if rain impedes you or you are sick. But take your precaution. God prepares for the disbelievers shameful punishment.

103. When you have performed the act of worship, remember God, standing, sitting, and reclining. And when you are in safety, observe proper worship. Worship at fixed hours has been enjoined on the believers.

104. Do not relent in pursuit of the enemy. If you are suffering, they suffer even as you suffer and you hope from God that for which they cannot hope. God is ever knower, wise.

105. We reveal to you the scripture with the truth, that you may judge between mankind by what God shows you. And do not be a pleader for the treacherous;

106. And seek forgiveness of God. God is ever forgiving, merciful.

107. And do not plead on behalf of (people) who deceive themselves. God does not love one who is treacherous and sinful.

108. They seek to hide from men and do not seek to hide from God. He is with them when by night they hold discourse displeasing to Him. God ever surrounds what they do.

109. You are they who pleaded for them in the life of the world. But who will plead with God for them on the day of resurrection, or who will then be their defender?

110. Yet whoever does evil or wrongs his own soul, then seeks pardon of God, will find God forgiving, merciful.

111. Whoever commits sin commits it only against himself. God is ever knower, wise.

112. And whoever commits a delinquency or crime, then throws (the blame) of it on the innocent, has burdened himself with falsehood and a flagrant crime.

113. But for the grace of God on you (Muḥammad), and His mercy, a party of them had resolved to mislead you, but they will mislead only themselves and they will not hurt you at all. God reveals to you the scripture and wisdom, and teaches you what you knew not. The grace of God toward you has been infinite.

114. There is no good in much of their secret conferences except (in) him who enjoins almsgiving and kindness and peacemaking among the people. Whoever does that, seeking the good pleasure of God, We shall bestow on him a vast reward.

115. And whoever opposes the messenger after the guidance (of God) has been manifested to him, and follows other than the believer's way, We appoint for him that to which he himself has turned, and expose him to hell—an unfortunate journey's end!

116. God does not pardon that partners should be ascribed to him. All except that He pardons to whom He will. Whoever ascribes partners to God has wandered far astray.

117. They invoke in His stead only females;[7] they pray to none else than Satan, a rebel

118. Whom God cursed, and he said: "I will take of Your servants an appointed portion,

119. And I will lead them astray, and I will arouse desires in them, and I will command them and they will cut the cattle's ears,[8] and surely I will command them and they will change God's creation." Whoever chooses Satan for a patron instead of God is a loser and his loss is manifest.

120. He promises them and stirs up desires in them, and Satan promises them only to beguile.

121. For such, their habitation will be hell, and they will find no refuge from it.

122. But as for those who believe and do good works We shall bring them into gardens underneath which rivers flow, in which they will abide for ever. It is a promise from God in truth; and who can be more truthful than God in utterance?

123. It will not be in accordance with your desires, nor the desires of the People of the Scripture.[9] He who does wrong will have the recompense of it, and will not find against God any protecting friend or helper.

124. And whoever does good works, whether male or female, and he (or she) is a believer, such will enter paradise and they will not be wronged the speck on a date stone.

125. Who is better in religion than he who surrenders his purpose to God while doing good (to men) and follows the tradition of Abraham, the upright? God (Himself) chose Abraham for friend.

126. To God belongs whatever is in the heavens and whatever is on the earth. God ever surrounds all things.

7. The idols which the pagan Arabs worshipped were all female [Pickthall's note].
8. A pre-Islamic practice to dedicate the animal to an idol.
9. Jews and Christians [Pickthall's note].

127. They consult you concerning women. Say: "God gives you a decree concerning them, and the scripture which has been recited to you (gives a decree), concerning female orphans to whom you do not give what is ordained for them though you desire to marry them,[1] and (concerning) the weak among children, and that you should deal justly with orphans." Whatever good you do, God is ever aware of it.

128. If a woman fears ill-treatment from her husband, or desertion, it is no sin for the two if they make terms of peace between themselves. Peace is better. But greed has been made present in the minds (of men). If you do good and keep from evil, God is ever informed of what you do.

129. You will not be able to deal equally between (your) wives, however much you wish (to do so). But do not turn altogether away (from one), leaving her as in suspense. If you do good and keep from evil, God is ever forgiving, merciful.

130. But if they separate, God will compensate each out of His abundance. God is ever all-embracing, all-knowing.

131. To God belongs whatever is in the heavens and whatever is on the earth. And We charged those who received the scripture before you, and (We charge) you, that you keep your duty toward God. And if you disbelieve, to God belongs whatever is in the heavens and whatever is on the earth, and God is ever absolute, owner of praise.

132. To God belongs whatever is in the heavens and whatever is on the earth. And God is sufficient as defender.

133. If He will, He can remove you, O people, and produce others (in your stead). God is able to do that.

134. Whoever desires the reward of the world, (let him know that) with God is the reward of the world and the hereafter. God is ever hearer, observer.

135. O you who believe! Be staunch in justice, witnesses for God, even though it be against yourselves or (your) parents or (your) kindred, whether (the case be of) a rich man or a poor man, for God is nearer to both (than you are). So do not follow passion for fear that you lapse (from truth) and if you lapse or fall away, then God is ever informed of what you do.

136. O you who believe! Believe in God and His messenger and the scripture which He has revealed to His messenger, and the scripture which He revealed before. Whoever disbelieves in God and His angels and His scriptures and His messengers and the last day, he has wandered far astray.

137. Those who believe, then disbelieve and then (again) believe, then disbelieve, and then increase in disbelief, God will never pardon them, nor will he guide them to a way.

138. Bear to the hypocrites the tidings that for them there is a painful doom;

139. Those who choose disbelievers for their friends instead of believers! Do they look for power at their hands? All power belongs to God.

140. He has already revealed to you in the scripture that when you hear the revelations of God rejected and derided, (you) do not sit with them (who

1. The Qur'ān often speaks about the duty to be just with orphans, imposed particularly on those in charge of an orphan's property. Here the warning is to a guardian who would unjustly hold on to a female orphan's wealth, either by refusing to allow her to marry or by marrying her himself.

disbelieve and mock) until they engage in some other conversation. In that case (if you stayed) you would be like them. God will gather hypocrites and disbelievers, all together, into hell;

141. Those who wait upon occasion in regard to you and, if a victory comes to you from God, say: "Are we not with you?" and if the disbelievers meet with a success say: "Had we not the mastery of you, and did we not protect you from the believers?" God will judge between you at the day of resurrection, and God will not give the disbelievers any way (of success) against the believers.

142. The hypocrites seek to beguile God, but it is God who beguiles them. When they stand up to worship they perform it languidly and to be seen by people, and are but little mindful of God;

143. Swaying between this (and that), (belonging) neither to these nor to those. He whom God causes to go astray, you (O Muḥammad) will not find a way for him:

144. O you who believe! Do not choose disbelievers for (your) friends in place of believers. Would you give God a clear warrant against you?

145. The hypocrites (will be) in the lowest deep of the fire, and you will find no helper for them;

146. Except those who repent and amend and hold fast to God and make their religion pure for God (only). Those are with the believers. And God will bestow on the believers an immense reward.

147. What concern has God for your punishment if you are thankful (for His mercies) and believe (in Him)? God was ever responsive, aware.

148. God does not love the utterance of harsh speech except by one who has been wronged. God is ever hearer, knower.

149. If you do good openly or keep it secret, or forgive evil, God is forgiving, powerful.

150. Those who disbelieve in God and His messengers, and seek to make distinction between God and His messengers, and say: "We believe in some and disbelieve in others, and seek to choose a way in between";

151. Such are disbelievers in truth; and for disbelievers We prepare a shameful doom.

152. But those who believe in God and His messengers and make no distinction between any of them, to them God will give their wages; and God was ever forgiving, merciful.

153. The People of the Scripture ask of you that you should cause an (actual) book to descend on them from heaven. They asked a greater thing of Moses before, for they said: "Show us God plainly." The storm of lightning seized them for their wickedness. Then (even after that) they chose the calf (for worship)[2] after clear proofs (of God's sovereignty) had come to them. And We forgave them that! And We bestowed on Moses evident authority.

154. And We caused the mount to tower above them at (the taking of) their covenant: and We bade them: "Enter the gate, prostrate!" and We bade them: "Do not transgress the Sabbath!" and We took from them a firm covenant.

155. Then because of their breaking of their covenant, and their disbelieving in the revelations of God, and their slaying of the prophets

2. For the golden calf, see Exodus 32:1–8.

wrongfully, and their saying: "Our hearts are hardened"—No, but God has set a seal upon them for their disbelief, so that only a few of them believe—

156. And because of their disbelief and of their speaking against Mary a tremendous calumny;[3]

157. And because of their saying: "We slew the Messiah Jesus son of Mary, God's messenger"—They did not kill him or crucify him, but it appeared so to them; and those who disagree concerning it are in doubt of it; they have no knowledge of it except pursuit of a conjecture; for certain they did not slay him,

158. But God took him up to Himself. God was ever mighty, wise.

159. There is not one of the People of the Scripture but will believe in Him before his death, and on the day of resurrection He will be a witness against them—

160. Because of the wrongdoing of the Jews We forbade them good things which were (before) made lawful to them, and because of their much hindering from God's way,

161. And of their taking usury when they were forbidden it, and of their devouring people's wealth by false pretences. We have prepared for those of them who disbelieve a painful doom.

162. But those of them who are firm in knowledge and the believers believe in what is revealed to you, and what was revealed before you, especially the diligent in prayer and those who pay the poor tax, the believers in God and the last day. Upon these We shall bestow immense reward.

163. We inspire you as We inspired Noah and the prophets after him, as We inspired Abraham and Ishmael and Isaac and Jacob and the tribes,[4] and Jesus and Job and Jonah and Aaron and Solomon, and as we imparted to David the Psalms;

164. And messengers We have mentioned to you before and messengers We have not mentioned to you; and God spoke directly to Moses;

165. Messengers of good cheer and of warning, in order that mankind might have no argument against God after the messengers. God was ever mighty, wise.

166. But God (Himself) testifies concerning what He has revealed to you; in His knowledge has He revealed it; and the angels also testify. And God is sufficient witness.

167. Those who disbelieve and hinder (others) from the way of God, they have wandered far astray.

168. Those who disbelieve and deal in wrong, God will never forgive them, neither will He guide them to a road,

169. Except the road of hell, in which they will abide for ever. And that is ever easy for God.

170. O mankind! The messenger has come to you with the truth from your Lord. Therefore believe; (it is) better for you. But if you disbelieve, still, to God belongs whatever is in the heavens and on the earth. God is ever knower, wise.

171. O People of the Scripture! Do not exaggerate in your religion nor utter anything concerning God except the truth. The Messiah, Jesus son of Mary, was only a messenger of God, and His word which He conveyed

3. This passage criticizes the Jews for insulting the chastity of Mary.
4. The twelve tribes of Israel, by tradition descendents of the twelve sons of Jacob.

to Mary, and a spirit from Him. So believe in God and His messengers, and say not "Three"—Cease! (it is) better for you!—God is only one god.[5] Far is it removed from His transcendent majesty that He should have a son. His is all that is in the heavens and all that is in the earth. And God is sufficient as defender.

172. The Messiah will never scorn to be a servant to God, nor will the favored angels. Whoever scorns His service and is proud, all such will He assemble to Him;

173. Then, as for those who believed and did good works, to them will He pay their wages in full, adding to them of His bounty; and as for those who were scornful and proud, them will He punish with a painful doom.

174. And they will not find for them, against God, any protecting friend or helper.

175. O mankind! Now has a proof from your Lord come to you, and We have sent down to you a clear light;

176. As for those who believe in God, and hold fast to Him, them He will cause to enter into His mercy and grace, and will guide them to Him by a straight road.

177. They ask you for a pronouncement. Say: "God has pronounced for you concerning distant kindred. If a man die childless and he has a sister, hers is half the heritage, and he would have inherited from her had she died childless. And if there are two sisters, then theirs are two-thirds of the heritage, and if they are brothers, men and women, to the male is the equivalent of the share of two females." God expounds to you, so that you do not err. God is knower of all things.

## Sūra 5

*Al-Mā'ida*, "The Table Spread," derives its name from verses 112ff., where it is told how the disciples of Jesus asked that a table spread with food might be sent down from heaven and their prayer was granted, a passage in which some have seen an allusion to the Eucharist. Many authorities regard it as the last sūra in order of revelation, and Rodwell[1] has so placed it in his chronological arrangement; but the claim can only be established in the case of verse 3, which announces the completion of their religion for the Muslims, and the choice for them of Islam (the surrender to God) as their religion. That verse is undoubtedly the latest of the whole Qur'ān. It was revealed during the Prophet's last pilgrimage ("the Farewell Pilgrimage," as it is called) to Mecca, and spoken by him in the course of his address to the assembled thousands at 'Arafāt, when all Arabia had embraced Islam, only a little while before his death. It is possible that, as Nöldeke supposes, two other verses near to it are of the same date, but the remainder of the revelations contained in this sūra belong rather to the period between the fourth and seventh years of the *hijra*. Its subject is observance of religious duties. The followers of former prophets had failed through breaking their covenant, and so the Muslims are adjured to keep their covenant with God and all their obligations watchfully, because God's covenant is only with those who do right. There is more mention of the Christians here than in the former sūras, from which some writers infer that this sūra must have been

5. A reference to the Christian belief in the Trinity (Father, Son, and Holy Spirit united in one Godhead).
1. John Medows Rodwell (1808–1900), English clergyman and Orientalist; he published a translation of the Qur'ān in 1861.

revealed at the time when the Prophet was at war with certain Christian tribes belonging to the Eastern Roman Empire. But there is no evidence for that either in tradition or in the text itself.

The period of revelation is between the fifth and tenth years of the *hijra*.

## The Table Spread

*Revealed at Medina*

In the name of God, the beneficent, the merciful.

1. O you who believe! Fulfill your undertakings. The beast of cattle is made lawful to you (for food) except what is announced to you (here), game being unlawful when you are on the pilgrimage. God ordains what pleases Him.

2. O you who believe! Do not profane God's monuments nor the sacred month nor the offerings nor the garlands, nor those repairing to the Sacred House,[2] seeking the grace and pleasure of their Lord. But when you have left the sacred territory, then go hunting (if you will). And let not your hatred of a people who (once) stopped your going to the Inviolable Place of Worship seduce you to transgress; but help one another to righteousness and pious duty. Do not help one another to sin and transgression, but keep your duty to God. God is severe in punishment.

3. Forbidden to you (for food) are carrion and blood and swine-flesh, and what has been dedicated to any other than God, and the strangled, and the dead through beating, and the dead through falling from a height, and what has been killed by (the goring of) horns, and devoured by wild beasts, except what you make lawful (by the deathstroke), and what has been immolated to idols. And (forbidden is it) that you swear by the divining arrows. This is an abomination. This day are those who disbelieve in despair of (ever harming) your religion; so do not fear them, fear Me! This day have I perfected your religion for you and completed My favor to you, and have chosen for you as religion al-Islām.[3] Whoever is forced by hunger, not by will, to sin: (for him) God is forgiving, merciful.

4. They ask you (O Muhammad) what is made lawful for them. Say: "(All) good things are made lawful for you. And those beasts and birds of prey which you have trained as hounds are trained, you teach them what God taught you; so eat of what they catch for you and mention God's name upon it, and observe your duty to God. God is swift to take account.

5. "This day are (all) good things made lawful for you. The food of those who have received the scripture is lawful for you, and your food is lawful for them. And so are the virtuous women of the believers and the virtuous women of those who received the scripture before you (lawful for you) when you give them their marriage portions and live with them in honor, not in fornication, nor taking them as secret concubines. Whoever denies the faith, his work is vain and he will be among the losers in the hereafter."

6. O you who believe! When you rise up for prayer, wash your faces, and your hands up to the elbows, and lightly rub your heads and (wash)

2. I.e. the Ka'ba at Mecca [Pickthall's note].
3. I.e. "The Surrender" to God. Thus solemnly the religion which the Prophet had established received its name [Pickthall's note]. Most scholars believe this to be the final verse of the revelation, which occurred during the Farewell Pilgrimage.

your feet up to the ankles.[4] And if you are unclean, purify yourselves. And if you are sick or on a journey, or one of you comes from the toilet, or you have had contact with women, and you do not find water, then go to clean, high ground and rub your faces and your hands with some of it. God would not place a burden on you, but He would purify you and would perfect His grace on you, that you may give thanks.

7. Remember God's grace upon you and His covenant by which He bound you when you said: "We hear and we obey"; and keep your duty to God. God knows what is in the breasts (of men).

8. O you who believe! Be steadfast witnesses for God in equity, and do not let hatred of any people seduce you so that you do not deal justly. Deal justly, that is nearer to your duty. Observe your duty to God. God is informed of what you do.

9. God has promised those who believe and do good works: Theirs will be forgiveness and immense reward.

10. And they who disbelieve and deny Our revelations, such are rightful owners of hell.

11. O you who believe! Remember God's favor to you, how a people were minded to stretch out their hands against you but He withheld their hands from you; and keep your duty to God. In God let believers put their trust.

12. God made a covenant of old with the Children of Israel and We raised among them twelve leaders, and God said: "I am with you. If you establish worship and pay the poor tax, and believe in My messengers and support them, and lend to God a kindly loan,[5] surely I shall remit your sins, and surely I shall bring you into gardens underneath which rivers flow. Whoever among you disbelieves after this will go astray from a plain road."

13. And because of their breaking their covenant, We have cursed them and made hard their hearts. They change words from their context and forget a part of that by which they were admonished. You will not cease to discover treachery from all except a few of them. But bear with them and pardon them. God loves the kindly.

14. And with those who say: "We are Christians," We made a covenant, but they forgot a part of that about which they were admonished. Therefore We have stirred up enmity and hatred among them until the day of resurrection, when God will inform them of their handiwork.

15. O People of the Scripture! Now has Our messenger come to you, expounding to you much of what you used to hide in the scripture, and forgiving much. Now has come to you light from God and a plain scripture,

16. By which God guides him who seeks His good pleasure to paths of peace. He brings them out of darkness into light by His decree, and guides them to a straight path.

17. They indeed have disbelieved who say: "God is the Messiah, son of Mary." Say: "Who then can do anything against God, if He had willed to destroy the Messiah son of Mary, and his mother and everyone on earth? God's is the sovereignty of the heavens and the earth and all that is between them. He creates what He will. And God is able to do all things."

4. The syntax of this verse suggests that the face and hands are to be washed, and the head and feet are to be wiped, and that is how Shī'ī scholars read it. Sunni scholars, arguing from grammar, extend the washing to the feet.

5. I.e. a loan without interest or thought of gain [Pickthall's note].

18. The Jews and Christians say: "We are sons of God and His loved ones." Say: "Why then does He chastise you for your sins? No, you are but mortals of His creating. He forgives whom He will, and chastises whom He will. God's is the sovereignty of the heavens and the earth and all that is between them, and to Him is the journeying."

19. O People of the Scripture! Now has Our messenger come to you to make things plain after an interval (of cessation) of the messengers, for fear that you should say: "There did not come to us a messenger of cheer nor any warner." Now has a messenger of cheer and a warner come to you. God is able to do all things.

20. And (remember) when Moses said to his people: "O my people! Remember God's favor to you, how He placed among you prophets, and He made you kings, and gave you that (which) He did not give to any (other) of (His) creatures.

21. "O my people! Go into the holy land which God has ordained for you. Do not turn in flight, for surely you turn back as losers":

22. They said: "O Moses! A giant people (dwell) there, and we do not go in until they go forth from there. When they go forth, then we will enter (not until then)."

23. Then two of those who feared (their Lord) to whom God had been gracious said: "Enter in upon them by the gate, for if you enter by it, you will be victorious. So put your trust (in God) if you are indeed believers."

24. They said: "O Moses! We will never enter (the land) while they are in it. So you and your Lord go and fight! We will sit here."

25. He said: "My Lord! I have control of none but myself and my brother, so distinguish between us and the wrongdoing people."

26. (Their Lord) said: "For this the land will surely be forbidden them for forty years that they will wander on the earth, bewildered. So do not grieve over the wrongdoing people."

27. But recite to them with truth the tale of the two sons of Adam, how they offered each a sacrifice, and it was accepted from the one of them and it was not accepted from the other. (The one) said: "I will surely kill you." (The other) answered: "God accepts only from those who ward off (evil).

28. "Even if you stretch out your hand against me to kill me, I shall not stretch out my hand against you to kill you, I fear God, the Lord of the worlds.

29. "I would rather you should bear the punishment of the sin against me and your own sin and become one of the owners of the fire. That is the reward of evildoers."

30. But (the other's) mind imposed on him the killing of his brother, so he slayed him and became one of the losers.

31. Then God sent a raven scratching up the ground, to show him how to hide his brother's naked corpse. He said: "Woe to me! Am I not able to be as this raven and so hide my brother's naked corpse?" And he became repentant.

32. For that cause We decreed for the Children of Israel that whoever kills a human being for other than manslaughter or corruption on the earth, it shall be as if he had killed all mankind, and whoever saves the life of one, it shall be as if he had saved the life of all mankind. Our messengers came to them of old with clear proofs (of God's sovereignty), but afterward many of them became prodigals on the earth.

33. The only reward of those who make war upon God and His messenger and strive after corruption in the land will be that they will be killed or crucified, or will have their hands and feet on alternate sides cut off, or will be expelled out of the land. Such will be their degradation in the world, and in the hereafter theirs will be an awful doom;

34. Except those who repent before you overpower them. For know that God is forgiving, merciful.

35. O you who believe! Be mindful of your duty to God, and seek the way of approach to Him, and strive in His way in order that you may succeed.

36. As for those who disbelieve, if all that is in the earth were theirs, and as much again along with it, to ransom them from the doom on the day of resurrection, it would not be accepted from them. Theirs will be a painful doom.

37. They will wish to come forth from the fire, but they will not come forth from it. Theirs will be a lasting doom.

38. As for the thief, both male and female, cut off their hands. It is the reward of their own deeds, an exemplary punishment from God. God is mighty, wise.

39. But whoever repents after his wrongdoing and amends, God will relent toward him. God is forgiving, merciful.

40. Do you not know that to God belongs the sovereignty of the heavens and the earth? He punishes whom He will, and forgives whom He will. God is able to do all things.

41. O Messenger! Do not let them grieve you who vie with one another in the race to disbelief, of such as say with their mouths: "We believe," but their hearts believe not, and of the Jews: listeners for the sake of falsehood, listeners on behalf of other people who do not come to you, changing words from their context and saying: "If this is given to you, receive it, but if this is not given to you, then beware!" He whom God dooms to sin, you (by your efforts) will avail him nothing against God. Those are they for whom the will of God is that He cleanse not their hearts. Theirs in the world will be ignominy, and in the hereafter an awful doom;

42. Listeners for the sake of falsehood! Greedy for illicit gain! If then they have recourse to you (Muḥammad) judge between them or disclaim jurisdiction. If you disclaim jurisdiction, then they cannot harm you at all. But if you judge, judge between them with equity. God loves the equitable.

43. Why do they come to you for judgment when they have the Torah, in which God has delivered judgment (for them)? Yet even after that they turn away. Such (people) are not believers.

44. We did reveal the Torah, in which is guidance and a light, by which the prophets who surrendered (to God) judged the Jews, and the rabbis and the priests (judged) by such of God's scripture as they were bidden to observe, and they were witnesses to it. So fear not mankind, but fear Me. And do not barter My revelations for a little gain. Whoever does not judge by what God has revealed: such are disbelievers.

45. And We prescribed for them in it: The life for the life, and the eye for the eye, and the nose for the nose, and the ear for the ear, and the tooth for the tooth,[6] and for wounds retaliation. But whoever forgoes it

6. See Exodus 21:23–25; Leviticus 24:20; Deuteronomy 19:21.

(in the way of charity) it shall be expiation for him. Whoever does not judge by what God has revealed: such are wrongdoers.

46. And We caused Jesus, son of Mary, to follow in their footsteps, confirming what was (revealed) before him in the Torah, and We bestowed on him the Gospel in which is guidance and a light, confirming what was (revealed) before it in the Torah—a guidance and an admonition to those who ward off (evil).

47. Let the people of the Gospel judge by what God has revealed in it. Whoever does not judge by what God has revealed, such are iniquitous.

48. And to you have We revealed the scripture with the truth, confirming whatever scripture was before it, and a watcher over it. So judge between them by what God has revealed, and do not follow their desires away from the truth which has come to you. For each We have appointed a divine law and a traced-out way. Had God willed He could have made you one community. But that He may try you by what He has given you (He has made you as you are). So vie with one another in good works. To God you will all return, and He will then inform you of that in which you differ.

49. So judge between them by what God has revealed, and do not follow their desires, but beware of them for fear that they seduce you from some part of what God has revealed to you. And if they turn away, then know that God's will is to strike them for some sin of theirs. Many of mankind are iniquitous.

50. Is it a judgment of the time of (pagan) ignorance that they are seeking? Who is better than God for judgment to a people who have certainty (in their belief)?

51. O you who believe! Do not take the Jews and the Christians for friends. They are friends of one another. He among you who takes them for friends is (one) of them. God does not guide wrongdoing people.

52. And you see those in whose heart is a disease race toward them, saying: "We fear that a change of fortune befall us." And it may happen that God will grant (to you) the victory, or a commandment from His presence. Then they will repent of their secret thoughts.

53. Then will the believers say (to the People of the Scripture): "Are these they who swore by God their most binding oaths that they were surely with you? Their works have failed, and they have become the losers."

54. O you who believe! Whoever of you becomes a renegade from his religion, (know that in his stead) God will bring a people whom He loves and who love Him, humble toward believers, stern toward disbelievers, striving in the way of God, and not fearing the blame of any blamer. Such is the grace of God which He gives to whom He will. God is all-embracing, all-knowing.

55. Your friend can be only God; and His messenger and those who believe, who establish worship and pay the poor tax, and bow down (in prayer).[7]

56. And whoever takes God and His messenger and those who believe for friend (will know that), the party of God, they are the victorious.

57. O you who believe! Do not choose for friends such of those who received the scripture before you, and of the disbelievers, as make a jest and sport of your religion. But keep your duty to God if you are true believers.

7. Shīʿī exegetes understand this verse to refer to ʿAlī ibn Abī Ṭālib.

58. And when you call to prayer they take it for a jest and sport. That is because they are a people who do not understand.

59. Say: "O, People of the Scripture! Do you blame us for anything else than that we believe in God and what is revealed to us and what was revealed before, and because most of you are iniquitous?"

60. Shall I tell you of a worse (case) than theirs for retribution with God? Worse (is the case of him) whom God has cursed, him on whom His wrath has fallen! Worse is he of whose sort God has turned some to apes and swine,[8] and who serves idols. Such are in worse plight and further astray from the plain road.

61. When they come to you (Muslims), they say: "We believe"; but they came in in unbelief and they went out in the same; and God knows best what they were hiding.

62. And you see many of them vying with one another in sin and transgression and their devouring of illicit gain. Evil is what they do.

63. Why do not the rabbis and the priests forbid their evil-speaking and their devouring of illicit gain? Evil is their handiwork.

64. The Jews say: "God's hand is fettered." Their hands are fettered and they are accursed for saying so. No, but both His hands are spread out wide in bounty. He bestows as He will. What has been revealed to you from your Lord is certain to increase the defiance and disbelief of many of them, and We have cast among them enmity and hatred until the day of resurrection. As often as they light a fire for war, God extinguishes it. Their effort is for corruption in the land, and God does not love corrupters.

65. If only the People of the Scripture would believe and ward off (evil), surely We would remit their sins from them and surely We would bring them into gardens of delight.

66. If they had observed the Torah and the Gospel and what was revealed to them from their Lord, they would surely have been nourished from above them and from beneath their feet. Among them there are people who are moderate, but many of them are of evil conduct.

67. O Messenger! Make known what has been revealed to you from your Lord, for if you do not, you will not have conveyed His message. God will protect you from mankind. God does not guide the disbelieving people.[9]

68. Say: "O People of the Scripture! You have nothing (of guidance) until you observe the Torah and the Gospel and what was revealed to you from your Lord." What is revealed to you (Muḥammad) from your Lord is certain to increase the defiance and disbelief of many of them. But do not grieve for the disbelieving people.

69. Those who believe, and those who are Jews, and Sabaeans, and Christians—whoever believes in God and the last day and does right—no fear shall come upon them, neither shall they grieve.[1]

70. We made a covenant of old with the Children of Israel and We sent to them messengers. As often as a messenger came to them with what their souls did not desire (they became rebellious). Some (of them) they denied and some they slayed.

8. While a literalist would understand God's wrath as physically transformative, many commentators have read this verse metaphorically.

9. According to Shīʿī scholars, this verse was revealed at the pool of Ghadīr Khumm during the Farewell Pilgrimage to indicate the succession of ʿAlī ibn Abī Ṭālib to Muḥammad.

1. Almost identical with Q 2:62 [Pickthall's note].

71. They thought no harm would come of it, so they were willfully blind and deaf. And afterward God turned (in mercy) toward them. Now (even after that) are many of them willfully blind and deaf. God is observer of what they do.

72. They surely disbelieve who say: "God is the Messiah, son of Mary." The Messiah (himself) said: "O Children of Israel, worship God, my Lord and your Lord." Whoever ascribes partners to God, for him God has forbidden paradise. His abode is the fire. For evildoers there will be no helpers.

73. They surely disbelieve who say: "God is the third of three"; when there is no God except the one God. If they do not desist from so saying a painful doom will fall on those of them who disbelieve.

74. Will they not rather turn to God and seek forgiveness of Him? For God is forgiving, merciful.

75. The Messiah, son of Mary, was no other than a messenger, messengers (the like of whom) had passed away before him. And his mother was a saintly woman. And they both used to eat (earthly) food. See how We make the revelations clear for them, and see how they are turned away!

76. Say: "Do you serve in place of God what has no power to hurt or benefit you?" God it is Who is the hearer, the knower.

77. Say: "O People of the Scripture! Do not stress in your religion other than the truth, and do not follow the vain desires of people who erred of old and led many astray, and erred from a plain road."

78. Those of the Children of Israel who went astray were cursed by the tongue of David, and of Jesus, son of Mary. That was because they rebelled and used to transgress.

79. They did not restrain one another from the wickedness they did. Evil was what they used to do!

80. You see many of them making friends with those who disbelieve. Surely ill for them is what they themselves send on before them: that God will be angry with them and in the doom they will abide.

81. If they believed in God and the Prophet and what is revealed to him, they would not choose them for their friends. But many of them are of evil conduct.

82. You will find the most vehement of mankind in hostility to those who believe (to be) the Jews and the idolaters. And you will find the nearest of them in affection to those who believe (to be) those who say: "We are Christians." That is because there are among them priests and monks,[2] and because they are not proud.

83. When they listen to what has been revealed to the messenger, you see their eyes overflow with tears because of their recognition of the truth. They say: "Our Lord, we believe. Inscribe us as among the witnesses.

84. "How should we not believe in God and what has come to us of the truth. And (how should we not) hope that our Lord will bring us in along with righteous people?"

85. God has rewarded them for their saying—gardens underneath which rivers flow, in which they will abide for ever. That is the reward of the good.

86. But those who disbelieve and deny Our revelations, they are owners of hellfire.

2. I.e. persons entirely devoted to the service of God, as were the Muslims [Pickthall's note].

87. O you who believe! Do not forbid the good things which God has made lawful for you, and do not transgress. God does not love transgressors.

88. Eat of what God has bestowed on you as food lawful and good, and keep your duty to God in whom you are believers.

89. God will not take you to task for what is unintentional in your oaths, but He will take you to task for the oaths which you swear in earnest. The expiation of it is the feeding of ten of the needy with the average of that with which you feed your own people, or the clothing of them, or the liberation of a slave, and for him who does not find (the means to do so) then a three days' fast. This is the expiation of your oaths when you have sworn; and keep your oaths. Thus God expounds to you His revelations in order that you may give thanks.

90. O you who believe! Strong drink and games of chance and idols and divining arrows are only an infamy of Satan's handiwork. Leave it aside in order that you may succeed.

91. Satan seeks only to cast among you enmity and hatred by means of strong drink and games of chance, and to turn you from remembrance of God and from (His) worship. Will you then have done?

92. Obey God and obey the messenger, and beware! But if you turn away, then know that the duty of Our messenger is only plain conveyance (of the message).

93. There shall be no sin (imputed) to those who believe and do good works for what they may have eaten (in the past). So be mindful of your duty (to God), and believe, and do good works; and again: be mindful of your duty, and believe; and once again: be mindful of your duty, and do right. God loves the good.

94. O you who believe! God will surely try you somewhat (in the matter) of the game which you take with your hands and your spears, that God may know him who fears Him in secret. Whoever transgresses after this, for him there is a painful doom.

95. O you who believe! Kill no wild game while you are on the pilgrimage. Whoever of you kills it of set purpose he shall pay its forfeit in the equivalent of what he has killed, of domestic animals, the judge to be two men among you known for justice, (the forfeit) to be brought as an offering to the Kaʿba; or, for expiation, he shall feed poor persons, or the equivalent of that in fasting, that he may taste the evil consequences of his deed. God forgives whatever (of this kind) may have happened in the past, but whoever relapses, God will take retribution from him. God is mighty, able to requite (the wrong).

96. To hunt and to eat the fish of the sea is made lawful for you, a provision for you and for seafarers; but to hunt on land is forbidden you so long as you are on the pilgrimage. Be mindful of your duty to God, to whom you will be gathered.

97. God has appointed the Kaʿba, the sacred house, a standard for mankind, and the sacred month and the offerings and the garlands. That is so that you may know that God knows whatever is in the heavens and whatever is on the earth, and that God is knower of all things.

98. Know that God is severe in punishment, but that God (also) is forgiving, merciful.

99. The duty of the messenger is only to convey (the message). God knows what you proclaim and what you hide.

100. Say: The evil and the good are not alike even though the abundance of the evil attracts you. So be mindful of your duty to God, O men of understanding, that you may succeed.

101. O you who believe! Do not ask of things which, if they were made known to you, would trouble you; but if you ask of them when the Qur'ān is being revealed, they will be made known to you. God pardons this, for God is forgiving, clement.

102. A people before you asked (for such disclosures) and then disbelieved in them.

103. God has not appointed anything in the nature of a *Baḥīra* or a *Sā'iba* or a *Waṣīla* or a *Ḥām*,[3] but those who disbelieve invent a lie against God. Most of them have no sense.

104. And when it is said to them: "Come to what God has revealed and to the messenger," they say: "That in which we found our fathers is enough for us." What! Even though their fathers had no knowledge whatever, and no guidance?

105. O you who believe! You have charge of your own souls. He who errs cannot injure you if you are rightly guided. To God you will all return; and then He will inform you of what you used to do.

106. O you who believe! Let there be witnesses between you when death draws near to one of you, at the time of bequest—two witnesses, just men from among you, or two others from another tribe, in case you are campaigning in the land and the calamity of death befalls you. You shall detain them both after the prayer, and, if you doubt, they shall be made to swear by God (saying): "We will not take a bribe, even though it were (on behalf of) a near kinsman nor will we hide the testimony of God, for then indeed we should be of the sinful."

107. But then, if it is afterward ascertained that both of them merit (the suspicion of) sin, let two others take their place of those nearly concerned, and let them swear by God, (saying): "Our testimony is truer than their testimony and we have not transgressed (the bounds of duty), for then indeed we should be of the evildoers."

108. Thus it is more likely that they will bear true witness or fear that after their oath the oath (of others) will be taken. So be mindful of your duty (to God) and listen. God guides not the obstinate people.

109. In the day when God gathers together the messengers, and says: "What was your response (from mankind)?" they say: "We have no knowledge. You, only You are the knower of things hidden."

110. When God says: "O Jesus, son of Mary! Remember My favor to you and to your mother; how I strengthened you with the holy spirit, so that you could speak to mankind in the cradle as in maturity; and how I taught you the scripture and wisdom and the Torah and the Gospel; and how you shaped of clay as it were the likeness of a bird by My permission, and blew upon it and it was a bird by My permission, and you healed him who was born blind and the leper by My permission; and how you raised the dead

3. Different classes of cattle liberated in honor of idols and reverenced by the pagan Arabs [Pickthall's note].

by My permission;[4] and how I restrained the Children of Israel from (harming) you when you came to them with clear proofs, and those of them who disbelieved exclaimed: 'This is nothing else than mere magic';

111. "And when I inspired the disciples, (saying): 'Believe in Me and in My messenger,' they said: 'We believe. Bear witness that we have surrendered[5] (to You).'"

112. When the disciples said: "O Jesus, son of Mary! Is your Lord able to send down for us a table spread with food from heaven?" He said: "Observe your duty to God, if you are true believers."

113. (They said:) "We wish to eat of it, that we may satisfy our hearts and know that you have spoken truth to us, and that of it we may be witnesses."

114. Jesus, son of Mary, said: "O God, Lord of us! Send down for us a table spread with food from heaven, that it may be a feast for us, for the first of us and for the last of us, and a sign from You. Give us sustenance, for You are the best of sustainers."

115. God said: "I send it down for you. And whoever disbelieves of you afterward, him I will punish with a punishment with which I have not punished any of (My) creatures."

116. And when God says: "O Jesus, son of Mary! Did you say to mankind: 'Take me and my mother for two gods beside God?'" he says: "Be glorified! It was not mine to utter that to which I had no right. If I used to say it, then You knew it. You know what is in my mind, and I do not know what is in Your mind. You, only You are the knower of things hidden."

117. I spoke to them only what You commanded me, (saying): "Worship God, my Lord and your Lord." I was a witness of them while I dwelt among them, and when You took me You were the watcher over them. You are witness over all things.

118. If You punish them, they are Your servants, and if You forgive them (they are Your servants). You, only You are the mighty, the wise.

119. God says: "This is a day in which their truthfulness profits the truthful, for theirs are gardens underneath which rivers flow, in which they are secure for ever, God taking pleasure in them and they in Him. That is the great triumph.

120. "To God belongs the sovereignty of the heavens and the earth and whatever is in it, and He is able to do all things."

## Sūra 6

*Al-An'ām*, "Cattle," takes its name from a word in verse 137, repeated in verses 139, 140, where cattle are mentioned in connection with superstitious practices condemned by Islam.

With the possible exception of nine verses, which some authorities—e.g. Ibn Salāma[1]—ascribe to the Medina period, the whole of this sūra belongs to the year before the *hijra*. It is related, on the authority of Ibn 'Abbās,[2] that it was revealed in a single visitation. It is placed here on account of the subject, vindication of the divine unity, which fittingly follows on the subjects of the previous sūras. The note of certain triumph is remarkable in the

4. See, e.g., Matthew 8–9.
5. Or "are Muslims" [Pickthall's note].
1. Hibāt Allah ibn Salāma (d. 1020), an authority on abrogation in the Qur'ān.
2. A Companion of Muḥammad (ca. 619–687/88), and one of the great scholars of early Islam.

circumstances of its revelation, when the Prophet, after thirteen years of effort, saw himself obliged to flee from Mecca and seek help from strangers.
A late Meccan sūra.

## Cattle

*Revealed at Mecca*

In the name of God, the beneficent, the merciful.

1. Praise be to God, who has created the heavens and the earth, and has appointed darkness and light. Yet those who disbelieve ascribe rivals to their Lord.

2. He it is who has created you from clay, and has decreed a term for you. A term is fixed with Him. Yet still you doubt!

3. He is God in the heavens and on the earth. He knows both your secret and your utterance, and He knows what you earn.

4. There never came to them a revelation of the revelations of God but they turned away from it.

5. And they denied the truth when it came to them. But there will come to them the tidings of that which they used to deride.

6. Do they not see how many a generation We destroyed before them, whom We had established on the earth more firmly than We have established you, and We shed on them abundant showers from the sky, and made the rivers flow beneath them? Yet We destroyed them for their sins, and created after them another generation.

7. Had we sent down to you (Muḥammad) (actual) writing upon parchment, so that they could feel it with their hands, those who disbelieve would have said: "This is nothing else than mere magic."

8. They say: "Why has an angel not been sent down to him?" If We sent down an angel, then the matter would be judged; no further time would be allowed them (for reflection).

9. Had We appointed an angel (Our messenger), We would have made him (as) a man (that he might speak to men); and (thus) obscured for them (the truth) they (now) obscure.

10. Messengers (of God) have been derided before you, but that at which they scoffed surrounded those of them who did deride.

11. Say (to the disbelievers): "Travel in the land, and see the nature of the consequence for the rejecters!"

12. Say: "To whom belongs whatever is in the heavens and the earth?" Say: To God. He has prescribed for Himself mercy, that He may bring you all together to the day of resurrection of which there is no doubt. Those who ruin their own souls will not believe.

13. To Him belongs whatever rests in the night and the day. He is the hearer, the knower.

14. Say: "Shall I choose for a protecting friend other than God, the originator of the heavens and the earth, who feeds and is never fed?" Say: "I am ordered to be the first to surrender (to Him)." And do not be (O Muḥammad) of the idolaters.

15. Say: "I fear, if I rebel against my Lord, the retribution of an awful day."

16. He from whom (such retribution) is averted on that day, (God) has in truth had mercy on him. That will be the signal triumph.

17. If God touches you with affliction, there is no one that can relieve (you) from it except Him, and if He touch you with good fortune (there is no one that can impair it); for He is able to do all things.

18. He is the omnipotent over His servants, and He is the wise, the knower.

19. Say (O Muḥammad): "What thing is of most weight in testimony?" Say: "God is witness between you and me. And this Qur'ān has been inspired in me, that I may warn you with it and whomever it may reach. Do you in truth bear witness that there are gods beside God?" Say: "I bear no such witness." Say: "He is only one God. I am innocent of what you associate (with Him)."

20. Those to whom We gave the scripture recognize (this revelation) as they recognize their sons. Those who ruin their own souls will not believe.

21. Who does greater wrong than he who invents a lie against God and denies His revelations? The wrongdoers will not be successful.

22. And on the day We gather them together We shall say to those who ascribed partners (to God): "Where are (now) those partners of your make-believe?"

23. Then they will have no contention except that they will say: "By God, our Lord, we were never idolaters."

24. See how they lie against themselves, and (how) the thing which they devised has failed them!

25. Of them are some who listen to you, but We have placed upon their hearts veils, for fear that they should understand, and in their ears a deafness. If they saw every sign they would not believe in it; to the point that, when they come to you to argue with you, the disbelievers say: "This is nothing other than fables of the men of old."

26. And they forbid (men) from it and avoid it, and they ruin no one but themselves, though they perceive not.

27. If you could see when they are set before the fire and say: "Oh, would that we might return! Then we would not deny the revelations of our Lord but we would be of the believers!"

28. No, but that has become clear to them which before they used to hide. And if they were sent back they would return to what they are forbidden. They are liars.

29. And they say: "There is nothing except our life of the world, and we shall not be raised (again)."

30. If you could see when they are set before their Lord! He will say: "Is not this real?" They will say: "Yes, by our Lord!" He will say: "Taste now the retribution because you used to disbelieve."

31. They indeed are losers who deny their meeting with God until, when the hour comes on them suddenly, they cry: "Alas for us, that we neglected it!" They bear upon their backs their burdens. Evil is what they bear!

32. The life of the world is nothing but a pastime and a sport. Better far is the abode of the hereafter for those who keep their duty (to God). Have you then no sense?

33. We know well how their talk grieves you, though in truth they do not deny you (Muḥammad), but evildoers flout the revelations of God.

34. Messengers indeed have been denied before you, and they were patient under the denial and the persecution until Our succor reached them. There is none to alter the decisions of God. Already there has reached you (somewhat) of the tidings of the messengers (We sent before).

35. And if their aversion is grievous to you, then, if you can, seek a way down into the earth or a ladder to the sky that you may bring to them a sign (to convince them all)!—If God willed, He could have brought them all together to the guidance—So be not among the foolish ones.

36. Only those can accept who hear. As for the dead, God will raise them up; then to Him they will be returned.

37. They say: "Why has no sign been sent down upon him from his Lord?" Say: "God is able to send down a sign. But most of them know not."

38. There is not an animal on the earth, nor a flying creature flying on two wings, but they are peoples like you. We have neglected nothing in the book (of Our decrees). Then to their Lord they will be gathered.

39. Those who deny our revelations are deaf and dumb in darkness. Whom God wills He sends astray, and whom He wills He places on a straight path.

40. Say: "Can you see yourselves, if the punishment of God comes upon you or the hour comes upon you, calling upon other than God? Do you then call (for help) to any other than God? (Answer that) if you are truthful.

41. "No, but to Him you call, and He removes that because of which you call to Him, if He will, and you forget whatever partners you ascribed to Him."

42. We have already sent to peoples who were before you, and We visited them with tribulation and adversity, in order that they might grow humble.

43. If only, when our disaster came on them, they had been humble! But their hearts were hardened and the devil made all that they used to do seem fair to them!

44. Then, when they forgot that of which they had been reminded, We opened to them the gates of all things until, even as they were rejoicing in what they were given, We seized them unawares, and they were dumbfounded.

45. So of the people who did wrong the last remnant was cut off. Praise be to God, Lord of the worlds!

46. Say: "Have you imagined, if God should take away your hearing and your sight and seal your hearts, who is the God who could restore it to you except God?" See how We display the revelations to them! Yet still they turn away.

47. Say: "Can you see yourselves, if the punishment of God comes upon you unawares or openly? Would any perish except wrongdoing people?"

48. We do not send the messengers except as bearers of good news and warners. Whoever believes and does right, no fear shall come upon them neither shall they grieve.

49. But as for those who deny Our revelations, torment will afflict them because they used to disobey.

50. Say (O Muḥammad, to the disbelievers): "I do not say to you (that) I possess the treasures of God, nor that I have knowledge of the unseen; and I do not say to you: 'I am an angel.' I follow only what is inspired in

me." Say: "Are the blind man and the one who sees equal? Will you not then take thought?"

51. Warn by it those who fear (because they know) that they will be gathered to their Lord, for whom there is no protecting friend nor intercessor beside Him, that they may ward off (evil).

52. Do not repel those who call upon their Lord at morning and evening, seeking His countenance. You are not accountable for them in anything, nor are they accountable for you in anything, such that you should repel them and be of the wrongdoers.

53. And even so We try some of them by others, that they say: "Are these they whom God favors among us? Is not God best aware of the thanksgivers?"

54. And when those who believe in Our revelations come to you, say: "Peace be to you! Your Lord has prescribed for Himself mercy, that whoever of you does evil through ignorance and repents of it afterward and does right, (for him) God is forgiving, merciful."

55. Thus We expound the revelations that the way of the unrighteous may be manifest.

56. Say: "I am forbidden to worship those on whom you call instead of God." Say: "I will not follow your desires, for then I should go astray and I should not be of the rightly guided."

57. Say: "I am (relying) on clear proof from my Lord, while you deny Him. I do not have that for which you are impatient. The decision is for God only. He tells the truth and He is the best of deciders."

58. Say: "If I had that for which you are impatient, then the case (before this) would have been decided between me and you. God is best aware of the wrongdoers.

59. "And with Him are the keys of the invisible. None but He knows them. And He knows what is in the land and the sea. Not a leaf falls but He knows it, not a grain amid the darkness of the earth, nothing of wet or dry but (it is noted) in a clear record.

60. "He it is Who gathers you at night and knows that which you commit by day. Then He raises you again to life in it, that the term appointed (for you) may be accomplished. And afterward to Him is your return. Then He will proclaim to you what you used to do.

61. "He is the omnipotent over His servants. He sends guardians over you until, when death comes to one of you, Our messengers[3] receive him, and they neglect not.

62. "Then are they restored to God, their Lord, the just. Surely His is the judgment. And He is the most swift of reckoners."

63. Say: "Who delivers you from the darkness of the land and the sea?" You call upon Him humbly and in secret, (saying): "If we are delivered from this (fear) we will be of the thankful."

64. Say: "God delivers you from this and from all affliction. Yet you attribute partners to Him."

65. Say: "He is able to send punishment upon you from above you or from beneath your feet, or to bewilder you with dissension and make you taste the tyranny one of another." See how We display the revelations so that they may understand.

3. I.e. angels. The same word *rusul* is used for angels and for prophets [Pickthall's note].

66. Your people (O Muḥammad) have denied it, though it is the truth. Say: "I am not put in charge of you."

67. For every announcement there is a term, and you will come to know.

68. And when you see those who meddle with Our revelations, withdraw from them until they meddle with another topic. And if the devil causes you to forget, do not sit, after the remembrance, with the congregation of wrongdoers.

69. Those who ward off (evil) are not accountable for them in anything, but the reminder (must be given them) that they (too) may ward off (evil).

70. And forsake those who take their religion for a pastime and a jest, and whom the life of the world beguiles. Remind (mankind) by it [the Qur'ān] for fear that a soul be destroyed by what it earns. It has no friend beside God nor intercessor, and though it offer every compensation it will not be accepted from it. Those are they who perish by their own deserts. For them is boiling water to drink[4] and a painful doom, because they disbelieved.

71. Say: "Shall we cry, instead of to God, to that which neither profits us nor hurts us, and shall we turn back after God has guided us, like one bewildered whom the devils have infatuated on the earth, who has companions who invite him to the guidance (saying): 'Come to us?'" Say: "The guidance of God is guidance, and we are ordered to surrender to the Lord of the worlds,"

72. And to establish worship and be dutiful to Him, and He it is to whom you will be gathered.

73. He it is who created the heavens and the earth in truth. In the day when He says: "Be!" it is.

74. His word is the truth, and His will be the sovereignty on the day when the trumpet is blown. Knower of the invisible and the visible, He is the wise, the aware.

75. (Remember) when Abraham said to his father Azar: "Do you take idols for gods?[5] I see you and your people in manifest error."

76. Thus We showed Abraham the kingdom of the heavens and the earth that he might be of those possessing certainty:

77. When the night grew dark upon him he beheld a star. He said: "This is my Lord." But when it set, he said: "I don't love things that set."

78. And when he saw the moon rising, he exclaimed: "This is my Lord." But when it set, he said: "Unless my Lord guide me, I surely shall become one of the people who are astray."

79. And when he saw the sun rising, he cried: "This is my Lord! This is greater!" And when it set he exclaimed: "O my people! I am free from all that you associate (with Him).

80. "I have turned my face toward Him Who created the heavens and the earth, as one by nature upright, and I am not of the idolaters."

81. His people argued with him. He said: "Do you dispute with me concerning God when He has guided me? I fear not at all what you set up beside Him unless my Lord wills. My Lord includes all things in His knowledge. Will you not remember?

4. One of the punishments of hell.
5. According to rabbinic tradition, Abraham's father (Terah) manufactured idols.

82. "How should I fear that which you set up beside Him, when you do not fear to set up beside God that for which He has revealed to you no warrant? Which of the two factions has more right to safety? (Answer me that) if you have knowledge."

83. Those who believe and do not obscure their belief by wrongdoing, theirs is safety; and they are rightly guided.

84. That is Our argument. We gave it to Abraham against his people. We raise to degrees of wisdom whom We will. Your Lord is wise, aware.

85. And We bestowed on him Isaac and Jacob; each of them We guided; and Noah We guided before; and of his seed (We guided) David and Solomon and Job and Joseph and Moses and Aaron. Thus We reward the good.

86. And Zechariah and John and Jesus and Elias. Each one (of them) was of the righteous.

87. And Ishmael and Elisha and Jonah and Lot. Each of them We preferred above (Our) creatures,

88. With some of their forefathers and their offspring and their brothers; and We chose them and guided them to a straight path.

89. Such is the guidance of God with which He guides whom He will of His servants. But if they had set up (for worship) anything beside Him, (all) that they did would have been vain.

90. Those are they to whom We gave the scripture and command and prophethood. But if these disbelieve in it, then indeed We shall entrust it to a people who will not be disbelievers in it.

91. Those are they whom God guides, so follow their guidance. Say (O Muḥammad, to mankind): "I ask of you no fee for it. It is nothing but a reminder to (His) creatures."

92. And they do not measure the power of God its true measure when they say: "God has revealed nothing to a human being." Say (to the Jews who speak thus): "Who revealed the book which Moses brought, a light and guidance for mankind, which you have put on parchments which you show, but you hide much (of it), and by which you were taught that which you knew not yourselves nor (did) your fathers (know it)?" Say: God. "Then leave them to their play of foolish chatter."

93. And this is a blessed scripture which We have revealed, confirming that which (was revealed) before it, that you may warn the mother of villages[6] and those around her. Those who believe in the hereafter believe in it (the scriptures), and they are careful of their worship.

94. Who is guilty of more wrong than he who forges a lie against God, or says: "I am inspired," when he is not inspired in anything; and who says: "I will reveal the like of what God has revealed"? If you could see, when the wrongdoers reach the pangs of death and the angels stretch their hands out, saying: "Deliver up your souls. This day you are awarded the punishment of degradation for what you used to say concerning God other than the truth, and scorned His signs."

95. Now you have come to Us singly as We created you at the first, and you have left behind you all that We bestowed upon you, and We do not see your intercessors with you, of whom you claimed that they possessed a share in you. Now is the bond between you severed, and that which you presumed has failed you.

6. I.e. Mecca [Pickthall's note].

96. God (it is) who splits the grain of corn and the date stone (for sprouting). He brings forth the living from the dead, and is the bringer-forth of the dead from the living. Such is God. How then are you perverted?

97. He is the cleaver of the daybreak, and He has appointed the night for stillness, and the sun and the moon for reckoning. That is the measuring of the mighty, the wise.

98. And He it is who has set for you the stars that you may guide your course by them amid the darkness of the land and the sea. We have detailed Our revelations for a people who have knowledge.

99. And He it is who has produced you from a single being, and (has given you) a habitation and a repository. We have detailed Our revelations for a people who have understanding.

100. He it is Who sends down water from the sky, and with it We bring forth buds of every kind; We bring forth the green blade from which We bring forth the thick-clustered grain; and from the date palm, from its pollen, spring pendant bunches; and (We bring forth) gardens of grapes, and the olive and the pomegranate, alike and unlike. Look upon its fruit, when they bear fruit, and upon its ripening. In this are signs for a people who believe.

101. Yet they ascribe as partners to Him the jinn,[7] although He did create them, and impute falsely, without knowledge, sons and daughters to Him. Glorified be He and high exalted above (all) that they ascribe (to Him).

102. The originator of the heavens and the earth! How can He have a child, when there is for Him no consort, when He created all things and is aware of all things?

103. Such is God, your Lord. There is no god except Him, the creator of all things, so worship Him. And He takes care of all things.

104. Vision does not comprehend Him, but He comprehends (all) vision. He is the subtle, the aware.

105. Proofs have come to you from your Lord, so whoever sees, it is for his own good, and whoever is blind is blind to his own hurt. And I am not a keeper over you.

106. Thus We display Our revelations that they may say (to you, Muḥammad): "You have studied," and that We may make (it) clear for people who have knowledge.

107. Follow that which is inspired in you from your Lord; there is no god except Him; and turn away from the idolaters.

108. Had God willed, they would not have been idolatrous. We have not set you as a keeper over them, nor are you responsible for them.

109. Do not revile those to whom they pray beside God for fear that they wrongfully revile God through ignorance. Thus to every nation have We made their deed seem fair. Then to their Lord is their return, and He will tell them what they used to do.

110. And they swear a solemn oath by God that if there comes to them a sign they will believe in it. Say: "Signs are with God and (so is) that which tells you that if such came to them they would not believe."

111. We confound their hearts and their eyes. As they did not believe in it at the first, We let them wander blindly on in their defiance.

7. The third class of intelligent beings (together with humans and angels) for whom salvation is possible. According to Q 55:15, God created them from smokeless fire.

112. And though We should send down the angels to them, and the dead should speak to them, and We should gather against them all things in array, they would not believe unless God so willed. Yet, most of them are ignorant.

113. Thus have We appointed to every prophet an adversary—devils of humankind and jinn who inspire in one another plausible discourse through guile. If your Lord willed, they would not do so; so leave them alone with their devising;

114. That the hearts of those who do not believe in the hereafter may incline to it, and that they may take pleasure in it, and that they may earn what they are earning.

115. Shall I seek other than God for judge, when He it is who has revealed to you (this) scripture, fully explained? Those to whom We gave the scripture (before) know that it is revealed from your Lord in truth. So be not (O Muḥammad) among the waverers.

116. Perfected is the Word of your Lord in truth and justice. There is nothing that can change His words. He is the hearer, the knower.

117. If you obeyed most of those on earth they would mislead you far from God's way. They follow nothing but an opinion, and they only guess.

118. Your Lord knows best who errs from His way; and He knows best (who are) the rightly guided.

119. Eat of that over which the name of God has been mentioned,[8] if you are believers in His revelations.

120. How should you not eat of that over which the name of God has been mentioned, when He has explained to you what is forbidden to you, unless you are compelled to do so. But many are led astray by their own lusts through ignorance. Your Lord, He is best aware of the transgressors.

121. Forsake the outwardness of sin and its inwardness. Those who garner sin will be awarded what they have earned.

122. And do not eat of that over which God's name has not been mentioned, for it is abomination. The devils inspire their minions to dispute with you. But if you obey them, in truth you will be idolaters.

123. Is he who was dead and We have raised him to life, and set for him a light in which he walks among men, as him whose similitude is in utter darkness from which he cannot emerge? Thus is their conduct made fair seeming for the disbelievers.

124. And thus have We made in every city great ones of its wicked ones, that they should plot in it. They plot only against themselves, though they perceive not.

125. And when a sign comes to them, they say: "We will not believe until we are given what God's messengers are given." God knows best with whom to place His message. Humiliation from God and heavy punishment will strike the guilty for their scheming.

126. And whomever it is God's will to guide, He expands his breast to the surrender,[9] and whomever it is His will to send astray, He makes his breast close and narrow as if he were engaged in sheer ascent. Thus God lays ignominy upon those who do not believe.

127. This is the path of your Lord, a straight path. We have detailed Our revelations for a people who take heed.

8. During slaughter.
9. Islam [Pickthall's note].

128. For them is the abode of peace with their Lord. He will be their protecting friend because of what they used to do.

129. In the day when He will gather them together (He will say): "O you assembly of the jinn! Many of humankind did you seduce." And their adherents among humankind will say: "Our Lord! We enjoyed one another, but now we have arrived at the appointed term which You appointed for us." He will say: "Fire is your home. Abide in it forever, except him whom God wills (to deliver). Your Lord is wise, aware."

130. Thus We let some of the wrongdoers have power over others because of what they are accustomed to earn.

131. O you assembly of the jinn and humankind! Did there not come to you messengers of your own who recounted to you My signs and warned you of the meeting of this your day? They will say: "We testify against ourselves." And the life of the world beguiled them. And they testify against themselves that they were disbelievers.

132. This is because your Lord does not destroy the townships arbitrarily while their people are unconscious (of the wrong they do).

133. For all there will be ranks from what they did. Your Lord is not unaware of what they do.

134. Your Lord is the absolute, the Lord of mercy. If He will, He can remove you and can cause what He will to follow after you, even as He raised you from the seed of other people.

135. That which you are promised will surely come to pass, and you cannot escape.

136. Say (O Muḥammad): "O my people! Work according to your power. I too am working. Thus you will come to know for which of us will be the happy sequel. The wrongdoers will not be successful."

137. They assign to God, of the crops and cattle which He created, a portion, and they say: "This is God's"—in their make-believe—"and this is for (His) partners in regard to us." Thus that which (they assign) to His partners in them does not reach God and that which (they assign) to God goes to their (so-called) partners. Evil is their ordinance.

138. Thus have their (so-called) partners (of God) made the killing of their children seem fair to many of the idolaters, that they may ruin them and make their faith obscure for them. Had God willed (it otherwise), they would not have done so. So leave them alone with their devices.

139. And they say: "Such cattle and crops are forbidden." No one is to eat of them except whom we will—in their make-believe—cattle whose backs are forbidden, cattle over which they do not mention the name of God. (All that is) a lie against Him. He will repay them for what they invent.

140. And they say: "What is in the bellies of such cattle is reserved for our males and is forbidden to our wives; but if it be born dead, then they (all) may be partakers of it." He will reward them for their attribution (of such ordinances to Him).[1] He is wise, aware.

141. They are losers who besottedly have slain their children without knowledge,[2] and have forbidden that which God bestowed upon them, inventing a lie against God. They indeed have gone astray and are not guided.

1. Verses 139 and 140 refer to customs of the pagan Arabs [Pickthall's note].
2. The reference is to the burial alive of female children who were deemed superfluous, and the practice of human sacrifice to idols [Pickthall's note].

142. He it is Who produces gardens trellised and untrellised, and the date palm, and crops of diverse flavor, and the olive and the pomegranate, like and unlike. Eat of its fruit when it flowers, and pay its due upon the harvest day, and do not be prodigal. God does not love the prodigals.

143. And of the cattle (He produces) some for burdens, some for food. Eat of what God has bestowed upon you, and do not follow the footsteps of the devil, for he is an open foe to you.

144. Eight pairs: Of the sheep two, and of the goats two. Say: "Has He forbidden the two males or the two females, or what the wombs of the two females contain? Expound to me (the case) with knowledge, if you are truthful."[3]

145. And of the camels two and of the oxen two. Say: "Has He forbidden the two males or the two females, or that which the wombs of the two females contain; or were you witnesses when God commanded you (all) this? Then who does greater wrong than he who devises a lie concerning God, that he may lead mankind astray without knowledge. God does not guide wrongdoing people."

146. Say: "I do not find in what is revealed to me anything prohibited to an eater of that which he eats, except carrion, or blood poured forth, or swine-flesh—for that is foul—or the abomination which was immolated to the name of other than God. But who is compelled (to that), neither craving nor transgressing, (for him) your Lord is forgiving, merciful."

147. To those who are Jews We forbade every animal with claws. And of the oxen and the sheep We forbade to them their fat except that on the backs or the entrails, or that which is mixed with the bone. That We awarded them for their rebellion. And We are truthful.

148. So if they give the lie to you (Muḥammad), say: "Your Lord is a Lord of all-embracing mercy, and His wrath will never be withdrawn from guilty people."

149. They who are idolaters will say: "Had God willed, we would not have ascribed (to Him) partners, neither would our fathers, nor would we have forbidden anything." Thus did those who were before them give the lie (to God's messengers) until they tasted of the fear of Us. Say: "Have you any knowledge that you can adduce for us? You follow nothing but an opinion, you only guess."

150. Say—for God's is the final argument—had He willed, He could indeed have guided all of you.

151. Say: "Come, bring your witnesses who can bear witness that God forbade (all) this." And if they bear witness, do not bear witness with them. Do not follow the whims of those who deny Our revelations, those who do not believe in the hereafter and think (others) equal with their Lord.

152. Say: "Come, I will recite to you what your Lord has made a sacred duty for you: that you ascribe no thing as partner to Him and that you do good to parents, and that you do not slay your children because of poverty—We provide for you and for them—and that you do not draw near to lewd things whether open or concealed. And that you do not slay

3. This and the following verses relate to superstitions of the pagan Arabs with regard to cattle used for food [Pickthall's note].

the life which God has made sacred, except in the course of justice. This He has commanded you, in order that you may discern."

153. And do not approach the wealth of the orphan except with what is better, until he reaches maturity. Give full measure and full weight, in justice. We do not task any soul beyond its scope. And if you give your word, do justice, even though it be (against) a kinsman; and fulfill the covenant of God. This He commands you that perhaps you may remember.

154. And (He commands you, saying): This is My straight path, so follow it. Do not follow other ways, for fear that you will be parted from His way. This has he ordained for you in order that you may ward off evil.

155. Again, We gave the scripture to Moses, complete for him who would do good, an explanation of all things, a guidance and a mercy, that they might believe in the meeting with their Lord.

156. And this is a blessed scripture which We have revealed. So follow it and ward off (evil), that you may find mercy.

157. For fear that you should say: "The scripture was revealed only to two groups before us, and we were unaware of what they read";

158. Or for fear that you should say: "If the scripture had been revealed to us, we surely would have been better guided than they." Now there has come to you a clear proof from your Lord, a guidance and a mercy; and who does greater wrong than he who denies the revelations of God, and turns away from them? We award to those who turn away from Our revelations an evil doom because of their aversion.

159. Do they wait, indeed, for nothing less than that the angels should come to them, or your Lord should come, or there should come one of the signs from your Lord? In the day when one of the signs from your Lord comes, its belief does not avail a soul which did not believe before, and in its belief did not earn good (by works). Say: "Wait!" We (too) are waiting.

160. As for those who sunder their religion and become schismatics, you have no concern at all with them. Their case will go to God, who then will tell them what they used to do.

161. Whoever brings a good deed will receive the like of it tenfold, while whoever brings an ill deed will be awarded only its like; and they will not be wronged.

162. Say: "As for me, my Lord has guided me to a straight path, a right religion, the community of Abraham, the upright, who was no idolater."

163. Say: "My worship and my sacrifice and my living and my dying are for God, Lord of the worlds.

164. "He has no partner. This I am commanded, and I am first of those who surrender (to Him)."

165. Say: "Shall I seek another than God for Lord, when He is Lord of all things?" Each soul earns only on its own account, nor does any laden bear another's load. Then to your Lord is your return and He will tell you in what you differed.

166. He it is who has placed you as viceroys of the earth and has exalted some of you in rank above others, that He may try you by (the test of) that which He has given you. Your Lord is swift in prosecution, and He is forgiving, merciful.

## Sūra 7

*Al*-Aʿrāf, "The Heights," takes its name from a word in verse 46, "And on the heights are men who know them all by their marks." The best authorities assign the whole of it to about the same period as Q 6, i.e. the Prophet's last year in Mecca, though some consider verses 163–167 to have been revealed at Medina. The subject may be said to be the opponents of God's will and purpose, from Satan onward, through the history of divine guidance.

A late Meccan sūra.

## The Heights

*Revealed at Mecca*

In the name of God, the beneficent, the merciful.

1. Alif. Lām. Mīm. Ṣād.[1]
2. (It is) a scripture that is revealed to you (Muḥammad)—so let there be no heaviness in your heart from it—that you may warn with it, and (it is) a reminder to believers.
3. (Saying): "Follow that which is sent down to you from your Lord, and follow no protecting friends beside Him. Little do you recollect!"
4. How many a township have We destroyed! As a raid by night, or while they slept at noon, Our terror came to them.
5. No plea had they, when Our terror came to them, except that they said: "We were wrongdoers."
6. Then We shall question those to whom (Our message) has been sent, and We shall question the messengers.
7. Then We shall narrate to them (the event) with knowledge, for We were not absent (when it came to pass).
8. The weighing on that day is the true (weighing). As for those whose scale is heavy, they are the successful.
9. And as for those whose scale is light: those are they who lose their souls because they used to reject Our revelations.
10. And We have given you (mankind) power on the earth, and appointed for you livelihoods in it. Little do you give thanks!
11. And We created you, then fashioned you, then told the angels: "Fall prostrate before Adam!" And they fell prostrate, all except Iblīs, who was not of those who make prostration.
12. He said: "What hindered you that you did not fall prostrate when I bade you?" (Iblīs) said: "I am better than him. You created me of fire while him You created of mud."
13. He said: "Then go down from here! It is not for you to show pride here, so go forth! You are of those degraded."
14. He said: "Reprieve me until the day when they are raised (from the dead)."
15. He said: "You are of those reprieved."
16. He said: "Now, because You have sent me astray, I shall lurk in ambush for them on Your right path.

1. See Q 2:1, footnote [Pickthall's note].

17. "Then I shall come upon them from before them and from behind them and from their right hands and from their left hands, and You will not find most of them beholden (to You)."

18. He said: "Go forth from here, degraded, banished. As for such of them as follow you, surely I will fill hell with all of you."

19. And (to man): "O Adam! You and your wife dwell in the garden and eat from where you will, but come not near this tree for fear that you become wrongdoers."[2]

20. Then Satan whispered to them that he might manifest to them that which was hidden from them of their shame, and he said: "Your Lord forbade you from this tree only for fear that you should become angels or become of the immortals."

21. And he swore to them (saying): "I am a sincere adviser to you."

22. Thus did he lead them on with guile. And when they tasted of the tree their shame was manifest to them and they began to hide (by heaping) on themselves some of the leaves of the garden. And their Lord called them, (saying): "Did I not forbid you from that tree and tell you: 'Satan is an open enemy to you?'"

23. They said: "Our Lord! We have wronged ourselves. If You do not forgive us and do not have mercy on us, surely we are of the lost!"

24. He said: "Go down (from here), one of you a foe to the other. There will be for you on earth a habitation and provision for a while."

25. He said: "There shall you live, and there shall you die, and from there shall you be brought forth.

26. "O Children of Adam! We have revealed to you garments to conceal your shame, and finery, but the garment of restraint from evil, that is best. This is of the revelations of God, that they may remember.

27. "O Children of Adam! Let not Satan seduce you as he caused your (first) parents to go forth from the garden and tore off from them their robe (of innocence) that he might manifest their shame to them. He sees you, he and his tribe, from where you do not see him. We have made the devils friends to protect those who do not believe."

28. And when they do some lewdness they say: "We found our fathers doing it and God has enjoined it on us." Say: "God does not enjoin lewdness. Do you tell concerning God that which you know not?"

29. Say: "My Lord enjoins justice." And set your faces, upright (toward Him) at every place of worship and call upon Him, making religion pure for Him (only). As He brought you into being, so return (to Him).

30. He has led a party aright, while error has just hold over (another) party, for they choose the devils for protecting friends instead of God and think that they are rightly guided.

31. O Children of Adam! Look to your adornment at every place of worship, and eat and drink, but do not be prodigal. He does not love the prodigals.

32. Say: "Who has forbidden the adornment of God which He has brought forth for His servants, and the good things of His providing?" Say: "Such, on the day of resurrection, will be only for those who believed during the life of the world." Thus do We detail Our revelations for people who have knowledge.

2. Cf. Genesis 3.

33. Say: "My Lord forbids only indecencies, such of them as are apparent and such as are within, and sin and wrongful oppression, and that you associate with God that for which no warrant has been revealed, and that you tell concerning God what you know not."

34. And every nation has its term, and when its term comes, they cannot put it off an hour nor yet advance (it).

35. O Children of Adam! If messengers of your own come to you who narrate to you My revelations, then whoever refrains from evil and amends—no fear shall come upon them, neither shall they grieve.

36. But they who deny Our revelations and scorn them—such are rightful owners of the fire; they will abide there.

37. Who does greater wrong than he who invents a lie concerning God or denies Our signs? (For such) their appointed portion of the book (of destiny) reaches them until, when Our messengers[3] come to gather them, they say: "Where (now) is that i.e. the gods to which you cried beside God?" They say: "They have departed from us." And they testify against themselves that they were disbelievers.

38. He says: "Enter into the fire among nations of the jinn and humankind who passed away before you." Every time a nation enters, it curses its sister (nation) until, when they have all been made to follow one another there, the last of them says to the first of them: "Our Lord! These led us astray, so give them double torment of the fire." He says: "For each one there is double (torment), but you know not."

39. And the first of them says to the last of them: "You were in no way better than us, so taste the doom for what you have earned."

40. They who deny Our revelations and scorn them, for them the gates of heaven will not be opened nor will they enter the garden until the camel goes through the needle's eye.[4] Thus do We requite the guilty.

41. Theirs will be a bed of hell, and over them coverings (of hell). Thus do We requite wrongdoers.

42. But (as for) those who believe and do good works—We tax not any soul beyond its scope—such are rightful owners of the garden. They abide in it.

43. And We remove whatever rancor may be in their hearts. Rivers flow beneath them. And they say: "Praise to God, Who has guided us to this. We could not truly have been led aright if God had not guided us." The messengers of our Lord did bring the truth. And it is cried to them: "This is the garden. You inherit it for what you used to do."

44. And the dwellers of the garden cry to the dwellers of the fire: "We have found that which our Lord promised us (to be) the truth. Have you (too) found that which your Lord promised the truth?" They say: "Yes." And a crier in between them cries: "The curse of God is on evildoers,

45. "Who debar (men) from the path of God and would have it crooked, and who are disbelievers in the last day."

46. Between them is a veil. And on the heights are men who know them all by their marks. And they call to the dwellers of the garden: "Peace be to you!" They do not enter it although they hope (to enter).

3. I.e. angels [Pickthall's note].
4. Compare Matthew 19:24.

47. And when their eyes are turned toward the dwellers of the fire, they say: "Our Lord! Do not place us with the wrongdoing people."

48. And the dwellers on the heights call to men whom they know by their marks, (saying): "What did your multitude and that in which you took your pride avail you?"

49. Are these they of whom you swore that God would not show them mercy? (To them it has been said): "Enter the garden. No fear shall come upon you nor is it you who will grieve."

50. And the dwellers of the fire cry out to the dwellers of the garden: "Pour on us some water or some of that with which God has provided you." They say: "God has forbidden both to disbelievers (in His guidance),

51. "Who took their religion for a sport and pastime, and whom the life of the world beguiled." So this day We have forgotten them even as they forgot the meeting of this day of theirs and as they used to deny Our signs.

52. We have brought them a scripture which We expound with knowledge, a guidance and a mercy for a people who believe.

53. Do they await anything except its fulfillment? On the day when its fulfillment comes, those who were before forgetful of it will say: "The messengers of our Lord did bring the truth! Have we any intercessors, that they may intercede for us? Or can we be returned (to life on earth), that we may act otherwise than we used to act?" They have lost their souls, and that which they devised has failed them.

54. Your Lord is God who created the heavens and the earth in six days, then He mounted the throne. He covers the night with the day, which is in haste to follow it, and has made the sun and the moon and the stars subservient by His command. His is all creation and commandment. Blessed be God, the Lord of the worlds!

55. (O mankind!) Call upon your Lord humbly and in secret. He does not love aggressors.

56. Do not work confusion on the earth after the fair ordering (of it), and call on Him in fear and hope. The mercy of God is near to the good.

57. And He it is who sends the winds as tidings heralding His mercy, until, when they bear a cloud heavy (with rain), We lead it to a dead land, and then cause water to descend on it and thereby bring forth fruits of every kind. Thus We bring forth the dead. Perhaps you may remember.

58. As for the good land, its vegetation comes forth by permission of its Lord; while as for that which is bad, only evil comes forth (from it). Thus do We recount the signs for people who give thanks.

59. We sent Noah (of old) to his people, and he said: "O my people! Serve God. You have no other god except Him. I fear for you the retribution of an awful day."

60. The leaders of his people said: "We see you in plain error."

61. He said: "O my people! There is no error in me, but I am a messenger from the Lord of the worlds.

62. "I convey to you the messages of my Lord and give good counsel to you, and know from God what you do not know."

63. Do you marvel that there should come to you a reminder from your Lord by means of a man among you, that he may warn you, and that you may keep from evil, and that perhaps you may find mercy?

64. But they denied him, so We saved him and those with him in the ship,[5] and We drowned those who denied Our signs. They were blind people.

65. And to (the tribe of) 'Ād (We sent) their brother, Hūd.[6] He said: "O my people! Serve God. You have no other god but Him. Will you not ward off (evil)?"

66. The leaders of his people, who were disbelieving, said: "We surely see you in foolishness, and we think you to be of the liars."

67. He said: "O my people! There is no foolishness in me, but I am a messenger from the Lord of the worlds.

68. "I convey to you the messages of my Lord and am for you a true adviser.

69. "Do you marvel that there should come to you a reminder from your Lord by means of a man among you, that he may warn you? Remember how He made you viceroys after Noah's people, and gave you growth of stature. Remember (all) the bounties of your Lord, that perhaps you may be successful."

70. They said: "Have you us that we should serve God alone, and forsake what our fathers worshipped? Then bring upon us that with which you threaten us if you are of the truthful!"

71. He said: "Terror and wrath from your Lord have already fallen on you. Would you wrangle with me over names which you have named, you and your fathers, for which no warrant from God has been revealed? Then await (the consequence), I (also) am of those awaiting (it)."

72. And We saved him and those with him by a mercy from Us, and We cut the root of those who denied Our revelations and were not believers.

73. And to (the tribe of) Thamūd (We sent) their brother Ṣāliḥ.[7] He said: "O my people! Serve God. You have no other god except Him. A wonder from your Lord has come to you. This is the camel of God, a sign to you; so let her feed in God's earth, and do not touch her with hurt for fear that painful torment seize you.

74. "And remember how He made you viceroys after 'Ād and gave you station on the earth. You choose castles in the plains and hew the mountains into dwellings. So remember (all) the bounties of God and do not do evil, making mischief on the earth."

75. The leaders of his people, who were scornful, said to those whom they despised, to such of them as believed: "Do you know that Ṣāliḥ is one sent from his Lord?" They said: "In that with which he has been sent we are believers."

76. Those who were scornful said: "In that which you believe we are disbelievers."

77. So they hamstrung the she-camel, and they flouted the commandment of their Lord, and they said: "O Ṣāliḥ! Bring upon us what you threaten if you are indeed of those sent (from God)."

78. So the earthquake seized them, and morning found them prostrate in their dwelling-place.

5. The story of Noah's ark and the flood is told in Exodus 6–8.
6. An ancient Arab prophet [Pickthall's note].
7. An ancient Arab prophet [Pickthall's note].

79. And Ṣāliḥ turned from them and said: "O my people! I delivered my Lord's message to you and gave you good advice, but you do not love good advisers."

80. And Lot! (Remember) when he said to his people: "Will you commit abomination such as no creature ever did before you?

81. You come with lust to men instead of women. No, but you are wanton people."

82. And the answer of his people was only that they said (one to another): "Turn them out of your township.[8] They are people, in truth, who keep pure."

83. And We rescued him and his household, except his wife, who was of those who stayed behind.[9]

84. And We rained a rain upon them. See now the nature of the consequence for evildoers!

85. And to Midian (We sent) their brother, Shu'ayb.[1] He said: "O my people! Serve God. You have no other god except Him. A clear proof has come to you from your Lord; so give full measure and full weight and do not wrong mankind in their goods, and do not work confusion on the earth after the fair ordering of it. That will be better for you, if you are believers.

86. "Do not lurk on every road to threaten (wayfarers), and to turn away from God's path him who believes in Him, and to seek to make it crooked. And remember, when you were but few, how He did multiply you. And see the nature of the consequence for the corrupters!

87. "And if there is a party of you who believes in that with which I have been sent, and there is a party who does not believe, then have patience until God judges between us. He is the best of all who deal in judgment."

88. The leaders of his people, who were scornful, said: "Surely we will drive you out, O Shu'ayb, and those who believe with you, from our township, unless you return to our religion." He said: "Even though we hate it?

89. "We should have invented a lie against God if we returned to your religion after God has rescued us from it. It is not for us to return to it unless God should (so) will. Our Lord comprehends all things in knowledge. In God we put our trust. Our Lord! Decide with truth between us and our people, for You are the best of those who make decision."

90. But the leaders of his people, who were disbelieving, said: "If you follow Shu'ayb, then you shall be the losers."

91. So the earthquake seized them, and morning found them prostrate in their dwelling-place.

92. Those who denied Shu'ayb became as though they had not dwelt there. Those who denied Shu'ayb, they were the losers.

93. So he turned from them and said: "O my people! I delivered my Lord's messages to you and gave you good advice; then how can I sorrow for a people that rejected (truth)?"

94. And We sent no prophet to any township but We afflicted its people with tribulation and adversity that perhaps they might grow humble.

8. The Arabic word *qarya* means originally a settled community, polity, or civilization [Pickthall's note].
9. Compare Genesis 19:11–26.
1. Identified with Jethro [Pickthall's note]. In the Hebrew Bible, the father-in-law of Moses (Exodus 3:1).

95. Then We changed the evil plight for good until they grew affluent and said: "Tribulation and distress touched our fathers." Then We seized them unawares, when they did not perceive.

96. And if the people of the townships had believed and kept from evil, surely We should have opened for them blessings from the sky and from the earth. But (to every messenger) they gave the lie, and so We seized them on account of what they used to earn.

97. Are the people of the townships then secure from the coming of Our wrath upon them as a night raid while they sleep?

98. Or are the people of the townships then secure from the coming of Our wrath upon them in the daytime while they play?

99. Are they then secure from God's scheme? None thinks himself secure from God's scheme except people that perish.

100. Is it not an indication to those who inherit the land after its people (who thus reaped the consequence of evildoing) that, if We will, We can strike them for their sins and print upon their hearts so that they do not hear?

101. Such were the townships. We relate some tidings of them to you (Muḥammad). Their messengers came to them with clear proofs (of God's sovereignty), but they could not believe because they had already denied. Thus does God print upon the hearts of disbelievers (that they hear not).

102. We found no (loyalty to any) covenant in most of them. No, most of them We found wrongdoers.

103. Then, after them, We sent Moses with our signs to Pharaoh and his leaders, but they repelled them. Now, see the nature of the consequence for the corrupters!

104. Moses said: "O Pharaoh! I am a messenger from the Lord of the worlds,

105. "Approved upon condition that I speak concerning God nothing but the truth. I come to you (lords of Egypt) with a clear proof from your Lord. So let the Children of Israel go with me."

106. (Pharaoh) said: "If you come with a sign, then produce it, if you are of those who speak the truth."

107. Then he flung down his staff and it was a serpent manifest;

108. And he drew forth his hand (from his breast), and it was white for the beholders.

109. The leaders of Pharaoh's people said: "This is some knowing sorcerer,

110. "Who would expel you from your land. Now what do you advise?"

111. They said (to Pharaoh): "Put him off (a while)—him and his brother—and send into the cities summoners,

112. "To bring each knowing sorcerer to you."

113. And the sorcerers came to Pharaoh, saying: "Surely there will be a reward for us if we are victors."

114. He answered: "Yes, and surely you shall be of those brought near (to me)."

115. They said: "O Moses! Either throw (first) or let us be the first throwers."

116. He said: "Throw!" And when they threw they cast a spell upon the people's eyes, and overawed them, and produced a mighty spell.

117. And We inspired Moses (saying): "Throw your staff!" And it swallowed up their lying show.

118. Thus was the truth vindicated and that which they were doing was made vain.

119. Thus were they there defeated and brought low.

120. And the sorcerers fell down prostrate,

121. Crying: "We believe in the Lord of the worlds,

122. "The Lord of Moses and Aaron."

123. Pharaoh said: "You believe in Him before I give you leave! This is the plot that you have plotted in the city that you may drive its people from it. But you shall come to know!

124. "Surely I shall have your hands and feet cut off upon alternate sides. Then I shall crucify you every one."

125. They said: "We are about to return to our Lord!

126. "You take vengeance on us only because we believed the signs of our Lord when they came to us. Our Lord! Grant to us steadfastness and make us die as men who have surrendered (to You)."

127. The leaders of Pharaoh's people said: "(O King), will you allow Moses and his people to make mischief in the land, and flout you and your gods?" He said: "We will slay their sons and spare their women, for we are in power over them."

128. And Moses said to his people: "Seek help in God and endure. The earth is God's. He gives it for an inheritance to whom He will. And the ultimate triumph is for those who keep their duty (to Him)."

129. They said: "We suffered hurt before you came to us, and since you have come to us." He said: "It may be that your Lord is going to destroy your adversary and make you viceroys on the earth, that He may see how you behave."

130. And We afflicted Pharaoh's people with famine and the dearth of fruits, that perhaps they might heed.

131. But whenever good befell them, they said: "This is ours"; and whenever evil smote them they ascribed it to the evil auspices of Moses and those with him. Surely their evil auspice was only with God. But most of them did not know.

132. And they said: "Whatever sign you bring with which to bewitch us, we shall not put faith in you."

133. So We sent them the flood and the locusts and the vermin and the frogs and the blood—a succession of clear signs. But they were arrogant and a guilty folk.

134. And when the terror fell on them they cried: "O Moses! Pray for us to your Lord, because He has a covenant with you. If you remove the terror from us we will trust you and will let the Children of Israel go with you."

135. But when We did remove from them the terror for a term which they must reach, they broke their covenant.

136. Therefore We took retribution from them; therefore We drowned them in the sea: because they denied Our revelations and were heedless of them.

137. And We caused the people who were despised to inherit the eastern parts of the land and its western parts which We had blessed. And

the fair word of your Lord was fulfilled for the Children of Israel because of their endurance; and We annihilated (all) that Pharaoh and his people had done and that they had contrived.

138. And We brought the Children of Israel across the sea, and they came to a people who were given up to idols which they had. They said; "O Moses! Make for us a god even as they have gods." He said: "You are a people who do not know.

139. "As for these, their way will be destroyed and all that they are doing is in vain."

140. He said: "Shall I seek for you a god other than God when He has favored you above (all) creatures?

141. "And (remember) when We delivered you from Pharaoh's people who were afflicting you with dreadful torment, slaughtering your sons and sparing your women. That was a tremendous trial from your Lord."

142. And when We appointed for Moses thirty nights (of solitude), and added to them ten, and he completed the whole time appointed by his Lord of forty nights; and Moses said to his brother, Aaron: "Take my place among the people. Do right, and do not follow the way of mischief-makers."

143. And when Moses came to Our appointed meeting and his Lord had spoken to him, he said: "My Lord! Show me (Your self), that I may gaze upon You." He said: "You will not see Me, but gaze upon the mountain! If it stands still in its place, then you will see Me." And when his Lord revealed (His) glory to the mountain He sent it crashing down. And Moses fell down senseless. And when he woke he said: "Glory to You! I turn to You repentant, and I am the first of (true) believers."

144. He said: "O Moses! I have preferred you above mankind by My messages and by My speaking (to you). So hold that which I have given you, and be among the thankful."

145. And We wrote for him, upon the tablets, the lesson to be drawn from all things and the explanation of all things, then (bade him): "Hold it fast; and command your people (saying): 'Take the better (course made clear) in it.' I shall show you the abode of the iniquitous.

146. "I shall turn away from My revelations those who magnify themselves wrongfully on the earth, and if they see each sign do not believe it, and if they see the way of righteousness do not choose it for (their) way, and if they see the way of error choose it for (their) way. That is because they deny Our revelations and are used to disregard them."

147. Those who deny Our revelations and the meeting of the hereafter, their works are fruitless. Are they requited anything except what they used to do?

148. And the people of Moses, after (he had left them), chose a calf (for worship), (made) out of their ornaments, of saffron hue,[2] which gave a lowing sound. Did they not see that it did not speak to them or guide them to any way? They chose it, and became wrongdoers.

149. And when they feared the consequences of that and saw that they had gone astray, they said: "Unless our Lord have mercy on us and forgive us, we are of the lost."

150. And when Moses returned to his people, angry and grieved, he said: "Evil is that (course) which you took after I had left you. Would you

2. Or *a body*. But, as the word in the Arabic (*jasad*) can only mean a body of flesh and blood, the meaning "saffron-colored" better fits the context [Pickthall's note].

hasten on the judgment of your Lord?" And he cast down the tablets, and he seized his brother by the head, dragging him toward him. He said: "Son of my mother! The people judged me weak and almost killed me. Oh, do not make my enemies to triumph over me and do not place me among the evildoers!"

151. He said: "My Lord! Have mercy on me and on my brother; bring us into Your mercy, You the most merciful of all who show mercy."

152. Those who chose the calf (for worship), terror from their Lord and humiliation will come upon them in the life of the world. Thus do We requite those who invent a lie.

153. But those who do ill deeds and afterward repent and believe—for them, afterward, God is forgiving, merciful.

154. Then, when the anger of Moses abated, he took up the tablets, and in their inscription there was guidance and mercy for all those who fear their Lord.

155. And Moses chose of his people seventy men for Our appointed meeting and, when the trembling came on them, he said: "My Lord! If You had willed You would have destroyed them long before, and me with them. Will You destroy us for that which the ignorant among us did? It is but Your trial (of us). You send whom You will astray and guide whom You will. You are our protecting friend, therefore forgive us and have mercy on us, You, the best of all who show forgiveness.

156. "And ordain for us in this world that which is good, and in the hereafter (that which is good), We have turned to you." He said: "I strike with My punishment whom I will, and My mercy embraces all things, therefore I shall ordain it for those who ward off (evil) and pay the poor tax, and those who believe Our revelations";

157. Those who follow the messenger, the Prophet who can neither read nor write, whom they will find described in the Torah and the Gospel[3] (which are) with them. He will enjoin on them that which is right and forbid them that which is wrong. He will make lawful for them all good things and prohibit for them only the foul; and he will relieve them of their burden and the fetters that they used to wear. Then those who believe in him, and honor him, and help him, and follow the light which is sent down with him: they are the successful.

158. Say (O Muḥammad): "O mankind! I am the messenger of God to you all—(the messenger of) Him to whom belongs the sovereignty of the heavens and the earth. There is no God except Him. He gives life and He gives death. So believe in God and His messenger, the Prophet who can neither read nor write,[4] who believes in God and in His words, and follow him that perhaps you may be led aright."

159. And of Moses' people there is a community who lead with truth and establish justice with it.

160. We divided them into twelve tribes, nations; and We inspired Moses, when his people asked him for water, saying: "Strike with your staff

3. Muslim exegetes claim that a number of passages from the Hebrew Bible and New Testament support this claim. In the view of the British Arabist Richard Bell (1876–1952), the connection to most of them, including Deut. 33:2, Matt. 13:31 and 21:34–40, Mark 12:1, Luke 20:9, and John 1:23, is tenuous, though Deut. 18:15–18 and John 14:16, 26 are likely referred to here.

4. I give the usual rendering. Some modern criticism, while not denying the comparative illiteracy of the Prophet, would prefer the rendering "who is not of those who read the Scriptures" or "Gentile" [Pickthall's note].

the rock!" And there gushed forth from it twelve springs, so that each tribe knew their drinking-place. And we caused the white cloud to overshadow them and sent down for them the manna and the quails (saying): "Eat of the good things with which We have provided you." They did not wrong Us, but they would wrong themselves.

161. And when it was said to them: "Dwell in this township and eat from it when you will, and say 'Repentance,'[5] and enter the gate prostrate; We shall forgive you your sins; We shall increase (reward) for the the right-doers."

162. But those of them who did wrong changed the word which had been told them for another saying, and We sent down upon them wrath from heaven for their wrongdoing.

163. Ask them (O Muḥammad) of the township that was by the sea, how they broke the sabbath, how their big fish came to them visibly upon their sabbath day and on a day when they did not keep sabbath they did not come to them. Thus did We test them because they were evil-livers.

164. And when a community among them said: "Why do you preach to a people whom God is about to destroy or punish with an awful doom?" they said: "In order to be free from guilt before your Lord, and that perhaps they may ward off (evil)."

165. And when they forgot that of which they had been reminded, We rescued those who forbade wrong, and visited those who did wrong with dreadful punishment because they were iniquitous.

166. So when they took pride in what they had been forbidden, We said to them: "Be apes despised and loathed!

167. "And (remember) when your Lord proclaimed that He would raise against them until the day of resurrection those who would lay on them a cruel torment. Your Lord is swift in prosecution and He is forgiving, merciful."

168. And We have sundered them on the earth as (separate) nations. Some of them are righteous, and some far from that. And We have tried them with good things and evil things that perhaps they might return.

169. And a generation has succeeded them who inherited the scriptures. They grasp the goods of this low life (as the price of evildoing) and say: "It will be forgiven us." And if there came to them (again) the offer of the like, they would accept it (and would sin again). Has not the covenant of the scripture been taken on their behalf that they should not speak anything concerning God except the truth? And they have studied that which is in it. And the abode of the hereafter is better, for those who ward off (evil). Have you then no sense?

170. And as for those who make (men) keep the scripture, and establish worship—We do not squander the wages of reformers.

171. And when We shook the mountain above them as though it were a covering, and they supposed that it was going to fall upon them (and We said): "Hold fast what We have given you, and remember what is in it, that you may ward off (evil).

172. "And (remember) when your Lord brought forth from the Children of Adam, from their loins, their seed, and made them testify of themselves, (saying): Am I not your Lord?" They said: "Yes. We testify." (That was) for

5. Q 2:58, footnote [Pickthall's note].

fear that you should say at the day of resurrection: "Of this we were unaware";

173. Or for fear that you should say: "(It is) only (that) our fathers ascribed partners to God of old and we were (their) seed after them. Will You destroy us on account of what those who follow falsehood did?"

174. Thus We detail Our revelations, that perhaps they may return.

175. Recite to them the tale of him to whom We gave Our revelations, but he sloughed them off, so Satan overtook him and he became of those who lead astray.

176. And had We willed We could have raised him by their means, but he clung to the earth and followed his own lust. Therefore his likeness is as the likeness of a dog: if you attack him he pants with his tongue out, and if you leave him he pants with his tongue out. Such is the likeness of the people who deny Our revelations. Narrate to them the history (of the men of old), that perhaps they may take thought.

177. Evil as an example are the people who denied Our revelations, and used to wrong themselves.

178. He whom God leads, he indeed is led aright, while he whom God sends astray—they indeed are losers.

179. Already have We urged to hell many of the jinn and humankind, having hearts with which they do not understand, and having eyes with which they do not see, and having ears with which they do not hear. These are as the cattle—no, but they are worse! These are the neglectful.

180. God's are the fairest names.[6] Invoke Him by them. And leave the company of those who blaspheme His names. They will be requited for what they do.

181. And of those whom We created there is a nation who guide with the truth and by it establish justice.

182. And those who deny Our revelations—step by step We lead them on from where they know not.

183. I give them rein (for) My scheme is strong.

184. Have they not thought (that) there is no madness in their comrade? He is but a plain warner.

185. Have they not considered the dominion of the heavens and the earth, and what things God has created, and that it may be that their own term draws near? In what fact after this will they believe?

186. Those whom God sends astray, there is no guide for them. He leaves them to wander blindly on in their defiance.

187. They ask you of the (destined) hour, when will it come to port. Say: "Knowledge of it is with my Lord only. He alone will manifest it at its proper time. It is heavy in the heavens and the earth. It comes to you only unawares." They question you as if you could be well informed of it. Say: "Knowledge of it is with God only, but most of mankind know not."

188. Say: "For myself I have no power to benefit, nor power to hurt, except what God wills. Had I knowledge of the unseen, I should have abundance of wealth, and adversity would not touch me. I am but a warner, and a bearer of good tidings to people who believe."

189. He it is who did create you from a single soul, and from it made his mate that he might take rest in her. And when he covered her she bore

6. The *al-asmāʾ al-ḥusnā*, or "beautiful names" of God. Traditionally held to number 99, these names describe aspects of God's being.

a light burden, and she passed (unnoticed) with it, but when it became heavy they cried to God, their Lord, saying: If You give to us a righteous child we shall be among the thankful.

190. But when He gave to them a righteous child, they ascribed to Him partners in respect of that which He had given them. He is exalted high above all that they associate (with Him).

191. Do they attribute as partners to God those who created nothing, but are themselves created,

192. And cannot give them help, nor can they help themselves?

193. And if you call them to the guidance, they do not follow you. Whether you call them or are silent is all one to you.

194. Those on whom you call beside God are servants like you. Call on them now, and let them answer you, if you are truthful!

195. Have they feet with which they walk, or have they hands with which they hold, or have they eyes with which they see, or have they ears with which they hear? Say: "Call upon your (so-called) partners (of God), and then contrive against me, spare me not!

196. "My protecting friend is God who reveals the scripture. He befriends the righteous.

197. "They on whom you call beside Him have no power to help you, nor can they help themselves."

198. And if you (Muslims) call them to the guidance they do not hear; and you (Muḥammad) see them looking toward you, but they do not see.

199. Keep to forgiveness (O Muḥammad), and enjoin kindness, and turn away from the ignorant.

200. And if a slander from the devil wound you, then seek refuge in God. He is hearer, knower.

201. Those who ward off (evil), when an apparition from the devil troubles them, they but remember (God's guidance) and behold them observers!

202. Their brothers plunge them further into error and do not cease.

203. And when you do not bring a verse for them they say: "Why have you not chosen it?" Say: "I follow only that which is inspired in me from my Lord." This (Qur'ān) is insight from your Lord, and a guidance and a mercy for a people that believe.

204. And when the Qur'ān is recited, give ear to it and pay heed, that you may obtain mercy.

205. And (O Muḥammad) remember your Lord within yourself humbly and with awe, below your breath, at morning and evening. And do not be of the neglectful.

206. Those who are with your Lord are not too proud to do Him service, but they praise Him and adore Him.

## Sūra 8

*Al-Anfāl*, "The Spoils," takes its name from the first verse by which it is proclaimed that property taken in war belongs "to God and His messenger"—that is to say, to the theocratic state, to be used for the common good. The date of the revelation of this sūra is established, from the nature of the contents, as the time that elapsed between the battle of Badr and the division of the spoils—a space of only one month—in the second year of the *hijra*. The concluding verses are of later date and lead up to the subject of Q 9.

A Meccan caravan was returning from Syria, and its leader, Abū Sufyān, fearing an attack from Medina, sent a camel rider on to Mecca with a frantic appeal for help; which must have come too late, considering the distances, if, as some writers even among Muslims have alleged, the Prophet had always intended to attack the caravan. Ibn Iṣḥāq[1] (*apud* Ibn Hishām), when treating of the Tabūk expedition, says that the Prophet announced the destination on that occasion, whereas it was his custom to hide his real objective. Was not the real objective hidden in this first campaign? It is a fact that he only advanced when the army sent to protect the caravan, or rather (it is probable) to punish the Muslims for having plundered it, was approaching Medina. His little army of three hundred and thirteen men, ill-armed and roughly equipped, traversed the desert for three days until, when they halted near the water of Badr, they had news that the army of Quraysh was approaching on the other side of the valley. Then rain fell—heavily upon Quraysh so that they could not advance further on account of the muddy state of the ground, lightly on the Muslims, who were able to advance to the water and secure it. At the same time Abū Sufyān, the leader of the caravan, which was also heading for the water of Badr, was warned by one of his scouts of the advance of the Muslims and turned back to the coast plain. Before the battle against what must have appeared to all men overwhelming odds, the Prophet gave the Anṣār, the men of Medina, whose oath of allegiance had not included fighting in the field, the chance of returning if they wished; but they were only hurt by the suggestion that they could possibly forsake him. On the other hand, several of Quraysh, including the whole Zuhrī clan, returned to Mecca when they heard the caravan was safe, having no grudge otherwise against the Prophet and his followers, whom they regarded as men who had been wronged.

Still the army of Quraysh outnumbered the Muslims by more than two to one, and was much better mounted and equipped, so that their leaders counted on an easy victory. When the Prophet saw them streaming down the sandhills, he cried: "O God! Here are Quraysh with all their chivalry and pomp, who oppose You and deny Your messenger. O God! Your help which You have promised me! O God! Make them bow this day!"

The Muslims were successful in the single combats with which Arab battles opened. But the mêlée at first went hard against them, and the Prophet stood and prayed under the shelter which they had put up to screen him from the sun, and cried: "O God! If this little company is destroyed, there will be none left in the land to worship You." Then he fell into a trance and, when he spoke again, he told Abū Bakr, who was with him, that the promised help had come. At this he went out to encourage his people. Taking up a handful of gravel, he ran toward Quraysh and flung it at them, saying: "The faces are confounded!" on which the tide of battle turned in favor of the Muslims. The leader of Quraysh and several of their greatest men were killed, many were taken prisoner, and their baggage and camels were captured by the Muslims. It was indeed a day to be remembered in the early history of Islam, and there was great rejoicing in Medina. But the Muslims are warned in this sūra that it is only the beginning of their struggle against heavy odds. In fact, in the following year at Mt. Uḥud (referred to in Q 3), the enemy came against them with an army of three thousand, and in the fifth year of the *hijra*, an allied army of the pagan clans,

1. Arab biographer of Muḥammad (ca. 704–767; see p. 359 below), known today in the edition of Ibn Hishām (d. 833).

amounting to 10,000, besieged Medina in the "War of the Trench" (see Q 33, "The Clans").

The date of revelation is the second year of the *hijra* for the most part. Some good Arabic authorities hold that verses 30–40, or some of them, were revealed at Mecca just before the *hijra*.

## The Spoils

*Revealed at Medina*

In the name of God, the beneficent, the merciful.

1. They ask you (O Muḥammad) of the spoils of war. "Say: The spoils of war belong to God and the messenger, so keep your duty to God, and adjust the matter of your difference, and obey God and His messenger, if you are (true) believers."

2. Only they are the (true) believers whose hearts feel fear when God is mentioned, and when His revelations are recited to them they increase their faith, and who trust in their Lord;

3. Who establish worship and spend of that We have bestowed on them.

4. Those are they who are in truth believers. For them are grades (of honor) with their Lord, and pardon, and a bountiful provision.

5. Even as your Lord caused you (Muḥammad) to go forth from your home with the truth, and a party of the believers were averse (to it),

6. Disputing with you of the truth after it had been made manifest, as if they were being driven to visible death.

7. And when God promised you one of the two bands[2] (of the enemy) that it should be yours, and you longed that other than the armed one might be yours. And God willed that He should cause the truth to triumph by His words, and cut the root of the disbelievers;

8. That He might cause the truth to triumph and bring vanity to nothing, however much the guilty might oppose;

9. When you sought help of your Lord and He answered you (saying): "I will help you with a thousand of the angels, rank on rank."

10. God appointed it only as good tidings, and that by it your hearts might be at rest. Victory comes only by the help of God. God is mighty, wise.

11. When He made the slumber fall on you as a reassurance from Him and sent down water from the sky on you, that by it He might purify you, and remove from you the fear of Satan, and make your hearts strong and by it make (your) feet firm.

12. When your Lord inspired the angels, (saying:) "I am with you." So make those who believe stand firm. I will throw fear into the hearts of those who disbelieve. Then strike the necks and strike of them each finger.

13. That is because they opposed God and His messenger. Whoever opposes God and His messenger, (for him) God is severe in punishment.

14. That (is the award), so taste it, and (know) that for disbelievers is the torment of the fire.

15. O you who believe! When you meet those who disbelieve in battle, do not turn your backs to them.

2. Either the army or the caravan [Pickthall's note].

16. Whoever on that day turns his back to them, unless maneuvering for battle or intent to join a company, he truly has incurred wrath from God, and his habitation will be hell, a wretched journey's-end.

17. You (Muslims) did not slay them, but God slayed them. And you (Muḥammad) did not throw when you threw, but God threw, that He might test the believers by a fair test from Him. God is hearer, knower.

18. That (is the case); and (know) that God (it is) who makes the plan of disbelievers weak.

19. (O Quraysh!) If you sought a judgment, the judgment has now come to you. And if you cease (from persecuting the believers) it will be better for you, but if you return (to the attack) We also shall return. And your host will avail you nothing, however numerous it be, and (know) that God is with the believers (in His guidance).

20. O you who believe! Obey God and His messenger, and do not turn away from him when you hear (him speak).

21. Do not be as those who say, We hear, and they hear not.

22. The worst of beasts in God's sight are the deaf, the dumb, who have no sense.

23. Had God known of any good in them He would have made them hear, but had He made them hear they would have turned away, averse.

24. O you who believe! Obey God, and the messenger when He calls you to what gives you life, and know that God comes in between the man and his own heart, and that it is He to whom you will be gathered.

25. And guard yourselves against a chastisement which cannot fall exclusively on those of you who are wrongdoers, and know that God is severe in punishment.

26. And remember, when you were few and reckoned feeble in the land, and were in fear that men should exterminate you, how He gave you refuge, and strengthened you with His help, and made provision of good things for you, so that perhaps you might be thankful.

27. O you who believe! Do not betray God and His messenger, nor knowingly betray your trusts.

28. And know that your possessions and your children are a test, and that with God is immense reward.

29. O you who believe! If you keep your duty to God, He will give you discrimination (between right and wrong) and will rid you of your evil thoughts and deeds, and will forgive you. God is of infinite bounty.

30. And when those who disbelieve plot against you (O Muḥammad) to wound you fatally, or to kill you or to drive you forth; they plot, but God (also) plots; and God is the best of plotters.

31. And when Our revelations are recited to them they say: "We have heard. If we wish we can speak the like of this. This is nothing but fables of the men of old."

32. And when they said: "O God! If this be indeed the truth from You, then rain down stones on us or bring on us some painful doom!"

33. But God would not punish them while you were with them, nor will He punish them while they seek forgiveness.

34. What (plea) have they that God should not punish them, when they debar (His servants) from the sacred mosque, though they are not its fitting guardians. Its fitting guardians are only those who keep their duty to God. But most of them do not know.

35. And their worship at the (holy) house is nothing but whistling and hand-clapping. Therefore (it is said to them): "Taste of the doom because you disbelieve."

36. Those who disbelieve spend their wealth in order that they may bar (men) from the way of God. They will spend it, then it will become an anguish for them, then they will be conquered. And those who disbelieve will be gathered to hell,

37. That God may separate the wicked from the good. The wicked He will place piece upon piece, and heap them all together, and consign them to hell. Such are the losers.

38. Tell those who disbelieve that if they cease (from persecution of believers) what is past will be forgiven them; but if they return (to it) then the example of the men of old has already gone (before them, for a warning).

39. And fight them until persecution is no more, and religion is all for God. But if they cease, then God is observer of what they do.

40. And if they turn away, then know that God is your befriender—a transcendent patron, a transcendent helper!

41. And know that whatever you take as spoils of war, a fifth of it is for God, and for the messenger[3] and for the relative (who has need) and orphans and the needy and the wayfarer, if you believe in God and what We revealed to Our servant on the day of discrimination, the day when the two armies met. And God is able to do all things.

42. When you were on the near bank (of the valley) and they were on the farther bank, and the caravan was below you (on the coast plain). And had you made an appointment to meet one another you surely would have failed to keep the meeting, but (it happened, as it did, without the forethought of either of you) that God might conclude a thing that must be done; that he who perished (on that day) might perish by a clear proof (of His sovereignty) and he who survived might survive by a clear proof (of His sovereignty). God in truth is hearer, knower.

43. When God showed them to you (O Muḥammad) in your dream as few in number, and if He had shown them to you as many, you (Muslims) would have faltered and would have quarreled over the affair. But God saved (you). He knows what is in the breasts (of men).

44. And when He made you (Muslims), when you met (them), see them with your eyes as few, and lessened you in their eyes, (it was) that God might conclude a thing that must be done. To God all things are brought back.

45. O you who believe! When you meet an army, hold firm and think of God much, that you may be successful.

46. And obey God and His messenger, and do not dispute with one another for fear that you falter and your strength depart from you; but be steadfast! God is with the steadfast.

47. Do not be as those who came forth from their dwellings boastfully and to be seen of men, and bar (men) from the way of God, while God is surrounding all they do.

48. And when Satan made their deeds seem fair to them and said: "No one of mankind can conquer you this day, for I am your protector." But when the armies came in sight of one another, he took flight, saying: "I am

3. I.e. for the state, to be used for the common good [Pickthall's note].

guiltless of you. I see what you see not. I fear God. And God is severe in punishment."

49. When the hypocrites and those in whose hearts is a disease said: "Their religion has deluded these." Whoever puts his trust in God (will find that) God is mighty, wise.

50. If you could see how the angels receive those who disbelieve, striking their faces and their backs and (saying): "Taste the punishment of burning!"

51. This is for what your own hands have sent before (to the judgment), and (know) that God is not a tyrant to His servants.

52. (Their way is) as the way of Pharaoh's people and those before them; they disbelieved the revelations of God, and God took them in their sins. God is strong, severe in punishment.

53. That is because God never changes the grace He has bestowed on any people until they first change what is in their hearts, and (that is) because God is hearer, knower.

54. (Their way is) as the way of Pharaoh's people and those before them; they denied the revelations of their Lord, so We destroyed them in their sins. And We drowned the people of Pharaoh. All were evildoers.

55. The worst of beasts in God's sight are the ungrateful who will not believe;

56. Those of them with whom you made a treaty, and then at every opportunity they break their treaty, and they do not keep duty (to God).

57. If you come on them in the war, deal with them so as to strike fear in those who are behind them, so that perhaps they may remember.

58. And if you fear treachery from any people, then throw back to them (their treaty) fairly. God does not love the treacherous.

59. And do not let those who disbelieve suppose that they can outstrip (God's purpose). They cannot escape.

60. Make ready for them all you can of (armed) force and of horses tethered, that thereby you may dismay the enemy of God and your enemy, and others beside them whom you do not know. God knows them. Whatever you spend in the way of God it will be repaid to you in full, and you will not be wronged.

61. And if they incline to peace, incline also to it, and trust in God. He is the hearer, the knower.

62. And if they would deceive you, then God is sufficient for you. It is He who supports you with His help and with the believers,

63. And (as for the believers) has made union between their hearts. If you had spent all that is on the earth you could not have attuned their hearts, but God has attuned them. He is mighty, wise.

64. O Prophet! God is sufficient for you and those of the believers who follow you.

65. O Prophet! Exhort the believers to fight. If of you there are twenty steadfast they shall overcome two hundred, and if of you there are a hundred (steadfast) they shall overcome a thousand of those who disbelieve, because they (the disbelievers) are a people without intelligence.

66. Now has God lightened your burden, for He knows that there is weakness in you. So if of you there are a steadfast hundred they shall overcome two hundred, and if of you there are a thousand (steadfast) they shall overcome two thousand by permission of God. God is with the steadfast.

67. It is not for any prophet to have captives until he has inflicted heavy damage in the land. You desire the lure of this world and God desires (for you) the hereafter, and God is mighty, wise.

68. Had it not been for an ordinance of God which had gone before, an awful doom would have come upon you on account of what you took.

69. Now enjoy what you have won, as lawful and good, and keep your duty to God. God is forgiving, merciful.[4]

70. O Prophet! Say to those captives who are in your hands: "If God knows any good in your hearts He will give you better than what has been taken from you, and will forgive you. God is forgiving, merciful."

71. And if they would betray you, they betrayed God before, and He gave (you) power over them. God is knower, wise.

72. Those who believed and left their homes and strove with their wealth and their lives for the cause of God, and those who took them in and helped them: these are protecting friends of one another.[5] And those who believed but did not leave their homes; you have no duty to protect them until they leave their homes; but if they seek help from you in the matter of religion then it is your duty to help (them) except against a people between whom and you there is a treaty. God is observer of what you do.

73. And those who disbelieve are protectors of one another—Unless you do the same, there will be confusion in the land, and great corruption.

74. Those who believed and left their homes and strove for the cause of God, and those who took them in and helped them—these are the believers in truth. For them is pardon, and a bountiful provision.

75. And those who afterward believed and left their homes and strove along with you, they are of you; and those who are akin are nearer to one another in the ordinance of God. God is knower of all things.

## Sūra 9

*Al-Tawba*, "Repentance," takes its name from verse 104. It is often called *al-Barā'a*, "The Immunity," from the first word. It is the only sūra which is without the *basmala* ("In the name of God the beneficent, the merciful"), which is generally considered to be on account of the stern commandments against idolaters which it contains. Verses 1–12, forming the proclamation of immunity from obligation toward the idolaters, were revealed after the pilgrims had started for Mecca in the ninth year of the *hijra* and sent by special messenger to Abū Bakr, leader of the pilgrimage, to be read out by 'Alī to the multitudes at Mecca. It signified the end of idolatry in Arabia. The Christian Byzantine Empire had begun to move against the growing Muslim power, and this sūra contains mention of a greater war to come, and instructions with regard to it. Verses 38–99 refer to the Tabūk campaign,[1] and especially to those Arab tribes who failed to join the Muslims in that campaign. The

4. Verses 67–69 were revealed when the Prophet had decided to spare the lives of the prisoners taken at Badr and hold them to ransom, against the wish of 'Umar, who would have executed them for their past crimes. The Prophet took the verses as a reproof, and they are generally understood to mean that no quarter ought to have been given in that first battle [Pickthall's note].

5. This verse is usually understood to refer to the Muslims who emigrated with Muḥammad from Mecca to Medina (the Emigrants, or *muhājirūn*) and Muslims of Medina who took them in (the Helpers, or *anṣār*).

1. A military expedition to northern Arabia, launched in October 630 CE (after the Muslim conquest of Mecca).

"Hypocrites," as the half-hearted supporters of Islam were called, had long been a thorn in the side of the Muslims. They had even at one time gone the length in dissent of forming a congregation and building a mosque of their own surreptitiously. On the Prophet's return from Tabūk they invited him to visit that mosque. This is referred to in verses 107ff.

The date of revelation is the ninth year of the *hijra*.

## Repentance

*Revealed at Medina*

1. Freedom from obligation (is proclaimed) from God and His messenger toward those of the idolaters with whom you made a treaty:

2. Travel freely in the land four months, and know that you cannot escape God and that God will confound the disbelievers (in His guidance).

3. And a proclamation from God and His messenger to all men on the day of the greater pilgrimage that God is free from obligation to the idolaters, and (so is) His messenger. So, if you repent, it will be better for you; but if you are averse, then know that you cannot escape God. Give tidings (O Muḥammad) of a painful doom to those who disbelieve,

4. Excepting those of the idolaters with whom you (Muslims) have a treaty, and who have since abated nothing of your right nor have supported anyone against you. (As for these), fulfill their treaty to them until their term. God loves those who keep their duty (to Him).

5. Then, when the sacred months have passed, slay the idolaters wherever you find them, and take them (captive), and besiege them, and prepare for them each ambush. But if they repent and establish worship and pay the poor tax, then leave their way free. God is forgiving, merciful.[2]

6. And if anyone of the idolaters seeks your protection (O Muḥammad), then protect him so that he may hear the word of God, and afterward convey him to his place of safety. That is because they are a people who do not know.

7. How can there be a treaty with God and with His messenger for the idolaters except those with whom you made a treaty at the Inviolable Place of Worship? So long as they are true to you, be true to them. God loves those who keep their duty.

8. How (can there be any treaty for the others) when, if they have the upper hand of you, they do not regard pact or honor in respect of you? They satisfy you with their mouths while their hearts refuse. And most of them are wrongdoers.

9. They have purchased with the revelations of God a little gain, so they debar (men) from His way. Evil is what they are used to doing.

10. And they observe toward a believer neither pact nor honor. These are they who are transgressors.

11. But if they repent and establish worship and pay the poor tax, then are they your brothers in religion. We detail Our revelations for a people who have knowledge.

2. Known as the "sword verse," this is often cited in discussions and debates about whether the Qur'ān advocates violence.

12. And if they break their pledges after their treaty (has been made with you) and assail your religion, then fight the heads of disbelief—they have no binding oaths—in order that they may desist.

13. Will you not fight a people who broke their solemn pledges, and purposed to drive out the messenger and did attack you first? What! Do you fear them? Now God has more right that you should fear Him, if you are believers.

14. Fight them! God will chastise them at your hands, and He will lay them low and give you victory over them, and He will heal the breasts of people who are believers.

15. And He will remove the anger of their hearts. God relents toward whom He will. God is knower, wise.

16. Or did you think that you would be left (in peace) when God does not yet know those of you who strive, choosing for familiar none except God and His messenger and the believers? God is informed of what you do.

17. It is not for the idolaters to tend God's sanctuaries, bearing witness against themselves of disbelief. As for such, their works are vain and in the fire they will abide.

18. He only shall tend God's sanctuaries who believes in God and the last day and observes proper worship and pays the poor tax and fears none except God. For such (only) is it possible that they can be of the rightly guided.

19. Do you count the slaking of a pilgrim's thirst and tending of the Inviolable Place of Worship as (equal to the worth of him) who believes in God and the last day, and strives in the way of God? They are not equal in the sight of God. God does not guide wrongdoing people.

20. Those who believe, and have left their homes and striven with their wealth and their lives in God's way, are of much greater worth in God's sight. These are they who are triumphant.

21. Their Lord gives them good tidings of mercy from Him, and acceptance, and gardens where enduring pleasure will be theirs;

22. There they will abide for ever. With God there is immense reward.

23. O you who believe! Do not choose your fathers or your brothers for friends if they take pleasure in disbelief rather than faith. Whoever of you takes them for friends, such are wrongdoers.

24. Say: "If your fathers, and your sons, and your brothers, and your wives, and your tribe, and the wealth you have acquired, and merchandise for which you fear that there will be no sale,[3] and dwellings you desire are dearer to you than God and His messenger and striving in His way: then wait until God brings His command to pass. God does not guide wrongdoing people.

25. "God has given you victory on many fields and on the day of Ḥunayn,[4] when you exulted in your multitude but it availed you nothing, and the earth, vast as it is, was constricted for you; then you turned back in flight;

26. "Then God sent His peace of reassurance down upon His messenger and upon the believers, and sent down hosts you could not see, and punished those who disbelieved. Such is the reward of disbelievers.

3. It was objected that if idolaters were forbidden to make the pilgrimage, the trade of Mecca would decline [Pickthall's note].

4. The Muslim army, ambushed at Ḥunayn [630 CE], gained a great victory after being nearly routed [Pickthall's note].

27. "Then afterward God will relent toward whom He will; for God is forgiving, merciful."

28. O you who believe! Only the idolaters are unclean. So do not let them come near the Inviolable Place of Worship after this their year. If you fear poverty (from the loss of their merchandise) God shall preserve you of His bounty if He will. God is knower, wise.

29. Fight against such of those who have been given the scripture as do not believe in God or the last day, and do not forbid what God has forbidden by His messenger, and do not follow the religion of truth, until they pay the tribute readily, being brought low.[5]

30. And the Jews say: "Ezra is the son of God," and the Christians say: "The Messiah is the son of God." That is their saying with their mouths. They imitate the saying of those who disbelieved of old. God (Himself) fights against them. How perverse they are!

31. They have taken as lords beside God their rabbis and their monks and the Messiah son of Mary, when they were commanded to worship only one God. There is no god except Him. Be He glorified from all that they ascribe as partner (to Him)!

32. Willingly would they put out the light of God with their mouths, but God disdains (anything) except that He shall perfect His light, however much the disbelievers are averse.

33. He it is who has sent His messenger with the guidance and the religion of truth, that He may cause it to prevail over all religion, however much the idolaters may be averse.

34. O you who believe! Many of the (Jewish) rabbis and the (Christian) monks devour the wealth of mankind wantonly and debar (men) from the way of God. They who hoard up gold and silver and do not spend it in the way of God, to them give tidings (O Muḥammad) of a painful doom,

35. On the day when it will (all) be heated in the fire of hell, and their foreheads and their flanks and their backs will be branded with it (and it will be said to them): "Here is what you hoarded for yourselves. Now taste of what you used to hoard."

36. The number of the months with God is twelve months by God's ordinance in the day that He created the heavens and the earth. Four of them are sacred: that is the right religion. So do not wrong yourselves in them. And wage war on all of the idolaters as they are waging war on all of you. And know that God is with those who keep their duty (to Him).

37. Postponement (of a sacred month)[6] is only an excess of disbelief by which those who disbelieve are misled; they allow it one year and forbid it (another) year, that they may make up the number of the months which God has hallowed, so that they allow what God has forbidden. The evil of their deeds is made attractive to them. God does not guide the disbelieving people.

38. O you who believe! What ails you that when it is said to you: "Go forth in the way of God," you are bowed down to the ground with heaviness. Do you take pleasure in the life of the world rather than in the hereafter? The comfort of the life of the world is but little in the hereafter.

5. This verse is the primary scriptural warrant for a poll tax (Ar. *jizya*) levied on People of the Book living in Muslim territories.

6. The idolaters would postpone a sacred month in which war was forbidden, when they wanted to make war, and make up for it by hallowing another month [Pickthall's note].

39. If you do not go forth He will afflict you with a painful doom, and will choose instead of you a people other than you. You cannot harm Him at all. God is able to do all things.

40. If you do not help him, still God helped him when those who disbelieve drove him forth, the second of two; when they two[7] were in the cave, when he said to his comrade: "Grieve not. God is with us." Then God caused His peace of reassurance to descend on him and supported him with forces you cannot see, and made the word of those who disbelieved the lowliest, while it was God's word that became the uppermost. God is mighty, wise.

41. Go forth, light-armed and heavy-armed, and strive with your wealth and your lives in the way of God! That is best for you if you only knew.

42. Had it been a near adventure and an easy journey they would have followed you, but the distance seemed too far for them.[8] Yet will they swear by God (saying): "If we had been able we would surely have set out with you." They destroy their souls, and God knows that they are liars.

43. God forgive you (O Muḥammad)! Why did you grant them leave before those who told the truth were manifest to you and you knew the liars?

44. Those who believe in God and the last day do not ask to be excused from striving with their wealth and their lives. God is aware of those who keep their duty (to Him).

45. They alone ask permission of you who do not believe in God and the last day, and whose hearts feel doubt, so in their doubt they waver.

46. And if they had wished to go forth they would assuredly have made ready some equipment, but God was averse to their being sent forth and held them back and (it was said to them): "Sit with the sedentary!"

47. Had they gone forth among you they would have added to you nothing except trouble and would have hurried to and fro among you, seeking to cause sedition among you; and among you there are some who would have listened to them. God is aware of evildoers.

48. Before they sought to cause sedition and raised difficulties for you until the truth came and the decree of God was made manifest, though they were averse.

49. Of them is he who says: "Grant me permission (to stay at home) and do not tempt me."[9] Surely it is into temptation that they (thus) have fallen. Hell is all around the disbelievers.

50. If good befalls you (O Muḥammad) it afflicts them, and if calamity befalls you, they say: "We took precaution," and they turn away well pleased.

51. Say: "Nothing befalls us except what God has decreed for us. He is our protecting friend. In God let believers put their trust!"

52. Say: "Can you await for us anything except one of two good things (death or victory in God's way)? while we await for you that God will afflict you with a doom from Him or at our hands. Await then! We are awaiting with you."

7. The Prophet and Abū Bakr during the flight from Mecca to Medina [Pickthall's note].
8. The reference is to the Tabūk expedition. Tabūk is halfway between Medina and Damascus [Pickthall's note].
9. The temptation here referred to is generally explained as being the beauty of the women of Syria, the country against which the campaign was directed [Pickthall's note].

53. Say: "Pay (your contribution), willingly or unwillingly, it will not be accepted from you. You were ever obstinate people."

54. And nothing prevents that their contributions should be accepted from them except that they have disbelieved in God and in His messenger, and they do not come to worship except as idlers, and do not pay (their contribution) except reluctantly.

55. So do not let their riches or their children please you (O Muḥammad). God thereby intends only to punish them in the life of the world and that their souls shall pass away while they are disbelievers.

56. And they swear by God that in truth they are of you, when they are not of you, but they are people who are afraid.

57. Had they only found a refuge, or caverns, or a place to enter, they surely would have dashed there swift as runaways.

58. And of them is he who defames you in the matter of the alms. If they are given part of them they are content, and if they are not given part of them, they are enraged.

59. (How much more seemly) had they been content with what God and His messenger had given them and had said: "God suffices us. God will give us of His bounty, and (also) His messenger. To God we are suppliants."

60. The alms are only for the poor and the needy, and those who collect them, and those whose hearts are to be reconciled,[1] and to free the captives and the debtors, and for the cause of God, and (for) the wayfarer; a duty imposed by God. God is knower, wise.

61. And of them are those who vex the Prophet and say: "He is only a hearer." Say: "A hearer of good for you, who believes in God and is true to the believers, and a mercy for such of you as believe." Those who vex the messenger of God, for them there is a painful doom.

62. They swear by God to you (Muslims) to please you, but God, with His messenger, has more right that they should please Him if they are believers.

63. Do they not know that whoever opposes God and His messenger, his portion is fire of hell, to abide there? That is the extreme abasement.

64. The hypocrites fear that a sūra should be revealed concerning them, proclaiming what is in their hearts. Say: "Scoff (your fill)! God is disclosing what you fear."

65. And if you ask them (O Muḥammad) they will say: "We only talked and jested." Say: "Was it at God and His revelations and His messenger that you scoffed?"

66. Make no excuse. You have disbelieved after your (confession of) belief. If We forgive a party of you, a party of you We shall punish because they have been guilty.

67. The hypocrites, both men and women, proceed one from another. They enjoin the wrong, and they forbid the right, and they withhold their hands (from spending for the cause of God). They forget God, so He has forgotten them. The hypocrites, they are the transgressors.

68. God promises the hypocrites, both men and women, and the disbelievers fire of hell for their abode. It will suffice them. God curses them, and theirs is lasting torment.

1. A special portion of the alms was allotted to the people of Mecca, the former enemies of Islam, who were converted en masse after the capture of the city, and whose "hearts were to be reconciled" [Pickthall's note].

69. Even as those before you who were mightier than you in strength, and more affluent than you in wealth and children. They enjoyed their lot awhile, so you enjoy your lot awhile even as those before you did enjoy their lot awhile. And you jabber even as they jabbered. Such are they whose works have perished in the world and the hereafter. Such are they who are the losers.

70. Has not the fame of those before them reached them—the people of Noah, 'Ād, Thamūd, the people of Abraham, the dwellers of Midian and the disasters (which befell them)? Their messengers (from God) came to them with proofs (of God's sovereignty). So God surely did not wrong them, but they wronged themselves.

71. And the believers, men and women, are friends protecting one another; they enjoin the right and forbid the wrong, and they establish worship and they pay the poor tax, and they obey God and His messenger. As for these, God will have mercy on them. God is mighty, wise.

72. God promises to the believers, men and women, gardens underneath which rivers flow, in which they will abide—blessed dwellings in gardens of Eden. And—greater (far)!—acceptance from God. That is the supreme triumph.

73. O Prophet! Strive against the disbelievers and the hypocrites! Be harsh with them. Their ultimate abode is hell, a wretched journey's end.

74. They swear by God that they said nothing (wrong), yet they did say the word of disbelief, and did disbelieve after their surrender (to God). And they intended what they could not attain, and they sought revenge only so that God by His messenger should enrich them of His bounty. If they repent it will be better for them; and if they turn away, God will afflict them with a painful doom in the world and the hereafter, and they have no protecting friend or helper on the earth.

75. And of them is he who made a covenant with God (saying): "If He give us of His bounty We will give alms and become of the righteous."

76. Yet when He gave them of His bounty, they hoarded it and turned away, averse;

77. So He has made the consequence (to be) hypocrisy in their hearts until the day when they shall meet Him, because they broke their word to God that they promised Him, and because they lied.

78. Do they not know that God knows both their secret and the thought that they confide, and that God is the knower of things hidden?

79. Those who point at such of the believers as give the alms willingly and such as can find nothing to give but their endeavors, and deride them—God (Himself) derides them. Theirs will be a painful doom.

80. Ask forgiveness for them (O Muḥammad), or do not ask forgiveness for them; though you ask forgiveness for them seventy times God will not forgive them. That is because they disbelieved in God and His messenger, and God does not guide wrongdoing people.

81. Those who were left behind rejoiced at sitting still behind the messenger of God, and were averse to striving with their wealth and their lives in God's way. And they said: "Do not go forth in the heat!" Say: "The fire of hell is more intense heat," if they but understood.

82. Then let them laugh a little: they will weep much, as the reward of what they used to earn.

83. If God brings you back (from the campaign) to a party of them and they ask of you leave to go out (to fight), then say to them: "You shall nevermore go out with me or fight with me against a foe. You were content with sitting still the first time. So sit still, with the useless."

84. And never (O Muḥammad) pray for one of them who dies, or stand by his grave. They disbelieved in God and His messenger, and they died while they were evildoers.

85. Do not let their wealth or their children please you! God intends only to punish them by it in the world, and that their souls shall pass away while they are disbelievers.

86. And when a sūra is revealed (which says): "Believe in God and strive along with His messenger," the men of wealth among them still ask leave of you and say: "Allow us to be with those who sit (at home)."

87. They are content that they should be with the useless and their hearts are sealed, so that they do not apprehend.

88. But the messenger and those who believe with him strive with their wealth and their lives. Such are they for whom are the good things. Such are they who are the successful.

89. God has made ready for them gardens underneath which rivers flow, in which they will abide. That is the supreme triumph.

90. And those among the wandering Arabs[2] who had an excuse came in order that permission might be granted them. And those who lied to God and His messenger sat at home. A painful doom will fall on those of them who disbelieve.

91. Not to the weak nor to the sick nor to those who can find nothing to spend is any fault (to be imputed though they stay at home) if they are true to God and His messenger. Not to the good is there any road (of blame). God is forgiving, merciful.

92. Nor to those whom, when they came to you (asking) that you should mount them, did you tell: "I cannot find (an animal) on which to mount you." They turned back with eyes flowing with tears, for sorrow that they could not find the means to spend.

93. The road (of blame) is only against those who ask for leave of you (to stay at home) when they are rich. They are content to be with the useless. God has sealed their hearts so that they do not know.

94. They will make excuse to you (Muslims) when you return to them. Say: "Make no excuse, for we shall not believe you. God has told us tidings of you. God and His messenger will see your conduct, and then you will be brought back to Him who knows the invisible as well as the visible, and He will tell you what you used to do."

95. They will swear by God to you, when you return to them, that you may let them be. Let them be, for they are unclean, and their abode is hell as the reward for what they used to earn.

96. They swear to you, that you may accept them. Though you accept them, God does not accept wrongdoing people.

97. The wandering Arabs are more hard in disbelief and hypocrisy, and more likely to be ignorant of the limits which God has revealed to His messenger. And God is knower, wise.

2. Ar. *al-a'rāb*, meaning the various Bedouin nomadic tribes, some of whom became allied to Muḥammad.

98. And of the wandering Arabs there is he who takes what he expends (for the cause of God) as a loss, and awaits (evil) turns of fortune for you (that he may be rid of it). The evil turn of fortune will be theirs. God is hearer, knower.

99. And of the wandering Arabs there is he who believes in God and the last day, and takes what he expends and also the prayers of the messenger as acceptable offerings in the sight of God. It is an acceptable offering for them. God will bring them into His mercy. God is forgiving, merciful.

100. And the first to lead the way, of the Muhājirūn[3] and the Anṣār,[4] and those who followed them in goodness—God is well pleased with them and they are well pleased with Him, and He has made ready for them gardens underneath which rivers flow, in which they will abide forever. That is the supreme triumph.

101. And among those around you of the wandering Arabs there are hypocrites, and among the townspeople of Medina (there are some who) persist in hypocrisy whom you (O Muḥammad) do not know. We, We know them, and We shall chastise them twice; then they will be relegated to a painful doom.

102. And (there are) others who have acknowledged their faults. They mixed a righteous action with another that was bad. It may be that God will relent toward them. God is forgiving, merciful.

103. Take alms of their wealth, with which you may purify them and may make them grow, and pray for them. Your prayer is an assuagement for them. God is hearer, knower.

104. Do they not know that God is He who accepts repentance from His servants and takes the alms, and that God is He who is the relenting, the merciful?

105. And say (to them): "Act! God will behold your actions, and (so will) His messenger and the believers, and you will be brought back to the knower of the invisible and the visible, and He will tell you what you used to do."

106. And (there are) others who await God's decree, whether He will punish them or will forgive them. God is knower, wise.

107. And as for those who chose a place of worship out of opposition and disbelief, and in order to cause dissent among the believers, and as an outpost for those who warred against God and His messenger before, they will surely swear: "We intended nothing except good." God bears witness that they verily are liars.

108. Never stand (to pray) there. A place of worship which was founded upon duty (to God) from the first day is more worthy for you to stand (to pray) there, in which are men who love to purify themselves. God loves the purifiers.

109. Is he who founded his building upon duty to God and His good pleasure better; or he who founded his building on the brink of a crumbling, overhanging precipice so that it toppled with him into the fire of hell? God does not guide wrongdoing people.

110. The building which they built will never cease to be a misgiving in their hearts unless their hearts be torn to pieces. God is knower, wise.

3. The fugitives from Mecca to Medina [Pickthall's note].
4. The Muslims of Medina who welcomed the fugitives from Mecca and helped the Prophet with their wealth and defended him with their lives [Pickthall's note].

111. God has bought from the believers their lives and their wealth because the garden will be theirs: they shall fight in the way of God and shall slay and be slain. It is a promise which is binding on Him in the Torah and the Gospel and the Qur'ān. Who fulfills His covenant better than God? Rejoice then in your bargain that you have made, for that is the supreme triumph.

112. (Triumphant) are those who turn repentant (to God), those who serve (Him), those who praise (Him), those who fast, those who bow down, those who fall prostrate (in worship), those who enjoin the right and who forbid the wrong, and those who keep the limits (ordained) of God—And give glad tidings to believers!

113. It is not for the Prophet, and those who believe, to pray for the forgiveness of idolaters even though they may be near of kin (to them) after it has become clear that they are people of hellfire.

114. The prayer of Abraham for the forgiveness of his father was only because of a promise he had promised him, but when it had become clear to him that he (his father) was an enemy to God he (Abraham) disowned him. Abraham was soft of heart, long suffering.

115. It was never God's (part) that he should send a people astray after He had guided them until He had made clear to them what they should avoid. God is aware of all things.

116. God! To Him belongs the sovereignty of the heavens and the earth. He gives life and He gives death. And you have, instead of God, no protecting friend or helper.

117. God has turned in mercy to the Prophet, and to the Muhājirūn and the Anṣār[5] who followed him in the hour of hardship. After the hearts of a party of them had almost swerved aside, then He turned to them in mercy. He is full of pity, merciful for them.

118. And to the three also (He turned in mercy) who were left behind, when the earth, vast as it is, was constricted for them, and their own souls were constricted for them until they thought that there is no refuge from God except toward Him. Then He turned to them in mercy that they (too) might turn (repentant to Him).[6] God! He is the relenting, the merciful.

119. O you who believe! Be careful of your duty to God, and be with the truthful.

120. It is not for the townspeople of Medina and for those around them of the wandering Arabs to stay behind the messenger of God and prefer their lives to his life. That is because neither thirst nor toil nor hunger afflicts them in the way of God, nor do they step any step that angers the disbelievers, nor do they gain from the enemy a gain, but a good deed is recorded for them therefore. God does not lose the wages of the good.

121. Nor do they spend any spending, small or great, nor do they cross a valley, but it is recorded for them, that God may repay them the best of what they used to do.

122. And the believers should not all go out to fight. Of every band of them, only a party should go forth, that they (who are left behind) may gain sound knowledge in religion, and that they may warn their people when they return to them, so that they may beware.

5. See v. 100, footnotes [Pickthall's note].
6. The reference is to three men of Medina who were ostracized on account of a misdeed, but afterward repented and were forgiven [Pickthall's note].

123. O you who believe! Fight those of the disbelievers who are near to you, and let them find harshness in you, and know that God is with those who keep their duty (to Him).

124. And whenever a sūra is revealed there are some of them who say: "Which one of you has thus increased in faith?" As for those who believe, it has increased them in faith and they rejoice (therefore).

125. But as for those in whose hearts is disease, it only adds wickedness to their wickedness, and they die while they are disbelievers.

126. Do they not see that they are tested once or twice in every year? Still they do not turn in repentance, neither do they pay heed.

127. And whenever a sūra is revealed, they look at one another (as who should say): "Does anybody see you?" Then they turn away. God turns away their hearts because they are a people who do not understand.

128. There has come to you a messenger, (one) of yourselves, for whom anything that you are overburdened is grievous, full of concern for you, for the believers full of pity, merciful.

129. Now, if they turn away (O Muḥammad) say: "God suffices me. There is no god except Him. In Him have I put my trust, and He is Lord of the tremendous throne."

## Sūra 10

Derives its title from verse 99. "If only there had been a community (of all those that were destroyed of old) that believed and profited by its belief as did the people of Jonah!" As is the case with nearly all the Meccan sūras, the date of revelation is uncertain, on account of the dearth of historical allusion. All that can with certainty be said is that it belongs to the latest group of Meccan sūras and must therefore have been revealed at some time during the last four years before the *hijra*.

A late Meccan sūra, with the exception of three verses revealed at Medina.

## Jonah

*Revealed at Mecca*

In the name of God the beneficent, the merciful.

1. Alif. Lām. Rā.[1]

2. These are verses of the wise scripture.[2]

3. Is it a wonder for mankind that We have inspired a man among them, saying: "Warn mankind and bring to those who believe the good tidings that they have a sure footing with their Lord"? The disbelievers say: "This is a mere wizard."

4. Your Lord is God who created the heavens and the earth in six days,[3] then He established Himself upon the throne, directing all things. There

1. See Q 2:1, footnote [Pickthall's note].
2. The Arabic *kitāb*, meaning "writing" or "book," refers to the Qur'ān's conception of itself as a scripture such as those revealed to the Jews and Christians.
3. See Q 22:47, 32:5, and 70:4 [Pickthall's note].

is no intercessor (with Him) except after His permission. That is God, your Lord, so worship Him. Oh, will you not pay heed?

5. To Him is the return of all of you; it is a promise of God in truth. He produces creation, then reproduces it, that He may reward those who believe and do good works with equity; while, as for those who disbelieve, theirs will be a boiling drink and painful doom because they disbelieved.

6. He it is who appointed the sun a splendor and the moon a light, and measured for her stages, that you might know the number of the years, and the reckoning. God did not create (all) that except in truth. He details the revelations for people who have knowledge.

7. In the difference of day and night and all that God has created in the heavens and the earth are signs for folk who ward off (evil).

8. Those who do not expect the meeting with Us but desire the life of the world and feel secure in it, and those who are neglectful of Our revelations,

9. Their home will be the fire because of what they used to earn.

10. Those who believe and do good works, their Lord guides them by their faith. Rivers will flow beneath them in the gardens of delight,

11. Their prayer in it will be: "Glory be to You, O God!" and their greeting in it will be: "Peace." And the conclusion of their prayer will be: "Praise be to God, Lord of the worlds!"

12. If God were to hasten on for men the ill (that they have earned) as they would hasten on the good, their respite would already have expired. But We suffer those who do not look for the meeting with Us to wander blindly on in their defiance.

13. And if misfortune touches a man he cries to Us, (while reclining) on his side, or sitting or standing, but when We have relieved him of the misfortune he goes his way as though he had not cried to us because of a misfortune that afflicted him. Thus is what they do made (apparently) fair to the prodigal.

14. We destroyed the generations before you when they did wrong; and their messengers (from God) came to them with clear proofs (of His sovereignty) but they would not believe. Thus do We reward the guilty people.

15. Then We appointed you successors on the earth after them, that We might see how you behave.

16. And when our clear revelations are recited to them, they who do not look for the meeting with Us say: "Bring a Lecture[4] other than this, or change it." Say (O Muḥammad): "It is not for me to change it of my own accord. I only follow that which is inspired in me. If I disobey my Lord I fear the retribution of an awful day."

17. Say: "If God had so willed I should not have recited it to you nor would He have made it known to you. I dwelt among you a whole lifetime before it (came to me). Have you then no sense?"

18. Who does greater wrong than he who invents a lie concerning God and denies His revelations? The guilty never are successful.

19. They worship beside God that which neither hurts them nor profits them, and they say: "These are our intercessors with God." Say: "Would you inform God of (something) that He does not know in the heavens or

4. Ar. *Qur'ān* [Pickthall's note].

on the earth? Praised be He and high exalted above all that you associate (with Him)!"

20. Mankind was but one community; then they differed; and had it not been for a word that had already gone forth from your Lord it would have been judged between them in respect of that in which they differ.

21. And they will say: "If only a sign were sent down upon him from his Lord!" Then say, (O Muḥammad): "The unseen belongs to God. So wait! I am waiting with you."

22. And when We cause mankind to taste of mercy after some adversity which had afflicted them, behold! they have some plot against Our revelations. Say: "God is more swift in plotting. Our messengers write down that which you plot."

23. He it is who makes you to go on the land and the sea until, when you are in the ships and they sail with them with a fair breeze and they are glad in them, a storm wind reaches them and the wave comes to them from every side and they deem that they are overwhelmed therein; (then) they cry to God, making their faith pure for Him only: "If You deliver us from this, we truly will be of the thankful."

24. Yet when He has delivered them, behold! they rebel on the earth wrongfully. O mankind! Your rebellion is only against yourselves. (You have) enjoyment of the life of the world; then to Us is your return and We shall proclaim to you what you used to do.

25. The similitude of the life of the world is only as water which We send down from the sky, then the earth's growth of that which men and cattle eat mingles with it until, when the earth has taken on her ornaments and is embellished, and her people deem that they are masters of her, Our commandment comes by night or by day and we make it as reaped corn as if it had not flourished yesterday. Thus do We expound the revelations for people who reflect.

26. And God summons to the abode of peace, and leads whom He will to a straight path.

27. For those who do good is the best (reward) and more (of it). Neither dust nor ignominy comes near their faces. Such are rightful owners of the garden; they will abide in it.

28. And those who earn ill deeds, (for them) requital of each ill deed by the like of it; and ignominy overtakes them—they have no protector from God—as if their faces had been covered with a cloak of darkest night. Such are rightful owners of the fire; they will abide there.

29. On the day when We gather them all together, then We say to those who ascribed partners (to Us): "Stand back, you and your (pretended) partners (of God)!" And We separate them, the one from the other, and their (pretended) partners say: "It was not us you worshipped."

30. God suffices as a witness between us and you, that we were unaware of your worship.

31. There does every soul experience that which it did before, and they are returned to God, their rightful Lord, and what they used to invent has failed them.

32. Say (unto them, O Muḥammad): "Who provides for you from the sky and the earth, or who owns hearing and sight; and who brings forth the living from the dead and brings forth the dead from the living; and who

directs the course?" They will say: "Will you not then keep your duty (to Him)?"

33. Such then is God, your rightful Lord. After the truth what is there but error? How then are you turned away!

34. Thus is the word of your Lord justified concerning those who do wrong: that they believe not.

35. Say: "Is there of your partners (whom you ascribe to God) one that produces creation and then reproduces it?" Say: "God produces creation, then reproduces it. How, then, are you misled!"

36. Say: "Is there of your partners (whom you ascribe to God) one that leads to the truth?" Say: "God leads to the truth. Is He who leads to the truth more deserving that He should be followed, or he who does not find the way unless he (himself) be guided? What ails you? How judge you?"

37. Most of them follow nothing but conjecture. Assuredly conjecture can by no means take the place of truth. God is aware of what they do.

38. And this Qur'ān is not such as could ever be invented except by God; but it is a confirmation of what was before it and an exposition of what is decreed for mankind—in it there is no doubt—from the Lord of the worlds.

39. Or do they say: "He has invented it?" Say: "Then bring a sūra like it, and call (for help) on all you can besides God, if you are truthful."

40. No, but they denied that, the knowledge of which they could not comprehend, and of which the interpretation (in events) has not yet come to them. Even so did those before them deny. Then see what was the consequence for the wrongdoers!

41. And of them is he who believes in it, and of them is he who does not believe in it, and your Lord is best aware of the corrupters.

42. And if they deny you, say: "To me my work, and to you your work. You are innocent of what I do, and I am innocent of what you do."

43. And of them are some who listen to you. But can you make the deaf to hear even though they do not apprehend?

44. And of them is he who looks toward you. But can you guide the blind even though they do not see?

45. God does not wrong mankind in anything, but mankind wrong themselves.

46. And on the day when He shall gather them together, (when it will seem) as though they had tarried but an hour of the day, recognizing one another, those will have perished who denied the meeting with God and were not guided.

47. Whether We let you (O Muḥammad) behold something of what We promise them or (whether We) cause you to die, still to Us is their return, and God, moreover, is witness over what they do.

48. And for every nation there is a messenger. And when their messenger comes (on the day of judgment) it will be judged between them fairly, and they will not be wronged.

49. And they say: "When will this promise be fulfilled, if you are truthful?"

50. Say: "I have no power to hurt or benefit myself, except what God wills. For every nation there is an appointed time. When their time comes, then they cannot put it off an hour, nor hasten (it)."

51. Say: "Have you thought: When His doom comes to you as a raid by night, or in the (busy) day; what is there of it that the guilty ones desire to hasten?

52. "Is it (only) then, when it has befallen you, that you will believe? What! (Believe) now, when (until now) you have been hastening it on (through disbelief)?"

53. Then will it be said to those who dealt unjustly, "Taste the torment of eternity. Are you requited anything except what you used to earn?"

54. And they ask you to inform them (saying): "Is it true?" Say: "Yes, by my Lord, it is true, and you cannot escape."

55. And if each soul that does wrong had all that is on the earth it would seek to ransom itself therewith; and they will feel remorse within them, when they see the doom. But it has been judged between them fairly and they are not wronged.

56. All that is in the heavens and the earth is God's. God's promise is true. But most of them do not know.

57. He quickens and gives death, and to Him you will be returned.

58. O mankind! There has come to you an exhortation from your Lord, a balm for that which is in the breasts, a guidance and a mercy for believers.

59. Say: "In the bounty of God and in His mercy: in that let them rejoice. It is better than what they hoard."

60. Say: "Have you considered what provision God has sent down for you, how you have made of it lawful and unlawful?" Say: "Has God permitted you, or do you invent a lie concerning God?"

61. And what do those think who invent a lie concerning God (will be their plight) upon the day of resurrection? God truly is bountiful toward mankind, but most of them do not give thanks.

62. And you (Muḥammad) are not occupied with any business and you do not recite a lecture[5] from this (scripture), and you (mankind) perform no act, but We are witness of you when you are engaged in it. And not an atom's weight on the earth or in the sky escapes your Lord, nor what is less than that or greater than that, but it is (written) in a clear book.

63. The friends of God are (those) on whom fear does not (come), nor do they grieve.

64. Those who believe and keep their duty (to God),

65. Theirs are good tidings in the life of the world and in the hereafter—there is no changing the words of God—that is the supreme triumph.

66. And do not let their speech grieve you (O Muḥammad). Power belongs wholly to God. He is the hearer, the knower.

67. Is it not to God that belongs whoever is in the heavens and whoever is on the earth? Those who follow anything instead of God do not follow (His) partners. They follow only a conjecture, and they only guess.

68. He it is who has appointed for you the night that you should rest in it and the day giving sight. Here are signs for a people that heed.

69. They say: "God has taken (to Him) a son"—Glorified be He! He has no needs! His is all that is in the heavens and all that is on the earth. You have no warrant for this. Do you tell concerning God what you know not?

70. Say: "Those who invent a lie concerning God will not succeed."

5. Ar. *Qur'ān* [Pickthall's note].

71. This world's portion (will be theirs), then to Us is their return. Then We make them taste a dreadful doom because they used to disbelieve.

72. Recite to them the story of Noah, when he told his people: "O my people! If my sojourn (here) and my reminding you by God's revelations are an offense to you, in God have I put my trust, so decide upon your course of action, you and your partners. Do not let your course of action be in doubt, for you. Then have at me, give me no respite.

73. "But if you are averse I have asked of you no wage. My wage is the concern of God only, and I am commanded to be of those who surrender (to Him)."

74. But they denied him, so We saved him and those with him in the ship, and made them successors (on the earth), while We drowned those who denied Our revelations. See then the nature of the consequence for those who had been warned.

75. Then, after him, We sent messengers to their people, and they brought them clear proofs. But they were not ready to believe in what they before denied. Thus do We print on the hearts of the transgressors.

76. Then, after them, We sent Moses and Aaron to Pharaoh and his chiefs with Our revelations, but they were arrogant and were a guilty people.

77. And when the truth from Our presence came to them, they said: "This is mere magic."

78. Moses said: "Do you speak (so) of the truth when it has come to you? Is this magic? Now magicians do not thrive."

79. They said: "Have you come to us to pervert us from that (faith) in which we found our fathers, and that you two may own the place of greatness in the land? We will not believe you two."

80. And Pharaoh said: "Bring every cunning wizard to me."

81. And when the wizards came, Moses said to them: "Cast your cast!"

82. And when they had cast, Moses said: "What you have brought is magic. God will make it vain. God upholds not the work of mischief-makers.

83. "And God will vindicate the truth by His words, however much the guilty be averse."

84. But none trusted Moses, except some scions of his people, (and they were) in fear of Pharaoh and their chiefs, that they would persecute them. Pharaoh was a tyrant in the land, and he was of the wanton.

85. And Moses said: "O my people! If you have believed in God then put trust in Him, if you have indeed surrendered (to Him)!"

86. They said: "In God we put trust. Our Lord! Oh, do not make us a lure for the wrongdoing people;

87. "And, of Your mercy, save us from the people that disbelieve."

88. And We inspired Moses and his brother, (saying): "Appoint houses for your people in Egypt and make your houses oratories, and establish worship. And give good news to the believers."

89. And Moses said: "Our Lord! You have given Pharaoh and his chiefs splendor and riches in the life of the world, Our Lord! that they may lead men astray from Your way. Our Lord! Destroy their riches and harden their hearts so that they do not believe until they see the painful doom."

90. He said: "Your prayer is heard. You and your brother keep to the straight path, and do not follow the road of those who have no knowledge."

91. And We brought the Children of Israel across the sea, and Pharaoh with his hosts pursued them in rebellion and transgression, until, when the (fate of) drowning overtook him, he exclaimed: "I believe that there is no God except Him in whom the Children of Israel believe, and I am of those who surrender (to Him)."

92. What! Now! When before you have rebelled and been of the wrongdoers?

93. But this day We save you in your body that you may be a sign for those after you. Most of mankind are heedless of Our signs.

94. And We allotted to the Children of Israel a fixed abode, and provided them with good things; and they did not differ until the knowledge came to them. Your Lord will judge between them on the day of resurrection concerning that in which they used to differ.

95. And if you (Muḥammad) are in doubt concerning that which We reveal to you, then question those who read the scripture (that was) before you. The truth from your Lord has come to you. So do not be of the waverers.

96. And do not be of those who deny the revelations of God, for then were you of the losers.

97. Those for whom the word of your Lord (concerning sinners) has effect will not believe,

98. Though every sign come to them, until they see the painful doom.

99. If only there had been a community (of all those that were destroyed of old) that believed and profited by its belief as did the people of Jonah! When they believed We drew off from them the torment of disgrace in the life of the world and gave them comfort for a while.

100. And if your Lord willed, all who are on the earth would have believed together. Would you (Muḥammad) compel men until they are believers?

101. It is not for any soul to believe except by the permission of God. He has set uncleanness upon those who have no sense.

102. Say: "Behold what is in the heavens and the earth!" But revelations and warnings do not avail people who will not believe.

103. What do they expect except the like of the days of those who passed away before them? Say: "Expect then! I am with you among the expectant."

104. Then shall We save Our messengers and the believers, in like manner (as of old). It is incumbent upon Us to save believers.

105. Say (O Muḥammad): "O mankind! If you are in doubt of my religion, then (know that) I do not worship those whom you worship instead of God, but I worship God who causes you to die, and I have been commanded to be of the believers."

106. And, (O Muḥammad) set your purpose resolutely for religion, as a man by nature upright, and be not of those who ascribe partners (to God).

107. And cry not, beside God, to what cannot profit you nor hurt you, for if you did so then were you of the wrongdoers.

108. If God afflicts you with some hurt, there is none who can remove it except Him; and if He desires good for you, there is none who can repel His bounty. He strikes with it whom He will of his servants. He is the forgiving, the merciful.

109. Say: "O mankind! Now has the truth from your Lord come to you. So whoever errs errs only against it. And I am not a warder over you."

110. And (O Muḥammad) follow what is inspired in you, and be patient until God gives judgment. And He is the best of judges.

## Sūra 11

*Hūd* takes its name from verse 50, which begins the story of Hūd, of the tribe of ʿĀd, one of the prophets of Arabia who are not mentioned in the Hebrew scriptures. The sūra also contains the stories of two other Arab prophets, Ṣāliḥ, of the tribe of Thamūd, and Shuʿayb of Midian (identified with Jethro), which, with those of Noah and Moses, are quoted as part of the history of divine revelation, the truth of which is here vindicated, in a manner supplementary to Q 10.

A late Meccan sūra, except verses 114ff., revealed at Medina.

## Hūd

*Revealed at Mecca*

In the name of God, the beneficent, the merciful.

1. Alif. Lām. Rā.[1] (This is) a scripture the revelations of which are perfected and then expounded. (It comes) from one wise, informed,

2. (Saying): Serve none but God. I am to you from Him a warner and a bringer of good tidings.

3. And (bidding you): Ask pardon of your Lord and turn to Him repentant. He will cause you to enjoy a fair estate until a time appointed. He gives His bounty to every bountiful one. But if you turn away, (then) I fear for you the retribution of an awful day.

4. To God is your return, and He is able to do all things.

5. Now they fold up their breasts that they may hide (their thoughts) from Him. At the very moment when they cover themselves with their clothing, God knows that which they keep hidden and that which they proclaim. He is aware of what is in the breasts (of men).

6. And there is not a beast on the earth but the sustenance of it depends on God. He knows its habitation and its repository. All is in a clear record.

7. And He it is who created the heavens and the earth in six days[2]—and His throne was upon the water—that He might try you, which of you is best in conduct. Yet if you (O Muḥammad) say: "You will be raised again after death!" those who disbelieve will surely say: "This is nothing but mere magic."

8. And if We delay for them the doom until a reckoned time, they will surely say: "What withholds it?" Truly on the day when it comes to them, it cannot be averted from them, and that which they derided will surround them.

9. And if We cause man to taste some mercy from Us and afterward withdraw it from him, he is despairing, thankless.

1. See Q 2:1, footnote [Pickthall's note].
2. Q 22:47, 32:5, and 70:4 [Pickthall's note].

10. And if We cause him to taste grace after some misfortune that had befallen him, he says: "The ills have gone from me." He is exultant, boastful;

11. Save those who persevere and do good works. Theirs will be forgiveness and a great reward.

12. A likely thing, that you would forsake anything of what has been revealed to you, and that your breast should be straightened for it, because they say: "Why has a treasure not been sent down for him, or an angel come with him?" You are but a warner, and God is in charge of all things.

13. Or they say: "He has invented it." Say: "Then bring ten sūras, the like of it, invented, and call on everyone you can beside God, if you are truthful!"

14. And if they do not answer your prayer, then know that it is revealed only in the knowledge of God; and that there is no god save Him. Will you then be (among) those who surrender?[3]

15. Whoever desires the life of the world and its pomp, We shall repay them their deeds in it, and in it they will not be wronged.

16. Those are they for whom there is nothing in the hereafter except the fire. (All) that they contrive here is vain and (all) that they are used to do is fruitless.

17. Is he (to be counted equal with them) who relies on a clear proof from his Lord, and a witness from Him recites it, and before it was the book of Moses, an example and a mercy? Such believe in it, and whoever of the clans disbelieves in it, the fire is his appointed place. So do not be in doubt concerning it. It is the truth from your Lord; but most of mankind believe not.

18. Who does greater wrong than he who invents a lie concerning God? Such will be brought before their Lord, and the witnesses will say: "These are they who lied concerning their Lord." Now the curse of God is upon wrongdoers,

19. Who debar (men) from the way of God and would have it crooked, and who are disbelievers in the hereafter.

20. Such will not escape on the earth, nor have they any protecting friends beside God. For them the torment will be double. They could not bear to hear, and they used not to see.

21. Such are they who have lost their souls, and that which they used to invent has failed them.

22. Assuredly in the hereafter they will be the greatest losers.

23. Those who believe and do good works and humble themselves before their Lord: such are rightful owners of the garden; they will abide there.

24. The similitude of the two parties is as the blind and the deaf and the one who sees and the one who hears. Are they equal in similitude? Will you not then be admonished?

25. And We sent Noah to his people (and he said): "I am a plain warner to you.

26. "That you serve none, except God. I fear for you the retribution of a painful day."

27. The leaders of his people, who disbelieved, said: "We see you but a mortal like us, and we do not see that any follow you except the most abject

3. Ar. *Muslimūn* [Pickthall's note].

among us, without reflection. We behold in you no merit above us—we deem you liars."

28. He said: "O my people! Do you think, if I rely on a clear proof from my Lord and there has come to me a mercy from His presence, and it has been made obscure to you, can we compel you to accept it when you are averse to it?"

29. And, "O my people! I ask of you no wealth for it. My reward is the concern only of God, and I am not going to thrust away those who believe—They have to meet their Lord—but I see that you are an ignorant people."

30. And, "O my people! who would deliver me from God if I thrust them away? Will you not then reflect?

31. "I do not say to you: 'I have the treasures of God' nor 'I have knowledge of the unseen,' nor do I say: 'I am an angel!' Nor do I say to those whom your eyes scorn that God will not give them good—God knows best what is in their hearts—Then indeed I should be of the wrongdoers."

32. They said: "O Noah! You have disputed with us and multiplied disputation with us; now bring upon us that with which you threaten us, if you are of the truthful."

33. He said: "Only God will bring it upon you if He will, and you can by no means escape.

34. "My counsel will not profit you if I were minded to advise you, if God's will is to keep you astray. He is your Lord and to Him you will be brought back."

35. Or they say (again): "He has invented it?" Say: "If I have invented it, upon me be my crimes, but I am innocent of (all) that you commit."

36. And it was inspired in Noah, (saying): "No one of your people will believe except him who has believed already. Do not be distressed because of what they do.

37. "Build the ship under Our eyes and by Our inspiration, and do not speak to Me on behalf of those who do wrong. They will be drowned."

38. And he was building the ship, and every time that leaders of his people passed him, they mocked of him. He said: "Though you mock us, yet we mock you even as you mock;

39. "And you shall know to whom a punishment that will confound him comes, and upon whom a lasting doom will fall."

40. (Thus it was) until, when Our commandment came to pass and the oven gushed forth water,[4] We said: "Load in it two of every kind, a pair (the male and female), and your household, except him against whom the word has gone forth already, and those who believe." And but a few were they who believed with him.

41. And he said: "Embark in it! In the name of God be its course and its mooring. My Lord is forgiving, merciful."

42. And it sailed with them amid waves like mountains, and Noah cried to his son—and he was standing aloof—"O my son! Come ride with us, and do not be with the disbelievers."

43. He said: "I shall take myself to some mountain that will save me from the water." (Noah) said: "This day there is none that saves from the

4. This was a sign of the deluge, water gushing up from underground as well as falling from the sky [Pickthall's note].

commandment of God except him on whom He has had mercy." And the wave came in between them, so he was among the drowned.

44. And it was said: "O earth! Swallow your water and, O sky! be cleared of clouds!" And the water was made to subside. And the commandment was fulfilled. And it (the ship) came to rest upon (the mount) al-Jūdī and it was said: "A far removal for wrong-doing people!"

45. And Noah cried to his Lord and said: "My Lord! My son is of my household! Surely Your promise is the truth and You are the most just of judges."

46. He said: "O Noah! He is not of your household; he is of evil conduct, so do not ask of Me that of which you have no knowledge. I admonish you for fear that you be among the ignorant."

47. He said: "My Lord! In You do I seek refuge (from the sin) that I should ask of You that of which I have no knowledge. Unless You forgive me and have mercy on me I shall be among the lost."

48. It was said (to him): "O Noah! Go down (from the mountain) with peace from Us and blessings upon you and some nations (that will spring) from those with you. (There will be other) nations to whom We shall give enjoyment a long while and then a painful doom from Us will overtake them."

49. This is of the tidings of the unseen which We inspire in you (Muḥammad). You yourself did not know it, nor did your people (know it) before this. Then have patience. The sequel is for those who ward off (evil).

50. And to (the tribe of) 'Ād (We sent) their brother, Hūd. He said: "O my people! Serve God! You have no other god except Him. You do but invent!

51. "O my people! I ask of you no reward for it. My reward is the concern only of Him who made me. Have you then no sense?"

52. And, "O my people! Ask forgiveness of your Lord, then turn to Him repentant; He will cause the sky to rain abundance on you and will add strength to your strength. Do not turn away, guilty!"

53. They said: "O Hūd! You have brought us no clear proof and we are not going to forsake our gods on your (mere) saying, and we are not believers in you.

54. "We say nothing except that one of our gods has possessed you in an evil way." He said: "I call God to witness, and do you (too) bear witness, that I am innocent of (all) that you ascribe as partners (to God)

55. "Beside Him. So (try to) circumvent me, all of you, give me no respite.

56. "I have put my trust in God, my Lord and your Lord. There is not an animal but He grasps it by the forelock![5] My Lord is on a straight path.

57. "And if you turn away, still I have conveyed to you that with which I was sent to you, and my Lord will set in place of you a people other than you. You cannot injure Him at all. My Lord is guardian over all things."

58. And when Our commandment came to pass We saved Hūd and those who believed with him by a mercy from Us; We saved them from a harsh doom.

59. And such were 'Ād. They denied the revelations of their Lord and flouted His messengers and followed the command of every obstinate potentate.

5. The sense is that God has control and power over all creatures.

60. And a curse was made to follow them in the world and on the day of resurrection. 'Ād disbelieved in their Lord. A far removal for 'Ād, the people of Hūd!

61. And to (the tribe of) Thamūd (We sent) their brother Ṣāliḥ. He said: "O my people! Serve God, You have no other god but Him. He brought you forth from the earth and has settled you in it. So ask forgiveness of Him and turn to Him repentant. My Lord is near, responsive."

62. They said: "O Ṣaliḥ! You have been among us before this as that in which our hope was placed. Do you ask us not to worship what our fathers worshipped? We verily are in grave doubt concerning that to which you call us."

63. He said: "O my people! Do you think if I am (acting) on clear proof from my Lord and there has come to me a mercy from Him, who will save me from God if I disobey Him? You would add to me nothing except perdition.

64. O my people! This is the camel of God, a token to you, so allow her to feed in God's earth, and do not touch her with harm lest a near torment seize you."

65. But they hamstrung her, and then he said: "Enjoy life in your dwelling-place three days! This is a threat that will not be belied."

66. So, when Our commandment came to pass, We saved Ṣāliḥ, and those who believed with him, by a mercy from Us, from the ignominy of that day. Your Lord! He is the strong, the mighty.

67. And the (awful) cry overtook those who did wrong, so that morning found them prostrate in their dwellings,

68. As though they had not dwelt there. Thamūd did not believe in their Lord. A far removal for Thamūd!

69. And Our messengers came to Abraham with good news. They said: "Peace!" He answered: "Peace!" and did not delay to bring a roasted calf.

70. And when he saw their hands did not reach to it, he mistrusted them and conceived a fear of them. They said: "Fear not! We are sent to the people of Lot."

71. And his wife, standing by, laughed when We gave her good tidings (of the birth) of Isaac, and, after Isaac, of Jacob.

72. She said: "Oh, woe is me! Shall I bear a child when I am an old woman, and this my husband is an old man? This is a strange thing!"

73. They said: "Do you wonder at the commandment of God? The mercy of God and His blessings be upon you, O people of the house! He is owner of praise, owner of glory!"

74. And when the awe departed from Abraham, and the glad news reached him, he pleaded with Us on behalf of the people of Lot.

75. Abraham was mild, imploring, penitent.

76. (It was said) "O Abraham! Forsake this! Your Lord's commandment has gone forth, and there comes to them a doom which cannot be repelled."

77. And when Our messengers came to Lot, he was distressed and knew not how to protect them. He said: "This is a distressful day."

78. And his people came to him, running toward him—and before then they used to commit abominations—He said: "O my people! Here are my daughters![6] They are purer for you. Beware of God, and do not

6. See Genesis 19:8.

degrade me in (the person of) my guests. Is there not among you any upright man?"

79. They said: "You know well that we have no right to your daughters, and you know well what we want."

80. He said: "Would that I had strength to resist you or had some strong support (among you)!"

81. (The messengers) said: "O Lot! We are messengers of your Lord; they shall not reach you. So travel with your people in a part of the night, and let not one of you turn round—(all) except your wife. That which strikes them will strike her (also). Their meeting is (for) the morning. Is not the morning near?"

82. So when Our commandment came to pass We overthrew (that township) and rained upon it stones of clay, one after another,

83. Marked with fire in the providence of your Lord (for the destruction of the wicked). And they are never far from the wrongdoers.

84. And to Midian (We sent) their brother Shuʿayb. He said: "O my people! Serve God. You have no other god except Him! And do not give short measure and short weight. I see you well-to-do, and I fear for you the doom of a devastating day.

85. "O my people! Give full measure and full weight in justice, and do not wrong people in respect of their goods. And do not evil on the earth, causing corruption.

86. "That which God leaves with you is better for you if you are believers; I am not a keeper over you."

87. They said: "O Shuʿayb! Does your way of prayer command you that we should forsake what our fathers (used to) worship, or that we (should leave off) doing what we will with our own property? You are the mild, the guide to right behavior."

88. He said: "O my people! Do you think that if I am (acting) on a clear proof from my Lord and He sustains me with fair sustenance from Him (how can I concede anything to you)? I do not desire to do behind your backs that which I ask you not to do. I desire nothing except reform so far as I am able. My welfare is only in God. In Him I trust and to Him I turn (repentant)."

89. And, "O my people! Do not let the schism with me cause you to sin so that there befalls you that which befell the people of Noah and the people of Hūd, and the people of Ṣāliḥ; and the people of Lot are not far off from you.

90. "Ask pardon of your Lord and then turn to Him (repentant). My Lord is merciful, loving."

91. They said: "O Shuʿayb! We do not understand much of what you tell, and we behold you weak among us. But for your family, we should have stoned you, for you are not strong against us."

92. He said: "O my people! Is my family more to be honored by you than God? And you put Him behind you, neglected! My Lord surrounds what you do."

93. And, "O my people! Act according to your power, I (too) am acting. You will soon know on whom there comes a doom that will abase him, and who it is that lies. And watch! I am a watcher with you."

94. And when Our commandment came to pass We saved Shuʿayb and those who believed with Him by a mercy from Us; and the (awful) cry

seized those who did injustice, and morning found them prostrate in their dwellings,

95. As though they had not dwelt there. A far removal for Midian, even as Thamūd had been removed afar!

96. And We sent Moses with Our revelations and a clear warrant

97. To Pharaoh and his chiefs, but they followed the command of Pharaoh, and the command of Pharaoh was no right guide.

98. He will go before his people on the day of resurrection and will lead them to the fire for watering-place. Unfortunate is the watering-place (to which they are) led.

99. A curse is made to follow them in the world and on the day of resurrection. Unfortunate is the gift (that will be) given (them).

100. That is (something) of the tidings of the townships[7] (which were destroyed of old) We relate it to you (Muḥammad). Some of them are standing and some (already) reaped.

101. We did not wrong them, but they wronged themselves; and their gods on whom they call beside God availed them nothing when your Lord's command came; they added to them nothing except ruin.

102. Even thus is the grasp of your Lord when he grasps the townships[8] while they are doing wrong. His grasp is painful, very strong.

103. In this there is a sign for those who fear the doom of the hereafter. That is a day to which mankind will be gathered, and that is a day that will be witnessed.

104. And We defer it only to a term already reckoned.

105. On the day when it comes no soul will speak except by His permission; some among them will be wretched, (others) glad.

106. As for those who will be wretched (on that day) they will be in the fire; sighing and wailing will be their portion there,

107. Abiding there so long as the heavens and the earth endure except for that which your Lord wills. Your Lord is doer of what He wills.

108. And as for those who will be glad (that day) they will be in the garden, abiding there so long as the heavens and the earth endure except for what your Lord wills: a gift unfailing.

109. So do not be in doubt concerning what these (people) worship. They worship only as their fathers worshipped before. We shall pay them their whole due unabated.

110. And We gave to Moses the scripture, and there was strife about it; and had it not been for a word that had already gone forth from your Lord, the case would have been judged between them, and they are in grave doubt concerning it.

111. And to each your Lord will repay his works in full. He is informed of what they do.

112. So tread the straight path as you are commanded, together with those who turn (to God) with you, and do not transgress. He is observer of what you do.

113. And do not incline toward those who do wrong for fear that the fire touch you, and you have no protecting friends against God, and afterward you would not be helped.

7. Or *communities* [Pickthall's note].
8. Or *communities* [Pickthall's note].

114. Establish worship at the two ends of the day and in some watches of the night. Good deeds annul ill deeds. This is a reminder for the mindful.
115. And have patience, (O Muḥammad), for God does not lose the wages of the good.
116. If only there had been among the generations before you men possessing a remnant (of good sense) to warn (their people) from corruption on the earth, as did a few of those whom We saved from them! The wrongdoers followed that by which they were made effete, and were guilty.
117. In truth your Lord did not destroy the townships tyrannously while their people were doing right.
118. And if your Lord had willed, He would have made mankind one nation, yet they do not cease differing,
119. Except him on whom your Lord has mercy; and for that He created them. And the word of your Lord has been fulfilled: "I shall fill hell with the jinn and mankind together."
120. And all that We relate to you of the story of the messengers is in order that by it We may make firm your heart. And in this the truth has come to you and an exhortation and a reminder for believers.
121. And say to those who believe not: "Act according to your power. We (too) are acting.
122. "And wait! We (too) are waiting."
123. And God's is the invisible of the heavens and the earth, and to Him the whole matter will be returned. So worship Him and put your trust in Him. Your Lord is not unaware of what you (mortals) do.

## Sūra 12

*Yūsuf* takes its name from its subject which is the life story of Joseph. It differs from all other sūras in having only one subject. The differences from the Bible narrative[1] are striking. Jacob is here a prophet, who is not deceived by the story of his son's death, but is distressed because, through a suspension of his clairvoyance, he cannot see what has become of Joseph. The real importance of the narrative, its psychic burden, is emphasized throughout, and the manner of narration, though astonishing to Western readers, is vivid.

Tradition says that it was recited by the Prophet at Mecca to the first converts from Yathrib (Medina), i.e. in the second year before the *hijra*; but that, as Nöldeke points out, does not mean that it was not revealed till then, but that it had been revealed by then.

A late Meccan sūra.

## Joseph

*Revealed at Mecca*

In the name of God the beneficent, the merciful.

1. Alif. Lām. Rā.[2] These are verses of the scripture that makes plain.
2. We have revealed it, a Qur'ān in Arabic, that you may understand.

1. See Genesis 37–46.
2. See Q 2:1, footnote [Pickthall's note].

3. We narrate to you (Muḥammad) the best of narratives in that We have inspired in you this Qur'ān, though before you were of the heedless.

4. When Joseph said to his father: "O my father! I saw in a dream eleven planets and the sun and the moon, I saw them prostrating themselves to me."

5. He said: "O my dear son! Do not tell your brothers of your vision, for fear that they plot a plot against you. Satan is for man an open foe.

6. "Thus your Lord will prefer you and will teach you the interpretation of events, and will perfect His grace upon you and upon the family of Jacob as he perfected it upon your forefathers, Abraham and Isaac. Your Lord is knower, wise."

7. In Joseph and his brothers are signs (of God's sovereignty) for the inquiring.

8. When they said: "Joseph and his brother are dearer to our father than we are, many though we be. Our father is in plain error."

9. (One said:) "Kill Joseph or cast him to some (other) land, so that your father's favor may be all for you, and (that) you may afterward be righteous people."

10. One among them said: "Do not kill Joseph but, if you must be doing, fling him into the depth of the pit; some caravan will find him."

11. They said: "O our father! Why will you not trust us with Joseph, when we are good friends to him?

12. "Send him with us tomorrow that he may enjoy himself and play. We shall take good care of him."

13. He said: "In truth it saddens me that you should take him with you, and I fear that the wolf may devour him while you are heedless of him."

14. They said: "If the wolf should devour him when we are (so strong) a band, then surely we should have already perished."

15. Then, when they led him off, and were of one mind that they should place him in the depth of the pit, We inspired in him: You will tell them of this deed of theirs when they know (you) not.

16. And they came weeping to their father in the evening.

17. Saying: "O our father! We went racing one with another, and left Joseph by our things, and the wolf devoured him, and you do not believe our saying even when we speak the truth."

18. And they came with false blood on his shirt. He said: "No, but your minds have beguiled you into something. (My course is) becoming patience. And God it is whose help is to be sought in that (predicament) which you describe."

19. And there came a caravan, and they sent their water drawer. He let down his pail (into the pit). He said: "Good luck! Here is a youth." And they hid him as a treasure, and God was aware of what they did.

20. And they sold him for a low price, a number of silver coins; and they attached no value to him.

21. And he of Egypt who purchased him said to his wife: "Receive him honorably. Perhaps he may prove useful to us or we may adopt him as a son." Thus We established Joseph in the land that We might teach him the interpretation of events. And God was predominant in his career, but most of mankind did not know.

22. And when he reached his prime We gave him wisdom and knowledge. Thus We reward the good.

23. And she, in whose house he was, asked of him an evil act. She bolted the doors and said: "Come!" He said: "I seek refuge in God! He is my Lord, who has treated me honorably. Wrongdoers never prosper."

24. She desired him, and he would have desired her if it had not been that he saw the illumination from his Lord. Thus it was, that We might ward off from him evil and lewdness. He was of Our chosen servants.

25. And they raced with one another to the door, and she tore his shirt from behind, and they met her lord and master at the door. She said: "What shall be his reward, who wishes evil to your people, except prison or a painful doom?"

26. (Joseph) said: "It was she who asked of me an evil act." And a witness of her own people testified: "If his shirt is torn from before, then she speaks truth and he is of the liars.

27. "And if his shirt is torn from behind, then she has lied and he is of the truthful."

28. So when he [Pharaoh] saw his shirt torn from behind, he said: "This is of the guile of you women. The guile of you is very great.

29. "O Joseph! Turn away from this, and you, (O woman), ask forgiveness for your sin. You are of the sinful."

30. And women in the city said: "The ruler's wife is asking of her slave-boy an ill deed. Indeed he has smitten her to the heart with love. We behold her in plain error."

31. And when she heard of their sly talk, she sent to them and prepared for them a cushioned couch (to lie on at the feast) and gave to every one of them a knife and said (to Joseph): "Come out to them!" And when they saw him they exalted him and cut their hands, exclaiming: "God forbid! This is not a human being. This is no other than some gracious angel."

32. She said: "This is he on whose account you blamed me. I asked of him an evil act, but he proved continent, but if he does not do my bidding he shall be imprisoned, and shall be of those brought low."

33. He said: "O my Lord! Prison is more dear than that to which they urge me, and if You do not fend off their wiles from me I shall incline to them and become of the foolish."

34. So his Lord heard his prayer and fended off their wiles from him. He is hearer, knower.

35. And it seemed good to them (the men) after they had seen the signs (of his innocence) to imprison him for a time.

36. And two young men went to prison with him. One of them said: "I dreamed that I was pressing wine." The other said: "I dreamed that I was carrying upon my head bread of which the birds were eating. Announce to us the interpretation, for we see you are among those good (at interpretation)."

37. He said: "The food which you are given (daily) shall not come to you but I shall tell you the interpretation before it comes to you. This is of what my Lord has taught me. I have forsaken the religion of people who do not believe in God and are disbelievers in the hereafter.

38. "And I have followed the religion of my fathers, Abraham and Isaac and Jacob. It never was for us to attribute anything as partner to God. This is of the bounty of God to us (the seed of Abraham) and to mankind; but most men do not give thanks.

39. "O my two fellow prisoners! Are diverse lords better, or God the one, the almighty?

40. "Those whom you worship beside Him are but names which you have named, you and your fathers. God has revealed no sanction for them. The decision rests with God only, Who has commanded you that you worship none except Him. This is the right religion, but most men know not.

41. "O my two fellow prisoners! As for one of you, he will pour out wine for his lord to drink; and as for the other, he will be crucified so that the birds will eat from his head. Thus is the case judged concerning which you did inquire."

42. And he said to him of the two who he knew would be released: "Mention me in the presence of your lord." But Satan caused him to forget to mention it to his lord, so he (Joseph) stayed in prison for some years.

43. And the king said: "I saw in a dream seven fat cows which seven lean were eating, and seven green ears of corn and another (seven) dry. O notables! Expound for me my vision, if you can interpret dreams."

44. They answered: "Jumbled dreams! And we are not knowledgeable in the interpretation of dreams."

45. And he of the two who was released, and (now) at length remembered, said: "I am going to announce to you the interpretation, therefore send me forth."

46. (And when he came to Joseph in the prison, he exclaimed): "Joseph! O you truthful one! Expound for us the seven fat cows which seven lean were eating and the seven green ears of corn and another (seven) dry, that I may return to the people, so that they may know."

47. He said: "You shall sow seven years as usual, but that which you reap, leave it on the ear, all except a little which you eat.

48. "Then after that will come seven hard years which will devour all that you have prepared for them, except a little of that which you have stored.

49. "Then, after that, will come a year when the people will have plenteous crops and when they will press (wine and oil)."

50. And the king said: "Bring him to me." And when the messenger came to him, he (Joseph) said: "Return to your lord and ask him what was the case of the women who cut their hands. My lord knows their guile."

51. He (the king) (then sent for those women and) said: "What happened when you asked an evil act of Joseph?" They answered: "God forbid! We know no evil of him." The wife of the ruler said: "Now the truth is out. I asked of him an evil act, and he is surely of the truthful."

52. (Then Joseph said: "I asked for) this, that he (my lord) may know that I did not betray him in secret, and that surely God does not guide the snare of the betrayers.

53. "I do not exculpate myself. The (human) soul enjoins to evil, except that on which my Lord has mercy. My Lord is forgiving, merciful."

54. And the king said: "Bring him to me that I may attach him to my person." And when he had talked with him he said: "You are today in our presence established and trusted."

55. He said: "Set me over the storehouses of the land. I am a skilled custodian."

56. Thus We gave power to Joseph in the land. He was the owner of it where he pleased. We reach with Our mercy whom We will. We do not lose the reward of the good.

57. And the reward of the hereafter is better, for those who believe and ward off (evil).

58. And Joseph's brothers came and presented themselves before him, and he knew them but they knew him not.

59. And when he provided them with their provision he said: "Bring to me a brother of yours from your father. Do you not see that I fill up the measure and I am the best of hosts?

60. "And if you do not bring him to me, then there shall be no measure for you with me, nor shall you draw near."

61. They said: "We will try to win him from his father: that we will surely do."

62. He said to his young men: "Place their merchandise in their saddlebags, so that they may know it when they go back to their people, and so will come again."

63. So when they went back to their father they said: "O our father! The measure is denied us, so send with us our brother that we may obtain the measure, surely we will guard him well."

64. He said: "Can I entrust him to you except as I entrusted his brother to you before? God is better at guarding, and He is the most merciful of those who show mercy."

65. And when they opened their belongings they discovered that their merchandise had been returned to them. They said: "O our father! What (more) can we ask? Here is our merchandise returned to us. We shall get provision for our people and guard our brother, and we shall have the extra measure of a camel (load). This (that we bring now) is a light measure."

66. He said: "I will not send him with you until you give me an undertaking in the name of God that you will bring him back to me, unless you are surrounded." And when they gave him their undertaking he said: "God is the warden over what we say."

67. And he said: "O my sons! Do not go in by one gate; go in by different gates. I can avail you nothing as against God. The decision rests with God only. In Him do I put my trust, and in Him let all the trusting put their trust."

68. And when they entered in the manner which their father had enjoined, it would have availed them nothing as against God; it was but a need of Jacob's soul which he thus satisfied;[3] and he was a lord of knowledge because We had taught him; but most of mankind do not know.

69. And when they went in before Joseph, he took his brother to himself, saying: "I, even I, am your brother, therefore do not sorrow for what they did."

70. And when he provided them with their provision, he put the drinking cup in his brother's saddlebag, and then a crier cried: "O camel riders! You are surely thieves!"

71. They cried, coming toward them: "What is it you have lost?"

3. There is a prevalent superstition in the East that the members of a large family ought not to appear all together, for fear of the ill luck that comes from envy in the hearts of others [Pickthall's note].

72. They said: "We have lost the king's cup, and he who brings it shall have a camel load," and "I" (said Joseph) "am answerable for it."

73. They said: "By God, well you know we did not come to do evil in the land, and are no thieves."

74. They said: "And what shall be the penalty for it, if you prove liars?"

75. They said: "The penalty for it! He in whose bag (the cup) is found, he is the penalty for it. Thus we requite wrongdoers."

76. Then he (Joseph) began the search with their bags before his brother's bag, then he produced it from his brother's bag. Thus did We contrive for Joseph. He could not have taken his brother according to the king's law unless God willed. We raise by grades (of mercy) whom We will, and over every lord of knowledge there is one more knowing.

77. They said: "If he steals, a brother of his stole before." But Joseph kept it secret in his soul and did not reveal it to them. He said (within himself): "You are in worse case, and God knows best (the truth of) that which you allege."

78. They said: "O ruler of the land! He has an aged father, so take one of us instead of him. We behold you to be of those who do kindness."

79. He said: "God forbid that we should seize anyone but him with whom we found our property; then truly we should be wrongdoers."

80. So, when they despaired of (moving) him, they conferred together apart. The eldest of them said: "Do you not know how your father took an undertaking from you in God's name and how you failed in the case of Joseph before? Therefore I shall not go forth from the land until my father gives leave or God judges for me. He is the best of judges.

81. "Return to your father and say: 'O our father! Your son has stolen. We testify only to that which we know; we are not guardians of the unseen.

82. "'Ask the township where we were, and the caravan with which we traveled here. We speak the truth.'"

83. (And when they came to their father and had spoken thus to him) he said: "No, but your minds have beguiled you into something. (My course is) becoming patience! It may be that God will bring them all to me. He, only He, is the knower, the wise."

84. And he turned away from them and said: "Alas, my grief for Joseph!" And his eyes were whitened with the sorrow that he was suppressing.

85. They said: "By God, you will never cease remembering Joseph until your health is ruined or you are of those who perish!"

86. He said: "I expose my distress and anguish only to God, and I know from God what you know not.

87. "Go, O my sons, and ascertain concerning Joseph and his brother, and do not despair of the spirit of God. None despairs of the spirit of God except disbelieving people."

88. And when they came (again) before him (Joseph) they said: "O ruler! Misfortune has touched us and our people, and we bring but poor merchandise, so fill for us the measure and be charitable to us. God will requite the charitable."

89. He said: "Do you know what you did to Joseph and his brother in your ignorance?"

90. They said: "Is it indeed you who are Joseph?" He said: "I am Joseph and this is my brother. God has shown us favor. He who wards off (evil) and endures (finds favor); for God does not lose the wages of the kindly."

91. They said: "By God, God has preferred you above us, and we were indeed sinful."

92. He said: "Have no fear this day! May God forgive you, and He is the most merciful of those who show mercy.

93. "Go with this shirt of mine and lay it on my father's face, he will become (again) one who sees; and come to me with all your people."

94. When the caravan departed their father had said: "Truly I am conscious of the scent of Joseph, though you call me a foolish babbler."

95. (Those around him) said: "By God, you are in your old error."

96. Then, when the bearer of glad tidings came, he laid it on his face and he became one who sees once more. He said: "Did I not say to you that I know from God what you know not?"

97. They said: "O our father! Ask forgiveness of our sins for us, for we were sinful."

98. He said: "I shall ask forgiveness for you of my Lord. He is the forgiving, the merciful."

99. And when they came in before Joseph, he took his parents to him, and said: "Come into Egypt safe, if God will!"

100. And he placed his parents on the daïs and they fell down before him prostrate, and he said: "O my father! This is the interpretation of my dream of old. My Lord has made it true, and He has shown me kindness, since He took me out of the prison and has brought you from the desert after Satan had made strife between me and my brethren. My Lord is tender to whom He will. He is the knower, the wise.

101. "O my Lord! You have given me (something) of sovereignty and have taught me (something) of the interpretation of events—creator of the heavens and the earth! You are my protecting friend in the world and the hereafter. Make me to die submissive (to You), and join me to the righteous."

102. This is of the tidings of the unseen which We inspire in you (Muḥammad). You were not present with them when they fixed their plan and they were scheming.

103. And though you try much, most men will not believe.

104. You ask them no fee for it. It is nothing else than a reminder to the peoples.

105. How many a sign is there in the heavens and the earth which they pass by with face averted!

106. And most of them do not believe in God except that they attribute partners (to Him).

107. Do they think themselves secure from the coming on them of a pall of God's punishment, or the coming of the hour suddenly while they are unaware?

108. Say: "This is my way: I call on God with sure knowledge, I and whoever follows me—Glory be to God!—and I am not of the idolaters."

109. We did not send before you (any messengers) except men whom We inspired from among the people of the townships—Have they not traveled in the land and seen the nature of the consequence for those who were before them? And the abode of the hereafter, for those who ward off (evil), is best. Have you then no sense?—

110. Until, when the messengers despaired and thought that they were denied, then Our help came to them, and whom We would was saved. And Our wrath cannot be warded from the guilty.

111. In their history there is a lesson for men of understanding. It is no invented story but a confirmation of the existing (scripture) and a detailed explanation of everything, and a guidance and a mercy for people who believe.

## Sūra 13

*Al-Ra'd*, "The Thunder," takes its name from a word in verse 13. The subject is divine guidance in relation to the law of consequences, it being explained here, as elsewhere in the Qur'ān, that there is no partiality or aversion on the part of God, but that reward and punishment are the result of obeying or rejecting natural (or divine) laws. According to some ancient authorities, it is a Meccan sūra with the exception of two verses revealed at Medina; according to others, a Medinan sūra with the exception of two verses revealed at Mecca. The very fact of such wholesale difference of opinion favors the Meccan attribution because there could be no such doubt about a complete Medinan sūra, owing to the great number of witnesses. The Medinan ascription may have arisen from the recognition of some verses by those witnesses as having been revealed at Medina on a certain occasion.

A late Meccan sūra for the most part.

## The Thunder

*Revealed at Mecca*

In the name of God, the beneficent, the merciful.

1. Alif. Lām. Mīm. Rā.[1] These are verses of the scripture. What is revealed to you from your Lord is the truth, but most of mankind do not believe.

2. It is God who raised up the heavens without visible supports, then mounted the throne, and compelled the sun and the moon to be of service; each runs to an appointed term; He orders the course; He details the revelations, that perhaps you may be certain of the meeting with your Lord.

3. And it is He who spread out the earth and placed on it firm hills and flowing streams, and of all fruits he placed in it two pairs (male and female). He covers the night with the day. In this are signs for people who take thought.

4. And on the earth are neighboring tracts, vineyards and ploughed lands, and date palms, like and unlike,[2] which are watered with one water. And We have made some of them to excel others in fruit. In this are signs for people who have sense.

5. And if you wonder, then wondrous is their saying: "When we are dust, are we then (to be raised) in a new creation?" Such are they who disbelieve in their Lord; such have iron rings on their necks; such are rightful owners of the fire, they will abide there.

6. And they bid you hasten on the evil rather than the good, when exemplary punishments have indeed occurred before them. But your Lord is

1. See Q 2:1, footnote [Pickthall's note].
2. Or it may be, "growing thickly or alone" [Pickthall's note].

rich in pardon for mankind despite their wrong, and your Lord is strong in punishment.

7. Those who disbelieve say: "If only some sign were sent down on him from his Lord!" You are a warner only, and for every people a guide.

8. God knows what every female bears and what the wombs absorb and what they grow. And everything with Him is measured.

9. He is the knower of the invisible and the visible, the great, the high exalted.

10. You are like he who hides the saying and he who noises it abroad, he who lurks in the night and he who goes freely in the daytime.

11. For him are angels ranged before him and behind him, who guard him by God's command.[3] God does not change the condition of a people until they (first) change what is in their hearts; and if God wills misfortune for a people there is none that can repel it, nor have they a defender beside Him.

12. It is He who shows you the lightning, a fear and a hope,[4] and raises the heavy clouds.

13. The thunder hymns His praise and (so do) the angels for awe of Him. He launches the thunderbolts and strikes with them whom He will while they dispute (in doubt) concerning God, and He is mighty in wrath.

14. To Him is the real prayer. Those to whom they pray beside God do not respond to them at all, except as (is the response to) one who stretches forth his hands toward water (asking) that it may come to his mouth, and it will never reach it. The prayer of disbelievers goes (far) astray.

15. And to God falls prostrate whoever is in the heavens and the earth, willingly or unwillingly, as do their shadows in the morning and the evening hours.

16. Say (O Muḥammad): "Who is Lord of the heavens and the earth?" Say: "God!" Say: "Do you then take (others) beside Him for protectors, which, even for themselves, have neither benefit nor hurt?" Say: "Is the blind man equal to the one who sees, or is darkness equal to light? Or do they assign to God partners who created the like of His creation so that the creation (which they made and His creation) seemed alike to them?" Say: "God is the creator of all things, and He is the one, the almighty."

17. He sends down water from the sky, so that valleys flow according to their measure, and the flood bears (on its surface) swelling foam—from what they smelt in the fire in order to make ornaments and tools rises a foam like it—thus God coins (the similitude of) the true and the false. Then, as for the foam, it passes away as scum upon the banks, while, as for what is of use to mankind, it remains on the earth. Thus God coins the similitudes.

18. For those who answered God's call is bliss; and for those who did not answer His call, if they had all that is on the earth, and the equal of its like, they would offer it as ransom. Such will have a woeful reckoning, and their habitation will be hell, a dire abode.

19. Is he who knows that what is revealed to you from your Lord is the truth like him who is blind? But only men of understanding heed;

3. This is taken by some commentators to refer to "him who goes freely in the daytime" in the previous verse. In that case it would read: "for whom are guards before him and behind him as if to guard him against God's commandment" [Pickthall's note].

4. The fear is of the lightning, and the hope is of the rain [Pickthall's note].

20. Such as keep the pact of God, and do not break the covenant;

21. Such as unite what God has commanded should be joined, and fear their Lord, and dread a woeful reckoning;

22. Such as persevere in seeking their Lord's countenance and are regular in prayer and spend of what We bestow on them secretly and openly, and overcome evil with good. Theirs will be the sequel of the (heavenly) home,

23. Gardens of Eden which they enter, along with all who do right among their fathers and their spouses and their progeny. The angels enter upon them from every gate,

24. (Saying): "Peace be to you because you persevered. Blessed of the ultimate (heavenly) home."

25. And those who break the covenant of God after ratifying it, and sever what God has commanded should be joined, and make mischief on the earth: theirs is the curse and theirs the ill abode.

26. God enlarges livelihood for whom He will, and restricts (it for whom He will); and they rejoice in the life of the world, whereas the life of the world is but brief comfort as compared with the hereafter.

27. Those who disbelieve say: "If only a sign were sent down upon him from his Lord!" Say: "God sends whom He will astray, and guides to Himself all who turn (to Him),"

28. Who have believed and whose hearts have rest in the remembrance of God. In the remembrance of God do hearts find rest!

29. Those who believe and do right: Joy is for them, and bliss (their) journey's end.

30. Thus We send you (O Muḥammad) to a nation, before whom other nations have passed away, that you may recite to them what We have inspired in you, while they are disbelievers in the beneficent. Say: "He is my Lord; there is no god except Him. In Him I put my trust and to Him is my recourse."

31. Had it been possible for a lecture[5] to cause the mountains to move, or the earth to be torn asunder, or the dead to speak, (this Qur'ān would have done so). No, but God's is the whole command. Do not those who believe know that, had God willed, He could have guided all mankind? As for those who disbelieve, disaster does not cease to strike them because of what they do, or it dwells near their home until the threat of God comes to pass. God does not fail to keep the meeting.

32. And messengers (of God) were mocked before you, but long I bore with those who disbelieved. At length I seized them, and how (awful) was My punishment!

33. Is He who is aware of the earnings of every soul (as he who is aware of nothing)? Yet they ascribe to God partners. Say: "Name them. Is it that you would inform Him of something which He knows not on the earth? Or is it but a way of speaking?" No, but their contrivance is made to seem for those who disbelieve and they are kept from the right road. He whom God sends astray, for him there is no guide.

34. For them is torment in the life of the world, and the doom of the hereafter is more painful, and they have no defender from God.

35. A similitude of the garden which is promised to those who keep their duty (to God): Underneath it rivers flow; its food is everlasting, and

5. Ar. *Qur'ān* [Pickthall's note].

its shade; this is the reward of those who keep their duty, while the reward of disbelievers is the fire.

36. Those to whom We gave the scripture rejoice in what is revealed to you. And of the clans there are who deny some of it. Say: "I am commanded only that I serve God and ascribe to Him no partner. To Him I cry, and to Him is my return."

37. Thus have We revealed it, a decisive utterance in Arabic; and if you should follow their desires after what has come to you of knowledge, then truly you would have from God no protecting friend nor defender.

38. And We sent messengers (to mankind) before you, and We appointed for them wives and offspring, and it was not (given) to any messenger that he should bring a sign except by God's leave. For everything there is a time prescribed.

39. God effaces what He will, and establishes (what He will), and with Him is the source of ordinance.

40. Whether We let you see something of what We have promised them, or make you die (before its happening), yours is but conveyance (of the message), Ours the reckoning.

41. Do they not see how We visit the land, reducing it of its outlying parts?[6] (When) God dooms there is none that can postpone His doom, and He is swift at reckoning.

42. Those who were before them plotted; but all plotting is God's. He knows what each soul earns. The disbelievers will come to know for whom will be the sequel of the (heavenly) home.

43. They who disbelieve say: "You are no messenger (of God)." Say: "God, and whoever has true knowledge of the scripture, is sufficient witness between me and you."

## Sūra 14

*Ibrāhīm*, so called from Abraham's prayer in verses 35–41, at the time when he was establishing his son Ishmael, the ancestor of the Arabs, in the "uncultivable valley" of Mecca. Otherwise the subject of the sūra is the same as that of other Meccan sūras revealed during the last three years before the *hijra*. The reference in verse 46 to the plot of the idolaters makes it probable that it is among the last of the Meccan revelations.

A late Meccan sūra; except verses 28–30, revealed at Medina.

## Abraham

*Revealed at Mecca*

In the name of God, the beneficent, the merciful.

1. Alif. Lām. Rā.[1] (This is) a scripture which We have revealed to you (Muḥammad) that by it you may bring forth mankind from darkness to light, by the permission of their Lord, to the path of the mighty, the owner of praise,

6. If this is a Medinan verse, the reference would be to the spread of Islam; if a Meccan verse it would be to the Persian and the Eastern Roman Empires encroaching on Arabia [Pickthall's note].

1. See Q 2:1, footnote [Pickthall's note].

2. God, to whom belongs whatever is in the heavens and whatever is on the earth. And woe to the disbelievers from an awful doom;

3. Those who love the life of the world more than the hereafter, and debar (men) from the way of God and would have it crooked: such are far astray.

4. And We never sent a messenger except with the language of his people, that he might make (the message) clear for them. Then God sends whom He will astray, and guides whom He will. He is the mighty, the wise.

5. We sent Moses with Our revelations, saying: "Bring your people forth from darkness to light. And remind them of the days of God. In that are revelations for each steadfast, thankful (heart)."

6. And (remind them) how Moses said to his people: "Remember God's favor to you when He delivered you from Pharaoh's people who were afflicting you with dreadful torment, and were slaying your sons and sparing your women; that was a tremendous trial from your Lord."

7. And when your Lord proclaimed: "If you give thanks, I will give you more; but if you are thankless, My punishment is dire."

8. And Moses said: "Though you and all who are on the earth prove thankless, God is absolute, owner of praise."

9. Has not the history of those before you reached you: the people of Noah, and (the tribes of) 'Ād and Thamūd, and those after them? None but God knows them. Their messengers came to them with clear proofs, but they thrust their hands into their mouths, and said: "We disbelieve in that with which you have been sent, and we are in grave doubt concerning that to which you call us."

10. Their messengers said: "Can there be doubt concerning God, the creator of the heavens and the earth? He calls you that He may forgive you your sins and reprieve you to an appointed term." They said. "You are but mortals like us, who would willingly turn us away from what our fathers used to worship. Then bring some clear warrant."

11. Their messengers said to them: "We are but mortals like you, but God gives grace to whom He will of His servants. It is not ours to bring you a warrant unless by the permission of God. In God let believers put their trust!

12. "How should we not put our trust in God when He has shown us our ways? We surely will endure the hurt you do us. In God let the trusting put their trust!"

13. And those who disbelieved said to their messengers: "We will drive you out from our land, unless you return to our religion." Then their Lord inspired them, (saying): "We shall destroy the wrongdoers,

14. "And We shall make you to dwell in the land after them." This is for him who fears My majesty and fears My threats.

15. And they sought help (from their Lord) and every obstinate potentate was brought to nothing;

16. Hell is before him, and he is made to drink a festering water,

17. Which he sips but can hardly swallow, and death comes to him from every side while yet he cannot die, and before him is a harsh doom.

18. A similitude of those who disbelieve in their Lord: Their works are as ashes which the wind blows hard upon a stormy day. They have no control of anything that they have earned. That is the extreme failure.

19. Have you not seen that God has created the heavens and the earth with truth? If He will, He can remove you and bring (in) some new creation;

20. And that is no great matter for God.

21. They all come forth to their Lord. Then those who were despised say to those who were scornful: "We were to you a following, can you then avert from us anything of God's doom?" They say: "Had God guided us, we should have guided you. Whether we rage or patiently endure is (now) all one for us; we have no place of refuge."

22. And Satan says, when the matter has been decided: "God promised you a promise of truth; and I promised you, then failed you. And I had no power over you except that I called to you and you obeyed me. So do not blame me, but blame yourselves. I cannot help you, nor can you help me. I disbelieved in what you ascribed to me before. For wrongdoers there is a painful doom."

23. And those who believed and did good works are made to enter gardens underneath which rivers flow, there abiding by permission of their Lord, their greeting there: "Peace!"

24. Do you not see how God coins a similitude: A goodly saying, as a goodly tree, its root set firm, its branches reaching into heaven,

25. Giving its fruit at every season by permission of its Lord? God coins the similitudes for mankind in order that they may reflect.

26. And the similitude of a bad saying is as a bad tree, uprooted from upon the earth, possessing no stability.

27. God confirms those who believe by a firm saying in the life of the world and in the hereafter, and God sends wrongdoers astray. And God does what He will.

28. Have you not seen those who gave the grace of God in exchange for thanklessness and led their people down to the abode of loss,

29. (Even to) hell? They are exposed to it. A wretched end!

30. And they set up rivals to God that they may mislead (men) from His way. Say: "Enjoy life (while you may) for your journey's end will be the fire."

31. Tell My servants who believe to establish worship and spend of that which We have given them, secretly and publicly, before a day comes in which there will be neither trading nor befriending.

32. God is He Who created the heavens and the earth, and causes water to descend from the sky, thereby producing fruits as food for you, and makes the ships to be of service to you, that they may run upon the sea at His command, and has made the rivers of service to you;

33. And makes the sun and the moon, constant in their courses, to be of service to you, and has made of service to you the night and the day.

34. And He gives you something of all you ask of Him, and if you would count the bounty of God you cannot reckon it. Man is a wrongdoer, an ingrate.

35. And when Abraham said: "My Lord! Make safe this territory, and preserve me and my sons from serving idols.

36. "My Lord! They have led many of mankind astray. But whoever follows me, he is of me. And whoever disobeys me—Still You are forgiving, merciful.

37. "Our Lord! I have settled some of my posterity in an uncultivable valley near to Your holy house,[2] our Lord! that they may establish proper worship; so incline some hearts of men that they may yearn toward them, and provide them with fruits in order that they may be thankful.

38. "Our Lord! You know what we hide and what we proclaim. Nothing on the earth or in the heaven is hidden from God.

39. "Praise be to God Who has given me, in my old age, Ishmael and Isaac! My Lord is indeed the hearer of prayer.

40. "My Lord! Make me establish proper worship, and some of my posterity (also); our Lord! and accept the prayer.

41. "Our Lord! Forgive me and my parents and believers on the day when the account is cast."

42. Do not think that God is unaware of what the wicked do. He only gives them a respite until a day when eyes will stare (in terror),

43. As they come hurrying on in fear, their heads upraised, their gaze not returning to them, and their hearts as air.

44. And warn mankind of a day when the doom will come upon them, and those who did wrong will say: "Our Lord! Reprieve us for a little while. We will obey Your call and will follow the messengers." (It will be answered): "Did you not swear before that there would be no end for you?

45. "And (have you not) dwelt in the dwellings of those who wronged themselves (of old) and (has it not) become plain to you how We dealt with them, and made examples for you?"

46. They have plotted their plot, and their plot is with God, though their plot were one by which the mountains should be moved.

47. So do not think that God will fail to keep His promise to His messengers. God is mighty, able to requite (the wrong).

48. On the day when the earth will be changed to other than the earth, and the heavens (also will be changed) and they will come forth to God, the one, the almighty,

49. You will see the guilty on that day linked together in chains,

50. Their raiment of pitch, and the fire covering their faces,

51. That God may repay each soul what it has earned. God is swift at reckoning.

52. This is a clear message for mankind in order that they may be warned by it, and that they may know that He is only one God, and that men of understanding may take heed.

## Sūra 15

*Al-Ḥijr* (which I take to be a place-name) is so called from verses 80–84, where the fate of the dwellers at that place is described. The date of revelation is earlier than that of any of the Meccan sūras which precede it in the arrangement of the book, though the subject and the tone are similar, which accounts for its position. Nöldeke places it in his middle group of Meccan sūras, that is (as far as one can judge from the inclusions), those revealed after the eighth year and before the third year before the *hijra*, and in so doing but

2. The valley of Mecca [Pickthall's note].

confirms the judgment of the best Muslim authorities, though some Muslim authorities would place it among the earliest revelations.

It belongs to the middle group of Meccan sūras.

## Al-Ḥijr

*Revealed at Mecca*

In the name of God, the beneficent, the merciful.

1. Alif. Lām. Rā.[1] These are verses of the scripture and a plain reading.[2]

2. It may be that those who disbelieve wish ardently that they were Muslims.[3]

3. Let them eat and enjoy life, and let (false) hope beguile them. They will come to know!

4. And We destroyed no township unless there was a known decree for it.

5. No nation can outstrip its term nor can they lag behind.

6. And they say: "O you to whom the reminder is revealed, you are indeed a madman!

7. "Why do you not bring angels to us, if you are of the truthful?"

8. We do not send down the angels except with the truth, and in that case (the disbelievers) would not be tolerated.

9. We, even We, reveal the reminder, and We are its guardian.

10. We sent (messengers) before you among the factions of the men of old.

11. And there never came to them a messenger but they mocked him.

12. Thus do We make it traverse the hearts of the guilty:

13. They do not believe in it, though the example of the men of old has gone before.

14. And even if We opened to them a gate of heaven and they kept mounting through it,

15. They would say: "Our sight is wrong—no, but we are people bewitched."

16. And in the heaven We have set mansions of the stars, and We have beautified it for beholders.

17. And We have guarded it from every outcast devil,

18. Except him who steals the hearing, and him a clear flame pursues.[4]

19. And the earth We have spread out, and placed in it firm hills, and caused each seemly thing to grow in it.

20. And We have given to you livelihoods in it, and to those for whom you do not provide.

21. And there is not a thing but with Us are its stored goods. And We do not send it down except in appointed measure.

22. And We send the winds fertilizing, and cause water to descend from the sky, and give it to you to drink. It is not you who are the ones who store it.

1. See Q 2:1, footnote [Pickthall's note].
2. Ar. *Qur'ān* [Pickthall's note].
3. Or "those who have surrendered" [Pickthall's note].
4. Muslim scholars understand this verse to refer to the ability of the jinn to reach the lowest heaven, where they attempt to overhear heavenly discussions. The jinn are repulsed by angels who throw shooting stars at them.

23. It is We, even We, Who quicken and give death, and We are the inheritor.

24. We know the eager among you and We know the laggards.

25. Your Lord will gather them together. He is wise, aware.

26. We created man of potter's clay of black mud altered,

27. And the jinn We created before of essential fire.

28. And (remember) when your Lord said to the angels: "I am creating a mortal out of potter's clay of black mud altered,

29. "So, when I have made him and have breathed into him of My spirit, fall down, prostrating yourselves to him."

30. So the angels fell prostrate, all of them together

31. Except Iblīs. He refused to be among the prostrate.

32. He said: "O Iblīs! What ails you that you are not among the prostrate?"

33. He said: "Why should I prostrate myself to a mortal whom you have created out of potter's clay of black mud altered?"

34. He said: "Then go forth from here, for you are outcast.

35. "And the curse shall be upon you until the day of judgment."

36. He said: "My Lord! Reprieve me until the day when they are raised."

37. He said: "You are of those reprieved

38. "Until the day of appointed time."

39. He said: "My Lord! Because You have sent me astray, I shall adorn the path of error for them in the earth, and shall mislead them every one,

40. "Except those of them as are Your perfectly devoted servants."

41. He said: "This is a right course incumbent upon Me:

42. "As for My servants, you have no power over any of them except those of the obstinate as follow you,

43. "For all those, hell will be the promised place.

44. "It has seven gates, and each gate has an appointed portion.

45. "Those who ward off (evil) are among gardens and watersprings.

46. "(And it is said to them): 'Enter them in peace, secure.'

47. "And We remove whatever rancor may be in their breasts. As brothers, face to face, (they rest) on couches raised.

48. "Toil does not come to them there, nor will they be expelled from there."

49. Announce, (O Muḥammad) to My servants that I am the forgiving, the merciful,

50. And that My doom is the dolorous doom.

51. And tell them of Abraham's guests,

52. (How) when they came in to him, and said: "Peace." He said: "We are afraid of you."

53. They said: "Be not afraid! We bring you good tidings of a boy possessing wisdom."

54. He said: "Do you bring me good tidings (of a son) when old age has overtaken me? Of what then can you bring good tidings?"

55. They said: "We bring you good tidings in truth. So do not be of the despairing."

56. He said: "And who despairs of the mercy of his Lord except those who are astray?"

57. He said: "And afterward what is your business, O you messengers (of God)?"

58. They said: "We have been sent to a guilty people,

59. "(All) except the family of Lot. Them we shall deliver everyone,

60. "Except his wife, of whom We had decreed that she should be of those who stay behind."

61. And when the messengers came to the family of Lot,

62. He said: "You are people unknown (to me)."

63. They said: "No, but we bring you that concerning which they keep disputing,

64. "And bring you the truth, and we are truth-tellers.

65. "So travel with your household in a portion of the night, and follow their backs. Let none of you turn round, but go where you are commanded."

66. And We made plain the case to him, that the root of them (who did wrong) was to be cut at early morn.

67. And the people of the city came, rejoicing at the news (of new arrivals).

68. He said: "They are my guests. Do not affront me!

69. "And keep your duty to God, and do not shame me!"

70. They said: "Have we not forbidden you from (entertaining) anyone?"

71. He said: "Here are my daughters, if you must be doing (so)."

72. By your life (O Muḥammad) they moved blindly in the frenzy of approaching death.

73. Then the (awful) cry overtook them at the sunrise.

74. And We utterly confounded them, and We rained on them stones of heated clay.

75. In this are signs for those who read the signs.

76. It is upon a road still uneffaced.

77. In this is indeed a sign for believers.

78. And the dwellers in the wood[5] were evildoers.

79. So We took vengeance on them; they both are on a high road plain to see.

80. And the dwellers in al-Ḥijr denied (Our) messengers.

81. And We gave them Our revelations, but they were averse to them.

82. And they used to hew out dwellings from the hills, (in which they dwelt) secure.

83. But the (awful) cry overtook them at the morning hour,

84. And what they were accustomed to count as gain availed them not.

85. We did not create the heavens and the earth and all that is between them except with truth, and the hour is surely coming. So forgive, O Muḥammad, with a gracious forgiveness.

86. Your Lord! He is the all-wise creator.

87. We have given you seven of the oft-repeated (verses)[6] and the great Qur'ān.

88. Do not strain your eyes toward what We cause some kinds among them to enjoy, and do not be grieved on their account, and lower your wing (in tenderness) for the believers.

89. And say: "I, even I, am a plain warner,"

90. Such as We send down for those who make division,

5. Another name for Midian [Pickthall's note].
6. According to a strong tradition, the reference is to Q 1, which consists of seven verses and forms a part of every Muslim prayer [Pickthall's note].

91. Those who break the Qur'ān into parts.
92. Them, by your Lord, We shall question, every one,
93. Of what they used to do.
94. So proclaim that which you are commanded, and withdraw from the idolaters.
95. We defend you from the scoffers,
96. Who set some other god along with God. But they will come to know.
97. We know well that your bosom is at times oppressed by what they say,
98. But hymn the praise of your Lord, and be of those who make prostration (to Him).
99. And serve your Lord until the inevitable[7] comes to you.

## Sūra 16

*Al-Naḥl*, "The Bee," takes its name from verse 68, where the activities of the bee are mentioned as a type of duty and of usefulness. It calls attention to God's providence for creation, and to His guidance to mankind as a necessary part of it, and warns disbelievers in that guidance that the folly in rejecting it as great as would be the rejection of food and drink. The sūra is ascribed to the last Meccan group, though some ancient authorities regard the ascription as valid only for verses 1–40, and consider the whole latter portion as revealed at Medina. The only verse in the sūra which is self-evidently of Medinan revelation is verse 110, where the fugitives from persecution are said to have fought; for in the Meccan period fighting was unlawful for the Muslims, though many of them fled from persecution, taking refuge in Abyssinia.

A late Meccan sūra, with the exception of verse 110, which must have been revealed at Medina not earlier than the year 2 AH, and possibly many other verses toward the end.

## The Bee

*Revealed at Mecca*

In the name of God, the beneficent, the merciful.

1. The commandment of God will come to pass, so do not seek to hasten it. Glorified and exalted be He above all that they associate (with Him).
2. He sends down the angels with the spirit of His command to whom He will of His servants, (saying): "Warn mankind that there is no god but Me, so keep your duty to Me."
3. He has created the heavens and the earth with truth. High be He exalted above all that they associate (with Him).
4. He has created man from a drop of fluid, yet behold! he is an open opponent.
5. And the cattle He has created, from which you have warm clothing and uses, and of which you eat;
6. And in which is beauty for you, when you bring them home, and when you take them out to pasture.
7. And they bear your loads for you to a land you could not reach except with great trouble to yourselves. Your Lord is full of pity, merciful.

7. I.e. death [Pickthall's note].

8. And horses and mules and asses (He has created) that you may ride them, and for ornament. And He creates that which you know not.

9. And God's is the direction of the way, and some (roads) do not go straight. And had He willed He would have led you all aright.

10. He it is who sends down water from the sky; from it you have drink, and from it are trees on which you send your beasts to pasture.[1]

11. He causes crops to grow for you by it, and the olive and the date palm and grapes and all kinds of fruit. Here is indeed a sign for people who reflect.

12. And he has constrained the night and the day and the sun and the moon to be of service to you, and the stars are made subservient by His command. Here indeed are signs for people who have sense.

13. And whatever He has created for you on the earth of diverse hues, in that is indeed a sign for people who take heed.

14. And He it is who has constrained the sea to be of service that you eat fresh meat from it, and bring forth from it ornaments which you wear. And you see the ships plowing it that you (mankind) may seek of His bounty, and that perhaps you may give thanks.

15. And He has cast into the earth firm hills that it quake not with you, and streams and roads that you may find a way.

16. And landmarks (too), and by the stars they find a way.

17. Is He then who creates as him who creates not? Will you not then remember?

18. And if you would count the favor of God you cannot reckon it. God is indeed forgiving, merciful.

19. And God knows that which you keep hidden and that which you proclaim.

20. Those to whom they cry beside God created nothing, but are themselves created.

21. (They are) dead, not living. And they do not know when they will be raised.

22. Your god is one God. But as for those who do not believe in the hereafter their hearts refuse to know, for they are proud.

23. Assuredly God knows that which they keep hidden and that which they proclaim. He does not love the proud.

24. And when it is said to them: "What has your Lord revealed?" they say: "(Mere) fables of the men of old,"

25. That they may bear their burdens undiminished on the day of resurrection, with some of the burdens of those whom they mislead without knowledge. Evil is that which they bear!

26. Those before them plotted, so God struck at the foundations of their building, and then the roof fell down upon them from above them, and the doom came on them from where they knew not;

27. Then on the day of resurrection He will disgrace them and will say: "Where are My partners, for whose sake you opposed (My guidance)?" Those who have been given knowledge will say: "Disgrace this day and evil are upon the disbelievers,

1. There being hardly any herbage in Arabia, the cattle eat the leaves of trees and shrubs [Pickthall's note].

28. "Whom the angels cause to die while they are wronging themselves." Then will they make full submission (saying): "We did not use to do any wrong." Surely God is knower of what you used to do.

29. So enter the gates of hell, to dwell there forever. Woeful indeed will be the lodging of the arrogant.

30. And it is said to those who ward off (evil): "What has your Lord revealed?" They say: "Good." For those who do good in this world there is a good (reward) and the home of the hereafter will be better. Pleasant indeed will be the home of those who ward off (evil)—

31. Gardens of Eden which they enter, underneath which rivers flow, where they have what they will. Thus God repays those who ward off (evil),

32. Those whom the angels cause to die (when they are) good. They say: "Peace be to you! Enter the garden because of what you used to do."

33. Do they await anything except that the angels should come to them or your Lord's command should come to pass? Even so did those before them. God did not wrong them, but they wronged themselves,

34. So that the evil of what they did struck them, and that which they used to mock surrounded them.

35. And the idolaters say: "Had God willed, we would not have worshipped anything beside Him, we and our fathers, nor would we have forbidden anything without (command from) Him." Even so did those before them. Are the messengers charged with anything save plain conveyance (of the message)?

36. And We have raised in every nation a messenger, (proclaiming): "Serve God and shun false gods." Then some of them (there were) whom God guided, and some of them (there were) upon whom error had just hold. Travel in the land and see the nature of the consequence for the deniers!

37. Even if you (O Muḥammad) desire their right guidance, still God assuredly will not guide him who misleads. Such have no helpers.

38. And they swear by God their most binding oaths (that) God will not raise up him who dies. No, but it is a promise (binding) upon Him in truth, but most of mankind know not,

39. That He may explain to them that in which they differ, and that those who disbelieved may know that they were liars.

40. And Our word to a thing, when We intend it, is only that We say to it: "Be!" and it is.

41. And those who became fugitives for the cause of God after they had been oppressed, We shall give them goodly lodging in the world, and surely the reward of the hereafter is greater, if they but knew;

42. Such as are steadfast and put their trust in God.

43. And We did not send (as Our messengers) before you other than men whom We inspired—Ask the followers of the remembrance if you do not know!—

44. With clear proofs and writings; and We have revealed to you the remembrance that you may explain to mankind that which has been revealed for them, and that perhaps they may reflect.

45. Are they who plan ill deeds then secure that God will not cause the earth to swallow them, or that the doom will not come on them from where they know not?

46. Or that He will not seize them in their going to and fro so that there be no escape for them?

47. Or that He will not seize them with a gradual wasting? Your Lord is indeed full of pity, merciful.

48. Have they not observed all things that God has created, how their shadows incline to the right and to the left, making prostration to God, and they are lowly?

49. And to God makes prostration whatever is in the heavens and whatever is on the earth of living creatures, and the angels (also), and they are not proud.

50. They fear their Lord above them, and do what they are bidden.

51. God has said: "Do not choose two gods. There is only one God. So of Me, Me only, be in awe."

52. To God belongs whatever is in the heavens and the earth, and religion is His forever. Will you then fear any other than God?

53. And whatever of comfort you enjoy, it is from God. Then, when misfortune reaches you, to Him you cry for help.

54. And afterward, when He has rid you of the misfortune, behold! a set of you attribute partners to their Lord,

55. So as to deny that which We have given them. Then enjoy life (while you may), for you will come to know.

56. And they assign a portion of that which We have given them to what they know not. By God! but you will indeed be asked concerning (all) that you used to invent.

57. And they assign to God daughters—be He glorified!—and to themselves what they desire;

58. When if one of them receives tidings of the birth of a female, his face remains darkened, and he is inwardly angry.

59. He hides himself from the people because of the evil of that of which he has had tidings, (asking himself): Shall he keep it in contempt, or bury it beneath the dust? Evil is their judgment.

60. For those who do not believe in the hereafter is an evil similitude, and God's is the sublime similitude. He is the mighty, the wise.

61. If God were to take mankind to task for their wrongdoing, he would not leave here a living creature, but He reprieves them to an appointed term, and when their term comes they cannot put (it) off an hour nor (yet) advance (it).

62. And they assign to God that which they (themselves) dislike, and their tongues expound the lie that the better portion will be theirs. Assuredly theirs will be the fire, and they will be abandoned.

63. By God, We sent messengers to the nations before you, but the devil made their deeds fair-seeming to them. So he is their patron this day, and theirs will be a painful doom.

64. And We have revealed the scripture to you only that you may explain to them that in which they differ, and (as) a guidance and a mercy for a people who believe.

65. God sends down water from the sky and with it revives the earth after her death. In this is indeed a sign for a people who hear.

66. And in the cattle there is a lesson for you. We give you to drink of what is in their bellies, from between the refuse and the blood, pure milk palatable to the drinkers.

67. And of the fruits of the date palm, and grapes, from which you derive strong drink and (also) good nourishment. In this is indeed a sign for people who have sense.

68. And your Lord inspired the bee, saying: "Choose habitations in the hills and in the trees and in that which they thatch;

69. "Then eat of all fruits, and follow the ways of your Lord, made smooth (for you)." There comes forth from their bellies a drink diverse of hues, in which is healing for mankind. In this is indeed a sign for people who reflect.

70. And God creates you, then causes you to die, and among you is he who is brought back to the most abject stage of life, so that he knows nothing after (having had) knowledge. God is knower, powerful.

71. And God has favored some of you above others in provision. Now those who are more favored will by no means hand over their provision to those (slaves) whom their right hands possess, so that they may be equal with them in respect of it. Is it then the grace of God that they deny?

72. And God has given you wives of your own kind, and has given you, from your wives, sons and grandsons, and has made provision of good things for you. Is it then in vanity that they believe and in the grace of God that they disbelieve?

73. And they worship beside God that which provides no provision whatever for them from the heavens or the earth, nor have they (whom they worship) any power.

74. So do not coin similitudes for God. God knows; you know not.

75. God coins a similitude: (on the one hand) a (mere) chattel slave, who has control of nothing, and (on the other hand) one on whom We have bestowed a fair provision from Us, and he spends of it secretly and openly. Are they equal? Praise be to God! But most of them know not.

76. And God coins a similitude: Two men, one of them dumb, having control of nothing, and he is a burden on his owner; wherever he directs him to go, he brings no good. Is he equal with one who enjoins justice and follows a straight path (of conduct)?

77. And to God belongs the unseen of the heavens and the earth, and the matter of the hour (of doom) is but as a twinkling of the eye, or it is nearer still. God is able to do all things.

78. And God brought you forth from the wombs of your mothers knowing nothing, and gave you hearing and sight and hearts that perhaps you might give thanks.

79. Have they not seen the birds obedient[2] in mid-air? None holds them except God. In this are signs for a people who believe.

80. And God has given you in your houses an abode, and has given you (also), of the hides of cattle, houses[3] which you find light (to carry) on the day of migration and on the day of pitching camp; and of their wool and their fur and their hair, furnishing and comfort for a while.

81. And God has given you, of what He has created, shelter from the sun; and has given you places of refuge in the mountains, and has given you coats to ward off the heat from you, and coats (of armor) to save you from your own foolhardiness. Thus He perfects His favor to you, in order that you may surrender (to Him).

2. Lit. "made subservient"—i.e. to the law of God [Pickthall's note].
3. I.e. tents [Pickthall's note].

82. Then, if they turn away, your duty (O Muḥammad) is but plain conveyance (of the message).

83. They know the favor of God and then deny it. Most of them are ingrates.

84. And (think about) the day when We raise up of every nation a witness, then there is no leave for disbelievers, nor are they allowed to make amends.

85. And when those who did wrong behold the doom, it will not be made light for them, nor will they be reprieved.

86. And when those who ascribed partners to God behold those partners of theirs, they will say: "Our Lord! these are our partners to whom we used to cry instead of You." But they will fling to them the saying: "You are liars!"

87. And they offer to God submission on that day, and all that they used to invent has failed them.

88. For those who disbelieve and debar (men) from the way of God, We add doom to doom because they wrought corruption,

89. And (think about) the day when We raise in every nation a witness against them of their own people, and We bring you (Muḥammad) as a witness against these. And We reveal the scripture to you as an exposition of all things, and a guidance and a mercy and good tidings for those who have surrendered (to God).

90. God enjoins justice and kindness, and giving to kinsfolk, and forbids lewdness and abomination and wickedness. He exhorts you in order that you may take heed.[4]

91. Fulfill the covenant of God when you have covenanted, and do not break your oaths after the affirmation of them, and after you have made God surety over you. God knows what you do.

92. And do not be like her who unravels the thread, after she has made it strong, to thin filaments, making your oaths a deceit between you because of a nation being more numerous than (another) nation. God only tries you by it, and He will explain to you on the day of resurrection that in which you differed.

93. Had God willed He could have made you (all) one nation, but He sends whom He will astray and guides whom He will, and you will indeed be asked about what you used to do.

94. Do not make your oaths a deceit between you, for fear that a foot should slip after being firmly planted and you should taste evil because you debarred (men) from the way of God, and yours should be an awful doom.

95. And do not purchase a small gain at the price of God's covenant. That which God has is better for you, if you only knew.

96. What you have wastes away, and what God has remains. And We shall pay those who are steadfast a recompense in proportion to the best of what they used to do.

97. Whoever does right, whether male or female, and is a believer, We shall quicken with good life, and We shall pay them a recompense in proportion to the best of what they used to do.

4. Since the time of ʿUmar II the Umayyad, this verse has been recited at the end of every weekly sermon in all Sunnī congregations [Pickthall's note]. ʿUmar ibn ʿAbd al-Azīz (682/83–720); the Umayyad caliphate was the first great Muslim dynasty (661–750).

98. And when you recite the Qur'ān, seek refuge in God from Satan the outcast.

99. He has no power over those who believe and put trust in their Lord.

100. His power is only over those who make a friend of him, and those who ascribe partners to Him (God).

101. And when We put a revelation in place of (another) revelation—and God knows best what He reveals—they say: "You are only inventing. Most of them know not."

102. Say: "The holy spirit[5] has revealed it from your Lord with truth, that it may confirm (the faith of) those who believe, and as guidance and good tidings for those who have surrendered[6] (to God)."

103. And We know well that they say: "Only a man teaches him." The speech of him at whom they falsely hint is outlandish, and this is clear Arabic speech.[7]

104. Those who disbelieve the revelations of God, God does not guide them and theirs will be a painful doom.

105. Only they invent falsehood who do not believe God's revelations, and (only) they are the liars.

106. Whoever disbelieves in God after his belief—except him who is forced and whose heart is still content with the faith—but whoever finds ease in disbelief: On them is wrath from God. Theirs will be an awful doom.

107. That is because they have chosen the life of the world rather than the hereafter, and because God does not guide the disbelieving folk.

108. Such are they whose hearts and ears and eyes God has sealed. And such are the heedless.

109. Assuredly in the hereafter they are the losers.

110. Then your Lord—for those who became fugitives after they had been persecuted, and then fought and were steadfast—your Lord afterward is (for them) indeed forgiving, merciful,

111. On the day when every soul will come pleading for itself, and every soul will be repaid what it did, and they will not be wronged.

112. God coins a similitude: a township that dwelt secure and well content, its provision coming to it in abundance from every side, but it disbelieved in God's favors, so God made it experience the garb of dearth and fear because of what they used to do.

113. And there had come to them a messenger from among them, but they had denied him, and so the torment seized them while they were wrongdoers.

114. So eat of the lawful and good food which God has provided for you, and thank the bounty of your Lord if it is Him you serve.

115. He has forbidden for you only carrion and blood and swine-flesh and what has been immolated in the name of any other than God; but he who is driven to it, neither craving nor transgressing, then God is forgiving, merciful.

116. And do not speak, concerning that which your own tongues qualify (as clean or unclean), the falsehood: "This is lawful, and this is forbidden,"

5. I.e. Gabriel [Pickthall's note].
6. Ar. *Muslimīn* [Pickthall's note].
7. Among the various attempts of the idolaters to deride the Qur'ān was the charge that a Christian slave among the earliest converts taught it to the Prophet. The same slave suffered cruel persecution for his belief in the divine inspiration of the Qur'ān [Pickthall's note].

so that you invent a lie against God. Those who invent a lie against God will not succeed.

117. A brief enjoyment (will be theirs); and theirs a painful doom.

118. And to those who are Jews We have forbidden what We have already related to you. And We did not wrong them, but they were used to wrong themselves.

119. Then your Lord—for those who do evil in ignorance and afterward repent and amend—(for them) your Lord is afterward indeed forgiving, merciful.

120. Abraham was a nation obedient to God, by nature upright, and he was not of the idolaters;

121. Thankful for His bounties; He chose him and He guided him to a straight path.

122. And We gave him good in the world, and in the hereafter he is among the righteous.

123. And afterward We inspired you (Muḥammad, saying): "Follow the religion of Abraham, as one by nature upright. He was not of the idolaters."

124. The sabbath was appointed only for those who differed concerning it, and your Lord will judge between them on the day of resurrection concerning that in which they used to differ.

125. Call to the way of your Lord with wisdom and fair exhortation, and debate with them in the better way. Your Lord is best aware of him who strays from His way, and He is best aware of those who go aright.

126. If you punish, then punish with the like of that with which you were afflicted. But if you endure patiently, it is better for the patient.

127. Endure (O Muḥammad). Your endurance is only by (the help of) God. Do not grieve for them, and do not be in distress because of what they devise.

128. God is with those who keep their duty to Him and those who are doers of good.

## Sūra 17

*Banū Isrā'īl*, "The Children of Israel," begins and ends with references to the Israelites. Verse 1 relates to the Prophet's vision, in which he was carried by night upon a heavenly steed to the Temple at Jerusalem, whence he was caught up through the seven heavens to the very presence of God. The sūra may be taken as belonging to the middle group of Meccan sūras, except verse 81, or, according to other commentators, verses 76–82, revealed at Medina.

## The Children of Israel

*Revealed at Mecca*

In the name of God, the beneficent, the merciful.

1. Glorified be He who carried His servant by night from the inviolable place of worship[1] to the far distant place of worship[2] the neighborhood of

1. Mecca [Pickthall's note].
2. Jerusalem [Pickthall's note].

which We have blessed, that We might show him of Our signs! He, only He, is the hearer, the observer.

2. We gave to Moses the scripture, and We appointed it a guidance for the Children of Israel, saying: "Choose no guardian beside Me."

3. They were the seed of those whom We carried (in the ship) along with Noah. He was a grateful servant.

4. And We decreed for the Children of Israel in the scripture: "You will work corruption in the earth twice,[3] and you will become great tyrants."

5. So when the time for the first of the two came, We roused against you servants of Ours of great might who ravaged (your) country, and it was a threat performed.

6. Then We gave you once again your turn against them, and We aided you with wealth and children and made you more in manpower,

7. (Saying): "If you do good, you do good for your own souls, and if you do evil, it is for them (in like manner)." So, when the time for the second (of the judgments) came (We roused against you others of Our servants) to ravage you, and to enter the temple even as they entered it the first time, and to lay waste all that they conquered with an utter wasting.

8. It may be that your Lord will have mercy on you, but if you repeat (the crime) We shall repeat (the punishment), and We have appointed hell a dungeon for the disbelievers.

9. This Qur'ān guides to that which is straightest, and gives tidings to the believers who do good works that theirs will be a great reward.

10. And that those who do not believe in the hereafter, for them We have prepared a painful doom.

11. Man prays for evil as he prays for good; for man was ever hasty.

12. And We appoint the night and the day two signs. Then We make dark the sign of the night, and We make the sign of the day sight-giving, that you may seek bounty from your Lord, and that you may know the computation of the years, and the reckoning; and everything We have expounded with a clear expounding.

13. And every man's augury We have fastened to his own neck, and We shall bring forth for him on the day of resurrection a book which he will find wide open.

14. (And it will be said to him): "Read your book. Your soul suffices as reckoner against you this day."

15. Whoever goes right, it is only for (the good of) his own soul that he goes right, and whoever errs, errs only to its hurt. No laden soul can bear another's load. We never punish until We have sent a messenger.

16. And when We would destroy a township We send a command to its people who live at ease, and afterward they commit abomination there, and so the word (of doom) has effect for it, and We annihilate it with complete annihilation.

17. How many generations have We destroyed since Noah! And God suffices as knower and beholder of the sins of His servants.

18. Whoever desires that (life) which hastens away, We hasten for him in it what We will for whom We please. And afterward We have appointed for him hell; he will endure the heat of it, condemned, rejected.

3. Muslim and non-Muslim commentators have suggested that this may refer to the destruction of the First Temple in 586 BCE and the Second Temple in 70 CE, understood as a divine punishment for the disobedience of the Israelites.

19. And whoever desires the hereafter and strives for it with the effort necessary, being a believer; for such, their effort finds favor (with their Lord).

20. Each do We supply, both these and those, from the bounty of your Lord. And the bounty of your Lord can never be walled up.

21. See how We prefer one above another, and the hereafter will be greater in degrees and greater in preferment.

22. Do not set up with God any other god (O man) for fear that you sit down reproved, forsaken.

23. Your Lord has decreed that you worship none save Him, and (that you show) kindness to parents. If one of them or both of them attain old age with you, do not speak disrespectfully to them or repulse them, but speak to them a gracious word.

24. And lower to them the wing of submission through mercy, and say: "My Lord! Have mercy on them both as they did care for me when I was little."

25. Your Lord is best aware of what is in your minds. If you are righteous, He was ever forgiving to those who turn (to Him).

26. Give the kinsman his due, and the needy, and the wayfarer, and do not squander (your wealth) in wantonness.

27. The squanderers were ever brothers of the devils, and the devil was ever an ingrate to his Lord.

28. But if you turn away from them, seeking mercy from your Lord, for which you hope, then speak to them a reasonable word.

29. And do not let your hand be chained to your neck or spread it open completely, for fear that you sit down rebuked, denuded.

30. Your Lord enlarges the provision for whom He will, and restricts (it for whom He will). He was ever knower, observer of His servants.

31. Do not slay your children, fearing a fall to poverty, We shall provide for them and for you. The slaying of them is great sin.

32. And do not come near to adultery. It is an abomination and an evil way.

33. And do not slay the life which God has forbidden except with right. Whoever is slain wrongfully, We have given power to his heir, but let him not commit excess in slaying. He will be helped.

34. Do not come near the wealth of the orphan except with what is better until he comes to strength; and keep the covenant. Of the covenant it will be asked.[4]

35. Fill the measure when you measure, and weigh with a right balance; that is fitting, and better in the end.

36. (O man), do not follow that of which you have no knowledge. The hearing and the sight and the heart—of each of these it will be asked.

37. And do not walk on the earth exultant. You cannot rend the earth, nor can you stretch to the height of the hills.

38. The evil of all that is hateful in the sight of your Lord.

39. This is (part) of that wisdom with which your Lord has inspired you (O Muḥammad). And do not set up with God any other god, for fear that you be cast into hell, reproved, abandoned.

4. I.e., humans will be judged on whether or not they keep their promises and commitments.

40. Has your Lord then distinguished you (O men of Mecca) by giving you sons, and has chosen for Himself females from among the angels? You speak an awful word!

41. We have displayed (Our warnings) in this Qur'ān that they may take heed, but it increases them in nothing except aversion.

42. Say (O Muḥammad, to the disbelievers): "If there were other gods along with Him, as they say, they would have sought a way against the Lord of the throne."

43. Glorified is He, and high exalted above what they say!

44. The seven heavens and the earth and all that is in them praise Him, and there is not a thing but hymns his praise; but you do not understand their praise. He is ever clement, forgiving.

45. And when you recite the Qur'ān We place between you and those who do not believe in the hereafter a hidden barrier;

46. And We place upon their hearts veils lest they should understand it, and in their ears a deafness; and when you make mention of your Lord alone in the Qur'ān, they turn their backs in aversion.

47. We are best aware of what they wish to hear when they give ear to you and when they take secret counsel, when the evildoers say: "You only follow a man bewitched."

48. See what similitudes they coin for you, and thus are all astray, and cannot find a road!

49. And they say: "When we are bones and fragments, shall we be raised up as a new creation?"

50. Say: "Be you stones or iron

51. "Or some created thing that is yet greater in your thoughts!" Then they will say: "Who shall bring us back (to life)?" Say: "He who created you at the first." Then will they shake their heads at you, and say: "When will it be?" Say: "It will perhaps be soon;

52. "A day when He will call you and you will answer with His praise, and you will think that you have tarried but a little while."

53. Tell My servants to speak what is kindlier. The devil sows discord among them. The devil is for man an open foe.

54. Your Lord is best aware of you. If He will, He will have mercy on you, or if He will, He will punish you. We have not sent you (O Muḥammad) as a warden over them.

55. And your Lord is best aware of all who are in the heavens and the earth. And We preferred some of the prophets above others, and to David We gave the Psalms.

56. Say: "Cry to those (saints and angels) whom you assume (to be gods) beside Him, yet they have no power to rid you of misfortune nor to change."

57. Those to whom they cry seek the way of approach to their Lord, which of them shall be the nearest; they hope for His mercy and they fear His doom. The doom of your Lord is to be shunned.

58. There is no township[5] that We shall not destroy before the day of resurrection, or punish with dire punishment. That is set forth in the book (of Our decrees).

5. Or *community* [Pickthall's note].

59. Nothing hinders Us from sending signs except that the people of old denied them. And We gave Thamūd the she-camel—a clear sign—but they did wrong in respect of her. We do not send signs except to warn.

60. And (it was a warning) when We told you: "Your Lord encompasses mankind," and We appointed the vision[6] which We showed you as an ordeal for mankind, and (likewise) the accursed tree in the Qur'ān.[7] We warn them, but it increases them in nothing save gross impiety.

61. And when We said to the angels: "Fall down prostrate before Adam" and they fell prostrate all except Iblīs, he said: "Shall I fall prostrate before that which You have created of clay?"

62. He said: "See this (creature) whom You have honored above me; if You give me grace until the day of resurrection I will seize his seed, except a few."

63. He said: "Go, and whoever of them follows you—hell will be your payment, ample payment.

64. "And excite any of them whom you can with your voice, and urge your horse and foot against them, and be a partner in their wealth and children, and promise them. Satan promises them only to deceive.

65. "My (faithful) servants—over them you have no power, and your Lord suffices as (their) guardian."

66. (O mankind), your Lord is He who drives for you the ship upon the sea that you may seek of His bounty. He was ever merciful toward you.

67. And when harm touches you upon the sea, all to whom you cry (for succor) fail except Him (alone), but when He brings you safe to land, you turn away, for man was ever thankless.

68. Do you feel secure then that He will not cause a slope of the land to engulf you, or send a sandstorm upon you, and then you will find that you have no protector?

69. Or do you feel secure that He will not return you to that (plight) a second time, and send against you a hurricane of wind and drown you for your thanklessness, and then you will not find there that you have any avenger against Us?

70. We have honored the children of Adam. We carry them on the land and the sea, and have made provision of good things for them, and have preferred them above many of those whom We created with a marked preferment.

71. On the day when We shall summon all men with their record, whoever is given his book in his right hand—such will read their book and they will not be wronged a shred.

72. Whoever is blind here will be blind in the hereafter, and yet further from the road.

73. And they indeed strove hard to beguile you (Muhammad) away from that with which We have inspired you, that you should invent other than it against Us; and then they would have accepted you as a friend.[8]

74. And if We had not made you wholly firm you might almost have inclined to them a little.

6. The Prophet's vision of his ascent through the seven heavens [Pickthall's note].
7. See Q 44:43–49 [Pickthall's note].
8. The idolaters more than once offered to compromise with the Prophet [Pickthall's note].

75. Then We would have made you taste a double (punishment) of living and a double (punishment) of dying, then you would have found no helper against Us.

76. And they indeed wished to scare you from the land that they might drive you forth from there, and then they would have stayed (there) but a little after you.[9]

77. (Such was Our) way in the case of those whom We sent before you (to mankind), and you will not find for Our way anything of power to change.

78. Establish worship at the going down of the sun until the dark of night, and (the recital of) the Qur'ān at dawn. (The recital of) the Qur'ān at dawn is ever witnessed.

79. And some part of the night awake for it, a largess for you. It may be that your Lord will raise you to a praised estate.

80. And say: "My Lord! Cause me to come in with a firm incoming and to go out with a firm outgoing. And give me from Your presence a sustaining power."

81. And say: "Truth has come and falsehood has vanished away. Falsehood is ever bound to vanish."[1]

82. And We reveal of the Qur'ān that which is a healing and a mercy for believers though it increases the evildoers in nothing but ruin.

83. And when We make life pleasant to man, he turns away and is averse; and when ill touches him he is in despair.

84. Say: "Each one does according to his rule of conduct, and your Lord is best aware of him whose way is right."

85. They will ask you concerning the Spirit. Say: "The Spirit is by command of my Lord, and of knowledge you have been vouchsafed but little."

86. And if We willed We could withdraw what We have revealed to you, then would you find no guardian for you against Us in respect to it.

87. (It is nothing) except mercy from your Lord. His kindness to you was ever great.[2]

88. Say: "Though mankind and the jinn should assemble to produce the like of this Qur'ān, they could not produce the like of it though they were helpers one of another."

89. And We have displayed for mankind in this Qur'ān all kinds of similitudes, but most of mankind refuse anything except disbelief.

90. And they say: "We will not put faith in you until you cause a spring to gush forth from the earth for us;

91. "Or you have a garden of date palms and grapes, and cause rivers to gush forth in it abundantly;

92. "Or you cause the heaven to fall upon us piecemeal, as you have pretended, or bring God and the angels as a warrant;

9. If, as the Jalālayn declare, verses 76–82 were revealed at Medina, the reference here is to the plotting of the Jews and Hypocrites [Pickthall's note]. *Tafsīr al-Jalālayn* (*Commentary of the Two Jalāls*), begun by Jalāl al-Dīn al-Maḥallī (1389–1459) and completed by Jalāl al-Dīn al-Suyūṭī (1445–1505).

1. These words were recited by the Prophet when he witnessed the destruction of the idols round the Ka'ba after the conquest of Mecca [Pickthall's note].

2. Verses 85, 86, and 87 are said to have been revealed in answer to the third question which some Jewish rabbis prompted the idolaters to ask, the first two questions being answered in the following sūra [Pickthall's note].

93. "Or you have a house of gold; or you ascend up into heaven, and even then we will put no faith in your ascension until you bring down for us a book that we can read." Say (O Muḥammad): "My Lord be glorified! Am I anything but a mortal messenger?"

94. And nothing prevented mankind from believing when the guidance came unto them except that they said: "Has God sent a mortal as (His) messenger?"

95. Say: "If there were on the earth angels walking secure, We would have sent down for them from heaven an angel as messenger."

96. Say: "God suffices for a witness between me and you. He is knower, observer of His servants."

97. And he whom God guides, he is led aright; while, as for him whom He sends astray, for them you will find no protecting friends beside Him, and We shall assemble them on the day of resurrection on their faces, blind, dumb and deaf; their habitation will be hell; whenever it abates, We increase the flame for them.

98. That is their reward because they disbelieved Our revelations and said: "When we are bones and fragments shall we be raised up as a new creation?"

99. Have they not seen that God who created the heavens and the earth is able to create the like of them, and has appointed for them an end of which there is no doubt? But the wrongdoers refuse anything but disbelief.

100. Say (to them): "If you possessed the treasures of the mercy of my Lord, you would surely hold them back for fear of spending, for man was ever grudging."

101. And We gave to Moses nine signs, clear proofs (of God's sovereignty).[3] Ask the Children of Israel how he came to them, then Pharaoh said to him: "I deem you one bewitched, O Moses."

102. He said: "In truth you know that none sent down these (signs) except the Lord of the heavens and the earth as proofs, and (for my part) I deem you lost, O Pharaoh."

103. And he wished to scare them from the land, but We drowned him and those with him, all together.

104. And We said to the Children of Israel after him: "Dwell in the land; but when the promise of the hereafter comes to pass We shall bring you as a crowd gathered out of various nations."[4]

105. With truth have We sent it down, and with truth has it descended. And We have sent you as nothing else but a bearer of good tidings and a warner.

106. And (it is) a Qur'ān that We have divided, that you may recite it to mankind at intervals, and We have revealed it by (successive) revelation.

107. Say: "Believe in it or believe not, those who were given knowledge before it, when it is read to them, fall down prostrate on their faces, adoring,

3. According to early commentators, these are the signs that Moses brings to Pharaoh and his people: flood, locusts, vermin, frogs, blood, his staff, his hand, destruction, and the enclosing waters.

4. A reference to the dispersal of the Jews as the consequence of their own deeds after God had established them in the land [Pickthall's note].

108. "Saying: 'Glory to our Lord! The promise of our Lord must be fulfilled.'"

109. They fall down on their faces, weeping, and it increases humility in them.

110. Say (to mankind): "Cry to God, or cry to the Beneficent,[5] to whomever you cry (it is the same). His are the most beautiful names." And you (Muḥammad), do not be loud voiced in your worship nor yet silent in it, but follow a way between.

111. And say: "Praise be to God, who has not taken to Himself a son, and who has no partner in the sovereignty, nor has He any protecting friend through dependence." And magnify Him with all magnificence.

## Sūra 18

*Al-Kahf*, "The Cave," takes its name from the story of the youths who took refuge from persecution in a cave (verses 10–27) and were preserved there as if asleep for a long period—a story which is generally identified by Western writers (e.g. Gibbon) with the legend of the Seven Sleepers of Ephesus.[1] But a strong tradition in the Muslim world asserts that this story and that of Dhū l-Qarnayn ("the Two-Horned One"), verses 83–98, possibly also that of Moses and the angel, verses 60–82, were revealed to the Prophet to enable him to answer the questions which the Jewish doctors of Yathrib had instructed the idolaters to ask him, as a test of prophethood.

The questions were three: "Ask him," said the rabbis, "of some youths who were of old, what was their fate, for they have a strange story; and ask him of a much-traveled man who reached the sunrise regions of the earth and its sunset regions, what was his history; and ask him of the spirit, what it is."

The tormentors of the Prophet, who had been to Yathrib to get hints from the Jews, on their return to Mecca put these questions to the Prophet, after having told the people that it was to be a crucial test. The Prophet said that he would surely answer them upon the morrow, without adding "if God will," as though he could command God's revelation. As a reproof for that omission, the wished-for revelation was withheld from him for some days, and when it came included the rebuke contained in verse 24.[2] There is no reason whatever to doubt the truth of the tradition which connects this chapter with three questions set by Jewish rabbis, and the answers must have been considered satisfying, or at least silencing, or the Jews would certainly have made fun of them when they were taunting the Prophet daily after his flight to Yathrib. That being so, it would seem rash to identify the story with that of the Christian Seven Sleepers; it must belong, as the story of the "Two-Horned One" actually does belong, to rabbinical lore. The third of the questions is answered in Q 17:85ff.

It belongs to the middle group of Meccan sūras.

5. The idolaters had a peculiar objection to the name *al-Raḥmān*, "the Beneficent," in the Qur'ān. They said: "We do not know this Raḥmān." Some of them thought that al-Raḥmān was a man living in Yamāma [Pickthall's note]. Yamāma: region in central Saudi Arabia.

1. In Christian legend, seven Christian men who hid in a cave near Ephesus, in modern-day Turkey, in 250 CE to escape Roman persecution; they awoke when Christianity was the religion of the empire, during the reign of Theodosius II (408–50). The story is told by the British historian Edward Gibbon (1737–1794) at the end of chapter 33 of his *The History of the Decline and Fall of the Roman Empire* (1776–88), where he cites this version among others.

2. Guillaume, *Life*, pp. 136–39 [Pickthall's note].

## The Cave

*Revealed at Mecca*

In the name of God, the beneficent, the merciful.

1. Praise be to God who has revealed the scripture to His servant, and has not placed in it any crookedness,

2. (But has made it) straight, to give warning of stern punishment from Him, and to bring to the believers who do good works the news that theirs will be a fair reward,

3. In which they will abide forever;

4. And to warn those who say: "God has chosen a son,"

5. (A thing) of which they have no knowledge, nor (had) their fathers. Dreadful is the word that comes out of their mouths. They speak nothing but a lie.

6. Yet it may be, if they do not believe in this statement, that you (Muḥammad) will torment your soul with grief over their footsteps.

7. We have placed all that is in the earth as an ornament for it that we may try them: which of them is best in conduct.

8. And We shall make all that is on it a barren mound.

9. Or do you consider that the People of the Cave and the inscription are a wonder among Our signs?

10. When the young men fled for refuge to the cave and said: "Our Lord! Give us mercy from Your presence, and shape for us right conduct in our plight."

11. Then We sealed up their hearing in the cave for a number of years.

12. And afterward We raised them up that We might know which of the two parties would best calculate the time that they had tarried.

13. We narrate to you their story with truth. They were young men who believed in their Lord, and We increased them in guidance.

14. And We made firm their hearts when they stood forth and said: "Our Lord is the Lord of the heavens and the earth. We cry to no god beside Him, for then should we utter an enormity.

15. "These, our people, have chosen (other) gods beside Him though they bring no clear warrant (vouchsafed) to them. And who does greater wrong than he who invents a lie concerning God?"

16. And when you withdraw from them and that which they worship except God, then seek refuge in the cave; your Lord will spread for you of His mercy and will prepare for you a pillow in your plight.

17. And you might have seen the sun when it rose move away from their cave to the right, and when it set go past them on the left, and they were in the cleft of it. That was (one) of the signs of God. He whom God guides, he indeed is led aright, and he whom He sends astray, for him you will not find a guiding friend.

18. And you would have considered them waking though they were asleep, and we caused them to turn over to the right and the left, and their dog stretching out his paws on the threshold.

19. If you had observed them closely you would have assuredly turned away from them in flight, and been filled with awe of them.

20. And in like manner We awakened them that they might question one another. A speaker from among them said: "How long have you tarried?" They said: "We have tarried a day or some part of a day." (Others) said: "Your Lord best knows how long you have tarried. Now send one of you with this your silver coin to the city, and let him see what food is purest there and bring you a supply of it. Let him be courteous and let no man know of you."

21. For they, if they should come to know of you, will stone you or turn you back to their religion; then you will never prosper.

22. And in like manner We disclosed them (to the people of the city) that they might know that the promise of God is true, and that, as for the hour, there is no doubt concerning it. When (the people of the city) disputed of their case among themselves, they said: "Build over them a building; their Lord knows best concerning them." Those who won their point said: "We shall build a place of worship over them."

23. (Some) will say: "They were three, their dog the fourth," and (some) say: "Five, their dog the sixth," guessing at random; and (some) say: "Seven, and their dog the eighth." Say (O Muḥammad): "My Lord is best aware of their number. None knows them except a few. So do not contend concerning them except with an outward contending, and do not ask any of them to pronounce concerning them."

24. And do not say of anything: "I shall do that tomorrow,"

25. Except if God will. And remember your Lord when you forget, and say: "It may be that my Lord guides me to a nearer way of truth than this."

26. And (it is said) they tarried in their cave three hundred years and add nine.

27. Say: "God is best aware how long they tarried." His is [the knowledge of] the invisible of the heavens and the earth. How clear of sight is He and keen of hearing! They have no protecting friend beside Him, and He makes none to share in His government.

28. And recite what has been revealed to you of the scripture of your Lord. There is none who can change His words, and you will find no refuge beside Him.

29. Restrain yourself along with those who cry to their Lord at morning and evening, seeking His countenance; and do not let your eyes overlook them, desiring the pomp of the life of the world; and do not obey him whose heart We have made heedless of Our remembrance, who follows his own lust and whose case has been abandoned.

30. Say: "(It is) the truth from the Lord of you (all)." Then whoever will, let him believe, and whoever will, let him disbelieve. We have prepared for disbelievers fire. Its tent encloses them. If they ask for showers, they will be showered with water like molten lead which burns the faces. Calamitous the drink and ill the resting-place!

31. As for those who believe and do good works—We do not suffer the reward of one whose work is goodly to be lost.

32. As for such, theirs will be gardens of Eden, in which rivers flow beneath them; there they will be given armlets of gold and will wear green robes of finest silk and gold embroidery, reclining upon thrones there. Blessed the reward, and fair the resting-place!

33. Coin for them a similitude: Two men, to one of whom We had assigned two gardens of grapes, and We had surrounded both with date palms and had put between them cropland.

34. Each of the gardens gave its fruit and withheld nothing thereof [i.e. did not fail]. And We caused a river to gush forth there.

35. And he had fruit. And he said to his comrade, when he spoke with him: "I am more than you in wealth, and stronger in respect of men."

36. And he went into his garden, while he (thus) wronged himself. He said: "I do not think that all this will ever perish.

37. "I do not think that the hour will ever come, and if indeed I am brought back to my Lord I surely shall find better than this as a resort."

38. And his comrade, while he disputed with him, exclaimed: "Do you disbelieve in Him who created you of dust, then of a drop (of seed), and then fashioned you a man?

39. "But He is God, my Lord, and I ascribe to my Lord no partner.

40. "If only, when you entered your garden, you had said: 'That which God wills (will come to pass)!' There is no strength save in God! Though you see me as less than you in wealth and children,

41. "Yet it may be that my Lord will give me better than your garden, and will send on it a bolt from heaven, and some morning it will be a smooth hillside,

42. "Or some morning the water of it will be lost in the earth so that you cannot make search for it."

43. And his fruit was beset (with destruction). Then he began to wring his hands for all that he had spent upon it, when (now) it was all ruined on its trellises, and to say: "Would that I had ascribed no partner to my Lord!"

44. And he had no troop of men to help him against God, nor could he save himself.

45. In this case is protection only from God, the true. He is best for reward, and best for consequence.

46. And coin for them the similitude of the life of the world as water which We send down from the sky, and the vegetation of the earth mingles with it and then becomes dry twigs that the winds scatter. God is able to do all things.

47. Wealth and children are an ornament of the life of the world. But the good deeds which endure are better in your Lord's sight for reward, and better in respect of hope.

48. And (think of) the day when We remove the hills and you see the earth emerging, and We gather them together so as not to leave one of them behind.

49. And they are set before your Lord in ranks (and it is said to them): "Now have you come to Us as We created you at the first. But you thought that We had set no meeting for you."

50. And the book is placed, and you see the guilty fearful of that which is in it, and they say: "What kind of a book is this that leaves not a small thing nor a great thing except that it has counted it!"[3] And they find all that they did confronting them, and your Lord wrongs no one.

51. And (remember) when We said to the angels: "Fall prostrate before Adam," and they fell prostrate, all except Iblīs. He was of the jinn,[4] so he

3. The sense is that God will hold people accountable for all of their actions.

4. The fact that Iblīs or Satan is of the jinn and not of the angels, though he was among the latter, explains his disobedience, since jinn, like men, can choose their path of conduct [Pickthall's note].

rebelled against his Lord's command. Will you choose him and his seed for your protecting friends instead of Me, when they are an enemy to you? Calamitous is the exchange for evildoers!

52. I did not make them to witness the creation of the heavens and the earth, nor their own creation; nor did I choose misleaders for (My) helpers.

53. And (be mindful of) the day when He will say: "Call those whom you pretended were partners of Mine." Then they will cry to them, but they will not hear their prayer, and We shall set a gulf of doom between them.

54. And the guilty behold the fire and know that they are about to fall into it, and they find no way of escape from it.

55. And We have displayed for mankind in this Qur'ān all manner of similitudes, but man is more than anything contentious.

56. And nothing hinders mankind from believing when the guidance comes to them, and from asking forgiveness of their Lord, unless (it be that they wish) that the judgment of the men of old should come upon them or (that) they should be confronted with the doom.

57. We do not send the messengers except as bearers of good news and warners. Those who disbelieve contend with falsehood in order to refute the truth by it. And they take Our revelations and that with which they are threatened as a jest.

58. And who does greater wrong than he who has been reminded of the revelations of his Lord, yet turns away from them and forgets what his hands send forward (to the judgment)? On their hearts We have placed coverings so that they do not understand, and in their ears a deafness. And though you call them to the guidance, in that case they can never be led aright.

59. Your Lord is the forgiver, full of mercy. If He took them to task (now) for what they earn, He would hasten on the doom for them; but theirs is an appointed term from which they will find no escape.

60. And (all) those townships! We destroyed them when they did wrong, and We appointed a fixed time for their destruction.

61. And when Moses said to his servant: "I will not give up until I reach the point where the two rivers meet, though I march on for ages."

62. And when they reached the point where the two met, they forgot their fish, and it took its way into the waters, being free.

63. And when they had gone further, he said to his servant: "Bring us our breakfast. We have found fatigue in this our journey."

64. He said: "Did you see, when we took refuge on the rock, and I forgot the fish—and none but Satan caused me to forget to mention it—it took its way into the waters by a marvel."

65. He said: "This is what we have been seeking." So they retraced their steps again.

66. Then they found one of Our servants, to whom We had given mercy from Us, and had taught him knowledge from Our presence.

67. Moses said to him: "May I follow you, to the end that you may teach me right conduct of that which you have been taught?"

68. He said: "You cannot bear with me.

69. "How can you bear with that of which you cannot compass any knowledge?"

70. He said: "God willing, you shall find me patient and I shall not in anything deny you."

71. He said: "Well, if you go with me, do not ask me concerning anything until I myself make mention of it to you."

72. So the two set out until, when they were in the ship, he made a hole in it. (Moses) said: "Have you made a hole in it to drown its people? You have done a dreadful thing."

73. He said: "Did I not tell you that you could not bear with me?"

74. (Moses) said: "Do not be angry with me that I forgot, and do not be hard upon me for my fault."

75. So the two journeyed on until, when they met a lad, he slew him. (Moses) said: "What! Have you slain an innocent soul who has slain no man? You have done a horrid thing."

76. He said: "Did I not tell you that you could not bear with me?"

77. (Moses) said: "If I ask you after this concerning anything, do not keep company with me. You have received an excuse from me."

78. So the two journeyed on until, when they came to the people of a certain township, they asked its people for food, but they refused to make them guests. And they found in it a wall on the point of falling into ruin, and he repaired it. (Moses) said: "If you had wished, you could have taken payment for it."

79. He said: "This is the parting between you and me! I will announce to you the interpretation of what you could not bear with patience.

80. "As for the ship, it belonged to poor people working on the river,[5] and I wished to damage it, for there was a king behind them who is taking every ship by force.

81. "And as for the lad, his parents were believers and We feared that he should oppress them by rebellion and disbelief.

82. "And We intended that their Lord should change him for them for one better in purity and nearer to mercy.

83. "And as for the wall, it belonged to two orphan boys in the city, and there was beneath it a treasure belonging to them, and their father had been righteous, and your Lord intended that they should come to their full strength and should bring forth their treasure as a mercy from their Lord; and I did it not upon my own command. Such is the interpretation of that with which you could not bear."

84. They will ask you of Dhū l-Qarnayn.[6] Say: "I shall recite to you a remembrance of him."

85. We made him strong in the land and gave him a road to everything.

86. And he followed a road

87. Until, when he reached the setting-place of the sun, he found it setting in a muddy spring, and found a people near it. We said: "O Dhū l-Qarnayn! Either punish or show them kindness."

88. He said: "As for him who does wrong, we shall punish him, and then he will be brought back to his Lord, who will punish him with awful punishment!

89. But as for him who believes and does right, good will be his reward, and We shall speak to him a mild command."

90. Then he followed a road

5. Or, it might be, "sea" [Pickthall's note].
6. Literally, "Two-Horned One."

91. Until, when he reached the rising-place of the sun, he found it rising on a people for whom We had appointed no shelter from it.

92. So (it was). And We knew all concerning him.

93. Then he followed a road

94. Until, when he came between the two mountains, he found beside them a people that scarce could understand a saying.

95. They said: "O Dhū l-Qarnayn! Gog and Magog[7] are spoiling the land. So may we pay you tribute on condition that you set a barrier between us and them?"

96. He said: "That in which my Lord has established me is better (than your tribute). But help me with strength (of men), I will set between you and them a bank.

97. Give me pieces of iron"—until, when he had leveled up (the gap) between the cliffs, he said: "Blow!"—until, when he had made it a fire, he said: "Bring me molten copper to pour on it."

98. And (Gog and Magog) were not able to surmount, nor could they pierce (it).

99. He said: "This is a mercy from my Lord; but when the promise of my Lord comes to pass, He will lay it low, for the promise of my Lord is true."

100. And on that day We shall let some of them surge against others, and the trumpet will be blown. Then We shall gather them together in one gathering.

101. On that day We shall present hell to the disbelievers, plain to view,

102. Those whose eyes were hoodwinked from My reminder, and who could not bear to hear.

103. Do the disbelievers reckon that they can choose My servants as protecting friends beside Me? We have prepared hell as a welcome for the disbelievers.

104. Say: "Shall We inform you who will be the greatest losers by their works?"

105. Those whose effort goes astray in the life of the world, and yet they reckon that they do good work.

106. Those are they who disbelieve in the revelations of their Lord and in the meeting with Him. Therefore their works are vain, and on the day of resurrection We assign no weight to them.

107. That is their reward: hell, because they disbelieved, and made a jest of Our revelations and Our messengers.

108. Those who believe and do good works, theirs are the gardens of paradise for welcome,

109. In which they will abide, with no desire to be removed from there.

110. Say: "Though the sea became ink for the words of my Lord, the sea would be used up before the words of my Lord were exhausted, even though We brought the like of it to help."

111. Say: "I am only a mortal like you. My Lord inspires in me that your God is only one God. And whoever hopes for the meeting with his Lord, let him do righteous work, and make none sharer of the worship due to his Lord."

7. Legendary peoples who wreaked havoc on the earth and will do so again on the last day (see Q 21:96).

## Sūra 19

*Maryam* takes its name from verses 16ff. That it is of quite early Meccan revelation is established by the following tradition:

In the fifth year of the Prophet's mission (the ninth before the *hijra*, or flight, to Medina) a number of the poorer converts were allowed by the Prophet to emigrate to Abyssinia, a Christian country where they would not be subject to persecution for their worship of the one God. This is known as the first *hijra*. The rulers of Mecca sent ambassadors to ask the Negus for their extradition, accusing them of having left the religion of their own people without entering the Christian religion, and of having done wrong in their own country. The Negus (against the wish of the envoys) sent for the spokesmen of the refugees and, in the presence of the bishops of his realm, questioned them of their religion. Ja'far ibn Abī Ṭālib, cousin of the Prophet, answered (I translate from the account given by Ibn Isḥāq):[1]

"We were people immersed in ignorance, worshipping idols, eating carrion, given to lewdness, severing the ties of kinship, bad neighbors, the strong among us preying on the weak; thus were we until God sent to us a messenger of our own, whose lineage, honesty, trustworthiness, and chastity we knew, and he called us to God that we should acknowledge His unity and worship Him and eschew all the stones and idols that we and our fathers used to worship beside Him; and ordered us to be truthful and to restore the pledge and observe the ties of kinship, and be good neighbors, and to abstain from things forbidden, and from blood, and forbade us lewdness and false speech, and to prey upon the wealth of orphans, and to accuse good women; and commanded us to worship God only, ascribing no thing to Him as partner, and enjoined upon us prayer and legal alms and fasting. (And he enumerated for him the teachings of Islam.)

"So we trusted him and we believed in him and followed that which he had brought from God, and we worshipped God only, and ascribed no thing as partner to Him. And we refrained from that which was forbidden to us, and indulged in that which was made lawful for us. And our people became hostile to us and tormented us, and sought to turn us from our religion that they might bring us back to the worship of idols from the worship of God most high, and that we might indulge in those iniquities which before we had deemed lawful.

"And when they persecuted and oppressed us, and hemmed us in, and kept us from the practice of our religion, we came forth to your land, and chose you above all others, and sought your protection, and hoped that we should not be troubled in your land, O King!

"Then the Negus asked him: 'Do you have with you anything of that which he brought from God?' Ja'far answered: 'Yes.' Then the Negus said: 'Relate it to me,' and Ja'far recited to him the beginning of Kāf, Hā, Yā, 'Ayn, Ṣād"—the Arabic letters with which this sūra begins, such letters being generally used instead of titles by the early Muslims. Therefore this sūra must have been revealed and well-known before the departure of the emigrants for Abyssinia.

An early Meccan sūra, with the possible exception of verses 59 and 60, which, according to some authorities, were revealed at Medina.

1. Guillaume, *Life*, pp. 151–52 [Pickthall's note].

# Mary

*Revealed at Mecca*

In the name of God, the beneficent, the merciful.

1. Kāf. Hā. Yā. ʿAyn. Ṣād.[2]
2. A mention of the mercy of your Lord to His servant Zachariah.
3. When he cried to his Lord a cry in secret,
4. Saying: "My Lord! My bones grow feeble and my head is shining with gray hair, and I have never been unblest in prayer to You, my Lord.
5. "I fear my kinsfolk after me, since my wife is barren. Oh, give me from Your presence a successor
6. "Who shall inherit of me and inherit (also) of the house of Jacob. And make him, my Lord, acceptable (to You)."
7. (It was said to him): "O Zachariah! We bring you tidings of a son whose name is John;[3] We have given the same name to none before (him)."
8. He said: "My Lord! How can I have a son when my wife is barren and I have reached infirm old age?"
9. He said: "So (it will be). Your Lord says: 'It is easy for Me, even as I created you before, when you were nothing.'"
10. He said: "My Lord! Appoint for me some sign." He said: "Your sign is that you, with no bodily defect, shall not speak to mankind three nights."
11. Then he came forth to his people from the sanctuary, and signified to them: "Glorify your Lord at break of day and fall of night."
12. (And it was said to his son): "O John! Hold fast the scripture." And We gave him wisdom when a child,
13. And compassion from Our presence, and purity; and he was devout,
14. And dutiful toward his parents. And he was not arrogant, rebellious.
15. Peace on him the day he was born, and the day he dies and the day he shall be raised alive!
16. And make mention of Mary in the scripture, when she had withdrawn from her people to a chamber looking east,
17. And had chosen seclusion from them. Then We sent to her Our spirit and it assumed for her the likeness of a perfect man.
18. She said: "I seek refuge in the Beneficent one from you, if you are God-fearing."
19. He said: "I am only a messenger of your Lord, that I may bestow on you a faultless son."
20. She said: "How can I have a son when no mortal has touched me, neither have I been unchaste?"
21. He said: "So (it will be). Your Lord says: 'It is easy for Me. And (it will be) that We may make of him a revelation for mankind and a mercy from Us, and it is a thing ordained.'"
22. And she conceived him, and she withdrew with him to a far place.
23. And the pangs of childbirth drove her to the trunk of the palm tree. She said: "Oh, would that I had died before this and had become as nothing, forgotten!"

2. See Q 2:1, footnote [Pickthall's note].
3. Ar. *Yaḥya* [Pickthall's note].

24. Then (one) cried to her from below her, saying: "Grieve not! Your Lord has placed a rivulet beneath you,

25. "And shake the trunk of the palm tree toward you, you will cause ripe dates to fall upon you.

26. "So eat and drink and be consoled. And if you meet any mortal, say: 'I have vowed a fast to the Beneficent, and may not speak this day to any mortal.'"

27. Then she brought him[4] to her own people, carrying him. They said: "O Mary! You have come with an amazing thing.

28. "O sister of Aaron![5] Your father was not a wicked man nor was your mother a harlot."

29. Then she pointed to him. They said: "How can we talk to one who is in the cradle, a young boy?"

30. He spoke: "I am the servant of God. He has given me the scripture and has appointed me a prophet,

31. "And has made me blessed wherever I may be, and has enjoined upon me prayer and almsgiving so long as I remain alive,

32. "And (has made me) dutiful toward her who bore me, and has not made me arrogant, unblest.

33. "Peace on me the day I was born, and the day I die, and the day I shall be raised alive!"

34. Such was Jesus, son of Mary: (this is) a statement of the truth concerning which they doubt.

35. It does not befit (the majesty of) God that He should take to Himself a son. Glory be to Him! When He decrees a thing, He says to it only: "Be!" and it is.

36. And God is my Lord and your Lord. So serve Him. That is the right path.

37. The sects among them differ: but woe to the disbelievers from the meeting of an awful day.

38. See and hear them on the day they come to Us! Yet the evildoers are today in error manifest.

39. And warn them of the day of anguish when the case has been decided. Now they are in a state of carelessness, and they do not believe.

40. We, only We, inherit the earth and all who are on it, and to Us they are returned.

41. And make mention (O Muḥammad) in the scripture of Abraham. He was a saint, a prophet.

42. When he said to his father: "O my father! Why worship that which hears not nor sees, nor can it avail you anything?

43. "O my father! There has come to me some knowledge that did not come to you. So follow me, and I will lead you on a right path.

44. "O my father! Do not serve the devil. The devil is a rebel to the Beneficent.

45. "O my father! I fear that a punishment from the Beneficent may overtake you so that you become a comrade of the devil."

46. He said: "Do you reject my gods, O Abraham? If you do not cease, I shall surely stone you. Depart from me a long while!"

4. Her son, Jesus.
5. See Q 3, introduction [Pickthall's note].

47. He said: "Peace be to you! I shall ask forgiveness of my Lord for you. He was ever gracious to me.

48. "I shall withdraw from you and that to which you pray beside God, and I shall pray to my Lord. It may be that, in prayer to my Lord, I shall not be unblest."

49. So, when he had withdrawn from them and what they were worshipping beside God, We gave him Isaac and Jacob. Each of them We made a prophet.

50. And We gave them of Our mercy, and assigned to them a high and true renown.

51. And make mention in the scripture of Moses. He was chosen, and he was a messenger (of God), a prophet.

52. We called him from the right slope of the mount, and brought him near in communion.

53. And We bestowed upon him of Our mercy his brother Aaron, a prophet (likewise).

54. And make mention in the scripture of Ishmael. He was a keeper of his promise, and he was a messenger (of God), a prophet.

55. He enjoined upon his people worship and almsgiving, and was acceptable in the sight of his Lord.

56. And make mention in the scripture of Idrīs.[6] He was a saint, a prophet;

57. And We raised him to high station.

58. These are they to whom God showed favor from among the prophets, of the seed of Adam and of those whom We carried (in the ship) with Noah, and of the seed of Abraham and Israel, and from among those whom We guided and chose. When the revelations of the Beneficent were recited to them, they fell down, adoring and weeping.

59. Now there has succeeded them a later generation who have ruined worship and have followed lusts. But they will meet deception,

60. Except him who shall repent and believe and do right. Such will enter the garden, and they will not be wronged in anything—

61. Gardens of Eden, which the Beneficent has promised to His servants in the unseen. His promise is ever sure of fulfillment—

62. They hear in it no idle talk, but only peace; and in it they have food for morning and evening.

63. Such is the garden which We cause the devout among Our servants to inherit.

64. We (angels) did not come down except by commandment of your Lord. To Him belongs all that is before us and all that is behind us and all that is between those two, and your Lord was never forgetful—

65. Lord of the heavens and the earth and all that is between them! Therefore, worship Him and be steadfast in His service. Do you know one that can be named along with Him?

66. And man says: "When I am dead, shall I be brought forth alive?"

67. Does man not remember that We created him before, when he was nothing?

68. And, by your Lord, We shall assemble them and the devils, then We shall bring them, crouching, around hell.

6. Identified with Enoch [Pickthall's note]. See Genesis 5:18–24.

69. Then We shall pluck out from every group whichever of them was most stubborn in rebellion to the Beneficent.

70. And surely We are best aware of those most worthy to be burned in it.

71. There is not one of you but shall approach it. That is a fixed ordinance of your Lord.

72. Then We shall rescue those who kept from evil, and leave the evildoers crouching there.

73. And when Our clear revelations are recited to them, those who disbelieve say to those who believe: "Which of the two parties (yours or ours) is better in position, and more imposing as an army?"

74. How many a generation have We destroyed before them, who were more imposing in respect of gear and outward seeming!

75. Say: "As for him who is in error, the Beneficent will prolong his span of life until, when they behold what they were promised, whether it be punishment (in the world) or the hour (of doom), they will know who is worse in position and who is weaker as an army."

76. God increases in right guidance those who walk aright, and the good deeds which endure are better in your Lord's sight for reward, and better for resort.

77. Have you seen him who disbelieves in Our revelations and says: "Assuredly I shall be given wealth and children"?

78. Has he perused the unseen, or has he made a pact with the Beneficent?

79. No, but We shall record what he says and prolong for him a span of torment.

80. And We shall inherit from him that of which he spoke, and he will come to Us, alone, (without his wealth and children).

81. And they have chosen (other) gods beside God that they may be a power for them.

82. No, but they will deny their worship of them, and become opponents to them.

83. Do you not see that We have set the devils on the disbelievers to confound them with confusion?

84. So make no haste against them (O Muḥammad). We do but number to them a sum (of days).

85. On the day when We shall gather the righteous to the Beneficent, a goodly company.

86. And drive the guilty to hell, a weary herd,

87. They will have no power of intercession, except him who has made a covenant with his Lord.

88. And they say: "The Beneficent has taken to Himself a son."

89. Assuredly you utter a disastrous thing,

90. Whereby almost the heavens are torn, and the earth is split asunder and the mountains fall in ruins,

91. That you ascribe to the Beneficent a son,

92. When it is not fitting for (the majesty of) the Beneficent that He should choose a son.

93. There is none in the heavens and the earth but comes to the Beneficent as a servant.

94. He knows them and numbers them with (right) numbering.

95. And each one of them will come to Him on the day of resurrection, alone.
96. Those who believe and do good works, the Beneficent will appoint for them love.
97. And We make (this scripture) easy on your tongue, (O Muḥammad) only that you may bear good tidings with it to those who ward off (evil), and warn with it the obstinate folk.
98. And how many a generation before them have We destroyed! Can you (Muḥammad) see a single man of them, or hear from them the slightest sound?

## Sūra 20

*Ṭā Hā* takes its name from the Arabic letters which form the first verse. As in the case of Q 19, the early date of revelation is established by a strong tradition.

ʿUmar b. al-Khaṭṭāb, who afterward became caliph, was among the bitterest opponents of Islām in early days. He set out one day, sword in hand, with the intention of killing the Prophet—"this Sabaean who has split the unity of Quraysh, calls their ideals foolish and their religion shameful, and blasphemes their gods"—when a friend who met him dissuaded him, reminding him that if he slew the Prophet he would have to reckon with the vengeance of a powerful clan: "Do you think that the Banū ʿAbd Munāf would let you walk on the earth if you had slain Muḥammad?" for tribal pride survived religious difference. "Is it not better for you to return to the people of your own house and keep them straight?" ʿUmar asked: "Which of the people of my house?" "Your brother-in-law and cousin, Saʿīd ibn Zayd, and your sister, Fāṭima daughter of al-Khaṭṭāb, for, by God, they have become Muslims and followers of Muḥammad in his religion, so look to them." Then ʿUmar returned, enraged against his sister and brother-in-law, and there was with them in the house Khabāb ibn ʿArit, having with him a leaf on which was written Ṭā Hā (this sūra) which he was reading aloud to them. When they heard the noise of ʿUmar's coming, Khabāb hid in a closet that they had in the house and Fāṭima took the leaf and hid it under her thigh. But ʿUmar had heard the sound of Khabāb's reading as he drew near the house, and when he entered he said: "What was that mumbling which I heard?" They said: "You heard nothing." ʿUmar said: "Yes, by God! And I have already been informed that you have become followers of Muḥammad in his religion." Then he attacked his brother-in-law Saʿīd ibn Zayd, but Fāṭima sprang to keep him off her husband and he struck and wounded her. And when he had done that, his sister and his brother-in-law said to him: "Yes, we are Muslims and we believe in God and His messenger, so do what you will!" But when ʿUmar saw the blood upon his sister he was sorry for what he had done, and he said to his sister: "Give me that leaf from which I heard you reading just now, that I may see what this is that Muḥammad has brought." And ʿUmar was a scribe. When he said that, his sister said: "We fear to trust you with it." He said: "Fear not!" and swore by his gods that he would return it to her when he had read it. And when he said that, she hoped for his conversion to al-Islām, but said: "O my brother, you are unclean on account of your idolatry and none may touch it save the purified." Then ʿUmar went out and washed himself, and she gave him the leaf on which Ṭā Hā was written and he read it. And when he had read it he said: "How excellent are these words!" and praised it highly. And when he heard that, Khabāb came out to him and said: "O ʿUmar, I hope that God has brought you in answer to the prayer of the Prophet, for only yesterday I heard him saying: O God! Strengthen al-Islām with Abu'l-Ḥukm ibn Hishām or ʿUmar ibn al-Khaṭṭāb; and God is God, O ʿUmar!" At that he said: "O Khabāb, direct me to Muḥammad that I may go to him and make surrender."[1]

The conversion of ʿUmar took place in the fifth year of the Prophet's mission (ninth before the *hijra*) soon after the departure of the emigrants to Abyssinia. At that time this sūra was already written down and in circulation.

An early Meccan sūra.

## Ṭā Hā

*Revealed at Mecca*

In the name of God, the beneficent, the merciful.

1. Ṭā Hā.
2. We have not revealed to you (Muḥammad) this Qurʾān that you should be distressed,
3. But as a reminder to him who fears,
4. A revelation from Him who created the earth and the high heavens,
5. The Beneficent one, who is established on the throne.
6. To Him belongs whatever is in the heavens and whatever is in the earth, and whatever is between them, and whatever is beneath the sod.
7. And if you speak aloud, then He knows the secret (thought) and (what is yet) more hidden.
8. God! There is no god but him. His are the most beautiful names.
9. Has there come to you the story of Moses?
10. When he saw a fire and said to his people: "Wait! I see a fire far off. Perhaps I may bring you a brand from it or may find guidance at the fire."
11. And when he reached it, he was called by name: "O Moses!
12. "I, even I, am your Lord. So take off your shoes, for you are in the holy valley of Tuwa.
13. "And I have chosen you, so listen to what is inspired.
14. "I, even I, am God. There is no god but Me. So serve Me and establish worship for My remembrance.
15. "The hour is surely coming. But I will to keep it hidden, that every soul may be rewarded for that which it strives (to achieve).
16. "Therefore, do not let him turn you aside from (the thought of) it who does not believe in it but follows his own desire, for fear that you perish.
17. "And what is that in your right hand, O Moses?"
18. He said: "This is my staff on which I lean, and with which I beat down branches for my sheep, and in which I find other uses."
19. He said: "Cast it down, O Moses!"
20. So he cast it down, and it was a serpent, gliding.[2]
21. He said: "Grasp it and fear not. We shall return it to its former state.
22. "And thrust your hand within your armpit, it will come forth white without hurt. (That will be) another token.
23. "That We may show you (some) of our greater signs,
24. "Go to Pharaoh! He has transgressed (the bounds)."
25. (Moses) said: "My Lord! Relieve my mind

1. Guillaume, *Life*, pp. 156–57 [Pickthall's note].
2. This transformation is a sign of God's power. See Q 28:31.

26. "And ease my task for me;
27. "And loose a knot from my tongue,
28. "That they may understand my speech.
29. "Appoint for me a henchman from my people,
30. "Aaron, my brother.
31. "Confirm my strength with him
32. "And let him share my task,
33. "That we may glorify You much
34. "And much remember You.
35. "You are ever seeing us."
36. He said: "You are granted your request, O Moses.
37. "And indeed, another time, already We have shown you favor,
38. "When We revealed to your mother what was revealed,
39. "Saying: 'Throw him into the ark, and throw it into the river, then the river shall throw it on to the bank, and there an enemy to me and an enemy to him shall take him.' And I endowed you with love from Me that you might be trained according to My will,
40. "When your sister went and said: 'Shall I show you one who will nurse him?' and We restored you to your mother that her eyes might be refreshed and might not sorrow. And you killed a man and We delivered you from great distress, and tried you with a heavy trial. And you tarried for years among the people of Midian. Then you came (hither) by (My) providence, O Moses,
41. "And I have attached you to Myself.
42. "Go, you and your brother, with my tokens, and do not be faint in remembrance of Me.
43. "Go, both of you, to Pharaoh. He has transgressed (the bounds).
44. "And speak to him a gentle word, that perhaps he may heed or fear."
45. They said: "Our Lord! We fear that he may do us harm or that he may play the tyrant."
46. He said: "Fear not. I am with you two, hearing and seeing.
47. "So go to him and say: 'We are two messengers of your Lord. So let the Children of Israel go with us, and torment them not. We bring you a token from your Lord. And peace will be for him who follows right guidance.
48. "'It has been revealed to us that the doom will be for him who denies and turns away.'"
49. (Pharaoh) said: "Who then is the Lord of you two, O Moses?"
50. He said: "Our Lord is He who gave to everything its nature, then guided it aright."
51. He said: "What then is the state of the generations of old?"
52. He said: "The knowledge of that is with my Lord in a record. My Lord neither errs nor forgets,
53. "Who has appointed the earth as a bed and has threaded roads for you in it and has sent down water from the sky with which We have brought forth various kinds of vegetation,
54. "(Saying): 'Eat and feed your cattle. In this are signs for men of thought.
55. "'Of that We created you, and to that We return you, and from that We bring you forth a second time.'"
56. And We showed him all our signs, but he denied them and refused.

57. He said: "Have you come to drive us out from our land by your magic, O Moses?

58. "But we surely can produce magic for you the like of it; so appoint a tryst between us and you, which neither we nor you shall fail to keep, at a place convenient (to us both)."

59. (Moses) said: "Your tryst shall be the day of the feast, and let the people assemble when the sun has risen high."

60. Then Pharaoh went and gathered his strength, then came (to the appointed tryst).

61. Moses said to them: "Woe to you! Do not invent a lie against God, for fear that he exterminate you by some punishment. He who lies fails miserably."

62. Then they debated with one another what they must do, and they kept their counsel secret.

63. They said: "These are two wizards who would drive you out from your country by their magic, and destroy your best traditions;

64. "So arrange your plan, and come in battle line. Whoever is uppermost this day will indeed be successful."

65. They said: "O Moses! Either throw first, or let us be the first to throw?"

66. He said: "No, you throw!" Then their cords and their staves, by their magic, appeared to him as though they ran.

67. And Moses conceived a fear in his mind.

68. We said: "Fear not! You are the higher.

69. "Throw what is in your right hand! It will eat up what they have made. What they have made is but a wizard's artifice, and a wizard shall not be successful to whatever point (of skill) he may attain."

70. Then the wizards were (all) flung down prostrate, crying: "We believe in the Lord of Aaron and Moses."

71. (Pharaoh) said: "You put faith in him before I give you leave. He is your chief who taught you magic. Now surely I shall cut off your hands and your feet alternately, and I shall crucify you on the trunks of palm trees, and you shall know for certain which of us has sterner and more lasting punishment."

72. They said: "We do not choose you above the clear proofs that have come to us, and above Him who created us. So decree what you will decree. You will end for us only the life of the world.

73. "We believe in our Lord, that He may forgive us our sins and the magic to which you forced us. God is better and more lasting.

74. "Whoever comes guilty to his Lord, for him is hell. There he will neither die nor live.

75. "But whoever comes to Him a believer, having done good works, for such are the high stations;

76. "Gardens of Eden underneath which rivers flow, in which they will abide forever. That is the reward of him who grows."

77. And We inspired Moses, saying: "Take away my servants by night and strike for them a dry path in the sea, fearing not to be overtaken, neither being afraid (of the sea)."

78. Then Pharaoh followed with his hosts and there covered them that which did cover them of the sea.

79. And Pharaoh led his folk astray, he did not guide them.

80. O Children of Israel! We delivered you from your enemy, and We made a covenant with you on the holy mountain's side, and sent down on you the manna and the quails,

81. (Saying): "Eat of the good things which We have provided you, and do not transgress with respect to it lest My wrath come upon you; and he on whom My wrath comes, he is lost indeed.

82. "And I am forgiving toward him who repents and believes and does good, and afterward walks aright."

83. And (it was said): "What has made you hasten from your people, O Moses?"

84. He said: "They are close upon my track. I hastened to you, my Lord, that you might be well pleased."

85. He said: "We have tried your people in your absence, and al-Sāmirī[3] has misled them."

86. Then Moses went back to his people, angry and sad. He said: "O my people! Has not your Lord promised you a fair promise? Did the time appointed then appear too long for you, or did you wish that wrath from your Lord should come upon you, that you broke your promise with me?"

87. They said: "We did not break our promise with you of our own will, but we were laden with burdens of ornaments of the people, then cast them (in the fire), for thus al-Sāmirī proposed."

88. Then he produced for them a calf, of saffron hue,[4] which gave forth a lowing sound. And they cried: "This is your god and the god of Moses, but he has forgotten."

89. Do they not see, then, that it returns no saying to them and possesses for them neither hurt nor use?

90. And Aaron indeed had told them beforehand: "O my people! You are but being seduced by it, for your Lord is the Beneficent, so follow me and obey my order."

91. They said: "We shall by no means cease to be its devotees until Moses returns to us."

92. He (Moses) said: "O Aaron! What held you back when you saw them gone astray,

93. "That you followed me not? Have you then disobeyed my order?"

94. He said: "O son of my mother! Clutch not my beard nor my head! I feared lest you should say: 'You have caused division among the Children of Israel, and have not waited for my word.'"

95. (Moses) said: "And what have you to say, O Sāmirī?"

96. He said: "I perceived what they do not perceive, so I seized a handful from the footsteps of the messenger, and then threw it in. Thus my soul commended to me."[5]

97. (Moses) said: "Then go! And in this life it is for you to say: 'Do not touch me!' and there is for you a promise you cannot break. Now look

3. Understood by Muslim scholars to mean the "Samaritan" who led the Israelites to worship the golden calf.
4. Or "a body." See Q 7:148, footnote [Pickthall's note].
5. The explanation usually given is that al-Sāmirī had seen the angel Gabriel pass by, and had taken some of the dust which he had hallowed, and thrown it into the image of the calf, thus giving it a semblance of life. Others say that al-Sāmirī was an adept of the Egyptian idolatry who had believed for a little while and halfheartedly in the God of Moses [Pickthall's note].

upon your god of which you have remained a devotee. We will burn it and will scatter its dust over the sea.

98. "Your god is only God, than whom there is no other god. He embraces all things in his knowledge."

99. Thus We relate to you (Muḥammad) some tidings of what happened of old, and we have given you from our presence a reminder.

100. Whoever turns away from it, he will bear a burden on the day of resurrection,

101. Abiding under it—an evil burden for them on the day of resurrection,

102. The day when the trumpet is blown. On that day We assemble the guilty white-eyed (with terror),

103. Murmuring among themselves: "You have tarried but ten (days)."

104. We are best aware of what they utter when their most exemplary say: "You have tarried but a day."

105. They will ask you of the mountains (on that day). Say: "My Lord will break them into scattered dust.

106. "And leave it as an empty plain,

107. "In which you see neither curve nor ruggedness."

108. On that day they follow the summoner who does not deceive, and voices are hushed for the Beneficent, and you hear but a faint murmur.

109. On that day no intercession avails except (that of) him to whom the Beneficent has given leave and whose word he accepts.

110. He knows (all) that is before them and (all) that is behind them, while they cannot compass it in knowledge.

111. And faces humble themselves before the living, the eternal. And he who bears (a burden of) wrongdoing is indeed a failure (on that day).

112. And he who has done some good works, being a believer, he does not fear injustice nor begrudging (of his wage).

113. Thus We have revealed it as a lecture[6] in Arabic, and have displayed in it certain threats, that perhaps they may keep from evil or that it may cause them to take heed.

114. Then exalted be God, the true king! And do not hasten (O Muḥammad) with the Qur'ān before its revelation has been perfected for you, and say: "My Lord! Increase me in knowledge."

115. And We made a covenant of old with Adam, but he forgot, and We found no constancy in him.

116. And when We said to the angels: "Fall prostrate before Adam," they fell prostrate (all) except Iblīs; he refused.

117. Therefore we said: "O Adam! This is an enemy to you and to your wife, so do not let him drive you both out of the garden so that you come to toil.

118. "It is (given) to you that you do not hunger there nor are naked,

119. "And that you do not thirst there nor are exposed to the sun's heat."

120. But the devil whispered to him, saying: "O Adam! Shall I show you the tree of immortality and power that does not waste away?"

121. Then they both ate of it, so that their shame became apparent to them, and they began to hide by heaping on themselves some of the leaves of the garden. And Adam disobeyed his Lord, so went astray.[7]

6. Ar. *Qur'ān* [Pickthall's note].
7. Cf. Q 7:20ff. [Pickthall's note].

122. Then his Lord chose him, and relented toward him, and guided him.

123. He said: "Go down from here, both of you, one of you a foe to the other. But if there comes to you from Me a guidance, then whoever follows my guidance, will not go astray nor come to grief.[8]

124. But he whoever turns away from remembrance of Me, his will be a narrow life, and I shall bring him blind to the assembly on the day of resurrection."

125. He will say: "My Lord! Why have you gathered me (hither) blind, when I used to see?"

126. He will say: "So (it must be). Our revelations came to you but you forgot them. In like manner you are forgotten this day."

127. Thus do We reward him who is prodigal and believes not the revelations of his Lord; and the doom of the hereafter will be sterner and more lasting.

128. Is it not a guidance for them (to know) how many generations We destroyed before them, amid whose dwellings they walk? In that are signs for men of thought.

129. But for a decree that had already gone forth from your Lord, and a term already fixed, the judgment would (have) been inevitable (in this world).

130. Therefore (O Muḥammad), bear with what they say, and celebrate the praises of your Lord before the rising of the sun and before its setting. And glorify Him some hours of the night and at the two ends of the day, that you may find acceptance.

131. And do not strain your eyes toward what We cause some wedded pairs among them to enjoy, the flower of the life of the world, that We may try them by it. The provision of your Lord is better and more lasting.

132. And enjoin upon your people worship, and be constant in it. We do ask not of you a provision; We provide for you. And the sequel is for righteousness.

133. And they say: "If only he would bring us a miracle from his Lord!" Has there not come to them the proof of what is in the former scriptures?

134. And if We had destroyed them with some punishment before it, they would assuredly have said: "Our Lord! If only You had sent us a messenger, so that we might have followed Your revelations before we were (thus) humbled and disgraced!"

135. Say: "Each is awaiting; so await! You will come to know who are the owners of the path of equity, and who is right."

## Sūra 21

*Al-Anbiyā'*, "The Prophets," is named from its subject, the history of the former prophets. The speaker in verse 4 and verse 112 is every prophet. There is no historical reference or tradition to enable us to fix the date. It is undoubtedly of Meccan revelation, and lacks the characteristics of the latest and earliest Meccan sūras. It may, therefore, be taken as belonging to the middle group of Meccan sūras.

8. Cf. Q 2:38, and the passage leading up to it [Pickthall's note].

## The Prophets

*Revealed at Mecca*

In the name of God, the beneficent, the merciful.

1. Their reckoning draws near for mankind, while they turn away in heedlessness.
2. There never comes to them a new reminder from their Lord but they listen to it while they play,
3. With hearts preoccupied. And they confer in secret. The wrongdoers say: "Is this other than a mortal like you? Will you then succumb to magic when you see (it)?"
4. He says: "My Lord knows what is spoken in the heaven and the earth. He is the hearer, the knower."
5. "No," they say, "(these are but) muddled dreams; no, he has only invented it; no, he is but a poet. Let him bring us a sign even as those of old (who were God's messengers) were sent (with signs)."
6. Not a township believed of those which We destroyed before them (though We sent them signs): would they then believe?
7. And We did not send (as Our messengers) before you other than men whom We inspired. Ask the followers of the reminder,[1] if you know not?
8. We did not give them bodies that would not eat food, nor were they immortals.
9. Then We fulfilled the promise to them. So We delivered them and whom We would, and We destroyed the prodigals.
10. Now We have revealed to you a scripture in which is your reminder. Have you then no sense?
11. How many a community that dealt unjustly have We shattered, and raised up after them another people!
12. And, when they felt Our might, behold them fleeing from it!
13. (But it was said to them): "Flee not, but return to that (existence) in which you enjoyed luxury and to your dwellings, that you may be questioned."
14. They cried: "Alas for us! We were wrongdoers."
15. And this their crying did not cease until We made them as reaped corn, extinct.
16. We did not create the heaven and the earth and all that is between them in play.
17. If We had wished to find a pastime, We could have found it in Our presence—if We ever did.
18. No, but We hurl the true against the false, and it breaks its head and it vanishes. And yours will be woe for that which you ascribe (to Him).
19. To Him belongs whoever is in the heavens and the earth. And those who dwell in His presence are not too proud to worship Him, nor do they weary;
20. They glorify (Him) night and day; they do not flag.
21. Or have they chosen gods from the earth who raise the dead?

1. I.e. the Jewish scripture [Pickthall's note]. "The followers of the reminder" (Ar. *ahl al-dhikr*) is usually understood to mean the Jews and Christians.

22. If in it there were gods beside God, then both (the heavens and the earth) would have been disordered. Glorified be God, the Lord of the throne, from all that they ascribe (to Him).

23. He will not be questioned as to what He does, but they will be questioned.

24. Or have they chosen other gods beside Him? Say: "Bring your proof (of their godhead)." This is the reminder of those with me and those before me, but most of them know not the truth and so they are averse.

25. And We sent no messenger before you but We inspired him, (saying): "There is no god save Me (God), so worship Me."

26. And they say: "The Beneficent has taken to Himself a son. Be He glorified!" No, but (those whom they call sons) are honored servants;

27. They do not speak until He has spoken, and they act by His command.

28. He knows what is before them and what is behind them, and they cannot intercede except for him whom He accepts, and they quake for awe of Him.

29. And one of them who should say: "I am a god beside Him," that one We should repay with hell. Thus We repay wrongdoers.

30. Have not those who disbelieve known that the heavens and the earth were of one piece, then We parted them, and We made every living thing of water? Will they not then believe?

31. And We have placed in the earth firm hills lest it quake with them, and We have placed in it ravines as roads that perhaps they may find their way.

32. And We have made the sky a roof withheld (from them). Yet they turn away from its signs.

33. And He it is Who created the night and the day, and the sun and the moon. They float, each in an orbit.

34. We appointed immortality for no mortal before you. What! if you die, can they be immortal?

35. Every soul must taste of death, and We try you with evil and with good, for ordeal. And to Us you will be returned.

36. And when those who disbelieve behold you, they only choose you out for mockery, (saying): "Is this he who makes mention of your gods?" And they would deny all mention of the Beneficent.

37. Man is made of haste. I shall show you My signs, but do not ask Me to hasten.

38. And they say: "When will this promise (be fulfilled), if you are truthful?"

39. If those who disbelieved but knew the time when they will not be able to drive off the fire from their faces and from their backs, and they will not be helped!

40. No, but it will come upon them unawares so that it will stupefy them, and they will be unable to repel it, neither will they be reprieved.

41. Messengers before you, indeed, were mocked, but that at which they mocked surrounded those who scoffed at them.

42. Say: "Who guards you in the night or in the day from the Beneficent?" No, but they turn away from mention of their Lord!

43. Or have they gods who can shield them from Us? They cannot help themselves nor can they be defended from Us.

44. No, but We gave these and their fathers ease until life grew long for them. Do they not see how We visit the land, reducing it of its outlying parts?[2] Can they then be the victors?

45. Say (O Muḥammad, to mankind): "I warn you only by the inspiration." But the deaf do not hear the call when they are warned.

46. And if a breath of your Lord's punishment were to touch them, they assuredly would say: "Alas for us! We were wrongdoers."

47. And We set a just balance for the day of resurrection so that no soul is wronged in anything. Though it be of the weight of a grain of mustard seed, We bring it. And We suffice for reckoners.

48. And We gave Moses and Aaron the Criterion[3] (of right and wrong) and a light and a reminder for those who keep from evil,

49. Those who fear their Lord in secret and who dread the hour (of doom).

50. There is a blessed reminder that We have revealed: Will you then reject it?

51. And We gave Abraham of old his proper course, and We were aware of him,

52. When he said to his father and his people: "What are these images to which you pay devotion?"

53. They said: "We found our fathers worshippers of them."

54. He said: "You and your fathers were in plain error."

55. They said: "Did you bring to us the truth, or are you some jester?"

56. He said: "No, but your Lord is the Lord of the heavens and the earth, Who created them; and I am of those who testify to that.

57. "And, by God, I shall outwit your idols after you have gone away and turned your backs."

58. Then he reduced them to fragments, all save the chief of them, that perhaps they might have recourse to it.

59. They said: "Who has done this to our gods? Surely it must be some evildoer."

60. They said: "We heard a youth make mention of them, who is called Abraham."

61. They said: "Then bring him (here) before the people's eyes that they may testify."

62. They said: "Is it you who has done this to our gods, O Abraham?"

63. He said: "But this, their chief has done it. So question them, if they can speak."

64. Then they gathered apart and said: "You yourselves are the wrongdoers."

65. And they were utterly confounded, and they said: "You know well that these do not speak."

66. He said: "Do you worship then instead of God that which cannot profit you at all, nor harm you?

67. "Fie on you and all that you worship instead of God! Have you then no sense?"

68. They cried: "Burn him and stand by your gods, if you will be doing."

69. We said: "O fire, be coolness and peace for Abraham."

2. See Q 13:41, note [Pickthall's note].
3. Ar. *al-furqān*, understood to be revelation that distinguishes right from wrong.

70. And they wished to set a snare for him, but We made them the greater losers.

71. And We rescued him and Lot (and brought them) to the land which We have blessed for (all) peoples.

72. And We bestowed upon him Isaac, and Jacob as a grandson. Each of them We made righteous.

73. And We made them leaders who guide by Our command, and We inspired in them the doing of good deeds and the right establishment of worship and the giving of alms, and they were worshippers of Us (alone).

74. And to Lot We gave judgment and knowledge, and We delivered him from the community that did abominations. They were people of evil, lewd.

75. And We brought him in to Our mercy. He was of the righteous.

76. And Noah, when he cried of old, We heard his prayer and saved him and his household from the great affliction.

77. And delivered him from the people who denied Our revelations. They were people of evil, therefore We drowned them all.

78. And David and Solomon, when they gave judgment concerning the field, when people's sheep had strayed and browsed in it by night; and We were witnesses to their judgment.

79. And We made Solomon to understand (the case); and to each of them We gave judgment and knowledge. And We subdued the hills and the birds to hymn (His) praise along with David. We were the doers (of it).

80. And We taught him the art of making garments (of mail) to protect you in your daring. Are you then thankful?

81. And to Solomon (We subdued) the wind in its raging. It set by His command toward the land which We had blessed. And of everything We are aware.

82. And of the evil ones[4] (We subdued to him) some who dived (for pearls) for him and did other work, and We were warders to them.

83. And Job, when he cried to his Lord, (saying): "Adversity afflicts me, and You are most merciful of all who show mercy."

84. Then We heard his prayer and removed that adversity from which he suffered, and We gave him his household (that he had lost) and the like of it along with them, a mercy from Our store, and a remembrance for the worshippers;

85. And (mention) Ishmael, and Idrīs, and Dhū l-Kifl.[5] All were of the steadfast.

86. And We brought them in to Our mercy. They are among the righteous.

87. And (mention) Dhū'n-Nūn,[6] when he went off in anger and deemed that We had no power over him, but he cried out in the darkness, saying: "There is no god but You. Be You glorified! I have been a wrongdoer."

88. Then We heard his prayer and saved him from the anguish. Thus We save believers.

89. And Zachariah, when he cried to his Lord: "My Lord! Leave me not childless, though You are the best of inheritors."

90. Then We heard his prayer, and bestowed upon him John, and adjusted his wife (to bear a child) for him. They used to vie one with the

4. Ar. *shayāṭīn*, lit. "devils" [Pickthall's note].
5. A prophet famous among the Arabs, whose story resembles that of Ezekiel [Pickthall's note].
6. Lit. "Lord of the Fish" = Jonah [Pickthall's note].

other in good deeds, and they cried to Us in longing and in fear, and were submissive to Us.

91. And she who was chaste,[7] therefore We breathed into her (something) of Our spirit and made her and her son a sign for (all) peoples.

92. This, your religion, is one religion,[8] and I am your Lord, so worship Me.

93. And they have broken their religion (into fragments) among them, (yet) all are returning to Us.

94. Then whoever does good works and is a believer, there will be no rejection of his effort. We record (it) for him.

95. And there is a ban upon any community which We have destroyed: that they shall not return,

96. Until, when Gog and Magog are let loose,[9] and they hasten out of every mound,

97. And the true promise draws near; then behold them, staring wide (in terror), the eyes of those who disbelieve! (They say): "Alas for us! We (lived) in forgetfulness of this. Ah, but we were wrongdoers!"

98. You (idolaters) and that which you worship beside God are fuel of hell. There you will come.

99. If these had been gods they would not have come there, but all will abide there.

100. In there wailing is their portion, and in there they do not hear.

101. Those to whom kindness has gone forth before from Us, they will be far removed from there.

102. They will not hear the slightest sound of it, while they abide in what their souls desire.

103. The supreme horror will not grieve them, and the angels will welcome them, (saying): "This is your day which you were promised;

104. "The day when We shall roll up the heavens as a recorder rolls up a written scroll. As We began the first creation, We shall repeat it. (It is) a promise (binding) upon Us. We are to perform it.

105. "And We have written in the scripture, after the reminder: 'My righteous slaves will inherit the earth'":

106. There is a plain statement for people who are devout.

107. We sent you only as a mercy for the peoples.

108. Say: I have only received revelation that your god is one God. Will you then surrender (to Him)?

109. But if they are averse, then say: "I have warned you all alike, although I know not whether near or far is that which you are promised.

110. "He knows what is said openly, and what you conceal.

111. "And I know only that this may be a trial for you, and enjoyment for a while."

112. He said: "My Lord! Judge with truth." Our Lord is the Beneficent, whose help is to be implored against what you ascribe (to Him).

7. The reference here is to the Virgin Mary [Pickthall's note].
8. The Arabic *umma* carries a range of meanings, including group, society, and religious community.
9. See Q 18:95, footnote.

## Sūra 22

*Al-Ḥajj*, "The Pilgrimage," takes its name from verses 26–38 relating to the pilgrimage to Mecca. This sūra is ascribed by some authorities to the Meccan, by others to the Medinan period. The copy of the Qur'ān which I have followed throughout has the Medinan ascription, and, as it was copied long before the days of "higher" criticism,[1] and was authorized for use throughout the Ottoman Empire, I retain that ascription. Verses 11–13, 25–30, 39–41, and 58–60 were, according to all authorities, revealed at Medina. Nöldeke, the greatest of the "higher" critics, says that the ascription is justified on account of the importance of the verses in this sūra which must, from the nature of their contents, have been revealed at Medina, while holding that much of the sūra belongs to the last Meccan period.

## The Pilgrimage

*Revealed at Medina*

In the name of God, the beneficent, the merciful.

1. O mankind! Fear your Lord. The earthquake of the hour (of doom) is a tremendous thing.

2. On the day when you behold it, every nursing mother will forget her nursling and every pregnant one will be delivered of her burden, and you (Muḥammad) will see mankind as drunken, yet they will not be drunken, but the doom of God will be strong (upon them).

3. Among mankind is he who disputes concerning God without knowledge, and follows each obstinate devil;

4. For him it is decreed that whoever takes him for friend, he will mislead him and will guide him to the punishment of the flame.

5. O mankind! If you are in doubt concerning the resurrection, then We have created you from dust, then from a drop of seed, then from a clot, then from a little lump of flesh shapely and shapeless, that We may make (it) clear for you. And We cause what We will to remain in the wombs for an appointed time, and afterward We bring you forth as infants, then (give you growth) that you attain your full strength. And among you there is he who dies (young), and among you there is he who is brought back to the most abject time of life, so that, after knowledge, he knows nothing.[2] And you (Muḥammad) see the earth barren, but when We send down water on it, it does thrill and swell and put forth every lovely kind[3] (of growth).

6. That is because God, He is the truth. He quickens the dead, and He is able to do all things;

7. And because the hour will come, there is no doubt of it; and because God will raise those who are in the graves.

1. Scholarly analysis of scripture for evidence about historical matters.
2. A reference to old age and senility.
3. Or "every lovely pair." Prof. Ghamrawi who helped me in the revision of the text kept exclaiming on the subtlety and wealth of meaning of every expression used in the Qur'ān concerning natural phenomena. Thus the word "pair" occurs often in the sense of "species," commemorating the fact that every growth of the earth exists as male and female. See particularly Q 36:35 [Pickthall's note]. Muḥammad Aḥmad al-Ghamrāwī, an Egyptian, was a lecturer in chemistry at the Cairo College of Medicine.

8. And among mankind is he who disputes concerning God without knowledge or guidance or a scripture giving light,

9. Turning away in pride to beguile (men) from the way of God. For him in this world is ignominy, and on the day of resurrection We make him taste the doom of burning.

10. (And to him it will be said): "This is for what your two hands have sent before, and because God is no oppressor of His servants."

11. And among mankind is he who worships God upon a narrow edge (of faith) so that if good befalls him he is content with it, but if a trial befalls him, he falls away utterly. He loses both the world and the hereafter. That is the sheer loss.[4]

12. He calls, beside God, to what neither hurts him nor benefits him. That is the far error.

13. He calls to him whose harm is nearer than his benefit; an evil patron and an evil friend!

14. God causes those who believe and do good works to enter gardens underneath which rivers flow. God does what He intends.

15. Whoever is used to thinking (through envy) that God will not give him (Muḥammad) victory in the world and the hereafter (and is enraged at the thought of his victory), let him stretch a rope up to the roof (of his dwelling), and let him hang himself. Then let him see whether his strategy dispells that at which he rages![5]

16. Thus We reveal it as plain revelations, and God guides whom He will.

17. Those who believe this revelation, and those who are Jews, and the Sabians and the Christians and the Magians[6] and the idolaters—God will decide among them on the day of resurrection. God is witness over all things.

18. Have you not seen that to God pays adoration whoever is in the heavens and whoever is on the earth, and the sun, and the moon, and the stars, and the hills, and the trees, and the beasts, and many of mankind, while there are many to whom the doom is justly due. He whom God scorns, there is none to give him honor. God does what He will.

19. These two (the believers and the disbelievers) are two opponents who contend concerning their Lord. But as for those who disbelieve, garments of fire will be cut out for them; boiling fluid will be poured down on their heads,

20. By which what is in their bellies, and their skins too, will be melted;

21. And for them are hooked rods of iron.

22. Whenever, in their anguish, they would go forth from there they are driven back into it and (it is said to them): "Taste the doom of burning."

23. God will cause those who believe and do good works to enter gardens underneath which rivers flow, in which they will be allowed armlets of gold, and pearls, and their garments there will be silk.

4. Tradition says that the reference is to certain Arabs who came to the Prophet at Medina and professed Islam; then, if they prospered in a worldly sense, they were content, but if they had to suffer at all they relapsed to idolatry [Pickthall's note].

5. The meaning is that God will undoubtedly cause the Prophet to triumph in both worlds, and therefore his opponents have no strategy except that of despair [Pickthall's note].

6. Members of a priestly caste in ancient Persia, later influenced by Zoroastrianism (the monotheistic religion of pre-Islamic Iran).

24. They are guided to gentle speech; they are guided to the path of the glorious one.

25. Those who disbelieve and bar (men) from the way of God and from the Inviolable Place of Worship, which We have appointed for mankind together, the dweller there and the nomad: whoever seeks wrongful partiality there, We shall cause him to taste a painful doom.

26. And (remember) when We prepared for Abraham the place of the (holy) house, saying: Do not ascribe anything as partner to Me, and purify My House for those who make the circumambulation there and those who stand and those who bow and make prostration.

27. And proclaim to mankind the pilgrimage.[7] They will come to you on foot and on every lean camel; they will come from every deep ravine,

28. That they may witness things that are of benefit to them, and mention the name of God on appointed days over the beast of cattle that He has bestowed on them. Then eat of it and feed with it the poor unfortunate.

29. Then let them make an end of their unkemptness and pay their vows and go around the ancient House.

30. That (is the command). And whoever magnifies the sacred things of God, it will be well for him in the sight of his Lord. The cattle are lawful to you except what has been told you. So shun the filth of idols, and shun lying speech,

31. Turning to God (only), not ascribing partners to Him; for whoever ascribes partners to God, it is as if he had fallen from the sky and the birds had snatched him or the wind had blown him to a far-off place.

32. That (is the command). And whoever magnifies the offerings consecrated to God, it surely is from devotion of the hearts.

33. In them are benefits for you for an appointed term; and afterward they are brought for sacrifice[8] to the ancient House.

34. And for every nation We have appointed a ritual, that they may mention the name of God over the beast of cattle that He has given them for food;[9] and your God is one God, therefore surrender to Him. And give good tidings (O Muḥammad) to the humble,

35. Whose hearts fear when God is mentioned, and those patient for whatever may befall them, and those who establish worship and who spend of that We have bestowed on them.

36. And the camels! We have appointed them among the ceremonies of God. In them you have much good. So mention the name of God over them when they are drawn up in lines. Then when their flanks fall (dead), eat of it and feed the beggar and the suppliant. Thus have We made them subject to you, that perhaps you may give thanks.

37. Their flesh and their blood do not reach God, but the devotion from you reaches Him. Thus have We made them subject to you that you may magnify God that He has guided you. And give good tidings (O Muḥammad) to the good.

7. Q 2:196ff. [Pickthall's note].
8. The slaughter of animals for food for the poor which is one of the ceremonies of the Muslim pilgrimage is not a propitiatory sacrifice, but is in commemoration of the sacrifice of Abraham which marked the end of human sacrifices for the Semitic race, and which made it clear that the only sacrifice which God requires of man is the surrender of his will and purpose—i.e. Islam [Pickthall's note].
9. In order that they may realize the awfulness of taking life, and the solemn nature of the trust which God has imposed on them in the permission to eat animal food [Pickthall's note].

38. God defends those who are true. God does not love each treacherous ingrate.

39. Sanction is given to those who fight because they have been wronged; and God is indeed able to give them victory;

40. Those who have been driven from their homes unjustly only because they said: "Our Lord is God"—For had it not been for God's repelling some men by means of others, cloisters and churches and oratories and mosques, in which the name of God is often mentioned, would assuredly have been pulled down. God helps one who helps Him. God is strong, almighty—

41. Those who, if We give them power in the land, establish worship and pay the poor-tax and enjoin kindness and forbid iniquity. And God's is the sequel of events.

42. If they deny you (Muḥammad), even so the people of Noah, and (the tribes of) 'Ād and Thamūd, before you, denied (Our messengers);

43. And the people of Abraham and the people of Lot;

44. (And) the dwellers in Midian. And Moses was denied; but I indulged the disbelievers a long while, then I seized them, and how (terrible) was My abhorrence!

45. How many a township have We destroyed while it was sinful, so that it lies (to this day) in ruins, and (how many) a deserted well and lofty tower!

46. Have they not traveled in the land, and have they hearts with which to feel and ears with which to hear? For it is not the eyes that grow blind, but it is the hearts, which are within the breasts, that grow blind.

47. And they will bid you hasten on the doom, and God does not fail His promise, but a day with God is as a thousand years of what you reckon.

48. And how many a township did I grant a reprieve long though it was sinful! Then I grasped it. To Me is the return.

49. Say: "O mankind! I am only a plain warner to you."

50. Those who believe and do good works, for them is pardon and a rich provision;

51. While those who strive to thwart Our revelations, such are rightful owners of the fire.

52. We never sent a messenger or a prophet before you but when He recited (the message) Satan proposed (opposition) in respect of what he recited of it. But God abolishes what Satan proposes. Then God establishes His revelations. God is knower, wise;

53. That He may make what the devil proposes a temptation for those in whose hearts is a disease, and those whose hearts are hardened—the evildoers are in open schism—

54. And that those who have been given knowledge may know that it is the truth from your Lord, so that they may believe in it and their hearts may submit humbly to Him. God is guiding those who believe to a right path.

55. And those who disbelieve will not cease to be in doubt of it until the hour comes upon them unawares, or there comes to them the doom of a disastrous day.

56. The sovereignty on that day will be God's, He will judge between them. Then those who believed and did good works will be in gardens of delight,

57. While those who disbelieved and denied Our revelations, for them will be a shameful doom.

58. Those who fled their homes for the cause of God and then were slain or died, God will provide for them a good provision. God, He is best of all who make provision.

59. Assuredly He will cause them to enter by an entry that they will love. God is knower, indulgent.

60. That (is so). And whoever has retaliated with the like of what he was made to suffer and then has (again) been wronged, God will help him. God is mild, forgiving.

61. That is because God makes the night to pass into the day and makes the day to pass into the night, and because God is hearer, observer.

62. That is because God, He is the true, and that on which they call instead of Him, it is the false, and because God, He is the high, the great.

63. Do you not see how God sends down water from the sky and then the earth becomes green in the morning? God is subtile, aware.

64. To Him belongs all that is in the heavens and all that is on the earth. God, He is the absolute, the owner of praise.

65. Have you not seen how God has made all that is on the earth subservient to you? And the ship runs upon the sea by His command, and He holds back the heaven from falling on the earth unless by His leave. God is, for mankind, full of pity, merciful.

66. And He it is who gave you life, then He will cause you to die, and then will give you life (again). Man is an ingrate.

67. To each nation We have given sacred rites which they are to perform; so let them not dispute with you on the matter, but summon you to your Lord. You indeed follow right guidance.

68. And if they wrangle with you, say: "God is best aware of what you do.

69. "God will judge between you on the day of resurrection concerning that in which you used to differ.

70. "Have you not known that God knows all that is in the heaven and the earth? It is in a record. That is easy for God."

71. And they worship instead of God that for which He has sent down no warrant, and that of which they have no knowledge. For evildoers there is no helper.

72. And when Our revelations are recited to them, you know the denial in the faces of those who disbelieve; they all but attack those who recite Our revelations to them. Say: "Shall I proclaim to you worse than that? The fire! God has promised it for those who disbelieve. A wretched journey's end!"

73. O mankind! A similitude is coined, so pay heed to it: Those on whom you call beside God will never create a fly though they combine together for the purpose. And if the fly took something from them, they could not rescue it from him. So weak are (both) the seeker and the sought!

74. They do not measure God His rightful measure. God is strong, almighty.

75. God chooses from the angels messengers, and (also) from mankind. God is hearer, observer.

76. He knows all that is before them and all that is behind them, and to God all things are returned.

77. O you who believe! Bow down and prostrate yourselves, and worship your Lord, and do good, that perhaps you may prosper.

78. And strive for God with the endeavor which is His right. He has chosen you and has not laid upon you in religion any hardship; the faith

of your father Abraham (is yours). He has named you Muslims[1] from before and in this (scripture), that the messenger may be a witness against you, and that you may be witnesses against mankind. So establish worship, pay the poor tax, and hold fast to God. He is your protecting friend. A blessed patron and a blessed helper!

## Sūra 23

*Al-Mu'minūn*, "The Believers," is so named from a word occurring in the first verse or, it may be said, from its subject, which is the triumph of believers. It is considered to be the last of the sūras revealed at Mecca, immediately before the Prophet's flight to Yathrib (Medina).

A late Meccan sūra.

## The Believers

*Revealed at Mecca*

In the name of God, the beneficent, the merciful.

1. Successful indeed are the believers
2. Who are humble in their prayers,
3. And who shun vain conversation,
4. And who are payers of the poor tax;
5. And who guard their modesty—
6. Except from their wives or the (slaves) whom their right hands possess, for then they are not blameworthy,
7. But whoever craves beyond that, such are transgressors—
8. And who are shepherds of their pledge and their covenant,
9. And who pay heed to their prayers.
10. These are the heirs
11. Who will inherit paradise. There they will abide.
12. We created man from a product of wet earth;
13. Then placed him as a drop (of seed) in a safe lodging;
14. Then We fashioned the drop a clot, then We fashioned the clot a little lump, then We fashioned the little lump bones, then clothed the bones with flesh, and then produced it as another creation. So blessed be God, the best of creators!
15. Then after that you surely die.
16. Then on the day of resurrection you are raised (again).
17. And We have created above you seven paths, and We are never unmindful of creation.
18. And We send down from the sky water in measure, and We give it lodging in the earth, and We are able to withdraw it.
19. Then by it We produce for you gardens of date palms and grapes, in which is much fruit for you and of which you eat;
20. And a tree that springs forth from Mount Sinai that grows oil and relish for the eaters.

1. "Those who have surrendered" [Pickthall's note].

21. In the cattle there is a lesson for you. We give you to drink of that which is in their bellies, and many uses have you in them, and of them do you eat;

22. And on them and on the ship you are carried.

23. And We sent Noah to his people, and he said: "O my people! Serve God. You have no other god except Him. Will you not ward off (evil)?"

24. But the leaders of his people, who disbelieved, said: "This is only a mortal like you who would make himself superior to you. Had God willed, He surely could have sent down angels. We did not hear of this in the case of our fathers of old.

25. "He is only a man in whom is a madness, so watch him for a while."

26. He said: "My Lord! Help me because they deny me."

27. Then We inspired in him, saying: "Make the ship under Our eyes and Our inspiration. Then, when Our command comes and the oven gushes water, introduce into it of every (kind) two spouses, and your household except him against whom the word has already gone forth. And do not plead with Me on behalf of those who have done wrong. They will be drowned.

28. "And when you are on board the ship, you and whoever is with you, then say: 'Praise be to God Who has saved us from the wrongdoing people!'"

29. And say: "My Lord! Cause me to land at a blessed landing-place, for You are best of all who bring to land."

30. In that are signs. We are ever putting (mankind) to the test.

31. Then, after them, We brought forth another generation;

32. And We sent among them a messenger of their own, saying: "Serve God. You have no other god save Him. Will you not ward off (evil)?"

33. And the leaders of his people, who disbelieved and denied the meeting of the hereafter, and whom We had made soft in the life of the world, said: "This is only a mortal like you, who eats of that of which you eat and drinks of that you drink.

34. "If you were to obey a mortal like yourselves, you surely would be losers.

35. "Does he promise you that you, when you are dead and have become dust and bones, will (again) be brought forth?

36. "Begone, begone, with that which you are promised!

37. "There is nothing but our life of the world; we die and we live, and we shall not be raised (again).

38. "He is only a man who has invented a lie about God. We are not going to put faith in him."

39. He said: "My Lord! Help me because they deny me."

40. He said: "In a little while they surely will become repentant."

41. So the (awful) cry overtook them rightfully, and We made them like wreckage (that a torrent hurls). A far removal for wrongdoing people!

42. Then after them We brought forth other generations.

43. No nation can outstrip its term, nor yet postpone it.

44. Then We sent our messengers one after another. Whenever its messenger came to a nation they denied him; so We caused them to follow one another (to disaster) and We made them bywords. A far removal for people who believe not!

45. Then We sent Moses and his brother Aaron with Our signs and a clear warrant

46. To Pharaoh and his chiefs, but they scorned (them) and they were despotic people.

47. And they said: "Shall we put faith in two mortals like ourselves, and whose people are servile to us?"

48. So they denied them, and became of those who were destroyed.

49. And We gave Moses the scripture, that perhaps they might go aright.

50. And We made the son of Mary and his mother a sign, and We gave them refuge on a height, a place of flocks and watersprings.

51. O you messengers! Eat of the good things, and do right. I am aware of what you do.

52. This your religion is one religion and I am your Lord, so keep your duty to Me.

53. But they (mankind) have broken their religion among them into sects,[1] each sect rejoicing in its tenets.

54. So leave them in their error until a time.

55. Do they think that in the wealth and sons with which We provide them

56. We hasten to them with good things? No, but they do not perceive.

57. Those who go in awe for fear of their Lord,

58. And those who believe in the revelations of their Lord,

59. And those who do not ascribe partners to their Lord,

60. And those who give what they give with hearts afraid because they are about to return to their Lord,

61. These race for the good things, and they shall win them in the race.

62. And We do not task any soul beyond its scope, and with Us is a record which speaks the truth, and they will not be wronged.

63. No, but their hearts are in ignorance of this (Qur'ān), and they have other works, besides, which they are doing;

64. Until when We grasp their affluent ones with the punishment, behold, they supplicate.

65. Do not supplicate this day! Assuredly you will not be helped by Us.

66. My revelations were recited to you, but you used to turn back on your heels,

67. In scorn. Nightly you raved together.

68. Have they not pondered the word, or has that come to them which did not come to their fathers of old?

69. Or do they not know their messenger, and so reject him?

70. Or do they say: "There is a madness in him"? No, but he brings them the truth; and most of them are haters of the truth.

71. And if the truth had followed their desires, the heavens and the earth and whoever is in them would have been corrupted. No, We have brought them their reminder, but from their reminder they now turn away.

72. Or do you ask of them (O Muḥammad) any tribute? But the bounty of your Lord is better, for He is best of all who make provision.

73. And you summon them to a straight path.

74. And those who do not believe in the hereafter are indeed astray from the path.

1. The Arabic *zubur* (groups, sects) contrasts the unity of the Muslim community to the splits among their opponents.

75. Though We had mercy on them and relieved them of the harm afflicting them, they still would wander blindly on in their recalcitrance.
76. Already We have grasped them with punishment, but they do not humble themselves to their Lord, nor do they pray,
77. Until, when We open for them the gate of extreme punishment, then indeed they are aghast at it.
78. He it is Who has created for you ears and eyes and hearts. Small thanks you give!
79. And He it is Who has multiplied you on the earth, and to Him you will be gathered.
80. And He it is Who gives life and causes death, and His is the difference of night and day. Have you then no sense?
81. No, but they say the like of that which the men of old said;
82. They say: "When we are dead and have become (mere) dust and bones, shall we then be raised again?
83. "We were already promised this, we and our forefathers. This is nothing but fables of the men of old."
84. Say: "To Whom (belongs) the earth and whoever is in it, if you have knowledge?"
85. They will say: "To God." Say: "Will you not then remember?"
86. Say: "Who is Lord of the seven heavens, and Lord of the tremendous throne?"
87. They will say: "To God (all that belongs)." Say: "Will you not then keep duty (to Him)?"
88. Say: "In whose hand is the dominion over all things and He protects, while against Him there is no protection, if you have knowledge?"
89. They will say: "To God (all that belongs)." Say: "How then are you bewitched?"
90. No, but We have brought them the truth, and they are liars.
91. God has not chosen any son, nor is there any god along with Him; otherwise each god would have assuredly championed that which he created, and some of them would assuredly have overcome others. Glorified be God above all that they allege.
92. Knower of the invisible and the visible! And exalted be He over all that they ascribe as partners (to Him)!
93. Say: "My Lord! If You should show me that which they are promised,
94. My Lord! then do not set me among the wrongdoing people."
95. And We are able to show you what We have promised them.
96. Repel evil with what is better. We are best aware of what they allege.
97. And say: "My Lord! I seek refuge in You from suggestions of the evil ones,
98. "And I seek refuge in You, my Lord, for fear that they be present with me,
99. "Until, when death comes to one of them, he says: 'My Lord! Send me back,
100. "'That I may do right in what I have left behind!'" But no! It is but a word that he speaks; and behind them is a barrier until the day when they are raised.
101. And when the trumpet is blown there will be no kinship among them that day, nor will they ask of one another.

102. Then those whose scales are heavy, they are the successful.
103. And those whose scales are light are those who lose their souls, in hell abiding.[2]
104. The fire burns their faces, and there they are glum.
105. (It will be said): "Were not My revelations recited to you, and then you used to deny them?"
106. They will say: "Our Lord! Our evil fortune conquered us, and we were erring people.
107. "Our Lord! Oh, bring us forth from here! If we return (to evil) then indeed we shall be wrongdoers."
108. He said: "Begone into it, and do not speak to Me.
109. "There was a party of My slaves who said: 'Our Lord! We believe, therefore forgive us and have mercy on us for You are best of all who show mercy';
110. "But you chose them for a laughingstock until they caused you to forget remembrance of Me, while you laughed at them.
111. "I have rewarded them this day because they were steadfast; and they are the triumphant."
112. He will say: "How long did you tarry on the earth, counting by years?"
113. They will say: "We tarried but a day or part of a day. Ask of those who keep count!"
114. He will say: "You tarried but a little if you only knew.
115. "Did you think then that We had created you for nothing, and that you would not be returned to Us?"
116. Now God be exalted, the true king! There is no god save Him, the Lord of the throne of grace.
117. He who cries to any other god along with God has no proof of it. His reckoning is only with his Lord. Disbelievers will not be successful.
118. And (O Muḥammad) say: "My Lord! Forgive and have mercy, for You are best of all who show mercy."

## Sūra 24

*Al-Nūr*, "Light," takes its name from verses 35–40, descriptive of the light of God as it should shine in the homes of believers, the greater part of the sūra being legislation for the purifying of home life. All its verses were revealed at Medina. Tradition says that verses 11–20 relate to the slanderers of 'Ā'isha[1] in connection with an incident which occurred in the fifth year of the *hijra* when the Prophet was returning from the campaign against the Banū l-Muṣṭaliq, 'Ā'isha having been left behind on a march, and found and brought back by a young soldier who let her mount his camel and himself led the camel. A weaker tradition places the revelation of verses 1–10 as late as the ninth year of the *hijra*.

The period of revelation is the fifth and sixth years of the *hijra*.

2. The scales of justice will weigh each person's deeds on the day of judgment.
1. Muḥammad's wife, daughter of the first caliph, and a source of authoritative knowledge in early Islam (ca. 614–678).

# Light

*Revealed at Medina*

In the name of God, the beneficent, the merciful.

1. (Here is) a sūra which We have revealed and enjoined, and in which We have revealed plain signs, that perhaps you may take heed.

2. The adulteress and the adulterer, scourge each one of them (with) a hundred stripes. And do not let pity for the two withhold you from obedience to God, if you believe in God and the last day. And let a party of believers witness their punishment.

3. The adulterer shall not marry except an adulteress or an idolatress, and the adulteress none shall marry except an adulterer or an idolater. All that is forbidden to believers.

4. And those who accuse honorable women but do not bring four witnesses, scourge them (with) eighty stripes and never (afterward) accept their testimony—they indeed are evildoers—

5. Except those who afterward repent and make amends. (For such) God is forgiving, merciful.

6. As for those who accuse their wives but have no witnesses except themselves; let the testimony of one of them be four testimonies, (swearing) by God that he is of those who speak the truth;

7. And yet a fifth, invoking the curse of God on him if he is of those who lie.

8. And it shall avert the punishment from her if she bear witness before God four times that the thing he says is indeed false,

9. And a fifth (time) that the wrath of God be upon her if he speaks truth.

10. And had it not been for the grace of God and His mercy to you, and that God is clement, wise, (you would have been undone).

11. They who spread the slander are a gang among you. Do not consider it a bad thing for you; it is good for you. To every man of them (will be paid) what he has earned of the sin; and as for him among them who had the greater share in it, his will be an awful doom.

12. Why did not the believers, men and women, when you heard it, think good of their own people, and say: "It is a manifest untruth?"

13. Why did they not produce four witnesses? Since they do not produce witnesses, they are liars in the sight of God.

14. Had it not been for the grace of God and His mercy to you in the world and the hereafter an awful doom would have overtaken you for that of which you murmured.

15. When you welcomed it with your tongues, and uttered with your mouths that of which you had no knowledge, you counted it a trifle. In the sight of God it is very great.

16. When you heard it, you did not say: "It is not for us to speak of this. Glory be to You (O God)! This is awful calumny."

17. God admonishes you that you not repeat the like of it ever, if you are (in truth) believers.

18. And He expounds to you the revelations. God is knower, wise.

19. Those who love that slander should be spread concerning those who believe, theirs will be a painful punishment in the world and the hereafter. God knows. You know not.

20. Had it not been for the grace of God and His mercy to you, and that God is clement, merciful, (you would have been undone).

21. O you who believe! Do not follow the footsteps of the devil. To whoever follows the footsteps of the devil, he commands filthiness and wrong. Had it not been for the grace of God and His mercy to you, not one of you would ever have grown pure. But God causes whom He will to grow. And God is hearer, knower.

22. And do not let those who possess dignity and ease among you swear not to give to the near of kin and to the needy, and to fugitives for the cause of God.[2] Let them forgive and show indulgence. Do you not yearn that God may forgive you? God is forgiving, merciful.

23. As for those who defame virtuous, believing women (who are) careless, cursed are they in the world and the hereafter. Theirs will be an awful doom

24. On the day when their tongues and their hands and their feet testify against them as to what they used to do,

25. On that day God will pay them their just due, and they will know that God, He is the manifest truth.

26. Vile women are for vile men, and vile men for vile women. Good women are for good men, and good men for good women; such are innocent of what people say: For them is pardon and a bountiful provision.

27. O you who believe! Do not enter houses other than your own without first announcing your presence and invoking peace upon its people. That is better for you, that you may be heedful.

28. And if you find no one within, still do not enter until permission has been given. And if it be said to you: "Go away again," then go away, for it is purer for you. God knows what you do.

29. (It is) no sin for you to enter uninhabited houses in which is comfort for you. God knows what you proclaim and what you hide.

30. Tell the believing men to lower their gaze and be modest. That is purer for them. God is aware of what they do.

31. And tell the believing women to lower their gaze and be modest, and to display of their adornment only what is apparent, and to draw their veils over their breasts, and not to reveal their adornment except to their own husbands or fathers or husbands' fathers, or their sons or their husbands' sons, or their brothers or their brothers' sons or sisters' sons, or their women, or their slaves, or male attendants who lack vigor, or children who know nothing of women's nakedness. And let them not stamp their feet so as to reveal what they hide of their adornment. And turn to God together, O believers, in order that you may succeed.

32. And marry such of you as are solitary and the pious of your slaves and maidservants. If they be poor, God will enrich them of His bounty. God is of ample means, aware.

33. And let those who cannot find a match keep chaste until God give them independence by His grace. And such of your slaves as seek a writing

2. Tradition says that Abū Bakr, when he heard that a kinsman of his own whom he had supported had been among the slanderers of his daughter 'Ā'isha, swore no longer to support him, and that this verse was revealed on that occasion [Pickthall's note].

(of emancipation), write it for them if you are aware of anything of good in them, and bestow upon them of the wealth of God which He has bestowed upon you. Do not force your slave-girls to whoredom that you may seek enjoyment of the life of the world, if they would preserve their chastity. And if one force them, then (to them), after their compulsion, God will be forgiving, merciful.

34. And We have sent down for you revelations that make plain, and the example of those who passed away before you. An admonition to those who ward off (evil).

35. God is the light of the heavens and the earth. The similitude of His light is as a niche in which there is a lamp. The lamp is in a glass. The glass is as it were a shining star. (This lamp is) kindled from a blessed tree, an olive neither of the east nor of the west, whose oil would almost glow forth (of itself) though no fire touched it. Light upon light. God guides to His light whom He will. And God speaks to mankind in allegories, for God is knower of all things.

36. (This lamp is found) in houses which God has allowed to be exalted and that His name shall be remembered there. Offer praise to Him there at morning and evening

37. Men whom neither merchandise nor sale beguiles from remembrance of God and constancy in prayer and paying to the poor their due; who fear a day when hearts and eyes will be overturned;

38. That God may reward them with the best of what they did, and increase reward for them of His bounty. God gives blessings without stint to whom He will.

39. As for those who disbelieve, their deeds are as a mirage in a desert. The thirsty one supposes it to be water until he comes to it and finds it nothing, and finds, in the place of it, God, who pays him his due; and God is swift at reckoning.

40. Or as darkness on a vast, abysmal sea. There covers him a wave, above which is a wave, above which is a cloud. Layer upon layer of darkness. When he holds out his hand he scarce can see it. And he for whom God has not appointed light, for him there is no light.

41. Have you not seen that God, He it is whom all who are in the heavens and the earth praise, and the birds in their flight? Of each He knows the worship and the praise; and God is aware of what they do.

42. And to God belongs the sovereignty of the heavens and the earth, and to God is the journeying.

43. Have you not seen how God wafts the clouds, then gathers them, then makes them layers, and you see the rain come forth from between them; He sends down from the heaven mountains in which is hail, and strikes with it whom He will, and averts it from whom He will. The flashing of His lightning all but snatches away the sight.

44. God causes the revolution of the day and the night. In this is indeed a lesson for those who see.

45. God has created every animal of water. Of them is (a kind) that goes upon its belly and (a kind) that goes upon two legs and (a kind) that goes upon four. God creates what He will. God is able to do all things.

46. We have sent down revelations and explained them. God guides whom He will to a straight path.

47. And they say: "We believe in God and the messenger, and we obey"; then after that a faction of them turn away. Such are not believers.
48. And when they appeal to God and His messenger to judge between them, a faction of them are averse;
49. But if right had been with them they would have come to him willingly.
50. Is there in their hearts a disease, or have they doubts, or fear they that God and His messenger should wrong them in judgment? No, but such are evildoers.
51. The saying of (all true) believers when they appeal to God and His messenger to judge between them is only that they say: "We hear and we obey." And such are the successful.
52. He who obeys God and His messenger, and fears God, and keeps duty (to Him): such indeed are the victorious.
53. They swear by God solemnly that, if you order them, they will go forth. Say: "Swear not; known obedience (is better). God is informed of what you do."
54. Say: "Obey God and obey the messenger. But if you turn away, then (it is) for him (to do) only that with which he has been charged, and for you (to do) only that with which you have been charged. If you obey him, you will go rightly." But the messenger has no other charge than to convey (the message) plainly.
55. God has promised such of you as believe and do good works that He will surely make them succeed (the present rulers) on the earth even as He caused those who were before them to succeed (others); and that He will surely establish for them their religion which He has approved for them, and will give them in exchange safety after their fear. They serve Me. They ascribe no thing as partner to Me. Those who disbelieve after that, they are the evildoers.
56. Establish worship and pay the poor tax and obey the messenger, that perhaps you may find mercy.
57. Do not think that the disbelievers can escape in the land. Fire will be their home—an unfortunate journey's end!
58. O you who believe! Let your slaves, and those of you who have not come to puberty, ask leave of you at three times (before they come into your presence): Before the prayer of dawn, and when you lay aside your garments for the heat of noon, and after the prayer of night.[3] Three times of privacy for you. It is no sin for them or for you at other times, when some of you go around attendant upon others (if they come into your presence without leave). Thus God makes clear the revelations for you. God is knower, wise.
59. And when the children among you come to puberty then let them ask leave even as those before them used to ask it. Thus God makes clear His revelations for you. God is knower, wise.
60. As for women past childbearing, who have no hope of marriage, it is no sin for them if they discard their (outer) clothing in such a way as not to show adornment. But to refrain is better for them. God is hearer, knower.
61. No blame is there upon the blind nor any blame upon the lame nor any blame upon the sick nor on yourselves if you eat from your houses, or the houses of your fathers, or the houses of your mothers, or the houses of

3. The prayer to be offered when the night has fully come [Pickthall's note].

your brothers, or the houses of your sisters, or the houses of your fathers' brothers, or the houses of your fathers' sisters, or the houses of your mothers' brothers, or the houses of your mothers' sisters, or (from that) of which you hold the keys, or (from the house) of a friend. No sin shall it be for you whether you eat together or apart. But when you enter houses, salute one another with a greeting from God, blessed and sweet. Thus God makes clear His revelations for you, that perhaps you may understand.

62. They only are the true believers who believe in God and His messenger and, when they are with him on some common errand, do not go away until they have asked leave of him. Those who ask leave of you, those are they who believe in God and His messenger. So, if they ask your leave for some affair of theirs, give leave to whom you will of them, and ask for them forgiveness of God. God is forgiving, merciful.

63. Do not make the calling of the messenger among you as your calling of one another. God knows those of you who steal away, hiding themselves. And let those who conspire to evade orders beware for fear that grief or painful punishment befall them.

64. To God belongs whatever is in the heavens and the earth. He knows your condition. And (He knows) the day when they are returned to Him so that He may inform them of what they did. God is knower of all things.

## Sūra 25

*Al-Furqān*, "The Criterion," takes its name from a word occurring in verse 1. The subject is the folly of superstition and the craving for miraculous events in face of the wonders of God's creation.

It belongs to the middle group of Meccan sūras, except verses 68–70 which were revealed at Medina.

# The Criterion (of Right and Wrong)

*Revealed at Mecca*

In the name of God, the beneficent, the merciful.

1. Blessed is He who has revealed to His servant the criterion (of right and wrong), that he may be a warner to the peoples.

2. He to whom belongs the sovereignty of the heavens and the earth, He has chosen no son nor has He any partner in the sovereignty. He has created everything and has apportioned out for it a measure.

3. Yet they choose beside Him other gods who create nothing but are themselves created, and possess not hurt nor profit for themselves, and possess not death nor life, nor power to raise the dead.

4. Those who disbelieve say: "This is nothing but a lie that he has invented, and other people have helped him with it, so that they have produced a slander and a lie."

5. And they say: "Fables of the men of old which he has had written down so that they are dictated to him morning and evening."

6. Say (to them, O Muḥammad): "He who knows the secret of the heavens and the earth has revealed it. He ever is forgiving, merciful."

7. And they say: "What ails this messenger (of God) that he eats food and walks in the markets? Why is not an angel sent down to him, to be a warner with him?

8. "Or (why is not) a treasure thrown down to him, or why does he not have a paradise from which to eat?" And the evildoers say: "You are only following a man bewitched."

9. See how they coin similitudes for you, so that they are all astray and cannot find a road!

10. Blessed is He who, if He will, will assign you better than (all) that—gardens underneath which rivers flow—and will assign you mansions.

11. No, but they deny (the coming of) the hour, and for those who deny (the coming of) the hour We have prepared a flame.

12. When it sees them from afar, they hear the crackling and the roar of it.

13. And when they are flung into a narrow place of it, chained together, they pray for destruction there.

14. Do not pray that day for one destruction, but pray for many destructions!

15. Say: "Is that (doom) better or the garden of immortality which is promised to those who ward off (evil)?" It will be their reward and journey's end.

16. There abiding, they have all that they desire. It is for your Lord a promise that must be fulfilled.

17. And on the day when He will assemble them and that which they worship instead of God and will say: "Was it you who misled these my servants or did they (themselves) wander from the way?"

18. They will say: "Be You glorified! It was not for us to choose any protecting friends beside You; but You gave them and their fathers ease until they forgot the warning and became lost people."

19. Thus they will give you the lie regarding what you say, then you can neither avert (the doom) nor obtain help. And whoever among you does wrong, We shall make him taste great torment.

20. We never sent before you any messengers except they ate food and walked in the markets. And We have appointed some of you a test for others: Will you be steadfast? And your Lord is ever observer.

21. And those who do not look for a meeting with Us say: "Why are angels not sent down to us and (why) do we not see our Lord?" Assuredly they think too highly of themselves and are scornful with great pride.

22. On the day when they behold the angels, on that day there will be no good tidings for the guilty; and they will cry: "A forbidding ban!"

23. And We shall turn to the work they did and make it scattered motes.

24. Those who have earned the garden on that day will be better in their home and happier in their place of noonday rest;

25. A day when the heaven with the clouds will be rent asunder and the angels will be sent down, a grand descent.

26. The sovereignty on that day will be the true (sovereignty) belonging to the Beneficent one, and it will be a hard day for disbelievers.

27. On the day when the wrongdoer gnaws his hands, he will say: "Ah, would that I had chosen a way together with the messenger (of God)!

28. "Alas for me! Ah, would that I had never taken such a one for friend!

29. "He led me astray from the reminder after it had reached me. Satan was ever man's deserter in the hour of need."

30. And the messenger says: "O my Lord! My own people make this Qur'ān of no account."

31. Even so have We appointed to every prophet an opponent from among the guilty; but God suffices for a guide and helper.

32. And those who disbelieve say: "Why is the Qur'ān not revealed to him all at once?" (It is revealed) thus that We may strengthen your heart with it; and We have arranged it in right order.

33. And they bring you no similitude but We bring you the truth (as against it), and better (than their similitude) as argument.

34. Those who will be gathered on their faces to hell: such are worse in plight and further from the right road.

35. We gave Moses the scripture and placed with him his brother Aaron as minister.

36. Then We said: "Go together to the people who have denied Our revelations." Then We destroyed them, a complete destruction.

37. And Noah's folk, when they denied the messengers, We drowned them and made of them a sign for mankind. We have prepared a painful doom for evildoers.

38. And (the tribes of) 'Ād and Thamūd, and the dwellers in al-Rass,[1] and many generations in between.

39. Each (of them) We warned by examples, and each (of them) We brought to utter ruin.

40. And indeed they have passed by the township on which was rained the fatal rain.[2] Can it be that they have not seen it? No, but they hope for no resurrection.

41. And when they see you (O Muḥammad) they treat you only as a jest (saying): "Is this he whom God sends as a messenger?

42. "He would have led us far away from our gods if we had not been staunch to them." They will know, when they behold the doom, who is more astray as to the road.

43. Have you seen him who chooses for his god his own lust? Would you then be guardian over him?

44. Or do you think that most of them hear or understand? They are but as the cattle—no, but they are farther astray!

45. Have you not seen how your Lord has spread the shade—and if He willed He could have made it still—then We have made the sun its pilot;

46. Then We withdraw it to Us, a gradual withdrawal?

47. And He it is who makes night a covering for you, and sleep repose, and makes day a resurrection.

48. And He it is who sends the winds, glad tidings heralding His mercy, and We send down purifying water from the sky,

49. That We may give life thereby to a dead land, and We give many beasts and men that We have created to drink of it.

50. And We have repeated it among them that they may remember, but most of mankind begrudge anything except ingratitude.

51. If We willed, We could raise up a warner in every village.

1. Said to have been a town in Yamāma [Pickthall's note].
2. The great trade caravans from Mecca into Syria passed by the Dead Sea [Pickthall's note].

52. So do not obey the disbelievers, but strive against them by it with a great endeavor.

53. And He it is who has given independence to the two seas[3] (though they meet); one palatable, sweet, and the other saltish, bitter; and has set a bar and a forbidding ban between them.

54. And He it is who has created man from water, and has appointed for him kindred by blood and kindred by marriage; for your Lord is ever powerful.

55. Yet they worship instead of God that which can neither benefit them nor hurt them. The disbeliever was ever a partisan against his Lord.

56. And We have sent you (O Muḥammad) only as a bearer of good tidings and a warner.

57. Say: "I ask of you no reward for this, except that whoever will may choose a way to his Lord."

58. And trust you in the Living One who does not die, and hymn His praise. He suffices as the knower of His servant's sins,

59. Who created the heavens and the earth and all that is between them in six days,[4] then He mounted the throne. The Beneficent! Ask any one informed concerning Him!

60. And when it is said to them: "Adore the Beneficent!" they say: "And what is the Beneficent? Are we to adore whatever you (Muḥammad) bid us?" And it increases aversion in them.

61. Blessed be He who has placed in the heaven mansions of the stars, and has placed in it a great lamp and a moon giving light!

62. And He it is who has appointed night and day in succession, for him who desires to remember, or desires thankfulness.

63. The (faithful) servants of the Beneficent are they who walk upon the earth modestly, and when the foolish ones address them answer: "Peace";

64. And who spend the night before their Lord, prostrate and standing,

65. And who say: "Our Lord! Avert from us the doom of hell"; the doom of it is anguish;

66. It is wretched as abode and station;

67. And those who, when they spend, are neither prodigal nor grudging; and there is ever a firm station between the two;

68. And those who do not cry to any other god along with God, nor take the life which God has forbidden except in (course of) justice, nor commit adultery—and whoever does this shall pay the penalty;

69. The doom will be doubled for him on the day of resurrection, and he will abide there disdained forever;

70. Except him who repents and believes and does righteous work; as for such, God will change their evil deeds to good deeds. God is ever forgiving, merciful.

71. And whoever repents and does good, he repents toward God with true repentance—

72. And those who will not witness vanity, but when they pass near senseless play, pass by with dignity.

73. And those who, when they are reminded of the revelations of their Lord, do not fall deaf and blind at it.

3. I.e. the two kinds of water on the earth [Pickthall's note].
4. See Q 22:47; 32:5, and 70:4 [Pickthall's note].

74. And who say: "Our Lord! Grant us comfort of our wives and of our offspring, and make us models for (all) those who ward off (evil)."
75. They will be awarded the high place because they were steadfast, and they will meet there with welcome and the word of peace,
76. Abiding there for ever. Happy is it as abode and station!
77. Say (O Muḥammad, to the disbelievers): "My Lord would not concern himself with you but for your prayer. But now you have denied (the truth), therefore there will be judgment."

## Sūra 26

*Al-Shuʿarāʾ*, "The Poets," takes its title from verses 224ff., where the difference between poets and a prophet is tersely pointed out; poets being those who say what they do not mean, while a prophet always practices what he preaches. The pagan Arabs and their poets believed the poetic inspiration to be the work of jinn.

The story of a number of former prophets is here given to console the believers at a time of persecution, with the assurance that it is no new thing for a messenger of God to be persecuted, but that the persecutors always suffer in the end. It shows also that all the messengers of God came with the same message.

It belongs to the middle group of Meccan sūras, with the exception of verses 224–227, which were revealed at Medina.

## The Poets

*Revealed at Mecca*

In the name of God, the beneficent, the merciful.

1. Ṭā. Sīn. Mīm.[1]
2. These are revelations of the scripture that makes plain.
3. It may be that you torment yourself (O Muḥammad) because they do not believe.
4. If We will, We can send down on them from the sky a sign so that their necks would remain bowed before it.
5. There never comes to them a fresh reminder from the Beneficent one, but they turn away from it.
6. Now they have denied (the truth); but there will come to them tidings of that at which they used to scoff.
7. Have they not seen the earth, how much of every fruitful kind We make to grow in it?
8. In this is indeed a sign; yet most of them are not believers.
9. Your Lord! He is indeed the mighty, the merciful.
10. And when your Lord called Moses, saying: "Go to the wrongdoing people,
11. "The people of Pharaoh. Will they not ward off (evil)?"
12. He said: "My Lord! I fear that they will deny me.

1. See Q 2:1, footnote [Pickthall's note].

13. "And I shall be embarrassed, and my tongue will not speak plainly, therefore send for Aaron (to help me).
14. "And they have a crime against me, so I fear that they will kill me."
15. "No," He said: "So you two go with Our tokens. We shall be with you, hearing.
16. "And come together to Pharaoh and say: 'We bear a message of the Lord of the Worlds,
17. "'(Saying): Let the Children of Israel go with us.'"
18. (Pharaoh) said (to Moses): "Did we not rear you among us as a child? And you dwelled many years of your life among us,
19. "And you did your deed which you did, and you were one of the ingrates."
20. He said: "I did it then, when I was of those who are astray.
21. "Then I fled from you when I feared you, and my Lord granted me a command and appointed me (of the number) of those sent (by Him).
22. "And this is the past favor with which you reproach me: that you have enslaved the Children of Israel."
23. Pharaoh said: "And what is the Lord of the worlds?"
24. (Moses) said: "Lord of the heavens and the earth and all that is between them, if you had sure belief."
25. (Pharaoh) said to those around him: "Do you not hear?"
26. He said: "Your Lord and the Lord of your fathers."
27. (Pharaoh) said: "Your messenger who has been sent to you is indeed a madman!"
28. He said: "Lord of the east and the west and all that is between them, if you did but understand."
29. (Pharaoh) said: "If you choose a god other than me, I assuredly shall place you among the prisoners."
30. He said: "Even though I show you something plain?"
31. (Pharaoh) said: "Produce it then, if you are of the truthful!"
32. Then he flung down his staff and it became a manifest serpent,
33. And he drew forth his hand and it was white to the beholders.
34. (Pharaoh) said to the chiefs about him: "This is a knowing wizard,
35. "Who would drive you out of your land by his magic. Now what do you counsel?"
36. They said: "Put him off, (him) and his brother, and send into the cities summoners
37. "Who shall bring to you every knowing wizard."
38. So the wizards were gathered together at a set time on a day appointed.
39. And it was said to the people: "Are you (also) gathering?"
40. (They said): "Yes, so that we may follow the wizards if they are the winners."
41. And when the wizards came they said to Pharaoh: "Will there be a reward for us if we are the winners?"
42. He said: "Yes, and you will then be of those brought near (to me)."
43. Moses said to them: "Throw what you are going to throw!"
44. Then they threw down their cords and their staves and said: "By Pharaoh's might, we are the winners."
45. Then Moses threw his staff and it swallowed that which they did falsely show.
46. And the wizards were flung prostrate,

47. Crying: "We believe in the Lord of the worlds,
48. "The Lord of Moses and Aaron."
49. (Pharaoh) said: "You put your faith in him before I give you leave. He doubtless is your chief who taught you magic! But you shall come to know. I will cut off your hands and your feet alternately, and I will crucify you every one."
50. They said: "It is no hurt, for to our Lord we shall return.
51. "We ardently hope that our Lord will forgive us our sins because we are the first of the believers."
52. And We inspired Moses, saying: "Take away My slaves by night, for you will be pursued."
53. Then Pharaoh sent into the cities summoners,
54. (Who said): "These are but a little band,
55. "And they are offenders against us.
56. "But we are a ready host."
57. Thus did We take them away from gardens and watersprings,
58. And treasures and a fair estate.
59. Thus (were those things taken from them) and We caused the Children of Israel to inherit them.
60. And they overtook them at sunrise.
61. And when the two hosts saw each other, those with Moses said: "We are caught,"
62. He said: "No, for my Lord is with me. He will guide me."
63. Then We inspired Moses, saying: "Smite the sea with your staff." And it parted, and each part was as a vast mountain.
64. Then We brought the others near to that place.
65. And We saved Moses and those with him, every one;
66. And We drowned the others.
67. In this is indeed a sign, yet most of them are not believers.
68. Your Lord! He is indeed the mighty, the merciful.
69. Recite to them the story of Abraham:
70. When he said to his father and his folk: "What do you worship?"
71. They said: "We worship idols, and are ever devoted to them."
72. He said: "Do they hear you when you cry?
73. "Or do they benefit or harm you?"
74. They said: "No, but we found our fathers acting in this way."
75. He said: "See now that which you worship,
76. "You and your forefathers!
77. "They are (all) an enemy to me, save the Lord of the worlds,
78. "Who created me, and He guides me,
79. "And Who feeds me and waters me.
80. "And when I sicken, then He heals me,
81. "And Who causes me to die, then gives me life (again),
82. "And Who, I ardently hope, will forgive me my sin on the day of judgment.
83. "My Lord! Grant me wisdom and unite me to the righteous.
84. "And give me a good reputation in later generations.
85. "And place me among the inheritors of the garden of delight,
86. "And forgive my father. He is of those who err.
87. "And do not abase me on the day when they are raised,
88. "The day when wealth and sons do not avail (any man)

89. "Except him who brings to God a whole heart.
90. "And the garden will be brought near for those who ward off (evil).
91. "And hell will appear plainly to the erring.
92. "And it will be said to them: 'Where is (all) that you used to worship
93. "'Instead of God? Can they help you or help themselves?'
94. "Then will they be hurled into it, they and the seducers
95. "And the hosts of Iblīs, together.
96. "And they will say, when they are quarreling there:
97. "'By God, of a truth we were in error manifest
98. "'When we made you equal with the Lord of the worlds.
99. "'It was but the guilty who misled us.
100. "'Now we have no intercessors
101. "'Nor any loving friend.
102. "'Oh, that we had another turn (on earth), that we might be of the believers!'"
103. In this is indeed a sign, yet most of them are not believers!
104. Your Lord! He is indeed the mighty, the merciful.
105. Noah's people denied the messengers (of God),
106. When their brother Noah said to them: "Will you not ward off (evil)?
107. "I am a faithful messenger to you,
108. "So keep your duty to God, and obey me.
109. "And I ask of you no wage for it; my wage is the concern only of the Lord of the worlds.
110. "So keep your duty to God, and obey me."
111. They said: "Shall we put faith in you, when the lowest (of the people) follow you?"
112. He said: "And what knowledge have I of what they may have been doing (in the past)?
113. "Their reckoning is my Lord's concern, if you but knew;
114. "And I am not (here) to repulse believers.
115. "I am only a plain warner."
116. They said: "If you do not cease, O Noah, you will surely be among those stoned (to death)."
117. He said: "My Lord! My own folk deny me.
118. "Therefore judge between us, a (conclusive) judgment, and save me and those believers who are with me."
119. And We saved him and those with him in the laden ship.
120. Then afterward We drowned the others.
121. In this is a sign, yet most of them are not believers.
122. Your Lord, He is indeed the mighty, the merciful.
123. (The tribe of) 'Ād denied the messengers (of God),
124. When their brother Hūd said to them: "Will you not ward off (evil)?
125. "I am a faithful messenger to you,
126. "So keep your duty to God and obey me.
127. "And I ask of you no wage for it; my wage is the concern only of the Lord of the worlds.
128. "Do you build on every high place a monument for vain delight?
129. "And do you seek out strongholds, that you may last for ever?
130. "And if you seize by force, do you seize as tyrants?
131. "Rather keep your duty to God, and obey me.

132. "Keep your duty toward Him who has aided you with (the good things) that you know,
133. "Has aided you with cattle and sons
134. "And gardens and watersprings.
135. "I fear for you the retribution of an awful day."
136. They said: "It is all one to us whether you preach or are not of those who preach;
137. "This is but a fable of the men of old,
138. "And we shall not be doomed."
139. And they denied him; therefore We destroyed them. In this is a sign, yet most of them are not believers.
140. And your Lord, He is indeed the mighty, the merciful.
141. (The tribe of) Thamūd denied the messengers (of God)
142. When their brother Ṣāliḥ said to them: "Will you not ward off (evil)?
143. "I am a faithful messenger to you,
144. "So keep your duty to God and obey me.
145. "And I ask of you no wage for it; my wage is the concern only of the Lord of the worlds.
146. "Will you be left secure in that which is here before us,
147. "In gardens and watersprings
148. "And tilled fields and heavy-sheathed palm trees,
149. "Though you hew out dwellings in the mountain, being skillful?
150. "Therefore keep your duty to God and obey me,
151. "And do not obey the command of the prodigal,
152. "Who spread corruption on the earth, and do not reform."
153. They said: "You are but one of the bewitched;
154. "You are but a mortal like us. So bring some sign if you are of the truthful."
155. He said: "(Behold) this she camel. She has the right to drink (at the well), and you have the right to drink, (each) on an appointed day.
156. "And do not touch her with ill for fear that there comes on you the retribution of an awful day."
157. But they hamstrung her, and then were penitent.
158. So the retribution came on them. In this is a sign, yet most of them are not believers.
159. Your Lord! He is indeed the mighty, the merciful.
160. The people of Lot denied the messengers (of God),
161. When their brother Lot said to them: "Will you not ward off (evil)?
162. "I am a faithful messenger to you,
163. "So keep your duty to God and obey me.
164. "And I ask of you no wage for it; my wage is the concern only of the Lord of the worlds.
165. "What! Of all creatures do you come to the males,
166. "And leave the wives your Lord created for you? No, but you are obstinate people."
167. They said: "If you do not cease, O Lot, you will soon be among the outcast."
168. He said: "I am in truth among those who hate your conduct.
169. "My Lord! Save me and my household from what they do."
170. So We saved him and his household, every one,
171. Except an old woman among those who stayed behind.

172. Then afterward We destroyed the others.

173. And We rained on them a rain. And dreadful is the rain of those who have been warned.

174. In this is a sign, yet most of them are not believers.

175. And your Lord, He is indeed the mighty, the merciful.

176. The dwellers in the wood (of Midian) denied the messengers (of God),

177. When Shu'ayb said to them: "Will you not ward off (evil)?

178. "I am a faithful messenger to you,

179. "So keep your duty to God and obey me.

180. "And I ask of you no wage for it; my wage is the concern only of the Lord of the worlds.

181. "Give full measure, and be not of those who give less (than the due).

182. "And weigh with the true balance.

183. "Do not wrong mankind in their goods, and do not evil, making mischief, on the earth.

184. "And keep your duty to Him Who created you and the generations of the men of old."

185. They said: "You are but one of the bewitched;

186. "You are but a mortal like us, and we deem you of the liars.

187. "Then make fragments of the heaven fall upon us, if you are of the truthful."

188. He said: "My Lord is best aware of what you do."

189. But they denied him, so there came on them the retribution of the day of gloom. It was the retribution of an awful day.

190. In this is indeed a sign; yet most of them are not believers.

191. Your Lord! He is indeed the mighty, the merciful.

192. And it is a revelation of the Lord of the worlds,

193. Which the true spirit has brought down

194. Upon your heart, that you may be (one) of the warners,

195. In plain Arabic speech.

196. It is in the scriptures of the men of old.

197. Is it not a sign for them that the learned men of the Children of Israel[2] know it?

198. And if We had revealed it to one of any other nation than the Arabs,

199. And he had read it to them, they would not have believed in it.

200. Thus do We make it traverse the hearts of the guilty.

201. They will not believe in it until they behold the painful doom,

202. So that it will come upon them suddenly, when they perceive not.

203. Then they will say: "Are we to be reprieved?"

204. Would they (now) hasten on Our doom?

205. Have you then seen, if We make them content for (long) years,

206. And then comes that which they were promised,

207. (How) that with which they were contented avails them not?

208. And We destroyed no township unless it had its warners

209. For reminder, for We never were oppressors.

210. The devils did not bring it down.

211. It is not fitting for them, nor is it in their power,

212. They are banished from the hearing.

2. The Jews knew, from their scripture, that a prophet had been promised to the Arabs [Pickthall's note]. See perhaps Deuteronomy 18:18–19.

213. Therefore do not invoke with God another god, for fear that you be one of the doomed.

214. And warn your tribe of near kindred,

215. And lower your wing (in kindness) to those believers who follow you.

216. And if they (your kinsfolk) disobey you, say: "I am innocent of what they do."

217. And put your trust in the mighty, the merciful.

218. Who sees you when you stand up (to pray)

219. And (sees) your abasement among those who fall prostrate (in worship).

220. He, only He, is the hearer, the knower.

221. Shall I inform you upon whom the devils descend?

222. They descend on every sinful, false one.

223. They listen eagerly, but most of them are liars.

224. As for poets, the erring follow them.

225. Have you not seen how they stray in every valley,

226. And how they say that which they do not?

227. Except those who believe and do good works, and remember God much, and vindicate themselves after they have been wronged. Those who do wrong will come to know by what a (great) reverse they will be overturned!

## Sūra 27

*Al-Naml*, "The Ants," takes its name from the ant mentioned in verse 18. Some commentators, objecting to the miraculous, seek to explain the ants, in the story of Solomon, as an old Arab tribe, the birds as cavalry, Hudhud (the hoopoe) as a man's name, and the jinn as foreign troops.

It belongs to the middle group of Meccan sūras.

# The Ants

*Revealed at Mecca*

In the name of God, the beneficent, the merciful.

1. Tā. Sīn.[1] These are revelations of the Qur'ān and a scripture that makes plain;

2. A guidance and good tidings for believers

3. Who establish worship and pay the poor tax and are sure of the hereafter.

4. As for those who do not believe in the hereafter, We have made their works seem attractive to them so that they are all astray.

5. Those are they for whom is the worst of punishment, and in the hereafter they will be the greatest losers.

6. As for you (Muḥammad), you receive the Qur'ān from the presence of one wise, aware.

7. (Remember) when Moses said to his household: "I spy a far-off fire; I will bring you tidings from there, or bring to you a borrowed flame that you may warm yourselves."

1. See Q 2:1, footnote [Pickthall's note].

8. But when he reached it, he was called, saying: "Blessed is whoever is in the fire and whoever is round about it! And glorified be God, the Lord of the worlds!

9. "O Moses! It is I, God, the mighty, the wise.

10. "And throw down your staff!" But when he saw it writhing as if it were a demon, he turned to flee headlong; (but it was said to him): "O Moses! Fear not! The emissaries do not fear in My presence,

11. "Except him who has done wrong and afterward has changed evil for good.[2] I am forgiving, merciful.

12. "And put your hand into the bosom of your robe, it will come forth white but unhurt. (This will be one) among nine signs to Pharaoh and his people. They were ever evil-living folk."

13. But when Our signs came to them, plain to see, they said: "This is mere magic,"

14. And they denied them, though their souls acknowledged them, for spite and arrogance. Then see the nature of the consequence for the wrongdoers!

15. And We gave knowledge to David and Solomon, and they said: "Praise be to God, Who has preferred us above many of His believing servants!"

16. And Solomon was David's heir. And he said: "O mankind! We have been taught the language of birds, and have been given (abundance) of all things. This surely is evident favor."

17. And there were gathered together to Solomon his armies of the jinn and humankind, and of the birds, and they were set in battle order;

18. Until, when they reached the Valley of the Ants, an ant exclaimed: "O ants! Enter your dwellings for fear that Solomon and his armies crush you, unperceiving."

19. And (Solomon) smiled, laughing at her speech, and said: "My Lord, arouse me to be thankful for Your favor with which You have favored me and my parents, and to do good that shall be pleasing to You, and include me in (the number of) Your righteous servants."

20. And he sought among the birds and said: "How is it that I do not see the hoopoe, or is he among the absent?

21. "I will punish him with hard punishment or I will slay him, or he shall bring me a plain excuse."

22. But he was not long in coming, and he said: "I have found out (a thing) that you do not apprehend, and I come to you from Sheba with sure tidings.

23. "I found a woman ruling over them, and she has been given (abundance) of all things, and hers is a mighty throne.

24. "I found her and her people worshipping the sun instead of God; and Satan makes their works fair-seeming to them, and debars them from the way (of truth), so that they do not go aright;

25. "So that they do not worship God, Who brings forth the hidden in the heavens and the earth, and knows what you hide and what you proclaim,

26. "God; there is no god but Him, the Lord of the tremendous throne."

27. (Solomon) said: "We shall see whether you speak truth or whether you are of the liars.

2. Moses had been guilty of a crime in Egypt [Pickthall's note]. See Q 26:19–21; Moses killed an Egyptian who was beating a Hebrew (Q 28:15).

28. "Go with this my letter and throw it down to them; then turn away and see what (answer) they return."

29. (The Queen of Sheba) said (when she received the letter): "O leaders! There has been thrown to me a noble letter.

30. "It is from Solomon, and it is: 'In the name of God, the beneficent, the merciful;

31. "'Do not exalt yourselves against me, but come to me as those who surrender.'"

32. She said: "O leaders! Pronounce for me in my case. I decide no case until you are present with me."

33. They said: "We are lords of might and lords of great prowess, but it is for you to command; so consider what you will command."

34. She said: "Kings, when they enter a township, ruin it and make the honor of its people shame. Thus will they do.

35. "I am going to send a present to them, and to see with what (answer) the messengers return."

36. So when (the envoy) came to Solomon, (the King) said: "What! Would you help me with wealth? But that which God has given me is better than that which He has given you. No it is you (and not I) who exult in your gift.

37. "Return to them. We shall come to them with hosts that they cannot resist, and we shall drive them out from there with shame, and they will be abased."

38. He said: "O chiefs! Which of you will bring me her throne before they come to me, surrendering?"

39. An *'ifrīt*[3] said: "I will bring it to you before you can rise from your place. I am strong and trusty for such work."

40. One who had some knowledge of the scripture said: "I will bring it to you before your gaze returns to you." And when he saw it set in his presence, (Solomon) said: "This is of the bounty of my Lord, that He may try me whether I give thanks or am ungrateful. Whoever gives thanks he only gives thanks for (the good of) his own soul; and whoever is ungrateful (is ungrateful only to his own soul's hurt). For my Lord is absolute in independence, bountiful."

41. He said: "Disguise her throne for her that we may see whether she will go aright or be of those not rightly guided."

42. So, when she came, it was said (to her): "Is your throne like this?" She said: "(It is) as though it were the very one." And (Solomon said): "We were given the knowledge before her and we had surrendered (to God).

43. "And (all) that she used to worship instead of God hindered her, for she came of disbelieving people."

44. It was said to her: "Enter the hall." And when she saw it she deemed it a pool and bared her legs. (Solomon) said: "It is a hall, made smooth, of glass." She said: "My Lord! I have wronged myself, and I surrender with Solomon to God, the Lord of the worlds."[4]

45. And We sent to Thamūd their brother Ṣāliḥ, saying: "Worship God." And they (then) became two parties quarreling.

46. He said: "O my people! Why will you hasten on the evil rather than the good? Why will you not ask pardon of God, that you may receive mercy."

3. A class of jinn.
4. Muslim commentators understand these verses as describing Solomon's tests of Bilqīs, the Queen of Sheba.

47. They said: "We predict evil of you and those with you." He said: "Your evil prediction is with God. No, but you are people that are being tested."

48. And there were in the city nine persons who made mischief in the land and did not reform.

49. They said: "Swear one to another by God that we will attack him and his household by night, and afterward we will surely say to his friend: 'We did not witness the destruction of his household. We are truthtellers.'"

50. So they plotted a plot and We plotted a plot, while they did not perceive.

51. Then see the nature of the consequence of their plotting, for We destroyed them and their people, every one.

52. See, yonder are their dwellings empty and in ruins because they did wrong. In this is indeed a sign for a people who have knowledge.

53. And we saved those who believed and used to ward off (evil).

54. And Lot! when he said to his folk: "Will you commit abomination knowingly?

55. "Must you lust after men instead of women? No, but you are people who act senselessly."

56. But the answer of his people was nothing but that they said: "Expel the household of Lot from your township, for they are people who would keep clean!"

57. Then We saved him and his household except his wife; We destined her to be of those who stayed behind.

58. And We rained a rain upon them. Dreadful is the rain of those who have been warned.

59. Say (O Muḥammad): "Praise be to God, and peace be on His servants whom He has chosen!" Is God best, or (all) that you ascribe as partners (to Him)?

60. Is not He (best) Who created the heavens and the earth, and sends down for you water from the sky with which We cause to spring forth joyous orchards, whose trees it never has been yours to cause to grow. Is there any God beside God? No, but they are people who ascribe equals (to Him)!

61. Is not He (best) who made the earth a fixed abode, and placed rivers in the folds of it, and placed firm hills in it, and has set a barrier between the two seas? Is there any god beside God? No, but most of them know not!

62. Is not He (best) who answers the wronged one when he cries to Him and removes the evil, and has made you viceroys of the earth? Is there any god beside God? Little do they reflect!

63. Is not He (best) who guides you in the darkness of the land and the sea, He who sends the winds as heralds of His mercy? Is there any god beside God? High exalted be God from all that they ascribe as partner (to Him)!

64. Is not He (best) who produces creation, then reproduces it, and Who provides for you from the heaven and the earth? Is there any god beside God? Say: "Bring your proof, if you are truthful!"

65. Say (O Muḥammad): "None in the heavens and the earth knows the Unseen except God; and they do not know when they will be raised (again)."

66. No, but does their knowledge reach to the hereafter? No, for they are in doubt concerning it. No, for they cannot see it.

67. Yet those who disbelieve say: "When we have become dust like our fathers, shall we be brought forth (again)?

68. "We were promised this, we and our fathers. (All) this is nothing but fables of the men of old."

69. Say (to them, O Muḥammad): "Travel in the land and see the nature of the sequel for the guilty!

70. "And do not grieve for them, nor be in distress because of what they plot (against you)."

71. And they say: "When (will) this promise (be fulfilled), if you are truthful?"

72. Say: "It may be that a part of that which you would hasten on is close behind you."

73. Your Lord is full of bounty for mankind, but most of them do not give thanks.

74. Your Lord knows surely all that their bosoms hide, and all that they proclaim.

75. And there is nothing hidden in the heaven or the earth but it is in a clear record.

76. This Qur'ān narrates to the Children of Israel most of that concerning which they differ.

77. It is a guidance and a mercy for believers.

78. Your Lord will judge between them of His wisdom, and He is the mighty, the wise.

79. Therefore (O Muḥammad) put your trust in God, for you (stand) on the plain truth.

80. You cannot make the dead to hear, nor can you make the deaf to hear the call when they have turned to flee;

81. Nor can you lead the blind out of their error. You can make none to hear, except those who believe Our revelations and who have surrendered.

82. And when the word is fulfilled concerning them, We shall bring forth a beast of the earth to speak to them because mankind did not have faith in Our revelations.

83. And (remind them of) the day when We shall gather out of every nation a host of those who denied Our revelations, and they will be set in array;

84. Until, when they come (before their Lord), He will say: "Did you deny My revelations when you could not compass them in knowledge, or what was it that you did?"

85. And the word will be fulfilled concerning them because they have done wrong, and they will not speak.

86. Have they not seen how We have appointed the night that they may rest in it, and the day sight-giving? In that are signs for a people who believe.

87. And (remind them of) the day when the trumpet will be blown, and all who are in the heavens and the earth will start in fear, except him whom God wills. And all come to Him, humbled.

88. And you see the hills you think to be solid flying with the flight of clouds: the doing of God who perfects all things. He is informed of what you do.

89. Whoever brings a good deed will have better than its worth; and such are safe from fear that day.

90. And whoever brings an ill deed, such will be flung down on their faces in the fire. Are you rewarded anything but what you did?

91. (Say): "I (Muḥammad) am commanded only to serve the Lord of this land which He has hallowed, and to Whom all things belong. And I am commanded to be of those who surrender (to Him),

92. "And to recite the Qur'ān." And whoever goes right, goes right only for (the good of) his own soul; and as for him who goes astray—(To him) say: "I am only a warner."

93. And say: "Praise be to God who will show you His signs so that you shall know them. And your Lord is not unaware of what you (mortals) do."

## Sūra 28

*Al-Qaṣaṣ*, "The Story," takes its name from a word in verse 25. The name is moreover justified by the nature of the sūra, which consists mostly of the story of Moses, his early struggles and ultimate triumph, revealed at a time when the Prophet's case seemed desperate. It is one of the last Meccan sūras. Some Arabic writers even say that it was revealed during the *hijra*, while others are of opinion that verse 85 only was revealed during the flight.

A late Meccan sūra, except verse 85 revealed during the Prophet's flight from Mecca to Medina, and verses 52–55 revealed at Medina.[1]

## The Story

*Revealed at Mecca*

In the name of God, the beneficent, the merciful.

1. Ṭā. Sīn. Mīm.[2]

2. These are revelations of the scripture that makes plain.

3. We narrate to you (somewhat) of the story of Moses and Pharaoh with truth, for people who believe.

4. Pharaoh exalted himself on the earth and made its people factions. A tribe among them he oppressed, killing their sons and sparing their women. He was of those who work corruption.

5. And We desired to show favor to those who were oppressed on the earth, and to make them examples and to make them the inheritors,

6. And to establish them on the earth, and to show Pharaoh and Hāmān and their hosts what they feared from them.

7. And We inspired the mother of Moses, saying: "Suckle him and, when you fear for him, then cast him into the river and do not fear nor grieve. We shall bring him back to you and shall make him (one) of Our messengers."

8. And the family of Pharaoh took him up, that he might become for them an enemy and a sorrow. Pharaoh and Hāmān and their hosts were ever sinning.

9. And the wife of Pharaoh said: "(He will be) a consolation for me and for you. Do not kill him. Perhaps he may be of use to us, or we may choose him for a son." And they did not perceive.

1. Jalāl al-Din Muḥammad b. Aḥmad al-Maḥallī and Jalāl al-Dīn al-Suyūṭī, *Tafsīr al-Jalālayn* (ca. 1505). [Pickthall's note].
2. See Q 2:1, footnote [Pickthall's note].

10. And the heart of the mother of Moses became void, and she would have betrayed him if We had not fortified her heart, that she might be of the believers.

11. And she said to his sister: "Trace him." So she observed him from afar, and they did not perceive.

12. And We had before forbidden fostermothers for him, so she said: "Shall I show you a household who will rear him for you and take care of him?"

13. So We restored him to his mother that she might be comforted and not grieve, and that she might know that the promise of God is true. But most of them know not.

14. And when he reached his full strength and was ripe, We gave him wisdom and knowledge. Thus do We reward the good.

15. And he entered the city at a time of carelessness of its people, and he found there two men fighting, one of his own faction, and the other of his enemies; and he who was of his faction asked him for help against him who was of his enemies. So Moses struck him with his fist and killed him. He said: "This is of the devil's doing. He is an enemy, a mere misleader."

16. He said: "My Lord! I have wronged my soul, so forgive me." Then He forgave him. He is the forgiving, the merciful.

17. He said: "My Lord! Because You have favored me, I will never again be a supporter of the guilty."

18. And morning found him in the city, fearing, vigilant, when behold! he who had appealed to him the day before cried out to him for help. Moses said to him: "You are indeed a mere hothead."

19. And when he would have fallen upon the man who was an enemy to them both, he said: "O Moses! Would you kill me as you killed a person yesterday. You would be nothing but a tyrant in the land, you would not be of the reformers."

20. And a man came from the farthest part of the city, running. He said: "O Moses! The chiefs take counsel against you to slay you; therefore escape. I am of those who give you good advice."

21. So he escaped from there, fearing, vigilant. He said: "My Lord! Deliver me from the wrongdoing people."

22. And when he turned his face toward Midian, he said: "Perhaps my Lord will guide me in the right road."

23. And when he came to the water of Midian he found there a whole tribe of men, watering. And he found apart from them two women keeping back (their flocks). He said: "What ails you?" The two said: "We cannot give (our flocks) to drink until the shepherds return from the water; and our father is a very old man."

24. So he watered (their flock) for them. Then he turned aside into the shade, and said: "My Lord! I am needy of whatever good You send down for me."

25. Then there came to him one of the two women, walking shyly. She said: "My father bids you, that he may reward you with a payment because you watered (the flock) for us." Then, when he came to him and told him the (whole) story, he said: "Fear not! You have escaped from the wrongdoing people."

26. One of the two women said: "O my father! Hire him! For the best (man) that you can hire is the strong, the trustworthy."

27. He said: "I would willingly marry you to one of these two daughters of mine on condition that you hire yourself to me for (the term of) eight pilgrimages. Then if you complete ten it will be of your own accord, for I would not make it hard for you. God willing, you will find me of the righteous."

28. He said: "That (is settled) between you and me. Whichever of the two terms I fulfill, there will be no injustice to me, and God is surety over what we say."

29. Then, when Moses had fulfilled the term, and was traveling with the people of his house, he saw in the distance a fire and said to his family: "Stay (here). I see in the distance a fire; perhaps I shall bring you tidings from there, or a brand from the fire that you may warm yourselves."

30. And when he reached it, he was called from the right side of the valley in the blessed field, from the tree: "O Moses! I, even I, am God, the Lord of the worlds;

31. "Throw down your staff." And when he saw it writhing as if it were a demon, he turned to flee headlong, (and it was said to him): "O Moses! Draw near and fear not. You are of those who are secure.

32. "Thrust your hand into the bosom of your robe, it will come forth white without hurt. And guard your heart from fear. Then these shall be two proofs from your Lord to Pharaoh and his chiefs. They are evil-living people."

33. He said: "My Lord! I killed a man among them and I fear that they will kill me.

34. "My brother Aaron is more eloquent than me in speech. Therefore send him with me as a helper to confirm me. I fear that they will call me a liar."

35. He said: "We will strengthen your arm with your brother, and We will give to you both power so that they cannot reach you for Our signs. You two, and those who follow you, will be the winners."

36. But when Moses came to them with Our clear signs, they said: "This is nothing but invented magic. We never heard of this among our fathers of old."

37. And Moses said: "My Lord is best aware of him who brings guidance from His presence, and whose will be the sequel of the home (of bliss). Wrongdoers will not be successful."

38. And Pharaoh said: "O chiefs! I do not know that you have a god other than me, so kindle for me (a fire), O Hāmān, to bake the mud; and set up for me a lofty tower in order that I may survey the God of Moses; and I consider him of the liars."

39. And he and his hosts were haughty in the land without right, and deemed that they would never be brought back to Us.

40. Therefore We seized him and his hosts, and abandoned them to the sea: Behold the nature of the consequence for evildoers!

41. And We made them leaders that invite to the fire, and on the day of resurrection they will not be helped.

42. And We made a curse to follow them in this world, and on the day of resurrection they will be among the hateful.

43. And We gave the scripture to Moses after We had destroyed the generations of old: clear testimonies for mankind, and a guidance and a mercy, that perhaps they might reflect.

44. And you (Muḥammad) were not on the western side (of the Mount) when We expounded to Moses the commandment, and you were not among those present;

45. But We brought forth generations, and their lives dragged on for them. And you were not a dweller in Midian, reciting to them Our revelations, but We kept sending (messengers to men).

46. And you were not beside the Mount when We called; but (the knowledge of it is) a mercy from your Lord that you may warn a people to whom no warner came before you, that perhaps they may give heed.

47. Otherwise, if disaster should afflict them because of what their own hands have sent before (them), they might say: "Our Lord! Why did You not send a messenger to us, that we might have followed Your revelations and been of the believers?"

48. But when there came to them the truth from Our presence, they said: "Why is he not given the like of what was given to Moses?" Did they not disbelieve in what was given to Moses of old? They say: "Two magics[3] that support each other"; and they say: "In both we are disbelievers."

49. Say (to them, O Muḥammad): "Then bring a scripture from the presence of God that gives clearer guidance than these two (that) I may follow it, if you are truthful."

50. And if they do not answer you, then know that what they follow is their lusts. And who goes farther astray than he who follows his lust without guidance from God? God does not guide wrongdoing folk.

51. And now We have caused the word to reach them, that perhaps they may give heed.

52. Those to whom We gave the scripture before it, they believe in it,

53. And when it is recited to them, they say: "We believe in it. It is the truth from our Lord. Even before it, we were of those who surrender (to Him)."

54. These will be given their reward twice over, because they are steadfast and repel evil with good, and spend of that with which We have provided them,

55. And when they hear vanity they withdraw from it and say: "To us our works and to you your works. Peace be to you! We do not desire the ignorant."

56. You (O Muḥammad) do not guide whom you love, but God guides whom He will. And He is best aware of those who walk aright.

57. And they say: "If we were to follow the guidance with you we should be torn out of our land." Have We not established for them a sure sanctuary,[4] to which the produce of all things is brought (in trade), a provision from Our presence? But most of them know not.

58. And how many a community have We destroyed that was thankless for its means of livelihood! And yonder are their dwellings, which have not been inhabited after them except a little. And We, even We, were the inheritors.

59. And your Lord never destroyed the townships, until He had raised up in their mother(-town) a messenger reciting to them Our revelations. And We never destroyed the townships unless their folk were evildoers.

3. I.e. the scripture of Moses and the Qur'ān [Pickthall's note].
4. The sacred territory of Mecca [Pickthall's note].

60. And whatever you have been given is a comfort of the life of the world and an ornament of it; and that which God has is better and more lasting. Have you then no sense?

61. Is he whom We have promised a fair promise which he will find (true) like him whom We allowed to enjoy awhile the comfort of the life of the world, then on the day of resurrection he will be of those summoned?

62. On the day when He will call to them and say: "Where are My partners whom you imagined?"

63. Those concerning whom the word will have come true will say: "Our Lord! These are they whom we led astray. We led them astray even as we ourselves were astray. We declare our innocence before You: us they never worshipped."

64. And it will be said: "Cry to your (so-called) partners (of God)." And they will cry to them, and they will give no answer to them, and they will see the doom. Ah, if they had but been guided!

65. And on the day when He will call to them and say: "What answer did you give to the messengers?"

66. On that day (all) tidings will be dimmed for them, nor will they ask one of another,

67. But as for him who shall repent and believe and do right, he perhaps may be one of the successful.

68. Your Lord brings to pass what He wills and chooses. They never have any choice. Glorified be God and exalted above all that they associate (with Him)!

69. And your Lord knows what their breasts conceal, and what they publish.

70. And He is God; there is no god but Him. His is all praise in the former and the latter (state), and His is the command, and to Him you will be brought back.

71. Say: "Have you thought, if God made night everlasting for you until the day of resurrection, who is a god beside God who could bring you light? Will you not then hear?"

72. Say: "Have you thought, if God made day everlasting for you until the day of resurrection, who is a god beside God who could bring you night in which you rest? Will you not then see?"

73. Of His mercy has He appointed for you night and day, that in that you may rest, and that you may seek His bounty, and that perhaps you may be thankful.

74. And on the day when He shall call to them and say: "Where are My partners whom you pretended?"

75. And We shall take out from every nation a witness and We shall say: "Bring your proof." Then they will know that God has the truth, and all that they invented will have failed them.

76. Now Korah was of Moses' people, but he oppressed them; and We gave him so much treasure that the stores of it would have been a burden for a troop of mighty men. When his own people said to him: "Do not exult; God does not love the exultant;

77. "But seek the abode of the hereafter in that which God has given you and do not neglect your portion of the world, and be kind even as God has been kind to you, and seek not corruption on the earth; God does not love corrupters,"

78. He said: "I have been given it only on account of knowledge I possess. "Did he not know that God had already destroyed of the generations before him men who were mightier than him in strength and greater in respect of following? The guilty are not questioned of their sins.

79. Then he went forth before his people in his pomp. Those who were desirous of the life of the world said: "Ah, would that we had the like of what has been given to Korah! He is lord of rare good fortune."

80. But those who had been given knowledge said: "Woe to you! The reward of God for him who believes and does right is better, and only the steadfast will obtain it."

81. So We caused the earth to swallow him and his dwelling-place. Then he had no host to help him against God, nor was he of those who can save themselves.

82. And morning found those who had coveted his place only yesterday crying: "Behold! God enlarges the provision for whom He will of His servants and straitens it (for whom He will). If God had not been gracious to us He would have caused it to swallow us (also). Behold! the disbelievers never prosper."

83. As for that abode of the hereafter We assign it to those who do not seek oppression on the earth, nor corruption. The sequel is for those who ward off (evil).

84. Whoever brings a good deed, he will have better than the same; while as for him who brings an ill deed, those who do ill deeds will be requited only what they did.

85. He Who has given you the Qur'ān for a law will surely bring you home again.[5] Say: "My Lord is best aware of him who brings guidance and him who is in error manifest."

86. You had no hope that the scripture would be inspired in you; but it is a mercy from your Lord, so never be a helper to the disbelievers.

87. And do not let them divert you from the revelations of God after they have been sent down to you; but call (mankind) to your Lord, and do not be of those who ascribe partners (to Him).

88. And do not cry to any other god along with God. There is no god but Him. Everything will perish except His countenance. His is the command, and to Him you will be brought back.

## Sūra 29

*Al-'Ankabūt*, "The Spider," takes its name from verse 41 where false beliefs are likened to the spider's web for frailty. Most of this sūra belongs to the middle or last Meccan period. Some authorities consider verses 7 and 8, others the whole latter portion of the sūra,[1] to have been revealed at Medina. It gives comfort to the Muslims in a time of persecution.

A late Meccan sūra.

5. A tradition says that this verse was revealed during the Prophet's flight from Mecca to Medina [Pickthall's note].
1. Hibat Allāh ibn Salāma [d. 1020], *Kitāb al-Nāsikh wa-l-mansūkh* [*The Book of the Abrogating and Abrogated (Verses)*] [Pickthall's note].

## The Spider

*Revealed at Mecca*

In the name of God, the beneficent, the merciful.

1. Alif. Lām. Mīm.[2]

2. Do men imagine that they will be left (at ease) because they say, "We believe," and will not be tested with affliction?

3. We tested those who were before you. Thus God knows those who are sincere, and knows those who feign.

4. Or do those who do ill deeds imagine that they can outstrip Us? Evil (for them) is that which they decide.

5. Whoever looks forward to the meeting with God (let him know that) God's reckoning is surely near, and He is the hearer, the knower.

6. And whoever strives, strives only for himself, for God is altogether independent of (His) creatures.

7. And as for those who believe and do good works, We shall remit from them their evil deeds and shall repay them the best that they did.

8. We have enjoined on man kindness to parents; but if they strive to make you join with Me that of which you have no knowledge, then do not obey them. To Me is your return and I shall tell you what you used to do.

9. And as for those who believe and do good works, We shall make them enter in among the righteous.

10. Of mankind is he who says: "We believe in God," but, if he be made to suffer for the sake of God, he mistakes the persecution of mankind for God's punishment; and then, if victory comes from your Lord, will say: "We were with you (all the while)." Is not God best aware of what is in the bosoms of (His) creatures?

11. God knows those who believe, and He knows the hypocrites.

12. Those who disbelieve say to those who believe: "Follow our way (of religion) and we will bear your sins (for you)." They cannot bear anything of their sins. They are liars.

13. But they will bear their own loads and other loads beside their own, and they will be questioned on the day of resurrection concerning that which they invented.

14. And We sent Noah (as Our messenger) to his people, and he continued with them for a thousand years less fifty years; and the flood engulfed them, for they were wrongdoers.

15. And We rescued him and those with him in the ship, and made of it a sign for the peoples.

16. And Abraham! (Remember) when he said to his people: "Serve God, and keep your duty to Him; that is better for you if you only knew.

17. "You serve instead of God only idols, and you only invent a lie. Those whom you serve instead of God own no provision for you. So seek your provision from God, and serve Him, and give thanks to Him, (for) to Him you will be brought back.

18. "But if you deny, then nations have denied before you. The messenger is only to convey (the message) plainly."

2. See Q 2:1, footnote [Pickthall's note].

19. Do they not see how God produces creation, then reproduces it? For God that is easy.

20. Say (O Muḥammad): "Travel in the land and see how He originated creation, then God brings forth the later growth. God is able to do all things.

21. "He punishes whom He will and shows mercy to whom He will, and to Him you will be turned.

22. "You cannot escape (from Him) on the earth or in the sky, and beside God there is for you no friend or helper."

23. Those who disbelieve in the revelations of God and in (their) meeting with Him, such have no hope of My mercy. For such there is a painful doom.

24. But the answer of his people was only that they said: "Kill him" or "Burn him." Then God saved him from the fire. In this are portents for people who believe.

25. He said: "You have chosen idols instead of God. The love between you is only in the life of the world. Then on the day of resurrection you will deny each other and curse each other, and your abode will be the fire, and you will have no helpers."

26. And Lot believed him, and said: "I am a fugitive to my Lord. He, only He, is the mighty, the wise."

27. And We bestowed on him Isaac and Jacob, and We established the Prophethood and the scripture among his seed, and We gave him his reward in the world, and in the hereafter he is among the righteous.

28. And Lot! (Remember) when he said to his people: "You commit lewdness such as no creature did before you.

29. "For do you not come to males, and do you not cut the road (for travelers), and do you not commit abomination in your meetings?" But the answer of his people was only that they said: "Bring God's doom upon us if you are a truthteller!"

30. He said: "My Lord! Give me victory over people who work corruption."

31. And when Our messengers brought Abraham the good news,[3] they said: "We are about to destroy the people of that township, for its people are wrongdoers."

32. He said: "Lot is there." They said: "We are best aware of who is there. We are to deliver him and his household, all save his wife, who is of those who stay behind."

33. And when Our messengers came to Lot, he was troubled upon their account, for he could not protect them; but they said: "Fear not, nor grieve! We are to deliver you and your household, (all) save your wife, who is of those who stay behind.

34. "We are about to bring down upon the people of this township a fury from the sky because they are iniquitous."

35. And of that We have left a clear sign for people who have sense.

36. And to Midian We sent Shu'ayb, their brother. He said: "O my people! Serve God, and look forward to the last day, and do not evil, making mischief, on the earth."

37. But they denied him, and the dreadful earthquake took them, and morning found them prostrate in their dwelling-place.

3. That he was to have a son [Pickthall's note].

38. And (the tribes of) 'Ād and Thamūd! (Their fate) is manifest to you from their (ruined and deserted) dwellings. Satan made their deeds seem fair to them and so debarred them from the way, though they were keen observers.

39. And Korah, Pharaoh, and Hāmān! Moses came to them with clear proofs (of God's sovereignty), but they were boastful in the land. And they were not winners (in the race).

40. So We took each one in his sin; of them was he on whom We sent a hurricane, and of them was he who was overtaken by the (awful) cry, and of them was he whom We caused the earth to swallow, and of them was he whom We drowned. It was not for God to wrong them, but they wronged themselves.

41. The likeness of those who choose other patrons than God is as the likeness of the spider when she takes to herself a house, and the frailest of all houses is the spider's house, if they but knew.

42. God knows what thing they invoke instead of Him. He is the mighty, the wise.

43. As for these similitudes, We coin them for mankind, but none will grasp their meaning except the wise.

44. God created the heavens and the earth with truth. In that there is indeed a sign for believers.

45. Recite that which has been inspired in you of the scripture, and establish worship. Worship preserves from lewdness and iniquity, but remembrance of God is more important. And God knows what you do.

46. And do not argue with the People of the Scripture unless it be in (a way) that is better, except with such of them as do wrong; and say: "We believe in that which has been revealed to us and revealed to you; our God and your God is One, and to Him we surrender."

47. In like manner We have revealed to you the scripture, and those to whom We gave the scripture before will believe in it; and of these (also)[4] there are some who believe in it. And none deny our revelations except the disbelievers.

48. And you (O Muḥammad) were not a reader of any scripture before it, nor did you write it with your right hand,[5] for then might those have doubted, who follow falsehood.

49. But it is clear revelations in the hearts of those who have been given knowledge, and none deny Our revelations except wrongdoers.

50. And they say: "Why are not signs sent down upon him from his Lord?" Say: "Signs are with God only, and I am but a plain warner."

51. Is it not enough for them that We have sent down to you the scripture which is read to them? In that is mercy, and a reminder for folk who believe.

52. Say (to them, O Muḥammad): "God suffices for witness between me and you. He knows whatever is in the heavens and the earth. And those who believe in vanity and disbelieve in God, they are the losers."

53. They bid you hasten on the doom (of God). And if a term had not been appointed, the doom would assuredly have come to them (before now). And it will come upon them suddenly when they perceive not.

4. I.e. the people of Mecca [Pickthall's note].
5. Understood as a confirmation that Muḥammad was illiterate and could not have written the Qur'ān himself.

54. They bid you hasten on the doom, when hell will encompass the disbelievers

55. On the day when the doom will overwhelm them from above them and from underneath their feet, and He will say: "Taste what you used to do!"

56. O my servants who believe! My earth is spacious. Therefore serve only Me.

57. Every soul will taste of death. Then to Us you will be returned.

58. Those who believe and do good works, them We shall house in lofty dwellings of the garden underneath which rivers flow. There they will dwell secure. How sweet the recompense of the toilers,

59. Who persevere, and put their trust in their Lord!

60. And how many an animal there is that does not bear its own provision! God provides for it and for you. He is the hearer, the knower.

61. And if you were to ask them: "Who created the heavens and the earth, and constrained the sun and the moon (to their appointed work)?" they would say: "God." How then are they turned away?

62. God makes the provision wide for whom He will of His servants, and restricts it for whom (He will). God is aware of all things.

63. And if you were to ask them: "Who causes water to come down from the sky, and therewith revives the earth after its death?" they would say: "God." Say: "Praise be to God!" But most of them have no sense.

64. This life of the world is but a pastime and a game. The home of the hereafter—that is life, if they but knew.

65. And when they mount upon the ships they pray to God, making their faith pure for Him only, but when He brings them safe to land, they ascribe partners (to Him),

66. That they may disbelieve in that which We have given them, and that they may take their ease. But they will come to know.

67. Have they not seen that We have appointed a sanctuary immune (from violence),[6] while mankind are ravaged all around them? Do they then believe in falsehood and disbelieve in the bounty of God?

68. Who does greater wrong than he who invents a lie concerning God, or denies the truth when it comes to him? Is not there a home in hell for disbelievers?

69. As for those who strive in Us, We surely guide them to Our paths, and God is with the good.

## Sūra 30

*Al-Rūm*, "The Romans," takes its name from a word in the second verse.

The armies of the Eastern Roman Empire had been defeated by the Persians in all the territories near Arabia. In the year 613 CE Jerusalem and Damascus fell, and in the following year Egypt. A Persian army invaded Anatolia and was threatening Constantinople itself in the year 615 or 616 CE (the sixth or seventh year before the *hijra*) when, according to the best authorities, this sūra was revealed at Mecca. The pagan Arabs triumphed in the news of Persian victories over the Prophet and his little band of followers, because the Christian Romans were believers in the one God, whereas the Persians were not. They

6. The territory of Mecca [Pickthall's note].

argued that the power of God could not be supreme and absolute, as the Prophet kept proclaiming it to be, since the forces of a pagan empire had been able to defeat His worshippers.

The Prophet's answer was provided for him in this grand assertion of theocracy, which shows the folly of all those who think of God as a partisan. It opens with two prophecies: that the Romans would be victorious over the Persians, and that the little persecuted company of Muslims in Arabia would have reason to rejoice, "within ten years."[1] In fact, in 624 CE the Roman armies entered purely Persian territory, and in the same year a little army of Muslims, led by the Prophet, overthrew the flower of Arab chivalry upon the field of Badr.

But the prophecies are only the prelude to a proclamation of God's universal kingdom, which is shown to be an actual sovereignty. The laws of nature are expounded as the laws of God in the physical sphere, and in the moral and political spheres mankind is informed that there are similar laws of life and death, of good and evil, action and inaction, and their consequences—laws which no one can escape by wisdom or by cunning. His mercy, like His law, surrounds all things, and the standard of His judgment is the same for all. He is not remote or indifferent, partial or capricious. Those who do good earn His favor, and those who do ill earn His wrath, no matter what may be their creed or race; and no one, by the lip profession of a creed, is able to escape His law of consequences.

It belongs to the middle group of Meccan sūras.

## The Romans

*Revealed at Mecca*

In the name of God, the beneficent, the merciful.

1. Alif. Lām. Mīm.[2]

2. The Romans have been defeated

3. In the nearer land, and they, after their defeat will be victorious

4. Within ten years—God's is the command in the former case and in the latter—and in that day believers will rejoice

5. In God's help to victory. He helps to victory whom He will. He is the mighty, the merciful.

6. It is a promise of God. God does not fail His promise, but most of mankind do not know.

7. They know only some appearance of the life of the world, and are heedless of the hereafter.

8. Have they not pondered upon themselves? God did not create the heavens and the earth, and that which is between them, except with truth and for a destined end. But truly many of mankind are disbelievers in the meeting with their Lord.

9. Have they not traveled in the land and seen the nature of the consequence for those who were before them?[3] They were stronger than these in power, and they dug the earth and built upon it more than these have built.

1. The word in the Arabic (*biḍa'*) implies a space of not less than three, and not more than nine, years [Pickthall's note].
2. See Q 2:1, footnote [Pickthall's note].
3. To those who journeyed out from Mecca, northward into Mesopotamia and Syria, or southward to the Yemen and Ḥaḍramawt, appeared the ruins of old civilizations which, tradition said, had been destroyed on account of their corruption and disobedience to the will of God [Pickthall's note].

Messengers of their own came to them with clear proofs (of God's sovereignty). Surely God did not wrong them, but they wronged themselves.

10. The evil was the consequence to those who dealt in evil, because they denied the revelations of God and made a mock of them.

11. God produces creation, then He reproduces it, then to Him you will be returned.

12. And in the day when the hour rises the unrighteous will despair.

13. There will be none to intercede for them of those whom they made equal with God. And they will reject their partners (whom they ascribed to Him).

14. In the day when the hour comes, in that day they will be sundered.

15. As for those who believed and did good works, they will be made happy in a garden.

16. But as for those who disbelieved and denied Our revelations, and denied the meeting of the hereafter, such will be brought to doom.

17. So glory be to God when you enter the night and when you enter the morning—

18. To Him be praise in the heavens and the earth!—and at the sun's decline and in the noonday.

19. He brings forth the living from the dead, and He brings forth the dead from the living, and He revives the earth after her death. And even so will you be brought forth.

20. And among His signs is this: He created you of dust, and behold you are human beings, ranging widely!

21. And among His signs is this: He created for you spouses from yourselves that you might find rest in them, and He ordained between you love and mercy. In this indeed are signs for people who reflect.

22. And among His signs is the creation of the heavens and the earth, and the difference of your languages and colors. In this indeed are signs for men of knowledge.

23. And among His signs is your slumber by night and by day, and your seeking of His bounty. In this indeed are signs for people who heed.

24. And among His signs is this: He shows you the lightning for a fear and for a hope, and sends down water from the sky, and thereby quickens the earth after her death. In this indeed are signs for people who understand.

25. And among His signs is this: The heavens and the earth stand fast by His command, and afterward, when He calls you, from the earth you will emerge.

26. To Him belongs whoever is in the heavens and the earth. All are obedient to Him.

27. He it is who produces creation, then reproduces it, and it is easier for Him. His is the sublime similitude in the heavens and in the earth. He is the mighty, the wise.

28. He coins for you a similitude of yourselves. Have you, from among those whom your right hands possess,[4] partners in the wealth We have bestowed upon you, equal with you in respect of it, so that you fear them as you fear each other (that you ascribe to Us partners out of that which We created)? Thus We display the revelations for people who have sense.

4. I.e. the slaves [Pickthall's note].

29. No, but those who do wrong follow their own lusts without knowledge. Who is able to guide him whom God has sent astray? For such there are no helpers.

30. So set your purpose (O Muḥammad) for religion as a man by nature upright—the nature (framed) of God, in which He has created man. There is no altering (the laws of) God's creation. That is the right religion, but most men know not—

31. Turning to Him (only); and be careful of your duty to Him, and establish worship, and do not be among those who ascribe partners (to Him);

32. Of those who split up their religion and became schismatics, each sect exulting in its tenets.

33. And when harm touches men they cry to their Lord, turning to Him in repentance; then, when they have tasted of His mercy, behold! some of them attribute partners to their Lord

34. So as to disbelieve in that which We have given them. (To such it is said): Enjoy yourselves awhile, but you will come to know.

35. Or have We revealed to them any warrant which speaks of that which they associate with Him?

36. And when We cause mankind to taste of mercy they rejoice in it; but if an evil thing befall them as the consequence of their own deeds, they are in despair!

37. Do they not see that God enlarges the provision for whom He will, and straightens (it for whom He will). In this indeed are signs for people who believe.

38. So give to the kinsman his due, and to the needy, and to the wayfarer. That is best for those who seek God's countenance. And such are they who are successful.

39. What you give in usury in order that it may increase on (other) people's property has no increase with God; but what you give in charity, seeking God's countenance, has increase manifold.

40. God is He who created you and then sustained you, then causes you to die, then gives life to you again. Is there any of your (so-called) partners (of God) that does anything of that? Praised and exalted be He above what they associate (with Him)!

41. Corruption appears on land and sea because of (the evil) which men's hands have done, that He may make them taste a part of what they have done, in order that they may return.

42. Say (O Muḥammad, to the disbelievers): "Travel in the land, and see the nature of the consequence for those who were before you! Most of them were idolaters."

43. So set your purpose resolutely for the right religion, before the inevitable day comes from God. On that day mankind will be sundered—

44. Whoever disbelieves must (then) bear the consequences of his disbelief, while those who do right make provision for themselves—

45. That He may reward out of His bounty those who believe and do good works. He does not love the disbelievers (in His guidance).

46. And of His signs is this: He sends herald winds to make you taste His mercy, and that the ships may sail at His command, and that you may seek His favor, and that perhaps you may be thankful.

47. We sent before you (Muḥammad) messengers to their own folk. They brought them clear proofs (of God's sovereignty). Then We took vengeance upon those who were guilty (in regard to them). To help believers is incumbent upon Us.

48. God is He who sends the winds so that they raise clouds, and spreads them along the sky as pleases Him, and causes them to break and you see the rain down-pouring from within them. And when He makes it to fall on whom He will of His servants, they rejoice;

49. Though before that, even before it was sent down upon them, they were in despair.

50. Look, therefore, at the prints of God's mercy (in creation): how He quickens the earth after her death. He is the quickener of the dead, and He is able to do all things.

51. And if We sent a wind and they beheld it yellow, they would still continue in their disbelief.

52. For you (Muḥammad) cannot make the dead to hear, nor can you make the deaf to hear the call when they have turned to flee.

53. Nor can you guide the blind out of their error. You can make none to hear except those who believe in Our revelations so that they surrender (to Him).

54. God is He who shaped you out of weakness, then appointed after weakness strength, then, after strength, appointed weakness and grey hair. He creates what He will. He is the knower, the mighty.

55. And on the day when the hour rises the guilty will vow that they tarried only an hour—thus were they ever deceived.

56. But those to whom knowledge and faith are given will say: "The truth is, you have tarried, by God's decree, until the day of resurrection. This is the day of resurrection, but you did not know."

57. In that day their excuses will not profit those who did injustice, nor will they be allowed to make amends.

58. We have coined for mankind in this Qur'ān all kinds of similitudes; and indeed if you came to them with a miracle, those who disbelieve would exclaim: "You are but tricksters!"

59. Thus does God seal the hearts of those who know not.

60. So have patience (O Muḥammad)! God's promise is the very truth, and let not those who have no certainty make you impatient.

## Sūra 31

*Luqmān* takes its name from verses 12ff., which contain mention of the wisdom of Luqmān, a sage whose memory the Arabs revered, but who is unknown to Jewish scripture. He is said to have been a Negro slave and the fables associated with his name are so like those of Aesop[1] that the usual identification seems justified. The sūra conveys assurance of success to the Muslims at a time of persecution.

It belongs to the middle or last group of Meccan sūras; except verses 27 and 28 which were revealed at Medina.

1. Legendary Greek creator of fables, believed to have been a slave (6th c. BCE).

## Luqmān

*Revealed at Mecca*

In the name of God, the beneficent, the merciful.

1. Alif. Lām. Mīm.[2]

2. These are revelations of the wise scripture,

3. A guidance and a mercy for the good,

4. Those who establish worship and pay the poor tax and have sure faith in the hereafter.

5. Such have guidance from their Lord. Such are the successful.

6. And of mankind is he who pays for mere pastime of discourse, that he may mislead from God's way without knowledge, and make it the butt of mockery. For such there is a shameful doom.

7. And when Our revelations are recited to him he turns away in his pride as if he had not heard them, as if there were a deafness in his ears. So give him tidings of a painful doom.

8. Those who believe and do good works, for them are the gardens of delight,

9. In which they will abide. It is a promise of God in truth. He is the mighty, the wise.

10. He has created the heavens without supports that you can see, and has cast into the earth firm hills, so that it does not quake with you; and He has dispersed in it all kinds of beasts. And We send down water from the sky and We cause (plants) of every goodly kind to grow in it.

11. This is the creation of God. Now show me what those (you worship) beside Him have created. No, but the wrongdoers are in manifest error!

12. And We gave Luqmān wisdom, saying: "Give thanks to God and whoever gives thanks, he gives thanks for (the good of) his soul. And whoever refuses—God is absolute, owner of praise."

13. And (remember) when Luqmān said to his son, when he was exhorting him: "O my dear son! Ascribe no partners to God. To ascribe partners (to Him) is a tremendous wrong"—

14. And We have enjoined upon man concerning his parents—his mother bears him in weakness upon weakness, and his weaning is in two years—give thanks to Me and to your parents. To Me is the journeying.

15. But if they strive with you to make you ascribe to Me as partner that of which you have no knowledge, then do not obey them. Consort with them in the world kindly, and follow the path of him who repents to Me. Then to Me will be your return, and I shall tell you what you used to do—

16. "O my dear son! Though it be but the weight of a grain of mustard seed, and though it be in a rock, or in the heavens, or on the earth, God will bring it forth. God is subtile, aware.

17. "O my dear son! Establish worship and enjoin kindness and forbid iniquity, and persevere whatever may befall you. That is of the steadfast heart of things.

18. "Do not turn your cheek in scorn toward people, nor walk with arrogant abandon in the land. God loves not each conceited boaster.

2. See Q 2:1, footnote [Pickthall's note].

19. "Be modest in your bearing and subdue your voice. The harshest of all voices is the voice of the ass."

20. Do you not see how God has made serviceable to you whatever is in the skies and whatever is on the earth and has loaded you with His favors both without and within? Yet of mankind is he who disputes concerning God, without knowledge or guidance or a scripture giving light.

21. And if it be said to them: "Follow what God has revealed," they say: "No, but we follow that in which we found our fathers." What! Even though the devil were inviting them to the doom of flame?

22. Whoever surrenders his purpose to God while doing good, he has grasped the firm handhold. To God belongs the sequel of all things.

23. And whoever disbelieves, let not his disbelief afflict you (O Muḥammad). To Us is their return, and We shall tell them what they did. God is aware of what is in the breasts (of men).

24. We give them comfort for a little, and then We drive them to a heavy doom.

25. If you should ask them: "Who created the heavens and the earth?" they would answer: "God." Say: "Praise be to God!" But most of them know not.

26. To God belongs whatever is in the heavens and the earth. God, He is the absolute, the owner of praise.

27. And if all the trees on the earth were pens, and the sea, with seven more seas to help it, (were ink), the words of God could not be exhausted. God is mighty, wise.

28. Your creation and your raising (from the dead) are only as (the creation and the raising of) a single soul. God is hearer, knower.

29. Have you not seen how God causes the night to pass into the day and causes the day to pass into the night, and has subdued the sun and the moon (to do their work), each running to an appointed term; and that God is informed of what you do?

30. That (is so) because God, He is the true, and that which they invoke beside Him is the false, and because God, He is the sublime, the great.

31. Have you not seen how the ships glide on the sea by God's grace, that He may show you of His wonders? In that indeed are signs for every steadfast, grateful (heart).

32. And if a wave enshrouds them like awnings, they cry to God, making their faith pure for Him only. But when He brings them safe to land, some of them compromise. None denies Our signs except every traitor ingrate.

33. O mankind! Keep your duty to your Lord and fear a day when the parent will not be able to avail the child in anything, nor the child to avail the parent. God's promise is the very truth. Let not the life of the world beguile you, nor let the deceiver beguile you, in regard to God.

34. God! With Him is knowledge of the hour. He sends down the rain, and knows what is in the wombs. No soul knows what it will earn tomorrow, and no soul knows in what land it will die. God is knower, aware.

## Sūra 32

*Al-Sajda*, "The Prostration," takes its name from a word in verse 15.
It belongs to the middle group of Meccan sūras.

## The Prostration

*Revealed at Mecca*

In the name of God, the beneficent, the merciful.

1. Alif. Lām. Mīm.[1]

2. The revelation of the scripture of which there is no doubt is from the Lord of the worlds.

3. Or do they say: "He has invented it"? No, but it is the truth from your Lord, that you may warn a people to whom no warner came before you, that perhaps they may walk aright.

4. God it is who created the heavens and the earth, and that which is between them, in six days. Then He mounted the throne. You have not, beside Him, a protecting friend or mediator. Will you not then remember?

5. He directs the ordinance from the heaven to the earth; then it ascends to Him in a day, of which the measure is a thousand years of that you reckon.

6. Such is the knower of the invisible and the visible, the mighty, the merciful,

7. Who made all things good which He created, and He began the creation of man from clay;

8. Then He made his seed from an extract of despised fluid;

9. Then He fashioned him and breathed into him of His spirit; and appointed for you hearing and sight and hearts. Small thanks give you!

10. And they say: "When we are lost on the earth, how can we then be re-created?" No but they are disbelievers in the meeting with their Lord.

11. Say: "The angel of death, who has charge concerning you, will gather you, and afterward to your Lord you will be returned."

12. Could you but see when the guilty hang their heads before their Lord, (and say): "Our Lord! We have now seen and heard, so send us back; we will do right, now we are sure."

13. And if We had so willed, We could have given every soul its guidance, but the word from Me concerning evildoers took effect: that I will fill hell with the jinn and mankind together.

14. So taste (the evil of your deeds). For as much as you forgot the meeting of this your day, We forget you. Taste the doom of immortality because of what you used to do.

15. Only those believe in Our revelations who, when they are reminded of them, fall down prostrate and hymn the praise of their Lord, and they are not scornful,

16. Who forsake their beds to cry to their Lord in fear and hope, and spend of what We have bestowed on them.

17. No soul knows what is kept hid for them of joy, as a reward for what they used to do.

18. Is he who is a believer like to him who is iniquitous? They are not alike.

19. But as for those who believe and do good works, for them are the gardens of retreat—a welcome (in reward) for what they used to do.

1. See Q 2:1, footnote [Pickthall's note].

20. And as for those who do evil, their retreat is the fire. Whenever they desire to issue forth from it, they are brought back to it. To them it is said: "Taste the torment of the fire which you used to deny."

21. And We make them taste the lower punishment[2] before the greater, that perhaps they may return.

22. And who does greater wrong than he who is reminded of the revelations of his Lord, then turns from them. We shall requite the guilty.

23. We gave Moses the scripture; so do not be in doubt of his receiving it; and We appointed it a guidance for the Children of Israel.

24. And when they became steadfast and believed firmly in Our revelations, We appointed from among them leaders who guided by Our command.

25. Your Lord will judge between them on the day of resurrection concerning that in which they used to differ.

26. Is it not a guidance for them (to observe) how many generations We destroyed before them, amid whose dwelling-places they walk? In that are signs! Will they not then heed?

27. Have they not seen how We lead the water to the barren land and by that bring forth crops of which their cattle eat, and they themselves? Will they not then see?

28. And they say: "When does this victory (of yours) come if you are truthful?"

29. Say (to them): "On the day of the victory the faith of those who disbelieve (and who then will believe) will not avail them, neither will they be reprieved."

30. So withdraw from them (O Muḥammad), and await (the event). They (also) are awaiting (it).

## Sūra 33

*Al-Ahzāb*, "The Clans," takes its name from the army of the allied clans which came against Yathrib (Medina) in the fifth year of the *hijra* (verses 9–25). Certain of the Banū Nadīr, a Jewish tribe whom the Prophet had expelled from Yathrib on the ground of treason (see Q 59), went first to the leaders of Quraysh in Mecca and then to the chiefs of the great desert tribe of Ghaṭafān, urging them to exterminate the Muslims and promising them help from the Jewish population of Yathrib. As a result of their efforts, Quraysh with all their clans and Ghaṭafān with all their clans marched to destroy Yathrib.

When the Prophet had news of their design, he ordered a trench to be dug before the city and himself led the work of digging it. The trench was finished when the clans arrived, 10,000 strong. The Prophet went out against them with his army of 3,000, the trench being between the two armies. For nearly a month the Muslims were exposed to showers of arrows, in constant expectation of attack by much superior forces; and, to make matters worse, news came that the Jewish tribe of Banū Qurayẓa in their rear had broken their alliance with the Muslims and made common cause with Quraysh.

The women and children had been put in strongholds—towers like the peel towers of northern England, of which every family of note had one for refuge in the time of raids. These were practically unguarded, and some of the Muslims asked permission of the Prophet to leave the battle front and go to guard them,

2. I.e. punishment in this world [Pickthall's note].

though they were not then in danger because the Banū Qurayẓa were not likely to show their treachery until the victory of the clans was certain.

The case of the Muslims seemed, humanly speaking, hopeless. But a secret sympathizer in the enemy camp managed to sow distrust between the Banū Qurayẓa and the chiefs of the clans, making both feel uneasy. The obstacle of the trench was unexpected and seemed formidable; and when a fierce, bitter wind from the sea blew for three days and nights so furiously that they could not keep a shelter up, or light a fire, or boil a pot, Abū Sufyān, the leader of Quraysh, raised the siege in disgust. And when Ghaṭafān one morning found Quraysh had gone, they too departed for their homes.

On the very day when the Muslims returned from the trench began the siege of the traitorous Banū Qurayẓa in their towers of refuge. It lasted for twenty-five days. When they at length surrendered some of the tribe of Aws, whose adherents they were, asked the Prophet to show them the same grace that he had shown to the tribe of Khazraj, in the case of Banū Naḍīr, in allowing them to intercede for their dependents.

The Prophet said: "Would you like that one of you should decide concerning them?" They said: "Yes," and he appointed Sa'd b. Mu'ādh, a great chief of Aws, who had been wounded and was being cared for in the mosque. Sa'd was sent for and he ordered their men to be put to death, their women and children to be made captive, and their property to be divided among the Muslims at the Prophet's will.

I have taken this account from the narrative of Ibn Khaldūn,[1] which is concise, rather than from that in Ibn Hishām, which is exceedingly diffuse, the two accounts being in absolute agreement. Verses 26 and 27 refer to the punishment of Banū Qurayẓa.

In verse 37 the reference is to the unhappy marriage of Zayd, the Prophet's freedman and adopted son, with Zaynab, the Prophet's cousin, a proud lady of Quraysh. The Prophet had arranged the marriage with the idea of breaking down the old barrier of pride of caste, and had shown but little consideration for Zaynab's feelings. Tradition says that both she and her brother were averse to the match, and that she had always wished to marry the Prophet. For Zayd, the marriage was nothing but a cause of embarrassment and humiliation. When the Prophet's attention was first called to their unhappiness, he urged Zayd to keep his wife and not divorce her, being apprehensive of the talk that would arise if it became known that a marriage arranged by him had proved unhappy. At last, Zayd did actually divorce Zaynab, and the Prophet was commanded to marry her in order, by his example, to disown the superstitious custom of the pagan Arabs, in such matters, of treating their adopted sons as their real sons, which was against the laws of God (i.e. the laws of nature); whereas in arranging a marriage, the woman's inclinations ought to be considered. Unhappy marriage was no part of God's ordinance, and was not to be held sacred in Islām.

The sūra contains further references to the wives of the Prophet in connection with which it may be mentioned that from the age of twenty-five until the age of fifty he had only one wife, Khadīja, fifteen years his senior, to whom he was devotedly attached and whose memory he cherished until his dying day. With the exception of 'Ā'isha, the daughter of his closest friend, Abū Bakr, whom he married at her father's request when she was still a child, all his later marriages were with widows whose state was pitiable for one reason or another. Some of them were widows of men killed in war. One was a captive, when he made the marriage the excuse for emancipating all the conquered tribe and restoring their property. Two were daughters of his

1. 'Abd al-Raḥmān ibn Muḥammad ibn Khaldūn (1332–1406), the preeminent Muslim historian and historiographer of the late medieval period.

enemies, and his alliance with them was a cause of peace. It is noteworthy that the period of these marriages was also the period of his greatest activity, when he had little rest from campaigning, and was always busy with the problems of a growing empire.

The period of revelation is between the end of the fifth and the end of the seventh years of the *hijra*.

## The Clans

*Revealed at Medina*

In the name of God, the beneficent, the merciful.

1. O Prophet! Keep your duty to God and do not obey the disbelievers and the hypocrites. God is knower, wise.

2. And follow what is inspired in you from your Lord. God is aware of what you do.

3. And put your trust in God, for God is sufficient as guardian.

4. God has not assigned to any man two hearts within his body, nor has he made your wives whom you declare (to be your mothers) your mothers,[2] nor has he made those whom you claim (to be your sons) your sons. This is only a saying of your mouths. But God says the truth and He shows the way.

5. Proclaim their real parentage. That will be more equitable in the sight of God. And if you do not know their fathers, then (they are) your brothers in the faith, and your clients. And there is no sin for you in the mistakes that you make unintentionally, but what your hearts intend (that will be a sin for you). God is forgiving, merciful.

6. The Prophet is closer to the believers than their selves, and his wives are (as) their mothers. And the blood relatives are closer to one another in the ordinance of God than (other) believers and the fugitives (who fled from Mecca), except that you should do kindness to your friends.[3] This is written in the book (of nature).

7. And when We exacted a covenant from the prophets, and from you (O Muḥammad) and from Noah and Abraham and Moses and Jesus son of Mary, We took from them a solemn covenant;

8. That He may ask the loyal of their loyalty. And He has prepared a painful doom for the unfaithful.

9. O you who believe! Remember God's favor to you when there came against you armies, and We sent against them a great wind and forces you could not see. And God is ever observer of what you do.

10. When they came upon you from above you and from below you, and when eyes grew wild and hearts reached to the throats, and you were imagining vain thoughts concerning God.

11. There were the believers sorely tried, and shaken with a mighty shock.

2. The reference is to a custom of the pagan Arabs by which a man could put away his wife by merely saying: "Your back is as my mother's back for me" [Pickthall's note].
3. The Prophet had ordained brotherhood between individuals of the Anṣār (Muslims of Medina) and the Muhājirūn (fugitives from Mecca), a brotherhood which was closer than kinship by blood. This verse abolished such brotherhood, insofar as inheritance was concerned [Pickthall's note].

12. And when the hypocrites, and those in whose hearts is a disease, were saying: "God and His messenger promised us nothing except delusion."

13. And when a party of them said: "O people of Yathrib! There is no stand (possible) for you, therefore turn back." And certain of them (even) sought permission of the Prophet, saying: "Our homes lie open (to the enemy)." And they did not lie open. They only wished to flee.

14. If the enemy had entered from all sides and they had been exhorted to treachery, they would have committed it, and would have hesitated over it little.

15. And they had already sworn to God that they would not turn their backs (to the foe). An oath to God must be answered for.

16. Say: "Flight will not avail you if you flee from death or killing, and then you dwell in comfort only a little while."

17. Say: "Who is he who can preserve you from God if He intends harm for you, or intends mercy for you?" They will not find that they have any friend or helper other than God.

18. God already knows those of you who hinder, and those who say to their brothers: "Come here to us!" and they do not come to the stress of battle except a little,

19. Being sparing of their help to you (believers). But when the fear comes, then you (Muḥammad) see them regarding you with rolling eyes like one who faints as if dead. Then, when the fear departs, they scald you with sharp tongues in their greed for wealth (from the spoil). Such have not believed. Therefore God makes their deeds fruitless. And that is easy for God.

20. They hold that the clans have not retired (for good); and if the clans should advance (again), they would rather be in the desert with the wandering Arabs, asking for the news of you; and if they were among you, they would not give battle, except a little.

21. In the messenger of God you have a good example for him who looks to God and the last day, and remembers God much.

22. And when the true believers saw the clans, they said: "This is what God and His messenger promised us. God and His messenger are true." It only confirmed them in their faith and resignation.

23. Among the believers are men who are true to what they covenanted with God. Some of them have paid their vow by death (in battle), and some of them still are waiting; and they have not altered in the least;

24. That God may reward the true men for their truth, and punish the hypocrites if He will, or relent toward them (if He will). God is forgiving, merciful.

25. And God repulsed the disbelievers in their wrath; they gained no good. God averted their attack from the believers. God is strong, mighty.

26. And He brought those of the People of the Scripture who supported them down from their strongholds, and cast panic into their hearts. Some you slew, and you made captive some.

27. And He caused you to inherit their land and their houses and their wealth, and land you have not trodden. God is able to do all things.

28. O Prophet! Say to your wives: "If you desire the world's life and its adornment, come! I will content you and will release you with a fair release.

29. "But if you desire God and His messenger and the abode of the hereafter, then God has prepared for the good among you an immense reward."

30. O you wives of the Prophet! Whoever of you commits manifest lewdness, the punishment for her will be doubled, and that is easy for God.

31. And whoever of you is submissive to God and His messenger and does right, We shall give her her reward twice over, and We have prepared for her a rich provision.

32. O you wives of the Prophet! you are not like any other women. If you keep your duty (to God), then do not be soft of speech, for fear that he in whose heart is a disease aspire (to you), but utter customary speech.

33. And stay in your houses. Do not adorn yourselves with the adornment of the time of ignorance. Be regular in prayer, and pay the poor tax and obey God and His messenger. God's wish is only to remove uncleanness far from you, O People of the House, and cleanse you with a thorough cleansing.

34. And bear in mind what is recited in your houses of the revelations of God and wisdom. God is subtile, aware.

35. Men who surrender to God, and women who surrender, and men who believe and women who believe, and men who obey and women who obey, and men who speak the truth and women who speak the truth, and men who persevere (in righteousness) and women who persevere, and men who are humble and women who are humble, and men who give alms and women who give alms, and men who fast and women who fast, and men who guard their modesty and women who guard (their modesty), and men who remember God much and women who remember—God has prepared for them forgiveness and a vast reward.

36. And it does not become a believing man or a believing woman, when God and His messenger have decided an affair (for them), that they should (after that) claim any say in their affair; and whoever is rebellious to God and His messenger, he goes astray in error manifest.

37. And when you said to him on whom God has conferred favor and you have conferred favor: "Keep your wife to yourself, and fear God." And you did hide in your mind what God was to bring to light, and you did fear mankind whereas God has a better right that you should fear Him. So when Zayd had performed the necessary formality (of divorce) from her, We gave her to you in marriage, so that (henceforth) there may be no sin for believers in respect of wives of their adopted sons, when the latter have performed the necessary formality (of release) from them. The commandment of God must be fulfilled.

38. There is no reproach for the Prophet in what God makes his due. That was God's way with those who passed away of old—and the commandment of God is certain destiny—

39. Who delivered the messages of God and feared Him, and feared none except God. God keeps good account.

40. Muḥammad is not the father of any man among you, but he is the messenger of God and the seal of the prophets; and God is aware of all things.

41. O you who believe! Remember God with much remembrance.

42. And glorify Him early and late.

43. He it is who blesses you, and His angels (bless you), that He may bring you forth from darkness to light; and He is merciful to the believers.

44. Their salutation on the day when they shall meet Him will be: "Peace." And He has prepared for them a goodly recompense.

45. O Prophet! We have sent you as a witness and a bringer of good tidings and a warner,

46. And as a summoner to God by His permission, and as a lamp that gives light.

47. And announce to the believers the good tidings that they will have great bounty from God.

48. And do not incline to the disbelievers and the hypocrites. Disregard their noxious talk, and put your trust in God. God is sufficient as trustee.

49. O you who believe! If you wed believing women and divorce them before you have touched them, then there is no period that you should reckon. But content them and release them handsomely.

50. O Prophet! We have made lawful to you your wives to whom you have paid their dowries, and those whom your right hand possesses of those whom God has given you as spoils of war, and the daughters of your uncle on the father's side and the daughters of your aunts on the father's side, and the daughters of your uncles on the mother's side and the daughters of your aunts on the mother's side who emigrated with you, and a believing woman if she give herself to the Prophet and the Prophet desire to ask her in marriage—a privilege for you only, not for the (rest of) believers—We are aware of what We enjoined on them concerning their wives and those whom their right hands possess—that you may be free from blame, for God is forgiving, merciful.

51. You can defer whom you will of them and receive to you whom you will, and whomever you desire of those whom you have set aside (temporarily), it is no sin for you (to receive her again); that is better; that they may be comforted and not grieve, and may all be pleased with what you give them. God knows what is in your hearts (O men) and God is forgiving, clement.

52. You are not allowed to take (other) women after, nor should you change them for other wives even though their beauty pleased you, except those whom your right hand possesses. And God is watcher over all things.

53. O you who believe! Do not enter the dwellings of the Prophet for a meal without waiting for the proper time, unless permission be granted you. But if you are invited, enter, and, when your meal is ended, then disperse. Do not linger for conversation. That would cause annoyance to the Prophet, and he would be shy of (asking) you (to go); but God is not shy of the truth. And when you ask of them (the wives of the Prophet) anything, ask it of them from behind a curtain. That is purer for your hearts and for their hearts. And it is not for you to cause annoyance to the messenger of God, nor that you should ever marry his wives after him. That in God's sight would be an enormity.

54. Whether you divulge a thing or keep it hidden, God is knower of all things.

55. It is no sin for them (your wives) (to converse freely) with their fathers, or their sons, or their brothers, or their brothers' sons, or the sons

of their sisters or of their own women, or their slaves. O women! Keep your duty to God. God is witness over all things.

56. God and His angels shower blessings on the Prophet. O you who believe! Ask blessings on him and salute him with a worthy salutation.

57. Those who malign God and His messenger, God has cursed them in the world and the hereafter, and has prepared for them the doom of the disdained.

58. And those who malign believing men and believing women undeservedly, they bear the guilt of slander and manifest sin.

59. O Prophet! Tell your wives and your daughters and the women of the believers to draw their cloaks close around themselves (when they go abroad). That will be better, so that they may be recognized and not annoyed. God is ever forgiving, merciful.

60. If the hypocrites, and those in whose hearts is a disease, and the alarmists in the city do not cease, We shall urge you on against them, then they will be your neighbors in it but a little while.

61. Accursed, they will be seized wherever found and slain with a (fierce) slaughter.

62. That was the way of God in the case of those who passed away of old; for the way of God you will not find anything of power to change.

63. Men ask of you the hour. Say: "The knowledge of it is with God only." What can convey (the knowledge) to you? It may be that the hour is near.

64. God has cursed the disbelievers, and has prepared for them a flaming fire,

65. Where they will abide forever. They will find (then) no protecting friend nor helper.

66. On the day when their faces are turned over in the fire, they say: "Oh, would that we had obeyed God and had obeyed His messenger!"

67. And they say: "Our Lord! We obeyed our princes and great men, and they misled us from the way."

68. "Our Lord! Oh, give them double torment and curse them with a mighty curse."

69. O you who believe! Do not be as those who slandered Moses, but God proved his innocence of what they alleged, and he was well esteemed in God's sight.

70. O you who believe! Guard your duty to God, and speak words straight to the point;

71. He will adjust your works for you and will forgive you your sins. Whoever obeys God and His messenger, he has gained a signal victory.

72. We offered the trust to the heavens and the earth and the hills, but they shrank from bearing it and were afraid of it. And man assumed it. He has proved a tyrant and a fool.

73. So God punishes hypocritical men and hypocritical women, and idolatrous men and idolatrous women. But God pardons believing men and believing women, and God is forgiving, merciful.

## Sūra 34

*Sabā'*, "Sheba," takes its name from verses 15ff., where Sheba (*Saba*), a region in Yemen, is mentioned as having been devastated by a flood. It warns of the effects of luxury.

An early Meccan sūra.

## Sabā'

*Revealed at Mecca*

In the name of God, the beneficent, the merciful.

1. Praise be to God, to whom belongs whatever is in the heavens and whatever is on the earth. His is the praise in the hereafter, and He is the wise, the aware.

2. He knows what goes into the earth and what comes forth from it, and what descends from the heaven and what ascends to it. He is the merciful, the forgiving.

3. Those who disbelieve say: "The hour will never come to us." Say: "No, by my Lord, but it is coming to you surely." (He is) the knower of the unseen. Not an atom's weight, or less than that or greater, escapes Him in the heavens or on the earth, but it is in a clear record,

4. That He may reward those who believe and do good works. For them is pardon and a rich provision.

5. But those who strive against Our revelations, challenging (Us), theirs will be a painful doom of wrath.

6. Those who have been given knowledge see that what is revealed to you from your Lord is the truth and leads to the path of the mighty, the owner of praise.

7. Those who disbelieve say: "Shall we show you a man who will tell you (that) when you have become dispersed in dust with most complete dispersal, still, even then, you will be created anew?"

8. Has he invented a lie concerning God, or is there in him a madness? No, but those who disbelieve in the hereafter are in torment and far error.

9. Have they not observed what is before them and what is behind them of the sky and the earth? If We will, We can make the earth swallow them, or cause obliteration from the sky to fall on them. In this surely is a sign for every servant who turns (to God) repentant.

10. And assuredly We gave David grace from Us, (saying): "O you hills and birds, echo his psalms of praise!" And We made the iron supple to him,

11. Saying: "Make long coats of mail and measure their links. And do right. I am observer of what you do."

12. And to Solomon (We gave) the wind, of which the morning course was a month's journey and the evening course a month's journey, and We caused the fount of copper to gush forth for him, and (We gave him) certain of the jinn who worked before him by permission of his Lord. And such of them as deviated from Our command, We caused to taste the punishment of flaming fire.

13. They made for him what he willed: synagogues and statues, basins like wells and boilers built into the ground. Give thanks, O House of David! Few of My servants are thankful.

14. And when We decreed death for him, nothing showed his death to them except a creeping creature of the earth which gnawed away his staff. And when he fell the jinn saw clearly how, if they had known the unseen, they would not have continued in despised toil.

15. There was indeed a sign for Sheba in their dwelling-place: Two gardens on the right hand and the left (as who should say): "Eat of the provision of your Lord and render thanks to Him. A fair land and an indulgent Lord!"

16. But they were obstinant, so We sent on them the flood of the dams,[1] and in exchange for their two gardens gave them two gardens bearing bitter fruit, the tamarisk and here and there a lote tree.[2]

17. This We awarded them because of their ingratitude. Do We ever punish any except the ingrates?

18. And We set, between them and the towns which We had blessed, towns easy to be seen, and We made the stage between them easy, (saying): "Travel in them safely both by night and day."

19. But they said: "Our Lord! Make the stage between our journeys longer." And they wronged themselves, therefore We made them bywords (in the land) and scattered them abroad, a total scattering. In this are signs for each steadfast, grateful (heart).

20. And Satan indeed found his calculation true concerning them, for they follow him, all except a group of true believers.

21. And he had no warrant whatever against them, except that We would know him who believes in the hereafter from him who is in doubt about it; and your Lord (O Muḥammad) takes note of all things.

22. Say (O Muḥammad): "Call on those whom you set up beside God!" They possess not an atom's weight either in the heavens or on the earth, nor have they any share in either, nor has He a helper among them.

23. No intercession avails with Him except for him whom He permits. Yet, when fear is banished from their hearts, they say: "What was it that your Lord said?" They say: "The truth. And He is the sublime, the great."

24. Say: "Who gives you provision from the sky and the earth?" Say: "God. We or you assuredly are rightly guided or in error manifest."

25. Say: "You will not be asked of what we committed, nor shall we be asked of what you do."

26. Say: "Our Lord will bring us all together, then He will judge between us with truth. He is the all-knowing judge."

27. Say: "Show me those whom you have joined to Him as partners." No (you dare not)! For He is God, the mighty, the wise.

28. And We have not sent you (O Muḥammad) except as a bringer of good tidings and a warner to all mankind; but most of mankind know not.

29. And they say: "When is this promise (to be fulfilled) if you are truthful?"

30. Say (O Muḥammad): "Yours is the promise of a day which you cannot postpone nor hasten by an hour."

1. Usually connected with the Dam of Ma'rib in the pre-Islamic kingdom of Sheba.
2. A thorny tree with a plum-like fruit.

31. And those who disbelieve say: "We do not believe in this Qur'ān or in that which was before it"; but oh, if you could see, when the wrongdoers are brought up before their Lord, how they cast the blame one to another; how those who were despised (on the earth) say to those who were proud: "But for you, we should have been believers."

32. And those who were proud say to those who were despised: "Did we drive you away from the guidance after it had come to you? No, but you were guilty."

33. Those who were despised say to those who were proud: "No, but (it was your) scheming night and day, when you commanded us to disbelieve in God and set up rivals to Him." And they are filled with remorse when they behold the doom; and We place chains on the necks of those who disbelieved. Are they requited anything except what they did?

34. And We did not send to any township a warner, but its pampered ones declared: "We are disbelievers in that with which you have been sent."

35. And they say: "We are more (than you) in wealth and children. We are not the punished!"

36. Say (O Muḥammad): "My Lord enlarges the provision for whom He will and narrows it (for whom He will). But most of mankind know not."

37. And it is not your wealth nor your children that will bring you near to Us, but he who believes and does good (he draws near). As for such, theirs will be twofold reward for what they did, and they will dwell secure in lofty halls.

38. And as for those who strive against Our revelations, challenging, they will be brought to the doom.

39. Say: "My Lord enlarges the provision for whom He will of His servants, and narrows (it) for him. And whatever you spend (for good) He replaces it. And He is the best of providers."

40. And on the day when He will gather them all together, He will say to the angels: "Did these worship you?"

41. They will say: "Be glorified. You are our protector from them! No, but they worshipped the jinn; most of them were believers in them."

42. That day you will possess no use nor hurt one for another. And We shall say to those who did wrong: "Taste the doom of the fire which you used to deny."

43. And if Our revelations are recited to them in plain terms, they say: "This is nothing else than a man who would turn you away from what your fathers used to worship"; and they say: "This is nothing else than an invented lie." Those who disbelieve say of the truth when it reaches them: "This is nothing else than mere magic."

44. And We have given them no scriptures which they study, nor did We send to them, before you, any warner.

45. Those before them denied, and these have not attained a tithe of what We bestowed on them (of old); yet they denied My messengers. How intense then was My abhorrence (of them)!

46. Say (to them, O Muḥammad): "I exhort you to one thing only: that you awake, for God's sake, by twos and singly, and then reflect: There is no madness in your comrade. He is nothing else than a warner to you in face of a terrific doom."

47. Say: "Whatever reward I might have asked of you is yours. My reward is the affair of God only. He is witness over all things."

48. Say: "My Lord hurls the truth. (He is) the knower of things hidden."

49. Say: "The truth has come, and falsehood shows not its face and will not return."

50. Say: "If I err, I err only to my own loss, and if I am rightly guided it is because of what my Lord has revealed to me. He is hearer, near."

51. Could you but see when they are terrified with no escape, and are seized from near at hand,

52. And say: "We (now) believe in it." But how can they reach (faith) from afar off,

53. When they disbelieved in it before? They aim at the unseen from afar off.

54. And a gulf is set between them and what they desire, as was done for people of their kind of old. They were in hopeless doubt.

## Sūra 35

*Al-Malā'ika*, "The Angels," also called *al-Fāṭir*, "The Creator," takes its name in either case from a word in verse 1.

An early Meccan sūra.

## The Angels

*Revealed at Mecca*

In the name of God, the beneficent, the merciful.

1. Praise be to God, the creator of the heavens and the earth, who appoints the angels messengers having wings two, three, and four. He multiplies in creation what He will. God is able to do all things.

2. That which God opens to mankind of mercy none can withhold it; and that which He withholds none can release thereafter. He is the mighty, the wise.

3. O mankind! Remember God's grace toward you! Is there any creator other than God who provides for you from the sky and the earth? There is no God except Him. Where then are you turned?

4. And if they deny you, (O Muḥammad), messengers (of God) were denied before you. To God all things are brought back.

5. O mankind! The promise of God is true. So let not the life of the world beguile you, and let not the (avowed) beguiler beguile you with regard to God.

6. The devil is an enemy for you, so treat him as an enemy. He only summons his faction to be owners of the flaming fire.

7. Those who disbelieve, theirs will be an awful doom; and those who believe and do good works, theirs will be forgiveness and a great reward.

8. Is he, the evil of whose deeds is made fair-seeming to him so that he thinks it good, (other than Satan's dupe)? God sends whom He will astray, and guides whom He will; so do not let your soul expire in sighings for them. God is aware of what they do!

9. And God it is who sends the winds and they raise a cloud; then We lead it to a dead land and by it revive the earth after its death. Such is the resurrection.

10. Whoever desires power (should know that) all power belongs to God. To Him good words ascend, and the pious deed He exalts; but those who plot iniquities, theirs will be an awful doom; and the plotting of such (people) will come to nothing.

11. God created you from dust, then from a little fluid, then He made you pairs (the male and female). No female bears or brings forth except with His knowledge. And no one grows old who grows old, nor is anything lessened of his life, but it is recorded in a book. That is easy for God.

12. And the two seas[1] are not alike: this, fresh, sweet, good to drink, this (other) bitter, salt. And from them both you eat fresh meat and derive the ornament that you wear. And you see the ship cleaving them with its prow that you may seek of His bounty, and that perhaps you may give thanks.

13. He makes the night to pass into the day and He makes the day to pass into the night. He has subdued the sun and moon to service. Each runs to an appointed term. Such is God, your Lord; His is the sovereignty; and those to whom you pray instead of Him do not own so much as the white spot on a date stone.

14. If you pray to them they do not hear your prayer, and if they heard they could not grant it to you. On the day of resurrection they will disown association with you. None can inform you like Him who is aware.

15. O mankind! You are the poor in your relation to God. And God! He is the absolute, the owner of praise.

16. If He will, He can be rid of you and bring (instead of you) some new creation.

17. That is not a hard thing for God.

18. And no burdened soul can bear another's burden, and if one heavy laden cries for (help with) his load, nothing of it will be lifted even though he (to whom he cries) be of kin. You warn only those who fear their Lord in secret, and have established worship. He who grows (in goodness), grows only for himself, (he cannot by his merit redeem others). To God is the journeying.

19. The blind man is not equal with the one who sees;

20. Nor is darkness (tantamount to) light;

21. Nor is the shadow equal with the sun's full heat;

22. Nor are the living equal with the dead. God makes whom He will to hear. You cannot reach those who are in the graves.

23. You are only a warner.

24. We have sent you with the truth, a bearer of glad tidings and a warner; and there is not a nation but a warner has passed among them.

25. And if they deny you, those before them also denied. Their messengers came to them with clear proofs (of God's sovereignty), and with the Psalms and the scripture giving light.

26. Then I seized those who disbelieved, and how intense was My abhorrence!

27. Have you not seen that God causes water to fall from the sky, and by it We produce fruit of diverse hues; and among the hills are streaks white and red, of diverse hues, and (others) raven black;

28. And of men and beasts and cattle, in like manner, diverse hues? The erudite among His servants fear God alone. God is mighty, forgiving.

1. I.e., the two kinds of water on the earth [Pickthall's note].

29. Those who read the scripture of God, and establish worship, and spend of what We have bestowed on them secretly and openly, they look forward to imperishable gain,

30. That He will pay them their wages and increase them of His grace. He is forgiving, responsive.

31. As for that which We inspire in you of the scripture, it is the truth confirming what was (revealed) before it. God is indeed observer, the one who sees his slaves.

32. Then We gave the scripture as inheritance to those whom We elected of our servants. But among them are some who wrong themselves and among them are some who are lukewarm, and among them are some who outstrip (others) through good deeds, by God's leave. That is the great favor!

33. Gardens of Eden! They enter them wearing armlets of gold and pearl and their garments there are silk.

34. And they say: "Praise be to God who has put grief away from us. Our Lord is forgiving, bountiful,

35. "Who, of His grace, has installed us in the mansion of eternity, where toil does not touch us not nor can weariness affect us."

36. But as for those who disbelieve, for them is fire of hell; it does not take complete effect upon them so that they can die, nor is its torment lightened for them. Thus We punish every ingrate.

37. And they cry for help there, (saying): "Our Lord! Release us; we will do right, not (the wrong) that we used to do." Did We not grant you a life long enough for him who reflected to reflect in it? And the warner came to you. Now taste (the flavor of your deeds), for evildoers have no helper.

38. God is the knower of the unseen of the heavens and the earth. He is aware of the secret of (men's) breasts.

39. He it is who has made you regents on the earth; so he who disbelieves, his disbelief be on his own head. Their disbelief increases for the disbelievers, in their Lord's sight, nothing except abhorrence. Their disbelief increases for the disbelievers nothing except loss.

40. Say: "Have you seen your partner-gods to whom you pray beside God? Show me what they created of the earth! Or have they any portion in the heavens? Or have We given them a scripture so that they act on clear proof from it?" No, the evildoers promise one another only to deceive.

41. God grasps the heavens and the earth so that they do not deviate, and if they were to deviate there is not one that could grasp them after Him. He is ever clement, forgiving.

42. And they swore by God, their most binding oath, that if a warner came to them they would be more tractable than any of the nations; yet, when a warner came to them it aroused in them nothing except repugnance,

43. (Shown in their) behaving arrogantly in the land and plotting evil; and the evil plot encloses only the men who make it. Then, can they expect anything except the treatment of the people of old? You will not find any change in God's way of treating (people). You will not find any deviation in God's way of treating (people).

44. Have they not traveled in the land and seen the nature of the consequence for those who were before them, and they were mightier than these in power? God is not such that anything in the heavens or on the earth escapes Him. He is the wise, the mighty.

45. If God took mankind to task by that which they deserve, He would not leave a living creature on the surface of the earth; but He reprieves them to an appointed term, and when their term comes—then (they will know that) God is ever observer of His servants.

## Sūra 36

*Yā' Sīn* takes its name from the two letters of the Arabic alphabet which stand as the first verse and are generally held to signify *Yā Insān* ("O Man"). This sūra is regarded with special reverence, and is recited in times of adversity, illness, fasting and on the approach of death.

It belongs to the middle group of Meccan sūras.

## Yā Sīn

*Revealed at Mecca*

In the name of God, the beneficent, the merciful.

1. Yā Sīn.
2. By the wise Qur'ān,
3. You are of those sent
4. On a straight path,
5. A revelation of the mighty, the merciful,
6. That you may warn a people whose fathers were not warned, so they are heedless.
7. Already has the word proved true of most of them, for they do not believe.
8. We have put on their necks chains reaching to the chins, so that they are made stiff-necked.
9. And We have set a bar before them and a bar behind them, and (thus) have covered them so that they do not see.
10. Whether you warn them or you warn them not, it is alike for them, for they do not believe.
11. You warn only him who follows the reminder and fears the Beneficent in secret. To him bear tidings of forgiveness and a rich reward.
12. It is We Who bring the dead to life. We record what they send before (them), and their footprints. And all things We have kept in a clear register.
13. Coin for them a similitude: The people of the city when those sent (from God) came to them;
14. When We sent to them two, and they denied them both, so We reinforced them with a third, and they said: "We have been sent to you."
15. They said: "You are but mortals like us. The Beneficent has revealed nothing. You only lie!"
16. They answered: "Our Lord knows that we are indeed sent to you.
17. "And our duty is but plain conveyance (of the message)."
18. (The people of the city) said: "We predict ill of you. If you do not desist, we shall surely stone you, and grievous torture will befall you at our hands."

19. They said: "Your evil augury be with you! Is it because you are reminded (of the truth)? No, but you are obstinate people!"
20. And there came from the farthest part of the city a man running. He cried: "O my people! Follow those who have been sent!
21. "Follow those who ask of you no fee, and who are rightly guided.
22. "For why should I not serve Him Who has created me, and to Whom you will be brought back?
23. "Shall I take (other) gods in place of Him when, if the Beneficent should wish me any harm, their intercession will avail me nothing, nor can they save?
24. "Then truly I should be in error manifest.
25. "I have believed in your Lord, so hear me!"
26. It was said (to him): "Enter paradise." He said: "Would that my people knew
27. "With what (munificence) my Lord pardoned me and made me of the honored ones!"
28. We did not send down against his people after him a host from heaven, nor do We ever send.
29. It was only one shout, and they were extinct.
30. Ah, the anguish for the servants! There never came to them a messenger except they mocked him!
31. Have they not seen how many generations We destroyed before them, which do not return to them?
32. But all, without exception, will be brought before Us.
33. A token to them is the dead earth. We revive it, and We bring forth from it grain so that they eat of it;
34. And We have placed in it gardens of the date palm and grapes, and We have caused springs of water to gush forth in it, that they may eat of the fruit of it, and their hands did not make it. Will they not, then, give thanks?
35. Glory be to Him Who created all the sexual pairs, of that which the earth grows, and of themselves, and of that which they know not!
36. A sign to them is night. We strip it of the day, and they are in darkness.
37. And the sun runs on to a resting-place for him. That is the measuring of the mighty, the wise.
38. And for the moon We have appointed mansions until she returns like an old shriveled palm leaf.
39. It is not for the sun to overtake the moon, nor does the night outstrip the day. They float each in an orbit.
40. And a sign to them is that We bear their offspring in the laden ship,
41. And have created for them of its like on which they ride.
42. And if We will, We drown them, and there is no help for them, neither can they be saved;
43. Unless by mercy from Us and as comfort for a while.
44. When it is said to them: "Beware of what is before you and what is behind you, that perhaps you may find mercy" (they are heedless).
45. A sign of the signs of their Lord never came to them, but they turned away from it!
46. And when it is said to them: "Spend out of what God has provided you," those who disbelieve say to those who believe: "Shall we feed those

whom God, if He willed, would feed?" You are in nothing else than error manifest.

47. And they say: "When will this promise be fulfilled, if you are truthful?"

48. They await only one shout, which will surprise them while they are disputing.

49. Then they cannot make bequest, nor can they return to their own people.

50. And the trumpet is blown and from the graves they hasten to their Lord,

51. Crying: "Woe upon us! Who has raised us from our place of sleep? This is that which the Beneficent promised, and the messengers spoke truth."

52. It is only one shout, and behold them brought together before Us!

53. This day no soul is wronged in anything; nor are you requited anything except what you used to do.

54. Those who merit paradise this day are happily employed,

55. They and their wives, in pleasant shade, on thrones reclining;

56. Theirs the fruit (of their good deeds) and theirs (all) that they ask;

57. The word from a merciful Lord (for them) is: "Peace!"

58. But begone, O you guilty, this day!

59. Did I not charge you, O you sons of Adam, that you not worship the devil—he is your open foe!—

60. But that you worship Me? That was the right path.

61. Yet he has led astray a great multitude of you. Had you then no sense?

62. This is hell which you were promised (if you followed him).

63. Burn in it this day for what you disbelieved.

64. This day We seal up mouths, and hands speak out to Us and their feet bear witness as to what they used to earn.

65. And had We willed, We could have quenched their eyesight so that they should struggle for the way. Then how could they have seen?

66. And had We willed, We could have fixed them in their place, making them powerless to go forward or turn back.[1]

67. He whom We bring to old age, We reverse him in creation (making him go back to weakness after strength). Have you then no sense?

68. And We have not taught him (Muḥammad) poetry, nor is it fitting for him. This is nothing else than a reminder and a lecture[2] making plain,

69. To warn whoever lives, and that the word may be fulfilled against the disbelievers.

70. Have they not seen how We have created for them of Our handiwork the cattle, so that they are their owners,

71. And have subdued them to them, so that some of them they have for riding, some for food?

72. Benefits and (various) drinks have they from them. Will they not then give thanks?

73. And they have taken (other) gods beside God, in order that they may be helped.

1. But they have sight and power of motion so can choose their way [Pickthall's note].
2. Ar. *Qur'ān* [Pickthall's note].

74. It is not in their power to help them; but they (the worshippers) are a host in arms to them.

75. So do not let their speech grieve you (O Muḥammad). We know what they conceal and what proclaim.

76. Has man not seen that We have created him from a drop of seed? Yet he is an open opponent.

77. And he has coined for Us a similitude, and has forgotten the fact of his creation, saying: "Who will revive these bones when they have rotted away?"

78. Say: "He will revive them Who produced them at the first, for He is knower of every creation,

79. "Who has appointed for you fire from the green tree, and behold! you kindle from it."

80. Is not He Who created the heavens and the earth able to create the like of them? Yes, that He is! For He is the All-Wise Creator,

81. But His command, when He intends a thing, is only that He says to it: "Be!" and it is.

82. Therefore glory be to Him in Whose hand is the dominion over all things! To Him you will be brought back.

## Sūra 37

*Al-Ṣāffāt* takes its name from a word in the first verse. The reference in the first three verses is to the angels, as is made clear by verses 164–166, where the revealing angel speaks in person. Tradition says that soothsayers and astrologers throughout the East were bewildered at the time of the Prophet's coming by the appearance in the heavens of a comet and many meteors which baffled all their science and made them afraid to sit at nights on high peaks to watch the stars, as was their general custom. They told enquirers that their familiars could no longer guide them, being themselves completely at a loss and terrified. This is the explanation usually given of verses 7–9, and of a passage of similar import in Q 72:8–10.

It stands early in the middle group of Meccan sūras.

## Those Who Set the Ranks

*Revealed at Mecca*

In the name of God, the beneficent, the merciful.

1. By those who set the ranks in battle order
2. And those who drive away (the wicked) with reproof
3. And those who read (the word) for a reminder,
4. Your Lord is surely one;
5. Lord of the heavens and of the earth and all that is between them, and Lord of the sun's risings.
6. We have adorned the lowest heaven with an ornament, the planets;
7. With security from every rebellious devil.
8. They cannot listen to those on high[1] for they are pelted from every side,

1. Ar. *al-mala' al-a'lā*, the assembly of angels in the heavenly court.

9. Outcast, and theirs is a perpetual torment;

10. Except him who snatches a fragment, and there pursues him a piercing flame.[2]

11. Then ask them (O Muḥammad): "Are they stronger as a creation, or those (others) whom We have created? We created them of plastic clay."

12. No, but you marvel when they mock

13. And do not heed when they are reminded,

14. And seek to scoff when they behold a sign.

15. And they say: "This is mere magic;

16. "When we are dead and have become dust and bones, shall we then be raised (again)?

17. "And our forefathers?"

18. Say (O Muḥammad): "Yes, in truth; and you will be brought low."

19. There is but one shout, and they behold,

20. And say: "Ah, woe for us! This is the day of judgment."

21. This is the day of separation,[3] which you used to deny.

22. (And it is said to the angels): "Assemble those who did wrong, together with their wives and what they used to worship

23. "Instead of God, and lead them to the path to hell;

24. "And stop them, for they must be questioned."

25. What ails you that you do not help one another?

26. No, but this day they make full submission.

27. And some of them draw near to others, mutually questioning.

28. They say: "You used to come to us, imposing, (swearing that you spoke the truth)."

29. They answer: "No, but you (yourselves) were not believers.

30. "We had no power over you, but you were wayward people.

31. "Now the word of our Lord has been fulfilled concerning us. We are about to taste (the doom).

32. "Thus we misled you. We were (ourselves) astray."

33. Then this day they (both) are sharers in the doom.

34. Thus do We deal with the guilty.

35. For when it was said to them, "There is no god but God," they were scornful

36. And said: "Shall we forsake our gods for a mad poet?"

37. No, but he brought the truth, and he confirmed those sent (before him).

38. (Now) you taste the painful doom—

39. You are requited for nothing but what you did—

40. Except single-minded servants of God;

41. For them there is a known provision,

42. Fruits. And they will be honored

43. In the gardens of delight,

44. On couches facing one another;

45. A cup from a gushing spring is brought round for them,

46. White, delicious to the drinkers,

47. In which there is no headache nor are they made mad thereby.

48. And with them are those of modest gaze, with lovely eyes,

2. Q 72:8–10; 67:5 [Pickthall's note].
3. Another name for the day of judgment when the righteous will be separated from the wicked.

49. (Pure) as if they were hidden eggs (of the ostrich).
50. And some of them draw near to others, mutually questioning.
51. A speaker of them said: "I had a comrade
52. "Who used to say: 'Are you in truth of those who put faith (in his words)?
53. "'Can we, when we are dead and have become mere dust and bones—can we (then) be brought to judgment?'
54. "He said: 'Will you look?'
55. "Then he looked and saw him in the depth of hell.
56. "He said: 'By God, you all but caused my ruin,
57. "'And had it not been for the favor of my Lord, I too would have been of those brought forward (to doom).'"
58. Are we then not to die
59. Except our former death, and are we not to be punished?
60. This is the supreme triumph.
61. For the like of this, then, let the workers work.
62. Is this better as a welcome, or the tree of Zaqqūm?[4]
63. We have appointed it a torment for wrongdoers.
64. It is a tree that springs in the heart of hell
65. Its crop is as it were the heads of devils
66. And they must eat of it, and fill (their) bellies with it.
67. And afterward, with it they have a drink of boiling water
68. And afterward, their return is surely to hell.
69. They indeed found their fathers astray,
70. But they make haste (to follow) in their footsteps.
71. And most of the men of old went astray before them,
72. And We sent among them warners.
73. Then see the nature of the consequence for those warned,
74. Except single-minded servants of God.
75. And Noah prayed to Us, and gracious was the hearer of his prayer
76. And We saved him and his household from the great distress,
77. And made his seed the survivors,
78. And left for him among the later people (the salutation):
79. "Peace be to Noah among the peoples!"
80. Thus do We reward the good.
81. He is one of Our believing slaves.
82. Then We drowned the others.
83. And of his persuasion was Abraham
84. When he came to his Lord with a whole heart;
85. When he said to his father and his folk: "What is it that you worship?
86. Is it a falsehood—gods beside God—that you desire?
87. What then is your opinion of the Lord of the worlds?"
88. And he glanced a glance at the stars
89. Then said: "I feel sick!"
90. And they turned their backs and went away from him.
91. Then he turned to their gods and said: "Will you not eat?
92. "What ails you that you speak not?"
93. Then he attacked them, striking with his right hand.
94. And (his people) came toward him, hastening.

4. Q 44:43; 56:52 [Pickthall's note].

95. He said: "Do you worship what you yourselves carve
96. "When God has created you and what you make?"
97. They said: "Build for him a pyre and fling him in the red-hot fire."[5]
98. And they designed a snare for him, but We made them the lowest.
99. And he said: "I am going to my Lord who will guide me.
100. "My Lord! Grant me one of the righteous."[6]
101. So We gave him tidings of a gentle son.
102. And when (his son) was old enough to walk with him, (Abraham) said: "O my dear son, I have seen in a dream that I must sacrifice you. So look, what do you think?" He said: "O my father! Do what you are commanded. God willing, you will find me of the steadfast."[7]
103. Then, when they had both surrendered (to God), and he had flung him down upon his face,
104. We called to him: "O Abraham!
105. "You have already fulfilled the vision. Thus do We reward the good."
106. That was a clear test.
107. Then We ransomed him with a tremendous victim.[8]
108. And We left for him among the later people (the salutation):
109. "Peace be to Abraham!"
110. Thus do We reward the good.
111. He is one of Our believing servants.
112. And We gave him tidings of the birth of Isaac, a prophet of the righteous.
113. And We blessed him and Isaac. And of their seed are some who do good, and some who plainly wrong themselves.
114. And We gave grace to Moses and Aaron,
115. And saved them and their people from the great distress,
116. And helped them so that they became the victors.
117. And We gave them the clear scripture
118. And showed them the right path.
119. And We left for them among the later people (the salutation):
120. "Peace be to Moses and Aaron!"
121. Thus do We reward the good.
122. They are two of our believing slaves.
123. And Elias[9] was of those sent (to warn),
124. When he said to his people: "Will you not ward off (evil)?
125. Will you cry to Baal[1] and forsake the best of creators,
126. God, your Lord and Lord of your forefathers?"
127. But they denied him, so they surely will be brought forward (to the doom)
128. Except single-minded servants of God.
129. And We left for him among the later folk (the salutation):
130. "Peace be to Elias!"

5. Abraham's people reject his call to monotheism and attempt to burn him alive. God cools the flame (cf. Q 21:69) so that Abraham can pass through unscathed.
6. A child.
7. Cf. Genesis 22.
8. Muslim commentators differ over why the sacrifice was a "tremendous victim." Some speculate that it was because of the size or bulk of the animal, or because it was accepted as a substitute for a prophet. Others, particularly Shīʿī commentators, have understood it as a reference to the sacrifice of Ḥusayn, Muḥammad's grandson, at Karbalāʾ (680 CE).
9. The Hebrew prophet Elijah (9th c. BCE); see 1 Kings 17–19; 2 Kings 1–2.
1. A god widely worshipped in the ancient Middle East.

131. Thus do We reward the good.
132. He is one of our believing servants.
133. And Lot was of those sent (to warn),
134. When We saved him and his household, every one,
135. Except an old woman among those who stayed behind;
136. Then We destroyed the others.
137. And you pass by (the ruin of) them in the morning
138. And at nighttime; have you then no sense?
139. And Jonah was of those sent (to warn)
140. When he fled to the laden ship,
141. And then drew lots and was of those rejected;
142. And the fish swallowed him while he was blameworthy;
143. And had he not been one of those who glorify (God)
144. He would have tarried in its belly until the day when they are raised;
145. Then We cast him on a desert shore while he was sick;
146. And We caused a tree of gourd to grow above him;
147. And We sent him to a hundred thousand (people) or more
148. And they believed, therefore We gave them comfort for a while.
149. Now ask them (O Muḥammad): "Has your Lord daughters whereas they have sons?
150. "Or did We create the angels females while they were present?"
151. It is of their falsehood that they say:
152. "God has begotten." And they tell a lie.
153. (And again of their falsehood): "He has preferred daughters to sons."
154. What ails you? How do you judge?
155. Will you not then reflect?
156. Or have you a clear warrant?
157. Then produce your book, if you are truthful.
158. And they imagine kinship between Him and the jinn, whereas the jinn know well that they will be brought before (Him).
159. Glorified be God from that which they attribute (to Him),
160. Except single-minded servants of God.
161. You and that which you worship,
162. You cannot excite (anyone) against Him
163. Except him who is to burn in hell.
164. There is not one of us[2] but has his known position.
165. We, even we are they who set the ranks.
166. We, even we are they who hymn his praise
167. And indeed they used to say:
168. "If we had but a reminder from the men of old
169. "We would be single-minded slaves of God."
170. Yet (now that it is come) they disbelieve in it; but they will come to know.
171. And Our word went forth of old to our messengers sent (to warn)
172. That they would be helped,
173. And that Our host, they would be the victors.
174. So withdraw from them (O Muḥammad) awhile,
175. And watch, for they will (soon) see.
176. Would they hasten on Our doom?

2. Here the revealing angel speaks in person [Pickthall's note].

177. But when it comes home to them, then it will be a wretched morn for those who have been warned.

178. Withdraw from them awhile

179. And watch, for they will (soon) see.

180. Glorified be your Lord, the Lord of majesty, from that which they attribute (to Him)

181. And peace be to those sent (to warn).

182. And praise be to God, Lord of the worlds!

## Sūra 38

*Ṣād.* This sūra takes its name from the letter of the Arabic alphabet which stands alone at the beginning of the first verse. Tradition says that the first ten verses were revealed when the leaders of Quraysh tried to persuade Abū Ṭālib[1] to withdraw his protection from the Prophet, or when Abū Ṭālib died. The former is the more probable.

Its place is early in the middle group of Meccan sūras.

## Ṣād

*Revealed at Mecca*

In the name of God, the beneficent, the merciful.

1. Ṣād. By the renowned Qur'ān,

2. No, but those who disbelieve are in false pride and schism.

3. How many a generation We destroyed before them, and they cried out when it was no longer the time for escape!

4. And they marvel that a warner from among themselves has come to them, and the disbelievers say: "This is a wizard, a charlatan.

5. "Does he make the gods one God? That is an astounding thing."

6. The chiefs among them go about, exhorting: "Go and be staunch to your gods! This is a thing to be desired.[2]

7. "We have not heard of this in later religion. This is nothing but an invention.

8. "Has the reminder been revealed to him (alone) among us?" No, but they are in doubt concerning My reminder; no, but they have not yet tasted My doom.

9. Or are theirs the treasures of the mercy of your Lord, the mighty, the bestower?

10. Or is the kingdom of the heavens and the earth and all that is between them theirs? Then let them ascend by ropes!

11. A defeated host are (all) the factions that are there.

12. The people of Noah before them denied (their messenger) and (so did the tribe of) 'Ād, and Pharaoh firmly planted,

13. And (the tribe of) Thamūd, and the people of Lot, and the dwellers in the wood:[3] these were the factions.

1. Muḥammad's uncle (d. 619).
2. I.e. that is what you must do.
3. Midian [Pickthall's note].

14. Not one of them but did deny the messengers, therefore My doom was justified;

15. These wait for only one shout, there will be no second.

16. They say: "Our Lord! Hasten on for us our fate before the day of reckoning."

17. Bear with what they say, and remember Our servant David, lord of might. He was ever turning in repentance (toward God).

18. We subdued the hills to hymn the praises (of their Lord) with him at nightfall and sunrise,

19. And the birds assembled; all were turning to Him.

20. We made his kingdom strong and gave him wisdom and decisive speech.

21. And has the story of the litigants come to you? How they climbed the wall into the royal chamber;

22. How they burst in upon David, and he was afraid of them. They said: "Be not afraid! (We are) two litigants, one of whom has wronged the other, therefore judge rightly between us; do not be unjust; and show us the fair way.

23. "This my brother has ninety-nine ewes while I had one ewe; and he said: 'Entrust it to me,' and he conquered me in speech."

24. (David) said: "He has wronged you in demanding your ewe in addition to his ewes, and many partners oppress one another, except those who believe and do good works, and they are few." And David guessed that We had tried him,[4] and he sought forgiveness of his Lord, and he bowed himself and fell down prostrate and repented.

25. So We forgave him that; and he had access to Our presence and a happy journey's end.

26. (And it was said to him): "O David! We have set you as a viceroy on the earth; therefore judge rightly between mankind, and do not follow desire that it beguile you from the way of God." Those who wander from the way of God have an awful doom, inasmuch as they forgot the day of reckoning.

27. And We did not create the heaven and the earth and all that is between them in vain. That is the opinion of those who disbelieve. And woe to those who disbelieve, from the fire!

28. Shall We treat those who believe and do good works as those who spread corruption on the earth; or shall We treat the pious as the wicked?

29. (This is) a scripture that We have revealed to you, full of blessing, that they may ponder its revelations, and that men of understanding may reflect.

30. And We bestowed on David, Solomon. How excellent a servant! He was ever turning in repentance (toward God).

31. When there were shown to him at evening light-footed steeds

32. And he said: "I have preferred the good things (of the world) to the remembrance of my Lord"; until they were taken out of sight behind the curtain.

33. (Then he said): "Bring them back to me," and fell to slashing (with his sword their) legs and necks.

34. And We tried Solomon, and set upon his throne a (mere) body. Then he repented.

4. Because he took Bathsheba, the wife of Uriah, as one of his wives.

35. He said: "My Lord! Forgive me and bestow on me sovereignty such as shall not belong to any after me. You are the bestower."

36. So We made the wind subservient to him, blowing softly by his command wherever he intended.

37. And the unruly,[5] every builder and diver (We made subservient),

38. And others linked together in chains,

39. (Saying): "This is Our gift, so bestow or withhold, without reckoning."

40. He has favor with Us, and a happy journey's end.

41. And make mention (O Muḥammad) of Our servant Job, when he cried to his Lord (saying): "The devil afflicts me with distress and torment."

42. (And it was said to him): "Strike the ground with your foot. This (spring) is a cool bath and a refreshing drink."

43. And We bestowed on him (again) his household and their like together with them, a mercy from Us, and a memorial for men of understanding.

44. And (it was said to him): "Take in your hand a branch and strike with it, and do not break your oath." We found him steadfast, how excellent a servant! He was ever turning in repentance (to his Lord).

45. And make mention of our servants, Abraham, Isaac and Jacob, men of power and vision.

46. We purified them with a pure thought, remembrance of the home (of the hereafter).

47. In Our sight they are of the elect, the excellent.

48. And make mention of Ishmael and Elisha and Dhū l-Kifl.[6] All are of the chosen.

49. This is a reminder. For those who ward off (evil) is a happy journey's end,

50. Gardens of Eden, whose gates are opened for them,

51. In which, reclining, they call for plenteous fruit and cool drink (that is) in it.

52. And with them are those of modest gaze, companions.

53. This it is what you are promised for the day of reckoning.

54. This in truth is Our provision, which will never waste away.

55. This (is for the righteous). For the transgressors there will be an evil journey's end,

56. Hell, where they will burn, an evil resting-place.

57. Here is a boiling and an ice-cold draught, so let them taste it,

58. And other (torment) of the kind in pairs (the two extremes)!

59. Here is an army rushing blindly with you. (Those who are already in the fire say): "No word of welcome for them. They will roast at the fire."

60. They say: "No, but you (misleaders), for you there is no word of welcome. You prepared this for us (by your misleading). Now unfortunate is the plight."

61. They say: "Our Lord! Whoever prepared this for us, oh, give him double portion of the fire!"

62. And they say: "What ails us that we do not behold men whom we used to count among the wicked?

5. Lit. "devils" [Pickthall's note].
6. A prophet of the Arabs whose story is like that of Ezekiel [Pickthall's note].

63. "Did we take them (wrongly) for a laughingstock, or have our eyes missed them?"

64. That is very truth: the wrangling of the dwellers in the fire.

65. Say (to them, O Muḥammad): "I am only a warner, and there is no god save God, the one, the absolute,

66. "Lord of the heavens and the earth and all that is between them, the mighty, the pardoning."

67. Say: "It is tremendous tidings

68. "From which you turn away!

69. "I had no knowledge of those on high when they disputed;

70. "It is revealed to me only that I may be a plain warner."

71. When your Lord said to the angels: "I am about to create a mortal out of mire,

72. "And when I have fashioned him and breathed into him of My spirit, then fall down before him prostrate,"

73. The angels fell down prostrate, every one,

74. Except Iblīs; he was scornful and became one of the disbelievers.

75. He said: "O Iblīs! What hinders you from falling prostrate before that which I have created with both My hands?[7] Are you too proud or are you of the high exalted?"

76. He said: "I am better than him. You created me of fire, while You created him of clay."

77. He said: "Go forth from here, for you are outcast,

78. "My curse is on you until the day of judgment."

79. He said: "My Lord! Reprieve me until the day when they are raised."

80. He said: "You are of those reprieved

81. "Until the day of the time appointed."

82. He said: "Then, by Your might, I surely will beguile them every one,

83. "Save Your single-minded servants among them."

84. He said: "The truth is, and the truth I speak,

85. "That I shall fill hell with you and with such of them as follow you, together."

86. Say (O Muḥammad, to mankind): "I ask of you no fee for this, and I am no impostor.

87. "It is nothing else than a reminder for all peoples

88. "And you will come in time to know the truth of it."

## Sūra 39

*Al-Zumar*, "The Troops," takes its name from a peculiar word, meaning troops or companies, which occurs in verse 71, and again in verse 73. Some authorities think that verses 53 and 54 were revealed at Medina.

It seems manifestly to belong to the middle group of Meccan sūras, though Nöldeke places it in his last group.

7. The Muslim mystics explain this as meaning with both the glorious and the terrific attributes of God, whereas the angels were created by the exercise of only one class of attributes [Pickthall's note].

## The Troops

*Revealed at Mecca*

In the name of God, the beneficent, the merciful.

1. The revelation of the scripture is from God, the mighty, the wise.
2. We have revealed the scripture to you (Muḥammad) with truth; so worship God, making religion pure for Him (only).
3. Surely pure religion is for God only. And those who choose protecting friends beside Him (say): "We worship them only that they may bring us near to God." God will judge between them concerning that in which they differ. God does not guide one who is a liar, an ingrate.
4. If God had willed to choose a son, he could have chosen what he would of that which He has created. Be He glorified! He is God, the one, the absolute.
5. He has created the heavens and the earth with truth. He makes night to succeed day, and He makes day to succeed night, and He constrains the sun and the moon to give service, each running on for an appointed term. Is not He the mighty, the forgiver?
6. He created you from one being, then from that (being) He made its mate; and He has provided for you of cattle eight kinds. He created you in the wombs of your mothers, creation after creation, in a threefold gloom. Such is God, your Lord. His is the sovereignty. There is no God but Him. How then are you turned away?
7. If you are thankless, yet God is independent of you, though He is not pleased with thanklessness for His servants; and if you are thankful He is pleased by it for you. No laden soul will bear another's load. Then to your Lord is your return; and He will tell you what you used to do. He knows what is in the breasts (of men).
8. And when some hurt touches man, he cries to his Lord, turning to Him (repentant). Then, when He grants him a boon from Him he forgets that for which he cried to Him before, and sets up rivals to God that he may beguile (men) from His way. Say (O Muḥammad, to such an one): "Take pleasure in your disbelief a while. You are among the owners of the fire."
9. Is he who pays adoration in the watches of the night, prostrate and standing, bewaring of the hereafter and hoping for the mercy of his Lord, (to be accounted equal with a disbeliever)? Say (to them, O Muḥammad): "Are those who know equal with those who know not?" But only men of understanding will pay heed.
10. Say: "O My servants who believe! Observe your duty to your Lord." For those who do good in this world there is good, and God's earth is spacious. The steadfast will be paid their wages without stint.
11. Say (O Muḥammad): "I am commanded to worship God, making religion pure for Him (only).
12. "And I am commanded to be the first of those who surrender[1] (to Him)."
13. Say: "If I should disobey my Lord, I fear the doom of a tremendous day."

1. Ar. *Muslimīn* [Pickthall's note].

14. Say: "God I worship, making my religion pure for Him (only).
15. "Then worship what you will beside Him." Say: "The losers will be those who lose themselves and their family on the day of resurrection." Ah, that will be the manifest loss!
16. They have an awning of fire above them and beneath them a dais (of fire). With this does God appall His servants. O My servants, therefore fear Me!
17. And those who put away false gods lest they should worship them and turn to God in repentance, for them there are glad tidings. Therefore give good tidings (O Muḥammad) to my servants
18. Who hear advice and follow the best of it. Such are those whom God guides, and such are men of understanding.
19. Is he on whom the word of doom is fulfilled (to be helped), and can you (O Muḥammad) rescue him who is in the fire?
20. But those who keep their duty to their Lord, for them are lofty halls with lofty halls above them, built (for them), beneath which rivers flow. (It is) a promise of God. God does not fail His promise.
21. Have you not seen how God has sent down water from the sky and has caused it to penetrate the earth as watersprings, and afterward thereby produces crops of diverse hues; and afterward they wither and you see them turn yellow; then He makes them chaff. In this is a reminder for men of understanding.
22. Is he whose bosom God has expanded for the surrender[2] (to Him), so that he follows a light from his Lord, (as he who disbelieves)? Then woe to those whose hearts are hardened against remembrance of God. Such are in plain error.
23. God has (now) revealed the fairest of statements, a scripture consistent, (in which are promises of reward) paired (with threats of punishment), with which the flesh of those who fear their Lord creep, so that their flesh and their hearts soften to God's reminder. Such is God's guidance, with which He guides whom He will. And him whom God sends astray, for him there is no guide.
24. Is he then, who will strike his face against the awful doom upon the day of resurrection (as he who does right)? And it will be said to the wrongdoers: "Taste what you used to earn."
25. Those before them denied, and so the doom came on them from where they knew not.
26. Thus God made them taste humiliation in the life of the world, and the doom of the hereafter will be greater if they only knew.
27. And We have coined for mankind in this Qur'ān all kinds of similitudes, that perhaps they may reflect;
28. A lecture[3] in Arabic, containing no crookedness, that perhaps they may ward off (evil).
29. God coins a similitude: A man in relation to whom are several part owners, quarreling, and a man belonging wholly to one man. Are the two equal in similitude? Praise be to God! But most of them know not.
30. You will die, and they will die;
31. Then on the day of resurrection, before your Lord you will dispute.

2. Ar. *al-Islām* [Pickthall's note].
3. Ar. *Qur'ān* [Pickthall's note].

32. And who does greater wrong than he who tells a lie against God, and denies the truth when it reaches him? Will not the home of disbelievers be in hell?

33. And whoever brings the truth and believes in it—such are the dutiful.

34. They shall have what they will of their Lord's bounty. That is the reward of the good:

35. That God will remit from them the worst of what they did, and will pay them for reward the best they used to do.

36. Will not God defend His servant? Yet they would frighten you with those beside Him. He whom God sends astray, for him there is no guide.

37. And he whom God guides, for him there can be no misleader. Is not God mighty, able to requite (the wrong)?

38. And if you should ask them: "Who created the heavens and the earth?" they will say: "God." Say: "Do you think then of those you worship beside God, if God willed some hurt for me, could they remove from me His hurt; or if He willed some mercy for me, could they restrain His mercy?" Say: "God is my all. In Him do (all) the trusting put their trust."

39. Say: "O my people! Act in your manner. I too am acting. Thus you will come to know

40. "Who it is to whom comes a doom that will abase him, and on whom there falls everlasting doom."

41. We have revealed to you (Muḥammad) the scripture for mankind with truth. Then whoever goes right it is for his soul, and whoever strays, strays only to its hurt. And you are not a warder over them.

42. God receives (men's) souls at the time of their death, and that (soul) which dies not (yet) in its sleep. He keeps that (soul) for which He has ordained death and dismisses the rest until an appointed term. In this are signs for people who reflect.

43. Or do they choose intercessors other than God? Say: "What! Even though they have power over nothing and have no intelligence?"

44. Say: "To God belongs all intercession. His is the sovereignty of the heavens and the earth. And afterward to Him you will be brought back."

45. And when God alone is mentioned, the hearts of those who do not believe in the hereafter are repelled, and when those (whom they worship) beside Him are mentioned, behold! they are glad.

46. Say: "O God! Creator of the heavens and the earth! Knower of the invisible and the visible! You will judge between Your servants concerning that in which they used to differ."

47. And though those who do wrong possess all that is on the earth, and as much again together with it, they will seek to ransom themselves with it on the day of resurrection from the awful doom; and there will appear to them, from their Lord, that with which they never reckoned.

48. And the evils that they earned will appear to them, and that at which they used to scoff will surround them.

49. Now when hurt touches a man he cries to Us, and afterward when We have granted him a boon from Us, he says: "Only by force of knowledge I obtained it." No, but it is a test. But most of them know not.

50. Those before them said it, yet (all) that they had earned availed them not;

51. But the evils that they earned smote them; and such of these as do wrong, the evils that they earn will smite them; they cannot escape.

52. Do they not know that God enlarges providence for whom He will, and restricts it (for whom He will). In this are signs for people who believe.

53. Say: "O My servants who have been prodigal to their own hurt! Do not despair of the mercy of God, Who forgives all sins. He is the forgiving, the merciful."

54. Turn to your Lord repentant, and surrender to Him, before there comes to you the doom, when you cannot be helped.

55. And follow the better (guidance) of that which is revealed to you from your Lord, before the doom comes on you suddenly when you know not,

56. For fear that any soul should say: "Alas, my grief that I was unmindful of God, and I was indeed among the scoffers!"

57. Or should say: "If God had but guided me I should have been among the dutiful!"

58. Or should say, when it sees the doom: "Oh, that I had but a second chance that I might be among the righteous!"

59. (But now the answer will be): "No, for My revelations came to you, but you denied them and were scornful and were among the disbelievers."

60. And on the day of resurrection you (Muḥammad) see those who lied concerning God with their faces blackened. Is not the home of the scorners in hell?

61. And God delivers those who ward off (evil) because of their deserts. Evil does not touch them, nor do they grieve.

62. God is creator of all things, and He is guardian over all things.

63. His are the keys of the heavens and the earth, and they who disbelieve the revelations of God—such are they who are the losers.

64. Say (O Muḥammad, to the disbelievers): "Do you bid me serve other than God? O you fools!

65. "And it has been revealed to you as to those before you (saying): 'If you ascribe a partner to God your work will fail and you indeed will be among the losers.'

66. "No, but God you must serve, and be among the thankful!"

67. And they do not esteem God as He has the right to be esteemed, when the whole earth is His handful on the day of resurrection, and the heavens are rolled in His right hand. Glorified is He and high exalted from all that they ascribe as partner (to Him).

68. And the trumpet is blown, and all who are in the heavens and on the earth swoon away, save him whom God wills. Then it is blown a second time, and behold them standing waiting!

69. And the earth shines with the light of her Lord, and the book is set up, and the prophets and the witnesses are brought, and it is judged between them with truth, and they are not wronged.

70. And each soul is paid in full for what it did. And He is best aware of what they do.

71. And those who disbelieve are driven to hell in troops until, when they reach it and its gates are opened, and its warders say to them: "Did there not come to you messengers of your own, reciting to you the revelations of your Lord and warning you of the meeting of this your day?" They say: "Yes." But the word of doom for disbelievers is fulfilled.

72. It is said (to them): "Enter the gates of hell to dwell there." Thus wretched is the journey's end of the scorners.

73. And those who keep their duty to their Lord are driven to the garden in troops until, when they reach it, and its gates are opened, and its warders say to them: "Peace be to you! You are good, so enter (the garden of delight), to dwell there";

74. They say: "Praise be to God, Who has fulfilled His promise to us and has made us inherit the land, sojourning in the garden where we will!" So bounteous is the wage of workers.

75. And you (O Muḥammad) see the angels thronging round the throne, hymning the praises of their Lord. And they are judged aright. And it is said: "Praise be to God, the Lord of the worlds!"

## Sūra 40

*Al-Mu'min*, "The Believer," takes its name from verses 28–45, which describe the attempt of a believer, in the house of Pharaoh, to dissuade his people from opposing Moses and Aaron. It is the first of seven sūras beginning with the Arabic letters Ḥā, Mīm, all of which are sometimes referred to as Ḥā Mīm.

It belongs to the middle group of Meccan sūras. Some authorities hold verses 56 and 57 to have been revealed at Medina.

## The Believer

*Revealed at Mecca*

In the name of God, the beneficent, the merciful.

1. Ḥā. Mīm.[1]

2. The revelation of the scripture is from God, the mighty, the knower,

3. The forgiver of sin, the accepter of repentance, the stern in punishment, the bountiful. There is no God but Him. To Him is the journeying.

4. None argue concerning the revelations of God except those who disbelieve, so do not let their turn of fortune in the land deceive you (O Muḥammad).

5. The people of Noah and the factions after them denied (their messengers) before these, and every nation intended to seize their messenger and argued falsely, (thinking) thereby to refute the truth. Then I seized them, and how (awful) was My punishment.

6. Thus was the word of your Lord concerning those who disbelieve fulfilled: that they are owners of the fire.

7. Those who bear the throne, and all who are round about it, hymn the praises of their Lord and believe in Him and ask forgiveness for those who believe (saying): "Our Lord! You comprehend all things in mercy and knowledge, therefore forgive those who repent and follow Your way. Ward off from them the punishment of hell.

8. "Our Lord! And make them enter the gardens of Eden which you have promised them, with such of their fathers and their wives and their descendants as do right. You, only You, are the mighty, the wise.

1. See Q 2:1, footnote [Pickthall's note].

9. "And ward off from them ill deeds; and he from whom You ward off ill deeds that day, him have You taken into mercy. That is the supreme triumph."

10. (On that day) those who disbelieve are informed by proclamation: God's abhorrence is more terrible than your abhorrence one of another, when you were called to the faith but did refuse.

11. They say: "Our Lord! Twice have You made us die, and twice have You made us live. Now we confess our sins. Is there any way to go out?"

12. (It is said to them): "This is (your plight) because, when God only was invoked, you disbelieved, but when some partner was ascribed to Him you were believing. But the command belongs only to God, the sublime, the majestic.

13. "He it is who shows you His signs, and sends down for you provision from the sky. None pays heed except him who turns (to Him) repentant.

14. "Therefore (O believers) pray to God, making religion pure for Him (only), however much the disbelievers be averse"—

15. The exalter of ranks, the Lord of the throne. He casts the Spirit of His command upon whom He will of His servants, that He may warn of the day of meeting,

16. The day when they come forth, nothing of them being hidden from God. Whose is the sovereignty this day? It is God's, the one, the almighty.

17. This day is each soul requited what it has earned; no wrong (is done) this day. God is swift at reckoning.

18. Warn them (O Muḥammad) of the day of the approaching (doom), when the hearts will be choking the throats, (when) there will be no friend for the wrongdoers, nor any intercessor who will be heard.

19. He knows the traitor of the eyes, and what the bosoms hide.

20. God judges with truth, while those to whom they cry instead of Him judge not at all. God, He is the hearer, the observer.

21. Have they not traveled in the land to see the nature of the consequence for those who disbelieved before them? They were mightier than these in power and (in the) traces (which they left behind them) on the earth. Yet God seized them for their sins, and they had no protector from God.

22. That was because their messengers kept bringing them clear proofs (of God's sovereignty) but they disbelieved; so God seized them. He is strong, severe in punishment.

23. And We sent Moses with Our revelations and a clear warrant

24. To Pharaoh and Hāmān and Korah,[2] but they said: "A lying sorcerer!"

25. And when he brought them the truth from Our presence, they said: "Slay the sons of those who believe with him, and spare their women." But the plot of disbelievers is in nothing but error.

26. And Pharaoh said: "Permit me to kill Moses, and let him cry to his Lord. I fear that he will alter your religion or that he will cause confusion in the land."

27. Moses said: "I seek refuge in my Lord and your Lord from every scorner who does not believe in a day of reckoning."

2. See Q 28:76.

28. And a believing man of Pharaoh's family, who hid his faith, said: "Would you kill a man because he says: 'My Lord is God,' and has brought you clear proofs from your Lord? If he is lying, then his lie is upon him; and if he is truthful, then some of that with which he threatens you will strike you. God guides not one who is a prodigal, a liar.

29. "O my people! Yours is the kingdom today, you being uppermost in the land. But who would save us from the wrath of God should it reach us?" Pharaoh said: "I only show you what I think, and I only guide you to wise policy."

30. And he who believed said: "O my people! I fear for you a fate like that of the factions (of old);

31. "A plight like that of Noah's people, and 'Ād and Thamūd, and those after them, and God wills no injustice for (His) servants.

32. "And, O my people! I fear for you a day of summoning,

33. "A day when you will turn to flee, having no preserver from God: and he whom God sends astray, for him there is no guide.

34. "And Joseph brought you of old clear proofs, yet you did not cease to be in doubt concerning what he brought you until, when he died, you said: 'God will not send any messenger after him. Thus God deceives him who is a prodigal, a doubter.'"

35. Those who wrangle concerning the revelations of God without any warrant that has come to them, it is greatly hateful in the sight of God and in the sight of those who believe. Thus does God print on every arrogant, disdainful heart.

36. And Pharaoh said: "O Hāmān! Build for me a tower that perhaps I may reach the roads,

37. "The roads of the heavens, and may look upon the God of Moses, though I think him a liar." Thus was the evil that he did made attractive to Pharaoh, and he was debarred from the (right) way. The plot of Pharaoh ended but in ruin.

38. "And he who believed said: "O my people! Follow me. I will show you the way of right conduct.

39. "O my people! This life of the world is but a passing comfort, and the hereafter, that is the enduring home.

40. "Whoever does an ill deed, he will be repaid the like of it, while whoever does right, whether male or female, and is a believer, (all) such will enter the garden, where they will be nourished without stint."

41. And, "O my people! What ails me that I call you to deliverance when you call me to the fire?

42. "You call me to disbelieve in God and ascribe to Him as partners that of which I have no knowledge, while I call you to the mighty, the forgiver.

43. "Assuredly that to which you call me has no claim in the world or in the hereafter, and our return will be to God, and the prodigals will be owners of the fire.

44. "And you will remember what I say to you. I confide my cause to God. God is observer of (His) servants."

45. So God warded off from him the evils which they plotted, while a dreadful doom encompassed Pharaoh's people,

46. The fire; they are exposed to it morning and evening; and on the day when the hour rises (it is said): "Cause Pharaoh's people to enter the most awful doom."

47. And when they wrangle in the fire, the weak say to those who were proud: "We were a following to you: will you therefore rid us of a portion of the fire?"

48. Those who were proud say: "We are all (together) here. God has judged between (His) servants."

49. And those in the fire say to the guards of hell: "Entreat your Lord that He relieve us of a day of the torment."

50. They say: "Did not your messengers come to you with clear proofs?" They say: "Yes." They say: "Then pray, although the prayer of disbelievers is in vain."

51. We do help Our messengers, and those who believe, in the life of the world and on the day when the witnesses arise,

52. The day when their excuse does not avail the evildoers, and theirs is the curse, and theirs the ill abode.

53. And We gave Moses the guidance, and We caused the Children of Israel to inherit the scripture,

54. A guide and a reminder for men of understanding.

55. Then have patience (O Muḥammad). The promise of God is true. And ask forgiveness of your sin, and hymn the praise of your Lord at fall of night and in the early hours.

56. Those who wrangle concerning the revelations of God without a warrant having come to them, there is nothing else in their breasts except pride which they will never attain. So take refuge in God. He, only He, is the hearer, the observer.

57. Assuredly the creation of the heavens and the earth is greater than the creation of mankind; but most of mankind know not.

58. And the blind man and the one who sees are not equal, neither are those who believe and do good works (equal with) the evildoer. Little do you reflect!

59. The hour is surely coming, there is no doubt of it; yet most of mankind believe not.

60. And your Lord has said: "Pray to me and I will hear your prayer. Those who scorn My service, they will enter hell, disgraced."

61. God it is who has appointed for you night that you may rest in it, and day for seeing. God is a Lord of bounty for mankind, yet most of mankind do not give thanks.

62. Such is God, your Lord, the creator of all things. There is no God except Him. How then are you perverted?

63. Thus are they perverted who deny the revelations of God.

64. God it is who appointed for you the earth for a dwelling-place and the sky for a canopy, and fashioned you and perfected your shapes, and has provided you with good things. Such is God, your Lord. Then blessed be God, the Lord of the worlds!

65. He is the living one. There is no God except Him. So pray to Him, making religion pure for Him (only). Praise be to God, the Lord of the worlds!

66. Say (O Muḥammad): "I am forbidden to worship those to whom you cry beside God since there have come to me clear proofs from my Lord, and I am commanded to surrender to the Lord of the worlds."

67. He it is who created you from dust, then from a drop (of seed), then from a clot, then brings you forth as a child, then (ordains) that you attain

full strength and afterward that you become old men—though some among you die before—and that you reach an appointed term, that perhaps you may understand.

68. He it is who quickens and gives death. When He ordains a thing, He says to it only: "Be!" and it is.

69. Have you not seen those who wrangle concerning the revelations of God, how they are turned away?—

70. Those who deny the scripture and that with which We send Our messengers. But they will come to know,

71. When shackles are about their necks and chains. They are dragged

72. Through boiling waters; then they are thrust into the fire.

73. Then it is said to them: "Where are (all) that you used to make partners (in the sovereignty)

74. "Beside God?" They say: "They have failed us; but we used not to pray to anything before." Thus does God send astray the disbelievers (in His guidance).

75. (And it is said to them): "This is because you exulted on the earth without right, and because you were petulant.

76. "Enter the gates of hell, to dwell there. Evil is the habitation of the scornful."

77. Then have patience (O Muḥammad). The promise of God is true. And whether we let you see a part of that which We promise them, or (whether) We cause you to die, still to Us they will be brought back.

78. We sent messengers before you, among them those of whom We have told you, and some of whom We have not told you; and it was not given to any messenger that he should bring a sign except by God's leave, but when God's commandment comes (the cause) is judged aright, and the followers of vanity will then be lost.

79. God it is who has appointed for you cattle, that you may ride on some of them, and eat of some—

80. (Many) benefits you have from them—and that you may satisfy by their means a need that is in your breasts, and may be borne upon them as upon the ship.

81. And He shows you His signs. Which, then, of the signs of God do you deny?

82. Have they not traveled in the land to see the nature of the consequence for those before them? They were more numerous than these, and mightier in power and (in the) traces (which they left behind them) on the earth. But all that they used to earn availed them not.

83. And when their messengers brought them clear proofs (of God's sovereignty) they exulted in the knowledge they (themselves) possessed. And that which they used to mock befell them.

84. Then, when they saw Our doom, they said: "We believe in God only and reject (all) that we used to associate (with Him)."

85. But their faith could not avail them when they saw Our doom. This is God's law which has ever taken course for His servants. And then the disbelievers will be ruined.

## Sūra 41

*Fuṣṣilat*, "They Are Expounded," derives its title from a word in verse 3. It is also often called *Ḥā-Mīm, al-Sajda*, from a word in verse 37, *Ḥā-Mīm* being added to distinguish it from Q 32, which is called *al-Sajda*.

It belongs to the middle group of Meccan sūras.

# They Are Expounded

*Revealed at Mecca*

In the name of God, the beneficent, the merciful.

1. Ḥā. Mīm.[1]

2. A revelation from the beneficent, the merciful,

3. A scripture of which the verses are expounded, a lecture[2] in Arabic for people who have knowledge,

4. Good tidings and a warning. But most of them turn away so that they do not hear.

5. And they say: "Our hearts are protected from that to which you (O Muḥammad) call us, and in our ears there is a deafness, and between us and you there is a veil. Act, then. We also shall be acting."

6. Say (to them O Muḥammad): "I am only a mortal like you. It is inspired in me that your god is one God; therefore take the straight path to Him and seek forgiveness of Him. And woe to the idolaters,

7. "Who do not give the poor tax, and who are disbelievers in the hereafter.

8. "As for those who believe and do good works, for them is a reward enduring."

9. Say (O Muḥammad, to the idolaters): "Do you disbelieve in Him who created the earth in two days,[3] and do you ascribe rivals to Him?" He (and none else) is the Lord of the worlds.

10. He placed in it firm hills rising above it, and blessed it and measured in it its sustenance in four days, alike for (all) who ask;

11. Then He turned to the heaven when it was smoke, and said to it and to the earth: "Come both of you, willingly or loth." They said: "We come, obedient."

12. Then He ordained them seven heavens in two days and inspired in each heaven its mandate; and we decked the nether heaven with lamps, and rendered it inviolable.[4] That is the measuring of the mighty, the knower.

13. But if they turn away, then say: "I warn you of a thunderbolt like the thunderbolt (which fell of old upon the tribes) of ʿĀd and Thamūd;

14. "When their messengers came to them from before them and behind them, saying: 'Worship none but God!' they said: 'If our Lord had willed, He surely would have sent down angels (to us), so we are disbelievers in that with which you have been sent.'"

1. See Q 2:1, footnote [Pickthall's note].
2. Ar. *Qurʾān* [Pickthall's note].
3. Q 22:47; 32:5; 70:4 [Pickthall's note].
4. Q 37:6–10; 72:8–10 [Pickthall's note].

15. As for ʿĀd, they were arrogant in the land without right, and they said: "Who is mightier than us in power?" Could they not see that God who created them, He was mightier than them in power? And they denied Our revelations.

16. Therefore We let loose on them a raging wind in evil days, that We might make them taste the torment of disgrace in the life of the world. And the doom of the hereafter will be more shameful, and they will not be helped.

17. And as for Thamūd, We gave them guidance, but they preferred blindness to the guidance, so the bolt of the doom of humiliation overtook them because of what they used to earn.

18. And We delivered those who believed and used to keep their duty to God.

19. And (make mention of) the day when the enemies of God are gathered to the fire, they are driven on

20. Until, when they reach it, their ears and their eyes and their skins testify against them as to what they used to do.

21. And they say to their skins: "Why do you testify against us?" They say: "God has given us speech who gives speech to all things, and who created you at the first, and to whom you are returned.

22. "You did not hide yourselves for fear that your ears and your eyes and your skins should testify against you, but you deemed that God did not know much of what you did.

23. "That, your thought which you did think about your Lord, has ruined you; and you find yourselves (this day) among the lost."

24. And though they are resigned, yet the fire is still their home; and if they ask for favor, yet they are not of those to whom favor can be shown.

25. And We assigned them comrades (in the world), who made their present and their past fair-seeming to them. And the word concerning nations of the jinn and humankind who passed away before them has repercussions for them. They were ever losers.

26. Those who disbelieve say: Do not heed this Qur'ān, and drown the hearing of it; perhaps you may conquer.

27. But We shall cause those who disbelieve to taste an awful doom, and We shall requite them the worst of what they used to do.

28. That is the reward of God's enemies: the fire. In it is their immortal home, payment because they denied Our revelations.

29. And those who disbelieve will say: "Our Lord! Show us those who beguiled us of the jinn and humankind. We will place them underneath our feet that they may be among the lowliest."

30. Those who say: "Our Lord is God," and afterward are upright, the angels descend upon them, saying: "Fear not nor grieve, but hear good tidings of the paradise which you are promised.

31. "We are your protecting friends in the life of the world and in the Hereafter. There you will have (all) that your souls desire, and there you will have (all) for which you pray.

32. "A gift of welcome from the forgiving, the merciful."

33. And who is better in speech than him who prays to his Lord and does right, and says: "I am of those who surrender[5] (to Him)."

5. Ar. *Muslimīn* [Pickthall's note].

34. The good deed and the evil deed are not alike. Repel the evil deed with one which is better; then he, between whom and you there was enmity (will become) as though he was a bosom friend.

35. But none is granted it except those who are steadfast, and none is granted it except the owner of great happiness.[6]

36. And if a whisper from the devil reach you (O Muḥammad) then seek refuge in God. He is the hearer, the knower.

37. And of His portents are the night and the day and the sun and the moon. Do not adore the sun nor the moon; but adore God who created them, if it is in truth Him whom you worship.

38. But if they are too proud—still those who are with your Lord glorify Him night and day, and tire not.

39. And of His signs (is this): that you see the earth lowly, but when We send down water on it it thrills and grows. He who quickens it is the quickener of the dead. He is able to do all things.

40. Those who distort Our revelations are not hid from Us. Is he who is hurled into the fire better, or he who comes secure on the day of resurrection? Do what you will. He is observer of what you do.

41. Those who disbelieve in the reminder when it comes to them (are guilty), for it is an unassailable scripture.

42. Falsehood cannot come at it from before it or behind it. (It is) a revelation from the wise, the owner of praise.

43. Nothing is said to you (Muhammad) except what was said to the messengers before you. Your Lord is owner of forgiveness, and owner (also) of dire punishment.

44. And if We had appointed it a lecture[7] in a foreign tongue they would assuredly have said: "If only its verses were expounded (so that we might understand)!" "What! A foreign tongue and an Arab?"—Say to them (O Muḥammad): "For those who believe it is a guidance and a healing; and as for those who disbelieve, there is a deafness in their ears, and it is blindness for them. Such are called to from afar."

45. And We gave Moses the scripture, but there has been dispute concerning it; and but for a word that had already gone forth from your Lord, it would before now have been judged between them; but they are in hopeless doubt concerning it.

46. Whoever does right it is for his soul, and whoever does wrong it is against it. And your Lord is not at all a tyrant to His servants.

47. To Him is referred (all) knowledge of the hour. And no fruits burst forth from their sheaths, and no female carries or brings forth except with His knowledge. And on the day when He calls to them: "Where are My partners now?" they will say: "We confess to You, not one of us is a witness (for them)."

48. And those to whom they used to cry of old have failed them, and they perceive they have no place of refuge.

49. Man does not tire of praying for good, and if ill touches him, then he is disheartened, desperate.

50. And if We cause him to taste mercy after some hurt that has touched him, he will say: "This is my own; and I do not think that the hour will ever

6. I.e. not everyone is able to practice such forgiveness [Pickthall's note].
7. Ar. *Qur'ān* [Pickthall's note].

rise, and if I am brought back to my Lord, I surely shall be better off with Him"—But We shall tell those who disbelieve (all) that they did, and We shall make them taste hard punishment.

51. When We show favor to man, he withdraws and turns aside, but when ill touches him then he abounds in prayer.

52. Do you think: If it is from God and you reject it—Who is further astray than one who is at open feud (with God)?

53. We shall show them Our signs on the horizons and within themselves until it will be manifest to them that it is the truth. Does not your Lord suffice, since He is witness over all things?

54. How! Are they still in doubt about the meeting with their Lord? Is not He surrounding all things?

## Sūra 42

*Al-Shūrā*, "Counsel," takes its name from a word in verse 38.
It belongs to the middle group of Meccan sūras.

## Counsel

*Revealed at Mecca*

In the name of God, the beneficent, the merciful.

1. Hā. Mīm.[1]

2. 'Ayn. Sīn. Qāf.

3. Thus God the mighty, the knower inspires you (Muḥammad) as (He inspired) those before you.

4. To Him belongs all that is in the heavens and all that is on the earth, and He is the sublime, the tremendous.

5. Almost might the heavens above be rent asunder while the angels hymn the praise of their Lord and ask forgiveness for those on the earth. God is the forgiver, the merciful.

6. And as for those who choose protecting friends beside Him, God is warden over them, and you are in no way a guardian over them.

7. And thus We have inspired in you a lecture[2] in Arabic, that you may warn the mother-town[3] and those around it, and may warn of a day of assembling of which there is no doubt. A host will be in the garden, and a host of them in the flame.

8. Had God willed, He could have made them one community, but God brings whom He will into His mercy. And the wrongdoers have no friend or helper.

9. Or have they chosen protecting friends besides Him? But God, He (alone) is the protecting friend. He quickens the dead, and He is able to do all things.

10. And in whatever you differ, the verdict in that belongs to God. Such is my Lord, in whom I put my trust, and to whom I turn,

1. See Q 2:1, footnote [Pickthall's note].
2. Ar. *Qur'ān* [Pickthall's note].
3. I.e. Mecca [Pickthall's note].

11. The creator of the heavens and the earth. He has made for you pairs of yourselves, and of the cattle also pairs, by which He multiplies you. Nothing is as His likeness; and He is the hearer, the observer.

12. His are the keys of the heavens and the earth. He enlarges providence for whom He will and restricts (it for whom He will). He is knower of all things.

13. He has ordained for you that religion which He commended to Noah, and what We inspire in you (Muḥammad), and what We commended to Abraham and Moses and Jesus, saying: "Establish the religion, and do not be divided in it. Dreadful for the idolaters is that to which you call them." God chooses for Himself whom He will, and guides to Himself him who turns (toward Him).

14. And they were not divided until after the knowledge came to them, through rivalry among themselves; and had it not been for a word that had already gone forth from your Lord for an appointed term, it surely would have been judged between them. And those who were made to inherit the scripture after them are in hopeless doubt concerning it.

15. To this, then, summon (O Muḥammad). And be you upright as you are commanded, and do not follow their lusts, but say: "I believe in whatever scripture God has sent down, and I am commanded to be just among you. God is our Lord and your Lord. To us our works and to you your works; no argument between us and you. God will bring us together, and to Him is the journeying."

16. And those who argue concerning God after He has been acknowledged, their argument has no weight with their Lord, and wrath is upon them and theirs will be an awful doom.

17. God it is who has revealed the scripture with truth, and the balance.[4] How can you know? It may be that the hour is near.

18. Those who do not believe in it seek to hasten it, while those who believe are fearful of it and know that it is the truth. Are not they who dispute, in doubt concerning the hour, far astray?

19. God is gracious to His servants. He provides for whom He will. And He is the strong, the mighty.

20. Whoever desires the harvest of the hereafter, We give him increase in its harvest. And whoever desires the harvest of the world, We give him of it, and he has no portion in the hereafter.

21. Or have they partners (of God) who have made lawful for them in religion what God did not allow? And but for a decisive word (gone forth already), it would have been judged between them. For wrongdoers is a painful doom.

22. You see the wrongdoers fearful of what they have earned, and it will surely befall them; while those who believe and do good works (will be) in flowering meadows of the gardens, having what they wish from their Lord. This is the great preferment.

23. This is what God announces to His servants who believe and do good works. Say (O Muḥammad, to mankind): "I ask of you no fee for it, save loving-kindness among kinsfolk." And whoever scores a good deed We add to its good for him. God is forgiving, responsive.

4. Ar. *mīzān*, understood as a symbol of justice or the scale God uses to weigh a person's deeds.

24. Or say they: "He has invented a lie concerning God"? If God willed, He could have sealed your heart (against them). And God will wipe out the lie and will vindicate the truth by His words. He is aware of what is hidden in the breasts (of men).

25. And He it is who accepts repentance from his servants, and pardons the evil deeds, and knows what you do,

26. And accepts those who do good works, and gives increase to them of His bounty. And as for disbelievers, theirs will be an awful doom.

27. And if God were to enlarge the provision for His servants they would surely rebel on the earth, but He sends down by measure as He wills. He is informed, an observer of His servants.

28. And He it is who sends down the saving rain after they have despaired, and spreads out His mercy. He is the protecting friend, the praiseworthy.

29. And of His signs is the creation of the heaven and the earth, and of whatever beasts He has dispersed in it. And He is able to gather them when He will.

30. Whatever of misfortune strikes you, it is what your right hands have earned. And He forgives much.

31. You cannot escape on the earth, for beside God you have no protecting friend nor any helper.

32. And of His signs are the ships, like banners on the sea;

33. If He will He calms the wind so that they keep still upon its surface—in this are signs for every steadfast grateful (heart)—

34. Or he causes them to perish on account of what they have earned—and He forgives much—

35. And that those who argue concerning Our revelations may know they have no refuge.

36. Now whatever you have been given is but a passing comfort for the life of the world, and what God has is better and more lasting for those who believe and put their trust in their Lord,

37. And those who shun the worst of sins and indecencies and, when they are angry, forgive,

38. And those who answer the call of their Lord and establish worship, and whose affairs are a matter of counsel, and who spend of what We have bestowed on them,

39. And those who, when great wrong is done to them, defend themselves,

40. The recompense of an ill deed is an ill the like of it. But whoever pardons and amends, his wage is the affair of God. He loves not wrongdoers.

41. And whoever defends himself after he has suffered wrong—for such, there is no way (of blame) against them.

42. The way (of blame) is only against those who oppress mankind, and wrongfully rebel on the earth. For such there is a painful doom.

43. And whoever is patient and forgives—that is (of) the steadfast heart of things.

44. He whom God sends astray, for him there is no protecting friend after Him. And you (Muḥammad) will see the evildoers when they see the doom, say: "Is there any way of return?"

45. And you will see them exposed to (the fire), made humble by disgrace, and looking with veiled eyes. And those who believe will say: "The

(eternal) losers are they who lose themselves and their family on the day of resurrection." Are not the wrongdoers in perpetual torment?

46. And they will have no protecting friends to help them instead of God. He whom God sends astray, for him there is no road.

47. Answer the call of your Lord before there comes to you from God a day which there is no averting. You have no refuge on that day, nor have you any (power of) refusal.

48. But if they are averse, We have not sent you as a warder over them. Yours is only to convey (the message). And when We cause man to taste of mercy from Us he exults in it. And if some evil strikes them because of what their own hands have sent before, then man is an ingrate.

49. To God belongs the sovereignty of the heavens and the earth. He creates what He will. He bestows female (offspring) on whom He will, and bestows male (offspring) on whom He will;

50. Or He mingles them, males and females, and He makes barren whom He will. He is knower, powerful.

51. And it was not (given) to any mortal that God should speak to him unless (it be) by revelation or from behind a veil, or (that) He sends a messenger to reveal what He will by His leave. He is exalted, wise.

52. And thus have We inspired in you (Muḥammad) a spirit of Our command. You knew not what the scripture was, nor what the faith. But We have made it a light by which We guide whom We will of Our servants. And you guide to a right path,

53. The path of God, to whom belongs whatever is in the heavens and whatever is on the earth. Do not all things reach God at last?

## Sūra 43

*Al-Zukhruf*, "Ornaments of Gold," is the fourth of the Ḥā Mīm sūras. It takes its name from a word meaning golden ornaments which occurs in verse 35.

It belongs to the middle group of Meccan sūras.

## Ornaments of Gold

*Revealed at Mecca*

In the name of God, the beneficent, the merciful.

1. Ḥā. Mīm.[1]
2. By the scripture which makes plain,
3. We have appointed it a lecture[2] in Arabic that perhaps you may understand.
4. And in the mother of the book,[3] which We possess, it is indeed sublime, decisive.
5. Shall We utterly ignore you because you are a wanton people?
6. How many prophets did We send among the men of old!

1. See Q 2:1, footnote [Pickthall's note].
2. Ar. *Qur'ān* [Pickthall's note].
3. Commentators generally understand the "mother of the book" (Ar. *umm al-kitāb*) to be the divine source of the revelations given to the prophets.

7. And there never came there to them a prophet except they used to mock him.

8. Then We destroyed men mightier than these in prowess; and the example of the men of old has gone (before them).

9. And if you (Muḥammad) ask them: "Who created the heavens and the earth?" they will surely answer: "The mighty, the knower" created them;

10. Who made the earth a resting-place for you, and placed roads for you in it, that perhaps you may find your way;

11. And who sends down water from the sky in (due) measure, and with it We revive a dead land. Even so will you be brought forth;

12. He who created all the pairs, and appointed for you ships and cattle on which you ride.

13. That you may mount upon their backs, and may remember your Lord's favor when you mount thereon, and may say: "Glorified be He Who has subdued these for us, and we were not capable (of subduing them);

14. "To our Lord we are returning."

15. And they allot to Him a portion of His servants! Man is a mere ingrate.

16. Or does he choose daughters of all that He has created, and does He honor you with sons?

17. And if one of them has tidings of that which he likens to the Beneficent one,[4] his countenance becomes black and he is full of inward rage.

18. (Do they then liken to God) what is bred up in outward show, and in dispute cannot make itself plain?

19. And they make the angels, who are the slaves of the Beneficent, females. Did they witness their creation? Their testimony will be recorded and they will be questioned.

20. And they say: "If the Beneficent one had (so) willed, we should not have worshipped them." They have no knowledge whatever of that. They but guess.

21. Or have We given them any scripture before (this Qur'ān) so that they are holding fast to it?

22. No, for they say only: "We found our fathers following a religion, and we are guided by their footprints."

23. And even so We did not send a warner before you (Muḥammad) into any township without its affluent ones saying, "We found our fathers following a religion, and we are following their footprints."

24. (And the warner) said: "What! Even though I bring you better guidance than that you found your fathers following?" They answered: "In what you bring we are disbelievers."

25. So We requited them. Then see the nature of the consequence for the rejecters!

26. And when Abraham said to his father and his people: "I am innocent of what you worship

27. "Except Him Who did create me, for He will surely guide me."

28. And he made it a word enduring among his seed, that perhaps they might return.

29. No, but I let these and their fathers enjoy life (only) until there should come to them the truth and a messenger making plain.

4. I.e. tidings of the birth of a girl-child [Pickthall's note].

30. And now that the Truth has come to them they say: "This is mere magic, and we are disbelievers in it."

31. And they say: "If only this Qur'ān had been revealed to some great man of the two towns!"[5]

32. Is it they who apportion your Lord's mercy? We have apportioned among them their livelihood in the life of the world, and raised some of them above others in rank that some of them may take labor from others; and the mercy of your Lord is better than (the wealth) that they amass.

33. And were it not that mankind would have become one community,[6] We might well have appointed, for those who disbelieve in the Beneficent, roofs of silver for their houses and stairs (of silver) with which to mount,

34. And for their houses doors (of silver) and couches of silver on which to recline,

35. And ornaments of gold. Yet all that would have been only a provision of the life of the world. And the hereafter with your Lord would have been for those who keep from evil.

36. And he whose sight is dim to the remembrance of the Beneficent, We assign him a devil who becomes his comrade;

37. They surely turn them from the way of God, and yet they deem that they are rightly guided;

38. Until, when he comes to Us, he says (to his comrade): "Ah, would that between me and you there were the distance of the two horizons"[7]—an evil comrade!

39. And it does not profit you this day, because you did wrong, that you will be sharers in the doom.

40. Can you (Muḥammad) make the deaf to hear, or can you guide the blind or him who is in error manifest?

41. And if We take you away, We surely shall take vengeance on them,

42. Or (if) We show you that with which We threaten them; for We have complete command of them.

43. So hold fast to what is inspired in you. You are on a right path.

44. It is in truth a reminder for you and for your people; and you will be questioned.

45. And ask those of Our messengers whom We sent before you: "Did We ever appoint gods to be worshipped beside the Beneficent?"

46. And We sent Moses with Our revelations to Pharaoh and his chiefs, and he said: "I am a messenger of the Lord of the Worlds."

47. But when he brought them Our signs, they laughed at them.

48. And every sign that We showed them was greater than its sister (sign), and we grasped them with the torment, that perhaps they might turn again.

49. And they said: "O wizard! Entreat your Lord for us by the pact that He has made with you. We will walk aright."

50. But when We eased them of the torment, they broke their word.

51. And Pharaoh caused a proclamation to be made among his people saying: "O my people! Is not mine the sovereignty of Egypt and these rivers flowing under me? Can you not then discern?

5. The two towns were Mecca and Ṭā'if [Pickthall's note].
6. Through love of riches [Pickthall's note].
7. Lit. "the two Easts" [Pickthall's note].

52. "I am surely better than this fellow, who is despicable and can hardly make (his meaning) plain!

53. "Why, then, have armlets of gold not been set upon him, or angels sent along with him?"

54. Thus he persuaded his people to make light (of Moses), and they obeyed him. They were a wanton people.

55. So, when they angered Us, We punished them and drowned them every one.

56. And We made them a thing past, and an example for those after (them).

57. And when the son of Mary is quoted as an example, the people laugh aloud,

58. And say: "Are our gods better, or is he?" They do not raise the objection except for argument. No! but they are a contentious folk.

59. He is nothing but a servant[8] on whom We bestowed favor, and We made him an example for the Children of Israel.

60. And had We willed We could have set among you angels to be viceroys on the earth.

61. And there is knowledge of the hour. So do not doubt concerning it, but follow Me. This is the right path.

62. And do not let Satan turn you aside. He is an open enemy for you.

63. When Jesus came with clear proofs (of God's sovereignty), he said: "I have come to you with wisdom, and to make plain some of that concerning which you differ. So keep your duty to God, and obey me.

64. "God, He is my Lord and your Lord. So worship Him. This is a right path."

65. But the factions among them differed. Then woe to those who do wrong from the doom of a painful day.

66. Do they await anything except the hour, that it shall come upon them suddenly, when they know not?

67. Friends on that day will be foes one to another, except those who kept their duty (to God).

68. O My servants! For you there is no fear this day, nor is it you who grieve;

69. (You) who believed Our revelations and were self-surrendered,

70. Enter the garden, you and your wives, to be made glad.

71. There are brought round for them trays of gold and goblets, and there is all that souls desire and eyes find sweet. And you are immortal there.

72. This is the Garden which you are made to inherit because of what you used to do.

73. There for you is fruit in plenty from which to eat.

74. The guilty are immortal in hell's torment.

75. It is not relaxed for them, and there they despair.

76. We did not wrong them, but they themselves did the wrong.

77. And they cry: "O master! Let your Lord make an end of us." He says: "Here you must remain.

78. "We brought the truth to you, but you were, most of you, averse to the truth."

8. 'Abd Allah, "slave of God," is a proud designation with the Muslims, bondage to Allah implying liberation from all earthly servitudes [Pickthall's note]. Most contemporary English translations give "servant of God."

79. Or do they determine anything (against the Prophet)? We (also) are determining.
80. Or do they deem that We cannot hear their secret thoughts and private confidences? No, but Our envoys, present with them, do record.
81. Say (O Muḥammad): "The Beneficent one has no son. I am first among the worshippers."
82. Glorified be the Lord of the heavens and the earth, the Lord of the throne, from that which they ascribe (to Him)!
83. So let them flounder (in their talk) and play until they meet the day which they are promised.
84. And He it is who in the heaven is God, and on the earth God. He is the wise, the knower.
85. And blessed be He to whom belongs the sovereignty of the heavens and the earth and all that is between them, and with whom is knowledge of the hour, and to whom you will be returned.
86. And those to whom they cry instead of Him possess no power of intercession, except him who bears witness to the truth knowingly.
87. And if you ask them who created them, they will say: "God." How then are they turned away?
88. And he says: "O my Lord! Those are a people who believe not."
89. Then bear with them (O Muḥammad) and say: "Peace." But they will come to know.

## Sūra 44

*Al-Dukhān*, "The Smoke," takes its name from a word in verse 10. Tradition says that smoke here refers prophetically to the haze of dust which surrounded Mecca at the time of the great drought and famine which preceded the Muslim conquest of Mecca and facilitated it.

It belongs to the middle group of Meccan sūras.

## The Smoke

*Revealed at Mecca*

In the name of God, the beneficent, the merciful.

1. Ḥā. Mīm.[1]
2. By the scripture that makes plain
3. We revealed it on a blessed night—We are ever warning—
4. In it every wise command is made clear
5. As a command from our presence—We are ever sending—
6. A mercy from your Lord. He, even He is the hearer, the knower,
7. Lord of the heavens and the earth and all that is between them, if you would be sure.
8. There is no God but Him. He gives life and gives death; your Lord and Lord of your forefathers.
9. No, but they play in doubt.
10. But watch (O Muḥammad) for the day when the sky will produce visible smoke

1. See Q 2:1, footnote [Pickthall's note].

11. That will envelop the people.[2] This will be a painful torment.
12. (Then they will say): "Our Lord relieve us of the torment. We are believers."
13. How can there be remembrance for them, when a messenger making plain (the truth) had already come to them,
14. And they had turned away from him and said: "One taught (by others), a madman?"
15. We withdraw the torment a little. You return (to disbelief).
16. On the day when We shall seize them with the greater seizure, (then) in truth We shall punish.
17. And We tried before them Pharaoh's people, when there came to them a noble messenger,
18. Saying: "Give up to me the servants of God. I am a faithful messenger to you."
19. And saying: "Be not proud against God. I bring you a clear warrant.
20. "And I have sought refuge in my Lord and your Lord for fear that you stone me to death.
21. "And if you put no faith in me, then let me go."
22. And he cried to his Lord, (saying): "These are guilty folk."
23. Then (his Lord commanded): "Take away my servants by night. You will be followed,
24. "And leave the sea behind at rest, for they are a drowned host."
25. How many were the gardens and the watersprings that they left behind,
26. And the cornlands and the goodly sites
27. And pleasant things in which they took delight!
28. Even so (it was), and We made it an inheritance for other people;
29. And the heaven and the earth did not weep for them, nor were they reprieved.
30. And We delivered the Children of Israel from the shameful doom;
31. (We delivered them) from Pharaoh. He was a tyrant of the wanton ones.
32. And We chose them, purposely, above (all) creatures.
33. And We gave them signs in which there was a clear trial.
34. These, in truth, are saying:
35. "There is nothing but our first death, and we shall not be raised again.
36. Bring back our fathers, if you speak the truth!"
37. Are they better, or the people of Tubb'a[3] and those before them? We destroyed them, for surely they were guilty.
38. And We did not create the heavens and the earth, and all that is between them, in play.
39. We did not create them except with truth; but most of them know not.
40. Assuredly the day of decision is the term for all of them,
41. A day when in nothing can a friend avail, nor can they be helped,
42. Except him on whom God has mercy. He is the mighty, the merciful.
43. The tree of Zaqqūm,[4]

2. Of Mecca [Pickthall's note].
3. A name for many kings of Ḥimyar (the south Arabians), each of whom was called Tubb'a just as every king of Egypt was called Pharaoh [Pickthall's note].
4. Q 37:62; 56:52 [Pickthall's note].

44. The food of the sinner!
45. Like molten brass, it seethes in their bellies
46. As the seething of boiling water.
47. (And it will be said): "Take him and drag him to the midst of hell,
48. "Then pour upon his head the torment of boiling water.
49. "(Saying): 'Taste! You were, in truth, the mighty, the noble!
50. "'This is that about which you used to doubt.'"
51. Those who kept their duty will be in a place secure
52. Amid gardens and watersprings,
53. Attired in silk and silk embroidery, facing one another.
54. Even so (it will be). And We shall wed them to fair ones with wide, lovely eyes.
55. They call there for every fruit in safety.
56. They do not taste death there, except the first death. And He has saved them from the doom of hell,
57. A bounty from your Lord. That is the supreme triumph.
58. And We have made (this scripture) easy in your language only that they may heed.
59. Wait then (O Muḥammad). They (too) are waiting.

## Sūra 45

*Al-Jāthiya*, "Crouching," takes its name from a word in verse 28.
It belongs to the middle group of Meccan sūras.

## Crouching

*Revealed at Mecca*

In the name of God, the beneficent, the merciful.

1. Ḥā. Mīm.[1]
2. The revelation of the scripture is from God, the mighty, the wise.
3. In the heavens and the earth are signs for believers.
4. And in your creation, and all the beasts that He scatters on the earth, are signs for a people whose faith is sure.
5. And the difference of night and day and the provision that God sends down from the sky and thereby quickens the earth after her death, and the ordering of the winds, are signs for a people who have sense.
6. These are the signs of God which We recite to you (Muḥammad) with truth. Then in what fact, after God and His signs, will they believe?
7. Woe to each sinful liar,
8. Who hears the revelations of God recited to him, and then continues in pride as though he had not heard them. Give him tidings of a painful doom.
9. And when he knows anything of Our revelations he makes it a jest. For such there is a shameful doom.

1. See Q 2:1, footnote [Pickthall's note].

10. Beyond them there is hell, and that which they have earned will avail them nothing, nor those whom they have chosen for protecting friends beside God. Theirs will be an awful doom.

11. This is guidance. And those who disbelieve the revelations of their Lord, for them there is a painful doom of wrath.

12. God it is who has made the sea of service to you that the ships may run on it by His command, and that you may seek of His bounty, and that perhaps you may be thankful;

13. And has made of service to you whatever is in the heavens and whatever is on the earth; it is all from Him. In that are signs for a people who reflect.

14. Tell those who believe to forgive those who do not hope for the days of God; in order that He may requite folk what they have earned.

15. Whoever does right, it is for his soul, and whoever does wrong, it is against it. And afterward to your Lord you will be brought back.

16. And We gave the Children of Israel the scripture and the command and the prophethood, and provided them with good things and favored them above (all) peoples;

17. And gave them plain commandments. And they did not differ until after the knowledge came to them, through rivalry among themselves. Your Lord will judge between them on the day of resurrection concerning that in which they used to differ.

18. And now We have set you (O Muḥammad) on a clear road of (Our) commandment; so follow it, and do not follow the whims of those who know not.

19. They can avail you nothing against God. And as for the wrongdoers, some of them are friends of others; and God is the friend of those who ward off (evil).

20. This is clear indication for mankind, and a guidance and a mercy for a people whose faith is sure.

21. Or do those who commit ill deeds suppose that We shall make them as those who believe and do good works, the same in life and death? Bad is their judgment!

22. And God has created the heavens and the earth with truth, and that every soul may be repaid what it has earned. And they will not be wronged.

23. Have you seen him who makes his desire his god, and God sends him astray purposely, and seals up his hearing and his heart, and sets on his sight a covering? Then who will lead him after God (has condemned him)? Will you not then heed?

24. And they say: "There is nothing but our life of the world; we die and we live, and nothing destroys us save time"; when they have no knowledge whatever of (all) that; they only guess.

25. And when Our clear revelations are recited to them their only argument is that they say: "Bring (back) our fathers then, if you are truthful."

26. Say (to them, O Muḥammad): "God gives life to you, then causes you to die, then gathers you to the day of resurrection of which there is no doubt. But most of mankind know not."

27. And to God belongs the sovereignty of the heavens and the earth; and on the day when the hour rises, on that day those who follow falsehood will be lost.

28. And you will see each nation crouching, each nation summoned to its record. (And it will be said to them): "This day you are requited for what you used to do.
29. "This Our book pronounces against you with truth. We have caused (all) that you did to be recorded."
30. Then, as for those who believed and did good works, their Lord will bring them in to His mercy. That is the evident triumph.
31. And as for those who disbelieved (it will be said to them): "Were not Our revelations recited to you? But you were scornful and became a guilty people.
32. "And when it was said: 'God's promise is the truth, and there is no doubt of the hour's coming,' you said: 'We do not know what the hour is. We deem it nothing but a conjecture, and we are by no means convinced.'"
33. And the evils of what they did will appear to them, and that which they used to deride will befall them.
34. And it will be said: "This day We forget you, even as you forgot the meeting of this your day; and your habitation is the fire, and there is none to help you."
35. This, since as you made the revelations of God a jest, and the life of the world beguiled you. Therefore this day they do not come forth from there, nor can they make amends.
36. Then praise be to God, Lord of the heavens and Lord of the earth, the Lord of the worlds.
37. And to Him (alone) belongs majesty in the heavens and the earth, and He is the mighty, the wise.

## Sūra 46

*Al-Aḥqāf*, "The Wind-Curved Sandhills" (a formation which will be familiar to all desert travelers, and which especially characterized the region in which the tribe of ʿĀd were said originally to have lived), takes its name from a word in verse 21 and is the last of the Ḥāʾ Mīm group.

It belongs to the middle group of Meccan sūras, with the exception of verse 10, verses 15–18, and verse 35, which were revealed at Medina.

## The Wind-Curved Sandhills

*Revealed at Mecca*

In the name of God, the beneficent, the merciful.

1. Ḥā. Mīm.[1]
2. The revelation of the scripture is from God the mighty, the wise.
3. We did not create the heavens and the earth and all that is between them except with truth, and for a term appointed. But those who disbelieve turn away from that of which they are warned.
4. Say (to them, O Muḥammad): "Have you considered all that you invoke beside God? Show me what they have created of the earth. Or

1. See Q 2:1, footnote [Pickthall's note].

have they any portion in the heavens? Bring me a scripture before this (scripture), or some vestige of knowledge (in support of what you say), if you are truthful."

5. And who is further astray than those who, instead of God, pray to such as do not hear their prayer until the day of resurrection, and are unconscious of their prayer,

6. And when mankind are gathered (to the judgment) will become enemies for them, and will become deniers of having been worshipped.

7. And when Our clear revelations are recited to them, those who disbelieve say of the truth when it reaches them: "This is mere magic."

8. Or they say: "He has invented it." Say (O Muḥammad): "If I have invented it, still you have no power to support me against God. He is best aware of what you say among yourselves concerning it. He suffices for a witness between me and you. And He is the forgiving, the merciful."

9. Say: "I am no new thing among the messengers (of God), nor do I know what will be done with me or with you. I but follow that which is inspired in me, and I am but a plain warner."

10. Do you think: If it is from God and you disbelieve in it, and a witness of the Children of Israel[2] has already testified to the like of it and has believed, and you are too proud (what plight is yours)? God does not guide wrongdoing people.

11. And those who disbelieve say of those who believe: "If it had been (any) good, they would not have been before us in attaining it." And since they will not be guided by it, they say: "This is an ancient lie";

12. When before it there was the scripture of Moses, an example and a mercy; and this is a confirming scripture in the Arabic language, that it may warn those who do wrong and bring good tidings for the righteous.

13. Those who say: "Our Lord is God," and afterward walk aright, no fear shall come upon them neither shall they grieve.

14. Such are rightful owners of the garden, immortal in it, as a reward for what they used to do.

15. And We have commended to man kindness toward parents. His mother bears him with reluctance, and brings him forth with reluctance, and the bearing of him and the weaning of him is thirty months, until, when he attains full strength and reaches forty years, he says: "My Lord! inspire me that I may give thanks for the favor with which You have favored me and my parents, and that I may do right acceptable to You. And be gracious to me in the matter of my seed. I have turned to You repentant, and I am of those who surrender[3] (to You)."

16. Those are they from whom We accept the best of what they do, and overlook their evil deeds. (They are) among the owners of the garden. This is the true promise which they were promised (in the world).

17. And whoever says to his parents: "Shame upon you both! Do you threaten me that I shall be brought forth (again) when generations before me have passed away?" And they (the two parents) cry to God for help (and say): "Woe to you! Believe! The promise of God is true." But he says: "This is nothing except fables of the men of old":

2. ʿAbdallāh b. Salām [d. 663/64], a learned Jew of Medina, who became a devout Muslim. This is the usual explanation, though the verse is still considered as of Meccan revelation [Pickthall's note].

3. Ar. *Muslimīn* [Pickthall's note].

18. Such are those on whom the word concerning nations of the jinn and mankind which have passed away before them has effect. They are the losers.

19. And for all there will be ranks from what they do, that He may pay them for their deeds; and they will not be wronged.

20. And on the day when those who disbelieve are exposed to the fire (it will be said): "You squandered your good things in the life of the world and sought comfort in it. Now this day you are rewarded with the doom of ignominy because you were disdainful in the land without a right, and because you used to transgress."

21. And make mention (O Muḥammad) of the brother of ʿĀd[4] when he warned his people among the wind-curved sandhills—and warners came and went before and after him—saying: "Serve none but God. I fear for you the doom of a tremendous day."

22. They said: "Have you come to turn us away from our gods? Then bring upon us that with which you threaten us, if you are of the truthful."

23. He said: "The knowledge is with God only. I convey to you that with which I have been sent, but I see you are a people that do not know."

24. Then, when they beheld it as a dense cloud coming toward their valleys, they said: "Here is a cloud bringing us rain." No, but it is what you sought to hasten, a wind in which is painful torment,

25. Destroying all things by commandment of its Lord. And morning found them so that nothing could be seen except their dwellings. Thus do We reward the guilty people.

26. And We had empowered them with what We have not empowered you, and had assigned them ears and eyes and hearts; but their ears and eyes and hearts availed them nothing since they denied the revelations of God; and what they used to mock befell them.

27. And We have destroyed townships around you, and displayed (for them) Our revelation, that perhaps they might return.

28. Then why did those whom they had chosen for gods as a way of approach (to God) not help them? No, but they failed them utterly. And (all) that was their lie, and what they used to invent.

29. And when We inclined toward you (Muḥammad) certain of the jinn, who wished to hear the Qurʾān and, when they were in its presence, said: "Give ear!" and, when it was finished, turned back to their people, warning.

30. They said: "O our people! We have heard a scripture which has been revealed after Moses,[5] confirming what was before it, guiding to the truth and a right road.

31. "O our people! respond to God's summoner and believe in Him. He will forgive you some of your sins and guard you from a painful doom."

32. And whoever does not respond to God's summoner cannot escape on the earth, and he has no protecting friends instead of Him. Such are in error manifest.

33. Have they not seen that God, Who created the heavens and the earth and was not wearied by their creation, is able to give life to the dead? Yes, He is able to do all things.

4. The prophet Hūd [Pickthall's note].

5. From the mention of Moses it has been conjectured by some commentators that these jinn were foreign (i.e. non-Arabian) Jews, the word *jinn* in old Arabic being often applied to clever foreigners [Pickthall's note].

34. And on the day when those who disbelieve are exposed to the fire (they will be asked): "Is not this real?" They will say: "Yes, by our Lord." He will say: "Then taste the doom because you disbelieved."

35. Then have patience (O Muḥammad) even as the stout of heart among the messengers (of old) had patience, and seek not to hasten on the doom for them. On the day when they see what they are promised (it will seem to them) as though they had tarried but an hour of daylight. A clear message. Shall any be destroyed except evil-living people?

## Sūra 47

*Muḥammad*. This sūra takes its name from the mention of the Prophet by name in verse 2. Most commentators agree that verse 18 was revealed when the Prophet, forced to flee from Mecca, looked back, weeping, for a last sight of his native city. Some have considered the whole sūra to be a Meccan revelation, but with no good reason.

It belongs to the first and second years after the *hijra*, with the exception of verse 18, which was revealed during the *hijra*.

## Muḥammad

*Revealed at Medina*

In the name of God, the beneficent, the merciful.

1. Those who disbelieve and turn (men) from the way of God, He renders their actions vain.

2. And those who believe and do good works and believe in what is revealed to Muḥammad—and it is the truth from their Lord—He rids them of their ill deeds and improves their state.

3. That is because those who disbelieve follow falsehood and because those who believe follow the truth from their Lord. Thus God coins their similitudes for mankind.

4. Now when you meet in battle those who disbelieve, then it is striking of the necks until, when you have routed them, then making fast of bonds; and afterward either grace or ransom until the war lays down its burdens. That (is the ordinance). And if God willed He could have punished them (without you) but (thus it is ordained) that He may try some of you by means of others. And those who are slain in the way of God, He does not render their actions vain.

5. He will guide them and improve their state,

6. And bring them in to the garden which He has made known to them.

7. O you who believe! If you help God, He will help you and will make your foothold firm.

8. And those who disbelieve, perdition is for them, and He will make their actions vain.

9. That is because they are averse to what God has revealed; therefore He makes their actions fruitless.

10. Have they not traveled in the land to see the nature of the consequence for those who were before them? God wiped them out. And for the disbelievers there will be the like of it.

11. That is because God is patron of those who believe, and because the disbelievers have no patron.

12. God will cause those who believe and do good works to enter gardens underneath which rivers flow; while those who disbelieve take their comfort in this life and eat even as the cattle eat, and the fire is their habitation.

13. And how many a township stronger than your township (O Muḥammad) which has cast you out have We destroyed, and they had no helper!

14. Is he who relies on a clear proof from his Lord like those for whom the evil that they do is beautified while they follow their own lusts?

15. A similitude of the garden which those who keep their duty (to God) are promised: In it are rivers of unpolluted water, and rivers of milk of which the flavor does not change, and rivers of wine delicious to the drinkers, and rivers of clear-run honey; in it is every kind of fruit for them, with pardon from their Lord. (Are those who enjoy all this) like those who are immortal in the fire and are given boiling water to drink so that it tears their bowels?

16. Among them are some who give ear to you (Muḥammad) until, when they go forth from your presence, they say to those who have been given knowledge: What was that he said just now? Those are they whose hearts God has sealed, and they follow their own lusts.

17. While as for those who walk rightly, He adds to their guidance, and gives them their protection (against evil).

18. Do they await anything except the hour, that it should come upon them unawares? And the beginnings of it have already come. But how, when it has come on them, can they take their warning?

19. So know (O Muḥammad) that there is no god except God, and ask forgiveness for your sin and for believing men and believing women. God knows (both) your place of turmoil and your place of rest.

20. And those who believe say: "If only a sūra were revealed!" But when a decisive sūra is revealed and war is mentioned in it, you see those in whose hearts is a disease looking at you with the look of men fainting to death. Therefore woe to them!

21. Obedience and a civil word. Then, when the matter is determined, if they are loyal to God it will be well for them.

22. Would you then, if you were given the command, work corruption in the land and sever your ties of kinship?

23. Such are they whom God curses so that he deafens them and makes blind their eyes.

24. Will they not then meditate on the Qur'ān, or are there locks on their hearts?

25. Those who turn back after the guidance has been manifested to them, Satan has seduced them, and He gives them the rein.

26. That is because they say to those who hate what God has revealed: "We will obey you in some matters"; and God knows their secret talk.

27. Then how (will it be with them) when the angels gather them, striking their faces and their backs!

28. That will be because they followed what angers God, and hated what pleases Him. Therefore He has made their actions vain.

29. Or do those in whose hearts is a disease think that God will not bring to light their (secret) hates?

30. And if We would, We could show them to you (Muḥammad) so that you should know them surely by their marks. And you shall know them by the burden of their talk. And God knows your deeds.

31. And We shall try you until We know those of you who strive hard (for the cause of God) and the steadfast, and until We test your record.

32. Those who disbelieve and turn from the way of God and oppose the messenger after the guidance has been manifested to them, they do not hurt God at all, and He will make their actions fruitless.

33. O you who believe! Obey God and obey the messenger, and do not render your actions vain.

34. Those who disbelieve and turn from the way of God and then die disbelievers, God will not pardon them.

35. So do not falter and cry out for peace when you (will be) the uppermost, and God is with you, and He will not grudge (the reward of) your actions.

36. The life of the world is only a sport and a pastime. And if you believe and ward off (evil), He will give you your wages, and will not ask of you your worldly wealth.

37. If He should ask it of you and importune you, you would hoard it, and He would bring to light your (secret) hates.

38. You are those who are called to spend in the way of God, yet among you there are some who hoard. And as for him who hoards, he hoards only from his soul. And God is the rich, and you are the poor. And if you turn away He will exchange you for some other people, and they will not be the likes of you.

## Sūra 48

*Al-Fatḥ* takes its name from the word *fatḥ* meaning "victory" which occurs several times, and refers not to the conquest of Mecca but to the truce of al-Ḥudaybiya, which, though at the time it seemed a setback to the Muslims, proved in fact the greatest victory for Islam.

In the sixth year of the *hijra*, the Prophet set out with some 1,400 Muslims from Medina and the surrounding country, in the garb of pilgrims, not for war but to visit the Kaʿba. When they drew near to Mecca, they were warned that Quraysh had gathered their allies against them, and that their cavalry under Khālid b. al-Walīd[1] was on the road before them. Making a detour through gullies of the hills, they escaped the cavalry and, coming into the valley of Mecca, encamped at al-Ḥudaybiya below the city. The Prophet resolutely refused to give battle and persisted in attempts to parley with Quraysh who had sworn not to let him reach the Kaʿba. The Muslims were all the while in a position of some danger. Finally ʿUthmān b. ʿAffān[2] was sent into the city, as the man most likely to be well received on account of his relationships. ʿUthmān was detained by the Meccans, and news that he had been murdered reached the Muslims in their camp.[3]

It was then that the Prophet, sitting under a tree, took from his comrades the oath (referred to in verse 18) that they would hold together and fight to the death.[4] Then it became known that the rumor of ʿUthmān's death was

1. A military leader who would soon thereafter convert to Islam (d. 642).
2. The third caliph (d. 656).
3. Guillaume, *Life*, pp. 499–503 [Pickthall's note].
4. Guillaume, *Life*, pp. 503–4 [Pickthall's note].

false, and Quraysh at length agreed to a truce of which the terms were favorable to them. The Prophet and his multitude were to give up the project of visiting the sanctuary for that year, but were to make the pilgrimage the following year when the idolaters undertook to evacuate Mecca for three days to allow them to do so. Fugitives from Quraysh to the Muslims were to be returned, but not fugitives from the Muslims to Quraysh; and there was to be no hostility between the parties for ten years.

"And there was never a victory," says Ibn Khaldūn, "greater than this victory; for, as al-Zuhrī says, when it was war the peoples did not meet, but when the truce came and war laid down its burdens and people felt safe one with another, then they met and indulged in conversation and discussion. And no man spoke of Islam to another but the latter espoused it, so that there entered Islam in those two years (i.e., between al-Ḥudaybiya and the breaking of the truce by Quraysh) as many as all those who had entered it before, or more."[5]

The date of revelation is the sixth year of the *hijra*.

## Victory

*Revealed at Medina*

In the name of God, the beneficent, the merciful.

1. We have given you (O Muḥammad) a signal victory,[6]

2. That God may forgive you of your sin, that which is past and that which is to come, and may perfect His favor to you, and may guide you on a right path,

3. And that God may help you with strong help—

4. He it is who sent down peace of reassurance into the hearts of the believers that they might add faith to their faith. God's are the hosts of the heavens and the earth, and God is ever knower, wise—

5. That He may bring the believing men and the believing women into gardens underneath which rivers flow, in which they will abide, and may remit from them their evil deeds—that, in the sight of God, is the supreme triumph—

6. And may punish the hypocritical men and the hypocritical women, and the idolatrous men and the idolatrous women, who think an evil thought concerning God. For them is the evil turn of fortune, and God is angry at them and has cursed them, and has made ready for them hell, a wretched journey's end.

7. God's are the hosts of the heavens and the earth, and God is ever mighty, wise.

8. We have sent you (O Muḥammad) as a witness and a bearer of good tidings and a warner,

9. That you (mankind) may believe in God and His messenger, and may honor Him, and may revere Him, and may glorify Him at early dawn and at the close of day.

5. 'Abd al-Raḥmān b. Khaldūn, *Kitāb al-'Ibar* [ca. 1406, *Book of Lessons*], 8 vols. (Beirut: Dār al-Kutub al-'Ilmiyya, 1427/2006), 2:434 [Pickthall's note].
6. Traditionally understood as the treaty with the Meccans in 628 CE or the conquest of Mecca in 630 CE.

10. Those who swear allegiance to you (Muḥammad), swear allegiance only to God. The hand of God is above their hands. So whoever breaks his oath, breaks it only to his soul's hurt; while whoever keeps his covenant with God, on him will He bestow immense reward.

11. Those of the wandering Arabs who were left behind will tell you: "Our possessions and our households occupied us, so ask forgiveness for us!" They speak with their tongues what is not in their hearts. Say: "Who can avail you anything against God, if he intends you hurt or intends you profit? No, but God is ever aware of what you do.

12. "No, but you thought that the messenger and the believers would never return to their own people, and that was made to appear desirable in your hearts, and you did think an evil thought, and you were worthless people."

13. And as for him who does not believe in God and His messenger—We have prepared a flame for disbelievers.

14. And God's is the sovereignty of the heavens and the earth. He forgives whom He will, and punishes whom He will. And God is ever forgiving, merciful.

15. Those who were left behind will say, when you set forth to capture booty: "Let us go with you." They would rather change the verdict of God. Say (to them, O Muḥammad): "You shall not go with us. Thus has God said before." Then they will say: "You are envious of us." No, but they do not understand, except a little.

16. Say to those of the wandering Arabs who were left behind: "You will be called against a people of mighty prowess,[7] to fight them until they surrender; and if you obey, God will give you a fair reward; but if you turn away as you turned away before, He will punish you with a painful doom."

17. There is no blame for the blind, nor is there blame for the lame, nor is there blame for the sick (that they do not go forth to war). And whoever obeys God and His messenger, He will make him enter gardens underneath which rivers flow; and whoever turns back, him will He punish with a painful doom.

18. God was well pleased with the believers when they swore allegiance to you beneath the tree,[8] and He knew what was in their hearts, and He sent down peace of reassurance on them, and has rewarded them with a near victory;

19. And much booty that they will capture. God is ever mighty, wise.

20. God promises you much booty that you will capture, and has given you this in advance, and has withheld men's hands from you, that it may be a sign for the believers, and that He may guide you on a right path.

21. And other (gain), which you have not been able to achieve, God will encompass it. God is able to do all things.

22. And if those who disbelieve join battle with you they will take to flight, and afterward they will find no protecting friend nor helper.

23. It is the law of God which has taken course before. You will not find for the law of God anything of power to change.

24. And He it is who has withheld men's hands from you, and has withheld your hands from them, in the valley of Mecca, after He had made you victors over them. God is observer of what you do.

7. This prophecy is taken to refer to the war with the Persian or the Byzantine Empire [Pickthall's note].

8. A pledge of fidelity that Muḥammad took from each of his followers on the plain of al-Ḥudaybiya on the outskirts of Mecca.

25. It was these who disbelieved and debarred you from the Inviolable Place of Worship, and debarred the offering from reaching its goal. And if it had not been for believing men and believing women, whom you do not know, for fear that you should tread them under foot and thus incur guilt for them unknowingly—that God might bring into His mercy whom He will—if (the believers and the disbelievers) had been clearly separated We would have punished those of them who disbelieved with painful punishment.

26. When those who disbelieve had set up zealotry in their hearts, the zealotry of the age of ignorance, then God sent down His peace of reassurance upon His messenger and upon the believers and imposed on them the word of self-restraint, for they were worthy of it and fitting for it. And God is aware of all things.

27. God has fulfilled the vision[9] for His messenger in truth. You shall indeed enter the Inviolable Place of Worship, if God will, secure, (having your hair) shaven and cut, not fearing. But He knows what you know not, and has given you a near victory beforehand.

28. He it is who has sent His messenger with the guidance and the religion of truth, that He may cause it to prevail over all religion. And God suffices as a witness.

29. Muḥammad is the messenger of God. And those with him are hard against the disbelievers and merciful among themselves. You (O Muḥammad) see them bowing and falling prostrate (in worship), seeking bounty from God and (His) acceptance. The mark of them is on their foreheads from the traces of prostration. Such is their likeness in the Torah and their likeness in the Gospel—like sown corn that sends forth its shoot and strengthens it and rises firm upon its stalk, delighting the sowers—that He may enrage the disbelievers with (the sight of) them. God has promised, to such of them as believe and do good works, forgiveness and immense reward.

## Sūra 49

*Al-Ḥujurāt* takes its name from verse 4, which, with the following verse, is said to refer to the behavior of a deputation at a time when deputations from all parts of Arabia were coming to Medina to profess allegiance to the Prophet. The whole sūra, dealing as it does with manners, and particularly with behavior toward the Prophet, evidently belongs to a period when there were many seeking audience, among them many who were quite uncivilized.

The date of revelation is the ninth year of the *hijra*, "the year of deputations," as it is called.

## The Private Apartments

*Revealed at Medina*

In the name of God, the beneficent, the merciful.

1. O you who believe! Do not be forward in the presence of God and His messenger, and keep your duty to God. God is hearer, knower.

9. The Prophet had had a vision that he was entering the sanctuary at Mecca in peace and safety [Pickthall's note].

2. O you who believe! Do not lift up your voices above the voice of the Prophet, nor shout when speaking to him as you shout to one another, for fear that your works be rendered vain while you do not perceive.

3. They who subdue their voices in the presence of the messenger of God, those are they whose hearts God has proven to righteousness. Theirs will be forgiveness and immense reward.

4. Those who call you from behind the private apartments, most of them have no sense.

5. And if they had had patience until you came forth to them, it would have been better for them. And God is forgiving, merciful.

6. O you who believe! If an iniquitous one brings you tidings,[1] verify it, for fear that you strike some people in ignorance and afterward repent of what you did.

7. And know that the messenger of God is among you. If he were to obey you in much of the government, you would surely be in trouble; but God has endeared the faith to you and has beautified it in your hearts, and has made disbelief and lewdness and rebellion hateful to you. Such are they who are the rightly guided.

8. (It is) a bounty and a grace from God; and God is knower, wise.

9. And if two parties of believers fall to fighting, then make peace between them. And if one party of them does wrong to the other, fight that which does wrong until it returns to the ordinance of God; then, if it returns, make peace between them justly, and act equitably. God loves the equitable.

10. The believers are nothing else than brothers. Therefore make peace between your brothers and observe your duty to God that perhaps you may obtain mercy.

11. O you who believe! Do not let a people deride a people who may be better than they (are), nor let women (deride) women who may be better than they are; neither defame one another, nor insult one another by nicknames. Bad is the name of lewdness after faith. And whoever does not turn in repentance, such are evildoers.

12. O you who believe! Shun much suspicion; for some suspicion is a crime. And do not spy on or backbite one another. Would one of you love to eat the flesh of his dead brother? You abhor that (so abhor the other)! And keep your duty (to God). God is relenting, merciful.

13. O mankind! We have created you male and female, and have made you nations and tribes that you may know one another. The noblest of you, in the sight of God, is the best in conduct. God is knower, aware.

14. The wandering Arabs say: "We believe." Say (to them, O Muḥammad): "You do not believe, but rather say 'We submit,' for the faith has not yet entered into your hearts. Yet, if you obey God and His messenger, He will not withhold from you anything of (the reward of) your deeds. God is forgiving, merciful."

15. The (true) believers are only those who believe in God and His messenger and afterward do not doubt, but strive with their wealth and their lives for the cause of God. Such are the sincere.

1. The reference is to a man who brought false news of a revolt of the subject Jews at Khaybar [Pickthall's note]. Khaybar, an oasis north of Medina, was conquered by Muslim forces in 629 CE.

16. Say (to them, O Muḥammad): "Would you teach God your religion, when God knows all that is in the heavens and all that is on the earth, and God is aware of all things?"

17. They make it a favor to you (Muḥammad) that they have surrendered (to Him). Say: "Do not consider your surrender a favor to me; no, but God does confer a favor on you, inasmuch as He has led you to the faith, if you are earnest.

18. "God knows the unseen of the heavens and the earth. And God is observer of what you do."

## Sūra 50

Takes its name from the letter of the Arabic alphabet which stands alone at the beginning of the first verse.

It belongs to the middle group of Meccan sūras.

## Qāf

*Revealed at Mecca*

In the name of God, the beneficent, the merciful.

1. Qaf. By the glorious Qur'ān.

2. No, but they marvel that a warner of their own has come to them; and the disbelievers say: "This is a strange thing:

3. "When we are dead and have become dust (shall we be brought back again)? That would be a far return!"

4. We know what the earth takes of them,[1] and with Us is a recording book.

5. No, but they have denied the truth when it came to them, therefore they are now in a troubled state.

6. Have they not then observed the sky above them, how We have constructed it and beautified it, and how there are no rifts in it?

7. And the earth have We spread out, and have flung firm hills on it, and have caused of every lovely kind to grow on it,

8. A vision and a reminder for every penitent servant.

9. And We send down from the sky blessed water whereby We give growth to gardens and the grain of crops,

10. And lofty date palms with ranged clusters,

11. Provision (made) for men; and with it We quicken a dead land. Even so will be the resurrection of the dead.

12. The people of Noah denied (the truth) before them, and (so did) the dwellers at al-Rass and (the tribe of) Thamūd,

13. And (the tribe of) 'Ād, and Pharaoh, and the brethren of Lot,

14. And the dwellers in the wood,[2] and the people of Tubb'a:[3] every one denied their messengers, therefore My threat took effect.

1. I.e. those of them who die and are buried in the earth [Pickthall's note].
2. Midian [Pickthall's note].
3. The name of a famous dynasty in Yemen [Pickthall's note].

15. Were We then worn out by the first creation? Yet they are in doubt about a new creation.

16. We created man and We know what his soul whispers to him, and We are nearer to him than his jugular vein.

17. When the two receivers[4] receive (him), seated on the right hand and on the left,

18. He utters no word but there is with him an observer ready.

19. And the agony of death comes in truth. (And it is said to him): This is what you were accustomed to shun.

20. And the trumpet is blown. This is the threatened day.

21. And every soul comes, along with it a driver and a witness

22. (And to the evildoer it is said): "You were in heedlessness of this. Now We have removed from you your covering, and piercing is your sight this day."

23. And (to the evildoer) his comrade says: "This is that which I have ready (as testimony)."

24. (And it is said): "You two[5] hurl to hell each rebel ingrate,

25. "Hinderer of good, transgressor, doubter,

26. "Who sets up another god along with God. You two hurl him to the dreadful doom."

27. His comrade says: "Our Lord! I did not cause him to rebel, but he was (himself) far gone in error."

28. He says: "Do not contend in My presence, when I had already offered to you the warning.

29. "The sentence that comes from Me cannot be changed, and I am not a tyrant to the servants."

30. On the day when We say to hell: "Are you filled?" and it says: "Can there be more to come?"

31. And the garden is brought near for those who kept from evil, no longer distant.

32. (And it is said): "This is what you were promised. (It is) for every penitent and heedful one,

33. "Who fears the beneficent in secret and comes with a contrite heart.

34. "Enter it in peace. This is the day of immortality."

35. There they have all that they desire, and there is more with Us.

36. And how many a generation We destroyed before them, who were mightier than these in prowess so that they overran the lands! Had they any place of refuge (when the judgment came)?

37. In that is a reminder for him who has a heart, or gives ear with full intelligence.

38. And We created the heavens and the earth, and all that is between them, in six days,[6] and nothing of weariness touched Us.

39. Therefore (O Muḥammad) bear with what they say, and hymn the praise of your Lord before the rising and before the setting of the sun;

40. And in the nighttime hymn His praise, and after the (prescribed) prostrations.

4. A reference to the two angels who sit on a person's shoulders and record both good and evil deeds.
5. The driver and the witness (verse 21) or the two receivers (verse 17) [Pickthall's note].
6. Q 22:47; 32:5; 70:4 [Pickthall's note].

41. And listen on the day when the crier cries from a near place,
42. The day when they will hear the (awful) cry in truth. That is the day of coming forth (from the graves).
43. It is We Who bring to life and give death, and to Us is the journeying.
44. On the day when the earth splits asunder from them, hastening forth (they come). That is a gathering easy for Us (to make).
45. We are best aware of what they say, and you (O Muḥammad) are not a compeller over them. But warn by the Qur'ān him who fears My threat.

## Sūra 51

*Al-Dhāriyāt*, "The Winnowing Winds," takes its name from a word in verse 1. I have followed the usual interpretation of the first four verses, but they may also be taken as all referring to winds or to angels.

An early Meccan sūra.

## The Winnowing Winds

*Revealed at Mecca*

In the name of God, the beneficent, the merciful.

1. By those that winnow with a winnowing
2. And those that bear the burden (of the rain)
3. And those that glide with ease (upon the sea)
4. And those who distribute (blessings) by command,
5. That with which you are threatened is indeed true,
6. And the judgment will indeed befall.
7. By the heaven full of paths,
8. You are of various opinion (concerning the truth).
9. He is made to turn away from it who is (himself) averse.
10. Accursed be the conjecturers
11. Who are careless in an abyss!
12. They ask: "When is the day of judgment?"
13. (It is) the day when they will be tormented at the fire,
14. (And it will be said to them): "Taste your torment (which you inflicted). This is what you sought to hasten."
15. Those who keep from evil will dwell amid gardens and watersprings,
16. Taking what their Lord gives them; for before they were doers of good;
17. They used to sleep but little of the night,
18. And at the dawning of each day would seek forgiveness,
19. And in their wealth the beggar and the outcast had due share.
20. And on the earth are portents for those whose faith is sure,
21. And (also) in yourselves. Can you then not see?
22. And in the heaven is your providence and that which you are promised;
23. And by the Lord of the heavens and the earth, it is the truth, even as (it is true) that you speak.

24. Has the story of Abraham's honored guests reached you (O Muḥammad)?

25. When they came in to him and said: "Peace!" he answered, "Peace!" (and thought): "People unknown (to me)."

26. Then he went apart to his housefolk so that they brought a fatted calf;

27. And he set it before them, saying: "Will you not eat?"

28. Then he conceived a fear of them. They said: "Fear not!" and gave him tidings of (the birth of) a wise son.

29. Then his wife came forward, making moan, and struck her face, and cried: "A barren old woman!"

30. They said: "Even so says your Lord. He is the wise, the knower."

31. (Abraham) said: "And (afterward) what is your errand, O you sent (from God)?"

32. They said: "We are sent to a guilty folk,

33. "That we may send upon them stones of clay,

34. "Marked by your Lord for (the destruction of) the wanton."

35. Then We brought forth such believers as were there.

36. But We found there but one house of those surrendered[1] (to God).

37. And We left behind there a sign for those who fear a painful doom.

38. And in Moses (too, there is a sign) when We sent him to Pharaoh with clear warrant,

39. But Pharaoh withdrew (confiding) in his might, and said: "A wizard or a madman."

40. So We seized him and his hosts and flung them in the sea, for he was reprobate.

41. And in (the tribe of) 'Ād (there is a sign) when We sent the fatal wind against them.

42. It spared nothing that it reached, but made it (all) as dust.

43. And in (the tribe of) Thamūd (there is a portent) when they were told: "Take your ease awhile."

44. But they rebelled against their Lord's decree, and so the thunderbolt overtook them even while they gazed;

45. And they were unable to rise up, nor could they help themselves.

46. And the people of Noah before that. They were a licentious people.

47. We have built the heaven with might, and We it is Who make the vast extent (of it).

48. And the earth have We laid out, how gracious is its spreader!

49. And all things We have created by pairs, that perhaps you may reflect.

50. Therefore flee to God; I[2] am a plain warner to you from Him.

51. And do not set any other god along with God; I am a plain warner to you from Him.

52. Even so there did not come a messenger to those before them but they said: "A wizard or a madman!"

53. Have they handed down (the saying) as an heirloom one to another? No, but they are obstinate people.

54. So withdraw from them (O Muḥammad), for you are in no way blameworthy,

1. Ar. *Muslimīn* [Pickthall's note].
2. The revealing angel, it would appear [Pickthall's note].

55. And warn, for warning profits believers.

56. I created the jinn and humankind only that they might worship Me.

57. I seek no livelihood from them, nor do I ask that they should feed Me.

58. God! He it is that gives livelihood, the Lord of unbreakable might.

59. And for those who (now) do wrong there is an evil day like the evil day (which came for) their likes (of old); so let them not ask Me to hasten on (that day).

60. And woe to those who disbelieve, from that day of theirs which they are promised.

## Sūra 52

*Al-Ṭūr*, "The Mount," takes its name from the opening verse.
An early Meccan sūra.

## The Mount

*Revealed at Mecca*

In the name of God, the beneficent, the merciful.

1. By the mount,
2. And a scripture inscribed
3. On fine parchment unrolled,
4. And the house frequented,
5. And the roof exalted,
6. And the sea kept filled,
7. The doom of your Lord will surely come to pass;
8. There is none that can ward it off.
9. On the day when the heaven will heave with (awful) heaving,
10. And the mountains move away with (awful) movement,
11. Then woe that day to the deniers
12. Who play in talk of grave matters;
13. The day when they are thrust with a (disdainful) thrust, into the fire of hell
14. (And it is said to them): "This is the fire which you used to deny.
15. "Is this magic, or do you not see?
16. "Endure the heat of it, and whether you are patient of it or impatient of it is all one for you. You are only being paid for what you used to do."
17. Those who kept their duty dwell in gardens and delight,
18. Happy because of what their Lord has given them, and (because) their Lord has warded off from them the torment of hellfire.
19. (And it is said to them): "Eat and drink in health (as a reward) for what you used to do,"
20. Reclining on ranged couches. And We wed them to fair ones with wide, lovely eyes.
21. And they who believe and whose seed follow them in faith, We cause their seed to join them (there), and We deprive them of nothing of their (life's) work. Every man is a pledge for that which he has earned.
22. And We provide them with fruit and meat such as they desire.

23. There they pass from hand to hand a cup in which is neither vanity nor cause of sin.

24. And there go round, waiting on them menservants of their own, as they were hidden pearls.

25. And some of them draw near to others, questioning,

26. Saying: "Of old, when we were with our families, we were ever anxious;

27. "But God has been gracious to us and has preserved us from the torment of the breath of fire.

28. "We used to pray to Him of old. He is the benign, the merciful."

29. Therefore warn (men, O Muḥammad). By the grace of God you are neither soothsayer nor madman.[1]

30. Or do they say: "(He is) a poet, (one) for whom we may expect the accident of time?"

31. Say (to them): "Expect (your fill)! I am with you among the expectant."

32. Do their minds command them to do this, or are they an outrageous people?

33. Or do they say: "He has invented it?" No, but they will not believe!

34. Then let them produce speech the like of it, if they are truthful.

35. Or were they created out of nothing? Or are they the creators?

36. Or did they create the heavens and the earth? No, but they are sure of nothing!

37. Or do they own the treasures of your Lord? Or have they been given charge (of them)?

38. Or have they any stairway (to heaven) by means of which they overhear (decrees). Then let their listener produce some warrant manifest!

39. Or has He daughters whereas you have sons?

40. Or do you ask (Muḥammad) a fee from them so that they are plunged in debt?

41. Or do they possess the unseen so that they can write (it) down?

42. Or do they seek to ensnare (the messenger)? But those who disbelieve, they are the ensnared!

43. Or have they any god beside God? Glorified be God from all that they ascribe as partner (to Him)!

44. And if they were to see a fragment of the heaven falling, they would say: "A heap of clouds."

45. Then let them be (O Muḥammad), until they meet their day, in which they will be thunderstricken,

46. A day in which their guile will avail them nothing, nor will they be helped.

47. And, for those who do wrong, there is a punishment beyond that. But most of them know not.

48. So wait patiently (O Muḥammad) for your Lord's decree, for surely you are in our sight; and hymn the praise of your Lord when you arise,

49. And in the nighttime also hymn His praise, and at the setting of the stars.

1. Some of Muḥammad's opponents charged that he was a sorcerer, a poet, or insane.

# Sūra 53

*Al-Najm*, "The Star," takes its name from a word in the first verse.
An early Meccan sūra.

## The Star

*Revealed at Mecca*

In the name of God, the beneficent, the merciful.

1. By the star when it sets,
2. Your comrade does not err, nor is deceived;
3. Nor does he speak of (his own) desire.
4. It is nothing but an inspiration that is inspired,
5. Which one of mighty powers has taught him,
6. One vigorous; and he grew clear to view[1]
7. When he was on the uppermost horizon.
8. Then he drew near and came down
9. Until he was (distant) two bows' length or even nearer,
10. And He revealed to His servant what he revealed.
11. The heart did not lie (in seeing) what it saw.
12. Will you then dispute with him concerning what he sees?
13. And he saw him yet another time[2]
14. By the lote tree of the utmost boundary,[3]
15. Near to which is the garden of abode.
16. When that which shrouds did enshroud the lote tree,
17. The eye turned not aside nor yet was overbold.
18. He saw one of the greater revelations of his Lord.
19. Have you thought about al-Lāt[4] and al-ʿUzzā[5]
20. And Manāt,[6] the third, the other?
21. Are yours the males and His the females?[7]
22. That indeed would be an unfair division!
23. They are but names which you have named, you and your fathers,
for which God has revealed no warrant. They follow but a guess and that
which (they) themselves desire. And now the guidance from their Lord has
come to them.
24. Or shall man have what he covets?
25. But to God belongs the after (life), and the former.
26. And how many angels are in the heavens whose intercession avails
nothing except after God gives leave to whom He chooses and accepts!

1. This and the five following verses are generally accepted as referring to the Prophet's vision on Mt. Ḥirāʾ [Pickthall's note]. The first revelation; see Q 96:1–5.
2. This is generally accepted as a reference to the Prophet's vision in which he ascended through the seven heavens [Pickthall's note].
3. Many commentators believe that the lote tree is the heavenly boundary beyond which angels cannot pass, while others see it as a reference to the shade and bliss of heaven.
4. An idol of the pagan Arabs [Pickthall's note].
5. An idol of the pagan Arabs [Pickthall's note].
6. An idol of the pagan Arabs [Pickthall's note].
7. The pagan Arabs pretended that their idols were daughters of God [Pickthall's note].

27. It is those who disbelieve in the hereafter who name the angels with the names of females.

28. And they have no knowledge of it. They follow but a guess, and a guess can never take the place of the truth.

29. Then withdraw (O Muhammad) from him who flees from Our remembrance and desires but the life of the world.

30. Such is their sum of knowledge. Your Lord is best aware of him who strays, and He is best aware of him who goes right.

31. And to God belongs whatever is in the heavens and whatever is on the earth, that He may reward those who do evil with that which they have done, and reward those who do good with goodness.

32. Those who avoid enormities of sin and abominations, except the unwilled offences—(for them) your Lord is of vast mercy. He is best aware of you (from the time) when He created you from the earth, and when you were hidden in the bellies of your mothers. Therefore do not ascribe purity to yourselves. He is best aware of him who wards off (evil).

33. Did you (O Muḥammad) observe him who turned away,

34. And gave a little, then was grudging?

35. Has he knowledge of the unseen so that he sees?

36. Or has he not had news of what is in the books of Moses

37. And Abraham who paid his debt:

38. That no laden one (soul) shall bear another's load,

39. And that man has only that for which he makes effort,

40. And that his effort will be seen,

41. And afterward he will be repaid for it with fullest payment;

42. And that your Lord, He is the goal;

43. And that He it is who makes (people) laugh, and makes (people) weep,

44. And that He it is who gives death and gives life;

45. And that He creates the two spouses, the male and the female,

46. From a drop (of seed) when it is poured forth;

47. And that He has ordained the second bringing forth;

48. And that He it is Who enriches and contents;

49. And that He it is Who is the Lord of Sirius;[8]

50. And that He destroyed the former (tribe of) 'Ād,[9]

51. And (the tribe of) Thamūd He did not spare;

52. And the people of Noah before that, they were more unjust and more rebellious;

53. And al-Mu'tafika[1] He destroyed

54. So that there covered them that which did cover.

55. Concerning which then, of the bounties of your Lord, can you dispute?

56. This is a warner of the warners of old.

57. The threatened hour is near.

58. None beside God can disclose it.

59. Marvel then at this statement,

60. And laugh and not weep,

61. While you amuse yourselves?

62. Rather prostrate yourselves before God and serve Him.

8. A star worshipped by some of the pagan Arabs.
9. There was still in existence a tribe of that name [Pickthall's note].
1. Generally supposed to be a name for the villages of the people of Lot [Pickthall's note].

# Sūra 54

*Al-Qamar*, "The Moon," takes its name from the first verse: "The hour drew near and the moon was rent in two." A strange appearance of the moon in the sky, as if it had been torn asunder, is recorded in the traditions of several Companions of the Prophet as having astonished the people of Mecca about the time when the idolaters were beginning to persecute the Muslims.

An early Meccan sūra.

## The Moon

*Revealed at Mecca*

In the name of God, the beneficent, the merciful.

1. The hour drew near and the moon was rent in two.
2. And if they behold a portent they turn away and say: "Prolonged illusion."
3. They denied (the truth) and followed their own lusts. Yet everything will come to a decision
4. And surely there has come to them news of which the purport should deter,
5. Effective wisdom; but warnings avail not.
6. So withdraw from them (O Muḥammad) on the day when the summoner summons to a painful thing.
7. With downcast eyes, they come forth from the graves as if they were locusts spread abroad,
8. Hastening toward the summoner; the disbelievers say: "This is a hard day."
9. The people of Noah denied before them, yes, they denied our servant[1] and said: "A madman"; and he was repulsed.
10. So he cried to his Lord, saying: "I am vanquished, so give help."
11. Then We opened the gates of heaven with pouring water
12. And caused the earth to gush forth springs, so that the waters met for a predestined purpose.
13. And We carried him upon a thing of planks and nails,
14. That ran (upon the waters) in Our sight, as a reward for him who was rejected.
15. And We left it as a token; but is there any that remembers?
16. Then see how (dreadful) was My punishment after My warnings!
17. And in truth We have made the Qur'ān easy to remember;[2] but is there any that remembers?
18. (The tribe of) 'Ād rejected warnings. Then how (dreadful) was My punishment after My warnings.
19. We let loose on them a raging wind on a day of constant calamity,

1. To be *'abd Allāh*, "a servant of God," is the proudest rank the Muslim can claim, bondage to God implying liberation from all other servitudes. All especially devoted men, all the chosen ones, are called servants of God in the Qur'ān [Pickthall's note].
2. It is a fact that the Qur'ān is marvelously easy for believers to commit to memory. Thousands of people in the East know the whole book by heart. The translator, who finds great difficulty in remembering well-known English quotations accurately, can remember page after page of the Qur'ān in Arabic with perfect accuracy [Pickthall's note].

20. Sweeping men away as though they were uprooted trunks of palm trees.

21. Then see how (dreadful) was My punishment after My warnings!

22. And in truth We have made the Qur'ān easy to remember; but is there any that remembers?

23. (The tribe of) Thamūd rejected warnings

24. For they said: "Is it a mortal man, alone among us, that we are to follow? Then indeed we should fall into error and madness.

25. "Has the remembrance been given to him alone among us? No, but he is a rash liar."

26. (To their warner it was said): "Tomorrow they will know who is the rash liar."

27. We are sending the she-camel as a test for them; so watch them and have patience;

28. And inform them that the water is to be shared between (her and) them. Every drinking will be witnessed.

29. But they called their comrade and he took and hamstrung (her).

30. Then see how (dreadful) was My punishment after My warnings!

31. We sent upon them one shout, and they became as the dry twigs (rejected by) the builder of a cattlefold.

32. And in truth We have made the Qur'ān easy to remember; but is there any that remembers?

33. The folk of Lot rejected warnings.

34. We sent a storm of stones upon them (all) except the family of Lot, whom we rescued in the last watch of the night,

35. As grace from Us. Thus We reward him who gives thanks.

36. And he indeed had warned them of Our blow, but they doubted the warnings.

37. They even asked of him his guests for an ill purpose. Then We blinded their eyes (and said): "Taste now my punishment after My warnings!"

38. And in truth the punishment decreed befell them early in the morning.

39. Now taste My punishment after My warnings!

40. And in truth We have made the Qur'ān easy to remember; but is there any that remembers?

41. And warnings came in truth to the house of Pharaoh

42. Who denied Our revelations, every one. Therefore We grasped them with the grasp of the mighty, the powerful.

43. Are your disbelievers better than those, or have you some immunity in the scriptures?

44. Or do they say: "We are a host victorious"?

45. The hosts will all be routed and will turn and flee.

46. No, but the hour (of doom) is their appointed tryst, and the hour will be more wretched and more bitter (than their earthly failure).

47. The guilty are in error and madness.

48. On the day when they are dragged into the fire on their faces (it is said to them): "Feel the touch of hell."

49. We have created everything by measure.

50. And Our commandment is but one (commandment), as the twinkling of an eye.

51. And We have destroyed your fellows; but is there any that remembers?
52. And everything they did is in the scriptures,
53. And every small and great thing is recorded.
54. The righteous will dwell among gardens and rivers,
55. Firmly established in the favor of a mighty king.

## Sūra 55

*Al-Raḥmān* takes its name from the first verse. In the refrain: "Which is it, of the favors of your Lord, that you deny?" *you* and the verb are in the dual form, and the question is generally believed to be addressed to mankind and the jinn. Some have held that verses 46–76 refer not to the paradise hereafter but to the later conquests of the Muslims, the four gardens being Egypt, Syria, Mesopotamia, and Persia. There may well be a double meaning.

An early Meccan sūra.

## The Beneficent

*Revealed at Mecca*

In the name of God, the beneficent, the merciful.

1. The Beneficent
2. Has made known the Qur'ān.
3. He has created man.
4. He has taught him utterance.
5. The sun and the moon are made punctual.
6. The stars and the trees adore.
7. And the sky He has uplifted; and He has set the measure,
8. That you exceed not the measure,
9. But observe the measure strictly, nor fall short of it.
10. And the earth He has appointed for (His) creatures,
11. In which are fruit and sheathed palm trees,
12. Husked grain and scented herb.
13. Which is it, of the favors of your Lord, that you deny?
14. He created man of clay like the potter's,
15. And the jinn he created of smokeless fire.
16. Which is it, of the favors of your Lord, that you deny?
17. Lord of the two easts,[1] and Lord of the two wests![2]
18. Which is it, of the favors of your Lord, that you deny?
19. He has loosed the two seas.[3] They meet.
20. There is a barrier between them. They do not encroach (one upon the other).
21. Which is it, of the favors of your Lord, that you deny?
22. There comes forth from both of them the pearl and coral-stone.

1. The two points where the sun rises in winter and in summer [Pickthall's note].
2. The two points where the sun sets in winter and in summer [Pickthall's note].
3. I.e. the salt water and the sweet [Pickthall's note].

23. Which is it, of the favors of your Lord, that you deny?
24. His are the ships displayed upon the sea, like banners.[4]
25. Which is it, of the favors of your Lord, that you deny?
26. Everyone that is on it will pass away;
27. There remains but the countenance of your Lord of might and glory.
28. Which is it, of the favors of your Lord, that you deny?
29. All that are in the heavens and the earth entreat Him. Every day He exercises (universal) power.
30. Which is it, of the favors of your Lord, that you deny?
31. We shall dispose of you, O you two dependents (man and jinn).
32. Which is it, of the favors of your Lord, that you deny?
33. O company of jinn and men, if you have power to penetrate (all) regions of the heavens and the earth, then penetrate (them)! You will never penetrate them except with (Our) sanction.
34. Which is it, of the favors of your Lord, that you deny?
35. There will be sent, against you both, heat of fire and flash of brass, and you will not escape.
36. Which is it, of the favors of your Lord, that you deny?
37. And when the heaven splits asunder and becomes rosy like red hide—
38. Which is it, of the favors of your Lord, that you deny?—
39. On that day neither man nor jinn will be questioned of his sin.
40. Which is it, of the favors of your Lord, that you deny?
41. The guilty will be known by their marks, and will be taken by the forelocks and the feet.
42. Which is it, of the favors of your Lord, that you deny?
43. This is hell which the guilty deny.
44. They go circling round between it and fierce, boiling water.
45. Which is it, of the favors of your Lord, that you deny?
46. But for him who fears the standing before his Lord there are two gardens.
47. Which is it, of the favors of your Lord, that you deny?
48. Of spreading branches.
49. Which is it, of the favors of your Lord, that you deny?
50. In which are two fountains flowing.
51. Which is it, of the favors of your Lord, that you deny?
52. In which is every kind of fruit in pairs.
53. Which is it, of the favors of your Lord, that you deny?
54. Reclining upon couches lined with silk brocade, the fruit of both the gardens near to hand.
55. Which is it, of the favors of your Lord, that you deny?
56. Therein are those of modest gaze, whom neither man nor jinn will have touched before them.
57. Which is it, of the favors of your Lord, that you deny?
58. (In beauty) like the jacinth and the coral-stone.
59. Which is it, of the favors of your Lord, that you deny?
60. Is the reward of goodness other than goodness?
61. Which is it, of the favors of your Lord, that you deny?

4. The usual explanation of the commentators is "built into the sea like mountains" [Pickthall's note].

62. And beside them are two other gardens,
63. Which is it, of the favors of your Lord, that you deny?
64. Dark green with foliage.
65. Which is it, of the favors of your Lord, that you deny?
66. In which are two abundant springs.
67. Which is it, of the favors of your Lord, that you deny?
68. In which is fruit, the date palm and pomegranate.
69. Which is it, of the favors of your Lord, that you deny?
70. In which (are found) the good and beautiful—
71. Which is it, of the favors of your Lord, that you deny?—
72. Fair ones, close-guarded in pavilions—
73. Which is it, of the favors of your Lord, that you deny?—
74. Whom neither man nor jinn will have touched before them—
75. Which is it, of the favors of your Lord, that you deny?—
76. Reclining on green cushions and fair carpets.
77. Which is it, of the favors of your Lord, that you deny?
78. Blessed be the name of your Lord, mighty and glorious!

## Sūra 56

*Al-Wāqi'a*, "The Event," takes its name from a word in verse 1.
An early Meccan sūra.

## The Event

*Revealed at Mecca*

In the name of God, the beneficent, the merciful.

1. When the event occurs—
2. There is no denying that it will occur—
3. Abasing (some), exalting (others);
4. When the earth is shaken with a shock
5. And the hills are ground to powder
6. So that they become a scattered dust,
7. And you will be three kinds:
8. (First) those on the right hand; what of those on the right hand?
9. And (then) those on the left hand; what of those on the left hand?
10. And the foremost in the race, the foremost in the race:
11. Those are they who will be brought near
12. In gardens of delight;
13. A multitude of those of old
14. And a few of those of later time,
15. On lined couches,
16. Reclining there face to face.
17. There wait on them immortal youths
18. With bowls and ewers and a cup from a pure spring
19. From which they get no aching of the head nor any madness,
20. And fruit that they prefer
21. And flesh of fowls that they desire.

22. And (there are) fair ones with wide, lovely eyes,
23. Like hidden pearls,
24. Reward for what they used to do.
25. There they hear no vain speaking or recrimination
26. (Nothing) but the saying: "Peace," (and again) "peace."
27. And those on the right hand; what of those on the right hand?
28. Among thornless lote trees
29. And clustered plantains,
30. And spreading shade,
31. And water gushing,
32. And fruit in plenty
33. Neither out of reach nor yet forbidden,
34. And raised couches;
35. We have created them a (new) creation
36. And made them virgins,
37. Lovers, friends,
38. For those on the right hand;
39. A multitude of those of old
40. And a multitude of those of later time.[1]
41. And those on the left hand: What of those on the left hand?
42. In scorching wind and scalding water
43. And shadow of black smoke,
44. Neither cool nor refreshing.
45. Before this they were effete with luxury
46. And used to persist in the awful sin.
47. And they used to say: "When we are dead and have become dust and bones, shall we then be raised again,
48. "And also our forefathers?"
49. Say (to them, O Muhammad): "Those of old and those of later time
50. "Will all be brought together to the tryst of an appointed day.
51. "Then you, the erring, the deniers,
52. "You will eat of a tree called Zaqqūm[2]
53. "And will fill your bellies from it;
54. "And you will drink of boiling water,
55. "Drinking even as the camel drinks."
56. This will be their welcome on the day of judgment.
57. We created you. Will you then admit the truth?
58. Have you seen what you emit?
59. Do you create it or are We the creator?
60. We mete out death among you, and We are not to be outrun,
61. That We may transfigure you and make you what you know not.
62. And you know the first creation. Why, then, do you not reflect?
63. Have you seen that which you cultivate?
64. Is it you who foster it, or are We the fosterer?
65. If We willed, We could make it chaff, then you would not cease to exclaim:
66. "We are laden with debt!

1. This verse is said to have been revealed at Medina [Pickthall's note].
2. See Q 37:62–66.

67. "No, but we are deprived!"
68. Have you observed the water which you drink?
69. Is it you who shed it from the raincloud, or are We the shedder?
70. If We willed We could make it bitter. Why, then, do you not give thanks?
71. Have you observed the fire which you kindle;
72. Was it you who made its tree to grow, or were We the grower?
73. We, even We, appointed it a memorial and a comfort for the dwellers in the wilderness.
74. Therefore (O Muḥammad), praise the name of your Lord, the tremendous.
75. No, I swear by the places of the stars—
76. And that is a tremendous oath, if you but knew—
77. That (this) is indeed a noble Qur'ān
78. In a book kept hidden
79. Which none touches except the purified,
80. A revelation from the Lord of the worlds.
81. Is it this statement that you scorn,
82. And make denial of it your livelihood?
83. Why, then, when (the soul) comes up to the throat (of the dying)
84. And you are at that moment looking—
85. And We are nearer to him than you are, but you do not see—
86. Why then, if you are not in bondage (to Us),
87. Do you not force it back, if you are truthful?
88. Thus if he is of those brought near,
89. Then breath of life, and plenty, and a garden of delight.
90. And if he is of those on the right hand,
91. Then (the greeting) "Peace be to you" from those on the right hand.
92. But if he is of the rejecters, the erring,
93. Then the welcome will be boiling water
94. And roasting at hellfire.
95. This is certain truth.
96. Therefore (O Muḥammad) praise the name of your Lord, the tremendous.

## Sūra 57

*Al-Ḥadīd*, "Iron," takes its name from a word in verse 25.

The reference in the word "victory" in verse 10, is undoubtedly to the conquest of Mecca, though Nöldeke[1] takes it to refer to the battle of Badr, and so would place the sūra in the fourth or fifth year of the *hijra*. The words of the verse are against such an assumption since no Muslims "spent and fought" before the battle at Badr, which was the beginning of their fighting.

The date of revelation must be the eighth or ninth year of the *hijra*.

1. Nöldeke, *Geschichte des Qorâns*, part 1, p. 195 [Pickthall's note]. Mecca surrendered to the Muslim forces in 630 CE.

## Iron

*Revealed at Medina*

In the name of God, the beneficent, the merciful.

1. All that is in the heavens and the earth glorifies God; and He is the mighty, the wise.

2. His is the sovereignty of the heavens and the earth; He gives life and He gives death; and He is able to do all things.

3. He is the first and the last, and the outward and the inward; and He is knower of all things.

4. He it is who created the heavens and the earth in six days;[2] then He mounted the throne. He knows all that enters the earth and all that emerges from it and all that comes down from the sky and all that ascends into it; and He is with you wherever you may be. And God is observer of what you do.

5. His is the sovereignty of the heavens and the earth, and to God (all) things are brought back.

6. He causes the night to pass into the day, and He causes the day to pass into the night, and He is knower of all that is in the breasts.

7. Believe in God and His messenger, and spend of what He has made you trustees; and such of you as believe and spend (rightly), theirs will be a great reward.

8. What ails you that you do not believe in God, when the messenger calls you to believe in your Lord, and He has already made a covenant with you, if you are believers?

9. He it is who sends down clear revelations to His servant, that He may bring you forth from darkness to light; and for you, God is full of pity, merciful.

10. And what ails you that you do not spend in the way of God, when to God belongs the inheritance of the heavens and the earth? Those who spent and fought before the victory are not on a level (with the rest of you). Such are greater in rank than those who spent and fought afterward. To each has God promised good. And God is informed of what you do.

11. Who is he that will lend to God a goodly loan,[3] that He may double it for him and his may be a rich reward?

12. On the day when you (Muḥammad) will see the believers, men and women, their light shining forth before them and on their right hands, (and will hear it said to them): "Glad news for you this day: Gardens underneath which rivers flow, in which you are immortal. That is the supreme triumph."

13. On the day when the hypocritical men and the hypocritical women will say to those who believe: "Look on us that we may borrow from your light!" it will be said: "Go back and seek for light!" Then there will separate them a wall in which there is a gate, the inner side of which contains mercy, while the outer side of it is toward the doom.

14. They will cry to them (saying): "Were we not with you?" They will say: "Yes; but you tempted one another, and hesitated, and doubted, and

2. Q 22:47; 32:5; 70:4 [Pickthall's note].
3. A loan without interest or any thought of gain or loss [Pickthall's note].

vain desires beguiled you until the ordinance of God came to pass; and the deceiver deceived you concerning God;

15. "So this day no ransom can be taken from you nor from those who disbelieved. Your home is the fire; that is your patron, and a wretched journey's end."

16. Is not the time ripe for the hearts of those who believe to submit to God's reminder and to the truth which is revealed, so that they do not become as those who received the scripture before but the term was prolonged for them and so their hearts were hardened, and many of them are iniquitous.

17. Know that God gives life to the earth after its death. We have made clear Our revelations for you, that perhaps you may understand.

18. Those who give alms, both men and women, and lend to God a goodly loan, it will be doubled for them, and theirs will be a rich reward.

19. And those who believe in God and His messengers, they are the loyal; and the martyrs are with their Lord; they have their reward and their light; while as for those who disbelieve and deny Our revelations, they are owners of hellfire.

20. Know that the life of the world is only play, and idle talk, and pageantry, and boasting among you, and rivalry in respect of wealth and children; as the likeness of vegetation after rain, of which the growth is pleasing to the husbandman,[4] but afterward it dries up and you see it turning yellow, then it becomes straw. And in the hereafter there is grievous punishment, and (also) forgiveness from God and His good pleasure, whereas the life of the world is but the stuff of illusion.

21. Race with one another for forgiveness from your Lord and a garden of which the breadth is as the breadth of the heavens and the earth, which is in store for those who believe in God and His messengers. Such is the bounty of God, which He bestows on whom He will, and God is of infinite bounty.

22. Nothing of disaster befalls on the earth or in yourselves unless it is in a book before We bring it into being—that is easy for God

23. That you do not grieve for the sake of what has escaped you, nor yet exult because of what has been given. God does not love all prideful boasters,

24. Who hoard and who enjoin on the people avarice. And whoever turns away, still God is the absolute, the owner of praise.

25. We sent Our messengers with clear proofs, and revealed with them the scripture and the balance, that mankind may observe right measure; and He revealed iron, in which is mighty power and (many) uses for mankind, and that God may know him who helps Him and His messengers, though unseen. God is strong, almighty.

26. And We sent Noah and Abraham and placed the prophethood and the scripture among their seed, and among them there is he who goes right, but many of them are iniquitous.

27. Then We caused Our messengers to follow in their footsteps; and We caused Jesus, son of Mary, to follow, and gave him the Gospel, and placed compassion and mercy in the hearts of those who followed him. But

4. Ar. *kuffār*, ordinarily translated as "unbelievers"; but some classical commentators, such as Ibn Qutayba (828–889) and al-Zamakhsharī (1075–1144), give "husbandman" or "farmer" (*zurrā'*) as a synonym.

monasticism they invented—We did not ordain it for them—only seeking God's pleasure, and they did not observe it with right observance.[5] So We give those of them who believe their reward, but many of them are iniquitous.

28. O you who believe! Be mindful of your duty to God and put faith in His messenger. He will give you twofold of His mercy and will appoint for you a light in which you shall walk, and will forgive you. God is forgiving, merciful;

29. That the People of the Book[6] may know that they control nothing of the bounty of God, but that the bounty is in God's hand to give to whom He will. And God is of infinite bounty.

## Sūra 58

*Al-Mujādila*, "She Who Disputes," takes its name from a word in verse 1.

A woman had complained to the Prophet that her husband had put her away for no good reason by employing an old formula of the pagan Arabs, saying that her back was for him as the back of his mother, and she "disputed" with the Prophet because he would take no action against the man before this revelation came to him. There is a brief reference to the same method of getting rid of wives in Q 33:4. This sūra must therefore have been revealed before Q 33.

The date of revelation is the fourth or fifth year of the *hijra*.

## She Who Disputes

*Revealed at Medina*

In the name of God, the beneficent, the merciful.

1. God has heard the saying of she who disputes with you (Muḥammad) concerning her husband, and complains to God. And God hears your conversing. God is hearer, knower.

2. Such of you as put away your wives (by saying they are as their mothers)—they are not their mothers;[1] none are their mothers except those who gave them birth—they utter an ill word and a lie. And God is forgiving; merciful.

3. Those who put away their wives (by saying they are as their mothers)[2] and afterward would go back on what they have said, (the penalty) in that case (is) the freeing of a slave before they touch one another. To this you are exhorted; and God is informed of what you do.

4. And he who does not find (the means), let him fast for two successive months before they touch one another; and for him who is unable to do so (the penance is) the feeding of sixty needy ones. This, that you may put trust in God and His messenger. Such are the limits (imposed by God); and for disbelievers is a painful doom.

5. Those who oppose God and His messenger will be abased even as those before them were abased; and We have sent down clear signs, and for disbelievers is a shameful doom

5. Most often understood as a rejection of monastic celibacy.
6. I.e. Jews and Christians [Pickthall's note].
1. Q 33:4 [Pickthall's note].
2. Q 33:4 [Pickthall's note].

6. On the day when God will raise them all together and inform them of what they did. God has kept account of it while they forgot it. And God is witness over all things.

7. Have you not seen that God knows all that is in the heavens and all that is on the earth? There is no secret conference of three but He is their fourth, nor of five but He is their sixth, nor of less than that or more but He is with them wherever they may be; and afterward, on the day of resurrection, He will inform them of what they did. God is knower of all things.

8. Have you not observed those who were forbidden conspiracy and afterward returned to what they had been forbidden, and (now) conspire together for crime and wrongdoing and disobedience toward the messenger? And when they come to you they greet you with a greeting with which God does not greet you, and say within themselves: "Why should God punish us for what we say?" Hell will suffice them; they will feel the heat of it—an unfortunate journey's end!

9. O you who believe! When you conspire together, do not conspire together for crime and wrongdoing and disobedience toward the messenger, but conspire together for righteousness and piety, and keep your duty toward God, to whom you will be gathered.

10. Conspiracy is only of the devil, that he may vex those who believe; but he can harm them not at all unless by God's leave. In God let believers put their trust.

11. O you who believe! When it is said to you, "Make room!" in assemblies, then make room; God will make way for you (hereafter). And when it is said, "Come up higher!" go up higher; God will exalt those who believe among you, and those who have knowledge, to high ranks. God is informed of what you do.

12. O you who believe! When you hold conference with the messenger, offer an alms before your conference. That is better and purer for you. But if you cannot find (the means) then God is forgiving, merciful.

13. Do you fear to offer alms before your conference? Then, when you do not do it and God has forgiven you, establish worship and pay the poor-tax and obey God and His messenger. And God is aware of what you do.

14. Have you not seen those who take for friends a people with whom God is angry? They are neither of you nor of them, and they swear a false oath knowingly.

15. God has prepared for them a dreadful doom. Evil is what they are used to doing.

16. They make a shelter of their oaths and turn (men) from the way of God; so theirs will be a shameful doom.

17. Their wealth and their children will avail them nothing against God. Such are rightful owners of the fire; they will abide in it.

18. On the day when God will raise them all together, then will they swear to Him as they (now) swear to you, and they will fancy that they have some standing. Is it not they who are the liars?

19. The devil has engrossed them and so has caused them to forget remembrance of God. They are the devil's party. Is it not the devil's party who will be the losers?

20. Those who oppose God and His messenger, they will be among the lowest.

21. God has decreed: I shall conquer, I and My messengers. God is strong, almighty.

22. You will not find people who believe in God and the last day loving those who oppose God and His messenger, even though they be their fathers or their sons or their brothers or their clan. As for such, He has written faith upon their hearts and has strengthened them with a spirit from Him, and He will bring them into gardens underneath which rivers flow, in which they will abide. God is well pleased with them, and they are well pleased with Him. They are God's party. Is it not God's party who are the successful?

## Sūra 59

*Al-Ḥashr*, "Exile," takes its name from verses 2–17, which refer to the exile of the Banū Naḍīr, a Jewish tribe of Medina (for treason and projected murder of the Prophet) and the confiscation of their property. The "Hypocrites," as the lukewarm Muslims were called, had secretly sympathized with these Jews, whose opposition had grown strong since the Muslim reverse at Mt. Uḥud, and had promised to side with them if it came to a collision with the Muslims; and to emigrate with them if they were forced to emigrate. But when the Muslims marched against the Banū Naḍīr, and the latter took refuge in their strong towers, the Hypocrites did nothing. And when at length they were reduced and exiled, the Hypocrites did not go with them into exile.

The date of revelation is the fourth year of the *hijra*.

## Exile

*Revealed at Medina*

In the name of God, the beneficent, the merciful.

1. All that is in the heavens and all that is on the earth glorifies God, and He is the mighty, the wise.

2. He it is who has caused those of the People of the Scripture[1] who disbelieved to go forth from their homes to the first exile. You did not think that they would go forth, while they thought that their strongholds would protect them from God. But God reached them from a place which they did not reckon, and cast terror in their hearts so that they ruined their houses with their own hands and the hands of the believers. So learn a lesson, O you who have eyes!

3. And if God had not decreed migration for them, He would have punished them in this world, and theirs in the hereafter is the punishment of the fire.

4. That is because they were opposed to God and His messenger; and whoever is opposed to God, (for him) God is stern in reprisal.

5. Whatever palm trees you cut down or left standing on their roots, it was by God's leave, in order that He might confound the iniquitous.

6. And what God gave as spoil to His messenger from them, you did not urge any horse or riding-camel for the sake of it, but God gives His messenger lordship over whom He will. God is able to do all things.

1. The term for Jews and Christians. In this case it refers to Jews [Pickthall's note].

7. That which God gives as spoil to His messenger from the people of the townships, it is for God and His messenger[2] and for the near of kin and the orphans and the needy and the wayfarer, that it does not become a commodity between the rich among you. And whatever the messenger gives you, take it. And whatever he forbids, abstain (from it). And keep your duty to God. God is stern in reprisal.

8. And (it is) for the poor fugitives who have been driven out from their homes and their belongings, who seek bounty from God and help God and His messenger. They are the loyal.

9. Those who entered the city and the faith before them love those who flee to them for refuge, and find in their breasts no need for what has been given them, but prefer (the fugitives) above themselves though poverty become their lot. And whoever is saved from his own avarice—such are they who are successful.

10. And those who came (into the faith) after them say: "Our Lord! Forgive us and our brothers who were before us in the faith, and do not place in our hearts any rancor toward those who believe. Our Lord! You are full of pity, merciful."

11. Have you not observed those who are hypocrites, (how) they tell their brothers who disbelieve among the People of the Scripture: If you are driven out, we surely will go out with you, and we will never obey anyone against you, and if you are attacked we will help you. And God bears witness that they are liars.

12. (For) indeed if they are driven out they do not go out with them, and if they are attacked they do not help them, and if they had helped them they would have turned and fled, and then they would not have been victorious.

13. You are more awful as a fear in their breasts than God. That is because they are a people who understand not.

14. They will not fight against you in a body except in fortified villages or from behind walls. Their adversity among themselves is very great. You think of them as a whole whereas their hearts are at variance. That is because they are a people who have no sense.

15. On the likeness of those (who suffered) a short time before them, they taste the ill effects of their own conduct, and theirs is painful punishment.

16. (And the hypocrites are) on the likeness of the devil when he tells man to disbelieve, then, when he disbelieves says: "I am quit of you. I fear God, the Lord of the worlds."

17. And the consequence for both will be that they are in the fire, there abiding. Such is the reward of evildoers.

18. O you who believe! Observe your duty to God. And let every soul look to what it sends on before for the morrow. And observe your duty to God. God is informed of what you do.

19. And be not as those who forgot God, therefore He caused them to forget their souls. Such are the evildoers.

20. Not equal are the owners of the fire and the owners of the garden. The owners of the garden, they are the victorious.

21. If We had caused this Qur'ān to descend upon a mountain, you (O Muḥammad) would have seen it humbled, rent asunder by the fear of God. Such similitudes We coin for mankind that perhaps they may reflect.

2. I.e. for the state [Pickthall's note].

22. He is God, than whom there is no other god, the knower of the invisible and the visible. He is the beneficent, the merciful.

23. He is God, than whom there is no other god, the sovereign Lord, the holy one, peace, the keeper of faith, the guardian, the majestic, the compeller, the superb. Glorified be God from all that they ascribe as partner (to Him).

24. He is God, the creator, the shaper out of nothing, the fashioner. His are the most beautiful names. All that is in the heavens and the earth glorifies Him, and He is the mighty, the wise.

## Sūra 60

*Al-Mumtaḥana*, "She Who Is to Be Examined," takes its name from verse 10, where the believers are told to examine women who come to them as fugitives from the idolaters and, if they find them sincere converts to Islam, not to return them to the idolaters. This marked a modification in the terms of the truce of al-Ḥudaybiya, by which the Prophet had engaged to return all fugitives, male and female, while the idolaters were not obliged to give up renegades from Islam. The more terrible persecution which women had to undergo, if extradited, and their helpless social condition were the causes of the change. Instead of giving up women refugees who were sincere, and not fugitives on account of crime or some family quarrel, the Muslims were to pay an indemnity for them; while as for Muslim husbands whose wives might flee to Quraysh, no indemnity was to be paid by the latter but, when some turn of fortune brought wealth to the Islamic state, they were to be repaid by the state what their wives had taken of their property. In verse 12 is the pledge which was to be taken from the women refugees after their examination.

The date of revelation is the eighth year of the *hijra*.

## She Who Is to Be Examined

*Revealed at Medina*

In the name of God, the beneficent, the merciful.

1. O you who believe! Do not choose My enemy and your enemy for friends. Do you give them friendship when they disbelieve in that truth which has come to you, driving out the messenger and you because you believe in God, your Lord? If you have come forth to strive in My way and seeking My good pleasure, (do not show them friendship). Do you show friendship to them in secret, when I am best aware of what you hide and what you proclaim? And whoever does it among you, he has strayed from the right way.

2. If they have the upper hand of you, they will be your foes, and will stretch out their hands and their tongues toward you with evil (intent), and they long for you to disbelieve.

3. Your ties of kindred and your children will avail you nothing on the day of resurrection. He will part you. God is observer of what you do.

4. There is a goodly pattern for you in Abraham and those with him, when they told their people: "We are guiltless of you and all that you worship beside God. We are done with you. And there has arisen between us and you hostility and hate forever until you believe in God only"—except

that which Abraham promised his father (when he said): "I will ask forgiveness for you, though I have no power for you from God"—Our Lord! In You we put our trust, and to You we turn repentant, and to You is the journeying.

5. Our Lord! "Do not make us a prey for those who disbelieve, and forgive us, our Lord! You, only You, are the mighty, the wise."

6. You have in them a goodly pattern for everyone who looks to God and the last day. And whoever may turn away, still God, He is the absolute, the owner of praise.

7. It may be that God will ordain love between you and those of them with whom you are at enmity. God is mighty, and God is forgiving, merciful.

8. God does not forbid you those who did not war against you on account of religion and did not drive you out from your homes, that you should show them kindness and deal justly with them. God loves the just dealers.

9. God forbids you only those who warred against you on account of religion and have driven you out from your homes and helped to drive you out, that you make friends of them. Whoever makes friends of them—(all) such are wrongdoers.

10. O you who believe! When believing women come to you as fugitives, examine them. God is best aware of their faith. Then, if you know them for true believers, do not send them back to the disbelievers. They are not lawful for the disbelievers, nor are the disbelievers lawful for them. And give the disbelievers what they have spent (on them). And it is no sin for you to marry such women when you have given them their dues. And do not hold to the ties of disbelieving women; and ask for (the return of) what you have spent; and let the disbelievers ask for what they have spent. That is the judgment of God. He judges between you. God is knower, wise.

11. And if any of your wives have gone from you to the disbelievers and afterward you have your turn (of triumph), then give to those whose wives have gone the like of what they have spent, and keep your duty to God in whom you are believers.

12. O Prophet! If believing women come to you, taking oath of allegiance to you that they will ascribe nothing as partner to God, and will neither steal nor commit adultery nor kill their children, nor produce any lie that they have devised between their hands and feet, nor disobey you in what is right,[1] then accept their allegiance and ask God to forgive them. God is forgiving, merciful.

13. O you who believe! Do not be friendly with a people with whom God is angry, (a people) who have despaired of the hereafter as the disbelievers despair of those who are in the graves.

## Sūra 61

*Al-Ṣaff*, "The Ranks," takes its name from a word in verse 4. In the copy of the Qur'ān which I have followed,[1] it is stated to have been revealed at Mecca, though its contents evidently refer to the Medina period. It may have

1. This is called the women's oath of allegiance. It was the oath exacted from men also until the second pact of al-'Aqaba when the duty of defense was added to the men's oath [Pickthall's note]. Al-'Aqaba is on the outskirts of Mecca; this pact was made shortly before the *hijra*.

1. A lithograph copy written by Muḥammad Shakarzādeh in 1833/34.

been revealed while the Prophet and his Companions were encamped in the valley of Mecca during the negotiations of the Truce of al-Ḥudaybiya, with which some of its verses are associated by tradition.

In that case the date of revelation would be the sixth year of the *hijra*.

## The Ranks

*Revealed at Medina*

In the name of God, the beneficent, the merciful.

1. All that is in the heavens and all that is on the earth glorifies God, and He is the mighty, the wise.
2. O you who believe! Why do you say what you do not do?
3. It is most hateful in the sight of God that you say what you do not do.
4. God loves those who battle for His cause in ranks, as if they were a solid structure.
5. And (remember) when Moses said to his people: "O my people! Why do you persecute me, when you know well that I am God's messenger to you?" So when they went astray God sent their hearts astray. And God does not guide the evil-living people.
6. And when Jesus son of Mary said: "O Children of Israel! I am the messenger of God to you, confirming what was (revealed) before me in the Torah, and bringing good tidings of a messenger who comes after me, whose name is "the praised one."[2] Yet when he has come to them with clear proofs, they say: 'This is mere magic.'"
7. And who does greater wrong than he who invents a lie against God when he is summoned to Islam?[3] And God does not guide wrongdoing people.
8. Willingly would they put out the light of God with their mouths, but God will perfect His light however much the disbelievers are averse.
9. He it is who has sent His messenger with the guidance and the religion of truth, that He may make it conqueror of all religion however much idolaters may be averse.
10. O you who believe! Shall I show you a commerce that will save you from a painful doom?
11. You should believe in God and His messenger, and should strive for the cause of God with your wealth and your lives. That is better for you, if you only knew.
12. He will forgive you your sins and bring you into gardens underneath which rivers flow, and pleasant dwellings in gardens of Eden. That is the supreme triumph.
13. And (He will give you) another (blessing) which you love: help from God and present victory. Give good tidings (O Muḥammad) to believers.
14. O you who believe! Be God's helpers, even as Jesus son of Mary said to the disciples: "Who are my helpers for God?" They said: "We are God's helpers." And a party of the Children of Israel believed, while a

2. Ar. *Aḥmad*. A name of the Prophet of Arabia. The promised "comforter" was believed by many Christian communities of the East to be a prophet yet to come, and most of them accepted Muḥammad as that prophet [Pickthall's note].
3. Lit. "the Surrender" [Pickthall's note].

party disbelieved. Then We strengthened those who believed against their foe, and they became the uppermost.

## Sūra 62

*Al-Jum'a*, "The Congregation," takes its name from a word in verse 9, where obedience to the call to congregational prayer is enjoined. Tradition says that verses 9–11 refer to an occasion when a caravan entered Medina with beating of drums at the time when the Prophet was preaching in the mosque, and that the congregation broke away to look at it except twelve men. If, as one version of the tradition says, the caravan was that of Diḥya al-Kalbī, the incident must have occurred before the fifth year of the *hijra*, because Diḥya was a Muslim in the fifth year AH.

The date of revelation is between the years 2 and 4 AH.

## The Congregation

*Revealed at Medina*

In the name of God, the beneficent, the merciful.

1. All that is in the heavens and all that is on the earth glorifies God, the sovereign Lord, the holy one, the mighty, the wise.

2. He it is who has sent among the unlettered ones a messenger of their own, to recite to them His revelations and to make them grow, and to teach them the scripture and wisdom, though before they were in error manifest,

3. Along with others of them who have not yet joined them. He is the mighty, the wise.

4. That is the bounty of God; which he gives to whom He will. God is of infinite bounty.

5. The likeness of those who are entrusted with the law of Moses, yet do not apply it, is as the likeness of the ass carrying books. Wretched is the likeness of people who deny the revelations of God. And God does not guide wrongdoing people.

6. Say (O Muḥammad): "O you who are Jews! If you claim that you are favored of God apart from (all) mankind, then long for death if you are truthful."

7. But they will never long for it because of all that their own hands have sent before, and God is aware of evildoers.

8. Say (to them, O Muḥammad): "The death from which you shrink will surely meet you, and afterward you will be returned to the knower of the invisible and the visible, and He will tell you what you used to do.

9. "O you who believe! When the call is heard for the prayer of the day of congregation, hasten to remembrance of God and leave your trading. That is better for you if you only knew.

10. "And when the prayer is ended, then disperse in the land and seek God's bounty, and remember God much, that you may be successful."

11. But when they spy some merchandise or pastime they break away to it and leave you standing. Say: "What God has is better than pastime and than merchandise, and God is the best of providers."

# Sūra 63

*Al-Munāfiqūn*, "The Hypocrites," takes its name from a word occurring in the first verse. Verse 8 refers to a remark of 'Abdallāh b. Ubayy, the "hypocrite" leader, expressing the desire that the old aristocracy of Yathrib, of which he had been the acknowledged chief, might regain the ascendancy and turn out the refugees from Mecca, whom he regarded as intruders.

The date of revelation is the fourth year of the *hijra*.

## The Hypocrites

*Revealed at Medina*

In the name of God, the beneficent, the merciful.

1. When the hypocrites come to you (O Muḥammad), they say: "We bear witness that you are indeed God's messenger." And God knows that you are indeed His messenger, and God bears witness that the hypocrites are speaking falsely.

2. They make their faith a pretext so that they may turn (men) from the way of God. Evil is what they are used to doing,

3. That is because they believed, then disbelieved, therefore their hearts are sealed so that they do not understand.

4. And when you see them their bodies please you; and if they speak you give ear to their speech. (They are) as though they were blocks of wood in striped cloaks.[1] They think every shout to be against them. They are the enemy, so beware of them. God confound them! How perverted they are!

5. And when it is said to them: "Come! The messenger of God will ask forgiveness for you!" they avert their faces and you see them turning away, disdainful.

6. Whether you ask forgiveness for them or do not ask forgiveness for them, God will not forgive them. God does not guide the evil-living people.

7. They are those who say: "Do not spend on behalf of those (who dwell) with God's messenger that they may disperse (and go away from you)," when God's are the treasures of the heavens and the earth; but the hypocrites do not comprehend.

8. They say: "Surely, if we return to Medina the mightier will soon drive out the weaker," when might belongs to God and to His messenger and the believers; but the hypocrites know not.

9. O you who believe! Let not your wealth or your children distract you from remembrance of God. Those who do so, they are the losers.

10. And spend of that with which We have provided you before death comes to one of you and he says: "My Lord! If only you would reprieve me for a little while, then I would give alms and be among the righteous."

11. But God reprieves no soul when its term comes, and God is aware of what you do.

1. Or *propped-up blocks of wood* [Pickthall's note].

## Sūra 64

*Al-Taghābun*, "Mutual Disillusion," takes its name from a word in verse 9.

The date of revelation is possibly the year 1 AH, though it is generally regarded as a late Meccan sūra, verses 14ff. being taken as referring to the pressure brought to bear by wives and families to prevent Muslims leaving Mecca at the time of the *hijra*.

## Mutual Disillusion

*Revealed at Mecca*

In the name of God, the beneficent, the merciful.

1. All that is in the heavens and all that is on the earth glorifies God; to Him belongs sovereignty and to Him belongs praise, and He is able to do all things.

2. He it is who created you, but one of you is a disbeliever and one of you is a believer, and God is observer of what you do.

3. He created the heavens and the earth with truth, and He shaped you and made good your shapes, and to Him is the journeying.

4. He knows all that is in the heavens and all that is on the earth, and He knows what you conceal and what you publish. And God is aware of what is in the breasts (of men).

5. Has not the story reached you of those who disbelieved of old and so tasted the ill effects of their conduct, and theirs will be a painful doom.

6. That was because their messengers (from God) kept coming to them with clear proofs (of God's sovereignty), but they said: Shall mere mortals guide us? So they disbelieved and turned away, and God was independent (of them). God is absolute, owner of praise.

7. Those who disbelieve assert that they will not be raised again. Say (to them, O Muḥammad): "Yes, by my Lord! you will be raised again and then you will be informed of what you did; and that is easy for God."

8. So believe in God and His messenger and the light which We have revealed. And God is aware of what you do.

9. The day when He shall gather you to the day of assembling, that will be a day of mutual disillusion. And whoever believes in God and does right, He will remit his evil deeds from him and will bring him into gardens underneath which rivers flow, there to abide for ever. That is the supreme triumph.

10. But those who disbelieve and deny Our revelations, such are owners of the fire; they will abide in it—a wretched journey's end!

11. No calamity befalls except by God's leave. And whoever believes in God, He guides his heart. And God is knower of all things.

12. Obey God and obey His messenger; but if you turn away, then the duty of Our messenger is only to convey (the message) plainly.

13. God! There is no god except Him. In God, therefore, let believers put their trust.

14. O you who believe! Among your wives and your children there are enemies for you, therefore beware of them. And if you pardon and overlook and forgive, then God is forgiving, merciful.
15. Your wealth and your children are only a temptation, whereas God! with Him is an immense reward.
16. So keep your duty to God as best you can, and listen, and obey, and spend; that is better for your souls. And whoever is saved from his own greed, such are the successful.
17. If you lend to God a goodly loan,[1] He will double it for you and will forgive you, for God is responsive, clement,
18. Knower of the invisible and the visible, the mighty, the wise.

## Sūra 65

*Al-Ṭalāq*, "Divorce," is so called from verses 1–7, which contain an amendment to the laws of divorce which are set forth in Q 2. This is generally referred traditionally to a mistake made by Ibn ʿUmar in divorcing his wife, which is said to have happened in the sixth year of the *hijra*. But others relate that the Prophet on that occasion only quoted this verse which had already been revealed.

The date of revelation is the sixth year of the *hijra* or a little earlier.

## Divorce

*Revealed at Medina*

In the name of God, the beneficent, the merciful.

1. O Prophet! When you (men) put away women, put them away for their (legal) period and reckon the period, and keep your duty to God, your Lord. Do not expel them from their houses or let them go forth unless they commit open immorality. Such are the limits (imposed by) God; and whoever transgresses God's limits, wrongs his soul. You do not know: it may be that God will afterward bring some new thing to pass.
2. Then, when they have reached their term, take them back in kindness or part from them in kindness, and call to witness two just men among you, and keep your testimony upright for God. Whoever believes in God and the last day is exhorted to act thus. And whoever keeps his duty to God, God will appoint a way out for him,
3. And will provide for him from (a quarter) where he has no expectation. And whoever puts his trust in God, He will suffice him. God brings His command to pass. God has set a measure for all things.
4. And for such of your women as despair of menstruation, if you doubt, their period (of waiting) shall be three months, along with those who do not have it.[1] And for those with child, their period shall be until they bring forth their burden. And whoever keeps his duty to God, He makes his course easy for him.
5. That is the commandment of God which He reveals to you. And whoever keeps his duty to God, He will remit from him his evil deeds and magnify reward for him.

1. I.e. a loan without interest or any thought of gain or loss [Pickthall's note].
1. Other divorced women must wait three menstrual cycles before remarrying.

6. Lodge them where you dwell, according to your wealth, and do not harass them so as to constrain life for them. And if they are with child, then spend for them until they bring forth their burden. Then, if they nurse for you, give them their due payment and consult together in kindness; but if you make difficulties for one another, then let some other woman nurse for him (the father of the child).

7. Let him who has abundance spend of his abundance, and he whose provision is measured, let him spend of what God has given him. God asks nothing of any soul except what He has given it. God will grant, after hardship, ease.

8. And how many a community revolted against the ordinance of its Lord and His messengers, and we called it to a stern account and punished it with dire punishment,

9. So that it tasted the ill effects of its conduct, and the consequence of its conduct was loss.

10. God has prepared for them stern punishment; so keep your duty to God, O men of understanding! O you who believe! Now God has sent down to you a reminder,

11. A messenger reciting to you the revelations of God made plain, that He may bring forth those who believe and do good works from darkness to light. And whoever believes in God and does right, He will bring him into gardens underneath which rivers flow, there to abide forever. God has made good provision for him.

12. God it is who has created seven heavens, and of the earth the like of it. The commandment comes down among them slowly, that you may know that God is able to do all things, and that God surrounds all things in knowledge.

## Sūra 66

*Al-Taḥrīm*, "The Banning," takes its name from a word in verse 1.

There are three traditions as to the occasion of verses 1–4:

(1) The Prophet was very fond of honey. One of his wives received a present of honey from a relative and by its means inveigled the Prophet into staying with her longer than was customary. The others felt aggrieved, and ʿĀʾisha devised a little plot. Knowing the Prophet's horror of unpleasant smells, she arranged with two other wives that they should hold their noses when he came to them after eating the honey, and accused him of having eaten the produce of a very rank-smelling tree. When they accused him of having eaten *maghāfīr*[1] the Prophet said that he had eaten only honey. They said: "The bees had fed on *maghāfīr*." The Prophet was dismayed and vowed to eat no more honey.

(2) Ḥafṣa found the Prophet in her room with Māriya—the Coptic girl, presented to him by the ruler of Egypt, who became the mother of his only male child, Ibrāhīm—on a day which custom had assigned to ʿĀʾisha. Moved by Ḥafṣa's distress, the Prophet vowed that he would have no more to do with Māriya, and asked her not to tell ʿĀʾisha. But Ḥafṣa's distress had been largely feigned. No sooner had the Prophet gone than she told ʿĀʾisha with glee how easily she had got rid of Māriya.

(3) Before Islam women had had no standing in Arabia. The Qurʾān gave them legal rights and an assured position, which some of them were inclined

1. A sweet-tasting tree resin with a noxious odor.

to exaggerate. The Prophet was extremely kind to his wives. One day 'Umar had to rebuke his wife for replying to him in a tone which he considered disrespectful. She assured him it was the tone in which his own daughter Ḥafṣa, 'Ā'isha, and others of the Prophet's wives answered the Prophet. 'Umar went at once and remonstrated with Ḥafṣa and with another of the Prophet's wives to whom he was related. He was told to mind his own business, which increased his horror and dismay. Soon afterward the Prophet separated from his wives for a time, and it was thought that he was going to divorce them. Then 'Umar ventured to tell the story of his own vain effort to reform them, at which the Prophet laughed heartily.

Traditions (1) and (3) are the better authenticated and are alone adduced by the great traditionists. But the commentators generally prefer (2) as more explanatory of the text. All allude to a tendency on the part of some of the wives of the Prophet to presume on their new status and the Prophet's well-known kindness—a tendency so marked that, if allowed to continue, it would have been a bad example to the whole community. The Qur'ān first rebukes the Prophet for yielding to their desires to the extent of undertaking to forgo a thing which God had made lawful for him—in the case of (2), fulfillment of his vow involved a wrong to Māriya—and then reproves the women for their double-dealing and intrigue.

The above traditions have been made by some non-Muslim writers the text for strictures which appear irrelevant because their ideology is altogether un-Islamic. The Prophet has never been regarded by Muslims as other than a human messenger of God; sanctity has never been identified with celibacy. For Christendom the strictest religious ideal has been celibacy; monogamy is already a concession to human nature. For Muslims, monogamy is the ideal, polygamy the concession to human nature. Polygamy is of the nature of some men in all countries, and of all men in some countries. Having set a great example of monogamic marriage, the Prophet was to set a great example of polygamic marriage, by following which men of that temperament could live righteous lives. He encountered all the difficulties inherent in the situation, and when he made mistakes the Qur'ān helped him to retrieve them. Islam did not institute polygamy. It restricted an existing institution by limiting the number of a man's legal wives, by giving to every woman a legal personality and legal rights which had to be respected, and making every man legally responsible for his conduct toward every woman. Whether monogamy or polygamy should prevail in a particular country or period is a matter of social and economic convenience. The Prophet himself was permitted to have more wives than were allowed to others because, as head of the state, he was responsible for the support of women who had no other protector. With the one exception of 'Ā'isha, all his wives had been widows.

## The Banning

*Revealed at Mecca*

In the name of God, the beneficent, the merciful.

1. O Prophet! Why do you ban what God has made lawful for you, seeking to please your wives? And God is forgiving, merciful.

2. God has made lawful for you (Muslims) absolution from your oaths (of such a kind), and God is your protector. He is the knower, the wise.

3. When the Prophet confided a fact to one of his wives and when she afterward divulged it and God apprised him of it, he made known (to her)

part of it and passed over part. And when he told it to her she said: "Who has told you?" He said: "The knower, the aware has told me."

4. If you two turn to God repentant, (you have cause to do so) for your hearts desired (the ban); and if you aid one another against him (Muḥammad) then God, even He, is his protecting friend, and Gabriel and the righteous among the believers; and furthermore the angels are his helpers.

5. It may happen that his Lord, if he divorce you, will give him in your stead wives better than you, submissive (to God), believing, pious, penitent, devout, inclined to fasting, widows and maids.

6. O you who believe! Ward off from yourselves and your families a fire of which the fuel is men and stones, over which are set angels strong, severe, who do not resist God in what He commands them, but do what they are commanded.

7. (Then it will be said): O you who disbelieve! Make no excuses for yourselves this day. You are only being paid for what you used to do.

8. O you who believe! Turn to God in sincere repentance! It may be that your Lord will remit from you your evil deeds and bring you into gardens underneath which rivers flow, on the day when God will not abase the Prophet and those who believe with him. Their light will run before them and on their right hands: they will say: "Our Lord! Perfect our light for us, and forgive us! You are able to do all things."

9. O Prophet! Strive against the disbelievers and the hypocrites, and be stern with them. Hell will be their home, a wretched journey's end.

10. God cites an example for those who disbelieve: the wife of Noah and the wife of Lot, who were under two of our righteous servants yet betrayed them so that they (the husbands) availed them nothing against God and it was said (to them): "Enter the fire along with those who enter."

11. And God cites an example for those who believe: the wife of Pharaoh when she said: My Lord! Build for me a home with you in the garden, and deliver me from Pharaoh and his work, and deliver me from evildoing people;

12. And Mary, daughter of 'Imrān, whose body was chaste, therefore We breathed into it something of Our spirit. And she put faith in the words of her Lord and His scriptures, and was of the obedient.

## Sūra 67

*Al-Mulk* takes its name from a word in the first verse.

It belongs to the middle group of Meccan sūras.

## The Sovereignty

*Revealed at Mecca*

In the name of God, the beneficent, the merciful.

1. Blessed is He in whose hand is the sovereignty, and He is able to do all things.

2. Who has created life and death that He may try you, which of you is best in conduct; and He is the mighty, the forgiving,

3. Who has created seven heavens in harmony. You (Muḥammad) can see no fault in the Beneficent one's creation; then look again: Can you see any rifts?

4. Then look again and yet again, your sight will return to you weakened and made dim.

5. And We have beautified the world's heaven with lamps, and We have made them missiles for the devils,[1] and for them We have prepared the doom of flame.

6. And for those who disbelieve in their Lord there is the doom of hell, an unfortunate journey's end!

7. When they are flung into it they hear its roaring as it boils up,

8. As it would burst with rage. Whenever a (fresh) host is flung into it its wardens ask them: "Did no warner come to you?"

9. They say: "A warner came to us; but we denied and said: 'God has revealed nothing; you are in nothing but a great error.'"

10. And they say: "Had we been accustomed to listen or have sense, we would not have been among the dwellers in the flames."

11. So they acknowledge their sins; but far removed (from mercy) are the dwellers in the flames.

12. Those who fear their Lord in secret, theirs will be forgiveness and a great reward.

13. And keep your opinion secret or proclaim it. He is knower of all that is in the breasts (of men).

14. Should He not know what He created? And He is the subtile, the aware.

15. He it is Who has made the earth subservient to you, so walk in its paths and eat of His providence. And to Him will be the resurrection (of the dead).

16. Have you taken security from Him Who is in the heaven that He will not cause the earth to swallow you when it is convulsed?

17. Or have you taken security from Him Who is in the heaven that He will not let loose on you a hurricane? But you shall know the manner of My warning.

18. And those before them denied, then (see) the manner of My wrath (with them)!

19. Have they not seen the birds above them spreading out their wings and closing them? Nothing upholds them except the Beneficent. He is observer of all things.

20. Or who is he that will be an army to you to help you instead of the Beneficent? The disbelievers are only in delusion.

21. Or who is he that will provide for you if He should withhold His providence? No, but they are set in pride and obstinacy.

22. Is he who goes groping on his face more rightly guided, or he who walks upright on a beaten road?

23. Say (to them, O Muḥammad): "He it is who gave you being, and has assigned to you ears and eyes and hearts. Small thanks you give!"

24. Say: "He it is who multiplies you on the earth, and to whom you will be gathered."

1. On the authority of a tradition going back to Ibn 'Abbās, the allusion is to the soothsayers and astrologers who saw the source of good and evil in the stars. See Q 72:9, footnote [Pickthall's note].

25. And they say: "When (will) this promise (be fulfilled), if you are truthful?"

26. Say: "The knowledge is with God only, and I am but a plain warner";

27. But when they see it near, the faces of those who disbelieve will be awry, and it will be said (to them): "This is that for which you used to call."

28. Say (O Muḥammad): "Have you thought: Whether God causes me (Muḥammad) and those with me to perish or has mercy on us, still, who will protect the disbelievers from a painful doom?"

29. Say: "He is the Beneficent. In Him we believe and in Him we put our trust. And you will soon know who it is that is in error manifest."

30. Say: "Have you thought: If (all) your water were to disappear into the earth, who then could bring you gushing water?"

## Sūra 68

*Al-Qalam*, "The Pen," takes its name from a word in the first verse.
A very early Meccan sūra.

## The Pen

*Revealed at Mecca*

In the name of God, the beneficent, the merciful.

1. Nūn.[1] By the pen and that which they write (with it),
2. You are not, for your Lord's favor to you, a madman.
3. And yours will be a reward unfailing.
4. And you are of a tremendous nature.
5. And you will see and they will see
6. Which of you is the demented.
7. Your Lord is best aware of him who strays from His way, and He is best aware of those who walk aright.
8. Therefore do not obey the rejecters
9. Who would have had you compromise, that they may compromise.
10. Neither obey each feeble oath-monger,
11. Detracter, spreader abroad of slanders,
12. Hinderer of the good, transgressor, malefactor,
13. Greedy, moreover, intrusive.
14. It is because he is possessed of wealth and children
15. That, when our revelations are recited to him, he says: "Mere fables of the men of old."
16. We shall brand him on the nose.
17. We have tried them as we tried the owners of the garden when they vowed that they would pluck its fruit next morning,
18. And made no exception (for the will of God);[2]
19. Then a visitation from your Lord came upon it while they slept
20. And in the morning it was as if plucked.
21. And they cried out to one another in the morning,

1. See Q 2:1, footnote [Pickthall's note].
2. I.e. they forgot to say: "If God wills" [Pickthall's note].

22. Saying: "Run to your field if you would pluck (the fruit)."
23. So they went off, saying to one another in low tones:
24. "No needy man shall enter it today against you."[3]
25. They went early, strong in (this) purpose.
26. But when they saw it, they said: "We are in error!
27. No, but we are desolate!"
28. The best among them said: "Did I not say to you: 'Why do you not glorify (God)?'"
29. They said: "Glorified be our Lord! We have been wrongdoers."
30. Then some of them drew near to others, self-reproaching.
31. They said: "Alas for us! In truth we were outrageous.
32. "It may be that our Lord will give us better than this in place of it. We beseech our Lord."
33. Such was the punishment. And the punishment of the hereafter is greater if they did but know.
34. For those who keep from evil are gardens of bliss with their Lord.
35. Shall We then treat those who have surrendered[4] as We treat the guilty?
36. What ails you? How foolishly you judge!
37. Or have you a scripture in which you learn
38. That you shall indeed have all that you choose?
39. Or have you a covenant on oath from Us that reaches to the day of judgment, that yours shall be all that you ordain?
40. Ask them (O Muḥammad) which of them will vouch for that!
41. Or have they other gods? Then let them bring their other gods if they are truthful
42. On the day when the fighting starts in earnest, and they are ordered to prostrate themselves but are not able,
43. With eyes downcast, abasement stupefying them. And they had been summoned to prostrate themselves while they were yet unhurt.
44. Leave Me (to deal) with those who give the lie to this pronouncement. We shall lead them on by steps from where they know not.
45. Yet I bear with them, for My scheme is firm.
46. Or do you (Muḥammad) ask a fee from them so that they are heavily taxed?
47. Or is the unseen theirs that they can write (of it)?
48. But wait for your Lord's decree, and do not be like him of the fish,[5] who cried out in despair.
49. Had it not been that favor from his Lord had reached him he surely would have been cast into the wilderness while he was reprobate.
50. But his Lord chose him and placed him among the righteous.
51. And those who disbelieve would willingly disconcert you with their eyes when they hear the reminder, and they say: "He is indeed mad";
52. When it is nothing else than a reminder to creation.

3. It was a custom throughout the East to allow the poor a gleaning of all harvests [Pickthall's note].
4. Ar. *Muslimīn* [Pickthall's note].
5. I.e. Jonah [Pickthall's note].

## Sūra 69

*Al-Ḥāqqa* takes its name from a word recurring in the first three verses. It belongs to the middle group of Meccan sūras.

## The Reality

*Revealed at Mecca*

In the name of God the beneficent, the merciful.

1. The reality!
2. What is the reality?
3. Ah, what will convey to you what the reality is!
4. (The tribes of) Thamūd and ʿĀd disbelieved in the judgment to come.
5. As for Thamūd, they were destroyed by the lightning.
6. And as for ʿĀd, they were destroyed by a fierce roaring wind,
7. Which He imposed on them for seven long nights and eight long days so that you might have seen men lying overthrown, as if they were hollow trunks of palm trees.
8. Can you (O Muḥammad) see any remnant of them?
9. And Pharaoh and those before him, and the communities that were destroyed, brought error,
10. And they disobeyed the messenger of their Lord, therefore He gripped them with a tightening grip.
11. When the waters rose, We carried you upon the ship
12. That We might make it a memorial for you, and that remembering ears (that heard the story) might remember.
13. And when the trumpet shall sound one blast
14. And the earth with the mountains shall be lifted up and crushed with one crash,
15. Then, on that day will the event befall.
16. And the heaven will split asunder, for that day it will be frail.
17. And the angels will be on its sides, and eight will uphold the throne of your Lord that day, above them.
18. On that day you will be exposed; not a secret of yours will be hidden.
19. Then, as for him who is given his record in his right hand, he will say: "Take, read my book!
20. "Surely I knew that I should have to meet my reckoning."
21. Then he will be in blissful state
22. In a high garden
23. Where the clusters are in easy reach.
24. (And it will be said to those there): "Eat and drink at ease for that which you sent on before you in past days."
25. But as for him who is given his record in his left hand, he will say: "Oh, would that I had not been given my book
26. "And did not know what will be my reckoning!
27. "Oh, would that it had been death!
28. "My wealth has not availed me,
29. "My power has gone from me."

30. (It will be said): "Take him and fetter him
31. "And then expose him to hellfire
32. "And then insert him in a chain whose length is seventy cubits.
33. "He used not to believe in God the tremendous,
34. "And did not urge the feeding of the wretched,
35. "Therefore he has no lover here this day.
36. "Nor any food save filth
37. "Which none but sinners eat."
38. But no! I swear by all that you see
39. And all that you do not see
40. That it is indeed the speech of an illustrious messenger.
41. It is not poet's speech—little is it that you believe!
42. Nor diviner's speech—little is it that you remember!
43. It is a revelation from the Lord of the worlds.
44. And if he had invented false sayings concerning Us,
45. We assuredly would have taken him by the right hand
46. And then severed his life-artery,
47. And not one of you could have held Us off from him.
48. And it is a warrant to those who ward off (evil).
49. And We know that some among you will deny (it),
50. And it is indeed an anguish for the disbelievers.
51. And it is absolute truth.
52. So glorify the name of your tremendous Lord.

## Sūra 70

*Al-Ma'ārij* takes its name from a word in verse 3.
An early Meccan sūra.

## The Ascending Stairways

*Revealed at Mecca*

In the name of God, the beneficent, the merciful.

1. A questioner questioned concerning the doom about to fall
2. Upon the disbelievers, which none can repel,
3. From God, Lord of the ascending stairways
4. (Whereby) the angels and the spirit ascend to Him in a day of which the span is fifty thousand years.
5. But be patient (O Muḥammad) with a patience fair to see.
6. They behold it afar off
7. While We behold it near:
8. The day when the sky will become as molten copper,
9. And the hills become as flakes of wool,
10. And no familiar friend will ask a question of his friend
11. Though they will be given sight of them. The guilty man will long to be able to ransom himself from the punishment of that day at the price of his children

12. And his spouse and his brother
13. And his kin that harbored him
14. And all that are on the earth, if then it might deliver him.
15. But no! for it is the fire of hell
16. Eager to roast;
17. It calls him who turned and fled (from truth),
18. And hoarded (wealth) and withheld it.
19. Man was created anxious,
20. Fretful when evil befalls him
21. And, when good befalls him, grudging;
22. Except worshippers
23. Who are constant at their worship
24. And in whose wealth there is a right acknowledged
25. For the beggar and the destitute;
26. And those who believe in the day of judgment,
27. And those who are fearful of their Lord's doom—
28. The doom of their Lord is that before which none can feel secure—
29. And those who preserve their chastity
30. Except with their wives and those whom their right hands possess, for thus they are not blameworthy;
31. But whoever seeks more than that, those are they who are transgressors;
32. And those who keep their pledges and their covenant,
33. And those who stand by their testimony
34. And those who are attentive at their worship,
35. These will dwell in gardens, honored.
36. What ails those who disbelieve, that they keep staring toward you (O Muḥammad), open-eyed,
37. On the right and on the left, in groups?
38. Does every man among them hope to enter the garden of delight?
39. No. We created them from what they know.
40. But no! I swear by the Lord of the rising-places and the setting-places of the planets that We are able
41. To replace them by (others) better than them. And We are not to be outrun.
42. So let them chat and play until they meet their day which they are promised,
43. The day when they come forth from the graves in haste, as racing to a goal,
44. With eyes aghast, abasement stupefying them: Such is the day which they are promised.

## Sūra 71

Takes its name from its subject, which is the preaching of the prophet Noah. An early Meccan sūra.

# Noah

*Revealed at Mecca*

In the name of God, the beneficent, the merciful.

1. We sent Noah to his people (saying): "Warn your people before the painful doom comes to them."
2. He said: "O my people! I am a plain warner to you
3. "(Bidding you): Serve God and keep your duty to Him and obey me,
4. "That He may forgive you somewhat of your sins and give you respite for an appointed term. The term of God, when it comes, cannot be delayed, if you but knew."
5. He said: "My Lord! I have called to my people night and day
6. "But all my calling only adds to their repugnance;
7. "And whenever I call to them that You may pardon them they thrust their fingers in their ears and cover themselves with their garments and persist (in their refusal) and magnify themselves in pride.
8. "And I have called to them aloud,
9. "And I have made public proclamation to them, and I have appealed to them in private.
10. "And I have said: 'Seek pardon of your Lord. He was ever forgiving.
11. "'He will let loose the sky for you in plenteous rain,
12. "'And will help you with wealth and sons, and will assign to you gardens and will assign to you rivers.
13. "'What ails you that you do not hope toward God for dignity
14. "'When He created you by (diverse) stages?
15. "'Do you not see how God has created seven heavens in harmony,
16. "'And has made the moon a light in them, and made the sun a lamp?
17. "'And God has caused you to grow as a growth from the earth,
18. "'And afterward He makes you return to it, and He will bring you forth again, a (new) forthbringing.
19. "'And God has made the earth a wide expanse for you
20. "'That you may thread its valley ways.'"
21. Noah said: "My Lord! They have disobeyed me and followed one whose wealth and children increase him in nothing but ruin;
22. "And they have plotted a mighty plot,
23. "And they have said: 'Do not forsake your gods. Do not forsake Wadd, or Suwā', or Yaghūth and Ya'ūq and Nasr.'[1]
24. "And they have led many astray, and You increase the wrongdoers in nothing but error."
25. Because of their sins they were drowned, then made to enter a fire. And they found they had no helpers in place of God.
26. And Noah said: "My Lord! Do not leave one of the disbelievers in the land.
27. "If You leave them, they will mislead your servants and will beget none but lewd ingrates.

1. Idols of the pagan Arabs [Pickthall's note].

28. "My Lord! Forgive me and my parents and him who enters my house believing, and believing men and believing women, and do not increase the wrongdoers in anything but ruin."

## Sūra 72

*Al-Jinn* takes its name from a word in the first verse, and also from the subject of verses 1–18. The meaning of the word *jinn* in the Qur'ān has exercised the minds of Muslim commentators, ancient and modern. Mr. Ya'qūb Ḥasan of Madras, in the first volume of a remarkable work in Urdu, *Kitābu l-Hudā*,[1] shows that it has at least three meanings in the Qur'ān and that one of those meanings is something akin to "clever foreigners" as in the case of the jinn who worked for Solomon. But undoubtedly the first and obvious meaning is "elemental spirits," to whom, as to mankind, the Qur'ān came as a guidance. The incident is said to have occurred during the Prophet's return from his unsuccessful missionary journey to Ṭā'if.

A late Meccan sūra.

## The Jinn

*Revealed at Mecca*

In the name of God, the beneficent, the merciful.

1. Say (O Muḥammad): "It is revealed to me that a company of the jinn gave ear, and they said: 'We have heard a marvelous Qur'ān,

2. "'Which guides to righteousness, so we believe in it and we ascribe no partner to our Lord.

3. "'And (we believe) that He—exalted be the glory of our Lord!—has taken neither wife nor son,

4. "'And that the foolish one among us used to speak concerning God an atrocious lie.

5. "'And we had supposed that humankind and jinn would not speak a lie concerning God'"—

6. And indeed (O Muḥammad) individuals of humankind used to invoke the protection of individuals of the jinn, so that they increased them in revolt (against God);

7. And indeed they supposed, even as you suppose, that God would not raise anyone (from the dead)—

8. And (the jinn who had listened to the Qur'ān said): "We had sought the heaven but had found it filled with strong warders and meteors.

9. "And we used to sit on (high) places there to listen. But he who listens now finds a flame in wait for him;[2]

10. "And we do not know whether harm is boded to all who are on the earth, or whether their Lord intends guidance for them.

11. "And among us there are righteous people and among us there are far from that. We are groups having different rules.

1. Published in Madras in 1928.
2. About the time of the Prophet's mission there were many meteors and other strange appearances in the heavens, which, tradition says, frightened the astrologers from the high observatories where they used to watch at night, and threw out all their calculations [Pickthall's note].

12. "And we know that we cannot escape from God on the earth, nor can we escape by flight.

13. "And when we heard the guidance, we believed in it, and whoever believes in his Lord, he fears neither loss nor oppression.

14. "And there are among us some who have surrendered (to God) and there are among us some who are unjust. And whoever has surrendered to God, such have taken the right path purposefully."

15. And as for those who are unjust, they are firewood for hell.

16. If they (the idolaters) tread the right path, We shall give them to drink of water in abundance

17. That We may test them thereby; and whoever turns away from the remembrance of his Lord, He will thrust him into ever-growing torment.

18. And the places of worship are only for God, so do not pray to anyone along with God.

19. And when the servant of God[3] stood up in prayer to Him, they crowded on him, almost stifling.[4]

20. Say (to them, O Muḥammad): "I pray to God only, and ascribe to Him no partner."

21. Say: "I control neither hurt nor benefit for you."

22. Say: "None can protect me from God, nor can I find any refuge beside Him.

23. "(Mine is) but conveyance (of the truth) from God, and His messages; and whoever disobeys God and His messenger, his is the fire of hell, in which such dwell forever.

24. "Until (the day) when they shall behold what they are promised (they may doubt); but then they will know (for certain) who is weaker in allies and less in multitude."

25. Say (O Muḥammad, to the disbelievers): "I do not know whether that which you are promised is near, or if my Lord has set a distant term for it.

26. "(He is) the knower of the unseen, and He reveals to none His secret,

27. "Except to every messenger whom He has chosen, and then He makes a guard to go before him and a guard behind him.

28. "That He may know that they have indeed conveyed the messages of their Lord. He surrounds all their doings, and He keeps count of all things."

## Sūra 73

*Al-Muzammil* takes its title from a word in verse 1. After his first trance and vision, the Prophet went to his wife Khadīja and told her to wrap him up in cloaks, and that was afterward his habit on such occasions, at any rate, in the early days at Mecca.

A very early Meccan revelation with the exception of the last verse, which all authorities assign to Medina.

3. I.e. the Prophet [Pickthall's note].
4. Generally taken to be an allusion to the rough treatment which the Prophet received at the hands of the people of Ṭā'if [Pickthall's note].

# The Enshrouded One

*Revealed at Mecca*

In the name of God, the beneficent, the merciful.

1. O you wrapped up in your raiment!
2. Keep vigil the night long, except a little—
3. A half of it, or abate a little of it
4. Or add (a little) to it—and chant the Qur'ān in measure,
5. For we shall charge you with a word of weight.
6. The vigil of the night is (a time) when impression is more keen and speech more certain.
7. You have by day a chain of business.
8. So remember the name of your Lord and devote yourself with a complete devotion—
9. Lord of the east and the west; there is no God but Him; so choose Him alone for your defender—
10. And bear with patience what they utter, and part from them with a fair leave-taking.
11. Leave me to deal with the deniers, lords of ease and comfort (in this life); and you bear with them awhile.
12. With us are heavy fetters and a raging fire,
13. And food which chokes (the partaker), and a painful doom
14. On the day when the earth and the hills rock, and the hills become a heap of running sand.
15. We have sent to you a messenger as witness against you, even as We sent to Pharaoh a messenger.
16. But Pharaoh rebelled against the messenger, whereupon We seized him with no gentle grip.
17. Then how, if you disbelieve, will you protect yourselves on the day which will turn children gray,
18. The very heaven being then rent asunder? His promise is to be fulfilled.
19. This is a reminder. Let him who will, then, choose a way to his Lord.
20. Your Lord knows how you keep vigil sometimes nearly two-thirds of the night, or (sometimes) half or a third of it, as do a party of those with you. God measures the night and the day. He knows that you count it not, and He turns to you in mercy. Recite, then, of the Qur'ān that which is easy for you. He knows that there are sick folk among you, while others travel in the land in search of God's bounty, and others (still) are fighting for the cause of God. So recite of it that which is easy (for you), and establish worship and pay the poor tax, and (so) lend to God a goodly loan.[1] Whatever good you send before you for your souls, you will surely find it with God, better and greater in the recompense. And seek forgiveness of God. God is forgiving, merciful.

1. I.e. a loan without interest or any thought of gain or loss [Pickthall's note].

## Sūra 74

*Al-Mudaththir* takes its name from a word in verse 1. The Prophet was accustomed to wrap himself in his cloak at the time of his trances. A tradition says that some time—about six months—elapsed between the first revelation (Q 96:1–5) and the second revelation in this sūra. Then the Prophet suddenly again beheld the angel who had appeared to him on Mt. Ḥirā', and wrapped himself in his cloak, whereupon this sūra was revealed to him. Another opinion is that by this sūra the Prophet was ordered to begin the public preaching of Islam, his preaching having until then been done privately among his family and intimates. He is said to have begun his public preaching three years after his call.

In either case this is a very early Meccan sūra.

## The Cloaked One

*Revealed at Mecca*

In the name of God, the beneficent, the merciful.

1. O you enveloped in your cloak,
2. Arise and warn!
3. Your Lord magnify,
4. Your garments purify,
5. Pollution shun!
6. And do not show favor, seeking worldly gain!
7. For the sake of your Lord, be patient!
8. For when the trumpet shall sound,
9. Surely that day will be a day of anguish,
10. Not of ease, for disbelievers.
11. Leave Me (to deal) with him whom I created lonely,
12. And then bestowed upon him ample means,
13. And sons abiding in his presence
14. And made (life) smooth for him.
15. Yet he desires that I should give more.
16. No! For he has been stubborn to Our revelations.
17. On him I shall impose a fearful doom.
18. For he did consider; then he planned—
19. Self-destroyed is he, how he planned!
20. Again self-destroyed is he, how he planned!
21. Then he looked,
22. Then he frowned and showed displeasure.
23. Then turned he away in pride
24. And said: "This is nothing else than magic from of old;
25. "This is nothing else than speech of mortal man."
26. Him shall I fling into the burning.[1]
27. Ah, what will convey to you what that burning is!
28. It leaves nothing; it spares nothing
29. It shrivels the man.

1. Ar. *saqar*—a name for hell [Pickthall's note].

30. Above it are nineteen.[2]

31. We have appointed only angels to be wardens of the fire, and their number have We made to be a stumbling block for those who disbelieve; that those to whom the scripture has been given may have certainty, and that believers may increase in faith; and that those to whom the scripture has been given and believers may not doubt; and that those in whose hearts there is disease, and disbelievers, may say: "What does God mean by this similitude?" Thus God sends astray whom He will, and guides whom He will. None knows the hosts of your Lord except Him. This is nothing else than a reminder for mortals.

32. No, by the moon
33. And the night when it withdraws
34. And the dawn when it shines forth,
35. This is one of the greatest (signs)
36. As a warning to men,
37. To him of you who will advance or hang back.
38. Every soul is a pledge for its own deeds;
39. Except those who will stand on the right hand.
40. In gardens they will ask one another
41. Concerning the guilty:
42. "What has brought you to this burning?"
43. They will answer: "We were not of those who prayed
44. "Nor did we feed the wretched.
45. "We used to wade (in vain dispute) with (all) waders,
46. "And we used to deny the day of judgment,
47. "Until the inevitable came to us."
48. The mediation of no mediators will avail them then.
49. Why do they now turn away from the admonishment,
50. As though they were frightened asses
51. Fleeing from a lion?

52. No, but every one of them desires that he should be given open pages (from God).

53. No. They do not fear the hereafter.
54. No. This is an admonishment.
55. So whoever wishes may heed.

56. And they will not heed unless God wills (it). He is the fount of fear. He is the fount of mercy.

## Sūra 75

*Al-Qiyāma* takes its name from a word in the first verse.

An early Meccan sūra.

2. The angels mentioned in the following verse.

## The Rising of the Dead

*Revealed at Mecca*

In the name of God, the beneficent, the merciful.

1. No, I swear by the day of resurrection;
2. No, I swear by the accusing soul (that this scripture is true).
3. Does man think that We shall not assemble his bones?
4. Yes. Yes, We are able to restore his very fingers!
5. But man would rather deny what is before him.
6. He asks: "When will be this day of resurrection?"
7. But when sight is confounded
8. And the moon is eclipsed
9. And sun and moon are united,
10. On that day man will cry: "Where to flee?"
11. Alas! No refuge!
12. To your Lord is the recourse that day.
13. On that day man is told the tale of that which he has sent before and left behind.
14. Oh, but man is a telling witness against himself,
15. Although he tender his excuses.
16. Do not stir your tongue with it to hasten it.[1]
17. On Us (rests) its putting together and its reading.
18. And when We read it, follow the reading;
19. Then upon Us (rests) its explanation.
20. No, but you do love the fleeting now
21. And neglect the hereafter.
22. That day will faces be resplendent,
23. Looking toward their Lord;
24. And that day will other faces be despondent,
25. You will know that some great disaster is about to fall on them.
26. No, but when the life comes up to the throat
27. And men say: "Where is the wizard (who can save him now)?"
28. And he knows that it is the parting;
29. And agony is heaped on agony;
30. To your Lord that day will be the driving.
31. For he neither trusted, nor prayed.
32. But he denied and flouted.
33. Then he went to his people with glee.
34. Nearer to you and nearer,
35. Again nearer to you and nearer (is the doom).
36. Does man think that he is to be left aimless?
37. Was he not a drop of fluid which gushed forth?
38. Then he became a clot; then (God) shaped and fashioned
39. And made of him a pair, the male and female.
40. Is not He (who does so) able to bring the dead to life?

1. I.e. the Qur'ān, which was revealed gradually, piece by piece [Pickthall's note].

## Sūra 76

*Al-Insān* or *al-Dahr* is, in either case, so called from a word in the first verse. An early Meccan sūra.

# "Man" or "Time"

*Revealed at Mecca*

In the name of God, the beneficent, the merciful.

1. Has there (ever) come upon man any period of time in which he was a thing unremembered?
2. We created man from a drop of thickened fluid to test him; so We made him hearing, knowing.
3. We have shown him the way, whether he is grateful or disbelieving.
4. We have prepared for disbelievers manacles and chains and a raging fire.
5. The righteous shall drink of a cup of which the mixture is of water of Kāfūr,[1]
6. A spring from which the servants of God drink, making it gush forth abundantly,
7. (Because) they perform the vow and fear a day of which the evil is wide-spreading,
8. And feed with food the needy wretch, the orphan and the prisoner, for love of him,
9. (Saying): "We feed you, for the sake of God only. We wish for no reward nor thanks from you;
10. "We fear from our Lord a day of frowning and of fate."
11. Therefore God has warded off from them the evil of that day, and has made them find brightness and joy;
12. And has awarded them for all that they endured, a garden and silk attire;
13. Reclining there upon couches, they will find there neither (heat of) a sun nor bitter cold.
14. The shade there is close upon them and its clustered fruits bow down.
15. Goblets of silver are brought round for them, and beakers (as) of glass
16. (Bright as) glass but (made) of silver, which they (themselves) have measured to the measure (of their deeds).
17. There are they watered with a cup whose mixture is of Zanjabīl,[2]
18. (The water of) a spring therein, named Salsabīl.[3]
19. There serve them youths of everlasting youth, whom, when you see them, you would take them for scattered pearls.
20. When you see you will see there bliss and high estate.
21. Their raiment will be fine green silk and gold embroidery. Bracelets of silver they will wear. Their Lord will slake their thirst with a pure drink.

1. Camphor, a tree resin used in scents, cooking, and medicine.
2. The spice ginger.
3. The name means "softly flowing."

22. (And it will be said to them): "This is a reward for you. Your endeavor (upon earth) has found acceptance."

23. We, even We, have revealed to you the Qur'ān, a revelation;

24. So submit patiently to your Lord's command, and do not obey any guilty one of them or disbeliever.

25. Remember the name of your Lord at morning and evening.

26. And worship Him (a portion) of the night, And glorify Him through the long night.

27. These love fleeting life, and put behind them (the remembrance of) a grievous day.

28. We, even We, created them, and strengthened their physique. And when We will, We can replace them, bringing others like them in their stead.

29. This is an admonishment, that whoever wishes may choose a way to his Lord.

30. Yet you will not, unless God wills. God is knower, wise.

31. He makes whom He wills to enter His mercy, and for evildoers has prepared a painful doom.

## Sūra 77

*Al-Mursalāt* takes its name from a word in the first verse. Verses 1, 2, and 3 are taken to refer to winds, verses 4 and 5 to angels.

An early Meccan sūra.

## The Emissaries

*Revealed at Mecca*

In the name of God, the beneficent, the merciful.

1. By the emissary winds, (sent) one after another
2. By the raging hurricanes,
3. By those which cause earth's vegetation to revive;
4. By those who winnow with a winnowing,
5. By those who bring down the reminder,
6. To excuse or to warn,
7. Surely that which you are promised will befall.
8. So when the stars are put out,
9. And when the sky is riven asunder,
10. And when the mountains are blown away,
11. And when the messengers are brought to their time appointed—
12. For what day is the time appointed?
13. For the day of decision.
14. And what will convey to you what the day of decision is!—
15. Woe to the repudiators on that day!
16. Did We not destroy the former folk,
17. Then caused the latter folk to follow after?
18. Thus do We ever deal with the guilty.
19. Woe to the repudiators on that day!

20. Did We not create you from a base fluid
21. Which We laid up in a safe abode
22. For a known term?
23. Thus We arranged. How excellent is our arranging!
24. Woe to the repudiators on that day!
25. Have We not made the earth a receptacle
26. Both for the living and the dead,
27. And placed in it high mountains and given you to drink sweet water there?
28. Woe to the repudiators on that day!
29. (It will be said to them:) Depart to that (doom) which you used to deny;
30. Depart to the shadow falling threefold,
31. (Which yet is) no relief or shelter from the flame.
32. It throws up sparks like the castles,
33. (Or) as it might be camels of bright yellow hue.
34. Woe to the repudiators on that day!
35. This is a day in which they do not speak,
36. Nor are they permitted to put forth excuses.
37. Woe to the repudiators on that day!
38. This is the day of decision, We have brought you and the men of old together.
39. If now you have any wit, outwit Me.
40. Woe to the repudiators on that day!
41. Those who kept their duty are amid shade and fountains,
42. And fruits such as they desire.
43. (To them it is said:) Eat, drink, and welcome, O you blessed, in return for what you did.
44. Thus do We reward the good.
45. Woe to the repudiators on that day!
46. Eat and take your ease (on earth) a little. You are guilty.
47. Woe to the repudiators on that day!
48. When it is said to them: "Bow down," they do not bow down!
49. Woe to the repudiators on that day!
50. In what statement, after this, will they believe?

## Sūra 78

*Al-Nabā'* takes its name from a word in the second verse.
An early Meccan sūra.

## The Tidings

*Revealed at Mecca*

In the name of God, the beneficent, the merciful.

1. About what do they question one another?
2. (It is) of the awful tidings,
3. Concerning which they are in disagreement.

4. No, but they will come to know!
5. No, again, but they will come to know!
6. Have We not made the earth an expanse,
7. And the high hills bulwarks?
8. And We have created you in pairs,
9. And have appointed your sleep for repose,
10. And have appointed the night as a cloak,
11. And have appointed the day for livelihood.
12. And We have built above you seven strong (heavens),
13. And have appointed a dazzling lamp,
14. And have sent down from the rainy clouds abundant water,
15. Thereby to produce grain and plant,
16. And gardens of thick foliage.
17. The day of decision is a fixed time,
18. A day when the trumpet is blown, and you come in multitudes,
19. And the heaven is opened and becomes as gates,
20. And the hills are set in motion and become as a mirage.
21. Hell lurks in ambush,
22. A home for the rebellious.
23. They will abide there for ages.
24. Therein they taste neither coolness nor (any) drink
25. Except boiling water and a paralyzing cold:
26. Reward proportioned (to their evil deeds).
27. For they did not look for a reckoning;
28. They called Our revelations false with strong denial.
29. Everything have We recorded in a book.
30. So taste (of what you have earned). No increase do We give you except of torment.
31. For the dutiful is achievement—
32. Gardens enclosed and vineyards,
33. And maidens for companions,
34. And a full cup.
35. There they hear neither vain discourse, nor lying—
36. Requital from your Lord—a gift in payment—
37. Lord of the heavens and the earth, and (all) that is between them, the Beneficent; with whom none can converse.
38. On the day when the angels and the spirit stand arrayed, they do not speak, except him whom the Beneficent allows and who speaks right.
39. That is the true day. So whoever will should seek recourse to his Lord.
40. We warn you of a doom at hand, a day in which a man will look on that which his own hands have sent before, and the disbeliever will cry: "Would that I were dust!"

## Sūra 79

*Al-Nāzi'āt* takes its name from a word in the first verse.
An early Meccan sūra.

# Those Who Drag Forth

*Revealed at Mecca*

In the name of God, the beneficent, the merciful.

1. By those who drag forth to destruction,
2. By the meteors rushing,
3. By the lone stars floating,[1]
4. By the angels hastening,
5. And those who govern the event,
6. On the day when the first trumpet resounds
7. And the second follows it,
8. On that day hearts beat painfully
9. While eyes are downcast
10. (Now) they are saying: "Shall we really be restored to our first state
11. "Even after we are crumbled bones?"
12. They say: "Then that would be a vain proceeding."
13. Surely it will need but one shout,
14. And they will be awakened.
15. Has there come to you the history of Moses?
16. How his Lord called him in the holy valley of Ṭuwa,
17. (Saying:) "Go you to Pharaoh—he has rebelled—
18. "And say (to him): 'Have you (will) to grow (in grace)?
19. "'Then I will guide you to your Lord and you shall fear (Him).'"
20. And he showed him the tremendous sign.
21. But he denied and disobeyed,
22. Then turned he away in haste,
23. Then gathered he and summoned
24. And proclaimed: "I (Pharaoh) am your lord the highest."
25. So God seized him (and made him) an example for the after (life) and for the former.
26. Here is indeed a lesson for him who fears.
27. Are you the harder to create, or is the heaven that He built?
28. He raised its height and ordered it;
29. And He made dark its night, and He brought forth its morn,
30. And after that He spread the earth,
31. And from it produced its water and its pasture,
32. And He made fast the hills,
33. A provision for you and for your cattle.
34. But when the great disaster comes,
35. The day when man will call to mind his (whole) endeavor,
36. And hell will stand forth visible to him who sees,
37. Then, as for him who rebelled
38. And chose the life of the world,
39. Hell will be his home.
40. But as for him who feared to stand before his Lord and restrained his soul from lust,

1. Some commentators take verses 2 and 3 also as referring to angels and explain them thus: "By those who console (the spirits of the righteous) tenderly." "By those who come floating (down from heaven with their Lord's command)." The rendering given in the text above is the more obvious [Pickthall's note].

41. The garden will be his home.
42. They ask you about the hour: "When will it come to port?"
43. Why (ask they)? What have you to tell of it?
44. To your Lord belongs (knowledge of) its term.
45. You are but a warner to him who fears it.
46. On the day when they behold it, it will be as if they had but tarried for an evening or the morning of it.

## Sūra 80

*'Abasa*, "He Frowned," takes its name from the first word. One day when the Prophet was in conversation with one of the great men of Quraysh (his own tribe), seeking to persuade him of the truth of Islam, a blind man came and asked a question concerning the faith. The Prophet was annoyed at the interruption, frowned and turned away from the blind man. In this sūra he is told that a man's importance is not to be judged from his appearance or worldly station.

An early Meccan sūra.

## He Frowned

*Revealed at Mecca*

In the name of God, the beneficent, the merciful.

1. He frowned and turned away
2. Because the blind man came to him.
3. What could inform you but that he might grow (in grace)
4. Or take heed and so the reminder might avail him?
5. As for him who thinks himself independent,
6. To him you pay regard.
7. Yet it is not your concern if he does not grow (in grace).
8. But as for him who comes to you with earnest purpose
9. And has fear,
10. From him you are distracted.
11. No, but it is an admonishment,
12. So let whoever wishes pay heed to it,
13. On honored leaves
14. Exalted, purified,
15. (Set down) by scribes
16. Noble and righteous.
17. Man is (self-)destroyed: how ungrateful!
18. From what thing does He create him?
19. From a drop of seed He creates him and proportions him,
20. Then makes the way easy for him,
21. Then causes him to die, and buries him;
22. Then, when He will, He brings him again to life.
23. No, but (man) has not done what He commanded him.
24. Let man consider his food:
25. How We pour water in showers
26. Then split the earth in clefts

27. And cause the grain to grow in it
28. And grapes and green fodder
29. And olive trees and palm trees
30. And garden closes of thick foliage
31. And fruits and grasses:
32. Provision for you and your cattle.
33. But when the shout comes
34. On the day when a man flees from his brother
35. And his mother and his father
36. And his wife and his children,
37. Every man that day will have concern enough to make him heedless (of others).
38. On that day faces will be bright as dawn,
39. Laughing, rejoicing at good news;
40. And other faces, on that day, with dust upon them,
41. Veiled in darkness,
42. Those are the disbelievers, the wicked.

## Sūra 81

*At-Takwīr* takes its name from a word in verse 1. Verses 8 and 9 contain an allusion to the practice of the pagan Arabs of burying alive girl-children whom they deemed superfluous.

An early Meccan sūra.

## The Overthrowing

*Revealed at Mecca*

In the name of God, the beneficent, the merciful.

1. When the sun is overthrown,
2. And when the stars fall,
3. And when the hills are moved,
4. And when the camels big with young are abandoned,
5. And when the wild beasts are herded together,
6. And when the seas rise,
7. And when souls are reunited,
8. And when the girl-child who was buried alive is asked
9. For what sin she was slain,
10. And when the pages are laid open,
11. And when the sky is torn away,
12. And when hell is lighted,
13. And when the garden is brought near,
14. (Then) every soul will know what it has made ready.
15. Oh, but I call to witness the planets,
16. The stars which rise and set,
17. And the close of night,[1]

1. Lit. "And the night when it closes" [Pickthall's note].

18. And the breath of morning[2]
19. That this is in truth the word of an honored messenger,
20. Mighty, established in the presence of the Lord of the throne,
21. (One) to be obeyed, and trustworthy;
22. And your comrade is not mad.
23. Surely he beheld him[3] on the clear horizon.[4]
24. And he is not a withholder of the unseen.
25. Nor is this the utterance of a devil worthy to be stoned.
26. Then where do you go?
27. This is nothing else than a reminder to creation,
28. To whoever of you wills to walk straight.
29. And you do not will, unless (it be) that God wills, the Lord of creation.

## Sūra 82

*Al-Infiṭār* takes its name from a word in verse 1.
An early Meccan sūra.

## The Cleaving

*Revealed at Mecca*

In the name of God, the beneficent, the merciful.

1. When the heaven is cleft asunder,
2. When the planets are dispersed,
3. When the seas are poured forth,
4. And the sepulchres are overturned,
5. A soul will know what it has sent before (it) and what left behind.
6. O man! What has made you careless concerning your Lord, the bountiful,
7. Who created you, then fashioned, then proportioned you?
8. Into whatever form He wills, He casts you.
9. No, but you deny the judgment.
10. There are above you guardians,
11. Generous and recording,
12. Who know (all) that you do.
13. The righteous will be in delight.
14. And the wicked will be in hell;
15. They will burn there on the day of judgment,
16. And will not be absent from it.
17. Ah, what will convey to you what the day of judgment is!
18. Again, what will convey to you what the day of judgment is!
19. A day on which no soul has power at all for any (other) soul. The (absolute) command on that day is God's.

2. Lit. "And the morning when it breathes" [Pickthall's note].
3. Usually understood to be the angel Gabriel.
4. The reference is to the Prophet's vision at Mt. Ḥirā' [Pickthall's note].

# Sūra 83

*Al-Taṭfīf*, "Defrauding," takes its name from a word in verse 1.
An early Meccan sūra.

## Defrauding

*Revealed at Mecca*

In the name of God, the beneficent, the merciful.

1. Woe to the defrauders:
2. Those who when they take the measure from mankind demand it full,
3. But if they measure for them or weigh for them, they cause them loss.
4. Do such (men) not consider that they will be raised again
5. To an awful day,
6. The day when (all) mankind stand before the Lord of the worlds?
7. No, but the record of the vile is in Sijjīn[1]—
8. Ah! what will convey to you what Sijjīn is!—
9. A written record.
10. Woe to the repudiators on that day!
11. Those who deny the day of judgment
12. Which none denies except each criminal transgressor,
13. Who, when you read to him Our revelations, say: "(Mere) fables of the men of old."
14. No, but that which they have earned is rust upon their hearts.
15. No, but surely on that day they will be covered from (the mercy of) their Lord.
16. Then they will burn in hell,
17. And it will be said (to them): "This is that which you used to deny."
18. No, but the record of the righteous is in 'Illiyīn[2]—
19. Ah, what will convey to you what 'Illiyīn is!—
20. A written record,
21. Attested by those who are brought near (to their Lord).
22. The righteous are in delight,
23. On couches, gazing,
24. You will know in their faces the radiance of delight.
25. They are given to drink of a pure wine, sealed,
26. Whose seal is musk—For this let (all) those strive who strive for bliss—
27. And mixed with water of Tasnīm,[3]
28. A spring from which those brought near (to God) drink.
29. The guilty used to laugh at those who believed,
30. And wink one to another when they passed them;
31. And when they returned to their own people, they returned jesting;
32. And when they saw them they said: "These have gone astray."
33. Yet they were not sent as guardians over them.
34. This day it is those who believe who have the laugh of disbelievers,

1. A pit in which the register of the deeds of the wicked is kept; also, the registry itself.
2. A celestial realm and, by extension, the register in which the deeds of the pious are written.
3. A well or fountain in paradise.

35. On high couches, gazing.
36. Are not the disbelievers paid for what they used to do?

## Sūra 84

*Al-Inshiqāq*, "The Sundering," takes its name from a word in verse 1.
An early Meccan sūra.

## The Sundering

*Revealed at Mecca*

In the name of God, the beneficent, the merciful.

1. When the heaven is split asunder
2. And attentive to her Lord in fear,
3. And when the earth is spread out
4. And has cast out all that was in her, and is empty
5. And attentive to her Lord in fear!
6. You, O man, are working toward your Lord a work which you will meet (in His presence).
7. Then whoever is given his account in his right hand
8. He truly will receive an easy reckoning
9. And will return to his folk in joy.
10. But whoever is given his account behind his back,
11. He surely will invoke destruction
12. And be thrown to scorching fire.
13. He lived joyous with his folk,
14. He thought that he would never return (to God).
15. No, but his Lord is ever looking on him!
16. Oh, I swear by the afterglow of sunset,
17. And by the night and all that it enshrouds,
18. And by the moon when she is at the full,
19. That you shall journey on from plane to plane.
20. What ails them, then, that they do not believe
21. And, when the Qur'ān is recited to them, do not worship (God)?
22. No, but those who disbelieve will deny;
23. And God knows best what they are hiding.
24. So give them tidings of a painful doom,
25. Except those who believe and do good works, for theirs is a reward unfailing.

## Sūra 85

*Al-Burūj* takes its name from a word in verse 1, which I have translated "mansions of the stars." The word has the meaning of towers or mansions and is applied to the signs of the zodiac. Verses 4 to 7 are generally taken to refer to the massacre of the Christians of Najrān in Yemen by a Jewish king Dhū Nawāṣ, an event of great historical importance since it caused the intervention of the Negus and led to the Abyssinian supremacy in the Yemen which lasted until the War of the Elephant (Q 105) in the Prophet's year of birth.[1] Professor Josef Horowitz thinks that the words "owners of the ditch, of the fuel-fed fire" refer not to any historical event but to the condition of all persecutors in the hereafter.[2]

An early Meccan sūra.

## The Mansions of the Stars

*Revealed at Mecca*

In the name of God, the beneficent, the merciful.

1. By the heaven, holding mansions of the stars,
2. And by the promised day.
3. And by the witness and that to which he bears testimony,
4. (Self-)destroyed were the owners of the ditch
5. Of the fuel-fed fire,
6. When they sat by it,
7. And were themselves the witnesses of what they did to the believers.[3]
8. They had nothing against them except that they believed in God, the mighty, the owner of praise,
9. Him to whom belongs the sovereignty of the heavens and the earth; and God is of all things the witness.
10. They who persecute believing men and believing women and do not repent, theirs will be the doom of hell, and theirs the doom of burning.
11. Those who believe and do good works, theirs will be gardens underneath which rivers flow. That is the great success.
12. The punishment of your Lord is stern.
13. He it is who produces, then reproduces,
14. And He is the forgiving, the loving,
15. Lord of the throne of glory,
16. Doer of what He will.
17. Has there come to you the story of the hosts
18. Of Pharaoh and (the tribe of) Thamūd?
19. No, but those who disbelieve live in denial
20. And God, all unseen, surrounds them.
21. No, but it is a glorious Qur'ān.
22. On a guarded tablet.

## Sūra 86

*Al-Ṭāriq* takes its name from a word in verse 1. There are other meanings to the word *ṭāriq*, but I have chosen that which must have occurred to every hearer of this sūra, especially as in verse 3 it is stated that a star is meant. The morning star has here a mystic sense, and is taken to refer to the Prophet

1. That is, 570 CE. The massacre occurred ca. 520.
2. See his "Judaeo-Arabic Relations in Pre-Islâmic Times," in *Islamic Culture* 3 (April 1929): 161–99 [Pickthall's note]. Josef Horovitz (1874–1931), German Orientalist.
3. Or it might be: "(Self-)destroyed were the owners of the trench of fuel-fed fire (i.e. hell) when they took their ease on earth and were themselves the witnesses," etc. [Pickthall's note].

himself. Some have thought that it refers to a comet which alarmed the East about the time of the Prophet's call. Others believe that this and other introductory verses, hard to elucidate, hide scientific facts unimagined at the period of revelation, and are related to the verses following them. Ghamrāwi Bey, my collaborator in the revision of this work, informed me that the late Dr. Ṣidqī[1] among others considered that the reference here is to the fertilizing germ penetrating the ovary, the subject being the same as verses 5–7.

An early Meccan sūra.

## The Morning Star

*Revealed at Mecca*

In the name of God, the beneficent, the merciful.

1. By the heaven and the morning star[2]—
2. Ah, what will tell you what the morning star is!—
3. The piercing star!
4. Every human soul has a guardian over it.
5. So let man consider from what he is created.
6. He is created from a gushing fluid
7. That issued from between the loins and ribs.
8. He is able to return him (to life)
9. On the day when hidden thoughts shall be searched out.
10. Then he will have no might or any helper.
11. By the heaven which gives the returning rain,
12. And the earth which splits (with the growth of trees and plants)
13. This (Qur'ān) is a conclusive word,
14. It is no pleasantry.
15. They plot a plot (against you, O Muḥammad)
16. And I plot a plot (against them).
17. So give a respite to the disbelievers. Deal gently with them for a while.

## Sūra 87

*Al-A'lā* takes its name from a word in verse 1.

An early Meccan sūra.

## The Most High

*Revealed at Mecca*

In the name of God, the beneficent, the merciful.

1. Praise the name of your Lord the most high,
2. Who creates, then disposes;
3. Who measures, then guides;
4. Who brings forth the pasturage,

1. Muḥammad Tawfiq Ṣidqī (d. 1920), Egyptian physician.
2. The Arabic word means originally "that which comes at night" or "one who knocks at the door" [Pickthall's note].

5. Then turns it to russet stubble.
6. We shall make you read (O Muḥammad) so that you shall not forget
7. Except that which God wills. He knows the disclosed and that which still is hidden;
8. And We shall ease your way to the state of ease.
9. Therefore remind (men), for of use is the reminder.
10. He who fears will heed,
11. But the most wretched will flout it,
12. He who will be flung to the great fire
13. In which he will neither die nor live.
14. He is successful who grows,
15. And remembers the name of his Lord, so prays.
16. But you prefer the life of the world
17. Although the hereafter is better and more lasting.
18. This is in the former scrolls,
19. The scrolls of Abraham and Moses.

## Sūra 88

*Al-Ghāshiya* takes its name from a word in verse 1.
An early Meccan sūra.

## The Overwhelming

*Revealed at Mecca*

In the name of God, the beneficent, the merciful.

1. Has there come to you tidings of the overwhelming?
2. On that day (many) faces will be downcast,
3. Toiling, weary,
4. Scorched by burning fire,
5. Drinking from a boiling spring,
6. No food for them but bitter thorn-fruit
7. Which does not nourish or release from hunger.
8. In that day other faces will be calm,
9. Glad for their effort past,
10. In a high garden
11. Where they hear no idle speech,
12. In which is a gushing spring,
13. In which are couches raised
14. And goblets set at hand
15. And cushions ranged
16. And silken carpets spread.
17. Will they not regard the camels, how they are created?
18. And the heaven, how it is raised?
19. And the hills, how they are set up?
20. And the earth, how it is spread?
21. Remind them, for you are but a reminder,

22. You are not at all a warder over them.
23. But whoever is averse and disbelieves,
24. God will punish him with direst punishment.
25. To Us is their return
26. And Ours their reckoning.

## Sūra 89

*Al-Fajr* takes its name from verse 1.
A very early Meccan sūra.

## The Dawn

*Revealed at Mecca*

In the name of God, the beneficent, the merciful.

1. By the dawn
2. And ten nights,[1]
3. And the even and the odd,
4. And the night when it departs,
5. There surely is an oath for a thinking man.
6. Do you not consider how your Lord dealt with (the tribe of) ʿĀd,
7. With many-columned[2] Iram,[3]
8. The like of which was not created in the lands;
9. And with (the tribe of) Thamūd, who clove the rocks in the valley;
10. And with Pharaoh, firm of might,
11. Who (all) were rebellious (to God) in these lands,
12. And multiplied iniquity in them?
13. Therefore your Lord poured on them the disaster of His punishment.
14. Your Lord is ever watchful.
15. As for man, whenever his Lord tests him by honoring him, and is gracious to him, he says: "My Lord honors me."
16. But whenever He tests him by restricting his means of life, he says: "My Lord despises me."
17. No, but you (for your part) do not honor the orphan
18. And do not urge the feeding of the poor,
19. And you devour heritages with devouring greed
20. And love wealth with abounding love.
21. No, but when the earth is ground to atoms, grinding, grinding,
22. And your Lord shall come with angels, rank on rank,
23. And hell is brought near that day; on that day man will remember, but how will the remembrance (then avail him)?

1. Of the month of pilgrimage [Pickthall's note].
2. I had written "many-columned," following the run of commentators, who take the word *ʿimād* to mean columns, pillars, when I happened upon Ibn Khaldūn's diatribe against that rendering and all the legends to which it has given rise, in the preface to the *Prolegomena*. The word meant "tent poles" to the Arabs of the Prophet's day, as Ibn Khaldūn points out. In view of recent discoveries in the Yemen, however, I prefer the usual rendering [Pickthall's note]. On Ibn Khaldūn's *Prolegomena* (*Muqaddimah*), see the introduction to the excerpt below, p. 478.
3. Variously identified as a location in Yemen or Syria.

24. He will say: "Ah, would that I had sent before me (some provision) for my life!"
25. None punishes as He will punish on that day!
26. None binds as He then will bind.
27. But ah! you soul at peace!
28. Return to your Lord, content in His good pleasure!
29. Enter among My bondmen!
30. Enter My garden!

## Sūra 90

*Al-Balad* takes its name from a word in verse 1.
A very early Meccan sūra.

## The City

*Revealed at Mecca*

In the name of God, the beneficent, the merciful.

1. No, I swear by this city—
2. And you are an indweller of this city[1]—
3. And the begetter and that which he begat,
4. We have created man in an atmosphere:[2]
5. Does he think that none has power over him?
6. And he says: "I have destroyed vast wealth,"
7. Does he think that none beholds him?
8. Did We not assign to him two eyes
9. And a tongue and two lips,
10. And guide him to the parting of the mountain ways?
11. But he has not attempted the ascent—
12. Ah, what will convey to you what the ascent is!—
13. (It is) to free a slave,
14. And to feed in the day of hunger
15. An orphan near of kin,
16. Or some poor wretch in misery,
17. And to be of those who believe and exhort one another to perseverance and exhort one another to pity.
18. Their place will be on the right hand.
19. But those who disbelieve our revelations, their place will be on the left hand.
20. Fire will be an awning over them.

## Sūra 91

*Al-Shams* takes its name from a word in verse 1.
A very early Meccan sūra.

1. Or "when you have control over this city" (prophetically) [Pickthall's note].
2. Or "in affliction" [Pickthall's note].

## The Sun

*Revealed at Mecca*

In the name of God, the beneficent, the merciful.

1. By the sun and its brightness,
2. And the moon when it follows it,
3. And the day when it reveals it,
4. And the night when it enshrouds it,
5. And the heaven and Him who built it,
6. And the earth and Him who spread it,
7. And a soul and Him who perfected it
8. And inspired it (with conscience of) what is wrong for it and (what is) right for it.
9. He is indeed successful who causes it to grow,
10. And he is indeed a failure who stunts it.
11. (The tribe of) Thamūd denied (the truth) in their rebellious pride,
12. When the basest of them broke forth
13. And the messenger of God said: "It is the she-camel of God, so let her drink!"
14. But they denied him, and they hamstrung her, so their Lord doomed them for their sin and razed (their dwellings).
15. He does not dread the sequel (of events).

## Sūra 92

*Al-Layl* takes its name from a word in verse 1.
A very early Meccan sūra.

## The Night

*Revealed at Mecca*

In the name of God, the beneficent, the merciful.

1. By the night enshrouding
2. And the day resplendent
3. And him who has created male and female,
4. Your effort is dispersed (toward diverse ends).
5. As for him who gives and is dutiful (toward God)
6. And believes in goodness;
7. Surely we will ease his way to the state of ease.
8. But as for him who hoards and thinks himself independent,
9. And denies goodness;
10. Surely we will ease his way to adversity.
11. His riches will not save him when he perishes.
12. Ours it is (to give) the guidance
13. And to Us belong the latter portion and the former.
14. Therefore have I warned you of the flaming fire

15. Which only the most wretched must endure,
16. He who denies and turns away.
17. Far removed from it will be the righteous
18. Who gives his wealth that he may grow (in goodness),
19. And none has with him any favor for reward,
20. Except as seeking (to fulfill) the purpose of his Lord most high.
21. He will be content.

## Sūra 93

*Al-Ḍuḥā*, "The Morning Hours," takes its name from the first verse. There was an interval during which the Prophet received no revelation and the idolaters mocked him, saying: "God, of whom we used to hear so much, has forsaken poor Muḥammad and now hates him." Then came this revelation. The Prophet had been a leading citizen of Mecca until he received his call. Now he was regarded as a madman. He was a man near fifty, and the prophecy in this sūra that "the latter portion would be better for him than the former" must have seemed absurd to those who heard it. Yet the latter portion of the Prophet's life, the last ten years, is the most wonderful record of success in human history.

An early Meccan sūra.

## The Morning Hours

*Revealed at Mecca*

In the name of God, the beneficent, the merciful.

1. By the morning hours
2. And by the night when it is stillest,
3. Your Lord has not forsaken you nor does He hate you,
4. And the latter portion will be better for you than the former,
5. And your Lord will give to you so that you will be content.
6. Did He not find you an orphan and protect (you)?
7. Did He not find you wandering and direct (you)?
8. Did He not find you destitute and enrich (you)?
9. Therefore do not oppress the orphan,
10. Therefore do not drive away the beggar,
11. Therefore of the bounty of your Lord be your discourse.

## Sūra 94

*Al-Inshirāḥ*, "Solace," takes its name from a word in verse 1, and also from its subject, which is relief from anxiety. It was probably revealed upon the same occasion as Q 93; and, at a time when the Prophet was derided and shunned after having been respected and courted, must have struck the disbelievers as ridiculous. It refers to the inward assurance which the Prophet had received by revelation, and speaks of future events as accomplished, as is usual in the Qur'ān, the revelation coming from a plane where time is not. Verse 4, speaking of his fame as exalted, must have seemed particularly absurd at that time of humiliation and persecution. But today, from every mosque in the world,

the Prophet's name is cried, as that of the messenger of God, five times a day, and every Muslim prays for blessings on him when his name is mentioned.
An early Meccan sūra.

## Solace

*Revealed at Mecca*

In the name of God, the beneficent, the merciful.

1. Have We not caused your breast to dilate,
2. And eased you of the burden
3. Which weighed down your back;
4. And exalted your fame?
5. But with hardship goes ease,
6. With hardship goes ease;
7. So when you are relieved, still toil
8. And strive to please your Lord.

## Sūra 95

*Al-Tīn*, "The Fig," takes its name from a word in verse 1. The sense is mystical, referring to man in relation to the revealed law of God and His judgment.
A very early Meccan sūra.

## The Fig

*Revealed at Mecca*

In the name of God, the beneficent, the merciful.

1. By the fig and the olive,
2. By Mount Sinai,
3. And by this land made safe;
4. Surely We created man of the best stature
5. Then We reduced him to the lowest of the low,
6. Except those who believe and do good works, and theirs is a reward unfailing.
7. So who[1] henceforth will give the lie to you about the judgment?
8. Is not God the most conclusive of all judges?

## Sūra 96

*Al-ʿAlaq* takes its name from a word in verse 2. Verses 1–5 are the words which the Prophet received in the vision at Mt. Ḥirāʾ, therefore the first of the Qurʾān to be revealed.
A very early Meccan sūra.

1. For another instance of *lo* meaning "who" instead of "what," see Q 91:5–7 [Pickthall's note].

## The Clot

*Revealed at Mecca*

In the name of God, the beneficent, the merciful.

1. Recite: In the name of your Lord who created,
2. Created man from a clot.
3. Recite: And your Lord is the most bounteous,
4. Who teaches by the pen,
5. Teaches man what he knew not.
6. No, but truly man is rebellious
7. That he thinks himself independent!
8. To your Lord is the return.
9. Have you seen him who dissuades
10. A servant (of God) when he prays?
11. Have you seen if he relies on the guidance (of God)
12. Or enjoins piety?
13. Have you seen if he denies (God's guidance) and turns away?
14. Is he then unaware that God sees?
15. No, but if he does not cease We will seize him by the forelock—
16. The lying, sinful forelock—
17. Then let him call upon his henchmen!
18. We will call the guards of hell.
19. No! Do not obey him. But prostrate yourself, and draw near (to God).

# Sūra 97

*Al-Qadr* takes its name from a word in verse 1. It refers to the night (one of the last nights of Ramaḍān) on which the Prophet received his call and the first verses of the Qur'ān were revealed in the vision of Mt. Ḥirā'. It is said to be the night on which God's decrees for the year are brought down to the earthly plane.

A very early Meccan sūra.

## Power

*Revealed at Mecca*

In the name of God, the beneficent, the merciful.

1. We revealed it on the night of power.
2. Ah, what will convey to you what the night of power is!
3. The night of power is better than a thousand months.
4. The angels and the spirit[1] descend in it, by the permission of their Lord, with all decrees.
5. (That night is) peace until the rising of the dawn.

1. I.e. Gabriel or, as some commentators think, a general term for angels of the highest rank [Pickthall's note].

## Sūra 98

*Al-Bayyina* takes its name from a word in the first verse. There is no certainty as to the period of revelation. Many regard it as a late Meccan sūra. I follow the attribution in the *muṣḥaf*[1] which I have followed throughout.

The probable date of revelation is the year 1 AH.

# The Clear Proof

*Revealed at Medina*

In the name of God, the beneficent, the merciful.

1. Those who disbelieve among the People of the Book and the idolaters could not have left off (erring) until the clear proof came to them,
2. A messenger from God, reading purified pages
3. Containing correct scriptures.
4. Nor were the People of the Book divided until after the clear proof came to them.
5. And they are ordered only to serve God, keeping religion pure for Him, as men by nature upright, and to establish worship and to pay the poor tax. That is true religion.
6. Those who disbelieve, among the People of the Book and the idolaters, will abide in hell's fire. They are the worst of created beings.
7. (And) those who believe and do good works are the best of created beings.
8. Their reward is with their Lord: gardens of Eden underneath which rivers flow, in which they dwell forever. God has pleasure in them and they have pleasure in Him. This is (in store) for him who fears his Lord.

## Sūra 99

*Al-Zilzāl* takes its name from a word in verse 1.

A very early Meccan sūra.

# The Earthquake

*Revealed at Mecca*

In the name of God, the beneficent, the merciful.

1. When earth is shaken with her (final) earthquake
2. And earth yields up her burdens,
3. And man says: "What ails her?"
4. That day she will relate her chronicles,
5. Because your Lord inspires her.
6. That day mankind will issue forth in scattered groups to be shown their deeds.

1. Codex.

7. And whoever does an atom's weight of good will see it then,
8. And whoever does an atom's weight of ill will see it then.

## Sūra 100

*Al-ʿĀdiyāt* takes its name from a word in the first verse.
A very early Meccan sūra.

## The Coursers

*Revealed at Mecca*

In the name of God, the beneficent, the merciful.

1. By the snorting coursers,[1]
2. Striking sparks of fire
3. And scouring to the raid at dawn,
4. Then, therewith, with their trail of dust,
5. Cleaving, as one, the center (of the foe),[2]
6. Man is an ingrate to his Lord
7. And he is a witness to that;
8. And in the love of wealth he is violent.
9. Does he not know that, when the contents of the graves are poured forth
10. And the secrets of the breasts are made known,
11. On that day will their Lord be perfectly informed concerning them.

## Sūra 101

*Al-Qāriʿa* takes its name from a word in verse 1 recurring in the next two verses.
A very early Meccan sūra.

## The Calamity

*Revealed at Mecca*

In the name of God, the beneficent, the merciful.

1. The calamity!
2. What is the calamity?
3. Ah, what will convey to you what the calamity is!
4. A day in which mankind will be as thickly scattered moths
5. And the mountains will become as carded wool.
6. Then, as for him whose scales are heavy (with good works),
7. He will live a pleasant life.
8. But as for him whose scales are light,

1. Fast-running horses.
2. The meaning of the first five verses is by no means clear. The above is a probable rendering [Pickthall's note].

9. The bereft and hungry one will be his mother.
10. Ah, what will convey to you what she is!—
11. Raging fire.

## Sūra 102

*Al-Takāthur* takes its name from a word in the first verse.
A very early Meccan sūra.

## Rivalry in Worldly Increase

*Revealed at Mecca*

In the name of God, the beneficent, the merciful.

1. Rivalry in worldly increase distracts you
2. Until you come to the graves.
3. No, but you will come to know!
4. No, but you will come to know!
5. No, would that you knew (now) with a sure knowledge!
6. For you will behold hellfire.
7. Yes, you will behold it with sure vision.
8. Then, on that day, you will be asked concerning pleasure.

## Sūra 103

*Al-'Aṣr* takes its name from a word in verse 1.
A very early Meccan sūra.

## The Declining Day

*Revealed at Mecca*

In the name of God, the beneficent, the merciful.

1. By the declining day,
2. Man is in a state of loss,
3. Except those who believe and do good works, and exhort one another to truth and exhort one another to endurance.

## Sūra 104

*Al-Humaza* takes its name from a word in verse 1. The idolaters waylaid all newcomers to Mecca and warned them against the Prophet, in order to prevent their listening to his preaching.
An early Meccan sūra.

## The Faultfinder

*Revealed at Mecca*

In the name of God, the beneficent, the merciful.

1. Woe to every slandering faultfinder,
2. Who has gathered wealth (of this world) and arranged it.
3. He thinks that his wealth will render him immortal.
4. No, but he will be flung to the consuming one.
5. Ah, what will convey to you what the consuming one is!
6. (It is) the fire of God, kindled,
7. Which leaps up over the hearts (of men).
8. It is closed in on them
9. In outstretched columns.

# Sūra 105

*Al-Fīl*, "The Elephant," takes its name from a word in the first verse. The allusion is to the campaign of Abraha, the Abyssinian ruler of Yemen, against Mecca, with the purpose of destroying the Ka'ba in the year of the Prophet's birth. He had with him an elephant which much impressed the Arabs. Tradition says that the elephant refused to advance on the last stage of the march, and that swarms of flying creatures pelted the Abyssinians with stones. Another tradition says that they retired in disorder owing to an outbreak of smallpox in the camp. At the time when this sūra was revealed, many men in Mecca must have known what happened. Dr. Krenkow,[1] a sound Arabic scholar, is of the opinion that the flying creatures may well have been swarms of insects carrying infection. In any case the Ka'ba was saved from destruction after its defenders had despaired.

A very early Meccan sūra.

## The Elephant

*Revealed at Mecca*

In the name of God, the beneficent, the merciful.

1. Have you not seen how your Lord dealt with the owners of the elephant?
2. Did he not bring their stratagem to nothing,
3. And send against them swarms of flying creatures,
4. Which pelted them with stones of baked clay,
5. And made them like green crops devoured (by cattle)?

1. Fritz Krenkow (1872–1953), German Orientalist.

## Sūra 106

*Al-Shitā'* is so called from a word occurring in verse 2. It is also often called *Quraysh*.

A very early Meccan sūra.

## "Winter" or "Quraysh"

*Revealed at Mecca*

In the name of God, the beneficent, the merciful.

1. For the taming[1] of Quraysh
2. For their taming (We cause) the caravans to set forth in winter and summer.
3. So let them worship the Lord of this house,
4. Who has fed them against hunger
5. And has made them safe from fear.

## Sūra 107

*Al-Mā'ūn* takes its name from a word in the last verse.

An early Meccan revelation.

## Small Kindnesses

*Revealed at Mecca*

In the name of God, the beneficent, the merciful.

1. Have you observed him who denies religion?
2. That is he who repells the orphan,
3. And does not urge the feeding of the needy.
4. Ah, woe to worshippers
5. Who are heedless of their prayer;
6. Who would be seen (at worship)
7. Yet refuse small kindnesses!

## Sūra 108

*Al-Kawthar* takes its name from a word in the first verse. The disbelievers used to taunt the Prophet with the fact that he had no son, and therefore none to uphold his religion after him.

1. I.e. "civilizing" [Pickthall's note].

## Abundance

*Revealed at Mecca*

In the name of God, the beneficent, the merciful.

1. We have given you abundance;
2. So pray to your Lord, and sacrifice.
3. It is your insulter (and not you) who is without posterity.

## Sūra 109

*Al-Kāfirūn* takes its name from a word in verse 1. It was revealed at a time when the idolaters had asked the Prophet to compromise in matters of religion.

## The Disbelievers

*Revealed at Mecca*

In the name of God, the beneficent, the merciful.

1. Say: O disbelievers!
2. I do not worship what you worship;
3. Nor do you worship what I worship.
4. And I shall not worship what you worship.
5. Nor will you worship what I worship.
6. To you your religion, and to me my religion.

## Sūra 110

*Al-Naṣr* takes its name from a word in the first verse. It is one of the very last revelations, having come to the Prophet only a few weeks before his death. Though ascribed always to Medina, tradition says that it was actually revealed at Mecca during the days the Prophet spent there when he made his farewell pilgrimage. It is described in Ibn Hishām and elsewhere as the first announcement that the Prophet received of his approaching death.

The date of revelation is the tenth year of the *hijra*.

## Help

*Revealed at Medina*

In the name of God, the beneficent, the merciful.

1. When God's help and the triumph comes
2. And you see mankind entering the religion of God in bands,
3. Then hymn the praises of your Lord, and seek forgiveness of Him. He is ever ready to show mercy.

## Sūra 111

*Al-Masad* takes its name from a word (to the Arabs a very homely word) in the last verse. It is the only passage in the whole Qur'ān where an opponent of the Prophet is denounced by name. Abū Lahab (the Father of Flame), whose real name was 'Abd al-'Uzzā, was a first cousin of the Prophet's grandfather and was the only member of his own clan who bitterly opposed the Prophet. He made it his business to torment the Prophet, and his wife took a pleasure in carrying thorn bushes and strewing them in the sand where she knew that the Prophet was sure to walk barefooted.

An early Meccan revelation.

## Palm Fibre

*Revealed at Mecca*

In the name of God, the beneficent, the merciful.

1. The power of Abū Lahab will perish, and he will perish.
2. His wealth and gains will not exempt him.
3. He will be plunged in flaming fire,
4. And his wife, the wood carrier,
5. Will have upon her neck a halter of palm fibre.

## Sūra 112

*Al-Tawḥīd*, "The Unity," takes its name from its subject.[1] It has been called the essence of the Qur'ān, of which it is really the last sūra. Some authorities ascribe this sūra to the Medinan period, and think that it was revealed in answer to a question of some Jewish doctors concerning the nature of God.

It is generally held to be an early Meccan sūra.

## The Unity

*Revealed at Mecca*

In the name of God, the beneficent, the merciful.

1. Say: He is God, the one!
2. God, the eternally besought of all!
3. He begets not nor was begotten.
4. And there is none comparable to Him.

## Sūra 113

*Al-Falaq*, "The Daybreak," takes its name from a word in the first verse. This and the following sūra are prayers for protection, this one being for protection

1. The sūra is more frequently known as *al-Ikhlāṣ* (Sincere Devotion)

from fears proceeding from the unknown. The two sūras are known as *al-Mu'awwadhatayn*, the two cries for refuge and protection.

An early Meccan sūra.

## The Daybreak

*Revealed at Mecca*

In the name of God, the beneficent, the merciful.

1. Say: I seek refuge in the Lord of the daybreak
2. From the evil of that which He created;
3. From the evil of the darkness when it is intense,
4. And from the evil of malignant witchcraft,[1]
5. And from the evil of the envier when he envies.

## Sūra 114

*Al-Nās*, the second of the two cries for refuge and protection, takes its name from a recurring word which marks the rhythm in the Arabic. In this case protection is sought especially from the evil in a man's own heart and in the hearts of other men.

An early Meccan revelation.

## Mankind

*Revealed at Mecca*

In the name of God, the beneficent, the merciful.

1. Say: I seek refuge in the Lord of mankind,
2. The king of mankind,
3. The God of mankind,
4. From the evil of the sneaking whisperer,
5. Who whispers in the hearts of mankind,
6. Of the jinn and of mankind.

1. Lit. "from the evil of blowers (feminine) upon knots," it having been a common form of witchcraft in Arabia for women to tie knots in a cord and blow upon them with an imprecation [Pickthall's note].

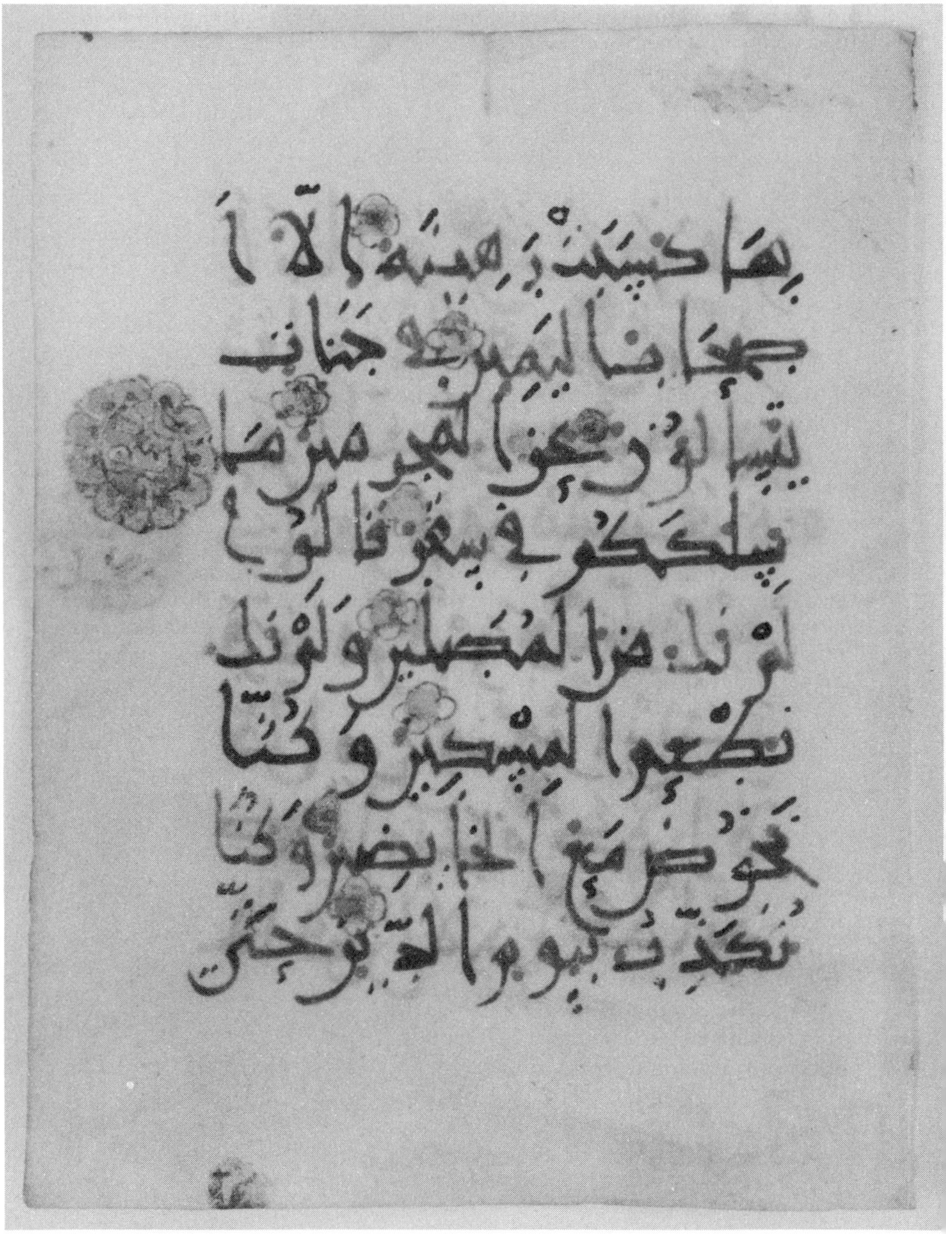

Folio of Q 74:38–54 (Iran 905). Freer Gallery of Art, Smithsonian Institution, Washington, D.C.: The Catherine and Ralph Benkaim Collection, S1997.92.

Mary and Jesus in an Indian miniature. Album of Persian and Indian calligraphy and paintings, Walters Manuscript W.668, fol.10b detail. Courtesy of The Walters Art Museum, Baltimore.

An older boy works on memorizing passages from the Qurʾān at the qurʾānic school of Tajir Ahmed in Timbuktu, Mali. © Alexandra Huddleston. Reproduced by permission of the photographer. Image courtesy of the Library of Congress Prints and Photographs Division.

The itinerant marabout Younoussa Ahamdou Djaroumba poses with a sheet of paper showing some of the mystical aspects of his studies of the Qurʾān. © Alexandra Huddleston. Reproduced by permission of the photographer. Image courtesy of the Library of Congress Prints and Photographs Division.

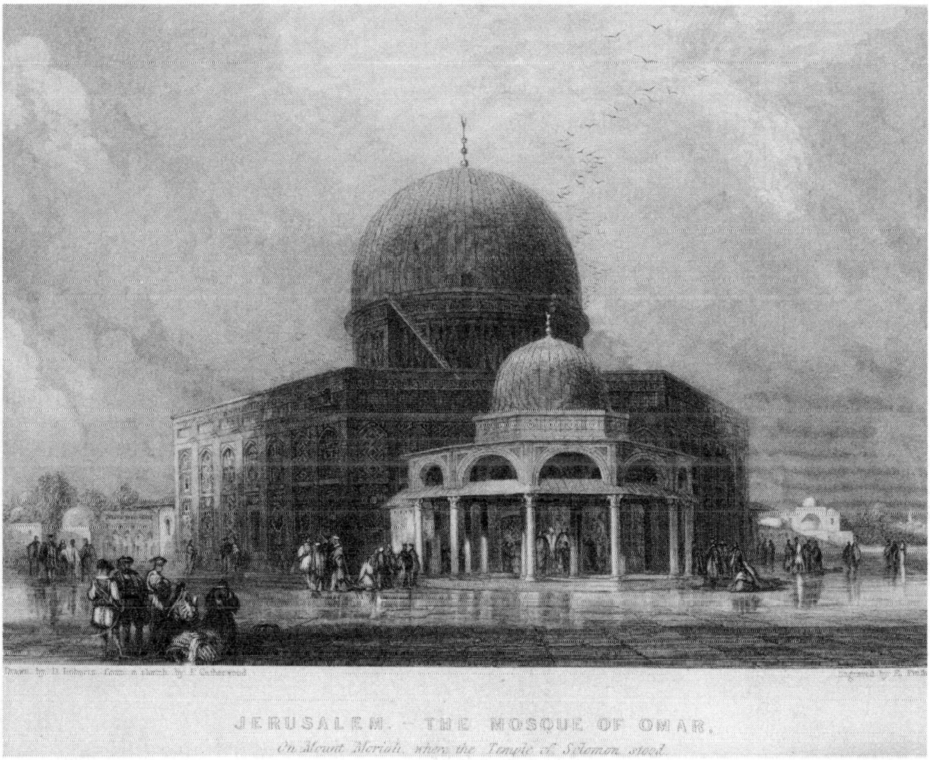
JERUSALEM. – THE MOSQUE OF OMAR.
On Mount Moriah, where the Temple of Solomon stood.

Dome of the Rock: Maps and drawings of Jerusalem and important sites by Frederick Catherwood (d. 1854). Courtesy of the Library of Congress.

Omar ibn Said (1770–1864). Portrait of Omar ibn Said from the DeRosset Family Papers #241, Southern Historical Collection, Louis Round Wilson Special Collections Library, University of North Carolina at Chapel Hill. Reproduced by permission.

Rep. Keith Ellison takes the oath of office on January 4, 2007, using the Qur'ān translation owned by Thomas Jefferson. Courtesy of the Library of Congress Office of Communications.

# ORIGINS

# Muḥammad

## IBN ISḤĀQ AND IBN HISHĀM

Muḥammad ibn Isḥāq ibn Yasār (ca. 704–767) was an early historian whose *Sīra*, or biography, of Muḥammad remains the standard source for information on the Prophet's life. Grandson of a prisoner of war, Ibn Isḥāq was born in Medina and followed the family vocation of memorizing and transmitting detailed genealogies of well-known personages, as well as stories of battles and military campaigns. The ʿAbbāsid caliph al-Manṣūr (r. 754–75) commissioned Ibn Isḥāq to write a universal history, beginning with creation of the world and ending with the author's own lifetime. The work originally comprised three sections—stories of the ancient peoples and rulers, the life and mission of Muḥammad, and the early community's raids and expeditions; although the first part has been lost, it can be reconstructed from later sources. A fourth volume—about Muḥammad's successors, the caliphs—was added later.

ʿAbd al-Malik ibn Hishām (d. 833), a scholar whose family was from southern Arabia, made an edition of Ibn Isḥāq's *Sīra* in which he omitted materials not relevant to Muḥammad's biography, corrected some of the poetry entries, and explained unusual words and references. Ibn Hishām's recension became the most popular version of Ibn Isḥāq's original work.

In his translation of this version, Alfred Guillaume (1888–1965), a British Arabist and university professor, included material attributed to Ibn Isḥāq from *The History of Prophets and Kings*, by Abū Jaʿfar ibn Jarīr al-Ṭabarī (ca. 839–923). These passages, which Guillaume indicated with a "Ṭ.," are not to be found in Ibn Hishām's recension of the *Sīra*.

Much of the narrative in the *Sīra* serves as exegesis or interpretation of the Qurʾān and has long been read as connecting specific qurʾānic citations to events in the life of Muḥammad.

### *From* The Life of Muhammad†

#### *The Prophet's Mission*

When Muhammad the apostle of God reached the age of forty God sent him in compassion to mankind, 'as an evangelist to all men.'[1] Now God had made a covenant with every prophet whom he had sent before him that he should believe in him, testify to his truth and help him against his adversaries, and he required of them that they should transmit that to everyone who believed in them, and they carried out their obligations in that respect. God said to Muhammad, 'When God made a covenant with the prophets (He said) this is the scripture and wisdom which I have given you,

† From *The Life of Muhammad: A Translation of Isḥāq's "Sīrat Rasūl Allāh,"* with introduction and notes by Alfred Guillaume (London: Oxford University Press, 1955), pp. 104–7, 111–13. Except as indicated, all notes are Guillaume's.

1. Q 34:27.

afterwards an apostle will come confirming what you know that you may believe in him and help him.' He said, 'Do you accept this and take up my burden?' i.e. the burden of my agreement which I have laid upon you. They said, 'We accept it.' He answered, 'Then bear witness and I am a witness with you.[2] Thus God made a covenant with all the prophets that they should testify to his truth and help him against his adversaries and they transmitted that obligation to those who believed in them among the two monotheistic religions.

* * *

ʿAbduʾl-Malik b. ʿUbaydullah b. Abū Sufyān b. al-ʿAlāʾ b. Jāriya the Thaqafite who had a retentive memory related to me from a certain scholar that the apostle at the time when Allah willed to bestow His grace upon him and endow him with prophethood would go forth for his affair and journey far afield until he reached the glens of Mecca and the beds of its valleys where no house was in sight; and not a stone or tree that he passed by but would say, 'Peace unto thee, O apostle of Allah.' And the apostle would turn to his right and left and look behind him and he would see naught but trees and stones. Thus he stayed seeing and hearing so long as it pleased Allah that he should stay. Then Gabriel came to him with the gift of God's grace whilst he was on Ḥirā'[3] in the month of Ramaḍān.

Wahb b. Kaisān a client of the family of al-Zubayr told me: I heard ʿAbdullah b. al-Zubayr say to ʿUbayd b. ʿUmayr b. Qatāda the Laythite, 'O ʿUbayd tell us how began the prophethood which was first bestowed on the apostle when Gabriel came to him.' And ʿUbayd in my presence related to ʿAbdullah and those with him as follows: The apostle would pray in seclusion on Ḥirā' every year for a month to practise *taḥannuth* as was the custom of Quraysh in heathen days. *Taḥannuth* is religious devotion. Abū Ṭālib[4] said:

> By Thaur and him who made Thabīr firm in its place
> And by those going up to ascend Ḥirāʾ and coming down.[5]

Wahb b. Kaisān told me that ʿUbayd said to him: Every year during that month the apostle would pray in seclusion and give food to the poor that came to him. And when he completed the month and returned from his seclusion, first of all before entering his house he would go to the Kaʿba[6] and walk round it seven times or as often as it pleased God; then he would go back to his house until in the year when God sent him, in the month of Ramaḍān in which God willed concerning him what He willed of His grace, the apostle set forth to Ḥirā' as was his wont, and his family with him. When it was the night on which God honoured him with his mission and showed mercy on His servants thereby, Gabriel brought him the command of God. 'He came to me,' said the apostle of God, 'while I was asleep, with a coverlet of brocade whereon was some writing, and said, "Read!" I said, "What shall I read?" He pressed me with it so tightly

2. Q 3:75.
3. A mountain about 2 miles from Mecca [editor's note].
4. Muḥammad's uncle (d. 619) [editor's note].
5. Thaur and Thabīr are mountains near Mecca.
6. Literally, "cube": the stone shrine in Mecca, believed to have been built by Adam and then rebuilt by Ibrāhīm (Abraham) and Ismāʿīl (Ishmael); central to both early pagan and Muslim pilgrimage rituals, it became the most important site in Islam [editor's note].

that I thought it was death; then he let me go and said, "Read!" I said, "What shall I read?" He pressed me with it again so that I thought it was death; then he let me go and said "Read!" I said, "What shall I read?" He pressed me with it the third time so that I thought it was death and said "Read!" I said, "What then shall I read?"—and this I said only to deliver myself from him, lest he should do the same to me again. He said:

"Read in the name of thy Lord who created,
Who created man of blood coagulated.
Read! Thy Lord is the most beneficent,
Who taught by the pen,
Taught that which they knew not unto men."[7]

So I read it, and he departed from me. And I awoke from my sleep, and it was as though these words were written on my heart. (Ṭ. Now none of God's creatures was more hateful to me than an (ecstatic) poet or a man possessed: I could not even look at them. I thought, Woe is me poet or possessed—Never shall Quraysh[8] say this of me! I will go to the top of the mountain and throw myself down that I may kill myself and gain rest. So I went forth to do so and then) when I was midway on the mountain, I heard a voice from heaven saying, "O Muhammad! thou art the apostle of God and I am Gabriel." I raised my head towards heaven to see (who was speaking), and lo, Gabriel in the form of a man with feet astride the horizon, saying, "O Muhammad! thou art the apostle of God and I am Gabriel." I stood gazing at him, (Ṭ. and that turned me from my purpose) moving neither forward nor backward; then I began to turn my face away from him, but towards whatever region of the sky I looked, I saw him as before. And I continued standing there, neither advancing nor turning back, until Khadīja sent her messengers in search of me and they gained the high ground above Mecca and returned to her while I was standing in the same place; then he parted from me and I from him, returning to my family. And I came to Khadīja[9] and sat by her thigh and drew close to her. She said, "O Abū'l-Qāsim,[1] where hast thou been? By God, I sent my messengers in search of thee, and they reached the high ground above Mecca and returned to me." (Ṭ. I said to her, "Woe is me poet or possessed." She said, "I take refuge in God from that O Abū'l-Qāsim. God would not treat you thus since he knows your truthfulness, your great trustworthiness, your fine character, and your kindness. This cannot be, my dear. Perhaps you did see something." "Yes, I did," I said.) Then I told her of what I had seen; and she said, "Rejoice, O son of my uncle, and be of good heart. Verily, by Him in whose hand is Khadīja's soul, I have hope that thou wilt be the prophet of this people."' Then she rose and gathered her garments about her and set forth to her cousin Waraqa b. Naufal b. Asad b. ʿAbdu'l-ʿUzzā b. Quṣayy, who had become a Christian and read the scriptures and learned from those that follow the Torah[2] and the Gospel. And when she related to him what the apostle of God told her he had seen and heard, Waraqa cried, 'Holy! Holy! Verily by Him in whose hand is Waraqa's soul, if thou hast spoken to me the truth, O Khadīja, there hath come unto him the greatest

7. Q 96:1–5.
8. The ruling tribe of Mecca [editor's note].
9. Muḥammad's first wife (ca. 554–619) [editor's note].
1. The *kunya* or "name of honor" of Muḥammad.
2. The first five books of the Hebrew Bible, traditionally ascribed to Moses [editor's note].

Nāmūs[3] (Ṭ. meaning Gabriel) who came to Moses aforetime, and lo, he is the prophet of this people. Bid him be of good heart.' So Khadīja returned to the apostle of God and told him what Waraqa had said. (Ṭ. and that calmed his fears somewhat.) And when the apostle of God had finished his period of seclusion and returned (to Mecca), in the first place he performed the circumambulation of the Ka'ba, as was his wont. While he was doing it, Waraqa met him and said, 'O son of my brother, tell me what thou hast seen and heard.' The apostle told him, and Waraqa said, 'Surely, by Him in whose hand is Waraqa's soul, thou art the prophet of this people. There hath come unto thee the greatest Nāmūs, who came unto Moses. Thou wilt be called a liar, and they will use thee despitefully and cast thee out and fight against thee. Verily, if I live to see that day, I will help God in such wise as He knoweth.' Then he brought his head near to him and kissed his forehead; and the apostle went to his own house. (Ṭ. Waraqa's words added to his confidence and lightened his anxiety.)

Ismā'īl b. Abū Ḥakīm, a freedman of the family of al-Zubayr, told me on Khadīja's authority that she said to the apostle of God, 'O son of my uncle, are you able to tell me about your visitant, when he comes to you?' He replied that he could, and she asked him to tell her when he came. So when Gabriel came to him, as he was wont, the apostle said to Khadīja, 'This is Gabriel who has just come to me.' 'Get up, O son of my uncle,' she said, 'and sit by my left thigh'. The apostle did so, and she said, 'Can you see him?' 'Yes,' he said. She said, 'Then turn round and sit on my right thigh.' He did so, and she said, 'Can you see him?' When he said that he could she asked him to move and sit in her lap. When he had done this she again asked if he could see him, and when he said yes, she disclosed her form and cast aside her veil while the apostle was sitting in her lap. Then she said, 'Can you see him?' And he replied, 'No.' She said, 'O son of my uncle, rejoice and be of good heart, by God he is an angel and not a satan.'

I told 'Abdullah b. Ḥasan this story and he said, 'I heard my mother Fāṭima, daughter of Ḥusayn, talking about this tradition from Khadīja, but as I heard it she made the apostle of God come inside her shift, and thereupon Gabriel departed, and she said to the apostle of God, "This verily is an angel and not a satan."'

* * *

## *The Beginning of the Sending Down of the Qurān*

The apostle began to receive revelations in the month of Ramaḍān. In the words of God, 'The month of Ramaḍān in which the Qurān was brought down as a guidance to men, and proofs of guidance and a decisive criterion.'[4] And again, 'Verily we have sent it down on the night of destiny, and what has shown you what the night of destiny is? The night of destiny is better than a thousand months. In it the angels and the spirit descend by their Lord's permission with every matter. It is peace until the rise of dawn.[5] Again, 'Ḥ.M.[6] by the perspicuous book, verily we have sent it down in a blessed night. Verily, we were warning. In it every wise matter is decided

3. Literally, "Law" [editor's note].
4. Q 2:181.
5. Q 97.
6. Ḥā. Mīm. (two letters of the Arabic alphabet) [editor's note].

as a command from us. Verily we sent it down.[7] And again, 'Had you believed in God and what we sent down to Our servant on the day of decision, the day on which the two parties met',[8] i.e. the meeting of the apostle with the polytheists in Badr.[9] Abū Ja'far Muhammad b. 'Alī b. al-Ḥusayn told me that the apostle of God met the polytheists in Badr on the morning of Friday, the 17th of Ramaḍān.

Then revelation came fully to the apostle while he was believing in Him and in the truth of His message. He received it willingly, and took upon himself what it entailed whether of man's goodwill or anger. Prophecy is a troublesome burden—only strong, resolute messengers can bear it by God's help and grace, because of the opposition which they meet from men in conveying God's message. The apostle carried out God's orders in spite of the opposition and ill treatment which he met with.

### *Khadīja, Daughter of Khuwaylid, Accepts Islam*

Khadīja believed in him and accepted as true what he brought from God, and helped him in his work. She was the first to believe in God and His apostle, and in the truth of his message. By her God lightened the burden of His prophet. He never met with contradiction and charges of falsehood, which saddened him, but God comforted him by her when he went home. She strengthened him, lightened his burden, proclaimed his truth, and belittled men's opposition. May God Almighty have mercy upon her!

* * *

Then revelations stopped for a time so that the apostle of God was distressed and grieved. Then Gabriel brought him the Sūra of the Morning, in which his Lord, who had so honoured him, swore that He had not forsaken him, and did not hate him. God said, 'By the morning and the night when it is still, thy Lord hath not forsaken nor hated thee,'[1] meaning that He has not left you and forsaken you, nor hated you after having loved you. 'And verily, the latter end is better for you than the beginning,'[2] i.e. What I have for you when you return to Me is better than the honour which I have given you in the world. 'And your Lord will give you and will satisfy you,' i.e. of victory in this world and reward in the next. 'Did he not find you an orphan and give you refuge, going astray and guided you, found you poor and made you rich?' God thus told him of how He had begun to honour him in his earthly life, and of His kindness to him as an orphan poor and wandering astray, and of His delivering him from all that by His compassion.

'Do not oppress the orphan and do not repel the beggar.' That is, do not be a tyrant or proud or harsh or mean towards the weakest of God's creatures.

'Speak of the kindness of thy Lord,' i.e. tell about the kindness of God in giving you prophecy, mention it and call men to it.

7. Q 44:1–4.
8. Q 8:42.
9. A town between Mecca and Medina; in 624 CE, it was the site of a decisive victory of the Muslims over the far more numerous Meccans [editor's note].
1. Q 93 [from which all the quotations in this section are taken—editor's note].
2. Q 93.

So the apostle began to mention secretly God's kindness to him and to his servants in the matter of prophecy to everyone among his people whom he could trust.

### *The Prescription of Prayer*

The apostle was ordered to pray and so he prayed. Ṣāliḥ b. Kaisān from ʿUrwa b. al-Zubayr from ʿĀʾisha[3] told me that she said, 'When prayer was first laid on the apostle it was with two prostrations for every prayer: then God raised it to four prostrations at home while on a journey the former ordinance of two prostrations held.'

A learned person told me that when prayer was laid on the apostle Gabriel came to him while he was on the heights of Mecca and dug a hole for him with his heel in the side of the valley from which a fountain gushed forth, and Gabriel performed the ritual ablution as the apostle watched him. This was in order to show him how to purify himself before prayer. Then the apostle performed the ritual ablution as he had seen Gabriel do it. Then Gabriel said a prayer with him while the apostle prayed with his prayer. Then Gabriel left him. The apostle came to Khadīja and performed the ritual for her as Gabriel had done for him, and she copied him. Then he prayed with her as Gabriel had prayed with him, and she prayed his prayer.

ʿUtba b. Muslim freedman of B. Taym from Nāfiʿ b. Jubayr b. Muṭʿim (who was prolific in relating tradition) from I. ʿAbbās[4] told me: 'When prayer was laid upon the apostle Gabriel came to him and prayed the noon prayer when the sun declined. Then he prayed the evening prayer when his shadow equalled his own length. Then he prayed the sunset prayer when the sun set. Then he prayed the last night prayer when the twilight had disappeared. Then he prayed with him the morning prayer when the dawn rose. Then he came to him and prayed the noon prayer on the morrow when his shadow equalled his height. Then he prayed the evening prayer when his shadow equalled the height of both of them. Then he prayed the sunset prayer when the sun set at the time it had the day before. Then he prayed with him the last night prayer when the first third of the night had passed. Then he prayed the dawn prayer when it was clear but the sun was not shining. Then he said, "O Muhammad, prayer is in what is between your prayer today and your prayer yesterday."[5] (Ṭ. Yūnus b. Bukayr said that Muhammad b. Isḥāq told him that Yaḥyā b. Abūʾl-Ashʿath al-Kindī of the people of Kūfa said that Ismāʿīl b. Iyās b. ʿAfif from his father from his grandfather said, 'When I was a merchant I came to al-ʿAbbās during the days of pilgrimage; and while we were together a man came out to pray and stood facing the Kaʿba; then a woman came out and stood praying with him; then a young man came out and stood praying with him. I said to

3. Muḥammad's wife (ca. 614–678), and daughter of the first caliph; she was a source of authoritative knowledge in early Islam [editor's note].
4. ʿAbdallāh ibn al-ʿAbbās (ca. 619–687/88), one of the greatest early Muslim scholars; he is often considered the founder of the qurʾānic exegetical tradition [editor's note].
5. Suhaylī takes the author to task for saying what he should not. Traditionists are agreed that this story belongs to the morrow of the prophet's night journey some 5 years later. Opinions differ as to whether this occurred 18 months or a year before the *hijra*, but that would have been long after the beginning of revelation. [ʿAbd Allah al-Suhaylī (1114–1185), Moroccan Islamic scholar—editor's note.]

'Abbās, "What is their religion? It is some thing new to me." He said, "This is Muhammad b. Abdullah who alleges that God has sent him with it and that the treasures of Chosrhoes and Caesar[6] will be opened to him. The woman is his wife Khadīja who believes in him, and this young man is his nephew 'Alī who believes in him." 'Afīf said, "Would that I could have believed that day and been a third!"[7])

## AL-ṬABARĪ

Abū Ja'far Muḥammad ibn Jarīr al-Ṭabarī (ca. 839–923) claims preeminence in two realms of Islamic intellectual renown—history and Qur'ān commentary. He was born in Amul, a provincial city in what is now Iran, making him one of the many Persian scholars who stand among the major thinkers of medieval Islam.

His precocity manifested itself early: according to his biographers, he had memorized the Qur'ān by the age of seven. Eventually his studies took him to Baghdad and then to other centers of Islamic learning, including Basra, Kūfa, and Cairo.

Al-Ṭabarī is remembered both for his erudition and for his unwillingness to seek court honors and offices. He was content with the life of scholar and teacher, and in those roles his influence was immense. His scholarly output was equally immense, and the biographical literature recounts stories of his students begging him to condense both his historical and his exegetical writings. A related series of tales divides his total literary output by the days of his life, calculating that on average he wrote fourteen—some versions say forty—pages a day.

The following selection has been drawn from al-Ṭabarī's universal history, *Ta'rīkh al-rusul wa-l-muluk* (*The History of Prophets and Kings*). This monumental chronicle begins with the creation of the world and concludes about a decade before the author's death. The English translation of *The History* has been published in thirty-nine volumes.

## *From* The History of al-Ṭabarī: Muḥammad at Mecca†

### *Signs of the Approach of Prophethood*

Abū Ja'far (al-Ṭabarī): Before Gabriel appeared to him to confer on him his mission as Messenger of God, it is said that he used to see signs and evidences indicating that God wished to ennoble him and to single him out for his favor. One of these is the account which I have previously given[1] of the two angels who came to him, opened up his breast, and removed the hatred and the impurity which were in it. This was when he was with his foster-mother, Ḥalīmah. Another is that it is said that whenever he passed along a road and passed by a tree or a stone, it would greet him.

6. That is, the Persian and Roman empires [editor's note].
7. This may be one of the traditions which Ibn Iṣhāq was accused of producing or recording in support of the 'Alids [i.e., Shī'īs]. It is certainly open to criticism.
† From Abū Ja'far Muḥammad ibn Jarīr al-Ṭabarī, *The History of al-Ṭabarī*, vol. 6, *Muḥammad at Mecca*, trans. W. Montgomery Watt and M. V. McDonald (Albany: State University of New York Press, 1988), pp. 63–67, 77–80.  Except as indicated, all notes are Watt and McDonald's.
1. Though Ṭabarī says "I have previously given," he appears to be referring to what comes subsequently [in a passage not included here—editor's note].

Al-Ḥārith b. Muḥammad—Muḥammad b. Saʿd—Muḥammad b. ʿUmar—ʿAlī b. Muḥammad b. ʿUbaydallāh b. ʿAbdallāh b. ʿUmar b. al-Khaṭṭāb—Manṣūr b. ʿAbd al-Raḥmān—his mother Barrah bt. Abī Tajrāh: When God willed that Muḥammad should be ennobled and should enter upon prophethood, it came about that whenever he went out to attend his business[2] he would go a great distance, out of sight of houses, and into the ravines and wādī-beds; and then every stone and tree he passed would say, "Peace be upon you, Messenger of God." He would turn to the right and the left and turn round, but could not see anyone.

### *Predictions of the Appearance of the Prophet*

Abū Jaʿfar (al-Ṭabarī): The various religious communities used to speak of his forthcoming mission, and the scholars of every community used to tell their people of it.

Al-Ḥārith—Muḥammad b. Saʿd—Muḥammad b. ʿUmar—ʿAlī b. ʿĪsā al-Ḥakamī—his father—ʿĀmir b. Rabīʿah: I heard Zayd b. ʿAmr b. Nufayl[3] saying, "I expect a prophet from the descendants of Ishmael, in particular from the descendants of ʿAbd al-Muṭṭalib. I do not think that I shall live to see him, but I believe in him, proclaim the truth of his message, and testify that he is a prophet. If you live long enough to see him, give him my greetings. I shall inform you of his description, so that he will not be hidden from you." I said, "Tell me, then," and he said, "He is a man who is neither short nor tall, whose hair is neither abundant nor sparse, whose eyes are always red, and who has the seal of prophethood between his shoulders. His name is Aḥmad,[4] and this town is his birthplace and the place in which he will commence his mission. Then his people will drive him out and hate the message which he brings, and he will emigrate to Yathrib and triumph. Beware lest you fail to recognize him. I have travelled around every land in search of the faith of Abraham. Every person whom I ask, whether Jew, Christian, or Magian,[5] says, 'This faith lies where you have come from,' and they describe him as I have described him to you. They say that no prophet remains but he."[6] ʿĀmir said, "When I became a Muslim, I told the Messenger of God what Zayd b. ʿAmr had said, and I gave him his greetings. He returned his greetings and said, 'May God have mercy on his soul. I saw him in Paradise dressed in flowing robes.'"

2. This seems to be the plain meaning of *al-ḥājah*; but "went out about his business" is also possible. The paragraph corresponds to Ibn Saʿd, *Ṭabaqāt*, 1:102.17–23 [*Kitāb al-ṭabaqāt al-kabīr* (*The Large Book of the Generations*), by Muḥammad ibn Saʿd (d. 845)—editor's note].
3. One of the four men mentioned by Ibn Isḥāq (143–49) as a *ḥanīf* or searcher for a pure monotheism; see Watt, *Muhammad at Mecca* [(Oxford: Clarendon Press, 1953)], 162–64. Ibn Saʿd, *Ṭabaqāt*, 1:105.23–106.8. [For the *Sīra* by Ibn Isḥāq (ca. 704–767), see above—editor's note.]
4. Aḥmad is commonly regarded as a variant form of Muḥammad, following the standard interpretation of Qurʾan 61:6, where Jesus says to the Israelites that he brings "good tidings of a messenger who comes after me, whose name is Aḥmad." (Aḥmad is, of course from the same root as Muḥammad, namely ḥ-m-d.) There are strong grounds, however, for thinking that for the first century or so of Islam the word *aḥmadu* was understood as an adjective meaning "more praiseworthy" and not as a proper name; see Watt, "His Name Is Aḥmad," *Muslim World* 43 (1953): 110–17.
5. A member of a priestly caste in ancient Persia, later influenced by Zoroastrianism (the monotheistic religion of pre-Islamic Iran) [editor's note].
6. This refers to the standard Muslim interpretation of the phrase "seal of the prophets" applied to Muḥammad in Qurʾan 33:40, namely, that he is the last prophet after whom there will be no other.

Ibn Ḥumayd—Salamah—Ibn Isḥāq—one who is above suspicion—'Abdallāh b. Ka'b the *mawlā* of 'Uthmān:[7] 'Umar b. al-Khattāb[8] was sitting with others in the Messenger of God's mosque one day when a beduin came up and entered the mosque looking for 'Umar (b. al-Khaṭṭāb). When 'Umar looked at him he said, "This man is still a polytheist, although at one point he abandoned polytheism. He was a soothsayer in the Jāhiliyyah."[9] The man greeted him and then sat down. 'Umar said to him, "Have you become a Muslim?" "Yes," he replied. "Were you a soothsayer in the Jāhiliyyah?" asked 'Umar. "Praise be to God," the man answered. "You have received me with words which I do not suppose that you have uttered to one of your subjects since you became Caliph." "God forgive me!" said 'Umar.[1] "During the Jāhiliyyah we used to do worse things than you. We used to worship idols and embrace graven images until God honored us with Islam." "Yes, by God, O Commander of the Faithful," answered the man. "I used to be a soothsayer in the Jāhiliyyah." "Tell me," said 'Umar, "what is the most amazing saying which your familiar spirit brought you?" "He came to me a month or a year before Islam," said the man, "and said to me:

Have you considered the Jinn[2] and their hopelessness
and their despair of their religion,
and their clinging to young female camels and their
saddle cloths?"

Then 'Umar said to the gathering, "By God, I was by one of the idols of the Jāhiliyyah with a number of men of Quraysh.[3] An Arab had sacrificed a calf to it, and we were waiting for it to be divided up in order to receive a share, when I heard coming from the belly of the calf a voice which was more penetrating than any voice I have ever heard—this was a month or a year before Islam—saying:

O people of Dharīḥ
A matter which has ended in success
A man shouting
Saying, "There is no deity but God."

Ibn Ḥumayd—'Alī b. Mujāhid—Ibn Ishāq—al-Zuhrī—'Abdallāh b. Ka'b the *mawlā* of 'Uthmān b. 'Affān: a similar account.

Al-Ḥārith—Muḥammad b. Sa'd—Muḥammad b. 'Umar—Muḥammad b. 'Abdallāh—al-Zuhrī—Muḥammad b. Jubayr b. Muṭ'im—his father: We were sitting by an idol at Buwānah a month before the Messenger of

7. 'Uthmān ibn 'Affān (d. 656), third caliph. *Mawlā*: client or supporter [editor's note].
8. Second caliph (ca. 586–644) [editor's note].
9. "The age of ignorance," the Muslim name for the time before God's revelation to Muḥammad [editor's note].
1. The point of this story appears to be that the Caliph 'Umar made a hasty judgement about this man's continuing polytheism, and then had to withdraw it. This account from Ibn Isḥaq is not in the standard text.
2. The jinn (plural; singular *jinnī*, formerly transliterated as "genie") are a third class of intelligent beings along with angels and humans. They are imperceptible to the senses, but may make appearances under different forms. They are capable of having a religion and believing in God; and the Qur'an (72:1–19; 46:29–32) speaks of Muḥammad preaching to them and of some being converted. In the present passage their "despair of their religion" may be intended as a sort of premonition of the coming of Islam; the reason for the reference to camels is unknown. The jinn play a large part in folklore. See $EI^2$ [*Encyclopaedia of Islam*, 2nd ed.], s.v. Djinn, first part.
3. The ruling tribe of Mecca [editor's note].

God commenced his mission, having slaughtered camels. Suddenly we heard a voice calling from the belly of one:[4]

> Listen to the wonder;
> There will be no more eavesdropping to overhear inspiration;
> We throw down shooting stars
> For a prophet in Mecca;
> His name is Aḥmad,
> His place of emigration is Yathrib.

We held back and marvelled; then the Messenger of God appeared (that is, he began his mission).

## *Proofs of Prophethood*

Aḥmad b. Sinān al-Qaṭṭān al-Wāṣiṭi—Abū Muʿāwiyah—Aʿmash—Abū Ẓibyān—Ibn ʿAbbās:[5] A man of the Banū ʿĀmir[6] came to the Prophet and said, "Show me the seal which is between your shoulders, and if you lie under any enchantment I will cure you, for I am the best enchanter of the Arabs." "Do you wish me to show you a sign?" asked the Prophet. "Yes," said the man, "summon that cluster of dates." So the Prophet looked at a cluster of dates hanging from a date palm and summoned it, and began to snap his fingers until it stood before him. Then the man said, "Tell it to go back," and it went back. The ʿĀmirī said, "O Banū ʿĀmir, I have never seen a greater magician than I have seen today."

Abū Jaʿfar (al-Ṭabarī): The stories of the proof of his prophethood are too numerous to be counted. We shall devote a book to this subject, if God wills.

* * *

## *The First Rituals of Islam Are Prescribed*

Abū Jaʿfar (al-Ṭabarī): The first of the duties of Islam to be prescribed for Muḥammad by God, after that of confessing God's oneness, disavowing graven images and idols, and repudiating false gods, is said to have been that of ritual prayer or worship *(ṣalāt)*.[7]

Ibn Humayd—Salamah—Muḥammad b. Ishāq—certain scholars:[8] When ritual prayer was prescribed for the Messenger of God, Gabriel came to him while he was in the upper part of Mecca, and dug his heel into the side of the wādī, whereupon a spring gushed out. While the Messenger of God watched him, Gabriel then performed the ritual ablution in order to show him how to purify himself for prayer. Then the Messenger of God performed the ritual ablution as he had seen Gabriel do. Next, Gabriel rose up and led him in prayer, and the Prophet followed his actions.

4. Reading *juzur* instead of *jazūr* with Ibn Saʿd, *Ṭabaqāt*, 1:105.12–17.
5. ʿAbdallāh ibn al-ʿAbbās (ca. 619–687/88), one of the greatest early Muslim scholars; he is often considered the founder of the qurʾānic exegetical tradition [editor's note].
6. A tribal confederation of western Arabia, initially hostile to Muḥammad [editor's note].
7. The word *ṣalāt* is commonly translated "prayer," although "worship" would be more appropriate, since there is virtually no petition or intercession. The *ṣalāt* consists of a series of acts accompanied by expressions of praise or adoration. The climax is touching the ground with the forehead in acknowledgement of God's majesty. Each Muslim is now required to accomplish the *ṣalāt* five times a day, though originally the number of times was probably not fixed.
8. Ibn Hishām [d. 833], *Sīrah*, 158.

Then Gabriel departed, and the Messenger of God went to Khadījah[9] and performed the ablution for her in order to show her how to purify herself for prayer, as Gabriel had shown him. She performed the ablution as he had done, and then he led her in prayer as Gabriel had led him, and she followed his actions.

### *The Prophet Ascends to the Seventh Heaven*

Ibn Ḥumayd—Hārūn b. al-Mughīrah and Ḥakkām b. Salm—ʿAnbasah—Abū Hāshim al-Wāṣiṭi—Maymūn b. Siyāh—Anas b. Mālik: At the time when the Prophet became a prophet, he used to sleep around the Kaʿbah[1] as did the Quraysh. On one occasion two angels, Gabriel and Michael, came to him and said, "Which of the Quraysh were we ordered to come to?" Then they said, "We were ordered to come to their chief," and went away. After this they came from the Qiblah[2] and there were three of them. They came upon him as he slept, turned him on his back, and opened his breast. Then they brought water from Zamzam and washed away the doubt, or polytheism, or pre-Islamic beliefs, or error, which was in his breast. Then they brought a golden basin full of faith and wisdom, and his breast and belly were filled with faith and wisdom.

Then he was taken up to the earthly heaven. Gabriel asked for admittance, and they said, "Who is it?" "Gabriel," he said. "Who is with you?" they said. "Muḥammad," he answered. "Has his mission commenced?" they asked. "Yes," he said. "Welcome," they said, and called down God's blessings on him. When he went in, he saw before him a huge and handsome man. "Who is this, Gabriel?" he asked. "This is your father, Adam," he replied. Then they took him to the second heaven. Gabriel asked for admission, and they said the same as before. Indeed, the same questions were asked and the same answers given in all the heavens. When Muḥammad went in to the second heaven he saw before him two men. "Who are these, Gabriel?" he asked. "John and Jesus, the two maternal cousins," he replied. Then he was taken to the third heaven, and when he went in he saw before him a man. "Who is this, Gabriel?" he asked. He replied, "Your brother Joseph who was given preeminence in beauty over other men as is the full moon over the stars at night." Then he was taken to the fourth heaven, and he saw before him a man and said, "Who is this, Gabriel?" "This is Idrīs,"[3] he said, and recited:

And we raised him to high station.[4]

Then he was taken to the fifth heaven, and he saw before him a man and said, "Who is this, Gabriel?" "This is Aaron," he said. Then he was taken to the sixth heaven, and he saw before him a man and said, "Who is this, Gabriel?" "This is Moses," he said. Then he was taken to the seventh heaven, and he saw before him a man and said, "Who is this, Gabriel?" "This is your father Abraham," he said.

9. Muḥammad's first wife (ca. 554–619) [editor's note].
1. Literally, "cube": the stone shrine in Mecca, believed to have been built by Adam and then rebuilt by Ibrāhīm (Abraham) and Ismāʿīl (Ishmael); central to both early pagan and Muslim pilgrimage rituals, it became the most important site in Islam [editor's note].
2. The direction of the Kaʿba, toward which Muslims face in prayer [editor's note].
3. A qurʾānic prophet who is sometimes identified with the biblical figure Enoch [editor's note].
4. Q 19:57.

Then he took him to Paradise, and there before him was a river whiter than milk and sweeter than honey, with pearly domes on either side of it. "What is this, Gabriel?" he asked. Gabriel replied, "This is al-Kawthar, which your Lord has given to you, and these are your dwellings." Then Gabriel took a handful of its earth and lo! it was fragrant musk. Then he went out to the Sidrat al-Muntahā,[5] which was a lote tree bearing fruits the largest of which were like earthenware jars and the smallest like eggs. Then his Lord drew nigh,

"Till he was distant two bows' length or nearer." Because of the nearness of its Lord the lote tree became covered by the like of such jewels as pearls, rubies, chrysolites, and colored pearls. God made revelation to his servant, caused him to understand and know, and prescribed for him fifty prayers (daily).

Then he went back past Moses, who said to him, "What did he impose your community?" "Fifty prayers," he said. "Go back to your Lord," said Moses, "and ask him to lighten the burden for your community, for your community is the weakest in strength and the shortest-lived." Then he told Muḥammad what he himself had suffered at the hands of the Children of Israel. The Messenger of God went back, and God reduced the number by ten. Then he passed Moses again, who said, "Go back to your Lord and ask him to lighten the burden further." This continued until he had gone back five times. Once more Moses said, "Go back to your Lord and ask him to lighten the burden," but the Messenger of God said, "I am not going back, although I do not wish to disobey you," for it had been put into his heart that he should not go back. God said, "My speech is not to be changed, and my decision and precept is not to be reversed, but he (Muḥammad) lightened the burden of prayer on my community to a tenth of what it was at first."[6]

Anas:[7] I never encountered any scent, not even the scent of a bride, more fragrant than the skin of the Messenger of God. I pressed my skin to his and smelt it.

## AL-BUṢĪRĪ

Born in Upper Egypt during the time of the Mamlūks, Sharaf al-Dīn Abū ʿAbdallāh Muḥammad al-Buṣīrī (ca. 1212–1294/97) spent time in Jerusalem, Mecca, and Medina but eventually returned to Egypt. He died in Cairo and is buried near the jurist al-Shāfiʿī (d. 820). As a youth he studied with a prominent master of the Shādhilliyya Ṣūfī order and later worked as a secretary and scribe. His renown, however, rests on a poem of 160 verses that has been recited and reproduced countless times.

5. The "lote tree of the utmost boundary" is spoken of in the description of Muḥammad's second vision in Sūrah 53:14. The following phrase about being "distant two bows' length or nearer" is from verse 9 describing the first vision. Though many Muslim scholars associate the second vision with Muḥammad's "night journey" or ascent to heaven, this is improbable since the main verse referring to the "night journey" (17:1) was revealed about the middle of the Meccan period, whereas the passage 53:13–18 almost certainly refers to a very early experience.
6. Literally, this runs: "he lightened the prayer for my community to a tenth." The translation adopted assumes that these words are a continuation of the speech of God, and seems to make best sense of "my"; but there are other possibilities.
7. Anas ibn Mālik (d. ca. 710), a Companion of the Prophet; he was given to Muḥammad as a servant at age ten [editor's note].

Al-Būṣīrī's *Burda* (*The Cloak* or *Mantle*), a poem in praise of Muḥammad, covers the standard topics of the Prophet's life, his virtues and his miracles. But its extraordinary popularity derives from its reputation for producing miracles, for possessing supernatural healing powers. The poet's dream vision of being wrapped in the Prophet's cloak and then awaking to find himself cured of his stroke ensured the abiding fame of this ode.

## *From* Mantle Ode†

### PART 3: PRAISE OF THE NOBLE MESSENGER

29. I have profaned the Path of him whose night prayers brought the darkness to life
Until his feet complained of pain and swelling,

30. Who tied a stone to his belly to blunt the hunger pangs,
Concealing beneath the stone his tender flank.

31. Haughty mountains of pure gold sought to tempt him,
But, oh, with what disdain he turned them down!

32. His need served only to strengthen his renunciation,
For necessity cannot prevail against the sinless.

33. How could need tempt with this world's vanities one who, but for him,
The world would never have emerged from nothingness?

34. Muḥammad, the master of all who dwell in both the seen and unseen worlds,
Of both corporeal species, men and jinn, of the two races, 'Arab and 'Ajam.[1]

35. Our Prophet, the commander of good and forbidder of evil;
No one was more just than he when he said "yes" or "no."

36. He is the beloved of God whose intercession is hoped for
In the face of every dread and unexpected horror.

37. He called mankind to God, so whoever clings to him
Clings to a rope that will never be broken.

38. He surpassed all other prophets in form and character;
They could not approach him in knowledge or in magnanimity.

39. Each of them beseeching God's Messenger
For a handful of the sea of his knowledge or a sip of the unceasing downpour of his munificence.

† From Suzanne Pinckney Stetkevych, trans., *The Mantle Odes: Arabic Praise Poems to the Prophet Muḥammad* (Bloomington: Indiana University Press, 2010), pp. 97–99. Reprinted with permission of Indiana University Press.

1. Literally, "barbarian" (Arabic *'Ajam*). It came to mean Persian, and then foreigner generally, as contrasted with *'Arab* (Arab). Jinn: in Muslim thought, the third class of intelligent beings for whom salvation is possible (the first two are humans and angels).

40. Standing before him, lined up by rank,
Like points on the letters of his knowledge or vowel-marks on the text[2] of his wisdom.

41. He is the one whose spirit and form were perfected,
Then the Creator of mankind chose him as His beloved.

42. In inner and outer beauty he is free from any partner,
For in him the essence of beauty is indivisible.

43. Don't claim what the Christians claim for their prophet,
But praise him as you judge best and proper.

44. Ascribe to him as much honor as you wish;
Assign him as much majesty as you desire,

45. For surely the merit of God's Messenger is without limit,
And so exceeds what any tongue could ever express.

46. If his miracles were as mighty as his rank, the mere mention of his name
Would bring decaying bones of dead men back to life.

47. He did not test us with more than human minds could grasp,
So we never harbored doubts nor fell into confusion.

48. But his true nature defies human understanding:
There is no one, near or far, who is not dumbfounded by it,

49. Like the sun that from afar seems small to the eye,
But is too bright to look at directly.

50. How can mankind in this world, asleep and distracted by dreams,
Comprehend the Prophet's true nature?

51. The utmost extent of our knowledge of him is that he is human,
And that he is the best of all of God's creation.

52. And all the miracles that other noble messengers have brought
Have reached them only through his light.

53. He is the sun in virtue; the others, stars
Whose lights appear to mankind only at night.

54. How noble is the form of a Prophet adorned with good morals,
Cloaked in comeliness, marked by a radiant face!

55. A tender blossom in complexion, the full moon in nobility,
The sea in magnanimity, in aspiration as limitless as time itself.

2. In written Arabic, points and other markings (not letters) represent vowels and distinguish consonants otherwise identical in form; the Qur'ān was initially written without them.

56. Even alone in his majesty, he seems, when you meet him,
Surrounded by an army and an entourage.

57. As if the pearls secreted in their oyster shells
Were from the two mines of his speech and of his smile.

58. No perfume is as redolent as the dust that holds his bones;
Whoever inhales or kisses it is blessed.

## DANTE

Dante Alighieri (1265–1321) was born in Florence, a city that rose to great prominence during his lifetime. After a traditional classical education he gained distinction as a poet and intellectual in his beloved city. He also became involved in its starkly divided politics—and before the age of forty, Dante found himself tried in absentia on false charges and banished for life. He died in the Adriatic city of Ravenna still an outcast.

His first important book, *La vita nuova* (ca. 1293, *The New Life*), couples poems dedicated to his idealized lover, Beatrice, with prose depictions of her abiding influence, her untimely death, and his shattering grief that followed.

In the early years of the fourteenth century, Dante began composing his most famous work, the three-part *Divine Comedy*. It has remained one of the most influential works in Western European literature. The three parts—titled *Hell*, *Purgatory*, and *Paradise*—trace the poet's imaginary journey through these cosmological realms, under the guidance first of the Roman poet Virgil and then of Dante's beloved Beatrice.

In hell, Dante meets a succession of famous sinners—as judged from the moral and theological perspectives of medieval Christianity—and each of these sinners endures an eternal punishment deemed suitable to the sin. Muḥammad's depiction, as a heretic and schismatic, reflects centuries of polemical writings in which Christian apologists accused Islam of being a Christian heresy. As schism cuts through a body of believers, so the bodies of the Prophet and of his son-in-law ʿAlī ibn Abī Ṭālib are continuously severed and torn asunder. For centuries, this gory portrayal of Muḥammad has proven grievously offensive to Muslims, who cannot utter the Prophet's name without invoking blessings upon him, but it demonstrates the harsh antipathy to a rival religion often found in medieval polemical discourse.

### *From* Inferno†

#### *Canto XXVIII*

Even in words not bounded by rhyme's law,
through many repetitions of the tale,
how could the blood and wounds that I now saw
be fully told? Every tongue would surely fail,
because our powers of speech and memory
are not meant to comprehend on such a scale.

† From Dante Alighieri, *Inferno*, trans. Michael Palma, ed. Giuseppe Mazzotta, Norton Critical Edition (New York: W. W. Norton, 2008), pp. 104–06. Except as indicated, all notes are Mazzotta's. 

If all of Apulia's battle dead[1] could be
assembled, those of that battered country who
bewailed blood spilled by Trojan infantry,
and those in the long war who fell victim to
the immense spoils of the rings (so does Livy say
in his history, where what he tells is true),[2]
and those who felt the heavy blows when they
resisted Robert Guiscard's[3] steady press,
and those whose bones are still piled up today
at Ceprano, failed by Apulian faithlessness,[4]
and there near Tagliacozzo where the old
Alardo won the victory weaponless,[5]
and one showed his pierced limb and one made bold
to display his stumps, it all would not begin
to approach the loathsomeness of the ninth hold.[6]
A cask, when its midboard or its cant has been
removed, is not so open as one I saw
whose body was split apart right from the chin
to the farthole. Down between his legs his raw
entrails spilled out, with his vitals visible
and the sorry sack where what goes through the maw
is turned to shit. I was looking at him, full
of awe and wonder, when he saw me stare
and spread his breast open, saying: "Watch me pull,
see mangled Mohammed tear himself![7] And there
walking before me and weeping is Alī,[8]
with his face split from his chin right to his hair.
And since all of these other sinners that you see
sowed scandal and schism in their lives, now they
are ripped apart in reciprocity.
Back there a devil waits to hack and flay
each one of us with the sharp edge of his blade,
cleaving anew, each time we pass his way,

1. Puglia is the southeastern corner of Italy, the heel of the boot. Dante uses the term, as was common in his time, to denote the entire southern portion of the peninsula. He alludes to several battles, ancient and modern, that were fought there, beginning with the invasion by Aeneas and his forces.
2. According to Livy (Titus Livius, 59 BCE–17 CE) in his monumental history of Rome, *Ab urbe condita*, Hannibal had his soldiers remove the rings of Roman officers they had killed at the battle of Cannae (216 BCE), an Apulian village, and sent them to the Carthaginian senate to demonstrate the magnitude of his victory. The "long war" was the second Punic War (218–201 BCE).
3. Robert Guiscard (1015–1085), brother of the duke of Normandy, was made ruler of Apulia and Calabria by Pope Nicholas II. He spent twenty years battling the Greeks and Saracens in southern Italy, and is cited in Canto XVIII of the *Paradiso* among warriors for the faith.
4. The forces of King Manfred of Sicily met the invading army of Charles of Anjou near Benevento (not Ceprano) on February 26, 1266. When his Apulian allies fled the field, Manfred chose to die in battle rather than flee. Because he had been excommunicated, he was buried in unconsecrated ground and subsequently disinterred (according to some, on the orders of Pope Clement IV).
5. In 1268, Charles of Anjou fought Conradin, nephew of Manfred and grandson of Frederick II, near Tagliacozzo. Charles was advised by the chevalier Érard de Valéry (ca. 1200–ca. 1277) to hold back his reserves as long as possible, which strategy turned the tide of battle in his favor.
6. Ditch; the schismatics are located in the 9th ditch of the 8th circle of hell [editor's note].
7. Ronald L. Martinez and Robert M. Durling state: "In the Christian polemics that were Dante's sources of information, Mohammed was said to have been a Nestorian Christian (the Nestorians denied that Christ's divine and human natures were united) before founding Islam; thus he was thought both a heretic and a schismatic, having drawn one third of the world's believers away from the true faith" (*The Divine Comedy of Dante Alighieri. Volume I: Inferno*, Oxford, 1996).
8. Ali (ca. 592–661) was Mohammed's cousin and son-in-law. Controversy over his assumption of the caliphate in 656 led to the splitting of Islam into the Sunni and Shiite sects.

every member of this miserable parade,
  for by the time we have circled the whole pit
  we are healed of the cuts he has already made.
But who are you? Are you putting off for a bit,
  by musing upon the bridge, the punishments
  pronounced on you for the sins you must admit?"
"Death has not found him," my guide[9] said. "No offense
  brings him here for torment, but in order to
  provide him with a full experience,
it is fitting that I, who am dead, conduct him through
  ring after ring of hell, and every word
  is as true as that I am speaking them to you."
More than a hundred in the ditch were stirred
  to gape at me, forgetting their agony
  as they stood amazed at what they had just heard.
"Tell Fra Dolcino, since you may shortly see
  the sun again, that if he still wants to live
  before joining me, he should fill his armory
with provisions, lest the grip of snow should give
  to the Novarese a victory that they
  might otherwise find difficult to achieve.[1]
Before Mohammed had turned to me to say
  these words, he had raised his foot into the air,
  and now he put it down and went away.

* * *

# WASHINGTON IRVING

The son of a Presbyterian elder, Washington Irving (1783–1859) wrote works ranging from satirical essays to short story collections, from biography to travel history, all of which enjoyed great popularity in his lifetime. His enduring legacy in American literature was assured by *The Sketchbook of Geoffrey Crayon, Gent.* (1819–20), a collection of essays and short fiction that includes "Rip Van Winkle" and "The Legend of Sleepy Hollow."

In 1826 Irving moved to Spain and in less than two years wrote a well-researched biography of Christopher Columbus that served scholars for the rest of the century. While there he explored the Alhambra in Granada, a palace complex of the Nasrid emirs that had suffered centuries of neglect. This stay inspired his *Tales of the Alhambra: A Series of Tales and Sketches of the Moors and Spaniards* (1832). As part of Irving's research for a possible history of Islamic Spain, he began collecting information on Islam's founder, the basis for what would later become his *Mahomet and His Successors* (1849–50).

9. The Roman poet Virgil (70–19 BCE), who guides Dante through hell and purgatory [editor's note].
1. Dolcino Tornielli of Novara was known as Fra Dolcino because of his association with the Apostolic Brethren, who sought to bring the Church back to the simplicity of its earliest times, the days of the Apostles. After the death of the group's founder, Gherardo Segarelli, Dolcino took command of the Brethren. He was accused of holding heretical views, and in 1305 Pope Clement V preached against the sect. Dolcino and a large group of his followers, including his companion and presumed mistress, Margaret of Trent, held out for some time in the hills between Novara and Vercelli, but were driven out by hunger and repeated attacks. Dolcino and Margaret were captured in June 1307 and burned at the stake.

In preparing this work, Irving clearly sought to introduce Muḥammad to the American public as a major historical figure. In his preface, he acknowledges a debt to the German professor Gustav Weil, whose *Mohammed der Prophet: Sein Leben und seine Lehre* (1843, *Muḥammad the Prophet: His Life and His Teaching*) would remain the standard scholarly source for several generations. Irving's intent was not to present new research but, as he explained, "to digest into an easy, perspicuous, and flowing narrative, the admitted facts concerning Mahomet, together with such legends and traditions as have been wrought into the whole system of Oriental literature; and at the same time to give such a summary of his faith as might be sufficient for the more general reader."

## *From* Mahomet and His Successors†

### *CHAPTER VI*

CONDUCT OF MAHOMET AFTER HIS MARRIAGE—BECOMES ANXIOUS FOR RELIGIOUS REFORM—HIS HABITS OF SOLITARY ABSTRACTION—THE VISION OF THE CAVE—HIS ANNUNCIATION AS A PROPHET

The marriage with Cadijah[1] placed Mahomet among the most wealthy of his native city. His moral worth also gave him great influence in the community. Allah, says the historian Abulfeda,[2] had endowed him with every gift necessary to accomplish and adorn an honest man; he was so pure and sincere; so free from every evil thought, that he was commonly known by the name of Al Amin, or The Faithful.

The great confidence reposed in his judgment and probity, caused him to be frequently referred to as arbiter in disputes between his townsmen. An anecdote is given as illustrative of his sagacity on such occasions. The Caaba[3] having been injured by fire, was undergoing repairs, in the course of which the sacred black stone was to be replaced. A dispute arose among the chiefs of the various tribes, as to which was entitled to perform so august an office, and they agreed to abide by the decision of the first person who should enter by the gate al Harâm.[4] That person happened to be Mahomet. Upon hearing their different claims, he directed that a great cloth should be spread upon the ground, and the stone laid thereon; and that a man from each tribe should take hold of the border of the cloth. In this way the sacred stone was raised equally and at the same time by them all to a level with its allotted place, in which Mahomet fixed it with his own hands.

Four daughters and one son, were the fruit of the marriage with Cadijah. The son was named Kasim, whence Mahomet was occasionally called Abu Kasim, or the father of Kasim, according to Arabian nomenclature. This son, however, died in his infancy.

For several years after his marriage he continued in commerce, visiting the great Arabian fairs, and making distant journeys with the caravans.

† From Washington Irving, *Mahomet and His Successors*, ed Henry A. Pochman and E. N. Feltskog (Madison: University of Wisconsin Press, 1970), pp. 29–33. Notes are by the editor of this Norton Critical Edition.

1. Khadīja bint al-Khuwaylid (ca. 554–619), Muḥammad's first wife.
2. Abū al-Fidā' Ismā'īl ibn 'Alī (1273–1331), a Syrian prince, polymath, and historian.
3. The Ka'ba (literally, "cube") is the stone shrine in Mecca, believed to have been built by Adam and then rebuilt by Ibrāhīm (Abraham) and Ismā'īl (Ishmael); central to both pre-Islamic and Muslim pilgrimage rituals, it became the most important site in Islam.
4. The *ḥaram* (adj, *ḥarām*; the holy, the sacred) is another name for the area surrounding the Ka'ba. The mosque there is often called al-Masjid al-Ḥarām.

His expeditions were not as profitable as in the days of his stewardship, and the wealth acquired with his wife diminished, rather than increased in the course of his operations. That wealth, in fact, had raised him above the necessity of toiling for subsistence, and given him leisure to indulge the original bias of his mind; a turn for reverie and religious speculation, which he had evinced from his earliest years. This had been fostered in the course of his journeyings, by his intercourse with Jews and Christians, originally fugitives from persecution, but now gathered into tribes, or forming part of the population of cities. The Arabian deserts too, rife as we have shown them with fanciful superstitions, had furnished aliment for his enthusiastic reveries. Since his marriage with Cadijah, also, he had a household oracle to influence him in his religious opinions. This was his wife's cousin Waraka,[5] a man of speculative mind and flexible faith; originally a Jew; subsequently a Christian; and withal a pretender to astrology. He is worthy of note as being the first on record to translate parts of the Old and New Testament into Arabic. From him Mahomet is supposed to have derived much of his information respecting those writings, and many of the traditions of the Mishnu and the Talmud,[6] on which he draws so copiously in his Koran.

The knowledge thus variously acquired and treasured up in an uncommonly retentive memory, was in direct hostility to the gross idolatry prevalent in Arabia, and practised at the Caaba. That sacred edifice had gradually become filled and surrounded by idols, to the number of three hundred and sixty, being one for every day of the Arab year. Hither had been brought idols from various parts, the deities of other nations, the chief of which, Hobal, was from Syria, and supposed to have the power of giving rain. Among these idols too, were Abraham and Ishmael, once revered as prophets and progenitors, now represented with divining arrows in their hands, symbols of magic.

Mahomet became more and more sensible of the grossness and absurdity of this idolatry, in proportion as his intelligent mind contrasted it with the spiritual religions, which had been the subjects of his inquiries. Various passages in the Koran show the ruling idea which gradually sprung up in his mind, until it engrossed his thoughts and influenced all his actions. That idea was a religious reform. It had become his fixed belief, deduced from all that he had learnt and meditated, that the only true religion had been revealed to Adam at his creation, and been promulgated and practised in the days of innocence. That religion inculcated the direct and spiritual worship of one true and only God, the creator of the universe.

It was his belief, furthermore, that this religion, so elevated and simple, had repeatedly been corrupted and debased by man, and especially outraged by idolatry; wherefore a succession of prophets, each inspired by a revelation from the Most High, had been sent from time to time, and at distant periods, to restore it to its original purity. Such was Noah, such was Abraham, such was Moses, and such was Jesus Christ. By each of these, the true religion had been reinstated upon earth, but had again been vitiated by their followers. The faith as taught and practised by Abraham when

5. Waraqa ibn Nawfal (d. before 622), the monotheist cousin of Khadīja. According to Muslim tradition, he confirmed Muḥammad's prophethood.
6. The Mishna is the oldest compilation of Jewish oral law (codified in the 3rd c. CE); rabbis' discussions and commentaries on it are collected in the Talmud (ca. 500 CE).

he came out of the land of Chaldea, seems especially to have formed a religious standard in his mind, from his veneration for the patriarch as the father of Ishmael, the progenitor of his race.

It appeared to Mahomet that the time for another reform was again arrived. The world had once more lapsed into blind idolatry. It needed the advent of another prophet, authorized by a mandate from on high, to restore the erring children of men to the right path, and to bring back the worship of the Caaba to what it had been in the days of Abraham and the patriarchs. The probability of such an advent, with its attendant reforms, seems to have taken possession of his mind, and produced habits of reverie and meditation, incompatible with the ordinary concerns of life and the bustle of the world. We are told that he gradually absented himself from society, and sought the solitude of a cavern on Mount Hara,[7] about three leagues north of Mecca, where, in emulation of the Christian anchorites of the desert, he would remain days and nights together, engaged in prayer and meditation. In this way he always passed the month of Ramadhan, the holy month of the Arabs. Such intense occupation of the mind on one subject, accompanied by fervent enthusiasm of spirit, could not but have a powerful effect upon his frame. He became subject to dreams, to ecstasies and trances. For six months successively, according to one of his historians, he had constant dreams bearing on the subject of his waking thoughts. Often he would lose all consciousness of surrounding objects, and lie upon the ground as if insensible. Cadijah, who was sometimes the faithful companion of his solitude, beheld these paroxysms with anxious solicitude, and entreated to know the cause; but he evaded her inquiries, or answered them mysteriously. Some of his adversaries have attributed them to epilepsy, but devout Moslems declare them to have been the workings of prophecy; for already, say they, the intimations of the Most High began to dawn, though vaguely, on his spirit; and his mind labored with conceptions too great for mortal thought. At length, say they, what had hitherto been shadowed out in dreams, was made apparent and distinct by an angelic apparition and a divine annunciation.

It was in the fortieth year of his age, when this famous revelation took place. Accounts are given of it by Moslem writers as if received from his own lips, and it is alluded to in certain passages of the Koran. He was passing, as was his wont, the month of Ramadhan in the cavern of Mount Hara, endeavoring by fasting, prayer, and solitary meditation, to elevate his thoughts to the contemplation of divine truth. It was on the night called by Arabs Al Kader,[8] or the Divine Decree; a night in which, according to the Koran, angels descend to earth, and Gabriel brings down the decrees of God. During that night there is peace on earth, and a holy quiet reigns over all nature until the rising of the morn.

As Mahomet, in the silent watches of the night, lay wrapped in his mantle, he heard a voice calling upon him; uncovering his head, a flood of light broke upon him of such intolerable splendor that he swooned away. On regaining his senses, he beheld an angel in a human form, which, approaching from a distance, displayed a silken cloth covered with written characters. "Read!" said the angel.

"I know not how to read!" replied Mahomet.

7. Mount Ḥirā, where Muḥammad received his first revelation in 610 CE.
8. Al-Qadr. This term also means "divine power"; see also Q 97.

"Read!" repeated the angel, "in the name of the Lord, who has created all things; who created man from a clot of blood. Read in the name of the Most High, who taught man the use of the pen; who sheds on his soul the ray of knowledge, and teaches him what before he knew not."[9]

Upon this Mahomet instantly felt his understanding illumined with celestial light, and read what was written on the cloth, which contained the decrees of God, as afterwards promulgated in the Koran. When he had finished the perusal, the heavenly messenger announced, "Oh Mahomet, of a verity, thou art the prophet of God! and I am his angel Gabriel."

Mahomet, we are told, came trembling and agitated to Cadijah in the morning, not knowing whether what he had heard and seen was indeed true, and that he was a prophet decreed to effect that reform so long the object of his meditations; or whether it might not be a mere vision, a delusion of the senses, or worse than all, the apparition of an evil spirit.

Cadijah, however, saw every thing with the eye of faith, and the credulity of an affectionate woman. She saw in it the fruition of her husband's wishes, and the end of his paroxysms and privations. "Joyful tidings dost thou bring!" exclaimed she. "By him, in whose hand is the soul of Cadijah, I will henceforth regard thee as the prophet of our nation. Rejoice," added she, seeing him still cast down; "Allah will not suffer thee to fall to shame. Hast thou not been loving to thy kinsfolk, kind to thy neighbors, charitable to the poor, hospitable to the stranger, faithful to thy word, and ever a defender of the truth?"

Cadijah hastened to communicate what she had heard to her cousin Waraka, the translator of the Scriptures; who, as we have shown, had been a household oracle of Mahomet in matters of religion. He caught at once, and with eagerness, at this miraculous annunciation. "By him in whose hand is the soul of Waraka," exclaimed he; "thou speakest true, oh Cadijah! The angel who has appeared to thy husband is the same who, in days of old, was sent to Moses the son of Amram. His annunciation is true. Thy husband is indeed a prophet!"

The zealous concurrence of the learned Waraka, is said to have had a powerful effect in fortifying the dubious mind of Mahomet.

NOTE—Dr. Gustav Weil, in a note to *Mohammed der Prophet*, discusses the question of Mahomet's being subject to attacks of epilepsy; which has generally been represented as a slander of his enemies and of Christian writers. It appears, however, to have been asserted by some of the oldest Moslem biographers, and given on the authority of persons about him. He would be seized, they said, with violent trembling, followed by a kind of swoon, or rather convulsion, during which perspiration would stream from his forehead in the coldest weather; he would lie with his eyes closed, foaming at the mouth and bellowing like a young camel. Ayesha[1] one of his wives, and Zeid one of his disciples, are among the persons cited as testifying to that effect. They considered him at such times as under the influence of a revelation. He had such attacks, however, in Mecca, before the Koran was revealed to him. Cadijah feared that he was possessed by evil spirits, and would have called in the aid of a conjurer to exorcise them, but he forbade her. He did not like that any one should see him

9. Q 96:1–5.
1. 'Ā'isha (ca. 614–678), daughter of the first caliph and a source of authoritative knowledge in early Islam.

during these paroxysms. His visions, however, were not always preceded by such attacks. Hareth Ibn Haschem,[2] it is said, once asked him in what manner the revelations were made. "Often," replied he, "the angel appears to me in a human form, and speaks to me. Sometimes I hear sounds like the tinkling of a bell, but see nothing. [A ringing in the ears is a symptom of epilepsy.][3] When the invisible angel has departed, I am possessed of what he has revealed." Some of his revelations he professed to receive direct from God, others in dreams; for the dreams of prophets, he used to say, are revelations.

The reader will find this note of service in throwing some degree of light upon the enigmatical career of this extraordinary man.

# FRED M. DONNER

## *From* Muhammad and the Believers' Movement†

* * *

### *The Problem of Sources*

* * *

Even if we accept the basic outlines of Muhammad's life as portrayed in traditional accounts, the historian is faced with many stubborn questions that the sources leave unaddressed. (For example, why were the pagans of Medina so readily won over to Muhammad's message, while the Quraysh[1] of Mecca resisted it so bitterly? What exactly was Muhammad's original status in Medina? What exactly was his relationship to the Jews of Medina?) Unfortunately, we have no original documents that might confirm unequivocally any of the traditional biography—no original copies of letters to or from or about Muhammad by his contemporaries, no inscriptions from his day written by members of his community, and so on.

These well-founded concerns about the limitations of the traditional Muslim accounts of Muhammad's life have caused some scholars to conclude that everything in these accounts is to be rejected. This, however, is surely going too far and in its way is just as uncritical an approach as unquestioning acceptance of everything in the traditional accounts. The truth must lie somewhere in between; and some recent work has begun to show that despite the vexing problems they pose, the traditional narratives do seem to contain some very early material about the life of Muhammad. A tolerably accurate and plausible account of the main events of Muhammad's life may someday be possible, when scholars learn more about how to sift the mass of traditional materials more effectively. However, such critical studies are just getting underway today, and for the present it remains prudent to utilize the traditional narratives sparingly and with caution.

Our situation as historians interested in Muhammad's life and the nature of his message is far from hopeless, however. A few seventh-century non-Muslim sources, from a slightly later time than that of Muhammad himself but much earlier than any of the traditional Muslim compilations, provide

2. Al-Ḥārith ibn Hishām, a Meccan who initially fought against Muḥammad.
3. Irving's brackets.
† From chapter 2 of Fred M. Donner, *Muhammad and the Believers: At the Origins of Islam* (Cambridge, MA: Belknap Press of Harvard University Press, 2010), pp. 52–54, 56–61, 68–71. 
1. The ruling tribe of Mecca [editor].

testimony that—although not strictly documentary in character—appears to be essentially reliable. Although these sources are few and provide very limited information, they are nonetheless invaluable. For example, an early Syriac source by the Christian writer Thomas the Presbyter, dated to around 640—that is, just a few years after Muhammad's death—provides the earliest mention of Muhammad and informs us that his followers made a raid around Gaza. This, at least, enables the historian to feel more confident that Muhammad is not completely a fiction of later pious imagination, as some have implied; we know that someone named Muhammad did exist, and that he led some kind of movement. And this fact, in turn, gives us greater confidence that further information in the massive body of traditional Muslim materials may also be rooted in historical fact. The difficulty is in deciding what is, and what is not, factual. * * *

Moreover, the most important source of information about the early community of Believers is still to be discussed: the text of the Qur'an itself, Islam's holy book. For Believing Muslims, the Qur'an is, of course, a transcript of God's word as revealed to Muhammad. Each of its 114 separate, named *suras* (chapters), containing altogether thousands of *ayas* (verses—literally, "signs" of God's presence) is, for the Believer, an utterance of eternal value that exists outside the framework of normal, mundane, historical time. Traditional Muslim exegesis developed an elaborate chronology for the Qur'an, connecting the revelation of each verse to a particular episode in the life of Muhammad—the so-called "occasions of revelation" literature (*asbab al-nuzul*). This literature, which was closely followed by traditional Western scholarship on the Qur'an, generally divided the text into verses considered, on grounds of both style and content, to hail from either the early Meccan, intermediate Meccan, late Meccan, or Medinese phases of Muhammad's career. Similarly, Muslim tradition preserves accounts of how the revelation came to take the form of a written book. According to this view, the various revelations that were first burned into the memory of their prophet were memorized by his followers; some passages were then written out by different people in the early community; finally, about twenty years after Muhammad's death, the scattered written and unwritten parts of the revelation were collected by an editorial committee and compiled in definitive written form.

The historian who questions the traditional narratives of Muhammad's life, however, is also likely to have difficulty accepting at face value this account of how the Qur'an text coalesced; but if we reject this account, we are left unsure of just what kind of text the Qur'an is and where it came from. Starting from this point, revisionist scholars using literary-critical approaches to the text have in recent years offered alternative theories on the origins and nature of the Qur'an as we now have it. One has suggested that the Qur'an originated as pre Islamic strophic hymns of Arabian Christian communities, which Muhammad adapted to form the Qur'an. Equally radical is the "late origins" hypothesis first circulated the late 1970s. According to this view, the Qur'an, far from being a product of western Arabia in the early seventh century C.E., actually crystallized slowly within the Muslim community over a period of two hundred years or more and mostly outside of Arabia, perhaps mainly in Iraq. In the opinion of this theory's advocates, the traditional story of the Qur'an's origins as revelations to Muhammad is merely a pious back-projection made by Muslims of later times who wished to root their beliefs and the existence of their community in the religious experience of an earlier prophetic figure.

If true, the "late origins" hypothesis of the Qur'an, in particular, would have devastating implications for the historian interested in reconstructing Muhammad's life or the beliefs of the early community. But the "late origins" hypothesis fails to explain many features of the Qur'an text, analysis of which suggests that in fact the Qur'an did coalesce very early in the history of Muhammad's community—within no more than three decades of Muhammad's death. For example, meticulous study of the text by generations of scholars has failed to turn up any plausible hint of anachronistic references to important events in the life of the later community, which would almost certainly be there had the text crystallized later than the early seventh century C.E. Moreover, some of the Qur'an's vocabulary suggests that the text, or significant parts of it, hailed from western Arabia. So we seem, after all, to be dealing with a Qur'an that is the product of the earliest stages in the life of the community in western Arabia.

This is not to say that we are all the way back to accepting the traditional view of the Qur'an's origins. Although the Qur'an itself claims to be in a "clear Arabic tongue," many passages in it remain far from clear, even in the most basic sense of knowing what the words might have meant in their original context, whatever it was. It may be that the Qur'an includes passages of older texts that have been revised and reused. The markedly different style and content of diverse parts of the Qur'an may be evidence that the text as we now have it is a composite of originally separate texts hailing from different communities of Believers in Arabia. Some recent studies suggest that the Qur'an text is not only aware of, but even in some ways reacting to, the theological debates of Syriac-speaking Christian communities of the Near East. Whether further work on the text will vindicate the close connection of particular passages in the Qur'an with specific episodes in Muhammad's life, as elaborated by both traditional Muslim and traditional Western scholarship, still remains to be seen. What we can say is that the Qur'an text is demonstrably early.

## *The Character of the Early Believers' Movement*

The fact that the Qur'an text dates to the earliest phase of the movement inaugurated by Muhammad means that the historian can use it to gain some insight into the beliefs and values of this early community. Later literary sources may then be used, with caution, to elaborate on what these earliest beliefs may have been, but the problem of interpolation and idealization in those later sources makes even their "supporting" role often quite uncertain. It is best, therefore, to stick very closely to what the Qur'an itself says for information.

### BASIC BELIEFS

What, then, does the Qur'an tell us about Muhammad and his early followers? To start, we notice that the Qur'an addresses overwhelmingly people whom it calls "Believers" (*mu'minun*). In this, it differs from the traditional Muslim narratives and from modern scholarly practice, both of which routinely refer to Muhammad and his followers mainly as "Muslims" (*muslimun*, literally, "those who submit") and refer to his movement as

"Islam." This later usage is, however, misleading when applied to the beginnings of the community as reflected in the Qur'an. It is of course true that the words *islam* and *muslim* are found in the Qur'an, and it is also true that these words are sometimes applied in the text to Muhammad and his followers. But those instances are dwarfed in number by cases in which Muhammad and his followers are referred to as *mu'minun*, "Believers"—which occurs almost a thousand times, compared with fewer than seventy-five instances of *muslim*, and so on. Later Muslim tradition, beginning about a century after Muhammad's time, came to emphasize the identity of Muhammad's followers as Muslims and attempted to neutralize the importance of the many passages in which they are called Believers by portraying the two terms as synonymous and interchangeable. * * *

If Muhammad and his followers thought of themselves first and foremost as Believers, in what did they believe? Above all, Believers were enjoined to recognize the oneness of God. (*Allah* is simply the Arabic word for "God.") The Qur'an tirelessly preaches the message of strict monotheism, exhorting its hearers to be ever mindful of God and obedient to His will. It rails against the sin of polytheism (*shirk*, literally "associating" something with God)—which, Muslim tradition tells us, was the dominant religious outlook in Mecca when Muhammad grew up there. From the Qur'an's or the Believers' perspective, failing to acknowledge the oneness of God, who created all things and gave us life, is the ultimate ingratitude and the essence of unbelief (*kufr*). But the Qur'an's strict monotheism also condemns the Christian doctrine of the Trinity as being incompatible with the idea of God's absolute unity: "Those who say that God is the third of three, disbelieve; there is no god but the one God . . ." (Q. 5:73).

As we have seen, the idea of monotheism was already well established throughout the Near East, including in Arabia, in Muhammad's day, and it has been plausibly suggested that the Qur'an's frequent invective against "polytheists" may actually be directed at trinitarian Christians and anyone else whom Muhammad considered only lukewarm monotheists. Be that as it may, the Qur'an makes it clear that the most basic requirement for the Believers was uncompromising acknowledgement of God's oneness. And, as we shall see, it was from this most fundamental concept, the idea of God's essential unity, that most other elements of true Belief flowed.

Also important to the Believers was belief in the Last Day or Day of Judgment (*yawm al-din*). Just as God was the creator of the world and of everything in it, and the giver of life, so too will He decree when it will all end—the physical world as we know it, time, everything. The Qur'an provides considerable detail on the Last Day: how it will come on us suddenly and without warning; how just before it the natural world will be in upheaval—mountains flowing like water, the heavens torn open, stars falling; how the dead from all past ages will be brought to life and raised from their graves; how all mankind will be brought before God to face final Judgment; and how we will then all be taken either to a paradise full of delights and ease, or to a hell full of torment and suffering, for eternity. But the Qur'an does not merely describe the coming Judgment for us—above all, it warns us of its approach, enjoining us to prepare ourselves for it by believing truly in God and by living righteously.

From the Qur'an we can also deduce that the Believers accepted the ideas of revelation and prophecy. The Qur'an makes clear that God has revealed His eternal Word to mankind many times, through the intermediacy of a series of messengers (singular, *rasul*) or prophets (singular, *nabi*). (The technical distinction between *rasul* and *nabi* will be discussed more fully later in this chapter.) The Qur'an offers many stories about, and lessons drawn from, the lives of these messengers and prophets. These include many figures familiar from the Old and New Testament—Adam, Noah, Job, Moses, Abraham, Lot, Zachariah, Jesus, and others—as well as a few otherwise unknown Arabian prophets (Hud, Salih) and, of course, Muhammad himself, to whom the Qur'an was revealed. Indeed, the Qur'an, as the most recent revelation of God's word, obviously supercedes earlier revelations, which were said to have become garbled over time. And the Believers are repeatedly enjoined to refer matters "to God and His messenger" Muhammad. Part of this complex of ideas, too, is the notion of "the book," referring in some cases to the heavenly archetype of God's word, of which the Qur'an is merely an exact transcript, and in other cases apparently to the Qur'an itself or to other, earlier scriptures.

Believers are also enjoined to believe in God's angels—creatures that assist God in various ways, most importantly by carrying God's word to His prophets at the moment of revelation, by serving as "orderlies" during the Last Judgment, and in various ways intervening in mundane affairs when it is God's will that they do so. Satan (also called Iblis) is, in Qur'anic doctrine, merely a fallen angel who always accompanies man and tries to seduce him into sin (Q. 7:11–22).

* * *

## ECUMENISM

The Qur'anic evidence suggests that the early Believers' movement was centered on the ideas of monotheism, preparing for the Last Day, belief in prophecy and revealed scripture, and observance of righteous behavior, including frequent prayer, expiation for sins committed, periodic fasting, and a charitable and humble demeanor toward others. All of these ideas and practices were quite well known in the Near East by the seventh century, although of course in the Qur'an they found a unique formulation (and one in a new literary idiom, Arabic). The earliest Believers thought of themselves as constituting a separate group or community of righteous, God-fearing monotheists, separate in their strict observance of righteousness from those around them—whether polytheists or imperfectly rigorous, or sinful, monotheists—who did not conform to their strict code.

On the other hand, there is no reason to think that the Believers viewed themselves as constituting a new or separate religious confession (for which the Qur'anic term seems to be *milla*, Q. 2:120). Indeed, some passages make it clear that Muhammad's message was the same as that brought by earlier apostles: "Say: I am no innovator among the apostles; and I do not know what will become of me or of you. I merely follow what is revealed to me; I am only a clear warner" (Q. 46:9). At this early stage in the history of the Believers' movement, then, it seems that Jews or Christians who were sufficiently pious could, if they wished, have participated in it because they recognized God's oneness already. Or, to put it the other way around, some of the early Believers were Christians or Jews—although surely not all were. The reason for this "confessionally open" or ecumenical quality was simply that the basic ideas of the Believers and their insistence on observance of strict piety were in no way antithetical to the beliefs and practices of some Christians and Jews. Indeed, the Qur'an itself sometimes notes a certain parallelism between the Believers and the established monotheistic faiths (often lumped together by the Qur'an in the term "people of the book," *ahl al-kitab*; Q. 48:29).

Closer examination of the Qur'an reveals a number of passages indicating that some Christians and Jews could belong to the Believers' movement—not simply by virtue of their being Christians or Jews, but because they were inclined to righteousness. For example, Q. 3:199 states, "There are among the people of the book those who Believe in God and what was sent down to you and was sent down to them . . ." Other verses, such as Q. 3:113–116, lay this out in greater detail. These passages and other like them suggest that some peoples of the book—Christians and Jews—were considered Believers. The line separating Believers from unbelievers did not, then, coincide simply with the boundaries of the peoples of the book. Rather, it cut across those communities, depending on their commitment to God and to observance of His law, so that some of them were to be considered Believers, while others were not.

Believers, then, whatever religious confession they may have belonged to—whether (non-trinitarian) Christians, Jews, or what we might call "Qur'anic monotheists," recent converts from paganism—were expected to live strictly by the law that God had revealed to their communities. Jews should obey the laws of the Torah; Christians those of the Gospels; and those who were not already members of one of the preexisting monotheist communities should obey the injunctions of the Qur'an.

* * *

# A Narrative Matrix

## PROTOEVANGELIUM OF JAMES

The Christian New Testament achieved its final form of twenty-seven individual books more than three hundred years after the death of Jesus. This New Testament "canon" emerged from centuries of debate over which of the writings that circulated among the earliest believers most faithfully reflected the teachings of Jesus and his first followers. Those works that were eventually excluded have come to be known, collectively, as the *pseudepigrapha* ("falsely ascribed") or *apocrypha* ("hidden writings"). Many of these writings languished for centuries in European and Middle Eastern monasteries and libraries. Others, often in fragmentary form, were discovered more recently through archaeological serendipity. Despite their noncanonical status, a number of the texts that fall within the fluid category of apocrypha exercised considerable influence on the art and literature of the Christian Middle Ages. Their influence on Islamic literature, both qur'ānic and post-qur'ānic, has long been a subject of scholarly study.

Among the most important apocryphal gospels is the *Protoevangelium*—literally, "Proto-Gospel"—*of James*, a work whose popularity is attested by the large number of extant Greek manuscripts and of translations into languages such as Syriac, Ethiopic, and Armenian. Its designation as a "protogospel" reflects its focus on events prior to Jesus' active ministry. The narrative opens with the tribulations of Anna, the mother of Mary, whose childlessness has humiliated her husband. Angels announce the impending birth of a child, and Anna vows to dedicate the child to God's service (Q 3:35–36). While still a toddler, Mary is taken to the temple—which is where the qur'ānic version of Mary's life finds her—and placed in the care of Zacharias (Zakariyyā; Q 3:37). At the age of twelve, when the onset of menstruation renders her impure for temple service, lots are drawn (Q 3:44) to determine who will become her guardian. The choice falls on Joseph; and while in his care, she is visited by the angel who tells her that she will conceive a son through the power of God (Q 3:45–49; 19:16–21).

### *From* The Protevangelium of James†

* * *

7. 1. The months passed, and the child grew. When she was two years old Joachim said, 'Let us take her up to the temple of the Lord, so that we may fulfil the promise which we made, lest the Lord send some evil to us and our gift be unacceptable.' And Anna replied, 'Let us wait until the third year, that the child may then no more long for her father and mother.'

† From J. K. Elliott, *The Apocryphal New Testament: A Collection of Apocryphal Christian Literature in an English Translation* (Oxford: Clarendon Press, 1993), pp. 60–65. Reprinted by permission of Oxford University Press. Except as indicated, all notes are Elliott's.

And Joachim said, 'Let us wait.' 2. And when the child was three years old Joachim said 'Call the undefiled daughters of the Hebrews, and let each one take a torch, and let these be burning, in order that the child may not turn back and her heart be tempted away from the temple of the Lord.' And they did so until they had gone up to the temple of the Lord. And the priest took her and kissed her and blessed her, saying, 'The Lord has magnified your name among all generations; because of you the Lord at the end of the days will reveal his redemption to the sons of Israel.' 3. And he placed her on the third step of the altar, and the Lord God put grace upon her and she danced with her feet, and the whole house of Israel loved her.

8. 1. And her parents returned marvelling, praising the Lord God because the child did not turn back. And Mary was in the temple of the Lord nurtured like a dove and received food from the hand of an angel. 2. When she was twelve[1] years old, there took place a council of the priests saying, 'Behold, Mary has become twelve years old in the temple of the Lord. What then shall we do with her lest she defile the temple of the Lord?' And they said to the high priest, 'You stand at the altar of the Lord; enter the sanctuary and pray concerning her, and that which the Lord shall reveal to you we will indeed do.' 3. And the high priest took the vestment with the twelve bells and went into the Holy of Holies and prayed concerning her. And behold, an angel of the Lord appeared and said to him, 'Zacharias, Zacharias, go out and assemble the widowers of the people, and to whomsoever the Lord shall give a sign she shall be a wife.' And the heralds went forth through all the country round about Judaea; the trumpet of the Lord sounded, and all came running.

9. 1. And Joseph threw down his adze and went out to their meeting. And when they were gathered together, they took the rods and went to the high priest. He took the rods from them all, entered the temple, and prayed. When he had finished the prayer he took the rods, and went out and gave them to them; but there was no sign on them. Joseph received the last rod, and behold, a dove came out of the rod and flew on to Joseph's head. And the priest said to Joseph, 'You have been chosen by lot to receive the virgin of the Lord as your ward.' 2. But Joseph answered him, 'I have sons and am old; she is but a girl. I object lest I should become a laughing-stock to the sons of Israel.' And the priest said to Joseph, 'Fear the Lord your God, and remember what God did to Dathan, Abiram, and Korah, how the earth was split in two and they were all swallowed up because of their rebellion.[2] And now beware, Joseph, lest these things happen in your house too.' And Joseph was afraid and received her as his ward. And Joseph said to Mary, 'I have received you from the temple of the Lord, and now I leave you in my house and go away to build my buildings. I will return to you; the Lord will guard you.'

10. 1. Now there was a council of the priests saying, 'Let us make a veil for the temple of the Lord.' And the priest said, 'Call to me pure virgins of the tribe of David.' And the officers departed and searched and they found seven virgins. And the priest remembered the child Mary, that she was of the tribe of David and was pure before God. And the officers went and fetched her. 2. Then they brought them into the temple of the Lord and the priest said, 'Cast lots to see who shall weave the gold, the

1. Variants: 'fourteen' or 'ten'.
2. See Numbers 16:1–33 [editor's note].

amiantus,[3] the linen, the silk, the hyacinth-blue, the scarlet, and the pure purple'. The pure purple and scarlet fell by lot to Mary. And she took them and went home. At that time Zacharias became dumb,[4] and Samuel took his place until Zacharias was able to speak again. Mary took the scarlet and spun it.

11. 1. And she took the pitcher and went out to draw water, and behold, a voice said, 'Hail, highly favoured one,[5] the Lord is with you, you are blessed among women.' And she looked around to the right and to the left to see where this voice came from. And, trembling, she went to her house and put down the pitcher and took the purple and sat down on her seat and drew out the thread. 2. And behold, an angel of the Lord stood before her and said, 'Do not fear, Mary; for you have found grace before the Lord of all things and shall conceive by his Word.' When she heard this she considered it and said, 'Shall I conceive by the Lord, the living God, and bear as every woman bears?' 3. And the angel of the Lord said, 'Not so, Mary; for the power of the Lord shall overshadow you; wherefore that holy one who is born of you shall be called the Son of the Most High. And you shall call his name Jesus; for he shall save his people from their sins.' And Mary said, 'Behold, (I am) the handmaid of the Lord before him: be it to me according to your word.[6]

12. 1. And she made ready the purple and the scarlet and brought them to the priest. And the priest blessed her and said, 'Mary, the Lord God has magnified your name, and you shall be blessed among all generations of the earth'.[7] 2. And Mary rejoiced and went to Elizabeth her kinswoman and knocked on the door. When Elizabeth heard it, she put down the scarlet and ran to the door and opened it, and when she saw Mary she blessed her and said, 'How is it that the mother of my Lord should come to me? For behold, that which is in me leaped and blessed you.'[8] But Mary forgot the mysteries which the archangel Gabriel had told her, and raised a sigh towards heaven and said, 'Who am I, Lord, that all generations of the earth count me blessed?' 3. And she remained three months with Elizabeth. Day by day her womb grew, and Mary was afraid and went into her house and hid herself from the children of Israel. And Mary was sixteen[9] years old when all these mysterious things happened.

13. 1. Now when she was in her sixth month, behold, Joseph came from his buildings and entered his house and found her with child. And he struck his face, threw himself down on the ground on sackcloth and wept bitterly saying, 'With what countenance shall I look towards the Lord my God? What prayer shall I offer for this maiden? For I received her as a virgin out of the temple of the Lord my God and have not protected her. Who has deceived me? Who has done this evil in my house and defiled the virgin? Has the story of Adam been repeated in me? For as Adam was absent in the hour of his prayer and the serpent came and found Eve alone and deceived her, so also has it happened to me.' 2. And Joseph arose from the sackcloth and called Mary and said to her, 'You who are cared for by

3. A fine, silky fabric made from the variety of asbestos of the same name [editor's note].
4. Cf. Luke 1:20–22, 64.
5. Luke 1:28.
6. Luke 1:31.
7. Luke 1:42, 48.
8. Luke 1:41–44.
9. Variants: 'fourteen' or 'fifteen'.

God, why have you done this and forgotten the Lord your God? Why have you humiliated your soul, you who were brought up in the Holy of Holies and received food from the hand of an angel?' 3. But she wept bitterly, saying, 'I am pure, and know not a man.' And Joseph said to her, 'As the Lord my God lives, I do not know whence it has come to me.'

14. 1. And Joseph feared greatly and parted from her, pondering what he should do with her. And Joseph said, 'If I conceal her sin, I shall be found to be in opposition to the law of the Lord. If I expose her to the children of Israel, I fear lest that which is in her may be from the angels and I should be found delivering innocent blood to the judgement of death. What then shall I do with her? I will put her away secretly.' And the night came upon him. 2. And behold, an angel of the Lord appeared to him in a dream, saying, 'Do not fear this child. For that which is in her is of the Holy Spirit. She shall bear a son, and you shall call his name Jesus; for he shall save his people from their sins.'[1] And Joseph arose from sleep and glorified the God of Israel who had bestowed his grace upon him, and he guarded her.

15. 1. And Annas the scribe came to him and said to him, 'Joseph, why have you not appeared in our assembly?' And Joseph said to him, 'Because I was weary from the journey and I rested the first day.' And Annas turned and saw that Mary was pregnant. 2. And he went running to the priest and said to him, 'Joseph, for whom you are a witness, has grievously transgressed.' And the high priest said, 'In what way?' And he said, 'The virgin, whom he received from the temple of the Lord, he has defiled, and has secretly consummated his marriage with her, and has not disclosed it to the children of Israel.' And the priest said to him, 'Has Joseph done this?' And Annas said to him, 'Send officers, and you will find the virgin pregnant.' And the officers went and found as he had said, and brought her and Joseph to the court. And the priest said, 'Mary, why have you done this? Why have you humiliated your soul and forgotten the Lord your God, you who were brought up in the Holy of Holies and received food from the hand of an angel, and heard hymns, and danced before him? Why have you done this?' But she wept bitterly saying, 'As the Lord my God lives, I am pure before him and I know not a man.' And the priest said to Joseph, 'Why have you done this?' And Joseph said, 'As the Lord my God lives, I am pure concerning her.' And the priest said, 'Do not give false witness, but speak the truth. You have consummated your marriage in secret, and have not disclosed it to the children of Israel, and have not bowed your head under the mighty hand in order that your seed might be blessed.' And Joseph was silent.

16. 1. And the priest said, 'Give back the virgin whom you have received from the temple of the Lord.' And Joseph began to weep. And the priest said, 'I will give you both to drink the water of the conviction of the Lord,[2] and it will make your sins manifest in your eyes.' 2. And the priest took it and gave it to Joseph to drink and sent him into the hill-country, and he returned whole. And he made Mary drink also, and sent her into the hill-country, and she returned whole. And all the people marvelled, because sin did not appear in them. And the priest said, 'If the Lord God has not revealed your sins, neither do I judge you.' And he released them. And

1. Cf. Matt. 1:20f.
2. See Numbers 5:11–31 [editor's note].

Joseph took Mary and departed to his house, rejoicing and glorifying the God of Israel.

17. 1. Now there went out a decree from the king Augustus that all those in Bethlehem in Judaea should be enrolled.[3] And Joseph said, 'I shall enrol my sons, but what shall I do with this child? How shall I enrol her? As my wife? I am ashamed to do that. Or as my daughter? But all the children of Israel know that she is not my daughter. On this day of the Lord the Lord will do as he wills.' 2. And he saddled his she-ass and sat her on it; his son led, and Joseph followed. And they drew near to the third milestone. And Joseph turned round and saw her sad and said within himself, 'Perhaps the child within her is paining her.' Another time Joseph turned round and saw her laughing and said to her, 'Mary, why is it that I see your face at one moment laughing and at another sad?' And Mary said to Joseph, 'I see with my eyes two peoples, one weeping and lamenting and one rejoicing and exulting.' 3. And having come half-way, Mary said to him, 'Joseph, take me down from the she-ass, for the child within me presses me to come forth.' And he took her down from the she-ass and said to her, 'Where shall I take you and hide your shame? For the place is desert.'

18. 1. And he found a cave there and brought her into it, and left her in the care of his sons and went out to seek for a Hebrew midwife in the region of Bethlehem. 2. Now I, Joseph, was walking, and yet I did not walk, and I looked up to the air and saw the air in amazement. And I looked up at the vault of heaven, and saw it standing still and the birds of the heaven motionless. And I looked down at the earth, and saw a dish placed there and workmen reclining, and their hands were in the dish. But those who chewed did not chew, and those who lifted up did not lift, and those who put something to their mouth put nothing to their mouth, but everybody looked upwards. And behold, sheep were being driven and they did not come forward but stood still; and the shepherd raised his hand to strike them with his staff but his hand remained upright. And I looked at the flow of the river, and saw the mouths of the kids over it and they did not drink. And then suddenly everything went on its course.

19. 1. And behold, a woman came down from the hill-country and said to me, 'Man, where are you going?' And I said, 'I seek a Hebrew midwife.' And she answered me, 'Are you from Israel?' And I said to her, 'Yes.' And she said, 'And who is she who brings forth in the cave?' And I said, 'My betrothed.' And she said to me, 'Is she not your wife?' And I said to her, 'She is Mary, who was brought up in the temple of the Lord, and I received her by lot as my wife, and she is not my wife, but she has conceived by the Holy Spirit.' And the midwife said to him, 'Is this true?' And Joseph said to her, 'Come and see.' And she went with him. 2. And they stopped at the entrance to the cave, and behold, a bright cloud overshadowed the cave. And the midwife said, 'My soul is magnified today, for my eyes have seen wonderful things; for salvation is born to Israel.' And immediately the cloud disappeared from the cave and a great light appeared, so that our eyes could not bear it. A short time afterwards that light withdrew until the baby appeared, and it came and took the breast of its mother Mary. And the midwife cried, 'This day is great for me, because I have seen this new sight.' 3. And the midwife came out of the cave, and Salome met her. And she said

3. Luke 2:1; Matt. 2:1.

to her, 'Salome, Salome, I have a new sight to tell you about; a virgin has brought forth, a thing which her condition does not allow.' And Salome said, 'As the Lord my God lives, unless I insert my finger and test her condition, I will not believe that a virgin has given birth.'

20. 1. And the midwife went in and said to Mary, 'Make yourself ready, for there is no small contention concerning you'. And Salome inserted her finger to test her condition. And she cried out, saying, 'Woe for my wickedness and my unbelief; for I have tempted the living God; and behold, my hand falls away from me, consumed by fire!' 2. And she bowed her knees before the Lord saying, 'O God of my fathers, remember me; for I am the seed of Abraham, Isaac, and Jacob; do not make me pilloried for the children of Israel, but restore me to the poor. For you know, Lord, that in your name I perform my duties and from you I have received my hire. 3. And behold, an angel of the Lord appeared and said to her, 'Salome, Salome, the Lord God has heard your prayer. Bring your hand to the child and touch him and salvation and joy will be yours.' 4. And Salome came near and touched him, saying, 'I will worship him, for a great king has been born to Israel.' And Salome was healed as she had requested, and she went out of the cave. And, behold, an angel of the Lord cried, 'Salome, Salome, do not report what marvels you have seen, until the child has come to Jerusalem.'

* * *

# SYRIAC DIALOGUE

Syriac—a dialect of Aramaic, the language that Jesus spoke—became the principal literary and liturgical language of the eastern Christian churches. It survives in the liturgies of Christian communities throughout the Middle East, particularly in Lebanon, Syria, and Iraq. As scholars have recently resumed their interest in qur'ānic source criticism, they have focused attention on Syriac texts that precede the Qur'ān's emergence. Mary, the mother of Jesus (and the only woman named in the Qur'ān), figures prominently in several genres of Syriac literature. One such genre is the *sughitho*, a dialogue poem in short verses that portrays an argument between two protagonists. Most of the extant dialogue poems are anonymous, and many date from around the fifth century CE. The one reproduced here imaginatively renders Mary's consternation at the announcement, or annunciation, that though a virgin she will conceive a son (Q 3:45–49; 19:16–21).

## Mary and the Angel†

The starting point is the Annunciation narrative in St Luke's Gospel (Luke 1:26–39), where Mary questions the angel Gabriel (Luke 1:34). In the course of the poem her 'wise questioning' is contrasted with Eve's failure to question the Serpent in Genesis. Significantly, it is only when the angel makes mention of the Holy Spirit that Mary finally accepts his message (Luke 1:38).

† From *Mary and Joseph and Other Dialogue Poems on Mary*, trans. Sebastian P. Brock (Piscataway, NJ: Gorgias Press, 2011), pp. 9–10, 12, 14, 16, 18, 20, 22, 24, 26, 28, 87–88. Reprinted by permission of the publisher. Except as indicated, all notes are Brock's.

**Refrain:** Praise to You, O Lord,
whom heaven and earth worship as they rejoice.

1. O Power[1] of the Father who came down and resided,[2]
compelled by His love,[3] in a virgin womb,
grant me utterance that I may speak
of this great deed of Yours which cannot be grasped.

2. O Son of the Bounteous One,[4] whose love so willed
that He resided in a poor girl's[5] womb,
grant me utterance and words
that in due wonder I may speak of You.

3. To speak of You the mouth is too small,
to describe You the tongue is quite inadequate;
voice and words are too feeble
to relate Your beauty, so please bid me tell of You!

4. Grant that I may approach, O Lord of all,[6]
in awe to that exalted place
of the chief of the watchers[7] when he announced
to the young mother Your coming.

5. You who are discerning, come, listen and give ear
to this episode so filled with wonder,
sing glory to Him who bent down[8]
to give life to Adam who had sinned and so died.

6. The Father in His mercy beckoned to His Son
to go down and deliver what He had fashioned,
and to Gabriel the angel He gave instructions
to prepare the path before His descent.

7. With David's daughter[9] did Mercy shine out,
for she was to be mother of Him

1. *Power*: Syriac writers usually differentiate 'the Power of the Most High' in Luke 1:35 from 'the Holy Spirit' (who precedes it), and identify the Power instead as the divine Word.
2. *resided* (*shro*): in early Syriac writings this verb (often in combination with 'came down', as here) is regularly used in paraphrases of Luke 1:35, even though all the Syriac versions employ a different verb (*aggen*) there. It seems likely that *shra* represents the very earliest Syriac term used to denote the Incarnation.
3. *compelled by His love*: the phrase occurs in a number of other *sughyotho* (e.g. the Dialogue between the Sinful Woman and Satan, stanza 1).
4. *Son of the Bounteous One* (*bar 'atiro*): the title already features in Ephrem, *Madroshe* on the Nativity 15:3 and 19:2. The paradox of rich/poor is based on 2 Cor. 8:9. [St. Ephrem the Syrian (ca. 306–373), a Christian theologian, poet, and doctor of the church. He wrote many hymns, or *madroshe*, and he described the ceding of Nisibis to the Persians in 363 in *Carmina Nisibina* (*Nisibine Hymns*)—editor's note.]
5. *poor girl*: in Ephrem, *Madroshe* on the Nativity 19:13 Christ is called 'son of poor parents'.
6. *Lord of all* (*Moro d-kul*): the title already occurs in the Acts of Thomas and Ephrem (*Madroshe* on Faith, 60:8). [The Acts of Thomas (early 3rd c. CE), an apocryphal work composed in Syriac, describes the journey of the apostle Thomas to and from India—editor's note.]
7. *watchers* (*'ire*): this term for angels derives from Daniel 4:13; it is more frequent in early Syriac writers than its synonym *mal'ake*.
8. *who bent down*: the verb is often used of the Incarnation in early writers (though it is absent from Aphrahat), e.g. Acts of Thomas, Ephrem, *Madroshe* against the Heresies 30:3. [The Syrian ascetic Aphrahat (fl. 4th c. CE), or Aphraates, the earliest-known Christian Syriac writer—editor's note.]
9. *David's daughter*: thus already, Ephrem, *Madroshe* on the Nativity 2:13, 16.

who had given birth to Adam and to the world,
and whose name is older than the sun.

8. That Will which cannot be reached flew down[1]
to summon the angel, sending him out
from the angelic ranks on his mission
to bring glad tidings to a pure virgin.

9. He brought a letter[2] that had been sealed
with the mystery that was hidden from all ages;
he filled it with greeting to the young girl,
and fair hope[3] for all the worlds.

10. The fiery being flew down until he reached
the destitute girl[4] to fill her with wealth;
he gave her a greeting, announcing to her too
concerning her conception, the cause of wonder to all.

11. ANGEL: To the Virgin the watcher says:
'Peace be with you, O mother of my Lord, Luke 1:28
blessed are you, young woman,
and blessed the Fruit[5] that is within you'. Luke 1:42

12. MARY: Says Mary, 'Who are you, sir?
And what is this that you utter?
What you are saying is remote from me,
and what it means, I have no idea'.

13. ANGEL: O blessed of women, in you has it pleased
the Most High to reside; have no fear,
for in you has Grace bent down
to pour mercy upon the world.

14. MARY: I beg you, sir, do not upset me;
you are clothed with coals of fire: mind you don't burn me.
What you are saying is alien to me
and I am unable to grasp what it means.

15. ANGEL: The Father has revealed to me, as I do so now to you,
this mystery which is shared
between Him and His Son, when He sent me to say
that from you will He shine out over the worlds.

16. MARY: You are made of flame, do not frighten me;
you are wrapped in coals of fire, do not terrify me.

1. *flew down* (*dol*): similarly in connection with the Incarnation in Ephrem, *Madroshe* on Faith 4:2.
2. *a letter*: Syriac poets make a great deal of use of letter imagery. * * * See further Brock, S.P. "Mary as a 'Letter', and Some Other Letter Imagery in Syriac Liturgical Texts." *Vox Patrum* (Festschrift for M. Starowieyski) 26 (2006): 89–99.
3. *fair hope*: the words translate Greek *eudokia* in the Peshitta at Luke 2:14. [The Peshitta (in Syriac, "Common" or "Simple") is the version of the Bible used in Syrian Christian churches—editor's note.]
4. *destitute girl*: similarly in stanza 42, below.
5. *blessed the Fruit . . .* : the anonymous author inadvertently puts these words of Elizabeth (Luke 1:42) into Gabriel's mouth!

O fiery being, why should I believe you
seeing that all you have spoken to me is utterly new?

17. ANGEL: It would be amazing in you if you were
to answer back,
annulling the message which I have brought to you
concerning the conception of the Most High,
whose will it is to reside in your womb.

18. MARY: I am afraid, sir, to accept you,
for when Eve my mother accepted
the serpent who spoke as a friend,
she was snatched away from her former glory.[6] Gen 3:1–7

19. ANGEL: My daughter, he certainly did use deception
on your mother Eve when he gave her the message,
but just as certainly I am not deceiving you now,
since it is from the True One that I have been sent.

20. MARY: All this that you have spoken
is most difficult, so do not find fault with me,
for it is not from a virgin that a son will appear,
nor from that fruit, a divine being![7]

21. ANGEL: The Father gave me this meeting with you here
to bring you greeting and to announce to you
that from your womb His Son will shine forth.
Do not answer back, disputing this.

22. MARY: This meeting with you and your presence here
is all very well,
if only the natural order of things did not stir me
to have doubts at your arrival,
for how can there be fruit in a virgin?

23. ANGEL: The angelic hosts quake at His word:
the moment He has commanded, they do not answer back;
how is it then that you are not afraid
to enquire into what the Father has willed?

24. MARY: I too quake, sir, and am terrified,
yet, though I am afraid, I find it hard to believe

6. *her former glory*: according to Syriac tradition (inherited from Judaism), Adam and Eve were created clothed in a 'garment of glory'; this was lost at the Fall, but made available again to humanity by Christ: at baptism Christians put on this garment of glory (or, of light) in potential, but it only at the end of time does it become a reality, that is, for those who have preserved this garment (linked with the wedding garment of Matthew 22:11) in purity. For this theme, see further "Clothing Metaphors as a Means of Theological Expression in Syriac Tradition," reprinted in Brock, *Studies in Syriac Christianity* (1992), chap. XI, and Brock, "The Robe of Glory: A Biblical Image in the Syriac Tradition," *The Way* 39 (1999): 247–59; Brock, *The Holy Spirit in the Syrian Baptismal Tradition* (Piscataway, NJ: Gorgias Press, 2008), pp. 61–67.
7. *a divine being*: or 'goddess'. In his Commentary on Genesis (II.20) Ephrem states that, prompted by the Serpent, Eve (and Adam) had wanted to attain to divinity by eating of the forbidden fruit of the Tree of Knowledge: 'Because she had believed the Serpent, she ate first, imagining that she would come back clothed in divinity . . .'. In the Nisibene *Madroshe* (69:12) he writes, 'The Most High knew that Adam had wanted to become a god, so He sent His Son who put him on in order to grant him his desire' (Adam here represents humanity).

since nature itself can well convince me
that virgins do not ever give birth.

25. ANGEL: It is the Father's love which has so willed
that in your virginity you should give birth to the Son.
It is appropriate you should keep silent,
and have faith too,
for the will of the Father cannot be gainsaid.

26. MARY: Your appearance is venerable, your message
full of awe,
your flames are leaping up.
Into the person of your Lord one cannot inquire,
but that I should believe all this is difficult for me.

27. ANGEL: It is glad tidings that I have brought you:
you shall give birth to your Lord, as I have explained.
O child, give thanks to Him who has held you worthy
to be His mother, while having Him as your Son.

28. MARY: I am but a girl and cannot
receive a man of fire.
The matter you speak of is hidden from me,
yet you proclaim that I should accept it.

29. ANGEL: Today for Adam hope has arrived,
for in you is the Lord of all pleased
to come down and release him, granting him liberty.
Accept my words, at the same time give thanks.

30. MARY: Today I wonder and am amazed
at all these things which you have said to me.
Yet I am afraid, sir, to accept you,
in case there is some deceit in your words.

31. ANGEL: When I was sent to announce to you
I heard His greeting and brought it to you.
My Lord is true, for thus He has willed
to shine forth from you over the worlds.

32. MARY: All your words astonish me;
I beg you, sir, do not blame me,
for a son in a virgin is not to be seen,
and no one has ever slept with me.

33. ANGEL: He will come to you, have no fear;
He will reside in your womb, do not ask how.
O woman full of blessings, sing praise
to Him who is pleased to be seen in you.

34. MARY: Sir, no man has ever known me,
nor has any ever slept with me.

How can this be in the way that you have said,
for without such a union there will never be any son?

35. ANGEL: From the Father was I sent
to bring you this message, for His love has
compelled Him
so that His Son should reside in your womb,
and over you the Holy Spirit will reside.[8] Luke 1:35

36. MARY: In that case, O watcher, I will not answer back:
if the Holy Spirit shall come to me,
I am His maidservant, and He has authority Luke 1:38
let it be to me, sir, in accordance with your word.

37. ANGEL: Let your head be raised up, O young girl,
let your heart rejoice, O virgin;
O Second Heaven,[9] let the earth Isa 65:17
rejoice at you, for in your Son it acquires peace.

38. MARY: Let my head be raised up, sir, as you say.
As I rejoice, I shall confess His name,
for if you, His servant, are so fair,
what might He be like—if you know?

39. ANGEL: This is something the angelic hosts are
unable to do,
to gaze on Him, for He is most fearful.
He is hidden within His Father's flame,
and the heavenly bands quake with fear at Him.

40. MARY: You greatly disturb me now,
for if, as you say, He is all flame,
how will my womb not be harmed
at the Fire residing there?

41. ANGEL: Your womb will be filled with sanctity,
sealed with the Hidden Divinity:
a place that is holy is greatly beloved
by God as a place in which to appear.

42. MARY: O watcher, reveal to me why it has pleased
your Lord to reside in a poor girl like me:
the world is full of kings' daughters,
so why does He want me who am quite destitute?

43. ANGEL: It would have been easy for Him to dwell
in a rich girl,
but it is with your poverty that He has fallen in love,

8. *over you the Holy Spirit will reside* (*shore*): at Luke 1:35 all the Syriac versions use a different verb (*naggen*).
9. *Second Heaven*: based on Isaiah 65:17, this became a frequent title for Mary in Patristic literature in every language.

so that He may become a companion to the poor,
and enrich them once He is revealed.

44. MARY: Explain to me, sir, if you know this,
when does He wish to come to me,
and will He appear to me like fire
when He resides in me, as you have said?

45. ANGEL: He has already so willed it, He is come
and is residing within you:
it was so as not to frighten you that you remained
unaware of Him.
I dare not look upon you
now that you are filled with the Fire that does not
consume. cp. Exod 3:2

46. MARY: I should like, sir, to put this question to you:
explain to me the ways of my Son
who resides in me without my being aware;
what should I do for Him so that He is not held in
contempt?

47. ANGEL: Cry out 'Holy, Holy, Holy', Isa 6:3
just as our heavenly legions do, adding nothing else,
for we have nothing besides this 'Holy';
this is all we utter concerning your Son.

48. MARY: Holy and glorious and blessed is his name,[1]
for He has looked upon His handmaid's low estate; Luke 1:48
henceforth all generations in the world
shall proclaim me blessed.

49. ANGEL: Height and depth shall hold Him in honour,
angels and human kind shall give Him praise,
for He, the Lord of all, has come down
and resided in a virgin, so as to make all things new.

50. MARY: Great is His mercy and not to be measured,
far beyond what lips can describe;
on high the heavens cannot contain Him,
yet below for Him a womb suffices!

51. Let heaven and earth call Him blessed;
let both the angel and the Virgin,
and all humanity too, call Him holy,
for in His love He has descended and become a
human being!

52. Let heaven and the watchers give thanks on high,
and let earth rejoice in the Virgin;

1. *blessed is his name* (*brik shmeh*): it is interesting that this features as a divine title in several Palmyrene inscriptions. [Palmyra (or Tadmur), in south-central Syria, is the site of thousands of Aramaic inscriptions—editor's note.]

let both sides, as they exult,
give praise to the Son of their Lord.

53. Let both sides be mingled in praise,
both watchers and human beings,
to the Son who has restored peace between them, Col 1:20–21
when there had been anger and disruption.

54. Thanks be to You, Lord, from all the fiery
and invisible worlds;
in this world, too, from every mouth
let the earth sing praises to You.

## MIDRASH RABBAH

The centuries-long interpretation of the Hebrew Bible, the homiletic and narrative amplification of biblical passages, is known as *midrash*. Halakhic *midrashim* are the parts of this vast literature that focus on legal prescriptions; the nonlegal portions fall in the category of aggadic *midrashim*, or simply *aggadah*. The largest volumes of the latter are often collectively designated as *Midrash Rabbah*. The following selection is drawn from the exegetical *midrash* to the second book of the Hebrew Bible, the book of Exodus. Although Exodus Rabbah was not redacted until about the tenth century CE, it draws on ancient sources and incorporates material from much earlier periods. In this selection, the biblical passage being treated is Exodus 7:9–12, a group of verses that recount the episode of Moses and his brother Aaron being brought before the Pharaoh of Egypt. When Pharaoh demands that they perform a miracle, Aaron throws his rod to the ground, where it is instantly transformed into a snake. Pharaoh then insists that his sorcerers perform the same feat—but when their rods turn to snakes, these are consumed by Aaron's. A version of this narrative can be found in Q 7:104–109 and Q 26:30–35, where it functions as one of the signs (*āyāt*) and evidences (*bayyināt*) of Moses' prophethood.

### Va'era†

1. When Pharaoh shall speak unto you, saying (vii, 9). R.[1] Phinehas, the priest, son of Ḥama, began his discourse thus: *Declaring the end from the beginning, and from ancient times things that are not yet done; saying: My counsel shall stand, and all My pleasure will I do* (Isa. xlvi, 10). God declares at the beginning what the end will be, for thus He told Moses: *And this people will rise up, and go astray after the foreign gods of the land* (Deut. xxxi, 16)—which they actually did after the death of Joshua. *And they will forsake Me, and break My covenant* (*ib.*): they did forsake the Lord and refused to serve Him,[2] which shows that '*He declareth the end from the beginning*'.[3] R. Phinehas, the priest, son of Ḥama, said: He who reads this

† From chapter 11 of *Midrash Rabbah: Exodus*, trans. S. M. Lehrman, 3rd ed. (New York: Soncino Press, 1983), pp. 120–25. Except as indicated, all notes are Lehrman's, and all brackets in the text are his. *Va'era*: And I appeared (Hebrew), spoken by God (Exodus 6:3) at the beginning of the 14th weekly portion (Exodus 6:2–9:35) in the annual cycle of reading the Torah.

1. Rabbi [editor's note].
2. Judg. 11, 12.
3. Even in such matters as are dependent on free will (Radal). [Radal: David Luria (1798–1855), a well-known Lithuanian rabbi—editor's note.]

verse will think: Is there a conflict of opinions[4] above [in heaven], that it says,'*My counsel shall stand, and all My pleasure will I do*'.[5] No, the meaning of '*And all My pleasure will I do*' is that He wishes to justify His creatures, as it says: *The Lord was pleased, for His righteousness' sake, to make the teaching great and glorious* (Isa. XLII, 21). He does not wish to condemn any creature, for it says: *I have no pleasure in the death of the wicked, but that the wicked turn from his way and live* (Ezek. XXXIII, 11); this is the meaning of '*And all My pleasures will I do*'. So also in the case of Moses, God told him the end at the beginning. Note that it does not say: *If* Pharaoh will speak unto you, but, *WHEN* HE SHALL SPEAK UNTO YOU, as if to say, Pharaoh *will* speak unto you thus. R. Judah, son of R. Shalom, said: [God said, 'Pharaoh] is quite right to say: SHOW A WONDER FOR YOU (VII, 9), for so you find in the case of Noah.' After all the miracles which God had performed for him in the ark, when He brought him forth and said to him: '*And the waters shall no more become a flood to destroy all flesh*' (Gen. IX, 15),[6] Noah began to demand a sign, and God had to assure him: *I have set My bow in the cloud, and it shall be for a token* (*ib.* 16).[7] If Noah who was righteous asked for a sign, shall not Pharaoh who is wicked certainly do so? Similarly, in the case of Hezekiah, when Isaiah came and said to him: '*Thus saith the Lord . . . behold, I will heal thee; on the third day thou shalt go up unto the house of the Lord*' (II Kings XX, 5), Hezekiah demanded a sign, as it says: *And Hezekiah said unto Isaiah: What shall be the sign that the Lord will heal me, and that I shall go up unto the house of the Lord the third day* (*ib.* 8). If Hezekiah who was righteous asked for a sign, shall not Pharaoh who is wicked certainly do so? Hananiah, Mishael, and Azariah only descended into the fiery furnace after a sign. Whence do we know this? *Not unto us, O Lord, not unto us* (Ps. CXVI, 1) was said by Hanania; *But unto Thy name give glory*, by Mishael; *For Thy mercy, and for Thy truth's sake* (*ib.*), by Azariah. Gabriel responded after them: *Wherefore should the nations say: Where is now their God?* (*ib.* 2).[8] When they found these verses fluent in their mouths the whole night,[9] they considered it a good sign and descended [into the furnace]. Should you not be satisfied to infer this from here, then you can derive it from another source, for it is written: *Hear now, O Joshua the high priest, thou and thy fellow that sit before thee; for they are men of*[1] *a sign* (Zech. III, 8). And who were they? R. Judah, son of R. Shalom, said: These are Hananiah, Mishael, and Azariah to whom this sign was given. Now if righteous men ask for a sign, then how much more so the wicked?

2. THEN SHALT THOU SAY UNTO AARON: TAKE THY ROD (VII, 8). Thus it is written: *The rod of thy strength the Lord will send out of Zion* (Ps. CX, 2). God rules over the wicked with a rod.[2] Why? Because they are compared to dogs, as it says: *They return at evening, they howl like a dog* (*ib.* LIX, 7),[3]

4. From the Gk. φιλονιχεία 'contentiousness'.
5. Text as emended by Rashash. As though He did it in spite of opposition. [Rashash: Shalom Sharabi (1720–1777), a rabbi who was born in Yemen and spent much of his life in Jerusalem—editor's note.]
6. Perhaps better: *neither shall there any more be a flood to destroy the earth* (Gen. IX, 11).
7. This implies that he had asked for a token.
8. Cf. *infra* XVIII, 5, where we are told that Gabriel saved them.
9. I.e. they found themselves repeatedly quoting these verses, or perhaps they dreamt of these verses (Radal).
1. Lit. translation, and so required here by the context. E.V. [English versions of the Bible] '*that are*'.
2. The verse concludes: *Rule thou in the midst of thine enemies.*
3. David is speaking of his enemies.

and just as one smites a dog with a stick, so will they be smitten. Hence does it say, '*The rod of thy strength.*' God said to them: 'Pharaoh is wicked; if he says to you: "*Show a wonder for you,*" smite him with a stick'; as it says: SAY UNTO AARON: TAKE THY ROD.

3. AND CAST IT DOWN BEFORE PHARAOH, THAT IT BECOME A SERPENT (VII, 9). We have learnt: One who is praying must not return the greeting even of a king; and even if a serpent has entwined itself round his heel, he must not cease. What made the Sages compare the twining of a snake to the kingdom of Egypt?[4] R. Simeon b. Pazzi said: Because it is written: *The sound thereof shall go like the serpents* (Jer. XLVI, 22).[5] Just as the serpent hisses and slays, so does the kingdom of Egypt hiss and slay, for they put men in prison and silently plan to slay them.[6] Another explanation: Why did God compare the kingdom of Egypt to a serpent? Just as a serpent is twisted, so does the kingdom of Egypt pervert her ways. Hence God said to Moses: 'Just as a serpent is crooked, so is Pharaoh; and when he begins being crooked, just tell Aaron to raise the rod in front of him, as if to say: "By this wilt thou be smitten."'

4. Another reason why he told him to perform the miracle of the serpent was because Pharaoh was like a serpent, as it is said: *The great dragon that lieth in the midst of his rivers* (Ezek. XXIX, 3).[7] When Moses departed from Pharaoh, the latter said: 'If this son of Amram should again come to me, I will slay him, I will crucify him, I will burn him.' But when Moses did come again, Pharaoh immediately became a rod.[8]

5. AND MOSES AND AARON WENT IN UNTO PHARAOH (VII, 10). Should not Aaron have gone in first, since he was his senior in years? Why Moses first? Because he was the greater in the land of Egypt, as it says: *Moreover the man Moses was very great in the land of Egypt* (XI, 3); alternatively, because God sent him in His stead over Aaron, as it says: *And thou shalt be to him in God's stead* (IV, 16). It is etiquette for the greater to enter first. AND THEY DID SO, AS THE LORD HAD COMMANDED THEM not performing their wonders before Pharaoh had asked for them, as God had said. As soon as he asked for a wonder, Aaron cast down his rod.

6. THEN PHARAOH ALSO CALLED FOR THE WISE MEN AND THE SORCERERS (VII, 11). Then did Pharaoh begin to mock them and crow at them like a cock, saying to them: 'So these be the signs of your God! It is usual for people to take goods to a place which has a shortage of them; but does one import murics[9] into Apamea[1] or fish into Acco? Are you not aware that all kinds of magic are within my province?' He then asked for children to be brought from school and they also performed these wonders; moreover, he called also his wife, and she did thus, for it says: THEN PHARAOH *ALSO* CALLED. Why '*also*'? Because his wife whom he called also did this. AND THE MAGICIANS OF EGYPT DID IN LIKE MANNER. Why the word '*gam*' (also)? Even children of four and five years of age whom he called did likewise.

4. This assumes that a non-Jewish king is meant.
5. The context refers to Egypt.
6. The original is in the singular. No particular person seems to be referred to, and this is a general description of Egypt's scrupulousness in judgment.
7. The prophecy is of Egypt.
8. The meaning here is probably * * * he became like a harmless rod, powerless to bite.
9. A pickle containing fish-hash and sometimes wine. M. Jastrow's *Dictionary of the Targumim, the Talmud Babli and Yerushalmi, and the Midrashic Liberature* [1886–1903].
1. There were several towns of that name in Bithynia, Mesopotamia, and Syria.

7. FOR THEY CAST DOWN EVERY MAN HIS ROD (VII, 12). Yohani and Mamre[2] said to Moses: 'Wouldst thou carry straw to Afarayim?[3] The reply was: 'To Herb-town carry herbs.[4] BUT AARON'S ROD SWALLOWED UP THEIR RODS. So it is written: *A fool spendeth all his spirit; but a wise man stilleth him at the last* (Prov. XXIX, 11). The fool, when he contends with his fellows, spendeth all his words at once, but the wise man, after it all, discomfits him.[5] Another meaning of: '*A fool spendeth all his spirit.*' After the wicked has spent all his counsel, the wise One of the Universe silenceth him at the end. This is what you find in the case of Ahasuerus, who, because he hindered the construction of the Temple,[6] only ruled over half the world. What is written of him? *When he showed the riches of his glorious kingdom* (Est. I, 4).[7] Our Sages have said: He showed them six collections of treasure every day and not two of them were alike. These he afterwards distributed among the nobles of his kingdom. R. Ḥiyya b. Abbu affirms that he showed them various expensive items.[8] R. Levi says that he displayed the priestly garments he had; because here it says: *And the honour of his excellent* (tifereth) *majesty*, and elsewhere we read: *And thou shalt make holy garments for Aaron thy brother, for splendour and for beauty*—tifereth (Ex. XXVIII, 2). Just as the word '*tifereth*' in this connection refers to the robes of the High Priest, so does the word '*tifereth*' mentioned in the story of Ahasuerus refer to the robes of the High Priest. '*But the wise One stilleth him at the last*': God frustrated his counsel, so that he slew Vashti.[9]

'*A fool spendeth all his spirit.*' This verse may also refer to Pharaoh, who scoffed at God, imagining that Moses and Aaron performed their wonder by witchcraft, and called the members of his household to do likewise. Thus '*a fool spendeth all his spirit*' refers to Pharaoh. But '*the wise One stilleth him at the last*' refers to God who is described as: *He is wise in heart, and mighty in strength* (Job IX, 4). God said at that time: 'If Aaron's serpent will swallow up the serpents of the Egyptians, there will be nothing remarkable in that, for serpents usually swallow each other. Therefore let it resume its original form and swallow up their serpents.' Hence what is the meaning of BUT AARON'S *ROD* SWALLOWED UP THEIR RODS? R. Eleazar said: To teach us that a double wonder occurred; the rod resuming its original form and then swallowing up their serpents. When Pharaoh beheld this, he was amazed and said: 'What will happen if he now says to his rod: "Swallow up Pharaoh and his throne"? It would at once swallow me up!' R. Jose b. Ḥanina said: A great miracle happened to that rod, for although it swallowed up all the rods that had been cast down, sufficient to make ten heaps, still the rod did not all become any thicker, and all who saw it recognised it as Aaron's rod. On this account, Aaron's rod became a good

2. The two chief Egyptian sorcerers.
3. I.e. 'carry coals to Newcastle'.
4. Such a place becomes a market-town for that particular commodity and you find ready purchasers there.
5. Lit. 'puts him aside'—and leaves him speechless.
6. Ezra IV, 6 and 21; this identifies Ahasuerus with Artaxerxes [king of Persia (r. 465–425 BCE); Ahasuerus is usually identified with his predecessor, Xerxes (r. 486–465 BCE)—editor's note].
7. So overjoyed was he at hindering the building of the Temple that he displayed all his treasures for 180 days.
8. That he spent on his militia and regalia.
9. By this quiet stroke, God effectively converted all his joy into grief. [According to the book of Esther, Vashti was Ahasuerus's first wife, repudiated by him for disobedience—editor's note.]

symbol for all the miracles and wonders which were to be performed for Israel throughout the generations.

* * *

# AL-THAʿLABĪ

While biblical figures and those from pre-Islamic lore populate the entire Qurʾān, the narrative segments about them are usually brief and elliptical. With the exception of the story of Joseph in Sūra Yūsuf (Q 12), there is no extended account of any of these earlier prophets and messengers. Rather, the qurʾānic references to prophets such as Abraham, Moses, and Jesus seem to presuppose an audience already familiar with their histories. As Islam spread beyond its original environment, the need to clearly identify and further elaborate the qurʾānic mentions generated a genre of storytelling called the "tales of the prophets" (*qiṣaṣ al-anbiyāʾ*).

Aḥmad ibn Muḥammad al-Thaʿlabī (d. 1035) was born in Nishapur, Iran, a thriving intellectual and cultural center of the Islamic empire that was eventually destroyed by Mongol invaders. In its glory days Nishapur counted among its illustrious inhabitants such figures as the great statesman Niẓām al-Mulk (ca. 1018–1092) and the poet and astronomer ʿOmar Khayyām (1048–1131). Al-Thaʿlabī, who eventually settled in Baghdad, won renown for writing one of the most important works of medieval commentary on the Qurʾān. While praising his expertise in exegesis, his biographers also laud his skill in literary genres beyond the strictly religious sciences. In addition, he was a powerful preacher and wove both qurʾānic and extra-qurʾānic material into sermons that sought to promote sound moral attitudes and actions. The same motivation underlies al-Thaʿlabī's collection of stories about the pre-Islamic prophets.

These selections from al-Thaʿlabī's *Lives of the Prophets* profile the prophet Abraham. One collection of narratives links the initial construction of the Kaʿba in Mecca to the first prophet, Adam, and describes how Abraham and his son Ishmael are entrusted with its later restoration and receive instruction on the *hajj* rituals from the angel Gabriel. Another set of stories recounts God's testing of Abraham by commanding that he sacrifice his son and then rescinding that command at the crucial instant.

## *From* Lives of the Prophets†

### *The Story of the Sacrifice, A Description of It, And What Abraham Did to His Son*

Al-Suddī[1] said, quoting his chain of authorities, (that) when Abraham, the Friend of God, fled his people and went to Syria, taking his creed with him, as the Lord has said, *And he said, "I am going away to my Lord Who will show me the way."*[2] He prayed to God to give him a pious son from

† From *"ʿArāʾis al-Majālis fī Qiṣaṣ al-Anbiyāʾ" or "Lives of the Prophets": As Recounted by Abū Isḥaq Aḥmad ibn Muḥammad ibn Ibrāhīm al-Thaʿlabī*, trans. and annot. William M. Brinner (Leiden: Brill, 2002), pp. 158–61. Reprinted by permission of Koninklijke Brill NV. All cites to the Qurʾān are Brinner's, and all the brackets in the text are his.

1. Ismāʿīl ibn ʿAbd al-Raḥmān (d. 745), preacher and commentator on the Qurʾan from Kūfa (in central Iraq).
2. 37:99.

Sarah and he said, *"O Lord, grant me a righteous son."*[3] When he was visited by his guests, the angels who were sent as messengers to al-Muʾtafikah, the city to be destroyed, they gave him tidings of a gentle son, and Abraham said, "He is, therefore, a sacrifice to God." When the boy was born *"and was old enough to go about with him,"*[4] people said to Abraham, "Now fulfill your vow that you made and offer your sacrifice to the Lord." This was the reason for God's command to His friend Abraham to sacrifice his son. Thereupon Abraham said to Isaac, "Come, let us depart and sacrifice to God," and he took a knife and a rope, then went with him until he brought him into the mountains. Then the boy said to him, *"Father, where is your sacrifice?" He replied, "O my son, I have seen (arā) in a dream that I must sacrifice you"* that is, meaning, *"I saw" (raʾaytu)*. He spoke in the future (*arā*) but his meaning was the past. *"Consider, what do you think?" He said, "Father, do as you are commanded. If God pleases, you will find me steadfast."*[5]

According to Ibn Isḥāq,[6] when Abraham visited Hagar and Ishmael he was carried on al-Burāq.[7] He would set out from Syria in the morning, hold the midday rest in Mecca and return from Mecca to spend the night with his family in Syria. When Ishmael "*was old enough to go about with him*" and Abraham became attached to him and had high hopes for him, as one who would worship his Lord and enhance the grandeur of His holy places, he saw in a dream that he was sacrificing him. After he was commanded to do so, he said, "My dear son, take the rope and the knife, let us go to this trail to gather firewood." When Abraham was alone with his son on the trail of Mount Thabīr, Abraham told him what he was ordered to do and said, *"My dear son, I have seen in a dream that I was sacrificing you. [Consider, what do you think?]"*[8]

And his son, whom he was about to sacrifice, said to him, "Father, bind me firmly so that I do not move about, and hold your garments away from me lest my blood splash them (which would lessen my reward), and lest my mother see them and be saddened. Sharpen your blade and pass your knife quickly over my throat so death will be easier for me. For death is harsh. When you come to my mother, give her my greetings, and return my shirt to her, if you think that this may comfort her for me." Abraham said to him, "How excellent is the Helper! My son, you are fulfilling what God has commanded." Abraham did as his son bade him. He bound him up, bent over him and kissed him while he was weeping and the son was weeping so their tears followed each other down his checks. Then he placed the knife on his throat, but he did not cut, nor did the knife do anything.

Al-Suddī relates that God cast a flat, thin sheet of copper over his throat, whereupon the boy said, "Father, turn me face down, for if you look into my face you will have mercy on me, and be overcome by compassion that will stand between you and God's commandment." Abraham did as he was asked, for that is His word, *When they submitted to the will of God and Abraham laid him down prostrate upon his brow.*[9] Then he placed the knife

3. 37:100.
4. 37:102.
5. 37:102.
6. Early Muslim authority upon whose work many later historians relied (ca. 704–767); see above.
7. The miraculous horse that the Prophet is said to have ridden on his ascent to heaven. Ishmael (Ismāʿīl) was Abraham's son borne by his wife's servant, Hagar.
8. 37:102. In Islamic tradition, Mount Thabīr is understood as the place where Ibrāhīm (Abraham) attempted to sacrifice his son.
9. 37:103.

on his nape, but the knife turned over and a voice called out to him, "*Abraham, you have fulfilled your dream. [Thus do We reward the good.]*[1] Here is what you should sacrifice as a ransom for your son, so sacrifice it instead of him." When Abraham looked up behold, there was Gabriel with a ram: white and black, with horns, the ram glorified (God), as did Abraham and Ishmael, for that is His word, "*So We ransomed him for a great sacrifice*."[2]

Saʿīd b. Jubayr[3] and others have said, on the authority of Ibn ʿAbbās,[4] that the ram came to Abraham from the Garden, having pastured there for forty autumns. Ibn ʿAbbās is also quoted as saying, "The ram that redeemed Abraham's son was the same that Abel, the son of Adam, sacrificed and was accepted from him. Abraham sent away his son to fetch the ram, then took it to the slaughtering-place of Minā and slaughtered it. By Him Who holds Ibn ʿAbbās' soul in his hand, this was in the early days of Islam, but the head of the ram is still hanging by its two horns from the water-spouts of the Kaʿbah,[5] and it had dried up.'"

ʿAmr b. ʿUbayd—al-Ḥasan[6]—his father, who was saying, "It was a female mountain goat by which Ishmael was ransomed: it was sent down to him near Mount Thabīr." This is the narration of Abū Ṣāliḥ—Ibn ʿAbbās, who said it was a mountain goat. Abū Hurayrah[7]—Kaʿb al-Aḥbār[8] and Ibn Isḥāq, quoting some men as saying that when Abraham saw in his dream that he was to sacrifice his son, Satan said, "By God, either I seduce the family of Abraham in this way, or I shall never be able to seduce any of them." So Satan presented himself to them as a man and came to the mother of the boy and said to her, "Do you know where Abraham took your son?" She replied, "He took him to gather firewood on this trail." He told her, "I swear that he took him for no other purpose than to sacrifice him." She said, "Certainly not! He is kinder to him than I, and loves him too much for such a deed." He said to her, "He claims that God commanded him." She said to him, "If this is true, he is right to continue on the path of obedience and submission to his Lord's command."

So Satan left her in a great hurry and caught up with the son, who was walking in his father's footsteps. He said to him, "Lad, do you know where your father is taking you?" He replied, "To gather wood for our family on this trail." He said, "No, by God, he wants to sacrifice you!" He asked, "Why?" He replied, "He claims that God commanded him to do so." He said to him, "Then let him follow God's command, for we must hear and obey the Lord." When the boy turned him down, Satan approached Abraham and said to him, "Where are you going, old man?" He replied, "I have something to do on that trail over there." He said, "By God, I think that Satan has come to you in your dream and commanded you to sacrifice this son of yours." But Abraham recognized him and said to him, "Get away

1. 37:105.
2. 37:107.
3. Kūfan scholar who was beheaded for having revolted against the Umayyad empire (d. 711/12).
4. A Companion of the Prophet and one of the greatest scholars of early Islam (ca. 619–687/88).
5. The Kaʿba (literally, "cube"), the stone shrine in Mecca, believed to have been built by Adam and then rebuilt by Abraham and Ishmael; central to both early pagan and Muslim pilgrimage rituals, it became the most important site in Islam.
6. Al-Ḥasan al-Baṣrī (d. 728), a famous scholar of the generation born just after the death of Muḥammad; he was often claimed by the Ṣūfīs as a spiritual authority.
7. Abū Hurayra (d. ca. 678), an impoverished early Companion who related many ḥadīth and eventually rose to (and was deposed from) the position of governor of Baḥrayn.
8. A Yemeni Jewish convert with extensive knowledge of biblical stories and legends (d. 652/53).

from me, cursed one! In the name of my God, I shall go forth to fulfill the command of my Lord." So Iblīs the cursed left in a great hurry, not having achieved anything that he wanted from Abraham and his family, for they had turned him down with God's help and assistance.

Abū l-Ṭufayl[9] quotes Ibn ʿAbbās as saying that when Abraham was commanded to sacrifice his son, Iblīs appeared to him at the pilgrimage station of al-Muzdalifah and tried to get ahead of him, but Abraham left him behind. Then he went to the western heap of stones, but Satan appeared to him there too, and Abraham threw seven stones at him and he went away. Then he appeared to him at the middle stone-heap, and again he threw seven pebbles at him until he left.[1] Thereafter Satan caught up with him at the large stone heap, but Abraham chased him away. Then Abraham set on his way to fulfill God's command, and this is the story of the sacrifice. Umayyah b. Abī Ṣalt[2] composed a poem about this story:

*And to Abraham, who kept the vow, willing to sacrifice,*
*I swear by Him Who praises selfless giving.*
*His own first-born son, he would never endure giving him up,*
*Not even if he had seen him in the troop of enemies.*
*"My son! I have vowed to slaughter you as an offering to the Lord so be steadfast, for I have no other way.*
*Be strong when I must draw the knife, as a prisoner is forced to drag his chains."*
*He had a knife which, as it moves, cuts into the flesh, vying for glory with a lad whose brow was like the new moon.*
*As he was pulling his garments away from his son, his Lord redeemed him with a ram fit for sacrifice.*
*"Fetch this one as a ransom for your son, for I surely do not dislike what the two of you have done."*
*Human souls often grieve at some matter that has a joyous end,*
*As if you are freed from your chains.*

## RABGHŪZĪ

Nāṣir al-Dīn ibn Burhān al-Dīn Rabghūzī was born in Transoxiana (western Turkestan) in the second half of the thirteenth century. The year of his death is likewise unknown, but the work that made him famous, *The Stories of the Prophets*, can be dated: his introduction to it notes its completion in 1310. Rabghūzī also tells the reader that the work was composed at the request of a Mongol prince, suggesting that he maintained good relations with the ruling elite of the Chaghatay khanate.

Rabghūzī's *Qiṣaṣ al-anbiyāʾ* combines qurʾānic commentary and ḥadīth with popular stories, epic themes, and poetry. As one of the few surviving prose works in the Khwarezmian Turkish literary language, it is of great interest to scholars of Turkish literature and linguistics. Rabghūzī drew on a tradition of religious works written in Turkish, including existing versions of the "tales of the prophets" genre. Though scholars have speculated about the connection between Rabghūzī's composition and earlier Arabic and Persian collections of such prophet stories, they have not been able to draw clear lines of textual influence.

9. A Companion of the Prophet (d. ca. 718).
1. This action is commemorated by pilgrims during the *ḥajj*, as they throw stones in a key ritual.
2. Pre-Islamic Arab poet (d. ca. 631).

This selection from Rabghūzī's *Stories of the Prophets* relates a story about the prophet Job, a figure of affliction also well known from the book in the Hebrew Bible that bears his name. Job's name (in Arabic, Ayyūb) is included among those listed as prophets in the Qur'ān (Q 6:83–90 and 4:163), but more specific elements of his story appear in Q 21:83–84 and Q 38:41–44.

## *From* The Stories of the Prophets†

At the edge of the city Job saw a person who was suffering; his flesh and body were covered with holes. He had sat down [before a house] intending to beg for something from the city's ruler when he passed by. The owner of the house said to the wretch: "Get out of my sight. I can't stand your stench any longer." Just then Job arrived. The poor wretch told Job: "I am at the roadside in the hope that the king may give me something when he passes by. This man tells me to go away from here." Job asked the other person: "Why are you telling this poor fellow to go away?" The man said: "He has been sitting on my doorstep for one year. I can't stand his stench any longer. I have told him to sit somewhere else for a month." Job said: "What he says is right. You have been sitting here for a year; sit somewhere else for a while." The poor wretch said: "This misfortune has been decreed for me by the judicious Lord." When Job had gone, the poor man said: "My Lord, afflict this messenger of Yours with a kind of misfortune that shows no mercy to anyone. My God, though Your messenger didn't have mercy on me, You at least show me mercy." When he had uttered this prayer, the Lord, *He is exalted*, granted him well-being. He stood up and went his way.

Gabriel arrived and said: "Oh Job, the Lord has deigned to ask: 'Why didn't you show mercy to that wretch?'" Job knew that the Lord, *He is exalted*, was reproaching him. He stood up and walked through the entire city of Nineveh.[1] Wherever he saw sick or afflicted persons, he assembled them all and offered them a meal by way of atonement. But it was of no avail.

It has been related: The prophet Job was very devoted to the Lord, *He is mighty and glorious*, and he was kind to the hungry and the naked. He had a farm with five hundred yoke of oxen. For each pair of oxen he owned one male and one female slave. Besides that, four hundred of his slaves traded with the help of four hundred donkeys. His wealth and affluence were unlimited. He didn't know the number of his male and female slaves. Job himself was of tall stature; he had a large head, attractive eyes and strong wrists. On his forehead was written: *The Patient Sufferer*. Job spent his life worshipping the Lord both day and night, and offering Him thanks. Meanwhile no one converted to the faith, exept for three men. One of them was a Yemenite called Narīf, the second was named Baldū and the third was called Sākhir. The latter two were from Nineveh. All three of them were old men.

The prophet Job was ninety-three years old. He had a son named Ḥaumal, who had a son named Bishr. The Lord, *He is exalted*, granted Bishr prophethood; and they say he was Dhū l-Kifl. But there is disagreement

† From Al-Rabghūzī, *The Stories of the Prophets: Qiṣaṣ al-Anbiyā': An Eastern Turkish Version*, trans. H.E. Boeschoten, J. O'Kane, and M. Vandamme (Leiden: Brill, 1995), 2:288–93. Reprinted with permission of Koninklijke Brill NV. All brackets in the text are the translators'.

1. An ancient Assyrian city on the east bank of the Tigris River.

about his being a prophet. Bishr's son was called ʿAbdān. Then after that Shuʿaib became a prophet.

The [A]mmārite scholars have related: The prophet Job had seven sons and seven daughters. Some have related: There are also those who say he had three sons and seven daughters.

Because Job's good deeds were so numerous, Satan envied him. Satan said: "My God, Job is obedient to you in affluence. He would not be obedient otherwise." The Lord, *He is exalted*, declared: "Oh cursed one, I hand over to you Job's prosperity." Satan went out in the countryside. He blew once from his mouth; from his mouth came fire. All Job's camels, oxen and sheep were consumed by it. Satan then took on the appearance of a camel-driver or a shepherd and, going before Job, he said: "Oh Job, all your camels, your oxen and your sheep have been destroyed; they have been burned." Job said: "The Lord has given and the Lord has taken away. Had you been any good, you would have been burned as well." The next day Satan returned and blew out of his mouth. All Job's grain was burned. Satan then took on the appearance of a farmer and went before Job: "Oh Job, all your grain has been burned." Job said: "Had you been any good, you would have been burned as well." The third day Satan destroyed all Job's male and female slaves. He came and told Job this. Job gave him the same answer as before. When he couldn't deal with Job's patience, Satan ascended to heaven.—At that time the demons could ascend to heaven. Since our Prophet Muḥammad the Chosen One was born of his mother, the demons can no longer do this and they stay down below.

Satan said: "My God, he can bear the loss of whatever cattle and livestock he possesses, but he will not be able to bear the loss of his sons and daughters. Give me power over his children." God declared: "I have given you the power." Job's fourteen sons and daughters were sitting in the palace with their teacher, reading books. Satan came and pulled away the palace's wooden props. The palace collapsed, and the children and their teacher remained beneath the rubble and died. Assuming the appearance of a schoolmaster, Satan went before Job and said: "Why are you worshipping? Come and have a look at your children. See how their bones are broken, how their brains flow out of their noses, how their eyes protrude. They have all fallen on their faces, and are lying under stone and dirt." Job repeated his previous reply. Once again Satan ascended to heaven and said: "My God, he bears the loss of any human being. But if his own body were afflicted, he would not bear it. Give me a free hand over Job's body." God declared: "I have given you a free hand." But whatever Satan did to Job, he couldn't break him. When Job lifted his bowed head during prayer, Satan blew a cold wind from his mouth into Job's face. Job felt comfort from that wind. Satan lifted Job's face upwards and struck his face once more with that wind. Satan's breath spread through Job's entire body, from his head to his feet. His flesh and body swelled up and began to itch. From each blister two worms appeared, one male and one female. They began to eat Job's flesh.

It has been related: There were two of these worms. Some have related: There were a thousand. Some have related: There were two thousand. And yet others have related: Their offspring increased to six thousand, and then to forty thousand. The worms ate his flesh and body; apart from his bones nothing remained. When they became hungry, the worms ate each other, and six thousand remained. After they had eaten each other this way, just two of them were left. Job's flesh stank. He had pupils who were studying with him; they ran away. They broke their pencils and burned their books. Only his wife Raḥma remained.

Satan arrived and called out: "Remove him from the city. Otherwise, he will infect all of you and you will perish." They removed him from the city and put him down in the shade at the foot of a wall. Later they took him away and put him in a mountain cave. During the daytime Raḥma went into town and cooked for the ladies there, and then she went and brought food for Job to eat. One day Satan mounted a high place in the city and called out: "Oh people, know that the wife of Job touches Job's blood and pus all day long. Then with her dirty hands she cooks meals and bread in your homes. This will bring you illness and disease." After that they didn't let Raḥma enter their homes. Then once again these worms increased to four thousand. The people exclaimed: "Oh Job, what a wicked deed you must have done for God to afflict you with such a misfortune."

It has been related: While a worm was eating of Job's flesh, it fell on the ground. The Lord gave it the power to speak. The worm said: "Oh Job, the Lord, *He is mighty and glorious*, has created us from you. Our daily bread rests with you." Job saw it and put it back in its place. When the worms fought while eating his flesh, Job would make peace amongst them, saying: "This food is yours. Eat it."

People would say: "Oh Job, can't you pray to the Lord, *He is mighty and glorious*, to deliver you from them?" Job replied: "Just as the Lord, *He is exalted*, has the power to send a calamity, so He has the might to remove it. When the proper time has come, He will do so."

It has been related: Once Satan took on the appearance of an old man and went before Job: "Oh Job, ask the Lord, *He is mighty and glorious*, to deliver you from the worms." Job said: "That is no concern of mine." Satan was sorely grieved and went away.

Again some people came and said: "Oh Job, we can't stand your stench any longer. Leave us!" Job replied: "I am unable to move. You must think of a way to take me away." They brought a rubbish basket, put Job in it and carried him out of the town. They made a shelter as wide as a millstone and set him down there. The worms ate away Job's flesh, muscles, veins and skin so vigorously that all his limbs were pierced. When the sun shone on one side of him, the light came out on the other side. None the less he worshipped the Lord, *He is mighty and glorious*. And his wife Raḥma went to the city of Nineveh to cook food and acquire food for Job to eat.

It has been related: Once Job, *peace be upon him*, said to Raḥma: "Oh Raḥma, womenfolk can bear up when there is affluence. But it is sometimes the case that they cannot bear misery. My suffering increases from day to day. If you find this hard to endure, I will divorce you. Or else I will transfer to you the right to divorce me. Whenever you wish you may have a divorce. In any case when I die, you will be delivered. But if the Lord grants me health, you can come back if you wish." Raḥma wept when she heard this. Then she replied: "Oh messenger of the Lord,[2] I stayed with you in affluence and comfort; how can I abandon you now that suffering has befallen you? I will not part from you until death separates us." Job said: "Oh Raḥma, I am content with you. May you be content with me."

2. A common title in the Qur'ān for a prophet.

Raḥma got up and went to the town. Satan assumed the appearance of a physician and approaching her, he said: "Bring me to Job, I will treat his disease." Raḥma brought Satan to Job and said: "I have brought a physician. He says he will treat you." Job replied: "This misfortune has been inflicted on me by the Lord. If He wishes, He will take it back. I have no need of a physician." Satan went away. When Raḥma went to town, she met him again, with a different appearance. He had wrapped a cotton cloth around his shoulders. Raḥma asked: "And who are you there?" He said: "I am God. I was angry at you and at Job, and therefore I have inflicted this misfortune on him. Now I order you to prostrate yourself before me once." Raḥma said: "I didn't know there was a god on earth." Satan said: "Do you want me to bring the livestock and cattle back to life? That way you will know that I am God." Just then the demons took on the appearance of cows and gathered together. Raḥma saw them. Satan asked: "Now do you believe that I am God?" And he said: "Prostrate yourself, and I will give them to you. I will deliver Job from his trial." Raḥma said: "I will tell this to Job first." Job was greatly displeased and said: "Oh Raḥma, that is Satan." Raḥma went and asked: "Are you Satan?" Satan replied: "Begone! You are free of me."

# INTERPRETATIONS AND ANALYSIS

# Classical and Modern Commentary

## AL-TUSTARĪ

Born in Tustar (in Persian, Shushtar) in southwestern Iran, Abū Muḥammad ibn ʿAbdallāh Sahl al-Tustarī (818–896) was an influential figure in the history of Islamic mysticism. His uncle introduced him to the formal study of his religion, overseeing his instruction in the fundamental areas of Islamic learning. For two decades, al-Tustarī adopted a rigorously ascetical lifestyle of Ṣūfī practices and devoted himself to the cultivation of his inner life. In midlife he began to accept disciples and to instruct them in his teachings. Among his most famous followers was the mystic al-Ḥusayn ibn Manṣūr al-Ḥallāj (ca. 858–922), who was cruelly executed after being accused of heresy. About twenty years before his death, al-Tustarī moved from Tustar to Baghdad, where he lived for the rest of his life.

Al-Tustarī's Qur'ān commentary, like his other writings, comes not from his own hand but from the memories and notes of his disciples. His exegetical reflections attended both to the literal, or outer, meaning and to the inner, allegorical sense. Examples of both interpretive modes may be found in the following selections from his *Tafsīr al-Qur'ān al-ʿaẓīm* (*Commentary on the Mighty Qur'an*). Often, as in his discussion of Q 55:19, he links a verse with phases on the mystic's path to enlightenment. Later Ṣūfī scholars, such as Abū Abd al Raḥmān al-Sulamī (ca. 940–1021), relied heavily on al-Tustarī's interpretations in drawing their own insights from the sacred text.

### *From* Tafsīr al-Tustarī†

#### 55 *Al-Raḥmān*

His words, Exalted is He:
[55:4] *and taught him [coherent] speech* (bayān).
He said:

> This means: He has taught him [mankind] speech (*kalām*) which pertains to the spiritual self (*nafs al-rūḥ*), understanding of the intellect (*fahm al-ʿaql*), discernment of the heart (*fiṭnat al-qalb*), natural intuition (*dhihn al-khulq*) and knowledge of the natural self (*ʿilm nafs al-ṭab*'). God granted Adam this [knowledge] through inspiration and then explained (*bayyana*) it to him.

† From Sahl b. ʿAbd Allāh al-Tustarī, *Tafsīr al-Tustarī*, trans. Annabel Keeler and Ali Keeler (Louisville, KY: Fons Vitae; Amman, Jordan: Royal Aal al-Bayt Institute for Islamic Thought, 2011), pp. 216–17, 318–19. Reprinted by permission of Fons Vitae. Except as indicated, all notes are the Keelers'; all brackets in the text are the Keelers'.

His words, Exalted is He:
[55:7] . . . *and has set up the balance,*
He said:

> Its inner meaning refers to commandments and prohibitions governing the bodily members [of a person].

His words, Exalted is He:
[55:17] *He is Lord of the two risings and Lord of the two settings.*
He said:

> Its inner meaning refers to the rising of the heart and its setting, the rising of the tongue and its setting, and the rising of the profession of His oneness, [whose] setting is the witnessing (*mushāhada*) of Him. And He also says, *[I swear] by the Lord of the risings and the settings* [70:40], meaning the risings of the bodily members through sincerity (*ikhlāṣ*), and their settings through subservience to people (*ṭāʿa liʾl-nās*) inwardly and outwardly.

His words, Exalted is He:
[55:19] *He has loosed the two seas, and they meet.*[1]
He said:

> One of these seas is the heart, which contains a variety of gems: the gem of faith, the gem of gnosis (*maʿrifa*), the gem of realising God's oneness, the gem of contentment (*riḍā*), the gem of love (*maḥabba*), the gem of longing (*shawq*), the gem of sorrow (*ḥuzn*), the gem of neediness [for God] (*faqr*), and other [gems]. The other sea is the self (*nafs*).

His words, Exalted is He:
[55:20] *Between them is a barrier [that] they do not overstep.*

> This is divine protection (*ʿiṣma*) and divinely-bestowed success (*tawfīq*).

His words, Exalted is He:
[55:46] *But for whosoever feared the standing [before] their Lord, there will be two gardens,*
Labīd[2] said:

> [Such a one] was on the point of [committing] a transgression, but then recalled the time when he will stand before God, Exalted is He, on the Day of Reckoning and refrained from that.
>
> I heard [the story of] a young man during the era of the caliphate of ʿUmar[3] who was endowed with beauty and had a striking appearance. ʿUmar was impressed with the young man and sensed that much good [would come] from him. One day the youth encountered a woman to

1. In his *Jāmiʿ al-bayān*, Ṭabarī presents a few possible interpretations of what the two seas might be, such as one sea being the Mediterranean Sea (Baḥr al-Rūm) and the other, the Persian Gulf (Baḥr al-Fārs). However, Ṭabarī prefers the view given in the majority of traditions that the two seas are the earthly and heavenly seas (*baḥr al-arḍ wa-baḥr al-samāʾ*). [On *The Comprehensive Clarification* (better known as his *Commentary on the Qurʾān*) by Abū Jaʿfar Muḥammad ibn Jarīr al-Ṭabarī (ca. 839–923), see below—editor's note.]
2. Perhaps this is Abū ʿAqil b. Rābiʿa Labīd (d. 40/661). The editor of the Dār al-Kutub al-ʿIlmiyya edition notes, however, that this tradition is attributed to Mujāhid in Aḥmad b. Ḥanbal's *Kitāb al-Waraʿ* (Beirut, 1983), p. 115.
3. ʿUmar ibn al-Khaṭṭāb (ca. 586–644), the second caliph (633–44) [editor's note].

whom he took a fancy. However, as soon as he was on the point of committing an indecent act, the divine protection descended upon him and he fell down on his face in a swoon. The woman then carried him to his house. He had a father who was an old man and it was his wont when evening fell to sit in front of his door waiting for his son's return. When the old man saw him he also fell into a swoon. When he regained his senses he asked his son about his condition. So he recounted the story, but then suddenly yelled with one cry and fell down dead. After he was buried ʿUmar stood up and recited over his grave: *But for whosoever feared the standing [before] their Lord, there will be two gardens*, upon which he [the young man] cried to him from the grave, 'God has given them to me and has granted me a third along with them.'

His words, Exalted is He:
[55:56] *In them are maidens of restrained glances . . .*
He said:

That is, they lower their gaze to all except their husbands. Thus whoever restrains his glances in this world from that which is forbidden and dubious, and from sensual delights and their attraction, will find that God grants him in Paradise maidens restraining their glances just as He has promised.

His words, Exalted is He:
[55:72] *Houris, secluded in pavilions.*

That is, kept in seclusion in pavilions. It was related from Muḥammad b. Sawwār,[4] on the authority of his chain of transmission, that Abū Mūsā al-Ashʿari[5] related that the Prophet said, 'Verily the believer will have in Paradise a pavilion made of white pearl, thirty miles in length, in which there are many inhabitants but they do not see one another.

*113 Al-Falaq*

His words, Exalted is He:
[113:1] *Say, 'I seek refuge in the Lord of the Daybreak,*
He said:

Truly God, Exalted is He, commanded him [the Prophet] in these two *sūras* [113 and 114] to take refuge (*iʿtiṣām*) in Him, seek help (*istiʿāna*) from Him, and show [his] need (*faqr*) for Him.

He was asked, 'What is showing [one's] need?' He replied:

It is the [substitution of one] state by another (*huwa'l-ḥāl bi'l-ḥāl*), for the natural disposition (*ṭabʿ*) is dead [in and of itself] and its life is in displaying this.[6]

He also said:

The best form of purification (*ṭahāra*)[7] is that the servant purifies himself from [the illusion of] his own power (*ḥawl*) and strength (*quwwa*).

4. The maternal uncle of al-Tustarī, from whom he received his basic education [editor's note].
5. A Companion of the Prophet (d. ca. 667); he later served as governor of first Basra and then Kūfa [editor's note].
6. Presumably what is meant here is that by displaying or acknowledging its neediness, life in the remembrance of God will be substituted for the death of our natural state.
7. The word *ṭahāra* is used in Islamic law to signify ritual purity.

Every act or saying that is not accompanied by the words: 'there is no power or strength save in God', will not have God's support, Mighty and Majestic is He. Furthermore, every saying which is not accompanied by the proviso,[8] will incur a punishment for [the person who said it], even if it was an act [or saying] of righteousness. And for every affliction (*muṣība*) which is received without being accompanied by the saying of 'return' (*istirjāʿ*),[9] the afflicted person will not be given steadfastness when facing it [affliction] on the Day of Resurrection.

He said:

According to Ibn ʿAbbās,[1] *al-falaq* means the morning (*subḥ*) while according to al-Ḍaḥḥāk[2] it refers to a valley in the Hellfire. [On the other hand], according to Wuhayb[3] it refers to a chamber in Hell, and according to Ḥasan[4] it refers to a well in Hell.

It has also been said that He intended by it all people (*iamīʿ al-khalq*). Or it has been said that it refers to the rock from which water springs forth.[5]

[113:2] *from the evil of that which He has created,*

from man and jinn.[6] This is because Labīd b. Aʿṣam al-Yahūdī cast into the well of Banū Bayāḍa a spell against the Prophet, who used to frequent it. [One day as] he headed towards [the well] the spell [cast against him] possessed him and the Prophet became affected by it, so God sent down the two *sūras* of seeking refuge (*muʿawwidhatayn*)[7] and the Angel Gabriel informed him of the magic spell. Then he sent two men among the Companions to [the well] and they took it [the knot] out of the well. They brought it to the Prophet, upon which he started to untie the knot reciting the verses the while, so that the Messenger was cured without delay after having completed the two *sūras*.

After this occurrence, Labīd used to go to the Prophet but he did not see any trace of [his spell] on the face of the Prophet, neither did he mention to him [what he had done].[8]

[113:3] *and from the evil of darkness when it gathers,*

That is to say, when night falls, or it has been said that it means when the darkness intensifies. It has also been said [that it means]: when night first encroaches on [lit. 'penetrates,' *dakhala*] the day, [that is],

8. Lit. 'exception' (*istithnāʾ*), that is, the proviso of saying 'God willing'.
9. *Istirjāʿ* being the utterance of the words: 'Truly, we belong to God and truly to Him we will return' (*innā liʾ Llāhi wa-innā ilayhi rājiʿūn*), which words are customarily said on hearing of the death of someone.
1. One of the greatest scholars of early Islam (ca. 619–687/88); he is often considered the founder of the qurʾānic exegetical tradition [editor's note].
2. Al-Ḍaḥḥāk ibn Muzāḥim al-Hilālī (d. 723/24), collector of ḥadīth and Qurʾān interpreter [editor's note].
3. Wuhayb b. al-Ward (d. 153/770).
4. Al-Ḥasan al-Baṣrī (642–728), a famously pious leader of early Islam [editor's note].
5. Most of these explanations of *al-falaq* may be found in Ṭabarī's *Jāmiʿ al-bayān*, as well as the opinion that it is a prison (*sijn*) within Hell, or that it is one of the names of Hell.
6. The third class of intelligent beings (together with humans and angels) for whom salvation is possible. According to Q 55:15, God created them from smokeless fire [editor's note].
7. Sūras 113 (*al-Falaq*) and 114 (*al-Nās*).
8. Bukhārī, *Ṣaḥīḥ*, 'Kitāb al-Ṭibb'. [Muḥammad ibn Ismāʿīl al-Bukhārī (810–870), one of the great compilers of ḥadīth whose main work was *Al-Jāmiʿ al-Ṣaḥīḥ* (*The Authentic Collection*); "Kitāb al-Ṭibb" means "Book of Medicine"—editor's note.]

when night is just beginning, devils among the jinn are released and anyone who is afflicted in that hour will not recover.

Sahl [also] said regarding *and from the evil of darkness when it gathers*:

Its inner meaning refers to remembrance, when regard for the self enters it, thereby screening it from sincerity towards God in the remembrance [purely] of Him.

[113:3] *and from the evil of the women-blowers*,

That is, the sorceresses who blow on knots.

[113:5] *and from the evil of the envier when he envies.*'

This means the Jews who envied the Prophet to the point that they practised sorcery against him.[9] Ibn ʿAbbās said: In this verse [is a reference to] the lower self of a human being [lit. son of Adam] ⌜and his eye (*wa ʿaynuhu*)⌝.

# AL-QUMMĪ

ʿAlī ibn Ibrāhīm al-Qummī (d. after 919) is credited with the first full-scale Shīʿī commentary on the Qurʾān. The details of his life are unclear, but he is known to have been a contemporary of the eleventh Shīʿī imam, al-Ḥasan al-ʿAskarī, who died in 873. While al-Qummī's family was originally from Kūfa, his father moved them to Qumm, a city that was to become a renowned center of Shīʿī learning. The only extant piece of writing from al-Qummī's pen is his Qurʾān commentary, a work that is important not only in its own right but also for what it contains of earlier strata of Shīʿī exegesis.

This selection from *Tafsīr al-Qummī* provides the interpretation of Q 24:35, the famous "Light Verse." In making an explicit connection between the symbolic language of the verse and the family of the Prophet, al-Qummī clearly manifests the Shīʿī orientation of his commentary.

## Light of the Heavens and the Earth†

Ṣāliḥ b. Sahl al-Hamadānī said, 'I heard Abū ʿAbd Allāh [Jaʿfar al-Ṣādiq][1] commenting on *God is the light of the heavens and the earth; the likeness of His light is as a niche*, that the niche is Fāṭima,[2] *wherein is a lamp, the lamp*, that is al-Ḥasan and al-Ḥusayn,[3] *in a glass, the glass as it were a*

9. In his commentary on this verse, Ṭabarī includes, among others, the opinion that what is meant by *the one who envies* is the Jew, and the tradition he cites adds that it was merely on account of envy that the Jews did not believe [in Muḥammad's message]. However, Ṭabarī himself opts for the opinion that the Prophet is being commanded to seek refuge from the evil of anyone who envies, and he discounts the view that it is specifically intended to refer to the Jews.

† From *An Anthology of Quranic Commentaries*, vol. 1, *On the Nature of the Divine*, ed. Feras Hamza and Sajjad Rizvi, with Farhana Mayer (Oxford: Oxford University Press; London: in association with the Institute of Ismaili Studies, 2008), pp. 353–56. Reprinted by permission of Oxford University Press. Except as indicated, all notes are theirs, and all brackets in the text are theirs.

1. Jaʿfar ibn Muḥammad al-Ṣādiq (702–765), the sixth Shīʿī imam [editor's note].
2. Muḥammad's daughter (ca. 605 or 616–633) and the only one of his children to survive him. She married his cousin, ʿAlī ibn Abī Ṭālib (ca. 599–661), the fourth caliph but first in the line of Shīʿī imams [editor's note].
3. Al-Ḥasan (624/25–670) and al-Ḥusayn (626–680) were the sons of Fāṭima and ʿAlī ibn Abi Ṭālib and the second and third Shīʿī imams, respectively [editor's note].

*glittering star*, that is to say, Fāṭima as it were a glittering star from among all the women of the earth; *kindled from a blessed tree*, that is, kindled from Abraham; *neither of the east nor of the west*, that is to say, neither Jewish nor Christian; *whose oil well-nigh would shine*, that is, knowledge would well-nigh exude profusely from it; *even if no fire touched it; light upon light*, that is, from it one imam[4] [succeeds] after another; *God guides to His light whom He will*, that is, God guides to the imams whom He wants to include within the light of their friendship (*wilāya*) with sincere devotion; *and God strikes similitudes for humankind, and God has knowledge of everything.*

Jaʿfar b. Muḥammad [al-Ṣādiq] said that his father [Muḥammad al-Bāqir][5] said about this verse,

> *God is the Light of the heavens and the earth*: God begins by [mentioning] His own Light; *the likeness of His light*, that is, the likeness of His guidance in the heart of the believer is *as a niche wherein is a lamp, the lamp*: the niche is the inner part of the believer, the lantern (*qindīl*) is the heart, the lamp (*miṣbāḥ*) is the light that God has placed in that heart; *kindled from a blessed tree*, the tree is the believer; *an olive that is neither of the east nor of the west*: atop a mountain, [facing] neither towards the east nor the west, and unaffected by the rising or setting of the sun; *whose oil well-nigh would shine*, that is, the light which God has placed in the [believer's] heart would well-nigh shine, even if he [the believer] were not to speak; *light upon light*: one obligation (*farīḍa*) after another, and one *sunna* after another, *God guides to His light whom He will*, that is, God guides to His precepts (*farāʾiḍ*) and ways (*sunan*) whom He wishes; *and God strikes similitudes for humankind*: this then is a similitude which God has struck for the believer, for the believer is exposed to five stages of light: his way in is light, his way out is light, his knowledge is light, his speech is light, and his path on the Day of Resurrection to Paradise is light.

I [Ṭalḥa b. Zayd] said to Jaʿfar b. Muḥammad [al-Ṣādiq], 'For the sake of God, master, they keep talking about the "likeness" of the Lord's light'; He replied, 'Glory be to God, He has no likeness. He says *strike not any similitudes for God* [Q. 16:74].'

ʿAlī b. Ibrāhīm [al-Qummī the commentator] said, with regard to *God is the Light of the heavens and the earth* [to the end of the verse]: My father related to me from ʿAbd Allāh b. Jundub that he [the latter] wrote to Abūʾl-Ḥasan al-Riḍā[6] asking him about the interpretation of this verse; he wrote back to me with the following response:

> Muḥammad was God's trustee (*amīn*) among His creatures. When Muḥammad died, we the People of the House[7] became the trustees of God on earth.[8] We had knowledge of all tribulations and fates of death, the genealogies of the Arabs and the birth of Islam.[9] We knew

4. In Shīʿism, one who is in the line of succession from the prophet Muḥammad [editor's note].
5. The fifth Shīʿī imam (d. 735) [editor's note].
6. ʿAlī al-Riḍā (765 or 768–818), the eighth Shiʿī imam [editor's note].
7. Muḥammad's family [editor's note].
8. The Shīʿī tradition considers the imams of the family of the Prophet to be the true *khulafāʾ* or trustees/vicegerents of God on earth.
9. A key feature of the Shīʿī doctrine of the imamate is the claim of special knowledge, especially knowledge of the beginning of the world and its eschaton.

whether a man was truly a believer or truly a hypocrite just by seeing him. The names [of the followers] of our party (*shīʿatunā*) have already been written down, together with those of their fathers.[1] God has put us under an obligation: they go where we go and they enter the places we enter. None except them and us are [true] followers of the creed of Abraham, the Intimate of the Merciful One (*khalīl al-raḥmān*). On the Day of Resurrection, we shall seek a means of holding fast to our Prophet, our Prophet shall seek the means of obtaining access to his Lord, and this means is light, and our party shall seek aid from us.[2] Whoever separates himself from us shall perish, and whoever follows us shall find salvation; the one who rejects closeness to us is an unbeliever, but our party and those who affiliate with us are believers; only an unbeliever hates us, and all [true] believers love us. Whoever dies loving us, God is bound to resurrect him alongside us. We are light for those that follow us and light for those who follow our example. Whoever rejects us does not belong with us, and whoever does not belong with us, has nothing to do with Islam.

With us, God began [creation] and with us He shall seal it. Through us God has given you to eat from the plants of this earth, and through us God has brought down rain for you from the heavens. Through us God has made you safe from drowning at sea and from being swallowed up by the ground. Through us God brings you benefits during your lifetimes, in your graves, at the Gathering (*al-ḥashr*), the Bridge (*al-ṣirāṭ*), the Scales (*al-mīzān*) and when you enter the Paradise. Our likeness in the Book of God is as a niche (*mishkāt*), and the *mishkāt* is a [place for the] lantern (*qindīl*); so we are the niche, *therein is a lamp* (*miṣbāḥ*), the lamp being Muḥammad; *the lamp in a glass*: we are that glass; *the glass as it were a glittering star kindled from a blessed tree, an olive that is neither of the east nor of the west*, i.e., it is neither unrecognised nor an impostor; *whose oil*, i.e., its light; *well-nigh would shine, even if no fire touched it; light upon light*, the light of the Criterion [*al-furqān*, sc. the Qurʾān]; *God guides to His light*, i.e., to our friendship, *whom He will [and God is omnipotent]*,[3] in guiding to our friendship whom He likes. It is incumbent upon God to resurrect the person who has affiliated with us with his face bright and shining, his evidence glorious and his proof from God. It is incumbent upon God that our enemy on the Day of Resurrection should arrive with his face blackened and his proof before God invalid. It is incumbent upon God to make the person who has affiliated with us the companion of the prophets, just men, martyrs and the righteous: good companions they are [cf. Q. 4:69]. It is incumbent upon God to make our enemy the companion of satans and unbelievers: evil companions they are. The martyr among us has four times the merit of other martyrs, and the martyr from our followers has seven times the merit of martyrs of other [groups].

We are of noble descent, the sons of the trustees (*awṣiyāʾ*), the foremost of people in [worshipping] God; we are the loyal ones, the

1. This reflects the deterministic tone of much early Twelver Imāmī material. [Followers of Twelver Shīʿīsm revere twelve successive leaders of the house of ʿAlī ibn Abī Ṭālib; other branches recognize only five or seven imams—editor's note.]
2. The imams are guarantors of salvation and intercessors for their faithful.
3. The Qurʾānic citation in square brackets is not actually part of Q. 24:35.

ones designated in God's Book, and we are the most deserving among people of [knowing] God's religion; we are the ones to whom God prescribed His religion, as God said, *He has laid down for you as religion that He charged Noah with and that We have revealed to you* [Q. 42:13], O Muḥammad, and that with which He charged Abraham, Ishmael, Isaac and Jacob. We have acquired the knowledge, we have passed on what we have learnt, and we have given over the knowledge for safekeeping. We are the heirs of the prophets, and we are the progeny of the men of knowledge. *Perform the religion* through the family of Muḥammad, and *scatter not regarding it*, be in consensus; *dreadful for the idolaters*—those who have committed *shirk* [association][4] with regard to loyalty to ʿAlī b. Abī Ṭālib—*is that to which you summon them*, that is, associating with ʿAlī; *God*, O Muḥammad, *chooses unto Himself whomsoever He will, and He guides to Himself whosoever turns, penitent* [Q. 42:13], i.e., the one who heeds your call to affiliate with ʿAlī b. Abī Ṭālib.

## AL-ṬABARĪ

Muḥammad ibn Jarīr al-Ṭabarī (ca. 839–923) was born in Ṭabaristān, the last part of the Sassanian Empire to be incorporated under Muslim rule. He began his studies in his native city of Āmul, and then he pursued them in Baghdad and, eventually, other parts of Iraq, as well as Syria and Egypt. One of the giants of medieval Muslim learning, al-Ṭabarī wrote on a wide range of subjects with masterly authority. His two major works are a history of the world (see above) and a commentary on the Qurʾān. Both continue to be read, studied, and frequently reprinted, despite their massive size. *The History of Messengers and Kings* (*Taʾrīkh al-rusul wa-al-mulūk*) covers the span from the creation of the world to the years of al-Ṭabarī's own lifetime. His commentary, *The Comprehensive Clarification of the Interpretation of the Verses of the Qurʾān* (*Jāmiʿ al-bayān ʿan taʾwīl āy al-Qurʾān*), encompasses the entire exegetical enterprise as it stood in his day. But al-Ṭabarī did far more than collect what went before. By judging among competing interpretations and using multiple angles of exegetical analysis, he ensured a comprehensive approach to commentary that would set the standard for centuries to come.

Reprinted below is al-Ṭabarī's exegesis of part of the *Fātiḥa*, "The Opening," the first sūra of the Qurʾān. This sūra is an essential element in Muslim worship, repeated at least twice in each set of daily prayers. It also figures prominently in other aspects of Muslim life, such as ratifying contracts and confirming marriage arrangements. Al-Ṭabarī's commentary has been slightly abridged by the translator, and most of the lengthy chains of transmission (*isnād*s)—indicated by the use of arrows—have been shortened.

4. That is, the sin of associating ʿAlī with the attributes of God [editor's note].

# *From* The Opening of the Book†

### *1:1*

*al-ḥamdu li-'llāhi rabbi 'l-'ālamīna*

*Praise belongs to Allāh, the Lord of the worlds,*

THE INTERPRETATION OF *AL-ḤAMDU LI-'LLĀH*

¶ Gratitude (*shukr*) belongs entirely to God, exalted is His praise—and not to anything else besides Him that might be worshipped, nor to anything which He has created—for the incalculable bounties He has bestowed on His servants, incalculable⌜, that is,⌝ to anyone but Him. ⌜He has blessed them⌝ by bringing health to the organs ⌜of the body⌝ so that He might be obeyed, and by strengthening the limbs of the body with which His ordinances must be performed; ⌜and He has also blessed them with⌝ the sustenance He has set forth for them in this present life of theirs, and ⌜with⌝ the gift of nourishment by which He feeds them—without their having any right to claim it from Him—as well as ⌜with⌝ the means, of which He has informed them and to which He has called them, which will lead ⌜them⌝ to everlasting eternity in the abode of remaining in the abiding blessing. Therefore, for all this, praise (*ḥamd*) is due to our Lord, first and last.

( . . . )

⇒ Ibn 'Abbās:[1]

Gabriel said to Muḥammad, may God bless both of them: 'O Muḥammad, say «*al ḥamdu li-'llāh*».' ( . . . ) ⌜It⌝ means: Gratitude to God, subservience (*al-istikhdhā'*) to God, the attestation of His bounties, His guidance, His initiative, and so on.

⇒ al-Ḥakam b. 'Umair:

The Prophet said: 'When you say «*al ḥamdu li-'llāhi rabbi 'l-'ālamīn*», you thank God, and He increases your bounty.

It is said that *al-ḥamdu li-'llāh* implies praising God for His Most Beautiful Names and Attributes, whereas *al-shukru li-'llāh* implies praising God for His bounties and favours; and it has been narrated from Ka'b al-Aḥbār[2] that he said that *al-ḥamdu li-'llāh* meant praising God, although it was not made clear in what was narrated from him which of the two senses of 'praise' which we have mentioned he intended.

⌜⇒ Ka'b b. al-Aḥbār:⌝

Whoever says *al-ḥamdu li-'llāh* ⌜means by⌝ that 'praise (*thanā'*) to God'. [153]

† From Abū Ja'far Muḥammad B. Jarīr al-Ṭabarī, *The Commentary on the Qur'ān*, [trans.] and annot. J. Cooper, general eds. W. F. Madelung and A. Jones, vol. 1 (London: Oxford University Press, 1987), pp. 61–66.

1. 'Abdallāh ibn al-Ābbās (619–687/88), one of the greatest scholars of early Islam; he is often considered the founder of the qur'ānic exegetical tradition.
2. A Yemeni Jewish convert with extensive knowledge of biblical stories and legends (d. 652/53).

⇒ al-Aswad b. Sarīʿ:[3]

The Prophet said: 'There is nothing with which praise has more affinity than God, which is why He praises Himself and says «*al-ḥamdu li-ʾllāh*».'

There is no disagreement among specialists in the Arabic language about the correctness of saying '*al-ḥamdu li ʾllāhi shukran*'. Since they all agree on this, it is clear that *al-ḥamd* and *al-shukr* can be used interchangeably⌜, i.e., that they have the same meaning⌝, for . . . it is a definite mistake to extract an ⌜intensifying⌝ abstract noun from *al-ḥamd* which does not have the same meaning or is not the same word.

QUESTION: Why is the definite article, *al-*, attached to *ḥamd*, instead of *ḥamdan li-ʾllāhi rabbi ʾl-ʿālamīn*?

REPLY: The use of the definite article gives a meaning which is not rendered by *ḥamdan*—leaving the article out—because its inclusion serves to convey the meaning 'All ⌜kinds of⌝ praise and complete gratitude belong to God', while its omission would serve to indicate only that the praising of the speaker, not all praisings, belonged to God. Someone saying '*ḥamdan li-ʾllāh*', then, would mean 'I praise God'; but the interpretation of «*al-ḥamdu li-ʾllāhi rabbi ʾl-ʿālamīn*» at the head of the first sura (*umm al-kitāb*) is not this, but rather what we have previously described, viz.: All praise belongs to God for His divinity (*ulūhīya*) and His bestowal on His creatures of those bounties He has bestowed on them, for ⌜all of⌝ which there is no match in religion, in this world, now or in the future.

OBJECTION: What does God mean by saying 'All praise belongs to God'? Does God praise Himself, and then teach us ⌜these words⌝ so that we might say them exactly as He did? If so, why then should He have said «You only do we serve; to You alone we pray for succour» (1: 4) when He is the One who is served, not one who serves? Are these ⌜perhaps⌝ the words of Gabriel or Muḥammad, the Messenger of God? For they cannot be the words of God.

REPLY: Indeed, all this is the word of God. But He praised and extolled Himself in terms befitting Him, then He taught this to His servants and imposed the recitation of it on them, making it a test and a trial for them. So He said to them: 'Say «Praise belongs to Allāh, the Lord of the realms of being», and say «Thee only do we serve; to Thee alone we pray for succour».' . . .

QUESTION: Where does He say: 'Say!'? How can the interpretation be as you say?

REPLY: We have previously pointed out that it is one of the characteristics of Arabic, when the position of a certain word is known, and there is no doubt that the hearer can understand what is omitted from the ostensive wording, to omit what the explicit words can convey on their own, especially if the word omitted is an utterance or the interpretation of an utterance. . . . This is the case with the omission ⌜of 'Say: . . .'⌝ from God's

3. A poet who went on numerous raids with the Prophet (d. 662).

words «Praise belongs to Allāh, the Lord of the worlds», since what He meant by this can be known from His saying «Thee only do we serve», i.e., that He orders His servants ⌜to recite⌝; and the meaning of the ostensive wording is adequate to bring out what has been omitted.

We narrated above the tradition from Ibn ʿAbbās . . . ⌜in which⌝ Gabriel told Muḥammad: 'O Muḥammad, say «*al-ḥamdu li-'llāhi rabbi 'l-ʿālamīn*». . . . And we have explained that Gabriel only taught Muḥammad what he was ordered to teach him. This tradition vindicates what we have said about the interpretation of this ⌜verse⌝.

### THE INTERPRETATION OF *RABB*

. . . In the speech of the Arabs, *rabb* has several meanings. A master (*saiyid*) who is obeyed is called *rabb* (=lord, master) . . . ; a man who puts something in order, puts it right, is called *rabb* . . . ; and the possessor of something is called its *rabb*. . . . Our Lord (*rabb*) is the Master without peer: nothing is equal to His dominion, ⌜He⌝ is the One who arranges the affair⌜s⌝ of His creatures through the bounties which He liberally bestows on them, ⌜He is⌝ the Owner to whom the creation and the command belong. [⇒ Ibn ʿAbbās]

### THE INTERPRETATION OF *ʿĀLAMĪN*

*ʿĀlamūn* is the plural of *ʿālam* (=cosmos, world), which is itself a collective noun like 'mankind', 'group', or 'army'. . . . *ʿĀlam* is the noun ⌜which stands⌝ for the ⌜different⌝ kinds of communities—each kind is an *ʿālam*. The members of each generation of each kind are the *ʿālam* of that generation and that time. Mankind is an *ʿālam*, and all the people of a period of time are the *ʿālam* of that time. The jinn[4] are an *ʿālam*, and so on with the other species of creation; each species is the *ʿālam* of its time.

( . . . )

This is our opinion as well as that of Ibn ʿAbbās and Saʿīd b. Jubair;[5] it is the meaning of what the commentators as a whole say.

(. .)

⇒Ibn ʿAbbās:

*Rabb al-ʿālamīn*: the jinn and mankind.

(. .)

⇒ Abu 'l-ʿĀliya:[6]

Mankind is one *ʿālam*, the jinn another, and apart from these ⌜there are⌝ eighteen thousand, or fourteen thousand—he was not sure—*ʿālams* of angels over earth. Moreover, there are four corners of the earth, in each of which are three thousand five hundred *ʿālams* which He has created to worship Him.

4. The third class of intelligent beings (together with humans and angels) for whom salvation is possible. According to Q 55:15, God created them from smokeless fire.
5. Saʿīd ibn Jubayr (d. 711/12), scholar from Kūfa (in central Iraq) who was beheaded for taking part in a revolt against the Umayyad empire.
6. Scholar from Basra (in southeastern Iraq) who collected ḥadīth from Companions of the Prophet (d. 708/9 or 714).

*1:2*

*al-raḥmāni 'l-raḥīmi*

*the Merciful, the Compassionate,*

The interpretation of *al-raḥmān al-raḥīm* was given in the exegesis of the *basmala*,[7] so there is no need to repeat it here. Nor is there any need to explain why ⌜this phrase⌝ is repeated here, since we did not consider the *basmala* to be a verse⌜, and so there is no repetition⌝. . . . ⌜The erroneous suggestion that it is repeated⌝ . . . with one verse being so near the other . . . is proof for us of the error in supposing the *basmala* to be a verse. For if it were, there would indeed be a repetition of a single verse ⌜within the same sura⌝ with the same meaning in precisely the same formulation, twice, with no separation. Such a thing does not exist in the Book of God, . . . and there is no space between God's pronouncement of His Names, 'the Merciful', 'the Compassionate', in the *basmala* and His pronouncement of them ⌜afterwards in the first sura⌝.

*Is this an example of repetition in the Qur'ān?*

OBJECTION: But «Praise belongs to God, the Lord of the worlds» separates them.

REPLY: A number of commentators denied this, saying that here it is a case of reversed word order, and that the meaning is: Praise belongs to God, the Merciful, the Compassionate, the Lord of the worlds, the Sovereign over the Day of Reckoning. They cited His words «*maliki yaumi 'l-dīn* (=Sovereign over the Day of Judgement)» as evidence for the correctness of what they claimed, and said that by ⌜this⌝ . . . God teaches His servant to ascribe sovereignty—according to the recitation of those who recite *malik*—, or possession—according to the recitation of those who recite *mālik*—, to Him. They said that the most appropriate thing to which His Attribute of sovereignty, or possession, could be adjacent was that Attribute which is similar to it, and that is «Lord of the worlds», which informs about His possession of all the species of creatures. ⌜They also said⌝ that the most appropriate thing to which His Attribute of greatness and divinity could be adjacent is the praise of Him which is similar to it, and that is «the Merciful, the Compassionate». So they claimed that this was a proof for them that «the Merciful, the Compassionate,» comes prior in meaning to «Lord of the worlds», although ostensively it follows it. They argued that similar cases of this ⌜kind of inversion⌝ . . . are widespread in Arabic speech, quite beyond count.

§ Ṭabarī gives further examples of inversion; one is from poetry, and another is from the Qur'ān (18:1), where one word («*qaiyiman*») has been put after the position dictated by the meaning.

This is further evidence for the correctness of the opinion of those who deny that the ⌜*basmala*⌝ . . . of the first sura ⌜counts as⌝ a verse.

* * *

7. "In the name of God, the beneficent, the merciful" (Q 1:1), the phrase that appears at the beginning of each sūra except the ninth.

# IBN AL-JAWZĪ

Abū Faraj ʿAbd al-Raḥmān ibn al-Jawzī (1116–1200) was born and lived his entire life in Baghdad. It was a difficult century for the city (though worse was to come with the devastating Mongol invasion of 1258), but Ibn al-Jawzī benefited from its rich intellectual and cultural resources. He studied with many of the best scholars of his day and eventually achieved or exceeded their prominence in history, Ḥanbalī jurisprudence (one of the four schools of Islamic law), qurʾānic exegesis, and literary prose. His extraordinary skill as a preacher was captured for posterity by the Andalusian travel writer Abū al-Ḥusayn ibn Jubayr (1145–1217), who attended and left a vivid account of three of Ibn al-Jawzī's sermons.

Ibn al-Jawzī called his commentary *Provisions for the Journey in the Science of Exegesis* (*Zād al-masīr fī ʿilm at-tafsīr*), intending to equip its readers with the exegetical essentials rather than the elaborations found in the more encyclopedic commentaries. In his introduction, reprinted below, Ibn al-Jawzī explains his methods and presents several topics that are foundational to the study and interpretation of the Qurʾān.

## The Introduction to *Zād al-masīr fī ʿilm al-tafsīr*†

In the name of God, the merciful, the compassionate, praise be to God who has honored us over other peoples with the illustrious Qurʾān and has called us, by granting us sound judgment, to a rightly guided state of life. By it He has set our souls firmly between promise and threat and He has protected it from change made by the ignorant and alternation by the obdurate: "Falsehood cannot enter it from before or behind, a sending down from a wise, a praiseworthy One".[1]

I praise Him for making the highest praise possible and thank Him for actualizing the affirmation of divine unity. I bear witness that there is no god but God alone, who has no complement—an act of witness whose stored treasure is continuously reinforced—and that Muḥammad is His servant and His messenger, sent to those both near and far, a herald to created beings and a warner, a lamp in the cosmos shining. From His abundance He gave him much bounty and set him ahead of all others, making him great, with no human his equal. Yet he forbade anyone to pray in his name as a way of glorifying and honoring him. God sent down on him a spoken revelation and confirmed the authenticity of His word by challenging to the production of its equivalent: "Say, in truth, if humans and jinn[2] agree to produce the equivalent of this Qurʾān, they will not be able to do so, even if they were to back each other up", *al-isrāʾ* (17), 88. So may God bless him and his family and his Companions and Followers[3] and his wives and his adherents and grant them great peace.

† From Jane Dammen McAuliffe, "Ibn al-Jawzī's Exegetical Propaedeutic: Introduction and Translation," *Alif: Journal of Comparative Poetics*, no. 8 (Spring 1988): 106–13. Reprinted by permission of the publisher. All brackets in the text are from this article, as are notes marked "McAuliffe's note."

1. This is a quote from *sūrat al-Fuṣṣilat* (41), 42 although not acknowledged as such in the text [McAuliffe's note].
2. The third class of intelligent beings (together with humans and angels) for whom salvation is possible. According to Q 55:15, God created them from smokeless fire.
3. Members of the generation after those who personally accompanied the Prophet (the Companions); they are also called "the Successors."

Since the mighty Qur'ān is the noblest fund of knowledge, understanding its ideas is the most perfect form of understanding. This is because the degree of eminence of the act of knowing lies in the eminence of that which is known. Yet I have carefully examined a whole range of commentaries and have found them either so vast as to induce despair in the (would-be) memorizer or so short as to preclude the full attainment of one's purpose. Those of average size, too, are of little benefit, being poorly arranged and sometimes neglecting the problematic while explaining the obvious. Therefore I offer you this simple compendium, containing knowledge in plenty, and have designated it "Provisions for the Journey on the Science of Exegesis". I have striven to keep it short so try, to the extent of your God-given capacity, to memorize it. God it is who aids in its realization, for He has never ceased generously to offer success.

### *On the Pre-eminence of the Science of Exegesis*

Abū 'Abd al-Raḥmān al-Sulamī reported on the authority of Ibn Mas'ūd:[4] "We would learn from the Messenger of God ten verses of the Qur'ān and would not go on to the next ten until we knew what they contained in the way of knowledge and action". Qatādah[5] reported that al-Ḥassan said: "God has sent down no verse for which I would not want to know why it was sent and what was intended by it". Īyās b. Mu'āwiyah[6] said: "The situation of one who can recite the Qur'ān and who knows how to interpret it (as opposed to not so knowing), is like that of a group to whom there comes at night a written message from one of their comrades, but who are without a lamp. With the message's arrival, fear at not knowing what is in it overcomes them. But when the lamp is brought to them they (immediately) recognise what is in it".

Those educated in the religious sciences have held various views on whether the terms *al-tafsīr* and *al-ta'wīl*[7] have the same meaning or two different meanings. A group whose proclivities were linguistic held the view that the two meant the same thing. This is the opinion of the generality of earlier exegetes (*mufassirūn*). A group with primarily legal interests were persuaded that the two terms differed in meaning. They defined *al-tafsīr* as 'moving something out of concealment into full view' and *al-ta'wīl* as 'shifting discourse from its conventional signification to some allusion which may even neglect the literal sense of the utterance'. Lexically, the term *ta'wīl* is derived from the stem 'WL in a sense synonymous with the stem ṢWR, i.e., 'to lead to', 'to arrive at'.

### *On the Duration of the Qur'an's Descent*

'Ikrimah reported from Ibn 'Abbās[8] saying "On the Night of Power the Qur'ān was sent down from the Preserved Tablet to the House of Splendour

4. Abdallāh ibn Mas'ūd (d. 652/53), famed early Companion who was noted for his integrity. In addition to being a transmitter of hadith, he was an expert in the recitation of the Qur'ān and was said to have his own codex; many variants to the orthodox reading are attributed to him. Al-Sulamī (ca. 940–1021), Ṣūfī scholar.
5. Qatāda ibn Di'ama ibn Qatada al-Sadūsī (d. ca. 735), a blind Successor who relayed much early thought on qur'ānic exegesis.
6. Basran judge (d. ca. 739).
7. Both terms basically mean "interpretation."
8. 'Abdallāh ibn al-'Abbās (619–687/88), one of the greatest early Islamic scholars; he is often considered the founder of the qur'ānic exegetical tradition. 'Ikrima (d. 723/24) was his former slave and transmitted much of his teaching.

as a single unit. After that it was sent down over a period of twenty years". Al-Shaʿbī said "God divided up the Qurʾān's revelation so that there were twenty years between the beginning and the end of it". Al-Ḥasan said: "Someone told us that between the beginning and end of it were eighteen years, eight of those elapsing in Mecca".

There has been a difference of opinion about what part of the Qurʾan came down first. The traditional view affirms that the first part to come down was: "Recite in the name of your Lord", *al-ʿalaq* (96), 1. ʿUrwah reported this on the authority of ʿĀʾishah.[9] Both Qatādah and Abū Ṣāliḥ held the same view. It has been reported from Jābir b. ʿAbdallāh[1] that the first thing that came down was "O, you who are encloaked", *al-muddaththir* (74), 1. The right view is that when "Recite in the name of your Lord" came down on him (*Muḥammad*), he went back and wrapped himself in a cloak. Then "O, you who are encloaked" came down. This is also suggested by the argument in the two *Ṣaḥīḥs*[2] from the *ḥadīth* of Jābir who said: "I heard the Prophet speak about the period of revelation, and in talking about it he said: 'While I was walking along I heard a sound from the heavens, so I raised my head. Lo and behold! The angel who had come to me on Mt. Ḥirāʾ[3] was sitting on a throne between heaven and earth. I was torn apart with fear (*juthiththu minhu ruʿban*). I went home and said: 'Keep close to me, keep close to me'. So they covered me with a cloak. Then God sent down 'O, you who are encloaked'". (The sense of *Juthiththu is furriqtu*. One can say a man is *majʾūth* or *majthūth*.)[4] Some professional transmitters have distorted it and said 'I shrank back (*jabuntu*), from cowardice (*jubn*). But the first reading is the valid one. It has been reported from al-Ḥasan and ʿIkrimah that the first part to come down was "In the name of God, the merciful, the compassionate".

There have been different views expressed about the last [part of the Qurʾān] to come down. Al-Bukhāri relates, in his section [of the *Ṣaḥīḥ*] on those *ḥadīth* with a single attestation, one such from Ibn ʿAbbās who said: "The last verse to be sent down on the Prophet was the verse about usury". In the uniquely attested *ḥadīths* from Muslim's collection there is one, also from Ibn ʿAbbās, which states: "The last *sūrah* to come down in its entirety was [the one which begins] 'When the help of God comes and the victory'", *al-naṣr* (110), 1. Al-Ḍaḥḥāk,[5] also reporting on the authority of Ibn ʿAbbās, said: "The last verse which was sent down was 'Beware the day in which you will be returned to God'", *al-baqarah* (2), 281. This is also the view of Saʿid b. Jubayr[6] and Abū Ṣāliḥ. On the authority of al-Barāʾ, Abū Isḥaq said: "The last verse sent down was 'They will seek legal judgments from you; say: God will decide for you about those who die without heirs'" *al-nisāʾ* (4), 176.

9. ʿĀʾisha bint Abī Bakr (ca. 614–678), daughter of the first caliph, Abū Bakr, and wife of Muḥammad; she was regarded as an important source in early Islam. ʿUrwa ibn al-Zubayr (ca. 643–ca. 712), her nephew, was a major preserver of prophetic traditions.
1. Jābir ibn ʿAbdullāh, a Companion of the Prophet.
2. A reference to the two ḥadīth collections by al-Bukhārī and Muslim, respectively [McAuliffe's note]. The compendium by Muḥammad ibn Ismāʿil al-Bukhārī (810–870) is the most widely recognized; the one by Muslim ibn al-Ḥajjāj (821–875) is also famous.
3. The site of Muḥammad's first revelation in 610.
4. As noted above, such interpolated lexical explanations are a commonplace of qurʾānic *tafsīr* [McAuliffe's note].
5. Al-Ḍaḥḥāk ibn Muzāḥim al-Hilālī (d. 723/24), collector of ḥadīth and Qurʾān interpreter.
6. Scholar from Kūfa (in central Iraq) who was beheaded for taking part in a revolt against the Umayyad empire (d. 711/12).

The last *sūrah* to be sent down was *al-barā'ah*.[7] It has been related from Ubayy b. Ka'b[8] that the last verse to come down was "Indeed there has come to you a messenger from among yourselves", *al-tawbah* (9), 128.[9]

Whereas I have seen most of the exegetes' works, scarcely a single one discloses the purport in a manner properly aspired to, so that one must study an individual verse in multiple sources. Many a *tafsīr* fails to provide full, or even partial, knowledge of the abrogating and abrogated verses. Again, if that *is* to be found therein, then information is lacking about all or most of the situations which occasioned revelation. If these latter are present, then a clear distinction as between which verses were revealed in Mecca, and which in Medina, is absent. If that clarification is to be found, then allusion to the prescriptive implication of the verse is missing. If such is there, then there is no attempt to deal with any ambiguity which occurs in the verse. All this is to say nothing of the various other areas of highly prized knowledge.

In this book, I have included of the subjects mentioned above (together with others not mentioned, but indispensable to exegesis) such matters as I hope will make this book sufficiently useful to avoid the need for most others of its sort. I have been very careful to repeat any elucidation of a previously-mentioned word only by brief allusion. Yet I have not omitted exegetical opinions with which I am well-acquainted, except those of (sufficiently doubtful) validity to accord uneasily with thoroughgoing brevity. Whenever you see in the whole range of verses something whose elucidation is not mentioned, its absence will be due to one of two reasons. Either it has already been presented or it is so clear that there is no need for elucidation. This book of ours has selected the choicest works of *tafsīr* and taken from them what is most sound, most fitting, and best preserved, and arranged it in concise form. This is the moment to enter upon what we have already undertaken, but God is the one who guarantees success.

### *On the 'Prayer for Protection (al-isti'ādhah)'*

God, who is mighty, exalted, commanded that the prayer for protection be said at the time of [scriptural] recitation by saying: "When you recite the Qur'ān, take refuge with God from the accursed Satan", *al-naḥl* (16), 98. It means 'when you *intend* to recite'. (Synonyms for *a'ūdhu* are *alja'a* and *alūdhu*.)

### *On the Basmalah*

Ibn 'Umar said that it (*basmalah*) came down in respect of each *sūrah*.[1] Those educated in religious matters have differed about whether it is a complete verse or not. Aḥmad [b. Ḥanbal][2] states two opinions on this. They have also held various opinions about whether it is part of *al-Fātiḥah* (the first *sūrah* of the Qur'ān) or not. Aḥmad gives two alternatives on this

7. "The Immunity" (Q 9).
8. Qur'ān reciter, personal secretary to Muḥammad, and participant in compiling a definitive version of the Qur'ān (d. ca. 650).
9. This verse is misidentified in the printed text as 138 [McAuliffe's note].
1. Ibn al-Jawzī does not note the exception to this, i.e., *sūrat al-tawbah* (9) [McAuliffe's note]. 'Abdullāh ibn 'Umar (ca. 612–693), a Companion of the Prophet. The *basmala* is "In the name of God, the beneficent, the merciful" (Q 1:1), the phrase that appears at the beginning of each sūra except the ninth.
2. Collector of ḥadīth and eponymous founder of the Ḥanbalī legal school (780–855).

as well. Those who hold that it is part of the *Fātiḥah* would make its recitation in formal prayer a requirement inasmuch as the *Fātiḥah* itself is obligatory. The one who does not deem it part of the *Fātiḥah* says that its recitation as part of the formal prayer is simply a matter of customary practice. The exceptional case is Mālik [b. Anas][3] who gives no commendation to its recitation in the prayer.

Scholars of the religious sciences have also differed about whether (the *basmalah*) is among those things pronounced aloud during the ritual prayer. A sizeable group have related on the authority of Aḥmad that its public pronouncement is not sanctioned by tradition. Such is the view of Abū Bakr, ʿUmar, ʿUthmān, ʿAlī, ibn Masʿūd, ʿAmmār b. Yāsir, Ibn Mughaffal, Ibn Zubayr and Ibn ʿAbbās. Among the eminent Followers and Successors who held to this judgment were al-Ḥasan, al-Shaʿbī, Saʿīd b. Jubayr, Ibrāhīm, Qatādah, ʿUmar b. ʿAbd al-ʿAzīz, al-Aʿmash, Sufyān al-Thawrī, Mālik, Abū Ḥanīfah and Abū ʿUbayd among others. Al-Shāfiʿī[4] was of the opinion that public pronouncement is sanctioned (merely) by traditional practice; this is also reported on the authority of Muʿāwiyah b. Abī Sufyān,[5] ʿAtāʾ, Tāwūs and Mujāhid.

As for the exegetical explanation of the *basmalah*, the expression "in the name of God *(bi-ism allāh)*" is a sort of short way of saying "I begin in the name" or "I have begun in the name of God". There are five ways of vocalizing the constituent letters *alif, sīn* and *mīm: ism* or *usm* when the word initiates a statement, or *sim, sum* and *sam*. Poetic attestation to the last set of variants may be found in the line:

wa-allāhu asmāka saman mubārakā
ātharaka allāhu bihi īthārakā[6]

The following invocation also attests to the shortened forms:

bi-ism alladhī fī kulli sūratin simuh[7]

Al-Farrāʾ[8] stated, some of the tribe of Qays say *simuh* meaning *ismahu*. Following the usage of some of the tribe of Qudāʿah, the vocalization would be *sumuh*. Some of them [said al-Farrāʾ] quoted to me:

wa-ʿamunā aʿjabanā muqaddamuh
yudʿā abā al-samḥi wa-qirḍābun sumuh[9]

(*Al-qirḍāb* equals *al-qaṭṭāʿ*, e.g. one says *sayfun qirḍābun* [a sharp-cutting sword]).

The religiously learned have differed about [lexical issues concerning] the name of God in the form *allāh*. One group has stated that it is derived *(mushtaqq)* while others have maintained that it is a proper name and so is not derived. Two views on the matters are reported on the authority of al-Khalīl.[1]

3. A scholar of jurisprudence and eponymous founder of the Maliki legal school (ca. 715–795).
4. Muḥammad ibn Idrīs al-Shafiʿī (767–820), a scholar of jurisprudence and eponymous founder of the Shafiʿī legal school.
5. First Umayyad caliph (ca. 602–680).
6. "God named you with an auspicious name / By it God favored you greatly" [McAuliffe's note].
7. "In the name of the one whose name is in every *sūrah*" [McAuliffe's note].
8. Abū Zakariyyāʾ Yaḥyā b. Ziyād al-Farrāʾ (761–822), an important grammarian from Kūfa.
9. "By [or And] our (present) year, whose first part we liked / And whose *kunyah* speaks of liberality while its personal name suggests hardship" [McAuliffe's note]. *Kunyah* or *kunya*: nickname, familiar name.
1. Al-Khalīl ibn Aḥmad al-Farāhidī (ca. 718–ca. 791), an important philologist and prosodist.

One: it is not derived and one cannot eliminate the definite article from it as may be done with the term *al-raḥmān*. Two: as Sībawayh[2] has recorded from al-Khalīl, it is derived. Abū Sulaymān al-Khaṭṭābī[3] has recounted on the authority of some of the religiously learned that it is derived from the first form of the root, ʻLH, as in *alaha al-rajulu* and *yaʼlahu*, to mean ʻhe took refuge with him from something which had befallen him'. Alternately, it could be from *alahahu* meaning protected him *(ajārahu)* and safeguarded him *(ammanahu)*, He (God) is also designated *ilāh* on the "pattern" of a man being called *imām*. Others say that its original form is *wilāh* with *wāw* having (later) been replaced by *hamzah*. So one would (equally well) say *ilāh* on the model of (such correlatives as) *wisādah* and *isādah* or of *wishāh* and *ishāh*.

[Another view is that] it has been derived from the stem WLH because the hearts of the worshippers yearn *(tuwallahu tūlahu)* towards Him, as when God says in *al-naḥl* (16), 53: "When harm befalls you, then to Him will you turn in supplication *(tajʼarūn)*".

Whereas the obvious passive participle for ʻLH would be *maʼlūh* on the analogy of *maʻbūd*, there has been a deviation from the normal process because it (the form actually used, i.e. *ilāh*) is a proper name. It is used in the same way that *kitāb* is commonly used in place of *maktūb* and *ḥisāb* for *maḥsūb*.

Some have maintained that the term *allāh* derives from the root ʻLH *(alaha al rajul, yaʼlahu)* in its signification of being perplexed or puzzled *(taḥayyara)*. This is because hearts feel such sentiments when reflecting upon God's majesty. According to some philologists the relevant forms of ʻLH are *alaha al-rajul, yaʼlahu* and *ilāhah* commensurate in meaning with *ʻabada, yaʻbudu* and *ʻibādah*. For *al-aʻrāf* (7), 127 the phrasing *wa-yadharaka wa-ilāhataka* with the meaning *ʻibādataka* has been recorded on the authority of Ibn ʻAbbās. He further stated that *al-taʼalluh* is equivalent to *al-taʻabbud*. A line by Rūʼbah [ibn al-ʻAjjāj][4] testifies to the usage:

> lillāhi darru al-ghāniyāti al-muddahi
> sabbaḥna wa-istarjaʻna min taʼalluhi[5]

The sense of *al-ilāh* is *al-maʻbūd* (object of worship).

As for the term *al-raḥmān*, most scholars have taken the position that it is an emphatic form derived from *al-raḥmah*, meaning ʻone who has no counterpart in the degree to which he possesses compassion *(al-raḥmah)*'. The form faʻlān is said by them [grammarians] to stand for emphasis as, in designating complete fullness *(imtilāʼ)*, one finds *malʼān* and for complete satiety *(al-shabʻ)*, *shabʻān*. Al-Khaṭṭābī spoke of *al-raḥmān* as ʻthe one who possesses all-encompassing compassion, sufficient for the daily needs and best interests of all humankind, including both believers and nonbelievers'.

The word *al-raḥīm*, however, is specific to the believers. In *al-aḥzāb* (33), 43 God exalted said: "He is *raḥīm* (merciful) to the believers". The significance of *al-raḥīm* is *al-raḥīm* (one who is merciful).

2. Abū Bishr ʻAmr ibn ʻUthmān Sībawayh (d. ca. 796), al-Khalīl's student and the author of an influential book on grammar, *al-Kitāb* (*The Book*).
3. Aḥmad ibn Muḥammad al-Khaṭṭābī (ca. 931–998), a collector of ḥadīth and poet.
4. A poet of the Tamīm tribe who settled in Basra, in southeastern Iraq (d. 762).
5. "How praiseworthy are the beautiful women / They glorified and invoked God from my adoration" [McAuliffe's note].

# FAKHR AL-DĪN AL-RĀZĪ

Muḥammad ibn ʿUmar Fakhr al-Dīn al-Rāzī (1149/50–1210) was born in Rayy, a city that is now part of the larger metropolitan area of Tehran. His early education ranged over the standard fields of Islamic intellectual discourse but also included philosophical studies. In adulthood, his fame as a teacher and preacher took him to far-flung areas of what is now Iran, Afghanistan, and Uzbekistan. A staunch adherent of Ashʿarī Sunnism, he frequently aimed his sermons at groups, such as the Muʿtazilīs and Karrāmīs, whom he considered to be theologically heterodox. Eventually, al-Rāzī settled in Herat, Afghanistan, where he secured significant patronage as well as intellectual renown.

While the more formal title of al-Rāzī's commentary is *The Keys of the Unseen* (*Mafātīḥ al-ghayb*), it is frequently published simply as *The Great Commentary* (*Al-Tafsīr al-kabīr*). And great it is—thirty-two volumes in the current printed edition. Al-Rāzī often divides his analysis of a particular verse into a series of subdivisions, each of which may undergo further segmentation. The following selection, which discuss one of the most famous verses in the Qurʾān (Q 24:35), exemplifies this methodology.

## *From* Light of the Heavens and the Earth†

The most important similitude [drawn] is God's statement *God is the Light of the heavens and the earth; the likeness of His light is as a niche wherein is alamp the lamp in a glass, the glass as it were a glittering star kindled from a blessed tree, an olive that is neither of the east nor of the west whose oil well-nigh would shine, even if no fire touched it; light upon light; God guides to His light whom He will. And God strikes similitudes for humankind, and God has knowledge of everything.*

Know that the discussion of this verse is organised in [four] parts.

### *Part I. Calling God 'The Light'*

Know that in Arabic the term 'light' (*nūr*) is used for that phenomenon which the sun, the moon and fire diffuse over the ground, [over] walls and [over] other things. According to various different points of view it is impossible that this phenomenon be a god.

**The first [point of view]** is that if this phenomenon is like a body, then the evidence that proves the incidence of the body [also] proves the incidence of this [phenomenon, i.e. light]. If it [this phenomenon] is an accidental contingent, then when the incidence [of this phenomenon, i.e. light] is established so is the incidence of all the [other] accidental contingents that come with it. However, this prefatory statement is only established after the evidence of the impossibility of imposing delimitations on God has [first] been established.

**The second [point of view]** is that, whether we say that light is a bodily form or is something present in the body, [the fact remains that] it is

† From *An Anthology of Quranic Commentaries*, vol. 1, *On the Nature of the Divine*, ed. Feras Hamza and Sajjad Rizvi, with Farhana Mayer (Oxford: Oxford University Press; London: in association with the Institute of Ismaili Studies, 2008), pp. 384–87, 399–401. Reprinted by permission of Oxford University Press. All brackets in the text are theirs.

divisible. [This is] because if it is a bodily form then it must be divisible, and if it is present in it [the body], then [its very] presence in that which is divisible [means it too] is divisible. According to two accounts, light is divisible, and everything that is divisible requires the existence of its parts in order to [itself] exist. Each one of its parts changes it, and each required part requires [parts] other than itself in order to exist. That which requires [the existence of] another is made possible by its essence, which is occasioned by [something] other than itself. Thus, light is something that is brought about [by another] and so is not a god.

**The third [point of view]** [is that] were this tangible light to be God, it could not vanish because it is impossible that God [ever] vanish.

**The fourth [point of view]** [is that] this tangible light arrives when the sun and stars appear, and this is not possible for God [since He is ever present].

**The fifth [point of view]** [is that] if these lights are eternal they would either move around or remain still. It is not possible that they be 'moving' since the meaning of movement is going from place to place. Movement precedes arrival in the initial place, and, [since] eternity cannot be preceded by anything else, so eternal movement is impossible. It is not possible that they [these lights] be motionless since, were motionlessness to be eternal, it would be impossible [for it] to [ever] come to an end. However, [the] motionlessness [of these lights] does end: we see lights moving from place to place and this proves that these lights occur [as opposed to being eternally in existence].

**The sixth [point of view]** [is that] light is either a bodily form or is a phenomenon that comes with bodies. The first [suggestion] is impossible since we understand the body to be a body regardless of [whether] it is illuminated, and because the body is enlightened after being in the dark [thus, it cannot have been always light]. The second [suggestion] holds true. However, a phenomenon that comes with the body requires the body, and that which requires something other than itself cannot be a god.

This evidence taken together proves false the statement of the Manicheans (*Mānuwiyya*)[1] who believe that God is the greatest light. The argument of those who say light is a bodily form is objected to by two points of view.

1. His [God's] statement *Like Him there is nothing* [Q. 42:11]. This would be false if He [God] were a light because all lights resemble one another.

2. God's statement *the likeness of His light* states unequivocally that His [God's] essence is not itself the light but rather light is attributed to Him [i.e., as one of His characteristics], thus [we have] His [God's] statement *God guides to His light whom He will*. It is said that His [God's] statement *God is the Light of the heavens and the earth* requires that His outward appearance itself be a light and His [God's] statement *the likeness of His light* requires that His [actual] essence is not a light [on account of the word '*likeness*'].

1. Mani (d. 276/889), the prophet founder of this sect, grew up in an Elchasian sect in southern Babylonia. He disseminated his teaching in the Sasanian empire, whence the mission spread to Egypt and the Roman empire. At the heart of Manichean theology is a dualist conception of two co-eval principles of light and darkness. The human soul is thus a spark or particle of divine light held captive in "dark" flesh [Hamza, Rizvi, and Mayer's note]. The Elchasaites were a heretical Christian sect, putatively founded by Elchasai (2nd c. CE?); the prophetic book attributed to him has been lost.

These [two statements] appear to be mutually incompatible. However, we would argue that when you say, 'Zayd. is [all] generosity and kindness', this would be analogous to this verse, since you [also] say 'People are invigorated by his [Zayd's] generosity and kindness.' In this way they do not contradict one another.

God's statement *And appointed the shadows and light* [Q. 6:1]. This states unequivocally that the essential nature of light is something that God has created, so it is impossible that God [Himself] be a light. It is established that [this] requires explanation and the religious experts mention various differing points of view about it.

**The first [point of view]** is that light causes [things] to become visible, and since guidance and light share this sense [i.e., since they are both understood to perform this function], it is correct that the name 'light' is often bestowed on 'guidance'. This is like God's statement, *God is the Protector of the believers; He brings them forth from the shadows into the light* [Q. 2:257]. His [God's] statement *Why, is he who was dead, and We gave him life, And appointed for him a light* [Q. 6:122]; His statement *but We made it a light, whereby We guide whom We will of Our servants* [Q. 42:52]; and His statement *God is the Light of the heavens and the earth* mean that the light of the heavens and the earth is His [God's]. The light is [God's] guidance and [this light] is found only with the inhabitants of the heavens. The gist [of this] implies that God is the Guide of the people of the heavens and the earth. This is the statement of Ibn ʿAbbās and the majority of commentators.

**The second [point of view]** is that the meaning [of the verse] is that He [God] is the truly just, competent and enlightening ruler of the heavens and the earth. He describes Himself like this just as the learned leader is described as being the light of [his] country. If their ruler rules well he is for them [i.e. for the inhabitants of a given region] like the light that guides to the ways of the right path. This [point of view] is preferred by al-Aṣamm and al-Zajjāj.[2]

**The third [point of view]** is that the meaning is He who organises the heavens and the earth according to the best system, and it may be that this system is interpreted as a light. It is said 'I see in this matter a light.'

**The fourth [point of view]** is that its meaning is enlightener of the heavens and earth. They [the commentators] recount three points of view concerning this statement:

1. He [God] enlightens the heavens through angels and the earth through prophets;
2. He [God] enlightens them with the sun, the moon and the stars;
3. [God] He adorns the heavens with the sun, the moon and the stars, and the earth with prophets and learned scholars, and this is related on the authority of Ubayy b. Kaʿb, al-Ḥasan [al-Baṣrī] and Abū'l-ʿĀliya.[3]

2. Abū Isḥāq Ibrāhīm al-Zajjāj (d. 923), a grammarian and author of a work on qur'ānic philology. Abū Bakr al-Aṣamm (d. 816/17), a theologian and commentator on the Qur'ān.
3. Three early Islamic scholars: Ubayy ibn Kaʿb (d. ca. 650), Qur'ān reciter, personal secretary to Muḥammad, and participant in compiling an authoritative version of the Qur'an; al-Ḥasan (642–728), a famous scholar of the generation after that of the prophet Muḥammad's Companions who was noted for his piety and asceticism; and Abū al-ʿĀliya Rufayʿ b. Mihrān al-Riyāḥī (d. 708/9 or 714), a collector of ḥadīth and transmitter of the Qur'ān.

The closest [to being correct], however, is the first of these statements, because He [God] said at the end of the verse that *God guides to His light whom He will*, indicating that the meaning of 'the light' is guidance towards knowledge and [best] action.

* * *

### *Part III. Explanation of the Nature of Drawing Comparisons*

Know that drawing comparisons requires two things: an object and something with which to compare it. People have different opinions here about what the object is. They [the commentators] recount several points of view.

**First [point of view]**: The majority of Muslim theologians, supported by al-Qāḍī [al-Bāqillānī],[4] state that what is meant by 'the guidance' (*hady*) is the verses that make [things] clear, and the meaning is that the clarifying and revealing nature of God's guidance extends to the utmost extremes; in this way it is the lamp (*mishkāt*) in which is found clear glass. In the glass is a niche (*miṣbāḥ*) that burns with the clearest possible oil. It is said it [God's guidance] cannot be compared with this [lamp's light] for we know that the light of the sun reaches a lot further than this. We say that God describes the perfect light that shines in the midst of darkness [as an analogy for His guidance] because most peoples thoughts and beliefs are vague, and thus are like darkness, while God's guidance is like the perfect light that reveals what is in darkness. This meaning does not apply to the light of the sun because when it [the sun's light] is visible, the world is filled with pure light, and when it vanishes the world is filled with pure darkness. So, the comparison [drawn between God's guidance and the lamp] is more fitting and appropriate [than making the same comparison between God's guidance and sunlight]. Know that in drawing this comparison, God considers those elements which make this light perfect:

1. The lamp (*miṣbāḥ*), because when it [the lamp] is not in the niche (*mishkāt*) its beams are dispersed, while when it is placed in a niche its beams come together and become one and give out a stronger light. This is proved by [the fact that] when a lamp (*miṣbāḥ*) is in a small house its light appears to be brighter than when it is seen in a big house.
2. When a lamp is in a clear glass, the beams that are separated from the lamp reflect from one side of the glass to the other because of the clearness and transparency of the glass. For this reason the light and glow are brighter. This is proved by [the fact that] when the sun's rays fall on a clear glass the visible light multiplies so that it appears that what it [the light] faces is the same as that light [i.e. the light is reflected on each side of the glass]. If these rays are reflected from all the sides of the glass to the other sides, the lights and glows grow more numerous, and this can go on endlessly.
3. The light of a lamp varies according to what is being used to burn it. If the oil is totally clear the light will be different to what it would be if [the oil] were murky. The clearest kind of oil is olive oil, which is perhaps as

4. Abū Bakr al-Bāqillānī (d. 1013), an Ash'arī theologian and author of a major work on the inimitability of the Qur'ān.

clear and thin as water with its extreme whiteness and the rays that are reflected from its parts.

4. This olive oil varies on account of the tree [from which it comes]. If [its tree] is neither east nor west, meaning that it is exposed to the sun in all conditions, its olives are the most ripe and succulent, and their oil is the most clear. It is easier to distinguish its clearness from its dirt because increased sunlight makes this possible.

If these four things come together at the same time they support one another, and the light [produced from the oil of the olives of the tree] is totally clear. Thus, it is appropriate to use this as a simile for God's guidance.

**Second [point of view]**: What is meant by the 'light' in His [God's] statement *the likeness of His light* is the Qur'ān, and this is suggested in God's statement *There has come to you from God a light* [Q. 5:15]. This is the statement of al-Ḥasan [al-Baṣrī], Sufyān b. 'Uyayna and Zayd b. Aslam.[5]

**Third [point of view]**: What is meant [by *the likeness of His light*] is the Messenger, because he [the Messenger] is the guide, and because God said describing him [Muḥammad] as *a radiant lamp* [Q. 33:46]. This is what 'Atā' [b. Abī Rabāḥ][6] says.

The latter two statements are implicit in the first statement, because the revelation of the Book [i.e. the Qur'ān] and the dispatching of the Message are each forms of guidance. God said, describing the Book, *Even so We have revealed to you a Spirit of Our bidding. You did not know what the Book was, nor [what is] faith* [Q. 42:52]; describing the Message, He said *Messengers bearing good tidings, and warning, so that mankind might have no argument against God, after the Messengers* [Q. 4:165].

**Fourth [point of view]**: What is meant [by *the likeness of His light*] is that which is in the heart of the believers in the way of acknowledgement of God and of the laws of Islam. This is proved by God's description of faith as light and of unbelief as darkness. He [God] said, *Is he whose breast God has expanded unto Islam, so he walks in a light from his Lord* [Q. 39:22]; God [also] said *that He may bring forth those who believe and do righteous deeds from the shadows into the light* [Q. 65:11]. The gist of this is that guidance leads to the right path, and the intention [of this] comparison is that the faith of the believer attains the same [effect] as the lamp in terms of clarifying obscurities and distinguishing [it] from the darkness of erring. This is what Ubayy b. Ka'b and Ibn 'Abbās[7] say. Ubayy [b. Ka'b] used to read [it as]: *mathalu nūr al-mu'min* (the likeness of the light of the believer). It is said that he used to read it as: *mathalu nūr man āmana bih* (the likeness of he who believes in Him). Ibn 'Abbās used to say: 'the likeness of the light in the heart of the believer'.

* * *

5. A Medinan narrator of ḥadīth (d. 753). Sufyān (725–811), a Meccan scholar of the third generation after that of the prophet Muḥammad.
6. A Meccan transmitter of ḥadīth (645–733).
7. 'Abdallāh ibn al-'Abbās (ca. 619–687/88), one of the greatest early Islamic scholars, and 'Aṭā's teacher; he is often considered the founder of the qur'ānic exegetical tradition.

# SAYYID QUTB

Born in a small city in Upper Egypt, Sayyid Qutb (1906–1966) became one of the most famous Egyptians of the twentieth- and twenty-first centuries. After earning a university degree in Cairo, he began his long career as an educator working for in the Ministry of Education. He also wrote novels, essays, political treatises, and poems, which developed a devoted following among the Cairene intelligentsia. Concerns about political corruption, social injustice, and moral drift in the Muslim world prompted him to join the reformist organization known as the Muslim Brotherhood, and he quickly assumed a leading position. Accused of an assassination attempt on Gamal Abdel Nasser, then president of Egypt, Qutb was arrested in 1954 and imprisoned for ten years. He was reincarcerated within a year of his release and, after a show trial, executed in 1966.

As a key concept of his political philosophy, Qutb extended the term *jāhiliyya* (Age of Ignorance), traditionally applied to the age before Islam, and gave it the meaning "un-Islamic" or "anti-Islamic." To term a Muslim society *jāhilī*, to call a Muslim leader *jāhil*, is tantamount to the accusation of apostasy—a charge punishable by death.

Qutb began his thirty-volume commentary, *In the Shade of the Qur'an* (Fī *zilāl al-Qur'ān*), before his arrest in 1954 but completed the work in prison. In the excerpt reproduced here he discusses Q 96, whose opening verses were, according to most traditional sources, the first to be revealed. Expanding beyond the usual exegetical themes, Qutb argues that this initiation of divine revelation was a transformative event for all humans.

## *From* Surah 96: The Blood Clots *(Al-Alaq)*†

In the name of Allah, the Beneficent, the Merciful.

Read in the name of your Lord who created,
created man from clots of blood.
Read! your Lord is the most Bounteous,
Who has taught the use of the pen,
has taught man what he did not know.
Indeed, man tyrannises, once he thinks himself self-sufficient.
Surely to your Lord all things return.
Observe the man who rebukes a servant of Allah when he prays!
Think: does he not follow the right guidance and enjoin true piety?
Think: if he denies the truth and turns his back,
does he not realise that Allah sees all?
Let him desist, or We will drag him by the forelock,
his lying, sinful forelock.
Then let him call his henchmen.
We will call the guards of Hell.
No, never obey him, but prostrate yourself and draw closer to Allah.

It is universally agreed that the opening of this *surah* was the first Qur'anic revelation. The accounts stating that other verses were revealed

† From Sayyid Qutb, *In the Shade of the Qur'ān*, vol. 30, trans. M. A. Salahi and A. A. Shamis (London: MWH, 1979), pp. 217–24. Reprinted by permission of the publisher.

first are not authentic. Imam Ahmad transmits the following *hadith* attributing it to Aisha,[1] the Prophet's wife:

> The first aspect of revelation to Allah's Messenger was that his dreams came true. Whatever vision he might have in his sleep would occur exactly as he had seen. Then, he began to enjoy seclusion. He used to retreat alone into the cave of Hira where he would spend several days in devotion before going back to his family. He used to take some food with him, and when he came back he would take a fresh supply for another period. He continued to do so until he received the truth while in the cave of Hira. The angel came to him and said, "Read." He replied, "I am not a reader." The Prophet says, "He held me and pressed hard until I was exhausted, then he released me and said, "Read." And I replied, "I am not a reader." So, he held me and pressed me hard a second time until I was exhausted, then he released me and said, "Read," I replied, "I am not a reader." He then held me and pressed me hard for the third time. Then he said, *"Read, in the name of your Lord Who created, created man from clots of blood. Read! your Lord is the most bounteous, Who has taught the use of the pen, has taught man what he did not know."* The Prophet returned home to Khadeeja[2] trembling and said, "Wrap me! Wrap me!" They wrapped him and his fear subsided. He turned to Khadeeja and exclaimed, "What has happened to me?" and related to her what had happened and said, "I fear for myself." And Khadeeja replied, "Fear not, be calm and relax. Allah will not let you suffer any humiliation, because you are kind to your relatives, you speak the truth, you assist anyone in need, you are hospitable to your guests and you help in every just cause." Then she took him to Waraqa ibn Nawfal,[3] her paternal cousin who was a Christian convert and a scholar with good knowledge of Arabic, Hebrew and the Bible. He had lost his eyesight as he had grown very old. Khadeeja said to Waraqa, "Cousin, would you like to hear what your nephew has to say?" Waraqa said, "Well, nephew,[4] what have you seen?" The Prophet related to him what he had seen. When he finished, Waraqa said, "It is the same revelation as was sent down to Moses. I wish I was a young man so that I might be alive when your people turn you away from this city." The Prophet exclaimed, "Would they turn me away?" Waraqa answered "Yes! No man has ever preached a message like yours but was met with enmity. If I live till that day, I will certainly give you all my support." But Waraqa died soon after that . . .

This *hadith* is transmitted in both of the most authentic books of the Prophet's traditions and was related by Al-Zuhri.[5]

Al-Tabari also transmitted the following tradition, related by Abdullah ibn Az-Zubair:[6]

1. ʿĀʾisha bint Abī Bakr (ca. 614–678), daughter of the first caliph, Abū Bakr (573–634), and a source of authoritative knowledge in early Islam. Aḥmad ibn Ḥanbal (780–855), collector of ḥadīth and eponymous founder of the Ḥanbalī legal school.
2. Khadīja bint al-Khuwaylid (ca. 554–619), Muḥammad's first wife.
3. Khadīja's monotheist cousin (d. before 622).
4. A courtesy title.
5. Ibn Shihāb al-Zuhrī (d. 742), an early legal authority responsible for the transmission of many ḥadīth.
6. ʿAbdallāh ibn al-Zubayr (624–692), the pious son of a famed Companion of the prophet; he set up a counter-caliphate at Mecca in rebellion against the Umayyads and was executed. Abū Jaʿfar Muḥammad ibn Jarīr al-Ṭabarī (ca. 839–923), scholar, exegete, and historian.

"The Prophet said, 'While I was asleep he came to me carrying a case of a very rich material in which there was a book. He said, 'Read.' I replied, 'I am not a reader.' He pressed me so hard that I felt I was about to die. Then he released me and said, 'Read.' I asked, 'What shall I read?' (and I said this only out of fear that he might repeat what he had done to me before.) He said, *'Read: In the name of your Lord who created . . . taught man what he did not know.'* I read it. He stopped, then left me and went away. I woke up feeling that it was actually written in my heart'." The Prophet went on to say, "No man was ever more loathsome to me than poets or deranged persons. I could not bear even looking at either. I thought, 'The man (meaning himself) is undoubtedly a poet or deranged. This shall not be said about me amongst the Quraish.[7] Let me climb high up in the mountain and throw myself and get rid of it all.' I went to carry out this intention. When I was half way up in the mountain I heard a voice coming from the heavens saying, 'Muhammad, you are the Messenger of Allah and I am Jibril.'[8] I raised my head up to the sky and I saw Jibril in the image of a man with his feet one next to the other, up on the horizon. He said again, 'Muhammad, you are the Messenger of Allah and I am Jibril.' I stood in my place looking up at him; this distracted me from my intention. I was standing there unable to move. I tried to turn my face away from him and to look up at the sky, but wherever I looked, I saw him in front of me. I stood still, moving neither forward nor backward. Kahdeeja sent her messengers looking for me and I remained standing in my place all the while until they went back to her. He then left me and I went back to my family . . .'"

This tradition is also related in more details by Ibn Ishaq, on the authority of Wahb ibn Kayssan.[9]

I reflected for a while upon this event. We all have read it many times in books; either those of the Prophet's biography or those explaining the meaning of the Qur'an. But we either read it casually or gave it little thought and went on with our reading.

Yet this is an event which has immense significance. It is an event which has important bearing on the life of humanity; but much as we try today to perceive its great value, many of its aspects will remain beyond our perception. It is no exaggeration to describe this event as the greatest in the long history of human existence.

The true nature of this event is that Allah, the Great, the Compeller, the Almighty, the Supreme, the Sovereign of the whole universe, out of His benevolence, has turned to that creation of His which is called "man", and which takes its abode in a hardly visible corner of the universe, the name of which is the "Earth". He has honoured this species of His creation by choosing one of its numbers to be the recipient of His Divine light and the guardian of His wisdom.

This is something infinitely great. Some aspects of its greatness become apparent when man tries, as best as he can, to perceive the essential qualities of Allah: absolute power, freedom from all limitations and

7. The Quraysh, the ruling tribe of Mecca.
8. The angel Gabriel (Ar. Jibrīl).
9. Wahb ibn Kaysān (d. 744), a Medinan scholar who related ḥadīth from earlier collectors. Ibn Isḥāq (ca. 704–767), author of the most authoritative life of Muḥammad (see above).

everlastingness; and when he reflects, in comparison, on the basic qualities of Allah's servants who are subject to certain limitations of power and life duration. One may then perceive the significance of this Divine care for man. He may realise the sweetness of this feeling and manifest his appreciation with thanksgiving, prayers and devotion. He feels that the whole universe shares in the general happiness spread by the revelation of Divine words to man in his obscure corner of the universe.

What is the significance of this event? With reference to Allah, it signifies that He is the source of all the great bounties and unfailing compassion. He is the Benevolent, the Loving, Who bestows His mercy and benefactions for no reason except that benevolence is one of His Divine attributes. As for man, this event signifies that Allah has bestowed on him an honour the greatness of which he can hardly ever appreciate and for which he can never show enough gratitude, not even if he spends all his life in devotion and prostration. This honour is that Allah has taken notice and care of him, established contact with him and chosen one of the human race as His messenger to reveal to him His words; that the earth, man's abode has become the recipient of these Divine words, which the whole universe echoes with submission and devotion.

This great event began to bear on the life of humanity as a whole right from the first moment. It marked a change in the course of history, following the change it brought about in the course followed by human conscience. It specified the source man should look up to in order to derive his ideals, values and criteria. The source is heaven and the Divine revelations, not this world and man's own desires. When this great event took place the people who recognised its true nature and adapted their lives accordingly enjoyed Allah's protection and manifest care. They looked up to Him directly for guidance in all their affairs, big and small. They lived and moved under His supervision. They expected that He would guide them along the road, step by step, stopping them from error and leading them to the right. Every night they expected to receive some Divine revelations concerning what they had on their minds, providing solutions for their problems and saying to them, "Do this and leave that."

The period which followed the event was certainly remarkable: twenty-three years of direct contact between the human race and the Highest Society. The true nature of this period cannot be recognised except by those who lived in that period and went through its experience, witnessed its start and its end, relished the sweet flavour of that contact and felt the Divine hand guiding them along the road. The distance which separates us from that reality is too great to be defined by any measure of length this world has known. It is a distance in the world of conscience incomparable to any distance in the material world, not even when we think of the gaps separating the stars or galaxies. It is a gap that separates the earth and the Heaven; a gap between human desires and Divine revelation as sources from which concepts and values are derived; a gap between *Ignorance* and Islam, the human and the Divine.

The people who lived in that period were fully aware of its uniqueness, recognised its special place in history and felt the great loss when the Prophet passed away to be in the company of the Supreme Companion. This marked the end of this remarkable period which our minds can hardly imagine but for its actual occurrence.

Anas related that Abu Bakr said to 'Umar[1] after the death of the Prophet "Let us go to visit Umm Ayman[2] as the Prophet used to do." When they went to her she burst into tears. They said, "What are you crying for? Don't you realise that Allah's company is far better for the Prophet?" She replied, "That is true, I am sure. I am only crying because revelation has ceased with his death." This made tears spring to their eyes and the three of them cried together. (Transmitted by Muslim[3]).

The impact of that period has been in evidence in the life of humanity ever since its beginning up to this moment, and it will remain in evidence until the day when Allah inherits the earth and all that walks on it. Man was reborn when he started to derive his values from Heaven rather than earth and his laws from the Divine revelation instead of his own desires. The course of history underwent a change the like of which has never been experienced before or since. That event, the commencement of revelation, was the point at which the roads crossed. Clear and permanent guidelines were established which cannot be changed by the passage of time or effaced by events. Human conscience developed a concept of existence, human life and its values unsurpassed in comprehensiveness, clarity and purity of all worldly considerations as well as its realism and practicability in human society. The foundations of this Divine code have been firmly established in the world and its various aspects and essential standards have been made clear, *"so that he who perishes may perish after having received a clear sign and he who lives may live after having received a clear sign."*[4]

The beginning of revelation was a unique event at a unique moment marking the end of one era and the start of another. It is the demarcation line in the history of mankind, not merely in the history of a certain nation or a particular generation. It has been recorded by the universe and echoed in all its corners. It has also been recorded in the conscience of man which today needs to be guided by what Allah has revealed and never to lose sight of it. It needs to remember that this event was a rebirth of humanity which can take place only once in history.

It is self evident that the rest of the *surah* was not revealed at the same time as its opening but at a later date. For it refers to a certain situation and to events in the life of the Prophet which took place later, after he was instructed to convey his message and commanded to offer his worship in public, and after he was met with opposition by the polytheists. This is indicated in the part of the *surah* which begins: *"Observe the man who rebukes a servant of Allah when he prays . . ."* Yet there is perfect harmony between all parts of the *surah*. The facts it relates after the opening part are also arranged in a perfect order. These two factors make the *surah* one perfectly harmonious unit.

*"Read in the name of your Lord Who created, created man from clots of blood. Read! your Lord is the most Bounteous, Who has taught the use of the pen, has taught man what he did not know."*

This is the first *surah* of the Qur'an so it starts with the name of Allah. It instructs the Messenger of Allah right at the very first moment of his blessed

1. 'Umar ibn al-Khaṭṭāb (ca. 586–644), the second caliph. Anas ibn Mālik (d. ca. 710), an early Companion of the Prophet and traditionist; he was given to Muḥammad as a servant at age ten.
2. Baraka (d. ca. 650), an Abyssinian freedwoman who was the nurse of the orphaned Muḥammad.
3. Muslim ibn al-Ḥajjāj (821–875), Persian scholar and one of the chief authorities on the ḥadīth.
4. Q 8:42.

contact with the Highest Society and before taking his very first step along the way of the message he was chosen to deliver, to read in the name of Allah, *"Read in the name of your Lord."* The first attribute of Allah it mentions is that of creation and initiation: *". . . your Lord Who created."* Then it speaks in particular of the creation of man and his origin: *"created man from clots of blood."* He is created from a dried drop of blood which sticks to the womb: a cheap and unsophisticated substance. This reflects the grace and mercy of the Creator as much as it reflects His power. It is out of His grace that He has elevated this clot of blood to the rank of man who can be taught and who can learn: *"Read! your Lord is the most Bounteous, Who has taught the use of the pen, has taught man what he did not know."* The gulf between the origin and the outcome is very wide indeed. But Allah is Able and He is Bounteous, hence this change which makes us dizzy with wonder.

Here also emerges the fact of the teaching of man by the Creator. The pen has always been the most widespread means of learning and it has always had the most far-reaching bearing on man's life. This fact was not as clear at the time of revelation as it is now. But Allah knows the value of the pen; hence, this reference to the pen at the beginning of this His final message to humanity, in the first *surah* of the Qur'an. Yet the Messenger charged with the conveyance of this message could not write. Had the Qur'an been his own composition, he would not have stressed this fact at the first moment. But the Qur'an is Allah's revelation and a message from the Divine.

The *surah* then states the source of learning, which is Allah. From Him man receives all his knowledge, past, present and future. From Him man learns any secret revealed to him about this universe, life and himself.

This single paragraph revealed at the very first moment of the Messenger's contact with the Highest Society states the comprehensive basis of faith and its concepts. Everything starts, works and moves in His name. He is the One Who creates, originates and teaches. Whatever man learns and whatever experience and knowledge he acquires come originally from Allah. He has taught man what he did not know. The Prophet recognised this basic Qur'anic fact. It governed his feelings, teachings and actions for the rest of his life because it is the principal fact of faith.

* * *

# Intellectual Amplification

## MUSLIM IBN AL-ḤAJJĀJ

Muslim ibn al-Ḥajjāj (821–875) died only five years after another famous traditionist, Muḥammad ibn Ismāʿīl al-Bukhārī (810–870). Their compendia of prophetic traditions, both titled *Ṣaḥīḥ*, are the most highly regarded of the six ḥadīth collections that became canonical. Muslim was born in the Iranian city of Nishapur, and biographers—as they do for so many classical scholars—list the many experts with whom he studied and the many places to which he journeyed in search of instruction. Travels through Iraq, Syria, Egypt, and Arabia enabled Muslim to learn ḥadīth from scholars who had been students of Mālik ibn Anas (ca. 715–795) and Muḥammad ibn Idrīs al-Shāfiʿī (767–820), founders of the legal schools that bear their names (Mālikī and Shāfiʿī), and to study directly with Aḥmad ibn Hanbal (780–855), who founded the Ḥanbalī school. Sources state that during these years of travel and study he compiled 300,000 ḥadīth, only a small fraction of which were included in his *Ṣaḥīḥ*.

The following selection, from the *Ṣaḥīḥ*'s "Book of Commentary" (*Kitāb al-Tafsīr*), treats several qurʾānic verses, drawn largely from the fourth sūra, "The Sūra of Women." Q 4:3–4 and 4:126 address the situation of orphan girls and the care they should receive from their male guardians. Q 4:128 is interpreted as showing that a wife can forestall a unilateral divorce by being willing to accept her husband's decision to marry another woman.

### *From* Book of Commentary†

#### *Chapter MCCXXXVI*

Hammām b. Munabbih reported: This is what Abū Huraira[1] reported to us from Allah's Messenger (may peace be upon him) and in this connection he narrated some of the aḥādīth[2] and Allah's Messenger (may peace be upon him) said: It was said to people of Israel: Enter this land saying *Ḥiṭṭa* (Remove Thou from us the burden of our sins), whereupon We would forgive you your sins, but they twisted (this statement) and entered the gate dragging upon their breech and said: The "grain in the ear."

Anas b. Mālik[3] reported that Allah, the Exalted and Glorious, sent revelation to Allah's Messenger (may peace be upon him) just before his death

† From Imām Muslim, *Ṣaḥīḥ Muslim: Being the Traditions of the Sayings and Doings of the Prophet Muḥammad as Narrated by His Companions and Compiled under the Title "Al-Jāmiʿ-uṣ-ṣaḥīḥ,"* trans. ʿAbdul Ḥamīd Ṣīddīqī (1971–75; reprint, Beirut: Dar al-Arabia, 2000), 4:1551–54.

1. Abū Hurayra (d. ca. 678), an impoverished early Companion of Muḥammad who related many ḥadīth; he eventually assumed (and was deposed from) the post of governor of Baḥrayn.
2. Traditions (sing. *ḥadīth*), the sayings of the prophet Muḥammad and his Companions.
3. An early Companion and traditionist (d. ca. 710); he was given to Muḥammad as a servant at age ten.

in quick succession until he left for his heavenly home, and the day when he died, he received the revelation profusely.

Ṭāriq b. Shihāb reported that a Jew said to ʿUmar:[4] You recite a verse which, if it had been revealed in relation to us, we would have taken that day as the day of rejoicing. Thereupon ʿUmar said: I know where it was revealed and on the day when it was revealed and where Allah's Messenger (may peace be upon him) had been at that time when it was revealed. It was revealed on the day of ʿArafa (ninth of Dhuʾl-Ḥijjah) and Allah's Messenger (may peace be upon him) had been staying in ʿArafāt.[5] Sufyān[6] said: I doubt, whether it was Friday or not (and the verse referred to) is this: "Today I have perfected your religion for you and completed My favours upon you" (v. 4).

Ṭāriq b. Shihāb reported that a Jew said to ʿUmar: If this verse were revealed in relation to the Jews (i.e. "This day I have perfected your religion for you and have completed My favours for you and have chosen for you al-Islām as religion") we would have taken the day of rejoicing on which this verse was revealed. Thereupon ʿUmar said: I know the day on which it was revealed and the hour when it was revealed and where Allah's Messenger (may peace be upon him) had been when it was revealed. It was revealed on the night of Friday and we were in ʿArafāt with Allah's Messenger (may peace be upon him) at that time.

Ṭāriq b. Shihāb reported that a Jew came to ʿUmar and said: Commander of the Faithful, there is a verse in your Book, which you recite. Had it been revealed in connection with the Jews, we would have taken it as the day of rejoicing. Thereupon he said: Which verse do you mean? He replied: "This day I have perfected your religion for you and I have completed My favours upon you and I have chosen al-Islam as religion for you." ʿUmar said, I know the day when it was revealed and the place where it was revealed. It was revealed to Allah's Messenger (may peace be upon him) at ʿArafāt on Friday.

ʿUrwa b. Zubair reported that he asked ʿĀʾisha[7] about the words of Allah: "If you fear that you will not be able to maintain equity amongst the orphan girls, then marry (those) you like from amongst the women two, three or four."[8] She said: O, the son of my sister, the orphan girl is one who is under the patronage of her guardian and she shares with him in his property and her property and beauty fascinate him and her guardian makes up his mind to marry her without giving her due share of the wedding money and is not prepared (to pay so much amount) which anyone else is prepared to pay and so Allah has forbidden to marry these girls but in case when equity is observed as regards the wedding money and they are prepared to pay them the full amount of the wedding money and Allah commanded to marry other women besides them according to the liking of their heart. ʿUrwa reported that ʿĀʾisha said that people began to seek verdict from

4. ʿUmar ibn al-Khaṭṭāb (ca. 586–644), the second caliph. Ṭāriq ibn Shihāb (d. 701/2), famed for taking part in battles during the first two caliphates.
5. A plain and low mountain about 13 miles east of Mecca, at which the pilgrims arrive on the day of ʿArafa, the 9th day of the hajj (performed in the month of Dhū al-Ḥijja). It is a key station in the pilgrimage ritual.
6. Sufyān ibn ʿUyayna (725–811), a Meccan scholar of the third generation after that of the prophet Muḥammad.
7. ʿĀʾisha bint Abī Bakr (ca. 614–678), daughter of the first caliph, Abū Bakr, and wife of Muḥammad; she is a source of authoritative knowledge in early Islam. ʿUrwa ibn al-Zubayr (ca. 643–ca. 712), her nephew, was a major preserver of prophetic traditions.
8. Q 4:3.

Allah's Messenger (may peace be upon him) after the revelation of this verse about them (orphan girls) and Allah, the Exalted and Glorious, revealed this verse: "They asked thee verdict about women; say: Allah gives verdict to you in regard to them and what is recited to you in the Book about orphan woman, whom you give not what is ordained for them while you like to marry them" (iv. 126). She said: The wording of Allah "what is recited to you" in the Book means the first verse, i.e. "if you fear that you may not be able to observe equity in case of an orphan woman, marry what you like in case of woman" (iv. 3). 'Ā'isha said: (And as for this verse [iv. 126], i.e. and you intend "to marry one of them from amongst the orphan girls") it pertains to one who is in charge (of orphans) having small amount of wealth and less beauty and they have been forbidden that they should marry what they like of her wealth and beauty out of the orphan girls, but with equity, because of their disliking for them.

'Urwa reported that he asked 'Ā'isha about the words of Allah: "If you fear that you will not be able to observe equity in case of orphan girls"; the rest of the ḥadīth is the same but with a slight variation of wording.

'Ā'isha said that as for the words of Allah: "If you fear that you would not be able to observe equity in case of orphan (girls)," it was revealed in reference to a person who had an orphan girl (as his ward) and he was her guardian, and her heir, and she possessed property, but there was none to contend on her behalf except her ownself. And he (her guardian) did not give her in marriage because of her property and he tortured her and ill-treated her, it was in relation to her that (Allah said:) "If you fear that you would not be able to observe equity in case of orphan girls, then marry whom you like among women," i.e. whatever I have made lawful for you and leave her whom you are putting to torture.

'Ā'isha said in connection with His words (those of Allah): "What is recited to you in the Book about orphan women whom you give not what is ordained for them, while you like to marry them," these were revealed in connection with an orphan girl who was in the charge of the person and she shared with him in his property and he was reluctant to marry her himself and was also unwilling to marry her to someone else (fearing) that (that person) would share in his property (as the husband of that girl), preventing her to marry, neither marrying her himself nor marrying her to another person.

Hishām[9] reported that 'Ā'isha said in connection with the words of Allah: "They ask thee the religious verdict about women, say: Allah gives you the verdict about them" (iv. 126), that these relate to an orphan girl who is in charge of the person and she shares with him in his property (as a heir) even in the date-palm trees and he is reluctant to give her hand in marriage to any other person lest he (her husband) should partake of his property, and thus keep her in a lingering state.

Hishām reported on the authority of his father that 'Ā'isha said in connection with His (Allah's) words: "And whoever is poor let him take reasonably (out of it)"[1] that it was revealed in connection with the custodian of the property of an orphan, who is in charge of her and looks after her; in case he is poor, he is allowed to eat out of that.

9. Hishām ibn 'Urwa ibn al-Zubayr (ca. 680–ca. 763), son of 'Urwa ibn al-Zubayr, from whom he relayed many traditions.
1. Q 4:6.

ʿĀʾisha reported in connection with the words of Allah, the Exalted: "He who is rich should abstain, and he who is poor may reasonably eat (out of it)" that this was revealed in relation to the guardian of an orphan who is poor; he may get out of that what is reasonable keeping in view his own status of solvency.

This ḥadīth has been narrated on the authority of Hishām with the same chain of transmitters.

ʿĀʾisha reported that these words of Allah: "When they came upon you from above you and from below you and when the eyes turned dull and the hearts rose up to the throats" (xxxiii. 10) pertain to the day of Ditch.[2]

ʿĀʾisha said in connection with the verse: "And if a woman has reason to fear ill-treatment from her husband or that he might turn away from her" (iv. 128) that it was revealed in case of a woman who had long association with a person (as his wife) and now he intends to divorce her and she says: Do not divorce me, but retain me (as wife in your house) and you are permitted to live with another wife. It is in this context that this verse was revealed.

ʿĀʾisha said in connection with these words of Allah, the Exalted and Glorious: "And if a woman has reason to fear ill-treatment from her husband or that he might turn away from her" that it was revealed in case of a woman who lived with a person and perhaps he does not want to prolong (his relationship with her) whereas she has had sexual relationship with him (and as a result thereof) she got a child from him and she does not like that she should be divorced, so she says to him: I permit you to live with the other wife.

ʿUrwa reported on the authority of his father that ʿĀʾisha said to him: O, the son of my sister, the Muslims were commanded to seek forgiveness for the Companions of Allah's Apostle (may peace be upon him) but they reviled him.

This ḥadith has been transmitted on the authority of Abū Usāma with the same chain of narrators.

Saʿīd b. Jubair[3] reported: The inhabitants of Kūfa differed in regard to this verse: "But whoever slays another believer intentionally, his requital shall be Hell" (iv. 92), so I went to Ibn ʿAbbās[4] and asked him about it, whereupon he said: This has been revealed and nothing abrogated it.

This ḥadīth has been transmitted on the authority of Shuʾba[5] with the same chain of narrators but with a slight variation of wording.

Saʾīd b. Jubair reported: ʿAbd al Raḥmān b. Abzā commanded me that I should ask Ibn ʿAbbās about these two verses: "He who slays a believer intentionally his requital shall be Hell where he would abide for ever" (iv. 92).[6] So, I asked him and he said: Nothing has abrogated it. And as for this verse: "And they who call not upon another god with Allah and slay not the soul which Allah has forbidden except in the cause of justice" (xxv. 68), he (Ibn ʿAbbās) said: This has been revealed in regard to the polytheists.

2. That is, the Battle of the Trench (627), when Muslim forces thwarted a Meccan attack by digging a deep ditch around parts of Medina.
3. Saʿīd ibn Jubayr (d. 711/12), a scholar from Kūfa (in central Iraq) who was beheaded for participating in a revolt against the Umayyad empire.
4. ʿAbdallāh ibn ʿAbbās (ca. 619–687/88), one of the greatest early Muslim scholars; he is often considered the founder of the qurʾānic exegetical tradition, and he was Saʿīd's teacher.
5. Shuʿba ibn al-Ḥajjāj (d. 776/77), prominent transmitter and critic of ḥadīth.
6. Q 4:93.

Ibn 'Abbās said: This verse was revealed in Mecca: "And they who call not upon another god with Allah and slay not the soul which Allah has forbidden except in the cause of justice" up to the word *Muhāna* (abased). Thereupon the polytheists said: Islam is of no avail to us for we have made peer with Allah and we killed the soul which Allah had forbidden to do and we committed debauchery, and it was (on this occasion) that Allah, the Exalted and Glorious, revealed this verse: "Except him who repents and believes and does good deeds"[7] up to the end. Ibn 'Abbā's says: He who enters the fold of Islam and understands its command and then kills the soul there is no repentance for him.

Sa'id b. Jubair reported: I said to Ibn 'Abbās: Will the repentance of that person be accepted who kills a believer intentionally? He said: No. I recited to him this verse of Sūra al-Furqān[8] (xix.): "And those who call not upon another god with Allah and slay not the soul which Allah has forbidden except in the cause of justice" to the end of the verse. He said: This is a Meccan verse which has been abrogated by a verse revealed at Medina: "He who slays a believer intentionally, for him is the requital of Hell-Fire where he would abide for ever," and in the narration of Ibn Hāshim (the words are): I recited to him this verse of Sūra al-Furqān: "Except one who made repentance."[9]

'Ubaidullah b. 'Abdallah b. 'Utba[1] reported: Ibn 'Abbās said to me: Do you know—and in the words of Hārūn (another narrator): Are you aware of—the last Sūra which was revealed in the Qur'ān as a whole? I said: Yes, "When came the help from Allah and the victory"[2] (cx.). Thereupon, he said: You have told the truth. And in the narration of Abū Shaiba (the words are): Do you know the Sūra? And he did not mention the words "the last one".

This ḥadith has been reported on the authority of Abū 'Umais through the same chain of transmitters but with a slight variation of wording.

* * *

# ABŪ ḤĀTIM AL-RĀZĪ

The *Proofs of Prophecy* (*A'lām al-nubuwwa*) recounts a memorable debate between two great Persian theologians of the tenth century. Because both were born in the region of Rayy, now a part of Tehran, they share the epithet "al-Rāzī." Abū Ḥātim al-Rāzī (d. ca. 934) was an Ismā'īlī, an adherent of that form of Shī'ism that acknowledges a succession of seven imams as the spiritual heirs to Muḥammad and achieved political ascendency during the Fatimid caliphate. Abū Ḥātim became a leader among the Ismā'īlīs of Rayy and a staunch defender of fundamental Muslim beliefs. His opponent, whom he dubbed "the heretic," is among the most famous philosopher-physicians of the medieval Islamic world. Abū Bakr Muḥammad

7. Q 25:70.
8. Sūra 25, "The Criterion."
9. Q 25:70.
1. 'Ubaydallāh ibn 'Abdallāh ibn 'Utba (d. 716/17); a collector of traditions from the Companions. He is credited with being one of the teachers of the third caliph, 'Umar ibn 'Abd al-Azīz, and is numbered among the "seven jurists of Medina," who helped found Islamic jurisprudence.
2. Q 110:1.

ibn Zakariyyā' al-Rāzī (ca. 854–ca. 935), known in the Latin-speaking world as Rhazes, drew on clinical experience in writing his medical works, revising the received wisdom of his day as required by his empirical observation.

The debate of these two "Rāzīs" covers topics ranging from basic philosophical premises to the evolution of the natural sciences. Abū Bakr is presented as a philosophical supremacist, utterly dismissive of prophets and their incoherent revelations, eager to defend the intelligent use of reason as sufficient for human guidance. He insists that the concept of divine benevolence cannot coexist with that of revelation made only to particular prophets and peoples, not to all of humanity. Abū Ḥātim, in turn, springs to the defense not only of the Qur'ān and Muḥammad but of previous prophets, like Moses and Jesus, and their scriptures.

## [On the Matter of the Qur'ān][†]

### *Part Three, Chapter One*

### *Regarding his statement, "We shall now examine the speech of these people and its contradictory nature"*

(1) We turn to his statement where he says: "Let us now examine the speech of these people and its contradictory nature"—he means the speech of prophets, upon whom peace. He continues: "Jesus claimed he was the son of God; Moses claimed that God had no son; Muḥammad claimed he was a creature, like all other humans; Mani and Zoroaster[1] disagreed with Moses, Jesus, and Muḥammad concerning the Eternal One, the creation of the world, and the origin of good and evil. Mani disagreed with Zoroaster regarding the two worlds and their causes. Muḥammad claimed that Jesus was not crucified. The Jews and Christians deny this and claim that he was killed and crucified."

(2) The heretic mentioned all these subjects, adding a great deal of extraneous material from the religious views of Magians[2] and Dualists and their heretical dogmas. He then added, "The Jews claimed that Moses said that God was all-powerful and neither composite nor created, and that He is not benefited by beneficial things nor harmed by harmful things; that the Torah[3] includes the following: 'that fat should be placed on the fire so that the Lord can smell the scent' [cf. Leviticus 1:9]; that the Ancient of Days is in the form of an old man with white hair and beard [cf. Daniel 7:9]. It also includes such things as: 'Why do you offer to me for sacrifice every lame or one-eyed beast? Were you to offer these as gifts to your friends, would they accept them unless these sacrifices were whole?' [cf. Leviticus 22:17]. In it also are such injunctions as: 'Bring to me a carpet of fine silk

† From *The Proofs of Prophecy*, trans. Tarif Khalidi (Provo, UT: Brigham Young University Press, 2011), pp. 50–56. Used by permission of Brigham Young University Press. All brackets in the text are Khalidi's.

1. Also known as Zarasthustra (ca. 628–ca. 551 BCE), an Iranian viewed as the prophet of Zoroastrianism (called in its later form Mazdaism): the religion has many dualist features but a monotheistic conception of God. Mani (216–274? CE), also Iranian, founded Manichaeism, a religion that envisions an absolute dualism of two opposed substances (light and darkness, good and evil).
2. That is, Zoroastrians.
3. The first five books of the Hebrew Bible, traditionally ascribed to Moses.

and delicate craftsmanship and a chest of box wood' [cf. Ezekiel 16:10; Exodus 37:1]."

(3) The heretic added, "This sort of speech is more appropriate to the speech of a pauper than to the speech of the Self-Sufficient and Praiseworthy." He then cited several passages in the Torah and ridiculed them, adding that the Christians claim that Jesus is eternal and not subject to the authority of the Lord and that he said, "I have come to fulfill the Torah" [cf. Matthew 5:17] but proceeded instead to abrogate its laws and change its rules and regulations; that the Christians claim that he is Father, Son, and Holy Spirit. He further mentioned what the Magians say regarding Zoroaster in the chapter on Ahriman and Ahura Mazda;[4] and the claims of Mani to the effect that the Word separated from the Father and killed the demons and scattered them, that the sky is made from the skins of demons, that thunder is the gurgling of demons, that earthquakes agitate the demons beneath the earth, that Mani elevated Shapur, for whom he had composed the Shāburgān,[5] into the sky and hid him there for a while, and that Mani used to be snatched away in spirit from their midst and would approach near to the sun disk, remaining there for perhaps an hour or for some days.

(4) He thus cited these and similar impossible events fabricated by Magian and Manichean heretics and mixed it with what is to be found in revealed books and the lore of prophets, ascribing them to God's blessed messengers, who are innocent of all this. He alleged that all this was part of their heritage and that this proves the existence of divergence and contradiction in their speech. Arguing thus, he denied prophecy, meaning to prove his point by referring to such ludicrous fables and to strengthen his logic with reference to these myths and silly tales.

(5) I affirm that he who wishes to extinguish the light of God through the impossible tales narrated by Manicheans, heretics, and other misguided people in every nation is impoverished indeed: "God shall perfect His light, even though the unbelievers detest it" [Q. 61:8].

(6) In answer we say: In what he mentioned regarding Magians and Manicheans, the heretic intended to malign religious communities. In citing these impossible stories fabricated by Magians and Manicheans, he has not thereby advanced any valid argument to disprove prophecy. For these stories are false fabrications, the like of which may be found in philosophy, and we shall return to this theme in its proper place, God willing.

(7) As regards what he cited from the Torah, the Gospels, and other revealed books, and what he claimed was contradictory in the Qur'ān, most of these are of the nature of common parables. Some are clear in meaning, and some are obscure. But there is in them neither divergence nor contradiction. All of it is right and true, and prophets have never differed. Their speech, although regarded by the ignorant as contradictory, is uniform in meaning, although divergent in verbal expression. This is because most of the speech of prophets and wise men was symbolic, and they would address the nations with wisdom and coin parables, heard by both elite and commoners. The scholars and the elite who could fathom

4. Wise Lord (Avestan), who appeared to Zoroaster in a vision; he is the creator, and Ahriman is the destructive spirit.
5. A book that, according to Muslim sources, Mani wrote for Shāpūr I (d. 272), Persian king of the Sasanian dynasty.

the secrets of prophets would understand them and then teach worthy people. This is so in order that the world should contain teachers and taught, elite and commoners, and in order that they be constantly tested in this way. He who examines the outward form of their speech and does not understand their true meaning would judge their speech to be contradictory and divergent.

(8) This is the heritage of the prophets. This too is the correct principle grasped by scholars of all religious communities: both those who passed away in ancient religions, and those who passed away in this, our Muslim community. Revealed books have made this clear, as have all the books of the sages and reports of scholars. This is also the case regarding the books of genuine and wise philosophers. In them, too, there is obscure speech where the student is in need of someone to clarify it for him until he can come to grasp it. He who misunderstands it and peddles his own opinion shall fall into error. This is how philosophers came to hold divergent views and to misinterpret the Ancients and criticize their opinions, as they diverged in the case of Aristotle.[6] Some judged from his speech that he believed in one god, while others judged differently, misunderstanding the symbolic nature of his discourse. Likewise, revealed books, the speech of prophets, and the reports narrated of them are of this nature.

(9) One must therefore examine with care the question of the revealed books and reports of prophets that the heretic claimed were impossible and contradictory. If the person to whom these reports are ascribed is truthful, rational, and well esteemed by men of his age, then the matter is as we have described. If the person to whom these books and reports are ascribed is a liar, or demented, or stupid in the opinion of his contemporaries and does not realize the import of what he is saying, then it is possible to pronounce them contradictory and deceitful, as claimed by the heretic. This is because a rational, discriminating, and superior human being cannot possibly produce speech that is contradictory, impossible, and divergent. Nor can a rational and discriminating person who testifies to the truth and prophecy of another and claims that he is following in his footsteps and that he wishes to defend his legacy, then turn and contradict his speech and undermine his achievement, as the heretic claimed was the case with the contradictions in the speech of prophets and the divergences among them and the undermining by some of the achievement of others. If these major religious figures—from whom these books were handed down and the reports transmitted from prophets like Moses, Jesus, and Muḥammad—were well known for their ignorance, stupidity, irrationality, and madness, then what the heretic claims is true, God forbid. In reality, these figures—whom believers in religious laws emulate, like Moses, Jesus, Muḥammad, or other prophets—were celebrated for their perfection, reason, discrimination, sound policy, and having embodied every praiseworthy virtue. How else can this be, seeing the manner in which they led mankind and got them to unite in obedience to their laws? In like manner, the countless numbers who saw Muḥammad all agreed that they found him to be perfect in mind, self-control, patience, and leadership qualities, in his behavior toward both elite and commoners, and in the perfection of all qualities needed by any leader of mankind.

6. Greek philosopher (384–322 BCE).

(10) Thus, the Quraysh[7] admitted that they found him to be the best man of his age, and the one who most embodied praiseworthy virtues. They used to call him truthful and trustworthy before he began his prophecy. So when they came to rebuild the Ka'bah,[8] which had fallen into ruin, the leaders of every clan of Quraysh came forward to join together in rebuilding it, so that this honor would not belong to some rather than others. When they came to lay the black stone in its place, they fell out among themselves and competed for that honor, but then agreed upon Muḥammad, saying, "We accept the verdict of the trustworthy one." Muḥammad came forward and ordered that a cloth be laid out and the stone placed upon it. Each clan leader would then take up a corner of this cloth and lift it up together. They did so, and then Muḥammad took the stone and placed it in its place. They accepted this from him because they trusted him and relied on his judgment, decency, reason, and truthfulness. This is how they viewed him until he declared his prophecy. When he announced his prophecy and rejected their religion, along with what they worshipped other than God, they grew hostile and aggressive and said to him, "O Muḥammad, we knew you as truthful and trustworthy, so what is this message that you bring to us?" Regarding this incident, God revealed the following verse: "It is not you they call the lie to, but the signs of God that the wrongdoers abjure" [Q. 6:33]. That is to say, they do not find you a liar; rather, they know you to be truthful. But they are unjust toward themselves and deny the truth and turn away from it. If someone says, "Why did they tell him, 'You are mad,' until God revealed, 'They turned their backs on him, saying, "He is tutored and crazed"' [Q. 44:14], and also, 'Or did they fail to recognize their Messenger and so denied him? Or do they say there is madness in him? Rather, he brought them the truth, but most of them detest the truth' [Q. 23:70]?" I answer: They did not mean that he is mad and infirm of mind. They simply claimed that he had a companion from the jinn[9] who taught him. It is in this sense that they said he is tainted with madness. For when they found out that the things he predicted of the Unseen turned out to be true as reported by him, they said that this was a vision granted him by the jinn and that he had a follower who instructed him in this manner.

(11) This charge was also leveled at earlier prophets, as revealed by God in the story of Noah: "He is but a man in whom there is madness, so watch him closely for a while" [Q. 23:25]. In the story of Moses, also, the following was revealed in the tongue of Pharaoh: "This your messenger, who has been sent to you, is mad" [Q. 26:27]. He then added, immediately after the miracle that Moses worked with the stick and the hand,[1] "This fellow is a most experienced sorcerer. He intends to drive you out of your land with his sorcery" [Q. 26:34]. So how can he mean by "mad" someone mentally infirm and then say that he is a skilled sorcerer who wants to make you leave your land through his magic? How can a madman be a skilled sorcerer? And how can Pharaoh be afraid of a madman

7. The tribe of the prophet Muḥammad, which ruled Mecca and which opposed Islam in its early years.
8. The stone shrine in Mecca (literally, "cube"), believed to have been built by Adam and then rebuilt by Ibrāhīm (Abraham) and Ismā'īl (Ishmael); central to both early pagan and Muslim pilgrimage rituals, it became the most important site in Islam.
9. The third class of intelligent beings (together with humans and angels) for whom salvation is possible. According to Q 55:15, God created them from smokeless fire.
1. He threw down his staff, and it turned into a snake; he put his hand into his armpit, and when he drew it out it was white but not harmed. See Q 20:17–22; 26:32–33.

who would drive him out of his land? By "mad," he meant someone granted a vision by the jinn. This is because he used to inform them of things that turned out to be true, and they said this was inspired by the jinn. Seeing the miracles, they said this was sorcery. So their saying to Muḥammad that he is one who is taught, mad, and tainted with madness, is not the equivalent of impugning his reason, perfection, perfect understanding, and discrimination. How can they think him mad after all the great and wonderful things they saw him perform? Do you not see how God says, "Or did they fail to recognize their Messenger and so denied him?"—that is to say, that they do not know him as honest and truthful and so deny his reason and accuse him of lying. But, in fact, they knew him well as an honest and trustworthy person. God also says, "You are not, by the grace of your Lord, a man possessed" [Q. 68:2]. The phrase "by the grace of your Lord" means, "You are not, thank God, mad." Immediately afterwards, God says, "And you are of a character most noble" [Q. 68:4]. In interpreting this phrase, some commentators say that the noble character is the Qurʾān, meaning that what you transmit is not from the jinn but is the noble Qurʾān that is inspired by the Almighty.

(12) If the religious leader [imām] is similar to Muḥammad in perfection and in combining all praiseworthy virtues to be found among mankind—such as truth, honesty, reason, self-restraint, sobriety, dignity, attractive demeanor, humility, generosity, faithfulness, courage, a soft heart, compassion for those who believe in and follow him, forgiveness toward those who blasphemed against or opposed him once he has captured them, as well as other praiseworthy qualities that exist among mankind—a person in such a situation cannot be accused of speaking in a manner that others recognize as contradictory and divergent, while the person himself is unaware of the import of his speech. Muḥammad combined in his person all these virtues. We shall mention only those virtues that are widely known, in order to prove the truth of our assertions, God willing.

## AL-QUSHAYRĪ

Abū al-Qāsim ʿAbd al-Karīm b. Hawāzin al-Qushayrī (986–1072) was born in an area of Khurasan that is now part of Iran. His first language was Persian, but as a youth he was schooled in Arabic language and literature. For more advanced education, he moved to Nishapur, where he became a disciple of the Ṣūfī master Abū ʿAlī al-Daqqāq (d. 1015 or 1021) and studied Shāfiʿī jurisprudence and Ashʿarite theology. Al-Qushayrī's most famous works are his commentary on the Qurʾān and his treatise on Sufism. His commentary, *Subtleties of the Allusions* (*Laṭāʾif al-ishārāt*), seeks to unveil mystical insights within the Qurʾān that are accessible only to the elect, God's special friends (*awliyāʾ*). With *The Epistle on Sufism* (*Al-Risāla al-Quyshayriyya fī ʿilm al-tasawwuf*), al-Qusayrī left to future generations a popular primer on the Ṣūfī path. The book combines the biographies of eighty-three famous Ṣūfīs with a handbook of special terminology and an exposition of the major "stations" (*maqāmāt*) of the Ṣūfī spiritual and experiential journey to God. The following excerpt, drawn from the third section, develops the concept of "trust in God" (*tawakkul*). Taking three qurʾānic verses as his proof texts, al-Qushayrī illustrates this concept with numerous Ṣūfī stories and sayings.

# *From* The Epistle on Sufism†

## TRUST IN GOD (*TAWAKKUL*)

God—may He be great and Exalted—said: "And whosoever puts his trust in God, He shall suffice him."[1] He also said: "And in God let the believers put all their trust."[2] [Finally,] He said: "Put all your trust in God, if you are believers."[3]

The imam Abu Bakr Muhammad b. al-Hasan b. Furak[4] said: ʿAbdallah b. Jaʿfar b. Ahmad al-Isbahani told us: Yunus b. Habib b. ʿAbd al-Qahir told us: Abu Dawud al-Tayalisi told us: Hammad b. Maslama[5] told us on the authority of ʿAsim b. Bahdala, on the authority of Zirr b. Hubaysh, on the authority of ʿAbdallah b. Masʿud[6]—may God be pleased with him—that: "The Messenger of God—may God bless and greet him—said: 'I was shown all the [religious] communities at the time of the pilgrimage. I saw that my community had filled both the valley and the plain [of ʿArafat].[7] I was pleased with their great number and their appearance. I was asked: "Are you satisfied?" I answered: "Yes."' [A voice] said [to me]: 'Among these there are seventy thousand who will enter Paradise without reckoning. They have never allowed themselves to be treated by cauterization, nor to divine the future by [observing] birds' flight, nor have resorted to [the magician's] charms. They have put their trust in God alone.' [When the Prophet said this] ʿUkkasha b. Muhsin al-Asadi stood up and requested: 'Messenger of God, pray to God that He would make me one of them!' The Messenger of God replied, saying: 'O God, make him one of them!' Another person stood up and asked: 'Pray to God that He would make me one of them!' The Messenger—may God bless and greet him—answered: 'ʿUkkasha has preceded you in this!'"

I heard ʿAbdallah b. Yusuf al-Isbahani say: I heard Abu Nasr al-Sarraj say: I heard Abu Bakr al-Wajihi say: I heard Abu ʿAli al-Rudhbari say: I asked ʿAmr b. Sinan to tell me a story about Sahl b. ʿAbdallah [al-Tustari].[8] ʿAmr said that Sahl once said: "One who trusts God is distinguished by three signs: he does not ask, does not refuse [when given], and does not hold on [to what was given to him]." I heard Shaykh Abu ʿAbd al-Rahman al-Sulami[9]—may God have mercy on him—say: I heard Mansur b. ʿAbdallah say: I heard Abu ʿAbdallah al-Shirazi say: "I heard Abu Musa al-Daylubi say that someone asked Abu Yazid al-Bistami[1] about trust in

† From Abu ʾl-Qasim al-Qushayri, *Al-Qushayri's Epistle on Sufism: Al-Risala al-qushayriyya fi ʿilm al-tasawwuf*, trans. Alexander D. Knysh, reviewed by Muhammad Eissa (Reading, UK: Garnet, 2007), pp. 178–83. Reprinted by permission of the publisher. All brackets in the text are Knysh's.

1. Q 65:3.
2. Q 14:11.
3. Q 5:23.
4. A famous Ashʿari theologian and teacher of al-Qushayrī, who resided in Nishapur. He died in 406/1015 [Knysh's note].
5. Or "ibn al-Salama" [Knysh's note].
6. ʿAbdallāh ibn Masʿūd (d. ca. 652/53), a Companion of the Prophet.
7. About 13 miles east of Mecca; it is a key station in the pilgrimage ritual, at which the pilgrims arrive on the 9th day of the *ḥajj*.
8. Sahl ibn ʿAbdallāh al-Tustarī (818–896), a Persian mystic who lived much of his life in Basra (Southeastern Iraq) and is famous for his Qurʾān interpretation.
9. Abū ʿAbd al-Raḥmān al-Sulāmī (ca. 940–1021), a famous Ṣūfī of Nishapur who wrote biographies of Ṣūfīs and commentaries on the Qurʾān.
1. Abū Yazīd al-Bisṭāmī (d. 874), Persian Ṣūfī mystic and poet.

God. He, in turn, asked me what I thought about it. I answered: 'My companions say: "Even if wild beasts and poisonous snakes were all around you, your innermost heart would still not be perturbed!"' Abu Yazid answered: 'Yes, this is close. But if you were to [observe] the people of Paradise enjoying themselves in its gardens and the people of Hell being tortured by its fires, and you would give preference to one over the other, you would leave the realm of trust in God altogether.'" Sahl b. ʿAbdallah said: "The beginning of trust in God is when the servant places himself before God as a dead corpse is placed before the washer of the dead, who turns it however he wishes, while the body has no moves nor will of its own." Hamdun al-Qassar[2] said: "Trust in God is taking refuge in God Most High."

I heard Muhammad b. al-Husayn say: I heard Abu Bakr Muhammad b. Ahmad al-Balkhi say: I heard Muhammad b. Hamid say: I heard Ahmad b. Khadrawayh say: "A man asked Hatim al-Asamm:[3] From where do you get your provisions?' He answered: 'To God belong the treasures of the heavens and of the earth, but the hypocrites do not understand.'"[4]

Know that the place of trust is in the heart. Outward action does not necessarily contradict trust in the heart. Once the servant has ascertained that determination comes from God Most High, he realizes that any hardship he experiences is pre-determined [by God] and any success he may have is also facilitated by God. ʿAli b. Ahmad b. ʿAbdan informed us: Ahmad b. ʿUbayd al-Basri told us: Ghaylan b. ʿAbd al-Samad told us: Ismaʿil b. Masʿud al-Jahdari told us: Khalid b. Yahya told us: "My uncle al-Mughira b. Abi Qurra recounted on the authority of Anas b. Malik[5] that a certain man came [to the Prophet] riding his she-came and asked him: 'Messenger of God, should I leave her loose and put my trust in God?' The Prophet responded: 'Tie her up and trust in God!'"

Ibrahim al-Khawwas[6] said: "He who trusts in God when dealing with himself will also trust God when dealing with others." Bishr al-Hafi[7] said: "One Sufi said: 'I have put my trust in God [and failed].' However, he lied to God Most High. If he were indeed to put his trust in God, he would have been content with what God did to him." Someone asked Yahya b. Muʿadh [al-Razi]:[8] "When can a man trust God?" He answered: "When he is content to have God as his trustee."

I heard Shaykh Abu ʿAbd al-Rahman al-Sulami—may God have mercy on him—say: I heard Muhammad b. ʿAli b. al-Husayn say: I heard ʿAbdallah b. Muhammad b. al-Samit say: I heard Ibrahim al-Khawwas say: "As I was journeying in the desert I heard someone speak. I looked around and saw a Bedouin walking along. He told me: 'Ibrahim, trust in God resides with us [people of the desert], so stay with us until your trust has become sound. Don't you see that you are driven to cities by the food that you hope to find there? Therefore, stop pinning your hopes on cities and put your trust in God instead!'" I also heard him [al-Sulami] say: I heard Muhammad b. Ahmad al-Farisi say: I heard Muhammad b. ʿAtaʾ[9] say that

2. Ḥamdūn al-Qaṣṣār (d. 844/85), founder of a Ṣūfī order that originated in Khurasan.
3. A Ṣūfī master of Khurasan (d. 852).
4. Q 63:7.
5. Anās ibn Mālik (d. ca. 710), an early Companion of the Prophet; he was given to Muḥammad as a servant at age ten.
6. Abū Isḥāq Ibrāhīm ibn Aḥmad al-Khawwās (d. 904), of Rayy.
7. Abu Nasr Bishr b. al-Ḥārith al-Ḥāfī (d. 842), of Baghdad.
8. Yaḥyā ibn Muʿādh al-Rāzī (d. 871/72), mystic and preacher of Balkh and Nishapur.
9. Muḥammad ibn ʿAṭāʾ (d. 921/22), a Ṣūfī master and scholar.

someone asked him about the true essence of trust in God. He answered: "It is when anxiety about things of this world does not prevail over you despite your dire need of them and when your reliance upon God prevails in you despite your dependence on such things."

I heard Abu Hatim al-Sijistani say: I heard Abu Nasr al-Sarraj say: "The condition for trust in God is what Abu Turab al-Nakhshabi had in mind when he said: 'To prostrate your body in worship, to attach your heart to lordship, and to find solace in sufficiency; when you are given, you are thankful and when you are denied, you persevere.'" Dhu 'l-Nun[1] said: "Trust in God is to give up planning for yourself and to abandon [reliance on your own] power and ability. The servant is capable of trust in God only when he has realized that God—may He be exalted—knows and sees his condition." I heard Muhammad b. al-Husayn say: I heard Abu 'l-Faraj al-Warathani say: I heard Ahmad b. Muhammad al-Qirmisini say: I heard al-Kattani say: I heard Abu Ja'far b. Abi 'l-Faraj say: "Once I saw a villain (*shatir*) nicknamed 'A'isha's Camel'[2] being whipped. I asked him: 'When will this lashing be easier for you?' He answered: 'When the one on whose account I am being whipped will see me.'" I heard 'Abdallah b. Muhammad say: I heard al-Husayn b. Mansur[3] say to Ibrahim al-Khawwas: "What have you achieved throughout all these travels of yours and your wanderings in the deserts?" He answered: "I have persevered in my trust in God, disciplining my soul thereby." Al-Husayn [b. Mansur] asked him: "So you have spent your entire life taking care of your inner self. What about annihilating your inner self through unifying it with God (*tawhid*)?"

I heard Abu Hatim al-Sijistani say: I heard Abu Nasr al-Sarraj say: "Trust in God is what Abu 'Ali al-Daqqaq[4] once said—that is, 'Limiting your livelihood's worth to one day only and giving up concern about what will happen [to you] tomorrow.'" Or, as Sahl b. 'Abdallah said: "Putting yourself in the hands of God, so that he would do with you what He wants." I heard Shaykh Abu 'Abd al-Rahman al-Sulami—may God have mercy on him—say: I heard Muhammad b. Ja'far b. Muhammad say: I heard Abu Bakr al-Bardha'i say: I heard Abu Ya'qub al-Nahrajuri say: "Trust in God in its perfect essence manifested itself in what happened to Abraham. [As he was flying through the air][5] he told Gabriel [who had offered him his help]: 'No, not from you!' For his [Abraham's] self had been annihilated in God [to such an extent that] he could see no one else but God alone—may He be great and exalted!"

I also heard him [al-Sulami] say: I heard Sa'id b. Ahmad b. Muhammad say: I heard Muhammad b. Ahmad b. Sahl say: I heard Sa'id b. 'Uthman al-Khayyat say: I heard Dhu 'l-Nun al-Misri say, when asked about trust in God: "Divesting oneself from all masters [other than God] and cutting one's attachment to all causes [other than God]." The inquirer asked him: "Tell me more!" Dhu 'l-Nun responded: "Throwing oneself into worship

1. Dhū al-Nūn al-Misrī (d. 861), an early Ṣūfī who was a master of asceticism and the teacher of many mystics.
2. 'Ā'isha bint Abī Bakr (ca. 614–678) was Muḥammad's wife and the daughter of Abū Bakr, the first caliph.
3. Al-Ḥusayn ibn Manṣūr al-Ḥallāj (ca. 858–922), Ṣūfī mystic and poet, executed for heresy and subversion.
4. Abū 'Alī Ḥasan al-Daqqāq (d. 1015 or 1021), a Ṣūfī master of Nishapur who was al-Qushayrī's teacher and father-in-law.
5. According to the biblical and qur'anic tradition, Abraham was thrown onto a bonfire by his infidel persecutors only to be miraculously rescued by the archangel Gabriel [Knysh's note].

and ridding oneself of any pretension to lordship." I also heard him say: I heard 'Abdallah b. Munazil say: I heard Hamdun al-Qassar say, when asked about trust in God: "It is as if you had ten thousand *dirhams* in your possession and one *daniq*[6] worth of debt, yet you would not be able to rest easy [fearing] that you might die without having this debt settled. Or as if you had a debt of ten thousand *dirhams* and no means to pay it back [after your death], yet you would not despair of God Most High's settling it for you." Someone asked Abu 'Abdallah al-Qurashi[7] about trust in God. He answered: "Holding on to God in every state." The inquirer asked: "Tell me more!" Al-Qurashi continued: "Giving up reliance on any cause that leads to another cause so as to render God the sole possessor of all causes." Sahl b. 'Abdallah said: "Trust in God is the [spiritual] state of the Prophet—may God bless and greet him—while earning is his custom (*sunna*). Whoever adheres to his [the Prophet's] state, will never depart from his custom." Abu Sa'id al-Kharraz[8] said: "Trust in God is agitation without rest and rest without agitation." It is also said: "Trust in God is when abundance and scarcity are one and the same to you." Ibn Masruq said: "Trust in God is to surrender oneself to the rule of divine commands and decrees."

I heard Muhammad b. al-Husayn say: I heard 'Abdallah al-Razi say: I heard Abu 'Uthman al-Hiri[9] say: "Trust in God is to be satisfied with and rely on God Most High." I also heard him [Muhammad b. al-Husayn] say: I heard Muhammad b. Muhammad b. Ghalib relate on the authority of al-Husayn b. Mansur, who said: "The true trust in God is when one does not eat anything in a land where there might be someone more deserving of food than him." I also heard him say: I heard 'Abdallah b. 'Ali say: I heard Mansur b. Ahmad al-Harbi say: Ibn Abi Shaykh related to us that he heard 'Umar b. Sinan say: "Once Ibrahim al-Khawwas passed us by. We asked him to tell us about the most wondrous thing he had ever seen during his travels. He answered: "[It is when] I met al-Khidr[1]—peace be on him—and he requested my companionship, yet I was afraid that I might compromise my trust in God by relying on him. So I left him."

Someone asked Sahl b. 'Abdallah about trust in God. He answered: "It is when a heart lives with God Most High alone without attaching itself to anything else." I heard the master Abu 'Ali al-Daqqaq—may God have mercy on him—say: "The one who puts his trust in God goes through three stages: trust in God, [self-]surrender [to God], and relegating [one's affairs to God]. The one who practices trust in God relies on His promise [of sustenance]; the one who surrenders himself [to God] is content with his knowledge [of God]; and the one who relegates his affairs [to God] is satisfied with His decree." I also heard him [al-Daqqaq] say: "Trust in God is the beginning, [self-]surrender is the middle and relegating [one's affairs to God] is the end." Someone asked al-Daqqaq about trust in God. He answered: "It is eating without appetite." Yahya b. Mu'adh said: "Putting on woolen clothing is [setting up] shop; discoursing about renunciation is a profession; and traveling with caravans [of pilgrims] is ostentation. All these are nothing but attachments [to this world]."

6. A coin worth one-sixth of the *dirham* [Knysh's note].
7. Abū 'Abdallāh al-Qurashī (d. 941), a Ṣūfī.
8. Abū Sa'īd Aḥmad ibn 'Īsā al-Kharrāz (d. ca. 895?), prominent in the Baghdad school of Ṣūfīs.
9. Abū 'Uthmān al-Ḥīrī (844–910), renowned Ṣūfī master of Khurasan.
1. Al-Khiḍr or al-Khaḍir ("the Green Man"), a figure of legend who is identified by most commentators with the servant of God whom Moses meets in the story recounted in Q 18:59–81.

A man came to al-Shibli[2] to complain to him about his large family. Al-Shibli retorted: "Go back to your house and expel from it anyone whose sustenance is not obligatory for God Most High!" I heard Shaykh Abu 'Abd al-Rahman al-Sulami—may God have mercy on him—say: I heard 'Abdallah b. 'Ali say: I heard Ahmad b. 'Ata' say: I learned from Muhammad b. al-Husayn that Sahl b. 'Abdallah said: "Whoever condemns stirring oneself [to earn a livelihood] condemns the Prophet's custom; and whoever condemns trust in God [to provide for him] condemns faith." I also heard him [al-Sulami] say: I heard Ahmad b. 'Ali b. Ja'far say: I heard Ja'far al-Khuldi say: Ibrahim al-Khawwas said: "I was on my way to Mecca, when I met a wild-looking person. I said to myself: 'Is this a man or a jinn?'[3] He answered: 'I am a jinn.' 'Where are you headed?' I asked him. He said that he was going to Mecca. I asked him: 'Do you travel without any provisions?' He said: 'Yes! Among us, too, are those who travel putting their trust in God.' I asked him: 'What, then, is trust in God?' He answered: 'Taking [your provisions] from God Most High.'" I heard him [al-Sulami] say: I heard Abu 'l-'Abbas al-Baghdadi say: I heard al-Farghani say: "Ibrahim al-Khawwas excelled in the art of trust and attained a great sophistication in it. However, he never parted with a needle and thread, a [begging] bowl,[4] and a pair of scissors. Someone asked him: 'Abu Ishaq, why do you carry all these things, while you abstain from all other things?' He answered: 'Things like these do not contradict trust in God, for God—may He be exalted—has made certain rules obligatory for everyone. Thus, a *dervish*[5] has but one piece of clothing, which may be torn. If he does not have a needle and thread, his private parts may be exposed and his prayer becomes invalid; and if he has no bowl, his ablutions may be corrupted. Therefore, if you see a poor man who has neither bowl nor needle and thread, be wary of the perfection of his prayer.'"

I heard the master Abu 'Ali al-Daqqaq—may God have mercy on him—say: "Trust in God is the characteristic of the [ordinary] believers; surrendering oneself to God is the characteristic of the elect; and relegating [one's affairs to God] is the characteristic of those who have achieved unity [with God]. [In other words], trust in God is the characteristic of the common folk; surrendering is the characteristic of the elect; and relegating is the characteristic of the elect of the elect." I also heard him [al-Daqqaq] say: "Trust is the characteristic of the friends of God (*awliya'*); surrendering is the characteristic of Abraham—peace be upon him—and relegating is the characteristic of our prophet Muhammad—may God bless and greet him."

I heard Muhammad b. al-Husayn say: I heard Abu 'l-Abbas al-Baghdadi say: I heard Muhammad b. 'Abdallah al-Farghani say: I heard Abu Ja'far al-Haddad say: "For more than ten years I lived in the state of trust in God, while working in the bazaar (*suq*). Every day I would receive my wages, but I did not use this money even to pay for a drink of water or for the admission fee to a public bath. Instead, I would bring this money to the poor folks who

2. Abū Bakr al-Shiblī (d. 945), an Abbasid court official who became a Ṣūfī in later life and was noted for his eccentricities and ecstatic utterances.
3. A member of the third class of intelligent beings (together with humans and angels) for whom salvation is possible. According to Q 55:15, God created them from smokeless fire.
4. A bowl that could be used for both begging and drinking [Knysh's note].
5. A member of a Ṣūfī mystic order.

resided at the al-Shuniziyya mosque.[6] In this way I preserved my state [of trust]."

I heard him [Muhammad b. al-Husayn] say: I heard Abu Bakr Muhammad b. ʿAbdallah b. Shadhan say: I heard al-Khawwas say: I heard al-Husayn, brother of Sinan, say: "I made fourteen pilgrimages [to Mecca] in the state of trust, barefoot. Whenever a thorn entered my foot I would remind myself that I had imposed trust in God upon myself, so I would rub it [the thorn] against the ground and walk on." I also heard him say: I heard Muhammad b. ʿAbdallah the Preacher (*waʿiz*) say: I heard Khayr al-Nassaj say: I heard Abu Hamza [al-Baghdadi][7] say: "When I have a vow to practice trust in God, I'd be ashamed before God Most High to enter the desert with a full stomach lest my journey should rely on my prior satiety with which I had equipped myself in advance."

Someone asked Hamdun al-Qassar about trust in God. He answered: "This is a stage that I have not reached yet. How can one who has not yet perfected his faith speak of trust in God?" They say that the one who trusts God is similar to an infant, who knows nothing but his mother's breast, which he always seeks. Likewise, one who trusts God is always led to his Lord Most High. One of the Sufis related: "I was in the desert walking before a caravan, when I saw someone in front of me. I hurried to catch up with him and saw a woman with a staff in her hand walking slowly. I thought that she was exhausted, so I reached into my pocket and brought out twenty *dirhams*. I told her: 'Take this and wait until the caravan catches up with you. You should then pay your fare with this money and catch up with me in the evening, so that I could arrange everything for you.' She said, as she raised her hand in the air like this and suddenly [I saw] *dinars*[8] in her palm: 'You take *dirhams* out of your pocket (*jayb*) and I take *dinars* out of the unseen (*ghayb*).' "

Once Abu Sulayman al-Darani[9] saw a man in Mecca who would live on nothing but some water from the Zamzam well.[1] Many days elapsed. One day Sulayman asked him: "If the water of Zamzam were to dry up, what would you drink?" The man jumped to his feet, kissed Sulayman's head and said: "May God give you a good reward! You have guided me aright, for I have nearly become a worshiper of Zamzam over the past few days!" Ibrahim al-Khawwas related: "Once on my way to Syria I saw a young man of good manners. He asked me: 'Would you like a companion?' When I told him that I was hungry, he replied: 'Whenever you are hungry, I will be hungry as well!' We had stayed together for four days, until something was given to us and I invited him to partake of it with me. He responded saying: 'I have made a vow not to accept anything from intermediaries.' I told him: 'You are meticulous indeed [in your trust in God]!' He answered: 'None of your idle words! The stern judge is watching [us]. What have you to do with trust in God?' He then added: 'The least [portion of] trust is when you encounter sources of satisfying your needs but your soul aspires toward nothing but Him Who holds all sufficiency!' "

6. In Baghdad.
7. Abū Ḥamza al-Baghdādī (d. 901/2), a Ṣūfī jurist and expert on Qurʾān recitation.
8. Gold coins; dirhams are silver.
9. Abū Sulaymān al-Raḥmān ibn ʿAṭiyya al-Dārānī (ca. 757–ca. 825), a Ṣūfī sage from Daran, a village near Damascus.
1. The sacred well located in the Meccan sanctuary [Knysh's note].

# AL-JUWAYNĪ

ʿAbd al-Malik ibn Muḥammad al-Juwaynī (1028–1085), a major theologian and jurisprudent of medieval Islam, was born near Nishapur, the intellectual and cultural center of the Persian province of Khurasan. After distinguishing himself as a student, he assumed his father's teaching responsibilities in Nishapur when his father died. Theologically, he became a leading figure among the Ashʿarites, and he was a proponent of the Shāfiʿī school of law. His most famous student was Abu Ḥamid Muḥammad al-Ghazālī (1058–1111).

A politically inspired denunciation of Ashʿarism forced al-Juwaynī to flee Nishapur and to live in exile for several years. He spent this period teaching and issuing legal opinions in Mecca and Medina, thereby earning his sobriquet, "leading master of the two holy cities" (*Imām al-Ḥaramayn*). With a change of political leadership in Nishapur, al-Juwaynī returned to his birthplace to teach at the newly created Niẓāmiyya, a school founded by the vizier Niẓām al-Mulk.

The full title of the work excerpted below clearly explains its purpose: *A Guide to Conclusive Proofs for the Principles of Belief* (*Irshād ilā qawāṭiʿ al-adilla fī uṣūl al-iʿtiqād*). Al-Juwaynī wanted to bolster belief with the best possible arguments, equipping his students and followers with the reasoned responses that destroy doubt and cancel conflicting interpretations. Within a larger discussion of theological propositions that have proven particularly controversial, he describes miracles, such as the inimitability of the Qurʾān, as proof of the prophetic mission.

## *From* The Doctrine about Proving the Prophecy of Our Prophet Muḥammad, God Bless Him and Keep Him†

* * *

### *Chapter: [On the miracles of Muḥammad, God bless him and keep him]*

It is best for us to begin this chapter with what applies to the Qurʾān and to confirm that it constitutes a miracle. Our goals are most clearly reached here by reviewing our responses to a number of questions.

Someone may inquire: What is your proof that your Prophet divulged the Qurʾān? And what assures you that it was not forged after him? We reply: One cannot argue against the self-evident. We know necessarily that our Prophet, on whom be peace, used to teach the Qurʾān and to recite it. He expounded it to his Companions and his followers. Whatever is proven by multiple concurring reports is known with self-evident certainty. To reject this is tantamount to denying that Muḥammad, God bless him and keep him, was ever in this world. That would be like denying the nations, events and times of those in bygone eras. There is no sense in going on about this at length.

Now it maybe said: Even if his divulging it in his own era were conceded to you, what is your proof of his having issued his prophetic challenge

† From Imām al-Ḥaramayn al-Juwaynī, *A Guide to Conclusive Proofs for the Principles of Belief: Kitāb al-irshād ilā qawāṭiʿ al-adilla fī uṣūl al-iʿtiqād*, trans. Paul E. Walker, reviewed by Muhammad S. Eissa (Reading, UK: Garnet, 2001), pp. 187–92. Reprinted by permission of the publisher. All brackets in the text are Walker's.

through it and having caused the nations summoned to contest with him not being able to do so? We respond to this: This also is known with self-evident certainty. The apostle of God, God bless him and keep him, never stopped speaking about the Qur'ān, applying it as evidence, insisting that he alone was singled out by having the Book of God, the Exalted, revealed to him. Those who deny the claim of his having been chosen for it and his being connected by the Lord God's specifically designating him with His Book, have rejected something attested by multiple and concordant reports.

What confirms what we say is that we know with intuitive certainty that, if one of the Arabs had produced—for the sake of argument—another Qur'ān like it, that would reject as unacceptable the pretension to a claim of prophecy, discredit the person making the claim and lower his status. This cannot be denied. If he had not issued his prophetic challenge in conjunction with it, the matter would not have been as it was. But there is no concealing what we have said; verses of the Qur'ān proclaim clearly the prophetic challenge and the resulting incapacity of the Arabs. Among them are the following words of God: "Say: if men and the jinn[1] joined together to produce the like of this Qur'ān, they could not produce its like, even if they backed one another" [17:88]. And there are other verses with the same meaning.

If someone says: It is not inconceivable to suppose divergences in these verses in their own right, since attaining the status of inimitability does not preclude assuming that they were themselves an invention, we reply: There is no verse of the Qur'ān whose transmission is not fully confirmed by multiple reports, since the reading of the later follows that of the preceding generations. The matter has been like this continuously; the younger generations transmit it from the older, going back without break in transmission to the reading of the Companions, may God be pleased with them. Nor did the number of readers in any given era decrease below the number that assures certainty. What further clarifies what we have just said is that, if we were to be able to doubt the origin of a given verse, this would extend to every verse and thereby invalidate the integrity of the transmission of the whole Qur'ān.

Someone may ask: What assures you that the Qur'ān was not contested and that what was contested in it was not subsequently hidden? We respond: This is absurd since, if it had happened like that, the matter would have been revealed and become well known. Circumstances so momentous as that could not be concealed over the course of time. Claiming what the questioner claims is tantamount to asserting that there was a caliph in charge of the Muslims prior to Abū Bakr,[2] may God be pleased with him. And that is self-evidently known to be false.

What supports our contention is that the unbelievers, from the time of the apostle of God, God bless him and keep him, until our era, have expended the utmost effort they have been capable of to destroy our religion. If the contestation had been possible and not completely unrealizable, over the past centuries and eras, they would have used every trick to

1. The third class of intelligent beings (together with humans and angels) for whom salvation is possible. According to Q 55:15, God created them from smokeless fire.
2. The first caliph (573–634), a position he assumed in 632 after the death of Muḥammad; he was Muḥammad's chief adviser and father-in-law.

achieve it. If the contesting of it were to have once been concealed, another instance of it or like it would have taken its place.

Furthermore, if this question or one like it were posed by those who uphold prophetic missions, one can turn against them all they advance with respect to the miracles of their own prophet. Say thus to the Jews: What assures you that Moses, on whom be peace, did not have his signs contested and that subsequently the tribe of Israel agreed among themselves to eradicate any information about occurrence of the contestation?

Someone may ask: How would you rebut those who insist that the Arabs did not refrain from contesting the Qurʾān because of an inability but rather they did not undertake it only because they had almost no interest in doing so? We reply: This is a weak argument indeed and one that no person with the least education would offer in public. The discussions and conferences of the Arabs were lively and animated, and they were vehement about disputing the weakness or strength of poetry. From this we know of necessity that the Qurʾān, in their belief, was not so inferior to the poetry of a poet or a work in prose that they took so little notice of it as to refrain even from discussing it.

How could this be when the Apostle, on whom be peace, and his supporters, said: "If you can contest successfully even one *sūra* of the Qurʾān, we will accord you peace; we will abandon the struggle and submit willingly to you. But, if it turns out to be otherwise, we will light the fire of war, devote our power entirely to it, make ourselves masters of its art, and desist neither from killing men nor violating freed Arab women." How could an intelligent person think, after the word of Islam had appeared and the flags and banners of the Muslims were waving, that the unbelievers would prefer to face horrors that turn forelocks white and events that make the immovable vanish, rather than to contest a *sūra* simply out of disdain for them?

Thus the miracle, the prophetic challenge, and the inability of anyone to contest it are proven. This evaluation suffices to accomplish what we wanted. And God alone is the guide to the truth.

## *Chapter: [On the various ways the Qurʾān is inimitable]*

If it is said: Explain to us in how, in what way, and to what degree the Qurʾān is inimitable, we respond: The doctrine approved by us is that the Qurʾān is inimitable because it combines eloquence with an elegance of form in an arrangement distinct from the ordinary speech of the Arabs. Hence the arrangement of words by itself does not yield the inimitability in it, nor does its eloquence alone.

The proof of this is for us to suppose simply that its eloquence is inimitable. This will not eliminate the following hypothetical challenge. Someone might say: If the Qurʾān were to be compared to the discourse of the Arabs, their prose, their grand poetry, and their poetry of short metres, the language of the masters of eloquence and rhetorical talents would not, in a manner that is clearly and decisively convincing, be judged inferior to the eloquence of the Qurʾān. On the other hand, if we claim that its inimitability resides solely in its form and an arrangement it has that differs from other modes of speech, one might direct against us examples of feeble utterances that resemble the order in Qurʾānic diction, such as in the shame speech of Musaylama,[3] the impostor, when he said: "The elephant! What is the elephant? And how can one grasp what an elephant is with its small thin tail and long trunk?" Something like this is not inimitable but is merely the condoning of absurdities and vile utterances designed to shock the ears. The sum of what we have just said forces us to tie together the inimitability in its wondrous order and in its eloquence.

Someone may say: What sort of rhetorical eloquence does the Qurʾān contain and in what way does its order differ from ordinary modes of speech? We answer: With respect to rhetorical eloquence, this is quite evident and obvious: Eloquence consists in expressing an appropriate meaning with a noble, apt and clear phrase, indicating what is to be said without superfluous additions. That is eloquent speech and precise discourse. Moreover, eloquence in speaking is comprised of several types.

Of them all, one consists of a discourse that indicates a multiplicity of meanings in few expressions. There are innumerable examples of this type in the Qurʾān.

One such example is God's providing, in only part of a verse, a lesson in the stories of bygone peoples about the future outcome reserved for those who exaggerate and the punishments for those who wreak destruction. He, the Mighty and Glorious, says: "[Each We seized for his sin]; and of them, against some We sent a storm of stones, some were caught by a mighty cry, some We caused the earth to swallow and some We drowned; God would never harm them but they wronged themselves" [29:40].

The Lord also said, at the beginning of the story of Noah's ark, of its floating above the waves and the destruction of the unbelievers, of its coming to rest and standing stationary, and of the commandment directed at the earth and the heavens to desist, and all that in His saying: "So he said, 'Embark in it, in God's name is its course and its berthing'" on to His words, "And it was said, 'Away with those who do evil'" [11:41–44].

God also teaches about the dead, the grief of separation, the life everlasting and its rewards and punishments, the good fortune of those who succeed, and the misfortune of those who commit sins. He warns against the deceptions of this world and describes its insignificance in relationship to that abode of permanent life. All of this He provides in His statement: "Every soul will taste of death; and only on the day of resurrection you will be paid your wages" (to the end of the verse) [3:185].

Another type of eloquent speech consists in telling a story without losing the elements of eloquence. Most masters of eloquence use an elevated style when they compose amorous praises of a beloved. But, if they are giving an intimate account of internal states, they employ threadbare language and scrawny words. If they were to try to use eloquent speech, one will be unable to perceive in it what they want to say in such a case.

Note, however, the story of Joseph, God bless him and keep him, which, despite comprising diverse and complex elements, was put together in the most pleasing arrangement and with the most elegant language, well ordered throughout, nicely assembled, as if its verses stood one on the neck of the other. Moreover, stories cannot be devoid of ambiguity

3. Musaylima ibn Ḥabīb (d. 633), a self-proclaimed prophet who controlled a section of eastern Arabia (Yamāma); he was killed in battle against the Muslims.

and redundancy, especially if the meanings are identical. But we have not imposed on ourselves in this handbook the task of draining an inexhaustible sea.

Among the most valid signs of the eloquence of the Qur'ān is its acknowledgment by the Arabs without exception, explicitly or implicitly. Some recognized it and declared so outright; others remained silent and did not speak about it. If there were in the Qur'ān the least inelegance, the ones with the most right to charge it with this weakness would have been the specialists in language.

If someone asks here: Is there in the Qur'ān any type of inimitability other than its arrangement and eloquence? We reply: Certainly, there are two other areas of its inimitability.

One is its relating of the stories about bygone peoples that are found to be in conformity to what exists in the other books that God revealed and yet the apostle of God, God bless him and keep him, was neither a scholar nor proficient at absorbing books. He was born among the Arabs and he had not undertaken trips abroad in which he could absorb knowledge and study literature. This is the truest of the signs of his veracity.

The Qur'ān, moreover, contains predictions that apply to future events and information about unseen matters, which might ordinarily come to pass once, perhaps, or twice. But when they follow in unerring succession, it constitutes a supernatural break in the habitual order. An example of secret matters in the Qur'ān is God's statement, "Say: if men and the jinn joined together . . ." (to the end of the verse) [17:88]; and His saying, "But if you do not—and certainly you will not . . ." [2:24]; and the Exalted saying, "You will enter the sacred mosque" [48:27]; His saying, "Alif, lām, mīm; the Roman Empire has been defeated" [30:2]; His saying, "God has promised you many spoils" [48:20] and others it would take too long to enumerate.

## *Chapter: [The miraculous signs of the apostle, God bless him and keep him, other than the Qur'ān]*

Aside from the Qur'ān, the apostle, God bless him and keep him, has innumerable miracles, such as the splitting of the moon, causing the mute to speak, water springing from between the fingers, the stone that glorified God and making much food out of only a little.

The view we approve is that any one of these miracles by itself has not been proven by sufficiently numerous reports, but the aggregate of them provides decisive knowledge of his having been distinguished by extraordinary supernatural events. It is similar to the individual acts of generosity done by Ḥatim,[4] which each by itself is not attested by sufficient reports but which together yield undeniable knowledge of his liberality. Like this are the reports about the courage of the Commander of the Faithful, 'Ali, may God be pleased with him, and his bravery. With respect to the splitting of the moon, it is related by verses of the Book of God whose transmission is confirmed by multiple and concordant reports. This evaluation should be effective and sufficient for what we hope to accomplish here.

4. Ḥātim al-Ṭā'ī was an Arab poet of the 6th century who is known proverbially as the paragon of generosity and hospitality [Walker's note].

# AL-GHAZĀLĪ

Born in the Persian city of Tūs, the orphan Abū Ḥāmid Muḥammad al-Ghazālī (1058–1111) was destined to become one of the greatest minds of medieval Islam and to make major and lasting contributions in the fields of law, philosophy, and theology.

He studied in Nishapur with ʿAbd al-Malik al-Juwaynī (1028–1085), "the leading master of the two holy cities [Mecca and Medina]," and later moved to Baghdad. There he eventually took a teaching position at the Niẓāmiyya, the *madrasa* (Islamic college) founded by the vizier Niẓām al-Mulk. In his late thirties, al-Ghazālī suffered an emotional crisis, driving him to renounce his professorship and leave Baghdad. For the next ten years, as his autobiographical work *Deliverance from Error* (*Al-Munqidh min al-Dalāl*) relates, he devoted himself to Ṣūfī asceticism, prayer, and spiritual seeking. During these years, as he traveled to Damascus, Jerusalem, Mecca, and Medina, he composed his greatest work, *The Revival of the Religious Sciences (Iḥyāʾ ʿulūm al-dīn)*, a comprehensive guide to the religious practices, forms of behavior, and interior dispositions essential for a devout life.

The excerpt below is from the eighth book of the *Iḥyāʾ*, "Recitation and Interpretation of the Qurʾan." Its detailed discussion of practices of qurʾānic recitation and reading underscores both the centrality of the scripture and the reverence with which it should be treated.

## *From* External Rules of Qurʾan Recitation†

> Only those who are clean can touch the Qurʾan.
>
> —Qurʾan 56:79
>
> Recite the Qurʾan in a slow and distinct manner.
>
> —Qurʾan 93:4
>
> One who does not chant with the Qurʾan is not one of us.
>
> —prophet Muḥammad
>
> Read the Qurʾan and weep. If you do not weep naturally, force yourselves to weep.
>
> —prophet Muḥammad

The external rules of Qurʾan-recitation are ten in number. [These rules together with a full illustration of them are as follows]:

[I]

The first rule concerns the condition of the Qurʾan-reciter.

It consists in the Qurʾan-reader's being in a state of ritual ablution (*wuḍūʾ*),[1] politeness and quietness, either standing or sitting, facing the *qibla* (i.e. the direction of the Kaʿba[2] in Mecca), with the head cast down,

† From Muhammad Abul Quasem, *The Recitation and Interpretation of the Qurʾan: Al-Ghazālī's Theory* (1979; reprint, London: Kegan Paul International, 1983), pp. 34–38, 41–44, 49–53. Reprinted by permission of Taylor and Francis Group, LLC, a division of Informa, plc. All brackets in the text are Quasem's; some parenthetical Arabic phrases have been omitted.

1. Literally, "cleanliness, purity"; *wuḍūʾ* are the ablutions required for ritual purity (without them, prayer is invalid). These consist of washing the hands, mouth, nose, face, and arms to the elbows, and lightly splashing the head, ears, and feet to the ankles.
2. The stone shrine in Mecca (literally, "cube"), believed to have been built by Adam and then rebuilt by Ibrāhīm (Abraham) and Ismāʿīl (Ishmael); central to both early pagan and Muslim pilgrimage rituals, it became the most important site in Islam.

neither sitting cross-legged nor leaning against anything nor sitting in a haughty manner. He should sit as he would when sitting in front of his teacher.

Of all the conditions [of the Qur'an-reader] the best is that he reads the Qur'an during ritual prayer standing and inside a mosque. This is one of the most excellent acts of man. If, however, he reads it without ritual ablution while reclining on his side on a bed, he has also excellence, but this excellence is of a lower grade.

[The proofs for these views are as follows:] God (exalted is He!) said, "[People of understanding are] those who remember God standing, sitting and lying on their sides, and ponder over the creation of the heavens and the earth."[3] Thus God has praised all three conditions; He has, however, mentioned first the condition of standing in remembrance of God, then the condition of sitting and then the remembrance of God lying on one's side. 'Alī[4] (may God be pleased with him!) said, "One who reads the Qur'an standing in ritual prayer will obtain [from God the reward of] one hundred good deeds for reading each letter of it. One who reads the Qur'an sitting in ritual prayer will obtain [the reward of] fifty good deeds for reading each letter. One who reads the Qur'an outside ritual prayer but being in a state of ritual ablution will obtain [the reward of] twenty-five good deeds. One who reads the Qur'an being without ritual ablution will obtain [the reward of] ten good deeds."

That reading of the Qur'an which constitutes part of keeping vigil at night (*qiyām bi l-layl*) is more excellent [than reading it during daytime] for at night the mind is most free [from other matters]. Abū Dharr al-Ghifārī[5] (may God by pleased with him!) said, "In daytime many prostrations, and at night keeping vigil for a long while are the most excellent."

[2]

The second rule concerns the amount of Qur'an-reading.

Qur'an-readers have formed different habits of considering how much they read. Some of them read the entire Qur'an right through in a day and night, some do this twice, and some even go so far as to do this thrice. Some Qur'an-readers read the Qur'an in its entirety once in a month.

The best thing in determining how much of the Qur'an to read is to rely upon the words of God's Messenger (may God bless him and greet him!), "One who has read the [entire] Qur'ran in less than three days has not understood it." This is because swift reading prevents the reader from reading in a slow and distinct manner (*tartīl*). When 'Ā'isha[6] (may God be pleased with her!) heard a man simply babbling over the Qur'an she remarked, "This man has neither read the Qur'an nor kept silent."

The Prophet (may God bless him and greet him!) ordered 'Abd Allāh Ibn 'Umar[7] (may God be pleased with them both!) to read the entire Qur'an once in every seven days. Likewise, a group of the Prophet's companions

3. Q 3:191.
4. 'Alī ibn Abī Ṭālib (ca. 599–661), the Prophet's cousin and son-in-law. He was one of the earliest to accept Islam and became the fourth caliph.
5. An early convert to Islam (d. 652/653), known for his piety and asceticism.
6. 'Ā'isha bint Abī Bakr (ca. 614–678), wife of Muḥammad, daughter of the first caliph, and a source of authoritative knowledge in early Islam.
7. 'Abdallāh ibn 'Umar ibn al-Khaṭṭāb (d. 693), son of the second caliph; he was highly regarded as a pious man and a source of traditions.

(may God be pleased with them!) used to complete the reading of the entire Qur'an on every Friday. This group consisted of such Companions as 'Uthmān, Zayd Ibn Thābit, Ibn Mas'ūd, and Ubayy Ibn Ka'b[8] (may God be pleased with them!).

There are, then, four grades of the reading of the Qur'an in its entirety: [a] To read the entire Qur'an once in a day and a night. A group [of religious scholars] has disliked this. [b] Reading the entire Qur'an [once] in every month—by reading every day one of its thirty parts. This seems to be an excessive reduction in the amount of reading, just as the first grade is an excess in over-reading, [c—d] Between these two grades are two moderate grades one of which consists in reading the entire Qur'an once in a week, and the other in reading it twice [or] nearly thrice in a week. [If twice a week] it is preferable to complete one reading of the entire Qur'an at night and the other at daytime. One should complete the reading at daytime on Monday in the two [obligatory] *rak'as*[9] of the Dawn Prayer or after them, and the reading at night on Friday night in the first two [obligatory] *rak'as* of the Sunset Prayer or after them. [This is the most preferable] because it welcomes the first part of the day and of the night with the completion of Qur'an-reading. The angels (may peace be upon them!) bless the Qur'an-reader until dawn, if his completion of Qur'an-reading occurs at night, and until evening, if it occurs during the daytime; thus the blessings of the two readings prevail throughout the day and throughout the night.

Details concerning the amount of Qur'an-reading are as follows. If the Qur'an-reader is one of the devotees traversing the ṣūfī path[1] by performing good acts of the body he should not do less than read the entire Qur'an twice a week. But if the reader is one of those who are traversing the ṣūfī path by performing actions of the soul and by different types of reflection, or one of those who are engaged in spreading [useful] knowledge, then there is nothing wrong in reducing the reading of the entire Qur'an to once a week. If the Qur'an-reader is making penetrating reflections on different meanings of the Qur'an it is sufficient for him to complete its reading once in a month, since he is much in need of repeating [the reading of verses] and reflecting [on them] many times.

* * *

[5]

The fifth rule is to read the Qur'an in a slow and distinct manner (*tartīl*). This manner of reading is praiseworthy (*mustaḥab*) in the case of the Qur'an because, as we shall soon discuss, the purpose of reading the Qur'an

8. Qur'ān reciter, secretary to Muḥammad, and participant in compiling an authoritative version of the Qur'ān (d. ca. 650). 'Uthmān ibn 'Affān (d. 656), son-in-law of the Prophet; he later became the third caliph (644–56). Zayd ibn Thābit (d. ca. 670), scribe to the Prophet and a key figure in the collection of the Qur'ān. 'Abdallāh ibn Mas'ūd (d. 653), an early Companion and transmitter of ḥadīth; he was an expert in the recitation of the Qur'ān, and a codex with many variants to the orthodox reading is attributed to him.
9. The cycle of bowing (the literal meaning of *rak'a*) and prostration—done 2, 3, or 4 times—that makes up the obligatory ritual prayer.
1. That is, those seeking inner meaning in the practice and rituals of Islam, in a mystical form of the religion.

is reflection [on its meaning] (*tafakkur*), and reading in a slow and distinct manner assists this. For this reason Umm Salama[2] (may God be pleased with her!) described the Qur'an-reading of the Messenger of God (may God bless him and greet him!), when she was asked concerning it; immediately [after being asked] she began to describe its recitation as clear and distinct in respect of every letter. 'Abd Allāh Ibn 'Abbās[3] (may God be pleased with them both!) said, "That I read the Sura of the Cow (*al-Baqara*) and the Sura of the House of 'Imrān (*Āl 'Imrān*)[4] in a slow and distinct manner while pondering over them, is better for me than to read the entire Qur'an babbling." He also said, "That I read [the sura beginning with] 'When the earth is shaken (*idhā zulzilat*) and the Sura of the Clatterer (*al-Qāri'a*),[5] reflecting over them, is better for me than to read the Sura of the Cow and the Sura of the House of 'Imrān babbling." Mujāhid[6] was asked concerning two men who started ritual prayer and who stood in that prayer for the same duration, but one of whom read only the Sura of the Cow and the other the Qur'an in its entirety. He replied, "They are equal in respect of merit."

Know that reading the Qur'an in a slow and distinct manner is praiseworthy not merely because it assists pondering (*tadabbur*) over it, since for a non-Arab (*'ajamī*) who does not understand the meaning of the Qur'an it is also praiseworthy to read it in a slow and distinct manner with pauses between the sentences, because this is nearer to the reverence and respect [which the Qur'an deserves] and stronger in its impression on the soul than babbling with haste.

[6]

The sixth rule is weeping [while reading the Qur'an].

Weeping while reading the Qur'an is praiseworthy (*mustaḥab*). The Messenger of God (may God bless him and greet him!) commanded, "Recite the Qur'an and weep. If you do not weep naturally, then force yourself to weep." The Prophet (may God bless him and greet him!) declared, "One who does not chant with the Qur'an is not one of us." Ṣāliḥ al-Murrī[7] said, "I read the Qur'an to the Messenger of God (may God bless him and greet him!) in my sleep. He asked me, 'Ṣāliḥ, this is only the reading of the Qur'an, but where is the weeping?'" 'Abd Allah Ibn 'Abbās (may God be pleased with them both!) said, "When you read [the Qur'anic verse of] prostration in which occurs the word *subḥāna*, do not hasten to prostrate until you weep. If the eyes of anyone of you do not weep his mind should weep [i.e. be filled with grief and fear of God]."

The method of forcing oneself to weep consists in bringing grief to the mind. From this grief will be produced weeping. The Prophet (may God bless him and greet him!) said, "Surely the Qur'an was revealed with grief.

2. Hind bint Abi Umayya (d. ca. 680), a widow who married the Prophet in 626; she was one of the earliest to accept Islam and was a significant transmitter of ḥadīth.
3. One of the greatest early Muslim scholars (ca. 619–687/88); he is often considered the founder of the qur'ānic exegetical tradition.
4. Sūras 2 and 3.
5. Sūras 99 and 101.
6. Mujāhid ibn Jabr (d. ca. 720), early exegete and scholar who studied with Ibn 'Abbās.
7. A Basran preacher, ascetic, and Qur'ān reciter (d. 792/93) who became famous for his "reading of sadness."

So when you read it you should force yourself to be aggrieved." The method of bringing grief [to the mind] of the Qur'an-reader is through reflecting on the threats, warnings covenants and promises which are contained in the Qur'an. Then he will reflect on his shortcomings in respect of the commandments of the Qur'an and its threats [of punishment]. Thus he will necessarily be aggrieved and will weep. Should he not feel grief and weep as do those who have purified souls, he should weep for his lack of grief and tears, because this is the greatest of all misfortunes.

* * *

[9]

The ninth rule concerns the reading of the Qur'an aloud.

There is no doubt that it is necessary to read the Qur'an loud enough so that the reader can hear it himself because reading means distinguishing clearly between sounds; thus sound is necessary, and the smallest degree of it is that which he can hear himself. If he cannot hear himself in a ritual prayer (*ṣalā*), his prayer is not correct.

As for reading so loud that he can be heard by others, it is to be considered praiseworthy in one respect and undesirable in another. The proofs that silent reading of the Qur'an is praiseworthy are [as follows]: It is related that the Prophet (may God bless him and greet him!) said, "The excellence of silent reading of the Qur'an compared with reading it aloud is like the excellence of secret almsgiving compared with public almsgiving." In other words this Tradition runs thus: "One who reads the Qur'an aloud is like one who gives alms publicly, and one who reads the Qur'an silently is like one who gives alms secretly." In a generally received Tradition [one finds that the Prophet said]: "A secret good act is more excellent than a public good act by seventy times." Likewise is the saying of the Prophet (may God bless him and greet him!): "The best measure of sustenance (*rizq*) is that which is sufficient, and the best mode of invocation of God (*dhikr*) is that which is secret."

In a Tradition [one finds that the Prophet warned]: "Some of you will not read the Qur'an aloud near others during the time between the Sunset Prayer (*Maghrib*) and the Evening Prayer (*'Ishā'*)." One night, in the Mosque of the Messenger of God (may God bless him and greet him!), Sa'īd Ibn al-Musayyab heard 'Umar Ibn 'Abd al-'Azīz[8] reading the Qur'an aloud in his ritual prayer—and he was a man of sweet voice. Sa'īd ordered his slave, "Go to this devotee and ask him to lower his voice." The slave said [to Sa'īd], "The mosque is not reserved for us only; that devotee has also a share in it." [Rejecting this argument of his slave] Sa'īd [himself] raised his voice, saying, "Devotee, if you intend to obtain the pleasure of God (great and mighty is He!) by your ritual prayer, then lower your voice. If, however, you intend to obtain the pleasure of people [you should know that] they will never be sufficient in respect of anything against God." 'Umar remained silent and shortened the *rak'a* of his ritual prayer. On salutation

8. Umayyad caliph (682/83–720; r. 717–20), renowned for his piety and asceticism. Sa'īd ibn al-Musayyab (d. 712/13), one of the earliest authorities on Islamic law; he was a traditionist and exegete of the second generation.

[to his right side and left side by which he withdrew from the ritual prayer], he took his shoes and departed. At that time he was the governor of Medina.

The proofs that reading the Qur'an aloud is praiseworthy are [as follows]: It is related that the Prophet (may God bless him and greet him!) once heard a group of his companions reading the Qur'an aloud in the supererogatory ritual prayer performed after midnight (*ṣālāt al-layl*) and approved of this. The Prophet (may God bless him and greet him!) [also] said, "If one of you keeps vigil at night performing supererogatory ritual prayers, he should read the Qur'an aloud, because the angels as well as those who are staying at his house listen to his Qur'an-reading and pray to God with his ritual prayer." Once the Prophet (may God bless him and greet him!) passed by three of his companions (may God be pleased with them!) who were engaged in different modes of Qur'an-reading: He passed by Abū Bakr[9] (may God be pleased with him!) who was reading the Qur'an silently. The Prophet asked him concerning the reason for this. He replied, "[I am reading silently because] the One to Whom I am whispering can hear me." The Prophet passed by 'Umar[1] (may God be pleased with him!) who was reading the Qur'an aloud. He asked him the reason for this. 'Umar replied. "[By reading aloud] I am awakening those who are asleep and [also] threatening Satan." The Prophet passed by Bilāl[2] who was reading some verses from one sura and other verses from other suras. The Prophet asked him the reason. He replied, "I am mingling [some] good things with other good things." The Prophet (may God bless him and greet him!) remarked, "Everyone of you has done good and right."

The method of reconciliation among these [apparently conflicting] Traditions is that the silent reading of the Qur'an is furthest from ostentation (*riyā'*) and affectation, and hence it is better [than reading aloud] in the case of a Qur'an-reader who is afraid of these for himself. If, however, he has no fear of these, and if loud reading of the Qur'an does not disturb (lit. confuse the time to) another devotee, then reading with a loud voice is better, [a] because it involves more effort, [b] because its benefit is also linked up with others—a good which involves other people is better than a good which cleaves to its agent only—, [c] because loud reading awakens the mind of the Qur'an-reader, unites his care for reflection on [the meaning of] the Qur'an and turns his ear to it, [d] because loud reading repels sleep by raising the voice, [e] because it adds to his energy for Qur'an-reading and lessens his laziness, [f] because waking a sleeping man can be expected from loud reading, in which case the Qur'an-reader will be the cause of the man's revival [from laziness which led him to sleep], and [g] because sometimes, having seen the loud reader, a workless, idle man gets energized because of his energy and encouraged to serve [God].

When one of these intentions is present loud reading of the Qur'an is better [than silent reading]. Should all these intentions join together the reward of Qur'an-reading would multiply. Because of many intentions

9. Muḥammad's chief adviser and father-in-law (573–634); he was the first caliph (632–34).
1. 'Umar ibn al-Khaṭṭāb (ca. 586–644), the second caliph (634–44).
2. Bilāl ibn Rabāḥ (d. ca. 640), a freed slave who became Muḥammad's servant and one of his most loyal companions; he was the first *mu'adhdhin*, or one who calls the faithful to prayer.

good acts of the pious grow, and the rewards they obtain multiply. If in a single act there are ten intentions ten rewards are to be obtained from it.

For this reason we say that reading from *muṣḥafs*[3] is better [than reading the Qur'an from memory], for, [in the former case], to the action of reading are added looking at the *muṣḥaf*, thinking about it, and carrying it; so the reward of Qur'an-reading will increase because of the addition of these. It is said that reading the entire Qur'an once from the *muṣḥaf* is equal [in value] to reading it in its entirety seven times from memory, because looking at a *muṣḥaf* is also an act of devotion to God (*'ibāda*). 'Uthmān (may God be pleased with him!) tore two *muṣḥafs* by reading much from them. Many Companions used to read from *muṣḥafs*, and they were unhappy when a day in which they did not look at *muṣḥafs* passed. A certain Egyption jurist (*faqīh*) visited ash-Shāfi'ī[4] (may God be pleased with him!) at dawn when he had in front of him a *muṣḥaf* [from which he was reading]. Ash-Shāfi'ī said to him, "Excessive study of jurisprudence has prevented you from reading the Qur'an. [For my part] I perform the Dawn Prayer in darkness and then put the *muṣḥaf* in front of me [for reading from it]; I do not shut it until there is day-light."

# AL-RŪMĪ

Jalāl al-Dīn Rūmī (1207–1273), later known as Mawlānā (in Arabic, "Our Master"), was born in Balkh, a thriving center of commerce and Persian culture in what is now northern Afghanistan that was destroyed by the Mongols in 1220. A few years before that catastrophe Rūmī's family left Balkh, stopping in Baghdad, Mecca, and other metropolises before eventually settling in the Turkish city of Konya. There, Jalāl al-Dīn entered the Ṣūfī path under the tutelage of one of his father's students; he ultimately became a teacher himself, taking on many *murīds*, or seekers of spiritual enlightenment. In 1244, Rūmī befriended a wandering holy man named Shams al-Dīn Muḥammad al-Tabrīzī. Shams became more than a friend to Rūmī, who adopted him as a spiritual guide and source of wisdom. But this attachment to Shams angered some of Rūmī's friends and family, and Shams unexpectedly vanished. Rūmī's infatuation expressed itself in renowned Persian lyrics that celebrated the rapture of lover and beloved as a metaphor for the human yearning for the divine.

*Signs of the Unseen* (*Fīhi mā fīhi*, literally "In It What Is in It"), a collection of al-Rūmī's homilies and lectures that was likely assembled only after his death, provides the clearest prose presentation of al-Rūmī's thought. The seventy-one sections reflect their genesis in Ṣūfī teaching sessions where topics could shift frequently. The section reprinted below focuses on reading the Qur'ān for its intrinsic meaning—specifically, on overcoming resistance to understanding the revelation more deeply.

3. Books, volumes (Arabic pl. *maṣāḥif*); here, the Qur'ān in book form.
4. Muḥammad ibn Idrīs al-Shāfi'ī (767–820), jurist and founder of the Shāfi'ī school of Islamic legal thought.

## *From* Signs of the Unseen†

### *Eighteen*

*Ibn Muqri*[1] reads the Koran correctly. That is, he reads the *form* of the Koran correctly, but he hasn't a clue as to the *meaning*. The proof of this lies in the fact that when he does come across a meaning he rejects it. He reads without insight, blindly. He is like a man who holds a sable in his hand. If offered a better sable he rejects it. We realize therefore that he does not know sable. Someone has told him that what he has is sable, and so he holds onto it in blind imitation. It is like children playing with walnuts; if offered walnut oil or walnut kernels, they will reject them because for them a walnut is something that rolls and makes a noise, and those other things do not roll or make noises.

God's treasure houses are many, and God's knowledge is vast. If a man reads *one* Koran knowledgeably, why should he reject any *other* Koran?

I once said to a Koran reader, "The Koran says: *Say, If the sea were ink to write the words of my Lord, verily the sea would fail, before the words of my Lord would fail.*[2] Now for fifty drams of ink one can write out the whole Koran. This is but a symbol of God's knowledge; it is not the whole of his knowledge. If a druggist put a pinch of medicine in a piece of paper, would you be so foolish as to say that the whole of the drugstore is in this paper? In the time of Moses, Jesus, and others, the Koran existed; that is, God's Word existed; it simply wasn't in Arabic." This is what I tried to make that Koran reader understand, but when I saw that it was having no effect on him I left.

* * *

It is said that during the time of the Apostle, the Companions who memorized a chapter or half a chapter of the Koran were deemed extraordinary and were objects of admiration. They did this because they "devoured" the Koran. Now anyone who can devour a pound or two of bread can be called extraordinary, but a person who just puts bread in his mouth and spits it out without chewing and swallowing can "devour" thousands of tons. It is about such a one that is said, "Many a reader of the Koran is cursed by the Koran," that is, one who is not aware of the real meaning. Yet it is well that this is so. God shut some people's eyes in heedlessness in order for them to make the world flourish. If some people were not heedless of the next world, then no world would be built up here. Such heedlessness initiates worldliness. A child grows up in heedlessness; when his mind reaches maturity, he does not grow any more. The cause and originator of his growing is heedlessness, while the cause for the lack of growth is awareness.

What we say does not go beyond two cases. We speak either out of envy or out of compassion. God forbid it be out of envy because what is worthy of being envied is so destroyed by envy that it is no longer enviable.

† From *Signs of the Unseen: The Discourses of Jalaluddin Rumi*, trans. W. M. Thackston Jr. (Putney, VT: Threshold Books, 1994), pp. 85–89. Reprinted by permission of the publisher.

1. Ṣā'in al-Dīn Muqri', a Qur'ān reciter who was a contemporary and eventual follower of Rūmī; his recitational practices are mentioned in *The Feats of the Knowers of God*, a biography of Rūmī by Shams al-Dīn Aḥmad Aflākī (ca. 1290–1360).
2. Q 18:109.

And then what is it? On the other hand, there are compassion and intercession, by means of which I wish to attract my dear friends to the concept.

The story is told of a man who wandered into the desert on his way to the pilgrimage and was overcome by great thirst. Finally, at a distance he saw a ragged little tent. Going there and seeing a woman, he cried out, "I can receive hospitality! Just what I needed!" And there he descended. He asked for water, but the water they gave him was hotter than fire and more brackish than salt, and it burned his throat as it went down. Out of compassion he began to advise the woman, saying, "I am obliged to you insofar as I have been comforted by you, and my compassion for you has been stirred. Take heed therefore of what I say to you. The cities of Baghdad, Kufah, and Wasit[3] are nearby. If you are in dire straits, you can get yourselves there in a few marches, where there is much sweet, cool water." And he also listed to her the great variety of foods, bathhouses, luxuries, and pleasures of those cities.

A moment later her Bedouin husband arrived. He had caught a few desert rats, which he told the woman to cook. They gave some to the guest, who, destitute as he was, could not refuse.

Later that night, while the guest was asleep outside the tent, the woman said to her husband, "You've never heard the likes of the tales this man had been telling." And she told her husband everything he had related to her.

"Don't listen to such things," the Bedouin said. "There are many envious people in the world, and when they see others enjoying ease and comfort they grow envious and want to deprive them of their enjoyment." People are just like that. When someone advises them out of compassion, they attribute it to envy.

If, on the other hand, one has a "basis," in the end one will turn to substance. Since on the Day of Alast[4] a drop was sprinkled on such a man, in the end that drop will deliver him from confusion and tribulation.

Come now, how long will you remain estranged from us in your confusion and melancholy? What, on the other hand, is one to say to a people who have never heard the likes of it, neither from him nor from their own teachers?

> There being no greatness among his forebears,
> He cannot abide to hear the great mentioned.

To turn to the substance of a thing, although not pleasant at first, becomes sweeter the further you go. In contrast, form appears beautiful at first, but the more you stay with it the more disenchanted with it you become. What is the form of the Koran in comparison with its substance? Look into a man to see what his form is and what his substance is. If the substance of a man's form were to go away, he would not be let loose in the house for even a moment.

3. Three major cities of Iraq: Baghdad, the center of the ʿAbbasid empire, built on both banks of the Tigris River in 762–63; Kūfa, on the Euphrates River, some 105 miles south of Baghdad, founded as a military garrison city in 638; and Wasit, in central Iraq on the west bank of the Tigris, which served as an administrative center of the Umayyad caliphate after its founding in 694.
4. The day of the primordial covenant, when God brought forth humankind and asked, "Am I not your Lord (*alastu bi-rabbikum*)?" (Q 7:172). Ṣūfīs believed that all souls were formed as sparks from the being of God, prior to the creation of the world, and they sought by overcoming the lower self to reunify with the divine being.

Mawlana Shamsuddin[5] used to tell of a large caravan, en route to a certain place, that could find neither settlement nor water. Suddenly they came across a well that had no means for drawing water. They brought a bucket and some rope and let the bucket down into the well. When they started to draw it up, the rope broke. They let down another bucket, but it too broke loose. Then they tied some of the members of the caravan to the rope and lowered them into the well, but they did not come back up either. An intelligent man among them said, "I'll go." So they lowered him down. When he was almost to the bottom, a horrible black thing appeared. "I'll never escape from this," said the man. "Yet, let me gather my wits and not go to pieces so I can see what is going to happen to me."

"There is no use making a ruckus," the black thing said. "You are my prisoner and will never go free unless you give me a correct answer."

"What is your question?"

"What is the best place?" it asked.

Here the intelligent man thought, "I am helpless as his prisoner. If I say Baghdad or any other place, it will be as though I have insulted his place." Therefore he said, "The best place is where one is at home. If it is in the depths of the earth, that's the best. If it's in a mousehole, that's the best."

"Well said!" said the thing, "You are free. You are a real man. I free not only you but also the others for your sake. Henceforth I will shed no more blood. Because of my love for you I bestow upon you the lives of all the men in the world." And he gave the people of the caravan all the water they wanted.

Now, the purport of all this is the intrinsic meaning. One can express this very same intrinsic meaning in another form, but those who adhere to convention can have it only their way. It is difficult to talk to them. If you say the same thing another way, they won't listen.

## AL-NAWAWĪ

Muḥyī al-Din Abū Zakariyya Yaḥyā ibn Sharaf al-Nawawī (1233–1277) was a Syrian jurist and scholar of ḥadīth. He was born in Nawa, a town south of Damascus, and his tomb there continues to attract pious pilgrims. Although his was not a long life—he died in his mid-forties—it was an unusually productive one. His legacy as a legal scholar has been enduring; commentaries on his major work on Shāfiʿī jurisprudence, *The Method of the Seekers* (*Minhāj al-Ṭālibīn*), continue to serve the Shāfiʿī school of law.

Al-Nawawī is equally well remembered for two collections of ḥadīth that are among the most popular ever compiled and circulated. His *Book of Forty* (*Kitāb al-arbaʿīn*) culled a few more than forty of the most important ḥadīth from the multivolume standard collections. It became the most popular of a whole subgenre of such abridged ḥadīth compilations.

His other famous collection, *Gardens of the Righteous* (*Riyāḍ al-Ṣāliḥīn*), serves as a handbook of pious behavior and practice. For many sections of *Gardens*, he cites an apposite verse from the Qur'ān, clearly underlining that both Qur'ān and ḥadīth are essential for Muslim life. The following excerpt concerns a subject to which al-Nawawī often returned: the practical importance of a believer's relationship with the Qur'ān. In these sections he presents

5. Muḥammad al-Shams al-Dīn Tabrīzī (d. 1247), Rūmī's friend and spiritual guide. The honorific "Mawlana" means "Our Master" (Arabic).

relevant traditions that bolster the believer's faith in the benefits of reading, reciting, and memorizing the Qur'ān.

## *From* Gardens of the Righteous[†]

### *179. On the Excellence of Reading the Quran*

**995.** Abu Umamah[1] relates that he heard the Holy Prophet say: Keep reading the Quran for it will intercede for its readers on the Day of Judgment (Muslim[2]).

**996.** Nawas ibn Sama'an relates that he heard the Holy Prophet say: The Quran will be summoned on the Day of Judgment along with those who kept it company in this life and acted in conformity with it. It will be heralded by the second and third chapters and these will plead on behalf of those who kept company with them (Muslim).

**997.** Uthman ibn Affan[3] relates that the Holy Prophet said: The best of you are those who learn the Quran and teach it (Bokhari[4]).

**998.** Ayesha[5] relates that the Holy Prophet said: He who recites the Quran fluently will be in the company of the noble and virtuous; and he who recites the Quran haltingly and with difficulty will have a double reward (Bokhari and Muslim).

**999.** Abu Musa Ash'ari[6] relates that the Holy Prophet said: The case of a believer who recites the Quran is that of fruit which is fragrant and delicious; and the case of a believer who does not recite the Quran is that of fruit which has no fragrance but is sweet to the taste; and the case of a hypocrite who recites the Quran is that of fruit which is fragrant but tastes bitter; and the case of a hypocrite who does not recite the Quran is that of fruit which has no fragrance and tastes bitter (Bokhari and Muslim).

**1000.** Umar ibn Khattab[7] relates that the Holy Prophet said: Allah will exalt many people through this Book, and will abase many because of it (Muslim).

**1001.** This *hadith* is the same as No. 575. [Ibn Umar[8] relates that the Holy Prophet said: Only two are to be envied: he upon whom Allah bestows the Quran and he conforms to it through the hours of the night and day; and he upon whom Allah bestows wealth and he spends it in the cause of Allah, through the hours of the night and day (Bokhari and Muslim).]

**1002.** Bra'a ibn 'Azib relates that a person was reciting *sura* Al-Kahf[9] (Chapter 18) while his horse was close to him secured by two ropes. A cloud

† From *Gardens of the Righteous: Riyadh as-Salahin of Imam Nawawi*, trans. Muhammad Zafrulla Khan (London: Curzon Press; Totowa, NJ: Rowman and Littlefield, 1975), pp. 185–89. Reprinted by permission of Rowman and Littlefield.

1. Abū Umāma al-Bāhilī (d. 700), a Companion of the Prophet.
2. Muslim ibn al-Ḥajjāj (821–875), one of the chief authorities on ḥadīth and author of the second most popular collection.
3. 'Uthmān ibn 'Affān (d. 656), son-in-law of the Prophet and the third caliph (644–56).
4. Muḥammad ibn Ismā'īl al-Bukhārī (810–870), compiler of the most widely accepted ḥadīth compendium in the Muslim intellectual tradition.
5. 'Ā'isha bint Abī Bakr (ca. 614–678), daughter of the first caliph, wife of Muḥammad, and a source of authoritative knowledge in early Islam.
6. Abū Mūsā al-Ash'arī (d. ca. 667), an early Companion of the Prophet who later served as governor of first Basra and then Kūfa.
7. 'Umar ibn al-Khaṭṭāb (ca. 586–644), the second caliph (634–44).
8. 'Abdallāh ibn 'Umar ibn al-Khaṭṭāb (d. 693), son of the second caliph; he was highly regarded as a pious man and a source of traditions.
9. The Cave.

spread over the horse and advanced towards it whereupon it began to frolic. In the morning the man came to the Holy Prophet and mentioned the incident to him. He said: This was comfort that descended by virtue of the recitation of the Quran (Bokhari and Muslim).

**1003.** Ibn Mas'ud[1] relates that the Holy Prohet said that when a person recites one letter from the Book of Allah that is one good deed equal to ten good deeds the like of it. I do not say that ALM[2] is a letter, but A is a letter, L is a letter and M is a letter (Tirmidhi[3]).

**1004.** Ibn Abbas[4] relates that the Holy Prophet said: He in whose heart there is nothing of the Quran is like a house in ruin (Tirmidhi).

**1005.** Abdullah ibn Amr ibn 'As[5] relates that the Holy Prophet said: One who is given to reciting the Quran will be told on the Day of Judgment: Go on reciting and ascending, and recite slowly as was thy wont in life, for thy station, will be where the last verse of thy recitation will end (Abu Daud[6] and Tirmidhi).

### *180. On Safeguarding the Quran*

**1006.** Abu Musa relates that the Holy Prophet said: Safeguard the Quran in your memories, for by Him in Whose hands is the life of Muhammad, it escapes sooner from memory than does a camel from its rope (Bokhari and Muslim).

**1007.** Ibn Umar relates that the Holy Prophet said: The case of one who has the Quran by heart is like that of one who has a camel secured by a rope. If he watches it, he retains it; and if he neglects it, it wanders away (Bokhari and Muslim).

### *181. On Good Recitation of the Quran*

**1008.** Abu Hurairah[7] relates that he heard the Holy Prophet say: Allah does not lend ear so joyously to anything as he does to the recitation of the Quran by a Prophet who has a beautiful voice and recites well and audibly (Bokhari and Muslim).

**1009.** Abu Musa Ash'ari relates that the Holy Prophet said to him: You have been granted one of the tunes of David (Bokhari and Muslim). Muslim has added: I wish you could have seen me when I was listening to your recitation last night.

**1010.** Bra'a ibn 'Azib relates: I heard the Holy Prophet recite *sura* Al-Tin[8] (Chapter 95) during the evening service. I have never heard anyone recite in a more beautiful voice than his (Bokhari and Muslim).

1. 'Abdallāh ibn Mas'ūd (d. 653), an early Companion and transmitter of ḥadīth; he was an expert in the recitation of the Qur'ān, and a codex with many variants to the orthodox reading is attributed to him.
2. A reference to the "mysterious letters" that precede 29 of the Qur'ān's chapters. Various theories exist to explain their significance, and they are always pronounced as individual letters.
3. Muḥammad ibn 'Īsā al-Tirmidhī (d. ca. 892), a traditionist who compiled one of the six canonical ḥadīth collections.
4. 'Abdallāh ibn al-'Abbās (ca. 619–687/88), one of the greatest early scholars of Islam; he is often considered the founder of the qur'ānic exegetical tradition.
5. 'Abdallāh ibn Amr ibn 'As (d. ca. 684), a Companion of the Prophet known for his asceticism.
6. Abū Dā'ūd al-Sijistānī (817–889), Persian traditionist who compiled one of the six canonical ḥadīth collections.
7. Abū Hurayra (d. ca. 678), an impoverished early Companion who related many ḥadīth; he eventually assumed (and was deposed from the post of) governor of Baḥrayn.
8. The Fig.

**1011.** Bashir ibn Abd al-Munzir relates that the Holy Prophet said: He who does not recite the Quran tunefully is not one of us (Abu Daud).

**1012.** This *hadith* is the same as No. 449. [Ibn Masʿud relates: The Holy Prophet asked me to recite the Quran to him. I said: Messenger of Allah, shall I recite the Quran to you, whereas it is to you to whom it has been revealed? He said: I like to hear it recited by another. So I recited to him a portion from the fourth Chapter till I came to the verse: How will it be when We shall bring a witness from every people, and shall bring thee as a witness against these (4.42) [4:41]? when he said: That is enough for now. I looked at him and saw that his eyes were running (Bokhari and Muslim).]

### *182. On Special Chapters and Verses*

**1013.** Abu Saʿid Rafiʾ relates: The Holy Prophet said to me: Shall I tell you before you go out of the mosque which is the greatest chapter of the Quran? and he took hold of my hand. When we were about to issue from the mosque I said to him: Messenger of Allah, you had said you would tell me which is the greatest chapter of the Quran. He answered: The opening chapter which contains the seven oft-repeated verses and the Great Quran which has been bestowed upon me (Bokhari).

**1014.** Abu Saʿid Khudri relates that the Holy Prophet said concerning the recitation of *sura* Al-Ikhlas (Chapter 112): By Him in Whose hands is my life, it is equal to the recitation of one third of the Quran. Another version is: The Holy Prophet inquired from his companions: Would any of you find it burdensome to recite one third of the Quran in the course of a night? They considered it difficult and said: Which of us would have the strength to do that, Messenger of Allah? He said: *sura* Al-Ikhlas is one third of the Quran (Bokhari).

**1015.** Abu Saʿid Khudri relates that a man heard another recite *sura* Al-Ikhlas[9] repeatedly. In the morning he came to the Holy Prophet and mentioned this to him belittling it. The Holy Prophet said to him: By Him in Whose hands is my life, it is equal to one third of the Quran (Bokhari).

**1016.** Abu Hurairah relates that the Holy Prophet said that the *sura* Al-Ikhlas (Chapter 112) equals one third of the Quran (Muslim).

**1017.** Anas[1] relates that a man said to the Holy Prophet: Messenger of Allah, I love *sura* Al-Ikhlas. He told him: Love of it will admit you to Paradise (Tirmidhi).

**1018.** Uqbah ibn ʿAmir relates that the Holy Prophet said: Know you not that last night certain verses were revealed the like of which has never been known; *sura* Al-Falaq and *sura* Al-Nas[2] (Chapters 113 and 114) (Muslim).

**1019.** Abu Saʿid Khudri relates that the Holy Prophet used to seek protection against the *jinn*[3] and the evil eye till *suras* Al-Falaq and Al-Nas were revealed. After they were revealed he took to them and discarded everything beside them (Tirmidhi).

**1020.** Abu Hurairah relates that the Holy Prophet said: There is a *sura* in the Quran comprising thirty verses which continued its intercession

9. Sincerity; also known as *Sūra al-Tawḥīd*, the Chapter of Unity.
1. Anas ibn Mālik (d. ca. 710), an early Companion of the Prophet; he was given to Muḥammad as a servant at age ten.
2. The Daybreak and Mankind, respectively.
3. The third class of intelligent beings (together with humans and angels) for whom salvation is possible. According to Q 55:15, God created them from smokeless fire.

on behalf of a man till he was forgiven. It is *sura* Al-Mulk[4] (Chapter 67) (Abu Daud and Tirmidhi).

**1021.** Abu Masʿud Badri relates that the Holy Prophet said: If a person recites the last two verses of *sura* Al-Baqarah[5] at night, they suffice him (Bokhari and Muslim).

**1022.** Abu Hurairah relates that the Holy Prophet admonished: Do not convert your houses into graves. Indeed, Satan runs away from a house in which *sura* Al-Baqarah is recited (Muslim).

**1023.** Ubayy ibn Ka'ab[6] relates: The Holy Prophet asked me: Abu Mundhir, do you know which verse of the Book of Allah is the grandest? I answered: the verse of the *Kursi*[7] (2.256). He poked me in the chest and said: Felicitations on your knowledge, Abu Mundhir (Muslim).

**1024.** Abu Hurairaḥ relates: The Holy Prophet had appointed me to watch over the Sadqa Fitr (alms given on the occasion of the Festival at the end of Ramadhan) and during the night one sneaked up and started stealing from the alms and I caught hold of him and said: I will take you to the Holy Prophet; but he pleaded: I am in need and I have a large family and we are in sore distress. So I let him go. Next morning the Holy Prophet asked me: Abu Hurairah, what did your prisoner do last night? I answered: Messenger of Allah, he pleaded his need and that of his family, so I took pity on him and let him go. The Holy Prophet said: He told you a lie and will return. So I realized that he would come back as the Holy Prophet had said and I kept watching for him. He sneaked up again and started taking from the alms and I said to him: I shall take you to the Holy Prophet. He pleaded: I am in need and have a large family; let me go and I shall not come back. So I took pity on him and let him go. Next morning the Holy Prophet said to me: Abu Hurairah, how did your prisoner of last night behave? I answered: Messenger of Allah, he pleaded his need and that of his family and I took pity on him and let him go. He said: He told you a lie and will come back again. So I watched for him a third time. He sneaked up to steal from the alms when I caught him and said: I shall take you to the Holy Prophet and this is the last of the three times you promised that you will not come back and you came back. He pleaded: Let me go, and I will tell you some phrases which will be of benefit to you before Allah. I asked him: What are they? He answered: When you go to bed recite the verse of the Chair (2.256) for it will be a guardian over you on behalf of Allah and Satan will not be able to approach you till morning. So I let him go. Next morning the Holy Prophet asked me: How did your prisoner behave last night? And I answered: Messenger of Allah, he said he would teach me some phrases which would be of benefit to me before Allah. So I let him go. He asked: What are those phrases? I answered: He said to me: When you go to bed recite the verse of the Chair from its beginning to its end and told me that this would guard me on behalf of Allah and Satan would not be able to approach me till the morning. The Holy Prophet observed: This time he told you the truth and yet he is a liar. Abu Hurairah, do you realise who was speaking to you during these three nights? I answered: No. The Holy Prophet answered: It was Satan (Bokhari).

4. The Sovereignty.
5. The Cow (chapter 2), the longest sūra in the Qur'ān.
6. Ubayy ibn Kaʿb (d. ca. 650), Qur'ān reciter, personal secretary to Muḥammad, and participant in compiling a definitive version of the Qur'ān.
7. The verse of the Throne or Chair (in most modern editions, 2:255).

**1025.** Abu Darda'[8] relates that the Holy Prophet said: He who commits to memory the first ten verses of *sura* Al-Kahf[9] (Chapter 18) will be secure against Anti-Christ. One version is: the last ten verses of *sura* Al-Kahf (Muslim).

**1026.** Ibn Abbas relates: While Gabriel was sitting with the Holy Prophet a sound was heard from above and Gabriel raised his head and said: A door has been opened from heaven which had not been opened up to this day. Then an angel descended from it and Gabriel said: This angel has descended to the earth and had not descended before till this day. He saluted the Holy Prophet and said: Be glad of the two lights that have been bestowed upon you which had not been bestowed upon any Prophet before you: The opening chapter of the Book and the last verses of *sura* Al-Baqarah (Chapter 2). Whenever you recite even a word of this it will be bestowed upon you (Muslim).

### *183. On Gathering together for Recitation of the Quran*

**1027.** Abu Hurairah relates that the Holy Prophet said: Whenever people gather together in one of the houses of Allah for recitation of the Quran and teaching it to one another, comfort descends upon them, mercy covers them, angels spread their wings over them and Allah makes mention of them to those around Him (Muslim).

## IBN KHALDŪN

In any intellectual history of the Muslim world, ʿAbd al-Raḥmān ibn Muḥammad ibn Khaldūn (1332–1406) will be cited as the preeminent historian and historiographer of the late medieval period. He came from a politically connected Arab family with roots in both Andalusia and North Africa. Born in Tunis, Ibn Khaldūn studied there and in Fez. His youth was marked by the tragedy of the Black Death: when the devastating plague struck Tunis in 1348–49, it took both of Ibn Khaldūn's parents as well as several of his teachers. Early in his life, his native intelligence as well as his family's status secured him positions in the courts of Fez and then Granada. Other such appointments followed but in 1382, in late middle age, he moved to Egypt, adopting Cairo as his new home. His final twenty-four years were largely spent teaching, writing, and filling a series of administrative posts. One eventful exception to this pattern was a journey on which he accompanied the Mamluk sultan, al-Naṣīr, to Damascus; there he met at length with the city's Turco-Mongol conqueror, Tīmūr (1336–1405).

The life of Ibn Khaldūn can be constructed in considerable detail because he left an autobiography and referred in other works to events from his life. His most noted writings, however, are his universal history (*Kitāb al-ʿIbar*) and what was originally its introduction (*muqaddima*), both the product of his final years. Even during his lifetime, the *Muqaddima* (*Introduction*), which runs to three volumes in the standard English translation, assumed an independent existence: Ibn Khaldūn's renown rests largely on the originality of its historiographical sociological reflections. In the following section from the *Muqaddima*, the author sketches the scholarly exercise of Qurʾān interpretation.

8. Abū al-Dardāʾ al-Anṣārī (d. 654/55), an early Companion who reported traditions and was known for piety and asceticism as well as expertise on the Qurʾān.
9. The Cave.

## *From* The Qur'ânic Sciences of Qur'ân Interpretation and Qur'ân Reading†

The Qur'ân is the word of God that was revealed to His Prophet and that is written down between the two covers of copies of the Qur'ân (*muṣḥaf*). Its transmission has been continuous in Islam. However, the men around Muḥammad transmitted it on the authority of the Messenger of God in different ways. These differences affect certain of the words in it and the manner in which the letters were pronounced. They were handed down and became famous. Eventually, seven specific ways of reading the Qur'ân became established. Transmission (of the Qur'ân readings), with their particular pronunciation, also was continuous. They came to be ascribed to certain men from among a large number of persons who had become famous as their transmitters.

The seven Qur'ân readings became the basis for reading the Qur'ân. Later on, other readings were occasionally added to the seven. However, they are not considered by the authorities on Qur'ân reading to be as reliably transmitted as (the seven).

The seven Qur'ân readings are well known from books which deal with them. Certain people have contested the continuity of their transmission. In their opinion, they are ways of indicating the pronunciation, and pronunciation is something that cannot definitely be fixed. This, however, they thought not to reflect upon the continuity of the transmission of the Qur'ân. The majority did not admit their view. They asserted the continuity of the transmission of the (seven readings). Others asserted the continuity (of all seven), except with regard to (the fine points of) pronunciation, such as the longer pronunciation of the long vowels and the weakening of the *alif*,[1] because the ear is not able to determine how it must be done. This is the correct opinion.

* * *

### *Qur'ân Interpretation*

It should be known that the Qur'ân was revealed in the language of the Arabs and according to their rhetorical methods. All Arabs understood it and knew the meaning of the individual words and composite statements. It was revealed in chapters and verses, in order to explain the oneness of God and the religious duties according to the (various) occasions.

Some passages of the Qur'ân concern articles of faith. Others concern the duties of the limbs of the body. Some are early and are followed by other, later passages that abrogate the earlier ones.

The Prophet used to explain these things, as it is said: "So that you may explain to the people that which was revealed to them."[2] He used to explain the unclear statements (in the Qur'ân) and to distinguish the abrogating statements from those abrogated by them, and to inform the men around

† From Ibn Khaldûn, *The Muqaddimah: An Introduction to History*, trans. Frans Rosenthal, 2nd ed. (Princeton: Princeton University Press, 1967), 2:439–40, 443–47. 

1. The first letter of the Arabic alphabet; usually pronounced "a" as in "cat."
2. Q 16:44.

him in this sense. The men around him, thus, became acquainted with (the subject). They knew why individual verses had been revealed, and the situation that had required them, directly on (Muḥammad's) authority. Thus, the verse of the Qur'ân, "When God's help comes and the victory,"[3] refers to the announcement of the Prophet's death, and similar things.

These (explanations) were transmitted on the authority of the men around Muḥammad and were circulated by the men of the second generation after them on their authority. They continued to be transmitted among the early Muslims, until knowledge became organized in scholarly disciplines and systematic scholarly works were written. At that time, most of these (explanations) were committed to writing. The traditional information concerning them, which had come down from the men around Muḥammad and the men of the second generation, was transmitted farther. That (material) reached aṭ-Ṭabarî, al-Wâqidî, ath-Tha'âlibî,[4] and other Qur'ân interpreters. They committed to writing as much of the traditional information as God wanted them to do.

The linguistic sciences then became technical discussions of the lexicographical meaning of words, the rules governing vowel endings (*i'râb*), and style (*balâghah*) in (the use of) word combinations. Systematic works were written on these subjects. Formerly, these subjects had been habits with the Arabs. No recourse to oral and written transmission had been necessary with respect to them. Now, that (state of affairs) was forgotten, and these subjects were learned from the books of philologists. They were needed for the interpretation of the Qur'ân, because the Qur'ân is in Arabic and follows the stylistic technique of the Arabs. Qur'ân interpretation thus came to be handled in two ways.

One (kind of Qur'ân interpretation) is traditional. It is based upon information received from the early Muslims. It consists of knowledge of the abrogating verses and of the verses that are abrogated by them, of the reasons why a (given) verse was revealed, and of the purposes of individual verses. All this can be known only through traditions based on the authority of the men around Muḥammad and the men of the second generation. The early scholars had already made complete compilations on the subject. However, their works and the information they transmit contain side by side important and unimportant matters, accepted and rejected statements. The reason is that the Arabs had no books or scholarship. The desert attitude and illiteracy prevailed among them. When they wanted to know certain things that human beings are usually curious to know, such as the reasons for the existing things, the beginning of creation, and the secrets of existence, they consulted the earlier People of the Book about it and got their information from them. The People of the Book were the Jews who had the Torah, and the Christians who followed the religion of (the Jews). Now, the people of the Torah who lived among the Arabs at that time were themselves Bedouins. They knew only as much about these matters as is known to ordinary People of the Book (in contrast to learned rabbis). The majority of those Jews were Ḥimyarites[5] who had adopted

3. Q 110:1.
4. Three important figures: Abū Ja'far Muḥammad ibn Jarīr al-Ṭabarī (ca. 839–923), a major exegete and historian; Muḥammad ibn 'Umar ibn al-Wāqidī (747–822), i.e., al-Wāqidī, a jurist and historian; and Aḥmad ibn Muḥammad al-Tha'labī (d. 1035), an exegete and compiler of a famed collection of legends about the biblical and qur'ānic prophets.
5. A people of southern Arabia, located mainly on the coast of modern Yemen.

Judaism. When they became Muslims, they clung to the (information) they possessed, such as information about the beginning of creation and information of the type of forecasts and predictions. That information had no connection with the (Jewish or Christian) religious laws they were preserving as theirs. Such men were Ka'b al-aḥbâr, Wahb b. Munabbih, 'Abdallâh b. Salâm,[6] and similar people. The Qur'ân commentaries were filled with material of such tendencies transmitted on their authority. It is information that entirely depends on them. It has no relation to (religious) laws, such that one might claim for it the soundness that would make it necessary to act (in accordance with it). The Qur'ân interpreters were not very rigorous in this respect. They filled the Qur'ân commentaries with such material, which originated, as we have stated, with the people of the Torah who lived in the desert and were not capable of verifying the information they transmitted. However, they were famous and highly esteemed, because they were people of rank in (their) religion and religious group. Therefore, their interpretation has been accepted from that time onwards.

Later, scholars applied themselves to verification and critical investigation. Abû Muḥammad b. 'Aṭîyah,[7] a recent Maghribî scholar, made his appearance. He abridged all the commentaries and selected the most likely interpretations. He set that material down in a good book, which is in general circulation among the inhabitants of the Maghrib and of Spain. Al-Qurṭubî[8] adopted his method in this respect in another work, which is well known in the East.

The other kind of Qur'ân interpretation has recourse to linguistic knowledge, such as lexicography and the stylistic form (*balâghah*) used for conveying meaning through the appropriate means and methods. This kind of Qur'ân interpretation rarely appears separately from the first kind. The first kind is the one that is wanted essentially. The second kind made its appearance only after language and the philological sciences had become crafts. However, it has become preponderant, as far as certain Qur'ân commentaries are concerned.

The commentary in which this discipline is best represented is the *Kitâb al-Kashshâf* by az-Zamakhsharî,[9] of Khuwârizm in the 'Irâq. However, its author is a Mu'tazilah[1] in his dogmatic views. Therefore, he uses the various methods of rhetoric (*balâghah*), arguing in favor of the pernicious doctrines of the Mu'tazilah, wherever he believed they occurred in the verses of the Qur'ân. Competent orthodox scholars have, therefore, come to disregard his work and to warn everyone against its pitfalls. However, they admit that he is on firm ground in everything relating to language and style (*balâghah*). If the student of the work is acquainted with the orthodox

6. 'Abdallāh ibn Salām (d. 663/64), a Medinan Jewish convert who was among Muḥammad's early defenders; Ka'b al-Aḥbār (d. 652/53), a Yemeni Jewish convert often cited as a source of biblical stories and legends; Wahb ibn Munabbih (d. 728 or 732), an expert in biblical traditions who belonged to the generation after that of Muḥammad's personal companions.
7. Abū Muḥammad ibn 'Aṭiyya (1088–1147/48), Granadan jurist and exegete (the Maghrib, which originally and today is limited to North Africa bordering the Mediterranean, at one time included Moorish Spain).
8. Abū 'Abdallāh al-Qurṭubī (1214–1273), Cordoban jurist of the Māliki school and author of a famous Qur'ān commentary.
9. Abū al-Qāsim Maḥmūd ibn 'Umar al-Zamakhsharī (1045–1144), Persian-born master of the Arabic language whose commentary, *Al-Kashshāf* (*The Discloser*), is admired for its grammatical expertise. Khwārezm is a region in present-day Turkmenistan and Uzbekistan.
1. A member of a school of Islamic speculative theology influenced by the methods of Hellenistic philosophy and condemned by more orthodox thinkers.

dogmas and knows the arguments in their defense, he is no doubt safe from its fallacies. Therefore, he should seize the opportunity to study it, because it contains remarkable and varied linguistic information.

Recently, a work by an ʿIrâqî scholar, Sharaf-ad-dîn aṭ-Ṭîbî,[2] of Tabrîz in the non-Arab ʿIrâq, has reached us. It is a commentary on the work of az-Zamakhsharî. Aṭ-Ṭîbî follows az-Zamakhsharî's work literally, but opposes its Muʿtazilah dogmas and arguments, showing their lack of validity and (always) explaining that an eloquent style exists in a given verse but it reflects the opinions of orthodox Muslims, and not the dogmas of the Muʿtazilah. He does that very well, and he also possesses all the various disciplines of rhetoric (*balâghah*).

"And He knows more than any scholar."[3]

2. Al-Husayn ibn ʿAbdallāh al-Ṭībī (d. 1343) [Rosenthal's identification].
3. Q 12:76.

# The Spectrum of Contemporary Scholarship

## TOSHIHIKO IZUTSU

### *From* The Basic Moral Dichotomy†

> Say, 'Listen, Kāfirs! I worship not what you worship.
> You are not worshipping what I worship.
> I am not worshipping what you worship.
> Nor will you worship what I worship.
> To you your religion, and to me my religion!'
> (CIX, 1–6, the whole Sūrah)

These words mark in a dramatic way the most radical break with the surrounding polytheism, to which Islām was led by its fundamental attitude in religious matters. This was, so to speak, the formal declaration of independence on the part of Islām from all that was essentially incompatible with the monotheistic belief which it proclaimed. In the domain of ethical practices, this declaration of independence involved a grave consequence. It suggested that henceforward all human values were to be measured by an absolutely reliable standard of evaluation.

The Qur'anic outlook divides all human qualities into two radically opposed categories, which—in view of the fact that they are too concrete and semantically too pregnant to be called 'good' and 'bad', or 'right' and 'wrong'—we might simply call the class of positive moral properties and the class of negative moral properties, respectively. The final yardstick by which this division is carried out is the belief in the one and only God, the Creator of all beings. In fact, throughout the Qur'ān there runs the keynote of dualism regarding the moral values of man: the basic dualism of believer and unbeliever. In this sense, the ethical system of Islām is of a very simple structure. For by the ultimate yardstick of 'belief' one can easily decide to which of the two categories a given person or a given act belongs.

The significance of this fact, however, was very great for the moral development of the Arabs, because it meant the first appearance of moral principle which was consistent enough to deserve the name of 'principle'. A whole practical code of conduct, though as yet largely unsystematic, was imposed upon the believer, the moment he truly believed in the oneness of God and the truth of the prophetic message. * * * [T]his was an

† From chapter 6 of Toshihiko Izutsu, *Ethico-Religious Concepts in the Qur'ān*, [rev. ed.] (Montreal: McGill University, Institute of Islamic Studies, McGill University Press, 1966), pp. 105–08. Reprinted by permission of McGill–Queen's University Press. All brackets in extracts are Toshihiko's.

unprecedented event in the spiritual history of the Arabs. In Jāhilīyah[1] there were * * * a number of recognized moral values. But they were just there as *membra disjecta*,[2] without any definite underlying principle to support them; they were based almost exclusively on an irrational sort of moral emotion, or rather, a blind and violent passion for the mode of life that had been handed down from generation to generation as a priceless tribal asset. Islām made it possible for the first time for the Arabs to judge and evaluate all human conduct with reference to a theoretically justifiable moral principle.

The basic dichotomy of moral properties to which I have just referred, appears in the Qurʾanic verses in a number of different forms. It may, to begin with, assume the form of an essential opposition of *kāfir* and *muʾmin* 'believer'.

> It is He who created you. But one of you is a *kāfir*, and one of you is a *muʾmin*. God sees everything you do. (LXIV, 2)

> Those who disbelieve (*kafarū*, a verbal form corresponding to *kāfir*) and turn men away from the way of God, He will surely make all their works vain and futile.
> Those, on the contrary, who believe (*āmanū*, verbal form corresponding to *muʾmin*) and do good works and believe in what is revealed unto Muḥammad inasmuch as it is the Truth from their Lord, He will surely remit from them their ill-deeds and improve their minds. All this is because those who disbelieve (*kafarū*) have adopted falsehood (*bāṭil*) whereas those who believe (*āmanū*) have adopted the Truth (*ḥaqq*) from their Lord. (XLVII, 1–3)

It may also take the form of an opposition of *kāfir* and *muttaqī* 'god-fearing'. The religious meaning of 'fear' of God (*taqwá*) in Islām was elucidated earlier.

> Verily, this Qurʾān is a reminder to the *muttaqīn* (pl. of *muttaqī*), but We know that there are amongst you some who cry lies to it. Verily, it is a cause of sorrow to the *kāfirīn* (pl. of *kāfir*), although in reality it is the absolute Truth. (LXIX, 48–51)

Or it may take the form of an opposition of *muslim*, 'he who has surrendered', and *mujrim*, 'sinful' or 'guilty'.

> Shall We treat the *muslimīn* in the same way as the *mujrimīn*? (LXVIII, 35)

Or, as an opposition of *ḍāll*, 'he who goes astray, errs', and *muhtadī*, 'he who is guided, who goes the right way'.

> Verily, thy Lord knows best who goes astray from His way, as He knows best those who are guided. (LIII, 31/30)

Or again, the 'positive' side may be called 'the Companions of Paradise' or 'the Fellows of the Right' and the 'negative' side 'the Companions of Hell' or 'the Fellows of the Left'.

1. Literally, "State of Ignorance": the period of time prior to Muhammad's 7th-century call to prophecy.
2. Scattered remains (Latin).

> Not equal are the Fellows of the Fire and the Fellows of Paradise. The Fellows of Paradise, they alone are the blissful. (LIX, 20)

As we shall see later, this fundamental dichotomy of human properties appears in still other forms. But they are all rather marginal variations within the bounds of the essential opposition of belief and unbelief; the most basic fact remains always the same.

Sometimes, the Qur'ān seems to divide men into not two but three classes, recognizing an intermediate state fluctuating between both ends. This unstable middle ground where belief and unbelief overlap and fuse, is formed by those who remain very lukewarm in their faith although they have formally accepted Islām and become Muslims.

> We conferred the Book [of Revelation] as an inheritance upon those whom We chose of Our servants. But of them some there are who wrong themselves [by rejecting it and crying lies to it], and of them are some who are lukewarm [though they have accepted it outwardly], and, again there are some who vie in good works by the leave of God. (XXXV, 29/32)

We should remark that it was mostly the nomadic Arabs of the desert that formed this middle class, though of course there were among them city-dwellers, too, people who remained lukewarm and always wavering between belief and *kufr.*[3] * * * The Qur'ān itself attests to this. In a remarkable passage (XLIX, 14–15), where the basic difference between *mu'min* 'believer' and *muslim* is brought out most clearly, it is declared that the Bedouins who have accepted Islām are not to be regarded, in virtue of that fact alone, as having become *mu'min* in the true sense of the word.

It must be admitted, nevertheless, that, semantically at least the class of such doubtful Muslims is after all but a borderline case, whose value is to be determined in terms of either the one extreme or the other of the common scale running from true belief to downright unbelief. The existence of those lukewarm believers in a great number was no doubt a tough practical problem for Muḥammad himself to solve, but there can be no doubt that they did not constitute in any way an independent category. In the eyes of Muḥammad, they were in the last resort a variation of the positive class. They represented, in other words, an imperfect type of the believer; very imperfect, and yet believers in the sense that they obeyed—at least outwardly—God and His Apostle; and, as such, they were not to be denied the reward of their deeds.

* * *

3. Unbelief, disbelief, denial (Arabic).

# NORMAN CALDER

## *Tafsīr* from Ṭabarī to Ibn Kathīr: Problems in the Description of a Genre, Illustrated with Reference to the Story of Abraham[†1]

1

*Tafsīr* is a literary genre with definable formal characteristics. The most fundamental of these is the presence of the complete canonical text of the Qurʾān (or at least a significant chunk of it), segmented for purposes of comment, and dealt with in canonical order. In a work of *tafsīr*, passages of comment invariably follow canonical segments. Canon and segmentation, lemma and comment: where these are not systematically present, then a work is not an example of the central tradition of *tafsīr*, though it may belong to the margins of that tradition. This formal structure is so fundamental as to require no exemplification. In sections 2 and 3 of this paper two further structures are proposed as constituting, together with this one, a sufficient description of *tafsīr*. Description is of course a mode of interpretation. The interpretation then which I set out in this paper is intended to be general, at least for the period under consideration, namely from Ṭabarī to Ibn Kathīr. Exemplification is restricted to commentary on verses which relate to the story of Abraham.[2] This does not impair the generality of the description, for, as will be evident, quranic narrative provoked more than merely narrative responses: in the hands of a skilled and sensitive exegete any quranic verse might be found to have implications ranging across the scholastic disciplines. * * * The structures which I propose as constitutive of the genre, and the tensions revealed by the varied manipulation of these structures, were recognized at least to a degree by participants in the tradition. * * *

2

> When Abraham said to his father *āzar* do you take idols as gods . . . (Qurʾān 6.74)

Without further reference and unpunctuated that verse permits a number of possible readings, the most obvious of which will take the word *āzar* to be the name of Abraham's father. But it was known from other narratives (historians, story-tellers, the Bible) that Abraham's father was called Terah (so in the English Bible; the Arabic versions were Tārah or Tārakh) and this prompted some creative reflection. Abraham's father had perhaps

† From Norman Calder, *Approaches to the Qurʾān*, ed. G. R. Hawting and Abdul-Kader A. Shareef (London: Routledge, 1993), pp. 101–6, 134–35, 138–40. Reprinted by permission of Taylor & Francis Books UK.

1. Selection of Ibn Kathīr to mark a period is justified in the course of this paper. Ṭabarī is conventionally recognized as marking both the end of the formative period and the beginning of classical *tafsīr*. The literary characteristics of *tafsīr* in its formative period are analysed in John Wansbrough, *Quranic Studies: Sources and Methods of Scriptural Interpretation*, London Oriental Series 31 (Oxford, 1977), pp. 118–246 [Calder's note]. Abū Jaʿfar Muḥammad ibn Jarīr al-Ṭabarī (ca. 839–923), scholar, exegete, and historian. Ismāʿīl ibn ʿUmar ibn Kathīr (ca. 1300–1373), historian and exegete.
2. The first of the Hebrew patriarchs (see Genesis 11–25), and the father of Jacob. According to rabbinic tradition, Abraham's father manufactured idols.

two names, just as Jacob was also called Israel. Or, in familiar idiom, Āzar was a *laqab* (nickname), Terah, an *ism* (proper name). Or vice-versa. Or, indeed, Āzar was the only correct name, a view ascribed to Ḥasan [al-Baṣrī].[3] ʿSulaymān al-Taymī[4] and others suggested that *āzar* was a word indicating abuse or insult, corresponding to Arabic *muʿwajj*: 'Fool, do you take idols . . . ?' Ḍaḥḥāk[5] suggested that *āzar* was Persian, meaning old man; Farrā'[6] that it corresponded to Arabic *mukhṭī'* (one who errs, wrong-doer). Jawharī[7] proposed that *āzar* was a foreign word (*aʿjamī*) derived from the Arabic (!) *āzara* meaning to help, and referred to the fact that Terah/Āzar helped his people to worship idols. Alternatively, it was related to an Arabic word meaning power or force (*quwwa*) and so generated the reading, 'Is it through force that you take idols . . . ?' For Mujāhid,[8] it was not the name of Abraham's father, but the name of an idol, and should be read in the accusative, hence, 'Do you take *āzar* as idols for gods?' Qurṭubī,[9] from whose *Tafsīr* all these readings are taken, adds a rare but helpful personal comment here, that in this case *āzar* is to be understood as a generic, *ism jins*. For Tha'labī,[1] Abraham's father was called Terah by his father but was given the name Āzar when he became overseer to the temple treasury under Nimrod.

All of these readings permitted the extra subtlety that they could be read either in the vocative or in the genitive after *li*: either, 'Abraham said to his father, Fool, do you take idols . . .' or, 'Abraham said to his father, a fool, Do you take idols . . .' In the first case, the word must be read *āzaru*, in the second case, *āzara* (not *āzari* since it was either a foreign proper name or an adjective of the form *afʿalu*, not permitting full declension). Ascribed to Ibn ʿAbbās[2] were two readings which propose a different word juncture without deviating from the consonantal outline of the quranic text: *a-izran tattakhidhu* or *a azran tattakhidhu*, meaning, 'Do you take Izr/Azr as idols . . . ?'

Commenting on this verse, Qurṭubī named a total of eighteen authorities, producing thereby a large variety of possible readings, while giving scarcely a hint as to his preferred reading amongst this amplitude. That amplitude was precisely the point might be inferred from his mode of approach. He began his commentary with a citation from Muḥammad b. Muḥammad al-Juwaynī[3] who claimed that there was no dispute (*ikht-ilāf*) on the name of Abraham's father, which was Terah. Juwaynī then gave two variants, both introduced by the anonymous *qīla*,[4] namely, (i) that *āzar* corresponds to *ya mukhtiʾ*, O wrong-doer, and is *marfūʿ*, in the nominative/vocative, and (ii) that it is the name of an idol and is in the accusative, with ellipsis of the verb. Qurṭubī

3. A famous scholar among the Successors (the generation after that of the Companions) of the Prophet, noted for his piety and asceticism (642–728).
4. Scholar of ḥadīth (d. 760).
5. Al-Ḍaḥḥāk ibn Muzāḥim al-Hilālī (d. 723/24), an outstanding exegete among the Successors.
6. Abū Zakariyyāʾ Yaḥyā b. Ziyād al-Farrāʾ (761–822), a prominent grammarian from Kūfa, in central Iraq.
7. Author of an influential Arabic dictionary (d. ca. 1005).
8. Mujāhid ibn Jabr (d. ca. 720), early exegete and scholar.
9. Abū ʿAbdallāh al-Qurṭubī (1214–1293), scholar of Cordoba, Spain, famous for his Qurʾān commentary.
1. Aḥmad ibn Muḥammad al-Thaʿlabī (d. 1035), author of one of the most important medieval commentaries on the Qurʾān.
2. One of the greatest early Muslim scholars (ca. 619–687/88), often considered the founder of the qurʾānic exegetical tradition.
3. ʿAbd al-Malik al-Juwaynī (1028–1085), Shāfiʿi jurist.
4. It is said (Arabic).

responds to this, first, by denying the claim that there is no dispute on the name of Abraham's father and then by multiplying the variant readings in the manner demonstrated above and providing them with named authorities. In effect, he rejects the over-simplified presentation of Juwaynī and affirms the need for named authorities and multiple readings.

This citation of named authorities and the consequent polyvalent reading of the text is the second structural characteristic of *tafsīr* which I propose as constitutive of the genre.[5] There were of course factors which limited the exploitation of this feature. Two such, open to all exegetes, were, simply, the exercise of choice (hiding variety) or the expression of preference (admitting while controlling variety). Amongst factors likely to strengthen the reductive tendency were a highly specialized concern with a particular (theological) message and/or a narrow focus on some scholastic disciplines and a consequent lack of interest in others. Zamakhsharī, for example, notoriously, combines a meticulous concern for grammatical nicety with a defence of Muʿtazilī theology.[6] These factors condition both his expressed preferences (admitting variety) and choices (implying eschewal of some possibilities). Polyvalent readings remain the norm, though named authorities are considerably reduced. Similar factors, if vastly different specific concerns, affect both Fakhr al-Dīn al-Rāzi[7] * * * and Ibn Kathīr * * * both of whom allow dogmatic considerations to restrict some readings, while admitting, variously, substantial polyvalent readings and sufficient named authorities to establish their participation within the genre—not just *tafsīr* but specifically Sunnī *tafsīr*.[8]

The process of citing authorities and providing multiple readings is in part a declaration of loyalty: it defines the tradition within which one works. It is also a means to establish the individuality or the artistry of a given *mufassir*:[9] the selection, presentation and organization of citations constitutes always a process that is unique to one writer. Finally, it is, of itself, one element in a theological message: the possibility of the community and the text to contain multiplicity while remaining one community and one text is thereby asserted.

Submission to polyvalent readings implied the danger of a tradition grown unmanageably large. Factors of choice, preference and scholarly or dogmatic exclusion worked continuously against centrifugal forces (temporal and spatial diffusion as well as scholarly imagination and development of sectarian and popular beliefs). If the main tradition embraced diversity and made it a means to various ends, the need for monovalent

5. Personal meditation on the text of the Qurʾān, even over a longish segment, is probably not *tafsīr*. The status of some works has been debated. "How elastic can the definition of *tafsīr* be?" John Burton asks ([review of *Approaches to the History of the Interpretation of the Qurʾān* by Andrew Rippin, in] *Bulletin of the School of Oriental and African Studies* 52 [1989]: 340) apropos of Todd Lawson on "The Qurʾān Commentary of the Bāb" (in *Approaches to the History of the Interpretation of the Qurʾān*, ed. Andrew Rippin [Oxford, 1988]). Lawson does not address himself systematically to the questions of form and structure which, in my view, alone might provide an answer [Calder's note].
6. A school of Islamic speculative theology influenced by the methods of Hellenistic philosophy and condemned by more orthodox thinkers. The commentary referred to is *Al-Kashshāf* (*The Discloser*), by Maḥmūd ibn ʿUmar al-Zamakhsharī (1075–1144).
7. A famous teacher and preacher (1149/50–1210), and author of a massive commentary on the Qurʾān.
8. Members of the Sunnī branch of Islam (today 90 percent of the world's Muslims) look only to the Qurʾān and canonical ḥadīth for authority; the Shīʿī also consider imams of specific lineages from Muḥammad's son-in-law ʿAlī to be authoritative.
9. An author of *tafsīr*.

readings—perhaps for very specific purposes—was not thereby cancelled. The work of Dīnawarī (308/920) within our period and the famous *Tafsīr al Jalālayn* of Suyūṭī and Maḥallī in the 9/15th century are firmly monovalent; as is one of the three *tafsīrs* by Wāḥidī (468/1076). Felicitously described by A. Rippin as 'Arabic translations' of the Qur'ān, these works probably reflect the needs of a curriculum (educational) and derive their larger meaning from the *tafsīr* tradition as a whole: in relation to this they are always either introduction or summary.[1]

3

For many contemporary scholars of philosophy and literary criticism, the concept of hermeneutics has become the focus for a highly generalized understanding of the relationship between the reader and the text/ the present and the past/ the individual and the world. For them the 'text' is either friend (to a degree, Gadamer) or enemy (Bloom) or just an indefinitely malleable system of signs without truth, without origins (Derrida); it is approached with prejudice (*Vorurteil*), or anxiety and misprision, or licence. Stimulating at certain levels of analysis, these ideas cannot be made to serve the immediate aim of assessing the forms or the content of *tafsīr*.[2] Refreshing, by contrast, is the assumption by G. Vermes that it is usually possible to distinguish between a problem that arises because of something in the text and a problem that emerges because something external to the text is imposed upon it: giving rise, respectively, in his terminology, to pure and applied exegesis.[3] This distinction has some value at a basic descriptive level but will hardly sustain the burden of precise systematic analysis. Does the exegetical problem related to *āzar* arise from a 'real' problem within the text or from an external idea or belief which is imposed upon the text? The question hardly seems appropriate. The problem arises because something within the text is recognized as being at odds with something outside the text. This must always be true of exegetical problems. Texts in isolation are not only unproblematic, they are meaningless. The text of the Qur'ān takes on meaning only when it is systematically

1. See Andrew Rippin, "Lexicographical Texts and the Qur'ān," in Rippin, ed., *Approaches*, p. 164. The work of Dīnawarī is the well-known *Tafsīr of Ibn 'Abbās*, also ascribed to Kalbī and now reassigned by Rippin; see "Al-Zukri, *naskh al-Qur'ān* and the Problem of Early *Tafsīr* Texts," *Bulletin of the School of Oriental and African Studies* 47 (1984): 23–24, and his forthcoming "Tafsīr Ibn 'Abbās," in *Jerusalem Studies in Arabic and Islam* [published as "Tafsīr Ibn 'Abbās and Criteria for Dating Early Tafsīr Texts," 18 (1994): 38–83; Calder's note]. Hishām ibn al-Kalbī (ca. 737–819/821), historian of the early Arabs.
2. The references are to Hans-Georg Gadamer, Harold Bloom and Jacques Derrida. It would of course be possible on the basis of the theoretical approaches to these (and other) writers to devise a typology of approaches to the hermeneutic task: Derrida-an, Bloomian etc. While no academic effort is free from a proselytising aspect, their programmes are probably too didactic and ideological for the normal (Anglo-Saxon!) approaches to literary description. In the field of Jewish, and, in particular, rabbinic studies, the central task of description—with all that implies of analysis and interpretation—has been consistently brought to the fore through the works of J. Neusner, A. Goldberg, P. Schäfer and P. Alexander (*inter alios*). It is worth remarking that my proposed description of *tafsīr* works also (with minor emendations) for *midrash*, reflecting, not influence, but common literary responses to the central role within a community of a divine book [Calder's note]. Calder names three major figures of 20th-century literary theory—the German philosopher Gadamer (1900–2002), the American literary critic Bloom (b. 1930), and the French philosopher Derrida (1930–2004)—and a number of contemporary scholars in Judaic studies: Jacob Neusner, Arnold Goldberg, Peter Schäfer, and Philip Alexander. *Midrash*: explanation (Hebrew), a collection of interpretations of biblical passages.
3. G. Vermes, "Bible and Midrash: Early Old Testament Exegesis," in *Cambridge History of the Bible*, vol. 1 (Cambridge, 1970) [Calder's note]. Géza Vermes (1924–2013), Hungarian-born British authority on the Dead Sea Scrolls.

juxtaposed to certain structures which exist independently (more or less) of the Qur'ān itself; notably the grammatical and rhetorical structures of the Arabic language, but also the scholastic disciplines of law, theology and prophetic narrative. In the case of *āzar*, the narrative structure within the text is apparently at odds with a known narrative structure external to the text. Resolution is achieved through such processes as (i) harmonization through narrative—Abraham's father had two names or he acquired one name later in life; (ii) differentiation: e. g. grammatical/lexical—*āzar* does not belong to the narrative structure but to the grammatical, being not a proper name but an adjective; or narrative/grammatical—*āzar* is the name of an idol or class of idols and the sentence exhibits transposition or ellision of a verb; and (iii) exclusion—the quranic narrative excludes the others. And so on. The problem is invariably one of bringing the internal structures and the external ones into some kind of harmony. (This was a process of course which prejudiced the independence of the scholastic discipines, not least those of grammar and rhetoric. In practice, the independent analogical structures of grammar and syntax were, just, preserved;[4] and so, marginally, and in spite of Ibn Kathīr, was the independent discipline of prophetic narrative.)

John Wansbrough, reacting in part to the weaknesses of established scholarship, proposed a typological approach to the historical development (diachronic) of *tafsīr*. His types are haggadic, halakhic, masoretic, rhetorical and allegorical.[5] The terminology is sectarian, though probably intended to reflect the universality of hermeneutic approaches. For purposes of synchronic description, of *tafsīr* in the classical, post-development, period, the hint is invaluable. The scholastic disciplines against which the quranic text must be measured are broadly incorporated in that list. Clearly, there is room for subdivision: it is usually possible to distinguish lexical, orthographic and syntactic devices under the heading masoretic (grammatical). And there is a minor usefulness in acknowledging a distinction between linguistic (instrumental) and theological (ideological) structures. In sum, I would propose that *tafsīr*, in the period up to Ibn Kathīr, can be described as a measuring of the quranic text against the following:

1 Instrumental structures:
orthography, lexis, syntax, rhetoric, symbol/allegory
2 Ideological structures:
prophetic history, theology, eschatology, law, *taṣawwuf*[6]

This is the third and most complex structural organization which constitutes the literary genre of *tafsīr*. The term 'prophetic history' is intended to cover the disciplines of prophetic biography, both *qiṣaṣ al-anbiyā'* and *sīrat al-nabī*.[7] 'Theology' covers the normal subject matter of *kalām*.

4. See further J. Wansbrough, *Studies*, pp. 100–102, 168–69, and 202ff. Also, illuminatingly, John Burton, "Linguistic Errors in the Qur'ān," *Journal of Semitic Studies* 33.2 (1988). Outside of the Qur'ān those linguistic problems in which Rāzī recognized a sign of the intellectual weakness of man would always be recognized as simply errors; ibid. p. 196 [Calder's note].
5. Wansbrough, *Studies*, pp. 119ff. [Calder's note]. Wansbrough (1928–2002), American-born historian of religion, borrowed the terms *haggadic* (narrative), *halakhic* (legal), and *masoretic* (linguistic) from traditional Jewish scholarship.
6. Islamic mysticism.
7. "Stories of the prophets" and "life of the Prophet," respectively. The first genre deals primarily with pre-Islamic prophets, while the second records Muḥammad's biography.

Orthography, lexis and syntax are the normal subject matter of the grammatical disciplines; allegory and symbol are most commonly dealt with in the Islamic intellectual tradition as a part of the discipline of rhetoric.[8] The list permits no doubt of finer articulation but adequately defines the standard and the marginal concerns both of *tafsīr* and of the Islamic scholastic disciplines. All of these subjects were independently studied for their own sake and permitted of indefinite extension beyond the constraints of the quranic text; and all were systematically subject to the centripetal force of the quranic text. The interplay of discipline and text was neither random nor absolutely constrained: it was controlled by the knowledge, interests, skills, sensitivity, imagination, even humour, of individual exegetes, as well as by their literary and sectarian loyalties. A *tafsīr*, after all, is a work of art. Symbolic and allegorical readings frequently coincide with *taṣawwuf*, but played a marginal role even in *kalām*-type discussions. On balance, they have only a limited role to play in the period discussed here, though capable of considerable expansion to serve the needs of a particular theological message (Rāzi[9]) and increasingly present in *tafsīr* works of the later period.

The claim advanced here is then that the three broad structures presented in the first three sections of this paper constitute the fundamental rules-of-the-game for *mufassirs*. The qualities which distinguish one *mufassir* from another lie less in their conclusions as to what the quranic text means than in their development and display of techniques which mark their participation in and mastery of a literary discipline. Just as the skill of, say, a football player can be recognized only in relation to a complex body of rules (variously constitued by such things as white lines on grass or a complex and developing off-side rule) so too the literary skills of a *mufassir* must be assessed not in terms of the end product (the Qur'ān explained) but in terms of their skilful participation in a rule-governed activity.

## MEIR M. BAR-ASHER

## *From* Scripture and Exegesis in Early Imāmī Shiism[†]

### *Introduction*

#### HISTORICAL AND RELIGIOUS BACKGROUND

The Shī'a[1] first made its appearance on the Muslim historical stage in the days that followed the death of the Prophet Muḥammad. The supporters of 'Alī ibn Abī Ṭālib, the Prophet's cousin and son-in-law, opposed the

8. For a general account of the Islamic disciplines in relation to *tafsīr*, Wansbrough, *Studies*, chapter 4 is invaluable; but see the specific discussion of symbol and allegory, pp. 239–46 [Calder's note].
9. Fakhr al-Dīn al-Rāzī (1149–1210), Persian-born theologian and scholar who wrote an authoritative commentary on the Qur'ān.
† From Meir M. Bar-Asher, *Scripture and Exegesis in Early Imāmī Shiism* (Leiden: Brill; Jerusalem: Magnes Press, Hebrew University, 1999), pp. 1–7, 12, 14–16, 87–93. Reprinted by permission of Koninklijke Brill NV. Except as indicated, all notes are Bar-Asher's, as are all brackets in the text. Some parenthetical Arabic phrases have been omitted.
1. In this study the terms "Shī'a" and "Shī'ī" refer to the Shī'a in general. Particular Shī'ī groups are identified by name—e.g. Imāmiyya (or Imāmī Shī'ism), Ismā'īliyya, Zaydiyya, Jārūdiyya, etc. The term "Twelver Shī'a" (or *Ithnā'ashariyya*) is used only in discussions of "twelver" aspects of Imāmi Shī'ism (see e.g. chap. 4, § 2.4.1.2, and chap. 6, § 2).

election of Abū Bakr as Muḥammad's heir and formed a separate sect known as *Shī'at 'Alī* (the party of 'Alī). Most Western scholars agree that this party did not initially display religious features different from those of the other Muslims and that the disagreement between the two rival camps—the majority, which eventually became known as the Sunna, and their opponents, the party of 'Alī—was merely political. Alongside this view there exists another, according to which this schism was characterized from the outset by both religious and political disputes.[2] In either case, the breach widened to a deep chasm in the wake of the rebellion against the Umayyads headed by 'Alī's son, Ḥusayn. This rebellion, which ended with the death of Ḥusayn and other descendants of the Prophet at Karbalā' (61/680), was a turning point in the history of Shī'ism. One can therefore point to two beginnings for Shī'ism: one at Medina, when the question of the Prophet's inheritance was disputed, and the other in Iraq (specifically in Kufa) following the failed revolt. Those killed at Karbalā' are regarded in Shī'ī tradition as martyrs, and their death opened a wide gulf between Shī'īs and Sunnīs (the latter represented by the Umayyad dynasty). All Shī'īs agreed that the Umayyad dynasty was evil, but they differed as to the approach to be adopted towards it. Disagreements on this and other issues led to further splits. The first occurred in 65/685, when a Shī'ī group headed by al-Mukhtār ibn Abī 'Ubayd, a *mawlā* of the tribe of Thaqīf,[3] once again took up arms against the Umayyads. Al-Mukhtār declared himself the representative of Muḥammad ibn al-Ḥanafiyya, Alī's son by his wife of the Ḥanīfa tribe. His objective was the establishment of a Shī'ī rule headed by the house of 'Alī. Two years later the governor of Baṣra, Muṣ'ab ibn al-Zubayr, killed al-Mukhtār and put down the rebellion. Armed resistance was then taken up by another Shī'ī group headed by Zayd ibn 'Alī (d. 122/740), a brother of the fifth Imam, Muḥammad al-Bāqir (d. 114/732 or 117/735). Armed rebellion henceforth became one of the prevalent features of Zaydī Shī'ism. The Ḥusaynī branch of the Shī'a, to which belonged some of the followers of Imam al-Bāqir, held the view that armed resistance should be abandoned. This group—which in fact constituted the kernel of the Imāmī sub-sect—adopted passive methods of protest that eventually became the hallmark of Imāmī Shī'ism. Its efforts were channelled toward the development of Imāmī Shī'ī doctrine, and its hopes of recompense for past and present evils were directed toward an apocalyptic future.

The rule of the Umayyad dynasty (41/661–132/750), especially following the Karbalā' uprising, was fraught with tension for the Shī'a, The harsh anti-Shī'ī policy adopted by most Umayyad caliphs provided fertile ground for Shī'ī unrest. In fact, many Shī'ī sub-sects, whose rise is recorded in the heresiographic literature[4] of both Sunnīs and Shī'īs, emerged during the days of the Umayyads.

The woeful situation of the Shī'īs did not change with the rise of the 'Abbāsids. The latter, who at first declared that their government would redress the wrongs inflicted on the Shī'a by the previous rulers, soon

2. A representative of this approach is the Shī'ī scholar S. H. M. Jafri; see his *Origins and Early Development of Shī'a Islam* (London, 1981), 1–23.
3. See G. R. Hawting, "al-Mukhtār b. Abī 'Ubayd," *EI*[2] [*Encyclopaedia of Islam*, 2nd ed.], 7, 521–4, and cf. H. Laoust, *Les schismes dans l'islam* (Paris, 1983), 2nd ed., 27–9. [*Mawlā*: client (Arabic)—editor's note.]
4. Writings on heresy [editor's note].

changed their tune.[5] Once the ʿAbbāsids realized that the Shīʿa presented a potential revolutionary threat and would never recognize the legitimacy of the ʿAbbāsid rule, they began to restrict the various Shīʿī sects. The proto-Imāmiyya[6] found itself in the position of a persecuted minority, and it was only during the caliphate of al-Maʾmūn (198/813–218/833) that the aspirations were temporarily raised. Al-Maʾmūn's marriage to the daughter of Imam ʿAlī al-Riḍā (d. 203/818),[7] as well as his promise to nominate al-Riḍā as heir apparent,[8] were seen by the proto-Imāmiyya as steps toward recognition of their claims to be the Prophet's successors. It seems that by these al-Maʾmūn intended to placate the opponents to ʿAbbāsid rule, given that a strong spirit of rebellion had manifested itself in the wake of the dynastic rivalry that had flared on the death of the Caliph Hārūn al-Rashīd (d. 193/809) between his two sons, al-Amīn and al-Maʾmūn. The Shīʿīs, particularly the Zaydī stream, took advantage of this dynastic squabble to stage a number of revolts.[9] The gestures toward the proto-Imāmiyya were thus intended to appease some of the potential opposition to the government. However, the hopes these gestures awoke in the proto-Imāmiyya were soon dispelled. With the death of al-Riḍā, who according to Shīʿī tradition was poisoned on the orders of the caliph, the proto-Imāmiyya reverted to its earlier position as a persecuted sect.[1] The ʿAbbāsids kept a careful eye on the Imams and on other descendants of the Prophet's family, whom their disciples considered to be the only legitimate candidates for leadership of the Muslim community. Most Shīʿī Imams living under ʿAbbāsid rule were kept under house arrest and died under unnatural circumstances.[2]

However, the political subjugation of the proto-Imāmiyya stood in inverse relationship to its development and flowering as a religious sect. This sect that had emerged in Kufa toward the end of the first/seventh century began toward the middle of the second/eighth century to exert an influence in important centres in the eastern provinces of the ʿAbbāsid state. Already in the days of the Umayyads, disciples of the Imam Jaʿfar al-Ṣādiq (d. 148/765) had arrived in Qumm, the earliest Shīʿī stronghold in Iran. This city, which was conquered in 23/644 by Arab forces led by Abū Mūsā l-Ashʿarī, became several decades later a haven for Arabs of the tribe of al-Ashʿar who had fled there from Kufa. As related in several sources, this emigration resulted from the failure of the revolt of ʿAbd al-Raḥmān b. al-Ashʿath in Kufa against the Umayyads (84/703); many of the rebels escaped to Qumm, conquered some of the surrounding towns by force, and settled there. According to other sources, the emigration occurred ten years later (94/713) and was carried out peacefully.[3] Be that

5. On the role played by Shīʿī groups in the ʿAbbāsid revolution see M. Sharon, *Black Banners from the East: The Establishment of the ʿAbbāsid State, Incubation of a Revolt* (Jerusalem, 1983), 41–5; M. Momen, *An Introduction to Shīʿī Islam* (New Haven and London, 1985), 71–4.
6. The first "followers of the imams," or Imāmī Shīʿa [editor's note].
7. See Momen, *An Introduction to Shīʿī Islam*, 72–3; J. Van Ess, *Theologie und Gesellschaft im 2. und 3. Jahrhundert Hidschra: eine Geschichte des religiösen Denkens im Frühen Islam* (Berlin, 1991–6) 3, 154–8; H. Modarressi, *Crisis and Consolidation in the Formative Period of Shiʿite Islam* (Princeton, 1993), 10–11.
8. See B. Lewis, " ʿAlī al-Riḍā," *EI*², 1, 399–400. See also Sharon, *Black Banners from the East*, 31; Laoust, *Les schismes dans l'islam*, 98.
9. See Momen, *An Introduction to Shīʿī Islam*, 71–2, and W. Madelung, *Religious Trends in Early Islamic Iran*, Columbia Lectures on Iranian Studies, 4 (New York, 1988), 87.
1. See B. Lewis, " ʿAlī al-Riḍā," *EI*², 1, 400.
2. See Momen, *An Introduction to Shīʿī Islam*, 39–45.
3. See Madelung, *Religious Trends in Early Islamic Iran*, 79.

as it may, these refugees, initially bound together only by their opposition to the Umayyads, became within a few decades faithful Shīʾīs, and the foundation was thus laid for the creation in Qumm, as of the second/eighth century, of one of the most important Shīʾī centres of all time.[4] The first of the Kūfī emigrants to become a follower of the Imam al-Ṣādiq was a son of ʿAbd Allāh b. Saʿd b. Mālik al-Ashʿarī.[5] He was followed by many of his generation. Toward the end of the second/eighth century Qumm became predominantly Imāmī-Shīʿī. Here, on the fringes of the Umayyad and ʿAbbāsid state, Imāmī Shīʿism fared better than it did in Kufa, its place of origin. While Kufa became, during the second/eighth century, a breeding ground for Shīʿī splits, in Qumm Imāmī Shīʿism managed to establish a firm stronghold.

In Kufa itself, the proto-Imāmiyya fought for hegemony with the Zaydiyya and with other sub-sects that broke away in the political and religious turmoil that usually erupted following the death of a particular Imam.[6] Some disciples of Jaʿfar al-Ṣādiq, for example, pledged support to his eldest son Ismāʿīl. This son is usually said to have predeceased his father. However, some of his supporters maintained that he had not died but was hidden away by his father and, further, that he would reappear as the Mahdī.[7] Others, known as the Mubārakiyya, recognized Ismāʿīl's son, Muḥammad, as their Imam.[8] The fate of these groups is unknown. About a century later an Ismāʿīlī movement emerged simultaneously in several centres of the ʿAbbāsid state; but there is no clear evidence as to a possible historical or doctrinal link between the early Ismāʿīlīs and the later movement. The sub-sect known as Faṭḥiyya (or Afṭaḥiyya)[9] regarded al-Ṣādiq's son ʿAbd Allāh al-Afṭaḥ as the rightful heir. A third group—those who viewed al-Ṣādiq's third son, Mūsā al-Kāẓim (d. 183/799), as the legitimate Imam—continued to constitute the nucleus of the Imāmiyya. A more serious split occurred following the death of al-Kāẓim. At that time many Shīʿī sects emerged, the largest being the Wāqifa, which denied al-Kāẓim's death; believing that he would return as the Mahdī, they refused to recognize the Imāma of his son ʿAlī al-Riḍā. Kufa became the centre of activity for these groups, as well as for extreme Shīʿī sects known as *ghulāt* (extremists). Among the leaders of these groups one may count, for example, two of the most prominent disciples of the Imam al-Ṣādiq—al-Mufaḍḍal b. ʿUmar al-Juʿfī (d. ca. 179/795) and Abū l-Khaṭṭāb (d. ca 138/755–6).[1]

4. See Momen, *An Introduction to Shīʿī Islam*, 78–81; Madelung, *Religious Trends in Early Islamic Iran*, 81–4.
5. As Madelung suggests (*Religious Trends in Early Islamic Iran*, 79), this was apparently his son ʿĪsā, mentioned in Shīʿī *rijāl* literature as a transmitter of traditions on the authority of Jaʿfar al-Ṣādiq and Mūsā al-Kāẓim. [*Rijāl* literature assesses the reliability of the narrators of ḥadīth—editor's note.]
6. On these schismastic developments following the death of the various Imams see e.g. Momen, *An Introduction to Shiʿi Islam*, 49–60.
7. The Guided One (Arabic): for the Shiʿa, the Twelfth Imam whose messianic return will herald the day of judgment [editor's note].
8. For details see F. Daftary, *The Ismāʿīlīs: Their History and Doctrines* (Cambridge, 1990), 102–3; and see also Madelung, *Religious Trends in Early Islamic Iran*, 93.
9. On this sect see Laoust, *Les schismes dans l'islam*, 68; al-Shahrastānī, *Kitāb al-Milal wa l-Niḥal: Livre des religions et des sectes*, edited by D. Gimaret and G. Monnot (Paris and Louvain, 1986), 1:488–9.
1. His full name is Muḥammad b. Abī Zaynab al-Asadī al-Ajdaʿ. On him see B. Lewis, *The Origins of Ismailism* (Cambridge, 1940), 32–7; H. Halm, *Die islamische Gnosis: Die extreme Schia und die ʿAlawiten* (Zürich, 1982), 199–206; and W. Madelung, "Khaṭṭābiyya," *EI*², 4, 1132–3.

Imāmī Shīʿism continued to spread to other regions of Iran, far from its place of origin in Kufa. Toward the end of the third/ninth century it reached Transoxania. * * *

* * * To sum up, during the period in which most of the commentators whose writings are dealt with in this study flourished—i.e. between the middle of the third/ninth century and the middle of the fourth/tenth century, Iraq and Iran, and more specifically Kufa and Qumm, served as the two major religious centres of Imāmī Shīʿism. This period corresponds roughly with the years between the two "Occultations" of the twelfth Imam:[2] "the Minor Occultation" (*al-ghayba al-ṣughrā*), which began, according to Imāmī tradition, in the year 260/874 (or 264/878), and "the Major Occultation" (*al-ghayba al-kubrā*) of 329/941.[3]

According to Imāmī belief, during the period of the Minor Occultation the twelfth Imam continued to lead his flock through four persons who served successively as his representatives (*sufarā'*)[4] whom he met secretly and through whom he instructed his believers. However, with the death of the fourth representative, the Imam disappeared altogether, and Shīʿīs believed that he will not reappear before his return as the Mahdī at the end of time.

* * *

The main issue of disagreement between Shīʿīs and other Muslims was that of the Imāma and the various doctrines derived from it. Two features characterized the Imāmī concept of the Imāma: one was the belief that the Imams were superior beings, endowed with a variety of supernatural qualities; the other was the belief that aside from the human attributes and qualities with which the leader of the Muslim community should be endowed, he should also be nominated as heir by his predecessor, through an explicit designation (*naṣṣ*). These questions, which gave rise to many others, were at the heart of most Shīʿī disputes. The fact that Imāmī Shīʿīs characterized their Imams as endowed with supernatural qualities, while Sunnīs refrained from ascribing those features even to Muḥammad, could not but widen the gulf between the two camps. On the other hand, it should be emphasized that what was eventually adopted by the Imāmiyya as part of its official dogma was achieved more often than not as the result of an internal struggle against even more extreme positions on the same issues.

* * *

The controversy over the question of the Prophet's inheritance, which had sparked the conflict between the Sunna and the Shīʿa in the first place, became ever more heated over the issue of the Imāma doctrine and

2. For a detailed periodization of the early Imāmiyya in direct relation to the development of its doctrine see E. Kohlberg, "The Attitude of the Imāmī Shīʿīs to the Companions of the Prophet" (Ph.D. dissertation, Oxford, 1971), v–vii; H. Modarressi, *An Introduction to Shīʿī Law: A Bibliographical Study* (London, 1984), 26–50.
3. The consequences of the Major Occultation and its effect on Imāmī literature are discussed in chap. 2. See also Kohlberg, "The Attitude of the Imāmī Shīʿīs to the Companions of the Prophet," v.
4. See E. Kohlberg, "Safīr", *EI*[2], 8, 811–2; Momen, *An Introduction to Shīʿī Islam*, 162–5; H. Halm, *Die Schia* (Darmstadt, 1988), 41–5 (=*Shiism*, translated by J. Watson [Edinburgh, 1991], 35–9).

its offshoots. But in other fields too, a deep chasm separated the rival camps from the inception of Shīʿism. A central issue was their differing attitudes toward the Qurʾān[5] and the prophetic tradition. Even in those traditions in which there had been no difference between the two camps, Shīʿī scholars avoided relying upon dicta not transmitted on the authority of the Imams or their disciples. It goes without saying that a dictum ascribed to most of the Companions of the Prophet—excluding those who were also supporters of ʿAlī—has no validity whatsoever in the eyes of Imāmī scholars. Those who denied ʿAlī's rights were vilified. They include the first three caliphs (Abū Bakr, ʿUmar and ʿUthmān), two of the Prophet's wives (ʿĀʾisha and Ḥafṣa) and other prominent Companions of the Prophet. In Sunnī tradition all Companions are considered worthy of respect and emulation; yet they are transformed in Imāmī tradition into evil figures whose actions are to be condemned and rejected. This attitude to the Companions of the Prophet and their disciples was not restricted to rejecting their traditions with regard to matters of religion; it included also the duty of dissociating from them and denigrating them. It is obvious that the dispute over these questions greatly inflamed the hostility and tension between the camps, with the Imāmiyya (as well as other Shīʿī sub-sects) venting feelings of outrage and frustration toward the Sunna and the Sunna viewing the positions taken by the Shīʿa as unforgivable heresies.

In contradistinction to these deep doctrinal divisions, there is considerable affinity between the two camps on questions of law. Aside from minor differences—similar to those found among the four Sunnī schools of law (*madhāhib al-fiqh*)—the common ground far outweighs the differences. Nevertheless, Sunnīs and Shīʿīs are deeply divided over three points of law, all of which relate to the status of woman: marriage, divorce and inheritance. As opposed to the Sunna, the Shīʿa permits pleasure (*mutʿa*) marriage—i.e. a marriage that is contracted for a fixed period, at the end of which it is automatically dissolved. The Sunna views all time-bound marriage contracts as null and void.[6] Divorce under Imāmī law is more difficult than under Sunnī law. Unlike the Sunnī schools, Imāmī law maintains that divorce formula must be pronounced explicitly in the presence of two witnesses. The two camps agree, however, that if a man divorces his wife three times, he is not allowed to marry her again unless she is first married to another. As for inheritance, here too Imāmī law is more favourably disposed towards women. For example, where there are males and females who are equally close in kinship to the deceased, Imāmī law does not exclude the females. In Sunnī law, by contrast, the males are preferred in such a case.[7]

5. On which see more below.
6. On *mutʿa* marriage see A. Gribetz, *Strange Bedfellows: Mutʿat al-nisāʾ and Mutʿat al-ḥajj—A Study Based on Sunnī and Shīʿī Sources of Tafsīr, Ḥadīth and Fiqh* (Berlin, 1994), esp. 48–50 and 161–7.
7. On the legal status of women in Shīʿī law see W. Madelung, "Shīʿī Attitudes toward Women as Reflected in Fiqh," in *Society and the Sexes in Medieval Islam*, Sixth Giorgio Della Vida Biennial Conference, edited by A. L. S. Marsot (Malibu, 1979), 69–79 (reprinted in *Religious Schools and Sects in Medieval Islam* [London, 1985], chapter 12).

## CHAPTER 3

### *The Methods of Exegesis*

* * *

The Imāmīyya, like any other religious group in Islam, sought to discover reference points (*loci probantes*) in the Qur'ān to which they could anchor their beliefs. Various beliefs that crystallized during the early phases of Shī'ism, and that later changed form and substance as a result of polemics with rival tendencies, are presented as though they were directly formulated in the Qur'ān. In this, Imāmī commentators are no different from their Sunnī counterparts, be they theologians, mystics, philosophers or others. Both Sunnīs and Shī'īs believe that the Qur'ān is many-faceted and that any idea or outlook can, with the help of various exegetical methods, be discovered within its pages.

The methods of exegesis used by the Imāmī commentators were in themselves not very different from those of the Sunnīs. Nevertheless pre-Buwayhid[8] Imāmī commentators consider their exegetical tradition to be superior to that of their Sunnī conterparts. They maintain that only the Shī'a possesses the keys to a correct understanding of the Qur'ān. A famous Imāmī tradition, which is also cited in Sunnī sources, ascribes the following words to Muḥammad: "There is one among you who will fight for the [correct] interpretation of the Qur'ān just as I myself fought for its revelation, and he is 'Alī b. Abī Ṭālib."

This tradition is one of many that elevates 'Alī's position as a Qur'ān interpreter, a position shared by his descendants, the Imams. The Imams' authority as interpreters is only one side of the coin, the other being the inferiority and even falsehood of non-Shī'ī interpretations.

* * *

The need to interpret the Qur'ān according to Imāmī principles is based on the assumption that the Qur'ān consists of much material pertaining to the Shī'a, its history and beliefs. This idea is found in many Imāmī traditions. In a well-known tradition, which appears in the writings of most early Imāmī commentators, the Imam al-Bāqir declares the following: "The Qur'ān was revealed [consisting of] four parts: One part concerning us [the Shī'a], one part concerning our enemies, one part commandments and regulations (*farā'iḍ wa aḥkām*) and one part customs and parables (*sunan wa amthāl*). And the exalted parts of the Qur'ān refer to us (*wa lanā karā'im al-qur'ān*).[9] Such a statement, which appears time and again in

8. Before the Buwayid or Būyid dynasty that ruled western Iran and Iraq (945–1055) [editor's note].
9. *T'A*, 1:9, 1, and also ibid, 3; ibid., 10, 7 (a tripartite division is suggested). Cf. also the following sources, in which a division into either three or four parts is alluded to: *TF*, 1:20–21; ibid., 2:5–6; 9–11; Abū Ja'far Muḥammad b. Ya'qūb al-Kulīnī, *al-Kāfī* (Tehran, 1375–6), 2:627–8; and see I. Goldziher, *Die Richtungen der islamischen Koranauslegung* (Leiden, 1920), 288. As for the expression *karā'im al-qur'ān*, see al-Majlisī's explanation in *Biḥār*², 23:76: "The exalted and most valuable verses, those which indicate excellence and praise" (*al-āyāt al-karīma wa nafā'ishuā wa hiya mā tadullu 'alā faḍl wa madḥ*). [*T'A*: Abū al-Naḍr Muḥammad b. Mas'ūd al-'Ayyāshī, *Tafsīr al-'Ayyāshī*, ed. Hāshim al-Rasūlī al-Maḥallātī (Qumm, 1960). *TF*: Furāt ibn Furāt ibn Ibrāhīm al-Kūfī, *Tafsīr Furāt* (Najaf, 1935). *Biḥār*²: Muḥammad Bāqir al-Majlisī, *Biḥār al-anwar*, new ed. (Beirut, 1403/1983)—editor's note.]

various forms in Imāmī works, raises the question: If indeed the Shīʿa is so central in the Qurʾān, why is it not mentioned explicitly? The following example indicates that this question was raised not only within Shīʿī circles but also from outside—by the rivals of the Shīʿa. One tradition sets out to interpret the verse 4/59: "Obey God, and obey the Messenger and those in authority among you" and maintains (as is usual in Imāmī exegesis) that the expression *ulī l-amr minkum* (those in authority among you) refers to the duty to obey ʿAlī and his descendants, the Imams. This commonplace interpretation, which is often repeated in Imāmī commentaries, induced Abū Baṣīr,[1] one of al-Bāqir's disciples, to raise the fundamental question: "People ask us: 'What prevented Him [God] from mentioning ʿAlī and his family in His book."[2] It is a question that was constantly on the minds of Imāmī commentators, as a result of both internal reflection and the Shīʿī need to defend its position against continual attacks on its excessive use of allegory and typology in its Qurʾān exegesis.[3]

Imāmī commentators use three arguments to explain the gap between the absence of any explicit mention of the Shīʿa in the Qurʾān and Shīʿī claims that the book is replete with such allusions:

a. The claim of forgery, i.e. issues relating to the Shīʿa, were deliberately omitted from the Qurʾān.

b. The Qurʾān contains hidden meanings, which the exegete should decipher.

c. The Qurʾān teaches principles while tradition expounds their details.

### THE CLAIM OF FORGERY

The claim that the ʿUthmānic Codex of the Qurʾān[4] had been falsified is one of the most common arguments to which early Imāmī tradition resorted in explaining the absence of any explicit reference to the Shīʿa in the Qurʾān. In the Qurʾānic commentary ascribed to the Imam Ḥasan al-ʿAskarī (d. 260-873-4) a tradition is found accusing the Companions of the Prophet of violating the integrity of the Qurʾānic text. "Those whose ambitions overcame their wisdom (i.e. the *Ṣaḥāba*[5]) falsified (*ḥarrafū*) the true meaning of God's book and altered it (*wa ghayyarūhu*)."[6] A similar tradition—which, however, does not blame the Companions of the Prophet for the falsification—is found in al-Ayyāshī's commentary on the Qurʾān: "Had the book of God not been subject to additions and omissions, our righteousness would not have been hidden from any [person] of wisdom."[7]

1. His full name is Abū Muḥammad Yaḥyā b. Abī l-Qāsim; he was also a disciple of the Imams al-Sādiq and al-Kāzim (Najāshī, 441; Kishshī, 402). According to Najāshī, ibid., Abū Baṣīr died in 150/767. [Abū al-ʿAbbās Aḥmad ibn ʿAlī al-Najāshī, *Rijāl al-Najāshī* (Qumm, 1986); Abū ʿAmr Muḥammad ibn ʿUmar al-Kishshī, *Kitāb al-rijāl* (Najaf, n.d.)—editor's note.]
2. *TʿA*, 1:249, 169; cf. *TF*, 34, 10–15. The Imam's answer is instructive and will be discussed later, together with other answers given to this question.
3. See e.g. the pointed criticism of Ibn Qutayba on this issue, *Taʾwīl mukhtalif al-ḥadīth*, 70–73, and *Taʾwīl mushkil al-qurʾān*, 260–263. [Abū Muḥammad ʿAbdallāh ibn Muslim ibn Qubtayba al-Dīnawarī (828–889), author of works on secular as well as religious topics; the two works cited here are *Taʾwīl mukhtalif al-ḥadīth* (Beirut, 1972) and *Taʾwīl mushkil al-Qurʾān*, ed. Muḥammad Ṣaqr (Medina, 1981)—editor's note.]
4. The authoritative written version of the Qurʾān, compiled at the direction of the third caliph, ʿUthmān ibn ʿAffān (d. 656) [editor's note].
5. Companions (Arabic) [editor's note].
6. See the Qurʾān commentary attributed to the Imam Ḥasan al-ʿAskarī, *Tafsīr al-ʿAskarī* (Qumm, 1409H), 95; cf. E. Kohlberg, "Some Notes on the Imamite Attitude to the Qurʾān," in *Islamic Philosophy and the Classical Tradition*, ed. S. M. Stern et al. (Oxford, 1972), 212 and n. 37.
7. *TʿA*, 1:13, 6.

In a similar tradition it is stated: "The [Qur'ān] contained the names of [various] persons, but these names have been removed."[8] The commentator does not attempt to verify this general claim with examples of texts that, in his opinion, have been altered.

* * *

This argument, which can be supported by a large number of additional texts, is essentially different from the two other explanations provided by the Shī'a for this problem, which will be discussed in the two following sections. The Shī'a maintain that the inconsistency between the Qur'ānic text and the Shī'ī outlook is not necessarily one that merely a "correct" interpretation can remedy. This inconsistency results from a textual gap between the incomplete Qur'ānic text found in the possession of all Islamic factions and the ideal text, which, according to Imāmī belief, is no longer in anyone's possession, but is kept with the Hidden Imam.[9]

### THE QUR'ĀN CONTAINS HIDDEN MEANINGS THAT THE EXEGETE SHOULD DECIPHER

The most common approach to the problem of the absence of references to the Shī'a in the Qur'ān is the assertion that it is in the nature of the Qur'ān to speak in symbols and codes. According to this approach it should come as no surprise that the Qur'ān does not mention the Shī'a explicitly, since those who know how to read the text itself correctly and to read between the lines can decipher the passages that allude to the Shī'a. This is the principle underlying the broad attempt to interpret many obscure (and even some quite clear) expressions in the Qur'ānic text as references to the Shī'a. This approach is exemplified by the following tradition ascribed to al-Bāqir. When addressing one of his disciples, Muḥammad b. Muslim (d. 150/767),[1] the Imam said: "Whenever you hear God [in the Qur'ān] mentioning someone of this nation in praise, it refers to us [i.e. the Shī'a]; and when you hear God denigrating people who flourished in the past, it refers to our enemies."[2] Even a cursory reading of the early Imāmī exegetical compositions reveals how wholeheartedly the concept embodied in this and similar traditions was embraced by the commentators.

### THE QUR'ĀN TEACHES PRINCIPLES WHILE TRADITION EXPOUNDS THEIR DETAILS

Another approach is expressed in the answer al-Bāqir gave to his disciple Abū Baṣīr concerning the reason why 'Alī is not mentioned in the Qur'ān:

Abū Ja'far said: Say to them:[3] God revealed to His Messenger [the verses about] prayer and did not [explicitly] mention three or four [prayers] until this was interpreted by the Messenger. So also He revealed [the verses about] the pilgrimage, but did not reveal the injunction 'encircle

8. Ibid.
9. For more on the Shī'ī claim regarding the falsification of the Qur'ān see Kohlberg, "Some Notes on the Imamite Attitude to the Qur'ān"; and H. Modarressi, "Early Debates on the Integrity of the Qur'ān: A Brief Survey," *Studia Islamica*, no. 77 (1993): 5–39.
1. A Kūfī scholar who was also a disciple of al-Ṣādiq and is considered a reliable source for traditions on the authority of the two Imams (Najāshī, 323–4).
2. *T'A*, 1:13, 3.
3. I.e. to those who put this question to you.

[the Ka'ba[4]] seven times.' So too is the meaning of the verse "Obey God and obey the Messenger and those in authority among you." This verse was revealed in relation to 'Alī, Ḥasan and Ḥusayn.[5]

In this tradition the reason that 'Alī and his disciples are not mentioned explicitly in the Qur'ān is based on the argument that the Qur'ān, by its very nature, restricts itself to general principles. It presents religious laws and general rulings yet does not go into details, a prerogative reserved for the interpreter. This tripartite division in no way suggests that these were three separate approaches to the problem, each exclusive of the other. Rather, the three together demonstrate the problems that Imāmī exegetes faced and the attempts they made to resolve them.

# AMINA WADUD

## How Perceptions of Woman Influence Interpretation of the Qur'an†

My objective in undertaking this research was to make a 'reading' of the Qur'an that would be meaningful to women living in the modern era. By 'reading' I mean the process of reviewing the words and their context in order to derive an understanding of the text. Every 'reading' reflects, in part, the intentions of the text, as well as the 'prior text' of the one who makes the 'reading'. Although each 'reading' is unique, the understanding of various readers of a single text will converge on many points.

In this Introduction * * * I will look at how the perception of woman influences the interpretations of the Qur'an's position on women. I will give an overview of my own perspective of woman and of the methods of interpretation I used in analysing the Qur'an which have led to some new conclusions.

No method of Qur'anic exegesis is fully objective. Each exegete makes some subjective choices. Some details of their interpretations reflect their subjective choices and not necessarily the intent of the text. Yet, often, no distinction is made between text and interpretation. I put interpretations of woman in the Qur'an into three categories: 'traditional', reactive, and holistic.

The first category of Qur'anic interpretation I call 'traditional'. Traditional *tafasir* (exegetical works) give interpretations of the entire Qur'an, whether from the modern or classical periods, with certain objectives in mind. Those objectives could be legal, esoteric, grammatical, rhetorical, or historical. Although these objectives may lead to differences in the *tafasir*, one similarity in these works is their atomistic methodology. They begin with the first verse of the first chapter and proceed to the second verse of the first chapter—one verse at a time—until the end of the Book. Little or

4. The stone shrine in Mecca (literally, "cube"), believed to have been built by Adam and then rebuilt by Ibrāhīm (Abraham) and Ismā'īl (Ishmael); central to both early pagan and Muslim pilgrimage rituals, it became the most important site in Islam.

5. *T'A*, 1:249, 169; *TF*, 24, 10–15 [Ḥasan (624/25–670), Ḥusayn's brother and the second Shī'ī Imam. See text at n. 2, p. 498—editor's note].

† From the introduction to Amina Wadud, *Qur'an and Woman: Rereading the Sacred Text from a Woman's Perspective* (New York: Oxford University Press, 1999), pp. 1–10, 13–14. Reprinted by permission of Oxford University Press. Except as indicated, all notes are Wadud's.

no effort is made to recognize themes and to discuss the relationship of the Qur'an to itself, thematically. A brief mention of one verse's relation to another verse may be rendered but these are haphazard with no underlying hermeneutical principle applied. A methodology for linking similar Qur'anic ideas, syntactical structures, principles, or themes together is almost non-existent.

However, what concerns me most about 'traditional' *tafasir* is that they were exclusively written by males. This means that men and men's experiences were included and women and women's experiences were either excluded or interpreted through the male vision, perspective, desire, or needs of woman. In the final analysis, the creation of the basic paradigms through which we examine and discuss the Qur'an and Qur'anic interpretation were generated without the participation and firsthand representation of women. Their voicelessness during critical periods of development in Qur'anic interpretation has not gone unnoticed, but it has been mistakenly equated with voicelessness in the text itself.

The second category of Qur'anic interpretation concerned with the issue of woman consists primarily of modern scholars' reactions to severe handicaps for woman as an individual and as a member of society which have been attributed to the text. In this category are many women and/or persons opposed to the Qur'anic message (or more precisely, to Islam) altogether. They use the poor status of women in Muslim societies as justification for their 'reactions'. These reactions have also failed to draw a distinction between the interpretation and the text.

The objectives sought and methods used, often come from feminist ideals and rationales. Although they are often concerned with valid issues, the absence of a comprehensive analysis of the Qur'an sometimes causes them to vindicate the position of women on grounds entirely incongruous with the Qur'anic position on woman. This shortcoming must be overcome in order to make use of a most effective tool for the liberation of Muslim women: demonstrating the link between that liberation and this primary source of Islamic ideology and theology.

The interpretations which reconsider the whole method of Qur'anic exegesis with regard to various modern social, moral, economic, and political concerns—including the issue of woman—represent the final category. It is in this category that I place this work. This category is relatively new, and there has been no substantial consideration of the particular issue of woman in the light of the entire Qur'an and its major principles.

I propose to make a 'reading' of the Qur'an from within the female experience and without the stereotypes which have been the framework for many of the male interpretations. In the final analysis, this reading will confront some of the conclusions drawn on this subject. Because I am analysing the text and not the interpretations of that text, my treatment of this issue differs from many of the existing works on this topic.

## *Background*

### METHODOLOGY: A HERMENEUTICAL MODEL

A hermeneutical model is concerned with three aspects of the text, in order to support its conclusions: 1. the context in which the text was written (in the case of the Qur'an, in which it was revealed); 2. the grammatical composition of the text (how it says what it says); and 3. the whole text, its *Weltanschauung* or world-view. Often, differences of opinion can be traced to variations in emphasis between these three aspects.

I argue against some conventional interpretations, especially about certain words used in the Qur'an to discuss and fulfil universal guidance. I render some discussions heretofore considered as gendered, into neutral terms. Other discussions, heretofore considered as universal, I render specific on the basis of their limitations and on the expression in terms specific to seventh-century Arabia. Some historical information with regard to occasions of revelation and the general period of revelation was considered here.

Thus, I attempt to use the method of Qur'anic interpretation proposed by Fazlur Rahman. He suggests that all Qur'anic passages, revealed as they were in a specific time in history and within certain general and particular circumstances, were given expression relative to those circumstances. However, the message is not limited to that time or those circumstances historically. A reader must understand the implications of the Qur'anic expressions during the time in which they were expressed in order to determine their proper meaning. That meaning gives the intention of the rulings or principles in the particular verse.

Believers from another circumstance must make practical applications in accordance with how that original intention is reflected or manifested in the new environments. In modern times this is what is meant by the 'spirit' of the Qur'an. To get at that 'spirit', however, there must be some comprehensible and organized hermeneutical model.[1]

The initial question behind my research was, why does the Qur'an specify males and females on some occasions (like 'Believing males and Believing females' [masculine plural followed by feminine plural forms]), while on other occasions it uses a more generic ('Oh you who believe . . .' [masculine plural]) form? From my perspective on the Qur'an, every usage of the masculine plural form is intended to include males and females, *equally*, unless it includes specific indication for its exclusive application to males.

The plural in Arabic is used to denote three or more rational beings. Thus the following Arabic sentences:

A. *Al-tullab fi al-ghurfah* (masculine plural form) means
  1. three or more students in the room—including at least one male
  2. three or more *exclusively* male students in the room.

B. *Al-talibat fi al-ghurfah* (feminine plural form) means
  1. three or more female students in the room.

As there is no form exclusively for males, the only way to determine if the masculine plural form (*al-tullab fi al-ghurfah* (A)) is exclusively for male (2) would be through some specific indication in the text. Thus:

C. *Al-tullab wa al-talibat fi al-ghurfah* indicates that the use of the masculine plural (*al-tullab*) refers *exclusively* to males since the

1. For details of Fazlur Rahman's discussion of the above double movement methodology—"from the present situation to Qur'anic times, then back to the present"—for particular communities, see his *Islam and Modernity: Transformation of an Intellectual Tradition* (Chicago: University of Chicago Press, 1982), introduction, especially pp. 4–9.

inclusion of the female plural form distinguishes the female students present.

All the verses which contained any reference to women, separately or together with men, were analysed with the traditional method of *tafsir al Qur'an bi al Qur'an* (interpretation of the Qur'an based on the Qur'an itself). However, I elaborated these particular terms of this method: each verse was analysed: 1. in its context; 2. in the context of discussions on similar topics in the Qur'an; 3. in the light of similar language and syntactical structures used elsewhere in the Qur'an; 4. in the light of overriding Qur'anic principles; and 5. within the context of the Qur'anic *Weltanschauung*, or world-view.

### LANGUAGE AND PRIOR TEXT

One unique element for reading and understanding any text is the prior text of the individual reader: the language and cultural context in which the text is read. It is inescapable and represents, on the one hand, the rich varieties that naturally occur between readers, and, on the other hand, the uniqueness of each.

Prior text adds considerably to the perspective and conclusions of the interpretation. It exposes the individuality of the exegete. This is neither good nor bad in and of itself. However, when one individual reader with a particular world-view and specific prior text asserts that his or her reading is the only possible or permissible one, it prevents readers in different contexts to come to terms with their own relationship to the text.

To avoid the potential of relativism, there is continuity and permanence in the Qur'anic text itself as exemplified even through various readings by their points of convergence. However, in order for the Qur'an to achieve its objective to act as a catalyst affecting behaviour in society, each social context must understand the fundamental and unchangeable principles of that text, and then implement them in their own unique reflection. It is not the text or its principles that change, but the capacity and particularity of the understanding and reflection of the principles of the text within a community of people.

Thus, each individual reader interacts with the text. However, the assertion that there is only one interpretation of the Qur'an limits the extent of the text. The Qur'an must be flexible enough to accommodate innumerable cultural situations because of its claims to be universally beneficial to those who believe. Therefore, to force it to have a single cultural perspective—even the cultural perspective of the original community of the Prophet—severely limits its application and contradicts the stated universal purpose of the Book itself.

### *THE PRIOR TEXT OF GENDER-SPECIFIC LANGUAGES*

The significance of masculine and feminine forms, whether used distinctively or to make generic indications, was an important part of my analysis. Perspectives on gender, particularly on the understanding of what constitutes feminine or masculine behaviour, and the roles of men and women in society, are based on one's cultural context. Gender-specific languages, such as Arabic, create a particular prior text for the speakers of that language. Everything is classified male or female. English, Malay, and other languages do not share this prior text with Arabic. This results in a distinction between the various readings of the Qur'an. This distinction becomes apparent in the interpretation of the text and the conclusions drawn from the function of the text with regard to gender.

With regard to Arabic, the language of the Qur'an, I approach the text from the outside. This frees me to make observations which are not imprisoned in the context of a gender-distinct language.

> There exists a very strong, but one-sided and thus untrustworthy, idea that in order better to understand a foreign culture, one must enter into it, forgetting one's own, and view the world through the eyes of this foreign culture. This idea, as I have said, is one-sided. Of course, a certain entry as a living being into a foreign culture, the possibility of seeing the world through its eyes, is a necessary part of the process of understanding it; but if this were the only aspect of this understanding, *it would merely be duplication and would not entail anything new or enriching.* Creative understanding does not renounce itself, its own place in time, its own culture; and it forgets nothing. In order to understand, it is immensely important for the person who understands to be located outside the object of his or her creative understanding—in time, in space, and in culture.[2] [emphasis mine]

A new look at Qur'anic language with regard to gender is especially necessary in the light of the absence of an Arabic neuter. Although each word in Arabic is designated as masculine or feminine, it does not follow that each use of masculine or feminine persons is necessarily restricted to the mentioned gender—from the perspective of universal Qur'anic guidance. A divine text must overcome the natural restrictions of the language of human communication. Those who argue that the Qur'an cannot be translated believe that there is some necessary correlation between Arabic and the message itself. I will demonstrate that gender distinction, an inherent flaw, necessary for human communication in the Arabic, is overcome by the text in order to fulfil its intention of universal guidance.

## PERSPECTIVES ON WOMEN

'Most men have at one time or another heard, or perhaps even believed, that women are "inferior" and "unequal" to men.'[3] I worked against the backdrop of common prejudices and attitudes among Muslims towards women which have not only affected the position of women in Muslim societies but also affected the interpretation of the position of women in the Qur'an. One such belief is that there are *essential* distinctions between men and women reflected in creation, capacity and function in society, accessibility to guidance (particularly to Qur'anic guidance), and in the rewards due to them in the Hereafter.

Although there are distinctions between women and men, I argue that they are not of their essential natures. More importantly, I argue against

2. M. M. Bakhtin, *Speech Genres and Other Late Essays*, trans. Vern W. McGee, (eds.) Caryl Emerson and Michael Holquist (Austin: University of Texas Press, 1986), pp. 6–7.
3. Alvin J. Schmidt, *Veiled and Silenced: How Culture Shaped Sexist Theology* (Macon, Georgia: Mercer University Press, 1989), Introduction, pp. xiii.

the *values* that have been attributed to these distinctions. Such attributed values describe women as weak, inferior, inherently evil, intellectually incapable, and spiritually lacking. These evaluations have been used to claim that women are unsuitable for performing certain tasks, or for functioning in some ways in society.

The woman has been restricted to functions related to her biology. The man, on the other hand, is evaluated as superior to and more significant than woman, an inherent leader and caretaker, with extensive capacity to perform tasks that the woman cannot. Consequently, men are *more* human, enjoying completely the choice of movement, employment, and social, political and economic participation on the basis of human individuality, motivation, and opportunity. This is actually an institutionalized compensation for the reverse situation:

> Woman alone gives birth to children, nurses them, and is their primary nurturer in their early formative years. Moreover, the social and economic roles that commonly have been defined as the province of the male have never been performed exclusively by men. Subconsciously, men are aware of this fact. . . . *The male has never had an exclusive social or economic role that woman could not participate in too. . . .*
>
> . . . Awareness of woman's monopoly was psychologically repressed and overshadowed by institutionalizing and socially legitimating male values that had the effect of creating self-fulfilling prophecies (emphasis mine).[4]

## *DISTINCTIONS BETWEEN MEN AND WOMEN*

The Qur'an acknowledges the anatomical distinction between male and female. It also acknowledges that members of each gender function in a manner which reflects the well-defined distinctions held by the culture to which those members belong. These distinctions are an important part of how cultures function. For this reason, it would be unwise if the Qur'an failed to acknowledge and, in fact, sympathize with culturally determined, functional distinctions.

> As they are divided, so genders are also interwoven differently in each culture and time. They can rule separate territories and rarely intertwine, or they can be knotted like the lines in the Book of Kells. Sometimes no basket can be plaited, no fire kindled, without the collaboration of two sets of hands. Each culture brings the genders together in its unique way.[5]

The Qur'an does not attempt to annihilate the differences between men and women or to erase the significance of functional gender distinctions which help every society to run smoothly and fulfil its needs. In fact, compatible mutually supportive functional relationships between men and women can be seen as part of the goal of the Qur'an with regard to

4. Ibid., pp. 59–60.
5. Ivan Illich, *Gender* (New York: Pantheon Books, 1982), pp. 106–7. [The elaborate decorations in the Book of Kells, an illuminated manuscript of the four Gospels (completed early 9th c.?), include many stylized representations of knots—editor's note.]

society.[6] However, the Qur'an does not propose or support a singular role or single definition of a set of roles, exclusively, for each gender across every culture.

The Qur'an acknowledges that men and women function as individuals and in society. However, there is no detailed prescription set on how to function, culturally. Such a specification would be an imposition that would reduce the Qur'an from a universal text to a culturally specific text—a claim that many have erroneously made. What the Qur'an proposes is transcendental in time and space.[7]

Gender distinctions and distinct gender functions contribute to the perceptions of morally appropriate behaviour in a given society. Since the Qur'an is moral guidance, it must relate to the perceptions of morality—no matter how gender-specified—which are held by individuals in various societies. Yet, the mere fact that the Qur'an was revealed in seventh-century Arabia when the Arabs held certain perceptions and misconceptions about women and were involved in certain specific lewd practices against them resulted in some injunctions specific to that culture.

Some prevailing practices were so bad they had to be prohibited explicitly and immediately: infanticide, sexual abuse of slave girls, denial of inheritance to women, *zihar*,[8] to name a few of the most common. Other practices had to be modified: polygamy, unconstrained divorce, conjugal violence, and concubinage, for example. With regard to some practices, the Qur'an seems to have remained neutral: social patriarchy, marital patriarchy, economic hierarchy, the division of labour between males and females within a particular family.

Some women activists today openly question this neutrality. Why didn't the Qur'an just explicitly prohibit these practises? If the evolution of the text and its **overall** objective is consumed under one—albeit important—aspect of social interaction, say consciousness raising with regard to women, then the Qur'an is made subservient to that aspect, rather than the other way around. There is an essential acknowledgement of the relationship between men and women as they function in society, but it is not the sole nor primary objective of the text.

In addition, certain practices encouraged by the Qur'an may be restricted to that society which practised them, but the Qur'an is 'not confined to, or exhausted by, (one) society and its history. . . . [9] Therefore, each new Islamic society must understand the principles intended by the particulars. Those principles are eternal and can be applied in various social contexts.

For example, in Arabia at the time of the revelation, women of wealthy and powerful tribes were veiled and secluded as an indication of protection.

6. See Sayyid Qutb, *Fi Zilal al-Qur'an* [*In the Shade of the Qur'ān*], 6 vols. (Cairo: Dar al-Shuruq, 1980), Vol. II, pp. 642–3, where he discusses the shared benefits and responsibility between men and women in the Islamic social system of justice.
7. Fazlur Rahman, *Islam and Modernity*, pp. 5–7, discusses the moral values of the Qur'an in 'extra-historical transcendental' terms, that is, the moral value extracted from a particular verse goes beyond the time and place of the specific instance at which that verse and its injunction was occasioned.
8. The practice of stating that one's wife was as 'the back of my mother', which would make conjugal relations impossible, but would not totally free the woman for remarriage.
9. Wan Mohd Nor Wan Daud, *The Concept of Knowledge in Islam and Its Implications for Education in a Developing Country* (London: Mansell Publisher Limited, 1989), p. 7.

The Qur'an acknowledges the virtue of modesty and demonstrates it through the prevailing practices. The principle of modesty is important—not the veiling and seclusion which were manifestations particular to that context. These were culturally and economically determined demonstrations of modesty.[1] Modesty is not a privilege of the economically advantaged only: all believing women deserve the utmost respect and protection of their modesty—however it is observed in various societies.

Modesty is beneficial for maintaining a certain moral fibre in various cultures and should therefore be maintained—but on the basis of faith: not economics, politics or other forms of access and coercion. This is perhaps why Yusuf Ali translates verse 24:31 'what (must ordinarily) appear'[2] (with regard to uncovered parts), to indicate that (ordinarily) there are culturally determined guidelines for modesty.

This method of restricting the particulars to a specific context, extracting the principles intended by the Qur'an through that particular, and then applying those principles to other particulars in various cultural contexts, forms a major variation from previous exegetical methodologies. The movement from principles to particulars can only be done by the members of whatever particular context a principle is to be applied. Therefore, interpretation of the Qur'an can never be final.

## HARALD MOTZKI

## *From* The Collection of the Qur'ān: A Reconsideration of Western Views in Light of Recent Methodological Developments†

*Dedicated to the memory of Ed de Moor*

### *I. The Qur'ān as a Historical Source*

Ever since the Qur'ān came into (earthly) existence, it has been used for different reasons. For Muslims it has always been a source of moral and religious inspiration and benefit. Muslim scholars have studied it chiefly as a basis for their system of legal and theological doctrines and seldom for purely historical reasons. The interest of modern Western (non-Muslim) scholars in the Qur'ān, however, has mainly been historical. It is used as a source for the preaching of Muḥammad and for details of his prophetic career, as a document of early Islam and even as a source for pre-Islamic religion and society of the Arabs.

If one decides to approach the Qur'ān as a historical source, it must be subjected to source criticism, which is one of the great methodological achievements of the modern study of history. The purpose of source criticism is to check the authenticity, originality and correctness of what a

1. See William Robertson Smith, *Kinship and Marriage in Early Arabia*, (ed.) Stanley A. Cook (London: A. & C. Black, 1907).
2. Translation by A. Yusuf Ali, *The Holy Qur'an: Text, Translation and Commentary*, US ed. (Elmhurst, N.Y.: Tahrike Tarsile Qur'an Inc., 1987).

† From *Der Islam: Zeitschrift für Geschichte und Kultur des islamischen Orients* 78 (2001): 1–5. Reprinted by permission of the publisher. Except as indicated, all notes are Motzki's.

source purports to be or is thought to inform us about. When trying to determine the reliability of a source, the first questions a historian usually asks are: How far away in time and space is the source from the event about which it informs us? Are the date and place of origin which the source claims for itself correct?

However, most scholars do not ask such questions any more. They take for granted that the Qur'ān is Muḥammad's prophecy and that even the time and place of origin of its parts can be determined with some certainty. Yet the fact that there are a few scholars who doubt this almost generally accepted view and wonder whether all parts of the Qur'ān really do have the same author, reminds us that historical insights are never final, but must be constantly reviewed. It is therefore legitimate to ask some source-critical questions concerning the Qur'ān once again. Taking as starting point the almost generally accepted view that the Qur'ān contains the revelations which Muḥammad announced during the first third of the 7th century AD at Mecca and Medina, we may ask: Where does this piece of information come from?

To answer this question in an empirically scientific way, we have three possible sources of knowledge at our disposal: early Qur'ānic manuscripts, the text of the Qur'ān itself, and the Islamic tradition relating to the Qur'ān. Let us first see whether these sources offer the necessary clues.

The question as to whether an early text really goes back to its reported author can be easily answered if we find its autograph. In the case of the Qur'ān, however, no discovery of an autograph has yet been made, neither one written by the Prophet himself nor by the scribes he may have had. Even early manuscripts of the Qur'ān are rare and their dating is controversial. There are, admittedly, some fragments of the Qur'ān written on papyrus or parchment dated by some scholars to the end of the 1st and the first half of the 2nd century AH, but these instances of dating are rejected by others and have not yet found general acknowledgment.[1] Additionally, the fragmentary character of most of the oldest Qur'ānic manuscripts does not allow us to conclude with certainty that the earliest Qur'āns must have had the exact same form, size and content as the later ones. Thus, manuscripts do not seem to be helpful (as yet) concerning our issue.

What about the text itself? Does the Qur'ān contain clear indications as to its author or its collectors? This is a controversial question, too. There are only very few concrete historical facts mentioned in the Qur'ān.[2] In most cases we are not able to grasp from the text itself what the historical circumstances are to which the text seems to refer.[3] The name Muḥammad is mentioned only four times and always in the third person.[4] Usually the text is only concerned with someone called 'the messenger' or 'the Prophet',

1. Cf. O. Pretzl, 'Die Koranhandschriften', in: Th. Nöldeke, *Geschichte des Qorāns*, part 3, Leipzig 1938², 249–274. A. Grohmann, 'The Problem of Dating Early Qur'āns', in: *Der Islam* 33 (1958), 213–231 and A. Neuwirth, 'Koran', in: H. Gätje (ed.), *Grundriß der arabischen Philologie*, vol. 2, Wiesbaden 1987, 112. Perhaps the Qur'ānic fragments found in Yemen in 1972 (cf. G.-R. Puin, 'Observations on Early Qur'ān Manuscripts in Ṣan'ā'', in: S. Wild (ed.), *The Qur'ān as Text*, Leiden 1996, 107–111) will produce specimens which can be dated with more certainty.
2. Cf. for a collection N. Robinson, *Discovering the Qur'an*, London 1996, 30–31.
3. Cf. for a summary of the Qur'ānic historical framework M. Cook, *Muhammad*, Oxford 1983, 69–70.
4. Some scholars have even suggested that the four verses were later additions, e.g. H. Hirschfeld, *New Researches into the Composition and Exegesis of the Qoran*, London 1902, 139.

who as a rule is taken to be this same Muḥammad in most places. However, it can be and has been argued that the person addressed in the Qur'ān in the second person singular is not necessarily always the messenger (and there are a few instances where this clearly cannot be the case), but can also be regarded in many places as the reader or reciter of the text in general.[5] If such a point of view is adopted, the issue of Muḥammad's authorship or transmission of the entire Qur'ān becomes questionable.

John Wansbrough advocated emphatically such a thesis in his *Quranic Studies.* He concluded on the basis of form-critical and other arguments that the Qur'ān had emerged out of pericopes of prophetic *logia* which developed independently during the first two Islamic centuries in Mesopotamia. The canonical collection, i.e., the Qur'ān as it now exists, cannot be dated, according to Wansbrough, before the beginning of the third century AH. Consequently, the Qur'ān loses much of its quality as a reliable historical source for Muḥammad's lifetime and environment and becomes instead a source for the development of one type of religious literature of the early Islamic communities elsewhere.[6] Wansbrough's conclusions can be and have been criticized for several reasons[7] and only a few scholars have accepted his views. Nevertheless, his contribution has reminded us that on the basis of the Qur'ānic text alone Muḥammad's 'authorship' of the whole text is difficult, if not impossible to prove.[8]

It seems then that the confidence of those scholars who believe that the Qur'ān is the collection of Muḥammad's revelations must be founded on something else. The only source which remains, if we exclude non-empirical sources of knowledge, is the Islamic tradition. 'Islamic tradition' is to be understood in a broad sense to include exegetical and historical traditions of any kind which purport to give background information on the Qur'ān and its details or are thought to provide such information. These sources, which are found in different types of literature, *tafsīr, sīra,* collections of *sunan*[9] or of historical traditions, can be labeled Ḥadīth.

We are faced here with a paradox in modern Western Islamic studies. Most Western scholars are highly skeptical about the historical reliability of the Ḥadīth but nevertheless accept on the basis of *ḥadīth* reports that the Qur'ān is the revelation preached by Muḥammad and that it reflects the historical circumstances of his life. Even scholars such as Ignaz Goldziher and Joseph Schacht,[1] who regarded most *ḥadīth* reports as fictitious

5. As argued by A. Rippin in, 'Muḥammad in the Qur'ān: Reading Scripture in the 21st Century', in: H. Motzki (ed.), "*The Biography of Muhammad: The Issue of the Sources*", Leiden 2000, 298–309.
6. J. Wansbrough, *Qur'anic Studies*, Oxford 1977, 1–52.
7. Cf. the reviews by G.H.A. Juynboll, in: *Journal of Semitic Studies* 24 (1979), 293–296; W.A. Graham, in: *Journal of the American Oriental Society* 100 (1980), 137–141, A. Neuwirth, in *Die Welt des Islams* 23–24 (1984), 539–542.
8. Cf. the contributions in H. Berg (ed.), 'Islamic Origins Reconsidered: John Wansbrough and the Study of Early Islam', in: *Method & Theory in the Study of Religion* 9/1 (Special Issue) 1997 for positive judgments of Wansbrough's studies.
9. Teachings, deeds, and sayings of Muḥammad. *Tafsīr*: Qur'ānic exegesis. *Sīra*: biography of Muḥammad [editor's note].
1. German-British scholar of Arabic and Islamic studies (1902–1969), who discussed ḥadīth in *The Origins of Muhammadan Jurisprudence* (1950). He built on the work of the Hungarian scholar Goldziher (1850–1921), who examined ḥadīth critically in *Muslim Studies* (1888–90) [editor's note].

and without any historical value for the time which they purport to reflect, did not contest the view that the Qur'ān went back to Muḥammad and they regarded it as the most reliable source of his life and preaching. This inconsistent position has been abandoned only recently by the followers of Schacht's radical opinions on the Ḥadīth such as Wansbrough, Michael Cook, Patricia Crone, Andrew Rippin, Gerald Hawting and others. They doubt that the Islamic tradition can be a historically reliable frame of reference for the Qur'ān, because it is generally uncertain whether the information in reports on Qur'ānic items is based on real knowledge independent of the Qur'ānic text itself and free of later apologetic, dogmatic and juridical preoccupations. Consequently, they also question the general conviction that the Qur'ān as a whole is a contemporary record of Muḥammad's utterances.

Is this the only way to escape the paradox? The obvious alternative would be to insist on the historical reliability of the Islamic tradition, at least in its essential points. This is the position which e.g. W. Montgomery Watt has adopted in assuming that the *Sīra* contains 'a basic core of material which is sound' and in thinking that 'it would be impossible to make sense of the historical material of the Qur'ān without assuming the truth of this core'.[2] But how can we know what the true core of the *sīra* tradition is? Watt's poor methodology in answering this question and in dismissing Schacht's objections to the Ḥadīth as not being applicable to the *sīra* material has not convinced critical minds and has brought upon himself the reproach of being gullible. To avoid such a reproach, scholars who are prepared to accept that the Qur'ān contains Muḥammad's preaching and thus to concede to the Islamic tradition a certain value, too, cannot but tackle the issue of the reliability of the Islamic traditions again. In the last decade several scholars—myself included—have devoted themselves to this task. I have designed different strategies to cope with the problem: a) a critical revaluation of the studies which deny to the *ḥadīth* reports a historical value for the first century, and b) an improvement of the methods to analyze and date traditions. Both strategies can be employed either on a more general level, e.g. concerning certain types of traditions, such as exegetical or legal ones,[3] or on a more specific level, e.g. with a single tradition or complex of traditions.[4]

* * *

2. W. Montgomery Watt, *Muhammad's Mecca*, Edinburgh 1988, 1.
3. Cf. for such an approach H. Motzki, *Die Anfänge der islamischen Jurisprudenz*, Stuttgart 1991; revised English edition: *The Origins of Islamic Jurisprudence. Meccan Fiqh before the Classical Schools*, Leiden 2001.
4. Examples are H. Motzki, 'Der Fiqh des -Zuhrī: die Quellenproblematik', in: *Der Islam* 68 (1991), 1–44; revised English edition: 'The Jurisprudence of Ibn Šihāb az-Zuhrī. A Source-critical Study', Nijmegen 2001, 1–55, http://webdoc.ubn.kun.nl/mono/m/motzki_h/juriofibs.pdf; idem, '*Quo vadis* Ḥadīt-Forschung?', in: *Der Islam* 73 (1996), 40–80, 193–231; revised English edition: 'Wither Ḥadīth Studies?', in: P. Hardy (ed.), *Traditions of Islam: Understanding, the Ḥadīth*, London 2002; idem, 'The Prophet and the Cat: On Dating Mālik's *Muwaṭṭa*' and Legal Traditions', in: *Jerusalem Studies in Arabic and Islam* 22 (1998), 18–83; and idem, 'The Murder of Ibn Abī l-Ḥuqayq: On the Origin and Reliability of some *Maghāzī*-Reports', in: idem (ed.), *The Biography of Muhammad: The Issue of the Sources*, Leiden 2000, 170–239.

# MANUELA MARÍN

## *From* Disciplining Wives: A Historical Reading of Qur'ân 4:34†

*And those you fear may be rebellious admonish; banish them to their couches, and beat them. If they then obey you, look not for any way against them; God is All-high, All-great.*

Qur'ân 4:34

In 2000 a book published in Spain caused a media scandal, followed by an official question addressed to the upper house of the Parliament and a lawsuit against the book's author. Entitled *La mujer en el islam* ("Women in Islam"), this book was written by Mohamed Kamal Mostafa, the imam in the mosque of Fuengirola, a seaside resort on the southern Spanish coast.

At the center of public attention and hostile reactions was the section of the book entitled "mistreatment of women."[1] Quotations from this section of the book appeared in national newspapers, and its author, M. K. Mostafa, was accused of advising husbands how to beat their wives without leaving any traces. Feminist associations led the protest against the book, and it was they who initiated legal actions against the imam. Not wanting to be seen as condoning violence against women, Muslim communities in Spain therefore disawoved the positions taken in the book. The whole affair contributed to creating a negative image of Islam, adding fresh fuel to the already heated controversy on the role of Muslims in Western societies. In the Spanish context, the "discovery" by a general public of Qur'ânic texts, as presented by M. K. Mostafa, that seemed to approve the beating of disobedient wives, has to be placed in the context of a new awareness concerning physical mistreatment of women—a social problem of growing relevance in a country where, in 2001 alone, 42 women were killed by their partners.[2]

The offending paragraphs in the book by M. K. Mostafa are hardly original. Similar statements can be found in Islamist literature all over the Arab-speaking world as well as in Western languages.[3] As a rule, this kind of literature offers literal readings of Qur'ân, 4:34, a verse used to justify male domination over women in the family as well as in the social sphere. Following the traditional exegesis of this verse, contemporary Islamists and conservative Muslim scholars understand it as God's will to

† From *Studia Islamica*, no. 97 (2003): 5–12. Reprinted by permission of Koninklijke Brill NV. Except as indicated, all notes are Marín's.

1. M. K. Mostafa, *La mujer en el islam*, Fuengirola, Centro Cultural Islámico Sohail, 2000, p. 85–87.
2. See Inés Alberdi and Natalia Matas, *La violencia doméstica. Informe sobre los malos tratos a mujeres en España*, 2002 (available online: www.estudios.lacaixa.es). The number of dead women is based on the statistics from the Spanish Ministry of Home Affairs. Women's associations give a higher number.
3. See, for instance, quotations of Maḥmûd Sha'bân, *Niẓâm al-usra bayna l-masîḥiya wa-l-islâm: dirâsa muqârana*, Cairo, 1983, in Y. Y. Haddad, "Islam and Gender: Dilemmas in the Changing Arab World", Y. Y. Haddad and J. L. Esposito (eds.), *Islam, Gender, and Social Change*, New York–Oxford, 1998, p. 3–25. A short but significant anthology of Arab authors on the same subject, in Ghassan Ascha, *Mariage, polygamie et répudiation en Islam. Justifications des auteurs arabo-musulmans contemporains*, Paris, 1998, p. 61–63. As for works published in the West, to quote only two among many titles, see H. 'Abd al-'Aṭi, *The Family Structure in Islam*, Brentwood (Maryland), 1977 and Nicholas Awde, *Women in Islam. An Anthology from the Qur'ân and Hadiths*, London, 2000.

give husbands the authority to beat their disobedient wives. Characteristically, this kind of commentary disregards the classical debate on the subject, and focuses instead on defining the essential inferiority of women, who need to be guided by the male members of their families and, if necessary, to be physically chastised by them.

At present, more liberal or even progressive interpretations of this controversial Qur'ânic verse are not uncommon. Western scholarship has welcomed and applauded the work of Fatima Mernissi, Riffat Hassan or Amina Wadud Muhsin, who have reacted against the "patriarchal" reading of Qur'ân 4:34.[4] Accordingly, the chapter on this verse in the commentary by the Tunisian historian Mohamed Talbi has been the object of a scholarly article in English, explaining Talbi's methodological approach in great detail.[5] Less known are works like that of Laylâ 'Abd al-Wahhâb on domestic violence, in which the author complains of the religious support given by the Qur'ânic verse to the dismissive opinion on women among Muslims in general.[6]

Methodologically, what distinguishes modern "progressive" exegesis from its conservative counterpart, is mainly the insistence on taking into account the historicity of the Qur'ân. For instance, in Talbi's interpretation, the universal message of any divine revelation has to be identified and separated from the historical circumstances in which it was sent to mankind. In the particular case of Qur'ân 4:34, Talbi proposes a reading set in the context of social and political circumstances in Medina, with the presence of two parties, the "feminist" and the "anti-feminist". Beyond the historical situation, a proper exegesis of the verse would therefore extract the true meaning of God's message, and the permissibility of disciplining a wife by beating expressed in the Qur'ân would be seen as nothing but a concession to circumstances.[7] For her part, Mernissi has also placed the controversial verse in the formative years of the Muslim community in Medina, emphasizing the difference of opinion between the Prophet and 'Umar b. al-Khaṭṭâb.[8]

This very short summary of the divergent contemporary views on Qur'ân 4:34 provides a general understanding of the problems believers face when trying to reconcile their faith with social changes and evolution. But if awareness of the problem of "battered wives" is a very recent one in Western societies, in Muslim societies it was already discussed from early times. These discussions have to be placed, as the Qur'ânic revelation itself, in their historical context. It should be noted that the emphasis on "historical circumstances" surrounding the revelation is not, by any means, new. In fact, a well developed part of the traditional curriculum in "Qur'ânic sciences" is that of *asbâb al-nuzûl* ("occasions of revelation"). In treatises specifically devoted to this genre, or in other exegetical works, explanations

4. Shaheen Sardar Ali, *Gender and Human Rights in Islam and International Law. Equal Before Allah, Unequal Before Man?*, The Hague-London-Boston, 2000, p. 39.
5. Ronald L. Nettler, "Mohamed Talbi's Commentary on Qur'ân IV: 34. A "historical reading" of a verse concerning the disciplining of women", *The Maghreb Review* 24 (1999), 19–33.
6. Laylâ 'Abd al-Wahhâb, *Al-'Unf al-usrî: al-jarîma wa-l-'unf ḍidd al-mar'a*, Beirut, 1994, p. 31ff.
7. I rely on Nettler's study, quoted above, as I had not been able to locate the original work in Arabic by Talbi.
8. Fatima Mernissi, *The Veil and the Male Elite: A Feminist Interpretation of Women's Rights in Islam*, Reading (Mass.), 1991, p. 153–160. See also Shaheen Sardar Ali, *Gender and Human Rights in Islam*, p. 69 and note 99. ['Umar (ca. 586–644), one of Muḥammad's chief advisers, and the second caliph—editor's note.]

of how, when and why a Qur'ânic verse was revealed to Muhammad are recorded with great precision.

### *The Revelation of Qur'ân 4:34 and Its Historical Circumstances*

The earliest commentary of the Qur'ân that I have been able to trace on this verse is that of Hûd b. Muḥkim al-Hawwârî (d. 258/871), which, according to its editor, is in fact an abstract of the commentary by Yaḥyâ b. Salâm al-Baṣrî (d. 200/815).[9] The text preserved by Hûd, says that a woman went to see the Prophet and complained that her husband had beat her. The Prophet's first intention was to ordain retaliation (*qiṣâṣ*) against the man, but he then received the revelation: "Men are the managers of the affairs (*qawwâmûn*) of women."[1]

In the first half of the 3rd/9th century, the Andalusian 'Abd al-Malik b. Ḥabîb (d. 238/853) was the author of a vast array of works, some still extant. One of them, is his collection of Prophetic Traditions on the "proper behaviour of women,"[2] in which Ibn Ḥabîb gathered early Islamic materials related to the ideal model of womanly modesty and virtues.[3] Occasionally Ibn Ḥabîb uses Traditions for exegetical purposes, as happens with the Qur'ânic verses under study. Ibn Ḥabîb's explanation of the circumstances surrounding the revelation of Qur'ân 4:34 is similar to that of Yaḥyâ b. Salâm and Hûd b. Muḥkim. The Prophet, on learning of a man who beat his wife, reprimands him; shortly thereafter he receives the revelation of the full text of Qur'ân 4:34.[4] A more developed and more historically located tradition is recorded by Ibn Ḥabîb in another section of his book, where he says: "I have been told that 'Abd Allâh b. 'Umar used to beat his wife, Safîya bt. Abî 'Ubayd, to the point of causing her pain. This is why the revelation was made in the Qur'ân on beating women if they are disobedient, rebellious and contradictory."[5]

Traditions circulating in the 3rd/9th century, as attested by the work of Yaḥyâ b. Salâm/Hûd b. Muḥkim and that of Ibn Ḥabîb, agree that the circumstances of the revelation of Qur'ân 4:34, involved a scene of physical violence against a woman by her husband. The reaction of the Prophet is in one case that of trying to apply the tribal law of retaliation and, in another, reprimanding the husband. In both situations, divine words received by the Prophet, imply a correction to his own position and establish a set of rules

9. Hud b. Muḥkim al-Hawwârî, *Tafsîr Kitâb Allâh al-'aziz*, ed. Bal-Hâjj b. Sa'îd Sharîfî, Beirut, 1990, p. 18–26 of the introduction. On Yaḥyâ b. Salâm, see F. Sezgin, *Geschichte des arabischen Shrifttums*, Leiden, 1967, I, p. 39.
1. Hûd b. Muḥkim, *Tafsîr Kitâb Allâh al-'aziz*, I, p. 377. The translation of *qawwâmûn* is from *The Koran Interpreted* by A. J. Arberry, Oxford, 1982. The sentence may be translated differently, as in "Men are in charge of women", "Men are responsible for women", or "Men are the protectors and maintainers of women". See, among others, S. Shaikh, "Exegetical violence: Nushuz in Qur'ânic Gender Ideology", *Journal for Islamic Studies* 17 (1997), 49–73, and M. Badran, "Islamic feminism: what's in a name?", *Al-Ahram Weekly Online*, 17–23 January 2002, Issue no. 569.
2. Ibn Ḥabîb, *Kitâb Adab al-nisâ' al-mawsûm bi-Kitâb al-Ghâya wa-l-nihâya*, ed. 'Abd al-Majid Turki, Beirut, 1992.
3. See on this work the introduction by its editor, and M. Marín, "Marriage and sexuality in Al-Andalus", *Marriage and Sexuality in Medieval and Early Modern Iberia*, ed. Eukene Lacarra Lanz, New York, 2002, 3–20.
4. Ibn Ḥabīb, *Kitâb Adab al-nisâ'*, no. 180.
5. *Idem*, n°. 182. 'Abd Allâh b. 'Umar (d. 73/693) was the son of the second Caliph, 'Umar b. al-Khaṭṭâb, and one of the most respected personalities of his time; see L. Veccia Vaglieri, "'Abd Allâh b. 'Umar b. al-Khaṭṭâb", *Encyclopaedia of Islam*, 2nd edition, 1, 53–54.

for disciplining women when necessary. But the last tradition recorded by Ibn Ḥabîb stands out from the rest, identifying, as it does, a well-known historical personality, while in the other cases, the husband remains anonymous.

The core of this "occasion of revelation" remained unchanged in later Qur'ânic commentaries but, as the specific genre of *asbâb al-nuzûl* took shape, a somewhat changed version of the events emerged and became authoritative. The name of ʿAbd Allâh b. ʿUmar b. al-Khaṭṭâb disappeared from the classical tradition related to Qur'ân 4:34, and the anonymous man who beat his wife in the Prophet's time both acquired a name and a place in the social structures of tribal and pre-Islamic Arabia. In the work of al-Wâḥidî (d. 468/975), the man is called Saʿd b. al-Rabiʿ and his wife, Ḥabîba bt. Zayd b. Abî Hurayra. Saʿd was one of the leaders (*nuqabâ*) of the *ansâr*.[6] When Ḥabîba behaved in a rebellious manner (*nashazat*), Saʿd struck her. Ḥabîba and her father went to see the Prophet complaining against Saʿd, and the Prophet allowed them to apply retaliation. Moments later, however, the Prophet received the revelation of Qur'ân 4:34, annulling the possibility of retaliation between husband and wife. The Prophet's comment was: "I wanted something, and God wanted something else. What God wanted is better."[7]

Saʿd b. al-Rabîʿ is mentioned by Ibn Saʿd as one of the participants in the battle of Uḥud, where he was killed.[8] His early death did not allow him to play any relevant role in later Islamic history, contrary to the fate of ʿAbd Allâh b. ʿUmar b. al-Khaṭṭâb. Introducing Saʿd as the main character in the story explaining the occasion of revelation was safer in more than one way for those who built up the tradition. Although, as will be shown later, there were other examples of chastised wives in the Prophet's immediate family, none of them were selected as the appropriate explanatory circumstance chosen by the divine word, to be announced. Saʿd b. al-Rabîʿ remained in later exegetical works the undoubted hero of the narrative.[9]

Two other significant aspects in al-Wâḥidî's account should be emphasised. First, the motif of retaliation, already present in the commentary of Yaḥyâ b.Salâm / Hûd b. Muḥkim, is strengthened here by the Prophet's admission of his own mistake—admitting it to a married man and, in consequence, favouring his wife. Thus the Qur'ânic revelation is the occasion, not only of establishing a new framework for the relationships between husband and wife, but also of abolishing the pre-islamic practice of retaliation within the life of a married couple. And secondly, it was Saʿd's

6. The "helpers" (Arabic): the inhabitants of Medina who supported Muḥammad after he left Mecca [editor's note].
7. Al-Wâḥidī al-Nîsâbûri, *Asbâb al-nuzûl*, Cairo, 1316 H, p. 111–112. This story is followed by two other and very similar accounts, in where the heroes are anonymous. On al-Wâḥidī and his work on the "occasions of revelation", see A. Rippin, "The Exegetical Genre *Asbâb al-nuzûl*: a Bibliographical and Terminological Survey", *Bulletin of the School of Oriental and African Studies* 48 (1985), 1–15, and R. Sellheim, "Al-Wâḥidī", *Encyclopedia of Islam*, 2nd edition, XI, p. 48.
8. Ibn Saʿd, *Kitâb al-Ṭabaqât al-kabîr*, ed. E. Sachau, Leiden, 1904, II, p. 25 and 30. On the circumstances of his death, see al-Dhahabî, *Tâʾrîkh al-islâm wa-wafayât al-mashâhir wa-l-aʿlâm: al-Maghâzî*, ed. U. A. Tadmurî, Beirut. 1990, p. 186. [At Uḥud, in one of the major battles of early Islam (625), the Meccans defeated Muḥammad's forces—editor's note.]
9. Saʿd's wife, Ḥabîba, was the daughter of Zayd b. Thâbit b. Abi Zuhayr/Abî Hurayra, whose son Khârija also died at the battle of Uḥud (al-Dhahabî, *Tâ'rîkh al-islâm*, p. 202). She is mentioned as the wife of Saʿd in the great majority of the works consulted, with the exception of a report quoted by al-Râzî on the authority of Ibn ʿAbbâs, where it is said that she was the daughter of Muḥammad b. Salama (see al-Râzî, *Al-Tafsîr al-kabîr*, Beirut, n.d., X, p. 87–91).

wife, Ḥabîba, who was responsible of her husband's behaviour, since she rebelled (*nashazat*) against him.

All these narrative strands and normative assertions were reunited, intertwined and polished by later commentators. Details were sometimes added, and personal opinions introduced, but the gist of the story, as told in al-Wâḥidî's treatise, did not undergo substantial alterations. The abrogation of retaliation between husband and wife attracted some attention, and al-Zamakhsharî (d. 528/1133-34) took firm stance on the issue, making a clear distinction between a slap in the face—not subjected to retaliation—and serious injuries or even death.[1] Ibn 'Aṭîya (d. 546/1151–52), commenting on the complaint presented by Ḥabība to the Prophet, says that this was the occasion for the Qur'ânic verse "on the correction (*ta'dîb*) of women to be revealed."[2] The well-known facts of the dispute between Sa'd b. al-Rabî' and his wife are accepted without discussion by other authors like Ibn Bashkuwâl (d. 578/1183),[3] al-Râzî (d. 606/1209),[4] and al-Balansî (d. 782/1380-81).[5] However, al-Suyûṭî (d. 911/1505-06) who wrote one of the most influencial treatises of *asbâb al-nuzûl*, did not identify the characters in the narrative.[6] The common elements remain present in a tradition expanding for more than seven centuries. Physical violence against a wife, usually motivated by her rebellious attitude, was the occasion for God's revelation.

The only exception to this mainstream tradition is linked to women themselves, asserting or trying to assert their own rights within the nascent Muslim community. Commentators are very cautious about these reports, and they present them succinctly and with some reservations about their authenticity. Ibn 'Aṭîya begins with an unsupported *qîlu* ("it was said") another explanation on the "occasion of revelation": it was received when women desired for themselves the same degree of treatment as that of men, and they had to accept that men were superior.[7] Al-Râzî, for his part, begins his commentary of 4:34 with a reference to "the occasion of this verse's revelation was that women spoke about the preference given by God to men in matters of inheritance. For this reason, God mentioned in this verse that the privilege accorded to men was due to the fact that they are the *qawwâmûn* of women."[8] After this opening, al-Râzî goes on reproducing the story of Ḥabîba and Sa'd b. Rabî', giving it a much longer development. That these two interpretations were indeed preserved is remarkable in itself, because they differ completely from the accepted and predominant version, and are lacking in any connection between physical violence against women and the revelation of Qur'ân 4:34.

* * *

1. Al-Zamakhshari, *Al-Kashshâf 'an ḥaqâ 'iq ghawâmiḍ al-tanzîl wa-'uyûn al-aqâwîl fi wujûh al-ta'wil*, Beirut, 1987, p. 505.
2. Ibn 'Aṭiya, *Al-Muḥarrar al-wajîz fi tafsîr al-kitâb al-'azîz*, Rabat, 1977, III, p. 103.
3. *Kitāb Ghawâmiḍ al-asmâ' al-mubhama al-wâqi'a fi mutûn al-ahâdîth al-musnada*, ed., I. al-Sayyid and M. K. 'Izz al-dîn, Beirut. 1987, II, p. 753–54.
4. See note 9, immediately above.
5. *Tafsîr mubhamât al-Qur'ân al-mawsûm bi-Ṣilat al-jam' wa-'â'id al-tadhyîl li-mawṣûl kitabây al-I'lâm wa-l-Takmîl*, ed. H. al-Qâsimî, Beirut, 1991, I, p. 326.
6. *Lubâb al-nuqûl fi asbâb al-nuzûl*, Tunis, 1984, p. 76. Al-Suyuṭi's commentary on the Qur'ân begins the exegesis of 4:34 by an account of the "occasions of the revelation", also with anonymous heroes in the story of a woman complaining against her husband's mistreatment of her (see *al-Durr al-manthûr fi l-tafsîr al-ma'thûr*, Beirut, 1990, II, p. 270).
7. Ibn 'Aṭiya, *Al-Muḥarrar*, III, p. 104.
8. Al-*Râzi*, *Tafsir*, X, p. 87.

# STEFAN WILD

## *From* Political Interpretation of the Qurʾān†

* * *

### *Exegesis and the West*

Much of modern Muslim exegesis of the Qurʾān is incomprehensible without an adequate understanding of the background of Western colonialism. At the beginning of the twentieth century, the majority of Muslims worldwide were under colonial rule: British, French, Dutch, etc. The Ottoman empire, the last multi-national Islamic state, had become the 'sick man of Europe'. The collapse of the empire after the First World War swept away the caliphate, the central symbol of Sunnī Islam, and brought large parts of the empire under European colonial rule. Islam was seen by many Muslims as the only effective weapon against the overwhelming cultural, economic and military superiority of 'the West'. The interest of Western, non-Muslim scholars in Islam and particularly in the Qurʾān, was usually viewed as either based on Christian missionary projects or a strategy to undermine Muslim political resistance, to demoralise Muslims and to ensure Western colonial dominance. The consequences of the Orientalist discourse, analysed in Edward W. Said's *Orientalism*,[1] are felt until today. Muslim scholars who try to develop new approaches to the qurʾānic text face the standard reproach that they have succumbed to the political enemy. Many traditional Muslim scholars see such innovative work as simply heretical. The differentiation between religious belief and traditional religious knowledge on the one hand, and scholarly research on a particular religion or a particular religious text on the other hand, is very often understood as part of a conspiracy against Islam and the Qurʾān. From the nineteenth century until today, the relation of Muslim exegesis and Muslim exegetes with the colonising West and its scholarly methods has sparked unending discussions.

A sensitive point for many contemporary Muslim exegetes is whether a scholarly co-operation between Muslim and non-Muslim academic work on the subject of qurʾānic exegesis is desirable or indeed possible. In intra-Muslim polemics, the suspected alignment with 'the West' and the related reproach of dependence on non-Muslim 'Western' scholarship in explaining the Qurʾān are even now leitmotivs of a considerable part of Muslim exegetical production, especially in the Arab world. Muhammad Mustafa al-Aʿzami (b. *c.* 1932), an Indian-born scholar who is close to the Saudi establishment and to the Meccan-based Islamic World League, includes in his most recent book an extra chapter entitled, 'An Appraisal of Orientalism'. In this chapter he deals with 'The Orientalist and the Qurʾān'. His judgement is clear: on Islamic topics like the Qurʾān 'only the writings of a practising Muslim are worthy of our attention'. Indeed, the Orientalists 'must . . . see Muhammad as a deluded madman or a liar bearing false

† From *The Cambridge Companion to the Qurʾān*, ed. Jane Dammen McAuliffe (Cambridge: Cambridge University Press, 2006), pp. 276–83, 287–89.  Except as indicated, all notes are Wild's.

1. E. Said, *Orientalism*, first ed. (New York: Pantheon Books, 1978).

claims of prophethood . . . If they did not set out to prove Muhammad's dishonesty or the Qur'ān's fallacy, what would hinder them from accepting Islam?[2] Al-A'zami can in no way claim to represent international Muslim scholarship, but he does stand for a widespread attitude, and one with a financially powerful support network. There are, of course, numerous Muslim scholars who collaborate with non-Muslim scholars in common projects dealing with the Qur'ān, one of the most recent examples being the *Encyclopaedia of the Qur'ān*.[3] On the other hand, many non-Muslim qur'ānic scholars remain unwilling to demythologise orthodox concepts of Islamic scripture—an idea advocated by Mohammed Arkoun (b. 1928).[4] In the shadow of the ill-fated anti-Islamic alliance between Western scholars, missionaries and colonialists in the nineteenth century they consider it inappropriate to enter an intra-Muslim debate.

Modern times have radically changed the form and content of Muslim exegesis. Sustaining continuity with the past, the traditional encyclopaedic verse-by-verse method remains alive. Such works may be revolutionary in content, but they follow the established exegetical form. There is, however, a growing number of works which follow a different model. They implicitly or explicitly reject the traditional comprehensive form and concentrate instead on only one aspect or one topic of the Qur'ān. Usually, hermeneutical discussions of the nature and meaning of the Qur'an in modern times are eclectic and interpret only a limited number of verses or passages; they refuse to produce a complete verse-by-verse commentary. The most important qualities of this new kind of exegesis seem to be several. The first of these is a growing interest in hermeneutics and method. This emphasis often considers the Qur'ān in relation to its historical embeddedness and sees the text as well as its reception as, at least partly, historically mediated. From this perspective, there is no 'objectively attainable' interpretation of the text valid for all ages and all social settings. A plurality of non-traditional methods to understand the text is as admissible as a plurality of understandings.

Secondly, this development runs parallel to the emergence of a new class of exegetes who deal with contemporary issues, such as physicians, engineers, journalists, as well as academics trained in fields like literature, history or the social sciences. These new commentators are either ignorant of or uninterested in the classical transmission of exegetical knowledge. Some of them claim that the preoccupations of classical exegesis are too far removed from the needs of present-day society. By speaking the language of modernity, they reach a non-specialist Muslim public.

Finally, attention should be drawn to the growing importance of scholarship by non-Arab Muslims. This has begun to balance the traditional predominance of work produced by those writing in Arabic. While an excellent knowledge of Arabic is a precondition for any scholarly approach to qur'ānic exegesis, more and more Turkish, Iranian, Indian, Pakistani, Indonesian, Malaysian, South African, etc., scholars address their own communities in their own languages. There is also a growing number of

2. M. M. al-A'zami, *The history of the qur'ānic text: From revelation to compilation: A comparative study with the Old and New Testaments* (Leicester: UK Islamic Academy, 2003), p. 341.
3. J. D. McAuliffe (ed.), *Encyclopaedia of the Qur'ān*, 5 vols. and index (Leiden: Brill, 2001–6).
4. M. Arkoun, *Lectures du Coran* (Paris: G. P. Maisonneuve et Larose, 1982), and his 'Contemporary critical practices and the Qur'ān', in McAuliffe (ed.), *Encyclopaedia of the Qur'ān*, vol. 1, pp. 412–31.

Muslim academics teaching Islam and related subjects in non-Muslim societies in North America, Europe and elsewhere. Normally they can publish their work under far fewer restrictions than those faced by their colleagues in Muslim countries. They also address an increasing number of Muslims in the West. The English language is rapidly becoming, in some ways, more important for a globalising Islam than Arabic.

Five voices can be considered fairly typical of an intentionally modernist approach. (1) Fazlur Rahman (d. 1988), a Pakistani by birth, who taught for decades in the United States, argues that contemporary Muslim scholarship on the Qurʾān faces two main problems: the lack of a genuine feel for the relevance of the Qurʾān today, which prevents presentation in terms adequate to the needs of contemporary society, and a fear that such a presentation might deviate on some points from traditionally received opinions.[5] (2) The Egyptian philosopher Ḥasan Ḥanafī (b. 1935) goes beyond criticism and identifies three important traits of what he considers to be modern exegesis, a genre which he calls 'thematic': (a) revelation is neither affirmed nor denied, exegesis begins with the text as given, without asking questions about its origin; (b) the Qurʾān is considered to be subject to the same rules of interpretation as any other text; (c) there is no true or false interpretation and the conflict over interpretation is a conflict of interest and, therefore, essentially a socio-political conflict, not a theoretical one.[6] (3) An even more radical example of political exegesis can be found in the work of the South African Muslim scholar Farid Esack. He bases his quest for a qurʾānic hermeneutic of liberation on the South African socio-political experience:

> Because every reader approaches the Qurʾān within a particular context it is impossible to speak of an interpretation of the Qurʾānic text applicable to the whole world . . . On this basis, I argue for the freedom to rethink the meanings and use of scripture in a racially divided, economically exploitative and patriarchal society and to forge hermeneutical keys that will enable us to read the text in such a way as to advance the liberation of all people.[7]

(4) The Iranian philosopher and scientist ʿAbd al-Karīm Sorūsh (b. 1945), who was for a time close to Imām Khomeini[8] and the Islamic Revolution in Iran, distinguishes in his work between 'religion' and the 'science of religion' and concludes: 'While revelation is true and without inner contradictions, scientific investigation of revelation is not. Religion is divine, its interpretation is completely mundane and human.[9] (5) And finally there is Mohammed Arkoun (professor emeritus at the Sorbonne), who opts for a rigorously multi-disciplinary approach, which involves the most advanced Western, particularly French, epistemological methods in order to deconstruct all types of orthodoxy. His revolutionary quest calls for

5. F. Rahman, *Major themes of the Qurʾān* (Minneapolis: Bibliotheca Islamica, 1980), ch. 12, passim.
6. H. Hanafi, 'Method of thematic interpretation of the Qurʾān', in S. Wild (ed.), *The Qurʾān as text* (Leiden: Brill, 1996), pp. 195–211.
7. F. Esack, *Qurʾān, liberation and pluralism: An Islamic perspective of interreligious solidarity against oppression* (Oxford: Oneworld, 1997), pp. 12, 78.
8. Ruhollah Khomeini (1902–1989), the Iranian Shīʿī cleric who led the 1979 revolution that overthrew Mohammad Reza Shah Pahlavi, the shah of Iran, and then led the Islamic Republic of Iran until his death [editor's note].
9. Cf. K. Amirpur, *Die Entpolitisierung des Islam: Abdolkarim Sorushs Denken und Wirken in der Islamischen Republik Iran* (Würzburg: Ergon Verlag, 2003).

structural anthropology, generative grammar, semiotics and many other approaches to open up a new epistemology within which to read the Qur'ān.[1] His ideas are fiercely critical and universalist; sometimes they transcend the visionary and border on the utopian. Such modern and modernist positions, however, co-exist with a mainstream exegesis which largely ignores hermeneutical problems.

## *Major Exegetical Issues*

### BELIEF AND KNOWLEDGE

One of the first concerns of modern Muslim exegetes was their demand that the Qur'ān be read as a text relevant for modernity. A basic tenet in the nineteenth century was the assertion that the Qur'ān could not but be in accord with progress and modern science, especially the natural sciences. Sayyid Aḥmad Khān (d. 1898), an Indian reformist scholar, taught that nothing in the Qur'ān contradicted the laws of nature. Where Copernican astronomy[2] seemed to be in conflict with a qur'ānic verse, the latter was not intended as an astronomical statement, but had to be taken metaphorically. One of his opponents, Muḥammad Qāsim Nānautvi (d. 1879), represented the diametrically opposed view, insisting that if human reason and scripture contradicted each other, reason should not be trusted.

One of the most influential commentaries of early modernity was the collective work of two pillars of reformist thought in Egypt, Muḥammad 'Abduh (d. 1905) and Rashid Riḍā (d. 1935), published initially in the prestigious Egyptian journal *al-Manār* (1927–35). Both authors agreed in theory that a complete commentary was unnecessary, because that work had already and often been done in an admirable manner. It was only necessary to explain certain verses. In practice, however, the *al-Manār* commentary did follow the 'verse-by-verse' model.

This *al-Manār* exegesis was characteristic of the reform movement in Egypt and also set out to prove to a colonised public that there was no contradiction between human reason and Western-dominated science, on the one hand, and the Islamic faith on the other. Wherever reason and the Qur'ān contradicted each other, reason should prevail. The commentary suggested, for example, that actions attributed in the Qur'ān to jinn[3] might in reality be caused by microbes. Rationalist scientific thought combined with Islam would lead to social reform and progress. The *al-Manār* commentary may have been the first to invoke Q 13:11 in this sense: 'God will never change [the condition of] a people until they change what is in themselves.' In the nineteenth century, Muslim exegesis also found allusions to inventions such as the telegraph, telephone and steamships in qur'ānic verses. Some exegetes like the Indo-Pakistani Ghulām Aḥmad

1. Cf. U. Günther, 'Mohammad Arkoun: Towards a radical rethinking of Islamic thought', in S. Taji-Farouki (ed.), *Modern Muslim intellectuals and the Qur'an* (Oxford: Oxford University Press, 2004), pp. 125–67; and also her *Mohammad Arkoun: Ein moderner Kritiker der islamischen Vernunft* (Würzburg: Ergon, 2004).
2. The theory, proposed by the Polish astronomer Nicolaus Copernicus (1473–1543), that the Sun is a fixed point around which the planets orbit; it replaced the system of the Egyptian astronomer Ptolemy (active 127–148 CE), in which each heavenly body is attached to its own solid sphere, nested with Earth at the center and the celestial sphere containing the stars at the outer edge [editor's note].
3. The third class of intelligent beings (together with humans and angels) for whom salvation is possible. According to Q 55:15, God created them from smokeless fire [editor's note].

Parvez (b. 1903), who wrote a book on qur'ānic terminology, discovered Darwin's evolutionary theory[4] in the Qur'ān. In the twentieth century, this list could be prolonged: nuclear power and AIDS were, according to some, also predicted in the holy text.

In the nineteenth and early twentieth centuries, most Muslim reformers deplored the fact that the rationalist Islam, which they propounded, was not the faith of most of their Muslim contemporaries. In the reformers' eyes most of these had lapsed into blind traditionalism. The genuine, but largely ignored, Islam was *the* religion of reason and it had to be re-established as the pure unadulterated Islam that existed at the time of the Prophet and of the four rightly guided caliphs.[5] Many Muslim exegetes of quite different persuasions followed and follow this kind of retrogressive utopian idea.

The concentration on natural sciences produced a separate sub-class of commentaries, which formed the school of 'scientific exegesis' (*tafsīr 'ilmī*). This school flourished especially in Egypt in the late nineteenth and early twentieth centuries, and is still not completely extinct. Its aim was to prove that the Qur'ān already contained all natural discoveries and laws of nature, aspects of creation which European science had come to know only in the nineteenth century and later. The authors were often physicians or journalists, not scholars versed in the traditional religious sciences. The Egyptian writer Tanṭāwī Jawhari (d. 1940) wrote such a commentary in twenty-six volumes, illustrated with drawings and photographs. Whether the Qur'ān validated modern sciences, or the other way around, the subtext of these and many other like-minded exegetical works was political: Islamic culture was equal to 'Western' culture, and the Qur'ān did not block but encouraged scientific and cultural progress. A Shī'ī commentary such as that of Ayatollah Abū l-Qāsim al-Mūsawī al-Khū'ī (d. 1992), 'Prolegomena to the Qur'ān' (*al-Bayān fī tafsīr al-Qur'ān*), written by the greatest Shī'ī authority of its time, also lists some of these 'mysteries of creation'.[6] This type of exegesis was popular but far from generally admitted. Jawharī's commentary, for example, was banned in several Muslim countries.

In the case of the earlier-mentioned Sayyid Aḥmad Khān the political side of this kind of exegesis is particularly clear. After the Indian mutiny (1857),[7] he devoted his life to a reconciliation between the British and the Indian Muslims. In his book on the 'roots of exegesis', written originally in Urdu, he developed, in advance of Muḥammad 'Abduh, the idea that there could be no contradiction between religion and science. At the same time he showed a sceptical attitude towards miracles and supernatural phenomena. For many of his Muslim contemporaries in India, however, this kind of anti-traditional exegesis was Anglophile, pro-Western and tantamount to a pact with colonialism.

4. That is, the theory of evolution by natural selection, proposed by the English naturalist Charles Darwin in *On the Origin of Species* (1859) [editor's note].
5. The first four caliphs who led the Muslim community after Muḥammad's death: Abū Bakr (r. 632–34), 'Umar ibn al-Khaṭṭāb (r. 634–44), 'Uthman ibn 'Affān (r. 644–56), and 'Alī ibn Abī Ṭālib (r. 656–61) [editor's note].
6. S. M. al-Khū'ī, *The prolegomena to the Qur'ān*, trans, and intro. A. A. Sachedina (New York: Oxford University Press, 1998), pp. 62ff.
7. An uprising against British rule in India, which began among Indian soldiers in the service of the British East India Company [editor's note].

### ISLAMIC LAW AND THE STATE

One of the most influential modern works of radical exegesis is the voluminous 'In the Shadow of the Qur'ān' of the Egyptian Sayyid Quṭb (1906–66).[8] This has become a 'book-icon'[9] for most of the Islamist movements, doubly sacred because it was written in prison and because the author was executed—in part for the exegesis put forward in this book—and was therefore venerated as a martyr. As a verse-by-verse commentary, Sayyid Quṭb's work resembles the commentary of *al-Manār* but he takes its authors to task: he accuses Muḥammad 'Abduh and Rashīd Riḍā of falling prey to the exegetical methods of the West, the methods of the Orientalists. Sayyid Quṭb's commentary is more than an example of an 'activist's exegesis'; it is directly anti-Western and anti-colonialist. For Quṭb, the Meccan part of the Qur'ān is a purely revolutionary message: there is one God and humans are his servants. The Medinan part of the Qur'ān is characterised by the experience of the emigration of the Prophet and his community from Mecca to Medina (*hijra*). The Muslim community in Mecca was in danger of succumbing to dissension and internal strife; therefore it had to leave Mecca. This *hijra* should be the model of all Muslim communities throughout history. A comprehensive Islamic state must be established—even by force—to give a home to the Muslim community. For Sayyid Quṭb, a key figure in the Egyptian Muslim Brothers,[1] this Islamic state did not yet exist anywhere. All states, including existing Muslim-majority nations, lived in a condition of practical paganism regardless of whether Islam was the religion of state or not. The leaders of these so-called Muslim states had to be viewed as apostates; their rule, even if legitimated by corrupt Muslim scholars, was illegitimate. Quṭb's ideas were important for the Muslim Brothers both within Egypt and beyond, and inspired splinter groups like 'The community of declaring infidel and emigration' (*Jamā'at al-takfīr wa-l-hijra*) and *al-Jihād*, which claimed responsibility for the assassination of the Egyptian president Anwar Sadat (1981).

Sayyid Quṭb's exegesis fights two major enemies: the powerful but spiritually bankrupt anti-Islamic West and the apostate Muslim societies and individuals, who are no better than pagan societies. In spite of his anti-Western rhetoric he does use Western concepts like 'revolution', 'democracy' and 'social justice'. His activist ideology was, and is, a source of inspiration for revolutionary Islamic movements fighting misrule and injustice in their societies. Officially banned in most Arab countries, these groups are active almost everywhere. Sayyid Quṭb's exegetical message was translated into Persian, Urdu, Turkish and English. It influenced the Iranian revolution (1979), the Shī'ī Hezbollah (*ḥizb Allāh*, 'party of God') in Lebanon and the Ḥamās in the West Bank and the Gaza strip. His most famous political exegesis dealt with Q 5:44–7: 'If any do fail to judge by what God has revealed, they are unbelievers, . . . wrongdoers, . . . rebels.' Quṭb interpreted the Arabic word 'to judge' (*yaḥkum*) as 'to rule'

8. S. Quṭb, *Fī ẓilāl al-Qur'ān*, 6 vols. (Cairo: Dār Iḥyā' al-Kutub al-'Arabiyya, (1959)); Eng. trans. M. A. Salahi and A. A. Khamis, *In the shade of the Qur'ān* (London: MWH, 1979).
9. O. Carré, *Mystique et politique: Lecture révolutionnaire du Coran par Sayyid Qutb, Frère musulman radicale* (Paris: Les Editions du Cerf, 1984), p. 20.
1. Also known as the Muslim Brotherhood, an Egyptian social and political organization founded in 1928 to promote a return to Islamic law; it was banned in Eygpt in 1954 [editor's note].

and built on this interpretation a complete theory of Islamic government establishing the 'Islamic order' in one all-embracing Islamic state. All Muslims were called upon to wage jihād against Muslim leaders who failed to strive for this Islamic state. Its main characteristic was the adoption of comprehensive Islamic law (*sharīʿa*). One of the favourite slogans of the Muslim Brothers was: 'The Qur'ān is our constitution.'

* * *

# HARTMUT BOBZIN

## *From* The "Seal of the Prophets": Towards an Understanding of Muhammad's Prophethood†

### *Introduction*

As is well known, Q 33:40 describes Muhammad as "the messenger of God and the seal of the prophets (*khātam an-nabiyyīn*)," a statement which today is generally understood in the sense of finality—in other words, as claiming that there will be no prophet after Muhammad.[1] Yet the mere fact that "prophetic" movements within Islam have arisen again and again shows that the word "seal" (*khātam*) has also been understood differently, not just as indicating the finality of Muhammad's prophethood, but also in the sense of confirmation, i.e., as a form of continuity with earlier prophets.

This is confirmed by an examination of as-Suyūṭī's (d. 1505) extensive commentary on the Qur'an *ad-Durr al-manthūr fī-tafsīr bi-l-maʾthūr*, which reveals a variety of interpretations of the term "seal." ʿĀʾisha,[2] for example, is reported to have said, "Say 'seal of the prophets' and not 'there will be no prophet after him'!" while another ḥadīth quoted by as-Suyūṭī states:

> A man once said in Mughīra (b. Shuʿba)'s presence: "God bless Muhammad, the seal of the prophets, there will be no further prophet after him!" Mughīra replied: "Content yourself with saying 'seal of the prophets.' For we have been told that Jesus, blessings be upon him, will come again, and if he comes, he would be both before Muhammad and after him (since he has already appeared earlier)!"[3]

The expression "seal of the prophets" has recently been examined by Carsten Colpe, who traces it back to Tertullian's (d. after 220) *Adversus Judaeos* (composed soon after 208).[4] Here, the expression refers to Jesus and is used polemically against the Jews; it appears in the interpretation of

† From *The Qur'ān in Context: Historical and Literary Investigations into the Qur'ānic Milieu*, ed. Angelika Neuwirth, Nicolai Sinai, and Michael Marx (Leiden: Brill, 2010), pp. 565–74, 582–83. Reprinted by permission of Koninklijke Brill NV. Except as indicated, all notes are Bobzin's.

1. Cf. the amusing anecdote in Aḥmad b. an-Nuwayrī, *Nihāyat al-ʿarab*, 31 vols. (Cairo, 1924–92), 11:14: "A woman who had been passing herself off as a prophetess was brought before the caliph. He asked her: 'Who are you?' She answered: 'I am the prophetess Fāṭima.'—'Do you believe in Muhammad's message?'—'Yes,' she replied, 'all that he preached is true!'—'But do you not know that Muhammad said: There will be no prophet after me (*lā nabiyya baʿdī*)?'—'I know it well; but did he also say: There will be no prophetess after me? (*lā nabiyyata baʿdī*)?"
2. Wife of Muḥammad and daughter of the first caliph (ca. 614–678), and a source of authoritative knowledge in early Islam [editor's note].
3. Jalāl ad-Din as-Suyūṭī, *Ad-Durr al-manthūr fī t-tafsīr bi-l-maʾthūr*, 6 vols. (Cairo, 1314 AH), ad loc.
4. *Against the Jews*, by the Christian theologian and polemicist Tertullian [editor's note].

an important passage from the Book of Daniel (9:24) that in early Christianity was frequently read in a messianic sense.[5] Without entering into the question of how plausible Colpe's derivation may be, I would like to add that very similar thinking in a very similar context can be found in some homilies by the Syrian theologian Aphraates (d. shortly after 345), who also applies the expression to Jesus and employs it against the Jews.[6] This appears particularly relevant given the significance of Aphraates' world of thought, and of Syrian monastic teaching in general, for Muhammad's early revelations, as pointed out long ago by Tor Andrae.[7] Thus, Aphraates regards Moses and Jesus as being the two greatest prophets—an understanding of prophethood reflected in the Qur'an, where Moses is shown as the leader of the "Children of Israel" (*banū Isrāʾīl*), and Jesus as that of the Christians (*naṣārā*). Quite characteristically, Aphraates also presents a typological exegesis of the Old Testament in which earlier prophets prefigure, and not merely foretell, the life of Jesus. The Qur'an interprets the traditional Judeo-Christian histories of the prophets in a similar fashion, yet does so with regard to Muhammad.

### *Messengers and Prophets: Some Statistical Observations*

In the following, I would like to focus on the second part of the "Seal Verse," which has hitherto been largely ignored by scholars, and in particular on the concept of "prophet" (*nabī*). What is immediately obvious is that Q 33:40 places *nabī* in close proximity to another concept that is also applied to Muhammad, namely, the term "messenger" (*rasul*). The entire verse reads:

> Muhammad is not the father of any of your men, but he is the messenger of God and the seal of the prophets (*mā kāna Muḥammadun aba aḥadin min rijālikum wa-lākin rasūla llāhi wa-khātama n-nabiyyīna*). God is cognizant of everything.

I should first like to examine more closely the two words "messenger" and "prophet." Today, both are used to refer to Muhammad, often without any discernible difference in meaning; Khoury's German translation of the Qur'an, for example, at one point even translates *rasūl* as "prophet" (Q 38:14)! The fact that the two are not always interchangeable can, however, be seen from certain everyday expressions. Thus Muhammad's birthday is referred to as *mawlid an-nabī*, "the birthday of the Prophet," and the call to pray for Muhammad is *ṣallū ʿalā n-nabī*, "pray for the Prophet." The *shahāda*,[8] the other hand, refers to Muhammad as a *rasūl*: "I confirm that there is no god other than God, and that Muhammad is

5. Carsten Colpe, "Das Siegel der Propheten," *Orientalica Suecana* 33–35 (1984–86): 77. Those interested in the entire spectrum of possible interpretations of the term "seal" should also consult Yohanan Friedmann's *Prophecy Continuous: Aspects of Aḥmadī Religious Thought and Its Medieval Background* (Berkeley, 1989), which debates the issue based on a wide range of source material, with particular regard to the modern "prophetic" movement of the Aḥmadiyya [an Islamic sect founded in India in 1889 by Mīrzā Ghulām Aḥmad].
6. Especially in the *Taḥwʾyāthā* against the Jews and concerning persecutions; cf. William Wright, ed., *The Homilies of Aphraates the Persian Sage* (London, 1869); German translation by Georg Bert, *Aphrahat's, des persischen Weisen, Homilien: Aus dem Syrischen übersetz und erläutert* (Leipzig, 1888), and recently by Peter Bruns, *Aphrahat, Unterweisungen*, 2 vols. (Freiburg i. Br., 1991). [*Taḥwʾyāthā* is Syriac for "demonstrations." The singular, *taḥwitā*, is the first word of the title of each of Aphraates' 23 homiles—editor's note.]
7. Andrae, *Mohammed: The Man and His Faith*, trans. T. Menzel (New York, 1960), chap. 6.
8. Testimony (Arabic); the Muslim profession of faith [editor's note].

the messenger of God." The *sīra* literature also describes Muhammad mainly as the "messenger of God" (*rasūlu llāh*). It may be briefly noted that the Qur'an does not use the expression "prophet of God" (*nabiyyu llāh*), the earliest occurrences of which I have discovered in ḥadīth literature[9] and in aṭ-Ṭabarī (d. 923).

Now it is a sound linguistic principle that two different expressions are likely to carry different meanings, so that it may be supposed that the expression "seal of the prophets" in the Seal Verse was not used without reason. In order to reach any further conclusion, one has to examine the complete text of the Qur'an for its use of the terms *nabī* and *rasūl*. The number of occurrences of each expression is recorded in the following table:

| *nabī* | | | *rasūl* | | |
|---|---|---|---|---|---|
| singular | *nabiyyun* | 54 | singular | *rasūlun* | 236 |
| plural | *nabiyyūna* | 16 | plural | *rusulan* | 96 |
| | 'anbiyā'u | 5 | | | |
| | total | 75 | | total | 332 |

Here, three things are noticeable: Firstly, the word "messenger" occurs 332 times, four times as often as "prophet" (75 occurrences). Secondly, on the basis of Nöldeke's chronology,[1] "prophet" appears predominantly in Medinan surahs and plays hardly any role in Muhammad's early revelations. Thirdly, the application of *nabī* to Muhammad himself also does not occur before the Medinan surahs.

If taken seriously therefore, the Qur'an's use of language stands in marked contradiction to the frequently held view that in Mecca Muhammad was primarily a "prophet," while in Medina he was primarily a "statesman." This division into periods has been adopted unquestioningly by a whole series of European biographies, from Karl Ahrens to Hans Heinrich Schaeder and W. M. Watt,[2] and is often accompanied by the assumption of a "break" in Muhammad's life. Yet such conceptions of Muhammad's actions are, to put it bluntly, closely linked to the understanding of prophethood current in modern Western theology, according to which a prophet is someone inspired or at least authorized by God and charged with the task of proclaiming a particular message concerning the future. This message can be socio-political in nature, as was the case with the classical biblical prophets such as Amos, Isaiah, or Hosea, yet it is insisted that the prophets were not themselves politicians. * * *

It will readily be admitted that attempting to understand the nature of Muhammad's prophethood on the basis of biblical precedents is a questionable method. It is, however, just as questionable to make uncritical

9. Cf. A. J. Wensinck et al., eds., *Concordance et Indices de la Tradition Musulmane*, 7 vols. (Leiden, 1936–70), vol. 6, s.v. *nabī*, pp. 332ff.

1. See Theodor Nöldeke, *Geschichte des Qorāns*, 2nd ed., vol. 1, rev. Friedrich Schwally (Leipzig, 1909).

2. See Ahrens, *Muhammed als Religionsstifter* (1935, *Muhammad as Religion Founder*); Schaeder, "Muhammed," in *Arabische Führergestalten*, ed. Schader, Walther Björkman, and Reinhard Hüber (1944); and Watt, *Muhammad at Mecca* (1953) and *Muhammad at Medina* (1956). [editor's note].

use of the understanding of prophethood advanced by Muslim biographers of Muhammad, since Ibn Iṣḥāq's *sīra*,[3] for example, is based on a definite concept of what a prophet ought to be like and of the course Muhammad's life must therefore have taken; it must therefore be used with the utmost caution when analyzing Qurʾanic notions of prophethood. The only legitimate method must be to begin with a scrupulous examination of the Qurʾan's own employment of the word. Whether it is thus possible to discover Muhammad's own self-understanding as a prophet must remain moot. To put it very briefly: Even though the Qurʾan does have indisputable value as a historical source, it remains a primarily kerygmatic text, that is, it represents the transmission of a religious message, it is a "proclamation."

### *The Early Qurʾanic Image of Muhammad*

How is Muhammad presented in the Qurʾan? As is well known, the earliest surahs contain purely descriptive references to Muhammad, the oldest and clearest of which is "warner" (*nadhīr, mundhir*; cf. Q 51:50.51, Q 79:45), followed by *mudhakkir* or "exhorter" (just once, in Q 88:21). Only later do we find "bearer of good news" (*bashīr* or *mubashshir*; see, for example, Q 35:24); interestingly enough, this designation is never used alone but always together with "warner." In addition, there is of course the word "messenger" (*rasul*), used twice together with the attribute *mubīn* (Q 44:13 and Q 43:29), which means "unambiguous, clearly understandable, evident." More frequently, this latter attribute appears in conjunction with "warner."

When regarded in the context of the "clarity" of Muhammad's task described in these expressions, the various Qurʾanic statements distinguishing him from other categories gain a new significance. Muhammad is said not to have been a "poet" (*shāʿir*, Q 69:41, Q 52:30) nor yet to have been "possessed" by a "spirit" (*jinn*)—in other words, *majnūn* (Q 68:2.51, Q 52:29), as poets were said to be (see Q 37:36: "Are we going to forsake our gods for the sake of a poet possessed?"). Nor was he a "magician" (*sāḥir*) or one of the ancient Arabian soothsayers (sg. *kāhin*). A summary of these distinguishing statements reveals two things. Firstly, that they cover the entire range of ancient Arabian ecstatics, who were defined by established expressions and associated with certain religious or social institutions; by contrast, this was not true of the terms "warner," and perhaps also, "messenger." Secondly, the mode of speech (*qawl*) these ecstatics employed was decidedly elaborate and in a certain sense artful. The poets' *qaṣīdas*[4] were metric and full of imagery and metaphor; as far as can be seen from the scant evidence available, this also holds true for the rhyming prose (*sajʿ*) of the soothsayers (*kuhhān*). In contrast to this, Muhammad's speech is described as being "clear."

A systematic compilation of all the imperatives and prohibitions which the Qurʾan describes as having been addressed to Muhammad by God reveals the singular nature of Muhammad's actions in Mecca in even

3. Biography; for Ibn Isḥāq (ca. 704–767), and an excerpt from this biography, see above [editor's note].
4. Instances of an elaborate poetic form developed in pre-Islamic Arabia [editor's note].

sharper focus. Two categories can be drawn up on the basis of content. On the one hand, there are commands defining Muhammad's public duties, described in terms corresponding with the functional definitions quoted above like "warner" and "exhorter": "Arise and warn" (Q 74:2), "So announce to them the good news of a very painful punishment" (*fa-bashshirhum bi-ʿadhābin ʾalīm*, Q 84:24), or simply the command to "remind" his audience (*dhakkir*, Q 87:9, 88:21, 51:55, 52:79). All of these imperatives define Muhammad's task as that of a preacher of penitence for his city (*qarya*) or people (*umma*). On the other hand, however, there is also a group of injunctions that refer to Muhammad as a person and to his relationship with God. These demand certain virtues of him, such as *ṣabr* (steadfastness, patience) or *tawakkul* (faith in God), or call on him to leave matters to God (*dharnī* . . . , cf. Q 68:44). In addition, they require a number of pious actions, as seen in the verbs *sabbaḥa* (to praise), *dhakara* (to mention), and *sajada* (to prostrate oneself): "Proclaim the praise of your Lord when you arise" (*sabbiḥ bi-ḥamdi rabbika ḥīna taqūm*, 52:48); "And mention (*wa-dhkur*) the name of your Lord morning and evening. And for part of the night, prostrate yourself (*fa-sjud*) to Him and glorify (*sabbiḥ*) Him all night long" (Q 76:25.26). These instructions in particular bear a clear resemblance to an ascetic, not to say monastic, ideal of piety. The closest parallels are to be found in Syriac Christian monasticism.

If one were therefore to seek to characterize Muhammad on the basis of the early Meccan surahs, it would be as an ascetic preacher of penitence. He warns of the coming Day of Judgment when there will be no one to plead man's case before the righteous Lord, the Creator, who has the power to kill and restore to life. Preaching this message to the Meccans, Muhammad met with disbelief and resistance. In order to legitimize his mission and to give it sufficient weight, the Qurʾan draws on the examples provided by earlier messengers of God (*rusul*). This happened by means of what Josef Horovitz has termed "Straflegenden," i.e., punishment narratives, according to which each "people" has its own messenger (*rasūl*) who is sent by God to "remind" it. In the six cases mentioned most frequently in the Qurʾan, the respective people accuse the messenger of lying, and meet with instant retribution. The people are destroyed, the messenger survives—sometimes, as in the case of Noah, accompanied by a small band of adherents faithful to him.[5]

### *The Qurʾanic Use of* nabī

It is in this context that the term *nabī* is first employed, most strikingly in Q 19, where it occurs in a sort of catalogue. On closer examination of the figures to whom the Qurʾan ascribes the titles "prophet" (*nabī*) or "messenger" (*rasūl/mursal*), the following picture emerges (brackets indicate non-explicit occurrences):

5. See Josef Horovitz, *Koranische Untersuchungen* (Berlin, 1926); cf. David Marshall, *God, Muhammad and the Unbelievers: A Qurʾanic Study* (Surrey, 1999).

| Name | nabī | rasūl |
|---|---|---|
| Adam (*Ādam*) | (x) | |
| Enoch (? *Idrīs*) | x | |
| Noah (*Nūḥ*) | x | x |
| Abraham (*Ibrāhīm*) | x | |
| Lot (*Lūṭ*) | (x) | x |
| Ishmael (*Ismāʿil*) | x | x |
| Isaac (*Isḥāq*) | x | |
| Jacob (*Yaʿqūb*) | x | |
| Joseph (*Yūsuf*) | (x) | |
| Moses (*Mūsā*) | x | x |
| Aaron (*Hārūn*) | x | x |
| Samuel | (x) | |
| David (*Dāʾūd*) | x | |
| Solomon (*Sulaymān*) | x | |
| Elijah (*Ilyās*) | (x) | x (*mursal*) |
| Elisha (*al-Yasaʿ*) | (x) | x (*mursal*) |
| Jonah (*Yūnus*) | x | |
| Job (*Ayyūb*) | x | |
| Zacharias (*Zakariyyā*) | (x) | |
| Hūd | | x |
| Ṣāliḥ | | x |
| Shuʿayb | | x |
| John the Baptist (*Yaḥyā*) | x | |
| Jesus (*ʿIsā*) | x | x |
| Muhammad | x | x |

As the table shows, all the figures described as *nabī* come from the Judeo-Christian tradition and have been aptly described by Arent Jan Wensinck as "biblical saints."[6] This link to Judeo-Christian tradition is not quite so generally the case for the "messengers"; there are also far fewer of them. The survey also shows that the oft-repeated rule of thumb "Not every *nabī* is a *rasūl*, but each *rasūl* is a *nabī*" is not strictly true.

An attempt to discover the characteristics of the two groups based purely on the Qurʾan reveals a number of features common to both prophets and messengers, such as a scripture (*kitāb*), miracles (*āyāt*), and inspiration (*waḥy*).[7] It is impossible to differentiate clearly between *rasūl* and *nabī* on the basis of just these characteristics. Having been sent to a specific people, on the other hand, is a constitutive feature of a *rasūl*. This cannot be true of prophets, not least because in contrast to the messengers, they are partly determined by their genealogy, that is, they all come from a particular lineage (*dhurriyya*).[8]

6. "Bibelheilige" in German; see A. J. Wensinck, "Muhammed und die Propheten," *Acta Orientalia* 2 (1924): 170.
7. Cf. W. A. Bijlefeld, "A Prophet and More than a Prophet? Some Observations on the Qurʾānic Use of the Terms 'Prophet' and 'Apostle,'" *Muslim World* 59 (1969): 1–28.
8. This genealogical aspect can be seen very clearly in Q 3:33: "God chose Adam, Noah, the family of Abraham and the family of ʿImrān above all mankind."

With this we have a further important characteristic for some of the prophets named in the Qur'an, namely, that of having been "chosen" by God. This was to have a significant effect on the veneration of Muhammad in later Islam as God's "Chosen One," *al-muṣṭafā* or *al-mukhtār*. * * * The "chosen ones" include almost all the figures to whom the title *nabī* applies. It is significant that they are joined by three groups: the "family of Abraham," the "Children of Israel," and the "family of ʿImrān," which correspond to the Jewish patriarchs or pre-Mosaic Jewry (= *āl Ibrāhīm*), Mosaic Jewry (*banū Isrāʾīl*), and post-Mosaic Jewry together with Christians and Jewish-Christians (= *āl ʿImrān*). Belonging to these "chosen ones" is therefore an essential attribute of the prophets and of their families as named in the Qur'an. The Qur'anic prophets all display one further characteristic. Each has given a "pledge" (*mīthāq*) that was accepted by God and thus has resulted in a "contract" or "covenant" (*ʿahd*). Such a covenant is not restricted to prophets but includes all of the "chosen ones" named above.

The Qur'anic notion of prophethood is thus closely bound up with the history of God's "chosen people" and with the concept of covenant. A closer examination of the terms "successor" (*khalīfa*, derived from the verb *khalafa*) and "inheritance" (the verb *waratha* and its various derivations) leads to a similar conclusion.[9] The title "messenger," on the other hand, does not exhibit this historical connotation, despite the fact that it does bear certain similarities to the concept of apostleship as found in the New Testament and the early Church. "Messenger" can without difficulty be applied to figures from Arabian history, such as Hūd, Ṣāliḥ, Shuʿayb—and, of course, Muhammad.

* * *

9. See Karl Prenner, *Muhammad und Musa: Strukturanalytische Untersuchungen zu den mekkanischen Musa-Perikopen im Qurʾān* (Altenberg, 1986). A similar conclusion was reached by Wolfdietrich Fischer, "Das geschichtliche Selbstverständnis Muhammads und seiner Gemeinde. Zur Interpretation von Vers 55 der 24 Sure des Koran," *Oriens* 36 (2001): 145–59.

# Literary Studies

## DEVIN J. STEWART

### *From Saj' in the Qur'ān: Prosody and Structure*†

From pre-Islamic times until the twentieth century, *saj'* has continuously occupied an important place in Arabic literature and in Arab society. It has been used in the sayings of the pre-Islamic *kuhhān*, in sermons and prayers, proverbs and aphorisms, epistles, *maqāmāt*,[1] biographies, and histories. From the tenth until the twentieth century, book titles were almost invariably written in *saj'*. Introductions to works of many genres were often written entirely in *saj'*. In short, *saj'* constitutes an extremely important feature of Arabic writing, including both elite and popular literature. It seems strange that a literary phenomenon of this dimension has received so little attention on the part of medieval and modern Arab literary critics.

What is *saj'*? The common English translation of the term is "rhymed prose", but is *saj'* simply that: prose which rhymes? A cursory reading of examples of *saj'* reveals that there are certain basic rules governing its composition, yet Arab critics wrote very little about these rules in contrast to their monumental efforts to record the rules of poetry. In his *Miftāḥ al-'ulūm*, which has been perhaps the most widely used text book of rhetoric for centuries, al-Sakkākī (d. 626/1228) devotes only two sentences to the topic of *saj'*. However, not all Arab critics ignored *saj'* to this degree. Abū Hilāl al-'Askarī (d. after 395/1005) discusses *saj'* in some detail in his *Kitāb al-ṣinā'atayn*, as does Ḍiyā' al-Dīn ibn al-Athīr (d. 637/1239) in his *al-Mathal al-sā'ir fī adab al-kātib wa-'l-shā'ir* and al-Qalqashandī (d. 821/1418) in his *Ṣubḥ al-a'shā fī ṣinā'at al-inshā*.[2] Many other medieval works on rhetoric and *i'jāz al-Qur'ān* treat the subject, but have received little attention from Western scholars. Modern Arab scholars appear to be more aware of medieval criticism of *saj'*, but do little more than report the opinions of their predecessors without criticizing or building on these ideas. These medieval sources ought to be examined in order to reach a satisfactory definition of *saj'* and to establish norms for the criticism of *saj'*.

This study will not include a detailed historical analysis of the development of *saj'* criticism, nor will it attempt to treat important topics such as

† From *Journal of Arabic Literature* 21 (1990): 101–8. A number of phrases in Arabic for which Stewart provides a translation are omitted. Reprinted by permission of Koninklijke Brill NV. Except as indicated, all notes are Stewart's.

1. An Arabic literary genre in which entertaining anecdotes are presented in alternating prose and verse. *Kuhhān*: soothsayers (sing. *kāhin*; Arabic) [editor's note].
2. The translations of these three titles are, respectively, *The Book of the Two Arts, Secretaryship and Poetry; Dawn of the Dim-Sighted in the Two Arts of [Official] Composition*; and *On the Stylistic Models Needed for Secretaries and Poets* [editor's note].

the development of *saj*ʿ in the *jāhiliyyah*,[3] the relationship of Qurʾānic *saj*ʿ to pre-Islamic *saj*ʿ, or the influence of Qurʾānic *saj*ʿ on later writers of *saj*ʿ. It will rather apply rules derived from medieval critical works to the Qurʾān in an attempt to analyze the structure of Qurʾānic *saj*ʿ, and thereby reach a better understanding of the formal rules governing this type of composition.

## *The Question of* Sajʿ *in the Qurʾān*

The most enduring examples of *saj*ʿ in Arabic are to be found in the Qurʾān. Much ink has been spilled over the question of whether or not the Qurʾān contains *saj*ʿ. According to Goldziher, *saj*ʿ is the oldest type of poetic speech in Arabic, pre-dating *rajaz* and the *qaṣidah*.[4] It was one of the prevalent types of eloquent speech in pre-Islamic Arabia, and was used specifically in orations and in statements with religious or metaphysical content. Muslim scholars concede that the Qurʾān was revealed in language consistent with that which was considered eloquent in the speech of the Arabs; as Ibn Sinān al-Khafājī (d. 466/1074) states, "The Qurʾān was revealed in the language of the Arabs, in accordance with their usage and custom".[5] Goldziher goes so far as to state that no Arab would have acknowledged utterances as coming from a divine source had they not been presented in *saj*ʿ.[6] It seems logical, therefore, that the Qurʾan would contain *saj*ʿ.

Diametrically opposed to this view is the doctrine of *iʿjaz al-Qurʾān*, the "inimitability" of the Qurʾān. For example, in his work entitled *Iʿjaz al-Qurʾān*, al-Bāqillānī (d. 403/1013) goes to great lengths to show that the Qurʾān does not contain *saj*ʿ, and he even attributes this opinion to al-Ashʿarī.[7] The doctrine of inimitability holds that the Qurʾān may not be compared to any type of sublunary composition, since the Qurʾān represents one of God's attributes—His speech. To call the Qurʾān *saj*ʿ would be to impute a mundane attribute to God.[8] Denial that the Qurʾān contained *saj*ʿ was part of a more general insistence that the Qurʾān was God's speech, not Muḥammad's. Enemies of Muḥammad tried to detract from the validity of his messages by labelling them the inventions of a poet or soothsayer.[9] To counter such attacks, many scholars chose to deny that the Qurʾān was a document of *saj*ʿ or that it contained *saj*ʿ, just as they denied that it contained poetry. It would appear that the rigidity of this doctrine left no room for the critic to exercise his skill, yet it is telling of the method of the Islamic sciences that the greatest advances in literary criticism and the study of rhetoric were made in the course of discussions

3. Literally, "ignorance" (Arabic): the period of time prior to Muḥammad's 7th-century call to prophecy [editor's note].
4. Ignaz Goldziher, *Abhandlungen zur arabischen Philologie* (Leiden: E. J. Brill, 1896), 2: 59. [*Rajaz*: the earliest examples of pre-Islamic poetry, written in a specific meter with short lines. *Qaṣīdah*: an elaborate poetic form of pre-Islamic Arabia—editor's note.]
5. Ibn Sinān al-Khafājī, ʿAbd Allāh b. Muḥammad, *Sirr al-faṣāḥah*, ed. ʿAbd al-Mutaʿāl al-Ṣaʿīdī (Cairo: Maṭbaʿat Muḥammad ʿAlī Ṣubayḥ, 1969), 167.
6. *Introduction to Islamic Theology and Law*, trans. Andras and Ruth Hamori, ed. Bernard Lewis (Princeton: Princeton University Press, 1981), 11.
7. See *Iʿjāz al-Qurʾān*, ed. Aḥmad Ṣaqr (Cairo: Dār al-maʿārif, 1954), 86–100. For the statement about al-Ashʿarī see 86. [Abū Mūsā al-Ashʿarī (d. ca. 667), an early Companion of the Prophet who later served as governor of first Basra and then Kūfa—editor's note.]
8. Jalāl al-Dīn al-Suyūṭī [1445–1505], *al-Itqān fī ʿulūm al-Qurʾān* (Cairo: al-Bābī ʾl-Ḥalabī, 1951), 2: 97.
9. On this subject, see Qurʾān 37:36, 52:30, 69:41.

of *iʿjaz al-Qurʾān*, and it was possible for Muslim scholars to hold a wide range of opinions on the issue of *sajʿ* without being judged heretical.

In the time of the Prophet, *sajʿ* was associated not only with eloquent speech in general, but also with the pronouncements of diviners and soothsayers.[1] The Arab critics report some of their often cryptic messages: "The sky and the earth, the loan and the debt, the flood and the trickle . . ."[2] These soothsayers were frequently thought to be in contact with the *jinn*[3] or familiar spirits and have magical powers. They used *sajʿ* to perform pagan functions such as foretelling the future, cursing enemies and warding off evil. To Muslims, the soothsayer's statements were necessarily ridiculous, false, or even heretical. As al-Bāqillānī states, "Soothsaying contradicts the prophecies."[4] The danger which the *kuhhān* could pose to the religion is demonstrated by the career of Musaylimah the Liar, a *kāhin* from the Banū Ḥanīfah tribe in Yamāmah contemporary to the Prophet Muḥammad, who held a rival claim to prophecy and formed his own community of believers. Their conflict with the Muslims, which began shortly after Muḥammad's death, culminated in the battle of ʿAqrabāʾ in year 12 of the *hijrah*, in which Musaylimah was killed and his forces defeated.[5]

Much discussion of *sajʿ* in the Qurʾān revolves around a *ḥadīth* known as the *ḥadīth* of the fetus. Abū Dāwūd (d. 275/889) gives three versions of this *ḥadīth* in *al-Sunan*. Though there are slight differences between the versions, the general context is as follows. Two women of the Hudhayl tribe quarreled, and one struck the other, who happened to be pregnant, in the belly with a staff or, according to another version, a stone. The wounded woman had a miscarriage before dying herself. She had been very close to giving birth, for the fetus, a male, had already begun to grow hair. The guardians of the two women disputed as to whether blood money should be paid for the fetus in addition to that paid for the mother. The dispute was brought before the Prophet, and when the Prophet gave the verdict that blood money should be paid for the fetus also, the guardian of the attacker remonstrated:

> "Oh Prophet of God! How can I pay blood money for him who has not yet drunk nor eaten, nor uttered a sound nor cried? Is blood money to be paid for such as this?"
>
> The Prophet replied, "This man is of the ilk of the *kuhhān* because of the *sajʿ* he has spoken".[6] * * *

The unwilling guardian phrased his question in *sajʿ*, and the Prophet expressed disapproval of this man's *sajʿ*, asking if it was like the *sajʿ* of the pre-Islamic soothsayers. Many critics have taken this *ḥadīth* as proof that

1. On soothsaying (*al-kihānah*) and the association of *sajʿ* with it, see Ibn Khaldūn, *al-Muqaddimah*, ed. M. Quatremère (Paris: Institut impériale de France, 1858), 1:181–5; Rosenthal translation, (New York: Pantheon, 1958), 1:202–7. [For ʿAbd al-Raḥmān ibn Muḥammad ibn Khaldūn (1332–1406) and his *Muqaddima* (*Introduction*), see above—editor's note.]
2. Abū Hilāl al-ʿAskarī, *Kitāb al-ṣināʿatayn*, ed. ʿAlī Maḥmūd al-Bajāwī and Muḥammad Abū ʾl-Faḍl Ibrāhīm (Cairo: Dār iḥyāʾ al-kutub al-ʿarabiyyah, 1952), 261.
3. The third class of intelligent beings (together with humans and angels) for whom salvation is possible. According to Q 55:15, God created them from smokeless fire [editor's note].
4. *Iʿjāz al-Qurʾān*, 87.
5. See Frantz Buhl in *The Encyclopaedia of Islam*, 1st edition, s.v. "Musailima". [This battle occurred in May 633 (12 AH)—editor's note.]
6. *al-Sunan*, ed. M. Muḥyī ʾl-Dīn ʿAbd al-Ḥamīd Hārūn (Cairo: Dār iḥyāʾ al-sunnah al-nabawiyyah, 1970), 4: 192–3.

the Prophet disapproved of *saj'* as such. Several critics refute this interpretation, on a variety of grounds. Both Abū Hilāl al-'Askarī and Ḍiya' al-Dīn ibn al-Athīr state that if the Prophet meant to criticize *saj'* per se, he would have said simply, "*a-saj'an*?" ("Is this *saj'*?") in his reply rather than "*a-saj'an ka-saj'i 'l-kuhhān*?"[7] Al-'Askarī's view is that the Prophet was not expressing a negative view of *saj'* in general, but of the *saj'* of the *kuhhān* in particular, because their *saj'* was very stilted or unnatural[.] * * *

Some critics used the issue of form and meaning to argue that the Qur'ān was not *saj'*. In doing so, they were thinking primarily of the ridiculous or incomprehensible statements attributed to the diviners. One of the early critics who argued this way is al-Rummānī (d. 384/994) in his *al-Nukat fī i'jāz al-Qur'ān*[.] * * * He states that using *saj'* in order to be eloquent is a waste of effort, like making a necklace for a dog.[8] He thought of *saj'* as being, by definition, a poetic mold for a worthless message. He gives an example attributed to Musaylimah the Liar:

> *O frog, croak away! You croak so much, but you don't muddy the water, and you don't leave the river.*[9]

Al-Rummānī attempts to justify the idea that in *saj'* the content is necessarily inane with his interpretation of the etymology of *saj'*. The term *saj'*, lexicographers agree, is derived from the cooing of doves. Al-Rummānī states that this is because they repeat sounds which are similar but have no meaning. Therefore, he holds that the original and true meaning of *saj'* is any nonsense which rhymes.[1]

Al-Rummānī's example evinces a biased view of the possibilities for the content of *saj'* to say the least, but his work was nevertheless influential. Al-Bāqillānī, who drew on al-Rummānī, argues similarly but syllogistically. In the Qur'ān, the form is subordinate to the meaning. In *saj'* the meaning is subordinate to the form. Therefore, the Qur'ān cannot be *saj'*.[2] The conclusion here follows logically from the two premises, but the premises are faulty. It is easy for a non-Muslim to say the first premise might be wrong, since there are many examples of the use of formal devices in the Qur'ān where the meaning is somewhat subordinated for aesthetic or rhetorical reasons. On the other hand, if we take the Qur'ān to be literally the word of God, could not God have the ability to express the desired meaning and mold it in an artistic form like *saj'* or poetry at the same time? Al-Bāqillānī, however, would probably have seen any attempt to say that God followed specific formal rules in the Qur'ān as an attempt to limit His power. The second premise is a disputed idea, and medieval critics pointed out that it was not necessarily true. In fact, Ibn al-Athīr turns al-Rummānī's idea on its head, stating that in order for *saj'* to be good, the form *must* be subordinate to the meaning and not vice-versa. If not, the *saj'* is like a gold scabbard enclosing a wooden blade.[3] Al-'Askarī insists that *saj'* is meritorious if it is not stilted,[4] and further states that Qur'ānic *saj'* is unlike human

7. Is this *saj'* like the *saj'* of the soothsayers? [editor's note].
8. *al-Nukat fī i'jāz al-Qur'ān*. In *Thalāth rasā'il fī i'jāz al-Qur'ān*, ed. Muḥammad Khalaf Allāh and Muḥammad Zaghlūt Salām (Cairo: al-Maṭba'ah al-taymūriyya, 1969), 97.
9. *Ibid.*, 97–98.
1. *Ibid.*, 98.
2. *I'jāz al-Qur'ān*, 88.
3. *al-Mathal al-sā'ir fī adab al-kātib wa-'l-shā'ir* (Cairo: Maktabat nahḍat Miṣr, 1959–62), 1: 276.
4. *Ibid.*, 261.

discourse for the very reason that it captures the fullest meaning and achieves elegance while adopting formal constraints.

* * *

The problem of *saj*ʿ in the Qurʾān has not been settled. The recent *Cambridge History of Arabic Literature* contains two statements on the issue which could not be farther apart. Paret baldly states: "The Qurʾān is written throughout in rhyming prose (*saj*ʿ)".[5] On the other hand, Abdulla el Tayib states:

> The rhythmic deviation by which it (the Qurʾān) departs from *saj*ʿ, *rajaz*, and verse eludes all probing because it is a fundamental tenet of Islam that the Qurʾān is by nature miraculous.[6]

The first statement takes a preconception to its furthest limit, forcing the text into a pre-determined mold through insensitive examination, and the second attempts to deny the value of investigation. This contradiction points to a serious problem. In investigating the problem of *saj*ʿ in the Qurʾān and in trying to define *saj*ʿ itself, it is wrong to impose existing conventions on the material, whether they be Arabic-Muslim or Western Orientalist, for this can only advance our understanding in a limited fashion. It is more important to understand the conventions within the tradition of criticism of the Qur'ān and of *saj*ʿ. Abdulla el Tayib's statement, in my view, reflects a lack of awareness of the variety of opinions held on the issue within the Arabic-Muslim tradition; he is not aware of the conventions, but rather is trapped by them. Is it not more fruitful to take the doctrine of *iʿjāz* as a challenge to investigation and comparison rather than a declaration of the futility of independent thinking? Did not the greatest Muslim literary critics do just that?

* * *

## ANGELIKA NEUWIRTH

## Some Remarks on the Special Linguistic and Literary Character of the Qurʾān†

In western research, the Qurʾān has had a fate similar to that of ancient Arabic poetry, in the sense that as a document of religious history and as evidence for matters of history and grammatical and linguistic studies, it has been made the object of so vast a literature that it can hardly any longer be comprehended. However, it has rarely been honored with an academic examination in terms of what it essentially is, and as what it was originally conceived to be: a liturgical oration, as a text for recitation.

5. "The Qurʾān - I", in *Cambridge History of Arabic Literature: Arabic Literature to the End of the Ummayyad Period*, ed. A.F.L. Beeston et. al. (Cambridge; Cambridge Univ. Press, 1983), 196.
6. "Pre-Islamic Poetry", *ibid*., 34.

† Translated by Gwendolin Goldbloom, in *The Qur'an: Style and Contents*, ed. Andrew Rippin (Brookfield, VT: Ashgate Variorum, 2001), pp. 253–57.  Except as indicated, all notes are Neuwirth's.

A literary study of the Qur'ān on the basis of its essential function is all the more pressing as the attempts up until now have misclassified the character of the Qur'ān and have applied criteria of judgment that produce a false image of its literary form. The Qur'ān evades the usual terms of classification on the grounds of its claims to be a text for recitation, which is clear from the self-testimony of the oldest *sūras*. It is neither to be classified as spiritual poetry nor as prophetic oration in the sense of the ancient Hebrew genre. Above all, it is not to be understood by the term "sermon" in the precise sense of rhetoric that expresses a truth that has already been announced and attempts to urge that truth upon the listener.[1] The Qur'ān may contain some elements of homily along with its many other elements, but it yields just as few examples of these as it yields of the catch-all categories of hymns, narratives or legislation. For the Qur'ān as a whole we are left with its own self-designation "text for recitation" until a description of the form can be devised that makes a more exact designation possible.

However, the subject of an examination of form cannot be the collection of texts entitled "al-Qur'ān", but rather must be the unit which was intended by the Prophet as the formal medium for his proclamation. I would like to point to the *sūra* as this medium. For although smaller thematic units may have come into being on the occasion of a specific "occasion of revelation" (*sabab al-nuzūl*), for the purposes of literary study it is not the external cause of a theme but rather the formation of the theme and its ordering in the total composition that is of interest. Therefore I would like to emphasize the unit of the *sūra* as a heuristic basis, a unit that is also ignored in the tendency towards atomization that predominates in recent investigation. It is the individual *sūra* that will serve as the textual foundation for literary study.

Fortunately, Mr. Gregor Schoeler will deal extensively in the following presentation with the application of the methods of modern literary study in Arabic studies.[2] Therefore I will only delve into a few of the specific demands of examination of the Qur'ān. The specific circumstances of the stratified genesis of various *sūras* on the one hand, and the collection and arrangement of the *sūras* by later redactors on the other, raise methodological problems that under normal circumstances do not arise in a literary work. This situation has its closest parallels in certain parts of the literature of the Old Testament, such as the prophetic books and some of the Psalms. Old Testament studies has therefore developed a series of methodological steps which also prove to be extremely useful for study of the Qur'ān. The most recent reflections on methods for the literary study of the Old Testament is offered by Wolfgang Richter in his *Exegese als Literaturwissenschaft. Entwurf einer alttestamentlichen Literaturtheorie und*

1. On the concept of sermon, see Leo Baeck, "Griechische und jüdische Predigt", in *Aus drei Jahrtausenden. Wissenschaftliche Untersuchungen und Abhandlungen zur Geschichte des jüdischen Glaubens* (Tübingen, 1958), 142: "Very early on, clarifications had to be given of the classical religious literature. Admonitions and edifying lectures were added. A special kind of instruction and discourse develops which no longer announces a new truth, but which seeks instead to depict and spread the already announced truth. Behind the seekers who saw godly faces and received voices from on high there now follow the speakers who possess their book and the seers and companions of the seers follow the preachers. For the term sermon, properly understood, cannot be used to refer to the prophetic word, but rather only to this eloquent imitation."
2. Gregor Schoeler, "Die Anwendung neuer literaturwissenschaftlicher Methoden in der Arabistik", the article following that of Angelika Neuwirth in the proceedings of the XIX. Deutscher Orientalistentag [(Stuttgart, 1977); translator's note].

*Methodologie* (Göttingen, 1971). Richter suggests the following methodological steps: literary investigation, investigation of form, investigation of genre, investigation of redaction. The literary investigation examines the text, in our case the *sura*, as an isolated unit: that is, in terms of its secondary composition. The investigation of form analyzes the exterior form, thereby yielding a description on the levels of sentence, word and individual phoneme. It then examines the collective structure of the individual text (*sūra*). Following this, the investigation of genre elaborates a typology of the structures of the individual text described in the previous two steps. The investigation of redaction examines the secondary composition of the text in terms of its literary compilation. In our case this would entail an analysis, on one hand, of those *sūras* that were not composed by the Prophet himself but were rather assembled during the process of redaction, and on the other hand, of the collection entitled "al-Qur'ān."

If one takes the term *sūra* not only as a proper name, a chapter heading reserved for a particular book, but rather as the name of a genre, then a quick glance at the literature to date shows that the genre of the *sūra* has almost never been recognized. In the works of Richard Bell[3] and Régis Blachère,[4] who have in recent times studied the composition of the Qur'ān, the *sūra* as a whole does not fall within the scope of study, which rather concerns the smaller components from which the *sūra* is composed. For them, the composition of a *sūra*, as a rule, is a later work undertaken by the Prophet himself or even by later redactors. In contrast to Bell and Blachère, Theodor Nöldeke, in his work of 1860, *Geschichte des Qorâns*, takes the *sūra* as a whole under consideration. He says that the relative chronology that he constructed is based on examination of the *sūra* in its entirety. And yet Nöldeke does not advance the term *sūra* as a genre. This is not because an interest in the "smallest components of revelation" draws his gaze away from the whole. Rather, his position of brusque rejection of the Islamic tradition makes it impossible for him to recognize the unique rules of Qur'ānic discourse. For in stark contrast to the strong tendency found in Islamic treatments of the Qur'ān as high above profane literature on the basis of the dogma of inimitability (*i'jāz*), Nöldeke refuses to consider the formal elements of the Qur'ān outside of a relation to the corresponding forms in poetry and rhymed prose. Nöldeke recognizes and describes numerous stylistic features of the Qur'an with the utmost exactness. Nonetheless, the technical and compositional function of these elements does not come into his field of observation because they possess no such function outside of the Qur'ān. Aside from a few examples with especially conspicuous composition, the *sūras* remain for him an amorphous construct and his few observations regarding form remain unutilized in terms of a concept of genre.

The fact that the treatments of the form of the Qur'ān to date have not been able to see the *sūra* as anything more than an external designation for the consequence of a more or less accidental division of the text has to do with the variety of the elements of the *sūra*. The *sūra* is a "mixed

3. Richard Bell, *The Qur'ān: Translated with a Critical Re-arrangement of the Sūras* (Edinburgh, 1937–39); idem, *Introduction to the Qur'ān* (Edinburgh, 1953).
4. Régis Blachère, *Introduction au Coran* (Paris, 1947); *idem, Le Coran. Traduction selon un essai de reclassement des sourates* (Paris, 1949–51); *idem, Histoire de la littérature arabe*, II (Paris, 1964), 187–230.

composition", that is to say, a complex later stage, coming after a longer process of religious and historical development. It is not a historical homogeneity but rather a secondary genre composed of elements that originally came from a variety of sources.

A comparison with the Hebrew Psalms serves to illuminate the subject. In the Psalter, along with longer and shorter pieces that belong to a single identifiable genre, there are also more complex compositions. Each of the individual Psalm genres, such as the hymn, proverb, oracle of salvation, eschatological song, and song of sacrifice among others, has, in itself, a different origin, a different context or Sitz im Leben[5] and a different style, vocabulary and set of conventions. These complex compositions in the Psalms, referred to in Old Testament studies as "Mischgedichte",[6] join together several of these originally separate genres into a larger unity. A portion of these Psalms can be called "liturgies" because they have to be understood as excerpts from liturgies if not as complete liturgies.[7] Of course, this typological comparison is not meant to suggest any direct influence of these Psalms on the Prophet. The aim is merely to compare the results of religio-historical developments that are in many ways parallel in order to cast light on phenomena in the Qurʾān, which are still poorly understood, through comparison with a better understood parallel.

The development of the Psalms took place within the same cult. The Arabian prophet, who stands on a much later stage of religio-historical development, found various religious groups already in existence. All of them have in common that their religious services are composed of various elements such as pericopes, songs that introduce or come between segments of the services and prayers among others. At this time, a variety of forms within a common framework is already a normal phenomenon. The prophet's awareness of form must have oriented itself according to such phenomena, if it developed at all in terms of liturgical form. This process by which a composition of elements that do not directly cohere thematically came into being could more naturally have been realized in this way than by way of that representative type of contemporary profane poetry, the *qaṣīda*.[8] The compound genre that we encounter in the case of the *sūra* becomes much more understandable when one takes into consideration that the complex form of liturgical discourse was "something natural" in the time of the Prophet.

Our methodological approach of taking the *sūra* to be a legitimate unit, and of seeing in individual *sūras*—as they now stand—various realizations of a single definable genre, can be proven if distinct categories of *sūras* can be demonstrated. Such categories do in fact exist. With the exception of a few examples that are still not entirely clear to me, all of the *sūras* of the middle and last Meccan period can be categorized according to distinct compositional schemes. Compared to this phase of development, the

5. Setting in life (German), or social context; a term used in German Form Criticism (an approach in early 20th-century biblical studies) [editor's note].
6. Mixed genre works (German) [editor's note].
7. S. Hermann Gunkel, *Die Psalmen* (Göttingen, 1926), *passim*; Hermann Gunkel and Joachim Begrich, *Einleitung in die Psalmen*, I (Neukirchen, 1961), lvvi: "One not infrequently has the impression that singers or poets, either arbitrarily or with a very definite tendency, put together individual elements from a 'liturgy' in the Psalms. A particular 'selection' is found, for example, in Psalm 132 or in Psalm 110."
8. An elaborate poetic form of pre-Islamic Arabia [editor's note].

*sūras* of the first Meccan period vary too drastically for one to be able to speak of distinct schemata. Nonetheless, even the early *sūras* show themselves to be distinct forms through their clearly proportioned composition. To demonstrate the division of the early Meccan *sūras* from the earlier-mentioned distinct compositional schemes of the middle and late Meccan *sūras* is not possible in the framework of this paper. However, this much can already be said: It is not only the study of the Qur'ān that stands to be greatly enriched through the use of the methods of general literary study. In the process, general literary study can also gain, in the *sūra*, a genre that cannot be found in such clear expression in other literatures.

# Qur'ān and Bible

## ANDREW RIPPIN

### *From* Interpreting the Bible through the Qur'ān†

It is commonly stated that Muslims approach the Bible with the attitude that when the biblical text agrees with the Qur'ān, the statements may be accepted, but when it disagrees, the Qur'ān is to be preferred.[1] The aim of this paper is to sketch out the ramifications this attitude has had in practice and to put it in historical perspective. This paper is no more than an attempt to outline a field of study and investigate some of its potential directions.[2] Clearly, there is a lot of work to be done here, both conceptually, in discovering new approaches to the material, and constructively, in bringing disparate sources together for analysis. It is significant to note that Muslims themselves have generally not separated out this field of biblical interpretation-allusion within their own intellectual systematizations; this is not a 'genre' of *tafsīr*.[3] From a Muslim perspective, it may well be said that this question cannot be separated from the notion of quranic interpretation in general. Yet, from a modern academic perspective, such a topic seems to have legitimacy by virtue of the way in which it reflects an investigator's own interests and construction of reality. That is, quranic studies as a modern, academic discipline cannot, even must not, stay within the intellectual constraints (as it often does) of what are frequently the medieval Muslim efforts towards the categorization of knowledge (as represented, for example, in the works of al-Suyūṭī[4]). Our intellectual efforts to make sense of the world around us must reflect our own understandings and form our knowledge into meaningful elements of our own world view.

I

There are essentially three areas of literature which need to be covered under the rubric of Muslim interpretation of the Bible: the use of biblical

† From *Approaches to the Qur'ān*, ed. G. R. Hawting and Abdul-Kader A. Shareef (London: Routledge, 1993), pp. 249–53, 257–59. Reprinted by Taylor and Francis Books UK. Except as indicated, all notes are Rippin's.

1. The idea clearly stems from the notion of *taḥrīf*, alteration of scripture; see further below.
2. This paper attempts to expand, and expose to a wider, specialist audience, my article called 'Muslim interpretation of the Bible', in R. Coggins, L. Houlden, eds, *Dictionary of biblical interpretation*, London 1990. All translations from the Qur'ān are from A. J. Arberry, *The Koran interpreted*, London 1955; Arberry's verse numbering is also used. Bible translations are from *The new English Bible* (unless translated from the Arabic). I should like to express my appreciation to Professor John Burton, University of St Andrews, for his detailed and helpful response to this paper at the *Colloquium*; his continued interest in, and encouragement of, my work is greatly appreciated.
3. Commentary on the Qur'ān (Arabic) [editor's note].
4. Jalāl al-Dīn al-Suyūṭī (1445–1505), Egyptian scholar who wrote on a wide variety of subjects [editor's note].

material in the Qur'ān itself, its use in *tafsīr* material especially the *qiṣaṣ al-anbiyā'*,[5] and its use in polemical literature. The modern context provides what might be considered an additional area for study, because of the manner in which it frequently brings all three of these elements together into one unit.

Within itself, the Qur'ān provides Muslims with a view of the Bible. Mention is made of the 'scrolls' of Abraham and Moses, the *Tawrāt* (Torah)[6] of Moses, the *Zabūr* (usually understood as the Psalms) of David and the *Injīl* (Gospel) of Jesus, all conceived as direct revelation from God to the prophet concerned: 'Surely We sent down the Torah, wherein is guidance and light' (Qur'ān 5.48); 'And We sent, following in their footsteps, Jesus son of Mary, confirming the Torah before him; and We gave to him the Gospel, wherein is guidance and light' (Qur'ān 5.50). In this way, all previous scriptures are pictured within the revelatory and compositional image of the Qur'ān itself. Additionally, the Muslim scripture is seen to be a confirmation of these earlier revelations; it also serves to make disputed matters clear: 'We have sent down to thee the Remembrance [i.e. the Qur'ān] that thou mayest make clear to mankind what was sent down to them' (Qur'ān 16.46). The Qur'ān also serves a correcting function: humans have misinterpreted and tampered with the works of Moses and Jesus especially; people have been 'perverting words from their meanings' (Qur'ān 5.45). The Qur'ān thus presents an uncorrupted version of the word of God and all scripture culminates in the Qur'ān, according to Muslim interpretation of these verses.[7]

The Qur'ān retells stories found in the Bible in a recognizable form but the accounts are always shorn of their overall biblical narrative context. Frequently the stories are truncated to such an extent that reference to the biblical tradition is necessary in order to make sense of the narrative elements provided in the Qur'ān. Some of the stories are clearly influenced by the exegetical tradition within Judaism and, to a lesser extent, Christianity.[8] The exact source of the stories—variously suggested to be Arabian Jews or Christians, Samaritans, remnants of the Qumran community, Jewish-Christian groups and so forth—remains a matter of debate,[9] but a great deal of emphasis in contemporary research falls on the oral nature of the transmission of the biblical material into the Arabic context in accounting for the form and the content of the narrative.[1]

5. Stories of the prophets (Arabic) [editor's note].
6. The first five books of the Hebrew Bible, traditionally ascribed to Moses.
7. A good treatment of the data related to this issue is to be found in A. Jeffery, 'The Qur'ān as scripture' *The Muslim World*, XL (1950), pp. 41–55, pp. 106–34, pp. 185–206, pp. 257–75; reprinted in book form with a supplement, *The Qur'ān as scripture*, New York 1952.
8. There are, of course, many works which attempt a summary and an analysis of the material. A concise treatment is to be found in J. Jomier, *The Bible and the Koran* (French original: *Bible et Coran*), New York 1964, chapter 10. Noteworthy for its general reflections is Franz Rosenthal, 'The influence of the Biblical tradition on Muslim historiography', in B. Lewis and P. M. Holt, eds, *Historians of the Middle East*, Oxford 1962, pp. 35–45. M. S. Seale, 'How the Qur'ān interprets the Bible: towards a Christian-Muslim dialogue' in his *Qur'ān and Bible: studies in interpretation and dialogue*, London 1978, pp. 71–7, is rather superficial.
9. See the excellent discussion of this subject, with extensive bibliography, in Tryggve Kronholm, 'Dependence and prophetic originality in the Koran,' *Orientalia Suecana*, XXXI–XXXII (1982–1983), pp. 47–70.
1. See e.g. M. R. Waldman, 'New approaches to "Biblical" materials in the Qur'ān', *The Muslim World*, LXXV (1985), pp. 1–13. Also see W. M. Brinner, S. Ricks (eds), *Studies in Islamic and Judaic traditions. Papers presented at the Institute for Islamic-Judaic Studies, Center for Judaic Studies, University of Denver*, Atlanta 1986; Haim Schwarzbaum, *Biblical and extra-biblical legends in Islamic folk-literature*, Beiträge zur Sprach-und Kulturgeschichte des Orients, Bd. 30, Walldorf-Hessen, H. Vorndran 1982; this work has an extensive bibliography.

Scholarship has not, as yet, it seems to me, paid much attention to the actual issue of the interpretation of the Bible from within the quranic perspective. Of far greater concern up to this point has been the attempt to establish the sources of the basic information itself. A few generalities may be suggested, however. It is clear that the biblical stories are cited not for their narrative or historical significance but for their spiritual and moral guidance, most especially in emphasizing the notion of God's determination of, and involvement in, history. The constant suggestion in the citation of the stories of the prophets of the past (starting with Adam and mentioning Noah, Isaac, Ishmael, Lot, Aaron, Ezra, Zechariah, John and so on, for example) is that God has sent messengers in the past with their message but the people have rejected both the message and the messengers. As a result, punishment has come down upon each community and God has thereby triumphed in the end. This stylized narrative plot line is illustrated by isolated episodes or single details from the life of individual prophets, stories which are familiar from the biblical tradition as a whole. Muḥammad's own career is frequently pictured in terms of this plot. Combined with this constant narrative element in the Qur'ān is a reworking of the Abrahamic tradition in the light of Muḥammad.[2] Abraham becomes the pivotal figure in the quranic picture of salvation history, seen as living before the Judaism of Moses and the Christianity of Jesus. This is the true faith, *ḥanīfiyya*, which Muḥammad revives in Makka, where Abraham had established the shrine known as the Ka'ba[3] to the glory of God. The sense in which the Qur'ān 'reworks' this biblical material is limited, however; for the most part, the quranic position on Abraham is assumed or hinted at, rather than explicitly detailed and proven on the basis of proof-texts or the like.

II

Because of the truncated and referential style in the quranic citation of biblical material which presupposed knowledge on the part of its audience of the actual details of the narratives,[4] the emergent Muslim community was faced with the problem of how to understand its own scripture once the original Judeo-Christian environment was left behind and Islam was established as the religion of the newly-formed and widespread Arab empire. On the evidence of extant literary sources, this matter became problematic some 150 years after the death of Muḥammad; at this time, we see the emergence of *tafsīr*: written works providing interpretation of the Qur'ān and thus, given the content of the scriptural text itself, providing a view of Muslim interpretation of the Bible.[5]

One of the earliest such works still extant is that ascribed to Muqātil ibn Sulaymān (d. 767), which clearly displays the way in which biblical

2. See A. Rippin, *Muslims, their religious beliefs and practices*, volume 1, *The formative period*, London 1990, chapter 3, for a discussion of this in the context of the mythic dimension of the Qur'ān.
3. Literally, "cube" (Arabic), the stone shrine in Mecca, believed to have been built by Adam and then rebuilt by Ibrāhīm (Abraham) and Ismā'īl (Ishmael); central to both early pagan and Muslim pilgrimage rituals, it became the most important site in Islam.
4. See the discussion of this in John Wansbrough, *Quranic studies: sources and methods of scriptural interpretation*, Oxford 1977, and A. Rippin, 'Literary analysis of Qur'ān, *sīra* and *tafsīr*: the methodologies of John Wansbrough', in R. C. Martin (ed.), *Approaches to Islam in religious studies*, Tucson 1985, pp. 151–63.
5. For a recent example of a study displaying this aspect of Muslim exegesis, see Reuven Firestone, 'Abraham's son as the intended sacrifice (*al-Dhabīḥ*, Qur'ān 37.99–113): issues in Qur'ānic exegesis', *Journal of Semitic Studies*, XXXIV (1989), pp. 95–131.

materials were interpreted and incorporated into the Muslim tradition in order to complete and supplement the bare bones of the Bible as presented in the Qurʾān.[6] The interpretation of the biblical text is generally left on the level of providing the narrative elements which were needed to embellish the Qurʾān text; certainly the Bible never becomes of relevance to legal issues within the Muslim community itself, nor, generally, for any theological judgements.[7]

Many early Muslim writers, including such people as Ibn Isḥāq (d. 767),[8] al-Jāḥiẓ (d. 869)[9] and Ibn Qutayba (d. 889),[1] display a certain measure of acquaintance with the actual text of the Bible itself. The recent publication of the book by Abū ʿUbayd (d. 838), *Kitāb al-khuṭab waʾl-mawāʿiẓ*,[2] provides an interesting illustration of this type of knowledge. In recounting various speeches of the ancient prophets, Abū ʿUbayd often indirectly cites biblical passages; sometimes these are cited as being 'quotations' from the 'scrolls of Abraham and Moses'[3] but on other, more interesting, occasions, the passages provide what might be best termed 'allusions':

> Abū ʿUbayd told us that Yazīd ibn Hārūn said on the authority of Abū Maʿshar on the authority of Saʿīd ibn Abī Saʿīd al-Maqburī that he said: 'A man came to Jesus, son of Mary, and said "O teacher of good deeds! Teach me something which you know but I do not, which will serve me well but not harm you." Jesus said, "What might that be?" The man said, "How can the servant be faithful to God?" Jesus replied, "That is simple. You should love God truly from your heart, work for God through your exertion and strength as much as you are able, and treat your brothers (*banū jinsika*) compassionately through your mercy and selflessness." The man said, "O teacher of good deeds! Who are my brothers?" Jesus replied, "All of the offspring of Adam. Whatever you consider to be inappropriate for yourself, do not inflict upon others. In this way, you are truly faithful to God."[4]

This sort of passage cannot be taken simply as imaginative quranic exegesis: its allusion to the New Testament is evident and while it may not prove the case for actual knowledge of the biblical text itself, it does demonstrate that Muslims were, at an early stage, working with more raw material in their elaborations of the Qurʾān than their imaginations. Indeed, one of the purposes of citing the Bible as these authors did, may have been to provide a check on the more imaginative embellishments which were being made in the interpretation of the Qurʾān in general which were often

6. *Tafsīr Muqātil ibn Sulaymān*, ed. A. M. Shihāta, Cairo [1969], volume 1 only, volumes 1–5 published Cairo 1979–89.
7. However, the 'biblical' elements of the Qurʾān text are certainly relevant in the overall scheme: see Roger Arnaldez, 'Les éléments bibliques du Coran comme sources de la théologie et de la mystique musulmanes', in *Aspects de la foi de l'Islam*, Brussels 1985, pp. 29–55.
8. See e.g. A. Guillaume, 'The version of the Gospels used in Medina circa 700 A. D.,' *Al-Andalus*, XV (1950), pp. 289–96.
9. See his *Kitāb al-radd ʿalāʾl-Naṣārā*, ed: J. Finkel, Cairo 1926 (under the title: *Thalāth rasāʾil li . . . al-Jāḥiẓ*), and J. Finkel, 'A Risāla of al-Jāḥiẓ', *Journal of the American Oriental Society*, XLVII (1927), pp. 311–34.
1. See G. Lecomte, 'Les citations de l'ancien et du nouveau testament dans l'oeuvre d'ibn Qutayba', *Arabica*, V (1958), pp. 34–46.
2. Edited by Ramaḍān ʿAbd al-Tawwāb, Cairo 1986. On the text see Claude Gilliot, 'Textes arabes anciens édités en Egypte au cours des années 1985 à 1987', *MIDEO*, XIX (1989), pp. 319–21.
3. E.g. *ibid.*, p. 125, paragraph 37.
4. *Ibid.*, p. 153, paragraph 73; the editor notes that this tradition, as with many others in this book, is found in Ibn Ḥanbal, *Kitāb al-Zuhd*. Cf. Matthew 22.34–40. [Aḥmad ibn Ḥanbal (780–855), Baghdadi jurist and collector of traditions—editor's note.]

claimed to stem from the Bible or Jewish and Christian sources. These exegetical excesses, at times, went to the extent of creating wholely spurious texts going under the name of *Tawrāt* or *Zabūr*, examples of which still exist.[5]

The tendency to incorporate biblical materials into the Islamic tradition, and to Islamicize them in doing so (and thus, it might be suggested, picking up on the Qur'ān's own way of retelling biblical stories), sees its ultimate manifestations in the genre of literature known as the *dalā'il al-nubuwwa*, the 'proofs of prophecy', and especially the *qiṣaṣ al-anbiyā'*, the 'stories of the prophets'. These latter tales, several of which are available in whole or in part in English translation,[6] display the end result of the exegetical process: a history of the prophets of the past, recounted in an order which for the most part accepts the biblical chronology, focused around passages of the Qur'ān supplemented by the biblical and most especially biblical-exegetical tradition. Much of this material has become known, pejoratively, as the *isrā'īliyyāt*, stories supposedly transmitted in the Islamic world by Jewish (and Christian) converts, although the material included within this term generally encompasses far more than that.[7] Frequently viewed with suspicion by Muslims, the material has provided the basis for the legendary expansion of the picture of the past prophets, but it is always filtered through a Muslim perspective: characteristics of the Islamic conception of prophets, for example their sinlessness, mould every image; the Arabian context becomes the focal point of many stories. The stories themselves must always agree with the quranic version of the events, even if this reconciliation requires a certain amount of interpretational ingenuity.[8] Overall, it may be said that the point of all these *qiṣaṣ al-anbiyā'* books is to demonstrate the continuity of the prophets from the time of Adam down to Muḥammad. In the recounting of the lives of the prophets, there is certainly a tendency to avoid any Christian symbolic prefigurements in the events of the 'Old Testament'. Likewise, there is no emphasis on Israel as a land and Judaism's connection to it. The stories are retold, once again, for their value in enhancing the spiritual and moral guidance implicit in the Qur'ān itself. Their function is always to interpret the Qur'ān by providing an authoritative, Muslim account of earlier history.

The end result of this writing down of the interpretational process—as embodied in the *tafsīr* works, the spurious bibles and the *qiṣaṣ al-anbiyā'* genre—was that it was never necessary for Muslims to consult the Bible

5. See J. Sadan, 'Some literary problems concerning Judaism and Jewry in medieval Arabic sources,' in M. Sharon, ed., *Studies in Islamic history and civilization in honour of Professor David Ayalon*, Jerusalem/Leiden 1989, esp. pp. 370ff. and the section entitled 'The "genuine" Pentateuch (*tawrāt*) of Moses, as rediscovered and reshaped by Islamic literature'.
6. See e.g., W. M. Thackston, Jr. (trans.), *The Tales of the Prophets of al-Kisa'i*, Boston 1978, and W. M. Brinner (trans.), *The History of al-Ṭabarī*, volume 2, *Prophets and Patriarchs*, Albany 1986.
7. The rise and employment of this term *isrā'iliyyāt* deserves a special study; my impression is that it comes into wide circulation as a pejorative term in *tafsīr*—material which is not to be accepted as valid in interpretation—only with writers as late as Ibn Taymiyya (d. 1328) and Ibn Kathīr (d. 1373). This fact seems to be ignored in works such as Gordon Newby 'Tafsir Isra'iliyat', *Journal of the American Academy of Religion*, XLVII (1979), supplement, pp. 658–97. On the rise of the term, see A. J. Johns, 'David and Bathsheba. A case study in the exegesis of Qur'anic storytelling', *MIDEO*, XIX (1989), p. 263, and Norman Calder's contribution to this volume ["Tafsīr from Ṭabarī to Ibn Kathīr: Problems in the Description of a Genre, Illustrated with Reference to the Story of Abraham," in *Approaches to the Our'ān*, pp. 101–40, excerpted above—editor's note].
8. See Norman Calder, 'From Midrash to Scripture: the sacrifice of Abraham in early Islamic tradition', *Le Muséon*, CI (1988), pp. 375–402, who points also to the status of the quranic narrative itself as a link in the centuries old interpretational process.

itself nor write commentaries upon it, for the necessary material had early on been incorporated into the Muslim exegetical literature. Another aspect of this is reflected in the way in which Muslim elaborations have then re-entered Jewish and Christian circles, especially in the exegetical material of those two religions,[9] but also, according to some, into translations of pseudepigraphical books such as the Ethiopic version of the *Life of Adam and Eve*.[1]

* * *

## SIDNEY H. GRIFFITH

### *From* The Bible in the Arabic Qurʾān[†]

The Qurʾān is very conscious of the Bible and sometimes presents itself as offering once again a revelation previously sent down in the Torah and the Gospel. One verse even seems to put the Qurʾān on a par with these earlier scriptures, when it speaks of the promise of paradise for those who fight in the way of God, as already truthfully recorded in "the Torah,[1] the Gospel, and the Qurʾān" (IX *at-Tawbah* 111). On the one hand, the Qurʾān's text insistently recalls the earlier biblical stories of the patriarchs and prophets, and even appeals to the books of the Torah, the Prophets, the Psalms, and the Gospel by name. On the other hand, Islamic scripture also pursues a reading of its own, often notably distinct from and sometimes even contrary to the biblical understandings of Jews or Christians. For the Qurʾān is in fact very selective in its approach to the Bible and to biblical lore. It ignores entirely portions of the scriptures that are very important to Jews or Christians. The New Testament Pauline epistles are a notable instance of this disinterest, as are large portions of the former and later prophets in the Hebrew Bible. What is notable is that the Qurʾān is not so much interested in the Bible per se, as it is in well-known accounts of the Bible's principal *dramatis personae*: Adam, Noah, Abraham, Ishmael, Isaac, Jacob, Joseph, Moses, Aaron, Miriam, David, Salomon, even Job and Jonah, along with Zachariah, John the Baptist, Mary and 'Jesus, son of Mary,' just to mention the major personalities. It interweaves recollections of the stories of these patriarchs and prophets into its own distinctive prophetology, culminating in Muḥammad, "the Messenger of God and the seal of the prophets" (XXXIII *al-Aḥzāb* 40), and in the presentation of God's message to the community of believers the prophet has summoned to hear it. The Qurʾān thus appears on the horizon of biblical history as a new paradigm for the reading, figuratively speaking, of a familiar scriptural narrative in an Arabic-speaking milieu, offering a new

9. See e.g., the *Encyclopaedia of Islam* 1st ed. articles of J. Heller on various biblical figures for illustrations.
1. See the references provided in J. Charlesworth, *The pseudopigrapha and modern research*, Missoula, MT 1976.

† From chapter 2 of Sidney H. Griffith, *The Bible in Arabic: The Scripture of the "People of the Book" in the Language of Islam* (Princeton: Princeton University Press, 2013), pp. 54–62, 71.  Except as indicated, all notes are Griffith's.

1. The first five books of the Hebrew Bible, traditionally ascribed to Moses [editor's note].

construal of a familiar salvation history, albeit not without echoes of earlier traditions.

The approach undertaken in this chapter is that of a historian of Judaism and Christianity in pursuit of understanding how the scriptural narratives and popular exegetical and communal traditions of the several Jewish and Christian communities, circulating orally in the first third of the seventh century CE in Arabic translation (from their original Hebrew, Aramaic, Greek, Syriac, and even Ethiopic expressions), came into the frame of reference of the Arabic Qur'ān. In other words, the chapter approaches the Qur'ān as a document in evidence of the history of Jews and Christians in Arabia, along with their scriptures and traditions, rather than as a document in Islamic history. For this purpose the inquiry respects the integrity of the Qur'ān in its canonical form, as Muslims actually have it, and recognizes its distinctive kerygma.[2] But it largely ignores later Islamic exegesis of the Qur'ān. It is an unusual approach in that almost all studies of the Qur'ān's incorporation of biblical material have heretofore come from an opposite perspective, that of a student of the Qur'ān itself and its Islamic interpretive tradition, engaged in either appreciatively or unappreciatively looking back from the Qur'ān's text on how well or ill, in the historian's opinion, the Islamic scripture has resumed earlier scriptural narratives.[3]

One of the first things that the historian of Arabian Judaism or Christianity notices on approaching the Qur'ān is that for all its obviously high degree of biblical awareness, the Qur'ān virtually never actually *quotes* the Bible. There are, of course, the exceptions that prove the rule. For example, scholars have long cited the passage from Psalm 37:29, evidently quoted in XXI *al-Anbiyā'* 105: "We have written in the Psalms after the reminder that 'My righteous servants will inherit the earth'."[4] And there is the phrase, "And God spoke directly with Moses" (*wakallama Allāh Musa taklīman*, IV *an-Nisā'* 164), which is hauntingly close to the oft-repeated Hebrew phrase in the Torah, "And God spoke all these things to Moses, saying . . ." (*waydabber Adonay 'el Mosheh kol-haddbārîm hā'ēllê lē'mōr*, e.g., Exodus 20:1).[5] From the Gospel there is the reminiscence of Jesus' saying, "It is easier for a camel to go through the eye of a needle than for a rich man to enter the kingdom of God" (Mt. 19:24) in the Qur'ān's dictum, "Indeed, those who have denied our revelations and rejected them arrogantly—the gates of heaven shall not be opened for them and they shall not enter paradise until the camel passes through the eye of the needle" (VII *al-A'rāf* 40). Otherwise, while there are passages in the Qur'ān that are somewhat hauntingly close to passages in the Hebrew Bible or the Gospels—in the story of the patriarch Joseph (XII *Yūsuf*), for example, or the accounts of the Annunciation (III *Āl 'Imrān*; XIX *Maryam*), they are actually, as we shall see, more paraphrases, allusions, and echoes than quotations in any strict sense of the word.

2. Proclamation of religious truth [editor's note].
3. See in this connection the observations of Tryggve Kronholm, "Dependence and Prophetic Originality in the Koran," *Orientalia Suecana* 31–32 (1982–1983), pp. 47–70.
4. See Anton Baumstark, "Arabische Übersetzung eines altsyrischen Evangelientextes und die Sure 21–105 zitierte Psalmenübersetzung," *Oriens Christianus* 9 (1931), pp. 164–188.
5. I am indebted to Prof. Meir Bar Asher, who pointed out this recurring biblical phrase to me and to Prof. Adele Berlin, who helped me find the particular instance of it at the beginning of the Torah's recitation of the Ten Commandments in Exodus.

For the past century and more, many Western scholars have studied the Bible in the Qur'ān, looking for its sources and the presumed influences on its text in both canonical and non-canonical, Jewish and Christian scriptures and apocryphal writings. Most often they declared the Qur'ānic readings to be garbled, confused, mistaken, or even corrupted when compared with the presumed originals. More recent scholars, however, some more sensitive than their academic ancestors to the oral character, as opposed to a 'written-text' interface between Bible and Qur'ān, have taken the point that the evident intertextuality that obtains in many places in the three sets of scriptures, Jewish, Christian, and Muslim (and in their associated literatures), reflects an oral intermingling of traditions, motifs, and histories in the days of the Qur'ān's origins. These various elements played a role in the several communities' interactions with one another within the ambience of Muḥammad's declamations of the messages he was conscious of having received for the purpose of proclaiming them in public. The Jewish and Christian texts in which scholars find them are not taken to be documentary evidences of the currency and availability of these elements in the Qur'ān's Arabic-speaking milieu. It is no longer a matter of sources and influences but of traditions, motifs, and histories retold within a different horizon of meaning. In this vein some scholars have even begun talking of the Qur'ān's role as a kind of biblical commentary in Arabic, reacting to the Bible, as one recent scholar has put it, as the Qur'ān's "biblical subtext,"[6] and developing many of its themes within its own interpretive framework.

Here the effort is not to contribute to the on-going study of individual units of the Qur'ān in which Bible-related material is to be found, but rather, from the point of view of one intent on consulting the Qur'ān as a document in evidence of Jewish and Christian history in its Arabic-speaking milieu, to study the modes of the Qur'ān's engagement, in its very formation, with the contemporary lore of the Jews and Christians, and with their biblical narratives in particular. With this purpose in mind, it is important to emphasize at the outset that one realizes that interaction with the 'People of the Book' and their scriptures is only one aspect of the Qur'ān's text in its integrity, albeit an important one. The Islamic scripture is certainly larger in scope and purpose than its interface with the Bible, albeit that its divine message is presented as continuous with the earlier scriptures.

Important recent studies of the major structures of the Qur'ān, concentrating on units of text within the framework of a given *sūrah*, well beyond the level of individual verses, where most traditional commentary, both Muslim and non-Muslim has long been focused, have called attention to the numerous prosodic features of the text. These include repeated ritual formulae, inclusions, and key indicative phrases that mark out passages of specific narrative or ritual intent.[7] * * *

6. Gabriel Said Reynolds, *The Qur'ān and Its Biblical Subtext* (Routledge Studies in the Qur'ān; London and New York: Routledge, 2010).
7. One has in mind in particular the studies of Angelika Neuwirth, *Studien zur Komposition der mekkanischen Suren: die literarische Form des Koran—ein Zeugnis seiner Historizität?* (2nd ed. Studien zur Geschichte und Kultur des islamischen Orients, Band 10 (NF); Berlin: De Gruyter, 2007) and Michel Cuypers, *Le Festin: une lecture de la sourate al-Mā'ida* (Paris: Lethielleux, 2007); Eng. trans., *The Banquet: A Reading of the Fifth Sura of the Qur'ān* (trans. Patricia Kelley, Series Rhetorica Semitica; Miami, FL: Convivium, 2009).

### *The Rubrics of Scriptural Recall*

In most of the places in the Qur'ān where narratives of biblical patriarchs or prophets are evoked, or earlier scriptural passages are recalled, the text may simply name a well-known biblical figure, or employ indicative vocabulary that sets the tone and sometimes forms the structure of the text in a given unit or *sūrah*. This usage functions on both a general and a more specific level, as we shall see, and indicates the purpose and the modality of a given instance of scriptural reminiscence. But the most basic thing one notices about the Qur'ān and its interface with the Bible is the Islamic scripture's unspoken and pervasive confidence that its audience is thoroughly familiar with the stories of the biblical patriarchs and prophets, so familiar in fact that there is no need for even the most rudimentary form of introduction. In what follows, the immediate purpose is to call attention to both the general and the more particular horizons within which biblical recall occurs in the Qur'ān, with a view to highlighting how the Arabic Qur'ān, which is the new scripture, and hence on its own terms the primary one, calls on the authority of the older scriptures to corroborate its revelatory message, in the process making the older scriptures secondary and, in that sense, servile to the new. Here we can furnish only sufficient examples of the modalities of this intertextual phenomenon to serve the general purpose of the present study, namely to show how the Bible comes into the Qur'ān's view.

#### THE WIDER HORIZON OF SCRIPTURAL RECALL IN THE QUR'ĀN

By the time the longer Medinan *sūrahs* had come into their final form, the general pattern of the Qur'ān's recall of the major figures and narratives in the Hebrew and Christian scriptures had been set, and the basic principles of their relationship had been enunciated. Succinctly put, the Qur'ān presents itself as confirming the truth that is in the previous scriptures and as safeguarding it. After speaking of the Torah, "in which there is guidance and light," and of Jesus, "as confirming the veracity of the Torah before him," and of the Gospel, "in which there is guidance and light," God says to Muḥammad regarding the Qur'ān: "We have sent down to you the scripture in truth, as a confirmation of the scripture before it, and as a safeguard for it" (V *al-Mā'idah* 44, 46, 48). The previous scriptures were, of course, in the Qur'ān's telling, principally the Torah and the Gospel, as is clear here and in other places, where the Qur'ān says to Muḥammad, "He has sent down to you the scripture in truth, as a confirmation of what was before it, and He sent down the Torah and the Gospel" (III *Āl 'Imrān* 3). In these and other passages one might cite, the position of the Qur'ān vis-à-vis the Jewish and Christian Bible is clear: the Qur'ān confirms the veracity of the earlier scriptures. In other words, the Qur'ān not only recognizes the Torah and the Gospel, and the Psalms too, as we shall see, as authentic scripture sent down earlier by God, but it now stands as the warrant for the truth they contain.

But the matter does not rest here. For while the Qur'ān, following both the then-current Jewish and Christian view, recognizes the Torah as the scripture God sent down to Moses—"We wrote for him in the Tablets about everything" (VII *al-A'rāf* 145)—the Gospel that the Qur'ān confirms is not the Gospel as Christians recognized it in the Qur'ān's own day. Rather, following the model of its own distinctive prophetology, the Qur'ān speaks of the Gospel as a scripture God gave to Jesus: "We gave him the Gospel, wherein is guidance and light, confirming what he had before him of the Torah" (V *al-Mā'idah* 46; LVII *al-Ḥadīd* 27). Here, as in other instances we have noted in the previous chapter, the Qur'ān apparently intends to criticize and correct what it regards as a mistaken Christian view of the Christians' own principal scripture. What is more, by the time of its collection, and principally in criticism of the behavior of the 'People of the Book' in regard to their scriptures, the Qur'ān is already speaking of the 'distortion' and 'alteration' of scriptural texts. This is to be found in the very passages (e.g., in II *al-Baqarah* 75–79; III *Āl 'Imrān* 78; IV *an-Nisā* 46; V *al-Mā'idah* 12–19) that in subsequent Islamic tradition will undergird the doctrine of the corruption of the earlier scriptures,[8] a development that would effectively discount the testimonies drawn by Jews or Christians from their scriptures in behalf of the verisimilitude of their teachings.

Against this background of familiarity with the major liturgical scriptures of the Jews and the Christians, the Torah and the Gospel, and the Psalms (*az-Zabūr*), "in which We wrote" (XXI *al-Anbiyā'* 105) and which "We brought to David" (IV *an-Nisā'* 163; XVII *al-Isrā'* 55), the Qur'ān even advises Muḥammad to consult "those who were reading the scripture (*al-kitāb*) before you" (X *Yūnus* 94). In context, the Qur'ān speaks of God's instructing the prophet in his discourse to his audience to "relate to them the story of Noah" (vs.71), and He goes on to speak of Moses and Aaron, the Pharaoh, the Exodus from Egypt, and the settlement of the Israelites. Within this frame of reference he also advises Muḥammad: "If you are in doubt about what We have sent down to you, ask those who were reading the scripture before you. The truth has come down to you from your Lord, so you should certainly not be in doubt" (X *Yūnus* 94). In a similar vein in another place, the Qur'ān records God's word to Muḥammad:

> We have sent out before you only men whom We have inspired, so ask the 'People of remembrance' (*ahl adh-dhikr*) if you do not know;[9] [We have inspired them] with clear evidences and texts (*az-zubur*) and We have sent down the remembrance (*adh-dhikr*) to you so that We might make clear to people what has been sent down to them; perhaps they will reflect. (XVI *an-Naḥl* 43–44)

In these passages the Qur'ān clearly commends recalling the message of the earlier scriptures, but what especially catches one's attention is the phrase 'People of remembrance' and the reference to what God sent down to Muḥammad as 'the remembrance'. Of note is the parallel between 'the remembrance' (*adh-dhikr*) and 'the scripture' (*al-kitāb*), so in this context the 'Scripture people'/'People of the Book' (*ahl al-kitāb*) are the 'People of remembrance', and what they remember or recall is God's dealings with the patriarchs and prophets as recorded in the scriptures, the very remembrance that is also recorded in the Qur'ān. This is one reason why the Qur'ān itself is referred to in its own text as a 'remembrance', here and in

8. See Jean-Marie Gaudeul and Robert Caspar, "Textes de la tradition musulmane concernant le *taḥrīf* (falsification) es écritures," *Islamochristiana* 6 (1980), pp. 61–104; Jane Dammen McAuliffe, "The Qur'ānic Context of Muslim Biblical Scholarship," *Islam and Christian Muslim Relations* 7 (1996), pp. 141–158.
9. This exact sentence is also found in XXI *al-Anbiyā'* 7.

the oath formula, "By the Qur'ān, possessed of remembrance (*dhī adh-dhikr*)" (XXXVIII *Ṣād* 1), and in such Qur'ānic epithets as "a blessed remembrance" (XXI *an-Anbiyā'* 50), and as being itself a "reminder" (*tadhkirah*) (XX *Ṭā Hā* 3), a 'reminder' (*dhikrā*) for the worlds "of the scripture, the judgment, and the prophethood God had previously sent down" (see VI *al-An'ām* 89–90).

On the face of it the remembrance and the recall seem to be recollections of earlier scriptures, given the repeated mention of terms such as 'book' or 'scripture' (*al-kitāb*) for the Qur'ān itself and for the earlier scriptures, as well as the use of such a term as *az-zubur,* in the sense of 'texts', as in "the texts of the ancients" (XXVI *ash-Shu'arā'* 196) or "the clear signs, the texts, and the illuminating scripture" that the messengers before Muḥammad brought (see XXXV *Fāṭir* 25). This can be seen even in the references to the 'scrolls' (*aṣ-ṣuḥuf*) of Moses, of Abraham, and of God's messengers in general, in which there are true scriptures (see, e.g., LIII *an-Najm* 36; LXXXVII *al-A'lā* 19; XCVIII *al-Bayyinah* 2–3). The same might even be said of the 'copy' (*nuskhah*) in which God's guidance and mercy appeared on Moses' tablets (VII *al-A'rāf* 154). But a closer look reveals that it is not books, texts, scrolls, or copies that the Qur'ān actually recalls, except in such general phrases as those just quoted. Rather, the Qur'ān's actual recollections are of biblical and other narratives of patriarchs and prophets, their words and actions, in the Qur'ān's own (re)telling of the stories, for, as we have said, there are virtually no quotations in the Qur'ān from the earlier scriptures.

### THE NEARER HORIZON OF BIBLICAL RECALL IN THE QUR'ĀN

When recollections of the biblical narratives and of the words and actions of the patriarchs and prophets actually come up in the Qur'ān, the first thing that strikes the reader is, as we have seen, the high degree of familiarity with the *dramatis personae* and their stories that the text presumes in its audience. This is a feature of Qur'ānic discourse that becomes immediately evident on one's approach to any passage that brings up a biblical reminiscence. For example, the very first mention of a biblical person that one encounters on opening the Qur'ān at its canonical beginning occurs in a verse that assumes a fairly wide-ranging knowledge not only of the particular person but of Jewish and Christian lore about the scenario in which the person's name is mentioned. The text evokes the memory of God's creation of Adam and of God's teaching him the names of creatures; it approaches the topic with the affirmation that God is the Creator of all things: "It is He who created for you everything on earth, then ascended to the heavens fashioning them into seven, and He has knowledge of all things" (II *al-Baqarah* 29). Already the scenario is familiar to the 'People of the Book' whom the text is addressing, who, as we shall see, are in this instance Jews. And the next verse moves immediately into the mode of narrative recall, utilizing a key term that recurs throughout the Qur'ān in such circumstances, the simple word 'when' (*idh*), implying a preceding admonition 'to remember'; "When your Lord said to the angels, "I am going to place a deputy on earth" (II *al-Baqarah* 30). The recollection proceeds to recall the story of Adam, Eve, and Iblīs[1] in the Garden (II *al-Baqarah*

1. In Islam, the devil (and so the counterpart of Satan) [editor's note].

29–38), and it does so without once quoting the scriptures, but nevertheless manages to evoke the biblical scene in details familiar not only from the Bible, but also from Jewish and Christian lore.[2] In the sequel, in the same *sūrah*, the text goes on for a hundred verses and more recalling Israelite salvation history through the remembrance of several of the major prophets, Moses in particular, three times exhorting the Israelites to *remember*, "O Sons of Israel, *remember* the grace I bestowed on you" (II *al-Baqarah* 40, 47, 122). Moreover, many subsequent verses begin with the tell-tale phrase, *wa'idh* (or *'idhā* or *lammā*), which in context many translators render as, "[Remember] when . . . ." (25x+). Often God then speaks in the imperative or recalls what He said or did on a given occasion, as in the sequence, "O Children of Israel, remember the grace I bestowed on you . . . beware of the day . . . and when Abraham was tried by his Lord . . . . And [remember] when We made the House. . . . And when Abraham said . . . And when Abraham and Ismā'īl raised the foundations of the house . . ." (II *al-Baqarah* 122, 123, 124, 125, 126, 127).

It is important to notice the prominence of the exhortation to remember or to recall, directly expressed (*idhkurū*), or implied, in Qur'ānic passages featuring the evocation of biblical figures and God's dealing with them.[3] Often, as in the instance just mentioned, the Qur'ān just mentions the name of a biblical person or the subject of a narrative event without any preamble, relying implicitly on its audience's ready recognition of the relevant scenario. The remembrance or recall of the tale is then most often freely phrased in its telling, or re-telling, as if from memory alone, and with no textual reference. Both narrative and dialogue on the part of both the speaker and the *dramatis personae* evoke a familiar scriptural account now woven into an almost iconic, even cinematic, narrative pattern of traditional exegetical or apocryphal details that are virtually midrashic in their generic character. What is more, even within a highly structured *sūrah*, these biblical recollections for the most part retain the feature of recalling well-known prophetic figures. In other words, it is the Qur'ān's distinctive prophetology that ultimately controls the process of scriptural recollection, determining which biblical narratives are recalled and which are ignored[.]

* * *

In short, the Qur'ān's distinctive prophetology, its *sunnah* as the Qur'ān itself speaks of it,[4] may be characterized as: universal (God's messengers have come to every people, not just to the people of Israel); recurrent (the pattern of prophetic experience recurs in the experience of each prophet);

2. For details and bibliography see Cornelia Schöck, "Adam and Eve," in Jane Dammen McAuliffe, ed., *Encyclopaedia of the Qur'ān*, 6 vols. (Leiden: Brill, 2001–06), vol. 1, pp. 22ff.
3. The evocation of biblical recollection is an aspect of the range of meaning of Qur'ānic *dhikr* that often goes unnoticed by modern scholarly commentators, most of whom put the accent simply on the recollection of God and of God's actions among men, an important subset of which is actually expressed in scriptural recall. See, e.g., Michael A. Sells, "Memory," in McAuliffe, *Encyclopaedia of the Qur'ān*, vol. 3, p. 372; Angelika Brodersen, "Remembrance," in McAuliffe, *Encyclopaedia of the Qur'ān*, vol. 4, pp. 419ff.
4. In reference to the messengers prior to Muḥammad, God speaks of "the *sunnah* of our messengers whom We have sent before you; you will not find that our *sunnah* has any change." XVII *al-Isrā'* 77. In other places the Qur'ān refers to this *sunnah* of the prophets and the '*sunnah* of the ancients' (*sunnat al-awwalīn*), as in XV *al-Ḥijr* 13; XXXV *Fāṭir* 43. See Zwettler, "A Mantic Manifesto," 106–109. [*Sunnah*: way, example (Arabic); the practice and behavior of the Prophet—editor's note.]

dialogical (the prophets interact in conversation with their people); singular in its message (there is one God, who rewards good and punishes evil on 'the Day of Judgment'); and triumphant (God vindicates His prophets in their struggles, i.e., in the so-called 'punishment stories').[5] There is also a corrective, even polemical dimension to the Qur'ān's prophetology vis-à-vis the biblical and other narratives of the Jews and Christians in its milieu. The Qur'ān means not to retell the biblical stories but to *recall* them, and to recollect them within the corrective framework of its own discourse. For this reason the Bible is not quoted; instead, the Qur'ān re-presents the stories of many of the Bible's major figures within the parameters of its own, distinctive prophetology, which is an apologetic typology in support of Muḥammad's mission. This phenomenon may best be observed by briefly reviewing several prominent instances of biblical recall in the Qur'ān, this in passages that have been widely studied by modern scholars and so may serve as briefcase studies, illustrative of how we find the Bible in the Qur'ān.

* * *

5. See David Marshall, "Punishment Stories," in McAuliffe, *Encyclopaedia of the Qur'ān*, vol. 4, pp. 318ff. See also David Marshall, *God, Muhammad and the Unbelievers: A Qur'ānic Study* (Richmond, Surrey: Qurzon Press, 1999).

# SIGHTS, SOUNDS, AND REMEDIES

# Learning, Reciting, and Memorizing

## TAHA HUSSEIN

Born in Upper Egypt, Taha Hussein (1889–1973) was the most important Egyptian writer and intellectual of his generation. Although he became blind as a small child, he was the first person to receive a PhD from the University of Cairo. He chose to write his thesis on the famous blind poet of classical Islam, Abū al-ʿAlāʾ al-Maʿarrī (973–1058). He then completed a PhD at the Sorbonne with a thesis on Ibn Khaldūn (1332–1406). Upon his return to Egypt, Hussein secured a faculty position at the University of Cairo and was soon appointed dean of the Faculty of Arts. Eventually, he was asked to head the Egyptian Ministry of Education. A prolific novelist and essayist, Hussein was the first Egyptian to be nominated for the Nobel Prize in Literature (finally awarded to an Egyptian writer, Naguib Mahfouz, in 1988).

Hussein's three-volume autobiography, *Al-Ayyām* (1929–67), is a landmark in modern Arabic literature: before its appearance, the genre of autobiography was virtually unknown. Translated into English as *The Days*, it achieved considerable success in the United States, Great Britain, and elsewhere. In this work Hussein creates a sense of personal distance and detachment by referring to himself as "the boy" and then as "the young man." In the excerpt that follows, he recounts the experience of memorizing the Qurʾān, forgetting it, and learning it again.

### *From* An Egyptian Childhood: The Autobiography of Taha Hussein†

*Five*

* * *

It is not to be wondered at that our friend[1] forgets how he learnt the Quran, since at the time of its completion he was not nine years old. He remembers very clearly the day on which he concluded his study of the Quran, and 'Our Master'[2] telling him some days before, how pleased his father would be with him and how he would make his stipulations for it and demand his past dues. For had he not taught four of our friend's brothers before him, of whom one had gone to Al-Azhar[3] and the others to various schools? So that our friend was the fifth. . . . Did 'Our Master' not have many claims upon the family?

† From *An Egyptian Childhood: The Autobiography of Taha Hussein*, trans. E. H. Paxton (1932; reprint, London: Heinemann; Washington, DC: Three Continents Press, 1981), pp. 15–21, 81.

1. The term that Hussein uses to refer to himself.
2. The teacher in his village school.
3. A university in Cairo (founded 970 CE), associated with a mosque of the same name, that has for centuries been the main center of Islamic learning in the world.

These claims 'Our Master' always detailed in terms of food, drink, clothes and money.

The first of all of these dues, of which he would demand payment, when our friend had finished the Quran, would be a rich supper; then a gown and caftan, a pair of shoes, a Maghraby tarbush,[4] a cotton cap of the material of which turbans are made and a golden guinea—he would not be satisfied with anything less than that . . . if they did not pay him all this, he would disown the family and would not take anything from them. Nor would he have any more to do with them. This he swore with the most binding oaths.

It was Wednesday, and 'Our Master' had announced in the morning that our friend would conclude the Quran that day. They set forth in the afternoon, 'Our Master' leading the way supported by his two companions, and behind him our friend, led by one of the orphans in the village. At last they reached the house and 'Our Master' gave the door a push and uttering the customary cry 'Ya Sattar' (O Veiler), made his way to the guest-room, where was the sheikh,[5] who had just finished his afternoon prayers and was reciting some private prayers as was his wont. He greeted them smilingly and confidently. His voice was soft and that of 'Our Master' raucous. Meanwhile our friend said nothing and the orphan was smiling from ear to ear.

The sheikh signed to 'Our Master' and his two companions to be seated, and placed a silver coin in the orphan's hand. Then having called the servant and bidden him take the orphan to a place where he would find something to eat, he patted his son on the head and said 'May God open his ways to you! Go and tell your mother that "Our Master" is here.'

His mother must have heard the voice of 'Our Master', for she had prepared such things as were necessary for an occasion like this: a tall and wide mug of unadulterated sugared water. It was brought to 'Our Master' and he gulped it down. His two companions also drank two mugs of sugared water. Then coffee was brought and then 'Our Master' urged the sheikh to examine the lad in the Quran, but the sheikh replied 'Leave him to play. He is yet young.' 'Our Master' got up to go, whereupon the sheikh said 'We will say the sunset prayer together, if God wills,' which was of course an invitation to supper.

I cannot recollect that 'Our Master' received any other reward in return for our friend completing the Quran, for he had known the family twenty years and received presents from them regularly, and did not stand on ceremony with them. Indeed he was confident that if he was unlucky with the family this time, he would not be so unlucky some other time.

## *Six*

From that day our small friend was a sheikh, although he was barely nine years old, because he had learnt the Quran by heart; for who memorises the Quran is a sheikh whatever age he be.

His father called him sheikh, his mother called him sheikh, and 'Our Master' used to call him sheikh in front of his parents. He also used to do

4. A fez. According to Paxton, a Maghraby ("Western," here North African) tarboosh was then "worn by sheikhs and some country people as distinct from the taller and stiffer Turkish fez worn by the majority of Egyptians."

5. Hussein's father. Sheikh (literally, "old man" in Arabic), an honorific often applied to secular leaders, can also be a general title of respect (especially for religious scholars).

so either when he was pleased with him or wanted to ask some favour of him. But apart from that he used to call him by his name and very often merely 'kid'.

Now our youthful sheikh was short, thin, pale and rather shabby. He had none of the dignity of sheikhs, and neither a large nor a small part of their reverent demeanour. Moreover his parents contented themselves with magnifying and exalting him by this epithet, which they attached to his name more out of pride and satisfaction with themselves than with the idea of pleasing or petting him.

As for himself, the epithet pleased him at first, but he expected something else, some outward and visible form of reward and encouragement.

He expected to become a real sheikh, and so don a turban and wear a gown and caftan, hence it was difficult to convince him that he was too small to carry a turban on his head or to get into a caftan.

How should he be convinced of it when he was a sheikh who had memorised the Quran! How could one so young be a sheikh! How could one who had memorised the Quran be so young! He was therefore unjustly treated . . . and what greater injustice could there be than that which came between him and his right to the turban, gown and caftan. . . .

It was not many days ere he became disgusted with the title of sheikh and hated to be called by it. He felt that life was full of injustice and deceit, and that mankind (including his parents) wronged him since parenthood did not prevent mothers and fathers from falsehood, trickery and deception.

This feeling soon gave place to one of contempt for the title of sheikh, and the feeling that his father and mother were full of pride and self admiration. Then it was not long before he forgot all this together with other things.

If the truth were known he was not worthy to be called sheikh, and in spite of his having learnt the Quran by heart he was only worthy to go to the village school as before, shabbily attired, with a cotton cap on his head that was only cleaned once a week, and wearing shoes that were renewed only once a year and not discarded until they were utterly worn out. Then he abandoned them and walked barefoot for a week or several weeks until God permitted him to have a new pair.

All this he richly deserved, because his knowledge of the Quran was not of long duration. . . . Was he alone to blame for that or was the blame equally divided between him and 'Our Master'? The truth was that 'Our Master' neglected him for a time, and concentrated his attention on others who had not yet finished the Quran. He neglected him in order to take a rest and also because he had not been paid for our friend's finishing the Quran.

Our friend rather enjoyed this neglect and began going to the village school and spending the entire day there in complete rest and uninterrupted play, waiting for the end of the year. Then his brother at Al-Azhar would come from Cairo, and when his holiday had come to an end, return to Cairo, taking our friend with him to become a sheikh in very truth and to study at Al-Azhar.

Months passed in this way. Our friend used to go to the village school and return from it without having done any work, confident that he had learnt the Quran by heart, while 'Our Master' was equally assured that he had learnt the Quran until the fatal day . . . and it certainly was a fatal day, in which for the first time our friend tasted the bitterness of failure, humiliation, degradation and hatred of life.

He returned from the school in the afternoon of that day, calm and self-assured, but he had hardly entered the house before his father called him, addressing him by the title of sheikh. He went to him and found him with two of his friends. His father came to meet him, bade him sit down in gentle tones and asked him some customary questions.

Then he asked him to recite 'The Sura of the Poets.[6] This request fell on him like a thunderbolt. He began to reflect and meditate. He uttered the customary phrase, 'I take refuge with God from the accursed Satan,' and also 'In the name of God the Beneficent, the Merciful,'[7] but after that all he could remember of 'The Sura of the Poets' was that it was one of the three that begin with Ta Sin Mim,[8] so he began to repeat Ta Sin Mim over and over again, without being able to arrive at what came after it. His father prompted him by telling him some of the words which followed, but in spite of that he could not proceed at all. So his father said, 'Recite the Sura of the Ant,[9] then.' Now he remembered that this Sura, like that of the Poets, began with Ta Sin Mim and he began to repeat this phrase. Again his father helped him, but he could not make any progress. . . . So his father said 'Read the Sura of the Stories,[1] then.' He remembered that this was the third that began with Ta Sin Mim and he began to repeat it again, but this time his father did not prompt him at all. Instead he said quietly, 'Go! I thought that you had learnt the Quran?'

Our friend stood ashamed while the perspiration poured forth. Meanwhile the two men began to make excuses for him on account of shyness and his tender age. So he went away wondering whether to blame himself because he had forgotten the Quran, or 'Our Master' for neglecting him or his father because he had examined him.

Whatever it was, the evening of this day was indeed a black one. He did not appear at the supper-table, and his father did not ask where he was. His mother came and asked him somewhat reluctantly to have supper with her, but he refused, so she left him, and he went to sleep.

On the whole this hateful evening was preferable to the morrow when he went to the village school, for then 'Our Master' called him roughly, 'What happened yesterday? How was it you were unable to recite the Sura of the Poets? Have you really forgotten it? Recite it to me!'

So our friend began to recite Ta Sin Mim. . . . It was the same story as had happened with his father the day before.

'Our Master' exclaimed, 'May God reward me well for all the time I have spent with you and for all the effort I have expended on your instruction, so you have forgotten the Quran and must learn it again. Not that I am to blame, nor you, but only your father; for if he had paid me my dues on the day you finished the Quran, then God would have blessed him by causing you to remember it, but he denied me my just dues, and so God has driven the Quran out of your head!'

6. Sūra 26 of the Qurʾān.
7. The phrase (known as the basmala) that appears at the beginning of every sūra except the ninth.
8. Many sūras begin with letters of the Arabic alphabet (these are transliterated *Ṭ, S, M*). See the note to Q 2:1, above.
9. Q 27.
1. Q 28.

Then he began to go through the Quran with him from the beginning, just as he did with those who were not sheikhs or had not learnt the Quran.

### *Seven*

There is no doubt that he learnt the Quran thoroughly after that in a very short time. He remembers that he returned from the village school on a certain day with 'Our Master', and on this day 'Our Master' made a point of going home with him. When they reached the house 'Our Master' bent and pushed the door, which opened to him. Then he uttered his familiar cry 'Ya Sattar!' (O Veiler!) The sheikh was in the guest-room as usual, and had just said the afternoon prayer. When 'Our Master' had seated himself, he said to the sheikh, 'So you averred that your son had forgotten the Quran and blamed me severely for that! Now I swore to you that he had not forgotten but was only nervous, but you contradicted me and mocked my beard. I have come to-day that you may put your son to a test in my presence, and I swear that should it appear that he has not learnt the Quran, I will shave off this beard of mine and become a laughing-stock among the fuqaha[2] in this town!' The sheikh replied, 'Don't get excited. Wouldn't it have been better to say "Well, he forgot the Quran, so I have been through it with him again"?' Said 'Our Master', 'I swear by God three times that he did not forget it, nor have I been through it with him again. I only heard him recite the Quran and he recited it to me like flowing water, neither stopping nor hesitating.'

Our friend listened to this dispute, knowing full well that his father was right and that 'Our Master' was lying, but he said nothing and stood waiting for the examination.

The examination was a very severe one, but on this occasion our friend was smart and intelligent, answering every question that was put to him without hesitation. Indeed he recited so quickly that his father said, 'Not so fast—it is a sin to gabble the Quran!' When at last he had finished, his father said to him, 'Well done! Go to your mother and tell her that you have really learnt the Quran this time.'

He went to his mother, but said nothing to her, nor did she ask him any questions.

On that day when 'Our Master' departed, he took with him a gown of broadcloth which the sheikh had presented to him.

## ANNE K. RASMUSSEN

## *From* The Qur'ân in Indonesian Daily Life: The Public Project of Musical Oratory†

In Indonesia, amidst a plethora of unique Southeast Asian popular and folk music, Western music, and traditional gamelan styles, the recitation of the Qur'ân pervades daily life as an archetype of Muslim authenticity.

2. *Fuqahā'* (sing, *faqīh*), those versed in religious jurisprudence (*fiqh*). According to Paxton, *faqīh* was "commonly used in Egypt for one who is versed in the study of the Quran."

† From *Ethnomusicology: Journal of the Society of Ethnomusicology* 45 (2001): 30–32, 40–41, 53. Reprinted by permission of The Society for Ethnomusicology.

Removed by thousands of miles and hundreds of years from the source of Islam, Indonesians perform and experience the Qur'ân in allegedly the same way as Muslims did during the time of the prophet, Muhammad. This article distills eight months of research as a student of professional male and female reciters of the Qur'ân in Jakarta, Indonesia, the capital city of the country that is home to more Muslims than any other in the world. It is a work in progress that foregrounds issues pertaining to: historical process; music learning, conceptualization, and performance; the role of ritual specialists in a community; the social construction of gender roles; and the congruence of political ideology and religious practice in contemporary Indonesia. How has the system of Arab musical modes that are employed for religious performance, been transmitted and perpetuated in Indonesia for nearly 400 years? What are the roles of professional male and female reciters (*Qari'* and *Qari'ah*) as they enable the continuity, through space and time, of this religious art? Why in Indonesia are women—school girls to national champions—participants in the public project of recitation when in the global Islamic *umma* (community) women's participation in religious life is often segregated and limited to the private domain? How has the project of New Order nationalism[1] served to support and create social and cultural structures that officially institutionalize the recitation of the Qur'ân, and how will the dynamic current of *Reformasi* (Reformation) effect this support? Each aspect of the investigation is seasoned with and limited by my own experiences as they were lived in the course of my work with those in Jakarta who practice *seni baca al-Qur'ân*, the art of reciting the Qur'ân.

## *The Ethnographic Setting*

A good deal of my ethnographic work took place at the Institut Ilmu al-Qur'ân (Arabic: 'Ilm al-Qur'ân), The Institute for the Study (or more literally, "Science") of the Qur'ân, a college for women in south Jakarta. On my first two visits I had caused something of a stir. After just a few minutes of instruction from our teacher, the recitation class had dissolved into a "show and tell with Ibu Anne."[2] The rigors of learning religious songs, called *tawâshîḥ* had been suspended at the direction of our guru (teacher); I was asked to come to the front of the class and talk about myself. Part of my "life story" for the class consisted of a little lecture demonstration on Arab music. I played the Arab lute, the 'ûd,[3] and sang songs in the Arabic language. I tried to explain how Arab music works and why it is related to the recitation of the Qur'ân in Jakarta. Through my performance, I aimed

1. The policy of Indonesia's second president, Suharto (1921–2008; president, 1967–98), who sought to distinguish his era from that of his predecessor; his rule was pro-Western and authoritarian.
2. A note on foreign terminology and transliteration: the title *Ibu* connotes maturity, marriage, and motherhood and is used in the Indonesian language (Bahasa Indonesia) for adult women. The term *Bapak* or Pak is used for adult men. Although I called professional reciters "Pak" and "Ibu," I use their professional titles *Qari'* and *Qari'ah* throughout the article. For Indonesian terms that are derived from the Arabic language, I generally use Indonesian spellings and provide, in parentheses, the transliteration of the Arabic term following the IJMES system (International Journal of Middle Eastern Studies) when there are obvious discrepancies in the transliteration systems [Rasmussen's note].
3. The 'ûd is pear-shaped fretless lute found throughout the Arab world and in parts of Central Asia and the circum-Mediterranean region. The lack of frets on the neck of the instrument enables a player to produce the non-tempered intervals, sometimes referred to as "neutral" or "quarter" tones, characteristic of Arab modes or *maqâmât* [Rasmussen's note].

to satisfy their curiosity with regard to my motivation for studying *seni baca al-Qur'ân*.

Following an indication from our guru, Haji Moersjied Qari' Indra, for my third visit to the Institute I had equipped myself with my first *busana Muslim* (Muslim fashion) outfit, complete with matching *jilbab* (head covering). My new Muslim fashion was greeted with unveiled enthusiasm. "Oh *cantik, cantik*" (beautiful, beautiful) the class chorused—"how nice you look in busana Muslim" (*busana Muslim cocok*)—"Why you look just like one of those Bosnian women on T.V." (*seperti wanita Bosnia*) one woman commented. At this point I was finally permitted to just sit and participate with the girls in the class as we imitated, in full singing voice, our guru line by line, phrase by phrase, in the music of the Qur'ân.

The opportunity to live for a year Indonesia arose when my husband was appointed advisor to the Indonesian Ministry of Environment. When my Dean approved my leave of absence I began to contemplate how I might go about studying the recitation of the Qur'ân. I hoped that my concentration for the past ten years on Arab music as a "first" area, through graduate studies, teaching, and performance, would give me a framework appropriate for research on this topic. I was curious about how the Qur'ân was learned and experienced in the non-Arab context of Indonesia. Qur'anic recitation in Jakarta sounded "Arab" I thought, as I identified strains of *maqâmât* (Arab modes) emanating from our neighborhood mosques or from our car radio. I was plagued by an urge to discover whether Indonesian reciters talked about the vocal artistry of the Qur'ân as "Arab music." What terminology did they use? How was musical practice described, articulated, conceptualized?

A chance meeting in November, 1995 with one of the judges at a competition for call to prayer (*adzân*), held at the month-long, government-sponsored, Islamic *Festival Istiqlâl* led to an invitation to the Institut Ilmu al-Qur'ân (IIQ). For the next eight months until my departure from Indonesia in July 1996, I attended weekly class and small group and private lessons at IIQ, an all female college dedicated to Qur'ânic studies. I engaged in formal interviews and conversations with the director (Kiyai Haji Ibrahim Hosen), with IIQ faculty, and Kiyai Haji Sayyid Mohammad Assirry, one of the premier reciters in Jakarta. I met reciters and scholars who visited from elsewhere in the Islamic Diaspora (i.e. Malaysia, Iran). I accompanied my two main teachers, one male (Dr. H. Moersjied Qari' Indra) and one female (Qari'ah Hajjah Maria Ulfah, M.A.), to many of their engagements. These teachers are in high demand as professional reciters in contexts that vary from official government events to the nightly evening-long prayers held during the month of Ramadan.[4] Furthermore, Qari' Moersjied and Qari'ah Maria are called upon regularly to judge the myriad competitions in Qur'anic recitation, *Musabaqah Tilawatil Qur'ân* (*Musâbaqat Tilawat al-Qur'ân*)—MTQ, that are held in every corner of Indonesian society, from neighborhood mosque to government ministry to national television studio. I also spent several days as a guest of Moersjied's family in residence at a *Pondok Pesantren* (religious boarding school) in South Sumatra. My visit coincided with their annual

4. The ninth month of the Islamic calendar and the Muslim month of fasting; according to Q 2:185, during this month the Qur'ān was first revealed.

graduation ceremonies as well as with the inauguration of a government program that attempts to combine the efforts of the local military with the needs of Islamic boarding schools (*ABRI Masuk Pondok Pesantren*—literally, "The Army Enters the Islamic Boarding School"). By the end of my first residence in Indonesia, my interest in studying *sent baca al-Qur'ân* had blossomed into a full schedule of classes, lessons, interviews, excursions, and invitations to competitions and evening activities.

* * *

### *Women's Voices*

* * *

Opportunities for women of all educational and social strata to learn and experience the performance of the Qur'ân are not limited to institutions like the IIQ or the Pondok Pesantren (religious boarding school). Once I had established a pattern of weekly lessons at IIQ I found women's groups all around me (or they found me). For example, one day the maid from the house across the street appeared to convey an invitation from her "woman of the house" to join her in her regular lessons. One of the mosques in my neighborhood held women's gatherings weekly during the year and daily during Ramadan. During these early morning meetings, various women recited from the Qur'ân, and a male *'alim* (religious leader) from the mosque gave a sermon. In one kampung (neighborhood), just walking distance from my house, I attended a very simple *madrasa* (religious school) of a neighborhood woman who tutored women in recitation and lead group meetings where the Qur'ân and other religious material was recited and sung in chorus. While it was exciting to be participant in this active and seemingly liberated Islamic "sisterhood," I occasionally questioned the extent to which official encouragement by the government, work place, family, and educational system for women to learn Qur'anic recitation is now part of a larger project of national conformity, a topic to which I will return below.

### *Standards of Excellence; Aesthetics of Performance*

Along with the rest of her students, I tape recorded each lesson with Qari'ah Hajjah Maria Ulfah, which I then practiced during the week by playing back the lessons *ad infinitum* and transcribing Ibu Maria's carefully-demonstrated musical phrases into musical notation. At the following lesson I would perform the recitation from the beginning, she would correct my mistakes, and we would move on to a new passage. By working on an entire ten-minute recitation, the norm for contests (*Sûrah* [chapter] *Al-Furqân*,[5] *Ayât* [verses] 64–78), I was able to experience the ways in which the melodic conventions of recitation—modal exposition, modulation, vocal timbre, and ornamentation—are matched to the text of the Qur'ân according to the rules of tajwîd.

Recitation is learned by the "100 times method." The teacher sings a phrase and names it using Arabic terms—for example *Bayâtî Shûrî* or *Bayâtî*

5. Sūra 25, "The Criterion."

*Jawâb*. The naming of phrases and sometimes the isolated repetition of musical sequences or ornaments are among the only analytical devices offered in the learning process. The techniques of vocal production are demanding. Women never break into their "head voice" but rather sing in a full if somewhat pinched chest voice through the top of their range. Our recitations covered an ambitus[6] from the D or C below middle-C—often just a rumble—to the F an octave and a fourth above middle-C; in other words, we sang a range of nearly two and a half octaves without breaking into a head voice. Qari'ah Maria would sometimes demonstrate a high passage in her head voice (*suara kecil*) but no "real" recitation, male or female, features a "falsetto" delivery. To break into a head voice, even in the highest passages, is to "break the rules."

Like instrumental *taqâsîm* (Arab modal improvisation) a recitation starts with relatively short and unornamented phrases in the lowest part of a singer's range and progresses to longer more fanciful phrases that are filled with ornamentation, sequences, and flourishes in the higher parts of a singer's range and that demand extraordinary breath control. While to Western ears the timbre of recitation may sound nasal throughout, a singer is also required to use nasalization (or extra nasalization) (Arabic: *ghunna*) as well as unvowelled consonants, for example singing a melismatic phrase on the consonant "nnnnnn," according to the multiple demands of tajwîd.[7]

*Seni baca al-Qur'ân* requires of a Qari' or Qari'ah the ability to have internalized all of these musical models and to have them available on "instant recall" as they recite any passage of the Qur'ân while simultaneously following the rules of tajwîd. Memorization of parts of the text of the Qur'ân can also be a goal for Qari' and Qari'ah. While recordings of men's and women's recitations can of course be distinguished, there is no effort on the part of women to sound like a woman, or to sound feminine, or to sound in any way different from a man. When they recite, Qari' and Qari'ah are channeling the archetypal recitation of the Qur'ân as it has been practiced, according to Muslim belief, for centuries.

* * *

## HELEN N. BOYLE

## *From* Embodying the Qur'an through Memorization: An Example from Morocco[†]

Because of their focus on rote memorization of the Qur'an, not to mention their use of corporal punishment, Qur'anic schools have often been described as backward, uninspiring to the student, and unproductive

6. The range of a melody or voice.
7. Defined by Rasmussen in a passage not included here as "the system which codifies the divine language and accent of Qur'anic recitation in terms of rhythm, timbre, the sectioning of the text, enunciation, and phonetics."
† From chapter 5 of Helen N. Boyle, *Quranic Schools: Agents of Preservation and Change* (New York: RoutledgeFalmer, 2004), pp. 89–90. Reprinted by permission of Taylor and Francis Group, LLC, a division of Informa, plc. Except as indicated, all notes are Boyle's; some of her references have been omitted.

socially. Memorization of the Qur'an, the defining mission of these schools, has for the most part been looked upon as a process whose only purpose is indoctrination into the practices and beliefs of Islam, and to promote sustained "discipline" over the child. I am suggesting, however, that Qur'anic memorization—the memorization of the penultimate and sacred text of Islam—is an educational process whereby the Qur'an becomes embodied within the person of the memorizer, usually a child. Memorization, in this case, is a process that seamlessly unites the physical and the mental in the formation and enactment of religious and cultural practice. Seen in this light, memorization is more than the following of tradition, more than sustained discipline or indoctrination, and even more than the passing on of religious rituals. The embodied Qur'an serves as a source of ongoing knowledge and protection to the child as he/she journeys through life. As such, Qur'anic memorization constitutes the beginning of an Islamic education; memorization is not the end goal of Islamic education, but its first step. Thus, embodiment, used as a conceptual framework for Qur'anic memorization, allows for a more complex and nuanced understanding of Islamic education and its use of memorization as a method of study.

### *Memorization as a Form of Learning*

Aisha, a mother whose child studied at a *kuttab* in Chefchouan,[1] when asked what she liked about the *kuttab*, attested to the value of memorization in and of itself, comparing the *kuttab* with a kindergarten to which she had sent some of her older children:

> I like everything. I swear, children *learn* the Qur'an. I sent my first children to a kindergarten but they didn't *memorize* the Qur'an. My daughter [at the *kuttab*] now is only three years old and she has *memorized* more than ten verses. In kindergarten, though we pay, they don't *memorize* this much [emphasis added].

While clearly valuing Qur'anic memorization and feeling that the kindergarten did not give the expected return, it is also very interesting to note that she uses the terms "learning" and "memorizing" synonymously. In her opinion, if her daughter did not memorize she did not learn. The ability to recite memorized material proved to Aisha that her daughter had learned something!

Likewise, the mother of the family that I spent a great deal of time with in Chefchouan, Khadija, was constantly scolding her kids to "go memorize your lessons." She was always referring to public school lessons—French, mathematics, science, etc. She too used the term memorization as synonymous with learning. She wanted her kids to learn their lessons so that they would be prepared to answer questions in class. Even though she used the verb "to memorize," it was clear that she was not telling her kids to commit every line of their lessons to memory, although there was probably some memorization involved. Thus, in an educational context in Morocco, memorization and learning are often used in the same sense.

1. A small city in the Rif mountain range of northern Morocco. *Kuttab* (i.e., *kuttāb*): school (Arabic); specifically, a Muslim elementary school [editor's note].

In order to understand the significance of Qur'anic memorization/learning and the still strong role of *kuttabs* in Chefchouan, the question of how understanding and reason relate to the idea of memorization is central.

### UNDERSTANDING

In Islamic education, memorization is generally considered the first step in understanding (not a substitute for it) as it ensures that sacred knowledge is passed on in proper form so that it can be understood later. Wagner quotes the philosopher Al Ghazali,[2] who pointed out five centuries ago that memorization of the Qur'an as a first step to learning did not necessarily preclude comprehension later on:

> [The] creed ought to be taught to a boy in the earliest childhood, so that he may hold it absolutely in memory. Thereafter, the meaning of it will keep gradually unfolding itself to him, point by point, as he grows older. So, first, is the committing to memory; then understanding; then belief and certainty and acceptance.[3]

Thus, memorization was the first step in a lifelong enterprise of seeking understanding and thus knowledge. It did not seek to replace understanding with dogmatism, but to plant the seeds that would lead to understanding. The same idea is echoed by historiographer Ibn Khaldun,[4] cited as part of a project report on *kuttab* innovations:

> Ibn Khaldoun suggests that this system took advantage of children's submissiveness in order to teach them what they would only be able to understand later: "Only children are capable of learning a text that they don't understand now and will understand later," he wrote.[5]

The idea that memorization did not preclude understanding but was a precursor to it is an important distinction since much of the criticism that is leveled at traditional Islamic education centers on the emphasis it places on memorization.

### REASON

Furthermore, in the Moroccan context, Qur'anic memorization equaled the exercise of reason, as did other exercises of mental discipline involved in being a good Muslim:

> Two features consistently associated with Islamic education are its rigorous discipline and the lack of explicit explanation of memorized material. Both of these features are congruent with the concept of essentially fixed knowledge which is at the base of Islamic education, at least in the Moroccan context, and the associated concept of "reason" (*'qal*) prevalent in Moroccan society. Reason is popularly conceived as man's ability to discipline his nature in order to act in accord with the arbitrary code of conduct laid down by God and

2. Abū Ḥāmid Muḥammad Al-Ghazālī (1058–1111), Iranian Muslim theologian, philosopher, and mystic [editor's note].
3. D. A. Wagner, "'Rediscovering Rote': Some Cognitive and Pedagogical Preliminaries," in *Human Assessment and Cultural Factors*, ed. S. H. Irvine and John W. Berry (New York: Plenum Press, 1983), p. 185.
4. 'Abd al-Raḥmān ibn Muḥammad ibn Khaldūn (1332–1406) [editor's note].
5. K. Bouzoubaa, *An Innovation in Morocco's Koranic Pre-Schools*, Working Papers in Early Childhood Development 23 (The Hague: Bernard van Leer Foundation, 1998), p. 3.

> epitomized by such acts of communal obedience as the fast of Ramadan.[6] Thus a firm discipline in the course of learning the Qur'an is culturally regarded as an integral part of socialization . . . In Moroccan towns and villages, the discipline of Qur'anic memorization is an integral part of learning to be human and Muslim.[7]

Reason is equated with discipline. Memorization is a form of discipline. Eickelman is speaking of traditional msids (another word for Qur'anic schools) from the early part of the twentieth century in the above quotation. Still, his observation rings true for today's kuttab students as well. The process of memorization of the Qur'an is a demonstration of behavior that involves mental discipline. This in turn is a manifestation of behavior based on reason. By contrast, hanging out in the street is the opposite of discipline, and many parents cite kuttabs as helping their children to avoid the danger of the streets.

### *Embodiment as a Framework*

The great precursors of embodiment as a theory are Merleau-Ponty and Bourdieu.[8] Although differing in theoretical orientation, what Merleau-Ponty and Bourdieu have in common is a conception of the body as a site of cultural production. Whether a perceptual setting in relation to the world or the site of unconscious practice (habitus), for both Merleau-Ponty and Bourdieu the body was not "a brute fact of nature"[9] but *a crossroads for cultural production.* Implicit in their theories is the elimination of the Cartesian mind/body separation that is characteristic of Western epistemological tradition. In this tradition, the body is associated with nature and the consciousness (mind) with culture.

* * *

In his 1988 Stirling Award Essay, Csordas picks up on this idea of the mindful body and extends it beyond medical anthropology or anthropology of the body to religious practice. His object is "to reformulate theories of culture, self, and experience, with the body at the center of analysis."[1] He refers to the body as "the existential ground of culture"[2] and illustrates this idea in talking about his work among charismatic Christians.

* * *

### *Embodying the Qur'an—How and Why*

In days past, when written literacy was not a common skill and when written texts were not plentiful or readily available, Qur'anic memorization had a very practical purpose. It preserved the Qur'an exactly as it was given

6. Dale F. Eickelman, *Moroccan Islam: Tradition and Society in a Pilgrimage Center* (Austin: University of Texas Press, 1976), pp. 130–38 [Eickelman's note].
7. Dale Eickelman, *Knowledge and Power in Morocco: The Education of a Twentieth-Century Notable* (Princeton: Princeton University Press, 1985), pp. 62–63.
8. Pierre Bourdieu (1930–2002), French sociologist. Maurice Merleau-Ponty (1908–1961), French phenomenologist [editor's note].
9. Thomas J. Csordas, "Introduction: The Body as Representation and Being-in-the-World," in *Embodiment and Experience: The Existential Ground of Culture and Self*, ed. Csordas (Cambridge: Cambridge University Press, 1994), p. 1.
1. Csordas, "Introduction," p. 4.
2. Thomas J. Csordas, "Embodiment as a Paradigm for Anthropology," *Ethos* 18 (1990): 5.

to the prophet Mohammed by God so that it could be shared with, and taught to, people who did not read or write. (Since the Qur'an is said to have come directly from God to Mohammed, it is considered in and of itself divine and therefore exact, immutable, and absolute.) Indeed, preservation of the Qur'an exactly as it was given to the prophet Mohammed was the key impetus for the widespread practice of memorization up until the middle of the twentieth century.

Qur'anic memorization has typically been associated with recitation. Someone who "knows" the Qur'an is generally someone who has memorized it; this knowledge is first demonstrated by being able to recite it. (This neither precludes nor assumes the ability to understand it as well.) In addition to demonstrating knowledge on the part of the reciter, the oral recitation of the Qur'an traditionally allowed it to be a presence in the lives of those who could not read it themselves. People could appreciate its beauty and power through hearing it being recited, and this is still true today. * * * One can recite from reading a text or from memory. When there were fewer texts available, recitation often depended on memory. With the wider availability (and affordability) of written and recorded texts and the increase in literacy rates, the ability to recite the Qur'an is not as dependent as it used to be on sheer memorization.

Memorization was important for other reasons beyond preservation and recitation. Memorization is also a part of religious practice, a necessity in being able to perform one's prayers, a means of learning a great deal about classical Arabic (through knowledge of its penultimate text), as well as a source of spirituality and pleasure.

In the current context of Chefchouan, one can regularly listen to the Qur'an being recited on TV or video, on cassette or CD. A significantly larger number of people are literate (43.7% of adults in 1995—56.6% of men and 30.97% of women—as compared to an overall adult literacy rate of 20.7% in 1970).[3] Islamic studies are taught in the public school system. In short, multiple delivery "channels" are available for people to listen to and to learn to recite the Qur'an.

Despite all this, my data suggest that in Chefchouan and in Morocco as a whole, it is still important to communities—as expressed through the voices of national decision makers or local experts, teachers, and parents—that children memorize some of the Qur'an. In Chefchouan, the demand for Qur'anic preschools is very high and growing. The *kuttab* more than holds its own in terms of attracting students.

It is true that Qur'anic memorization in the contemporary *kuttab* is much abridged from days past, with pupils memorizing at most the first *hizb* (chapter)[4] of the Qur'an. Nevertheless, parental interviews attest to the importance that parents still attach to their children correctly memorizing some of the Qur'an. For example, the majority of Qur'anic school parents, when asked if they would send their children to a modern *rawd* (kindergarten) in Chefchouan if cost were not a consideration, said no. The main reason parents gave was that the children do not memorize as well in the

3. United Nations Development Program, "Human Development Report—Gender Related Development Index," 1998; United Nations Development Program, "Trends in Human Development," 1998.
4. In the standard terminology of qur'ānic recitation, a *hizb* is one-sixtieth of the Qur'ān [editor's note].

*rawds*. The significance accorded to both memorization and the institution of the *kuttab* in Chefchouan has remained and perhaps increased.

While many would argue that the value of Qur'anic memorization is religious indoctrination, this argument folds back upon itself, since one major criticism of the *kuttabs* is that children do not understand what they are memorizing and teachers do not even attempt to explain the material. Hence, there are no points—rules, practices, beliefs—contained in the memorized materials that are drilled into children so as to indoctrinate them. At most, in the schools observed for this study, "indoctrination" went as far as touting reverence of God and love of the Prophet Mohammed, which are equally emphasized in public school religion classes in Morocco as well as in community and family life. Clearly, then, the memorization of Qur'anic verses on the part of preschool children observed did not serve to indoctrinate them into an uncritical acceptance of the tenets and beliefs of Islam. That being the case, Qur'anic memorization had to serve another, more nuanced purpose with respect to the education of children in Morocco.

In short, my research leads me to suggest that memorization of the Qur'an, even in this abridged form that one finds in the *kuttab*, is significant not because children understand what they have memorized, nor because it is a step on the road to memorizing the full Qur'an, but because this relatively brief exercise in learning has the lasting effect of embodying the Qur'an in the beings of these *kuttab* students. The embodied Qur'an preserves not just the words or the grammar, which are not in danger of being lost or mixed up, but the living spirit of the document vis-à-vis Moroccan practice. In this sense, I use embodiment as a conceptual bridge to reconcile the ongoing significance accorded to memorization and the schools that facilitate it, with the widely diminished practical need for memorization as a means of textual preservation or as a means of indoctrination.

Interview respondents, in particular, often used bodily expression to convey the level of bodily-rootedness of the Qur'an within the beings of those who memorize it. Typical were references to the Qur'an's presence in the mind or the heart of the child. The Qur'an is embodied in the interaction between the minds and bodies of the *kuttab* students; it is embodied in their ability to recall and bring to life in recitation whole chapters of the sacred text. More importantly, the memorized text stays with the children as a part of their beings and as a source of knowledge and spiritual renewal as they grow older and more consciously assume their places as practitioners in a community of practice.

How does this embodiment occur? How can we understand it? I use two metaphors that came through quite consistently in my research: children who memorize something early in life never lose it because it is engraved in their consciousness as something engraved in stone; and children who have memorized some of the Qur'an have been given an inner compass that can provide them with direction later in life.

Fatima, a Chouani mother with three preschool-aged daughters, expresses the core of these two ideas—permanence and direction—which were also expressed by GZA[5] administrators, other parents, and Qur'anic

5. The Green Zawiya Association for Education and Culture, which runs many qur'ānic preschools [editor's note].

school alumni from different eras. Fatima was asked the reasons as to why she considered *kuttabs* as important institutions:

> I have many reasons. The first one is that I like the Qur'an very much and all that is related to it, such as *Tafssir* [commentaries] and *Ahadith* [sayings of the prophet]. Also, since we are Muslims, the first thing children should know is that Allah the Gracious is our God and our creator and that Mohammed (peace be upon him) is our prophet and our model in life, and that the holy Qur'an is our constitution. *Although children won't perceive things as such, they should learn some verses of the Qur'an so as to adapt themselves to it. If they learn the Qur'an at an early age, they will always yearn for it when they become old.* Moreover, if they memorize something at an early age, they will never forget about it, in spite of the fact that [public] schools cut [some time devoted to] this learning of the Qur'an. At the beginning, I forgot what I learned, but when I grew up and started to know that as Muslims we should conserve these verses, I returned to the Qur'an and I didn't find any difficulties in memorizing it. Actually, I rememorized what I had forgotten and I improved [emphasis added].

This quotation eloquently sums up the idea of embodying the Qur'an. Children habituate themselves to it early and it serves to guide them later on; it comes back to them since it is preserved within them. Fatima suggests that even without understanding the Qur'an at first, the child will look at what he/she has memorized and this memorized text will answer some longing in the child-turned-adult.

* * *

## ANNA M. GADE

## *From* Recitation†

* * *

### *The Qur'ān and the* Sunna *on the Recited Qur'ān*

Throughout the development of traditions of Qur'ān recitation and up until the present, Muslims have based the theory and practice of the recited Qur'ān on the two most authoritative sources in Islamic tradition: the Qur'ān itself and, second, material in *ḥadīth* reports. The latter comprise the *sunna* or exemplary model of comportment of Muḥammad. The ethico-legal injunctions to recite the Qur'ān and the norms for how to recite it are expanded in other authoritative material such as information on how influential early Muslims recited and other normative guidelines for the technique and practice of recitation. Within this material, however, it is the Qur'ān and the *sunna* that carry the most authoritative force because of their status in tradition.

† From *The Blackwell Companion to the Qur'ān*, ed. Andrew Rippin (Malden, MA: Blackwell, 2006), pp. 481–89. Reprinted by permission of John Wiley and Sons Inc. All brackets in the text are Gade's.

As a highly self-referential text, the Qur'ān includes many descriptions of its own recitation and the power of hearing and voicing the text. The Qur'ān discusses its own recitation in general terms, and only somewhat less so in specific or technical terms. Because of the Qur'ān's unique authority in Islamic systems to guide Islamic thought and action, these descriptions of the recited Qur'ān function also as a kind of instruction to believers. The verses of the Qur'ān that have been said to be among the first revealed to Muḥammad, the beginning verses of *sūra* 96, *al-'Alaq*, are often interpreted as a command, specifically directed to the prophet while also directed to Muslims in general, to voice the Qur'ān, "Recite! In the name of your Lord who created humanity from a clot." The Qur'ān also gives guidelines about how to perform its own recitation, as in Q 73:4, "Recite the Qur'ān with *tartīl* [slowly, deliberately]." Muslims often cite Q 75:16 as instruction on Qur'ān recitation: "Do not hasten your tongue with it; it is for Us [God] to collect and to read it: when We recite it, follow then its recitation." The Qur'ān includes many recommendations about its own recitation, such as to concentrate fully, to recite as an act of supererogatory piety especially at night, and to "remember" and to "preserve" its message.

Many of the Qur'ānic directives concerning recitation found in the Qur'ān are descriptions of the effect of the recited Qur'ān on its listeners. The Qur'ān often expresses the embodied, emotive responses of believers to its own recitation. For example, the Qur'ān describes these reactions as "shivering" skin and "trembling" heart (for example Q 19:58 and 39:23). Weeping as a recognition of the message of the recited Qur'ān is a common Qur'ānic theme, as in Q 5:83, "And when they hear what has been sent down to the messenger [of the Qur'ān], you see their eyes overflow with tears because of what they have recognized of truth. They shout: 'Our Lord! We believe; so You will write us down among the witnesses to the Truth'." The Qur'ān often links such descriptions of affective response to the altered moral state of the believer who is receptive to the message. An example is Q 17:107–9, "When it [the Qur'ān] is recited to them, they fall down upon their faces, prostrating, and say: 'Glory be to our Lord. Our Lord's promise is fulfilled.' And they fall down upon their faces, weeping, and it increases them in humility."

*Ḥadīth* material enhances Qur'ānic prescription and description by conveying the ideal intensity of Qur'ānic engagement through the injunction to follow the model of Muḥammad. This is because the *sunna*, in the form of the sayings, actions, and tacit approvals and disapprovals of the prophet, is preserved in *ḥadīth* "traditions." *Ḥadīth* material contains many separate accounts that relate what kind of recitation Muḥammad favored, how he reacted to hearing the recited Qur'ān, as well as some information on how the prophet himself recited the Qur'ān. For example, there are many reports of statements made by Muḥammad that he valued beautiful voices in Qur'ān reading in the collection of al-Bukhārī (d. 256/870) and others, such as the following, "God has not heard anything more pleasing than listening to a prophet reciting the Qur'ān in a sweet, loud voice" (al-Bukhārī n.d.:[1] VI, Book 61, no. 541). *Ḥadīth* litera-

1. Muḥammad ibn Ismā'īl al-Bukhārī, *Ṣaḥīḥ al-Bukhārī*, English trans. Muḥammad Muḥsin Khān, 9 vols. (1971–76; reprint, Beirut: Dar al-Arabia, n.d.). Bukhārī's collection is the most widely recognized.

ture also includes many descriptions of the prophet weeping and shedding tears when he heard recitation that was especially affecting.

* * *

### *Systems for Reading the Qurʾān:* Qirāʾāt *and* Tajwīd

The recitation of the Qurʾān (*tilāwat al-Qurʾān*) is part of the fundamental branches of Qurʾānic study and learning. As such, it is a field within of the overall sciences of the "readings" (*qirāʾāt*) of the Qurʾān. The term *tilāwa* appears often in the Qurʾān in both the forms of a noun and a verb. In the Qurʾān it refers, for example, to the signs of God that are "rehearsed" in the Qurʾān, the accounts of previous messengers and communities in sacred history, as well as the actual practice of rendering the Qurʾān in voice. Usually, when the word refers to the reading of the Qurʾān, *tilāwa* conveys a sense of "following" the Qurʾānic message in voice. The practice of reading the Qurʾān follows a set of guidelines known as *tajwīd*. *Tajwīd*, although not a Qurʾānic term, is the basic system for the correct pronunciation and rendition of the speech of the Qurʾān; these guidelines are understood to have been revealed to the prophet by the angel Gabriel along with the Qurʾān itself. Recitation of the Qurʾān according to the rules of *tajwīd* has many names across the Muslim-majority world. Some of these are forms of the Qurʾānic expression *tartīl*, which conveys a sense of "measuring out" the recited Qurʾān in a careful way.

* * *

In its more technical and restricted usage, the term *qirāʾāt* usually denotes the idea of the variant accepted readings of the Qurʾān. These differing readings do not relate to pitch variation nor any substantive textual variants. Instead, all of the readings pertain to minor differences in the vocalization of the same ʿUthmānic text:[2] they all employ the same rules of sound production (*tajwīd*). There are said to be seven accepted readings in the system of *qirāʾāt*. This number has been disputed at times in the past. The number seven is based on a well-known *ḥadīth* transmitted in several versions. One states that Muḥammad said, "This Qurʾān has been revealed to be recited in seven different modes [*aḥruf*], so recite of it whichever is easiest for you." (al-Bukhārī n.d.: VI, Book 61, no. 561) Some variants of this report give an "occasion of revelation" or context for the verse, which was a question about the proper reading of Q 25; another *ḥadīth* report states that Muḥammad said that the angel Gabriel would recite in different ways for him. The idea of the "seven modes" has been open to a variety of interpretations in Islamic tradition, including the possibility that the *aḥruf* may refer to differing dialects among the Arabs at the time of the revelation of the Qurʾan. The standard interpretation, however, is that the *aḥruf* refer to what became known as the "seven readings" (*qirāʾāt*) of the Qurʾān. The reasons given for the diversity of these accepted readings include the idea that they afford an easier reception of the Qurʾān for learners, as well as the suggestion that they may enhance the multifaceted semantic layers of Qurʾānic meanings.

2. The authoritative written version of the Qurʾān, compiled at the direction of the third caliph, ʿUthmān ibn ʿAffān (d. 656).

The establishment of the accepted range of variation in "readings" is credited to Abū Bakr b. Mujāhid (d. 324/936). The seven readings that were standardized in the time of Ibn Mujāhid as the accepted *qirāʾāt* represented prominent traditions of reading in five centers of Muslim learning in that period: Mecca, Medina, Damascus, Basra, and Kufa. A list corresponding to this selection includes the following seven readers: Ibn Kathīr (Mecca, d. 120/737), Nāfiʿ (Medina, d. 169/785), Ibn ʿĀmir (Damascus, d. 118/736), Abū ʿAmr (Basra, d. 154/770). ʿĀṣim (Kufa, d. 128/745), Ḥamza (Kufa, d. 156/772), and al-Kisāʾī (Kufa, d. 189/804). A rationale behind this authoritative selection was to take independent lines of authoritative transmission going back to Muḥammad, and thereby minimize the possibility of error. There was, however, some controversy over the selection at the time. In addition, the "science of readings" continued to develop after this time as well; the later, influential scholar, Ibn al-Jazarī (d. 833/1429), describes ten variant readings, while other scholars have cited fourteen. Nevertheless, Ibn Mujāhid's system of seven *qirāʾāt* has been accepted as the standard. Today, the most popular readings are those transmitted from ʿĀṣim by Ḥafṣ (d. 180/796), along with Nāfiʿ transmitted by Warsh (d. 197/812).

In general, when recitation of the Qurʾān is begun in one of the seven readings, the reciter must continue with that reading consistently until he or she has finished the entire selection. In other words, it is not permissible to mix up the readings within a single performance. The differences in readings are, in general, minor differences in vocalizing particular words as well as stylistic variation. An example of accepted variation among the readings is found in the first *sūra* of the Qurʾān. The first word in the third verse may be rendered either as *māliki* or *maliki*. Both versions convey the same sense of meaning, which is God's dominion over the day of judgment. In another example, one that has led to differences of opinion on ritual law for ablution, Q 5:6 may carry two meanings about how to purify the area of the feet, depending on vocalization; it may be understood as "wash" (according to Nāfiʿ and Ḥafṣ) or "wipe" (according to Ibn Kathīr and Abū ʿAmr). These parameters of diversity among the standard readings have been seen by some, including those in European traditions of textual analysis, as important sources of information about Qurʾānic expression and the history of its reception.

There are two key terms for the applied aspects of the recitation of the Qurʾān: *tartīl* and *tajwīd*. These are technical components of *tilāwa*, aspects of any reading (*qirāʾa*). *Tartīl* and *tajwīd* are closely related terms; for example, the Qurʾān's own instruction, "Recite the Qurʾān with *tartīl*" (Q 73:4) is often considered to mean, "Recite the Qurʾān according to the rules of *tajwīd*." *Tajwīd* refers to a rigorous system of guidelines that determine the proper vocalization of the Qurʾān and thereby shape its characteristic rhythm and specific sound. It does not pertain to pitch variation, however, which is always improvised.

The root meaning of the word *tajwīd* carries senses of "beautifying" and "making correct." *Tajwīd* is part if the wider "science of readings" (*qirāʾāt*) within the classic "Qurʾānic sciences." It is often defined in Muslim sources by some variant of the expression, "giving each sound its correct weight and measure." The formal system of *tajwīd* provides instruction on the correct articulation of phonetic sounds, the assimilation of vowels and consonants in juxtaposition, and the proper rhythmic duration of vowel sounds. It also includes parameters for nonmelodic improvisational flexibility, since it governs, for example, pauses and starts in reading; these allow the reader to emphasize certain words, phrases, or sections. One of the reasons for the development of this Qur'ānic science alongside grammar and exegesis was the standardization of style and sound across the growing linguistic diversity of the Islamic world in the early period. The rules of *tajwīd* assure uniformity and consistency in the vocalization of God's speech through clear guidelines.

By determining the unique sound of Qur'ān recitation in these ways, *tajwīd* distinguishes the recited Qur'ān from ordinary Arabic speech and singing. Shaping cadences and rhythms of recitation, *tajwīd* also "musicalizes" the recited Qur'ān to some degree, although the recited Qur'ān is never to be understood in terms of a human product such as "music." It is one of the first areas of study of the Qur'ān, since children need to learn to recite the Qur'ān properly in order to fulfill one of the most basic ritual obligations, canonical prayer. For the four-fifths of the Muslim world that is not Arabic-speaking, this study also doubles as an introduction to the Arabic language. Native speakers of Arabic must study *tajwīd*, since the rules of *tajwīd* concern much more than grammatical and intelligible pronunciation. In some cases, the end of the formal study of *tajwīd* is the successful reading of the entire Qur'ān text with a teacher; known as *khatm al-Qur'an*, this achievement is marked with a life-cycle celebration in parts of the Muslim world.

* * *

### *Norms of Qur'ānic Worship, Preservation, and Piety*

The practice of reciting the Qur'ān is a foundational element of Islamic education, practice, and piety. During the fasting month of Ramaḍān,[3] the Qur'ān is read throughout the course of the month in nighttime prayers called *tarāwīḥ*. One of the standard divisions of the Qur'ān is its partition into thirty equal, consecutive parts, or *juz'*; this sectioning facilitates complete recitation of the Qur'ān over the course of a month. In addition, during Ramaḍān or during the days of *ḥajj*, the whole Qur'ān may be recited through in one night by pious Muslims. Muslims read the Qur'ān frequently as an act of supererogatory piety, and recitation especially at night is performed by committed Muslims.

Reciting the Qur'ān is required as a part of one of the fundamental acts of worship in Islam, *ṣalāt* (canonical prayer). The recitation of the opening *sūra* (*al-Fātiḥa*[4]) is carried out seventeen times a day by practicing Muslims due to its liturgical use as a component of *ṣalāt*. This chapter of the Qur'ān is also read in other contexts, such as the sealing of contractual agreements and blessings. During canonical prayer, Muslims are required to read another, unspecified part of the Qur'ān besides *surat al-fātiḥa*. When prayer is conducted individually, this is often a *sūra* selected from among the short Meccan *sūras* that are the thirtieth *juz'* of the Qur'ān; if the prayer is led by a prayer leader (*imām*) this reading will be according to

3. The ninth month of the Islamic calendar; according to Q 2:185, during this month the Qur'ān was first revealed.
4. The Opening.

the leader's choice. In addition, it is common in worship and other practices of Muslim piety to hear the well known "light verse" (Q 24:35) or the "throne verse" (Q 2:255). The final *juz'* of the Qur'ān, as well as other passages like these, are commonly memorized by Muslims. *Sūras* 49 and 67 are also often committed to memory. Other parts of the Qur'ān that are also well known and read on certain occasions include *sūra* 12 especially for life-cycle observances, and *sūra* 36, read for the deceased or dying in a sometimes controversial practice. *Sūra* 18 is often read communally as well.

The recitation of the Qur'ān is a prototype for the practice of *dhikr*, a Qur'ānic word for "reminder" and a practice associated with Ṣūfī piety.[5] The Qur'ān is the basis for the formulae used for such recitational piety as well as the recitation of the ninety-nine names of God (*al-asmā'al-ḥusnā*). These "beautiful names" are mentioned in Q 17:110, part of which reads, "Say: Call on Allāh or call on al-Raḥmān. By whatever name you call [Him], His are the most beautiful names (*al-asmā'al-ḥusnā*)." Not all of the names are given in the Qur'ān, however. The Qur'ān's brief listing of some of the names is found in Q 59:22–4.

* * *

The memorization of the complete Qur'ān, which is known as its "preservation" (*taḥfīẓ*), was encouraged ever since the earliest period of Islam. Among those known especially for memorizing and preserving the Qur'ān in the time of the prophet were his wives. There are many *ḥadīth* reports that encourage Muslims to read the Qur'ān and to know it by heart. Traditionally, formal education begins with the memorization of the Qur'ān at an early age and then branches out from there to other subjects; this institutionalized practice continues in many Muslim-majority societies. The memorization of the Qur'ān is a life-long pursuit, however, because readers must continually repeat the text so that no part of it is forgotten. The non-linear structure of the Qur'ān demands this continual rehearsal in order to commit to memory since it is, as a *ḥadīth* on memorization transmitted from Muḥammad has it, "like a camel that is always trying to run away." Memorizers who have made the commitment to "preserving" the Qur'ān often repeat one-seventh of it each day of the week. Students who are memorizing the Qur'ān for the first time study handbooks on difficult aspects of the Qur'ān, such as verses that closely resemble one another. For Muslim men and women who do not attempt the challenge of memorizing the entire Qur'ān, and then keeping it memorized, many are able to meet the goal of having memorized the final *juz'* (thirtieth) of the Qur'ān.

* * *

Material on the proper behavior and comportment with the Qur'ān is known as *adab al-Qur'ān*. This literature continues the precedent of collecting reports about the recitational practice of Muḥammad, while it also includes further information about the recitational customs of other pious persons and other norms of practice. These include respectful silence when listening, sitting facing the *qibla* (the direction of prayer)[6]

5. In this practice, a short phrase or prayer is repeated (often, the names of God).
6. Toward Mecca.

if possible, meeting the standards of ritual purity, repeating verses, and reciting the standard opening and closing formulae. These latter formulae are the opening statement, the *ta'awwudh* ("I take refuge in God from the accursed Satan") which is followed by the *basmala* ("In the name of God, the Merciful, the Compassionate"),[7] no matter where in the Qur'ān the reader begins. The reciter always closes a reading with the formula *ṣadaqa 'llāh al-'aẓīm*, meaning "Thus God the All-mighty has spoken truly." If the reciter is interrupted by a greeting (*salām*) while reading, he or she is to stop to return the greeting; he or she is also to stop when hearing the *adhān* (call to prayer). Reciters and listeners may observe *sajdat al-tilāwa*, which is the prostration that is to be performed at fourteen or fifteen verses (according to different traditions) in the Qur'ān that refer to created beings who bow before their Creator. Only in some parts of the Muslim world is there concern over men listening to the voices of women reciting the Qur'ān: in other regions, such as Indonesia, women reciters are very popular.

* * *

In addition to describing the peace and tranquility (*sakīna*) that descend when the Qur'ān is read in this world, the effects of recitation and of studying and teaching the recited Qur'ān are also described in terms of the accounting on the day of judgment and the consequences in the world to come. In an eschatological mode of piety, rewards for reciting the Qur'ān are often accounted *sūra* by *sura* in this literature, or even letter by letter. Early traditions of ascetic and Qur'ānic piety elaborated such material within Islamic tradition, and Ṣūfīs, among the heirs to this pious tradition, developed especially the soteriological and interiorized Qur'ānic dimensions of piety. In this tradition, a close relationship to the Qur'ān is depicted as an ongoing intimacy, at times framed in terms of the key Ṣufi concept of "friendship." Engaging the Qur'ān in practice should also conform to the reader's close and immediate experience of following (*tilāwa*) the Qur'ān in the "heart," and this pious ideal is central to the tradition of the recited Qur'ān within any pious Islamic orientation.

* * *

## CHARLES HIRSCHKIND

### *From* The Ethics of Listening[†]

Ahmad was one of the men with whom I listened to sermon tapes on a regular basis when I was in Cairo. He lived with his mother and sister in the lower-middle-class neighborhood of Ain Shams and worked in an aluminum processing plant on the outskirts of Cairo. Ahmad's father had

7. The phrase that appears at the beginning of every sūra except the ninth.
† From chapter 3 of Charles Hirschkind, *The Ethical Soundscape: Cassette Sermons and Islamic Counterpublics* (New York: Columbia University Press, 2006), pp. 67–76, 226–27.  All brackets in the text are Hirschkind's.

abandoned the family and gone off to work in Germany some years earlier, and for years now, his father's sole contribution to their family was an occasional phone call and the long-unfulfilled promise that he would someday bring Ahmad to Europe and set him up with a job. After her husband's departure, Ahmad's mother took up a job as a clerk in a government office; her salary, combined with Ahmad's, just barely covered basic expenses. Like many Egyptians in their late twenties and early thirties, Ahmad was desperately trying to put enough money aside to afford marriage, an issue all the more pressing given the increasing impatience of his prospective bride.

Ahmad had become involved in *daʿwa*[1] activities as a student during his years at Ain Shams University, from which he had graduated the year before I met him. Approached by other students, he had joined a small group that met regularly in a mosque not far from his house where they received instruction from the resident shaykh.[2] The mosque provided the group with sermon tapes, sheets with devotional sayings, and other instructional materials. The group followed a program aimed at strengthening their knowledge of Islam and their ability to live in accord with its precepts, a program that included the stipulation that they listen to a sermon tape at least twice a week. During one of the many government sweeps aimed at uncovering Islamic militants, a number of the group members were arrested, though most were released after two weeks. This experience led Ahmad to distance himself somewhat from the group and to generally steer clear of Islamist associations on campus. He still had a circle of friends with whom he would exchange tapes, and when they visited his house while I was there, we often listened to a tape together. Thus, while he continued to ascribe great importance to religious practice in his life—praying regularly and attending to his other religious duties, as well as listening to sermon tapes and reading current publications from Islamist presses—he no longer engaged in organized *daʿwa* activities or participated in Islamist political associations.

As with other sermon listeners I came to know in Cairo, Ahmad emphasized the utility of sermon tapes as a form of pious relaxation, similar to reading or listening to the Quran, a practice that calmed the mind and body while fortifying the soul. As he described it during one of our meetings:

> Remember when we were sitting at Muhammad's once and we played a tape of [the *khatib*[3]] Muhammad Hassan, you felt relaxed [*istirkhaʾ*]? This is what can happen, this is the opening of the heart [literally, "chest": *inshirah al-sadr*], the tranquility [*itmiʾnan*] that makes you want to pray, read the Quran, makes you want to get closer to God, to think [*tafakkir*] more about religion [*din*]. When you listen to a sermon, it helps you put aside all of your worries about work and money by reminding you of God. You remember that you will be judged and that fills you with fear [*khawf*] and makes you feel humility [*khushuʿ*]

1. Summons, call (Arabic); "*daʿwa* activities" are intended to morally guide and improve the Muslim community.
2. Religious scholar.
3. *Khaṭīb*, preacher (pl. *khuṭabāʾ*; Arabic).

and repentance [*nadam*]. The shaykh teaches you about Islam, what it requires of you, so you won't make errors.

As with most of those I met in Cairo who listened to sermon tapes, Ahmad seldom employed them in an exact or rigorous manner. Rarely, for example, would he listen at precise times of the day according to a fixed schedule. He most often put on tapes in the evenings, after he had returned from work, sometimes inviting a friend from the neighborhood to join him, especially if he had a new tape to play. On such occasions I would often be invited as well. We would usually sit in his small living room, drinking tea while listening to the tape on his portable tape player. While listening, Ahmad or someone else would often interject comments on the content of the sermon: "Can that be true?" or "The shaykh's going to get in trouble for saying that!" or "I heard that *hadith* was inauthentic." During the more passional moments of the sermon, however, such verbal interjections were rare.

Often someone would light up a cigarette. When I asked Ahmad about the compatibility of smoking with sermon audition, he commented: "Of course smoking is wrong [*ghalat*]: you are hurting yourself, one of God's creations, and that is forbidden [*haram*]; and to do it while listening to a sermon, you know, that is especially bad: in the presence of Quranic verses, words about God and the prophets?!" Then, cracking a smile, and making a gesture of resignation with his hands, he added: "Yes, of course I know I shouldn't do it, but sometimes I still do. That's the kind of times we're living in!" While many of the people I met rejected cigarettes outright as *haram*, perhaps an equal number expressed views similar to Ahmad's.

Ahmad's brother, Hisham, who lived nearby with his wife and young child and who would drop by on occasion to listen to a tape, would criticize the group for not listening with the appropriate gravity. Hisham worked in the same plant as Ahmad, and the two of them would frequently undertake the one-hour bus trip to the work site together. He had spent many years in a sort of apprenticeship to a shaykh at a local mosque, where he had studied Quranic recitation (*tajwid*), the *hadith*, and various classical exegetical and doctrinal texts. Ahmad would often turn to him whenever he was unsure about the meaning of a particular Quranic verse, the correct form of a ritual act, or the validity of a statement made by a *khatib* on a tape. Hisham was particularly emphatic about questions of ritual practice, and, at our first meeting, spent twenty minutes explaining to me how most Egyptians fail to wash their ankles correctly when doing ablutions. He had begun listening to tapes while under the guidance of his shaykh. He greatly appreciated passionate oratory but also emphasized the benefit of more explicitly pedagogical tapes, those that provide information about such issues as the correct enactment of prayer, the responsibilities of husbands and wives, and the cleansing and burial of the dead, as well as on the proper interpretation of Quranic verses and *hadiths*. Given his taxing work schedule, Hisham could not devote as much time to his study with the shaykh as he used to, but he still liked to listen to sermon tapes in the evening together with his wife and children.

During one of his visits to Ahmad's house, Hisham commented that "most people only listen [*yasmaʿu*] to tapes, whereas to really benefit from them you need to listen carefully [*yunsit*—literally, to incline one's ear toward] to the preacher's words." The distinction invoked by Hisham is most commonly elaborated in relation to the audition of the Quran. The two terms he contrasts (*yasmaʿ* and *yunsit*), for example, often appear in those *fatawi* (nonbinding legal opinions, sing. *fatwa*) concerned with the proper attitude and state of mind to be assumed when listening to recitations of the Quran. The following, taken from an official publication of al-Azhar *fatawi*, is characteristic:

> One need listen intently [*yunsit*] rather than just hear [*yasmaʿ*], so it is done with intention [*qasd wa niyya*], and directing the senses [*hiss*] to the words in order to understand them, to comprehend their intentions and their meanings. As far as hearing [*al-samʿ*], it is what occurs without intention. Close attention [*al-insat*] entails a stillness [*sukun*] in order to listen so as not to be distracted by surrounding words. . . . God ordered man to listen to the Quran with attention . . . [and] listening intently is the means to ponder over [*tadabbar*] the meanings of the Quran. . . . It is a duty on all Muslims to educate themselves, and be guided by the etiquette [*adab*] of al-Quran.[4]

"Listening with attention," *al-insat*, is figured here as a complex sensory skill, one opposed to mere hearing (*samʿ*), understood as a passive and spontaneous receptivity. According to Hisham, such was the kind of attentiveness appropriate to those moments when one's heart is inclined toward God, as should be the case in sermon listening: "Many people in Egypt listen to sermon tapes for entertainment [*ka tasliyya*], as if it were popular music, or they play a tape while doing something else, driving a car, or selling groceries: they don't really follow the sermon with their hearts."

Ahmad disagreed with Hisham. While he concurred that some concentration was required, he argued that the state of ethical receptivity that enabled one to benefit from tape audition did not demand the sort of active concentration indicated by Hisham: "Of course, if you listen as one would read a newspaper or watch the television, distractedly or indifferently, which many do, then the benefit is much less. What is most important, however, is to listen with humility [*khushuʿ*], with a pious fear [*bi'l-taqwa*]. If you listen with a sensitive heart, filled with humility and faith [*iman*], then even if you are momentarily distracted, or the phone rings, or your thoughts stray for a moment, you will still benefit [*tastafid minu*]. And if the shaykh is good, he will incite in you these feelings, and keep you close to God." Thus, for Ahmad, sermon tapes afford the listener a type of relaxation from which one can nonetheless expect an enriching of one's knowledge and a purifying operation on the soul. For people like Ahmad, tapes enable a strengthening of the will and what many people refer to as an ability to resist the devil's whispers (*wasawis*). With repeated and sensitive listening, they can also help lead a listener to change his or her ways. In short, for Ahmad and others, listening to sermon tapes is understood as a means by which a range of Islamic virtues could be sedimented in one's character, enabling one to live more piously and avoid moral transgressions.

4. Shaykh Hasnain Muhammed Makhluf, "Salat al-jum 'a khalf al-mudhiaʿ ghayr ja'iza," in *al-Fatawa al-islamiyya*, al-Azhar (Cairo: al-Majlis al-aʿla li al-shu'un al-islamiyya, wizarat al-awqaf, 1950) [Hirschkind's note].

For many sermon listeners, the regular practice of audition also serves as a constant reminder to monitor their behavior for vices and virtues. Tapes help one to maintain a level of self-scrutiny (*muraqaba*) in regard to one's day-to-day activities and, when possible, to change or modify one's behavior. As Beha, a taxi driver with whom I would often exchange sermon tapes, told me:

> One of the main things gained from listening is that one is reminded what Islam really entails. It then becomes more likely that one will correct one's behavior and be guided from one's state of being astray. See, I am not very Islamic [pointing to his cigarette], I smoke, but when I hear these things on tape, I am encouraged, steered toward correct practice [*a'mal saliha*]. I gain enthusiasm [*hamas*] for doing what is right.

Beha lived in Imbaba, which is one of the poorest quarters of Cairo and is often viewed as a hotbed of Islamic militancy (see chapter 4, note 35[5]). He frequently put in eighteen-hour days behind the wheel in an attempt to feed his wife and two kids, and on such long days sermon tapes were his constant companion. As his comments suggest, Beha recognized that he often acted in ways that contradicted what he held to be morally appropriate behavior. While he viewed such contradictions as moral lapses of greater and lesser degrees, they were lapses he sought to overcome within a teleological process of learning, one that included, among other things, the audition of sermon tapes. Many of the young men I worked with in Egypt related their decision to become diligent in the performance of their Islamic duties to having been moved by a particularly powerful sermon, heard either on tape or live at the mosque.

There are other pleasures and benefits that sermon tapes provide as well. For example, for those who work in public transportation, sermon audition may simultaneously help them to achieve a state of closeness to God and allow them to remain calm and relaxed in the face of Cairo's maddening traffic conditions. As Beha commented on another occasion:

> I listen to sermons while I am driving because it soothes and relaxes me. So I don't get upset and begin to shout at the other drivers. Reading the Quran is even better, but I can't read and drive. Sometimes music works as well, but sermons are better. They give you religious knowledge, and make me remember God when I get too caught up in making a living. When I hear the tape while I am driving, and the shaykh talks about the Quran, or the Prophet, or death, or the grave, then I start to remember that everything I do will be judged, that my money, work, children all will be gone, and I will be judged for my good works alone. Then I say "I fear God in His Glory [*ataq allah 'azim*]." "May God forgive me [*astaghfar allah*]." This gives me strength, and calms me and leaves my heart open [*munsharih*].

5. As spaces of political opposition, some of these neighborhoods became radicalized to the extent that they sought to forcibly eject the state from what they defined as "their territories." The most striking case of this occurred in Imbaba, a neighborhood of over one million people where a self-proclaimed Islamic government attempted to oversee the administration of the area. In 1992, the state sent a military contingent of fourteen thousand soldiers to "retake" the neighborhood. While this is an extreme example, forms of neighborhood solidarity in opposition to the state have become widespread in Egypt in recent decades [Hirschkind's note].

The tape produces in those already rightly disposed the sensorially rich experience of *inshirah*—the Quranic concept referring to the opening of the heart that accompanies drawing near to God—and in doing so, allows one to better meet the stress and monotony of urban labor. In contexts where reading the Quran or praying is impractical, a sermon tape on the Death of the Prophet or the Heavenly Pool of Kawthar that awaits the virtuous in the hereafter delivers diversion with a mild ethical elixir to the right place at the right time.

Muhammad Subhi, the *khatib* from whom I took lessons in the art of preaching for over a year, would often emphasize this calming and bolstering effect of recorded sermons, at least sermons by those *khutaba'* he considered masterful at the art.

> Listening to the Quran or sermon tapes, it leads you to a state of relaxation, or *sakina*. What does *sakina* mean? It means the calm one feels knowing that only God can determine when one will die. A calm by which one can stand firm before all oppression. It means one can let the winds of the mass media blow—all their silly words about Islamic terrorists, the [Islamic militant organization] *al-gam'at al-islamiyya*, all the lies they throw out, all of the seductive images they surround us with—one can live in this swirl of falsehoods but not follow or be moved by them, remain calm and sure before them.

Here, the modulation of affect performed by the preacher on the tape enacts an ethical therapy on the listener, both relaxing the body and enhancing the listener's capacity for discernment in the face of moral danger—in Muhammad's example, the danger of being deceived by state propaganda and corrupted by impious entertainment. Muhammad, like many of those I worked with, would frequently put on a tape upon coming home from work after a day of frustrations and difficulties. The mechanical manipulation and modulation of affective-kinesthetic experience enacted by the tape made him feel, in his words, lighter, fresh, and relieved, and turned his thoughts to God and religion. In this way, cassette sermons offer a portable, self-administered technology of moral health and Islamic virtue, one easily adapted to the rhythms, movements, and social contexts characteristic of contemporary forms of work and leisure.

In addition, sermon tapes may even serve to automatically reorient the heart in relation to God when one has inadvertently committed a moral error. One of the men I met once while visiting Cairo University was a twenty-three-year-old student named Saif. Saif had grown up with sermons: his father had been a *khatib*, though he now worked as a censor (*mufattish*) for the Ministry of Religious Affairs, which sent him round to different mosques each week to ensure that preachers were not straying into "sensitive" (*hassassi*) topics. Despite his father's official position, both Saif and his father emphasized to me on a number of occasions their strong preference for the more oppositional *khutaba'* associated with the *da'wa* movement. On one occasion Saif explained to me why he made a point of regularly listening to sermon tapes:

> Let's say that you looked at a woman desirously during the day, without even being aware you were doing it. In other words, you committed an act of disobedience to God. You should immediately ask for God's forgiveness, but let's say you are rushing somewhere and by

> the time you get there you don't even remember what you did. Well when you hear the shaykh in the bus on the way home talking about Judgment Day, or the tortures of the grave you get worried and start to fear. Your predicament becomes clear: you are going to die. You had forgotten to fear, and without it, you were probably preparing a place for yourself in hell. Then you will say, God, I seek your forgiveness for my disobedience. Of course, you don't need a tape to do this, and you should do it automatically. But the tape helps if you forget. Especially if the tape is a really scary one.

Here, sermon media sustain one of the primary affective conditions of virtuous conduct, an active fear of God, consumed as both ethics and entertainment. As a device for the reanimation, modulation, and embodiment of pious sensibilities, cassette technology may be seen as a prosthetic of the modern virtuous subject: a mnemonic instrument that both enhances and supplements the capacity for memory, ethical feeling, and moral discernment while providing many of the pleasures of popular entertainment.

### *The Physiology of the Quran*

As I discuss in chapter 2, the utility of tape audition for the task of ethical self-improvement is founded on a language ideology foregrounding the performative dimension of godly speech and its capacity to reform and attune a rightly disposed heart.[6] The effect of sermon speech on a "rusted heart," as the *khatib* and prolific writer on the craft of sermons, Ali Mahfuz, describes it, is not just one of cleansing. Sermons are understood to evoke in the sensitive listener a particular set of ethical responses, foremost among them, fear (*khawf*), humility (*khushu'*), regret (*nadam*), repentance (*tawba*), and tranquility (*itmi'nan* or *sakina*). These terms appeared constantly in the descriptions of the people I worked with, as in the following comment by Beha:

> Tapes are always of benefit, whether on the torment of the grave ['*adhab al-qabr*], Judgment Day [*yawm al-qiyama*], death [*al-mawt*], on the most dangerous of sins [*kaba'ir*], or the headscarf [*hijab*]. You learn things you didn't know, and this is useful. And they restore you to [moral] health [*biyas-hfuna*]. Listening to a tape of a sermon you've already heard is a way of reinforcing what you've learned, strengthening the fear of God's punishments, so you won't commit a moral error [*ma'asi*]. This leaves your heart calm [*mutma'in*]. There are some people who just do what they should. Many others, however, they realize that the devil [*shaytan*] has got into their heads [*yuwaswasu*—literally, whispers to them], and is making them think that what is evil [*haram*] is actually good [*halal*]. By listening, they strengthen themselves against this, as it gets them to pray and read the Quran. Then they begin to regret [*nadam*] what they have done, and ask God for forgiveness [*istighfar*]. The tape, in other words, helps them to fight [*bijahiduna*] against the devil.

6. By "godly speech," I refer not only to the Quran but to a vast range of locutions. As Constance Padwick (*Muslim Devotions: A Study of Prayer-Manuals in Common Use* [Oxford: Oneworld Publications, 1996]) shows in her analysis of popular Islamic devotional sayings drawn from both Middle Eastern and South Asian materials, many of the expressions used in ordinary speech (prayers, supplications, and other pious locutions) are commonly understood to bestow ethical benefit to both speakers and listeners [Hirschkind's note].

As elaborated within classical Islamic moral doctrine, the affective dispositions Beha describes that endow a believer's heart with the capacities of moral discrimination necessary for proper conduct.[7] They are both virtues and states of emotional receptivity and response. Traditional texts on the task of moral refinement (*tahdhib al-nafs*) elaborate these dispositions extensively, as does contemporary *da'wa* literature. In order to understand how this terminology of ethical affect was employed by the men I worked with, however, it will be useful to draw on some of the contemporary writings that they themselves used and frequently referred to. The following discussion comes from an article published in *al-Tawhid*, a monthly journal put out by the *da'wa* association al-Ansar al-Sunna al-Muhammadiyya, and often purchased or referred to by those I worked with. The article focuses on the effect of particular Quranic verses, when used by a *khatib*, on the moral condition of a faithful Muslim listener. Drawing from the exegetical works of classical scholars in regard to the interpretation of a verse from the Quranic chapter entitled "al-Zumar" (The throngs),[8] the author notes:

> What is meant here is that when the true people of faith, the people of the eternal and deeply rooted doctrine [*al-'aqida*] hear the verses of warning [*al-wa'id*] their flesh trembles in fear, their hearts are filled with despair [*inqabadat qulubuhum*], a violent angst shakes their backs [*irta'adat fara'isahum*], and their hearts become intoxicated with fear and dread. But if they then hear the verses of mercy [*al-rahma*] and forgiveness [*istighfar*], their flesh becomes filled with delight [*inbasatat juluduhum*], their chests are opened and relaxed [*insharahat suduruhum*], and their hearts are left tranquil [*itma'annat qulubuhum*].[9]

What is described here is a kind of moral physiology, the affective-kinesthetic experience of a body permeated by faith (*iman*) when listening to a *khatib*'s discourse. The description is derived directly from numerous verses of the Quran depicting the impact of godly speech on a rightly disposed listener, as in the following verse from the chapter entitled "al-Anfal" (Spoils of war): "Believers are only they whose hearts tremble whenever God is mentioned, and whose faith is strengthened whenever his messages are conveyed unto them" (Quran 8:2). This particular responsiveness constitutes what might be termed a Quranically tuned body and soul. This attunement, according to Badawi, is a characteristic of a person who is close to God. For such a person, auditory reception involves the flesh, back, chest, and heart—in short, the entire moral person as a unity of body and soul. To listen properly, one might say, is to engage in a performance, the articulated gestures of a dance.

The moral physiology that is invoked and refined in the context of sermon listening is elaborated in a plethora of visually striking images, found both in the Quran and in a vast body of exegetical and ethical writings.

7. See Majid Fakhry, *A History of Islamic Philosophy* (New York: Columbia University Press, 1983); Toshihiko Izutsu, *Ethico-Religious Concepts in the Quran* (Montreal: McGill University Press, 1966) and *The Concept of Belief in Islamic Theology* (Salem, NH: Ayer, 1988); and Mohamed Ahmed Sherif, *Ghazali's Theory of Virtue* (Albany: State University of New York Press, 1975) [Hirschkind's note].
8. Q 39.
9. Abdul Nazim Badawi, "Al-Quran wa atharihi fi al-qulub," *Al-Tawhid* 25 (3): 11–12 [Hirschkind's note].

Note, for example, the author's description above of how one relaxes in the process of hearing the verses of mercy and thus moves closer to God. The term used both here and by those I worked with in Cairo to denote this state of calm and relaxation is *inshirah* (literally, opening of the chest). As an ethical concept indicating the joyous relaxation that often follows acts of supplication or seeking forgiveness, it embeds strong affective and kinesthetic contours: to convey its meaning to others almost always involves an act of opening up the arms, raising and relaxing the chest, turning the face upward. The experience of *inshirah* has its origins in an event mentioned both in the Quran (in the chapter entitled al-Sharh)[1] and in many *hadiths*. It is recounted that on the night of the Prophet Muhammad's ascension to heaven (*al-isra'*), God opened his chest and took from his heart all the resentment, rancor, and lust and replaced them with virtues of faith and knowledge. The account, in other words, connects the purity of the soul with the powerful image of God opening up the chest—what Muhammad, the *khatib* I studied with, described to me as a "surgical operation" (*'amaliyya jirahiyya*). This connection provides the authoritative textual basis upon which a particular pattern of gestural and kinesthetic reponse is both conceptually *and experientially* linked to a moral state (*inshirah*).[2] For insomuch as the reading—or rather, recitation—of the event occurs within the disciplinary context of a Quranic education, it contributes to the training and inculcation of sensory habits. The account is not a dispassionate description but a story whose contours are learned with the body, in all of its kinesthetic and synaesthetic dimensions.

* * *

# MAIMUNA HUQ

## *From* Reading the Qur'an in Bangladesh: The Politics of "Belief" among Islamist Women[†]

### *Introduction*

In Muslim communities in contemporary South Asia and other Muslim-majority areas, informal religious lesson circles are proliferating rapidly as mass higher education brings more Muslims under the umbrella of

1. The first verse of "al-Sharh" ("The Opening-Up of the Heart," Quran 94) begins: "Have we not opened up thy heart, and lifted from thee the burden that had weighed so heavily on thy back?" [Hirschkind's note].
2. My argument here bears a certain similarity to that put forward by a number of cognitive linguists. In *Metaphors We Live By* (Chicago: University of Chicago Press, 1980), George Lakoff and Mark Johnson suggest that metaphor, as a process by which we characterize one domain of meaning in terms of another, is fundamental to much of our everyday discourse and not simply a creative literary device. In later writings, these authors argue that such cross-domain mapping involves what they refer to as "image schemata," cognitive constructs grounded in repeated patterns of bodily experience that are then applied to other regions of discourse and experience (Lakoff and Johnson, *Philosophy in the Flesh: The Embodied Mind and Its Challenge to Western Thought* [New York: Basic Books, 1999]; Johnson, *The Body in the Mind: The Bodily Basis of Meaning, Imagination, and Reason* [Chicago: University of Chicago Press, 1987]). * * * Where my argument here departs from these authors is in its focus on the specific methods of inculcation through which such perceptual patterning is learned [Hirschkind's note].

† From *Modern Asian Studies* 42 (2008): 457–60, 465–71. Copyright © 2008 Cambridge University Press. Reprinted with permission of Cambridge University Press. Except as indicated, all notes are Huq's.

standardized, nationalized education systems. These study circles often revolve around the study of compendia of Qur'anic commentary or exegesis, *hadith* (written records of sayings and acts attributed to the Prophet Muhammad) such as the thirteenth-century *Riyad al-Salihin*, as well as Qur'anic commentaries and theological texts produced by authoritative traditional religious scholars, contemporary or recent.[1]

While some scholars have discussed contemporary commentaries on the Qur'an and their authors, fewer have focused on the users of these commentaries and of other Islamic literature, or on the specifics of audience engagement with these texts.[2] Thus, for instance, while the works of Sayyid Qutb (which are central to the Muslim Brotherhood, the leading Islamic movement in the Middle East and North Africa) have been analysed by several scholars,[3] some important questions are left unanswered: How are Qutb's ideas explained to adherents on the ground? What styles of discourse are employed in lesson circles? Which ideas are emphasized and which marginalized, and what kinds of techniques are used to do so? Do lesson circles actually shape how individual members feel, think, express themselves, and act? If so, how, and to what extent? Which groups are reading which texts or selections from texts?[4]

As some scholars have noted, many contemporary Islamic activists are not recipients of traditional religious education. Rather, they are studying, or have studied, the sciences and humanities in nonreligious public schools and universities.[5] What, then, are the specific processes whereby such activists become familiar with Islamic texts and learn to view their own experiences and duties in the light of this religious literature? How, in turn, do they view this literature through the prism of their experiences?

1. One example of such a text, popular among devout Muslims in the Arab world and increasingly among diasporic Muslims, is the seminal work of the medieval Salafi theologian Abu Hamid al-Ghazali [1058–1111], *On Disciplining the Soul and on Breaking the Two Desires*. An example of an authoritative Islamic text popular among literate pious Muslim communities in South Asia, particularly Muslim women, is the reformist prescriptive treatise or advice manual *Heavenly Ornaments*, written in northern India in the early 1900s by Ashraf Ali Thanawi (1864–1943), a scholar trained in the Deobandi tradition of orthodox Islamic education in South Asia.
2. Dale F. Eickelman, 'Islamic religious commentary and lesson circles: Is there a Copernican revolution?' *Aporemata*, 4 (2004), 121–146.
3. See, for example, Gilles Kepel, *Muslim Extremism in Egypt: The Prophet and the Pharaoh*, translated by Jon Rothschild (Berkeley and Los Angeles: University of California Press, 1993 [1985]); Ahmad S. Moussalli, *Radical Islamic Fundamentalism: The Ideological and Political Discourse of Sayyid Qutb* (Beirut: American University of Beirut, 1992); Olivier Carré, *Mysticism and Politics: A Critical Reading of Fi Zilal al-Qur'an by Sayyid Qutb (1906–1966)*, translated from the French by Carol Artigues and revised by W. Shepard (Leiden; Boston: Brill, 2003); Sayed Khatab, *The Power of Sovereignty: The Political and Ideological Philosophy of Sayyid Qutb* (New York, NY: Routledge, 2006). [Qutb (1906–1996), an Egyptian Qur'ān scholar, has helped inspire later militant Sunni movements—editor's note.]
4. For an unusual and rich description of specific texts read by participants in a particular Islamic movement, in this case the transnational Islamic revivalist group Tabligh Jamaat, see Barbara D. Metcalf, 'Living Hadith in the Tablighi Jama'at,' *The Journal of Asian Studies*, 52, 3 (1993), 584–608.
5. This has been noted for Islamic activism from South Asia to Southeast Asia to the Middle East and North Africa. For example, see Fadwa El-Guindi, 'Veiling infitah with Muslim ethic: Egypt's contemporary Islamic movement,' *Social Problems*, 28 (1981), 465–83; Dale F. Eickelman, 'Mass higher education and the religious imagination in contemporary Arab societies,' *American Ethnologist*, 19, 4 (November 1992); 643–55; Razia Akhter Banu, *Islam in Bangladesh* (Leiden, New York, Koln: E. J. Brill, 1992); Seyyed Vali Reza Nasr, *The Vanguard of the Islamic Revolution* (Berkeley and Los Angeles: University of California Press, 1994); Suzanne Brenner, 'Reconstructing self and society: Javanese Muslim women and "the veil",' *American Ethnologist* 23, 4 (1996), 673–97; Nilufer Göle, *The Forbidden Modern* (Ann Arbor: The University of Michigan Press, 1996). [*Infitāḥ* (opening, Arabic) was the program of economic liberalization begun in Egypt by its then president, Anwar Sadat—editor's note.]

I will outline answers to some of the foregoing questions in the context of a particular women's Islamist student organization in Bangladesh, BICSa (Bangladesh Islamic Chatri Sangstha, i.e., Bangladesh Female Students' Islamic Association). This group actively harnesses Qur'anic verses to re-cultivate young, educated Bangladeshi Muslim women as activists committed to the task of Islamizing self, community and state. By focusing on this process, I will show that such Islamist lesson circles can be a key site for the production of a particular form of Islamic subjectivity. In fact, I will argue that lesson circles play a central role in the sustenance and expansion of Islamic movements in Bangladesh. They do so by helping reshape activists' conceptions of self, religious duty and others through a rhetoric that deploys specific notions of religiosity and religious identity, culture, state, the global Muslim community or *ummah*, and the current world order.

It is often in lesson circles that a lay-educated Bangladeshi trained in nominally secular public schools first engages the contents of the BICSa movement's message, especially notions of pristine Muslimhood and those interpretations of Qur'anic and *hadith* teachings privileged by the organization. Yet, as I will also show, a lesson circle not only manufactures consent but also generates, authorizes and equips dissent from the same body of belief.

*Lesson Circles, Education and Print: The BICSa Setting*

BICSa lesson circles, especially those centred around *tafsir* (Qur'anic exegesis), are designed to attract recruits to the organization, deepen the knowledge and enhance the faith of the active members BICSa calls 'workers', and train workers in the art of disseminating Islamic knowledge.[6] BICSa lesson circles are part of a range of practices identified by some scholars as increasingly constitutive of 'public Islam'[7] and are enabled, in part, by the advent of mass higher education and media technologies.

* * *

*Background Islamic Knowledge*

Some Qur'anic commentary or exegesis is part of the background knowledge of many Muslims in Muslim-majority societies.[8] In Bangladesh (as in many other Muslim countries), the primary site at which this knowledge is gained is the *madrasa* or traditional religious school, where jurisprudence

6. It is important to note, however, that some lesson circles, particularly those conducted by and for women, are not formally connected to any Islamic organization but by individual persons as acts of piety. Such circles centre more on Qur'anic commentary delivered by the group leader than on group discussion. The goal of such grassroots circles is less to train participants in authoritative Islamic knowledge than to re-moralize individuals and families in a particular neighbourhood (and often in specific socio-economic groups) by imparting a basic knowledge of Qur'anic prescriptions, and to do so by 'returning to the source'—i.e., the Qur'an, as opposed to popular manual-style works such as *Heavenly Ornaments* (see note 1 supra).
7. For example, see the collection of essays edited by Armando Salvatore and Mark LeVine, *Religion, Social Practice, and Contested Hegemonies: Reconstructing the Public Sphere in Muslim Majority Societies* (New York: Palgrave Macmillan, 2005). Also see the volume edited by Armando Salvatore and Dale F. Eickelman, *Public Islam and the Common Good* (Leiden, Boston: Brill, 2004).
8. Eickelman, 'Islamic Religious Commentary and Lesson Circles: Is There a Copernican Revolution?', 121.

studies (*fiqh*) and commentaries on the Qur'an and *ahadith* are the core of the curriculum. An important secondary site is the modern public school, where Islam is one among the many subjects taught within a set national curriculum in first through tenth grade.[9] While this subject is not generally considered important, since it has little bearing on educational or career success, it is taught as part of the state's effort to produce morally upright subjects with a basic knowledge of the religion of 88% of Bangladeshis. Parents are thus relieved of some of the responsibility for religious education. Friday sermons at the mosque, popular public preaching (*waaz mahfil*), and a few weekly religious programs on radio and television are tertiary sites for the production of generalized public religious knowledge.

One reason for the effectiveness of Qur'anic lesson circles, I suggest, is that these creatively exploit the 'background' or 'informal' Islamic knowledge to which many Bangladeshis are exposed. Qur'anic lesson circles build and elaborate on the kind of Qur'anic exegesis and the modern and rigorously classificatory or compartmentalized style of religious discourse introduced early on, albeit sketchily, in the non-religious public schools that most students from the relatively well-to-do families in Bangladesh attend.

## *The Structure of a Qur'anic Lesson Circle*

The lesson circle (*qoraner pat chakra*) is one of the two basic styles of pedagogy that BICSa employs to confer Qur'anic knowledge. The Qur'anic lesson circle—other varieties include the 'book lesson circle' and 'topic-based lesson circle'—often lasts 2 h or more, allowing for a relatively detailed exploration of Qur'anic verses (pre-assigned for study at the end of the previous meeting) in the light of exegetical texts, usually Mawdudi's[1] exegetical work *Tafheemul Qur'an*. In the course of such a circle, individuals are prompted by a group leader to discuss different assigned verses. Each person's micro-presentation or commentary may be followed by discussion. The overall result is a round-table conversation, formal in tone and interspersed with questions, answers and comments.

A Qur'anic lesson circle is supposed to emphasize practical examples over theoretical discussions and citations from the Qur'an and *ahadith*. As a BICSa leader explained to a group participating in a Qur'anic lesson circle for the first time, 'The main purpose of a group meeting is to transform theoretical Islamic knowledge into practical knowledge so that we can use this knowledge constantly in molding ourselves (*atyagatan*) and in drawing others to the movement and molding them well as future Islamic workers (*karmigatan*).'[2] In the course of a lesson circle, references are made primarily to texts by Mawdudi and secondarily to those by other

9. In Bangladesh, even though traditional religious schools have continued to receive some state aid, partly in order not to alienate the *ulamas* and partly to limit educational expenses, state support has been increasingly confined to public schools, with funds and key privileges (such as access to government jobs) shifting increasingly to graduates of nonreligious state schools. The majority of students, especially from the urban middle and upper classes, therefore attend modern, non-religious public schools. [*Ulamas*: the learned of Islam, members of the religious hierarchy—editor's note.]
1. Abū al-A'lā' Mawdūdī (1903–1979), Indian-Pakistani Islamic ideologue who helped guide the formation of Pakistan as an Islamic state. In 1941, he founded the political party Jamā'at-i Islāmī (the Islamic Party) [editor's note].
2. Fieldnotes, Qur'anic lesson circle at a training program for members of the 'worker' cadre from all over the country, Dhaka, 15 July 2000.

leading Jamaat thinkers. Top-level Jamaat leaders in Bangladesh such as Golam Azam and Matiyur Rahman Nizami are also occasionally cited as authorities. These leaders sometimes deliver lectures and conduct lesson circles for members of the highest cadre in BICSa. These members, called *sadasyas*, are considered sufficiently qualified to oversee group meetings and lesson circles.

### *Group Study of* Surah as-Saff

The Qur'anic verses preassigned for the meeting I am about to describe are among the most widely studied in BICSa, namely, verses 1–4 and 10–13 of a *Surah* (a chapter in the Qur'an) named *as-Saff.*[3] I have also chosen to describe this particular lesson circle because the themes extracted from these verses in the circle relate to three key concepts of BICSa's discursive regime. Most BICSa training programmes and the micro-technologies that constitute them—the 'lesson', 'lesson circle', 'report preservation' and supererogatory prayers—are oriented around the conceptual triad of 'belief' (*iman*), 'hypocrisy' (*monafeqi*) and 'struggle in the path of Allah' (*jihaad fii sabiilillah*). Below, I describe how these key concepts, particularly 'belief' and 'hypocrisy', are explained and discussed in a Qur'anic framework and are harnessed to the task of reforming oneself and others as subjects of an Islamic ideology. This details how the practice of lesson circles within the Islamist movement in Bangladesh embodies a conceptual domain that is simultaneously deliberative and disciplinary.[4]

The organizational context for the meeting I am about to describe is as follows: In the capital city Dhaka, where BICSa is strongest and where I conducted most of my field research, lesson circles are often led by senior BICSa leaders who usually occupy the highest administrative positions and therefore spend much time in the organization's headquarters or central office. The meeting concerned took place in a room in this office in Dhaka, which was simply furnished with a bed, a wardrobe, a desk and chair, and a valet stand for headscarves and *borkha* overcoats. The presence of the bed and wardrobe is explained by the fact that senior activists must occasionally work late at the office and so find it convenient occasionally to spend the night there. It is also used by activists from outside Dhaka who use the office as a temporary home till they can find more permanent housing in overcrowded dormitories. Following occasional episodes of especially violent conflict involving dominant, leftist–nationalist student groups and the Bangladesh Islami Chatra Shibir—BICSa's male counterpart, the openly political student wing of the Islamist party Jamaate Islami—BICSa women who fear violent retaliation from opposite groups on college and university campuses use the office as a temporary abode till tensions subside.

On the hot, hazy afternoon of 24 March 2003, I was in this room with Nabila, the lesson circle leader or moderator, waiting for the other seven participants to arrive. Since a group meeting is often 2–3 h long, it must begin early enough in the afternoon so that participants can reach home before dusk, at which time parents begin to worry for their daughters'

3. *Al-Ṣaff,* "The Ranks" (Q 61) [editor's note].
4. Charles Hirschkind, 'Civic virtue and religious reason: An Islamic counter public,' *Cultural Anthropology* 16/1 (2001).

safety. Participants whose classes continue beyond noon must therefore come directly from school. Some of these women may grab a quick bite if they reach the office before the meeting (the office also has a kitchen). Resident women cook several times a week, so there is always some cooked food in the refrigerator, but meeting participants must go hungry if they arrive at the office too late to eat. BICSa women sometimes joke among themselves that almost every activist they know suffers from 'gastric', an unpleasant stomach condition that can result from going without food for long hours. On the day in question, Nabila herself had arrived hungry from her part-time job as a schoolteacher. She did not eat even as we waited, eager to begin the meeting as soon as most of the participants arrived so that she could let them go home before dusk. All study-circle attendees are junior in rank to the moderator and most are younger as well, so often the moderator feels responsible for the well-being of the women in her group and develops a relationship of affection and concern towards them.

* * *

Nabila is a petite, slender woman no more than 5 feet tall, but used to talking to audiences. She began with a ritual invocation of the name of God (*basmalah*), invocations of blessings upon the Prophet Muhammad (*darud shareef*), and thanks to God for enabling the participants to gather for the meeting. She then chose a member, Bilkis, to recite the assigned Qur'anic verses (Surah as-Saff: 1–4, 10–13) from memory in the original Arabic. Bilkis did so. Once the various aspects of her recitation had been diligently critiqued—fluidity of recitation, correct or incorrect joining of the last letter of a particular word to the first letter of the next, pronunciation of individual letters—Nabila asked another member, Nargis, to read out the Bangla translation of the same verses from Mawdudi's *Tafheemul Qur'an* (*Tafheem* for short). Nargis was then asked to discuss, according to the standard order of points, the 'naming' (*namkaran*) of the *surah*, the context of its revelation (*naziler sthankal* or, more traditionally, *shaane nuzul*), and its gist or 'subject matter' (*mool bishaybastu*). Bilkis was also requested to discuss each verse in the set in a numerical order. Having attended numerous 'worker meetings' designed for initiates, to which the study of Qur'anic exegesis is central, lesson circle participants who are relatively advanced are well familiar with these discursive categories (e.g., 'naming' and 'context for revelation'), which are also commonly found in modern Qur'anic exegetical works such as *Tafheemul Qur'an*. Below, let us follow the activists' and the group's handling of these categories in order.

#### SIGNIFICANCE OF DISCUSSION OF NAMING AND CONTEXT OF SURAH

In study circles, discussion of the naming of a Surah and of the place, time and socio-historical context of its revelation (i.e., whether during the Prophet Muhammad's stay in Makka or Madina and prevailing circumstances) establishes continuity with the authoritative style of Mawdudi's exegesis. More traditional forms of Qur'anic exegesis tend to ignore historical and socio-political contexts and application to personal life and to focus instead on the philological aspects of the text and its underlying values, which are understood as eternal, impervious to time and place.[5] In BICSa's Mawdudi-derived style of exegesis, an emphasis on the 'sociopolitical context' of the revelation (*shaane nuzul*) of a particular set of verses enables BICSa to privilege certain verses by drawing analogies between events experienced by the Prophet with his companions and by contemporary Islamic activists. BICSa thus legitimizes the narrative frame it uses to interpret current events and its strategies for coping with these events. The eternal nature of Qur'anic guidance, especially as embodied in its numerous verses concerning the struggle between 'good' and 'evil', is reaffirmed but in such a way as to establish its relevance to the flux of history, a way which increases the plausibility of the Islamist project. Moreover, only certain sections of certain Qur'anic chapters (*surahs*) are included in the BICSa syllabus, a selectiveness that implicitly passes a distinctly human set of judgments on the relevance of various scriptures for the present time. However, few BICSa activists would acknowledge this selectiveness.[6]

### DISCUSSION OF SUBJECT MATTER

Nargis described the subject matter of the two groups of verses, drawing on *Tafheem*, as follows:

> Verses 1 through 4 describe the greatness of Allah. These also mention a particular quality found among the believers that Allah dislikes and the kind of dedication Allah favors. Verses 10 through 13 state that the only way to success both in this world and in the hereafter is to have sincere belief in Allah and in His Prophet, and to wage *jihad* in the cause of Allah through sacrificing life and property. The obedient will be rewarded in the Hereafter with paradise, and in this world with Allah's help and victory.

These remarks were followed by an extended discussion in which Nabila asked one member after another to discuss a single verse or sometimes two verses.[7] The explanation of each verse offered by the chosen participant—based on Tafheem, other Qur'anic verses, *ahadith*, and

5. Dale F. Eickelman, 'Qur'anic Commentary, Public Space, and Religious Intellectuals in the Writings of Said Nursi,' in *Islam at the Crossroads: On the Life and Thought of Bediuzzaman Said Nursi*, ed. Ibrahim M. Abu-Rabi (Albany: State University of New York Press, 2003), 54.
6. This is not to say that BICSa considers the other parts of the Qur'an to be less important; as BICSa activists advance in levels of piety and knowledge, the syllabus broadens accordingly, and one is expected to study an increasing number of Qur'anic verses and chapters. For the most advanced BICSa activists, who are usually a small group and comprise the core organizational leadership, the ideal is to study each and every chapter of the Qur'an. What is at stake here, therefore, is BICSa's ability to familiarize low- and mid-level activists working under significant time constraints with a selection of materials. BICSa sees itself as racing against time—the duration of each member's academic career—to produce authentic Muslims who will counter what it sees as the growing secularization of Muslim Bangali (Bengali) society and culture specifically and the global Muslim community of the *ummah* generally. For mid-level activists such as lesson-circle participants, BICSa's syllabus therefore features verses and chapters that equally emphasize both the cultivation of virtuous dispositions and the integral necessity of striving in the path of God both personally (in private, within oneself) and sociopolitically (in relations with others, especially Muslims, and in the public sphere).
7. Some study-circle leaders employ another method, which is to group two or more verses thematically for discussion. They feel that this forces an activist, trained to follow Mawdudi's *Tafheem* closely, to develop her own approach to the study of the Qur'an by beginning to think about the verses for herself instead of simply paraphrasing Mawdudi. Nabila felt that paraphrasing Mawdudi's exegesis for each verse and then supplementing that exegesis with knowledge derived from other sources was a more thorough approach; this way, the material 'becomes truly imprinted on the heart' (*mone genthe jai*). However, sometimes even Nabila would resort to a discussion organized around thematically grouped verses when there was too little time for the quantity of verses being considered.

practical examples—was followed by supplementary or critical comments by other participants, including the moderator. At the end of the discussion of each verse, Nabila would prompt individual activists for questions and then close with responses to questions raised and comments offered.

* * *

# Pharmacology and Fortune-telling

ABDULLAHI OSMAN EL-TOM

## *From* Drinking the Koran: The Meaning of Koranic Verses in Berti Erasure†

Islam, probably more than any other religion, connotes the image of a great tradition which has imposed itself on culturally diverse populations and gradually united them in a monolithic belief whose basic tenets stem from the Koran and the prophetic tradition. This image is bolstered by the fact that, despite the recognized cultural diversity of the Muslim world[1] which has been perpetuated through the differing interpretations of Islam embodied in its holy text, little research has been done on the meaning of the Koranic text at the local level. The lack of such research, in its own turn, perpetuates the false image of a uniform meaning of the Koranic text throughout the Muslim world.

This article is concerned with the meaning imposed on the Koranic text by graduates of Koranic schools (*khalwa*) among the Berti of the northern Darfur Province of the Republic of the Sudan.

* * *

* * * As in other parts of Muslim Black Africa, Berti Islam is a fusion of orthodox beliefs and practices and elements belonging to the indigenous pre-Islamic religious system. Indeed, Islam and the pagan cults form a dual axis constituting different recipes for social action. In general, Berti adherence to Islam is more emphasized at the collective level manifested in public rituals such as religious festival prayers, rain prayers, etc. At the individual level, as in the case of the daily Muslim prayers and ritual of ablution, Islam is grossly neglected by the Berti. Women in general are more pagan than men.[2]

Islam has also been promoted by the traditional Koranic schools, which are geared towards the memorizing of the Koran: the literacy which is taught in them is seen as means to this end. Successful graduates of these schools who claim to have committed the entire Koran to memory are

† From *Popular Islam South of the Sahara*, ed. J. D. Y. Peel and Charles C. Stuart (Manchester: Manchester University Press, in association with *Africa*: Journal of the International African Institute, [1987]), pp. 414–19, 429–30. Copyright © 1985 International African Institute. Reprinted with the permission of Cambridge University Press. El-Tom includes a note of acknowledgment: "Fieldwork for this paper was carried out between June 1980 and June 1981 and sponsored by the University of Gezira. I am grateful to it for its general assistance and to L. Holy for his comments on this paper." Except as indicated, all notes are his.

1. See C. Geertz, *Islam Observed* (New Haven: Yale University Press, 1968).
2. See J. S. Trimingham, *The Influence of Islam upon Africa* (London: Longman, 1968), p. 46.

known as *fakis*.[3] * * * Among the Berti they act as religious leaders of individual village communities, Koranic teachers, healers, diviners and providers of amulets. There are at least one or two fakis in each Berti village, one of whom is collectively contracted by village members to lead their religious rituals. He commands his people in all public prayers and attendance at *rites de passage* in the village is also among his duties.

* * *

Berti religious medication is almost entirely causal and the particular force which produces diseases with different symptoms can always be dealt with using the same Koranic verses. Symptomatic treatment of disease is also known and is applied particularly in the case of diseases which are attributed to 'natural' causes such as the weather, ordinary accidents, etc. Another important activity of the faki is to write some Koranic verses on both sides of a wooden slate (*lōh*) using a pen made of a sharpened millet stalk and ink (*dawāi*) made of a fermented paste of soot and gum arabic. The written text is then washed off with water which is drunk by the faki's clients. The water is referred to as *mihāi* (from the verb *yamha*, to erase) and, following Al-Safi,[4] I have translated this term as 'erasure'.

The use of both amulets and erasure derives from the belief in the power of the Koranic verses, the names of God and the other divine inscriptions which they contain. These are believed to cure diseases, to protect against specific malevolent forces and to enable the client to achieve various desirable goals.

Although the drinking of the Koranic texts seems to be widespread only on the periphery of the Islamic world,[5] the view that the Koran has a medical value is not merely the invention of Black Africans.

It is contained in the Koran itself:

> We send down (stage by stage)
> In the Koran that which
> Is a healing and a mercy . . .
> [sura 7: 82][6]

The notion of uttering the divine names for various purposes is similarly borrowed from the Koran:

> The most beautiful names
> Belong to God:
> So call on Him by them . . .
> [sura 7: 180]

The phrase 'call on Him' is perhaps better translated as 'invoke Him' (by His attributes). The original word is *udū* (invoke) which derives from the word *du'ā* (invoking), and the latter term is used by the Berti in referring to rain prayers or any prayers performed to ensure welfare or to alleviate

3. The term *faki* may be a corruption of either the word *faqīh* (jurisprudent), or the word *faqīr* (Sufi mendicant) [editor's note].
4. Ahmed al-Safi, *Native Medicine in the Sudan* (Khartoum: Khartoum University Press, 1970), p. 30.
5. For West Africa, see Lamin O. Sanneh, *The Jakhanke: The History of an Islamic Clerical People of the Senegambia* (London: International African Institute, 1979).
6. [Abdullah Yusuf] Ali's edition of the Koran (1958), published at Lahore, is used for all Koranic verses quoted in this paper. [All bracketed citations in the text are El-Tom's—editor's note.]

misfortune at the communal level. Although it is spiritual healing which is meant here according to the theological interpretation of the Koran,[7] the Berti understand these verses as recommending and justifying the use of erasure as medicine.

The Koran is regarded as containing divine power; thus, to possess the Koranic texts renders an individual powerful and protects him against misfortunes and malevolent forces. The highest form of the possession of the Koran is its commitment to memory, which amounts to its internalization in the head, the superior part of the body, whence it can be instantly reproduced by recitation. But the Koran can also be internalized in the body by being drunk. Although drinking the Koran is seen as being far less effective than memorizing it, it is superior to carrying it on the body through the use of amulets. A major disadvantage of amulets is that they are liable to be lost, left behind or rendered ineffective by exposure to ritual pollution.

Which particular Koranic verses are to be used for erasure or amulets is not taught in the Koranic schools. A faki has to gather such knowledge from his associates or from published books which are available in the local markets and which are used exclusively by fakis. The majority of these books are recent reprints of literature originally written during the early Islamic civilization and most of them are currently imported from Egypt, Iran, Lebanon and Saudi Arabia. Their contents are centred on early Islamic medicine with particular emphasis on the 'magical' use of the Koran and other divine inscriptions. A few of these books are exclusively devoted to the description of Islamic rituals.

In addition to at least one handwritten copy of the Koran, each faki keeps a small library containing some of these published books as well as a handwritten private book, referred to as umbatri, which consists of a collection of extracts copied from other handwritten or printed sources. Apart from Koranic verses or sometimes whole chapters, both amulets and erasure use various signs and tables of letters, numbers and names of prophets, jinns[8] and devils or specific adversaries of the client. The following discussion of erasure ignores these signs and tables, the main concern being with explaining the indigenous reasons for the selection of particular Koranic verses and the meanings imposed on them.

Most Berti villagers drink erasures once or twice a year for one reason or another. The decision to ask a faki to prepare an erasure may be triggered off by an illness, starting a business, getting involved in a dispute, setting out on a journey, etc. There are, indeed, countless situations which might prompt someone to drink an erasure and different people are obviously motivated by different concerns.

* * *

Depending on the length of the text and the number of times it has to be written, writing an erasure can take anything from a few hours to several weeks. As an erasure is given to the client in small portions, he has to consume each dose before he gets the next one. There is no strict

7. Abdulla Yusuf Ali, *The Holy Qurān Text: Translation and Commentary*, 3 vols. (Lahore: Imperial Printing Works, 1938), pp. 718 and 396.
8. The third class of intelligent beings (together with humans and angels) for whom salvation is possible. According to Q 55:15, God created them from smokeless fire [editor's note].

timing for taking it. An erasure is normally received in a small bowl or bottle and the client can either drink the whole lot at once or take it in small doses during the course of the day. The next day he asks the faki for more until the whole prescription has been drunk. An erasure can be prepared for and shared by more than one client and it is a quite common practice to order one erasure for all one's children. Despite the worry about the exact number of times each Koranic verse must be copied in the erasure, sharing the erasure takes place in a relaxed manner and no effort is made to ensure its equal distribution, which would easily be possible if, for example, teacups were used for measuring it. The erasure is taken from the same container by a number of people in exactly the same way as ordinary food and drink is consumed. During the time when he is taking an erasure the client must not commit adultery and, according to some people, he also has to refrain from sexual intercourse and from drinking beer. In spite of their view that drinking beer does not contravene any Islamic proscription, the Berti believe that, if beer and erasure are taken on the same day, the latter will not be blessed by God and consequently will not function.

A few Koranic chapters or verses used in erasures are known, at least by their titles, to most Berti adults. These are used for the most common complaints which require erasures and the client can order them by name. Other less frequently used Koranic passages are not widely known. With these, the client may describe his situation, leaving the choice of the appropriate verses to the faki. The common Koranic chapters which are generally known to most adults include the Unity chapter (used to counter the evil eye), the Mankind and Dawn chapters[9] (used against sorcery), and the Throne verses[1] (used as a protection against devils).[2] The Throne verses are also used when the erasure is ordered simply to ensure the client's good health and for protection against any unforeseen misfortune in the future. Their appropriateness for this purpose derives from the fact that they are considered to be the most powerful in the Koran. Ghazali, the Arab philosopher, treated them as a single verse, which he referred to as the 'chief' of the Koranic verses.[3] They demonstrate the ultimate power of God, His superiority and His constant alertness which is neither disrupted by fatigue nor terminated by sleep. God is omniscient and nothing can occur to His creatures (including the client) without His will. Misfortune, including sickness, is conceived of as issuing from malignant acts which are not blessed by God, and the client who drinks the Throne verses is taking refuge with God so that He will protect him against such malevolent disturbances.

The Exordium chapter,[4] which is reputed to guarantee success in new undertakings (like trade, travel, etc.), is also generally known. The reason why some Koranic verses are better known than others derives from the fact that the forces against which they are believed to be effective are seen as major causes of disease or misfortune in general. As knowledge is

9. Chapters 112, 114, and 113, respectively [editor's note].
1. Qur'ān 2:255 [editor's note].
2. Ali, *The Holy Qurān Text*, pp. 102–3.
3. Mohammed Abul Quasem, *The Jewels of the Koran: Al-Ghazālī's Theory* (Kuala Lumpur: University of Malaya Press, 1979), pp. 75–78. [Abū Ḥāmid Muḥammad Al-Ghazālī (1058–1111), Iranian Muslim theologian, philosopher, and mystic—editor's note.]
4. Sūra 1, "The Opening" (*al-Fātiḥa*) [editor's note].

unequally distributed in any given society,[5] it is hardly surprising that those who are in close contact with fakis and their clients are better informed than other Berti about which Koranic verses should be used in erasure. Berti women are particularly ill-informed and they show comparatively little interest in these matters. They have less contact with fakis and are expected to be represented by their male protectors when they need their service. At the same time, women are discouraged from attending Koranic schools, except for short periods, and are, therefore, deprived of the chance of becoming professional fakis. Their poor knowledge of the Koran in general can also be related to their lack of participation in the parts of rituals which require the use of the Koran, such as rain and funeral prayers.[6]

All erasure writings start with the verse 'In the name of God the Most Gracious, the Most Merciful'. This verse appears at the beginning of all but one of the chapters of the Koran. The verse or a part of it is frequently uttered by the Berti to ensure blessing, to avoid bad luck or to ward off any malevolent influences; it is uttered, for example, before eating, drinking, weeding or any other similar activity.

### *Koranic Verses Used in Erasures*

In the Berti view, specific verses have the power to bring about specific desirable outcomes. Sometimes a certain Koranic verse is used in erasure because the purpose for which the erasure was prepared is understood as being mentioned in the verse itself (Erasures 1–3);[7] in other cases the connection between the verse chosen and the purpose of the erasure is not that direct. The connection is, nevertheless, established through the imposition of a certain meaning on the verse used.

#### ERASURE 1 (FOR INDUCING PREGNANCY)

The following verses are seen as having the power to induce pregnancy in a woman who has failed to bear children, because they directly recall God's power to create life.

He it is Who shapes you
In the wombs as He pleases.
[sura 3: 6]

There is no god but He,
The Exalted in Power,
The Wise.
[sura 18]

#### ERASURE 2 (FOR SORE LEGS)

And the servants of [God]
Most Gracious are those

5. L. Holy and M. Stuchlik, "The Structure of Folk Models," in *The Structure of Folk Models*, ed. Holy and Stuchlik, ASA Monograph 20 (London: Academic Press, 1981), pp. 17–18.
6. Abdullah Osman El-Tom, "Religious Men and Literacy in Berti Society" (PhD thesis, University of St. Andrews, 1983), chap. 7.
7. Erasure 3 is not included here [editor's note].

Who walk on earth
In humility, and when the ignorants
Address them, they say,
'Peace!';
Those who spend the night
In adoration of their Lord
Prostrate and standing;
Those who say, 'Our Lord!
Avert from us the Wrath
Of Hell, for its Wrath
Is indeed an affliction grievous,
Evil indeed is it
As an abode, and as
A place to rest in.

[sura 25: 63–6]

These verses are obviously selected for their reference to walking. At the same time they portray the patient as humble, peaceful and spending the night praying. Prayers are normally associated with the physical movement of the body in which the legs are crucial. The selected verses give the impression that the legs are either incapacitated by excessive prayers or that they are required to be restored to health to allow the resumption of religious practice.

* * *

## JOYCE BURKHALTER FLUECKIGER

### *From* 'The Vision Was of Written Words': Negotiating Authority as a Female Muslim Healer in South India†

'Once you come to me, it will be cured—there's no question of "failure".'[1] The words are spoken by a female Muslim folk healer called Pirānimā or Amma by her patients, to a distressed mother whose teenage son has run away from home; they are repeated with variations throughout the day to patients with fevers, infertility and marital problems, failing businesses, or just general 'trouble' (*pareśānī*) in the house. Amma is a fifty-five-year-old healer who lives and works in a residential neighbourhood on the campus of Osmania University, in the south Indian city of Hyderabad. The stream of patients to the small healing room attached to her house is evidence

† From *Syllables of Sky: Studies in South Indian Civilization: In Honour of Velcheru Narayana Rao*, ed. David Shulman (Delhi: Oxford University Press, 1995), pp. 249, 251–58, 281–82. Reprinted by permission of Joyce Burkhalter Flueckiger. Except as indicated, all notes are Flueckiger's, and all brackets in the text are hers.

1. I first met Amma in January 1989, when I conducted a three-week workshop with Margaret Mills on 'Women and Folklore Fieldwork' in Hyderabad, Andhra Pradesh, sponsored by the Ford Foundation. I returned to Hyderabad to work intensively with Amma for seven weeks from December 1990 through January 1991, under the auspices of the American Institute of Indian Studies. An earlier version of this paper was presented at an SSRC-sponsored conference titled 'Authoritative Words: Strategies of Communication in South and Southeast Asia', May 1991, Madison, Wisconsin. Words in double quotation marks indicate that the English word was used by the speaker in an otherwise Urdu or Telugu conversation or narrative. [SSRC: Social Science Research Council—editor's note.]

of her reputation as a successful healer. Amma proudly testifies, 'Patients come by auto, foot and bus—from villages, Bombay and Pune. My *falītā* [paper wicks on which are written Qur'anic verses] are even taken to Dubai. . . .'

Amma's authoritative voice in a healing practice such as this, in which she meets both male and female, Muslim and Hindu patients, subverts traditional gender roles and hierarchy assumed by the male-dominated public discourse of the Muslim–Hindu community in which she lives. After sitting in her healing room for only a few hours, it becomes clear that both the healing power itself and the healer's authority to dispense that power derive from her mastery over words, both written and oral. As a healer in a public domain for which there is no clear female model, however, Amma's authority must be continually negotiated. These negotiations are the subject of this essay.

Visually, the written word dominates Amma's healing room—particularly striking for someone familiar with Hindu folk-healing contexts. Amma asserts that her healing power is based solely on the Qur'an, and throughout the day she continually *writes:* Qur'anic verses, numbers and symbolic geometric shapes on slips of paper to be folded into amulets (*tāvīz*) or rolled into wicks to be burned or immersed in drinking water (*falītā*), on saucers, unleavened breads, gourds and even pieces of uncured leather. Her table is lined with stacks of tāvīz and falītā, held down by glass paper weights; a pen is always in her hand. As Amma once exclaimed: 'There would be no world without paper and pen!'

Amma's healing rhetoric and vocabulary for ritual are also dominated by images of the written word. She uses the Urdu word *paṛnā*, literally 'to read', to describe *namāz* (ritual prayer), intercessory prayer (*dua*), meditation and the interpretation of dreams (*sapnā paṛnā*) and visions (*nazar*), as well as for the recitation of the Qur'an. Although the Qur'an is read from directly only infrequently, it stands as the base from which Amma derives her healing authority and is the basis for her diagnosis and treatment of patients. The healing setting is, in Shirley Heath's words, a 'literacy event . . . [an] occasion in which a piece of writing is integral to the nature of the participants' interactions and their interpretive processes.'[2]

But control over literal and figurative written words is not enough to make Amma a successful healer. She herself says: 'Even a parrot can read. It's understanding [that's the thing].' Patients come to Amma over other healers who possess similar mastery over the written word because of what several patients voiced as her unique *muhabbat* (love) and *bhakti* (devotion); and these qualities, as well as her *understanding* of the written word, are expressed through ritual performance and the spoken word.

Amma's is not the only voice of authority in the healing room. A unique dynamism is added to the room through the presence of her husband, Abba, storekeeper of the small provisions store that occupies one side of the room. He is a Sufi spiritual guide/teacher, a *murśid*, whose calling is to 'show and teach the right path' to his disciples. He is able to fulfil some of the obligations of this role while tending the store by giving oral teachings to the healing audience, some of whom are his own initiated disciples (as

2. Shirley Brice Heath, "Protean Shapes in Literacy Events: Ever-shifting Oral and Literate Traditions," in *Spoken and Written Language*, ed. Deborah Tannen (Norwood, NJ: Ablex, 1982), p. 100.

well as frequently taking it upon himself to answer the questions I was asking directly to Amma, a role she was usually content to let him assume).[3] Although learned in the popular Sufi tradition of which he is a part, Abba is not literate in the Arabic script, nor does tradition require such literacy of its murśid. Amma's position as healer, in contrast, is directly dependent upon well-developed skills in both reading and writing. Thus, the healing room becomes the focal point for negotiations between the authorities conferred by oral and written traditions, between hereditary and innovative religious roles, complicated by the non-traditional gender roles assumed and shared by Amma and Abba.

### *The Healing Setting*

Patients are 'called' to Amma's courtyard by the green flag flying above her courtyard, indicating that below is a site of Islamic ritual activity. The walls of the courtyard are decorated with bright murals of a roaring tiger, a horse with the head of a woman (the Burāq who carried the Prophet on his night journey and ascent to heaven) and a second horse carrying an open hand (symbolic of the Prophet's family)—all images common to popular Islam in India. Small groups of women (many of whom wear a black *burqā*), children and a few men are seated in the courtyard, exchanging news and gossip. Others are crowded around the doorway of the healing room as they await their turn, leaning over each other to hear the voice inside.

Amma meets patients in her healing room six days a week, eight to ten hours a day. She says her calling is to 'serve the "public" during the day and to remember Allah at night'. The room in which she sits is small and crowded with patients. When their number grows beyond five or six, they are given plastic, numbered discs indicating their position in the waiting line. Amma sits on a large chair behind a folding table, which is covered with the tools of her trade: slips of paper on which are written Qur'anic verses and geometric shapes, scissors and a pen. Her voice often competes with that of the screeching parrot sitting in a cage hanging above the courtyard or the whirring of two dilapidated floor fans.

Amma dresses in a simple nylon sari and a long-sleeved white blouse. Her graying hair is covered by the end of her sari when she prays over a patient; her burqā hangs in another room to be worn only when she leaves the neighbourhood. She takes pride in the fact that she does not 'need' jewellery to indicate her status and wears only simple glass bangles; her ears are lined with empty holes which once had gold earrings in them.[4] She puts on a pair of horn-rimmed glasses whenever she writes prescriptions for her patients. Her rounded face carries a jovial expression; her laugh is

3. Outside the healing room, the authority of Abba's position as a murśid is most visibly expressed in monthly samā ('concerts', for which *qawwālī* singers are hired) held in his courtyard, attended by his murīd (disciples) (see Regula B. Qureshi, *Sufi Music of India and Pakistan: Sound, Context and Meaning in Qawwali* [New York: Cambridge University Press, 1986]). The spiritual hierarchy of a murśid/murīd is made apparent through the honoured seat occupied by Abba, gifts of flowers offered to him by the murīd and the order in which disciples take turns dancing/twirling with him as they enter a trance state (*hāl*).

4. She recently wore earrings gifted to her by her niece, but her heart told her: 'No, take them out', and she obeyed. Her lack of jewellery is particularly striking when compared to the pirānimā I met at a 'women's *dargāh*' [shrine], who was often dressed in a fancy, auspicious green sari and *dupaṭṭā* (scarf), who wore a dozen glitzy green bangles on each arm and a heavy necklace, and whose eyes were rimmed with heavy kohl.

frequent and vigorous. At least once in an hour, she stops all healing activity, relaxes and pulls out a motley assortment of small tin boxes whose contents she uses to make herself *pān* (betel leaf), to which she admits an addiction.[5] Abba frequently reprimands Amma for taking time out to make pān when the room is filled with patients. However, these breaks from healing action are often occasions for a story. The stories are not frivolous; as we shall see later in the essay, they are carefully chosen to reinforce Amma's healing authority and to nurture her relationship with her patients.

One-third of the healing room is taken up by the small provisions store in which Abba sits. Abba, a retired university office assistant, is a distinguished seventy-five year old. His face is framed by shoulder-length hair and a long beard; his deeply wise eyes are subtly outlined with kohl (*kājal*) and periodically framed with black-rimmed glasses. Seated on the ground, he is barely visible behind the veil of bags of cheap candy, snacks and biscuits hanging from the ceiling. Soap, matches, incense and cigarettes line the shelves on the wall behind him; clay pots, whose lids hold lemons and eggs, and small wooden drawers filled with spices surround him.

Although Abba's physical presence in the healing room is somewhat obscured, he does not sit there quietly; his expressive voice frequently interjects into Amma's healing rhetoric, giving religious teachings or commentary relevant to the situation at hand. Interestingly, two of Amma and Abba's daughters frequently substitute for him in the store, as well as one of his trusted male disciples, while two of his sons assist Amma at the healing table and are learning her skills. The gender roles in the second generation reassert the normative model of *male* public healing in South Asian Islam. In this context, the continual negotiations between Amma and Abba of healing/teaching roles, as well as gender roles and their accompanying authorities, are palpable.

### *The Healing Practice*

Amma's healing practice is literally and figuratively based on the Qur'an. She asserts that everything she needs for her practice is found in what she calls the 'Book of Service' (*khidmatwālī kitab*).[6] Abba calls the Qur'an 'powerful magic' (*baṛā jādū*).[7] Amma and Abba both make clear, however, that Amma's healing power and use of the Qur'an are effective only against spiritual illnesses and problems caused by the evil eye (*asrat*) or the devil (*śaitān*), which frequently manifest themselves in the imbalance of the four elements of which the human body is made (earth, water, air, fire). These problems include infertility, miscarriage and stillbirth, fevers, general weakness and wasting away (particularly of children), failing

5. Amma's pān-chewing addiction is a source of seemingly jovial contention between her husband and herself. He insists that she chews too much and spends too much money on the habit, reportedly up to Rs 400 per month. Her answer to this accusation was: 'Allah provides', to which he retorted, 'If he provides, why do you ask me for money?'
6. See Fazlur Rahman, "Islam and Health/Medicine: A Historical Perspective," in *Healing and Restoring: Health and Medicine in the World's Religious Traditions*, ed. Lawrence E. Sullivan (New York: Macmillan, 1989), p. 150, for a discussion on the use of amulets in pre-Islamic Arabia and the Prophet's reluctant allowance of the practice 'with the proviso that writings on amulets consist only of verses from the Qur'an. He did this to safeguard against the possibility that some amulets might invoke powers to achieve healing other than the one unique God of Islam'.
7. *Jādū* in the Hindu context generally has negative connotations of black magic; however, used here by Abba, the word connotes 'power' in a more generalized sense.

businesses, abusive and/or lazy husbands and disobedient children. Amma identifies cancer, typhoid and polio as examples of illnesses that are beyond her control, outside the spiritual domain. Many patients, especially babies and young children with fevers, are brought to Amma only after they have already received treatment by a doctor that has failed; and I heard frequent, bitter complaints about the money wasted on such treatments.[8] In a discussion of the differences between the illnesses which doctors are able to control and those which Amma cures, Abba stated that the latter were all 'troubles for which doctors' medicines are useless. The medicine for these are this [pointing to Amma's table full of slips of paper]. We could say that they're killed by the very letters of "Arabi".'

Amma calls her standard diagnostic procedure *afjūd* (literally, 'adding'), in which she asks for the patient's name and that of his or her mother. She writes the name of each in the Arabic script. Each letter of the Arabic alphabet has been assigned a numerical value by the *abjād* tradition;[9] Amma adds up the values for each name, divides their individual totals by the day of the week or some other astrological number and then compares them. The numerical difference between the two indicates whether or not the patient's composition is weighted too far in the direction of any one of the four elements and determines the treatment.

On the surface, the primary mathematical diagnostic procedure of afjūd is relatively objective and straightforward. Several of Amma's disciples are able to aid her in carrying out the additions and divisions of afjūd, leaving only the final diagnosis to her. Determining the treatment is less simple, however, particularly deciding what should be written on specific tāvīz (amulets). What distinguishes Amma from her disciples and others who may be able to make the appropriate calculations is the authority with which she names the problem, determines its treatment and pronounces its cure.

Amma's treatment and diagnostic procedure of afjūd require an active use of the Arabic script. Letters of and numerical symbols for Qur'anic verses (*sūra*) are written on the slips of paper that are folded into amulets (tāvīz) to be worn around the neck or waist, carried in a wallet, smashed by a rock, hung above a doorway to flutter in the wind; or as stated earlier, they are rolled and burned as wicks or immersed in drinking water (falītā). Abba describes the number/verse substitution as one equivalent to degrees on a thermometer or kilometres in measuring distance. Words and numbers are written on saucers from which a patient drinks; they are written on

8. Members of Amma's own family frequently went to 'modern' medical practitioners for general flu symptoms such as fevers, coughs and colds, that others brought to Amma for treatment. Amma's eldest daughter was awaiting heart surgery in January 1991; the surgery was unsuccessful and she died later that summer.

9. See also T. Fahd, "Hurūf," in *Encyclopaedia of Islam*, 2nd ed., vol. 3 (Leiden: Brill, 1971), on *hurūf*.

The standard Urdu term for this technique is called abjād, referred to by Ja'far Sharif in his *Islam in India or Qanum-i-Islam* (trans. G. A. Herklots [1921; reprint, London: Curzon, 1972]). Sharif states that the numerical value ascertained by adding the values of the letters in the names is divided by twelve. The resulting number indicates which astrological sign will dominate the life of the patient. Amma's calculations appear to be somewhat different from this description. Nowhere in the author's descriptions of what the translator has rendered 'magicians' is mention made of female practitioners.

The differences between Amma's terminology and pronunciation and 'standard' Urdu terminology are frequent in her speech. One young, male Muslim M. Phil. graduate in Urdu literature, while listening to some tapes of Amma's healing rhetoric, exclaimed: 'This isn't Urdu!' (And, after listening for some time,) 'This isn't Islam!'

unleavened bread (*capātī*) fed to dogs as surrogates for errant husbands or disobedient children, on gourds that serve as substitutes for the weakened body of a child,[1] and on bits of animal skin burned in the fire to 'close the mouth' of an adversary. The written word reaches across distances and compels in ways that the oral word is unable to do, as Abba describes:

> [It's] like if I write a letter to you and tell you to come; it's "urgent"—a telegram. You can't refuse. Like that, there's a 'mantra'. And on [your] name, like if we know the name of your mother. Reading that and reading your name, we make an "attack".

Although Amma repeatedly asserts that all she needs for her practice is the Qur'an, there are several other books to which she refers for specific treatments and from which she copies sample geometric diagrams for use in specialized amulets. She was not eager to show these to me or reveal their contents, perhaps realizing the apparent contradiction between their use and her statement that the Qur'an is all she needs. It was only on one of the last days I spent in her healing room that she reluctantly showed me two of these books and told me their names: *Bangāl Aur Cīn Ke Jādū* (The Magic of Bengal and China) and *Mohinī Tantra* (A Collection of Charms/Incantations). When I asked about their contents, she answered: 'First practise and fully embrace what I have taught you [oral recitation]; then read the books.'[2]

When Amma reads from the Qur'an as part of her healing practice, she recites to herself in barely a whisper; the words are inaudible to her patients. Even if they were heard, most of her patients would not comprehend the Arabic, particularly the Hindu patients who constitute nearly half of the healing community. The Qur'anic words and number substitutes written on slips of paper are also incomprehensible to Amma's patients; not once did I see a patient try to read the words or ask what was written. The words lose their semantic content even for those who are literate in Arabic as they are spatially manipulated within various diagrams or written in such haste as to be illegible. In this setting, their power lies in their actual physical manifestation. The words on the tāvīz literally deflect the evil eye, falītā are burned and the smoke 'of the words' inhaled by the patient, or they are immersed in water and the ink which washes off is drunk by the patient.[3] They become graphic representations of power. They are understood to be, quite literally, the very words of God.

* * *

1. The power of transference behind these treatments is: in the same way that a dog is faithful to the person who feeds it, the husband or child will be faithful to the woman; as the gourd dries up, its life force will transfer to the weak child.
2. The discussion was occasioned by the arrival by mail of one of the above-mentioned books. It had been ordered by one of Amma's disciples. When I asked if I could see it, he handed me the wrapping paper on which was written the address and told me that I could buy one for myself in Delhi. Amma strongly objected, saying that I might be harmed or cause others harm if I read the wrong thing without appropriate training.
3. An interesting distinction is made in the physical production of tāvīz and falītā. Amma xeroxes falītā, except those that have to be drunk, which must be written in ink that can wash off in water. The more powerful tāvīz must be handwritten each time, with the allowable convenience of carbon paper (so that six copies of a single tāvīz can be made at one time).

# Manuscripts, Monuments, and Material Culture

## OLEG GRABAR

### *From* The Dome of the Rock†

The Dome of the Rock is the earliest work of Islamic architecture still standing in more or less its original shape and with much of its original decoration. Even in the contemporary setting of a modern city with its tall, massive buildings all over the hilly landscape, the Dome of the Rock still dominates much of the Old City of Jerusalem, the magnet of advertisements for tourism and the state of Israel and the central image of posters in Palestinian-owned shops all over the world.

It is a deceptively simple building located on a high platform that was erected at some indeterminate time on the large esplanade in the southeastern corner of the city. Its wooden gilt dome is slightly over twenty meters in diameter and rises like a tall cylinder to a height of some thirty meters over the surrounding stone-paved platform. It is supported by a circular arcade of four piers and twelve columns. An octagon of two ambulatories on eight piers and sixteen columns holds the cylinder tightly, as in a ring. The ambulatory is fourteen meters deep, thus giving to the whole building a diameter of forty-eight meters; it rises to only eleven meters inside and thirteen outside, thus strengthening the impact of the cupola, especially from afar. There are four doors, one at each of the cardinal points corresponding only approximately to the main axes of the Haram al-Sharif,[1] even less so to those of the higher platform on which the Dome of the Rock stands. An extensive decoration of mosaics, painted wood, marble, multi-colored tiles, carpets, and carved stone covers most of the building, inside and outside. This decoration comes from many different periods and has often been repaired with varying success, as the ravages of time and changes in taste affected the maintenance of the building.

It is important to recall that, in addition to its continuing forceful presence, the Dome of the Rock was the first monument sponsored by a Muslim ruler that was conceived as a work of art, a monument deliberately transcending its function by the quality of its forms and expression. An often quoted later text by Muqaddasi,[2] a native of Jerusalem, acknowledges with

† From chapter 2 of Oleg Grabar, *The Shape of the Holy: Early Islamic Jerusalem* (Princeton: Princeton University Press, 1996), pp. 52–61, 199. © 1996 Princeton University Press. Reprinted by permission of Princeton University Press. Except as indicated, all notes are Grabar's, and all brackets in the text are his. Figures and his references to them have been omitted.

1. Al-Ḥaram al-Sharīf (the Noble Sanctuary; Arabic), the Temple Mount, on which the Dome of the Rock was built [editor's note].
2. Muḥammad ibn Aḥmad al-Maqdisī (ca. 946–ca. 1000), Arab traveler and geographer [editor's note].

pride the aesthetic ambition of the building and thereby identifies one of the possible reasons for its construction. Muqaddasi's story deserves to be given in full, as it signals many of the themes that will recur more than once in what follows.

> Now one day I said, speaking to my father's brother: "O my uncle, verily it was not well of the caliph al-Walid [Abd al-Malik's successor who ruled from 705 to 715 and who ordered the building of the Great Mosque of Damascus] to expend so much of the wealth of the Muslims on the Mosque of Damascus. Had he expended the same on making roads, or in caravanserais, or in the restoration of the frontier fortresses, it would have been more fitting and more excellent of him." But my uncle said to me in answer: "O my little son, you have no understanding. Verily al-Walid was right and he was prompted to a worthy work. For he beheld Syria to be a country that had long been occupied by the Christians, and he noted there the beautiful churches still belonging to them, so enchantingly fair and so renowned for their splendor, as are the Qumamah [*refuse*, a vulgar pun on *qiyamah* or *resurrection*, the Arabic term for the church of the Holy Sepulchre in Jerusalem] and the churches of Lydda and Edessa. So he sought to build for the Muslims a mosque that should prevent their gazing at these [i.e., the Christian churches] and that should be unique and a wonder to the world. And in this manner is it not evident how the caliph Abd al-Malik, noting the greatness of the dome of the Qumamah and its magnificence, was moved, lest it should dazzle the minds of the Muslims, and hence erected above the Rock the Dome which is seen there?[3]

Without excluding other interpretations, Muqaddasi puts the Dome of the Rock in the thick of a competition, almost a confrontation, between Christianity and Islam or, perhaps more accurately, between Christians and Muslims. The question for the historian is whether a judgment expressed in the latter part of the tenth century which can easily be explained by the specific conditions of that time, should legitimately be extended to the time of the Dome's construction. Outside of the building itself, there is no more or less contemporary document from a Muslim source that could confirm or contradict Muqaddasi's assertions.

There are, on the other hand, a few Christian and Jewish sources, some somewhat later than the event and others nearly contemporary, that testify to the importance of the new building within the consciousness and the memory of the non-Muslim population. Sa'id ibn Bitriq,[4] a later Christian source, relates that the cupola of the Dome of the Rock (whose construction he attributes to al-Walid, 'Abd al-Malik's son) was taken from a Christian church in Baalbek in Lebanon and removed to Jerusalem.[5]

3. Al-Muqaddasi, *Aḥsan al-Taqāsīm fī Maʿrifāt al-Aqalīm*, ed. Michael Jan de Goeje, *Bibliotheca Geographorum Arabicarum*, vol. 3 (Leiden, 1906), text on p. 159. I have adopted the translation by Guy Le Strange, *Palestine under the Muslims: A Description of Syria and the Holy Land from A.D. 650 to 1500* (1890; reprint, Beirut, 1965), pp. 117–18, which is most complete; short excerpts from this text are found in many manuals on Islamic architecture.
4. The Arab name for Eutychius of Alexandria (877–940), physician, historian, and patriarch of Alexandria [editor's note].
5. Moshe Gil, *A History of Palestine, 634–1099* (Cambridge, 1992, from a Hebrew edition in 1983), p. 92.

Within a group of moralizing stories written in Creek around 680, one Anastasius of Sinai, a Christian monk, writes that he witnessed in Jerusalem the "clearing of the high place [most likely the area of the Haram today] by Egyptians helped by demons at night. Now, the rumor is that the Temple of God [i.e., the Jewish Temple] is being built there."[6] A Syriac chronicle dated in 716 relates that al-Walid "assembled all the treasures of the Saracens, . . . putting them into a single treasury in Jerusalem." The latest student of this text argues, quite reasonably, that the treasury is a reference to the Dome of the Rock completed some twenty years earlier.[7] And a medieval Jewish midrash, as usual almost impossible to date, reports that Abd al-Malik "shall build the house of the God of Israel," certainly a reflection of the presence of the Dome of the Rock on the site associated for centuries with the destroyed temple.[8] I shall suggest later an explanation for how all these texts may be understood, but the point is clear, even from these partial and fragmentary sources, that Christianity and Judaism were somehow involved in shaping the original perception of the Dome of the Rock.

All these examples, even Muqaddasi's text, are short references or inferences from the evidence of outsiders, to the construction or utilization of the building. The building itself, however, contains four documents that are, by physical necessity or because of the existence of a date, more or less contemporary with the time of its completion. In the order in which we perceive them today, these documents comprise its location, its architectural forms, its mosaic decoration (as well as a few other decorative fragments that belong to the original building), and the inscriptions from two of its entrances and in the frieze on the octagonal arcade. By dealing with the inscriptions first and then, in sequence, with the mosaics and other forms of surface decoration, the shape, and the location, I shall present the documents in their order of informational specificity, the precision and accuracy with which they can be defined, described, and explained. It is what Max van Berchem[9] called the "archaeological index" of a document, the range of its value in elucidating a monument. As we shall see, even the inscriptions, the clearest document involved, lead to questions without immediate answers.

* * *

## *The Inscriptions*

The most important and most spectacular inscription is located inside the building, as a continuous mosaic frieze of some 240 meters just below a cornice that supports the ceiling on either side of the octagonal arcade. It was thought by some that the inscription originally continued on the outer side of the circular arcade. This is not very likely, because the text as it stands delivers a rhetorically completed argument and does not seem to require a continuation. Still, the possibility cannot be excluded that some additional statement on either or both sides of the arcade disappeared when the Crusaders refurbished the building for their own

6. Bernard Flusin, "Démons et Sarrasins," *Travaux et Mémoires* 11 (1991): 386.
7. Andrew Palmer, *The Seventh Century in the West-Syrian Chronicles* (Liverpool, 1993), pp. 45–48.
8. Gil, *Palestine*, p. 92.
9. Swiss scholar of Arabic inscriptions (1863–1921) [editor's note].

purposes, or during the numerous repairs of Mamluk and Ottoman times.[1]

The inscription was read, for the most part, by Melchior de Vogüé, the first scholar and explorer allowed to work inside the building. It was then carefully reviewed and published by Max van Berchem and is included in the *Répertoire Chronologique d'Epigraphie Arabe.*[2] Considering the conditions under which he worked, with a ladder and candles, Max van Berchem's readings are remarkably accurate and only a few of his guesses turned out to be wrong. During the restorations carried out in the 1960s, Dr. Christel Kessler was able to study the inscription at close quarters. She corrected some of van Berchem's readings and pointed out the unexpectedly large number of diacritical marks found in the text on the inner face of the octagon. She published some of her findings and included in particular a very useful drawing of the inscription which gives a sense of its actual appearance and its idiosyncracies.[3]

Over twenty years later, Sheila Blair published a full translation of the inscription in the context of her interpretation of when the construction of the building was begun[4] and Heribert Busse included complete German translations in several of his numerous studies on early Islamic Jerusalem. Because of the importance of the inscription as a source for understanding the monument, an appendix to this book contains the Arabic text with a few technical observations. I am also providing a translation immediately below, with the passages that are also found in the Koran capitalized. Koranic quotations are identified according to the standard "Egyptian" version and the numbering of verses is, therefore, different from the ones in the *Répertoire.* I have not tried to give a literary flavor to the translation, and have made it as literal as possible. * * *

The inscription begins on the outer side of the octagon, just at the corner between the southeastern and southern sides (338°), where the rosette ending the outer sequence of the inscription is visible around the corner. There are only two words with some diacritical marking on the outer side: *tattakhidu* on the northwestern face (113°) and *taqabilu* on the southeastern one (308°). Rosettes serve to separate segments of the inscription from each other; there does not seem to have been any attempt to make them fit with architectural parts, except the south face of the octagon which includes one whole section of the inscription. The inner face of the octagon contains a single, continuous statement without rosette or other means to divide it into parts, and some fifty letters are provided with diacritical marks. It begins on the upper right corner of pier 22.

1. In the late 12th century, John of Würzburg is one of several writers giving the lengthy texts of Latin inscriptions located somewhere in the building; see John Wilkinson, *Jerusalem Pilgrimage, 1099–1185* (London, 1988), pp. 245–48, 289ff. One of those texts also alludes to older Arabic inscriptions which may have been covered up by the Latin ones.
2. Max van Berchem, *Matériaux pour un Corpus Inscriptionum Arabicum*, pt. 2, *Syrie du Sud*, vol. 2, *Jérusalem, "Haram," Mémoirs publiés par les membres de l'Institut Français d'Archéologie Orientale du Caire* 44 (1927), pp. 225ff.; see also *Répertoire chronologique d'Épigraphie arabe*, ed. Etienne Combe, Jean Sauvaget, and Gaston Wiet (Cairo, 1931–), no. 9.
3. Christel Kessler, "Abd al-Malik's Inscription in The Dome of the Rock, a Reconsideration," *Journal of the Royal Asiatic Society* (1970).
4. Sheila Blair, "What Is the Date of the Dome of the Rock," in *Bayt al-Maqdis, Abd al-Malik's Jerusalem I*, ed. Julian Raby and Jeremy Johns (Oxford, 1992), pp. 86–87. Heribert Busse, "Monotheismus und islamische Christologie in der Bauiuschrift der Felsendoms in Jerusalem," *Theologische Quartalschrift* 161 (1981), and "Die arabischen Inschriften im und am Felsendom," *Das Heilige Land* 109 (1977).

### THE OUTER FACE

"In the name of God, the Compassionate, the Merciful, there is no god but God, One, without associate. SAY HE IS GOD, ALONE,[5] GOD THE ETERNAL, HE DOES NOT BEGET NOR IS HE BEGOTTEN AND THERE IS NO ONE LIKE HIM [K 112]. Muhammad is the envoy of God, may God bless him. [ROSETTE] In the name of God, the Compassionate, the Merciful, there is no God but God, One, without associate. Muhammad is the envoy of God. INDEED GOD AND HIS ANGELS BLESS THE PROPHET; O YOU WHO BELIEVE SEND BLESSINGS ON HIM AND SALUTE HIM WITH FULL SALUTATION [K 33:56]. [ROSETTE] In the name of God, the Compassionate, the Merciful, there is no god but God, One. PRAISE TO GOD WHO BEGETS NO SON AND WHO HAS NO ASSOCIATE IN POWER AND WHO HAS NO SURROGATE FOR (PROTECTION FROM) HUMILIATION AND MAGNIFY HIS GREATNESS [K 17:111]. Muhammad is the envoy of God, may God bless him and His angels and His envoys and peace unto him and the mercy of God. [ROSETTE] In the name of God the Compassionate, the Merciful, there is no god but God, One and without associate. TO HIM IS DOMINION AND TO HIM IS PRAISE; HE GIVES LIFE OR DEATH AND HE HAS POWER OVER ALL THINGS [combination of K 64:1 and K 57:2]. Muhammad is the envoy of God, may God bless him and grant his intercession on the day of resurrection for his community. [ROSETTE] In the name of God, the Compassionate, the Merciful, there is no god but God, One, without associate. Muhammad is the envoy of God, God bless him. [ROSETTE] Has built this domed structure the servant of God, Abdallah, the imam al-Ma'mun, Commander of the Faithful, in the year seventy-two.[6] May God accept it from him and be satisfied with him. Amen. Lord of the worlds, to God is praise. [ROSETTE]." (It is obvious from logic and from the evidence of mosaic cubes that the name of the caliph Abd al-Malik had been replaced, while the date has remained the same.)

### THE INNER FACE

"In the name of God, the Compassionate, the Merciful, there is no god but God, One, without associate. TO HIM IS DOMINION AND TO HIM IS PRAISE, HE GIVES LIFE OR DEATH AND HE HAS POWER OVER ALL THINGS [combination of K 64:1 and K 57:2]. Muhammad is the servant of God and His envoy. Verily God and His angels send blessings to the Prophet. O YOU WHO BELIEVE SEND BLESSING ON HIM AND SALUTE HIM WITH FULL SALUTATION [K 33:54]. May God bless him and peace upon him and the mercy of God. O PEOPLE OF THE BOOK, DO NOT GO BEYOND THE BOUNDS OF YOUR RELIGION AND DO NOT SAY ABOUT GOD EXCEPT THE TRUTH. INDEED THE MESSIAH JESUS SON OF MARY WAS AN ENVOY OF GOD AND HIS WORD HE BESTOWED ON HER AS WELL AS A SPIRIT FROM HIM. SO BELIEVE IN GOD AND IN HIS ENVOYS AND DO NOT SAY 'THREE'; 'DESIST, IT IS BETTER FOR YOU. FOR INDEED GOD IS ONE GOD, GLORY BE TO HIM THAT HE SHOULD HAVE A SON. TO HIM BELONG WHAT IS IN HEAVEN AND WHAT IS ON EARTH AND IT IS SUFFICIENT FOR HIM

5. The exact meaning of the word *al-samad* used in this celebrated surah, *al-Ikhlas* ("Purity of Faith"), is difficult to determine; see Régis Blachère, *Le Coran Traduction* (Paris, 1949), 2:122–24. I finally decided on "alone" rather than "eternal" or "incorporeal," because of the broader meaning I give to the inscription and because it seems to conform with a meaning clearly attested in early times.
6. 691/92 CE [editor's note].

TO BE A GUARDIAN.[7] THE MESSIAH DOES NOT DISDAIN TO BE A SERVANT OF GOD, NOR DO THE ANGELS NEAREST (TO HIM). THOSE WHO DISDAIN SERVING HIM AND WHO ARE ARROGANT, HE WILL GATHER ALL TO HIMSELF [K 4:171–172]. Bless your envoy and your servant Jesus son of Mary AND PEACE UPON HIM ON THE DAY OF BIRTH AND ON THE DAY OF DEATH AND ON THE DAY HE IS RAISED UP AGAIN. THIS IS JESUS SON OF MARY. IT IS A WORD OF TRUTH IN WHICH THEY DOUBT. IT IS NOT FOR GOD TO TAKE A SON. GLORY BE TO HIM WHEN HE DECREES A THING HE ONLY SAYS 'BE' AND IT IS. INDEED GOD IS MY LORD AND YOUR LORD, THEREFORE SERVE HIM; THIS IS THE STRAIGHT PATH [K 19:33–36].[8] GOD BEARS WITNESS THAT THERE IS NO GOD BUT HE, (AS DO) THE ANGELS AND THOSE WISE IN JUSTICE. THERE IS NO GOD BUT HE, THE ALL-MIGHTY, THE ALL-WISE. INDEED THE RELIGION OF GOD IS ISLAM. THOSE WHO WERE GIVEN THE BOOK DID NOT DISSENT EXCEPT AFTER KNOWLEDGE CAME TO THEM (AND THEY BECAME) ENVIOUS OF EACH OTHER. WHOSOEVER DISBELIEVES IN THE SIGNS OF GOD, INDEED GOD IS SWIFT IN RECKONING [K 3:18–19]."

In addition to the long mosaic inscription, there were plaques with writing nailed on the wooden beam above the doors of the Dome of the Rock, two of which, on the eastern and northern doorways, have been preserved. The text was painted in gold over a blue background. Whether already done at the time of Abd al-Malik in the late seventh century, the effect of gold over blue may have represented or imitated the mosaics inside the building, although the notion of writing the text of the Revelation in gold met with opposition in the earliest *Books on Koranic Leaves* (*Kitab al-Masahif*) from the tenth century. Such opposition usually indicates common practice and there may not be any need to connect the execution of these door inscriptions with the mosaics inside.[9] The inscriptions were still *in situ* at the turn of the century, one over the eastern doorway, the other one, only partially preserved, over the northern one. Today both are kept in one of the small Mamluk sanctuaries in the Haram. Max van Berchem, who published the inscriptions, argued that the eastern one had seven lines from the Umayyad period,[1] most likely the time of Abd al-Malik, while the last two lines, which contain the historical information about the sponsorship of the work, were replacements from the time of al Ma'mun at the beginning of the ninth century. For reasons that are not at all clear, these historical lines are repeated and appear as two sets of two lines set next to each other. The northern plaque is incomplete, and it is some twenty centimeters shorter than the eastern one; it also repeats the historical statement and its pious first part is close to the eastern one, but not identical. It is likely that each of the building's four doors was provided with such inscriptions containing the same historical information, but with variations in their religious content. The texts of these inscriptions as read by van Berchem are also found in the Appendix.

7. Other readings of these words are possible, but the differences between them do not seem important to our understanding of the building.
8. There is a significant change here, as the Koran has Jesus speaking in the first person when referring to his birth, death, and Resurrection; or else the passage could be an earlier alternate version. This is also the location of three large dots set above each other, spandrel 98, as though indicating a clear separation in value between quoted passages from the Holy Text.
9. Arthur Jeffery, *Materials for the History of the Text of the Quran* (Leiden, 1937), pp. 150ff.
1. The Umayyad was the first dynasty to rule the caliphate (661–750) [editor's note].

### THE EAST DOOR

"In the name of God, the Compassionate, the Merciful, PRAISE BE TO GOD EXCEPT WHOM THERE IS NO GOD, THE LIVING, THE EVERLASTING, THE CREATOR OF HEAVEN AND OF EARTH, AND THE LIGHT OF HEAVEN AND OF EARTH [K 2:255, partly, or 3:1; 2:112 or 6:101, both in part], the Upholder of Heaven and earth, ONE, UNIQUE, HE DOES NOT BEGET NOR IS HE BEGOTTEN AND THERE IS NONE LIKE HIM [K 112, minus one word], One, LORD OF POWER, YOU GIVE POWER TO WHOM YOU PLEASE AND YOU TAKE AWAY POWER FROM WHOMEVER YOU PLEASE [K 3:26]. All power is to You and comes from You, our Master, and it returns to You, Master of power, Merciful, Compassionate. HE HAS WRITTEN MERCY FOR HIMSELF, HIS MERCY EXTENDS TO ALL THINGS (K 6:12 and K 7:156].[2] Glory to Him and may He be exalted over what polytheists associate [to Him]. We ask you, our God, by Your mercy, by Your beautiful names, by Your noble face, by Your immense power, by Your perfect word by which heaven and earth stand together and by which, and with Your mercy, we are preserved from the devil and we are all saved from Your punishment on the day of resurrection, by Your abundant grace, by Your great nobility, by Your clemency, Your power, Your forgiveness, and Your kindness, that You bless Muhammad, Your servant and Your Prophet, and that You accept his intercession for his community. May God bless him and give him peace and the mercy of God. And this is what was ordered by the servant of God Abdallah, the imam al-Ma'mun, Commander of the Faithful, may God prolong his life, under the rule of the brother of the Commander of the Faithful Abu Ishaq, son of the Commander of the Faithful al-Rashid, may God prolong him. By the hand of Salih ibn Yahya, client of the Commander of the Faithful, in *rabi' II* 216 [May–June 831]."

### THE NORTH DOOR

"In the name of God, the Compassionate, the Merciful, PRAISE BE TO GOD EXCEPT WHOM THERE IS NO GOD, THE LIVING, THE EVERLASTING [K 2:255, in part, or 3:1]. There is no partner to Him, One, UNIQUE, HE DOES NOT BEGET NOR IS HE BEGOTTEN AND THERE IS NONE LIKE HIM [K 112, except for first words). Muhammad is the servant of God and His envoy, WHOM HE SENT WITH GUIDANCE AND THE RELIGION OF TRUTH TO PROCLAIM IT OVER ALL RELIGIONS, EVEN THOUGH THE POLYTHEISTS HATE IT [K 9:33 or 61:9]. Let us believe in God and what was revealed to Muhammad and IN WHAT WAS GIVEN TO THE PROPHETS FROM THEIR LORD; WE MADE NO DIFFERENCE BETWEEN ONE AND THE OTHER AND WE ARE MUSLIMS TO HIM [K 2:139 or 3:78, slightly modified]. God bless Muhammad, His servant and His prophet, and peace upon him and the mercy of God, His grace, His forgiveness, and His pleasure." This is followed by a statement with the name of the caliph al-Ma'mun and the date of 831, as on the eastern door.

* * *

2. Here as well, the Koranic model, if it is one, was adapted to the inscription by putting the text of the quote in third instead of first person.

DORIS BEHRENS-ABOUSEIF

# *From* Beyond the Secular and the Sacred: Qur'anic Inscriptions in Medieval Islamic Art and Material Culture†

Qur'anic inscriptions appear in a variety of contexts in medieval Islamic art and material culture. With their literal references to the Holy Book, such inscriptions seem a direct invocation of religious intent. But to what extent can the presence of Qur'anic inscriptions be used to determine whether a particular material artefact or building should be considered as religious or secular within the arts and material culture of the pre-modern Muslim world?

Islam is traditionally conceived as *dunyā wa dīn*, that is, as an all-pervasive worldly and religious system that seems to deny a separation between the secular and religious aspects of life. The Western categorisation of 'religious' versus 'secular', therefore, poses a problem when applied in the context of pre-modern Islamic cultures. This is due, in part, to the dual role adopted by Muslim rulers in the early periods of Islamic history, which combined both political and religious authority.[1] Conversely, the Christian church in Europe set up autonomous clerical institutions that ultimately led to the separation between religion and the state. And yet pre-modern Muslim societies were aware of a distinction, albeit not necessarily a separation, between religious and non-religious matters. For example, Muslim political thought distinguished between *siyāsa*, meaning statecraft or politics, and *dīn*, or religion, a distinction that was conditioned, however, by the imperative that *siyāsa* must not conflict with religion, but rather be in accordance with it. The ruler was required to be guided by the shari'a (Islamic law) while applying the *siyāsa*.[2]

Muslim scholars also dealt with secular and religious categorisations in the process of the classification of the sciences. Muslim culture inherited and initially applied ancient Greek classifications of the sciences which were later replaced with a Muslim classification that distinguished between the Islamic sciences (*'ulūm shar'iyya*), dealing directly or indirectly with religious matters, and the non-Islamic ones (*'ulūm 'aqliyya*), the rational and natural sciences, including philosophy.[3] Historiography, for example, was often classified among the religious sciences but occasionally also among the rational ones, because of its subject matter that could deal either with Islamic or with pre-Islamic and other non-Muslim subjects.[4] This did not prevent Greek sciences such as medicine, geography and astronomy from being taught in religious institutions, and many

† From *Word of God, Art of Man: The Qur'an and Its Creative Expressions*, ed. Fahmida Suleman (London: Oxford University Press in association with the Institute of Ismaili Studies, 2007), pp. 41–45, 48–49. Reprinted by permission of Oxford University Press. A number of phrases in Arabic are omitted. Except as indicated, all notes are Behrens-Abouseif's.

1. See Dominique Sourdel, *et al.*, 'Khalīfa', $EI^2$, vol. IV, pp. 937–53. [$EI^2$: *Encyclopaedia of Islam*, 2nd ed., 12 vols. (Leiden: Brill, 1954–2005)—editor's note.]
2. Bernard Lewis, 'Siyāsa' in Arnold H. Green, ed., *In Quest of an Islamic Humanism* (Cairo, 1984), pp. 3–14.
3. Abu Hamid Muhammad al-Ghazali [1058–1111], *Iḥyā' 'ulūm al-dīn*, 5 vols. (Beirut, n.d.), pp. 18ff.
4. Ali Oumlil, *Histoire et son discours: essai sur la méthodologie d'Ibn Khaldoun* (Rabat, 1979), pp. 50ff.

Greek texts were translated into Arabic and Persian and circulated within Muslim societies until modern times. Philosophy, however, became controversial in the later period because it was viewed as contradicting Islam. In contrast, poetry of all types maintained the status of a secular art in the Arab world and was tolerated by the religious establishment because of its inherited high status among the pre-Islamic Arabs.

As part of an interpretation of the arts and material culture of the pre-modern Islamic period, historians and art historians often assign an object to a sacred or secular context based on the artefact's perceived religious significance. But how is religious significance to be judged? The presence or absence of figural representations in the material arts cannot be considered as a reliable criterion for making this distinction since figural art is relatively rare in certain regions, such as in North Africa, while it is abundant in other areas, such as in Iran, where it even occurs in starkly religious contexts. Considering the significance of epigraphy in Islamic art, one may argue that the presence of Qur'anic inscriptions in Islamic material culture is likely to be a more reliable criterion in distinguishing between religious and non-religious contexts of artefacts. Or is it?

In the Qur'an, God advises the believer to remember Him and mention His Names, and implicitly, His words, in all situations of life. In *Sūrat Āl 'Imrān* (Q. 3:191) Allah promises to reward those who mention Him when standing, sitting and reclining. The recitation of Qur'anic verses, especially the often repeated *basmala*,[5] is omnipresent in the everyday language of Muslims because they convey God's mercy.[6] Yet if we examine pre-modern objects of Islamic art and material culture, it is obvious that the written Qur'anic text is far from ubiquitous on these objects and was clearly not applied indiscriminately to all items of daily life.

In comparison with the presence of formulaic good wishes, poetic verses and historical labelling, Qur'anic verses seldom appear on vessels, and this seems to suggest a premeditated reservation against exposing the Qur'an to profane uses. Indeed, it appears that the Word of God was not used to advertise the work of Man. This reservation shows a discrepancy between the orally recited Qur'an, omnipresent in everyday life, and the written Qur'an in its tangible or palpable form as a book or as an inscription that might be exposed to impure surroundings. In fact, the purity of the written Qur'an in its material book form is emphasised in the Holy Book itself in *Sūrat al-Wāqi'a* (Q. 56:77–9): 'This is a glorious Qur'an safeguarded in a hidden Book which none may touch except the purified'. I am not aware of such requirements of physical purification when uttering phrases or reciting passages from the Qur'an. In compliance with this sura, there is a common attitude among Muslims to avoid exposing the written word of God to physical impurities. Hence, by analogy, what applies to the Qur'anic codex must then apply to its inscriptions.

The thirteenth-century Maliki jurist, Ibn al-Hajj, stipulated that a calligrapher of the Qur'an must not be involved in any other kind of calligraphy

5. The phrase that appears at the beginning of every sūra except the ninth: 'In the name of God, the beneficent, the merciful' [editor's note].
6. In general the Qur'anic translations in this chapter are taken from Mohammad Marmaduke Pickthall, *The Glorious Qur'an. Text and Explanatory Translation by Mohammad M. Pickthall* (Chicago, n.d.), with minor modifications [first published in 1930—editor's note].

save that of the Holy Book and he most certainly was not to engage in the writing of fiction, such as epics and anecdotes.[7] Moreover, Ibn al-Hajj also stated that the Maliki school of law opposed the recitation of the Qur'an on market streets, thus extending the principle of safeguarding the purity of the Qur'an to its oral form as well.[8]

Inscriptions in general are rarely found on vessels from the early Islamic period; however, their occurrence begins to increase in the tenth century. The content of such inscriptions evolved over time, although they rarely included Qur'anic verses. Conversely, the use of Qur'anic inscriptions in religious buildings is a more universal phenomenon, although the extent of such a use differed according to the geographical context. In Ibadi mosques in Oman, for example, the *miḥrāb* (prayer niche) is the only part of the mosque that is adorned with inscriptions.[9] Moreover, the definition of what constitutes a religious building is not so straightforward in a Muslim context. For example, Mamluk *sabīls* (water-houses) were pious endowments (*waqfs*) that did not directly fulfil a religious function, and yet they can be understood within a spiritual context. They were appropriately inscribed with various Qur'anic verses referring to water, such as the verse from *Sūrat al-Insān* (Q. 76:21): 'Their Lord will quench their thirst with a pure drink'.[1] Ottoman fountains were mostly inscribed with poetry, although occasionally short Qur'anic phrases with reference to water were included, such as '(and) We made every living thing of water' from *Sūrat al-Anbiyā'* (Q. 21:30).[2]

Interestingly, the Nilometer on the island of Rawda, facing Fustat, which was constructed for the Abbasid Caliph al-Mutawakkil[3] in AH 248/AD 861–62, is adorned with Qur'anic verses although it did not have any pious or charitable function. Rather, it was constructed to fulfil an administrative task by measuring the level of the flooding of the Nile, which was crucial for the evaluation of the state's annual taxes. In this particular case, historical sources tell us that the verses chosen for this structure (Q. 14:37) were meant to invoke a good flood and prosperous crops.[4] This latter example is comparable to the use of the Qur'an for talismanic purposes. However, there is further significance for the use of Qur'anic verses on the Nilometer. This monument, commissioned by and inscribed with the name of the caliph in Baghdad, was a symbol of the central caliphal authority, a domain in which Qur'anic inscriptions were regularly utilised, from coinage and textiles to official seals. Since the reign of the Umayyad caliph ʿAbd al-Malik (r. AH 65–86/AD 685–705), Muslim coinage was

7. Muhammad b. Muhammad b. al-Hajj, *Kitāb al-Madkhal*, 4 vols. (Beirut, 1981), vol. IV, p. 83ff.
8. Ibn al-Hajj, *al-Madhkal*, vol. II, p. 301.
9. Irus Baldisira, *al-Kitābāt fi'l-masājid al-ʿumāniyyah al-qadīma* (Oman, 1994). [The Ibāḍī imamate (beginning in the mid-8th century) unified Oman politically—editor's note.]
1. Max van Berchem, *Materiaux pour un corpus inscriptionum arabicarum, partie I: Égypte* (Paris, 1894–1930), vols. II–III, pp. 229, 333, 375.
2. The entire verse (Q. 21:30) reads: 'Are the disbelievers unaware that the heavens and the earth were of one piece, then We parted them, and We made every living thing of water? Will they not then believe?'
3. Caliph 847–61; the ʿAbbāsid dynasty (750–1258) was the second of the Muslim dynasties, following the Umayyads (661–750) [editor's note].
4. K.A.C. [Keppel Archibald Cameron] Creswell, *Early Muslim Architecture*, 2 vols. (Oxford, 1932–40; reprinted New York. 1979), vol. II, pp. 200ff. The verse in question (Q. 14.37) from *Sūrat Ibrāhīm* reads: 'Our Lord: I have settled some of my posterity in an uncultivable valley near Your holy house (i.e. the Meccan valley), Lord that they may establish proper worship; so incline some hearts of men so that they may yearn toward them, and provide them with fruits in order that they may be thankful'.

inscribed with brief Qur'anic phrases, and this practice, although not universal, continued into later periods under various dynasties.

Funerary architecture and implements associated with Muslim funerary contexts were generally inscribed with Qur'anic verses in spite of the opposition against this practice or against any kind of elaborate form of burial by Muslim *madhhabs* (schools of law). Ibn al-Hajj condemned the practice of inscribing tombs with Qur'anic inscriptions as *bid'a* (innovation) because of the danger of exposing them to impurities and pollution.[5] The Maliki *madhhab* forbids funerary prayers in the mosque, thus limiting the religious character of the burial ceremony.[6] And yet, royal mausoleums were generally treated as religious monuments and often equipped with *miḥrābs*. Mamluk royal mausoleums were integrated into mosques and hosted religious services, thus acquiring the status of a *masjid*.[7]

Medieval tombstones, cenotaphs and textile tomb-covers were often inscribed with Qur'anic texts. A very complex picture emerges if we examine various published tombstones dated from the ninth century onwards. Wiet's catalogue of Egyptian tombstones of the ninth to tenth centuries mentions at least 25 different verses from the Qur'an and Hadith inscribed in combination or alone. There is also a group of tombstones without Qur'an texts, which simply indicate that the deceased was a Muslim who acknowledged the *shahāda*.[8] Thirteenth- and fourteenth-century tombstones from Ahlat, in Eastern Anatolia, often carried either the so-called Throne Verse (*Āyat al-Kursī*, Q. 2:255) or the phrase 'Every soul shall taste death' from *Sūrat Āl 'Imrān* (Q. 3:185). However, this was not a rule and Hadith inscriptions are equally frequent.[9] Besides biographical data, Ottoman tombstones regularly included prayers and a request addressed to the visitor to 'Recite the *Fātiḥa*[1] for the soul of the deceased'. Sometimes the epitaph started with the word *Fātiḥa* without including its text.[2]

Implements of warfare such as weapons, armour, banners and talismanic shirts were often inscribed with verses from the Qur'an and other religious formulae. Two common verses found on implements of warfare include the Throne Verse (Q. 2:255) and 'Help from Allah and a speedy victory. Proclaim good tidings to the faithful' from *Sūrat al-Ṣaff* (Q. 61:13). Such verses applied on implements of war embodied notions of Islamic *jihād* (religious warfare) in which armed struggle was sanctioned against the enemies of Islam. Protective talismanic shirts inscribed with Qur'anic verses were worn by soldiers under their armour and their function can also be understood in the context of *jihād*; however, these shirts also belong to the broader category of prophylactic objects. Talismans and amulets of various forms as well as magical healing bowls are commonly inscribed with Qur'anic verses and are often prepared and administered by shaykhs or holy men. Surprisingly even Ibn al-Hajj, a purist, approves

5. Ibn al-Hajj, *al-Madhkal*, vol. III, p. 273.
6. Ibid., p. 252.
7. House of worship (Arabic) [editor's note].
8. Gaston Wiet, *Catalogue général du musée arabe du Caire: stèles funéraires*, vols. IV–IX (Cairo, 1936–41). [*Shahāda*: the Muslim profession of faith, "There is no god but God (Allāh); Muḥammad is the prophet of God"—editor's note].
9. Beyhan Karamağarali, *Ahlat Mezartaşlari* (Ankara, 1972).
1. "The Opening," Q 1 [editor's note].
2. İlhan M. Mehdi, 'Diyarbakir *Mezar Kitabeleri* (*Les inscriptions funéraires de Diyarbakir*)' in Jean-Louis Bacqué-Grammont and Aksel Tibet, eds., *Cimetières et traditions funéraires dans le monde islamique*, 2 vols. (Ankara, 1996), vol. I, pp. 179–212.

the use of Qur'anic verses for apotropaic purposes, such as on healing bowls, and he mentions specific verses with healing powers to be used in amulets against various diseases. Moreover, he recommends that the patient should drink a solution consisting of a paper inscribed with Qur'anic verses that is dissolved in water.[3]

The *basmala* occasionally appears on caskets made of ivory and metal from Umayyad Spain, mostly in the short form of *Bismillāh* (In the Name of God).[4] Another example of a secular object that incorporates a reference to the Qur'an is a late-Ottoman ceramic fireplace in the Victoria and Albert Museum which includes in its decoration the names of the 'Seven Sleepers of Ephesus'[5] who were identified by medieval Qur'anic commentators with the un-named 'Companions of the Cave' (*Aṣḥāb al-Kahf*) mentioned in *Sūrat al-Kahf* (Q. 18:9–26).[6] These types of objects that list the names of the *Aṣḥāb* were perhaps inspired by inscriptions with the names of the twelve Shi'i imams which were often engraved on bronze and silver vessels of the Safavid period. These vessels were more likely used in religious establishments by dervishes or students rather than in a secular environment.[7]

Finally, another secular setting, the ruler's palace, also contained Qur'anic inscriptions, particularly in the throne room. However, based on the available evidence it appears that the holy text did not predominate in these settings and poetical verses were the most widespread form of inscription in the palace. This applies to the Alhambra[8] in Granada as well as to the royal residences in Syria and Egypt from the Mamluk and Ottoman periods.

* * *

## SHEILA S. BLAIR

### *From* Transcribing God's Word: Qur'an Codices in Context[†]

The Qur'an is the most important book in the Islamic lands, comparable to the Bible in the Western tradition.[1] Transmitted orally, the text was soon committed to writing, and manuscripts—usually in the codex

3. Ibn al-Hajj, *al-Madhkal*, vol. IV, pp. 121ff.
4. Jerrilynn D. Dodds, ed., *Al-Andalus: The Art of Islamic Spain* (New York, 1992), pp. 192, 198, 202, 206, 208.
5. In Christian legend, seven Christian men who hid in a cave near Ephesus, in modern-day Turkey, in 250 CE to escape Roman persecution; they awoke when Christianity was the religion of the empire, during the reign of Theodosius II (408–50) [editor's note].
6. Rudi Paret, 'Aṣḥāb al-kahf', *EI*², vol. I, p. 691. For an image of the Ottoman fireplace see Tim Stanley, *Palace and Mosque: Islamic Art from the Middle East* (London, 2004), p. 107. The names of the *Aṣḥāb al-Kahf* are found inscribed on various Islamic amulets.
7. Asadullah Souren Melikian-Chirvani, *Islamic Metalwork from the Iranian World, 8th–18th Centuries* (London, 1982), pp. 289ff.
8. The fortress and palace (largely built 1238–1358) of the Moorish rulers of Granada, Spain [editor's note].

† From *Journal of Qur'anic Studies* 10 (2008): 72–97. Reprinted by permission of Edinburgh University Press and the author. Except as indicated, all notes are Blair's; all figures and her references to them have been omitted.

1. A preliminary version of this paper was first presented at the international conference on the manuscripts of the Qur'an held in September 2002 in Bologna and was published as "Uses and Functions of the Koranic Text" in *Mélanges de l'Université Saint-Joseph* 59 (2006): 183–201. An

format—became the most common written work in circulation.[2] Despite, or perhaps because of, this ubiquity, written versions of the text vary enormously in materials, format, and aspect. This paper presents a broad overview of the forms that Qur'anic transcriptions have assumed over the first millennium of Islamic history, examining these codices as both physical objects and cultural signifiers. Approaching the subject functionally, the essay relates physical changes such as differing format and materials used to transcribe the Qur'anic text to social and historical ones such as differences in the status of copyists and illuminators who made these manuscripts, differences in the types of people or institutions for whom these written versions were made, and differences in the ways that these manuscripts were used. It concentrates on the finest examples, thereby showing how the study of art can help us understand the changing nature of Muslim societies, particularly at the highest levels.

To sketch these developments, I have selected three types of Qur'anic text made for different purposes over the first thousand years of Islam: (1) parchment manuscripts made for recitation in the first centuries of Islam; (2) small paper codices made for sectarian use from the tenth century; and (3) behemoth multi-volume sets made for funerary complexes from the fourteenth century. To illustrate each type, I have selected a well published and readily dated or datable example that can stand for the group and that can be keyed to an architectural monument to illustrate the physical and intellectual setting for which these written versions were made. These three examples are not the only types of Qur'anic text, but they are some of the most important, and they show the wide range of uses and functions of the Qur'anic codex over the centuries. Taken together, they also give a good idea of the history of scholarship on Qur'anic manuscripts.

## *The Amājūr Qur'an*

The manuscript I have selected to exemplify the first group—parchment manuscripts made as aides-mémoire for recitation—is the so-called Amājūr Qur'an. It gets its common name because it was—according to notes on the recto of every folio—endowed by Amājūr, who served the 'Abbāsid[3] governor of Damascus from 256/870 to 264/878. The manuscript is now dispersed. A handful of folios are scattered across the world from Tokyo, Riyadh and Cairo to Cambridge University Library and the

expanded version was the subject of a seminar presented in May 2005 at the École des Hautes Études en Sciences Sociales in Paris at the kind invitation of Houari Touati. That seminar, in turn, was the genesis of lectures given at the conference "Qur'an: Text, Translation and Interpretation" held at the School of Oriental and African Studies, London, in November 2005, at the Netherlands-Flemish Institute in Cairo in December 2006, and at the University of Arizona in January 2007. Much of the material has been taken from my recent study *Islamic Calligraphy* (Edinburgh: Edinburgh University Press, 2006). The early history of the Bible as written text was the subject of a splendid exhibition held recently in Washington, DC: see Michelle P. Brown, ed., *In the Beginning: Bibles Before the Year 1000* (Washington, DC: Smithsonian Institution, 2006).

2. The exact dating and process of the change from oral to written is still unclear and a subject of great controversy. See, for example, John Burton, "The Collection of the Qur'ān," in *Encyclopaedia of the Qur'ān*. For an up to date view of the subject, see William Graham and Navid Kermani, "Recitation and Aesthetic Reception," in *The Cambridge Companion to the Qur'ān*, ed. Jane Dammen McAuliffe (Cambridge: Cambridge University Press, 2006), pp. 115–43. For an overview of Qur'an manuscripts, see François Déroche, "Manuscripts of the Qur'ān," in *Encyclopaedia of the Qur'an*; François Déroche, "Codices of the Qur'ān," in *Encyclopaedia of the Qur'ān*.
3. The second of the Muslim dynasties (750–1258), following the Umayyads (661–750) [editor's note].

Ashmolean Museum at Oxford, but the bulk of the manuscript—242 folios—survives in the Türk ve Islam Eserleri Müzesi in Istanbul.[4]

The Amājūr Qur'an is relatively well published from several different perspectives that illustrate the different methodologies and approaches scholars have used to investigate Qur'an manuscripts over the course of the twentieth and even the twenty-first century. The manuscript was first brought to scholarly attention in the West in 1913 when Bernhard Moritz included a photograph of one page from the Khedival Library in Cairo to illustrate his article 'Arabia' in the first edition of the *Encyclopaedia of Islam*.[5] Afterward, the manuscript, like much of the field of Qur'anic manuscript studies, languished for some 70 years until the work of François Déroche, who has single-handedly moved the subject from a backwater into the mainstream.[6] As part of his research in Istanbul, Déroche uncovered the large chunk of the Amājūr Qur'an in the Türk ve Islam Eserleri Müzesi in Istanbul. He mentioned his discoveries in several articles published in the 1980s, and in 1990 devoted a brief article to the manuscript in the journal *Manuscripts of the Middle East*.[7] There, he drew attention to the further written documentation he had found in the manuscript itself, including two *waqfiyyāt*, or endowment deeds, with the date 262/876 and a note that Amājūr had endowed the thirty-part manuscript to an unidentified mosque in the city of Tyre, now in Lebanon. And finally, in a presentation given in London in 2003 and published in the same year in the journal *Muqarnas*, Alain Fouad George analysed the layout and proportions used in transcribing individual bifolios like the one at Oxford.[8] In contrast to Déroche's work that concentrates on the manuscript's codicology, George's focuses on visual analysis of the individual pages.

The Amājūr Qur'an illustrates the physical standard for Qur'an manuscripts made in the early period.[9] It is copied in brownish tannin-based ink on parchment, known in Arabic as *raqq*, *riqq* or *jild* and referring to the

4. This repository holds probably the largest collection of early Islamic manuscripts and fragments, amounting to over 200,000 folios. Many of these had been stored in the courtyard of the Great Mosque of Damascus in Syria until the disastrous fire there at the end of the 19th century. For safekeeping, the manuscripts were then removed to Istanbul, capital of the Ottomans who ruled Syria at the time. The finest went to the Topkapi Library, the rest to the Evkaf Museum (literally the Museum of Pious Endowments), later renamed the Türk ve Islam Eserleri Müzesi (the Museum of Turkish and Islamic Art).
5. Bernhard Moritz, "Arabia," in *Encyclopaedia of Islam*, 1st ed.
6. His books on Qur'an manuscripts include catalogs of those in the Bibliothèque Nationale (*Les Manuscrits du coran, aux origines de la calligraphic coranique* (Paris: Bibliothèque Nationale, Département des Manuscrits, Catalogue des Manuscrits Arabes, 1983); *Les Manuscrits du coran, du Maghreb à l'Insulinde* (Paris: Bibliothèque Nationale, Département des Manuscrits, Catalogue des Manuscrits Arabes, 1985), and in the Nasser D. Khalili Collection (*The Abbasid Tradition: Qur'ans of the 8th to the 10th Centuries AD*, ed. Julian Raby, The Nasser D. Khalili Collection of Islamic Art, 1 (London: The Nour Foundation in association with Azimuth Editions and Oxford University Press, 1992)) in addition to his comprehensive *Manuel de codicologie des manuscrits en écriture arabe*, with contributions by Annie Berthier et al. (Paris: Bibliothèque Nationale de France. 2000), as well as his recent survey *Le livre manuscrit arabe: préludes à une historie* (Paris: Bibliothèque Nationale de France, 2004).
7. François Déroche, "Les écritures coraniques anciennes: bilan et perspectives," *Revue des études islamiques* 48 (1980): 207–44; "Les manuscrits arabes datés du IIIe/IXe siècle," *Revue des études islamiques* 55–57 (1987–89): 343–79; "The Qur'ān of Amğūr," *Manuscripts of the Middle East* 5 (1990–91): 59–66.
8. Alain Fouad George, "The Geometry of the Qur'ān of Amājūr: A Preliminary Study of Proportion in Early Arabic Calligraphy," *Muqarnas* 20 (2003): 1–16; "Geometry of Early Qur'anic Manuscripts," *Journal of Qur'anic Studies* 9.1 (2007): 78–110. See also his forthcoming book, *The Rise of Arabic Calligraphy*, to be published in London in 2009 [London: Sage, 2010]. I thank him for generously sharing the typescript with me.
9. Ursula Dreibholz, *Frühe Koranfragmente aus der Grossen Moschee in Sanaa/Early Quran Fragments from the Great Mosque in Sanaa*, Hefte zur Kulturgeschichte des Jemen, 2 (Sanaa:

skin of various animals.[1] Written sources mention various types, ranging from sheepskin to goat, calf, donkey, and even gazelle. But such a range may be more imaginary than real, wishful thinking designed to enhance the prestige of such precious items rather than a description of physical reality. As Ursula Dreibholz has pointed out, the skin of animals that are slaughtered must have been preferable, for the skin of wild animals such as gazelles is prone to scars and scratches from thorns, insect bites, and other wounds, flaws that would render it unsuitable for precious manuscripts.[2] Furthermore, no tests have established the presence of any of these other exotic materials. Sheepskin was undoubtedly the most common support for early Qur'an manuscripts, perhaps even the only one. Typically, these manuscripts were made from the skin of lambs, as that from older sheep is too thick.

To make a suitable surface for writing, the skin had to be prepared carefully.[3] First it was soaked in limewater for weeks to loosen the hair. After rinsing, it was then stretched on wooden frames to dry. To remove any remaining fat or flesh, the flesh side was then scraped with a special rounded knife while applying strong pressure to make the collagen fibers in the skin collapse from a rounded into a ribbon-like shape. While drying, both sides of the skin were also rubbed several times with pumice stone and chalk.

Surviving manuscripts show that the parchment for Qur'an manuscripts was prepared differently than that used in Christian manuscripts. In the latter the two sides of the parchment folio are often indistinguishable. By contrast, in Islamic manuscripts the two sides differ markedly, as shown by the bifolio from the Amājūr Qur'an now in Oxford. The hair side often shows traces of follicles, while the flesh side is generally whiter and velvety to the touch. The ink adheres better to the naturally smoother hair side, but flakes from the flesh side. The unequal condition shows that parchment makers in the Islamic lands did not rub down the flesh sides to make them as smooth as the hair sides.

* * *

Like many other early Qur'an manuscripts, the individual volumes in the Amājūr Qur'an were probably bound in leather. The bindings may have resembled the few surviving from early manuscripts preserved in the Yemen.[4] The 30 volumes of the Amājūr Qur'an were then further protected in boxes or chests. We know this because the more complete of the two

Deutsches Archäologisches Institut Orient-Abteilung Aussenstelle Sanaa, 2003), in which this conservator who is working on the extraordinary cache of manuscripts found in the Yemen and still basically unpublished, provides detailed information about the technical aspects of Qur'an manuscripts from the early Islamic period.

1. The generic term *parchment*, which refers to any type of animal skin, is preferable to the specialised term *vellum*, which refers specifically to calfskin.
2. Dreibholz, *Frühe Koranfragmente*, p. 45.
3. For a general description of the preparation of parchment, see Nicholas Pickwoad, "Parchment," in *The Dictionary of Art*, ed. Jane Turner (London: Macmillan Publishers Limited, 1996). For more specific remarks about the parchment used in Islamic manuscripts, see François Déroche, "L'emploi du parchemin dans les manuscrits islamiques: Quelques remarques preliminaries," in *The Codicology of Islamic Manuscripts: Proceedings of the Second Conference of al-Furqān Islamic Heritage Foundation, 4–5 December 1993*, ed. Yasin Dutton (London: Al-Furqan Islamic Heritage Foundation, 1995), pp. 17–57; Déroche, *Manuel*, pp. 36–51.
4. Ursula Dreibholz, "Some Aspects of Early Islamic Bookbindings from the Great Mosque of Sana'a, Yemen," in *Scribes et manuscrits du Moyen-Orient*, ed. François Déroche and Francis Richard (Paris: Bibliothèque Nationale de France, 1997), pp. 15–34.

endowment notices added to the manuscript, the one at the end of part (*juz'*) 16,[5] says that the manuscript was preserved in two trunks (*ṣundūqayn*). Such boxes were standard. According to al-Samhūdī (d. 891/1507), citing a passage by Ibn Zabāla (d. early third/ninth century) on the authority of his teacher, the famous jurist Mālik ibn Anas (d. 179/796), the large Qur'an manuscript that the Umayyad governor of Iraq, al-Ḥajjāj ibn Yūsuf, sent to the mosque in Medina was similarly stored in a box (*ṣundūq*) set next to the right side of the column (*usṭuwāna*) built for the tomb of the Prophet. The box would be opened on Friday and Saturday, and people would recite from it for the morning prayer.[6] Perhaps these were elaborate wooden or even metal boxes like the ones used in the Mamlūk period.[7] The steps taken to protect the text show how expensive the Amājūr Qur'an was in its own time.

The page layout of the Amājūr Qur'an confirms its preciousness. The writing is unusually spacious, with only three lines of script per page meticulously penned freehand without rulings made by a drypoint. Using the published pages as samples, we can calculate that each of the 30 volumes comprised some 100 bifolios.[8] The total manuscript would then have consumed the skins of some 750 sheep. In terms of consumption of sheepskin, the Amājūr Qur'an is therefore comparable to other larger manuscripts of the Qur'an made in early Islamic times. Déroche noted that several large Qur'an manuscripts (e.g. BN MS Arabe 324) had folios measuring 68×53 cm, each of which would have required the hide of a single animal, and that 600 folios (and therefore sheep) would have been required for these enormous copies.[9]

We can compare the Amājūr Qur'an and other large Qur'an manuscripts to contemporary presentation copies of the Bible, such as the so-called *Codex Amiatinus* (Florence, Biblioteca Medicea-Laurenziana, cod. *Aminatino* 1). The earliest surviving manuscript of the complete Bible in the Latin vulgate, it was one of three Bibles commissioned by Ceolfrith, Abbot of the Northumbrian monasteries of Monkwearmouth and Jarrow, and prepared under the supervision of the Venerable Bede. The Abbot took the manuscript as a gift for the shrine of Saint Peter in Rome, but died en route at Langress in 716.[1] The large volume weighs some 35 kilos without covers and contains 1030 folios, each measuring 49×34 cm and containing 43 or 44 lines of uncial script written in two columns by some nine scribes trained to a high standard. The total production thus required the skins of 515 young calves, forcing the

5. Each *juz'* (part; Arabic) is roughly one-thirtieth of the Qur'ān; these units of division facilitate recitation of the text in a single month [editor's note].
6. George, *Rise of Arabic Calligraphy*, p. 80.
7. The Mamlūk metal boxes, such as one made in the early 8th/14th century and now in the Museum of Islamic Art in Cairo (cat. no. 183), illustrated in Sheila S. Blair and Jonathan M. Bloom, *The Art and Architecture of Islam, 1250–1800*, Pelican History of Art (New Haven: Yale University Press, 1994), fig. 130, measure some 45 cm square and are subdivided on the interior into two compartments, each partitioned to hold fifteen slender volumes that would have measured some 20×15×3 cm, approximately the same size as the individual volumes in the Amājūr Qur'an and other early manuscripts.
8. Large sheets that were each folded to make two pages (folios) [editor's note].
9. Déroche, "Manuscripts of the Qur'an."
1. There is a lengthy body of scholarly literature about this long and complex volume. One of the most accessible and recent articles is Lawrence Nees, "Problems of Form and Function in Early Medieval Illustrated Bibles from Northwest Europe," in *Imaging the Early Medieval Bible*, ed. John Williams (University Park: Pennsylvania State University Press, 1999), pp. 121–78.

monastery to secure a grant of additional land to raise the head of cattle needed.[2]

Like the materials, the calligraphy of the Amājūr Qur'an is typical of early Islamic times. It is penned using the angular script known generally as Kufic, a script used almost exclusively for Qur'an manuscripts.[3] Déroche put the script in his Group D1, a type notable for the crescent-shaped bowl on *alif* and the returning stroke of final *nūn* whose upstroke widens slightly towards the end.[4] The same style is used in other contemporary Qur'an manuscripts, such as the well known one endowed by 'Abd al-Mu'nim in Dhū'l-Qa'da 298/July 911.[5] The Amājūr Qur'an is one of the largest examples of this style, with a height of 29 mm from the base of one line to the base of the next, the standard adopted by Déroche for measuring the calligraphy in these early Qur'an manuscripts.

* * *

Both format and script therefore make the Amājūr Qur'an representative of early Qur'an manuscripts. Its endowment notice in the name of Amājūr, 'Abbāsid governor of Damascus, further shows that it belongs to a group dating from the third/ninth century. * * *

This information about the identity of the people who endowed these manuscripts helps us to place the Amājūr Qur'an (and its fellow manuscripts) in context. As is well known, manuscripts like these with 30 parts could be used during the month of Ramaḍān,[6] with the reader (or reciter) completing one part per day, thereby finishing the entire text within the month. But I think that we can go further and speculate as to why these manuscripts were made for (or at least endowed by) people connected to the 'Abbāsid court at this particular time.

The endowment of these monumental thirty-part manuscripts of the Qur'an corresponds, it seems to me, to the consolidations carried out by the 'Abbāsids in the third/ninth century, a time that Claude Gilliot has recently called the 'moment impériale', when fields such as grammar, poetry, literature, exegesis and jurisprudence were codified.[7] The same regularisation took place in the field of architecture and art.[8] Congregational mosques were increasingly separated from palaces, which were hidden behind blank walls, while mosques became visually distinct. * * *

2. I take my information from Nees, "Problems of Form and Function," p. 149, following R. L. S. Bruce-Mitford, "The Art of the Codex Amiatinus, Jarrow Lecture 1967," reprinted in *Journal of the British Archaeological Association* 32 (1969). Nees notes also that the manuscript informs us about the Northumbrian diet, following up a suggestion by Christopher De Hamel (*A History of Illuminated Manuscripts* (Boston: Godine, 1986), p. 84) that the lack of Carthusian manuscripts might be tied to their vegetarian diet.
3. Rare exceptions include a fragmentary genealogical work now divided between the Bibliothèque Nationale (MS Arabe 2047, 13 folios) and the Staatsbibliothek, Berlin (MS Or. 379, 2 folios) and a copy of the Acts of the Apostles transcribed by the monk Musa al-Rahib, probably in Palestine in the 3rd/9th century, which is now in the Monastery of St. Catherine on Mt. Sinai, except for one quire in the Bibliothèque Nationale (MS Arabe 6725; Marie-Geneviève Guesdon and Annie Vernay-Nouri, eds., *L'art du livre arabe: du manuscrit au livre d'artiste* (Paris: Bibliothèque Nationale de France, 2001), no. 13).
4. Déroche, *The Abbasid Tradition*, table 4.
5. See, for example, the folios illustrated in Estelle Whelan, "Writing the Word of God: Some Early Qur'ān Manuscripts and Their Milieux, Part I," *Ars Orientalis* 20 (1990): 113–47, figs. 15–16.
6. The ninth month of the Islamic calendar and the Muslim month of fasting; according to Q 2:185, during this month the Qur'ān was first revealed.
7. Claude Gilliot, "Creation of a Fixed Text," in McAuliffe, ed., *The Cambridge Companion to the Qur'ān*, pp. 41–57.
8. These developments can be followed in Richard Ettinghausen, Oleg Grabar, and Marilyn Jenkins-Madina, *Islamic Art and Architecture, 650–1250* (New Haven: Yale University Press, 2001).

Mosques became signifiers of the caliphs as rulers of the Muslim community, and these multi-part manuscripts endowed to them would have commemorated the religious ceremonies that took place there, activities that justified the caliphs' right to rule. The endowment of such Qur'an manuscripts should be seen in this context of extending an imperial style. Over the course of the fourth/tenth century, however, Muslim society became increasingly diverse and fragmented (there were, for example, three rival claimants to the caliphate at one time: an 'Abbāsīd, a neo-Umayyad, and a Fāṭimid[9]), a change that we can follow in the second of our exemplars, the Qur'an penned by Ibn al-Bawwāb.

### *The Ibn al-Bawwāb Qur'an*

Like the Amājūr Qur'an, the manuscript copied by Ibn al-Bawwāb is well known and well published. The intact volume, now in the Chester Beatty Library in Dublin, was the subject of a monograph published by D.S. Rice more than a half-century ago.[1] Pages from the codex are illustrated in virtually every book on Islamic art and calligraphy. Part of its importance stems from the unusually complete documentation in the colophon, which says that 'Alī ibn Ḥilāl, better known as Ibn al-Bawwāb (literally, the son of a doorman), transcribed the complete text (*jāmi'*) at Madīnat al-Salām (referring to Baghdad) in 391/1000–1.

In materials and format, the Ibn al-Bawwāb Qur'an differs markedly from the one endowed by Amājūr. First, the support has changed from parchment to paper. Paper had been invented in China several centuries before the Common Era, and both the material and the technology to make it traveled westward along the Silk Road.[2] By the second/eighth century both were exploited in Central Asia, and under the 'Abbāsids in the third/ninth century, paper replaced papyrus and parchment for record keeping in the chancery. Paper had one great advantage over other supports: since paper absorbed ink, the writing on it could not easily be erased, as was the case with papyrus and parchment. Documents written on paper were therefore more secure from forgery.

* * *

Along with the new material came a new format. Although basically the same size as the Amājūr Qur'an (now trimmed, the pages in the codex penned by Ibn al-Bawwāb measure 19×14 cm, as compared to the parchment folios in the Amājūr Qur'an which measure 12.5×19.5 cm), the pages in the Ibn al-Bawwāb Qur'an are oriented differently. The format has switched from horizontal to vertical or, in computer parlance, from landscape to portrait.

The new support and format were accompanied by new ink and script. Instead of the brownish tannin-based ink used for parchment codices in rectilinear script, Ibn al-Bawwāb used a black carbon-based ink for his copy in round script. The visual aspect of the page has changed as well.

9. A political and religious dynasty of North Africa and the Middle East (909–1171); it tried to take control of the Islamic world from the 'Abbāsid caliphs [editor's note].
1. D. S. Rice, *The Unique Ibn al-Bawwāb Manuscript in the Chester Beatty Library* (Dublin: Chester Beatty Library, 1955).
2. Jonathan M. Bloom, *Paper Before Print: The History and Impact of Paper in the Islamic World* (New Haven: Yale University Press, 2001).

The spacious three-line layout has been replaced by a more compact one with 26 lines per page, allowing the complete text of the Qur'an to be sandwiched into a single volume.

Despite its compactness, the text in Ibn al-Bawwāb's copy is readily readable. Words are meticulously pointed, with relatively clear division and spacing between words. The text is written in the *scriptio plena*,[3] fully vocalised with vowels and consonants written throughout in the same ink. Unpointed[4] (*muhmala*) letters—*ḥā'*, *ṣad* and *'ayn*—are distinguished by small versions of the same letters written below. The letters *sīn* and *rā'* are marked above by an inverted circumflex that distinguishes them from *shīn* and *zā'*.

Ibn al-Bawwāb's flowing script is graceful and elegant. Letters are pitched just to the left of vertical, and individual words and letters like *kāf* slope downward from right to left, a movement echoed in the pairs of dots which are written on the same right-to-left downward slope. The slope imparts a forward movement to the script, a flow that is enhanced by the strong sublinear rhythm created by the swooping tails of final *nūn*, *yā'*, and similar letters which extend beneath the next word and sometimes encircle other descending tails before tapering to a point.

* * *

As opposed to the Amājūr Qur'an and its mates, which were designed for recitation by someone who already knew the text by heart, these single-volume manuscripts in round hands were made for reading. Insular scribes copying the Bible introduced similar changes such as word separation, punctuation and decorated initials in order to clarify legibility and meaning.[5] These Western scribes were stimulated by the reforms of Pope Gregory (d. 604), Isidore of Seville (d. 636), and the Venerable Bede (d. 735), the greatest scholar of the medieval West, all of whom promoted silent reading to facilitate meditation and comprehension, supplementing the classical emphasis upon reading aloud to foster oratory and rhetoric. In the same way, Ibn al-Bawwāb was responding to a need for reading the Qur'an rather than reciting it orally, a change necessitated by the full conversion of the population to Islam by the third/tenth century.[6]

In addition to adapting the script, Ibn al-Bawwāb also added fine illumination to enhance readability. Text pages are decorated in the traditional blue, gold and sepia, and the opening and closing pages include decoration in brown, white, green and red as well. * * *

The small paper codex penned by Ibn al-Bawwāb also shows other aids introduced to enhance the practicality of this handy volume. The Amājūr Qur'an had a single page of illumination at beginning and end of individual volumes. In the Ibn al-Bawwāb Qur'an, by contrast, there are multiple sets of frontis- and finispieces (five in all). The two closest to the text, like those in the Amājūr Qur'an, are solely decorative. They seem to act metaphorically as guardians of the sacred text. Such pages are an inheritance

3. Literally, "full writing" (Latin) [editor's note].
4. Lacking the marks to indicate vowels or to distinguish consonants otherwise identical in form [editor's note].
5. Brown, *In the Beginning*, pp. 51–52.
6. On the rate of conversion, see Richard W. Bulliet, *Conversion to Islam in the Medieval Period: An Essay in Quantitative History* (Cambridge, MA: Harvard University Press, 1979).

from classical Antiquity and were likewise passed down in the Western tradition of luxury books. Similar ones can be seen in such Western manuscripts as the Lindisfarne Gospels made in the early second/eighth century.[7]

The three other sets of illuminated pages in the Ibn al-Bawwāb Qur'an provide other information. The ones at the beginning tells us that this codex contains 114 chapters with 6,236 ayas[8] made up of 77,460 words or 321,250 letters and 156,051 diacritical points (fol. 6b–7a) following the reading of 'Alī[9] used at Kufa (fol. 7b–8a). The set at the end gives a count of the 29 individual letters of the alphabet used in this version. The letters are arranged in an older sequence that ends with *wāw, hā', lām-alif* and then the last letter, *yā'*, which is written in the marginal roundel. As Yasser Tabbaa showed, these tables with verse and letter counts reflect the variant readings that proliferated at this time.[1] In the early fourth/tenth century the reforms of Ibn Mujāhid (d. 324/936) had led to the adoption of seven canonical readings. Other scholars such as Ibn Khālawayh (d. 370/980) expanded the list to ten, sometimes supplemented by four 'irregular' variants after the ten.

* * *

These tables in the Ibn al-Bawwāb Qur'an, along with the colophon, also suggest that it was intended for a Shī'ī clientele. According to the frontispiece, the manuscript follows the reading followed by the Kufans on the authority of 'Alā ibn Abī Ṭālib.[2] The colophon also invokes blessings on the Prophet's 'pure family', a phrase of special relevance to Shī'īs. The manuscript may have been intended for a buyer who shared the Shī'ī leanings of Ibn al-Bawwāb's patrons, the Buwayhids.

Such reverence for the Prophet's family helps us to fit the Ibn al-Bawwāb into its historical and social milieu. The same type of Shī'ī eulogy occurs in architectural inscriptions of the time. References to the Prophet's 'pure family' are found, for example, in the congregational mosque at Nā'īn in central Iran.[3] * * * Such eulogies in both the Ibn al-Bawwāb Qur'an and the mosque at Nā'īn suggest that in Iraq and Iran during the late fourth/tenth and early fifth/eleventh centuries mosques were renovated and Qur'an manuscripts copied to serve a new clientele, who happened to be Shī'īs and who also commissioned large palaces and great libraries that have not survived.

The Ibn al-Bawwāb Qur'an was probably not made for public reading in a mosque. Rather its small single-volume format suggests that it was a personal copy. The lack of a dedication might even indicate that it was

7. Often illustrated, as, for example, in Brown, *In the Beginning*, p. 59.
8. Verses [editor's note].
9. 'Alī ibn Abī Ṭālib (ca. 599–661), Muḥammad's cousin and son-in-law, and the fourth caliph; his supporters became the Shī'a [editor's note].
1. Yasser Tabbaa, "The Transformation of Arabic Writing: Part 1 Qur'ānic Calligraphy," *Ars Orientalis* 21 (1991): 119–48.
2. The statement is somewhat perplexing, as Yasin Dutton, 'Red Dots, Green Dots, Yellow Dots and Blue: Some Reflections on the Vocalisation of Early Qur'anic Manuscripts (Part II)," *Journal of Qur'anic Studies* 2.1 (2000): 17, pointed out that the text actually follows the verse count of the Basran Abū 'Amr. [Abū 'Amr ibn al-'Alā' (d. ca. 770–72), founder of the Basran school of Arabic philology—editor's note.]
3. Sheila S. Blair, *The Monumental Inscriptions from Early Islamic Iran and Transoxiana*, Supplements to *Muqarnas* (Leiden: E. J. Brill, 1992), no. 9.

made for the market. It was a private copy, as distinct from the Amājūr Qur'an and from our third example, a large multi-part manuscript made for a funerary complex in the early eighth/fourteenth century.

### *The Aḥmad al-Suhrawardī Qur'an*

The monumental manuscript penned by Aḥmad al-Suhrawardī at the beginning of the eighth/fourteenth century is—like the Amājūr Qur'an—dispersed, with seven sections and the colophon scattered in collections ranging from Tehran to New York.[4] Like the other two Qur'an manuscripts discussed here, the copy by Aḥmad al-Suhrawardī bears internal documentation, in this case multiple signatures and colophons, including this one from *juz'* 28 signed by Aḥmad al-Suhrawardī at Baghdad during the year 707/1307–08.

Like the Amājūr Qur'an, Aḥmad al-Suhrawardī's copy comprises 30 volumes, but instead of parchment, it, like the manuscript by Ibn al-Bawwāb, is copied on paper. In this case, however, the sheets are very large. Each page measures 50×35 cm, with bifolios measuring 50×70 cm. Each page in this large manuscript is thus five times the area of the pages in the small manuscripts for Amājūr and by Ibn al-Bawwāb.

In addition to its large size, the paper in Aḥmad al-Suhrawardī's Qur'an manuscript is notable for its quality. Unlike the brownish and rather coarse paper used by Ibn al-Bawwāb, the paper used by Aḥmad al-Suhrawardī is particularly white. It is also thinner and stronger than that produced earlier and often has a slight sheen from the polished size.[5] When viewed under a microscope, the page copied by Aḥmad al-Suhrawardī shows well-beaten long white fibers under a flawless size.[6] The smooth surface meant that the calligrapher's pen glided smoothly across the surface, producing strokes of a uniform blackness. Such manuscripts represent the pinnacle of technical perfection of paper and ink.

These large and fine sheets came in standard sizes. At least one other Qur'an manuscript made at this time—another thirty-volume Qur'an manuscript probably also copied by Aḥmad al-Suhrawardī—is twice this size.[7] Its enormous bifolios, each measuring 70 x 100 cm, correspond to what the fifteenth-century Mamlūk chronicler al-Qalqashandī called the full *Baghdādī* size. The large size may have been possible by the introduction of hammer mills, possibly from China. Such paper represents the limit of what a single person can lift from the mould. It must have been a Herculean task to lift the wet sheets of paper, especially as over 1,000 bifolios were needed for this colossal Qur'an manuscript.

* * *

Just as the size of the paper has changed in the three centuries since Ibn al-Bawwāb, so has the script. Each page in Aḥmad al-Suhrawardī's

4. The basic publication is David James, *Qur'ans of the Mamlūks* (London: Alexandria Press and Thames & Hudson, 1988), no. 39. He calls it the "Anonymous Baghdad Qur'an." Folios from it were also included in Linda Komaroff and Stefano Carboni, eds., *The Legacy of Genghis Khan: Courtly Art and Culture in Western Asia, 1256–1353* (New Haven: Yale University Press in association with the Metropolitan Museum of Art, 2002), nos. 63–64.
5. Glutinous material used to fill the pores in the paper's surface [editor's note].
6. See Blair, *Islamic Calligraphy*, fig. 7.4.
7. James, *Qur'ans of the Mamlūks*, no. 40.

large Qur'an has five lines of black *muḥaqqaq*[8] script, with black for vowels and orthographic signs. The monochrome black ink contrasts with the vivid polychrome paint used for the decoration. * * *

Like Ibn al-Bawwāb, Aḥmad al-Suhrawardī was one of the most famous calligraphers of his time, but surviving manuscripts and written chronicles allow us to flesh out his career in much more detail than that of his predecessor and to see how the status of calligraphers had changed in the intervening three centuries.[9] In contrast to Ibn al-Bawwāb, the son of a gatekeeper who had begun life as a housepainter in Baghdad, Aḥmad al-Suhrawardī was an aristocrat who came from one of the most highly respected families in the same city. His great grandfather Abū Ḥafṣ 'Umar al-Suhrawardī was a renowned Ṣūfī, author of the comprehensive handbook, *'Awārif al-ma'ārif*, and founder of the Suhrawardiyya, one of the main Ṣūfī *ṭuruq*[1] under the 'Abbāsid caliph al-Nāṣir. A renowned calligrapher who became the most famous pupil of Yāqūt al-Musta'ṣimī,[2] Aḥmad al-Suhrawardī left multiple surviving works on paper ranging in date over three decades from 701/1301–2 (a single-volume Qur'an codex) or 702/1302–3 (a calligraphic specimen) to 732/1331–32 (a copy of his great-grandfather's Ṣūfī handbook). According to the seventeenth-century chronicler Qaḍī Aḥmad, Aḥmad al-Suhrawardī also designed most of the texts inscribed on buildings in Baghdad, though none has survived. This information points to a major change in this period: the use of paper patterns and stencils allowing calligraphic designs to be transferred to other media, including stone, brick and tile. Such designs became a hallmark of architectural decoration until modern times.[3]

Not only was Aḥmad al-Suhrawardī of more important lineage than his predecessor, but he was also more of a specialist. Whereas Ibn al-Bawwāb had done both calligraphy and illumination in his small manuscript, signatures in Aḥmad al-Suhrawardī's multi-volume copy and others like it tell us that calligraphers in this period worked in teams with specialist illuminators. Aḥmad al-Suhrawardī's partner was Muḥammad ibn Aybak ibn 'Abd Allāh. He also signed the enormous Qur'an manuscript, which has similar calligraphy and may well have been the work of Aḥmad al-Suhrawardī. The increasing importance of illumination in these Qur'an manuscripts made at the turn of the seventh/thirteenth to eighth/fourteenth century coincides with the rising importance of painting. The Qur'an manuscripts are particularly important in documenting this change, for the repeated signatures and dates gives us some idea about methods of manuscript production in the period, revealing in what order the work was carried out and how long it took. From these facts, we can deduce how prestigious (and expensive) it was.[4]

* * *

8. A type of cursive calligraphic Arabic script (literally, "clear" or "fully realized"), said to have been invented by Ibn al-Bawwāb [editor's note].
9. Brief biography in Blair, *Islamic Calligraphy*, p. 249.
1. Schools or orders (sing, *tarīqa*; Arabic) [editor's note].
2. Calligrapher (d. 1298) who served the last 'Abbāsid caliph [editor's note].
3. On this shift, see Jonathan M. Bloom, "Paper: The Transformative Medium in Ilkhanid Art," in *Beyond the Legacy of Genghis Khan*, ed. Linda Komaroff (Leiden: E. J. Brill, 2006), pp. 289–302.
4. Sheila S. Blair, "Calligraphers, Illuminators, and Painters in the Ilkhanid Scriptorium," in Komaroff, ed., *Beyond the Legacy of Genghis Khan*, pp. 167–82.

Format and signatures allow us to speculate about the original context for the very large Qur'an manuscript penned by Aḥmad al-Suhrawardī. Although it lacks a certificate of commissioning, its large size and lavish illumination bespeak court patronage. These magnificent multi-part manuscripts were endowed to the tomb complexes that developed in Iran under the Īlkhānids.[5] Their pious foundations often comprised several structures, including a mosque, *madrasa*, hospital, hospice for Ṣūfīs, guest hospice, and residence for descendants of the Prophet, all grouped around the patron's tomb. In at least one case, we can match a specific manuscript with a particular tomb. The largest of all the Qur'an manuscripts made for the Īlkhānids—the one copied on full-*Baghdādī* sheets—was endowed by Sultan Uljaytū to his tomb complex at Sulṭāniyya.[6]

* * *

Contemporary chronicles, some with illustrations, give us an idea of how these multi-part Qur'an manuscripts were used in the eighth/fourteenth century. According to the endowment deed for the pious foundation established by the vizier Rashīd al-Dīn[7] outside Tabrīz at the Khwānd Baraka and Rab'-i Rashīdī, the focus of the complex was the tomb where the Qur'an was recited around the clock and where feasts and special readings were held on holidays.[8] The tomb was separated from the mosque by a lattice screen secured with two chains and strong locks to safeguard the precious manuscripts and other objects kept inside. Near the latticed screen a trio of Qur'an readers took turns reading on small minbars. The tomb was lighted by four hanging lamps and four beeswax candles set in large candle stands. Incense perfumed the air and the reciters' noses.

* * *

These three Qur'an codices, then, show us some of the changes that took place in manuscript production during the first seven centuries of Islam. They are not the only types of Qur'an manuscript: we could equally well discuss bilingual copies, scrolls, or printed editions. Yet these examples show us that the manuscripts themselves have much to offer to tell us not only about transcription of the Qur'an but also about the evolution of Muslim religion and society over time.

5. A Mongol dynasty that ruled in Iran, 1256–1335 [editor's note].
6. For a discussion of the tomb complex there, see Sheila S. Blair, "The Mongol Capital of Sulṭāniyya, 'the Imperial,'" *Iran* 24 (1986): 139–51. [Uljaytū or Öljeitü (r. 1304–16), the 8th Īlkhānid ruler—editor's note.]
7. Persian statesman and historian (1247–1318); he was vizier to Uljaytū and his predecessor, Maḥmūd Ghāzān (r. 1295–1304) [editor's note].
8. Sheila S. Blair, "Ilkhanid Architecture and Society: An Analysis of the Endowment Deed of the Rab'-i Rashidi," *Iran* 22 (1984): pp. 67–90.

# THE QUR'ĀN IN AMERICA

# OMAR IBN SAID

In recent decades, the study of Islam in America has increasingly turned to the history of those long forgotten or ignored: the Muslims who came to this country in the slave ships that sailed from west Africa. While reliable statistics do not exist, scholars have estimated that eventually the number of African Muslims and their descendants who lived in colonial and antebellum America could be numbered in the tens of thousands.

Omar ibn Said (ca. 1770–1864), a Fulbe from Futa Toro (northern Senegal), was enslaved during a military conflict and transported to the Carolinas around 1807. Just over twenty years later, in response to the request of his final master—James Owens of Fayetteville, North Carolina—he wrote about his capture and deportation and about his harsh treatment at the hands of earlier owners. Omar's manuscript, which begins with Sūra *al-Mulk* ("The Sovereignty," Q 67), was written in Arabic, clear evidence of his education and former status as a scholar. Translations in English soon followed, and their broad dissemination increased Ibn Said's popularity and renown. The manuscript itself, long thought to be lost, was rediscovered in 1995 in Alexandria, Virginia. Today the mosque in Fayetteville is named after Omar ibn Said.

## The Life of Omar Ibn Said, Written by Himself†

The Life of Omar ben Saeed, called Morro, a Fullah Slave, in Fayatteville, N.C., Owned by Governor Owen, Written by himself in 1831 & sent to Old Paul, or Lahmen Kebby, in New York, in 1836, Presented to Theodore Dwight by Paul in 1836, Translated by Hon. Cotheal, Esq., 1848.[1] In the name of God, the merciful, the compassionate.[2] May God bless our Lord (*sayyidina*)[3] Mohammad:

Blessed be He in whose hand is the *mulk* and who has power over all things.

He created death and life that He might put you to the proof and find out which of you had the best work. He is the Mighty, the Forgiving One.

He created seven heavens arrayed one above the other. You will not see a flaw in the Merciful's creation. Turn up your eyes: can you detect a single crack?

Then look once more and yet again: your eyes in the end will grow dim and weary.

We have adorned the lowest heaven with lamps, missiles to pelt the devils with. We have prepared the scourge of Fire for these, and the scourge of Hell for those who deny their Lord: an evil fate!

† From *A Muslim American Slave: The Life of Omar Ibn Said*, trans. and ed. Ala Alryyes (Madison: University of Wisconsin Press, 2011), pp. 41–77. Reprinted by permission of the University of Wisconsin Press. Except as indicated, all notes are Alryyes's; all brackets in the text are his.

1. A nearly identical version of this translation and a short introduction were published as *The Life of Omar Ibn Said, Written by Himself* in *The Multilingual Anthology of American Literature: A Reader of Original Texts with English Translations*, ed. Marc Shell and Werner Sollors (New York: New York University Press, 2000), 58–93. [Dwight (1764–1846), lawyer, author, and newspaper editor—editor's note.]
2. Omar does not identify this Qur'anic fragment as *Surat al-Mulk* ["The Sovereignty," Q 67]. This is noteworthy in the context of a slave narrative. The noun *al-mulk* comes from the tripartite Arabic root: "malaka," meaning both to own and to have dominion. The title of the *sura* is therefore the perfect allusion to slavery: absolute power through ownership. The verb and the noun conflate persons and things.
3. I misread *sayyidina* in the earlier translation.

When they are flung into its flames, they shall hear it roaring and seething, as though bursting with rage. And every time a multitude is thrown therein, its keepers will say to them: "Did no one come to warn you?"

"Yes," they will reply, "he did come, but we rejected him and said: 'Allah has revealed nothing: you are in grave error.'"

And they will say: "If only we listened and understood, we should not now be among the heirs of the Fire."

Thus shall they confess their sin. Far from God's mercy are the heirs of the Fire.

But those that fear their Lord although they cannot see Him shall be forgiven and richly rewarded.

Whether you speak in secret or aloud, He knows your innermost thoughts. Shall He who created all things not know them all? Gracious is He and all-knowing.

It is He who has made the earth subservient to you. Walk about its regions and eat of His provisions. To Him all shall return at the Resurrection.

Are you confident that He who is in heaven will not cause the earth to cave in beneath you, so that it will shake to pieces and overwhelm you? [so that it will shake to pieces and overwhelm you?]

Are you confident that He who is in heaven will not let loose on you a sandy whirlwind? You shall before long know the truth of my warning.

Those who have gone before them likewise disbelieved: but how grievous was the way I rejected them!

Do they not see the birds above their heads, spreading their wings and closing them? None save the Merciful sustains them. He observes all things.

Who is it that will defend you like an army, if not the Merciful? Truly, the unbelievers are in error.

Who will provide for you if He withholds His sustenance? Yet they persist in arrogance and in rebellion.

Who is more rightly guided, he that goes groveling on his face, or he that walks upright upon a straight path?

Say: "It is He who has brought you into being, and given you ears and eyes and hearts. Yet you are seldom thankful."

Say: "It is He who placed you on the earth, and before him you shall all be assembled."

They ask: "When will this promise be fulfilled, if what you say is true?"

Say: "God alone has knowledge of that. My mission is but to warn you plainly."

But when they see it drawing near, the unbelievers' faces will turn black with gloom, and a voice will say: "This is the doom which you have challenged."

[Say: "Consider if all the water that you have were to sink down into the earth, who][4]

Say: "Consider whether Allah destroys me and all my followers or has mercy upon us, who will protect the unbelievers from a woeful scourge?"

[Say: "God alone has knowledge of that.][5]

4. Omar here inserts a fragment from the last verse of the *sura*.

5. Omar repeats a part of an earlier verse above, and omits the subsequent verse which reads: "Say: 'He is the Lord of Mercy: in Him we believe, and in Him we put our trust. You shall soon know who is in evident error.'"

Say: "Consider: if all the water that you have were to sink down into the earth, who would give you running water in its place?"

O Sheikh Hunter[6] (*Hanta*) I cannot write my life, I have forgotten much of my talk as well as the talk of the Maghreb.[7] O my brothers, do not blame me.

Praise be to Allah, much praise, He grants of bounty in abundance.

In the name of Allah, the Gracious, the Merciful. Thanks be to Allah, for his goodness of old, his generosity and favor. To him is majesty due. Thanks be to Him who created the creation for His worship, so He may judge their deeds and words.

From Omar to Sheikh Hunter: You asked me to write my life. I cannot write my life for I have forgotten much of my talk [language] as well as the talk of the Arabs. Also I know little grammar and little vocabulary. O my brothers, I ask you in the name of Allah, not to blame me for my eye is weak and so is my body.

My name is Omar Ibn Said; my birthplace is Fut Tur, between the two rivers [or seas].[8] I sought knowledge in Bundu and Futa with a Sheikh called Mohammad Said, my brother, and Sheikh Suleiman Kimba and Sheikh Jebril [i.e., Gabriel] Abdal. I continued seeking knowledge for twenty five years, [then] I came to my place [and stayed] for six years. [Then there] came to our country a big army. It killed many people. It took me, and walked me to the big Sea, and sold me into the hand of a Christian man (*Nasrani*) who bought me and walked me to the big Ship in the big Sea.[9]

We sailed in the big Sea for a month and a half until we came to a place called Charleston. And in a Christian language, they sold me. A weak, small, evil man called Johnson, an infidel (*Kafir*) who did not fear Allah at all, bought me.

I am a small man who cannot do hard work; I escape[d], from the hands of Johnson after a month, and walked to a place called Faydel.[1] I saw houses after a month; I entered the houses to pray. I saw a young man who was riding horses, then his father came to the place. He spoke to his father that he saw a Sudanese man in the house.[2] A man called Hindah together with another man riding a horse with many dogs took me walking with them for twelve miles to a place called Faydel.[3] They took me to a big

6. Words indicating English names of persons and places have been transliterated from Arabic by the translator.
7. Presumably Arabic. [The Maghreb: literally, "the west" (Arabic); the region of North Africa bordering the Mediterranean—editor's note.]
8. Fut Tur, or Futa Toro, lies between the Senegal and the Gambia rivers in western Africa. Michael A. Gomez notes that "In the middle Senegal valley a strong Muslim polity was established as early as the eleventh century. Subsequently, a dynasty of fluctuating loyalty to Islam was founded in the early sixteenth century, but it was overthrown in 1776 by a militant Islamic theocracy. Futa Toro, as the state came to be known, was ethnically Fulbe." Michael A. Gomez, "Muslims in Early America," *Journal of Southern History* 60, no. 4 (November 1994): 677. * * * The title-page of the manuscript refers to the author (in English) as "Omar ben Saeed, called Morro, a Fullah slave."
9. If consent and the freedom of movement are inextricably related, how poignantly ironic Omar's intense repetition of the verb "walk" is. The repetition of the word calls forth the processions of chained slaves—the physical repetition of nameless slaves—to which he probably submitted.
1. Fayetteville, North Carolina? Some of the Arabized names are difficult to interpret; for example, "Hindah," the leader of the chase party.
2. It was, and is, common to refer to black people in Arabic as "Sudanese" even if they did not hail from the Sudan. *Aswad* in Arabic means black.
3. The description of the group that "escorts" him, with mounted men and dogs, indicates perhaps a chase posse for escaped slaves.

house [building]. I could not come out of the big house—called *jeel* [i.e., jail] in the Christian language—for sixteen days and nights.

On Friday,[4] a man came and opened the door of the big house, and I saw many men whose language was Christian. They called to me: is not your name Omar, is it not Said? I did not understand [hear] the Christian language. I saw a man called Bob Mumford speaking [to the jailer?]. He took me out of the big house. I consented very much to walk with them to their place. I stayed in Mumford's place for four days and nights. A man called Jim Owen, the husband of Mumford's daughter, Betsy Mumford, asked me: "Do you consent to walk to a place called Bladen?"[5] I said, "Yes." I agreed to walk with them. I have stayed in Jim Owen's place until now.

Before I came into the hands of General Owen, a man called Mitchell came to buy me. Mitchell asked me: "Would you walk to a place called Charleston?" I said: "No, no, no, no, no, no, no—I will not walk to the place Charleston; I will stay in the hands of Jim Owen."

O, people of North Carolina; O, people of South Carolina; O, people of America, all of you: are there among you men as good as Jim Owen and John Owen?[6] They are good men for whatever they eat, I eat; and whatever they wear they give me to wear. Jim with his brother read from the Bible (*Ingeel*) that Allah is our Lord, our Creator, and our Owner and the restorer of our condition, health and wealth by grace and not duty. [According?] to my ability, open my heart to the right path, to the path of Jesus Christ, to a great light.

Before I came to the Christian country, my religion was/is the religion of Mohammad, the prophet of Allah, may Allah bless him and grant him peace.[7] I used to walk to the mosque (*masjid*) before dawn, and to wash my face, head, hands, feet. I [also] used to hold the noon prayers, the afternoon prayers, the sunset prayers, the night prayers.

I used to give alms (*zakat*) every year in gold, silver, harvest, cattle, sheep, goats, rice, wheat and barley—all I used to give in alms. I used to join the *Jihad* every year against the infidels (*Kuffar*). I used to walk to Mecca and Medinah as did those who were able.[8] My father had six sons and five daughters, and my mother had three sons and one daughter. When I left my country, I was thirty-seven years old. I have been residing in the Christian country for twenty four years.

In the year eight hundred and thirty and one (1831) [after] Jesus Christ.

O, people of North Carolina; O, people of South Carolina; O, people of America, all of you: The first son of Jim Owen is called Thomas and his sister is called Maas Jen [Martha Jane?]

4. Or could it be Sunday, the Christian Sabbath?
5. Bladen County, North Carolina, is south of Fayetteville.
6. John Owen (1787–1841), brother of Jim Owen, governor of North Carolina from December 1828 to December 1830.
7. Omar's construction is ambiguous; he does not use the past construction (*kana*) to indicate his previous religion. A literal translation would read: "Before . . . my religion is the religion of Mohammad, etc."
8. Omar seems here to enumerate some of the tenets and duties, or *arkan* and *furod*, of Islam, respectively, rather than assert what he has done. More precisely, I think he is mixing a description of his particular deeds, such as giving alms, with catechizing, such as "one should go to Mecca and Medinah if able."

This is a good generation (*Geel*). Tom Owen and Nell Owen had two sons and one daughter. The first boy is called Jim and the other John; the girl is called Melissa. Master (*Sayyid*) Jim and his wife Betsy Owen have two sons and five daughters. They are Tom, John, Martha, Miriam, Sophia, Margaret and Lisa. This generation is a very good generation.

And John Owen's wife is called Lucy. A good wife, she had three children and then two. Three died and two remained.

O, people of America; O, people of North Carolina: do you have, do you have, do you have, do you have such a good generation that fears Allah so much?

I am Omar, I love to read the book, the Great Qur'an.

General Jim Owen and his wife used to read the Bible, they used to read the Bible to me a lot. Allah is our Lord, our Creator, and our Owner and the restorer of our condition, health and wealth by grace and not duty. [According?] to my ability, open my heart to the Bible, to the path of righteousness. Praise be to Allah, the Lord of Worlds, many thanks for he grants bounty in abundance.

Because the law (*Shar'a*) was to Moses given, but grace and truth were by Jesus the Messiah.

First, [following] Mohammed. To pray, I said: "Praise be to Allah, Lord of the Worlds; the Compassionate, the Merciful; Sovereign (*Malik*) of the Day of Judgment; It is you we worship, and to you we turn for help; Guide us to the straight path; The path of those whom you have favored with grace; Not of those who have incurred Your wrath; Nor of those who have strayed. Amen."

And [but?] now,[9] I pray in the words of our Lord Jesus the Messiah: "Our Father, who art in heaven, hallowed be thy name, thy Kingdom come, thy Will be done, on earth as it is in Heaven. Give us this day our daily bread and forgive us our trespasses as we forgive those who trespass against us, and lead us not into temptation but deliver us from the evil one for thine is the Kingdom, the power, and the glory for ever and ever. Amen."[1]

I reside in our country here because of the great harm. The infidels took me unjustly and sold me into the hands of the Christian man (*Nasrani*) who bought me. We sailed on the big sea for a month and a half to a place called Charleston in the Christian language. I fell into the hands of a small, weak, and wicked man who did not fear Allah at all, nor did he read nor pray. I was afraid to stay with such a wicked man who committed many evil deeds so I escaped. After a month, Allah our Lord presented us into the hands of a righteous man who fears Allah, and who loves to do good deeds and whose name is General Jim Owen and whose brother is called Colonel John Owen. These are two righteous men. I am in a place called Bladen County.

9. The Arabic construction *wa alān* is ambiguous in that it can be translated as the inclusive "and now" or the exclusive "but now."

1. I give here, of course, a translation of Omar's Arabic rendering of the Lord's Prayer [Matthew 6:9–13]. Noteworthy is the fact that Omar uses the Protestant version.

# DENISE A. SPELLBERG

## *From* What Jefferson Learned—and Didn't—from His Qurʾan†

To be acquainted with the various laws and constitutions of civilized nations, especially those who flourish in our own time, is, perhaps, the most useful part of knowledge.

—George Sale, from the "Preliminary Discourse" to his English translation of the Qurʾan, 1734

[T]hat our civil rights have no dependance on our religious opinions . . . that therefore the proscribing any citizen as unworthy the public confidence by laying upon him an incapacity of being called to offices of trust and emolument, unless he profess or renounce this or that religious opinion, is depriving him injuriously of those privileges and advantages to which, in common with his fellow citizens, he has a natural right.

—Jefferson's Bill for Establishing Religious Freedom, drafted in 1777; proposed in Virginia, 1779; made state law, 1786

In 1765, the *Virginia Gazette*, the local newspaper in Williamsburg, which also served as the only bookseller in the colony, recorded a purchase by Thomas Jefferson.[1] The item at the bottom of page 2, under the heading "Williamsburg October 1765," indicates Jefferson acquired "Sale's Koran," in "2 Vols," for sixteen shillings.[2] The books had been shipped from London, where in 1734 George Sale had first published his translation of what in English was commonly called "the Alcoran of Mohammed."[3] Jefferson would have bought the third edition, printed in 1764.[4]

† From chapter 3 of Denise A. Spellberg, *Thomas Jefferson's Qurʾan: Islam and the Founders* (New York: Alfred A. Knopf, 2013), pp. 81–86, 91–92, 326–28, 330.  All notes are Spellberg's.

1. Paul P. Hoffman, ed., *Virginia Gazette Daybooks, 1750–1752 and 1764–1766*, (Charlottesville: University of Virginia Library Microfilm Publications, 1967), Segment 2, folio 202. The text is described as "Sali's [*sic*] *Koran*" that was "interspersed among his purchases of law books in 1764 and 1765" by Frank L. Dewey, *Thomas Jefferson, Lawyer* (Charlottesville: University Press of Virginia, 1986), 14. See also James Gilreath and Douglas L. Wilson, eds., *Thomas Jefferson's Library: A Catalog with the Entries in His Own Order* (Washington, DC: Library of Congress, 1989), 58; Kevin J. Hayes, "How Thomas Jefferson Read the Qurʾan," *Early American Literature* 39, no. 2 (2004): 247; Kevin J. Hayes, *The Road to Monticello: The Life and Mind of Thomas Jefferson* (New York: Oxford University Press, 2008), 9, 130, 201, 258–59, 316; E. Millicent Sowerby, ed., *Catalogue of the Library of Thomas Jefferson*, 5 vols. (Washington, DC: Library of Congress, 1952–53) 2:90, catalog #1457.
2. The original *Gazette* entry has after his name the word "Note," which appears but indicates no further information.
3. George Sale, trans., *The Koran, commonly called the Alcoran of Mohammed, Translated into English from the Original Arabic; with Explanatory Notes, taken from the Most Approved Commentators, to which is prefixed a Preliminary Discourse*, 2 vols. (London: L. Hawes, W. Clarke, R. Collins, and T. Wilcox, 1764). Rare Books and Special Collections Division, Library of Congress. I will refer to Jefferson's first volume of the Qurʾan through xvi as Sale, "To the Reader," or "Preliminary Discourse," or "To the Right Honourable John Lord Carteret (Dedication)," *Koran (1764)*. All other references to "To the Reader" or "Preliminary Discourse" refer to the 1734 first-edition facsimile of a Harvard manuscript in one volume, George Sale, trans., *The Koran* (New York: Garland, 1984), cited hereafter as Sale, "To the Reader," or "Preliminary Discourse," *Koran (1734)*. There are no substantial differences between the two editions, except that Jefferson's version is in two volumes rather than the initial one.
4. Arnoud Vrolijk, "Sale, George (b. in or after 1696–d. 1736)," in *Oxford Dictionary of National Biography*, 58 vols. (New York: Oxford University Press, 2004), 48:685–87. Vrolijk asserts that 1746 was the second edition in opposition to 1764, as stated by Sebastian R. Prange, "Thomas

Jefferson was not the only one to possess Sale's Qur'an in eighteenth-century Virginia. In 1781, Dr. James Bryden of Goochland County would claim that British troops during the Revolutionary War had seized not just his many medical books but also what he listed as "Al Coran of Mahomet" in two volumes, whose value he estimated at one pound, more than Jefferson had paid sixteen years before. Dr. Bryden did not mention Sale as translator, but that the book was in two volumes with the title "the Alcoran of Mohammed" makes the identification certain.[5] Whether Bryden was ever reimbursed for his loss is unknown, but the more important question remains: What happened to Jefferson's Qur'an of 1765?

### *One Qur'an—or Two? 1770*

In February 1770, five years after his purchase of the Qur'an, Thomas Jefferson wrote his friend John Page with calamitous news: "My late loss may perhaps have reached you by this time, I mean the loss of my mother's house by fire, and in it, of every paper I had in the world, and almost every book."[6] (The *Virginia Gazette* would also confirm that Jefferson "lost all his furniture, a valuable collection of books, and what is perhaps worse, his papers.")[7] A true bibliophile, Jefferson lamented, "Would to God it had been the money; then had it never cost me a sigh!"[8] What was worse, the loss "fell principally" on his "books of Common Law, of which [he had] but one left, at that time lent out."[9] The answers to the questions of how many and which books were lost remain elusive, but for the lawyer-in-training, the books were all critical.[1] There would have been additional losses too, as recorded purchases from the accounts of the *Virginia Gazette* attest, including the Acts of Parliament and British Common and Chancery law, and the works of Machiavelli and Milton.[2] All these were purchased around the same time he acquired the Qur'an.

When he bought the Qur'an in 1765, Jefferson was an impassioned law student engaged in criticizing the recently passed British Stamp Act.[3] The most immediate reason for wishing to study the Qur'an would have

Jefferson's Qur'an," *Saudi Aramco World* 62, no. 4 (July/August 2011): 5. Four editions are mentioned, without dates, by Hartmut Bobzin, "Translations of the Qur'an," in *Encyclopaedia of the Qur'an*, ed. Jane D. McAuliffe, 6 vols. (Leiden: E. J. Brill, 2006), 5:348.

5. My thanks for this important reference belong to two University of Texas at Austin graduate students: Sharon Silzell, whose own research interest in the Qur'an alerted me to the importance of this reference, which she heard about from her graduate colleague Ben Breen. He located the citation while researching for Professors James Sidbury of Rice University and Cassandra Pybus of the University of Sydney. I am grateful to the latter two historians for allowing me to cite this document, headed "Property Taken from Dr. James Bryden by the British Troops, '81." Library of Virginia, among a box of uncataloged documents referred to as "the British Depredations" of Goochland County, Virginia, 1782, call number BC 114 7038.
6. Thomas Jefferson, "Letter to John Page," February 21, 1770, in *The Papers of Thomas Jefferson*, ed. Julian P. Boyd et al., 40 vols. (Princeton: Princeton University Press, 1950–), 1:548. Hereafter cited as *Papers of Thomas Jefferson*.
7. Dewey, *Thomas Jefferson*, 154 n. 25.
8. *Papers of Thomas Jefferson*, 1:35.
9. Dewey, *Thomas Jefferson*, 154 n. 2; *Papers of Thomas Jefferson*, 1:35.
1. Although Jefferson may have lost between three hundred and five hundred volumes, this letter to Page may have been "an exaggeration," according to Hayes, *Road to Monticello*, 2–3, 8; quote on 2–3.
2. Hoffman, *Virginia Gazette Daybooks*, Segment 2, folios 7, 11, 12, 13, 28, 159, 175.
3. Prange, "Thomas Jefferson's Qur'an," 4. Jefferson's study of religion and law are paramount in the explanation for his interest in the Qur'an; see Hayes, "How Thomas Jefferson Read the Qur'an," 247, 252; Hayes, *Road to Monticello*, 9.

been to gain an insight into Islamic law and religion.[4] These may have interested him per se—Jefferson had an immense curiosity and a cosmopolitan outlook—but he may have had a more immediate purpose, for in seeking legal precedents for local Virginia cases, he would often look to other cultures around the world.

After the fire, Jefferson made no mention of the fate of the Qur'an he had purchased five years earlier. Did it perish in the flames, or was it miraculously spared? We will never know. During the mid-1760s, Jefferson had taken detailed notes on the texts he'd read with particular interest; these notes too, however, were lost in the fire at Shadwell, his mother's house. But if Jefferson's Qur'an was destroyed in 1770, then what are we to make of the two volumes of Sale's Qur'an he initialed, now at the Library of Congress in Washington, D.C.?[5]

There are two possibilities: The original Qur'an either survived the fire, or it was later replaced with another copy of the same edition.[6] If Jefferson did indeed buy the Qur'an twice, it would be an extraordinary testament to his desire to understand Islam. But even if he purchased the text only once, Jefferson remains unique among America's Founders in his desire to understand Islam on its own terms, looking directly to its most sacred source. In fact, his purchase of the Qur'an marked only the beginning of his study of Islam. After the 1770 fire, as he immediately began to reconstruct his lost library, Jefferson undertook to acquire numerous volumes about Middle Eastern languages,[7] history, and travel, and he continued doing so for the rest of his life.[8]

* * *

## *George Sale's Qur'an and the Problem of Translation*

George Sale (c. 1696–1736), a lawyer and an Anglican, described the Prophet Muhammad on the first page of his translation as "the legislator of the Arabs," words that would have appealed to Jefferson the lawyer.[9] Since the twelfth century, Christian translators of the Qur'an had commonly defined the text not as divine revelation but as a repository of Islamic law. Robert Ketton's first Latin translation in 1143 was entitled *Lex Saracenorum*, or *Law of the Saracens*.[1] The translations from the

4. An emphasis on Jefferson's interest in Islamic law is offered by Azizah Y. al-Hibri, "Islamic and American Constitutional Law: Borrowing Possibilities or a History of Borrowing?" *University of Pennsylvania Journal of Constitutional Law* 1, no. 3 (1999): 499–500.
5. Jefferson initialed volume 1, page 113, of the Qur'an, Rare Books and Special Collections Division, Library of Congress, with a "T" and "I" rather than a "T" and "J." On the commonality of Jefferson's use of his initials in his books, see Hayes, *Road to Monticello*, 6–8.
6. The first person to assert that "most likely Jefferson owned two copies of the Qur'an" because of the Shadwell fire was al-Hibri, "Islamic and American Constitutional Law," 498 n. 30.
7. Hayes, "How Thomas Jefferson Read the Qur'an," 251, 257–58.
8. Edwin S. Gaustad, *Sworn on the Altar of God: A Religious Biography of Thomas Jefferson* (Grand Rapids, MI: William B. Eerdmans, 1996), 18–19. I would like to commend the generosity of the late Shearer Davis (Dave) Bowman, a historian and colleague who recommended this work when he kindly shared his brief overview of Jefferson's views of Christianity with me.
9. Sale, "Preliminary Discourse," *Koran (1764)*, 1:A; Hayes, "How Thomas Jefferson Read the Qur'an," 247–48, 251–52; Hayes, *Road to Monticello*, 9.
1. Ziad Elmarsafy, *The Enlightenment Qur'an: The Politics of Translation and the Construction of Islam* (Oxford: Oneworld Press, 2009), 1–2. For a more in-depth assessment of medieval translations of the Qur'an, see Thomas E. Burman, *Reading the Qur'an in Latin Christendom, 1140–1560* (Philadelphia: University of Pennsylvania Press, 2007).

twelfth to the eighteenth century served primarily Christian polemics rather than scholarly interest in the accurate representation of Islamic beliefs.[2]

* * *

Sale's translation was commissioned by the Society for Promoting Christian Knowledge, a British Anglican Protestant group dedicated to "missionary and educational goals."[3] As the group also had an anti-Catholic bent,[4] Sale inextricably linked Catholicism with Islam, a connection previously expounded in the Whig treatise *Cato's Letters*.[5] Sale's immediate goal was to remind his Christian readers that Islam was a false religion, but he also intended his work to help convert Muslims to Protestant Christianity, which, like preceding translators of the Qur'an, Sale believed to be their only hope of salvation.[6]

But Sale also seemed determined to present his translation as a rigorously scholarly work, referring to it as "an impartial version."[7] He acknowledged a debt to earlier Christian translations, but did not neglect to criticize their mistakes. Having, for instance, made a careful study of the seventeenth-century Latin translation by the Catholic priest Ludovico Maracci (d. 1700), who worked from several manuscripts in the Vatican,[8] Sale rejected many of what he termed Maracci's "impertinent" interpretations, claiming that "Protestants alone are able to attack the Koran with success."[9]

The first English translation of the Qur'an was published almost a century before Sale's appeared in 1734. Alexander Ross's dubious effort of 1649 was translated not from the original Arabic but from a French edition published two years earlier by the diplomat André du Ryer.[1] And yet Ross's work was deemed explosive: Even before publication, his publisher was imprisoned and all copies were seized. After Ross's testimony at a hearing before the Council of State, the charges were dropped. When the book was finally published on May 7, 1649,[2] a cautionary disclaimer was added. The Qur'an, it declared, may be "dangerous and scandalous" to a few weak Christians, but true believers would not be "swayed from their faith."[3]

Ross's translation was also the first to cross the Atlantic, read by colonists such as Cotton Mather, who branded the Prophet the Anti-christ.[4] When Sale's Qur'an appeared in the American colonies, it was deemed

2. For the best account of translation as a "political act," see Elmarsafy, *Enlightenment Qur'an*, ix–xii, 1–80; Bobzin, "Translations of the Qur'an," 5:340, 344–49.
3. Elmarsafy, *Enlightenment Qur'an*, 22 (quote).
4. Ibid.
5. Thomas S. Kidd, "'Is it Worse to Follow Mahomet Than the Devil?' Early American Uses of Islam," *Church History* 72, no. 4 (December 2003): 767.
6. Sale, "To the Reader," *Koran (1764)*, 1.vii.
7. Ibid.
8. Bobzin, "Translations of the Qur'an," 5:345; Elmarsafy, *Enlightenment Qur'an*, 10–14, 37–63.
9. Elmarsafy, *Enlightenment Qur'an*, 74–75; Sale, "To the Reader," *Koran (1764)*, 1:vii.
1. Elmarsafy, *Enlightenment Qur'an*, 8–9; Bobzin, "Translations of the Qur'an," 5:346–47.
2. Nabil Matar, *Islam in Britain, 1558–1685* (New York: Cambridge University Press, 1998), 8, 76–82; Bobzin "Translations of the Qur'an," 5:347; Elmarsafy, *Enlightenment Qur'an*, 8.
3. Quoted in Matar, *Islam in Britain*, 79.
4. Elmarsafy, *Enlightenment Qur'an*, 9. The translation by Alexander Ross is considered by Nabil Matar, "Alexander Ross and the First English Translation of the Qur'an," *Muslim World* 88 (January 1998): 81–92. See also Matar, *Islam in Britain*, 76, 81.

the most informative and accurate translation then available, which indeed it was, for Sale had attempted to correct some of the most egregious distortions about Islam, out of a sincere desire for accuracy.[5] Sale also critiqued Ross's translation as "utterly unacquainted with the Arabic, and no great matter of French," filled with "fresh mistakes."[6]

* * *

An enormous success throughout Europe, Sale's translation was reprinted four times during the eighteenth century, and was translated into German, French, Russian, and Dutch.[7] It would remain the best available English version of the Qur'an into the nineteenth century.[8]

* * *

The first volume of Sale's 1764 edition contained a two-hundred-page "Preliminary Discourse" on the history of Islam. What Jefferson may have learned from the "Preliminary Discourse" remains critical because Sale, despite his missionary objectives, had collected a substantial amount of relevant, accurate information on Islamic history, ritual practice, and law. Sale sought to approach the conversion of Muslims in much the same manner as that of the Jews: with well informed reason.

* * *

### *The Importance of Sale's Qur'an in Jefferson's Library*

Committed as he was to cultivating an awareness of law and culture beyond those of Britain and continental Europe,[9] Jefferson probably would have approved of Sale's introductory statement: "To be acquainted with the various laws and constitutions of civilized nations, especially those who flourish in our own time, is, perhaps, the most useful part of knowledge."[1] In his *Notes on Virginia*, published in 1784 in Paris and 1787 in London, he had a rather similar recommendation for students in America: "History, by apprizing them of the past, will enable them to judge of the future; it will avail them of the experience of other times and other nations."[2]

But is there evidence that Jefferson gleaned anything from Sale's work to enhance his own knowledge and judgment? Jefferson's voluminous writings, including legislation and correspondence from 1765 to 1776, offer virtually none. Although Jefferson owned a Qur'an, there is no indication that he scrutinized the text verse by verse, as he would the New Testament much later, to create two expurgated volumes of Gospel selections he could accept as true, a version known after his death as the Jefferson Bible.[3]

5. Hayes, "How Thomas Jefferson Read the Qur'an," 251; Elmarsafy, *Enlightenment Qur'an*, 22–23.
6. Sale, "To the Reader," *Koran (1764)*, vi.
7. Elmarsafy, *Enlightenment Qur'an*, 35–36; Bobzin, "Translations of the Qur'an," 5:348.
8. Bobzin, "Translations of the Qur'an," 5:348; Hayes, "How Thomas Jefferson Read the Qur'an," 257–59.
9. Hayes, "How Thomas Jefferson Read the Qur'an," 248; al-Hibri, "Islamic and American Constitutional Law," 498, 501.
1. Sale, "To the Right Honourable John Lord Carteret (Dedication)," *Koran (1764)*, 1:A4.
2. Thomas Jefferson, *Notes on Virginia*, in *The Life and Selected Writings of Thomas Jefferson*, ed. Adrienne Koch and William Peden (New York: Modern Library, 1998), 246.
3. Jefferson actually compiled two separate collections of extracts from the New Testament, the first in 1804, the second in 1819–20. See Thomas Jefferson, *The Jefferson Bible: The Life and Morals of Jesus of Nazareth* (Boston: Beacon, 1989).

The phrase "Thomas Jefferson's Qur'an" implies no such interest in creating a version of the Islamic text he could approve, but it symbolizes a pivotal starting point in his lifelong exploration of Islamic belief and history. His direct references to the Qur'an, with one exception, appear neither as numerous, detailed, or systematic as those issuing from his lifelong engagement with Christianity. Indeed, Jefferson has been criticized for his "many unfair, unnuanced, and shallow caricatures" of several faiths, including Calvinism, Catholicism, Judaism, and Islam.[4] Such a sweeping assertion does not reflect the totality of his views about Islam. At this juncture, suffice it to say, Jefferson did subscribe to the anti-Islamic views of most of his contemporaries, and in politics he made effective use of the rhetoric they inspired.

In the absence of any notes of Jefferson's on Sale's translation of the Qur'an, we can only speculate how Sale's views would have struck him. Although both men were lawyers and Anglicans, Jefferson privately rejected the theological doctrines that Sale unquestioningly accepted. But they had in common a rejection of coercion or violence against religious minorities on account of their faith, and this alone puts them both within an alternative strain of European thought endorsing religious toleration; Jefferson would go even further, calling for the guarantee of individual rights regardless of religion.

* * *

4. Peter K. Conkin, "The Religious Pilgrimage of Thomas Jefferson," in *Jeffersonian Legacies*, ed. Peter Onuf (Charlottesville: University Press of Virginia, 1993), 30.

# Selected Bibliography

## *Reference Works*


Ambros, Arne A., and Stephan Prochazka. *A Concise Dictionary of Koranic Arabic*. Wiesbaden: Reichert, 2004.

Badawi, Elsaid M., and Muhammad Abdel Haleem. *Arabic-English Dictionary of Qur'anic Usage*. Leiden: Brill, 2007.

Bearman, P. J., Th. Bianquia, C. E. Bosworth, E. van Donzel, and W. P. Heinrichs, eds. *Encyclopaedia of Islam*, 2nd ed. 12 vols. with indexes. Leiden: Brill, 1954–2005. The 3rd ed. (ed. Kate Fleet, Gudrun Krämer, Denis Matringe, John Nawas, and Everett Rowson) is being published in print and online (2007–): http://referenceworks.brillonline.com/browse/encyclopaedia-of-islam-3.

Kassis, Hanna E. *A Concordance of the Qur'an*. Berkeley: University of California Press, 1983.

McAuliffe, Jane Dammen, gen. ed. *The Encyclopaedia of the Qur'ān*. 6 vols. Leiden: Brill, 2001–06.

Mir, Mustansir. *Dictionary of Qur'ānic Terms and Concepts*. New York: Garland, 1987.

Penrice, John. *A Dictionary and Glossary of the Kor-ân, with Copious Grammatical References and Explanations of the Text*. 1873. Reprint, New York: Praeger Publishers, 1971. With a new introduction by R. B. Serjeant.

Sherif, Faruq. *A Guide to the Contents of the Qur'an*. London: Ithaca Press, 1985.

Tadrus, Fawzi M. *The Holy Koran in the Library of Congress: A Bibliography*. Washington, DC: Library of Congress, 1993.


## *Translations*


Ali, Abdullah Yusuf, trans. *The Holy Quran: Text, Translation and Commentary*. New York: Hafner, 1946.

Ali, Ahmed, trans. *Al-Qur'an: A Contemporary Translation*. 2nd rev. ed. Princeton: Princeton University Press, 1988.

Arberry, Arthur J., trans. *The Koran Interpreted*. New York: Macmillan, 1955.

Asad, Muhammad, trans. *The Message of the Qur'ān*. Mecca: Muslim World League, 1964.

Bell, Richard, trans. and ed. *The Qur'ān: Translated, with a Critical Re-Arrangement of the Surahs*. 2 vols. Edinburgh: T. & T. Clark, 1937–39.

Fakhry, Majid. *The Qur'ān: A Modern English Version*. Reading, UK: Garnet, 1996.

Haleem, M. A. S. Abdel, trans. *The Qur'an: A New Translation*. New York: Oxford University Press, 2004.

Irving, T. B. *The Qur'ān: The First American Version*. Brattleboro, VT: Amana Books, 1985.

Khalidi, Tarif. *The Qur'an: A New Translation*. London: Penguin Classics, 2008.

Palmer, E. H., trans. *The Qur'ān*. Sacred Books of the East, ed. F. Max Müller, vols. 6 and 9. Oxford: Clarendon, 1880.

Rodwell, J. M. *The Koran: Translated from the Arabic, the Suras Arranged in Chronological Order; with Notes and Index*. London: Williams and Norgate, 1861.

Sells, Michael A. *Approaching the Qur'ān: The Early Revelations*. 2nd ed. Ashland, OR: White Cloud Press, 2007. (Includes a CD with Qur'ān recitations.)


## *Bibliographies of Qur'ān Translations*


Binark, Ismet, and Halit Eren. *World Bibliography of Translations of the Meanings of the Holy Qur'an: Printed Translations, 1515–1980*. Ed. Ekmeleddin İhsanoğlu. Istanbul: Research Centre for Islamic History, Art, and Culture, 1986.

Hamidullah, Muhammad. "Liste des traductions du Coran en langues européennes." In his *Le Coran*, pp. xxxix–l. Paris: Club Français du Livre, 1959.

Pearson, J. D. "Bibliography of Translations of the Qur'ān into European Languages." In his *Arabic Literature to the End of the Umayyad Period*, ed. A. F. L. Beeston, T. M. Johnstone, R. B. Serjeant, and G. R. Smith, pp. 502–20. Cambridge: Cambridge University Press, 1983.

Sefercioğlu, Mustafa Nejat. *World Bibliography of Translations of the Holy Qur'an in Manuscript Form*, ed. Ekmeleddin Ihsanoğlu. Vol. 1, *Turkish, Persian, and Urdu Translations Excluded*. Istanbul: Research Centre for Islamic History, Art, and Culture, 2000.

## *Introductions*

Bell, Richard. *Bell's Introduction to the Qur'an*. Revised and enlarged by W. Montgomery Watt. Edinburgh: Edinburgh University Press, 1970. (First published in 1953 as *Introduction to the Qur'an*.)

Cook, Michael. *The Koran: A Very Short Introduction*. Oxford: Oxford University Press, 2000.

Ernst, Carl W. *How to Read the Qur'an: A New Guide, with Select Translations*. Chapel Hill: University of North Carolina Press, 2011.

Esack, Farid. *The Qur'an: A Short Introduction*. Oxford: Oneworld, 2002.

Lawrence, Bruce. *The Qur'an: A Biography*. New York: Atlantic Monthly Press, 2006.

Mattson, Ingrid. *The Story of the Qur'an: Its History and Place in Muslim Life*. Chichester, West Sussex: Wiley-Blackwell, 2013.

McAuliffe, Jane Dammen, ed. *Cambridge Companion to the Qur'ān*. Cambridge: Cambridge University Press, 2006.

Rippin, Andrew, ed. *The Blackwell Companion to the Qur'ān*. Malden, MA: Blackwell, 2006.

Robinson, Neal. *Discovering the Qur'an: A Contemporary Approach to a Veiled Text*. London: SCM Press, 1996.

Saeed, Abdullah. *The Qur'an: An Introduction*. Abingdon: Routledge, 2008.

## *Studies*

Baljon, J. M. S. *Modern Muslim Koran Interpretation (1880–1960)*. 1961. Reprint, Leiden: Brill, 1968.

Bar-Asher, Meir M. *Scripture and Exegesis in Early Imāmī Shiism*. Leiden: Brill; Jerusalem: Magnes Press, the Hebrew University, 1999.

Barlas, Asma. *"Believing Women" in Islam: Unreading Patriarchal Interpretations of the Qur'an*. Austin: University of Texas Press, 2002.

Bell, Richard. *A Commentary on the Qur'an*. Ed. C. Edmund Bosworth and M. E. J. Richardson. 2 vols. Manchester: University of Manchester, 1991.

Berg, Herbert. *The Development of Exegesis in Early Islam: The Authenticity of Muslim Literature from the Formative Period*. Richmond, Surrey: RoutledgeCurzon, 2000.

Blair, Sheila S. *Islamic Calligraphy*. Edinburgh: Edinburgh University Press, 2006.

Boullata, Issa J., ed. *Literary Structures of Religious Meaning in the Qur'an*. Richmond, Surrey: Curzon, 2000.

Böwering, Gerhard. *The Mystical Vision of Existence in Classical Islam: The Qur'ānic Hermeneutics of the Ṣūfī At-Tustarī (d. 283/896)*. Berlin: Walter de Gruyter, 1980.

Brockopp, Jonathan E., ed. *The Cambridge Companion to Muḥammad*. Cambridge: Cambridge University Press, 2010.

Burman, Thomas E. *Reading the Qur'ān in Latin Christendom, 1140–1560*. Philadelphia: University of Pennsylvania Press, 2007.

Burton, John. *The Collection of the Qur'ān*. Cambridge: Cambridge University Press, 1977.

Elmarsafy, Ziad. *The Enlightenment Qur'an: The Politics of Translation and the Construction of Islam*. Oxford: Oneworld, 2009.

Firestone, Reuven. *Journeys in Holy Lands: The Evolution of the Abraham-Ishmael Legends in Islamic Exegesis*. Albany: State University of New York Press, 1990.

Goldziher, Ignaz. *Schools of Koranic Commentators*. Ed. and trans. Wolfgang H. Behn. Weisbaden: Harrassowitz, 2006. (Originally published in German in 1920.)

Graham, William A. *Beyond the Written Word: Oral Aspects of Scripture in the History of Religion*. Cambridge: Cambridge University Press, 1987.

Gwynne, Rosalind Ward. *Logic, Rhetoric, and Legal Reasoning in the Qur'ān: God's Arguments*. London: RoutledgeCurzon, 2004.

Hawting, G. R., and Abdul-Kader A. Shareef, eds. *Approaches to the Qur'ān*. London: Routledge, 1993.
Izutsu, Toshihiko. *God and Man in the Koran: Semantics of the Koranic Weltanschauung*. Tokyo: Keio Institute of Cultural and Linguistic Studies, 1964.
Jansen, J. J. G. *The Interpretation of the Koran in Modern Egypt*. Leiden: Brill, 1974.
Jeffery, Arthur. *The Foreign Vocabulary of the Qur'ān*. 1938. Reprint, Leiden: Brill, 2007. With a new foreword by Gerhard Böwering and Jane Dammen McAuliffe.
———, ed. *Materials for the History of the Text of the Qur'ān*. Leiden: Brill, 1937.
Jomier, Jacques. *The Great Themes of the Qur'an*. Trans. Zoe Hersov. London: SCM Press, 1997. (Originally published in French in 1978.)
Kropp, Manfred, ed. *Results of Contemporary Research on the Qur'ān: The Question of a Historio-Critical Text of the Qur'ān*. Beirut: Orient-Institut; Würzburg: Ergon in Kommission, 2007.
Lane, Andrew. *A Traditional Mu'tazilite Qur'ān Commentary: The Kashshāf of Jār Allāh al-Zamakhsharī (d. 538/1144)*. Leiden: Brill, 2006.
Lings, Martin. *The Quranic Art of Calligraphy and Illumination*. London: World of Islam Festival Trust, 1976.
Lüling, Günther. *A Challenge to Islam for Reformation: The Rediscovery and Reliable Reconstruction of a Comprehensive Pre-Islamic Christian Hymnal Hidden in the Koran under Earliest Islamic Reinterpretations*. Delhi: Motilal Banarsidass, 2003.
Luxenberg, Christoph. *The Syro-Aramaic Reading of the Koran: A Contribution to the Decoding of the Language of the Koran*. Berlin: Schiler, 2007.
Madigan, Daniel A. *The Qur'ân's Self-Image: Writing and Authority in Islam's Scripture*. Princeton: Princeton University Press, 2001.
Marshall, David. *God, Muhammad and the Unbelievers: A Qur'anic Study*. Richmond, Surrey: Curzon, 1999.
McAuliffe, Jane Dammen. *Qur'anic Christians: An Analysis of Classical and Modern Exegesis*. Cambridge: Cambridge University Press, 1991.
McAuliffe, Jane Dammen, Barry D. Walfish, and Joseph W. Goering, eds. *With Reverence for the Word: Medieval Scriptural Exegesis in Judaism, Christianity and Islam*. New York: Oxford University Press, 2003.
Motzki, Harald, ed. *The Biography of Muḥammad: The Issue of the Sources*. Leiden: Brill, 2000.
Nasser, Shady Hekmat. *The Transmission of the Variant Readings of the Qur'ān: The Problem of Tawātur and the Emergence of Shawādhdh*. Leiden: Brill, 2012.
Nelson, Kristina. *The Art of Reciting the Qur'an*. Austin: University of Texas Press, 1985.
Neuwirth, Angelika, Nicolai Sinai, and Michael Marx, eds. *The Qur'ān in Context: Historical and Literary Investigations into the Qur'ānic Milieu*. Leiden: Brill, 2010.
Nguyen, Martin. *Sufi Master and Qur'an Scholar: Abū'l-Qāsim al-Qushayrī and the "Laṭā'if al-ishārāt."* Oxford: Oxford University Press; London: Institute of Ismaili Studies, 2012.
Nöldeke, Theodor, Friedrich Schwally, Gotthelf Bergsträsser, and Otto Pretzl. *The History of the Qur'ān*. Ed. and trans. Wolfgang H. Behn. Leiden: Brill, 2013. (Nöldeke's 1st ed. was published in German in 1860; this translation is of the 2nd ed. [1909–38].)
Peters, F. E. *Muhammad and the Origins of Islam*. Albany: State University of New York Press, 1994.
Rahman, Fazlur. *Major Themes of the Qur'an*. Minneapolis: Bibliotheca Islamica, 1980.
Reynolds, Gabriel Said, ed. *New Perspectives on the Qur'ān: The Qur'ān in Its Historical Context 2*. London: Routledge, 2011.
———. *The Qur'ān and Its Biblical Subtext*. London: Routledge, 2010.
———, ed. *The Qur'ān in Its Historical Context*. London: Routledge, 2008.
Rippin, Andrew, ed. *Approaches to the History of the Interpretation of the Qur'ān*. Oxford: Clarendon Press; New York: Oxford University Press, 1988.
———, ed. *The Qur'an: Formative Interpretation*. Aldershot: Ashgate, 1999.
———, ed. *The Qur'an: Style and Contents*. Aldershot: Ashgate Variorum, 2001.
———. *The Qur'ān and Its Interpretative Tradition*. Aldershot: Ashgate Variorum, 2001.
Rubin, Uri. *The Eye of the Beholder: The Life of Muhammad as Viewed by the Early Muslims: A Textual Analysis*. Princeton: Darwin Press, 1995.
Saleh, Walid A. *The Formation of the Classical "Tafsīr" Tradition: The Qur'ān Commentary of al-Tha'labī (d. 427/1035)*. Leiden: Brill, 2004.

Sands, Kristin Zahra. *Ṣūfī Commentaries on the Qur'ān in Classical Islam*. London: Routledge, 2006.
Shah, Mustafa, ed. *Tafsīr: Interpreting the Qur'ān*. 4 vols. London: Routledge, 2013.
Small, Keith E. *Textual Criticism and Qur'ān Manuscripts*. Lanham, MD: Lexington Books, 2011.
Stowasser, Barbara Freyer. *Women in the Qur'an, Traditions, and Interpretation*. New York: Oxford University Press, 1994.
Taji-Farouki, Suha, ed. *Modern Muslim Intellectuals and the Qur'an*. Oxford: Oxford University Press; London: in association with the Institute of Ismaili Studies, 2004.
Tottoli, Roberto. *Biblical Prophets in the Qur'ān and Muslim Literature*. Trans. Michael Robertson. Richmond, Surrey: Curzon, 2002.
Versteegh, C. H. M. *Arabic Grammar and Qur'ānic Exegesis in Early Islam*. Leiden: Brill, 1993.
Wansbrough, John. *Quranic Studies: Sources and Methods of Scriptural Interpretation*. Oxford: Oxford University Press, 1977.
Wheeler, Brannon M. *Moses in the Quran and Islamic Exegesis*. London: Routledge-Curzon, 2002.
Wild, Stefan, ed. *The Qur'ān as Text*. Leiden: Brill, 1996.
———, ed. *Self-referentiality in the Qur'ān*. Wiesbaden: Harrassowitz, 2006.
Zadeh, Travis. *The Vernacular Qur'an: Translation and the Rise of Persian Exegesis*. Oxford: Oxford University Press; London: Institute of Ismaili Studies, 2012.

## *Online Resources*

*The Noble Qur'an*: http://quran.com
This site offers verse and sūra search of several English translations as well as those in a number of other languages.

*Quran Explorer*: www.quranexplorer.com/quran/
Searchable by sūra and verse, it offers several English translations and a large number of recitations. Click on a verse to hear it recited in Arabic or English.

*Tanzil—Quran Navigator*: http://tanzil.net/#l:l
Mouse over the Arabic text to see an English translation or to hear recitation.

*USC Qur'an*: www.usc.edu/org/cmje/religious-texts/quran/
A initiative of the Center for Muslim-Jewish Engagement at the University of Southern California, it includes several English translations and a useful index of the Qur'ān.

*Altafsir.com*: www.altafsir.com
A project of Jordan's Royal Aal al-Bayt Institute for Islamic Thought, it includes Qur'āns, recitations, and several commentaries in English translation.

*The Quranic Arabic Corpus*: http://corpus.quran.com
Hosted by the Language Research Group at the University of Leeds, this site provides the Arabic grammar, syntax, and morphology for each word in the Qur'ān.

*ReciteQuran.com*: www.recitequran.com
One of several websites that introduce qur'ānic recitation. There are also countless YouTube videos of well-known reciters.

*Quranflash*: www.quranflash.com/home?en
An interactive version that allows a choice of textual calligraphy and highlights the passage being recited.

*World Digital Library*: http://www.wdl.org/en/
This collaborative project by the Library of Congress, UNESCO, and libraries and museums from around the world includes an extensive archive of Qur'ān manuscripts photographed in high resolution.

Apps: hundreds of apps for smart phones and tablets are available, and the number increases continually. Use search terms such as "quran" and "tajweed" to pull these up.

*International Qur'anic Studies Association* (IQSA): http://iqsaweb.wordpress.com
On its website this scholarly association posts discussions of qur'ānic topics, book reviews, and notices of forthcoming conferences.